THIRD EDITION

SEXUALITY TODAY: *THE HUMAN PERSPECTIVE*

For my family—Betsy, Casey, and Chelsea—my companions in learning about life and love. There is nothing more wonderful in my life than being with each of you.

Gary F. Kelly has been a sex educator for over 25 years. He is currently Associate Dean of Students for Student Development at Clarkson University, where he works with students as a counselor and teaches the sexuality section of the Personal Wellness course. He is also headmaster of the Clarkson School, a special division of the university for talented high school students. Kelly is a lecturer in the counseling and human development program at St. Lawrence University, where he teaches graduate courses in human sexuality and transpersonal counseling. During 1991–1992 he served on a 15-member committee to advise The New York State Board of Regents and Commissioner of Education on curriculum for science, mathematics, and technology. As a person who strongly believes that young people must have solid basic information about sex and their own sexuality to make rational and responsible decisions, Kelly presents here a balanced approach to the physical as well as the psychological and sociologi-

cal aspects of human sexuality. His work with high school students received national recognition with his election to the board of directors of the Sex Information and Education Council of the United States (SIECUS). Kelly served for eight years as editor of the *Journal of Sex Education and Therapy* and is presently a consulting editor with that journal. Kelly is certified by the American Association of Sex Educators, Counselors, and Therapists (AASECT), and is a diplomate of the American Board of Sexology. He maintains a limited private practice in partnership/marriage counseling and sex therapy. He believes that his work with individuals in therapy has enlarged his personal and professional perspective on how people integrate their sexuality into their lives. The case studies in this book reflect that perspective.

THIRD EDITION

SEXUALITY TODAY
The Human Perspective

Gary F. Kelly

Clarkson University

DPG

The Dushkin Publishing Group, Inc.

Sexuality Today: The Human Perspective, 3rd Edition

Printed in the United States of America

Library of Congress Catalog Card Number: 91-77532

International Standard Book Number (ISBN) 1-56134-062-6

First Printing

The Dushkin Publishing Group, Inc., Sluice Dock, Guilford, Connecticut 06437

Preface

Matthew Arnold noted: "Not a having and a resting, but a growing and a becoming is the character of perfection as culture conceives it." During my lifetime I have spent a good deal of time working to understand the nature of my own sexuality. I have come to realize that my sexual feelings are at times among my most intense feelings and that they are capable of yielding great pleasure in my life. I have also learned that my sexual feelings and behaviors can sometimes create problems and cause worries. Although my sexual values have shifted and changed through the years, some of them have remained stable and form the basis of my philosophical approach to this book. First, I believe sexual feelings, behaviors, and fantasies are healthy and good. Decisions, however, about sex must be made with careful thought, because the potential for negative consequences also exists. Second, each individual must spend time understanding the place and importance of sex in his or her life. Third, each of us has a responsibility to show concern for other people who come into our lives in a romantic or sexual encounter. Sex ceases to be healthy and positive when it is exploitative or hurtful. Fourth, people differ greatly in their sexual orientations and behaviors. I try not to judge the morality of any of these preferences or actions. Instead, I hope all persons will find the sexual life-styles that will yield the most happiness, satisfaction, peacefulness, and fulfillment for them.

At this time I feel secure in my basic sexual and personal values, yet I also realize that as I have tried to be open to changing sexual values in the past, I must also be open to them in the future. Through the writing of this book I am reaffirming my belief in the importance of increased awareness and understanding of the many aspects of human sexuality.

I have included several features in this textbook to help make it an effective learning tool. For this third edition, I have been able to integrate the suggestions of instructors and students who have used the text over the past four years, and that has enhanced its usefulness even more. I am particularly pleased with the improvements in this edition. Many illustrations have been refined; new to this edition is a two-page insert of full-color illustrations covering development of a fetus; the text information is extremely up to date; and the supplementary boxed material in the chapters have some especially interesting new additions. The text is now more thorough and well-organized than ever before.

CHAPTER OUTLINES At the beginning of each chapter I give a brief outline of its major headings, to provide students a preview of the topics covered. Students may use the Chapter Outline along with the Chapter Summary to review the material effectively.

INTRODUCTORY QUOTES Each chapter begins with a brief quote. Some of these come from my own counseling sessions or classes, and some from other sources. They are carefully selected statements, opinions, and ideas intended to give students a personal, direct approach to the major concepts discussed in the chapter.

CASE STUDIES There is usually at least one case study in every chapter. Each case study illustrates in some detail a sexual problem or dilemma raised by the issues in the chapter. For the most part I have drawn these anecdotes from my own experiences as a sex educator and sex therapist. A few have been provided by other professionals. Readers are cautioned not to draw any generalized conclusions from the case studies, since they are statements about specific persons rather than about research studies on groups of people.

BOXED MATERIAL In nearly every chapter I have included one or more boxes that contain material intended to give students a broad humanitarian perspective on the concept being discussed. These boxes differ from case studies in that they are excerpts from various literary, philosophical, and biographical sources, or from current articles in magazines and newspapers. A great deal of new boxed material has been included in this edition.

FIGURES The figures were selected to clarify and extend the material in the text. Charts, graphs, and tables provide data for the most recent research available. The photographs and drawings were chosen to illustrate concepts in a practical yet caring manner. Figures are expressly cited in the text when they contain specific or scientific information, and otherwise appear near the material they illustrate.

GLOSSARY Important terms and concepts are underlined in the text and defined on the page where they occur, for quick and easy reference. Other important concepts are in italics. A pronunciation guide is included in the glossary for those terms that would probably be difficult for most students. The accent is indicated in capital letters. A complete alphabetized glossary appears at the end of the book.

CHAPTER SUMMARY At the end of each chapter is a numbered summary of the main ideas discussed. As a study aid, students may coordinate the summary with the outline at the beginning of the chapter in order to review the material effectively.

ANNOTATED READINGS I have included a carefully selected list of readings at the end of each chapter. I have briefly indicated the type of material and the approach of the book so that students can assess its usefulness. This is an excellent resource for those students seeking more information on a given topic.

SELF-EVALUATIONS Sexuality is not a topic to be considered apart from the self or separate from the nuances of human relationships. In fact, I believe that we should take the time to understand our own sexuality and its place in our personality. To this end I have included, in selected chapters, questionnaires, self-awareness exercises, and values clarification devices, under the heading of Self-Evaluation. By completing these activities, students may discover some things they did not know about themselves and sexuality, and clarify what they can expect to learn from this book.

APPENDIX As an additional resource for those students who might need to seek help for a specific problem, or who want additional information on a given topic, I have included a list of national organizations and federal agencies, with addresses and telephone numbers if available. Students should also note that numerous state agencies exist that can give them information or help them with a problem. These would be too numerous to list here.

SEXUALITY AND RELATIONSHIPS The chapter on Sexuality, Communication, and Relationships (chapter 8) was added to the second edition, and has been widely praised by users of the text. This chapter has been expanded and updated, and provides a practical guide to making relationships work, including ways in which sexual sharing may be responsibly integrated into a relationship. There is also an emphasis on the different personality characteristics that individuals bring to a relationship. It is generally recognized that effective communication is an important key to keeping loving relationships healthy and viable, and this chapter draws on the latest research in describing the elements of a dynamic communication process.

HIV AND AIDS

It has been suggested that so much recent emphasis on the relationship between sex and disease might turn young people away from sexuality and intimacy. That would be tragic. I believe that sexuality is such an integral part of our personality that we need to deal realistically with any problem rather than avoid it. In deciding to devote the whole of chapter 15 to HIV and AIDS, I realized that I was running the risk of being labeled an alarmist, but I make no apology for doing so. It seemed to me that it was my duty as an educator to summarize the data and to give readers the information they would need to make intelligent decisions about their sexual behavior. Both teachers and students should be aware that the latest information available is contained in this chapter, but since the HIV/AIDS crisis is volatile and research is ongoing, new information becomes available daily. This edition includes entirely updated information on HIV infection and AIDS and their implications for human sexuality.

ACCURACY, RESEARCH

As the editor of the *Journal of Sex Education and Therapy,* I often found it disconcerting to note how many authors quote statements from other authors as fact, when they were only hypotheses or generalizations based on limited personal observations, and I have taken this into account in preparing this book. It seems that surrounding every sex-related issue there is controversy. One of my major concerns has been to document these controversies as objectively as possible. Ideas such as the biological or environmental causes of homosexuality in chapter 11, the effectiveness of the IUD as a birth control method versus its possible physical dangers to women in chapter 5, the differences and similarities between genders in chapter 6, and the psychological effects of pornography versus the rights of the individual in chapter 17 are examples of several topics for which there is really not enough empirical evidence now to justify definitive conclusions.

This third edition includes information from nearly 400 new references, providing the most up-to-date facts and research studies available. Most of these references were published in the 1990s. Many older bibliographic references have been eliminated.

Throughout the book I have followed the style of the American Psychological Association, so that authors are cited and enclosed within parentheses; you will find full bibliographical details in the References.

I would welcome comments or suggestions for future editions from readers. I like to make contact with those who have connected with my words. If the spirit moves you, let me hear from you.

SUPPLEMENTS

The textbook is the core of a complete teaching/learning program. A teaching resource manual is available and contains a variety of aids for using this textbook effectively. A testbank contains a wide array of test items for measuring student accomplishments in learning the material in the course. A microcomputer test program, *EZ-TEST® to Accompany Sexuality Today: The Human Perspective, 3rd Edition,* which is keyed to the testbank, gives instructors the flexibility and ease of designing different tests for different classes. In addition, there is now available *Study Guide to Accompany Sexuality Today: The Human Perspective, 3rd Edition,* which includes both learning and self-testing activities for the student designed to reinforce and extend the material in the textbook.

ACKNOWLEDGMENTS

More people than I can properly recall have given me encouragement and suggestions for writing this book and revising it for the present edition. A number of them have offered specific help toward its improvement. These professionals and colleagues deserve thanks and acknowledgment. Before I began to write an earlier version, helpful suggestions were given me by Mary S. Calderone, founder and former president of the Sex Information and Education Council of the United States (SIECUS); Michael Carrera, Hunter College, CUNY; Patricia Schiller of the International Council of Sex Education and Parenthood at American University, founder of AASECT; Haskell Coplin, Amherst College; and Margie Strait, St. Lawrence University.

Several other professionals read portions of the first draft manuscript and took the time to offer their comments. These included Donald Auster and Fritz Renick, St. Lawrence University; Jack Annon, University of Hawaii; Jane Hart, University of Massachusetts; Joseph Norton, SUNY at Albany; and Ronald Gold of the National Gay Task Force. I am greatly indebted to a number of my distinguished colleagues who gave their professional advice and helpful comments in reviewing editions of this book:

Janice and John Baldwin, University of California, Santa Barbara
Karen R. Blaisure, Virginia Polytechnic Institute and State University
Sheila D. Brandick, University of Regina
Peggy Brick, Planned Parenthood, Inc., of Bergen County
Vern L. Bullough, State University College at Buffalo
T. Jean Byrne, Kent State University
Sandra L. Caron, University of Maine, Orono
Carol Cassell, Institute for Sexuality Education and Equity
Edward E. Coates, Judge Ely Family Healthcare
Geri Falconer-Ferneau, Arizona State University
Jane F. Gilgun, University of Minnesota
Susan E. Hetherington, University of Maryland
Karen M. Hicks, Lehigh University
Peter T. Knoepfler, sex therapist in private practice
Brian R. McNaught, consultant to corporations and universities on the effects of
    homophobia, trainer, author
Owen Morgan, Arizona State University
Marilyn Myerson, University of South Florida
Robert Pollack, University of Georgia
John Preston
James H. Price, University of Toledo
Laurna Rubinson, University of Illinois
Robin Sawyer, University of Maryland
Kay F. Schepp, University of Vermont
Dick Skeen, Northern Arizona University
Stephen Southern, The Sexual Medicine Institute of Southeast Louisiana
Marilyn Story, University of Northern Iowa
Karen S. Tee, Vanier College
Robert F. Valois, University of Texas at Austin
Patricia Whelehan, Potsdam College of the State University of New York
William L. Yarber, Indiana University

The bulk of the original manuscript—which was formidable indeed—was typed by my friend and former secretary Barbara Simpkins. Thanks are due to my secretaries Laurie Gagne and Connie Basham for their efficient handling of many of the revisions for the second and third editions, and for helping me meet my deadlines.

My wife Betsy was a constant source of good ideas. She read each chapter and offered many suggestions for making the book more readable and interesting.

Several friends and colleagues provided specific information and suggestions for the most recent two editions of this text. They are Helen Hutchinson of Planned Parenthood of Northern New York; Tobin Hart, University of Massachusetts; Frances Campbell and Terry de la Vega, nurse practictioners; Mary Theis, Jennifer Berkman, Art Siebert, Gail Berry, Cathy Siematkowski, Byron Whitney, and Steve Camp, all of Clarkson University; Jennifer Bixby, Citizens Against Violent Actions; Susan Horne, John Preston, and Shirley Tirrell. For this third edition, I appreciated the help of my student research assistant, Michael Shepard, and the suggestions of several Clarkson School students: Todd Haskell, Zarguhn Karim, Abe Maritime, Andy Mullin, Steve Sablan, and Allison Woodruff.

My publisher, Rick Connelly, deserves special mention here, for without his patient persistence in obtaining the publication rights for the book, it would not exist. His faith in the project has been an inspiration. I am also indebted to those at The Dushkin Publishing Group who were so helpful in all stages of production, especially John Holland and Robert Mill, who skillfully edited the third edition, and Pamela Carley Petersen, who carefully selected the photographs and other illustrations.

Finally, I want to thank my clients and students for the unending learning experiences they provide for me. Their willingness to share their lives and feelings is a continuing highlight of my life.

Gary F. Kelly
Clarkson University
Potsdam, NY 13699-5645

CONTENTS IN BRIEF

Preface   v

PART I   SEXOLOGY AND SEXUAL BIOLOGY   1

   1. Historical and Research Perspectives on Sexuality   3
   2. Sexual Systems   29
   3. Human Sexual Response   61

PART II   REPRODUCTIVE ASPECTS OF HUMAN SEXUALITY   79

   4. Reproduction and Birthing   81
   5. Birth Control and Unintended Pregnancy   103

PART III   SEXUALITY, PERSONALITY, AND RELATIONSHIPS   133

   6. Gender-Identity/Role and Society   135
   7. Sexuality Through the Life Cycle   165
   8. Sexuality, Communication, and Relationships   195

PART IV   HUMAN SEXUAL BEHAVIOR   225

   9. Sexual Individuality and Sexual Values   227
   10. Solitary Sex and Shared Sex   255
   11. Homosexuality and Bisexuality   275
   12. The Spectrum of Human Sexual Behavior   309

PART V   DEALING WITH SEXUAL PROBLEMS   339

   13. Sexual Abuse and Other Sexual Problems   341
   14. Sexually Transmitted Diseases and Other Physical Problems   375
   15. The AIDS Crisis and Sexual Decisions   401
   16. Sexual Dysfunctions and Their Treatment   431

PART VI   SEX AND CONTEMPORARY SOCIETY   459

   17. Sex, Art, the Media, and the Law   461

Appendix: Resources on Human Sexuality   487
Glossary   493
References   505
Index   529

CONTENTS

PREFACE v

PART I   SEXOLOGY AND SEXUAL BIOLOGY 1

ONE

HISTORICAL AND RESEARCH PERSPECTIVES ON SEXUALITY 3

The Sexual Revolution 4
  Roots of Change 5
    New approaches to morality 5
    Changing roles of women and men 6
    Increased leisure time and affluence 6
    Research into human sexuality 7
    Developments in science and technology 7
    AIDS as an agent for value change 7
  The Next Sexual Revolution 7
Milestones in Sex Research: A Brief Historical Survey 8
  Emerging From the 19th Century 8
  Richard von Krafft-Ebing 8
  Sigmund Freud 9
  Henry Havelock Ellis 9
  Sexual Studies in the Early 20th Century 10
  Mid-Century Sex Research 11
  Recent Directions in Sex Research 12
  Surveys of the Seventies and Eighties 13
    The Hunt Report 13
    The Hite reports 13
    Research on childhood sexuality 14
    Other surveys 14
  Research Trends for the Nineties 15
Sexological Research Today 16
  Collecting Research Data on Human Sexuality 16
    Selecting population samples 17
    Taking surveys 17

       Case studies and clinical research 18
       Observational research 18
       Experimental research 18
    Ethical Issues in Sex Research 19
  New Attitudes Toward Sexuality 19
    Attitudes Toward Masturbation 19
    Attitudes Toward Premarital Sex 20
    Attitudes Toward Homosexuality and Other Sexual Orientations 21
    Attitudes Toward the Body and Nudity 21
    Attitudes Toward the Double Standard 22
    Attitudes Toward Sex and Romance 22
    Attitudes Toward Sex Education 23
Self-Evaluation: You and Your Sexuality 24
Chapter Summary 27
Annotated Readings 27

TWO

SEXUAL SYSTEMS 29

Female Sex Organs 29
  Vulva 30
  Clitoris 31
  Clitoridectomy and Infibulation 32
  Vagina 33
  The Hymen 34
  Genital Self-Examination for Women 35
  Uterus 35
  Pelvic Examination 36
  Ovaries and Fallopian Tubes 36
  Female Breasts 37
  Breast Self-Examination 38
    Visual examination 38
    Manual examination 38
The Menstrual Cycle 39
  Preovulatory Preparation or Follicular Phase 40
  Ovulation 40
  Luteal Secretion 40
  Menstruation 41
  Premenstrual Syndrome 44
Male Sex Organs 44
  Testes and Scrotum 44
  Male Genital and Testicular Self-Examination 46
  Penis 47
  Erection 47
    Penis size 48
    Male circumcision: The debate 48
  Internal Male Organs 50
  Sperm Production and Ejaculation 50
  Hormonal Cycles in Men 53
Menopause and the Male Climacteric: The Sexual Systems Age 53
  Female Menopause 53
    Implications for women's sexuality 55

The Male Climacteric   55
  Surviving the male climacteric   56
Self-Evaluation: Your Sex Education: Past, Present, and Future   57
Chapter Summary   58
Annotated Readings   59

THREE

HUMAN SEXUAL RESPONSE   61

Models of Human Sexual Response   62
  The Masters and Johnson Four-Phase Model   62
  Kaplan's Three-Phase Model   62
Individual Differences in the Sexual Response Cycle   63
  Women, Men, and Sexual Arousal   65
Female Sexual Response   67
  Excitement Phase   67
  Plateau Phase   67
  Orgasm   68
  Resolution Phase   68
  Recent Controversies in Female Sexual Response   69
    Orgasms   69
    The G spot   69
    Ejaculation   69
  Kegel Exercises and Sexual Response   70
Male Sexual Response   70
  Excitement Phase   70
  Plateau Phase   70
  Orgasm   71
  Resolution   72
  Refractory Period   72
  Multiple Orgasms in Men   73
Hormonal Regulation of Sexual Response   73
Effects of Aging on Sexual Response   73
  Aging and Female Sexual Response   74
  Aging and Male Sexual Response   74
Self-Evaluation: Your Sexual Myths and Misconceptions   75
Chapter Summary   77
Annotated Readings   77

PART II   *REPRODUCTIVE ASPECTS OF HUMAN SEXUALITY   79*

FOUR

REPRODUCTION AND BIRTHING   81

Reproduction: Fertilization and Fetal Development   81
    Twinning and other multiples   82
  Development of the Embryo/Fetus   83
Reproductive and Fetal Technology   84
  Genetic Engineering   85

Artificial Insemination and Storage of Gametes and Embryos   88
In Vitro Fertilization and Related Techniques   89
Choosing the Sex of a Fetus   90
Will Human Cloning Become Possible?   91
Surrogate Motherhood   92
Fetal Technology   93
Amniocentesis   93
Chorionic villi sampling   93
Sonograms   94
Fetal surgery   94
Infertility and Sexuality   94
Pregnancy and Birthing   95
The Biology of Pregnancy   96
Pregnancy tests   96
Alcohol, drugs, and smoking   96
Sex during pregnancy   97
The Birth Process   97
Birthing Alternatives   98
Natural childbirth   98
The Lamaze method   98
Home birth   99
Birthing rooms   99
Problems During Pregnancy   99
Pregnancy-induced hypertension   99
Premature birth   99
Rh incompatibility   100
Chapter Summary   100
Annotated Readings   101

FIVE

BIRTH CONTROL AND UNINTENDED PREGNANCY   103

Historical Perspectives   103
Choosing to Become a Parent   104
Birth Control Today   105
Deciding About Contraceptives   105
Ethical and Religious Influences   106
Health Considerations   107
Psychological and Social Factors   108
Preparing the Way for Effective Contraception   110
Choosing the "Right" Contraceptive   110
Methods of Birth Control   114
Understanding Contraceptive Effectiveness   114
Sharing the Responsibility for Birth Control   114
Abstinence, Sex Without Intercourse, and Withdrawal   115
Oral Contraceptives: The Pill   115
Norplant Implants and Progestin Injections   116
Spermicides, Sponges, and Suppositories   117
Barrier Methods   117
Diaphragms and cervical caps   117
Condoms   119
Intrauterine Devices (IUDs)   120
Natural Family Planning/Fertility Awareness   121

Voluntary Sterilization   121
New Contraceptives for Males?   123
Postcoital Contraception   124
Self-Evaluation: Contraceptive Comfort and Confidence Scale   125
Unintended Pregnancy: The Options   125
Keeping the Baby   126
Adoption   126
Termination of Pregnancy   127
Methods of Abortion   127
Vacuum curettage   128
Dilation and evacuation or dilation and curettage   128
Procedure used later in pregnancy   129
Use of Fetal Tissue   129
Safety of Abortion for the Woman   129
Psychological Considerations   129
Chapter Summary   130
Annotated Readings   131

PART III   *SEXUALITY, PERSONALITY, AND RELATIONSHIPS*   133

SIX

GENDER-IDENTITY/ROLE AND SOCIETY   135

Gender-Identity/Role   135
Separating Women and Men   136
1. Prenatal factors   136
2. Factors of infancy and childhood   136
3. Factors at puberty   136
Prenatal Factors   136
Chromosomes   136
Fetal gonads or sex glands   137
Fetal hormones   138
Development of male or female genitals   138
Fetal hormones and the brain   139
Fetally androgenized females   140
Androgen insensitivity syndrome   140
DHT-deficiency syndrome   140
Factors of Infancy and Childhood   141
Sex assignment at birth   141
Rearing a child as girl or boy   142
The child's own body image   142
Factors at Puberty   143
Hormones at puberty   143
Physical changes during puberty and adolescence   144
Changes in sexual drive and behavior at puberty   145
Adult Gender-Identity/Role   146
Expressing Gender-Identity/Role   146
Occasional cross-dressing   147
Transvestism   147
Transgenderism (or cross-genderism)   147
Transsexualism   148

Masculinity and Femininity Today   148
    Traditionally masculine traits   149
    Traditionally feminine traits   149
  Learning Sex Roles   150
    Psychoanalytic tradition   150
    Social learning theory   150
    Cognitive-developmental   150
    Gender schema theory   151
  Women Rebel—The Feminist Movement   151
  Growing Up Female and Male   152
  Men React   156
  Gender Aware Therapy   158
  Androgyny: Bridging the Gap?   160
Self-Evaluation: Masculinity and Femininity in Your Life   161
Chapter Summary   162
Annotated Readings   163

SEVEN

SEXUALITY THROUGH THE LIFE CYCLE   165

Psychosexual Development   165
  Inborn Sexual Instinct Theory   166
  Psychoanalytic Theory   166
  Integrated Social Factors Theory   167
  Conditioning and Social Learning Theory   168
  Social Script Theory   170
  A Unified Theoretical Model of Sexual Development   170
Sexuality in Infancy and Childhood   171
  Sexual Curiosity Grows in Childhood   172
  Love and Romance in Childhood   174
Sexuality in Adolescence   174
  Sexual Behavior in Adolescence   175
  Self-Centered Early Adolescent Sex   175
  Adolescent Homosexual Activity   176
  Masturbation in Adolescence   177
  Adolescent Heterosexual Activity   177
  Social Relationships   180
Adult Sexuality and Relationships   180
  Intimacy and Sexuality   181
  Marriage, Cohabitation, Singles, and Sex   182
  Monogamy Versus Non-Monogamy   183
  Trends in Marriage   184
  Divorce   184
Sexuality and Aging   185
  Myths and Attitudes About Sex and Aging   186
    Loving and sexual feelings are experienced only during youth   186
    Sex is primarily for reproduction   187
    Remarriage after loss of a spouse should be discouraged   187
    Older men remain more sexually interesting to younger partners than do older women   187
    Aged people lose interest in sex   187
  Institutional Prohibitions on Sexual Expression   188
  Special Sexual Problems and Patterns of Aging   188

The individual's or couple's sexual history 189
Partner availability 189
Sexual values and attitudes 189
Knowledge about sexuality 189
Maintenance of self-esteem and a sense of identity 189
Masturbation and Heterosexual Intercourse in Old Age 189
Maximizing Sexual Expression During the Later Years 190
Self-Evaluation: Looking Ahead: Sex in Later Years 192
Chapter Summary 192
Annotated Readings 193

EIGHT

SEXUALITY, COMMUNICATION, AND RELATIONSHIPS 195

Communicating About Sex 195
The Communication Process 196
The Words We Use to Talk About Sex 196
Contemporary Myths About Communication 198
The Sexual Games We Play 199
The power games 199
The relationship games 199
The communication games 199
Effective Communication 200
The Ground Rules 200
Making It Happen 200
Demonstrate an attitude of warmth, caring, and respect 200
Avoid making snap judgments and "all-ness statements" 201
Listen carefully and really hear 201
Empathize and understand that feelings need to be felt 201
Be genuine 201
Make sense and ask for clarification 201
Don't let silence scare you 201
Beware of the "I don't want to hurt you" copout 202
Use self-talk effectively 202
The Pros and Cons of Quarreling 202
Resolving Conflicts Effectively 203
People Have Different Personality Types for Communicating 204
Communication Differences Between Women and Men 205
Talking over problems 205
Asking for directions 205
Expressing needs 205
Talking and listening 206
Loving Relationships and Sexuality 208
The "Other" Risks of Sex 208
Risk: Modeling your sexuality only after external standards rather than your own 208
Risk: Confusing romantic attachments and sexual attractions 208
Risk: Not allowing yourself to be vulnerable enough to accept the risks inherent in loving relationships 208
Risk: Being in a situation in which you feel bound to do something sexual that just doesn't feel quite right to you 208
What Is Love? 209
Infatuation and Being in Love 209
Sternberg's Triangular Theory of Love 210

Establishing Sensual and Sexual Intimacy 213
Confusion About Love and Sex in Relationships 214
Friendship and Sexuality 215
Jealousy and Possessiveness 217
Dealing With the Loss of a Loving Relationship 218
Self-Evaluation: Communicating About Sex 219
Chapter Summary 222
Annotated Readings 223

PART IV   *HUMAN SEXUAL BEHAVIOR*   225

NINE

SEXUAL INDIVIDUALITY AND SEXUAL VALUES   227

Labeling Sex: Cross-Cultural and Historical Perspectives 227
Sociocultural Standards for Sexual Arousal and Behavior 230
The heterosexual standard 230
The coital standard 230
The orgasmic standard 230
The two-person standard 230
The romantic standard 230
Sexual Standards in Other Cultures 231
Who Is Normal? 233
Statistical normalcy 233
Normalcy by expert opinion 233
Moral normalcy 233
A continuum of normalcy 233
Limits and Misuses of Labels 233
Sexual Individuality 234
How Does Sexual Individuality Develop? 235
Making Sexual Choices 238
Sex and Values 238
Dealing With Sex as a Moral Issue 239
Adherence to divinely established natural laws 239
The existence of a religious covenant between humankind and a God 239
Situation ethics 240
Hedonistic and ascetic traditions 240
Religion and Sex 240
Aligning Yourself With Social and Cultural Values 241
Finding Healthy Sexual Values 243
Sex Education 244
Current Trends in Sex Education 245
Technical advances 245
Distinguishing sexual expression from procreation 245
Debating the "just say no" philosophy 246
Increased emphasis on developing decision-making skills and loving relationships 246
Recognizing the need for sex education as a coordinated effort 246
The necessity of dealing with the AIDS crisis 247
What Sex Education Can and Cannot Accomplish 247
Sex Education for Professionals 247

Sex and Disability Groups 247
    Mental Retardation 249
    Visual and Auditory Disabilities 250
    Spinal Cord Injuries 250
    Other Physical and Mental Disabilities 251
    Institutions 252
Chapter Summary 252
Annotated Readings 253

TEN

SOLITARY SEX AND SHARED SEX 255

Solitary Sex: Masturbation 256
    How Girls and Women Masturbate 256
    How Boys and Men Masturbate 257
    Fantasy and Pictures in Masturbation 258
    Facts and Fallacies About Masturbation 258
    Masturbation and Morality 260
Shared Sexual Behavior 260
    Nongenital Oral Stimulation 261
    Stimulation of Erogenous Zones 261
    Oral-Genital and Oral-Anal Sex 262
    Mutual Manual Stimulation and Masturbation 263
    Interfemoral and Anal Intercourse 263
    Vibrators, Pornography, and Fantasies 263
    Chemical Aphrodisiacs 264
Heterosexual Intercourse 264
Sexual Intercourse and AIDS 264
Intromission 265
    Intercourse 265
    Positions for Intercourse 266
    Reclining Face-to-Face 266
        Man on top, women supine 267
        Woman on top, man supine 267
        Side-by-side 267
    Other Variations on Face-to-Face 268
        Woman on edge of bed or chair 268
        Both partners seated 268
        Both partners standing 269
    Rear Vaginal Entry 269
        Both partners kneeling, rear entry 269
        Man on top, woman lying on her abdomen, rear entry 270
        Side-by-side, rear entry 270
        Both partners seated or standing, rear entry 270
    After Sexual Relations 271
    Intercourse and Marriage 271
Chapter Summary 272
Annotated Readings 273

ELEVEN

HOMOSEXUALITY AND BISEXUALITY 275

Perspectives on Homosexuality 275
    The Kinsey Scale and Its Limitations 276
    Incidence of Homosexuality 278
    Cross-Cultural Comparisons 279
    Studying Homosexual Behavior 280
    Homophobia 281
Models of Homosexuality 282
    Moral Model 283
    Biological Determinants Model 283
    Psychoanalytic Models 285
    The Normal Variant Model 285
    The Bell, Weinberg, and Hammersmith Study on Sexual Preference 286
    Finding the Facts 287
    Perspectives on Therapy and Prevention 287
Homosexual Identity Formation 288
    Stages of Homosexual Identity Formation 288
        Stage 1: Identity confusion 289
        Stage II: Identity comparison 289
        Stage III: Identity tolerance 290
        Stage IV: Identity acceptance 290
        Stage V: Identity pride 292
        Stage VI: Identity synthesis 292
    Male-Female Differences in Identity Formation 292
    Bisexual People 293
    Comparing Same-Sex Behavior in Males and Females 294
    Same-Sex Relationships 295
    Aging and Homosexuality 296
Myths and Fallacies About Homosexuality 297
Homosexuality and Society 299
    Homosexual Subculture 299
    AIDS and Homosexuals 301
    Homosexuality and Religion 302
    Homosexuality and the Law 303
    Homosexuality and Marriage 304
Conclusion 306
Chapter Summary 306
Annotated Readings 307

TWELVE

THE SPECTRUM OF HUMAN SEXUAL BEHAVIOR 309

Varying Degrees of Sexual Interest and Activity 310
    Celibacy as a Choice 313
    The Variability of Sexual Individuality 313
Expressing Gender-Identity/Role 314
    Cross-Dressing: Transvestism 314
    Transgenderists 316
    Transsexualism 316
    Sex Reassignment 317
    Implications of Treating and Predicting Gender Transpositions 319

The Need to Enhance Sexual Arousal   320
   Use of Erotica and Pornography   321
   Sexual Devices and Gadgets   321
   Sexual Fantasy: Our Internal Pornography   322
   Fetishism   323
   Varying the Numbers   324
Atypical and Potentially Problematic Sexual Connections   325
   Extramarital Sex   326
   Paying for Sex   327
   Close Encounters   329
      Obscene telephone calls   329
      Frottage   329
      Exhibitionism   329
      Voyeurism   330
   Sadomasochism   331
   Sex With Animals   332
   Sex With the Dead   333
   The Emergence of Casual Sex and Pansexualism   333
Conclusion   334
Self-Evaluation: Your Sexual Fantasies   334
Chapter Summary   336
Annotated Readings   337

PART IV   *DEALING WITH SEXUAL PROBLEMS   339*

THIRTEEN

SEXUAL ABUSE AND OTHER SEXUAL PROBLEMS   341

When and How Does Sex Become a Problem?   341
   Negative Self-Attitudes   342
   Self-Destructive Behaviors   343
   Harm or Exploitation of Others   344
   Results of Prejudice and Ignorance   344
   When the Body Does Not Function as Expected or Desired   344
   The Sexual Addiction Controversy   344
Sexual Harassment   345
Sexual Abuse by Professionals   349
Rape   349
   Acquaintance Rape   355
   Marital Rape   357
   Rape of Men   357
   The Aftermath of Rape   359
Sex Between Adults and Children   360
   Effects of Child Sexual Abuse   363
Sex Between Family Members   364
Preventing and Dealing With Problematic Sex   366
   Learning About Sex   366
   Knowing How to Communicate   367
   Having Realistic Expectations   368
   Being Cautious and Responsible   368
   Finding Sex Counseling and Therapy   368

Conclusion   369
Self-Evaluation: Your Sexual Concerns and Problems   370
Chapter Summary   372
Annotated Readings   373

FOURTEEN

SEXUALLY TRANSMITTED DISEASES AND OTHER PHYSICAL PROBLEMS   375

Sexually Transmitted Diseases and Their Prevention   375
  Gonorrhea   375
    Symptoms   377
    Diagnosis   377
    Treatment   377
  Syphilis   378
    Symptoms   378
    Diagnosis and treatment   378
  Chlamydia   379
    Symptoms   379
    Diagnosis and treatment   379
  Nongonococcal Urethritis (NGU) in Males   380
  Vulvovaginal Infections   380
    Symptoms   381
    Types   381
    Prevention of vaginal infections   381
  Genital Herpes   382
    Symptoms   382
    Diagnosis and treatment   383
  Genital Warts   383
    Symptoms   384
    Treatment   384
  Viral Hepatitis   384
    Symptoms   384
    Treatment   384
  Pubic Lice   384
    Treatment   385
  Other Sexually Transmitted Diseases   385
  Preventing Sexually Transmitted Diseases   386
  Legal Aspects of Sexually Transmitted Diseases   387
Other Sex-Related Medical Problems   387
  Disorders of the Male Sex Organs   387
  Disorders of the Female Sex Organs   391
  Sexual Effects of Debilitating Illnesses   395
Self-Evaluation: Examining Your Attitudes Toward STDs   396
Chapter Summary   398
Annotated Readings   399

FIFTEEN

THE AIDS CRISIS AND SEXUAL DECISIONS 401

The Evolution of a New Disease 401
  The Origin of AIDS 403
  Discovery of HIV 404
  Statistics on the Prevalence of the AIDS and HIV Infection 404
  Risks of Infection 405
HIV: The Infection and the Virus 408
  Mechanism of HIV Action 409
  How HIV Is Spread 410
  Does Infection With HIV Mean AIDS? 411
HIV Testing, Treatment, and Vaccines 412
  Controversy over HIV Testing 414
  Treatment for HIV-Infected Patients 415
  Vaccines for HIV 416
AIDS and Society 417
  Individual Freedom vs. Public Health Interests 418
  Other Ethical Issues and AIDS 418
  Witch-Hunting Mentality 421
AIDS and Personal Decisions About Sex 422
  AIDS and HIV Education 422
  Can Sex Be Safe and Satisfying? 424
  Minimizing the Sexual Risks of Contracting HIV 425
Conclusion 427
Chapter Summary 428
Annotated Readings 429

SIXTEEN

SEXUAL DYSFUNCTIONS AND THEIR TREATMENT 431

Understanding Sexual Dysfunctions 431
  When Is a Dysfunction a Dysfunction? 432
    Mythical performance standards for men 432
    Mythical performance standards for women 432
  What Labels Tell Us 432
  The Sexual Response Cycle 433
  Desire Phase Problems 433
  Arousal Difficulties 435
  Vaginismus 437
  Orgasmic Dysfunctions 438
  Lack of Ejaculatory Control 439
  Post-Ejaculatory Pain 440
  Sexual Problems of Homosexuals 440
Causes of Sexual Dysfunctions 440
  Ruling Out Organic Causes 440
  Drugs and Alcohol 442
  The Pressure to Perform 443
  Relationships and Sexual Functioning 443
  Other Causes 444
Treating Sexual Dysfunctions 444
  Folk Remedies 445

Modes of Treatment   446
What Is a Sex Therapist?   448
Behavioral Approaches to Sex Therapy   448
Basic Goals of Behavioral Sex Therapy   448
Gaining a sense of permission to value one's sexuality   *448*
Taking more time to make sexual activity a priority   *449*
Eliminating elements that are blocking full sexual response   *449*
Reducing performance pressures   *449*
Using specific sexual exercises to develop more positive ways of functioning sexually   *449*
Self-Help Approaches   449
Partnership Approaches   450
Some Specific Behavioral Methods   452
A Critical Look at Sex Therapy   453
Is Sex Therapy Effective?   454
Ethical Issues in Sex Therapy   455
Conclusion   456
Chapter Summary   456
Annotated Readings   457

PART VI   *SEX IN CONTEMPORARY SOCIETY*   459

SEVENTEEN

SEX, ART, THE MEDIA, AND THE LAW   461

Pornography: A Definition   461
Nudity and Sex in Art   462
Historical Foundations of Erotic Art   462
Sex and the Printed Page   464
The Evolution of Literary Pornography   464
Victorian Pornography   464
Themes in Contemporary Literature   465
Magazines and Tabloids   465
Sex in the Media   468
Films   468
Homosexuality   *470*
Hard-core pornography   *471*
Video   471
Telephone   471
Computers and Sex Information   473
Television   473
Advertising   474
Child Pornography   475
Effects of Pornography   475
Pornography, the Courts, and the Law   477
Presidential Commission on Obscenity and Pornography, 1970   478
United States Attorney General's Commission on Pornography, 1986   478
Legal Aspects of Sexual Behavior   479
Sex and the Constitution   479
Special Issues and the Law   482
Sex education   *482*
Rape   *482*

Prostitution and nude dancing   483
Birth control, sterilization, and abortion   483
The rights and responsibilities of sexual partners   483
Conclusion   484
Chapter Summary   484
Annotated Readings   485

APPENDIX: RESOURCES ON HUMAN SEXUALITY   487

GLOSSARY   493

REFERENCES   505

INDEX   529

PART I

SEXOLOGY
AND SEXUAL BIOLOGY

I once heard a teacher say that sex is a biological function and love is a psychological function, thus distinguishing and separating these two aspects of human life with a slash of a semantic sword. But things are just not that simple when we try to understand human sexuality and its multidimensional place in our lives. Our sexuality cannot be relegated to a strictly biological realm, because it relates to our attitudes and feelings, our social relationships, our cultural expectations, and our history.

In terms of recorded human history, scientific inquiry and the scientific way of thinking represent relatively new approaches to perceiving the world and human nature. Until very recently, openly studying sexuality and all of its ramifications was taboo. It took several brave pioneers to venture into the pursuit of human sexual truths, and we still have a great deal of uncharted territory to explore. The first chapter of this book previews what is to follow. It deals with how Western society has been shifting its sexual attitudes and values in recent years, and examines how some of the pioneers of sexology—the science of sexuality—have opened up new paths of understanding. It also explores the different methodologies of sex research, each with its unique perspective to offer.

Chapters 2 and 3 introduce the biological foundations of human sexuality: the anatomical structures that make us physically sexual and our physiological responses to sexual arousal. While most of us no longer accept without qualification that "biology is destiny," the biological dimensions of our sexuality are inescapable. When we look at our bodies in the mirror, we see the evidence of our sex. When we begin menstruating or ejaculating semen, we are reminded of our biology. When we experience the arousal of the sexual response cycle, we encounter the power of our sexuality. It is a force to be reckoned with on many different levels: it is deeply personal, it affects culture in general, and it has a direct impact on such global issues as controlling population growth and stopping the spread of AIDS. To secure a firm grounding of understanding about human sexual biology is to prepare for the broader perspective that will follow in this book.

CHAPTER ONE
HISTORICAL AND RESEARCH PERSPECTIVES ON SEXUALITY

Traditional sexual values and attitudes are being challenged by several factors, including advances in medical science, greater amounts of leisure time, changing roles of men and women, new knowledge about sex, and growing concerns about sexually transmitted diseases. Understanding the behavior patterns of society and one's own sexuality is the goal of many types of research.

CHAPTER TWO
SEXUAL SYSTEMS

The human sex organs are an essential part of the complete human being. An awareness and understanding of the biological function of these organs and their effects on personality are important factors in feeling comfortable with oneself and in developing meaningful sexual relationships with others.

CHAPTER THREE
HUMAN SEXUAL RESPONSE

The female and the male have different cyles of sexual response. Masters and Johnson categorize the biological response as occurring in four phases. Helen Kaplan includes desire as an important part of her three-phase cycle. Hormones and aging affect sexual response.

CHAPTER ONE

THE SEXUAL REVOLUTION
  Roots of Change
  The Next Sexual Revolution

**MILESTONES IN SEX RESEARCH: A BRIEF
  HISTORICAL SURVEY**
  Emerging From the 19th Century
  Richard von Krafft-Ebing
  Sigmund Freud
  Henry Havelock Ellis
  Sexual Studies in the Early 20th Century
  Mid-Century Sex Research
  Recent Directions in Sex Research
  Surveys of the Seventies and Eighties
  Research Trends for the Nineties

SEXOLOGICAL RESEARCH TODAY
  Collecting Research Data on Human Sexuality
  Ethical Issues in Sex Research

NEW ATTITUDES TOWARD SEXUALITY
  Attitudes Toward Masturbation
  Attitudes Toward Premarital Sex
  Attitudes Toward Homosexuality and Other Sexual
    Orientations
  Attitudes Toward the Body and Nudity
  Attitudes Toward the Double Standard
  Attitudes Toward Sex and Romance
  Attitudes Toward Sex Education

SELF-EVALUATION: YOU AND YOUR SEXUALITY

CHAPTER SUMMARY

The vast majority of history books seem to imply that offspring just happen. Historians have often reported the existence of mistresses, mentioned prostitutes, and made clear the needs of kings and other rulers to beget male heirs, but until recently they rarely mentioned homosexuality, neglected topics such as contraception, and in fact generally ignored sex, even though it has to be regarded as one of the major, if not the most important, forces in shaping history.

—From the preface by V.L. Bullough in Sexual Variance in Society and History

HISTORICAL AND RESEARCH PERSPECTIVES ON SEXUALITY

Why do we study human sexuality? Isn't one's sexuality part of one's life that happens naturally? Can we learn to be better lovers? Better spouses? Better parents? In recent years, sexuality has been a popular subject. Perhaps all the interest in formerly taboo topics stems from the fact that most of us grew up with some rather confusing and conflicting messages about sex. On the one hand there were suggestions that sex was somehow "dirty," and on the other hand we were encouraged to save it for someone we really loved. Or we got the impression that sex was sacred and beautiful, but the less young people know about it, the better. With topics and emotions that can be as powerful and intimate as those associated with sexuality, it is no wonder that most of us are anxious to sort it out for ourselves.

Close attention to the nuances of full sexual expression is a luxury not afforded to all people of the world. For many, sex is a furtive release of tension or a way of producing offspring that are sometimes wanted, sometimes not. It may provide a brief, pleasurable escape from a life of hardship and struggling for survival. Western culture, however, in its relative affluence, has elevated sex to an almost religious status. It is studied, perfected, worshipped, and

preached about. The mass media are saturated with images of sex, and people with sexual problems seek help by the thousands. Sex has been made a central aspect of life at all ages. It may strike some of us from time to time that sex has been overrated and over-studied. But I believe that sexuality is an avenue to a complete understanding of human nature. To understand fully the many implications of human sexuality, we must look closely at the human condition. In its broadest sense, sexuality is interwoven with all aspects of being human. The biology of sex is complex, and it has only been within the past three decades that reliable facts concerning the physiology of sexual response have been available. The psychology of sex includes the spectrum of sexual orientations, behaviors, emotions, and interpersonal connections. The sociology and anthropology of sex mirror the many social, legal, and cultural patterns that play a role in human sexuality. In short, to study sexuality is to dissolve disciplinary boundaries.

In more affluent areas of the world, people will continue to use their leisure time to explore sex more fully and their money to seek information and help for sexual problems. Whenever sex takes on such social significance, sexual prowess becomes associated with one's status as a woman or a man, and the pressures for outstanding "performance" in sex become greater. As you explore the pages ahead, you will be opening yourself to areas of study that not long ago were ignored or forbidden because of cultural mores. You will be tapping into some information that will have a direct bearing on your own life and relationships. The fact of the matter is that sexuality is an inseparable part of being human.

The Sexual Revolution

During the 1960s the term sexual revolution was in vogue, carrying with it the implication that there had been significant and relatively abrupt changes in sexual attitudes, values, and behaviors during that period. Yet there is much disagreement among professionals over the alleged revolution: whether there indeed ever was a revolution, and if so, when it started, what its causes were, and what changes it generated.

Sociologist Ira Reiss (1977) suggested that the changes were not so radical or cataclysmic as the term *revolution* might imply, and instead represented a gradual emergence from the repression and tyranny of traditional sexual attitudes toward a more normal level of functioning. He preferred the term *sexual renaissance*. Others have seen the changes as a gradual process of growth and development toward a new system of sexual ethics—a sexual evolution. Still others claim we are going through a phase of moral degeneracy that will lead to the downfall of civilization as we know it.

A controversy over the magnitude of a "sexual revolution" erupted after a recently published examination of 1970 attitudes (Klassen, Williams, & Levitt, 1989) concluded that there had not been marked changes in sex-related attitudes in recent years. However, there is evidence that rapid and significant changes in some sexual attitudes and behaviors did indeed occur during the decades of the seventies and eighties. For example, a study conducted in 1963 by the National Opinion Research Center (NORC) found that 80 percent of people in the United States disapproved of premarital sex, even when the partners were in love. In a 1970 NORC study, between a third and a half of the respondents disapproved. By 1988, another NORC survey found that only 26 percent felt premarital intercourse was "always wrong" (Libby, 1990). These and other similar data suggest that changes have been occurring in some areas of attitudes and values. However, it has also been suggested that when it comes to attitudes about such issues as pornography, homosexuality, and extramarital sex, there has not been any marked shift toward more liberal attitudes (Smith, 1990).

Eminent sex researcher and social commentator John Money (1991) believes that a "sexual reform movement" began in the middle part of this century, characterized by the sexual liberation of women and homosexuals, a move toward more sex education, and the advent of sex therapy. He also contends that we are currently seeing a sexual counterreformation that began to gain steam in the late seventies. There was a growing sense of apprehension and dread about what the sexual reformation had wrought. There were rising concerns, reflected in various media blitzes, about genital herpes, teen pregnancy, the effects of women's liberation, and, eventually, AIDS. Money sees cycles of reformation and counterreformation reflected in changing social norms and policies.

Whether we call it revolution or renaissance, moral degeneracy or counterreformation, something has been going on during the past 3 or 4 decades with regard to our ways of thinking about sex (Selverstone, 1989). Consider the following excerpts from a sex education booklet published in 1934 called *The Mysteries of Life:*

> Up to the age of puberty, the sexual instinct may be said to be neutral. Boys and girls play innocently together, unconscious of the dominating force that is slumbering within. As puberty approaches, the boy assumes a more masterful attitude . . . his desires become stronger, his actions more gallant and his thoughts more sensual than formerly. The girl becomes more timid and shy than she has hitherto been.
>
> Too great stress cannot be laid upon the importance of caring for the child [during puberty]. . . . Too often schoolmates are the only instructors which many children have, their parents . . . allowing their minds to become inculcated with evil teachings before implanting the good . . . the natural tendencies toward sexual excitement are great during this period. . . . It is, therefore, of the utmost importance that the child is given a thorough education in self-control and instructed in regard to the irreparable dangers arising from a violation of the important laws of nature.

Most informed persons today scoff at the inaccuracy, sexism, and tone that was typical of much of the "informative" writing about human sexuality in the past. Most contemporary professionals would consider the attitudes expressed in the preceding excerpt to be unsound—even dangerous—approaches to raising children who will have a healthy perspective on sexuality.

Some of the most significant changes to grow out of the recent past have involved the attitudes and

---

sexual revolution: the changes in thinking about sexuality and sexual behavior in society that occurred in the 1960s and 1970s.

behaviors of women. As the availability of effective contraception increased and abortion was legalized, women were freed to acknowledge and participate in their sexuality more fully. Both men and women equally have begun to accept the fact that sexual behavior can be enjoyed. There has been an increased democratization of sex and greater acceptance of sexual differences among individuals and groups. However, some negative changes that have taken place include an increase in some sexually transmitted diseases, more obsessiveness about sex, and new waves of censorship and repression (Ellis, 1990).

It is obvious that there have been some changes in our views of human sexuality and that more are in progress. Unfortunately, there are many obstacles that prevent accurate assessment and analysis of these changes. One very significant impediment has been the mood in our society that change is very desirable, and that to be "with it" individuals must adopt more permissive sexual attitudes. This attitude clouds our ability to judge accurately how much fundamental change there has been. A second handicap is the lack of reliable scientific data on most aspects of human sexual behavior. Without research data, we are left with opinion, prejudice, and fantasy. To compound the difficulty, available information is interpreted through an intellectual framework that often assumes the sex drive to be a powerful and autonomous set of impulses that must be kept in check by social and cultural controls. It might just as legitimately be assumed that either there is no such thing as a sex drive or that it is not very powerful at all in many people and can easily be controlled and directed by inner checks exerted by the individual (Gagnon, 1990a).

A final obstacle to an accurate view of what today's sexual change is all about is the bias of many social commentators and advertisers. It serves the interests of both the sexual conservative and the sexual liberal to find the world increasingly permissive in sexual matters. The conservative can condemn the dangers of increased sexual freedom and the lowering of social constraints, while the liberal can praise the movement toward a more natural, self-directed way of sexual living. Advertisers create anxiety about sex appeal by suggesting that sex is all-important. As a consequence of all these obstacles, our present view of what is happening to sexual life-styles is often unrealistically distorted.

ROOTS OF CHANGE

Just as the sexual revolution (if we can agree on this term) has witnessed a variety of complex and interrelated changes, the very factors that led to these changes are themselves interwoven and complicated. These causative factors may be grouped into the following six main categories.

New Approaches to Morality Moral and ethical philosophies are usually in a state of flux, and they vary from culture to culture, family to family. They are influenced by and connected with political, academic, and religious ideologies. It is simplistic to blame Victorian sexual codes for all sexual problems of today, but it cannot be denied that many of the changes in moral outlooks during the past 60 years have been attempts at finding something more natural and spontaneous than the rigid, repressive Victorian approach to sex. (One extremist, though uncommon, Victorian policy demanded that librarians refrain from placing books by male and female authors next to one another on the same shelf.) Whatever physical enjoyment might have been found in sex was often marred by the guilt that sexual behavior generated. Many of today's moral codes incorporate the possibilities for situation ethics and recreation.

One of the most striking trends of Western society in the late 1960s and 1970s was increased resistance toward centralized, institutionalized authority. A counterculture movement questioned rules, regulations, and decisions that were set forth without thorough explanation or rationale. Young people challenged established values and norms that they felt robbed them of personal responsibility and the right of decision-making. The concept of Big Brotherism was feared and rejected. The mobility of our society, along with the decreasing stability of the nuclear family, created conditions that demanded more independence and self-reliance. There was a call for a return to innocence, spontaneity, and what was "natural" (Keen, 1983).

All of these developments led to a great deal of questioning of established values concerning sexual behavior. Legal restrictions on sexual activity between consenting adults gradually began to give way. Established religious restraints on sex began to shift. A number of religious groups adopted positive approaches to human sexuality in place of their restrictive, moralistic stances of the past. Academic institutions responded to the pressure by giving up their in loco parentis positions and liberalizing their residence hall policies on curfews, visits by members of the opposite sex, and privacy. Many young people no longer accepted without question the sexual values of their parents and began to develop their own standards of sexual behavior, creating conflict in some families. Before long the dominant culture began to integrate this counterculture movement into a consumption-oriented economy, and advertising picked up on the themes of naturalness, sex appeal, and instant gratification. Enjoyment of oneself

Case Study

SARAH: A GENERATION GAP IN SEXUAL VALUES

Sarah was a 17-year-old high school honor student. She was popular with her peers, respected by her teachers as an intelligent and creative young woman, and involved in school, church, and community activities. Her parents were not fond of her 20-year-old boyfriend, Jason, but they tolerated what they considered to be a puppy-love relationship. One afternoon, while cleaning Sarah's bedroom, her mother discovered birth control pills. She and her husband confronted Sarah, who admitted freely that she and Jason had been having sexual intercourse regularly. Her furious parents made arrangements for Sarah to see a counselor and forbade her from seeing the boyfriend again.

Sarah explained to the counselor, and later to her parents, that she felt she had made her sexual decisions carefully and responsibly and that she had no intentions of avoiding either her boyfriend or sex. Her parents, shocked and hurt, felt that her actions were immoral and that she was

too young to make such decisions on her own. They went through a painful questioning process attempting to understand what they had done wrong.

After several weeks of struggling at communication, including discussions with their minister, Sarah's counselor, and Jason, the parents decided that even though they could not agree with her decision or condone her actions, they would not interfere with the relationship. They decided that she would have to be free to make her own decision, whether or not they perceived it to be a mistake.

Eventually, Sarah ended her relationship with Jason, although apparently not from any parental pressure. Sarah and her parents became closer and communicated more openly following the difficult period, despite her parents' continued feeling that her decision was wrong. Sarah did not regret her relationship or the sexual experience that it had included.

and of one's own body was no longer condemned automatically as being immoral. New attitudes about sexuality moved into the mainstream of American life (Keen, 1983).

During the 1990s there has been some return to sexual values of former eras. The 1980s saw the accelerated development of conservative political and religious factions, such as the Right to Life movement and the Moral Majority, that have condemned sexual intercourse outside of marriage, many forms of sexual behavior and orientation, abortion, sex education in schools, and provision of contraception to minors without parental consent. This has resulted in some polarization in attitudes about how much personal freedom our society should allow in the sexual realm, and increased confusion for people who are trying to form their personal values and choices about sexual behavior (Hacker, 1990).

Changing Roles of Women and Men Another significant factor in sexual change has been in our shifting attitudes toward what men and women should be. Many women are no longer willing to be subjugated by

men. The traditional roles of the man as aggressive protector and provider and the woman as passive homemaker and servant have been moving toward roles that are individualized to each person's needs. Out of the renewed emancipation of women has come the realization that women have strong sexual feelings and can consider sex to be important to their lives. Women are demanding their share of sexual enjoyment and are allowing themselves the freedom to be the initiators of sexual activity (Kelley, 1987) (see chapter 6, "Gender-Identity/Role and Society").

Increased Leisure Time and Affluence For many people life today is no longer the day-to-day struggle for survival it once was. Timesaving conveniences have increased our amount of leisure time, and some people have enough money to live in comfort. In addition, the Puritan work ethic has loosened its grip, so that many individuals may use their leisure time for pleasurable pursuits without feeling profound guilt. It is not surprising, then, that many persons now feel free to spend more time—and money—on learning about sex and the development of sex appeal. Books on human sexuality abound, some valuable and carefully researched, others silly and essentially unsubstantiated.

Research Into Human Sexuality Of special importance in recent years has been the gradual increase in reliable information about human sexuality, resulting from the work of several new researchers.

During the nineteenth century, sexual matters were perceived as debased and animalistic. Consequently, many people attempted to ignore sexual needs as part of the human personality and assumed that "normal" was predominantly nonsexual. As studies on human sexual behavior began to appear, people began to realize that the sexual feelings, preferences, and behaviors they had tried so hard to ignore and hide were part of a good many other people's lives as well. This realization continues to lead us toward a greater acceptance of the normalcy of our sexual individuality, and it also has removed much of the element of secrecy from sexuality.

Research into sexual behavior has helped us to realize that "sex" does not equal sexual intercourse only. There are many other forms of sensual and sexual sharing that may enhance physical pleasure and expression of caring between people. This is of special importance at a time when AIDS makes some forms of sex, including intercourse, less safe (Hacker, 1990).

Developments in Science and Technology Two of the most significant fears that tended to dissuade people from participating in sexual activity in the past were the fear of pregnancy and the fear of venereal disease. A large part of sex education in former times consisted of reminders of these "dangers." With new advances in contraception, the risks of pregnancy have been greatly reduced. Liberalized approaches to abortion in some areas of the United States have further lessened the threat of unwanted pregnancy. The issue of legalized abortion is still being hotly debated.

While many of the venereal diseases of the past, such as syphilis and gonorrhea, have been treated and cured with antibiotics, a number of the remaining sexually transmitted diseases (STDs) of today, such as herpes, chlamydia, and AIDS, are highly contagious and resistant to treatment. AIDS itself has become a worldwide threat to life.

AIDS as an Agent for Value Change Acquired immunodeficiency syndrome, or AIDS, is widely recognized as a deadly disease that is already changing some of the fundamental ways in which people view sexual behavior. In the United States AIDS was first identified in 1981 among male homosexuals, and its virus was initially thought to be transmitted especially by sexual practices such as anal intercourse. It quickly became another excuse for prejudice, anger, and moral judgments about homosexuality.

It has now become clear that the human immunodeficiency virus (HIV) that causes this fatal disease can also be spread through heterosexual intercourse and infected blood and blood products. Caution about sex is becoming increasingly essential as the number of AIDS cases continues to rise. Whenever a choice is made to share intercourse or oral sex with anyone who has been sexually active within recent years, there is at least some risk of contracting HIV. As the awareness and fear about AIDS build, our values about sex are bound to shift. It is likely that casual sex will be seen increasingly in a negative light, and that condoms will become a required part of male homosexual and heterosexual encounters as never before (Griggs, 1987). In 1989 one study found that 58 percent of sexually active males aged 15 to 19 had used a condom during their most recent sexual intercourse, as compared to only 21 percent in 1979 (Sonenstein & Pleck, 1989). Another study of college students indicates that while they recognize AIDS as a problem objectively, that knowledge does not necessarily have much effect on their likelihood of using condoms (Ishii-Kuntz, Whitbeck, & Simons, 1990). This may reflect a prevalent attitude among younger people that "it won't happen to me." For a more complete discussion of AIDS and its implications, see chapter 15, "The AIDS Crisis and Sexual Decisions."

THE NEXT SEXUAL REVOLUTION

Ira Reiss (1990), a sociologist who has long studied sexual values and behaviors in the United States, has suggested that it is time for a new revolution in our approaches to human sexuality. He feels that far too much emphasis has been put on the "just say no" approach, which he believes is unrealistic and unsafe. While young people may once again be persuaded into promises of abstinence from sex, Reiss claims that "vows of abstinence break far more easily than do condoms." Instead, he believes that it is time for increased acceptance of a variety of sexual choices in our culture, based on values of honesty, equality, and responsibility. For example, statistics indicate that teenagers are not refraining from sexual intercourse. In fact, more adolescents than ever before are choosing to engage in sex. Reiss warns that as long as we emphasize a negative approach to sexual decision-making, people will only be less likely to take responsibility for protecting themselves from sexually transmitted disease and unintended pregnancy through the use of condoms, spermicides, and contraception.

7

His observations provide a sharp contrast to the growing emphasis on sexual abstinence at the national governmental level. In late 1990 the U.S. Department of Health and Human Services established public health goals to be met by the year 2000. Two of those goals were clearly directed at reducing sexual activity among the young. One was to "reduce the proportion of adolescents who have engaged in sexual intercourse by 50 percent for young teens and 20 percent for older teens." A second objective was to increase "to at least 40 percent the proportion of sexually-active adolescents, aged 17 and younger, who have abstained from sexual activity for the previous three months." Thus, some governmental agencies such as DHHS are now defining success in sex education and the maturity and responsibility of individual young people in terms of sexual abstinence and self-discipline (Haffner, 1991).

Reiss's call for a new revolution is not meant to be a recommendation that "anything goes" sexually. Instead, he is advocating pluralism in sexual morality (see box on p. 237). Pluralism means that there is tolerance for more than one way of believing and behaving. It totally rejects the kind of force or manipulation that results in rape or child sexual abuse. Instead it demands that people be responsible in their sexual choosing: being open and honest about what is going on, recognizing that the other person has an equal right to choose what will happen sexually, and being responsible for avoiding unwanted consequences such as pregnancy or the transmission of a disease. Pluralism recognizes that sexuality has both pleasurable and dangerous components, and that choices about sex must recognize that fact.

We have a long way to go before people may be assured that they will be treated fairly and considerately by others in sexual matters. There are more rapes and other violent sexual crimes in the United States than in most other countries, and yet we still often relegate discussion about sexuality to jokes and banter, and are reluctant to bring sex-related topics out into the open with frankness and honesty. As long as we are fettered by sexual ignorance, avoidance of sexual realities, and irresponsible sexual behavior, any sexual revolution will have been misdirected and misused.

Milestones in Sex Research: A Brief Historical Survey

Until the mid-twentieth century, serious attempts at research in sexual behavior were seldom made. A few researchers cautiously ventured into the realm of sexuality, sometimes risking their personal and professional reputations to do so. In the past 2 decades, sex research

has come of age and is considered a respectable—even attractive—pursuit. In this section I will give you a brief historical summary of some of the major advances in sex research.

EMERGING FROM THE 19TH CENTURY

The earliest sex research had to rely on historical case studies, since there were almost no other data about human sexual behavior, and it was not considered permissible to ask people about such things. Early in the nineteenth century there were some historical studies published about sexuality in classical Greek and Roman times. There was a major change in methodology, however, when in 1906 a German physician by the name of Iwan Bloch coined the term "sexual science" and began studying the history of prostitution and what he called "strange" sexual practices. Bloch's work was the first to conceive of history as an important foundation for understanding human sexuality. It has not been until quite recently that historians have accepted sexuality as a legitimate area for historical study (Bullough, 1990).

During the nineteenth century three other individuals, Richard von Krafft-Ebing, Sigmund Freud, and Henry Havelock Ellis, focused new attention on human sexuality.

In the last quarter of the nineteenth century the exploration into the subject by Krafft-Ebing, a German, and Freud, an Austrian, resulted in temporary professional ostracism for them both. The two were physicians who devoted much study to the understanding of mental disorders. Quite predictably, in a period of European history when an intensely repressive moral code governed sexual behavior and attitudes, both of these physicians found sex to be a major factor in causing emotional and mental disturbances. When sexual feelings or behaviors inevitably produced guilt, fear, and self-loathing, it might be expected that they would be at the root of many disorders.

RICHARD VON KRAFFT-EBING

The more extreme position of the two was taken by Krafft-Ebing (1840–1902), a German-born neurologist and psychiatrist who eventually became a prestigious teacher and practitioner in Vienna.

Krafft-Ebing's book *Psychopathia Sexualis*, revised through 12 editions, became a widely circulated medical text that portrayed most forms of sexual behavior and arousal as being disgusting and pathological. Krafft-Ebing grouped most sexual deviations into four classifications of pathology: sadism, masochism,

FIGURE 1.1   Sigmund Freud

Freud (1856–1939) was an Austrian neurologist who first theorized that sexuality existed throughout the life cycle and was the basic motivating factor in human behavior. He identified the basic stages of sexual emotional development as the oral, the anal, and the phallic.

fetishism, and homosexuality. Of special significance was his declaration that masturbation was the cause of all these sexual deviations. This is one example of how opinion and speculation, without a sound research basis, can be questionable and misleading. He illustrated his theories with case studies demonstrating the dire effects of masturbation. His case studies were highly sensational for the times, and they did call attention to the variety of human sexual orientations and activities. Unfortunately, his biased writings tainted most sexual behavior as being sick and unnatural. Even though Krafft-Ebing was not viewed as a mainstream sex researcher by his professional contemporaries, his perspective pervaded the medical and psychiatric professions for many years after, and still has some adherents today.

SIGMUND FREUD

Freud (1856–1939) lived nearly all of his life in Vienna and focused much of his work on the study of the psychosexual development of children and how it affected adult life and mental condition. Freud's contributions had far more influence on psychology than those of Krafft-Ebing, although they also perpetuated a decidedly negative attitude toward most aspects of human sexuality (see Fig. 1.1). In 1895 Freud published the epochal *Studies in Hysteria,* written in collaboration with Josef Breuer. The book contained discussion of the unconscious mind, repression, and free association, concepts that became the foundation for psychoanalysis. Freud had also become convinced that neuroses were produced by unconscious conflicts of a sexual nature, an idea that alienated most scientists of his time. In 1905 his *Three Essays on the Theory of Sexuality* precipitated another storm of protest. It was in this work that Freud developed his theory of infantile sexuality and attempted to demonstrate how adult sexual perversions were distortions of childhood sexual expressions (see chapter 7, "Sexuality Through the Life Cycle").

Many of his European contemporaries considered Freud's ideas marginal. His work was highly influential in the United States, however, where for a time publishing in the area of human sexuality was dominated by psychoanalysts who espoused Freudian theories of psychosexual development. There is today much disagreement as to the value of psychoanalysis and Freud's theories of sexuality, particularly his views about female sexuality. His emphasis, for example, on the superiority of vaginal orgasms—and of the women who experience them—has caused unwarranted frustration and self-devaluation for many women. This idea of Freud's has not been supported as accurate by research. He has also been accused of trying to deny and suppress the occurrence of incestual sexual relationships between fathers and daughters (Taynen, 1990). His work, nonetheless, led to an increased interest in sex and a willingness to think and talk about sexuality. Although he called most forms of sexual variance "perversions" and considered them to be signs of immaturity, Freud did not brand sexual behaviors as immoral, criminal, or pathological (Brecher, 1979). Through his work, sexuality became a legitimate concern of medicine and psychology.

HENRY HAVELOCK ELLIS

At the end of the nineteenth century an English sex researcher with a new perspective made his presence known. Henry Havelock Ellis (1859–1939) spent several decades studying all available information on human sexuality in the Western world and the sexual mores of other cultures (see Fig. 1.2). As a physician he studied the sex lives of his contemporaries and

9

FIGURE 1.2 Henry Havelock Ellis

Ellis (1859–1939), an English physician, invented the term *autoeroticism* to indicate the occurrence of masturbation in both sexes and all ages. He was farsighted in his views, particularly of the way sexuality affects women and the way mental attitude affects physical behavior.

carefully recorded what he learned. Eventually he began writing about his findings and published them in six volumes between 1896 and 1910 as *Studies in the Psychology of Sex.* A seventh volume was added in 1928 (Ellis, 1936).

If there has been a sexual revolution since Victorian times, Ellis certainly played a major role in effecting it. His *Studies* recognized that human beings exhibited great variety in their sexual inclinations and behaviors and that sexual mores are determined by cultural and social influences. His conclusions were radical by Victorian standards, amazingly farsighted by present-day standards. Ellis noted that masturbation was a common practice in males and females at all ages. He realized that homosexuality and heterosexuality in people existed in degrees rather than as absolutes. He legitimized the idea that women could have as great a sexual desire as men, and he pointed out that the orgasms of men and women were remarkably similar. Anticipating later trends in sex therapy, Ellis recognized that difficulties in achieving erection or orgasm were generally psychological problems

rather than physical. Here we can see a swing of the pendulum toward increasing attention given to physical bases for some sexual dysfunctions, such as erectile difficulty. Ellis emphasized what most professionals today accept, that "the range of variation within fairly normal limits is immense" when considering the sexual needs and behaviors of humans.

SEXUAL STUDIES IN THE EARLY 20TH CENTURY

In 1926 a Dutch physician by the name of Theodoor van de Velde (1873–1937) published the first edition of his book *Ideal Marriage.* Although it was not the only sex manual available at the time, it was significant because van de Velde intuitively knew how to balance the permission to be sexually responsive against the inhibitions left over from Victorianism (Brecher, 1979). A revised edition of the book is still available for those interested in this aspect of history.

Although van de Velde's suggestions for a more fulfilling sexual relationship were described in a marriage-oriented framework with some moralistic boundaries, and with an almost obsessive attention to cleanliness, he put forth a generally positive outlook, for which people by this time were ready. His book described a variety of coital positions, the use of oral sex in foreplay, and suggestions for dealing with some sexual problems. Because of the popularity of *Ideal Marriage,* his ideas played an important role in helping thousands of couples to achieve more sexual enjoyment.

One of the outstanding sex research efforts of the early twentieth century was a study published in 1932 by Robert Latou Dickinson called *A Thousand Marriages.* Between 1882 and 1924 Dickinson gathered 5,200 case studies of women he had treated while he was a gynecologist in New York City. In his analysis of the cases, he documented how the repressive sexual attitudes of childhood led to disastrous effects on adult sexual functioning—one of the earliest attempts at a better understanding of female sexuality. He also studied the physiological responses of the clitoris, vagina, and cervix during sexual stimulation and orgasm. Realizing that once a woman has been able to experience the pleasure of a self-induced orgasm she is more likely to have orgasm during intercourse, he introduced the use of electrical vibrators for women.

Another pioneer in the sexual liberation of women was Helena Wright, who began her gynecological medical practice in London in the 1920s. She discovered that most women found no enjoyment in sex and instead considered it to be a marital duty. She began publishing books that instructed women on how to achieve orgasm, through both intercourse and masturbation. The first of her books was *The Sex Factor in Marriage,* published in 1930. Subsequent editions of the book and Wright's other publications continued for decades to give explicit instructions to women on becoming fully acquainted with their sex organs and sexual responses.

MID-CENTURY SEX RESEARCH

The outstanding sex researcher at mid-century was Alfred C. Kinsey (1894–1956), a successful zoologist who gradually moved into research on human sexual behavior (see Fig. 1.3). It was through Kinsey's work that sex research became a more legitimate scientific pursuit than it had been, for he applied statistical analysis to sexual behavior instead of drawing conclusions solely from personal observations as most of his predecessors had done. In 1937 as a conservative and highly respected biology professor at Indiana University, Kinsey was selected to teach a new course in sexuality and marriage. In preparing lectures and attempting to answer the questions of his students, Kinsey began to realize that there was little reliable information about sexuality. He began gathering information by interviewing people about their sex lives, eventually involving associates in the interviews. By the end of 1949 he had gathered detailed histories on the sexual lives of more than 16,000 people.

Kinsey founded and directed Indiana University's Institute for Sex Research. Now called the Kinsey Institute for Research in Sex, Gender, and Reproduction (commonly known as the Kinsey Institute for Sex Research, or, more simply, the Kinsey Institute), it remains a major center for reliable sex research. Paul Gebhard (Gebhard & Johnson, 1979) and Wardell Pomeroy (1972) became Kinsey's principal collaborators and have described in detail the statistical approaches and skillful interview techniques that have rendered the Kinsey studies so valuable. The two studies that brought Kinsey wide recognition and notoriety were *Sexual Behavior in the Human Male*, published in 1948, and *Sexual Behavior in the Human Female*, published in 1953, both of which still serve as major sources of statistics on sexual behavior and are considered milestones in this field. Some of his findings are described throughout the chapters of this book.

There are numerous other sex researchers who made important contributions midway through this century. Among them are Niles Newton and Mary Jane Sherfey. Both have been influential in helping to further the understanding of female sexuality. In the mid-1950s Niles Newton published an important book,

FIGURE 1.3   Alfred C. Kinsey

Kinsey (1894–1956), above, was a zoologist, later a biology professor, who was instrumental in compiling face-to-face interviews with thousands of people about their sexual behavior. His work, not highly regarded in his lifetime, has come to be regarded as comprehensive, systematic, and the model upon which all other studies are based.

Maternal Emotions, emphasizing the intricate relationship between sexual feelings and a woman's reactions to menstruation, pregnancy, childbirth, breast-feeding, infant care, and sexual intercourse. Her study was based on interviews with many women. Later work done in collaboration with her husband, Michael Newton, demonstrated a close correlation between the female body's physiological responses during coitus and those during breast-feeding of infants (Newton & Newton, 1967). The research of the Newtons demonstrated how a woman's sexuality is often intimately related to many aspects of being a woman and a mother.

Mary Jane Sherfey studied under Alfred Kinsey at Indiana University, and this was a major influence behind her decision to study female sexuality. She has meticulously examined the sexual patterns of primates and attempted to understand the evolutionary, psychological, and physiological determinants of female sexual responsiveness (and the lack of it). To the

11

professional world, she argued against the old Freud-ian concept of the clitoris as an undersized, inadequate penis, showing the entire inner clitoral system of the female to be as powerful and sexually responsive as the male penis, perhaps more so. Sherfey went on to offer a comprehensive theory explaining why so many women find little enjoyment in sex, implicating West-ern society's long-standing repressive attitudes toward female sexuality (Sherfey, 1972). She also speculated on the cultural implications of the repression: that the male power structure feared the strength of female sexuality and therefore had a stake in repressing it. This aspect of her work has received less support. Regardless of the anthropological accuracy of her ideas, Mary Jane Sherfey opened up new perspectives on the sexual potential of women.

RECENT DIRECTIONS IN SEX RESEARCH

Recent milestones in sex research are too numerous to detail in this book, except for some highlights. Impor-tant studies on human sexuality continue to come from the Kinsey Institute for Research in Sex, Gender, and Reproduction. Paul Gebhard took over as director of the Institute after Kinsey's death and was succeeded in 1982 by June Reinisch. The Institute has contributed important studies on homosexuality, nudism, sexual deviance, sex offenders, sexual development in chil-dren and adolescents, prostitution, the development of sexual orientation, and many other topics.

During the early 1990s the Institute published several important collections of sex research, and Reinisch has attempted to bring up-to-date sex infor-mation to the general public through her syndicated newspaper column.

Another extensive study of human sexual behav-ior was carried out by Kinsey Institute researchers in 1970. Because of delays in analyzing the data and arguments over authorship of the book in which the data are described, publication of the results of the study was delayed for years. When the book finally appeared (Klassen, Williams, & Levitt, 1989), the study turned out to be an examination of sexual attitudes of 3,018 people, most of whom were married. There were suggestions from the data that our conclu-sions about sexual liberation during the late sixties were somewhat exaggerated. Critics of the study have maintained that conclusions about behavior based on attitude preferences are risky, since people sometimes behave sexually in ways that violate their own attitudes and values.

Another particularly significant area of research has been centered on studies of masculinity and femi-ninity. What are the factors that cause us to be born as

FIGURE 1.4 Virginia E. Johnson and William H. Masters

Masters and Johnson were the first researchers to actually observe, monitor, and film the physiological responses of people engaged in coitus or masturbation. This initial research led them to develop techniques for treating sexual dysfunction effectively.

males or females, and then mold our identities as men, women, or something in between? A pioneering sex researcher who has been attempting to answer these questions is John Money at the Johns Hopkins Hospital in Baltimore, Maryland. He and others who have followed his lead have explored the role of chromo-somes, hormones, and social factors in the develop-ment of gender identity. This work will be discussed in more detail in chapter 6, "Gender-Identity/Role and Society."

The two recent researchers who have contributed more to our knowledge of sexual functioning than any predecessor are William H. Masters and Virginia E. Johnson (see Fig. 1.4), now co-directors of the Masters and Johnson Institute in St. Louis, Missouri. Their work has focused on two major areas: the physiology of human sexual response and the treatment of sexual dysfunctioning.

From 1855 to 1955 several studies were published that described measurements of various human physi-ological responses during intercourse and masturba-tion. During the 1940s even Kinsey and his associates had observed intercourse and recorded the physiologi-cal responses of the participants. Yet many questions remained unanswered. William Masters launched his research study in 1954 and hired Virginia Johnson as an interviewer soon after. In the decade that followed, Masters and Johnson and their associates used sophisticated instrumentation to measure the physiological responses during masturbation and coitus of 694 individuals. In total, they studied more than 10,000 orgasms in these laboratory conditions. The detailed account of their work is in *Human Sexual Response* (Masters & Johnson, 1966).

Their second major research effort began in 1959, proceeding simultaneously with the studies on sexual response. For 5 years Masters and Johnson developed and perfected clinical techniques for the treatment of male and female sexual dysfunctioning. In 1965 they considered that their therapy methods were demonstrably effective and began to charge fees for the 2-week treatment that had been developed. In 1970 their revolutionary treatment format was described in *Human Sexual Inadequacy,* a book that inaugurated the age of sex therapy. Numerous other workers have now modified and enlarged upon the Masters and Johnson work, and sex therapy has become a distinct discipline of medicine and psychology.

During the mid-1970s Masters and Johnson also studied the sexual responsiveness and case histories of homosexual men and women. The results of this study were published in *Homosexuality in Perspective* (Masters & Johnson, 1979). Not unexpectedly, they discovered (after observing the physiological sexual responses of 94 homosexual men and 82 homosexual women) that the physiological responses were the same as in the heterosexuals they had studied earlier. They also confirmed what had long been assumed by observers of human sexual behavior: homosexuals who are motivated to do so can function sexually with members of the opposite sex as well. This study provided further substantiation for how significantly social and cultural factors can influence sexual response. While some basic aspects of sexual orientation are established early in ways we do not yet fully understand, specific *behavior* can sometimes be influenced by personal choice. Critics of the work have emphasized that motivation was a crucial element with the subjects in this research. There were people who very much *wanted* to have sex with members of the other gender, regardless of their primary orientation. Even Masters and Johnson did not want their work misconstrued as an indication that homosexual orientation was a matter of choice or that all homosexuals could change their behavior.

SURVEYS OF THE SEVENTIES AND EIGHTIES

As information about human sexuality began to proliferate, curiosity about the sexual behaviors of others began to increase. It became obvious that there were few reliable facts about what people felt, wanted, did, or fantasized about sexuality. The seventies became the decade of the sex survey, and books and magazines were filled with new peeks at the most private details of sex lives in the United States. Some of the surveys were conducted with methods reliable enough to lend the results credibility, while others suffered from serious inadequacies.

The Hunt Report   The largest survey on sexual behavior since the Kinsey studies was commissioned in the early 1970s by the Playboy Foundation. A private research foundation selected people from telephone books in 24 U.S. cities at random. Twenty percent of these individuals then agreed to complete a questionnaire, and data were gathered from 982 men and 1,044 women. The results were reported by professional journalist Morton Hunt in the book *Sexual Behavior in the 1970s,* which was published in 1975. The questionnaire employed in the survey asked over 1,000 questions about people's sexual histories and attitudes. There were four different versions of the questionnaire designed for men and women, married and unmarried. In addition to the written questionnaire, there were small-group discussions among participants on trends in sexual behavior in this country. There have been criticisms of the statistical validity of the Hunt Report, and the results should certainly be interpreted with care. However, the study did provide the most comprehensive data since Kinsey and is cited frequently in discussions of human sexual behavior. There was enough similarity between Hunt's study and Kinsey's research, conducted a quarter of a century earlier, to provide a basis for noting changes in patterns of sexual living that had occurred over this period of time. I have used statistics from the Hunt Report in this book.

The Hite Reports   In 1976 Shere Hite's report on female sexuality, *The Hite Report,* became a best-seller and opened up several issues for debate and discussion, including the degree of dissatisfaction women tended to express about their sexual relationships. Hite received completed questionnaires from 3,019 women (a very small proportion of the questionnaires she had distributed) concerning many aspects of their sexuality. The questionnaire asked for essay-type answers and therefore provided much anecdotal information as well as data that could be quantified. Hite later surveyed 7,239 men with a similar questionnaire, the results of which became *The Hite Report on Male Sexuality* (Hite, 1981). The results of this survey provided new insights into how men view their sexuality and sexual behavior. Her recent study, *Women and Love* (Hite, 1987), claims that women are generally unhappy with their loving relationships and that more than 70 percent

of the female respondents had experienced an affair. The response rate to the questionnaire used in this study was only 4 percent, considered very small.

The Hite studies have been criticized for being unrepresentative samples and for their lack of hard statistical analysis. Some critics have also claimed that the questions on the surveys were leading and thus biased the answers. While most sexologists recognize the limitations and methodological weaknesses of this type of research, the Hite reports are still rich with information and personal stories about the sex lives of several thousand people. Regardless of whether they represent all people, their anecdotes and answers surely represent the feelings, fears, and behaviors of some. Like all research, the Hite survey results must be weighed carefully with other information available.

Research on Childhood Sexuality Two international studies have been crucial in providing new understandings about sexuality during childhood, a much-neglected area until quite recently. Ronald and Juliette Goldman (1982) interviewed 838 children in Australia, North America, England, and Sweden concerning what they thought about sex, their relationships with others, and their sex education. The researchers found North American children to be the least well-informed about sex-related facts and issues.

The German researcher Ernest Borneman (1983) has been researching childhood sexuality for over 30 years, mostly through various types of interview surveys. Some of this work was longitudinal in scope, with several hundred research subjects being studied over a period of 20 years or more. His findings have tended to discount some of the widely held Freudian views of children's psychosexual development. Both the Goldman and Borneman studies have concluded that there is no evidence to support the existence of the latency period in children, a stage in development that Freud claimed was characterized by little interest in or awareness of sexual feelings. All recent research tends to support the notion that children are sexual from birth and have a diversity of sexual feelings, behaviors, and interests as they grow.

Other Surveys There have been several other important surveys since 1970. Robert Sorensen (1973) published *Adolescent Sexuality in Contemporary America,* based on answers from several hundred adolescents. Melvin Zelnik and John Kantner (1980) have used sophisticated research designs and methods of statisti-

latency period: a stage in human development characterized, in Freud's theory, by little interest in or awareness of sexual feelings.

14

cal analysis to study the sexual and contraceptive behaviors of teenagers. Their surveys have represented some of the most reliable data available today on teenage sexual behavior.

In the mid-1970s *Redbook Magazine* published a questionnaire about female sexuality to which over 100,000 women responded. While the results could not be considered representative of the general female population, the study constituted one of the largest samples of women's attitudes and behaviors ever attempted. The *Redbook* survey conveyed a picture of U.S. women as having active sex lives and often initiating sexual activities with their partners. Most of the women expressed relative satisfaction with their marital sex, although one-third had said they had experienced extramarital sexual relations. Nearly all of the women had, at one time or another, participated in oral-genital sex. The more religious the women in the study considered themselves, the more satisfied they were with their marital sex, and the less likely they were to have cohabited with a partner prior to marriage (Tavris & Sadd, 1977).

Alan Bell, Martin Weinberg, and Sue Kiefer Hammersmith (1981), of the Kinsey Institute, published the results of a unique study of homosexuality called *Sexual Preference—Its Development in Men and Women*. From a pool of 4,639 homosexual individuals, they conducted extensive interviews with 979, obtaining the most in-depth data of any study on homosexuality ever conducted. Although the research focused on homosexual people in only one area of the country, the San Francisco Bay area, it is still recognized as crucial to our understanding of sexual orientation and its development.

Philip Blumstein and Pepper Schwartz (1983), sociologists at the University of Washington, studied completed questionnaires from 4,314 heterosexual couples, 969 gay male couples, and 788 lesbian couples on various aspects of their relationships. Their report, titled *American Couples,* is considered to be a strong and important sociological study because of its large and diverse sample and its complicated research design. It provided a fresh perspective on the ways in which modern couples were approaching their sexual and loving relationships.

A 1990 survey from the Kinsey Institute (Reinisch & Beasley, 1990) examined the basic sexual knowledge of Americans and their sources of sex information while growing up. Eighteen questions about human sexuality were developed from the most frequently asked questions in letters to the Institute. Participants in the study were 1,974 women and men, selected randomly to represent a national sample. Although there have been criticisms about the questions asked in the survey, 55 percent of the participants failed the test, calling into question just how knowledgeable about sexuality Americans really are. Men tended to be better informed about general sexual matters such as intercourse and masturbation, while women performed better on questions relating to sexual health and birth control. The most common sources of sex information during the respondents' formative years were friends (42 percent), mothers (29 percent), and books (22 percent). Formalized sex education and fathers trailed behind the other sources cited.

RESEARCH TRENDS FOR THE NINETIES

The Kinsey Institute has been placing increased emphasis on the public's right to know about sexual matters. The Institute's director, June Reinisch, has a special interest in studying the effects that the hormones and drugs a child is exposed to during prenatal development can have on later behavior. There is also research planned to examine masculine and feminine roles and the development of the biological determinants of the psychological characteristics associated with adult maleness and femaleness. Reinisch would like to find funding to re-interview 2,000 members of the original Kinsey research population sample, to determine more about the reliability of retrospective studies (Hall, 1986).

Research funds for the next few years will be available to scientists who wish to study the implications of various forms of sexual behavior for the spread of the AIDS virus. This is one of the motivations behind an extensive new study of human sexual behavior being proposed by the National Institute on Child Health and Human Development. The research would involve the questioning of some 20,000 people about their sexual activities. However, opponents of the study in Congress and the Administration have managed to block any progress with this research through a series of political moves (Marshall, 1991). They have also expressed concerns over invasion of privacy and have wanted to limit the questions to information concerning sexual behaviors specifically linked to the transmission of AIDS. The researchers hope to survey broader aspects of sexual behavior. This study would cost over $15 million and would attempt to work with a population sample representative of the entire United States. If this study is eventually funded, its results would constitute the most extensive data since the Kinsey studies of 1948 and 1953, and the largest research project on human sexual behavior ever attempted (Booth, 1989a; Libby, 1990).

Puzzled by the many variations in the way AIDS may be spread, the World Health Organization (WHO) is conducting a major study on sexual behavior in at least 20

15

countries. Some scientists have noted the irony of the fact that Third World countries are ready to study sexual activity in depth, while proposals for such study in the United States have become mired in political debates. One of the major methodological difficulties of the international project will be designing a questionnaire that can be translated into many different languages, so that anyone may understand the sexual issues being addressed. Cross-cultural differences must also be considered. For example, in some regions of Nigeria, polygamy (marriage to more than one spouse) is accepted as part of the culture. If a man there reports having had sex with several different women during a certain time period, it should not be assumed that the man has been promiscuous. It may instead mean that he has several wives. The WHO study will gather information on religious attitudes, educational levels, condom use, knowledge about AIDS, and premarital and extramarital sex. It will represent the only coordinated international research on sexual behavior ever conducted on a major scale (Booth, 1989b).

As sex research gains in popularity and respectability, its future surely holds exciting new prospects for understanding human sexuality. As the next section shows, there are many issues to be considered when embarking on a project in sex research.

Sexological Research Today

Today the scientific method is considered the most reliable basis for establishing new knowledge in any field. Research into the interdisciplinary realm of sexology has been increasing, and now several professional journals are devoted exclusively to new concepts, controversies, and information relating to human sexuality. It has taken a long time, but the study of sexuality is finally gaining respect as a scholarly and academically respectable pursuit.

It is important to remember that scientific research does not take place in a social vacuum. Scientists and what they study are influenced by social and cultural circumstances. People learn how to be sexual, *and* learn how to be scientists, within specific cultures. The study of sexuality must take that fact into consideration (Gagnon, 1990a).

Theories about human sexuality represent a consensus among researchers in the field about the best ways to observe and explain things relating to sex. There is a great deal of confusion between what Money (1991) terms *sexology*, or the science of sex, and what he calls *sexosophy*, the ideology or philosophy of sex. He asserts that much of what is passed off without question as scientific information regarding human sexuality is actually ideological statement with-

out real scientific merit. Political agendas are often at the root of claims that use scientific information to exaggerate apprehensions and misconceptions about what is really going on in society. In the years to come, we will have to learn how to become more astute at separating valid sex research from ideological hype.

Considering the controversial nature of the pioneering sex research they wanted to undertake, earlier workers such as Alfred Kinsey and William Masters had built solid reputations for themselves in other areas before actually venturing into sexology. They recognized that establishing their own respectability was essential to eventual acceptance of their findings. Their cautious and deliberate approaches paved the way for the sex research of the future.

Aside from having to be concerned about the respectability of researching sex-related topics, there are other problems in establishing oneself as a sex researcher. Foremost among these is finding necessary funds to support research. Comprehensive scientific study tends to require substantial amounts of money, and such money is more available for work that has clear-cut practical applications. Governmental agencies, private foundations, and industry are generally more interested in funding research that will either lead to money-saving solutions to social problems or generate money from selling a new product. Scientists doing research designed to yield basic scientific data about sexual attitudes, the physiology of sexual response, or the origins of human sexual orientation will often find financing more difficult. This is one of the reasons why much attitudinal research today is conducted with college students—usually those taking psychology courses—which creates a somewhat distorted view of some issues.

Political climates may also determine how fundable sex research can be in the future. If an issue such as pornography becomes a significant topic for political debate, as it did in the Nixon and Reagan administrations, government funding may suddenly emerge to carry out scientific research. Unfortunately, political agendas and political philosophies only too often have a way of biasing the interpretations of scientific data and conclusions, as happened with the Attorney General's Commission on Pornography established by President Reagan (Lynn, 1986). We look at this subject further in chapter 17, "Sex, Art, the Media, and the Law."

COLLECTING RESEARCH DATA ON HUMAN SEXUALITY

One of the goals of scientific research is to find information that can then be generalized to the real world outside of the study. Science offers hope of being able to under-

" Another of those damned sex surveys, I suppose."   © Punch ROTHCO

stand, predict, and perhaps control various phenomena. Obviously, using human beings as research subjects creates many problems, for we are not as easily categorized or experimentally controlled as mice or molecules. Here are some of the particular methodological strategies used in conducting sex research.

Selecting Population Samples   When attempting to answer some questions about human sexuality, we would obviously find it impossible to get information about all human beings. Therefore, it is necessary to select a sample of the human population from which the results may be generalized to the larger population. The more people that can be included in the sample, and the more proportionally representative they can be to the various characteristics in the total population, the more statistically reliable the study may be considered to be. The best population sample is a random sample, in which individuals are selected at random from the whole population. If a significant enough number of persons is selected, the sample can be assumed to be very representative of the whole. However, such studies must also be large and expensive, so very little research of this sort has been conducted for groups as big as the entire U.S. population.

The Kinsey sex research published in 1948 and 1953 is still considered among the most reliable statistical research on human sexual behavior, since Kinsey's workers conducted carefully structured interviews with 12,000 people from many different segments of the population. Nevertheless, there has been a great deal of debate about the usefulness and reliability of his findings (Cochran, Mosteller, & Tukey, 1953; Gebhard & Johnson, 1979).

There are various forms of bias that may enter human research studies and influence the results and conclusions. Researchers may inadvertently bias a study by failing to select an adequately representative sample. On the other side of the coin, not everyone may be willing to participate in a study on sexuality, or be honest even if he or she agrees to participate. This creates volunteer bias that is bound to affect the outcome of research (Clement, 1990). The volunteer basis of subject participation is especially limiting. Robert Sorenson's study of adolescent sexuality, cited earlier, provides a good example of this limitation. He first asked parents' permission to interview their youngsters. Most agreed, but some did not. He then sought the cooperation of the youngsters themselves. Again, most, but not all, cooperated. Thus, there was some inaccuracy in the conclusions, especially as they might have been generalized to the general adolescent population.

Taking Surveys   Asking people questions about some aspect of their sexual attitudes or behaviors is one of the most common methods employed by sex researchers. This may be accomplished either in face-to-face interviews, telephone interviews, or through completion of questionnaires. The most-surveyed group in the United States has been college students. They are often asked to complete questionnaires on sexuality, since they represent a population accessible to faculty working on research. Care must be taken in generalizing such data to other populations.

Kinsey used a very detailed face-to-face interviewing procedure, in which researchers were carefully

sample: a representative group of a population that is the focus of a scientific poll or study.
random sample: a representative group of the larger population that is the focus of a scientific poll or study in which care is taken to select participants without a pattern that might sway research results.

trained in techniques to establish an accepting attitude and to avoid "leading" people into answers, thus attempting to minimize dishonesty and other forms of research bias. Printed questionnaires are an efficient and economical way of gathering information from large numbers of people, but it is much more difficult to detect dishonest answers, misunderstandings, exaggeration, or frivolity than in face-to-face interviews. Also, research has shown that people willing to complete sexuality questionnaires tend to have less guilt and fear about sex, and to have more heterosexual experience, than those who do not volunteer for such surveys (Clement, 1990). In other words, the results may reflect a certain type of personality rather than the total population. Therefore, results from most surveys and generalizations drawn from them must be interpreted cautiously.

Case Studies and Clinical Research   Professional counselors, physicians, psychologists, and other clinicians often work with an individual who is experiencing some sexual concern or problem. They employ various treatment strategies to help the individual, and may devise new methods. These professionals may discover that these strategies and methods are effective for large numbers of clients or patients and will sort out the characteristics that are most effective. Case studies may then be published, giving an in-depth look at particular individual circumstances. While it is risky to overgeneralize from case studies, these studies offer new ideas and perspectives to be considered. Some valuable and useful insights have been presented to the professional community from case study research.

When some sort of treatment strategy is tested with larger numbers of people, it is called clinical research. The study may consider the cause, treatment, and prevention of a disease or condition. For example, Masters and Johnson (1970) conducted clinical studies for several years on nearly 800 individuals who complained of various forms of sexual dysfunction, categorizing and labeling the problems, looking for possible causes, and trying out a variety of treatment methods. They then did follow-up studies with some of the individuals over a 5-year period. While, again, generalizations to the entire population must be done with great caution in such a study, the studies offered a conceptual framework on which the new field of sex therapy has been built. Clinical studies of this sort provide a foundation to which further research can add. Only too often, however, generalizations from clinical studies have been applied erroneously and broadly to larger populations. This is risky, since clinical populations represent people who have problems. Until recently most of our assumptions about homosexuality came from clinical work, and those assumptions were largely flawed, since only homosexual persons who had problems were being considered.

Observational Research   Some researchers have chosen to observe an aspect of human sexual behavior directly, thus eliminating the biases characteristic of research in which people report on themselves. Observational studies may take place in laboratory settings or in the field. Anthropologists, for example, tend to study groups of people in their natural settings. The Masters and Johnson (1966) research on human sexual response, discussed earlier in this chapter, is an example of a classic laboratory-based observational study. Various types of instrumentation were used to measure the physiological reactions of 694 people when they were aroused sexually. It was the first large-scale research in which observations were made in a systematic manner of the body's sexual responses.

Masters and Johnson have always been careful to point out that their findings may not apply to the responses of all human beings. Since it is especially difficult to bring a random sample to this kind of observational research, it is often criticized for its narrowness. Correctly or not, however, physiologists have typically assumed when dealing with the processes of the human body that such activities really are very similar among different people. There is, of course, little means by which to determine how much—if at all—the laboratory setting might affect people's functioning. Most sexologists, nevertheless, have accepted the findings of Masters and Johnson, and many other observational researchers, as fundamental to our understanding of human sexuality.

Experimental Research   A keystone of science is the use of the controlled experiment. In this type of research, the investigator examines what happens to a particular variable being studied and manipulated, while an attempt is made to control all other variables and keep them constant. The researcher may then draw inferences about cause-and-effect relationships that are difficult or impossible to draw from other kinds of research.

However, well-controlled experiments are difficult to design for human subjects, whose complexity

case study: an in-depth look at a particular individual and how he or she might have been helped to solve a sexual or other problem. Case studies may offer new and useful ideas for counselors to use with other patients.

clinical research: the study of the cause, treatment, or prevention of a disease or condition by testing large numbers of people.

controlled experiment: research in which the investigator examines what is happening to one variable while all other variables are kept constant.

variable: an aspect of a scientific study that is subject to change.

makes it nearly impossible to control all possible variables. Additionally, there is always the chance that the artificiality of a controlled experimental setting may influence the outcome of research with humans. For these reasons, experimental research evidence in human sexuality is sparse and ultimately open to the same sorts of shortcomings and criticisms found in other methods of study.

ETHICAL ISSUES IN SEX RESEARCH

In recent years a great deal of attention has focused on the need to protect and respect those people who participate as subjects in any form of human research. Because sexuality is viewed as such a private aspect of life, the ethical issues involved in sex research are particularly evident and crucial.

Since the 1970s, scientific groups have affirmed the right of informed consent, meaning that human research subjects deserve to have complete prior information about the purpose of the study and how they will be asked to participate. It has been generally agreed that researchers do not have the right to coerce people into participation or to be dishonest in presenting information about the research. Similarly, scientists have the obligation to protect the confidentiality of their participants, making certain that personal, private facts can never be connected with a particular individual. They must also protect subjects from physical and psychological harm. Researchers use a variety of methods to provide for anonymity in collecting data and to prevent inappropriate release of confidential information at some later time (Masters et al., 1980).

Universities and governmental agencies usually have human-research committees that must approve any research design that will involve human participation. What often must be carefully weighed by these committees is the potential value of the research to society versus any inherent stresses, risks, or dangers for the participants. The decision to allow an investigator to proceed with such research is not always an easy one.

New Attitudes Toward Sexuality

We can now take a closer look at some of the more specific changes that have taken place concerning how people think about their sexuality. It is important to emphasize that not all people have experienced changes in their attitudes toward sex. However, whether or not they have felt the changes in an inner personal sense, nearly everyone has been affected by them in one way or another. The changes are a part of our social and cultural growth.

As sex-related issues receive more publicity and research clarifies the diversity of human sexual behavior, the old taboos gradually slip away. The body is again being viewed as something of beauty and pleasure, with positive value. Many individuals who have felt that they were different, and therefore were lonely, feel less alienated as they find that a significant number of other people share their inclinations and feelings.

We seem to be in an era of transition, during which two sets of attitudes are existing side by side. One continues to encourage increased freedom in sexual matters. The other is decidedly uncomfortable with sexual freedom and tends to deny the existence of sexual feelings and behaviors. It is probably not appropriate to describe contemporary society as sexually "permissive," since there is no clear societal or cultural norm of permissiveness. In fact, our culture presently lacks any clearly identifiable sexual norm and continues to send mixed messages of sexual permission and restriction (Hacker, 1990). Nevertheless, there have been some gradual shifts in sex-related attitudes over recent decades.

ATTITUDES TOWARD MASTURBATION

Fears about masturbation seem to have stemmed originally from biblical references to the "sin" of Onan. Mentioned only briefly in biblical texts, Onan had been directed by God to have intercourse with the widow of his brother, to produce children. Because Onan instead "spilled the semen on the ground," God slew him (Genesis 38:9). Some interpreted that as God's displeasure with an act of masturbation. In the late eighteenth century, two observations compounded this negative attitude. One was that individuals with many sexual partners were more likely to have diseases of the sex organs. The other was that mental patients and other institutionalized people were sometimes seen masturbating, because they were afforded little privacy for any sort of sexual activity. Since the germ theory of disease had not yet been formulated, and little was known either about human sexual behavior or the causes of mental illness, it was assumed that sexual activity was to blame for physical and mental disorders because it overstimulated the nervous system. From

informed consent: the consent given by research subjects, indicating their willingness to participate in a study, after they are informed about the purpose of the study and how they will be asked to participate.

these contexts came the early idea that sexual self-stimulation was immoral and/or unhealthy.

In Richard von Krafft-Ebing's standard medical text of the Victorian period, *Psychopathia Sexualis,* the typical 1880s European attitude toward masturbation was expressed as follows:

> Nothing is so prone to contaminate . . . the source of all noble and ideal sentiments . . . as the practice of masturbation in early years. It despoils the unfolding bud of perfume and beauty, and leaves behind only the coarse, animal desire for sexual satisfaction. . . . The glow of sensual sensibility wanes, and the inclination toward the opposite sex is weakened. This defect influences the morals, the character, fancy, feeling and instinct of the youthful masturbator, male or female, in an unfavorable manner, even causing, under certain circumstances, the desire for the opposite sex to sink to nil. (Krafft-Ebing, 1965 translation, pp. 188–89)

This was a pretty gruesome outlook on masturbation, and it influenced the attitudes of the medical profession and laypersons for many years. It reflected the predominant value of the time, which held that the only normal, nonpathological sex was intercourse between a married man and woman, and the less said or done about that the better. Masturbation was blamed for homosexuality, insanity, sterility, and a variety of other conditions. Parents were so frightened by the possible consequences of masturbation that they purchased metal hand mitts and contraptions to cover the genitals to prevent masturbation in their children.

Gradually, throughout the twentieth century, the attitude toward masturbation became more tolerant. Eventually it was accepted that very occasional masturbation might not have any long-lasting effects, but it was still assumed that frequent masturbation could be debilitating. When Alfred Kinsey's (1948, 1953) statistics appeared, it was realized that masturbation was an extremely prevalent practice. Nearly all males (92 percent) reported masturbating to orgasm at some time in their lives, most of them many times. Of the females, 58 percent reported masturbating to orgasm, with an additional 4 percent masturbating without reaching orgasm.

Today prevailing professional opinion seems to be that masturbation is a very normal part of human sexual expression, common in youngsters and usually continuing to some extent well into adulthood and old age. It is often viewed as a healthy outlet for sexual tension and as a desirable way to learn about sexual responsiveness. It is now known to be a self-limiting phenomenon, and the general consensus is that, from a medical point of view, there is no such thing as too much masturbation. It seems to hold true even today, however, that masturbation is a more positively sanctioned behavior for males in our

society than it is for females (Story, 1985). There is more about masturbation in chapter 10, "Solitary Sex and Shared Sex."

ATTITUDES TOWARD PREMARITAL SEX

One of the strongest of the traditional sexual standards used to be that of premarital chastity. Until very recently the predominant attitude held that it was wrong on moral and religious grounds for a couple to have intercourse without the bond of marriage, a view still held by some.

To a degree, however, the double standard was always operative, making premarital sex less of an infraction for males than it was for females. Males were assumed to have uncontrollable sexual urges that a "good girl" would not allow to progress beyond the point where coitus became inevitable. Young women who "made a mistake" and were exposed by pregnancy or gossip generally suffered some negative social sanctions. Among college students well into the 1950s and 1960s, many women chose to be technical virgins, participating in sexual acts to orgasm but not allowing intercourse to occur.

Current studies show that among young people the attitudes toward premarital sex have changed. The majority of young men and women no longer condemn premarital sex, regardless of whether or not they have chosen to have coitus before marriage. Technical virginity is increasingly being seen as hypocritical and unsatisfactory among college students, although there is now greater emphasis on the importance of a loving emotional relationship between sexual partners. So now couples who would have stopped just short of intercourse in former years, and instead petted to orgasm, are choosing to have intercourse. At the same time, however, there is increased legitimacy for a variety of sexual interactions that do not include intercourse but still often lead to orgasm (Lawrance, Rubinson, & O'Rourke, 1984; Story, 1985).

Changes in attitudes and values do not necessarily lead to concomitant changes in behavior. More people favor the idea of sexual intercourse before marriage than actually participate in the behavior. The evidence indicates, however, that there are not only high percentages of young people who are experiencing coitus but that they are experiencing it at earlier ages (Singh & Forrest, 1990). The most significant upsurge in sexual activity has taken place in women since the mid-1960s. Studies of college women show a much higher percentage of nonvirgins in the 1980s than during the middle sixties or seventies (Daher, Greaves, & Supton, 1988; Robinson & Jedlicka, 1982; Story, 1985). The proportion of adolescent females aged 15 to 19 who indicate they have experienced sexual intercourse has now reached 53 percent, up from only 28.6 percent in 1970 and 47 percent in 1982 (Singh & Forrest, 1990).

ATTITUDES TOWARD HOMOSEXUALITY AND OTHER SEXUAL ORIENTATIONS

Any behavior that deviated from the accepted norm of heterosexual intercourse—man on top facing woman on the bottom—was until recently considered by many to be perverse or unnatural. Although significant numbers of people admitted having different sexual preferences, medical and mental health professionals generally classified them as sick; laws made them criminals; religions branded them as sinners; and the general populace feared, hated, or pitied them. Many of these attitudes still exist, but in the 1990s there has been a gradual trend toward somewhat more tolerance and acceptance of a diversity of sexual orientations (Gramick, 1991).

The change in attitude toward homosexual and bisexual behaviors has been particularly evident, especially among the helping professional groups and among younger people. The changes are not unanimous, however, in any of these groups. Many groups of professionals—including the American Psychiatric Association—no longer consider homosexual preferences to be a sickness but instead an alternative mode of sexual functioning. Homosexual individuals have grouped together to form organizations designed to educate the public about homosexuality, work toward equal rights for homosexuals, and gain more political influence (Voeller, 1990).

Other sexual behaviors have gained greater social acceptance in recent times. Sadomasochism, transvestism, oral sex, and a variety of other sexual practices no longer shock as many people as in previous times. There has been increased tolerance and acceptance of others' sexual preferences, rather than condemnation. A typical philosophy has been that every person should be free to enjoy his or her sexual inclinations, providing that other people are not harmed, exploited, or forced to participate without their consent. The emphasis for a time seemed to be moving toward the belief that sexual expression—its quality and quantity—was a personal matter.

With the new surge of political and religious conservatism of the 1980s came some marked reversals of this trend, however. The problems of acquired immunodeficiency syndrome (AIDS) in the gay men's community began to provide new ammunition for antihomosexual zealots. The 1986 Commission on Pornography tended to focus on the depiction of more unusual forms of sexual behavior in its attempt to show that such pornography led to violent and antisocial sexual offenses (Lynn, 1986). The U.S. Supreme Court upheld a Georgia law in 1986 that made sodomy (in this case oral sex shared by two adult males) a felony even between consenting adults. A poll conducted by *Newsweek* magazine indicated that a slim majority of Americans disapproved of the ruling, with the greatest negative reaction among middle-aged people. In the same poll, however, 61 percent of all respondents said they did not regard homosexuality as an acceptable life-style. These are all indications that there may well be some important shifts in the social and political climates that will show less tolerance for sexual orientations that do not conform with the heterosexual norm in our society.

ATTITUDES TOWARD THE BODY AND NUDITY

Early in the twentieth century the human body was thought to be a rather loathsome thing that was best kept covered to the greatest extent possible. It was also

FIGURE 1.5 Late 19th-Century Swimwear

In various cultures and various times it has been socially acceptable to either clothe or expose the body depending on the activity. In the United States late in the nineteenth century, swimwear for both men and women covered the body almost completely.

21

a source of shame, and nudity was frowned upon. The organs that protruded from the human torso—the male genitals and the female breasts—were kept under protective support and camouflage (see Fig. 1.5).

The picture in recent years has been very different. Many styles of clothing now expose much of the body; some swimwear only scantily covers the genitals and female breasts. Nudity is much more acceptable, and total frontal nudity of both women and men is accepted in a variety of popular magazines. The courts generally no longer consider simple exposure of the genitals in photographs to represent obscenity or pornography. Nudist camps have operated for many years, although they are often governed by very strict codes of behavior. One recent study showed that "social nudists" draw a sharp distinction between nudity and sex, viewing the naked human body as natural and pure rather than as sexually arousing. The nudists tend to be actually more sexually conservative than those who are clothed (Story, 1987). In a few areas of the United States, nudity is now being allowed on sections of beaches, and this is being accepted as natural and comfortable.

ATTITUDES TOWARD THE DOUBLE STANDARD

Sexual double standards of one sort or another are a part of many societies. Western culture's oldest double standard was founded on the assumption that men need and enjoy sexual pleasure more than women do. Additionally, men were expected to be more experienced in sexual matters and to be able to educate women. This double standard is deeply ingrained in our society and will continue for some time to shape relationships and sexual conduct for a large segment of the population (Clement, 1990).

While it is no longer assumed that it is crucial for women to be virgins until they marry, there is still a persistent attitude that it is more acceptable for men to be sexually active with a variety of partners than it is for women. College students continue to be in touch with a "conditional" double standard that limits the acceptable number of sexual partners for women to a very few and then only within the context of a meaningful loving relationship. One research study indicated that women were judged more negatively than men if they had experienced sexual intercourse as a teenager, or in a casual manner rather than in a steady relationship (Sprecher, McKinney, & Orbuch, 1987). Men, on the other hand, are permitted more casual sexual encounters at younger ages and are even respected by their peers for their sexual prowess. Research continues to show that men engage in more

sexual behavior, both in terms of quantity and variety, than do women (Story, 1985).

Many young people are realizing that there are healthy and fair standards that can provide bases for interpersonal relationships. As the strong sexual potentials of women continue to be realized and expressed, fewer women are feeling sexually inferior to men and fewer women are allowing themselves to be subjugated in double-standard relationships. Many men are also realizing that they need not be caught in a mentality emphasizing only the genital aspects of sex. Instead they are now free to enjoy a broader context of sensuality, friendship, and romance.

ATTITUDES TOWARD SEX AND ROMANCE

Philosophers since the time of the ancient Greeks have suggested that sexual desire is one type of loving and that love is fundamentally a desire for wholeness, the need to unify with the parts of ourselves we find in others. In most non-Western cultures and historical periods, infatuation and romantic love have been viewed as something quite separate from, even unrelated to, sexual longing. While in our culture marriage is the social institution that springs from romance and sexual desire and appears to bond them together, in most other cultures marriage is viewed as too significant a step to be determined by such passing fancies as romantic or sexual love. We are one of the first cultures to idealize romance, build it into the very fabric of our political and social structure, and make its link to sex and marriage a basic requirement for a satisfactory adult life (Keen, 1983).

In sex education lessons today, nearly anyone can spout the expected answer to the question "When is it all right for two people to have sex?" That answer is some variation on the theme: *When they love each other.* The counterculture's movement toward an instant gratification, do-it-if-it-feels-good mentality in the sixties and seventies never fit particularly well with the predominant values of the Western world. Before long everyone realized that things could not really be that simple. There were complicated consequences of instant sex: an increase in the incidence of sexually transmitted disease, unwanted pregnancy, and shattered emotions. The 1980s saw a great deal more about the "return" to intimacy, love, and romance, with many books and magazine articles on these topics. We now have the opportunity to examine more closely the many faces of love, the intricacies of human commitment and spirituality, and the complications of intimacy. Integrating romance and sex is not as simple or "natural" as it may seem (Kelly, 1984).

Case Study

JULIE: A STRUGGLE FOR NONEXCLUSIVE SEX

Julie, a 22-year-old college senior, had given a great deal of thought to the meaning of love and the place of sex in loving relationships. She decided that healthy love should place no restrictions on a loved one and that jealousy is a symptom of insecurity and stifling possessiveness. Julie enjoyed sex and felt that women should be as free as the double standard had allowed men to be, except she felt that honesty about sex was a necessary part of a good relationship.

After establishing a deep loving bond with Peter, also a college student, Julie moved into his apartment. A fundamental agreement for the relationship was that both would be free to love and have sex with others. Before long Julie was also seeing Carson and occasionally having sex with him. She continued to consider her relationship with Peter to be the primary one. Although he knew it was a violation of their original agreement, Peter began to react to Julie's other relationship with contempt and anger. They be-

gan to argue frequently, but Julie continued to maintain that healthy love and sex should be nonexclusive.

As Peter's hurt and jealousy grew, he felt alienated toward Julie. He began to intensify a friendship with a young woman he had known for several months. Eventually, their relationship included sexual intercourse. Surprisingly for Julie, she found herself reacting negatively to Peter's new relationship. Her emotions were in direct opposition to her philosophies, a state that left her frustrated and depressed.

Although Julie and Peter struggled for several months in an attempt to make their nonexclusive love and sex work, the relationship was unable to withstand the strain. Julie left Peter dejectedly, saying that she had learned a great deal from the experience. She continued to maintain that her philosophy of love and sex was sound, although she now had doubts that she was personally ready to make nonexclusive sex work for her own life.

ATTITUDES TOWARD SEX EDUCATION

For the first half of the twentieth century, human sexuality was subject to a great conspiracy of silence. Except for the off-color joke and double entendre, discussion of sexuality was rare among "nice" people. Sex education in schools seldom went beyond the discussion of the role of sperm and egg cells in reproduction; sex education in churches was usually a list of things not to do; sex education in the home was practically nonexistent. Even the professionals to whom people were referred for discussion of sex problems—physicians, religious counselors, and mental health workers—seldom had any special academic preparation in sexuality.

In the early 1960s more publicity began to appear about sex education in public schools and colleges. Organizations were formed that encouraged and supported sex education programs. The most influential group was chartered in 1964 as the Sex Information and Education Council of the United States (SIECUS). One of the cofounders of SIECUS, and its first executive director, was Dr. Mary S. Calderone, a woman

who became one of the world's leading advocates of sex education. In the late sixties and again in the mid-1980s, SIECUS and other pro-sex education groups came under attack by extremist political groups that used the sex education issue to gain attention for their causes or control over various boards of education. Although some fine sex education programs folded, the storm was weathered, and the trend toward more courses in sex education continues. The state of New Jersey was one of the first to mandate sex education for its public schools in the mid-1980s. By 1991, 21 states required all school districts to provide sex education, and 33 required AIDS education in their schools. An additional 24 states had recommended sex education in their schools.

In 1973 the SIECUS Board of Directors adopted a position statement that summarized the growing new attitude toward sex education:

Free access to full and accurate information on all aspects of sexuality is a basic right for everyone, children as well as adults. (Calderone, 1974, p. 1)

Another professional organization was formed in the late 1960s, the American Association of Sex Educators, Counselors, and Therapists (AASECT). It has worked to establish standards for these fields, and now certifies individuals who meet training criteria in the three different sexology fields: sex education, counseling, and therapy.

Sex education classes and programs have appeared in public schools, colleges, religious sects, and professional schools around the world. It is now recognized that people of all ages want and need information about human sexuality. The vast majority of Americans support sex education (de Mauro & Haffner, 1988). As the home continues to be recognized as the ideal location for effective sex education, some parents are better preparing themselves to be the sex educators of their own children. These efforts are indeed helping children and young people today learn basic facts about sex at much younger ages than did their parents and grandparents.

In considering these recent shifts in attitudes about sex, it should be clear that some important changes have been in progress. However, it is again necessary to emphasize that not all people have adopted new attitudes about sexuality or they may have adopted only some of them. The result is that we are living in times when many different sex ethics exist. The differences not only create confusion for individuals but conflicts among groups of people. It is still uncertain what effects these changes in attitude have had and will have on sexual behavior, but the remaining years of the twentieth century will surely represent a period of increased sexual awareness and controversy. ■

SELF-EVALUATION

You and Your Sexuality

The real significance of changing sexual attitudes rests on the influences that they have upon the lives of individuals. The questionnaires in this section are designed to help you take stock of your own sexual attitudes and their changes throughout your lifetime. They will also help you evaluate some of your sexual background and its meaning for your life today as a sexual human being. I hope that taking a closer look at your sexuality now will provide a more personal context for exploring the remainder of this book. Although there may be a variety of ways to use these questionnaires for classroom and group awareness activities, I have intended them for your own personal use.

SEXUAL ATTITUDES IN YOUR LIFE

In the questionnaire on the following page, I ask you to compare your present sexual attitudes with those of your parents (or the primary people who raised you) and with your own values of 4 to 6 years ago. It might be interesting to ask one of your parents* to complete the questionnaire. Otherwise complete the column for your parents with the responses that you feel accurately represent their attitudes.

Analysis: The final totals shown give a rough standard for comparison of your present attitudes with your attitudes of a few years ago and with those of the parents (or others) who gave you your earliest attitudes. Generally speaking, the higher the total score, the more liberal the attitudes (highest possible score = 100). There are no right or wrong responses or good or bad scores. Examine the individual responses and totals to get a clearer picture of how your sexual attitudes compare with those of your parents and how your own attitudes have or have not changed in the past few years.

*The term *parent(s)* as used in this book refers to a child's principal caregiver(s) and is therefore not limited only to biological parents nor just to two-parent households.

Attitude Questionnaire

Rate each attitude with one of the following numbers:

0 = uncertain   2 = somewhat disagree   4 = somewhat agree
1 = strongly disagree   3 = relatively neutral   5 = strongly agree

Attitude Statement	Rating for Your Parents	Rating for Yourself 4–6 Years Ago	Your Present Rating
1. Masturbation is a healthy, normal mode of sexual expression.	_____	_____	_____
2. Young people should be encouraged to use masturbation as a way of exploring their sexual feelings.	_____	_____	_____
3. Sexual activity without marriage is all right for a couple who share a loving relationship.	_____	_____	_____
4. Sexual activity solely for physical pleasure is all right if both partners agree to it.	_____	_____	_____
5. In a loving partnership, having sex with others outside the primary relationship is all right if both partners agree.	_____	_____	_____
6. Homosexuality is an acceptable sexual life-style.	_____	_____	_____
7. Homosexuals should not be discriminated against because of their sexual orientation.	_____	_____	_____
8. Pornography depicting sexual activity between adults should be available for other adults who wish to purchase and use it.	_____	_____	_____
9. Any sexual behavior is acceptable between consenting adults.	_____	_____	_____
10. At a beach, I would not be offended or made uncomfortable by having others around me in the nude.	_____	_____	_____
11. I would not be uncomfortable being nude myself with other nude people at the beach.	_____	_____	_____
12. The naked human body should be considered a source of beauty and pleasure, and not a source of shame.	_____	_____	_____
13. Women should have the same access and rights to sexual experience as men do.	_____	_____	_____
14. Women can enjoy sex and get as much pleasure from it as men do.	_____	_____	_____
15. Women should be as sexually assertive as men in initiating sexual activity.	_____	_____	_____
16. Accurate sex information should be available to all young people and adults.	_____	_____	_____
17. Birth control information and devices should be available to minors without parental consent.	_____	_____	_____
18. Physicians should be able to treat minors for sexually transmitted diseases without notification of parents.	_____	_____	_____
19. I support abortion as an alternative in cases of unplanned pregnancy.	_____	_____	_____
20. Women should have free choice about and access to abortion.	_____	_____	_____
TOTALS:	_____	_____	_____

25

YOUR SEXUAL HISTORY

The following questions are intended to provide further means of exploring where you have been as a sexual person and where you are now. It may help to write the answers down or to talk about the answers with someone you trust.

1. *Nudity*
   a. How often, when you were young, did you see your parents in the nude? What was your family's attitude toward nudity?
   b. If you ever have children (or if you have children now), do you hope to be (or are you now) more accepting of nudity in your family than your parents were, less accepting, or about the same?

2. *Masturbation*
   a. How did you first learn about or discover masturbation, and how did you feel about it at first?
   b. If you masturbated when you were younger, did you ever let anyone else know about it?
   c. If you masturbate now, how do you feel about the practice? Are you guilty? Ashamed? Happy? Proud? Disgusted? Satisfied?

3. *Sex Slang—"Dirty Words"*
   a. Make a list of the sex-related slang terms that you feel comfortable using, if any (e.g., screwing, fuck, cock, suck, cunt, etc.)
   b. Which of the words on the list would your parents have been comfortable using?
   c. Which of the words on the list would be offensive to you if you heard them being spoken by a friend of the other sex? Of the same sex?

4. *First Sexual Experiences*
   a. What is the first explicit sexual experience with another person that you can remember?
   b. What were your reactions to that first erotic experience?
   c. Has that initial experience affected your feelings about yourself as a sexual person or about sex in general even until today? How?

5. *Heterosexual Intercourse*
   a. How did you first learn about heterosexual intercourse, and what were your reactions and feelings when you did learn about it?
   b. If you have experienced sexual intercourse with someone of the other sex, what were your feelings following the first experience?
   c. Are your attitudes toward sex different now from what they were when you first had intercourse? In what ways?

6. *Same-Sex Activities*
   a. How did you first learn about homosexuality, and what were your reactions and feelings when you did learn about it?
   b. If you have ever participated in a sexual experience (even as a youngster) with someone of your same sex, what are your feelings about the experience?

7. *Sexual Behavior*
   a. In thinking about sexual contact, or during sexual involvement with another person, which of the following are most exciting for you and which are turn-offs?
      1. oral sex performed on you
      2. oral sex performed on partner (by you)
      3. anal sex
      4. kissing and being together nude
      5. intercourse
      6. touching and caressing
      7. using some painful stimulation
      8. acting out a sexual fantasy
      9. mutual masturbation
   b. If you have had intense shared sexual experiences, what things about the experience(s) have pleased and satisfied you most? Which have displeased or frustrated you most?
   c. What qualities do you desire in your ideal sexual partner?

YOU AND YOUR BODY

When you have sufficient privacy, remove all of your clothing and stand before the largest mirror available, preferably a full-length one. Try to relax and take some time to look over your body carefully. Consider the following questions as you look at your body with as much objectivity as you can muster:

1. Do you enjoy looking at and touching your body? Why or why not?
2. What aspects of your body do you like most? Least?
3. If you are a male, how do you feel about your general body shape, your penis, and your testicles, as compared to other male bodies you have seen?
4. If you are a female, how do you feel about your general body shape, your breasts, and your external genitals as compared to other female bodies you have seen?
5. Does your body conform to your ideas of what a (feminine or masculine) body should look like?
6. Do you think your nude body is (or would be) sexually attractive to members of the other sex? Of the same sex?

The next two chapters may help you to understand better your own sexual anatomy and physiological sexual responses.

CHAPTER SUMMARY

1. The study of human sexuality has become increasingly popular and complex. It is a significant way to understand many different aspects of human behavior and social interaction.
2. Whether a "sexual revolution" ever occurred has been subject to debate. However, there have been ongoing shifts in attitudes and values regarding sex and resulting changes in how people make their own decisions about sexual behavior.
3. Factors that have led to changed attitudes about human sexuality include advances in medical science, greater emphasis on individuality and personal freedom, changing codes of morality, new attitudes toward the roles of men and women, greater amounts of leisure time, new knowledge about sex, and growing concern over AIDS.
4. Three significant pioneers in nineteenth-century studies of human sexuality were Richard von Krafft-Ebing, Sigmund Freud, and Henry Havelock Ellis. Their work established fundamental perspectives on sexuality that persisted well into the twentieth century.
5. The early twentieth century was heavily influenced by Victorian values about sex and romance. The Kinsey studies opened new vistas concerning the spectrum of sexual behavior, and Masters and Johnson pioneered work in understanding sexual physiology and the treatment of sexual dysfunctions.
6. Several surveys about sex conducted in the 1970s, 1980s, and 1990s gained worldwide attention and brought new perspectives to female and male sexuality, childhood and adolescent sexuality, sexual orientation, knowledgability about sex, and the place of sex in relationships. A major new survey on sexual behavior in the United States has been proposed but not yet funded.
7. Scientific study of sex can be approached with various methods: population samples, surveys, working with case studies and clinical data, observing behavior directly, or through the use of controlled experiments. Scientific research raises numerous ethical issues.
8. Attitudes toward sexuality are always changing. Masturbation and premarital sex have become more accepted in recent years; there is greater openness about homosexuality and other orientations although still a significant degree of debate about their acceptability.
9. Nudity has become far more acceptable in the past two decades, and the former sexual double standard has given way to a "new" double standard that still finds sexual behavior more acceptable for men than for women.
10. Sexual desire and behavior have become closely intertwined with romantic love in recent generations.
11. Sex education seems to wax and wane in significance at various educational institutions. It is not yet mandated in most public schools.
12. Understanding ourselves as sexual human beings requires some introspection and self-questioning. Parental attitudes and values often influence the development of our own sexuality.

ANNOTATED READINGS

Brecher, E. (1979). *The sex researchers.* San Francisco: Specific Press. A highly readable survey of some of the most significant sex researchers and their work.

Bullough, V. L. (1979). *The frontiers of sex research.* Buffalo, NY: Prometheus Books. An overview of the methods and implications of sex research.

D'Emilio, J. D. & Freeman, E. B. (1988). *Intimate matters: A history of sexuality in America.* New York: Harper & Row. One of the most insightful discussions of sexuality and sexual attitudes during 200 years of the American experience.

Gilman, S. L. (1989). *Sexuality: An illustrated history.* Somerset, NJ: John Wiley & Sons. Makes use of pictorial representations to trace the evolutions of sexual values and myths. Examines concepts of beauty and ugliness, health and sickness, sexual ethics and politics from the Middle Ages to modern times.

Reinisch, J. M. & Beasley, R. (1990). *The Kinsey Institute new report on sex: What you must know to be sexually literate.* New York: St. Martin's Press. Survey of sex-related knowledge that confirms a high degree of sexual ignorance in the United States. Provides a source of information for some of our most misunderstood sexual concepts.

27

CHAPTER TWO

FEMALE SEX ORGANS
Vulva
Clitoris
Clitoridectomy and Infibulation
Vagina
Hymen
Genital Self-Examination for Women
Uterus
Pelvic Examination
Ovaries and Fallopian Tubes
Female Breasts
Breast Self-Examination

THE MENSTRUAL CYCLE
Preovulatory Preparation or Follicular Phase
Ovulation
Luteal Secretion
Menstruation
Premenstrual Syndrome

MALE SEX ORGANS
Testes and Scrotum
Male Genital and Testicular Self-Examination
Penis
Erection
Internal Male Organs
Sperm Production and Ejaculation
Hormonal Cycles in Men

**MENOPAUSE AND THE MALE CLIMACTERIC:
THE SEXUAL SYSTEMS AGE**
Female Menopause
The Male Climacteric

**SELF-EVALUATION: YOUR SEX EDUCATION:
PAST, PRESENT, AND FUTURE**

CHAPTER SUMMARY

Only two times during my childhood did my mother ever have to refer to my genitals, and both times all she could say was "down there." After I grew up, I guess she must have decided there was no need to refer to that region at all, so she never even said "down there." She said nothing at all. It wasn't until I took this course that I said the word vagina out loud myself. It feels as though I had to take 21 years to legitimize the entire sexual part of my body enough to make it part of me.

—From a student's essay

SEXUAL SYSTEMS

Before moving on to further consideration of the place of sexuality in the personality and in society, it is essential to discuss some anatomy and physiology of the human sex organs. The basic anatomy of the male and female sexual systems has been known for centuries. Reliable information on the sex organs and how they function has not been available until recently.

Sex education efforts have traditionally emphasized the role of the sex organs in human reproduction. At least in formalized sex education, the potential for gaining sexual pleasure from those organs—without the intent of procreation—was devalued or ignored until about the mid-1950s. Until recently sex education for teenagers has almost completely favored the reproductive aspects of sex.

In this book I will consider the sexual systems of men and women to have various functions in procreation, recreation, and as one form of intimate sharing and communication within a loving relationship. Current concerns about overpopulation, along with birth statistics, make it evident that sex is seldom used solely for reproduction. The high interest in effective birth control and achieving full sexual functioning shows that a great many people are practicing sex in nonprocreative ways.

In sex education today male sex organs are usually given recognition for their capability of generating pleasant feelings, while their role in reproduction has often been seen as a by-product of that pleasure. In the study of female sex organs, the emphasis clearly continues to be the reproductive functions of the uterus, ovaries, and fallopian tubes. The important roles of the vagina, clitoris, and other external structures have typically been neglected (Kelly, 1986). In fact, efforts to emphasize female sexuality more fully in sex education may be met with discomfort and resistance (Snowden, 1989). This chapter and the next recognize the sex organs of both women and men as potential sources of sexual pleasure and interpersonal intimacy as well as of babies. I cover the reproductive aspects of sex in chapter 4, "Reproduction and Birthing."

Female Sex Organs

The female sex organs are not confined to the inner body (see Fig. 2.1). There are many important structures located externally. These external structures play an important role in sexual arousal, while the internal organs tend to be more important in reproduction.

29

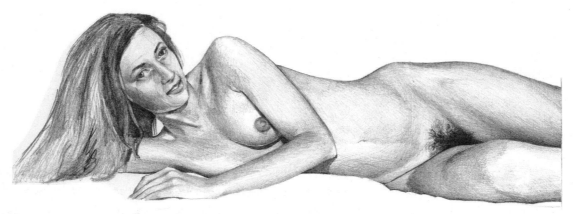

FIGURE 2.1 External Female Anatomy

The human sex organs are important for both procreation and recreation. Historically sex educators focused on the internal sex organs and reproduction, especially in women. In recent years, they have also focused on the pleasurable aspects of sexual behavior and the external sex organs.

VULVA

The external sex organs of the female, located between the legs, below and in front of the pubic symphysis, are collectively called the vulva (see Fig. 2.2). Especially visible are the mons and the major lips (labia majora). The mons, sometimes termed the mons pubis or mons veneris, is a rounded pad of fatty tissue just above the other sex organs on the pubic bone. During puberty the mons becomes covered with pubic hair, usually arranged in a roughly triangular pattern. The mons is

well endowed with nerve endings, and most women find that rubbing or exerting pressure on this area leads to sexual arousal.

The major lips are two folds of skin that extend from the mons down between the legs. They are relatively flat and indistinct in some women and thick and bulging in others. During puberty the skin of the major lips darkens slightly, and hair grows on their outer surfaces. The major lips cover and protect the inner, more sensitive sex organs of the woman. The inner structures cannot be seen unless the major lips are parted, so women may find it useful to position a mirror in such a way that they are able to see the other structures.

When the major lips are separated, another pair of smaller folds of skin become visible, the minor lips (labia minora). They are observed as pink, hairless, irregular and asymmetrical ridges that meet at the top to form a sheath of skin covering the clitoris called the prepuce or clitoral hood (see Fig. 2.3). Both the major and minor lips are sensitive to stimulation and are important in sexual arousal. Just inside each minor lip is the opening to a duct connected to Bartholin's gland.

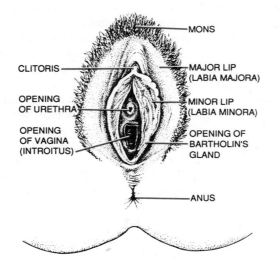

MONS

CLITORIS

OPENING
OF URETHRA

OPENING
OF VAGINA
(INTROITUS)

MAJOR LIP
(LABIA MAJORA)

MINOR LIP
(LABIA MINORA)

OPENING OF
BARTHOLIN'S
GLAND

ANUS

FIGURE 2.2 Vulva

The external female sex organs consist of the mons, labia, and clitoris. They have numerous nerve endings and are, therefore, sensitive to stimulation. In shape, size, and color the external sex organs vary greatly from woman to woman.

vulva: external sex organs of the female, including the mons, major and minor lips, clitoris, and opening of the vagina.

mons: cushion of fatty tissue located over the female's pubic bone.

major lips: two outer folds of skin covering the minor lips, clitoris, urethral opening, and vaginal opening.

minor lips: two inner folds of skin that join above the clitoris and extend along the sides of the vaginal and urethral openings.

prepuce (PREE-peus): in the female, tissue of the upper vulva that covers the clitoral shaft.

Bartholin's glands (BAR-tha-lenz): small glands located in the opening through the minor lips that produce some secretion during sexual arousal.

30

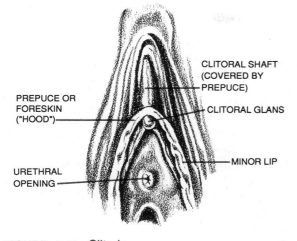

PREPUCE OR FORESKIN ("HOOD")

CLITORAL SHAFT (COVERED BY PREPUCE)

CLITORAL GLANS

MINOR LIP

URETHRAL OPENING

FIGURE 2.3 Clitoris

The most sensitive area of a female's genitals, the clitoris is located just beneath the point where the top of the minor lips meet. It is unique in that it is the only organ of either sex whose sole function is to provide sexual sensation and pleasure.

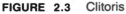

The gland produces a small amount of secretion during sexual arousal that may help moisten the entrance to the vagina and to some extent the labia. This secretion does not play a major role in lubrication of the vagina during arousal, however, and any other functions these glands may have are not known. Bartholin's glands can occasionally become infected with bacteria from feces or other sources and may require medical treatment.

Often the minor lips must be separated before the two openings between them may be seen. Just below the clitoris, a tiny hole is visible that is the urinary meatus or urethral opening. It is through this opening that urine leaves the body. Below the urethra a larger orifice is seen, the vaginal opening (introitus), which leads into the vagina. The opening of the vagina does not usually seem to be a hole, and in fact may only be recognized as an opening when something is inserted into it. In some women, particularly in younger age groups, the vaginal opening is partly covered by membranous tissue called the hymen (discussed later in the section on the vagina).

The entire area of the vulva is considered to be a major erogenous zone of females, since it is generally very sensitive to sexual stimulation.

CLITORIS

The clitoris is the most sexually sensitive female sex organ. Appropriate stimulation of the clitoris is usually necessary for women to reach orgasm, although the manner in which that stimulation is best applied varies

from woman to woman. The clitoris is usually observed as a small nub protruding from the cover of skin created by the merging of the minor lips. For many years it has been compared to the penis since it is sensitive to sexual stimulation and capable of erection. It has also been inaccurately viewed as a poorly developed, nonfunctional penis. On the contrary, the clitoris and the entire internal clitoral system of blood vessels, nerves, and erectile tissue constitute a very functional and important sex organ (Ladas, 1989).

The external body of the clitoris consists of the exposed, rounded tip, called the glans, and the shaft, which extends back under the covering of foreskin, or prepuce. The glans is the only part of the clitoris that hangs free, although it is usually too small to be very movable (see Fig. 2.3). The clitoral shaft is attached to the body along its entire underside. The clitoris contains two columns of spongy tissue, which become engorged with blood during sexual excitement, causing the entire structure to become hardened or erect. When not erect, the clitoris is rarely more than an inch in length, only the tip (glans) of which is external and visible, but during erection it may enlarge considerably, especially in diameter. Typically, in earlier stages of arousal the clitoris protrudes more than it does in an unaroused state. But as arousal proceeds it retracts again.

The tiny glands lining the prepuce produce oil that may mix with other secretions to form a substance called smegma. If this material collects around the shaft, mild infections may result. An infection could cause some pain or discomfort, especially during sexual activity. If smegma accumulations become a problem, they may be removed by a physician who inserts a small probe under the prepuce. A minor surgical procedure is sometimes used to cut the prepuce slightly, further exposing the clitoral glans and shaft. The procedure, called circumcision in Western culture, is not common in females, and the medical profession has found little legitimacy for it.

urethral opening: opening through which urine passes to the outside of the body.

introitus (in-TROID-us): the outer opening of the vagina.

hymen: membranous tissue that can cover part of the vaginal opening.

clitoris (KLIT-a-rus): sexually sensitive organ found in the female vulva; it becomes engorged with blood during arousal.

glans: sensitive head of the female clitoris, visible between the upper folds of the minor lips.

shaft: in the female, the longer body of the clitoris, containing erectile tissue.

smegma: thick, oily substance that may accumulate under the prepuce of the clitoris or penis.

circumcision: of clitoris—surgical procedure that cuts the prepuce, exposing the clitoral shaft.

Case Study

EMILY: A YOUNG WOMAN LEARNS ABOUT HER SEXUALITY

Emily was a college sophomore when she consulted a female counselor. She complained to the counselor that she felt very confused about her sexual values and generally ignorant about sex information. She had no previous sexual experience and was not certain that she would ever participate in intercourse or other sexual activities before marriage, but wanted to think about her values in that area carefully and learn more about her own sexual response.

In discussing masturbation with Emily, the counselor discovered that the young woman had talked with others about masturbation, but had never attempted to masturbate herself. Emily expressed a real desire to masturbate and experience the sensation of orgasm, but she knew almost nothing about her sexual functions and seemed afraid of injuring herself in some way. The counselor loaned her a book on sexuality and arranged to talk with her further about sex.

After two more sessions, Emily asked if the counselor could arrange for a visit to a physician who would be willing to help her understand her

sexual functions by pointing out and explaining her important sex organs. The counselor telephoned a female physician who was known for her knowledge and understanding about sexual matters and arranged a visit for the young woman. Using a mirror and some detailed diagrams, the physician carefully pointed out Emily's external sex organs to her and explained their respective roles in sexual arousal. Without attempting to persuade Emily to action, the physician also explained various ways in which women masturbate and gave reassurance on the safety of various methods.

In later counseling sessions, Emily expressed elation at her new self-awareness about her sexuality and reported that she had experienced orgasm. She was very pleased with "feeling more at home" with her body and her sexual feelings. She also continued to explore her sex-related values and tentatively concluded that she could not participate in shared sexual activity until a strong, loving relationship had developed.

CLITORIDECTOMY AND INFIBULATION

In other cultures and other historical periods, the clitoris has been subjected to various types of surgery and mutilation. With the fears of masturbation that were rife from the mid-nineteenth century to about 1935, it was not unusual for physicians to perform female circumcision or remove part or all of the clitoris, a surgical procedure called clitoridectomy. These measures were thought to "cure" masturbation and prevent insanity. In some African and Eastern Asian cultures and religions, clitoridectomy is still practiced as a rite of passage into adulthood. It is believed that millions of Islamic women in Egypt have undergone various forms of clitoral surgery. This may take the form of a traditional circumcision, in which the "hood" of tissue covering the clitoris is removed, along with the clitoral glans. Sometimes a more extensive clitoridectomy is performed, involving removal of the entire clitoris and much of the labial tissue sur-

rounding it. The effect of these procedures is to reduce sexual pleasure.

Some cultures also practice infibulation, in which the labia minora and sometimes the labia majora are removed and the sides of the external portion of the vagina are sewn together, assuring that the woman will not have intercourse prior to marriage. The threads are cut at the time of marriage, although in some cultures the procedure may be repeated if the husband is going to be absent for long periods of time (Frayser, 1985).

These rites were once often carried out with crude instruments, without sterile conditions or anesthetic. Women could get serious infections from such procedures, and there are cases in which women have bled to death following clitoridectomy. There is also a

clitoridectomy: surgical removal of the clitoris; practiced routinely in some cultures.
infibulation: surgical procedure, performed in some cultures, that seals the opening of the vagina.

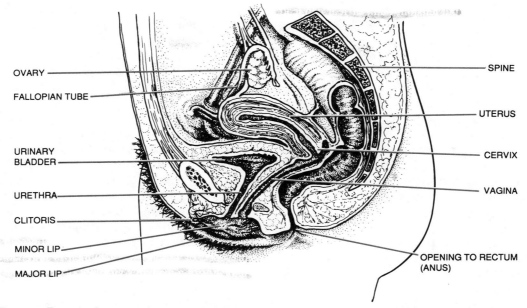

OVARY

FALLOPIAN TUBE

URINARY
BLADDER

URETHRA

CLITORIS

MINOR LIP

MAJOR LIP

SPINE

UTERUS

CERVIX

VAGINA

OPENING TO RECTUM
(ANUS)

FIGURE 2.4   Female Sexual and Reproductive Organs

The external and internal sexual and reproductive organs of the female are shown here in what is called a longitudinal section: this is a view through the middle of the body, from the side. Sex education often ignores the female organs of sexual pleasure, emphasizing instead the internal reproductive structures.

growing body of evidence that ritualized surgical practices can create psychological trauma, with far-reaching effects on people's sexuality, marriages, and the childbirth process (Lightfoot-Klein, 1989). Cultural changes have tended to alter traditional procedures so that in some places aseptic methods are now used. Some groups condemn the practice as barbaric and sexist. Others maintain that these are cultural practices in which outsiders do not have a right to interfere. At the Sixth World Congress of Sexology, held in Washington, D.C., in 1983, a resolution was proposed calling for professional opposition to clitoridectomy. However, since many delegates felt that such customs were not the business of professional groups from outside a particular culture, the measure was defeated.

Female circumcision, clitoridectomy, and infibulation are practices that are often deeply embedded in a particular culture's way of life. They may be seen as fundamental rites of passage to adulthood, and even looked upon with pride by the adult woman. Even though many societies have converted to more safe procedures for these rites, including hospitalization, there is a growing international movement that is calling for the banning of genital mutilation. Feminists in Western cultures have been particularly outspoken on this issue. However, the Association of African Women for Research and Development has claimed that Westerners do not fully comprehend the social complexities of the problem. They insist that African women themselves must take a more active political

and educational role, no longer allowing themselves to be subjected to mutilations that have potentially serious—even fatal—medical implications (Boston Women's Health Collective, 1984).

VAGINA

The vagina is a muscular, flat tube that is important as a female organ of reproduction and sexual pleasure and is where semen is deposited in penile-vaginal intercourse (see Fig. 2.4). The muscular walls of the vagina, which are very elastic, are collapsed together except when something is inserted into the cavity, so the inner cavity is best described as a "potential" space. The vagina is usually about 4 inches deep, although during sexual arousal it deepens even more. The inner lining of the vagina is fleshy and soft, and is corrugated by thin ridges of tissue. Except for the outer third and the area around its opening, the vagina is not particularly sensitive. The outer area, however, has many nerve endings and stimulation easily leads to sexual arousal.

There are two sets of muscles surrounding the vaginal opening, the *sphincter vaginae* and *levator ani* muscles. Women can exert some degree of control

vagina (vu-JI-na): muscular canal in the female that is responsive to sexual arousal; it receives semen during heterosexual intercourse for reproduction.

over these muscles, but tension, pain, or fear can lead to involuntary contraction of the outer vaginal muscles so that insertion of anything becomes difficult or painful for the woman. This condition is called vaginismus and is discussed in more detail in chapter 15, "Sexual Dysfunctions and Their Treatment." Women can also exert some control over the inner pubococcygeus (PC) muscle, much the same as the anal sphincter may be contracted or relaxed. This muscle may play a role in orgasmic response, and its tone can be improved by exercises, as is true of all voluntary muscles (see Kegel Exercises in chapter 3, "Human Sexual Response"). It is important to note that the vagina cannot contract to the extent that the penis might be trapped inside (penis captivus), even though some people have heard rumors to the contrary. When dogs mate, the penis erects in such a way that it is caught inside the vagina until erection subsides, but this is important to successful mating in canines. Nothing similar occurs in humans.

During sexual arousal in a woman, a lubricating substance is secreted through the inner lining of the vagina. This is discussed in chapter 3, "Human Sexual Response."

THE HYMEN

The hymen, usually present in the vaginal opening from birth, is a tissue usually having one or more openings in it. There are many different shapes of hymens that cover varying amounts of the introitus (see Fig. 2.5). Most hymens have a large enough opening to admit a finger or tampon. Attempting to insert anything larger, such as the erect penis, usually results in some tearing of the hymen. There are many ways other than sexual activity in which a hymen may be ruptured. While it is often stated that some girls are born without a hymen, the assumption has recently been called into question. A pediatric team at the University of Washington examined 1,131 infant girls, and found every one to have an intact hymen. They concluded that the absence of a hymen at birth is an unlikely occurrence, if it occurs at all. This suggests that when hymenal tissue cannot be identified in a young girl, some sort of trauma may have been the cause (Jenny, Huhns, & Arakawa, 1987).

Some hymens are apparently flexible enough so that they can even withstand coitus. Consequently the presence or absence of a hymen is unreliable as an indicator of a woman's virginity or nonvirginity. Some societies place special significance on the presence of the hymen and hold rituals for the rupturing of the hymen before a girl's first intercourse. Many people in Western societies today still believe that the presence of a hymen proves a female's virginity—a naive outlook at best. In fact the only way to determine physically whether or not a woman has experienced sexual intercourse is by finding sperm in a vaginal smear,

vaginismus (vaj-uh-NIZ-mus): involuntary spasm of the outer vaginal musculature, making penetration of the vagina difficult or impossible.

pubococcygeus (PC) muscle (pyub-o-kox-a-JEE-us): part of the supporting musculature of the vagina that is involved in orgasmic response and over which a woman can exert some control.

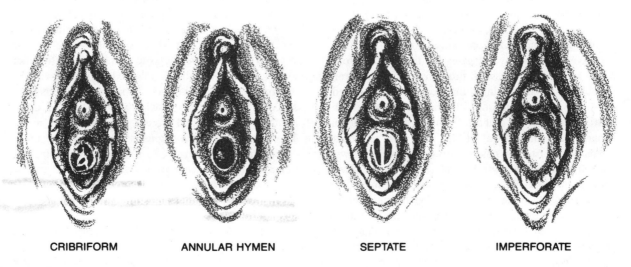

CRIBRIFORM   ANNULAR HYMEN   SEPTATE   IMPERFORATE

FIGURE 2.5 Hymen

A thin, delicate membrane, the hymen partially covers the vaginal opening in a variety of ways. It may bridge the vagina, surround it, or have several different shapes and sizes in the opening to the outside of the body. It has no known physiological function but historically has had psychological and cultural significance as a sign of virginity.

examined through a microscope. This procedure must be done within a few hours after intercourse and is sometimes used in rape cases as proof that coitus has occurred.

If the hymen is still present at the time of first sexual intercourse, penetration of the vagina by the penis may produce discomfort or pain and possibly some bleeding when the hymen is torn. The degree of pain varies in different women from slight to severe. If a woman is concerned about this, she may spend some time prior to the first coitus inserting fingers into the opening of the hymen, gradually widening it. A physician may also cut the hymen or stretch its opening with dilators of gradually increasing size. Usually there is little trouble inserting the penis through the hymen if the male partner persists with careful and gentle prodding with the erect penis. The woman may also take responsibility for guiding her partner's penis and controlling the timing and depth of penetration.

GENITAL SELF-EXAMINATION FOR WOMEN

After acquainting themselves with their basic external anatomy, it is a good idea for women to examine their genitals monthly, checking for any unusual signs or symptoms. Using a mirror and adequate light, look through pubic hairs to the underlying skin, and pull back the clitoral prepuce or hood. Then part the minor lips, exposing the area around the urethral and vaginal openings more fully.

Look for any unusual bumps, sores, or blisters. They may be red or light-colored, or may be more easily felt than seen. Be sure to look on the inside of each major and minor lip for similar signs. It is a good idea to become aware of what your normal vaginal discharge looks like, so you will notice any changes in its color, odor, or consistency. While such changes may occur normally over the course of the monthly menstrual cycle, some diseases cause distinct changes in vaginal discharge.

Anytime you find unusual bumps or discharges from the genitals, it is a good idea to consult a physician or other clinician specializing in women's health concerns. Often these symptoms do not even need treatment, but they may also signal the beginnings of an infection requiring medical attention. It is important to report any pain or burning upon urination, bleeding between menstrual periods, pain in the pelvic region, or an itchy rash around the vagina.

UTERUS

The neck of the uterus (or womb) protrudes into the deepest part of the vagina. The uterus is a thick-walled, muscular organ that provides a nourishing

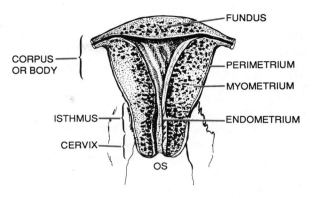

FIGURE 2.6 Uterus

The uterus is a hollow, muscular organ in which an embryo grows and is nourished until its birth. The uterus is held loosely in place in the pelvic cavity by several ligaments. Its walls are of varying thicknesses and consist of three layers, the perimetrium, the myometrium, and the endometrium.

environment for the developing embryo during pregnancy. It is usually about 3 inches long and pear-shaped, roughly 2½ to 3 inches in diameter at the top and narrowing to a 1-inch diameter at the end that extends into the vagina. During pregnancy it gradually expands to a much larger size. When a woman is standing, her uterus is almost horizontal and at a right angle to the vagina (see Fig. 2.4).

The two main parts of the uterus are the body and the cervix or neck, connected by a narrow isthmus. The top of the uterus is called the fundus. While the cervix is not especially sensitive to superficial touch, it is sensitive to pressure. The opening in the cervix is called the os. The inner cavity of the uterus has varying widths in different sections (see Fig. 2.6). The walls of the uterus are composed of three layers: the thin outer cover or perimetrium; the thick middle layer of muscular tissue called the myometrium; and the inner layer, which is rich in blood vessels and glands, the endometrium. It is the endometrium that plays a vital role in the menstrual cycle (discussed later in this chapter) and in the nourishment of a developing embryo (discussed in chapter 4, "Reproduction and Birthing").

uterus (YUTE-a-rus): muscular organ of the female reproductive system; a fertilized egg implants itself within the uterus.
cervix (SERV-ix): lower "neck" of the uterus that extends into the back part of the vagina.
os: opening in the cervix that leads into the hollow interior of the uterus.
perimetrium: outer covering of the uterus.
myometrium: middle, muscular layer of the uterine wall.
endometrium: interior lining of the uterus, innermost of three layers.

PELVIC EXAMINATION

The uterus, particularly the cervix, is a common site of cancer in women. Since cancer of the uterus often presents no symptoms for many years, it is especially dangerous. Women should have an internal, or pelvic, examination periodically, along with a Pap smear test, by a qualified gynecologist or other clinician. There is disagreement among health professionals as to the most desirable frequency for such exams, but most health experts recommend an annual examination. For a pelvic examination a speculum is first inserted into the vagina for a visual inspection. Then, using a rubber glove and lubricant, two fingers are inserted into the vagina and pressed on the cervix. The other hand is placed on the abdomen. The clinician is then able to feel the basic shape and size of the uterus and associated structures. To obtain a Pap smear (named for its developer, Dr. Papanicolaou) a speculum is carefully inserted into the vagina to hold open its walls. A thin spatula or a cotton swab is used to remove some cells painlessly from the area of the cervix. A smear is made from the material, which is fixed, stained, and examined under a microscope for any indications of abnormal cellular changes that might warn of cancer.

A new, self-administered home version of the Pap test may be available by prescription in the near future. Preliminary research shows that the home test has an accuracy rate almost as high as the clinical version. The test is presently awaiting approval by the Food and Drug Administration.

If suspicious cells are detected in a Pap smear, then more aggressive diagnostic procedures may be recommended. There first may be a biopsy to determine if there is a malignancy present. If growth of abnormal cells proves to be advanced, another procedure may be performed called a dilation and curettage, or D & C (see also chapter 5, "Birth Control and Unintended Pregnancy"). The opening of the cervix is dilated or widened, so that a metal instrument called a curette may be inserted into the inner cavity of the uterus. Some of the uterine lining is gently scraped away and then examined for malignant cells. The D & C is occasionally used to terminate a pregnancy, as an induced abortion, and is typically used to cleanse the uterus of dead tissue following a miscarriage (spontaneous abortion).

OVARIES AND FALLOPIAN TUBES

On either side of the uterus, and attached to it, are two almond-shaped glands called the ovaries (see Fig. 2.7). Ovarian ligaments attach the ovaries to the uterus. The ovaries have two primary functions: secretion of two

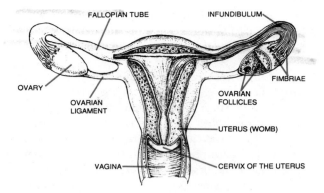

FIGURE 2.7 *Female Reproductive Organs*

About the size of unshelled almonds, the ovaries are the female reproductive glands or gonads. They are located one on each side of the uterus and have two separate functions: manufacturing the hormones estrogen and progesterone and producing and releasing eggs.

female sex hormones, estrogen and progesterone, and the production of the egg cells (ova) necessary for reproduction. Each ovary is about an inch long and weighs about one-fourth of an ounce.

Inside each ovary at a female's birth are tens of thousands of microscopic chambers called follicles, each of which contains a cell that has the potential to develop into an ovum. These cells are called oocytes. By the time of puberty it is believed that only a few thousand follicles remain in each ovary. Only a small percentage of these (400 to 500) will ever mature into ova.

In a mature woman the surface of the ovaries is irregular and pitted, evidence of the many ova that have pushed their way through the ovary walls in the process of ovulation, described on page 40. When the internal structure of an ovary is observed, follicles are seen in various stages of development. Two distinct parts of the ovary are also visible: the central medulla and its thick outer layer, the cortex (see Fig. 2.8).

Extending from one end of the ovaries to the upper portion of the uterus are the two fallopian tubes. The end of each fallopian tube nearest the ovary has a

Pap smear: medical test that examines a smear of cervical cells, to detect any cellular abnormalities.

ovaries: pair of female gonads, located in the abdominal cavity, that produce ova and female hormones.

ova: egg cells produced in the ovary. One cell is an ovum; in reproduction, it is fertilized by a sperm cell.

follicles: capsules of cells in which an ovum matures.

oocytes (OH-a-sites): cells that mature to become ova.

fallopian tubes: structures that are connected to the uterus and lead the ovum from an ovary to the inner cavity of the uterus.

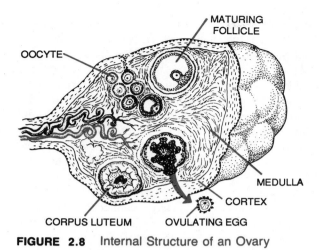

FIGURE 2.8 Internal Structure of an Ovary

This cross section of an ovary shows its cortex, the thick outer layer, and its central medulla as well as the various stages of ovum development. The first cell in the process of maturation is an oocyte, which with its surrounding cells is called the follicle.

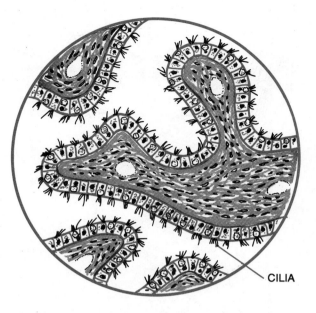

FIGURE 2.9 Cilia of Fallopian Tubes

This is a microscopic view of the cilia, the hairlike filaments that line the fallopian tubes. Their movement helps propel the ovum through the fallopian tube to the uterus.

number of fingerlike projections called *fimbriae,* which are not attached to the ovary but rather lie loosely around it. The fimbriae lead into the thickest end of the fallopian tube, the *infundibulum.* There is a narrow, irregular cavity that extends throughout each fallopian tube. The inner cavity gets progressively smaller in the sections of the tube closest to the uterus.

The inner lining of the fallopian tubes is covered by microscopic hairlike projections called cilia. It is by movements of these cilia that an ovum is carried through the tube from the ovary to the uterus (see Fig. 2.9). If fertilization is to occur, it is in the fallopian tubes that the sperm meets and enters the ovum. In this case the cilia in the tubes must then transport the tiny fertilized ovum to the uterus where it will implant itself and grow into a fetus (see the section on reproduction in chapter 4).

FEMALE BREASTS

The female breast is not a sex organ, but it has taken on sexual meanings in our society. Many people find women's breasts to be sources of sexual arousal, and many women find that stimulation of their breasts, especially the nipple, is sexually arousing. There are many individual differences in this respect. There may also be varying degrees of sensitivity depending on the woman's stage in her menstrual cycle.

Each breast (see Fig. 2.10) is composed of from 15 to 20 clusters of milk glands, each cluster having a milk duct that leads to the nipple. There are deposits of fatty tissue just under the skin of the breast. The

darkened circular area of skin surrounding the nipple is called the areola. There are often a few smaller nubs of skin on the areola.

During pregnancy, the breasts go through distinct changes as they prepare for nourishing a newborn infant. Within 2 or 3 days after a woman gives birth, her breasts begin to produce milk, the process of lactation. The pituitary hormone prolactin stimulates milk production. When the baby sucks at the nipple, the pituitary is stimulated to produce another hormone, oxytocin, which leads to the ejection of milk from the breast.

Concern about breast size and shape seems to be one of the most common bodily worries of women. Our culture has exaggeratedly created the impression that large breasts are sexy and desirable, and advertisers have capitalized on the anxieties of women by offering a wide variety of questionable breast enlargement techniques and devices. They not only are ineffective in enlarging the breasts but also may even be unsafe. Of course, female breasts can be in a great

cilia: microscopic hairlike projections that help move the ovum through the fallopian tube.
areola (a-REE-a-la): darkened, circular area of skin surrounding the nipple of the breast.
lactation: production of milk by the milk glands of the breasts.
prolactin: pituitary hormone that stimulates the process of lactation.
oxytocin: pituitary hormone that plays a role in lactation and in uterine contractions.

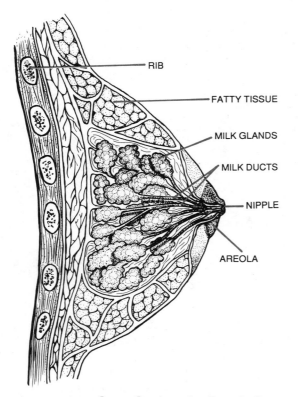

FIGURE 2.10 Cross Section of a Female Breast

The female breast has erotic and reproductive significance. The mammary or milk gland produces nourishment, which flows through the ducts to the nipple. The nipple is highly sensitive to stimulation, thereby playing a part in sexual arousal.

many sizes, shapes, and positions. It is typical for one of a woman's breasts to be slightly differently sized or shaped than the other. Larger breasts can be uncomfortable or even feel unattractive to some women. Smaller breasts may indeed be more sensitive to sexual stimulation, since the nerve endings in the skin are less dispersed.

BREAST SELF-EXAMINATION

Cancer of the breast is one of the more common types of malignancy, and about 1 in 9 women will have breast cancer at some time in their lives. Nearly 45,000 women died of the disease and its complications in 1991 in the United States. As with any form of cancer, early detection greatly increases the chances of complete cure. When breast cancer is detected in its early, localized stages, the survival rate after 5 years is 91 percent. However, survival rates for breast cancer detected in all stages drops to about 75 percent after 5 years (American Cancer Society, 1991). A test that is

recommended on a regular basis for women over the age of 35 is mammography. A special X-ray picture is taken of the breast and can detect even small lumps. Only low-level radiation is used to produce the image, called a mammogram. A recent study indicated that in spite of the fact that mammography is a significant way of detecting breast cancer at its earliest stages, nearly one-third of American women over 50 have never had the test. Some women are fearful of the test, even though it is relatively painless and poses no hazards (Wallis, 1991).

The breasts are easily examined by oneself, and the American Cancer Society recommends that breast self-examination be done once each month. Women who examine their breasts regularly become familiar with the natural contours of their breast tissue. Therefore they are likely to notice any unfamiliar lump that might develop there.

Breast self-examination should include both a visual inspection in a mirror and careful exploration of each breast with a hand. It is not a good idea to do this examination just before or during menstruation, since there tend to be more natural lumps during these phases. The best time for self-exam is midway through the menstrual cycle, around the time of ovulation. This would be approximately 12 to 16 days following the first day of the woman's last period. A systematic approach should be followed, as described below:

Visual Examination Stand before a mirror with your arms at your sides and examine the appearance of both breasts. Then raise your arms high above your head and look for any changes in the contour or skin of either breast. Look for any swelling or dimpling of the skin, or for any unusual signs in either nipple. Next, place your hands on your hips and flex the chest muscles, again looking for any unusual signs.

Manual Examination The breasts may be easily examined during a bath or shower, since the hands can glide easily over the wet skin. Another way is to examine them while lying down. Place a pillow under the shoulder on the same side as the breast to be examined and place that hand under your head. Use the hand from the opposite side for the actual examination. The fingers should be held together, forming a flat surface. Begin on the outer part of the breast, and move in complete, clockwise circles around the outer regions, checking for lumps, hard knots, or any unusual thickening. Then move inward toward the nipple about an inch and circle the breast again. Usually at least four concentric circles will have to be made to

mammography: sensitive X-ray technique used to discover small breast tumors.

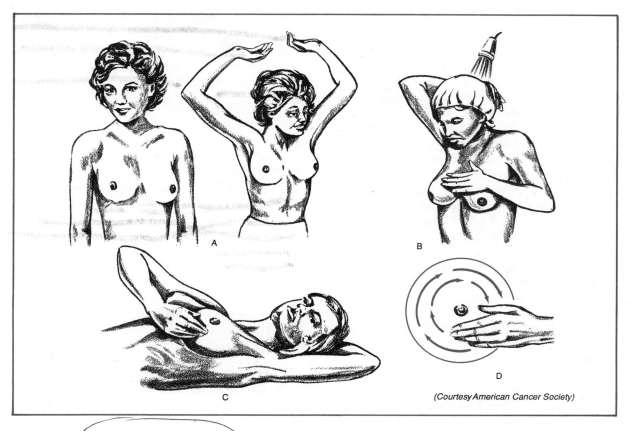

(Courtesy American Cancer Society)

FIGURE 2.11 Breast Self-Examination

It is important for a woman to examine her breasts regularly. She should look at her breasts in the mirror, first with her arms at her sides, then with them raised over her head (A). In the shower, her hands can easily move over the wet skin (B). When she is lying down, a woman can easily examine her breast tissue (C), and should repeat the procedure when in an upright position. The fingers should be held flat and move in complete clockwise circles around the outer portion of the breast, then move progressively inward toward the nipple (D).

examine every part of the breast. It is a good idea to repeat this procedure while sitting or standing, since the upright position redistributes breast tissue. Finally, squeeze each nipple to see if there is any discharge from either breast (see Fig. 2.11).

If you find any unusual features in a breast, *do not panic*. There are many nonmalignant conditions that can cause lumps, swelling, and discharge, but you should not take any chances. Always consult a physician, who can then prescribe further testing, such as a mammogram, to determine if the abnormality represents a malignancy. Even if a malignant tumor is discovered, modern medicine has made great strides in treatment and cure. Various combinations of radiation therapy, chemotherapy, and administration of hormones can be used. It is sometimes necessary to remove the entire breast in a surgical procedure called a mastectomy, but current research indicates that removal of only the lump itself and some surrounding tissue, a lumpectomy, is often sufficient (Henaham,

1984). Again, early discovery of unusual growths in the breast is a woman's best protection.

The Menstrual Cycle

Of special importance to the female's role in reproduction is the menstrual cycle. From the time of first menstruation, called menarche, to the period of life when her menstruation ceases, called menopause (or

mastectomy: surgical removal of all or part of a breast.
lumpectomy: surgical removal of a breast lump, along with a small amount of surrounding tissue.
menstrual cycle: the hormonal interactions that prepare a woman's body for possible pregnancy at roughly monthly intervals.
menarche (MEN-are-kee): onset of menstruation at puberty.
menopause (MEN-a-poz): time in mid-life when menstruation ceases.

39

climacteric), a woman's body goes through a periodic cycle that involves hormonal, psychological, and physical changes. This menstrual cycle involves the production of an ovum and the periodic preparation of the uterus for pregnancy, followed by a gradual return to the "unprepared" state if pregnancy does not occur.

Today menarche usually occurs sometime between the ages of 9 and 16, although variations from this range are normal. The onset of menopause is typically between the ages of 45 and 55 (Greenwood, 1988). So the years between menarche and menopause constitute a woman's potential child-bearing years, although she is actually able to conceive only for a day or two usually once a month. Women in their teenage years who bear children have a greater risk of experiencing physical complications and having children with birth defects. Likewise, the older a woman (or a man) is when having children, especially beyond the age of 35, the greater the possibility is of the offspring having birth defects. In the average mature woman, a single entire menstrual cycle usually lasts about 28 days. In teenaged girls, the length of the cycle tends to be more irregular and slightly longer, close to 31 days.

The menstrual cycle is regulated by a complex interaction of hormones secreted by the *pituitary gland,* located at the base of the brain; a portion of the brain itself called the *hypothalamus;* and the ovaries. The pituitary gland acts as a sort of relay station between the hypothalamus and ovaries. The hypothalamus produces gonadotropin releasing hormone (GnRH), which stimulates the pituitary gland to produce two hormones, follicle-stimulating hormone and luteinizing hormone, which in turn regulate hormonal secretion by the ovaries. How these hormones control the reproductive organs is described in the following section. Although the menstrual cycle is continuous, it will be divided into four stages, or phases, for ease of explanation: the follicular phase, ovulation, luteal secretion, and menstruation.

PREOVULATORY PREPARATION OR FOLLICULAR PHASE

During the first stage of the menstrual cycle (see Fig. 2.12), two important things must take place: the maturation of an ovum in one of the ovarian follicles and the beginning preparation of the uterus for the nourishment of an embryo, in case the ovum is fertilized. These developments are initiated by the secretion of follicle-stimulating hormone (FSH) from the pituitary gland into the bloodstream. The FSH influences the ovaries to "ripen" one or more of the ova in a follicle and also to increase their production of estrogen. The estrogen works directly on the inner lining of the

uterus (endometrium), causing it to thicken gradually, with enlargement of its many small glands and blood vessels. The estrogen also exerts a "feedback" effect on the pituitary gland, so that as the estrogen level in the blood increases, the production of FSH by the pituitary decreases.

OVULATION

When a high concentration of estrogen is reached (see Fig. 2.13), the hypothalamus triggers the release of luteinizing hormone (LH) from the pituitary. This hormone causes development of the egg to stop and is primarily responsible for the rupturing of the mature ovum through the outer wall of one ovary, the process of ovulation. After the ovum has left the ovary, the follicle remains as a tiny mass of cells called the corpus luteum. Under the influence of LH, the corpus luteum becomes many small glands.

LUTEAL SECRETION

With stimulation by LH, the corpus luteum begins secreting another essential hormone, progesterone, along with more estrogen (see Fig. 2.14). These hormones further thicken the uterine lining and cause it to begin secreting its own nutrient fluids that can nourish an early embryo if pregnancy occurs. The progesterone also has a "feedback" effect on the hypothalamus, so that it shuts off the production of GnRH. This in turn further decreases the production of LH and FSH. While these developments are happening, the ovum is slowly being moved through one of the fallopian tubes toward the uterus, a journey of 3 or 4 days. If the ovum is fertilized by a sperm, the fertilization will occur in the fallopian tube. If the ovum is not fertilized, it disintegrates.

gonadotropin releasing hormone (GnRH) (go-nad-a-TRO-pen): hormone from the hypothalamus that stimulates the release of FSH and LH by the pituitary.
follicle-stimulating hormone (FSH): pituitary hormone that stimulates the ovaries or testes.
estrogen (ES-tro-jen): hormone produced abundantly by the ovaries; it plays an important role in the menstrual cycle.
luteinizing hormone (LH): pituitary hormone that triggers ovulation in the ovaries and stimulates sperm production in the testes.
ovulation: release of a mature ovum through the wall of an ovary.
corpus luteum: cell cluster of the follicle that remains after the ovum is released, secreting hormones that help regulate the menstrual cycle.
progesterone (pro-JES-ter-one): ovarian hormone that causes the uterine lining to thicken.

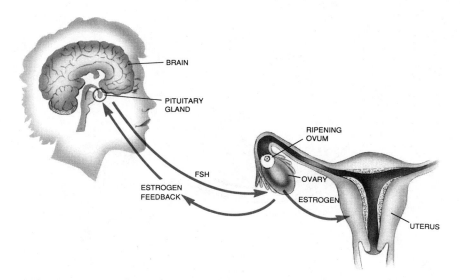

FIGURE 2.12 Preovulatory Preparation

In the first stage of the menstrual cycle, the maturation of the ovum begins. The follicle-stimulating hormone from the pituitary gland influences the production of estrogen by the ovaries that causes the lining of the uterus to thicken in preparation for a fertilized ovum.

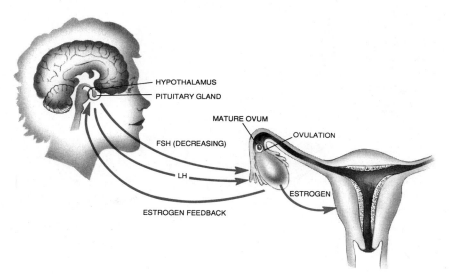

FIGURE 2.13 Ovulation

The pituitary gland is stimulated to release the luteinizing hormone by the presence of estrogen. This in turn causes the mature ovum to rupture through the outer wall of one ovary (the process of ovulation). The follicle that remains becomes an active gland, the corpus luteum.

MENSTRUATION

If the ovum is not fertilized, the corpus luteum degenerates, and the production of progesterone ceases. Estrogen level in the bloodstream begins to fall, and the thickened lining of the uterus begins to degenerate. Uterine cellular material, fluids, and a small amount of blood (usually about 2 to 5 ounces) are then lost through the vagina over a period of from 3 to 7 days. This is called menstruation or the menstrual period (see Fig. 2.15). The estrogen level continues to fall and eventually becomes low enough so that the pituitary

menstruation (men-stru-AY-shun): phase of menstrual cycle in which the inner uterine lining breaks down and sloughs off; the tissue, along with some blood, flows out through the vagina; also called the period.

41

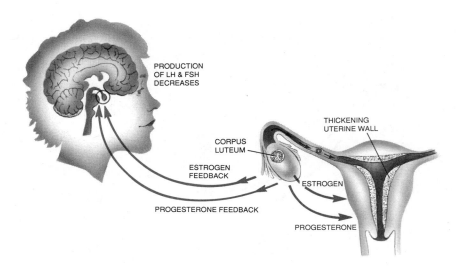

FIGURE 2.14 Luteal Secretion

The corpus luteum begins secreting progesterone as well as more estrogen, which further thickens the uterine lining in preparation for the possibility that the ovum will be fertilized as it moves through the fallopian tube.

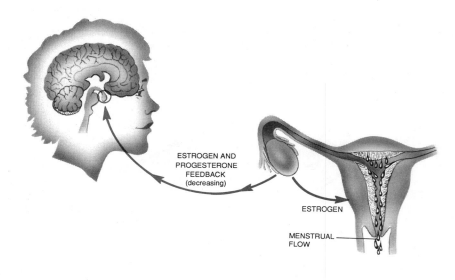

FIGURE 2.15 Menstruation

If the ovum is not fertilized, the corpus luteum degenerates and the progesterone and estrogen levels begin to fall. The portion of the uterus that had begun to thicken now begins to slough off and is lost through the vagina over a period of days.

again begins to produce FSH. The menstrual cycle is thus initiated all over again (see Table 2.1).

Unless a woman experiences pain during menstruation, called <u>dysmenorrhea</u>, or some other medical problem, there is no need to curtail any activities during menstruation. There are a number of products that can be used to absorb the menstrual flow. These include various sizes of absorbent pads that are held over the vaginal opening by adhesive that sticks to the underpants. Tampons are cylinders of absorbent mate-

rial and may be inserted directly into the vagina. Tampons do not stretch the vagina and usually cause no damage to an intact hymen, so they are favored by many women who prefer not to wear a pad externally. Since tampons may cause toxic shock syndrome, particularly if used for prolonged periods of time, care must be taken in their use (see chapter 5, p. 118).

dysmenorrhea (dis-men-a-REE-a): painful menstruation.

TABLE 2.1

Summary of the Menstrual Cycle

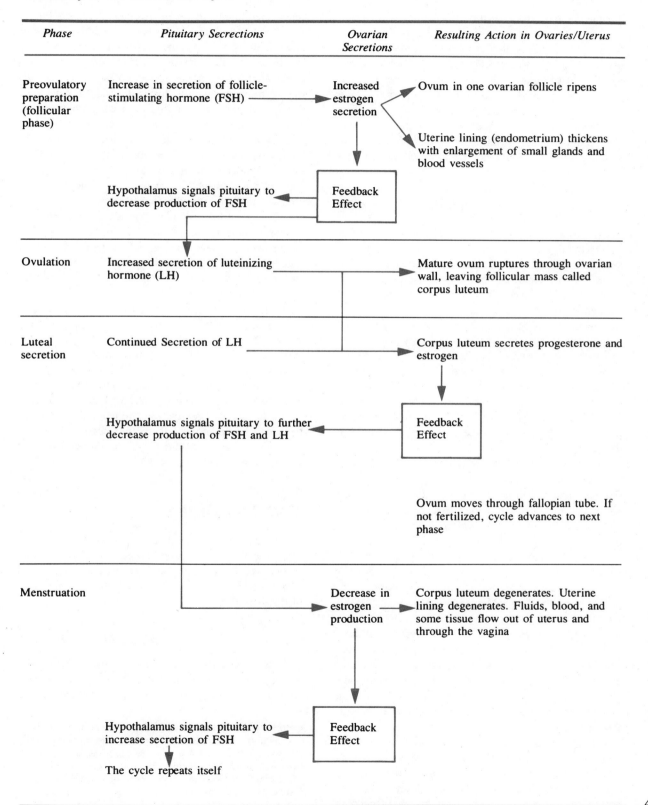

In some Native American and Eastern cultures the male hierarchy, primarily, considers the menstruating female unclean and sexual intercourse is prohibited during the menstrual period. Even though men and women in these cultures may subscribe to these social imperatives publicly, they do not necessarily do so in private. There is no medical reason for not having sex while menstruating; there is nothing wrong or dangerous about sexual activity during the period. Some women even experience a marked increase in sex drive before and during menstruation. Although there is less chance of pregnancy resulting from intercourse during menstruation, it should not be assumed that it is a totally "safe" time.

PREMENSTRUAL SYNDROME

Many women experience some physical discomfort and psychological shifts just prior to or during menstruation. These include headaches, backaches, fatigue, fluid retention, uterine cramping, anxiety, depression, and irritability. In 5 to 10 percent of women, these symptoms may become severe enough to interfere with daily activities. The discomfort and unpleasant symptoms are now generally collectively termed premenstrual syndrome, or PMS (Keye, 1983). However, there are many individual differences in how women experience and react to these symptoms.

Two hormones are believed to be involved in producing PMS. There is a decrease in the level of progesterone prior to menstruation and an increase in the amount of the substance called prostaglandin, a hormonelike chemical whose source in the body is as yet unidentified. These changes may lead to physiological and resulting psychological effects, since some research has confirmed that mood shifts can correlate with varying levels of hormones in the body. Some evidence suggests that psychological pressures may play a role in accentuating PMS symptoms. Two studies have shown that women who have been sexually traumatized or abused tend to have more severe problems with PMS (Miccio-Fonseca et al., 1990; Paddison et al., 1990).

There is a great deal of controversy over how PMS should be treated. Over-the-counter drugs that are advertised for menstrual cramping are generally antiprostaglandins that interfere with that hormone's contracting effects on the uterus. British physician Katharina Dalton (1979) has advocated the administration of progesterone to relieve PMS symptoms, but this has not been considered acceptable treatment by the medical community in the United States because of possible risks associated with progesterone. In two carefully controlled studies, it was found that progesterone was not more effective than a placebo in reducing premenstrual discomfort (Blume, 1983; Freeman, 1990). The debate continues, however, and some medical workers still believe that this hormone represents a legitimate treatment (Rolker-Dolinsky, 1987).

Some authorities have recommended changes in diet to help with PMS. The most common suggestions are to reduce the intake of salt, refined sugar, and caffeinated foods such as coffee, colas, and chocolate. Eating more frequently during the day, taking high dosages of certain vitamins, increasing fiber intake, and drinking herbal teas have been recommended (Harrison, 1982). More recently, exposure to bright lights relieved depression in women who were suffering from a certain type of PMS (Perry, 1989). In general, however, physicians remain skeptical over the efficacy of many remedies for PMS.

The controversy over premenstrual syndrome echoes a long-standing difference in our culture between women's needs and a male-dominated medical establishment. For decades women had reported a spectrum of symptoms associated with the menstrual cycle. Physicians have often failed to take these symptoms seriously or have been at a loss to know how to treat them. Women have often ended up feeling as though they are being perceived as complainers or hypochondriacs looking for attention.

Wherever the debate over PMS takes us, it is clear that the physical symptoms and mood shifts prior to menstruation are very real. It is also clear that before adequate, effective, and reliable treatment for PMS can be developed, there will need to be more high-quality research into all of the complexities involved (Rolker-Dolinsky, 1987).

Male Sex Organs

Just as in the female, the external sex organs of the male (see Fig. 2.16) are often seen as organs of sexual arousal, while the internal structures are associated more with reproduction. In males, however, the lines of distinction are much more vague.

TESTES AND SCROTUM

The two male sex glands, the testes (or testicles), develop within the abdominal cavity during fetal life. A few weeks before birth, the testes gradually move

premenstrual syndrome (PMS): symptoms of physical discomfort, moodiness, and emotional tensions that occur in some women for a few days prior to menstruation.

prostaglandin: hormonelike chemical whose concentrations increase in a woman's body just prior to menstruation.

testes (TEST-ees): pair of male gonads that produce sperm and male hormones.

FIGURE 2.16 External Male Anatomy

The external male sex organs are more visible and accessible than the female's. As with the female, the external organs are the primary source of sexual pleasure, while the internal organs are the source of reproduction, but the distinction is not as clearly defined in males.

downward through the *inguinal canal* into an external pouch of skin, the scrotum. In a small percentage of male infants, the testes do not descend into the scrotum properly, and a few of these cases require medical treatment. The testes have two major functions after puberty: the production of the male sex hormone testosterone, and formation of millions of sperm, the sex cells necessary for human reproduction.

Each testis (see Fig. 2.17) is subdivided internally into several lobes. The lobes are filled with a tangled mass of tiny seminiferous tubules, inside of which the sperm cells are formed. Each of the threadlike tubules is 1 to 3 feet long if extended. Between the tubules are interstitial cells (or Leydig cells) that produce testosterone. They are close to blood vessels, so that the hormone is secreted efficiently into the bloodstream. The seminiferous tubules combine at their ends to form larger ducts, and these empty into a series of even larger tubes, the *vasa efferentia*. Immature sperm from the seminiferous tubules are moved along by wavelike contractions into the vasa efferentia, and then into a coiled tubing network folded against the back and part of the top of each testis, the epididymis. It is in this area that the sperm mature and become ready to leave the body. The epididymis opens into a large duct that leads up into the abdominal cavity from each testis. This duct is called the vas deferens and transports the sperm up to the *seminal vesicle* during sexual activity.

The scrotum of a prepubescent male is quite smooth and light in color. At puberty the testes and scrotum grow, and the outer skin darkens and becomes somewhat wrinkled. The location of the testes in this external pouch is essential, since sperm production can only occur at temperatures slightly below inner body temperature. The *cremasteric muscles* suspend the testes in the scrotum and help to regulate their temperature. In cold surroundings (such as swimming in cold water) or stressful situations, these muscles and the scrotal tissue itself contract, pulling the testes up close to the body to keep them warmer and protected. In warmer surroundings (such as a hot bath), the muscles and scrotal tissue relax so the testes are lowered away from the body to keep them cooler. The adult male testes are about $1^{1}/_{2}$ inches in length and 1 inch in diameter. They are slightly movable in the scrotum. One testis usually hangs slightly lower than

scrotum (SKROTE-um): pouch of skin in which the testes are contained.
testosterone (tes-TAS-ter-one): major male hormone produced by the testes; it helps to produce male secondary sex characteristics.
sperm: reproductive cells produced in the testes; in fertilization, one sperm unites with an ovum.
seminiferous tubules (sem-a-NIF-a-rus): tightly coiled tubules in the testes in which sperm cells are formed.
interstitial cells: cells between the seminiferous tubules that secrete testosterone and other male hormones.
epididymis (ep-a-DID-a-mus): tubular structure on each testis in which sperm cells mature.
vas deferens: tube that leads sperm upward from each testis to the seminal vesicles.

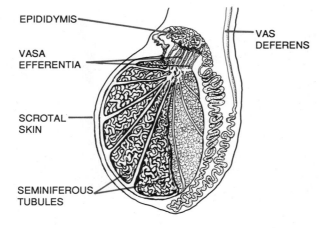

FIGURE 2.17 Testes

The testes are the male gonads or reproductive glands. They are paired structures located in the scrotum and their purpose is to produce sperm and the hormone testosterone that controls male sexual development. The word "testis" is based on the root word for "witness"; the ancient custom in taking an oath was to place a hand on the genitals— "testify."

FIGURE 2.18 Testicular Self-Examination

The best time for a man to examine his testes is right after a hot bath or shower because the testicles descend and the scrotal skin relaxes in the heat. He should place his index and middle fingers on the underside of each testicle and his thumbs on top (A). He should gently roll the testicle between his fingers and thumb. Any abnormal lump would be most likely at the front or the side of the testicle (B).

the other, and in the majority of men, it is the left testis that is lower. In left-handed men, the right testis tends to hang lower. There seems to be no particular significance either way. The scrotal area is well supplied with nerves, and the testes are very sensitive to pressure or sharp blows. Most men find gentle stimulation of the testes and scrotum to be sexually arousing.

During sports or other strenuous activity, increases in body temperature cause the testes to lower away from the body, making them more vulnerable to injury. An athletic supporter or jockstrap holds them up closer to the body, providing support and a measure of protection.

There is some thought that wearing underwear that holds the testicles close to the body can result in interference with sperm production. However, this theory is not consistently supported.

MALE GENITAL AND TESTICULAR SELF-EXAMINATION

Men should also take time at least monthly to examine their genital organs. Adequate lighting, and sometimes a mirror, can help with the self-examination process. Look through the pubic hair to the skin underneath, and examine the head and shaft of the penis carefully. If you are not circumcised, this will require pulling back the foreskin to expose the penile glans. Check for any bumps, sores, or blisters anywhere in the region. They may be reddish or light in color. It is important to

lift up the penis and look underneath, for this is an area that is often overlooked. Also be alert to any soreness in the genitals, or to any itching or burning sensations during urination or around the urethral opening. While many of these symptoms do not indicate serious conditions, you should have them checked by a physician or other clinician who specializes in men's health concerns.

Cancer of the testes is a relatively rare disease, with fewer than 5,000 new cases being diagnosed each year in the United States. It is primarily a disease of younger men, especially between the ages of 20 and 35. When detected and treated early, the chances of survival are excellent. However, if it is not treated within the first 3 months, the survival rate falls dramatically to only about 25 percent. Therefore it is crucial for men to get into the habit of checking their testes regularly for any lumps or other unusual symptoms (Smith, 1980).

Here is the best way to proceed with testicular self-examination. Choose a time after a hot shower or bath, so that the testes are lowered away from the body. Roll each testicle gently between the thumb and fingers, especially looking for any small hard lumps that may be found directly on the front or side surface of a testis (see Fig. 2.18). Such a lump is usually painless. Don't be alarmed at feeling the epididymis toward the top and back of each testis. Although not all lumps are malignant, any growth of this sort should be reported to a physician immediately for further investigation. Other symptoms that a man should consider suspicious and worth reporting include any "heavy" feeling in a testicle, accumulation of fluid in the scrotum, swelling of lymph nodes or other discomfort in the groin area, and any swelling or tenderness in the breasts.

If testicular cancer is diagnosed, the usual treatment involves surgical removal of the entire testis. The other testis is left in place and can easily produce enough male hormones on its own. Sexual functioning is typically not impaired in any way. An artificial, gel-filled testis can be placed in the scrotum for cosmetic reasons. Men should become comfortable with this self-examination procedure as a potentially lifesaving measure.

PENIS

Just above the scrotal sac is the male sex organ called the penis. The sensitive smooth and rounded head of the penis is called the glans. The glans is filled with nerve endings and is particularly sensitive to sexual stimulation. The two most sensitive areas of the glans are the frenulum, a thin, tightly stretched band of skin on its underside connecting the glans with the shaft (body) of the penis; and the corona, which is the ridge around the edge of the glans. The urethral opening or urinary meatus is found at the tip of the glans. When a male is born, the head of the penis is partly covered by a fold of skin called the prepuce or foreskin.

The longer body of the penis is called the shaft. The skin on the shaft is quite loose, allowing erection to occur. Inside the penile shaft are three cylinders of erectile tissue, each full of nerves and blood vessels (see Fig. 2.19). The two cylinders of tissues lying parallel along the top and sides of the penis are called the *corpora cavernosa*. The third, slightly narrower cylinder extends along the underside of the penis and is called the *corpus spongiosum*.

The penis is not only important as the male organ for sexual activity and reproduction, but it also is the organ through which urine leaves the body. The tube that carries both sperm and urine in the penis is the urethra, located in the corpus spongiosum, which extends back to the urinary bladder and connects with the sperm-carrying ducts.

ERECTION

During sexual arousal, the three cylinders inside the penis become engorged with blood so that the penis expands in circumference, becomes longer and harder, and stands out from the body. This is erection, and it is usually necessary for successful sexual intercourse. It is possible, however, for some men to have orgasm

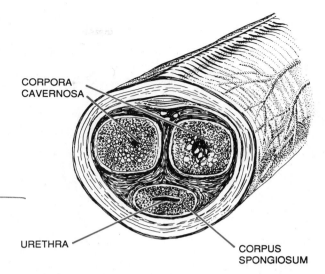

CORPORA CAVERNOSA

URETHRA

CORPUS SPONGIOSUM

FIGURE 2.19 Cross Section of a Penis

The penis is the male organ of urination and copulation. This cross section shows the three internal structures of the penis, all cylindrical in shape. The *corpus spongiosum* contains the urethra through which pass semen and urine. All three have spongelike tissue dotted with small blood vessels.

without erection. During erection, the three cylinders of erectile tissue may be felt distinctly. Penile erection occurs in several phases, involving increased blood flow into the erectile tissue and decreased flow out of the tissue. The penis elongates and expands to its maximum capacity, eventually becoming highly rigid as stimulation continues (Batra & Lue, 1990).

Sometimes there is a slight curvature in the erect penis, often toward the left. Unless the curvature is caused by some injury or disease (which is quite rare), it will not interfere with sexual performance (Horton & Devine, 1975).

Erection of the penis is controlled by a spinal reflex and is mostly an involuntary reaction (see Fig.

penis: male sexual organ that can become erect when stimulated; it leads urine and sperm to the outside of the body.

glans: in the male, the sensitive head of the penis.

frenulum (FREN-yu-lum): thin, tightly-drawn fold of skin on the underside of the penile glans; it is highly sensitive.

corona: the ridge around the penile glans.

foreskin: fold of skin covering the penile glans; also called prepuce.

urethra (yu-REE-thrah): tube that passes from the urinary bladder to the outside of the body.

shaft: in the male, cylindrical base of penis that contains three columns of spongy tissue: two corpora cavernosa and a corpus spongiosum.

erection: enlargement and stiffening of the penis as blood engorges the columns of spongy tissue and internal muscles contract.

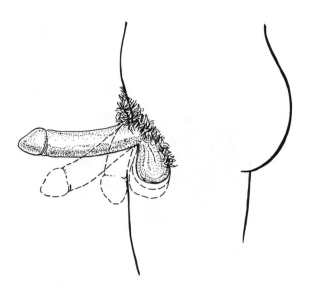

FIGURE 2.20 Penile Erection

Penile erection is achieved primarily by the increase in blood flow through the *corpus spongiosum* and the *corpora cavernosa* during sexual arousal. Other factors, such as spinal reflex and emotion, enter into the physical act of erection.

2.20). However, the cerebral cortex of the brain also has input and is intricately connected to the "erection center" of the spinal cord. So both reflexive and thought processes can work together to stimulate or inhibit erections. Even in men whose spinal cords have been severed, breaking the connection between the erection center and the brain, physical stimulation of the penis generates erection, although the brain has no awareness of feeling in the penis (Sporer, 1991).

The actual mechanism of erection is not fully understood. It is known that two muscles in the perineal area (below the scrotum), the *bulbocavernosus* and *ischiocavernosus muscles,* show bursts of activity just prior to erection. This activity is apparently closely related to increases in arterial blood flow into the penis, and the muscles and circulatory vessels then work together in maintaining erection (Batra & Lue, 1990). There is no evidence from research to date that the veins "close down" to keep blood trapped in the penis (Karacan, Aslan, & Hirshkowitz, 1983).

Penis Size Penis size is a nearly universal concern of men. The average nonerect penis is 2^1/2 to 4 inches long, and the erect penis is usually 5^1/2 to slightly more than 6 inches long. Yet normal penises may be much shorter or much longer than average, the nonerect range being roughly from 2 to 6 inches, and the erect range being roughly 3^1/2 to 13 inches (Masters & Johnson, 1966; Dickinson, 1949). Penis diameter is

usually about 1^1/2 inches during erection. Masters and Johnson have found that erection seems to have an equalizing effect, since smaller penises gain proportionately more size than larger penises upon erection. This equalizing effect was confirmed through a reanalysis of some of the original Kinsey work, in which 2,770 men measured their penises in both the flaccid and erect states. The more recent researchers (Jamison & Gebhard, 1988) divided flaccid penises into two categories: short (averaging 3.1 inches) and long (averaging 4.4 inches). They found that shorter penises tended to gain about 85 percent in size during erection, to an average of 5.8 inches; while the longer penises grew only by 47 percent, to an average of 6.5 inches. Likewise, narrower penises gain more in circumference during erection.

Penises vary in length, width, and shape, all being perfectly functional, perfectly normal. Although some men and women prefer larger penises for sexual activity, there is no basis for believing that any factors of penile size affect a man's ability to be a fully satisfactory sexual partner. There are specific physiological reasons for this. The inner two-thirds of the vagina expand (balloon) during sexual arousal. The outer third (nearest to the external opening) becomes smaller, embracing the penis. It is in this outer portion of the vagina that the greater sexual sensitivity is centered. Additionally, women can contract the vaginal muscles. There is no demonstrated relationship between general body size or the size of other particular organs and penis size.

Male Circumcision: The Debate When a male is born, the parents may decide to have the foreskin of the penis removed in a surgical procedure called circumcision, leaving the glans fully exposed (see Fig. 2.21). Until recently, most males in the United States were circumcised. The procedure, however, has been much less commonly used in Europe and Canada. Circumcision has sometimes been a part of a religious custom, as in the Jewish faith. The other most frequently stated reason for circumcision involves hygiene. It has been assumed that young males will find it troublesome to learn how to pull back the foreskin and wash the glans, thus permitting the buildup of a material called smegma that can then lead to infection.

There has been a growing controversy over the widespread practice of circumcising male infants. Some have complained that there are usually no legitimate reasons to justify circumcision, especially since there are risks in any such surgery (Ritter, 1980; Potter, 1989). Because the procedure was once per-

circumcision: in the male, surgical removal of the foreskin from the penis.

Case Study

ANDY: A YOUNG MAN CONCERNED ABOUT PENIS SIZE

Andy, a college freshman, shared with a counselor a concern that had plagued him since the age of 13. He was convinced that his penis was abnormally short in comparison to other men of his age. This embarrassed him to such an extent that he avoided all situations where he might be nude in the presence of other men, and he found it impossible to urinate in lavatories when other men stood next to him. Although he dated frequently and had an active sex life, Andy avoided allowing young women to see his penis or to touch it with their hands. During sexual intercourse, he would occasionally think himself to be inadequate, often resulting in difficulty in sustaining erection or in reaching orgasms. This problem contributed to a poor self-image.

Through questioning Andy and showing him photographs of typical male genitals, it became clear to the counselor that Andy's penis was within the limits of normal size. His body seemed to have matured normally. Andy was

then referred to a physician who confirmed that there was no physical problem and that Andy's penis was indeed very typical with regard to size. In further counseling, Andy was reminded that looking down onto one's own penis may lead to unfair comparison with other penises, which are viewed from the front or side. It was suggested that he look at his penis in a mirror. He was also assured that there was no reason why he should not be able to function perfectly well sexually.

Talking about his concerns and getting professional confirmation of the normalcy of his penis seemed to reduce the pressure Andy had felt. Gradually he let himself be seen in the nude by other males in the shower room, and he allowed his female sexual partners to see his penis. When no one expressed any special surprise at his organ's size, he gained further confidence concerning his normalcy.

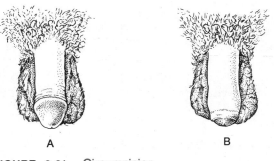

A   B

FIGURE 2.21 Circumcision

The surgical removal of the penile foreskin has a history that goes back as far as 4000 B.C. in Egypt. Its justification has been ritualistic, religious, and medical. The circumcised penis (A) leaves the glans exposed, supposedly making it easier to keep the penis clean and prevent the possibility of cancer. The uncircumcised penis (B) in a very few instances may have a condition called *phimosis* in which the foreskin cannot be retracted over the glans.

formed without anesthesia in infants, there was probably a fair amount of pain. Anticircumcision groups feel that this pain is an unnecessary trauma for a newborn, and claim that it can have continuing negative psycho-

logical consequences. More recently, however, it has become standard procedure to use a form of anesthesia called the dorsal penile nerve block, permitting pain-free surgery (Schoen, 1990; Williamson, 1990).

One study showed that a sample of 145 new mothers of boys tended to favor circumcised partners for the following by a substantial margin: intercourse (71 percent), attractiveness (76 percent), manual stimulation (75 percent), and oral sex (83 percent). Not surprisingly, 89 percent of these women had had their sons circumcised. The women cited reasons such as visual appeal, hygiene, and smell as the most typical reasons for their preference. Even the majority of women who had grown up with uncircumcised brothers preferred circumcised sexual partners (Williamson & Williamson, 1988).

One medical problem that has been cited as a good reason for circumcision is phimosis, or a too-tight foreskin, making it difficult to retract. Yet opponents of circumcision insist that spontaneous erections begin even before birth and gradually stretch the

phimosis (fy-MOS-us): a condition in which the penile foreskin is too tight to retract easily.

foreskin, so that by 6 years of age it can be retracted without difficulty in almost 100 percent of cases. If a real problem exists at some later stage in life, circumcision can then be performed. Opponents also believe that in infants the foreskin should be tight and nonretractable to protect the urethral opening from exposure to fecal material or other possible irritants. They further suggest that circumcision reduces the sensitivity of the glans and cuts away 25 percent of what could have been sensitive penile skin (Wallerstein, 1980). However, there is no evidence that circumcision affects male sexual responsiveness in any way.

In the 1960s, 95 percent of boys in the United States were circumcised. The American Academy of Pediatrics first took a position on male circumcision in 1971, stating that there were "no valid medical indications" for routine circumcision of newborns. During the 1980s there was a distinct decline in the procedure, so that by the end of 1986 only 59.4 percent of male infants were being circumcised (*SIECUS Report*, 1987). However, later in that decade, there was mounting evidence that this trend was leading to an increase in urinary tract infections in infant boys, a condition that can cause kidney complications. A review of the health records of 427,698 infants born in U.S. army hospitals over a 10-year period showed that lack of circumcision raised a boy's risk of such infection elevenfold (Wiswell et al., 1987). In early 1989 the American Academy of Pediatrics reconsidered their earlier position, stating that circumcision "has potential medical benefits and advantages," although they stopped short of recommending the procedure routinely. The chairman of the AAP's task force on circumcision has gone on record as supporting routine circumcision. He believes that the long-term disease-prevention potentials of the procedure outweigh its risks (Schoen, 1990).

Some men dissatisfied with having been circumcised have undergone reconstructive surgery to restore a foreskin. During the procedure, scrotal skin is transplanted over the glans in a series of operations. Although the newly created foreskin is somewhat different in color and texture from the skin on the penile shaft, those who have undergone the surgery have expressed satisfaction with the results (Greer et al., 1982).

INTERNAL MALE ORGANS

Located at the underside of the urinary bladder, and surrounding the urethra where it enters the bladder, is the prostate gland (see Fig. 2.22). This gland, a little larger than a walnut, has three lobes of muscular and glandular tissue. Along with the seminal vesicles, it produces secretions that help to transport the sperm through the penis. This fluid is called semen, or seminal fluid, and it is a milky, sticky, alkaline substance composed of proteins, citric acid, calcium, fats, and some enzymes. Semen may be quite thick and gelatinous when it leaves the penis, or it may be thin and watery. It usually becomes thicker soon after ejaculation, but then liquefies in 15 to 25 minutes.

The vas deferens of each testis carries sperm up into the body cavity, around to the back of the bladder, and back down to the prostate. Near the junction of the two vas deferens into a single ejaculatory duct, each vas deferens joins with a saclike structure called the seminal vesicle. Both seminal vesicles are about 2 inches long. The seminal vesicles produce secretions that help to activate the sperm and make them motile. Secretions from the vesicles, which constitute about 70 percent of the seminal fluid, join with the sperm and empty into the ejaculatory duct, which then joins the urethra within the prostate gland.

Below the prostate gland, located at the base of the penis and on each side of the urethra, are two pea-sized glands called Cowper's glands or bulbourethral glands. When a male is sexually aroused, these two glands secrete a clear, sticky alkaline substance, or preejaculatory fluid, that coats the inner lining of the urethra. Some of it may appear as a droplet at the tip of the penis during arousal. The secretion has often been called a lubricant, and indeed, if present in sufficient amounts it can serve as a lubricant for sexual activity. However, it is not always produced in such copious amounts and is believed instead primarily to help neutralize acids in the urethra and thus permit safe passage of sperm. Although the primary function of Cowper's gland secretion is not to carry sperm, it often does, and therefore can be responsible for pregnancy even if ejaculation does not occur within the vagina.

SPERM PRODUCTION AND EJACULATION

From puberty to old age, the male testes produce large amounts of sperm cells. The testes are partially controlled by two pituitary hormones, two of the same hormones found in females. One is luteinizing hor-

---

prostate: gland located beneath the urinary bladder in the male; it produces some of the secretions in semen.

semen (SEE-men): mixture of fluids and sperm cells that is ejaculated through the penis.

seminal vesicle (SEM-un-al): gland at the end of each vas deferens that secretes a chemical that helps sperm to become motile.

Cowper's glands: two small glands in the male that secrete an alkaline fluid into the urethra during sexual arousal.

bulbourethral glands: also called Cowper's glands.

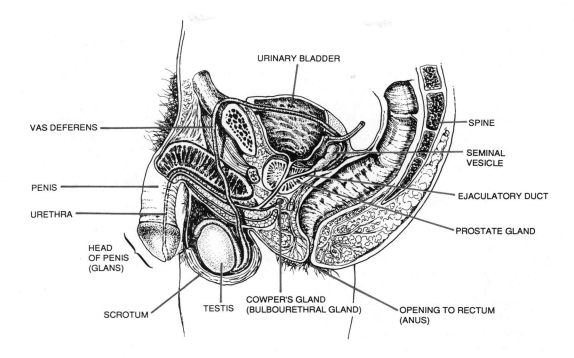

URINARY BLADDER

VAS DEFERENS

SPINE

SEMINAL VESICLE

PENIS

EJACULATORY DUCT

URETHRA

PROSTATE GLAND

HEAD OF PENIS (GLANS)

SCROTUM

TESTIS

COWPER'S GLAND (BULBOURETHRAL GLAND)

OPENING TO RECTUM (ANUS)

FIGURE 2.22 Male Sexual and Reproductive Organs

The external and internal sexual and reproductive organs of the male are shown here in longitudinal section. Although men are familiar with their more obvious external sex organs, they are often less well informed about their internal reproductive and sexual anatomy.

mone or LH, called interstitial-cell-stimulating hormone (ICSH) in males, and the other is follicle-stimulating hormone or FSH. The ICSH begins to be produced at puberty and stimulates the interstitial cells of the testes to produce the male hormone testosterone. The FSH helps to stimulate the sperm-producing cells—spermatocytes—in the linings of the seminiferous tubules to produce sperm.

Each mature sperm consists of a head and tail, separated by a short thickened area (see Fig. 2.23 on page 52). The head contains the male's genetic material, and the thickened middle area contains an energy-releasing mechanism that will help move the tail. Sperm are usually about 55 microns long (0.0021 inch or 0.055 millimeter) and can only be seen through a microscope. It is believed that an adult male produces about 15 to 30 billion sperm each month.

During sexual excitement and activity, the sperm are moved from the epididymis in the testes up to the ejaculatory duct through each vas deferens. Their tails are probably activated into a lashing movement by the secretions of the seminal vesicles. Stimulation of the erect penis sends nerve impulses to the ejaculatory center of the spinal cord. When these impulses have built to a certain threshold, the ejaculatory response is triggered. Sperm from the ejaculatory duct are moved into the urethra, along with fluids from both the

seminal vesicles and the prostate that form the semen. There are then contractions in the muscles surrounding the ejaculatory duct and urethra, forcing the semen to be ejaculated through the end of the penis. This is usually accompanied by the pleasurable sensations of orgasm, or sexual climax, although the two phenomena, ejaculation and orgasm, can occur separately (see chapter 3, "Human Sexual Response").

The amount of semen ejaculated depends on many factors—age, amount of sexual stimulation, general health, and interval of time since the last ejaculation—but typically there are 3 to 5 cubic centimeters of semen, about a teaspoonful or less. As much as 11 cubic centimeters of semen can be ejaculated. In the typical ejaculate, there are 150 million to 600 million sperm. Many men subjectively report that the more intense the sensation of orgasm, the more semen ejaculated and the more force with which it is propelled out of the penis. Most often the semen oozes out

interstitial-cell-stimulating hormone (ICSH): pituitary hormone that stimulates the testes to secrete testosterone; known as luteinizing hormone (LH) in females.

spermatocytes (sper-MAT-o-sites): cells lining the seminiferous tubules from which sperm cells are produced.

ejaculation: muscular expulsion of semen from the penis.

orgasm: pleasurable sensations and series of contractions that release sexual tension, usually accompanied by ejaculation in men.

Male Medicine

When a woman has a problem that involves urination, menstruation, contraception, reproduction, abortion, breast development, or sexuality, she is likely to see a gynecologist. Unfortunately there is no single specialist who can offer us men such a wide range of services. Urologists do specialize in problems of the male urogenital system, but it is rare to find one who is equally familiar with reproductive and sexual disorders as well. The average urologist is no more of an expert on sexuality than the average family doctor—neither of whom is likely to have had any special training in sexuality. The urologist is only now beginning to gain special knowledge of hormones, which are essential to our sexuality and reproduction.

The need for specialists in male medicine is becoming recognized among many professionals in the fields of urology, reproduction, sexuality, and endocrinology. The doctor whose knowledge will encompass all of these areas may be called an "andrologist." At the present time no one doctor has established himself as a practicing andrologist—due to current medical licensing which has not yet recognized this specialty as well as the way in which "male medicine" is traditionally taught. Those involved in the study of male medicine are mostly researchers and a few practicing urologists. But hopefully men will soon have a counterpart to the gynecologist to attend to the complex problems of the male urogenital system.

Until people stop responding with, "A what?" when you mention your last visit to your andrologist, we will have to take our urogenital difficulties to the urologist. Since the urinary tract and the reproductive system are separate and highly complicated systems, men have to make sure that the urologist we choose or have been referred to has special familiarity with the area in which our troubles lie.

—Sam Julty, *Men's Bodies, Men's Lives,* 1979, New York: Delta Books

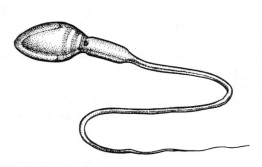

FIGURE 2.23 Sperm

A mature sperm consists of a head, middle piece, and tail. The head contains the chromosomes and is the part involved in fertilization. The tail moves the sperm from the ejaculatory duct into the urethra prior to ejaculation. If all the ova needed to repopulate the world would fit into two gallons, the sperm for the same purpose would fit into an aspirin tablet.

of the penis under some pressure, but it can sometimes spurt several inches.

Although ejaculation is a reflexive phenomenon, it is quite possible for men to learn how to control the length of time it takes to reach orgasm and ejaculation.

This usually involves learning how to modulate sexual excitement or to control inner musculature so that when ejaculation is near, stimulation to the penis is reduced until the sensation subsides. There is more about controlling ejaculation in chapter 5, "Birth Control and Unintended Pregnancy."

As a result of certain illnesses or the effects of some tranquilizing drugs, the semen may be ejaculated into the urinary bladder. The muscles at the base of the bladder that normally close the bladder off during ejaculation apparently do not contract, so that semen is permitted to enter the bladder. There is the full sensation of orgasm, but no semen leaves the penis. This phenomenon is called retrograde ejaculation. There are also organic problems that simply lead to the absence of semen and a resultant dry orgasm called anejaculation.

Under ideal laboratory conditions, sperm may be kept alive for up to 2 weeks after ejaculation. However, after ejaculation into the vagina during sexual

retrograde ejaculation: abnormal passage of semen into the urinary bladder at the time of ejaculation.
anejaculation: lack of ejaculation at the time of orgasm.

intercourse, it is unlikely that many sperm remain motile for more than 2 or 3 days. Once semen has been deposited in the vagina, some of it begins to seep into the uterus and the sperm swim against mucous currents and gravitational pull. Healthy sperm can swim about 3 to 7 inches in an hour, and following ejaculation some sperm can be expected to reach the female's fallopian tubes in 1 to 2 hours. Despite the many millions of sperm deposited in the vagina, only a very few thousand actually reach the fallopian tubes, where fertilization of the ovum can take place.

HORMONAL CYCLES IN MEN

Men do not undergo, so far as we know, predictable cyclical changes in hormonal levels, such as the female menstrual cycle, that affect their fertility. Some medical conditions, such as epileptic seizures, seem to worsen on roughly monthly cycles, and this might be traced to subtle shifts in hormonal concentrations. There have also been suggestions that men experience periodic emotional ups and downs that seem to follow cyclical patterns, but this has been difficult to substantiate in research. In one study the testosterone levels of 20 men were measured over a period of 60 days, the results indicating that most of the men had measurable testosterone cycles ranging from 3 to 30 days. The majority had cycles of around 22 days. The testosterone levels were also correlated with moods, but the only identifiable connection was between high testosterone levels and a greater degree of depression (Doering et al., 1978). Perhaps further evidence will emerge that men have cycles relating to their sexual or reproductive physiology.

Menopause and the Male Climacteric: The Sexual Systems Age

Aging is a natural process among living things, with predictable physiological changes occurring over time at all levels from the cellular to the organismic. For humans, it is apparently a process that is largely genetically controlled. Various degenerative physiological aspects of aging are triggered by genes, while our bodies also experience other effects of normal wear and tear. There are wide individual differences, but each of us experiences a gradual process of slowing down and becoming physically less pliable. While its rate may be affected by heredity, the environment, and personal health habits, the aging process is inevitable and irreversible.

The sexual implications of aging stem from both psychological and biological changes. In a society that places a high premium on the sexual attractiveness and power of the young, there is bound to be some discouragement as one sees oneself age. Yet, aging bodies may also be perceived as having beauty and strength if they can be approached with a positive psychological attitude.

FEMALE MENOPAUSE

The female body is genetically programmed to cease menstruating sometime in middle age, usually between the ages of 45 and 55. This is called menopause, and the years surrounding menopause are usually termed the climacteric. In popular usage, this is sometimes called the "change of life," or simply "the change." Modifications in ovarian function usually begin prior to age 30, and there is a gradual decline in the hormonal output of these glands. Eventually there is increased irregularity in ovulation and menstrual periods. There are usually unpredictable sequences of scanty menstrual flow and increased flow, but a few women just stop menstruating quite abruptly, never having it happen again. Although the pituitary gland continues to produce its follicle stimulating hormone (FSH) and luteinizing hormone (LH) that help control the woman's menstrual cycle, the ovaries apparently become increasingly insensitive to their stimulation. The hormone-producing tissues of the ovary atrophy until their output of estrogen and progesterone becomes minimal.

As the woman's hormonal levels drop, the most noticeable result is the gradual cessation of menstruation. This results from the lack of hormonal stimulation to the inner lining of the uterus, the endometrium. This means, of course, that the woman is no longer able to conceive, although most physicians recommend using birth control for a full year after the last menstrual period. However, there are other effects on the body as well. Very gradually, the uterus and breasts decrease somewhat in size. The inner walls of the vagina become thinner, and reduction in the number of small blood vessels in the pelvic region may result in reduced vaginal lubrication. There may also be changes in the texture and color of the skin and hair, and an increased tendency to gain weight, especially on the hips.

Another consequence of decreased estrogen production in some women is a weakening of bones,

climacteric: mid-life period experienced by both men and women when there is greater emotional stress than usual and sometimes physical symptoms.

Case Study

CONNIE: A WOMAN FACES MENOPAUSE

Connie considered herself to be a stable woman who had faced life crises with equanimity. She had raised three children, maintained a happy marriage, and found success in her ownership of a small bookshop. As she looks back on her menopause now, she says, "The one thing I wasn't ready for was a major change in my body."

At the age of 48 she began to experience increased irregularity of her menstrual periods, and her gynecologist assured her that it was the normal onset of menopause. She also experienced occasional "hot flashes" that would take her by surprise, and increased swings between emotional extremes. But the psychological stresses she encountered were the most difficult to handle.

In her words, "What I wasn't prepared for was how I began to feel about myself. While I had never considered menstruation to be any great privilege, as it began to cease altogether, I was faced with the realization that my reproductive years were over. As my husband reminded me, we certainly were never going to want more children, but for me that wasn't really the point. It represented an important passage for me. I

was leaving the longest and most eventful period of my entire life behind.

"I had never paid much attention to age, mine or others. Suddenly I began to feel as though I were heading toward the latter stages of middle age and was soon to be old.

"I sought out a few women I knew and also talked with a female counselor about my feelings. I know that a lot of what I went through in menopause was the result of the many hormonal changes going on in my body. But some of it was also a very natural psychological reaction that I simply hadn't anticipated. I talked it through, worked it through, and eventually began to feel more like myself again. The support of my husband and children made a huge difference.

"Now, 3 years later, I feel happier sexually than I've been in a long time. We don't have to worry about birth control anymore, and my husband and I have a loving bond that is always very reassuring for me. I know I have moved into a new phase of my life, but it is one that is also filled with potential for growth and new directions. I'm not just getting older—I'm getting wiser."

called osteoporosis. This condition most frequently strikes postmenopausal women who are slender and slight, and who have led sedentary lives. Women suffering from osteoporosis are predisposed to fractures of the hip and arm, and often suffer chronic back pain because of vertebral collapse. Although this condition cannot be completely cured, it may be treated to reduce the amount of bone weakness. The usual treatments involve the prescription of Vitamin D, calcium supplements, estrogen replacement and/or exercise (Neaman, 1981).

Menopausal changes in the body's hormonal balances may also cause mood alterations and other psychological effects. Some women complain of depression, irritability, or other emotional symptoms. Some experience unpredictable dilation of the blood vessels in the skin, causing a flushed, sweaty feeling. This is called a "hot flash," and its exact cause is unknown (Willis, 1988).

Menopausal women who are treated with dosages of estrogen hormone experience a reversal of the physical changes that accompany menopause (Walling, Andersen, & Johnson, 1990). However, estrogen replacement therapy (ERT) has been a highly controversial form of medical treatment. First popularized by Robert Wilson (1964) as a way of staying youthful and "feminine" for life, ERT eventually came under attack as a risky procedure. A number of studies in the 1970s began to demonstrate a statistical relationship between

osteoporosis (ah-stee-o-po-ROW-sus): disease caused by loss of calcium from the bones in postmenopausal women, leading to brittle bones and stooped posture.

hot flash: a flushed, sweaty feeling in the skin caused by dilated blood vessels, often associated with menopause.

estrogen replacement therapy (ERT): controversial treatment of the physical changes of menopause by administering dosages of the hormone estrogen.

ERT and the incidence of uterine and breast cancer. Several conditions were found to represent increased risk of complications with this therapy: a family history of blood clotting disorders, high blood pressure, heart disease, liver disease, and diabetes. So while ERT may well reduce some of the more unpleasant side effects of the climacteric, most authorities felt that in the majority of women the long-term risks outweighed the short-term benefits (Rayner, 1986).

A recent study of older women who have received estrogen, however, has again suggested that the advantages of ERT outweigh the risks. The study examined questionnaires and medical records of 8,881 women, finding that those who received estrogen actually tended to live longer than those who did not, and that they experienced less heart disease, stroke, and broken bones. Lower dosages of the hormone—about half of what was once considered necessary—over a long period of time seemed to have the most positive effects (Henderson et al., 1991). Again there have been cautionary statements indicating that women on estrogen therapy should be alert to breast lumps and uterine bleeding, and that the therapy would not be suitable for all aging women.

Implications for Women's Sexuality Females are typically raised to think of menstruation as a sign of being a woman, with its additional symbolic implications of fertility, femininity, and sexual readiness. Menarche is often heralded as the beginning of womanhood. Consequently, for many women menopause represents a loss of an important facet of womanhood and femininity. They fall prey to some of the menopause-related myths: that it is the beginning of the end of life, that sexual attractiveness and arousal deteriorate after menopause, and that one's purpose as a woman (that is, reproduction) has been lost (Smallwood & VanDyck, 1979).

Research studies generally confirm that menopause need not markedly affect a woman's sexual functioning, although there is research to indicate that over 25 percent of women experience some decrease in sexual desire during middle life anyway (Hallstrom & Samuelsson, 1990). As a woman faces the physical and psychological changes of menopause, there may be a temporary shift in sexual desire. It may increase or decrease, but there are usually no major, long-lasting changes. Some women perceive menopause as a release from concern about intercourse resulting in an unwanted pregnancy, thus freeing them to be more relaxed sexually. As women approach menopause, they sometimes assume that they are no longer at risk for pregnancy. About 25 percent of women aged 40 to 44 are at risk of unwanted pregnancy, and one in five of the at-risk group uses no birth control. This probably explains why women over 40 have some 18,000 abortions a year, giving them a ratio of abortions to live births second only to young teenage girls (Fortney, 1989).

Much of how a woman's sexual life is affected depends on how she views herself and menopause. It is influenced by the woman's cultural background, values about sex, social environment, overall health, and her fantasies and expectations regarding menopause.

It is therefore crucial that women get accurate information and emotional support through their menopausal experiences. There are counselors, women's centers, and trained social workers who may provide such help. Women need to be able to communicate their fears, doubts, and insecurities while being reassured that menopause is simply a natural stage of human development (Greenwood, 1988). It is important for the woman's partner to receive information and counseling about her menopausal experience as well.

THE MALE CLIMACTERIC

Men do not seem to have well-defined cyclical changes in hormonal balance, or reproductive or sexual capabilities, related to aging. They usually continue to produce sperm cells all of their lives, even into very old age, although the risk of genetic abnormalities in the sperm also increases with age. There have been several studies of testosterone production in aging males (Silny, 1980), but their significance is debatable. There are very gradual declines in the concentrations of male hormones found in the body through the mid-40s, and by age 75, testosterone levels often drop up to 90 percent compared with levels before the age of 30.

More significantly, biochemical changes in the body cause more testosterone to become chemically bound to blood proteins, or plasma, as a man ages. This results in a lower free testosterone index (FTI), and it is the free, unbound testosterone that seems to have the most important influence on the body. A study conducted by the National Institute on Aging (1979) found that age did not seem to have a major effect on several hormone levels in men, including testosterone. The study did find, however, that higher FTIs seem to correlate with higher levels of sexual activity in men.

More recent research indicates that optimal sexual functioning in males may be dependent on the presence of a minimum amount of free testosterone in the body. For men in which the FTI is low, administration of extra testosterone seems to improve sexual interest and potency (Carani et al., 1990). Testosterone replacement therapy carries some risks as well, and must be prescribed with caution.

Since there is usually no marked decrease in hormonal levels, and no loss of reproductive capacity, there really is nothing in males similar to menopause. Nevertheless, popular magazines continue to publish articles about "male menopause." Although it is less predictable, and its symptoms more variable, men often do experience a period of stress. It is often called mid-life crisis or transition, or the male climacteric (Moss, 1978), and is characterized by increased anxiety, depression, insomnia, hypochondria, loss of appetite, and/or chronic fatigue. Men often tend to smoke and drink more, develop high blood pressure, and pursue extramarital affairs at this stage of life (Henker, 1977).

This time in a man's life is often characterized by major changes and realizations. Most professionals believe that it is these psychological stresses that constitute the male climacteric. Again, in a youth-oriented culture, men must face the fact that they are aging. Men with wives and families are sharing the menopausal changes of their spouses and having their children leave home. In more traditional family structures, in which the man has been a primary breadwinner, he may begin to feel weary of the years of responsibility for wife and children. Middle age may be a time when a career plateau has been reached, and further vocational opportunities become more limited. Physical changes and stress-generated tension may produce alterations in sexual interest and behavior,

resulting in even more worry and discouragement. Psychological stress in middle-aged men has been shown to be greater when there are tensions in their marriages or in relationships with adolescent children (Julian, McKenry, & Arnold, 1990). The male climacteric largely seems to be a vicious cycle of middle-age stresses that feed on one another.

Surviving the Male Climacteric Because menopause has been more specifically identified, women often receive more support and understanding for their difficult physical and psychological symptoms. Men may need the same kind of supportive help through their mid-life crises as well. Counseling can help a man express his concerns and deal with his confusing emotions, but men may be reluctant to seek this sort of help. They may need guidance to help them realize that finding appropriate support during life's various crises is a strength, not a weakness. It is important for men to be cautioned about making major life changes during the throes of such a crisis. They may be better advised to try sticking with their present careers and relationships, while working to resolve any conflicts or tensions within those important areas of life. Then as things are brought into a more rational perspective, sensible changes in life-style and goals may be considered. ■

testosterone replacement therapy: administering testosterone injections to increase sexual interest or potency in older men; not considered safe for routine use.

SELF-EVALUATION

Your Sex Education: Past, Present, and Future

Sex education is far more than learning about the body's reproductive system. It is also an exercise in self-awareness—becoming acquainted with one's own sexual feelings, needs, and values. Sex education is also a lifelong process that must constantly integrate new information and changing personal situations. The exercises that follow ask you to examine the process of sex education as it relates to your life.

1. *Looking back.* Spend some time thinking about your answers to the following questions. They will help clarify some of the background of your sex education. You many want to discuss your answers with another trusted person.

   a. Can you recall your first discussions about sex with another child, a parent, or an adult? If so, can you remember any feelings or attitudes that you developed in relationship to that time and the topic of sex?

   b. How and when did you first learn what you consider to be the important information about the sex organs, reproduction, and other aspects of human sexuality? Would you say that the information was conveyed to you in a relatively positive, negative, or neutral atmosphere emotionally?

   c. Do you remember the first book or magazine you read that had factual information about sex? How did you react to it? Did it have illustrations, and if so, how did you react to those illustrations?

   d. In addition to this book, what other books on human sexuality have you at least partially read recently?

2. In the next column is a list of topics relating to human sexuality. You may be better informed on some of them than on others. Using the rating standards shown, rate each topic as to your level of competence with it, using appropriate checkmarks.

3. As you reexamine the checkmarks you made in question 2, pay attention to those topics you need to know more about. For each of them, indicate what your course of action, if any, will be:

   a. Will you seek further information on the topic? Why or why not?

   b. Where will you begin the search for the information?

   c. Are there some personal implications involved in your wanting to understand the topic better?

4. Do you expect to have children (or do you have children) for whom you will have some responsibility to provide effective sex education? If so, consider the following:

   a. Have you already made some attempts at educating children about sex? If so, how successful do you think you were and on what criteria do you base that evaluation?

   b. Make a list of goals that you feel are important to the sex education of children at different age levels; choose those goals in which you may play an active part. What would you not want to be a part of your children's sex education?

   c. What resources can you have available to assist with the sex education process? Consider books, films, television programs, other people (including professionals), and your own skills and competencies.

   d. Now, either alone or with another adult, try explaining aloud some of the things you would want your child to know about sex, considering the child's age and level of maturity. You might want to tape your talk so you can evaluate its effectiveness later, or you might have the other adult make comments and suggestions. This is an exercise to see how clearly and accurately you can express concepts about sex.

Are you aware of institutional sex education programs that might be available in your local schools, churches, or other agencies? If none exist, you might consider becoming instrumental in working for effective sex education. If programs already exist, you might want to help evaluate their effectiveness. First of all, you should clarify how you feel about sex education and get as much information about various programs as you can.

CHAPTER SUMMARY

1. The human sex organs have always been recognized for their procreative (reproductive) functions, but their potentials for pleasure and intimate communication have become increasingly recognized.

2. The female vulva consists of the external sex organs known as the mons, the major and minor labia, the clitoris, and the openings to the urethra and vagina.

3. The clitoris has a sensitive tip, or glans, and a shaft that extends back under a covering of tissue, the prepuce. Some cultures, religions, or social customs require surgical procedures such as clitoridectomy or infibulation to be performed as rites of passage.

4. The vagina is a muscular-walled organ of sexual pleasure and reproduction that extends into the woman's body. Its opening may be partially covered by tissue called a hymen.

5. Regular genital self-examination for women is a good way to assure early detection of infections or irritations.

6. The uterus is the organ in which fetal development takes place. Its cervix extends into the posterior part of the vagina. The Pap smear examines cells from the cervical area for suspicious (precancerous) signs.

7. The ovaries produce female hormones and eggs (ova). The fallopian tubes transport ova down toward the uterus, and it is in these tubes that fertilization of an egg by a sperm can take place.

8. The female breasts are strongly connected with sex in our culture. Their milk glands produce milk after a woman gives birth. Regular breast self-examination is essential to the detection of potentially malignant lumps.

9. Between menarche and menopause, a woman's fertility is regulated by the menstrual cycle. At roughly 4-week intervals, an ovum ripens in one ovary as the result of increased levels of follicle-stimulating hormone (FSH). Estrogen thickens the uterine wall, producing a suitable location for fetal growth. The ovum breaks through the ovary wall at ovulation. If the ovum is not fertilized, extra blood and tissue are shed from the uterus in menstruation. Hormones from the pituitary and hypothalamus help to regulate the menstrual cycle.

10. Premenstrual syndrome (PMS) consists of uncomfortable physical and emotional symptoms that affect some women prior to the menstrual period.

11. The male testes, located in the scrotum, produce male hormones and sperm. Sperm cells develop best at a temperature slightly lower than inner body temperature, mature in tubes called the epididymis, and will travel upward through the vas deferens.

12. Regular self-examination of the genitals and testes is an effective way to detect infections, or growths that could be testicular cancer.

13. The penis has a sensitive, rounded head called the glans, and a shaft attached to the man's body. Three columns of spongy tissue compose the interior of the shaft, and become filled with blood during erection. Sperm and urine are conducted through the penis by the urethra.

14. Circumcision is a surgical procedure in which the penile foreskin, or prepuce, is removed. Currently there is debate over whether circumcision should be performed routinely.

15. The prostate gland and seminal vesicles of the male produce secretions that mix with sperm to produce the semen that is ejaculated through the penis. Cowper's glands produce a clear secretion that lines the urethra during sexual arousal.

16. Sperm production is controlled by the secretion of FSH. Interstitial-cell-stimulating hormone (ICSH) stimulates the testes to produce testosterone. Up to 30 billion sperm are produced by the testes each month.

17. Sexual stimulation of the penis can lead to ejaculation of semen. The ejaculate can contain between 150 million and 600 million sperm.

18. Men do not seem to have predictable hormonal cycles, although their emotions may follow cyclical patterns.

19. Menstruation in women ceases at menopause, a period of life with physical and emotional changes. Estrogen replacement therapy (ERT) for uncomfortable menopausal symptoms has generally not been favored in the United States.

20. Men experience less-defined male climacteric, involving mood changes. It may or may not be correlated with the changing levels of male hormones.

ANNOTATED READINGS

Annual editions: Human sexuality. (1991). Guilford, CT: The Dushkin Publishing Group. This volume contains selected current articles by health educators, psychologists, sexologists, and sociologists, presenting their views on how and why sexual attitudes and behaviors are developed, maintained, and changed. Updated annually.

Briggs, A. (1984). *Circumcision: What every parent should know.* Minneapolis, MN: International Childbirth Education Association. Makes a case against routine circumcision for boys by exploring myths and misinformation about it.

Boston Women's Health Book Collective. (1984). *The new our bodies, ourselves: A book by and for women.* New York: Simon & Schuster. A revision of one of the best-known books about women's bodies and health. The tone is sometimes political, the information accurate.

Federation of Feminist Women's Health Centers. (1981). *A new view of woman's body: A fully illustrated guide.* New York: Simon & Schuster. Comprehensive feminist guide to women's sexuality and health issues.

Fromer, M. J. (1985). *Menopause: What it is, why it happens, how you can deal with it.* New York: Pinnacle. An interesting overview of menopause, encouraging women to be responsible for their own health care during mid-life.

Golub, S. (Ed.) (1983). *Lifting the curse of menstruation: A feminist appraisal of the influence of menstruation on women's lives.* New York: Haworth Press. An overview of social and medical values relating to menstruation. The book offers a great deal of information about a topic that often receives too little attention.

Greenwood, S. (1988). *Menopause, naturally: Preparing for the second half of life.* San Francisco: Volcano Press. This book provides a holistic approach to preparing for menopause with an emphasis on nutrition, exercise, and good health habits. It also discusses the physical and psychological changes of mid-life.

Harrison, M. (1982). *Self-help for premenstrual syndrome.* Cambridge, MA: Matrix Press. Describes dietary and life-style changes that may help relieve symptoms of PMS for some women. Provides a hopeful, proactive perspective, with plenty of useful suggestions.

Julty, S. (1979). *Men's bodies, men's selves.* New York: Dell Publishing. A comprehensive book on being male in today's world, with good descriptions of male sexual anatomy and health.

Lauerson, J., & Stukane, E. (1982). *Listen to your body: A gynecologist answers women's most intimate questions.* New York: Simon & Schuster. An informative survey of topics relating to women's bodies and sexual health.

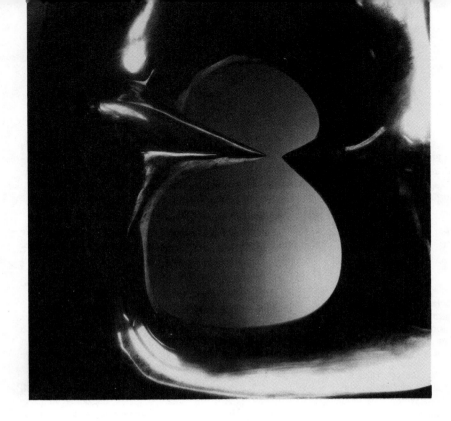

CHAPTER THREE

MODELS OF HUMAN SEXUAL RESPONSE
    The Masters and Johnson Four-Phase Model
    Kaplan's Three-Phase Model

**INDIVIDUAL DIFFERENCES IN THE SEXUAL
RESPONSE CYCLE**
    Women, Men, and Sexual Arousal

FEMALE SEXUAL RESPONSE
    Excitement Phase
    Plateau Phase
    Orgasm
    Resolution Phase
    Recent Controversies in Female Sexual Response
    Kegel Exercises and Sexual Response

MALE SEXUAL RESPONSE
    Excitement Phase
    Plateau Phase
    Orgasm
    Resolution
    Refractory Period
    Multiple Orgasms in Men

HORMONAL REGULATION OF SEXUAL RESPONSE

EFFECTS OF AGING ON SEXUAL RESPONSE
    Aging and Female Sexual Response
    Aging and Male Sexual Response

**SELF-EVALUATION: YOUR SEXUAL MYTHS AND
MISCONCEPTIONS**

CHAPTER SUMMARY

My first year in high school I was having erections all the time, always unpredictable and usually without any good reason. I could get a hard-on from putting a notebook in my locker or riding on the bus. Worst of all were the ones I would get during oral reports up in front of the class. Fortunately, the thing is a lot more under control now—most of the time.

—From a student's essay

HUMAN SEXUAL RESPONSE

Over the centuries the human body's sexual responses have been explained and interpreted in many different ways. They have been assigned religious significance in some cultures and shunned as unclean in others. Guides to the enhancement of sexual satisfaction have been written since ancient times, and "marriage manuals" have been popular in the United States since the 1940s.

Sexual responsiveness, and how it is perceived and expressed, cannot be understood outside the context of the culture in which a person lives. When Margaret Mead studied the Mundugumor of New Guinea, she remarked that lovemaking was conducted "like the first round of a prizefight," with scratching and biting as part of the foreplay. She later found that in Samoa, men preceded sexual activity by singing romantic songs and reciting poetry for their women, first preparing their minds with sensual thoughts and then their bodies with sensual touching (Konner, 1988).

In Eastern Tantric traditions of yoga and Buddhism, sexual response is intertwined with the spiritual dimensions of being human. It is believed that the energy of life and the spirit may be focused in different ways in the body, and that properly used sexual energy can help convey people to the highest levels of spiritual consciousness. In these traditions, men work to avoid orgasm, using various techniques to prolong states of intense sexual arousal for hours. It is in this way that they believe they can realize the full potential of their sexual energy (Devi, 1977). The emphasis is on the sensual and spiritual aspects of sex rather than immediate gratification or satisfaction.

Western cultural imperatives provide a predictable framework for sexual response; it tends to be goal-oriented, with orgasm and satisfying release its primary objectives. Rather than viewing sexual response as a holistic experience involving mind, body, emotions, and spirit, North Americans more typically view it as an act of the genitals. Therefore, the objective study of sexual response in our culture reflects this somewhat one-dimensional perspective on sex, focusing for the most part on measurable physiological responses of the body's organs and their functions.

With all of the attention that sexual response has received, it is surprising that much of what has been explained as "fact" has actually been myth and misin-

61

formation. It was not until 1966, in their pioneering book *Human Sexual Response,* that William Masters and Virginia Johnson provided the most thoroughly researched information on how the human body responds to sexual stimulation. Their study concentrated on careful observation and instrumental monitoring of men and women who were engaging in sexual activity. The 694 people who participated in the study were carefully interviewed and screened to obtain as "average" a sample as possible. These individuals were helped to feel comfortable with sexual activity alone in the laboratory setting before they were observed by the research team. Although Masters and Johnson saw their work as an incomplete, preliminary step to understanding human sexual response, and despite the fact that some controversies have grown out of their study, the findings have gained general acceptance among professionals.

Models of Human Sexual Response

It is clear that human response to sexual arousal is not confined to reactions of the sex organs, but involves marked changes throughout the body, especially in the muscular and circulatory systems. The human mind, with its personality traits, learned responses, and perceptions, plays a crucial role in sexual response. For easier understanding, the body's sexual responses have often been divided into separate phases.

THE MASTERS AND JOHNSON FOUR-PHASE MODEL

As Masters and Johnson observed the sexual response cycles of men and women in their laboratory, they realized that there were many similarities in responses between the two sexes. After gathering a great deal of data, they divided the sexual response process into four phases (see Fig. 3.1). The first phase they labeled excitement, during which the body begins to show signs of arousal. Blood is routed to the pelvic region, resulting in the earliest signs of arousal such as erection of the penis and clitoris, and vaginal lubrication. A wide range of physical and psychological stimuli can initiate this excitement phase. The intensity of the body's reactions to sexual arousal gradually builds to a higher level and is maintained at that level for varying lengths of time. Masters and Johnson labeled this the plateau phase because of its stable, or level, state of arousal.

The plateau phase, if held for sufficient periods of time, can be a major highlight of sexual response. The intensity of plateau may ebb and flow somewhat during sustained sexual activity, and thus provide some special "highs" of sensual enjoyment. This phase builds the body's tension toward triggering the pleasurable release of sexual tension called orgasm, or climax. It is a brief phase, lasting a few seconds to slightly less than a minute, but one in which thought is momentarily suspended, and the mind becomes focused inward on a rush of pleasurable physical sensations. Almost immediately after orgasm the body relaxes and begins to return to its unexcited state. Masters and Johnson termed this the resolution phase. Some women experience orgasm more than once in a single sexual experience, and so their bodies may return to plateau level and then reach orgasm again. This may even happen several times before entering the resolution phase.

The Masters and Johnson four-phase model is used in this chapter to describe female and male sexual response. More detail may be obtained by consulting their original study (Masters & Johnson, 1966). It should be understood, however, that their way of organizing these responses is only one way of viewing the phenomenon. Other researchers have raised legitimate criticisms and alternative models that remain open for consideration and further study. For example, there really is not a clear demarcation between excitement and plateau phases in males. Instead, there tends to be a steady and continuous buildup of sexual tension that is not readily divided into stages. Perhaps the Masters and Johnson approach attempts to impose a model on male sexual response that is far more applicable to women only (Goettsch, 1987).

KAPLAN'S THREE-PHASE MODEL

Another sex researcher and therapist, Helen Singer Kaplan (1974), first proposed that it makes more sense, from the standpoint of the body's actual neurophysiological mechanisms, to view sexual response as occurring in two phases. The first phase is charac-

---

excitement: the arousal phase of Masters and Johnson's four-phase model of the sexual response cycle.

plateau phase: the stable, leveled-off phase of Masters and Johnson's four-phase model of the sexual response cycle.

orgasm (OR-gaz-em): a rush of pleasurable physical sensations associated with the release of sexual tension.

climax: another term for orgasm.

resolution phase: the term for the return of a body to its unexcited state following orgasm.

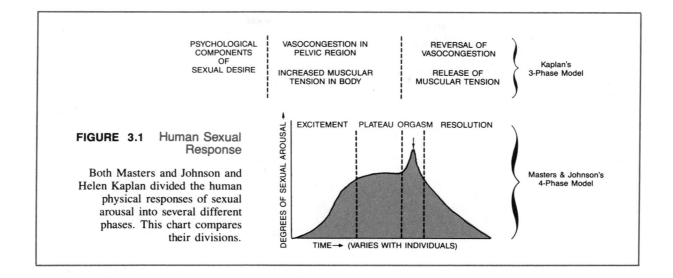

PSYCHOLOGICAL COMPONENTS OF SEXUAL DESIRE

VASOCONGESTION IN PELVIC REGION

INCREASED MUSCULAR TENSION IN BODY

REVERSAL OF VASOCONGESTION

RELEASE OF MUSCULAR TENSION

Kaplan's 3-Phase Model

EXCITEMENT PLATEAU ORGASM RESOLUTION

DEGREES OF SEXUAL AROUSAL

TIME→ (VARIES WITH INDIVIDUALS)

Masters & Johnson's 4-Phase Model

FIGURE 3.1 Human Sexual Response

Both Masters and Johnson and Helen Kaplan divided the human physical responses of sexual arousal into several different phases. This chart compares their divisions.

terized by vasocongestion, or buildup of blood in the pelvic area, and an accumulation of muscular tension throughout the body causing increases in heart rate, breathing, blood pressure, and other involuntary functions. Then orgasm acts as the trigger for the second phase, orgasmic release, in which the vasocongestion and muscular tension are released through the sudden orgasmic bursts and then more gradually as the body returns to normal levels of functioning.

However, as Kaplan worked with people's problems in sexual arousal, often referred to generally as sexual dysfunctions, she realized that some people simply did not seem to have much desire to become sexually aroused. This led her to suggest that a desire phase might well precede the body's physiological responses to arousal (Kaplan, 1979). The desire phase represents a psychological component that can lead to physical response. It was a modification of the Masters and Johnson model, focusing on the subjective, emotional approach to sexual arousal. Sexual desire is experienced as a specific sensation that moves the individual to seek out, or become receptive to, sexual experiences. These physical sensations are produced by the activation of a specific neural system in the brain. When this system is active a person may feel genital sensations or may feel vaguely sexy, interested in sex, open to sex, or even just restless. These sensations cease after sexual gratification, i.e., orgasm (Kaplan, 1979, p. 10).

What has become known as Kaplan's three-phase model has special validity when considering the various dysfunctions that can interfere with sexual responsiveness. These problems may involve inhibited sexual desire, sexual aversion, erectile dysfunction, vaginismus, or painful intercourse and are usually centered either in the desire phase, the vasocongestive

phase, or the orgasmic-release phase of the sexual response cycle (see chapter 16, "Sexual Dysfunctions and Their Treatment").

Individual Differences in the Sexual Response Cycle

It is clear that there are more physiological similarities in the sexual responses of males and females than there are differences. Both males and females experience pelvic vasocongestion and a general buildup of muscular tension. Orgasm is very similar in both sexes. Table 3.1 summarizes the sexual response cycles of females and males. It is also evident that, within certain bounds, there is great variation in sexual response among individuals. On the average, males tend to reach orgasm more rapidly than females during intercourse, but this phenomenon may well be influenced by the kind of stimulation and by the past learning of the individual. Many women respond with orgasm more quickly during masturbation than in intercourse. In fact, it is not unusual for women to respond almost as quickly as men via masturbation. It may be that during intercourse, it is typical for men to have more direct control over the kinds of stimulation being experienced, therefore bringing themselves to orgasm more quickly. They may adjust their position and rate

orgasmic release: reversal of the vasocongestion and muscular tension of sexual arousal, triggered by orgasm.

sexual dysfunctions: difficulties people have in achieving sexual arousal.

desire phase: Kaplan's term for the psychological interest in sex that precedes a physiological, sexual arousal.

TABLE 3.1

Female and Male Sexual Response

Phase	Female Responses	Male Responses
EXCITEMENT	Clitoris swells in diameter and length.	Penis becomes erect; urethral diameter begins to widen.
	Vagina lubricates, becomes expanded and lengthened, darker in color.	Scrotal skin tenses and thickens.
	Major and minor lips thicken and may open slightly.	Testes elevate slightly within scrotum.
	Breasts increase in size and nipples become erect.	Nipples become erect in some males.
	Appearance of sex flush in some females.	
	Increase in muscular tension.	Increase in muscular tension.
	Heart rate begins to increase.	Heart rate begins to increase.
	Blood pressure begins to rise.	Blood pressure begins to rise.
PLATEAU	Clitoris retracts under prepuce.	Penis increases in diameter and becomes fully erect.
	Vagina expands and lengthens more; orgasmic platform develops.	Scrotum has no changes.
	Uterus is completely elevated.	Testes enlarge and elevate up toward body.
	Major and minor lips swell more; minor lips have deeper red coloration.	Cowper's glands secrete a few drops of fluid.
	Breasts further increase in size and nipples become turgid.	Nipples become erect and more turgid.
	Sex flush has appeared in most females, and spreads.	Sex flush appears in some males and may spread.
	Further increase in muscular tension.	Further increase in muscular tension.
	Respiration and heart rates increase.	Respiration and heart rates increase.
	Marked elevation in blood pressure.	Marked elevation in blood pressure.
ORGASM	No changes in clitoris.	Penis and urethra undergo contractions that expel semen.
	Uterus undergoes wavelike contractions.	There are no changes in the scrotum or testes.
	There are no changes in the major and minor lips.	
	Breasts and nipples show no changes during orgasm.	Nipples remain erect.
	Sex flush deepens.	Sex flush deepens.
	Loss of voluntary muscle control; spasms of some muscles.	Loss of voluntary muscle control; spasms of some muscles.
	Respiration and heart rates reach peak intensity.	Respiration and heart rates reach peak intensity.
	Blood pressure reaches its peak.	Blood pressure reaches its peak.
RESOLUTION	Clitoris returns to nonaroused position and loses its erection.	Penis erection is lost, rapidly at first, then more slowly.
	Vaginal walls relax and return to nonaroused coloration.	Scrotal skin relaxes and returns to nonaroused thickness.
	Uterus lowers to usual position and cervical opening widens for 20–30 minutes.	Testes return to nonaroused size and position in scrotum.
	Major and minor lips return to nonaroused size, position, and color.	There is a period (refractory period) during which the male cannot be restimulated to orgasm.
	Breasts and nipples return to nonaroused size, position, and color.	Nipples return to nonaroused size.
	Disappearance of sex flush.	Disappearance of sex flush.
	Rapid relaxation of muscles.	Rapid relaxation of muscles.
	Respiration, heart rate, and blood pressure return to normal.	Respiration, heart rate, and blood pressure return to normal.
	Film of perspiration may appear on skin.	Film of perspiration may appear on skin, usually confined to soles of feet and palms of hands.

Source: W. Masters and V. E. Johnson, *Human Sexual Response,* 1966, Boston: Little, Brown. Adapted by permission.

of movement to increase localized stimulation to the penis. The amount of time for completion of the entire cycle varies with learning, the sexual situation, the kind and intensity of stimulation, and age. An entire cycle from excitement through resolution may take only a few minutes or last for several hours.

There seem to be subjective differences in the orgasms of males and females. Although male orgasms may vary in intensity and degree of pleasure, the experience is relatively standard among all males. Women often report experiencing different physical and psychological reactions during different orgasms. Some women even appear to have a very pleasurable feeling of sexual satisfaction but do not exhibit the usual physiological responses associated with orgasm.

Women can fake orgasm and some women feel that faking is necessary to please their sexual partners. Even though faking orgasm is less easy for men because of ejaculation, some men do fake orgasm from time to time. When such a deception enters a relationship, it can establish conditions for eventual problems. Openness and honesty about sex are a crucial part of a healthy relationship (see chapter 7, "Sexuality Through the Life Cycle").

Many North American males tend to be orgasm-oriented and feel that a sexual experience is incomplete without orgasm. This is not true of males in some other cultures and of some women in our own culture. These women apparently enjoy the physical intimacy of sex but do not strive for orgasmic release. For some women this seems to represent a dysfunctional problem (see chapter 16) but for others it apparently represents normal, healthy sexual functioning.

Individual differences in sexual response patterns make it all the more important for sexual partners to take time to learn about one another's responsiveness. This will also require developing effective lines of communication about emotions, needs, and sex.

WOMEN, MEN, AND SEXUAL AROUSAL

Of all the purported differences between men and women, the differences in sexual arousal are among the most rigidly believed. Until recently sex education books described the differences as natural human qualities. The main distinctions between male and female sexual arousal usually are described with the following stereotypes. Women become sexually aroused less often and less rapidly than men, apparently because they have a lower sex drive than men. Women become sexually aroused by different stimuli—while men are turned on by physical sex, pictures of nude women, and pictures of sexual acts, women are supposedly more aroused by the romantic aspects of

loving relationships. The nude male genitals for them are purported to be uninteresting or even repellent.

These differences in sexual arousal are not without some statistical validity. Kinsey and his associates (1953) reported that it was "characteristic of women in general" not to be sexually aroused by seeing a male's genitals or pictures of nude bodies. They also found that women were strongly aroused by romantic movies. However, the Kinsey report was conducted long before the so-called revolution of the 1960s and may have less scientific relevance in the 1980s or 1990s. One recent study of college students tested how well they remembered the romantic, erotic, and neutral elements of a story describing a heterosexual encounter. Women tended to remember romantic passages better, while men were more likely to remember the more sexual aspects of the story (Geer & McGlone, 1990).

The controversy now lies in whether these apparent differences are culturally conditioned or whether they represent innate distinctions between female and male sexual arousal. The former view is receiving plenty of support as many people argue that part of the socialization process for men is teaching them that viewing parts of the female anatomy or pictures of sex acts should be sexually stimulating for them, and that our society has always produced massive amounts of pictorial matter designed for this purpose. It is also proposed that women have been taught that they should not be aroused by this type of stimulus, and that very little pornography has ever been aimed at women. Often the argument includes a reminder that some men are not aroused by explicit pictures and some women are. Presumably these men and women have been more resistant to that aspect of the socialization process.

Some research indicates that there is probably less difference in male and female sexual arousal than formerly believed. One study compared the self-reported responses of nearly 600 German men and women to photographs of nude people and sexual acts and to reading stories depicting sexual experiences. No significant differences in the numbers of men and women reporting sexual arousal in response to these stimuli were found. Although it was found that there was a slightly greater tendency for the women to be repelled by the pornographic materials, many of those who reacted negatively apparently still were sexually aroused by the material. This would suggest that they had learned that they should not respond positively to such pictures and stories. Most of the men (80–91 percent) and women (70–83 percent) in the study experienced physiological signs of arousal, such as penile erection, sensations in the genital area, and vaginal lubrication (Schmidt & Sigusch, 1973). Similar

Case Study

ROGER AND ELLEN: A SEXUAL RELATIONSHIP EVOLVES

Ellen and Roger met in their college cafeteria, where they often sat with friends. They began dating early during their junior year. Neither had been particularly active in dating prior to that time. They worked at developing open patterns of communication and agreed that they wanted their relationship to be one of openness and emotional expression.

As their loving feelings deepened they began to consider sexual involvement, but they also both felt relatively inexperienced sexually. Together they decided to talk over their relationship with a head resident in one of the dormitories, a woman in her late twenties whom they both liked and trusted.

The woman loaned the couple several books on sexuality and talked with them at length about their decision-making. Since neither had previously had sexual intercourse, and there were no other likely ways in which they might have contracted the AIDS virus or other sexually transmitted diseases, they were not very con-

cerned about possible infection of one by the other. The head resident referred them to the local family-planning clinic to talk over possible means of contraception.

Although Roger and Ellen were already engaging in mutual sexual activities, they decided to postpone intercourse for the time being. Ellen did start taking birth control pills, a choice with which both of them were comfortable, since they felt eventually they would choose intercourse.

After 3 months, during which the two became increasingly familiar with one another's sexual responsiveness and particular preferences for sexual stimulation, they began to share intercourse occasionally. They continued to communicate openly about the sorts of sexual activities they enjoyed and those they preferred to avoid. Ellen was not orgasmic during the first two times they had intercourse, but with the third experience provided herself with some clitoral stimulation that helped her reach orgasm.

results have been found in American and Danish students. Schmidt and Sigusch believed that as women become "resexualized," the differences in sexual arousal patterns would lessen, gradually being "unmasked as [examples] of sexual prejudice."

Other researchers designed studies that did not rely on the self-reports of the subjects. Julia Heiman (1977) developed ways of measuring physiological sexual response while women and men listened to taped excerpts of explicit sexual reading material and romance-oriented material. One device she developed was a mercury-filled strain gauge that was attached to the penis and measured the degree of penile erection in the men. Another device was a probe she developed that could be inserted into the women's vaginas to measure increased blood volume there, a sign of sexual arousal in females. These two devices gave convincing evidence that both the men and the women were generally more sexually aroused by the explicitly sexual excerpts than by the romance-oriented material. It was also found that some women did not verbally report sexual arousal even though the instruments indicated they were aroused. Heiman suggested that

this may have resulted from the women's learned reactions to sexual excitement, conditioning them to deny arousal, even to themselves.

Even though these vasocongestion-measuring devices provided reliable data on two phenomena—penile erection and vaginal blood volume—they did not allow for direct comparison of degree of arousal between males and females. Another instrument, called a thermograph, has been used to measure changes in tissue temperature in the genitals caused by blood engorgement. This is believed to represent a better measurement for comparison between the sexes (Abramson et al., 1981). People have also been asked to report on their own subjective awarenesses of their bodies' responses and sensations. Women have been asked to report on sensations in their breasts and genitals, as well as vaginal lubrication and orgasm. Men have been asked for reports about their degree of erection, appearance of preejaculatory fluid, and ejaculation. Such information has been used to distinguish different degrees of sexual arousal between women and men.

Much evidence from recent research has been confusing and contradictory. The older evidence suggesting that males are far more easily and quickly sexually aroused than women has not been supported, perhaps indicating some important changes in social influences on women concerning their sexual feelings. Women's self-reported feelings about sexual arousal and their evaluations of their own sexual responses tend to be consistently more negative than the self-reported feelings and evaluations of men. Males still seem to value sex and sexual stimuli more positively than women, and therefore pursue them more actively and comfortably. Men also apparently dream to the point of orgasm more than women do (Griffitt, 1987).

At this point it is difficult to make further generalizations about how similar—or how different—the patterns of sexual arousal in women and men really are. There do seem to be strong indications that there is not so much difference between the two sexes as had been believed originally. Yet it also appears that because of sociological or biological differences, or a combination of both factors, males are somewhat more easily triggered to respond sexually by a variety of stimuli (Griffitt, 1987). Regardless of the eventual research findings, it is clear that many men and women do not fit conveniently into the traditional stereotypes of sexual arousal.

Female Sexual Response

EXCITEMENT PHASE

When the female body begins to respond sexually, changes are often first noticed in the vagina. As blood begins to build up (vasocongestion) in the blood vessels of the genital region, the vaginal walls darken in color, a change that is not visible externally.

This vasocongestion causes a slippery, alkaline fluid to seep through the lining of the vagina. This substance functions as a lubricant for sexual activity and may also help to create alkaline conditions in the vagina that are beneficial to sperm. The amount of lubrication in the vagina is not, however, necessarily a sign of how sexually aroused the woman is or how ready she might be for sexual activity.

Another change during the excitement phase is the lengthening and distention of the inner one-third of the vagina. The uterus is also pulled upward from its usual position (see Fig. 3.2). The vasocongestion causes changes in the major and minor lips, as they begin to enlarge and sometimes to open slightly. The clitoris begins to swell somewhat and its shaft may elongate slightly. Some of the vaginal lubrication may

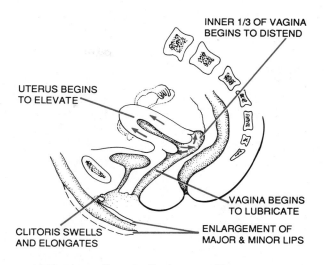

FIGURE 3.2 Female Excitement Phase

In the female, the first sign of sexual arousal is often the lubrication of the vagina. This is accompanied by the enlargement of the vaginal area including the clitoris and the major and minor lips, and a darkening of the color of the vaginal walls.

flow out onto the labia and clitoris, depending on its copiousness and if the particular sexual activity is apt to bring internal secretions to the exterior.

Other areas of the body respond to sexual excitement as well. Often the nipples become harder and erect, although this response also may result from nonsexual stimuli. Many women show a darkening of the skin through the neck, breasts, and upper abdomen during sexual excitement; this is termed the "sex flush." General muscular tension begins to build throughout the body as heart rate and blood pressure increase.

PLATEAU PHASE

The second stage of the female sexual response cycle leads to further changes in the vagina. The outer third of the vaginal wall becomes swollen with blood, narrowing the space within the vagina slightly. The inner two-thirds of the vagina show slightly more lengthening and expansion. The minor lips also become engorged with blood, causing thickening and a flaring outward. The swelling of the outer third of the vagina and the minor lips seems to create the tension that is an important precursor of orgasm, so together they are termed the "orgasmic platform" (see Fig. 3.3). During plateau phase the clitoris undergoes some major changes, retracting back under its foreskin so that it no longer receives any direct stimulation. By the

67

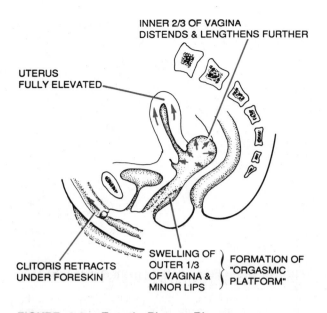

FIGURE 3.3 Female Plateau Phase

In the plateau phase of sexual response, high levels of arousal are maintained. In the female, the orgasmic platform is caused by swelling of the tissues in the outer third of the vagina, which causes the entrance to it to narrow. The clitoris retracts under its foreskin.

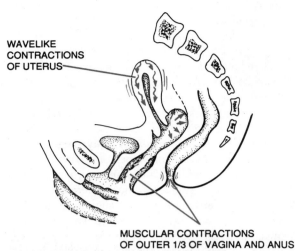

FIGURE 3.4 Female Orgasmic Phase

Orgasm is the release of sexual tension involving a total body response. The female physical response is marked by simultaneous rhythmic muscular contractions of the uterus, the outer third of the vagina, and the anal sphincter.

end of plateau the length of the clitoris is decreased by about 50 percent.

The breasts have usually expanded by this time and nipple erection may be maintained. Increase in breast size is not as pronounced in women who have breast-fed a baby. The sex flush, if present, sometimes spreads to the shoulders, back, buttocks, and thighs during the plateau phase. Muscular tension continues to increase, along with heart rate, respiration rate, and blood pressure. The heart rate usually increases to between 110 and 175 beats per minute.

ORGASM

The pleasurable release of sexual tension occurs during the sexual climax or orgasm. It is an intense experience, both physically and emotionally, and in females is immediately preceded by a sensation of "suspension," at which time the pulse rate reaches its peak. Then there is a feeling of increased sexual awareness in the area of the clitoris, which spreads upward, and a "suffusion" of warmth which spreads from the pelvis throughout the body. Many women also experience a sensation of throbbing in the lower pelvic area.

During the pleasurable feelings of the orgasmic phase, there are muscular contractions in the outer third of the vagina and in the anal area. Following the

initial contraction, which may last 2 to 4 seconds, there are three or four rhythmic contractions at intervals of about 0.8 second. There may be up to 15 such contractions, the interval between them gradually lengthening, and their intensity gradually decreasing. Two to 4 seconds after orgasm begins, the uterus has some mild wavelike contractions that move from its top to the cervix (see Fig. 3.4).

During orgasm, muscles throughout the body may contract involuntarily, causing pelvic thrusting and spastic movements of the neck, hands, arms, feet, and legs. The woman may scream, gasp, moan, or shout out words during the orgasmic experience. The heart and respiratory rates and blood pressure have all reached their peaks. The pulse rate may be twice as high as normal.

RESOLUTION PHASE

Following the release of sexual tension through orgasm, the body gradually returns to its unexcited state. As blood leaves the pelvic region, the vagina returns to its usual size and color, and the labia return to their prearoused state. Within 10 seconds, the clitoris emerges from the foreskin to its typical position, and within 15 to 30 minutes has returned to its usual size. The uterus also lowers to its prearoused position.

During resolution, the other signs of sexual arousal also gradually disappear. The breasts decrease in size and the nipples lose their erection. The sex flush leaves the body in the reverse order from which it developed, and respiration, pulse, and blood pressure soon return to their normal levels. It is quite common for the body to become wet with perspiration during resolution. As the muscles throughout the body relax, there is often a feeling of drowsiness that may lead to sleep.

During the resolution phase of sexual response, many females may be restimulated to orgasm. Unlike males, who go through a period when they cannot be restimulated to climax, some females are capable of experiencing numerous orgasms during a single sexual experience. Kinsey and his coworkers (1953) reported that 14 percent of women regularly experience sequential (or multiple) orgasms during sexual encounters, and the Masters and Johnson (1966) work suggests that most, if not all, women have the potential for more than one orgasm.

RECENT CONTROVERSIES IN FEMALE SEXUAL RESPONSE

Orgasms For many years there has been a controversy over the existence of two types of female orgasm: clitoral and vaginal. Masters and Johnson (1966) concluded that regardless of how it is produced, female orgasm proceeds physiologically in basically the same manner as previously described. They believe that, at least from a biological viewpoint, the clitoral-vaginal dichotomy was unfounded. However, the controversy continues as researchers report that there are distinct differences in how women experience orgasm produced by clitoral or vulval stimulation and that produced by deeper vaginal stimulation. Some women experience orgasm as the result of stimulation of the cervix. This has been called a "uterine orgasm." It has also been suggested that some women experience a "blended orgasm," which is a combination of the clitoral-vulval experience and the uterine orgasm (Whipple, 1991). The difference in orgasmic responses could be due to the two different nerve pathways that serve the sex organs, the *pudendal nerves* and the *pelvic nerves*. The pudendal nerve system connects with the clitoris, while the *pelvic system* innervates the vagina, cervix, and uterus. It is therefore hypothesized that there may be two different neurological routes to producing orgasm (Mahoney, 1983).

This controversy may well represent one of those cases in which it is difficult to reconcile the objective measures of science and the subjective reports of people's experiences. It has not been completely resolved whether orgasm is primarily a physiological or psychological phenomenon (Konner, 1988). Regardless of what sort of orgasm a woman might experience, the most important issue is that she is able to feel that a sexual interaction has been fulfilling to her personally.

The G Spot There is a possibility that there is a particularly sexually sensitive area on the inner front wall of the vagina. The existence of such an area was proposed years ago by a German physician named Gräfenberg (1950). The idea was revived in the 1980s by other researchers who claimed that there is indeed a mass of tissue in the anterior vagina that swells during sexual arousal and can lead to intense orgasmic experiences. They named this area the G spot, after Gräfenberg (Ladas, Whipple, & Perry, 1983). Some scientists have objected, feeling that such a sensitive area is not found in a large percentage of women, and that, when it is present, it is not in a clearly defined location that could legitimately be called a "spot" (Alzate, 1990; Hoch, 1983). The one thing that this controversy has confirmed is that many women are sensitive to vaginal stimulation, thus laying to rest a traditional view of the vagina as a rather insensitive organ (Perry, 1983; Ladas, 1989). It may also remind us of individual differences in sexual response, emphasizing the need for good patterns of communication between sexual partners.

Ejaculation Gräfenberg also suggested in his 1950 article that some women might ejaculate a semen-like substance from their urethras at the time of orgasm. This contention has also seen a recent revival, and it has been hypothesized that Skene's glands, located inside the urethra, might be similar to the prostate of males (Sevely, 1987). During particularly intense orgasms, some women report that a liquid is expelled from their urethras. A survey of 1,230 women in North America found that 40 percent of them had experienced such ejaculation. Those who had ejaculated were more likely to report their sexual responsiveness as above average (Darling, Davidson, & Conway-Welch, 1990). Some women seem to assume that the fluid is urine and are therefore reluctant to pursue the matter. Some of those women may even try to prevent themselves from experiencing intense orgasms in an effort to reduce the chances of emitting this fluid. The controversy now revolves around whether the liquid substance is actually a secretion produced internally

G spot: a vaginal area that some researchers feel is particularly sensitive to sexual stimulation.
Skene's glands: secretory cells located inside the female urethra.

69

during sexual arousal or is instead urine pressed out of the bladder by muscular pressure during orgasm. A recent study found that 10 out of 27 women expelled a whitish, opalescent fluid from the urethra after the anterior part of the vagina was stimulated (Zaviacic, 1988). Again, the different nerve systems serving the clitoris and vagina have been proposed as a possible explanation for how women can have clitorally-based orgasms without any ejaculatory response, and inner vaginally-based (G spot) orgasms that might produce some form of ejaculation (Mahoney, 1983). Other researchers insist that the evidence for female ejaculation is weak and questionable, and that release of urine during orgasm has been documented (Alzate, 1990). Only further research will finally resolve these issues.

It has been suggested that social factors play an important role in how legitimized such issues as female orgasm, the G spot, and female ejaculation become in our culture. There may well be male power issues involved. If the sexual focus in our society has traditionally been on what pleases men, it may be difficult to shift that focus toward those places in women that are associated with intense sexual pleasure (Winton, 1989).

KEGEL EXERCISES AND SEXUAL RESPONSE

In the early 1950s a surgeon by the name of Arnold Kegel developed exercises for the pubococcygeal muscle (PC) that surrounds the vagina. He originally intended the exercises for girls and women who had difficulty with urine leaking from their bladders. Eventually, Kegel found that in some of his subjects a well-toned PC muscle increased the ability to experience orgasmic satisfaction. Kegel exercises have also been recommended for pregnant women, and seem to help the vagina and uterus return to normal shape and tone more quickly after the delivery of a baby. It has been suggested that men keep their PC muscles in good shape to assure good orgasms as well. In men, the PC muscle is located in the penis.

Kegel exercises are accomplished by first locating the PC muscle. This is best accomplished by stopping and starting the flow of urine during urination, for the same muscle is involved. Once the individual is familiar with its location, it is usually suggested that the muscle be contracted firmly for 2 or 3 seconds and then released. While it has been recommended that these contractions be done in sets of tens, building up to several sets each day, some experts now believe that it is unnecessary, or even unwise, to exercise the PC muscle too much.

Recent studies have called into question whether Kegel exercises actually improve the orgasmic response by making it more intense (Sultan & Chambles, 1982). It has also been proposed, however, that such exercises may improve the subjective qualities of sex for women simply by creating increased sensitivity in the vagina (Messé & Geer, 1985).

Male Sexual Response

EXCITEMENT PHASE

Vasocongestion in the pelvic area during early sexual arousal contributes to erection of the penis, the first sign of the excitement phase in males. The degree of erection during this phase depends on the intensity of sexual stimuli. Eventually the inner diameter of the urethra doubles. Vasocongestion also causes thickening of the scrotal tissue and the scrotum pulls upward toward the body. The testes become elevated within the scrotum, although if the excitement phase continues for more than 5 or 10 minutes, the testes return to their original position (see Fig. 3.5).

Nipple erection and appearance of the sex flush are less common in males than in females, but both phenomena are usually first observed during excitement phase if they occur at all. Muscular tension increases throughout the body during late excitement phase, and heart rate and blood pressure both increase. Sometimes secretion from Cowper's glands appears during this stage, or can even precede erection.

PLATEAU PHASE

The penis does not change markedly during the second stage of sexual response, although it is less likely for a man to lose his erection if distracted during plateau phase than during excitement. As orgasm nears, the corona of the glans of the penis becomes more swollen and the glans itself may take on a deeper, often reddish purple color. There are no further changes in the scrotum, but the testes increase in size by 50 percent or more and become elevated up toward the body. During plateau, Cowper's glands secrete a few drops of fluid, some of which may appear at the tip of the penis. The longer plateau stimulation is maintained, the more fluid produced (see Fig. 3.6).

Muscular tension heightens considerably during plateau phase and involuntary body movements increase as orgasm approaches. The nipples may become erect. Males often have clutching or grasping movements of the hands in late plateau. Heart rate increases

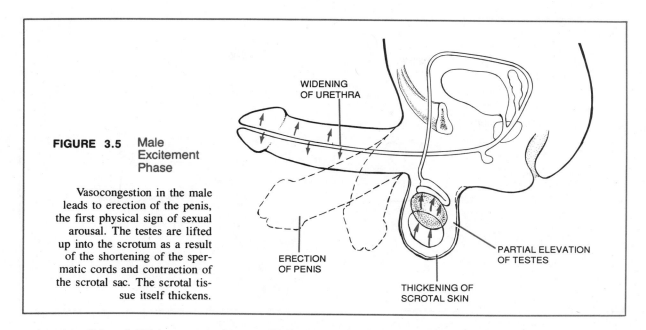

FIGURE 3.5 Male Excitement Phase

Vasocongestion in the male leads to erection of the penis, the first physical sign of sexual arousal. The testes are lifted up into the scrotum as a result of the shortening of the spermatic cords and contraction of the scrotal sac. The scrotal tissue itself thickens.

WIDENING OF URETHRA

ERECTION OF PENIS

THICKENING OF SCROTAL SKIN

PARTIAL ELEVATION OF TESTES

to between 100 and 175 beats per minute and blood pressure increases. Respiratory rate also increases, especially in latter plateau phase. If the sex flush is present, it may spread to the neck, back, and buttocks.

ORGASM

In males, actual climax and ejaculation are preceded by a distinct inner sensation that orgasm is imminent. This has been called ejaculatory inevitability. Almost immediately after that feeling is reached, the male senses that ejaculation cannot be stopped. The most noticeable change in the penis during orgasm is the ejaculation of semen. The muscles at the base of the penis and around the anus contract rhythmically, with intervals of about 0.8 second between the first three or four contractions. This varies in different individuals. The intensity of the contractions then diminishes and the interval between contractions lengthens. It is the first few contractions that expel the largest amount of semen. The testes are held at their maximum elevation throughout orgasm, and some sexologists believe that ejaculation is unlikely to occur unless the testes remain in this position (see Fig. 3.7).

ejaculatory inevitability: the sensation in the male that ejaculation is imminent.

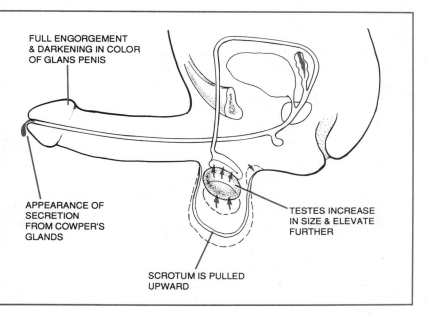

FIGURE 3.6 Male Plateau Phase

A generalized increase in neuromuscular tension is experienced in both males and females in the plateau phase. In the male, the head of the penis increases slightly in size and deepens in color. The testes swell by 50 to 100 percent of their unstimulated state. The testes continue to elevate. A secretion from Cowper's glands may appear from the male urethra and may carry live sperm.

FULL ENGORGEMENT & DARKENING IN COLOR OF GLANS PENIS

APPEARANCE OF SECRETION FROM COWPER'S GLANDS

SCROTUM IS PULLED UPWARD

TESTES INCREASE IN SIZE & ELEVATE FURTHER

71

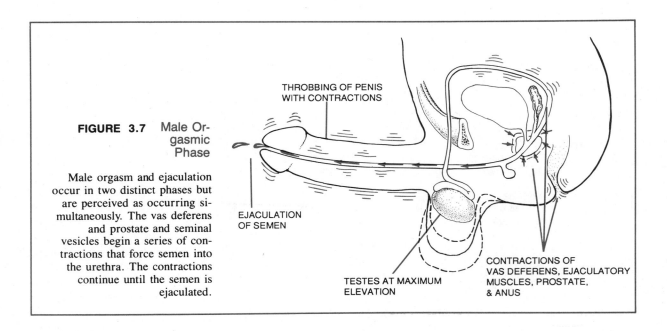

FIGURE 3.7 Male Orgasmic Phase

Male orgasm and ejaculation occur in two distinct phases but are perceived as occurring simultaneously. The vas deferens and prostate and seminal vesicles begin a series of contractions that force semen into the urethra. The contractions continue until the semen is ejaculated.

THROBBING OF PENIS WITH CONTRACTIONS

EJACULATION OF SEMEN

TESTES AT MAXIMUM ELEVATION

CONTRACTIONS OF VAS DEFERENS, EJACULATORY MUSCLES, PROSTATE, & ANUS

Males often have strong involuntary muscle contractions throughout the body during orgasm and usually exhibit involuntary pelvic thrusting. The hands and feet show spastic contractions and the entire body may arch backward or contract in a clutching manner. Many men moan or yell during orgasm and have a grimacing facial expression. Breathing, heart rate, and blood pressure all reach a peak during orgasm, and some men begin perspiring during this stage.

Men also have two different nerve pathways to different parts of their sex organs. The pudendal nerve system connects with the penile glans, while the pelvic nerve system serves the base of the penis and prostate gland. This could explain why orgasm is not necessarily always accompanied by ejaculation of semen. Orgasm produced from localized stimulation of the glans may be somewhat less likely to be accompanied by ejaculation (Mahoney, 1983). In any case, male orgasm and ejaculation should be viewed as two essentially separate sexual responses that most often happen at the same time.

RESOLUTION

Immediately following ejaculation, the male body begins to return to its unexcited state. About 50 percent of the penile erection is lost right away, and the remainder of the erection is lost over a longer period of time, depending on the degree of stimulation and nonsexual activity. Urination, walking, and other distracting activities usually lead to a more rapid return of the penis to its fully flaccid state. The diameter of the urethra returns to its usual width. The scrotum begins to relax as vasocongestion decreases, and the testes return to their prearoused size and position. Resolution in the scrotum and testes takes varying lengths of time, depending on the individual.

If nipple erection and sex flush have appeared, they gradually diminish. Muscular tension usually is fully dissipated within 5 minutes after orgasm, and the male feels relaxed and drowsy. Many men fall asleep quickly during the resolution phase. About one-third of men begin a perspiration reaction during this stage. Heart rate, respiration rate, and blood pressure rapidly return to normal. Resolution is a gradual process that may take as long as 2 hours.

REFRACTORY PERIOD

During resolution, most males experience a period of time during which they cannot be restimulated to ejaculation. This period of time is known as the refractory period. The duration of the refractory period depends on a variety of factors, including the amount of available sexual stimulation, the man's mood, and his age. On the average, men in their late thirties cannot be restimulated to orgasm for 30 minutes or more. The period gradually increases with age. Very few men beyond their teenage years are capable of more than one orgasm during sexual encounters, except occasionally. Most men feel sexually satiated with one orgasm.

refractory period: time following orgasm during which a man cannot be restimulated to orgasm.

MULTIPLE ORGASMS IN MEN

There have always been tales of men who are capable of experiencing more than one orgasm during a single sexual experience, presumably without experiencing a refractory period. Two studies have reported on small numbers of men who claim to be able to experience multiple orgasms, and some laboratory measures of their responses have been taken (Robbins & Jensen, 1978; Hartman & Fithian, 1984). These studies suggest that some men seem able to delay ejaculation but still experience some internal contractions and pleasurable sensations associated with orgasm. It has been suggested that men can learn to develop the muscle control enabling them to separate orgasm from ejaculation. Some men, especially at younger ages, may have a brief refractory period and may experience a second ejaculation quite rapidly, sometimes without losing their erections. The best evidence at present indicates that once ejaculation has occurred, a refractory period follows. For a few men (5 percent or less), there does seem to be the possibility of experiencing pleasurable orgasmic reactions two or more times prior to ejaculation. When ejaculation does not occur, the refractory period tends not to occur and so further orgasmic response is possible.

Hormonal Regulation of Sexual Response

There is a popular notion that it is sex hormones that control our levels of interest in sexual activity. This assumption would have us believe that the more "hormones" people produce in their bodies, the stronger their sex drives. The picture of how hormones affect sexual behavior is not all that clear, but we can conclude that the popular assumptions about a direct correlation between hormone levels and sexual activity are not accurate.

The secretions of endocrine glands can have two types of effects on an individual. One is called an organizing effect, and refers to ways in which hormones control patterns of early development in the body, playing a crucial role in the structure and function of particular organs. In chapter 6, "Gender-Identity/Role and Society," for example, I will describe how certain hormones control the development of sex glands and external genitals in the fetus, and how they may lead to some differences in how the nervous systems of males and females develop.

Another influence that hormones can exert is referred to as an activating effect. This describes the potential some hormones can have for affecting an actual behavior, either by activating or deactivating it.

In the matter of sexual response, it has been tempting to assume that levels of particular sex hormones in the bloodstream might increase or decrease a person's level of sexual activity, but the evidence for such a model does not hold up well (Feder, 1984).

There is a great deal of research with lower mammals indicating that their sexual behaviors are controlled quite directly by hormonal concentrations in their bodies. As a general rule, however, the behavior of higher species of mammals including humans is less influenced by hormones and more by the brain. For both men and women, the only hormone that has been shown to have much effect on sexual desire and behavior is testosterone. Although this is an androgen, or "male" hormone, it is produced by both males and females in the sex glands (testes or ovaries) and the adrenal glands. Men's bodies, however, tend to produce 10 to 15 times more testosterone than do women's bodies.

For both men and women, testosterone apparently has an activating effect on sexual interest. It might be viewed as a "switch" for sexual desire, and human beings seem to require some minimal levels of testosterone in order to have any potential for sexual desire. What that minimum must be seems to vary with different individuals. However, increased levels of testosterone beyond this minimal activating level do not result in increased interest in sex or amounts of sexual activity (Sporer, 1991). It is a mistake to conclude that because women produce generally lower levels of testosterone, they have a naturally lower interest in sex. It appears instead that women have a greater degree of sensitivity to testosterone, and therefore their bodies respond to smaller quantities of the hormone (Bancroft, 1984).

The "female" hormones, or estrogens, have little effect on sexual desire or activity, particularly in females. If males are given doses of estrogen, their interest in sex tends to decrease.

Effects of Aging on Sexual Response

There is a prevalent attitude in our culture that aging puts an end to responding sexually. Older people who accept this myth may allow their beliefs to become

organizing effect: manner in which hormones control patterns of early development in the body.

activating effect: the direct influence some hormones can have on activating or deactivating sexual behavior.

androgen: a male hormone, such as testosterone, that affects physical development, sexual desire, and behavior. It is produced by both male and female sex glands and influences each sex in varying degrees.

self-fulfilling prophecy. Attitudes toward one's own sexual functioning can play an important role in maintaining that functioning into old age.

Masters and Johnson (1966) interviewed 212 men beyond 50 years of age concerning their sexual lives. Thirty-nine of these men, the oldest of whom was 89, agreed to have their sexual responses observed by the research team. Thirty-four women over the age of 50 were also observed, and another 118 interviews were conducted with women between 51 and 80 years of age. The following discussion is based on these interviews and observations.

AGING AND FEMALE SEXUAL RESPONSE

Two manifestations of postmenopausal hormonal imbalance can cause unpleasant sensations during sexual activity in some older women. First, since the vaginal lining has thinned, and vaginal lubrication possibly reduced, intercourse may produce irritation that persists as burning or itching afterward. Water-soluble lubricants such as K-Y jelly can relieve such problems and estrogen-based creams may also help by increasing natural vaginal secretions. Second, some women also experience uterine cramping during and after orgasm. Masters and Johnson reported that some women beyond the age of 60 were so distressed by these sensations that they began to avoid coitus and orgasm. We know now that these unpleasant symptoms may be relieved by proper medical treatment.

As women age, there seems to be a general tempering of the usual physiological responses to sexual arousal. This is a very gradual process of change and is somewhat dependent on how sexually active a particular woman remains. For heterosexual women over the age of 70 who have been involved in long-term relationships, their degree of sexual involvement may have a great deal to do with the availability and capability of their male partners. Because of social conventions, their partners are an average of 4 years older and frequently suffer from debilitating conditions that interfere with sex. Older people of either sex whose bodies undergo regular sexual stimulation seem to maintain more intense levels of sexual response than do those who seldom participate in sex.

One effect of aging on female sexual response is a lengthening of the time for vaginal lubrication and other early signs of sexual arousal to take place. There is also less enlargement of the clitoris, labia, uterus, and breasts during sexual arousal. Orgasm takes a bit longer to occur in older women, and there are usually fewer orgasmic contractions of the vagina, uterus, and pelvic floor. However, women who have a history of multiple orgasms apparently retain this capability even

into very old age (Kaplan & Sager, 1971). The resolution phase of female sexual response, during which the body returns to its unexcited state, appears to be relatively unaffected by the aging process.

Again, it is important to emphasize that how much of a decline in sexual response patterns an older woman experiences seems to depend on how sexually involved she remains. This in turn depends on factors such as the woman's health, availability of a partner, the amount of privacy she is afforded, her attitudes and values about sexuality, and the degree of priority she has always placed on her sexual feelings and behaviors. For these reasons, some women remain sexually vital until the end of their lives, while others forgo sexual pleasures long before that time and gradually lose their abilities to respond sexually. Put in simple and direct language, this concept is often summarized by the phrase "use it or lose it."

AGING AND MALE SEXUAL RESPONSE

How responsive men remain in their older years seems to depend on a variety of physical, social, and psychological factors. Socially, they may lose their long-standing sexual partner, or live in a setting that provides little privacy for sexual expression. Since there is a natural "slowing down" process, some men begin to feel insecure about their sexual capabilities. They may fear sexual "failure," usually meaning erection problems of various sorts, and eventually withdraw from sexual activities. Once some men have experienced even a single erectile failure, they cease attempting sexual intercourse. They may assume that aging is rendering them incapable of sexual performance. As a result, the amount of sexual stimulation they seek is drastically reduced, and the priority they assign to sex is lowered. This can eventually lead to at least a temporary loss of the ability to respond. Men who are in good general physical health may eventually re-stimulate their sexual interests and response patterns, should a change in life situation make this appropriate. This might include the availability of a new sexual partner, a renewed sense of personal self-worth, or sex education that makes the man aware of how his responses can naturally be expected to change (Whitbourne, 1990).

There are three aspects of male sexual response that undergo predictable changes as men age. The first is erection. It takes two to three times longer for a man in his seventies to achieve full penile erection than it did in his younger years and he may require direct penile stimulation. Although during prolonged sexual arousal it is perfectly normal for men of any age to experience waxing and waning of erection, it is more difficult for older men to reestablish full rigidity once erection has been partially lost.

The second change relates to male orgasm and ejaculation. Older men take longer to reach orgasm than they did earlier in their lives. The strength of the orgasmic contractions is reduced, so that semen is ejaculated with less force, sometimes just seeping out of the urethra. The frequency with which men desire orgasm also seems to decline somewhat as they age. Except in rare instances, men over 60 are completely satisfied by one or, at the most, two orgasms in a week. They may enjoy participating in sexual behavior more frequently than that, experiencing full erection but no orgasm. The urge to achieve orgasm seems to be reduced with age.

The third change is a lengthening of the male refractory period, so that by their late fifties or early sixties most men cannot achieve erections again for 12 to 24 hours after ejaculation (Schiavi et al., 1990).

There are also decreases in other aspects of the aging male's sexual response. There is a reduction in the amount of preejaculatory secretion from the Cowper's glands and in the amount of semen produced. The testes and scrotum do not enlarge as much during sexual arousal, nor do the testes elevate so much within the scrotum. The resolution phase of men tends to occur more rapidly with age, and the penis may lose its erection after ejaculation much more rapidly (Schiavi, 1990).

It is important to point out that these changes in female and male sexual response are not necessarily negative developments for people's sexual lives. In fact many find increased enjoyment in the moderating responses brought about by aging. There is more about sexuality and aging in chapter 7, "Sexuality Through the Life Cycle." ■

SELF-EVALUATION

Your Sexual Myths and Misconceptions

Because human beings have had so little accurate, objective information about sex, many myths and fallacies have arisen about human sexuality. In recent years, with an increase in sex research, many of the old myths have died away—only to be replaced by new ones. The following test may help you to explore the myths and inaccuracies about sex that you still hold. It also may help you to decide in what areas of human sexuality you could use further study. Remember: this test is not for grading; it is for you to evaluate yourself.

Indicate whether each of the following statements relating to sexuality is true or false. (Answers are found at the end of the questionnaire on the next page.)

1. Participation in sexual activity prior to athletic activity will lower an athlete's performance level. **T F**
2. Sexually fulfilled, mature adults do not masturbate. **T F**
3. Alcohol enhances the body's sexual responsiveness. **T F**
4. Women may have as strong sexual needs as men. **T F**
5. Both men and women have sex hormones of the opposite sex in their bodies. **T F**
6. On psychological tests of creativity, girls on the average score better than boys. **T F**
7. Romance is more important to most women than to most men. **T F**
8. Women who use vibrators to produce orgasm are likely to become dependent on the vibrator. **T F**
9. Men who get their sexual kicks from dressing up in women's clothes are most likely homosexual. **T F**
10. Viewing pornography probably has no effect on most people. **T F**
11. It is the sex chromosome found in the male's sperm that determines whether a baby will be a boy or a girl. **T F**
12. There is no risk of pregnancy when sexual intercourse takes place during the woman's menstrual period. **T F**
13. Having a vasectomy in no way physically affects a man's sexual functioning. **T F**
14. A woman who takes birth control pills increases the risks of dangerous side effects if she smokes. **T F**
15. Generally, intercourse should be avoided during the last month or two of pregnancy. **T F**
16. As people grow older they are more apt to remain

sexually active if they have tried for sexual moderation and abstinence in their younger years. **T F**

17. Women must reach orgasm in order to become pregnant. **T F**

18. Adults who become involved in sexual contacts with children are usually known by the child. **T F**

19. If continuing impotence in a man does not respond to psychotherapy, it is often caused by some organic problem. **T F**

20. Homosexuals are more prone than heterosexuals to various personality disturbances. **T F**

21. Most adults do not masturbate. **T F**

22. As men grow older their need for orgasm during sexual activity often decreases. **T F**

23. A person who has sexual contact with an animal must have a serious mental or emotional disturbance. **T F**

24. Women are naturally more nurturing and gentle with children than are men. **T F**

25. The larger the penis in its nonerect state, the larger it will be when erect. **T F**

26. If a man loses both of his testes, he also loses his sex drive and becomes impotent. **T F**

27. Circumcision does not produce premature ejaculation in males. **T F**

28. After menopause a woman's sex drive usually begins to decline. **T F**

29. Male homosexuals usually come from families with a dominating mother and a submissive father. **T F**

30. Not all boys and men have nocturnal emissions (wet dreams). **T F**

31. For many women, perhaps the majority, sexual intercourse without other stimulation is not the best form of activity for producing orgasm. **T F**

32. Some women eject a fluid from their vaginas or urethras when they have orgasm. **T F**

33. Women who continue to seek sexual contact with a variety of sexual partners are usually nymphomaniacs. **T F**

34. Gonorrhea and syphilis are no longer common sexually transmitted diseases. **T F**

35. Vaginismus—the tensing of the outer vaginal musculature, making vaginal entry painful or impossible—is usually caused by psychological rather than physical factors. **T F**

36. Most women who are raped have placed themselves in compromising situations where rape is a likely outcome. **T F**

37. The AIDS virus is rarely transmitted by heterosexual intercourse. **T F**

38. Most physicians are well equipped to treat the routine sexual problems of their patients such as impotence or lack of orgasm. **T F**

39. Blacks generally have a stronger sex drive than whites. **T F**

40. There are several documented cases of men and women becoming stuck together during sexual intercourse. **T F**

41. If a woman lacks a hymen, it does not necessarily mean she has already experienced sexual intercourse. **T F**

42. The sperm that produce male babies come from one testis, while the female-producing sperm come from the other testis. **T F**

43. Sexual molesters of children are usually elderly males. **T F**

44. A man who enjoys inserting a finger into his anus during masturbation is displaying homosexual tendencies. **T F**

45. Even if people are paralyzed from the waist or neck down, they may still respond sexually with erection, lubrication, and/or orgasm. **T F**

46. Women tend to experience multiple orgasms during a single sexual encounter more often than men. **T F**

47. Most prostitutes are nymphomaniacs. **T F**

48. Children under the age of 8 can have romantic and sexual feelings. **T F**

49. Certain drugs can cause a condition in which a male experiences orgasm without ejaculation of semen. **T F**

50. During sexual arousal, the male's testicles can increase in size up to 50 percent more than their unexcited size. **T F**

Answers

1.	F	11.	T	21.	F	31.	T	41.	T
2.	F	12.	F	22.	T	32.	T	42.	F
3.	F	13.	T	23.	F	33.	F	43.	F
4.	T	14.	T	24.	F	34.	F	44.	F
5.	T	15.	F	25.	F	35.	T	45.	T
6.	T	16.	F	26.	F	36.	F	46.	T
7.	F	17.	F	27.	T	37.	F	47.	F
8.	F	18.	T	28.	F	38.	F	48.	T
9.	F	19.	T	29.	F	39.	F	49.	T
10.	F	20.	F	30.	T	40.	F	50.	T

CHAPTER SUMMARY

1. Masters and Johnson were among the first researchers to study scientifically the body's physiological changes during sexual response. They developed a four-phase model involving excitement, plateau, orgasm, and resolution.

2. A three-phase model proposed by Kaplan views sexual response as beginning with psychological desire with a subsequent buildup of blood and muscular tension, followed by reversal of these states as triggered by orgasm.

3. The term *desire phase* refers to the level of interest in sexual activity an individual may experience.

4. There are many individual differences in human sexual response, and good communication is essential to developing mutual understanding in a sexual relationship.

5. Devices have been used in research to measure and compare the degree of sexual arousal in women and men. There do not appear to be as many differences in their arousal patterns as once believed, and the differences that do exist may well be the result of socialization.

6. In females, the vagina becomes lubricated during sexual excitement, and an orgasmic platform develops with the swelling of the clitoris and labia. The clitoris eventually retracts under its foreskin.

7. Some researchers claim that there is a particularly sensitive spot on the inner front part of the vagina that swells during female arousal. This has been called the "G spot."

8. Kegel exercises can keep the urogenital musculature in good tone and may increase the intensity or pleasure of orgasm.

9. In males, penile erection is a major sign of excitement, and there are also increases in the size of the testes and scrotum. The testes move upward in the scrotum.

10. In both women and men, sexual response involves increases in respiration, heart rate, blood pressure, and general muscular tension. A reddish "sex flush" appears on the skin of the upper body in some individuals, and nipple erection may also occur.

11. Orgasm is the pleasurable release of sexual tension, involving a series of muscular contractions in both sexes. Ejaculation usually accompanies orgasm in men; some women may expel some fluids during orgasm as well. Some women, and a few men, have the capacity for more than one orgasm during a single period of sexual stimulation.

12. During resolution, at the end of sexual response, the body relaxes and returns to its unexcited state. In men, there is generally a refractory period during which there can be no restimulation to orgasm.

13. It is still not clear what role hormones may play in regulating sexual response. Testosterone, present in both men and women, may act as an activator for sexual desire.

14. The aging process causes changes in sexual response. Both men and women may experience slower arousal and somewhat less intensity of response. People who have been more sexually active during their younger years will tend to maintain a higher level of sexual activity during their later years.

ANNOTATED READINGS

Brecher, E., & Brecher, R. (1966). *An analysis of human sexual response.* New York: New American Library. This book was written as a simplified version of Masters and Johnson's studies of sexual response. Although new knowledge has since been added in the field, this book still represents an excellent introduction to the subject.

Masters, W., & Johnson, V. (1966). *Human sexual response.* Boston: Little, Brown. Although this original text describing Masters and Johnson's pioneering work is more difficult than the Brecher book above, it is complete. For any serious student wanting thorough information on the sexual response cycle, this book is a must.

Perper, T. (1985). *Sex signals: The biology of love.* Philadelphia: ISI Press. An interesting treatment concerning the relationship of love and intimacy, suggesting that they are rooted in human biology.

Wellness: Healthful aging. (1992). Guilford, CT: The Dushkin Publishing Group. This volume was designed as a place to begin to understand the relationship between life-style and good health throughout the life span, and to help readers think critically about the claims and counterclaims made about the aging process.

Sexuality is clearly linked to the process of reproduction. Human biology gives most people the capability of producing offspring. However, as the human mind and civilization have evolved, reproduction has become a far more complex issue than propagation of the species. Chapter 4 first deals with the mechanisms of fertilization and development of the fetus. For individuals who choose to have children, medical specialists now offer many forms of technological assistance. Some futurists are beginning to wonder if reproductive technology may eventually replace the most basic reproductive functions of sex, rendering them unnecessary to continuation of the species.

The *Brave New World* scenarios are still in their earliest phases, however, and society is just beginning to weigh the complicated ethical and legal issues they bring forth. For most individuals, heterosexual intercourse will carry with it the risks and choices relating to pregnancy. As chapter 5 describes, there are many ways in which the probability of pregnancy may be reduced. Yet, we are hardly living in the golden age of contraception. Development of new, more effective, and safer methods of birth control has lagged markedly in recent years, largely because research funding has been unavailable.

For a variety of reasons, there is still a high rate of unintended pregnancy in our society as well. People fail to use contraception, or they use it incorrectly, or it fails, and people are left with the difficult choices of how to resolve the situation. This chapter also deals with the options available to those facing an unintended pregnancy. It is one of those life situations in which making a choice is inescapable. Any action taken or not taken represents a choice. The issue becomes how much responsibility for the decision-making the individual is willing to take.

The reproductive aspects of human sexuality are an important part of sexuality's complex role in society, and should not be taken lightly. The issues surrounding reproduction, contraception, and termination of pregnancy have become highly politicized in recent years. The United States has become polarized in its debate and political struggles about abortion. Human sexual reproduction is far more than a biological phenomenon; it is a social and cultural controversy.

CHAPTER FOUR
REPRODUCTION AND BIRTHING

Modern technology has revolutionized reproduction for childless couples and for couples at high risk for a difficult pregnancy and/or delivery. Artificial insemination, in vitro fertilization, and surrogate motherhood give childless couples more options for having a child than they previously had. Amniocentesis, chorionic villi sampling, and sonograms help identify fetal difficulties in the womb.

CHAPTER FIVE
BIRTH CONTROL AND UNINTENDED PREGNANCY

Ethical, moral, and religious factors affect people's decisions about the use of contraceptives. The type of contraceptive used varies in effectiveness and a couple should consider together which method is best for them.

The decision to abort an unwanted pregnancy is difficult for most couples. Physical as well as moral issues must be considered, and counseling can help both the woman and the man deal with guilt, a sense of loss, or other psychological conflicts they may experience if they decide to abort.

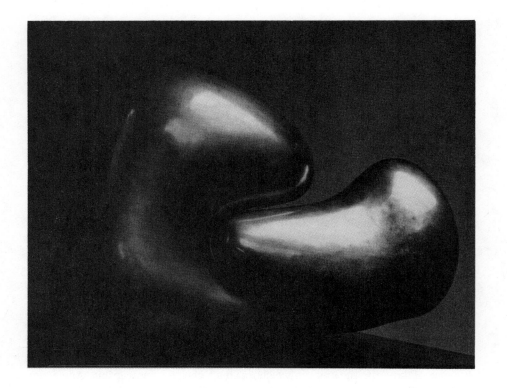

CHAPTER FOUR

REPRODUCTION: FERTILIZATION AND FETAL DEVELOPMENT
Development of the Embryo/Fetus

REPRODUCTIVE AND FETAL TECHNOLOGY
Genetic Engineering
Artificial Insemination and Storage of Gametes and Embryos
In Vitro Fertilization and Related Techniques
Choosing the Sex of a Fetus
Will Human Cloning Become Possible?

Surrogate Motherhood
Fetal Technology
Infertility and Sexuality

PREGNANCY AND BIRTHING
The Biology of Pregnancy
The Birth Process
Birthing Alternatives
Problems During Pregnancy

CHAPTER SUMMARY

When I got pregnant with my second child, I knew I wanted the whole experience to be different from the first time. I found a doctor who would let me be in charge. When I gave birth to my first child, I was a patient—plain and simple. Nobody told me anything. I was mostly alone and numbed with drugs. Giving birth to my second little girl was wonderful. I was awake and clear-headed. My husband was right with me the whole time. And I did it. My body gave birth to a baby just like it was meant to. Nobody tried to take over and do it for me.

—From a former student of a Lamaze childbirth class

REPRODUCTION AND BIRTHING

Sex and human reproduction are obviously linked closely together, biologically and socially. There are still many people who believe that the primary purpose of sexual intercourse between a woman and a man is procreation. With few exceptions, every time heterosexual intercourse occurs prior to a woman's menopause, there is at least a small chance of a pregnancy occurring.

Until recently it would have been quite accurate to state that reproduction of the human species could not take place without sex, without the transfer of semen into the vagina through sexual intercourse or some activity close to it. However, reproductive technology has developed a number of new ways of bringing sperm and egg together that do not necessarily depend on sexual contact between a man and a woman.

This chapter focuses on the facts about reproduction, the effects of new technology on fetal development, and the various approaches to assisting the birth process.

Reproduction: Fertilization and Fetal Development

During the menstrual cycle an ovum matures and is released from one of the female's ovaries. Fertilization of the ovum by a sperm must occur within 48 hours after ovulation while the ovum is being moved through the fallopian tube. As soon as semen is ejaculated from the penis into the vagina, the sperm begin their journey into the uterus. A few thousand usually reach the fallopian tubes. The more sperm present, the greater the probability that fertilization, or conception, will occur. It has long been wondered if eggs have some mechanism for communicating with sperm. Recent research suggests that a sperm-attracting chemical is released either by the egg itself or by the pocket of cells, or follicle, that it leaves behind in the ovary (Roberts, 1991). The sperm cells that come into contact with the ovum are believed to secrete an enzyme that may aid in the penetration of the outer membrane of

81

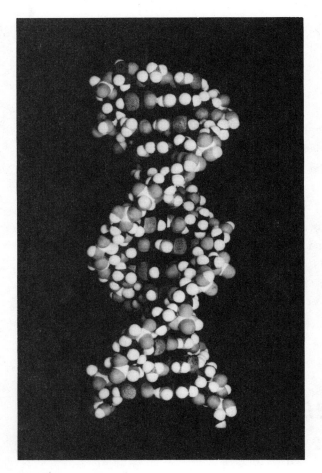

FIGURE 4.1 DNA

This model of a molecule of deoxyribonucleic acid (DNA) shows clearly its double helix shape. DNA is the building block of heredity containing within it the genetic code that produces a specific type of offspring. Scientists hope that by learning more about DNA they will be able to prevent genetic diseases and control some aspects of the reproductive process. On the other hand, skeptics point to some of the risks involved in manipulating the structure of genes.

the ovum, the zona pellucida. Usually only one sperm manages to burrow its way into the interior of the ovum (see four-color insert). Tiny outgrowths from the surface of the ovum reach out and hold tightly to the one sperm, and a hard protein surface develops that prevents further sperm from entering. The actual mechanisms of sperm penetration and exclusion of other sperm are poorly understood at this time. Probably an extra sperm occasionally fertilizes an ovum, but the fertilized ovum apparently dies in such cases because of the extra number of chromosomes that would result.

Fertilization is an extremely important event in human development. Not only does it initiate the growth of a new human being, but inherited traits are

determined at the moment of conception. Both the ovum and the sperm contain 23 chromosomes, each bearing genes that contain hereditary information stored in the form of deoxyribonucleic acid (DNA). In the combining and pairing of these 46 chromosomes, essential programs for the individual's heredity are initiated. It is the pairing of sex chromosomes at fertilization that determines the sex of the developing embryo—XX for female and XY for male. This is discussed in more detail in chapter 6, "Gender-Identity/Role and Society."

Twinning and Other Multiples Giving birth to twins, triplets, and other multiples always creates attention and excitement: the more babies born, the more excitement. Twins occur in slightly more than 1 percent of births in the United States, and triplets occur about once in 9,000 births. Twins may be either fraternal, formed from two separate ova being fertilized by two separate sperm, or identical, formed by a

zona pellucida (ZO-nah pe-LOO-sa-da): the transparent, outer membrane of an ovum.
deoxyribonucleic acid (DNA) (dee-AK-see-rye-bow-new-KLEE-ik): the chemical in each cell that carries the genetic code.
fraternal twin: a twin formed from two separate ova that were fertilized by two separate sperm.
identical twin: a twin formed by a single ovum that was fertilized by a single sperm before the cell divided in two.

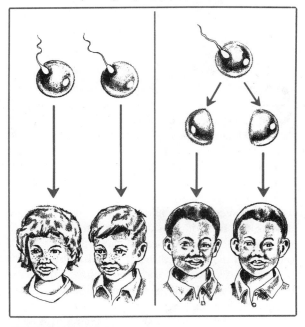

FIGURE 4.2 Twins

Fraternal or dizygotic twins are formed from the fertilization of two ova by two separate sperm. Identical or monozygotic twins are formed from the same fertilized ovum that divides before implantation in the uterus.

Case Study

GIVING BIRTH: A PERSONAL PERSPECTIVE

The distinct moments of giving birth to my two children were the most powerful and profound acts I have ever performed. At no other time in life does the planning, waiting, physical exertion, and time devoted to a task end with such magnificent results, the beginning of life for a whole new person. Both times, Gary and I were rendered speechless when our daughters emerged. You always know intellectually that the processes of reproduction and birth are supposed to result in the birth of a child. But not until you see that little body with eyes wide and staring with a powerful intensity are you struck with a miracle that has become reality.

The physical aspects of pregnancy and birth are the most obvious, but the psychological and relational aspects have the most profound effect. During the pregnancy there were times when I very deeply needed to feel loved and protected by my husband. There were times before and after the birth I needed some proof of autonomy from the child that was a physical part of me for 9 months. Gary and I both vacillated between periods of wanting to escape the whole thing and feeling certain that this experience would bind us together forever. The most crucial thing about facing all of our conflicting emotions was that each of us allowed the other to feel whatever was surfacing and offered support.

When I gave that final draining, straining push and my husband seemed so proud of me and what we had created together, it was a moment like no other in my life. Every rich detail will be forever woven into my memory. To be part of the life-giving forces of the universe is truly an awesome experience.

—Betsy A. Kelly

---

single ovum and sperm. In fraternal twins, the two fertilized ova develop separately, and the twins look no more alike than any other siblings in the family. They may be of the same or different sexes. In identical twins, when the first division of the fertilized ovum occurs, the two cells separate and develop as two individuals. Since they have exactly the same chromosomes, however, they are of the same sex and identical in appearance (see Fig. 4.2). Triplets, quadruplets, and other multiple fetuses may all be fraternal or may include one or more sets of identical twins. Identical triplets are extremely rare.

Multiple fetuses increase the risk of premature birth, birth defects, and other problems for the pregnant woman. The higher the number of fetuses, the greater the risk. Twenty-one percent of triplets die. For quadruplets the fatality rate is 43 percent, and for sextuplets it is 91 percent. For the mother, there is increased risk of serious bleeding, high blood pressure, and metabolic disturbances. Some fertility drugs used to stimulate production of ova in women have a tendency to produce multiple fetuses. For all of these reasons, a controversial new procedure has become available in medical practice. Selective reduction involves selectively aborting one or more of the fetuses so that a lower-risk number of two or three remains. In the past, when multiple fetuses were discovered, the couple had the option of either doing nothing and taking their chances on a successful outcome, or terminating the entire pregnancy. They now have this third option available, although it obviously represents a difficult choice. So far, the selective reduction technique has successfully reduced the number of premature multiple births and their accompanying complications (Hobbins, 1988).

DEVELOPMENT OF THE EMBRYO / FETUS

After the ovum has been fertilized, it begins a process of cell division as it continues to move toward the uterus. The first division produces two cells; these both divide to form four, and so on. With each cell division, the chromosomes are replicated so that every new cell has a full complement of hereditary material. Within 3 days, a spherical, solid mass of cells has been formed, called the morula. By the end of the 5th day

selective reduction: use of abortion techniques to reduce the number of fetuses when there are more than three in a pregnancy, thus increasing the chances of survival for the remaining fetuses.

morula (MOR-yul-a): a spherical, solid mass of cells formed after 3 days of embryonic cell division.

83

after fertilization the sphere has developed a fluid-filled cavity in its interior and is termed the blastocyst. By this time the mass of dividing cells has left the fallopian tube and entered the uterine cavity. Since there is no rich source of nourishment, the cells are not growing and the blastocyst is not appreciably larger than the original ovum.

Around a week after fertilization, the blastocyst comes into contact with the uterine lining (the endometrium) and secretes enzymes that help it to burrow into the lining. It eventually reaches the deeper blood vessels and nourishing tissues of the uterine lining and the burrowing stops. The blastocyst is implanted in the uterine wall and is now considered an embryo, about to undergo a series of dramatic changes in growth and development (see Fig. 4.3). Occasionally a blastocyst becomes implanted in a fallopian tube or strays into the abdominal cavity and attaches itself to some other tissue where it continues to develop as an embryo. This is called an ectopic pregnancy, and the embryo should be surgically removed to prevent rupture of the tube and bleeding. Complications of ectopic pregnancy constitute the seventh leading cause of death during pregnancy.

Typically, a baby is born after about 266 days (approximately 9 months) of development in the uterus. There are wide variations in the length of pregnancy, however. During that period the fertilized ovum develops into an infant capable of living outside the uterus and weighing about 6 billion times more at birth than it did at the time of fertilization.

Early in embryonic development several extra-embryonic membranes are formed; these are essential to the embryo's survival. The membrane that creates a sac to enclose the embryo is called the amnion. The sac is filled with amniotic fluid, which keeps the embryonic tissues moist and protectively cushions the embryo. The amniotic sac is called the bag of waters, and just before birth it breaks, releasing its clear watery fluid through the vagina. There are two membranes, the *yolk sac* and the *allantois*, that seem to function only in early embryonic development and gradually become partly incorporated into the umbilical cord. The outermost extraembryonic membrane is the chorion. It plays an essential role in the formation of the placenta, the structure that provides nourishment for the embryo. The chorion produces small fingerlike projections, called villi, that grow into the uterine tissue and form a major part of the placenta. It is within the placenta that blood vessels from the embryo come into close contact with blood vessels from the mother, although there is no actual intermingling of the two bloodstreams. While the blood vessels are in close proximity, however, food molecules and oxygen from the maternal blood diffuse into the embryo's blood.

Carbon dioxide and other metabolic wastes diffuse from the embryo's blood into the mother's blood, and her body then disposes of them through the lungs and kidneys. The embryo is connected to the placenta by the umbilical cord, which forms during the 5th week of pregnancy. It is through the umbilical cord that the embryo's blood vessels pass into and out of the placenta (see Fig. 4.4).

Usually after 2 months of development, the embryo is called the fetus. It is beyond the scope of this book to detail embryonic and fetal development. However, from the moment of conception to the time a baby is born, remarkable changes occur. An entire human body develops, with internal systems that can function to support life and enable the fetus to move and react to stimuli. Figure 4.5, pages 86–87, summarizes some of the important stages of fetal development.

Reproductive and Fetal Technology

In recent years many important social, legal, religious, personal, and ethical questions have been raised by biological research into the areas of sex, reproduction, and genetics. Some of Aldous Huxley's *Brave New World* imaginings of 1932 no longer seem so farfetched. Many medical and technological advancements are already being employed: artificial insemination, frozen sperm banks, in vitro fertilization, genetic selection and modification, predetermination of fetal sex, and surrogate

blastocyst: the morula, after 5 days of cell division, that has developed a fluid-filled cavity in its interior; it has entered the uterine cavity.

embryo (EM-bree-o): the term applied to the developing cells when, about a week after fertilization, the blastocyst implants itself in the uterine wall.

ectopic pregnancy (ek-TOP-ik): the implantation of a blastocyst somewhere other than in the uterus, usually in the fallopian tube.

amnion (AM-nee-on): a thin membrane that forms a closed sac around the embryo; the sac is filled with amniotic fluid that protects and cushions the embryo.

chorion (KOR-ee-on): the outermost extraembryonic membrane, essential in the formation of the placenta.

placenta (pla-SENT-a): the organ that unites the fetus to the mother by bringing their blood vessels closer together; it provides nourishment and removes waste for the developing baby.

villi: fingerlike projections of the chorion; they form a major part of the placenta.

umbilical cord: the tubelike tissues and blood vessels arising from the embryo's navel connecting it to the placenta.

fetus: the term given to the embryo after 2 months of development in the womb.

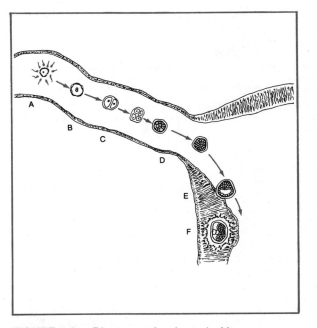

FIGURE 4.3 Blastocyst Implants in Uterus

After hundreds of sperm surround the ovum (A), one penetrates and fertilizes it (B). Cell division begins (C), and after 3 days produces a spherical mass called a morula (D). The 5th day after fertilization, the mass develops a sphere of cells called a blastocyst (E), and within a week implants in the uterine lining (F); it is now considered an embryo.

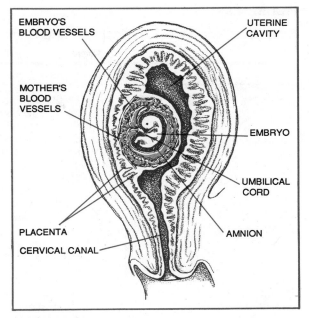

FIGURE 4.4 Placenta

The developing baby receives nourishment and oxygen from the mother's blood through the placenta and returns his or her waste products back through it. This exchange takes place through the umbilical cord, which connects the fetal and maternal circulatory systems.

motherhood (Baruch, D'Adamo, & Seager, 1989). Many of our culture's long-standing values about the roles of parents are being challenged by these developments. We are also realizing that different people make their ethical and moral decisions from different perspectives (Hendrixson, 1989).

We are moving beyond the time when we have to rely exclusively on chance in reproductive sex. Scientists are developing means by which we can manipulate genes and reproduction so that many new choices may soon be possible. Yet this work has been controversial because of its dangers. Genetic manipulation might create totally new life forms. The bypassing of natural reproductive functions may have implications that will raise serious doubts about the roles that men and women will play in procreation.

GENETIC ENGINEERING

Research has yielded significant information on how genes function. The types of offspring produced by sexual reproduction depend on the gene combinations made during the fertilization of a randomly selected sperm and egg. Genes give chemical messages to cells, causing them to carry on particular functions for which the cells are responsible. We now know that the genetic code that determines the traits of the offspring is contained in strands of DNA. The characteristics of a human being are essentially the result of that random combination and indeed are at the mercy of the process.

Molecular geneticists continue to learn more about how genes work and how they may be modified. Much of the early research was done with single-celled bacteria. Scientists succeeded in removing some genetic material from one cell, combining it with genes from another, and implanting the recombinant DNA into a host cell. The result was that the cell had a new genetic makeup and took on new characteristics. Similar experimentation has proceeded with recombinant DNA between different species of organisms, sometimes even producing entirely new species.

An especially important experiment culminated in 1976, after 9 years of work, with the actual creation of a gene by a team of scientists in Cambridge, Massachusetts, headed by Nobel laureate Har Gobind Khorana. The Khorana team was able to construct a gene biochemically in the laboratory, then insert it into a bacterial cell and have the cell function normally.

85

(continued on p. 88)

FIGURE 4.5

Embryonic and Fetal Development and Changes in the Mother's Body

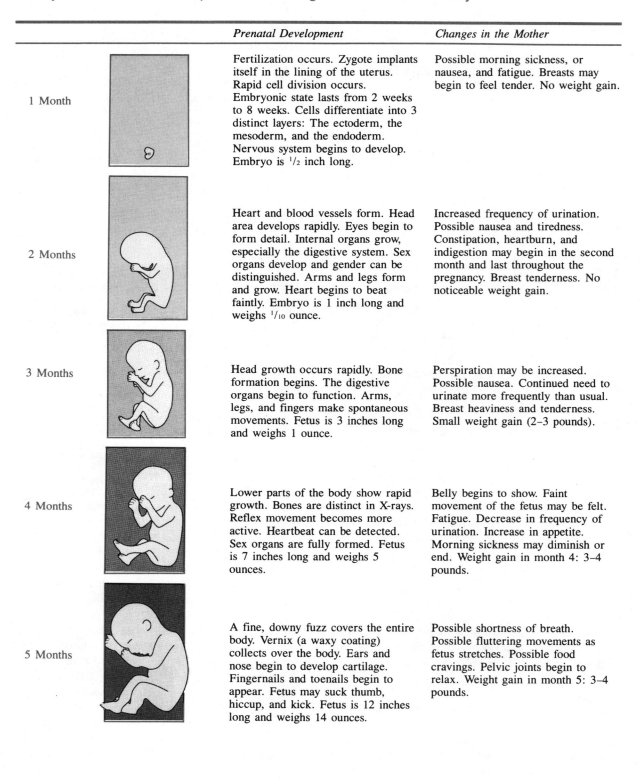

	Prenatal Development	Changes in the Mother
1 Month	Fertilization occurs. Zygote implants itself in the lining of the uterus. Rapid cell division occurs. Embryonic state lasts from 2 weeks to 8 weeks. Cells differentiate into 3 distinct layers: The ectoderm, the mesoderm, and the endoderm. Nervous system begins to develop. Embryo is 1/2 inch long.	Possible morning sickness, or nausea, and fatigue. Breasts may begin to feel tender. No weight gain.
2 Months	Heart and blood vessels form. Head area develops rapidly. Eyes begin to form detail. Internal organs grow, especially the digestive system. Sex organs develop and gender can be distinguished. Arms and legs form and grow. Heart begins to beat faintly. Embryo is 1 inch long and weighs 1/10 ounce.	Increased frequency of urination. Possible nausea and tiredness. Constipation, heartburn, and indigestion may begin in the second month and last throughout the pregnancy. Breast tenderness. No noticeable weight gain.
3 Months	Head growth occurs rapidly. Bone formation begins. The digestive organs begin to function. Arms, legs, and fingers make spontaneous movements. Fetus is 3 inches long and weighs 1 ounce.	Perspiration may be increased. Possible nausea. Continued need to urinate more frequently than usual. Breast heaviness and tenderness. Small weight gain (2–3 pounds).
4 Months	Lower parts of the body show rapid growth. Bones are distinct in X-rays. Reflex movement becomes more active. Heartbeat can be detected. Sex organs are fully formed. Fetus is 7 inches long and weighs 5 ounces.	Belly begins to show. Faint movement of the fetus may be felt. Fatigue. Decrease in frequency of urination. Increase in appetite. Morning sickness may diminish or end. Weight gain in month 4: 3–4 pounds.
5 Months	A fine, downy fuzz covers the entire body. Vernix (a waxy coating) collects over the body. Ears and nose begin to develop cartilage. Fingernails and toenails begin to appear. Fetus may suck thumb, hiccup, and kick. Fetus is 12 inches long and weighs 14 ounces.	Possible shortness of breath. Possible fluttering movements as fetus stretches. Possible food cravings. Pelvic joints begin to relax. Weight gain in month 5: 3–4 pounds.

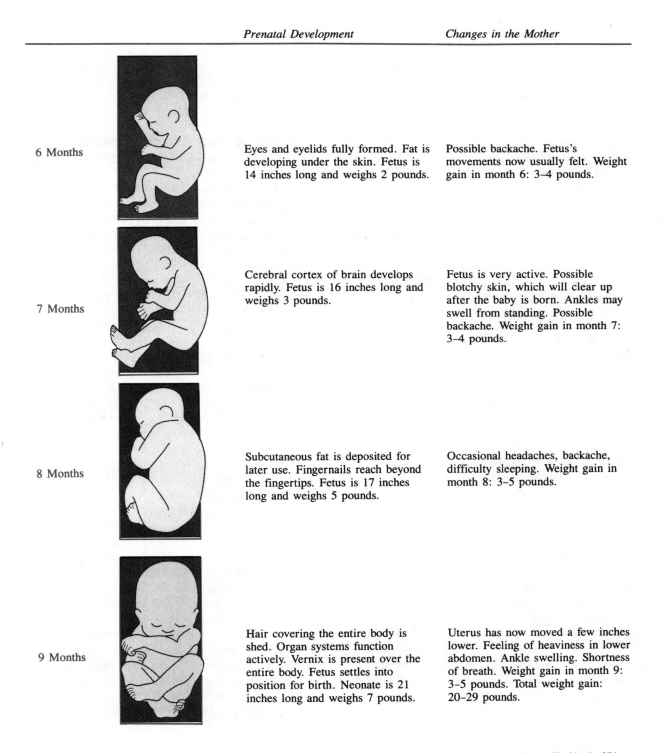

	Prenatal Development	*Changes in the Mother*
6 Months	Eyes and eyelids fully formed. Fat is developing under the skin. Fetus is 14 inches long and weighs 2 pounds.	Possible backache. Fetus's movements now usually felt. Weight gain in month 6: 3–4 pounds.
7 Months	Cerebral cortex of brain develops rapidly. Fetus is 16 inches long and weighs 3 pounds.	Fetus is very active. Possible blotchy skin, which will clear up after the baby is born. Ankles may swell from standing. Possible backache. Weight gain in month 7: 3–4 pounds.
8 Months	Subcutaneous fat is deposited for later use. Fingernails reach beyond the fingertips. Fetus is 17 inches long and weighs 5 pounds.	Occasional headaches, backache, difficulty sleeping. Weight gain in month 8: 3–5 pounds.
9 Months	Hair covering the entire body is shed. Organ systems function actively. Vernix is present over the entire body. Fetus settles into position for birth. Neonate is 21 inches long and weighs 7 pounds.	Uterus has now moved a few inches lower. Feeling of heaviness in lower abdomen. Ankle swelling. Shortness of breath. Weight gain in month 9: 3–5 pounds. Total weight gain: 20–29 pounds.

Sources: Terry F. Pettijohn, *Psychology: A Concise Introduction* (3rd Edition), 1992, Guilford, CT: The Dushkin Publishing Group; The March of Dimes; and *Earth Surface Graphics.*

All of this work in controlling cellular functioning has been termed <u>genetic engineering</u>, and the scientists involved see the potential for tremendous benefits. There are already a number of agricultural uses envisioned. More farsighted uses are being planned in the treatment of the more than 3,000 human disorders that have genetic causes. Principles of genetic engineering represent one avenue for developing a vaccine to destroy the AIDS virus or prevent it from infecting humans. There is now the long-term possibility that genetic engineering could prevent or treat such conditions as hemophilia, sickle-cell anemia, disorders of the immune system, certain types of diabetes and mental retardation, or a variety of other conditions caused by inherited faulty genes.

Scientists have recently begun a $3 billion project to create a complete map of the human genome, or DNA structure that makes a human being (Jaroff, 1989). Researchers have proposed that, by using a technique called gene transfer, healthy genes could be transplanted into enough cells of a person's body to overcome the effects of some genetic condition. Eventually, as tests to detect hereditary diseases become more highly perfected, such gene transfers could be made during embryonic development, as they already are in some animal experiments. The very aspects of genetic chance that have been considered basic to reproduction could actually be reversed and controlled. Companies engaged in potentially profitable gene technology have become big businesses and have seen their share of profits and losses. Already there are pharmaceutical products available that have been produced by genetic engineering, including a type of insulin for use by diabetics. However, much work remains to be done. We are moving toward new approaches for treating genetically linked diseases and modification of mutant genes (Friedmann, 1989).

Yet for some scientists, these possibilities raise other, more frightening ones. For example, what if one of the experimental microorganisms develops severe disease-causing, antibiotic-resistant properties and then escapes from controlled laboratory conditions? Or what if a powerful dictator decides to employ genetic engineering to modify human life in some way? Some prestigious molecular biologists called for a cessation of experiments in genetic engineering until risks could be assessed and guidelines formulated. By the late 1970s the National Institutes of Health had established strict guidelines for recombinant DNA research. Local and state governments began calling for controls on genetic research as well. The International Council of Scientific Unions established a Committee on Genetic Experimentation (COGENE) to encourage governments to establish uniform policies regulating recombinant DNA research. While the de-

bate about gene therapy continues, the federal government has approved the introduction of a foreign gene into humans (Roberts, 1989).

Genetic engineering is a science still in its infancy. Some scientists feel that fears about such research have been overblown, and that the potential benefits outweigh imagined risks. Nevertheless, scientists and laypersons alike must continue to sort through some of the potential ethical issues of the future.

ARTIFICIAL INSEMINATION AND STORAGE OF GAMETES AND EMBRYOS

<u>Artificial insemination</u>, or placing donated semen in the woman's vagina or uterus without intercourse, has been available for over 200 years, although it was not considered standard medical practice until the 1930s. During the following decade it was discovered that human semen could be frozen quickly in liquid nitrogen without damaging sperm cells. The first baby conceived from frozen semen was born in 1954 (Francoeur, 1985).

This method of impregnation is most typically used with couples in which the man's sperm count is low (less than 40 million sperm per cubic centimeter of semen) or, in extreme cases, zero, rendering it difficult or impossible for him to impregnate his partner. Although concentrating the sperm count from several of the man's own semen specimens has been one approach, it has not proven especially successful. A more common method is to use semen contributed by an anonymous donor, chosen for characteristics of good health, intelligence, and physical traits similar to those of the intended "father." The semen may be frozen or used fresh. It is inserted by a physician into the back of the woman's vagina, near the cervix. The pregnancy rate in artificial insemination ranges from 60 percent to 75 percent.

The preservation of sperm by quick-freezing techniques was a major advance in artificial insemination, since men could donate semen for storage in sperm banks, to be used later as needed. This added efficiency and convenience to the procedure for all involved. Eventually human eggs may be widely stored in the same way. In the early 1980s Australian scientists began experimenting with freezing human embryos for use in in vitro fertilization. This was for the purpose of convenience and efficiency as well, since several eggs could be withdrawn in a single

genetic engineering: the modification of the gene structure of cells to change cellular functioning.
artificial insemination: injecting the sperm cells of a male into a woman's vagina, with the intention of conceiving a child.

surgical procedure, fertilized, and then saved for future use. If one IVF fails, another embryo may then be tried, bypassing all of the earlier stages of the technique. The first baby from a frozen embryo implant was born in 1987.

Already a number of ethical issues have arisen about the storage of gametes (sperm and eggs) and embryos. In California a man by the name of Robert Graham originated a sperm bank intended to strengthen the human gene pool. He proposed freezing semen from Nobel Prize winners, to be used in the insemination of particularly bright women. The question of eugenics, or selecting human traits for improvement of the species, is one that has always created controversy. It becomes a question of who has the right to determine which characteristics should be preserved and fostered and which should be eliminated. For some it is a reminder that Hitler and his associates decided that an entire ethnic group was undesirable and were to be eliminated in a eugenic effort to create a "master race." For others it is seen as a legitimate attempt to direct human evolution.

A wealthy Australian couple who had preserved two embryos for possible later implantation were killed in an airplane crash. Legal and ethical questions arose about the fate of the embryos. There was debate over whether attempts should be made to implant the embryos, or to permit them instead to be discarded. The courts eventually allowed the frozen embryos to be destroyed, but it is interesting to speculate about the rights of the infants that might have been produced if they had been allowed to develop. Would they have been the legal heirs, thus entitling them to inherit the couple's considerable wealth?

Lesbian couples have been using artificial insemination in order to have children. In a classic case one woman used a relative's semen to inseminate her female lover artificially. Since she had carried out the act of insemination (with a basting syringe), she was listed as the father on the baby's birth certificate. When the couple eventually separated she fought for paternal visiting rights in the courts and won (Francoeur, 1985).

Society is just beginning to grapple with the complex ethical and legal ramifications of storage banks for gametes and embryos. There are many precedents yet to be established that can help guide decisionmakers of the future. Since the need for these decisions will multiply as reproductive technology is perfected, these issues must eventually be resolved. It has been suggested that we are on the verge of a biotechnical revolution in reproduction, with as profound implications as the Industrial Revolution, and that we are as unprepared for it as we were for the Industrial Revolution (Morris, 1991).

IN VITRO FERTILIZATION AND RELATED TECHNIQUES

Since the beginning of human life on this planet, it has seemed that nothing could replace the ability of the human body to produce more of its own kind. The male deposited sperm in the vagina, fertilization of the ovum took place in the fallopian tubes, and gestation of the fetus occurred in the uterus. Talk of "test-tube babies" once seemed to be imaginative science fiction, and yet now has become a reality.

In 1959 an Italian scientist, Dr. Daniele Petrucci, reported that he had achieved *in vitro* (in laboratory glassware) fertilization of a human egg and sperm. The embryo was being grown in the laboratory until the research was condemned by the Pope and Petrucci brought the experiment to a halt.

In the late 1960s a team of English scientists began further work with in vitro fertilization (IVF), and in 1978 the first "test-tube baby," Louise Brown, was born in Oldham, England. Her mother, like many infertile women, had blockages in the fallopian tubes that prevented the sperm and egg from meeting. IVF permits a woman who would otherwise be unable to conceive to have her own child. Ova are removed from one of her ovaries by a simple microsurgical technique and are then mixed with sperm cells from her partner, usually obtained through masturbation. Fertilization can be confirmed by microscopic examination, and a fertilized egg is then placed in the woman's uterus, which has been appropriately readied by hormonal treatment. If the process is successful, the embryo will implant in the uterine wall as would happen under natural conditions, and development of the fetus continues. There are now numerous clinics in the United States that offer this process to infertile couples. Several thousand babies have now been produced by the IVF method.

However, couples who are interested in IVF need to ask questions carefully to determine the odds of conceiving and giving birth to a full-term baby. The U.S. Office of Technology Assessment surveyed clinics in the mid-1980s and found that, of 170 IVF clinics, at least half had never sent a couple home with a baby. Patients who have special risk factors, such as being older or having a history of repeated miscarriages, are less likely to be successful. The actual sperm-ovum fertilization is achieved about 60 percent of the time, but the chances of clinical pregnancy occurring are only about 1 in 6 or 16.9 percent. Beyond that, however, there is still a one-third risk that

in vitro fertilization (IVF): a process whereby the union of the sperm and egg occurs outside the mother's body.

"I already know about the birds and the bees, Mom; I want to know about artificial insemination, in vitro fertilization, and surrogate mothering!"

the pregnancy will be ectopic or end in miscarriage. It is therefore crucial that couples investigate any IVF clinic's length of service, success rates, costs, and manner of producing statistics on "success." It is important to know whether all attempts to achieve IVF are included in the statistics, or only those that result in actual fertilization and transfer of the embryo to the uterus. The stakes can be high. A single IVF attempt may cost several thousand dollars, and there may be a significant emotional toll in continuing disappointment (Ferre Institute, 1988).

Physicians at Yale–New Haven Hospital recently developed an alternative fertilization method that is particularly useful for couples in which the male has a low sperm count. Eggs are removed from the ovary and injected through a catheter into the woman's fallopian tube. Sperm cells that have been separated from the partner's semen, thus concentrating them, are then injected directly into the same area, making fertilization a more likely result. This procedure is called gamete intra-fallopian transfer (GIFT).

Work is now proceeding with techniques that would allow one woman to donate eggs to another woman, whose mate's sperm could be used for fertilization. The embryo could then be implanted into the uterus of the woman unable to produce eggs of her own. This is called ovum transfer (Garner, 1987). The Cleveland Clinic in Ohio established an "egg bank" in 1987, so that eggs can be made available to sterile

women. In another procedure, called artificial embryonation, a developing embryo is flushed from the uterus of the donor woman 5 days after fertilization and transferred to another woman's uterus (Francoeur, 1985). This technique has the potential for allowing otherwise infertile couples to go through a pregnancy and birth, even though the child would not genetically be their own. In 1990, this technique was attempted with several women aged 41 to 44 who had already reached menopause. Four of seven women had healthy babies. The study shows that even women past menopause may be able to become pregnant through technological means (Sauer et al., 1990).

For the time being, these procedures are expensive or in experimental stages. It is not likely that the expense and inconvenience would persuade anyone to use the procedure as a substitute for procreative sexual intercourse. Yet if the techniques were perfected and made more affordable, it is conceivable that they could be used by women who want their own babies but are unwilling to be pregnant. Their embryos could be transferred to another woman for gestation.

An even more startling step would be the complete in vitro gestation of a fetus in a laboratory, until it could be removed and be self-sustaining. Some scientists believe that it will only be a matter of time and continued experimentation before someone produces a full-term, living baby outside of the human body—a real test-tube baby.

Today's dream (or nightmare) can be tomorrow's reality. Even today some women are saying that total liberation of women can only come from the total liberation from childbearing, through the use of these techniques. Yet we must also be prepared for innumerable ethical, moral, and legal questions that will develop. Perhaps many years from now, sex for reproduction will be replaced by techniques of fertilization and gestation that will permit careful selection and control of the reproductive process.

CHOOSING THE SEX OF A FETUS

It seems that some people have always wished they could choose the sex of their child ahead of time. Folk

gamete intra-fallopian transfer (GIFT): direct placement of ovum and concentrated sperm cells into the woman's fallopian tube to increase the chances of fertilization.

ovum transfer: use of an egg from another woman for conception, with the fertilized ovum then being implanted in the uterus of the woman wanting to become pregnant.

artificial embryonation: a process in which the developing embryo is flushed from the uterus of the donor woman 5 days after fertilization and placed in another woman's uterus.

cultures have invented their own techniques for predetermining a child's sex. These have included the man leaving his boots on during intercourse or hanging his trousers on the left side of the bed in order to conceive a girl; and removing his boots or hanging trousers on the right side for a boy (Singer & Wells, 1985). Approaches to selecting an infant's sex have emerged in modern technology. The techniques that identify the sex of a fetus within a few weeks after conception involve taking fetal cells through chorionic villi sampling or amniocentesis, then identifying the sex chromosomes. Beyond simply knowing the sex of the expected child, parents have the option of early abortion if the sex of the child is not what they had hoped for. This has become a common practice in China, where couples are generally allowed only one child. Other approaches involve choosing the baby's sex prior to conception. There are techniques by which either the X-bearing or Y-bearing sperm may be sorted out before artificial insemination or in vitro fertilization to increase the chances of the baby being a girl or a boy. The process that produces males is now over 80 percent effective, and the process for producing females is reported to be between 75 and 94 percent effective (Jancin, 1988). Other techniques have been suggested as well, including changing the diet prior to conception, timing of intercourse to be slightly before or slightly after ovulation in the menstrual cycle, and modifying the pH of the vagina. Kits are sold to help with the planning, although the Food and Drug Administration claims they are deceptive and of questionable worth.

Studies in this country have indicated that more than half of U.S. geneticists would be willing either to perform prenatal tests to determine the sex of a fetus, or to refer a patient to someone who would perform such a test. Over 10 percent of obstetricians in one survey indicated that abortion would be morally acceptable for reasons of sex selection. A prevalent view in the medical community is that patients should have the right to make choices that they feel are in their best interests (Wertz & Fletcher, 1991).

Again, the ability to choose the sex of a child raises some important ethical issues. In 1972 a Utah physician expressed strong disapproval to the American Medical Association concerning the morality of having an abortion simply because a child is of the "wrong" sex. Studies in the United States consistently demonstrate that couples tend to have preferences for sons, especially as their first child. The preference for male children is, in fact, found in many cultures and frequently translates into prejudice and sexism (Corea, 1985). This has caused some scientists to fear that predetermination of gender will create a population overweighted by males and infused with sexist values favoring men. Others feel that the process could be

monitored to prevent such imbalances, and that couples should be free to use available technology for choosing the sex of their children (Singer & Wells, 1985).

Sex predetermination is already a fact, and there are already about 60 centers in the United States that are using a patented sperm-separating technique to give parents a choice in the sex of their child (Jancin, 1988). The debates about it must continue. Supporters are seeing it as a way to make happier parents, produce smaller families (since there will be no need to keep trying for a girl or a boy), lower the incidence of sex-linked diseases, and keep the population under control. Opponents are charging that the world will be inundated with males, and that dangerous new forms of sexism and discrimination will arise. Regardless of what rules and regulations develop, preselection of a child's sex is probably here to stay, another example of the way in which biological chance in sexual reproduction is being overcome.

WILL HUMAN CLONING BECOME POSSIBLE?

Cloning is a type of reproduction that bypasses even the fertilization stage. In 1968 Oxford University scientist J. B. Gurdon succeeded in replacing the nucleus of a frog's egg with the nucleus of an intestinal cell from another frog. The egg divided normally and eventually formed a tadpole that became an adult frog. Because the new frog's cells contained exactly the same set of chromosomes as the frog that donated the intestinal cell, the two frogs were genetically identical. The process is called cloning and the exact-copy offspring is called a clone.

It is now beginning to become clear that techniques could be developed to permit the cloning of human beings. The nucleus of some body cell from a donor would be used to replace the nucleus of a human egg. The egg could then be implanted in the uterus of the woman who donated the egg, or that of another woman, (or grown in vitro if the possibility exists) and gestated there until birth. The clone would be genetically identical to the person who donated the original cell nucleus, since their chromosomes would be the same. It would have none of the characteristics from

cloning: a process involving the transfer of a full complement of chromosomes from a body cell of an organism into an ovum from which the chromosomal material has been removed; if allowed to develop into a new organism, it is an exact genetic duplicate of the one from which the original body cell was taken; the process is not yet used for humans, but has been performed in lower animal species.

clone: the genetic-duplicate organism produced by the cloning process.

91

the host mother's egg, since the egg's chromosomes would have been replaced (Singer & Wells, 1985).

The prospect of cloning raises some of the most fascinating and frightening questions concerning the future of sex. Could fatherhood (and men) be eliminated? No sperm would be required for cloning—only an egg cell and a uterus to grow it in would be necessary. If only women were used as nucleus donors, no males would be produced. Would a dictator or fanatic want to produce an entire army of look-alikes, picked for special characteristics? Would society decide to replicate its most valued citizens through cloning? Would people's egos drive them to seek a measure of immortality by cloning duplicates of themselves? Some observers believe that human cloning will be possible in the not-too-distant future. We must prepare now to look ahead at the implications this could have for human sexuality and human life.

SURROGATE MOTHERHOOD

In the 1980s surrogate motherhood, also called gestational surrogacy, became a reproductive phenomenon. Typically in these cases, a couple in which the woman is unable to bear children pays another woman up to $12,000 to be inseminated by the first woman's husband and then bear the child. A legal agreement is drawn up among the parties involved in which the woman who is to be impregnated promises to give the child to the couple when it is born. Laws to govern such situations have been scarce, and questions have been raised about how legally binding the contracts really are (Andrews, 1981). A variation on the gestational surrogacy theme that may well become a reality will involve the use of artificial embryonation, in which a surrogate mother will agree to gestating and giving birth to a baby for a couple who purchased the embryo from medical personnel, not contributing either sperm or egg.

The issues were put to a legal test in the 1987 "Baby M" case when a surrogate mother asked for the return of the child she had borne for another couple. The surrogate mother claimed in court that the other woman had paid her to have the child because she had not wanted pregnancy to interfere with her own career. The woman and her husband, who had contributed the sperm for the child, argued that they had opted for surrogate motherhood because the woman suffered from multiple sclerosis. When serious questions were raised about the mental health and emotional stability of the surrogate mother, the court allowed the couple to adopt the child legally, even denying visitation rights to the surrogate. Later, the decision not to allow visitation was overturned. This was the first major

FIGURE 4.6 Surrogate Motherhood

The first controversial surrogate-mother case centered around "Baby M." Mary Beth Whitehead agreed to be impregnated by the father's sperm, to carry the developing fetus, and to give birth to it for a childless couple. After the birth she refused to give up the baby. Here the father, William Stern, picks up his child after she visits her surrogate mother.

court precedent set for such cases, and it has stimulated numerous state legislatures to consider developing statutes to regulate gestational surrogacy.

In another legal battle, a surrogate mother gave birth to a baby that had resulted from another couple's egg and sperm. The woman who donated the egg lacked a uterus and was therefore unable to carry the fetus. The surrogate mother, however, refused to relinquish the child to the couple. In late 1990 a California court ruled that since the couple who donated the egg and sperm were actually the child's genetic parents, they should be given full custody of the child. In this case, genetics were given precedence over surrogacy, and the surrogate mother was denied any visitation privileges.

While some have hailed gestational surrogacy as a significant advance for childless couples, others have argued that it is nothing more than reproductive prostitution. After the Baby M test case, leading feminists, including Gloria Steinem and Betty Friedan, suggested that gestational surrogacy could represent the first step toward creating a caste of poor female breeders who would bear genetically improved children for upperclass couples. The entire procedure, including payment of the surrogate, today costs over $25,000. Opponents feel there is little difference between this procedure and the long-prohibited practice of selling babies for private adoption. It has also been claimed that the legal protections for the surrogate mother are slim compared with those of the couple, further escalating the argument that surrogate motherhood represents a form of exploitation for women (Neuhaus, 1991).

This new reproductive alternative of using one woman's body to gestate and give birth to a baby for another couple raises some of the most complex issues in reproductive technology. The courts have been ill-prepared to face the judgments they will continue to have to make about the contracts involved. It is a clear-cut example of natural reproductive processes moving out of their usual realms of biology and sexuality into socio-legal territory. Gestational surrogacy is surely headed for more controversy.

FETAL TECHNOLOGY

Problems can occur during fetal development. Great strides are being made in diagnosing, and even treating, medical difficulties in the fetus.

Amniocentesis A well-known technique is amniocentesis, used to detect certain genetic disorders such as Down's syndrome or muscular dystrophy as well as to monitor fetal development. Down's syndrome becomes an increasing risk in the children of women who become pregnant after age 35. In this procedure a needle is inserted through the abdominal wall, into the uterus and the amniotic sac, so that amniotic fluid may be withdrawn. Cells from the developing fetus may be found in this fluid and their chromosomes studied for possible abnormalities. If some birth defect is identified, the parents can make a decision about whether to continue or terminate the pregnancy. Analysis of chromosomes also can determine whether the fetus is female or male, although since there is a 1 percent risk of causing a miscarriage, amniocentesis is not used routinely for sex determination. A new and safer way of examining fetal blood cells is now being tested. It involves the sifting out of fetal blood cells from the mother's bloodstream, so there is no need to penetrate the amnion. The technique is expected to be perfected during the 1990s.

Chorionic Villi Sampling Whereas amniocentesis cannot be used until the end of the 4th month of

amniocentesis: a process whereby medical problems with a fetus can be determined while it is still in the womb; a needle is inserted into the amniotic sac, amniotic fluid is withdrawn, and its cells examined.

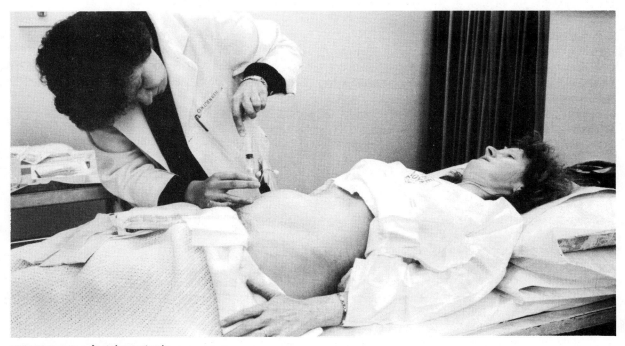

FIGURE 4.7 Amniocentesis

A woman, 16 weeks pregnant, undergoes the procedure of amniocentesis. The amniotic fluid is extracted from the uterus and analyzed. It will indicate the gender of the child as well as possible birth defects.

pregnancy, there is another diagnostic technique called chorionic villi sampling (CVS), which can be used as early as the 8th week. A thin catheter is inserted through the cervix, and a small sample of tissue from the chorionic membrane is withdrawn. The chromosomes in these cells may then be analyzed.

Sonograms One of the techniques that has made amniocentesis and other fetal diagnostic methods possible is the use of ultrasound pictures or sonograms. It is dangerous to expose a mother and fetus to X rays, and so ultrasonic waves are used instead to project a picture of internal structures. This assists in the positioning of the needle for amniocentesis and may also be used for finding certain birth defects, determining the position of a fetus, or checking to see if more than one fetus is present.

Fetal Surgery Ultrasound pictures are also crucial in one of the newest technological advances, fetal surgery. At a few major medical centers techniques are being used to perform actual surgical procedures on a fetus while it is still in the uterus. This has been most successful with urinary tract problems that can be diagnosed during pregnancy. During 1990 there were several successful surgeries on fetuses that had actually been removed from the uterus and then replaced following surgery. They were then born normally. This technique has been used to repair diaphragmatic hernia. In London, the first successful fetal heart surgery has been carried out. Fetal surgery represents one of the frontiers of reproductive and fetal technology that will see dramatic strides during the 1990s.

INFERTILITY AND SEXUALITY

Not all couples who want to have children are able to conceive. If pregnancy has not occurred after a period of a year or more of intercourse without contraception, there may be an infertility problem. It is believed to be a concern for up to 15 percent of couples. Great strides are being made in finding the causes of infertility in men and women and in correcting them. Studies have suggested, however, that even without treatment, many (up to 65 percent) presumably infertile couples eventually do become pregnant (Collins et al., 1983).

In women, there may be diseases, hormonal disturbances, or nutritional factors that lead to infrequent, or lack of, ovulation. Chronic pelvic infections can cause blockages in the fallopian tubes. There are various medications that can be used to stimulate ovulation, although they also increase the chances of multiple births. Surgical procedures can be used to remove blockages in fallopian tubes, although they are successful only in half the cases or less.

Male infertility usually is caused by a low sperm count, which can be less than 40 million sperm per cubic centimeter of semen, or by sluggish motility of the sperm. While low sperm counts do not make conception impossible, they do reduce the chances of it occurring. There are several infections and injuries of the testes that may damage the sperm-producing tubules and lead to this problem. Certain drugs, alcohol, and tobacco have also been implicated. While some medical and surgical treatments have been tried with male infertility, the results have been poor. One recommended method is to avoid ejaculation for 48 hours prior to intercourse in an attempt to raise the number of sperm in the ejaculate. It is also typically suggested that men with low sperm counts avoid lengthy submersion in very warm water, which may temporarily interfere with sperm production. Sperm are produced at a temperature slightly below internal body temperature, due to the external location of the testes.

Some infertile men have sperm that lack the viability to fertilize an ovum. A test has been developed to pinpoint this difficulty. It involves mixing the sperm with a hamster's egg, the only nonhuman ovum that can be fertilized by human sperm. If the sperm are able to penetrate the hamster egg, physicians know that they must search elsewhere for the infertility problem. There are a number of techniques under development to help with male infertility. One is injection of a sperm directly into an ovum, a method that has worked in animal tests. Several chemicals are also being tested that seem to increase motility of sperm. For men who are paralyzed below the waist and cannot ejaculate, electronic devices may be used to stimulate ejaculation of semen (Garner, 1987). Another experimental technique now in the early stages of testing is partial zona dissection (PZD). The ova are extracted from the woman, and then a microscopic incision is made in the zona pellucida that surrounds each one. This makes it easier for a sperm to penetrate the zona and fertilize the egg. By early 1990, several couples had achieved pregnancies using PZD.

chorionic villi sampling (CVS): a technique for diagnosing medical problems in the fetus as early as the 8th week of pregnancy; a sample of the chorionic membrane is removed through the cervix and studied.

sonograms: ultrasonic rays used to project a picture of internal structures such as the fetus; often used in conjunction with amniocentesis or fetal surgery.

fetal surgery: a surgical procedure performed on the fetus while it is still in the uterus.

infertility: the inability to produce offspring.

partial zona dissection (PZD): a technique used to increase the chances of fertilization by making a microscopic incision in the zona pellucida of an ovum. This creates a passageway through which sperm may enter the egg more easily.

Case Study

LORI AND JOHN: DEALING WITH INFERTILITY

After 5 years of trying to get pregnant, Lori was discouraged and frustrated. She and her husband John had waited 3 years after marrying to have children, since they wanted adequate time to adjust to married life themselves. They had planned to have a baby by the end of the next year, and Lori had made career adjustments accordingly. She would stay home with her child for at least 2 years.

As months had gone by without pregnancy, and then years, their disappointment mounted. As Lori now looks back on those times, she recalls the many reactions they both had to the situation.

"Every month when I got my period it was another defeat, and each time it got harder to face. Without fully realizing it, the tension was building between us. I got all the supplies to take my temperature and chart my cervical mucus, so we could time intercourse just right to be close to ovulation. Our whole sex life became built around trying to get pregnant. It seemed more like we had a task to complete, a goal to reach, rather than an opportunity to share intimacy and pleasure. Christmas and Halloween and Mother's Day always felt empty and depressing because we had planned to share them with children.

"John wasn't much at talking about the situation. He just had the attitude that we would try

again. Sometimes I felt as though he didn't care as much as I did, and then I would start feeling resentful. He didn't want to consider adoption either. First I would blame him for our not getting pregnant, and then I would think it must all be my fault. I didn't ever go to a doctor about it, partly I think because I was afraid of what I might find out.

"A new gynecologist started a practice in our town and advertised that he treated fertility concerns. After having agonized over this for 5 years, I decided it was time to get some professional help."

Lori and John both underwent a series of tests to determine if there were specific causes of the infertility. It was discovered that she might have some blockage in her fallopian tubes, and that John had a somewhat low sperm count, possibly due to a condition of varicose veins in his testicles. On her physician's recommendation, Lori underwent a procedure in which air was forced into her tubes in an attempt to unblock them. Six months later she became pregnant but faced further disappointment when the pregnancy ended in a miscarriage. Within another 6 months, she was pregnant again and eventually gave birth to a baby girl. The couple has since had a second child.

Infertility causes a great many pressures for a couple hoping to have a child. They feel a sense of deprivation that can lead to a range of difficult emotions, and then the emotions become difficult to face. Guilt, anger, loneliness, and frustration may create new tensions for the relationship. Some people begin to feel guilt over experiencing pleasure when they are in such turmoil, thus upsetting their lives even further. Professional counseling may be needed to prevent a sense of defeat from setting in (Donnis, 1984) and to help deal with the sense of loss an infertile couple is experiencing. The loss of self-esteem and fantasies of parenthood and the perceived loss of status in the eyes of others involve a very real process of grieving to be confronted. However, when a couple accepts the grieving process and works on it, they may find a rich opportunity for growth in their relationship (Mahlstedt, 1987).

Difficulties with infertility may also create sexual problems for couples. Since bearing children is viewed as a "validation" of sex and marriage by some in our society, couples who remain childless may begin to feel a sense of failure (Golden, 1983). This in turn can lead to disillusionment with sex and to particular sexual dysfunctions (see chapter 15, "Sexual Dysfunctions and Their Treatment").

Pregnancy and Birthing

Prompt diagnosis of pregnancy is crucial for a woman who anticipates giving birth to a healthy child. It is important to seek prenatal care as early as possible in a pregnancy to ensure the best chances of having an uncomplicated pregnancy and normal fetal development. Choosing a clinician with whom the woman can feel comfortable is always helpful. In addition, nurse-midwives are in private practice in some areas who can also provide care during pregnancy and the birthing process, with physician backup for complicated cases. At least 250,000 babies are born with birth defects each year in the United States. The cause for the majority of these defects is not known. However, there is growing evidence that toxins and radiation in the environment may damage sperm cells, leading to possible damage to the developing fetus (Blakeslee, 1991). Women who become pregnant in their late thirties or forties may face some special risk factors that should be investigated and explained with care (Mansfield, 1986). However, it should be noted that women who become pregnant at age 35 or over for the first time seem to adjust quite well in general. One study showed that they experienced less anxiety, depression, and other adverse symptoms than did their younger counterparts (Robinson et al., 1987).

Both women and men can have a wide range of reactions to pregnancy. There often are periods of elation and excitement alternating with feelings of apprehension and concern. It is a stressful time for everyone, with many unknowns. Fathers-to-be often have difficulty sorting out their reactions to pregnancy and feel some shifting in the relationship to the woman. Mothers-to-be may feel somewhat trapped in the "pregnant woman" role and resent that their former individual sense of identity seems to slip away at times. Both parents wonder what it will be like to have a new child in the family and worry about any potential problems with the pregnancy, birth, or the baby. They may vacillate between being irritable with each other and feeling the special closeness of sharing the pregnancy.

THE BIOLOGY OF PREGNANCY

There are many initial signs of pregnancy, although all of them may be caused by other factors. One of the first symptoms is usually the missing of a menstrual period; however, this can have a variety of other causes—including illness, emotional upsets, changes in living conditions. Also, about 20 percent of women continue having some menstrual flow even during the early stages of pregnancy. Other typical early signs of pregnancy are enlargement and tenderness of the breasts, increased frequency of urination, fatigue, and the experiencing of nausea and vomiting, especially upon waking in the morning. If most or all these symptoms are present, pregnancy should be at least suspected. There are other signs for which a clinician can look, such as softening of the lower uterine segment, color changes in the cervical tissues, and enlargement of the uterus.

Pregnancy Tests   Most laboratory tests for pregnancy involve analysis of the woman's urine or blood to detect the presence of the hormone human chorionic gonadotropin (HCG), produced by the fertilized egg and the placenta. There are even home versions of these tests that may be purchased in drugstores. Directions should be read and followed very carefully. Research indicates that the accuracy of home test prediction ranges from 62 percent to 84 percent, indicating that a substantial number of women may be misled by their results (Hatcher et al., 1990). Therefore, even if a home test is positive, most clinics or physicians will still do a repeat test to confirm the pregnancy. According to Planned Parenthood, laboratory diagnostic procedures are considered to be 95 to 98 percent accurate 2 weeks after a missed period. There is also a laboratory blood test that can be almost 100 percent accurate within 7 days after conception.

Pregnant women are usually given advice on diet, proper rest, clothing, and moderation of activities. Good nutrition is essential to healthy fetal development, and research is indicating that smoking, alcohol, and drugs play a role in creating birth defects and endangering the fetus's life.

Alcohol, Drugs, and Smoking   Heavy alcohol consumption can lead to fetal alcohol syndrome (FAS), characterized by abnormal fetal growth, neurological damage, and facial distortion. The Centers for Disease Control now indicate that FAS is the leading cause of birth defects in the United States. It can also cause miscarriage, death of the fetus, and premature birth. In infants, FAS can be manifested as brain damage, heart problems, and behavioral difficulties such as hyperactivity. Pregnant women are generally advised to avoid drinking alcohol because of these risks (Hingson et al., 1982). Smoking has been associated with complications in pregnancy, lower birth weights in babies, lowered intellectual abilities, and later behavior disorders in children.

Use of other drugs—whether prescription, over-the-counter, or illegal—is also ill-advised during pregnancy. Mothers who are addicted to drugs such as heroin, amphetamines, or barbiturates give birth to

human chorionic gonadotropin (HCG): a hormone detectable in the urine of a pregnant woman.
fetal alcohol syndrome (FAS): a condition in a fetus characterized by abnormal growth, neurological damage, and facial distortion caused by the mother's heavy alcohol consumption.

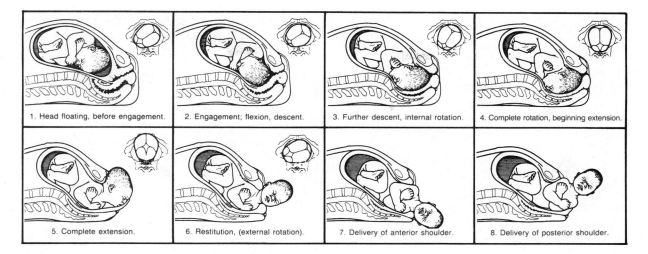

1. Head floating, before engagement.
2. Engagement; flexion, descent.
3. Further descent, internal rotation.
4. Complete rotation, beginning extension.
5. Complete extension.
6. Restitution, (external rotation).
7. Delivery of anterior shoulder.
8. Delivery of posterior shoulder.

FIGURE 4.8 Major Stages in the Birth Process

The fetus is shown in the uterus as labor contractions begin and the fetus progresses through the stages of birth.

babies who are already addicted and actually experience dangerous withdrawal symptoms. Use of marijuana may well affect fetal development. One study has demonstrated that heavy, frequent marijuana use can cause defects similar to those in fetal alcohol syndrome (Hingson et al., 1982).

Sex During Pregnancy Unless there are specific problems, there are few limitations placed on the woman during pregnancy. Many clinicians neglect to discuss sexual activity with their patients, however, and many myths have evolved concerning sex during pregnancy. Research shows that unless there is a medical problem there is no particular reason to prohibit sexual intercourse at any time during pregnancy, up until the birth process has begun. In the final months of pregnancy, the woman's abdomen is often distended enough so that the couple's usual intercourse positions may have to be modified. If coitus is uncomfortable or impossible for either partner, other forms of sexual activity may be engaged in. When the baby has been born, there seems to be no medical reason to prohibit intercourse after vaginal bleeding has stopped and any tears in the vaginal opening have healed.

THE BIRTH PROCESS

The birth process (see Fig. 4.8) is complex, and its controlling mechanisms are not fully understood. The hormone *oxytocin,* manufactured by the pituitary gland, is believed to play some part in the process. About a month before birth, the fetus shifts to a lower position in the abdomen. By this time it is normally in

its head-downward position. The most common signal that the birth process is beginning is the initiation of uterine contractions experienced as labor. The mucous plug that blocked the opening of the cervix is usually expelled just before birth begins and is sometimes seen as a small amount of bloody discharge. At some point in the process the amniotic sac ruptures, and its fluid pours or dribbles out of the vagina. The labor contractions are relatively mild at first, occurring at intervals of 15 to 20 minutes. They gradually increase in strength and frequency as the fetus moves downward in the uterus and the cervix is dilated to a diameter of about 10 centimeters. This first stage of labor takes several hours.

The second stage lasts an hour or two and involves the movement of the fetus through the vagina, now called the birth canal. The mother can help with this process by pushing with her abdominal muscles. Eventually the fetus's head appears at the vaginal opening, followed by one shoulder, then the other shoulder, and the rest of the body. The clinician assisting with the birth generally does not pull on the baby, but gently guides it out of the birth canal. If there is a chance of the fetus tearing the vaginal opening, a cut is made in some of the tissue, a procedure called an episiotomy. The incision is later sutured and usually

labor: uterine contractions in a pregnant woman; an indication that the birth process is beginning.
birth canal: term applied to the vagina during the birth process.
episiotomy (ee-piz-ee-OTT-a-mee): a surgical incision in the vaginal opening made by the clinician or obstetrician if it appears that the baby will tear the opening in the process of being born.

97

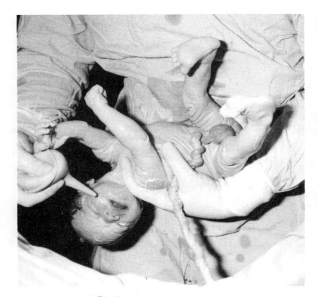

FIGURE 4.9 Birth

The delivery of the baby requires the efforts of both the mother and a clinician, nurse midwife, or physician. The newborn is held above the mother's body and fluids are suctioned from the mouth and nose to aid in breathing. The umbilical cord is then clamped and cut about 1¼ inches from the baby's body.

heals without problems. However, it sometimes becomes infected and may take up to 4 weeks to heal completely. About 16 percent of women experience pain or discomfort in the episiotomy scar even a year after giving birth (Hetherington, 1988).

When serious problems affect the birth process or the fetus seems too large for the woman's pelvis, a surgical procedure can be performed in which the child is removed through an incision in the abdominal wall and uterus. This is called a cesarian section, and the method has been used increasingly in recent years to lower the risks of complications for the mother and baby. This increase has been the subject of controversy, and some authorities believe that a substantial proportion of cesarian births are unnecessary. While it was almost standard practice through the late 1980s to perform cesarian sections on women who had given birth to an earlier child in this manner, the American College of Obstetricians and Gynecologists have now indicated that vaginal birth following a cesarian should be the procedure of choice unless some medical condition mitigates against it.

Within about an hour after the baby has been born, the third stage of the birth process occurs. The placenta, now a disc of tissue about 8 inches in diameter and 2 inches thick, pulls away from the uterine wall. The uterus expels the placenta, along with the remaining section of umbilical cord and the

fetal membranes, through the birth canal. The expelled tissues are collectively called the afterbirth.

BIRTHING ALTERNATIVES

In many cultures giving birth to a baby is viewed as a natural phenomenon not requiring fanfare or special attention. Over the past century, in more developed countries, medical intervention became increasingly a part of the birthing process. It became viewed in a perspective similar to illness, with an emphasis on using drugs and anesthetics to reduce pain and a prolonged period of complete bed rest as "convalescence." Delivery of a baby became a mysterious process, best left to doctors and nurses in a hospital setting.

Natural Childbirth   In 1932 a British physician named Grantly Dick-Read published a book called *Childbirth Without Fear.* He believed that the fear of the birthing process generated by medical interventions only created more tension and pain. He educated women thoroughly about labor and delivery and developed relaxation techniques to reduce their tension, calling his method natural childbirth. He started a trend toward returning control of the birth process to women and their partners that continues today (Feldman, 1978).

The Lamaze Method   In the 1950s a similar approach was introduced by a French obstetrician, Fernand Lamaze. The Lamaze method of "prepared" childbirth is very popular today and makes use of the baby's father or some other willing participant as a coach for the woman. In prenatal classes the couple is taught how to use different relaxation and breathing techniques through increasing levels of intensity during labor. While the Lamaze approach does not prohibit the use of pain-killing medications during labor, it usually reduces the need for them. The woman is able to remain an alert and active participant in giving birth to her baby, a process that her body is well equipped to accomplish.

cesarian section: a surgical method of childbirth in which delivery occurs through an incision in the abdominal wall and uterus.
afterbirth: the tissues expelled after childbirth, including the placenta, the remains of the umbilical cord, and fetal membranes.
natural childbirth: a birthing process that encourages the mother to take control, thus minimizing medical intervention.
Lamaze method (la-MAHZ): a birthing process based on relaxation techniques practiced by the expectant mother; her partner coaches her throughout the birth.

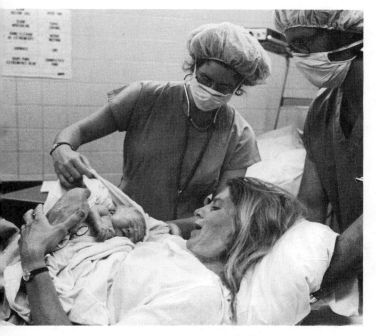

FIGURE 4.10 Cooperative Delivery

In some uncomplicated births the father is not only present at the birth of his child, but also may help in the process by coaching the mother in relaxing and breathing techniques. Here, the nurse-midwife looks on as a mother and father cuddle a 1-minute-old baby.

Home Birth Although most professionals still recommend hospital delivery, so that appropriate care can be available in case of complications, some couples choose to have a baby born at home. Trained and licensed midwives or certified nurse-midwives may assist, and it is usually recommended that a cooperative physician at least be on call in case of emergency.

Birthing Rooms Responding to the new trend to have birthing be a cooperative process, many hospitals have established birthing rooms. These are usually decorated and furnished in nonhospital fashion, and sometimes other children or family members are allowed to be present for the birth. When a birthing room is used, the woman remains in the same room and bed for labor and delivery, rather than being taken to a special delivery room for the actual delivery.

After delivery a baby is checked for any signs of distress, measured, and kept very warm. French physician Frederick Leboyer (1975) has advocated methods for reducing the shock of coming into a bright, noisy delivery area for a baby. He recommends that birth take place in a quiet, dimly lit, warm setting, and that time be taken for the baby to lie on the mother's abdomen before the umbilical cord is cut. He also suggests giving a newborn baby a gentle, warm bath.

It is widely believed that newborn babies are quite alert for the first hour or two immediately following birth and that time should be given for the parents to bond with their new infants. This early bonding may well provide more security and comfort for the baby's adjustment and growth processes, although research evidence to confirm this contention is presently incomplete.

PROBLEMS DURING PREGNANCY

All the possible problems of pregnancy will not be explored in detail here, but a few common ones will be at least mentioned.

Pregnancy-Induced Hypertension One disorder that occurs in women in less than 10 percent of pregnancies is pregnancy-induced hypertension, formerly called toxemia or eclampsia. This begins with a rise in blood pressure, swelling in the ankles and other parts of the body, and protein appearing in the urine. Usually this can be treated by bed rest, diet, and medication, but it sometimes progresses to serious or life-threatening conditions for the mother such as blindness, convulsions, or coma.

Premature Birth Any birth that takes place prior to the 36th week of pregnancy is considered a premature birth. The more premature a baby is born, the lower its chances of survival. Respiratory problems and their complications are particularly common among "preemies." Often, care in an isolette (formerly called an incubator) is necessary for a time. While the cause of a premature birth is not always known, a mother's illness or smoking habits can play a role. Prematurity is particularly common among teenage mothers, among women who smoke during their pregnancies, and in those who have experienced high stress, inadequate nutrition, or lack of proper medical care.

midwives: medical professionals, both women and men, trained to assist with the birthing process.
birthing rooms: special areas in the hospital, decorated and furnished in a nonhospital way, set aside for giving birth; the woman remains here to give birth rather than being taken to a separate delivery room.
bond: the emotional link between parent and child created by cuddling, cooing, physical and eye contact early in the newborn's life.
pregnancy-induced hypertension: a disorder that can occur in the latter half of pregnancy, marked by a swelling in the ankles and other parts of the body, high blood pressure, and protein in the urine; can progress to coma and death if not treated.
premature birth: a birth that takes place prior to the 36th week of pregnancy.

Rh Incompatibility A major risk for pregnancies in former times was Rh incompatibility. The Rh factor is a blood protein; blood may be either Rh positive if it contains this factor or Rh negative if it does not. A baby has its own blood type as the result of a genetic combination from its mother and father, and so it often will not have the same blood type as the mother. If a mother has Rh negative blood and her baby is Rh positive, the mother's body will begin producing antibodies that destroy red blood cells in the fetus, especially in second and subsequent pregnancies. Administering a medication called Rho GAM to the mother can now prevent the formation of these antibodies and has effectively eliminated many of the risks of Rh incompatibility. However, the potential for the problem must be noted in prenatal blood tests, another reason why good prenatal care is so crucial to a pregnant woman and her child-to-be. ■

Rh incompatibility: condition in which a blood protein of the infant is not the same as the mother's; antibodies formed in the mother can destroy red blood cells in the fetus.

Rho GAM: medication administered to a mother to prevent formation of antibodies when the baby is Rh positive and its mother Rh negative.

CHAPTER SUMMARY

1. When a sperm fertilizes an ovum within the fallopian tube, 23 chromosomes from both the sperm and the egg combine to form a total of 46. The DNA in these chromosomes establishes the genetic instructions for developing the new organism.

2. Fraternal twins result from the fertilization of two separate ova by two sperm. Identical twins are formed when a single fertilized egg divides into two cells that separate and develop into the embryos. Since they have exactly the same chromosomes, they are identical in appearance.

3. The fertilized egg divides into increasing numbers of cells eventually forming a spherical blastocyst. A few days after fertilization, the blastocyst implants itself in the inner lining (endometrium) of the uterus, where embryonic and fetal development will continue.

4. The embryo forms several extraembryonic membranes for its protection and nourishment. The amnion is a fluid-filled sac to keep the embryo moist and cushioned. The yolk sac and allantois become partly incorporated into the umbilical cord that connects the fetus with the placenta. It is in the placenta that blood systems of the fetus and the mother come close enough to permit exchange (by diffusion) of nutrients and wastes.

5. Advances in reproductive technology are revolutionizing the processes of conception and gestation. In cases where one man has a low or nonexistent sperm count, artificial insemination permits sperm from another man to be used for fertilization. Gametes (sperm and eggs) and embryos may now be frozen and kept for long periods for later use in various reproductive technologies. In vitro fertilization (IVF) allows for fertilization outside a woman's body with the developing embryo then implanted into the uterus afterward.

6. While emerging technologies may increase the accuracy of choosing the sex of a fetus ahead of time, this possibility has raised many ethical concerns.

7. Cloning has the potential for bypassing sexual reproduction altogether, making a copy of one individual by using the genes of one of that person's cells. While this is not yet possible for humans, the prospect of human cloning also raises ethical, social, and legal complications.

8. Surrogate motherhood is a controversial approach in which one woman agrees for a fee to be impregnated by the sperm of a man whose partner cannot become pregnant. The surrogate carries and gives birth to the baby, then gives it to the couple. Newer methods of IVF now permit transfer of an embryo produced from the egg and sperm of one couple into the uterus of the paid surrogate.

9. There are several methods used to diagnose potential medical problems in a fetus. Amniocentesis withdraws fetal cells from the amniotic sac so that possible chromosome abnormalities may be discovered. Chorionic villi sampling (CVS) also examines chromosomes, but may be used as early as the 8th week in the pregnancy. Ultrasound pictures, or sonograms, are an alternative to X rays for examining the features of the developing fetus. Fetal surgery is a developing technology that can be used to treat some medical difficulties.

10. Infertility can have many causes and often creates turmoil for couples who are anxious to have children.

11. Pregnancy may be signaled by many symptoms, including cessation of menstruation. Pregnancy tests used today detect a hormone produced by the embryo and placenta called human chorionic gonadotropin (HCG).

PLATE 1   Sperm Penetrating Egg

A sperm, with its oval head and long tail, approaches the egg, or ovum. Having been capacitated during its journey through the female reproductive tract, the sperm will secrete an enzyme that will help it penetrate the outer membrane of the ovum.

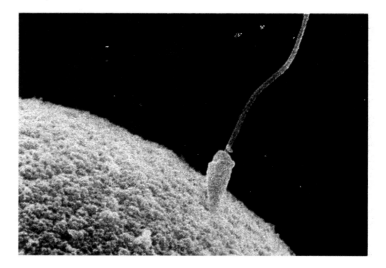

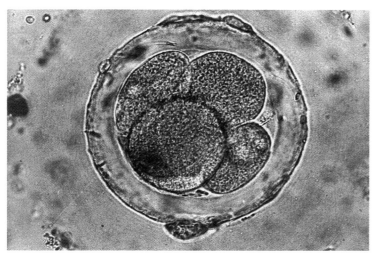

PLATE 2   Cell Division

Four new cells of the forming embryo. Following fertilization of the ovum by the sperm, their chromosomes join and the genetic plan to produce an embryo is set into motion. The zygote, or fertilized ovum, begins to undergo cell division, first producing 2 cells, then 4, and so on. Each new cell receives a complete set of 46 human chromosomes, programmed to produce an entirely new human being.

PLATE 3   Spine of Embryo at 6 Weeks

At 6 weeks of development, the embryo floats in the fluid of its amnion. In this rear view of the embryo, its developing spinal cord may be clearly seen, flanked by its two red vertebral arteries. The yolk sac, seen at the lower left of the photograph, will eventually become incorporated into the umbilical cord.

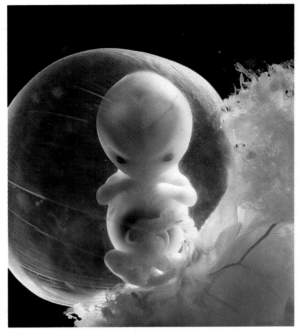

PLATE 4 Embryo at 7 Weeks

At 7 weeks, the embryo is nearly an inch long, and both its internal and external organs are rapidly forming. Facial features are beginning to take shape, and the skeleton is developing internally. The fontanel, or soft area in the center of the developing skull, is clearly visible in this picture.

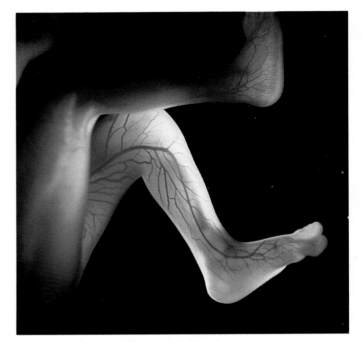

PLATE 5 Legs of Fetus at 4 Months

The blood vessels and developing bones are visible in the legs of this 4-month (6.4-inch) fetus. The skeleton is first formed from cartilage. Bone tissue then begins to grow out from the middle of the cartilage toward both ends. Bone development is not fully completed until an individual reaches the age of about 25 years.

PLATE 6 Fetus Sucking Thumb at 4½ Months

At 4½ months, the fetus has formed its human features and proportions. Survival reflexes, such as the sucking reflex, are already able to function. This photograph provides a startling demonstration of the potential for thumb-sucking in a fetus that is only halfway to being full-term.

PLATE 7 Pregnancy

Throughout the processes of pregnancy and birth, a woman's body goes through many internal and external changes. Maintaining an optimal level of health during this time is crucial for the well-being of both woman and child.

12. It is crucial that women take care of themselves during pregnancy, with proper rest and diet, and avoidance of smoking, alcohol, and drugs.

13. The birth process begins with contractions of the uterus, or labor. Gradually the baby is moved through the birth canal and is born. The placenta, umbilical cord, and fetal membranes follow as the afterbirth.

14. There are now many approaches to birthing, including those that emphasize full awareness and participation on the mother's part, such as the Lamaze method. Leboyer has advocated a quiet, warm, and comfortable area for the baby's delivery.

15. Pregnancy-induced hypertension is a complication of pregnancy that occurs occasionally. It involves a rise in the mother's blood pressure and a buildup of fluids in her body, sometimes with life-threatening consequences.

16. Prenatal blood tests are crucial, so any dangers of Rh incompatibility may be eliminated with medical treatment.

ANNOTATED READINGS

Andrews, L. B. (1984). *New conceptions: A consumer's guide to the newest fertility treatments.* New York: Ballantine Books. An excellent overview of the causes of infertility and the newer techniques that can increase the chances of getting pregnant.

Baruch, E. H., D'Adamo, A. F., & Seager, J. (1989). *Embryos, ethics, and women's rights: Exploring the new reproductive technologies.* Binghamton, NY: Haworth Press. This collection examines the controversial aspects of reproductive technologies from both personal and clinical perspectives. It covers legal, ethical, religious, social, psychological, and political issues.

Bing, E., & Coleman, L. (1982). *Making love during pregnancy.* New York: Bantam Books. This is a worrisome issue for many couples, even if they have been reassured by medical personnel. The book deals with all of the questions about sex that can trouble a couple during the months of a pregnancy.

Field, M. (1990). *Surrogate motherhood.* Cambridge, MA: Harvard University Press. A scholarly investigation of the many ethical, social, and political implications of surrogate motherhood in a timely and readable volume.

Herzfeld, J. (1985). *Sense and sensibility in childbirth.* New York: W. W. Norton. Examines childbirth methods and offers help in making decisions regarding the birthing process.

Kime, R. (1992). *Wellness: Pregnancy, childbirth, & parenting.* Guilford, CT: The Dushkin Publishing Group. The purpose of this volume is to help readers become informed health consumers on the subjects of pregnancy, childbirth, and parenting; and to enable readers to think critically about the health-related aspects of these topics.

Lesko, W., & Lesko, M. (1984). *The maternity sourcebook: 230 basic decisions for pregnancy, birth, and baby care.* New York: Warner Books. A comprehensive guide for expectant and new parents. The book surveys different approaches to giving birth, and helps parents to be more fully informed in making the many choices that will face them.

Mattis, M. (1986). *Sex and the single parent: How you can have happy and healthy kids—and an active social life.* New York: Henry Holt. As its title suggests, this book deals with the concerns of increasing numbers of single parents.

Rothman, B. K. (1990). *Recreating motherhood: Ideology and technology in a patriarchal society.* New York: W. W. Norton. Takes a critical and careful look at the developing issues surrounding the new reproductive technologies.

CHAPTER FIVE

HISTORICAL PERSPECTIVES
  Choosing to Become a Parent
  Birth Control Today

DECIDING ABOUT CONTRACEPTIVES
  Ethical and Religious Influences
  Health Considerations
  Psychological and Social Factors
  Preparing the Way for Effective Contraception
  Choosing the "Right" Contraceptive

METHODS OF BIRTH CONTROL
  Understanding Contraceptive Effectiveness
  Sharing the Responsibility for Birth Control
  Abstinence, Sex Without Intercourse, and Withdrawal
  Oral Contraceptives: The Pill
  Norplant Implants and Progestin Injections
  Spermicides, Sponges, and Suppositories
  Barrier Methods

  Intrauterine Devices (IUDs)
  Natural Family Planning/Fertility Awareness
  Voluntary Sterilization
  New Contraceptives for Males?
  Postcoital Contraception

SELF-EVALUATION: CONTRACEPTIVE COMFORT AND CONFIDENCE SCALE

UNINTENDED PREGNANCY: THE OPTIONS
  Keeping the Baby
  Adoption
  Termination of Pregnancy
  Methods of Abortion
  Use of Fetal Tissue
  Safety of Abortion for the Woman
  Psychological Considerations

CHAPTER SUMMARY

I got pregnant when I was fifteen. It's not like I didn't know about birth control or couldn't get it. I just didn't think it could happen to me—especially the first time. The boy was sixteen, but he was even more ignorant and immature than I was. To this day he doesn't know I got pregnant and had an abortion. Believe me, I grew up fast that year—too fast.

—From a student's essay

BIRTH CONTROL AND UNINTENDED PREGNANCY

Bringing children into the world carries important responsibilities—not only to the child, but to a dangerously overpopulated world. Children have become less of a status symbol than in former times and less of a necessity in terms of helping the family maintain a home, farm, or business. Many young couples are thinking more carefully about making a decision to have children, and many are particularly concerned about limiting the size of their families. Still, society expects married people to have children. There are family and social pressures to procreate, and couples who choose childlessness must often face the critical judgment of others (Linder, 1987). Many couples now share responsibility for generating income, and give much energy to their careers. Research continues to confirm that unwanted children experience more developmental difficulties and psychological problems than wanted youngsters (Holden, 1989). Having children should indeed be a choice, and one that is not made lightly.

After World War II, the birth rate in the United States went up dramatically. From 1945 to 1947, annual births jumped more than 30 percent. This period of increased birth rates reached its peak during the 1950s, when women of child-bearing age were having an average of 3.7 children. This has been called the "baby boom." The birth rate then tapered off to a low point in the mid-1970s, when women were averaging about 2 children. The National Center for Health Statistics reported that during the late 1980s and early 1990s there was a gradual increase in the birth rate again, sometimes averaging close to 5 percent during a half year. Demographers have been hard pressed to explain why the birth rate seems to be on the upswing, but the figures are dramatically higher than they have been for some time.

Historical Perspectives

Throughout history people have found that the practicalities of life sometimes necessitate the limiting of family size. Folk methods of contraception, often spiced with liberal doses of superstition, were developed. Insertion of substances into the vagina (such as crocodile dung) was frequently used in some ancient cultures, and may have offered the first "barrier" method of contraception. By the seventeenth century in Europe, condoms made from internal sheep membranes had been developed to contain the ejaculate during intercourse. However, condoms were originally designed to protect against syphilis, not pregnancy.

Historically, birth control was often discouraged by sociocultural values and religious teaching. Sexual intercourse was viewed as a procreative act, and so to use contraception was an indication that sex was being used for the gratification of nonprocreative desires. In many periods of history pleasures of the flesh were considered at the least improper and at the most evil.

As the mores of Victorian England filtered through to the United States in the 1860s, a great deal of attention was focused on sexual vices. A New York grocery clerk by the name of Anthony Comstock was incensed by the distribution of information about birth control methods and set out to suppress it. He became secretary of the New York Society for the Suppression of Vice and lobbied in Washington to have the federal mail act prohibit the mailing of contraceptive information, placing it in the same category as obscene materials. In the 1870s these federal regulations became known as the Comstock Laws. This represented governmental sanction of the idea that abstinence was the only permissible form of birth control.

The birth control movement in the United States was spurred on by an activist named Margaret Sanger, who was a nurse and worked in a section of Brooklyn where poor people lived. She saw women who were almost constantly pregnant, often resulting in serious consequences to their health, and women who had so many children they couldn't effectively raise them. Many of these women resorted to self-induced abortions or abortions performed in unsanitary conditions by illegal abortionists, frequently resulting in the women's deaths. Sanger became determined to remedy this problem and in 1914 founded the National Birth Control League. In her protests she deliberately violated the Comstock Laws and fought against attitudes that discouraged advertising about use of contraceptive devices, eventually opening her own birth control clinic in Brooklyn. She was arrested numerous times. After a number of court battles, physicians were finally given the right to give contraceptive information to women. In time contraception became increasingly socially acceptable, and new methods were developed. However, it was not until 1966 that the last major law concerning the sale of contraceptives was repealed.

CHOOSING TO BECOME A PARENT

Bringing a child into the world and caring for it through its years of growing up represent major life responsibilities. Experts agree that it is best for any couple to choose to become pregnant through a pro-

FIGURE 5.1 Margaret Sanger

Sanger (1883–1966) was instrumental in causing changes in the availability of birth control information and contraceptive devices in the United States. She believed every woman has the right to control her own fertility and was the first president of the International Planned Parenthood Federation.

cess of discussion and mutual agreement, carefully weighing all of the new obligations that parenthood will entail. There are many pressures and expectations in our culture to have children, especially after a man and woman have married and "settled down." Yet, these are also complicated times in which to become parents. Raising a child is not only filled with social requirements, it is very expensive. As of 1990 it was estimated that the average cost of raising a child to the age of 18 in the midwestern United States, including housing, clothes, food, medical care, public education, and transportation, was about $100,000 (U.S. Department of Education, 1991).

There are many *wrong* reasons to become a parent. For example, to have kids because your parents want grandchildren, or because you want a sibling for a first child, do not represent good reasons in themselves. Neither is it appropriate to have a child in order to save or refresh a shaky relationship. Sometimes a person is anxious to have a baby in order to have something to love or possess, but this is obviously reflective of other issues in the person's life that need work and resolution; it is not fair to ask a new baby to fill all of those emotional gaps.

Comstock Laws: enacted in the 1870s, this federal legislation prohibited the mailing of information about contraception.
National Birth Control League: an organization founded in 1914 by Margaret Sanger to promote use of contraceptives.

The choice to become a parent should be made with careful consideration given to all of the positive *and* negative aspects of what parenthood will be all about. Every stage of child development places demands on parents and requires exercising appropriate parenting skills. None of us is born knowing those skills, and they take time to develop. While it may be a thrill to anticipate the arrival of a baby, any parent can testify that the realities are at times exhausting, nerve-wracking, and confusing. To be a parent requires a level of maturity and commitment to long-term efforts. Having children also changes the relationship between the two parents, creating new pressures and complications. Most parents have found that their sexual lives change markedly with pregnancy and having a child in their lives. It takes real work and communication to maintain a happy and healthy relationship with the new pressures of parenthood (Mayer, 1990).

Of course, being a parent carries great satisfactions and rewards as well. It not only can help individuals to become more mature and responsible, but it may strengthen the bonds between the child's parents. That is especially true of couples who make their decision to have children carefully and with full knowledge of what implications parenthood will have for them. Choosing if and when to have a child will mean that contraception must be part of planning for heterosexual intercourse. Any couple that shares intercourse must also give some thought and planning to the possibility that birth control might fail. The information in this chapter is basic to thinking and deciding about these issues.

BIRTH CONTROL TODAY

Until quite recently pregnancy was considered one of the inevitable risks of sexual intercourse, or coitus (see chapter 10, "Solitary Sex and Shared Sex"). As such, it was one of the major arguments used by those who wished to discourage premarital coitus. Although coitus always carries some degree of pregnancy risk, modern methods of birth control have minimized this risk to the point where many couples have pursued their sexual activities with less concern for unintended pregnancy.

The modern contraceptive scene is deceptive, however. Of the 31.8 million women in the United States at risk of unintended pregnancy, 13 percent are not using any form of contraception. Few pharmaceutical companies are investigating any contraceptive drugs or devices at all, and there has been a steady decline in the availability of research funds to develop new contraceptives (Schroeder & Snowe, 1989). Fear of lawsuits has persuaded some pharmaceutical companies to remove particular methods from the market.

Religious and political groups have brought pressure to limit the availability of birth control to some groups, especially teenagers (Connell, 1987). Whereas in the early 1980s opinion polls indicated that most Americans expected a major breakthrough in contraceptive technology, in the early 1990s we expect to have no more choices than we did 20 years ago, and no appreciably greater degree of safety or effectiveness in the methods available (Sweet, 1988).

In fact, the 1980s have been called a "decade of disaster" for family planning (Swirling, 1990a). Funding for family planning clinics, especially for lower-income women, has declined by over 20 percent. Administrative restrictions greatly curtailed contraceptive research. Funding of surveys to gather data about pregnancy prevention and sexual behavior has been almost nonexistent. Legislation to provide family planning services to the poor has been vetoed. Family planning services represent one area relating to sexual behavior in which political agendas have become particularly evident.

For individuals who do not wish to be parents, either intercourse should be avoided or an adequate means of birth control should be employed. Different methods of birth control are best suited for different people and situations. It is often wise to consult a gynecologist or family planning specialist to determine which method(s) will hold the most potential effectiveness for a particular couple's life-style and sexual choices. The information that follows is meant to be a brief guide to various methods of birth control. It is a summary, and for those wishing more detailed information, a number of excellent resources are listed at the end of the chapter.

Deciding About Contraceptives

Making decisions about whether or not to use a means of birth control, and which method to use, can be very complicated. However, it is not difficult to minimize the risk of an unwanted pregnancy. There are at least five or six methods of contraception that, if used consistently and properly, will mean that less than five women in one hundred will conceive over the period of a year.

A recent survey of 344 women, aged 18 to 49, suggests that two-thirds of women use at least two different methods of birth control during their reproductive years, and 36 percent use at least three methods. It is typical for the first method to be selected on the basis of its effectiveness, but second and third selections are more likely to be made on the basis of health concerns and potential effects on the body. For example, it is common for women to choose the birth

Margaret Sanger

In her autobiography Margaret Sanger told of an incident during her nursing career that convinced her of the direction her life would have to take. In July of 1912 she tended a 28-year-old woman who had nearly died from the effects of a self-induced abortion. The woman and her husband, Jake Sachs, already had three children for whom she was barely able to care on her husband's truck-driver wages. Sanger nursed Mrs. Sachs back to health, although the patient often seemed lost in thought. Finally the woman was able to deal openly with her concerns:

At the end of three weeks, as I was preparing to leave and the fragile patient [preparing] to take up her difficult life once more, she finally voiced her fears, "Another baby will finish me, I suppose?"

"It's too early to talk about that," I temporized.

But when the doctor came to make his last call, I drew him aside. "Mrs. Sachs is worried about having another baby."

"She may well be," replied the doctor, and then he stood before her and said, "Any more such capers, young woman, and there'll be no need to send for me."

"I know, doctor," she replied timidly, "but," and she hesitated as though it took all her courage to say it, "what can I do to prevent it?"

The doctor was a kindly man, and he had worked hard to save her, but such incidents had become so familiar to him that he had long since lost whatever delicacy he might once have had. He laughed good-naturedly, "You want to have your cake and eat it too, do you? Well, it can't be done."

Then picking up his hat to depart, he said, "Tell Jake to sleep on the roof."

I glanced quickly at Mrs. Sachs. Even through my sudden tears I could see stamped on her face an expression of absolute despair. We simply looked at each other, saying no word until the door had closed behind the doctor. Then she lifted her thin, blue-veined hands and clasped them beseechingly, "He can't understand. He's only a man. But you do, don't you? Please tell me the secret, and I'll never breathe it to a soul. *Please!*"

What was I to do? I could not speak the conventionally comforting phrases which would be of no comfort. . . . A little later, when she slept, I tiptoed away.

control pill at first because of its effectiveness. Later on, they are more likely to change to barrier methods, such as the condom or diaphragm, because of their lesser health risks (Gallup Survey, 1990). It seems clear that there are many different factors to be weighed and considered in making a decision about contraception. Sorting through the complexities of the decision-making process is preferable to choosing to have sex without considering the risks of pregnancy or what the consequences of such a pregnancy might be.

ETHICAL AND RELIGIOUS INFLUENCES

For many people contraception is an ethical issue. It is often still related to the question of the "purpose" of sex. Some insist that sexual intercourse is meant to be a biological function, of which the major outcome is reproduction. They believe that a sexual act should always leave open the possibility of procreation. In

recent years it has become increasingly acceptable to perceive sex as an act of shared pleasure and communication within a loving relationship, with reproduction another aspect of sex to be chosen only when the time is right.

The Roman Catholic church officially forbids the use of "artificial" means of birth control and sanctions only abstinence or the use of the natural family planning/fertility awareness approach (see p. 121). Studies make it clear that the vast majority of Roman Catholic women in the United States (88.3 percent) use some other contraceptive method (Bachrach, 1984). Many times this use is even sanctioned by a sympathetic priest. In visits to American cities in 1987, Pope John Paul II clarified that the Vatican expects Roman Catholics throughout the world—including the United States—to follow the Church's teachings.

At least one method of birth control presents ethical dilemmas to individuals who hold that a human life begins at the moment of conception. The intra-

Night after night the wistful image of Mrs. Sachs appeared before me. I made all sorts of excuses to myself for not going back. I was busy on other cases; I really did not know what to say to her or how to convince her of my own ignorance; I was helpless to avert such monstrous atrocities. Time rolled by and I did nothing.

The telephone rang one evening three months later, and Jake Sachs's agitated voice begged me to come at once; his wife was sick again and from the same cause. . . . I turned into the dingy doorway and climbed the familiar stairs once more. The children were there, young little things.

Mrs. Sachs was in a coma and died within ten minutes. I drew a sheet over her pallid face. Jake was sobbing, running his hands through his hair and pulling it out like an insane person. Over and over again he wailed, "My God! My God! My God!"

I left him pacing desperately back and forth, and for hours I myself walked and walked and walked through the hushed streets. . . . [The city's] pains and griefs crowded in upon me: women writhing in travail to bring forth little babies; the babies themselves naked and hungry, wrapped in newspapers to keep them from the cold; six-year-old children with pinched, pale, wrinkled faces, old in concentrated wretchedness, pushed into gray and fetid cellars, crouching on stone floors, their small scrawny hands scuttling through rags, making lamp shades, artificial flowers; white coffins, black coffins, coffins, coffins interminably passing in never-ending succession. The scenes piled one upon another on another. I could bear it no longer.

As I stood there the darkness faded. It was the dawn of a new day in my life also. The doubt and questioning, the experimenting and trying, were now to be put behind me. I knew I could not go back merely to keeping people alive.

I went to bed, knowing that no matter what it might cost, I was finished with palliatives and superficial cures; I was resolved to seek out the root of evil, to change the destiny of mothers whose miseries were vast as the sky.

—Margaret Sanger, *Margaret Sanger: An Autobiography,* 1938,
New York: W. W. Norton & Co.

uterine device (IUD) is believed to interfere with implantation of the blastocyst in the uterus, which occurs after fertilization of the ovum by a sperm. It is, therefore, suggested by some to be a type of abortion. However, the American College of Obstetricians and Gynecologists defines pregnancy as the implantation of a blastocyst and thus the action of the IUD would not be considered an abortion.

In making any sex-related decision, we must examine the ethical and religious values that we hold to be important in our lives. Sometimes decisions require an internal balancing act to sort out how much weight we will give to our various beliefs, opinions, emotions, practical difficulties, and inner drives. Nevertheless, contraception is never an issue that can be ignored.

HEALTH CONSIDERATIONS

Anytime various methods of birth control are considered, possible effects on one's health must be weighed.

While several methods (such as condoms or diaphragms) have minimal implications for health, others such as hormonal methods or the IUD can affect a woman's health. Examining the potential effects on health should be an integral part of the decision-making process.

Part of the difficulty here, however, is that accurate information on potential health effects can be difficult to obtain. Pharmaceutical companies anxious to market a particular method may popularize research studies that have not fully met rigorous evaluative standards. Myths develop as well that may take time to sort through. Many people, for example, still have many misconceptions and fears about the possible dangers of birth control pills. In fact, recent research tends to show that, when properly prescribed, the pill is actually quite safe for nonsmokers and may even provide some health advantages. Research on health implications of the pill and other contraceptive methods continues to become available. Prior to making a

FIGURE 5.2 Pregnancy or Birth Control?

Deciding to have a child is a complicated issue for most people. Consideration must be given to health. Pregnancy itself may have greater risks than any particular method of birth control.

decision about birth control, one should become updated on current medical knowledge available.

Any potential risks of the method of contraception must be balanced against the risks inherent in pregnancy. Being pregnant has potential dangers to a woman's health as well, and they may outweigh any risks that would be faced in using a particular method of birth control.

The key issue is making sure that the chosen contraceptive method is fully understood by the user and properly prescribed if it requires a medical professional's approval. When methods such as the pill or IUD are possibilities, a thorough medical history must be taken and a careful evaluation made of any potential health risks. Most of all, women and men should take the responsibility of becoming fully informed about all health considerations, so that they can make the most careful and safe decisions possible.

PSYCHOLOGICAL AND SOCIAL FACTORS

How people feel about contraception themselves, and how they believe their society would view their choices, are also a part of the decision-making process. We live in a culture that often finds it difficult to legitimize and accept sexual expression. Both women and men are often placed in the position of feeling that sexual activity is acceptable only if it is spontaneous and unplanned (Cassell, 1985). Therefore, to plan ahead—to choose and have available a method of contraception "just in case"—can be a difficult step to take. It may call into question their views of personal morality, and this has important implications for how they feel about themselves. Some men may feel uncomfortable with women who are decisive and assertive enough to have taken steps to obtain a birth control method. On the other hand, it is not unusual for men to see contraception as the woman's responsibility. All of these factors can generate a good deal of tension and result in the blaming of one another should an unwanted pregnancy occur.

Research on the psychological and social factors that determine contraceptive behavior continues to show that negative emotions and attitudes toward sex often lead to inadequate use of birth control. When women feel guilty about sex or have other anxieties surrounding their sexual activities, they tend to have less accurate information about contraception, to select more ineffective contraceptive methods, and tend to use them much less consistently. They are more apt to leave decisions about birth control to their male partners.

On the surface this outcome does not seem to make much sense. It would seem more reasonable to assume that women who feel guilty or fearful about sex would be even more cautious and conscientious about using birth control. However, to avoid pregnancy requires the successful completion of numerous steps. There must be an acceptance on the woman's part that she is sexually active and that she is therefore at risk of pregnancy. Then she must obtain appropriate information about birth control methods and decide which

Cost Rules Out Birth Control for Many

In about three-fourths of the world's developing countries, birth control methods are so expensive that the average family cannot afford them, according to a study made public today.

The issue of cost is important now because some nations are seeking to turn over to charities and commercial suppliers the distribution of birth control methods to poor people, now done chiefly by governments.

This "social marketing" concept holds that selling birth control devices may be a more effective way of distributing them than giving them out in government clinics, which are often crowded and widely separated.

"This study debunks the idea," said Dr. Sharon L. Camp, senior vice president of the Population Crisis Committee, a nonprofit group here that made the study public today.

The report gives the cost of various methods of contraception in 110 countries and estimates what percentage of couples can afford them.

The social marketing idea, popular among many United States foreign aid experts, suggests that only private, profit-making concerns can provide affordable contraception to the hundreds of millions of low-income couples who want it, Dr. Camp said. But the study reports that private concerns charge such high prices that they exclude many of the people they are trying to reach.

In Ethiopia, for example, a year's supply of condoms or birth control pills at a pharmacy costs 30 percent of the average annual income for an individual, $120. Free or low-cost government distribution of the methods there reaches from 3 to 30 percent of the people, depending on the type of contraception and the geographic area, the study said.

In Kenya, a relatively more prosperous African nation, a year's supply of condoms costs 7 percent of an individual's annual income, and pills cost 37 percent. Low-cost distribution there reaches from 20 to 55 percent of the population.

In Lebanon, condoms cost 20 percent of a person's income for a year, and pills cost about 14 percent. From 15 to 29 percent of the people there get inexpensive supplies from the Government.

The study concluded that if contraceptives cost more than 1 percent of a couple's annual income, they are too expensive, and that if couples had to spend more than two hours a month in travel and waiting to get contraceptives, they were not easily accessible.

In most developed countries, more than 95 percent of the people have access to contraceptives at a price that is one-tenth of 1 percent to eight-tenths of 1 percent of an individual's annual income, the study said. Among developed countries, the United States was found to have the highest cost of contraceptives, at more than 1 percent of annual income. This country also has a comparatively low access rate, with 78 percent of the people able to get easy and affordable access to abortion, 80 percent to sterilization and 90 percent to birth control pills.

Among the nations with the most remarkable rise in access are Thailand, where there is 95 percent access and the cost is nearly 1 percent of annual income; Singapore, where the supplies are free and access is 100 percent; Bangladesh, where cost is less than seven-tenths of 1 percent of a year's income and access is from 86 percent to 95 percent for various birth control methods.

—Philip J. Hilts, *New York Times,* July 2, 1991

Case Study

FELICIA AND BILL: A COUPLE DECIDES ON A BIRTH CONTROL METHOD

Felicia and Bill began sharing sexual intercourse after they had been dating for about 2 months. Concerned about pregnancy and protection from AIDS for the two of them, Bill had used condoms. However, they wanted to explore other means of birth control after a series of AIDS tests indicated they were both free of the virus. Felicia kept meaning to visit the local birth control clinic, but delayed making an appointment. For several weeks, Bill tried to be careful, withdrawing before he ejaculated.

Felicia became worried when her menstrual period did not occur on schedule. She feared she might be pregnant. Bill took the initiative to set a time for visiting the clinic, and they went together for the appointment. The pregnancy test done at the clinic was negative, much to their relief, and they were more than happy to agree to the counselor's suggestion that they consider choosing a contraceptive method. They were

asked to view a film describing the various forms of birth control, and the counselor then talked more specifically about each one. Bill, who had always thought the birth control pill to be dangerous, was surprised to learn that pills currently available were quite safe and could even offer some other health benefits. Felicia, who had always thought an IUD would be ideal, found out that its risks made it unsuitable for someone her age who still might want to have children. They talked about using a diaphragm, but were both dissatisfied with its degree of risk.

After Felicia's thorough medical examination and her reporting a complete health history to the nurse, the couple decided that the pill represented an acceptable form of contraception for them. Felicia was given a 3-month supply of pills and was asked to return for a follow-up check toward the end of that time.

method to acquire and use. Ultimately she must then use the contraceptive method consistently and properly. Negative attitudes about sex and one's own sexual feelings can cause difficulty in negotiating any or all of these steps (Gerrard, 1987).

PREPARING THE WAY FOR EFFECTIVE CONTRACEPTION

In view of all the evidence, it would appear that sexual responsibility can entail some personal work to ensure that you are ready to approach sexual intercourse with effective contraception, providing you are not ready to be a parent. Here are some of the necessary factors to consider and steps to take in becoming an effective user of birth control:

1. Consider your ethical and moral values about sex, pregnancy, and contraception. What sorts of social, family, and religious influences do you have to take into consideration in your decision-making process?
2. What are the health concerns that you might have regarding contraception? What resources will you

use to become more fully informed about available facts?
3. Weigh carefully your attitude about your own sexual feelings and potential sexual activities. If you find a good deal of guilt or anxiety, you may want to rethink the decisions you have made. In particular, consider how you may have been ignoring or neglecting the whole issue of birth control.
4. Can you give yourself permission to be sexual? (This does not have to mean intercourse.) If not, consider how your inner reluctance may interfere with your sexual life.
5. Be prepared to talk with your partner about contraception and the possibility of pregnancy before engaging in sexual intercourse. Sharing mutual concerns, hesitations, and values is the best way to prepare for effective contraception.

CHOOSING THE "RIGHT" CONTRACEPTIVE

The goal of people who use some method of birth control is to prevent pregnancy. They have decided

(continued on p. 113)

TABLE 5.1

Contraceptive Methods: Failure Rates, Advantages,
Causes of Failure, and Side Effects

Method	Theoretical Failure Rate*	Actual Use Failure Rate in Typical Users*	Potential Advantages to Users	Possible Causes of Failure That Could Result in Pregnancy	Potential Negative Side Effects
Abstinence	0%	?	No cost or health risks. Freedom from worry about pregnancy.	Inability to continue abstaining.	Sexual frustration. Avoiding planning for eventual use of contraception.
Withdrawal (coitus interruptus)	4%	18%	No cost or preparation involved. No risks to health (if sexually transmitted diseases are absent). Available even if no other methods are.	Sperm present in preejaculatory fluid from the penis (even more likely if intercourse is repeated within a few hours). Lack of ejaculatory control, causing ejaculation in vagina. Ejaculating semen too close to vaginal opening after withdrawal.	Inability to fully relax during sexual intercourse and not be on guard. Frustration created by inability to ejaculate in the vagina.
Natural Family Planning/ Fertility Awareness	1-9%	20%	Accepted by Roman Catholic church. May be used to increase chances of pregnancy if that choice is made. No health risks.	Inadequate time devoted to charting female's menstrual cycle or misunderstanding of method. Ovulation at an unexpected time in the cycle. Deciding to have intercourse during the unsafe period of the cycle, without other contraception.	Sexual frustration during periods of abstinence.
Combination Oral Contraceptive Triphasic Pill (birth control pill containing estrogen & progestin)	0.1%	3%	Reliable; offers protection all the time. Brings increased regularity to menstrual cycle. Tends to reduce menstrual cramping. Associated with lower incidence of breast & ovarian cysts, pelvic inflammatory disease, and ovarian cancer.	Not taking pills as directed or skipping a pill. Improper supervision by clinician. Ceasing taking the pills for any reason.	Nausea, weight gain, fluid retention, breast tenderness, headaches, missed menstrual periods, acne. Mood changes, depression, anxiety, fatigue, decreased sex drive. Circulatory diseases.
Minipill (progestin only)	0.5%	3%	Safer for older women. Reliable; offers protection all the time. Brings increased regularity to menstrual cycle. Tends to reduce menstrual cramping. Associated with lower incidence of breast cysts, pelvic inflammatory disease, and ovarian cancer.	Not taking pills as directed or skipping a pill. Improper supervision by clinician. Ceasing taking the pills for any reason.	Irregular menstrual periods are a common side effect. Bleeding between menstrual periods. Appearance of ovarian cysts.
Norplant implants	0.04%	0.1-3%	Long-term protection. Extremely reliable. Requires no attention after initial treatment. Easily reversible. May have same benefits as pills.	Use beyond a 5-year period. Gaining a significant amount of weight (less effective in women over 155 lbs.).	Slight visibility of implants. Menstrual cycle irregularities. Improper insertion or difficult removal. May have risks similar to pills, but research is incomplete.

111

(continued on next page)

Method	Theoretical Failure Rate*	Actual Use Failure Rate in Typical Users*	Potential Advantages to Users	Possible Causes of Failure That Could Result in Pregnancy	Potential Negative Side Effects
Sponge (contains spermicide)	9%	18-28%	Ease of use. Relatively inexpensive. Protection over 24 hours, several acts of intercourse. No odor or taste. Available without prescription.	Difficulty in proper insertion and placement. Internal anatomical abnormalities that interfere with placement or retention.	Increased risk of toxic shock syndrome. Allergic reaction to polyurethane or spermicide. Vaginal dryness. Increased risk of vaginal yeast infections.
Cervical Cap with Spermicide	6%	18%	Can be left in place for long periods of time.	Improper fitting or insertion/placement. Deterioration by oil-based lubricants or vaginal medications.	Possible risk of toxic shock syndrome. Allergic reaction to rubber or spermicide. Abrasions or irritation to vagina or cervix.
Spermicidal Foam, Cream, Jelly, Suppositories, or Film	3%	21%	Available without prescription. Minimal health risks. Easy to carry and use. Does not require partner involvement. Provides lubrication for intercourse.	Not using enough spermicide or running out of a supply. Failure to use spermicide out of desire not to interrupt the sexual act. Placing spermicide in vagina too long before intercourse begins. Douching within 6–8 hours after intercourse. Failure of suppositories or film to melt or foam properly.	Allergic reactions to the chemical. Unpleasant taste of chemical during oral-genital sex.
Condom	2%	12%	Available without prescription. Offers protection from sexually transmitted diseases. A method for which the man can take full responsibility. Easy to carry and use.	Breakage of condom. Not leaving space at tip of condom to collect semen. Lubrication with petroleum jelly, or presence of some vaginal medications, weakening rubber condom. Seepage of semen around opening of condom or condom slipping off in the vagina after coitus. Storing of condom for more than 2 years or in temperature extremes. Not placing condom on penis at beginning of intercourse.	Allergic reactions to rubber (natural "skin" condoms are also available). Some reduction in sensation on the penis.
Diaphragm (with spermicide)	3%	18%	Negative side effects are rare. Inexpensive; can be re-used.	Improper fitting or insertion of the diaphragm. Removal of diaphragm too soon (within 6–8 hours after coitus). Not using sufficient amount of spermicidal jelly with the diaphragm. Leakage in or around diaphragm or slippage of diaphragm. Deterioration by oil-based lubricants or vaginal medications.	Allergic reaction to the rubber (plastic diaphragms are also available) or spermicide. Increased risk of toxic shock syndrome. Bladder infection or vaginal soreness because of pressure from rim.

Method	Theoretical Failure Rate*	Actual Use Failure Rate in Typical Users*	Potential Advantages to Users	Possible Causes of Failure That Could Result in Pregnancy	Potential Negative Side Effects
Intrauterine Device (IUD)	0.8-2%	3%	Reliable. Can be left in place, so that nothing must be remembered or prepared immediately prior to intercourse.	Failure to notice that IUD has been expelled by uterus.	Uterine cramping, abnormal bleeding, and heavy menstrual flow. Pelvic inflammatory disease or perforation of the uterus during insertion of the IUD; also violent allergic reaction; infection of the ovaries.
Vasectomy	0.1%	0.15%	Permanent; no other preparations. Very reliable. Minimal health risks.	Having unprotected intercourse before reproductive tract is fully cleared of sperm following vasectomy (may be several months). Healing together of the two cut ends of the vas.	Psychological implications of being infertile can sometimes lead to some sexual problems.
Tubal Ligation	0.2%	0.4%	Permanent; no other preparations. Very reliable. Minimal health risks.	The procedure not being properly done by the physician.	Rarely, postsurgical infection or other complications. Psychological implications of being infertile.

*See explanation of failure rates in text. Figures based on R. A. Hatcher et al., *Contraceptive Technology, 1990–1992* (15th edition), 1990, New York: Irvington Publishers. Reprinted by permission.

they do not want to be parents, at least for the time being. On the surface of things, then, it might seem most reasonable to look at a chart, find the method that shows the lowest rate of failure, and use it. However, choosing a contraceptive is just not that simple. Several other issues should be discussed by both partners, preferably with a family planning counselor.

In choosing a contraceptive method, people usually want to know the risks involved—the risks that pregnancy may still occur and the risks of any possible side effects to their health. It is true that some methods are more effective or safer than others. When choosing a method, you should have as much accurate information as possible. However, there are many other issues to be considered when choosing a contraceptive that go beyond statistics:

1. *Age and amount of protection needed.* Age relates to fertility. Younger women may need a higher degree of contraceptive reliability than older women. For example, vaginal barrier methods (diaphragm, cervical cap, sponge) are less effective for women under the age of 25. The minipill (discussed on p. 115) is particularly effective for older women and women who are breast-feeding (Hatcher et al., 1990). Similarly, a person who has sexual intercourse frequently may want to consider different forms of contraception than some-

one who has intercourse only occasionally. Also to be weighed are the potential side effects of a particular method versus the extent of complication or crisis a pregnancy would provide.

2. *Safety.* Some birth control methods are not recommended for women with histories of particular medical conditions in themselves or their families. Therefore, the woman's suitability for a contraceptive method should be evaluated in cooperation with a trained professional.

3. *Factors that might inhibit use.* In choosing a contraceptive method, you should know yourself and any influences that might hinder regular use of the method. Are there any fears or hesitancies about side effects that create reluctance on your part about its use? Do you find it difficult to remember daily routines, which are necessary in taking birth control pills? Would you be embarrassed to buy supplies in a drug store or to interrupt sexual activity to put a condom or diaphragm in place? Will your religious values make use uncomfortable for you? Are you reluctant to touch your sex organs or, if you are a woman, to insert something into your vagina? Would you avoid a method where a visit to a physician or family planning clinic were necessary, possibly with follow-up visits?

113

4. *Cost.* You will need to choose a method that you know you will be able to afford on a consistent basis.

Research indicates that a large percentage of pregnancies are unplanned (Hatcher et al., 1990). It is also safe to extrapolate that a substantial number of those unintended pregnancies are unwanted. Sexual intercourse in which the partners do not regularly make use of some form of contraception runs an extremely high risk (about 90 percent chance) over a year's time of incurring pregnancy. The most common methods of birth control are summarized in the sections that follow. Their effectiveness, advantages, causes of failure, and potential side effects are listed in Table 5.1. The Self-Evaluation activity on page 125 may help you sort through some of your own personal issues and concerns.

Methods of Birth Control

No method of contraception is foolproof or without both positive and negative aspects. This section focuses on the various methods of birth control currently available and evaluates their effectiveness, advantages, and risks.

UNDERSTANDING CONTRACEPTIVE EFFECTIVENESS

It is important to understand that there is a difference between the theoretical failure rate and the actual use failure rate of any contraceptive method. The theoretical failure rate or "lowest observed failure rate" refers to its effectiveness when used exactly according to directions and without error or technical failures. Actual use failure rate looks at typical users and takes into account human error, carelessness, and technical failure.

Failure rates are typically given as percentages. The failure rates used in this book reflect the percentage of times that pregnancy could be expected to occur when 100 couples are using the method during a 1-year period of average frequency intercourse; this takes into consideration the total number of times the women were susceptible to pregnancy. The rates given are based on research studies considered to be the best designed and most statistically valid by the widely respected resource *Contraceptive Technology* (Hatcher et al., 1990). The chances of any contraceptive method being effective are increased when the method is used correctly and consistently.

Some forms of birth control cause unpleasant or unhealthy side effects in a few individuals. As with any kind of medical treatment, there is even a small risk of fatal side effects in the use of oral contraceptives (the pill), intrauterine devices (IUDs), surgical sterilization of the female, or induced abortion. Most professionals agree, however, that the risks are minimal enough that these methods should be made fully available to those who wish to use them. Research has also demonstrated repeatedly that the risks inherent in all methods of birth control are markedly less than the risks associated with pregnancy and childbirth. Nevertheless, methods such as the diaphragm or condom have fewer health-related side effects than some other methods, such as the pill or IUD.

SHARING THE RESPONSIBILITY FOR BIRTH CONTROL

It is clear that decision-making about the type of birth control to be used, and then the responsibility for using it, can be shared by the woman and man. While some people feel that contraception is more the woman's responsibility because she is the one who could become pregnant, others have accepted that it takes two to make a pregnancy.

For now, only two methods of birth control are available for use exclusively by males. One is the condom, and the other is vasectomy. The latter choice, since it is a permanent form of sterilization, is not usually considered an option until later in life when a man has either fathered all the children he might want or has decided with certainty that he never will want to have children.

Even though most available methods are used by women, there are still many ways in which they may be shared. For example, male partners can participate in the decision about which method to use, and couples can go together for clinical counseling and care. The purchasing of the contraceptives can be shared by both partners. Another form of sharing can be in the actual use of the method. The man can help insert spermicidal foam into his partner's vagina, or he can prepare the diaphragm with spermicidal jelly prior to insertion. Men can play a role in reminding their partners to take a birth control pill each day. A woman can put her partner's condom on him as a part of sexual foreplay.

theoretical failure rate: a measure of how often a birth control method can be expected to fail, when used without error or technical problems.

actual use failure rate: a measure of how often a birth control method can be expected to fail when human error and technical failure are considered.

The most crucial way of sharing contraceptive responsibility is by deliberate, open communication about all of the issues between the partners. This should also include discussion of what avenues could be pursued should contraception fail. Each partner should be ready to discuss how he or she would want to deal with an unintended pregnancy. If serious conflicts develop over this issue, it may call into question the advisability of sharing sexual intercourse at all.

ABSTINENCE, SEX WITHOUT INTERCOURSE, AND WITHDRAWAL

One obvious approach to birth control is to avoid the depositing of semen in the vagina. Some couples, especially unmarried teenagers, choose abstinence—refraining from sexual intercourse—for this reason. This, of course, does not have to mean that other forms of sex are avoided. There are varieties of sexual behaviors that couples may find pleasurable and satisfying without having intercourse. These include massage, mutual masturbation, oral sex, and all sorts of physical intimacy not involving penetration. The alternatives to intercourse have been called "outercourse," and it has been praised as a form of birth control that is simple to use, free of side effects, and that may reduce the risks of giving or getting sexually transmitted diseases (Greenwood & Margolis, 1981).

Withdrawal, also known as coitus interruptus, is a method that is sometimes used among couples who have not yet obtained some safer method. The risk of pregnancy with the withdrawal method is high. The penis is withdrawn from the vagina prior to ejaculation, and it is crucial that ejaculation not take place near the opening of the vagina. Withdrawal can prove frustrating for couples who use it frequently. There are a number of reasons why its failure rate is high. One complication is the possibility that sperm may be present in fluids that are sometimes secreted from the penis during intercourse well before ejaculation. There is a greater likelihood of sperm being present in these secretions if the man has experienced ejaculation within the previous few hours. Of course, not all men have the ejaculatory control to withdraw in time, and some may simply choose not to do so after all. Nevertheless, when intercourse has been chosen and no other method is to be used, withdrawal is preferable to using no birth control at all.

ORAL CONTRACEPTIVES: THE PILL

Birth control pills were introduced in 1960 and rapidly gained in popularity. By the late 1980s nearly 13.8 million women in the United States were using oral contraceptives. Another 47 million women around the world take "the pill."

Three types of oral contraceptives are in use. The *combination type* of oral contraceptive contains a combination of two hormones, estrogen and progestin, taken in constant dosage levels for 21 days during the menstrual cycle. Many manufacturers provide seven "inert" pills to be taken on the remaining days of the 28-day cycle. There are also *minipills,* containing only a low dosage of progestin, and *triphasic pills* that provide varying levels of estrogen and progestin dosages over the cycle. They are said to be more consistent with the natural menstrual cycle and reduce side effects (Pasquale, 1984). However, the three companies who market triphasic pills apparently interpret the menstrual cycle differently, since they have differing concentrations of estrogen and progestin in their pills. This calls into question how "natural" they may be (Hatcher et al., 1990).

Pills create changes in the menstrual cycle that interrupt normal patterns of ovulation and implantation, thus preventing pregnancy. With combination and triphasic pills, the estrogen level is kept artificially high, thus inhibiting the release of FSH and LH, two hormones that control ovulation (see chapter 2, "Sexual Systems"). Progestin changes the consistency of the cervical mucus so that sperm cannot pass as easily into the uterus and also makes the uterine lining less receptive to implantation by an embryo. The minipill apparently works in this latter manner, as well as occasionally preventing ovulation.

It is crucial that birth control pills be taken each day at about the same time. If one is mistakenly skipped, it should be taken as soon as possible. If an entire day goes by without taking the skipped pill, however, it is advisable to use an alternative method of birth control for the remainder of the cycle, while continuing to take the rest of the pills.

The amounts of synthetic hormones contained in oral contraceptives have been markedly reduced since the earlier days of their use, and this has also reduced the frequency and intensity of their side effects. More recently, a number of noncontraceptive benefits of the pill have been identified. It usually makes menstrual periods lighter and more regular, with less cramping. Users of the pill have a lower incidence of breast cysts, ovarian cysts, and pelvic inflammatory disease. It also offers protection against both uterine and ovarian cancer (Hatcher et al., 1990). Current research seems to indicate that for healthy women under the age of 35 who do not smoke the benefits of the pill outweigh the

coitus interruptus (ko-EET-us *or* KO-ut-us): a method of birth control in which the penis is withdrawn from the vagina prior to ejaculation.

risks. While smoking increases the risk of heart attack and stroke for anyone, using the pill seems to compound the risk of these disorders even more. Therefore it is usually inadvisable for a woman who smokes to take birth control pills. According to research evidence to date, the pill does not seem to increase the risk for breast cancer, even for women who might have an inherited susceptibility to the disease (Stadel, 1989).

A very important consideration in obtaining oral contraceptives is to receive a good physical examination and have a complete health history taken. There are certain conditions, such as a history of blood clotting disorders or high blood pressure, that indicate to family planning specialists that the pill should not be prescribed. Follow-up checks that include blood pressure readings and an annual Pap test should also be required of anyone taking birth control pills.

There are a few symptoms that a pill user should consider to be warning signals worth checking out with a health professional. Pain in the abdomen, chest, or legs can signal the development of conditions that can become dangerous, including gall bladder or liver disease, heart conditions, or blood clots. Severe headaches or marked changes in vision can mean that the pill may have produced high blood pressure or other conditions that can increase the risk of stroke and cardiovascular disease.

There can be other troublesome side effects of contraceptive pills, although they are not usually dangerous. These include the possibility of depression, acne, fluid retention and associated weight gain, abnormal bleeding, or absence of menstrual periods. Another cautionary note was recently sounded with regard to effectiveness of the pill. Certain antibiotics, including ampicillin and tetracycline, interfere with internal absorption of the pill. Tranquilizers, barbiturates, sleeping pills, some anti-inflammatory medications, and some sulfa drugs may also reduce its contraceptive effectiveness (Lipman, 1987). Nevertheless, the contraceptive pill continues to represent a particularly effective and relatively safe form of birth control for many women. Risks associated with its use are lower than the risks inherent in pregnancy and giving birth.

NORPLANT IMPLANTS AND PROGESTIN INJECTIONS

After years of use and research in other countries, Norplant implants were approved by the Federal Drug Administration in December 1990 for use in the United States. They represent the first substantially new contraceptive method to become available in the United States for many years. They consist of six slender silicone rubber capsules, each about the size of a matchstick. The capsules contain a contraceptive steroid called levonorgestrol. They are placed under the skin on the inside of the woman's upper arm, in a fan-shaped configuration, and the drug very slowly diffuses through the walls of the capsules into the body. Like other forms of hormonally induced contraception, the Norplant hormone prevents ovulation and causes cervical mucus to thicken so that sperm may not penetrate into the uterus easily (Bruce, 1990).

These implants represent a particularly reliable means of birth control, and since they are implanted under the skin they cannot be used incorrectly. The effectiveness of this method very gradually decreases over a 5-year period so that the highest rate of failure tends to be toward the end of that period, but they are considered reliable for use during an entire 5 years. Implants are slightly less effective in women who weigh more than 155 pounds. They do require careful insertion by a trained clinician. Six tiny incisions are made in the skin, after a local anesthetic has been used to numb the area. The tubes are then slipped into place, and the incisions are covered by small bandages for a few days. No stitches are required since the openings in the skin are so tiny. The implants are slightly visible as six raised lines under the skin. At the end of 5 years, they must be replaced. If at any time a pregnancy is desired, they may be removed by a clinician, and fertility returns right away. The implants themselves are relatively expensive and they do require insertion and removal by a trained professional. Therefore, the one-time cost of up to $300 may be prohibitive for some people. They do not require other costs over the 5-year period of their effectiveness.

The most common side effect of Norplant implants is irregularity in the menstrual cycle, including prolonged bleeding or spotting between periods. A small percentage of women have the implant removed within the first 2 years because of these irregularities. There may also be mood changes, weight fluctuations, or other symptoms associated with the hormonal methods of birth control. The side effects vary with women's individual body chemistry. However, they generally subside after the first year of use (Sivin, 1988; Waldman, 1991).

Injections of long-acting progestin have also been used for contraception, although this method is not currently approved for use in the United States. There is some controversy over side effects of progestin injections, but current professional opinion seems to

Norplant implants: contraceptive method in which hormone-releasing rubber containers are surgically inserted under the skin.

progestin injection: use of injected hormone that can prevent pregnancy for several months; not yet approved for use in the United States.

be leaning toward offering them as an option for American women.

In other countries work is being done to examine the effectiveness of progestin implanted in IUDs or rings to fit on the cervix. These are birth control methods that may well achieve popularity in years to come (Hatcher et al., 1990).

SPERMICIDES, SPONGES, AND SUPPOSITORIES

Spermicides, or chemicals that kill sperm, are available without prescription as foams, creams, jellies, or implanted in a sponge or suppository. The two spermicidal chemicals usually used are nonoxynol-9 or octoxynol. They are generally not considered to be a highly effective method of contraception when used alone, but are very effective when used with other methods such as condoms or diaphragms. Used alone, they must be inserted deeply into the vagina so they will cover the cervical opening. Some spermicides have an unpleasant taste that can limit the pleasure of oral sexual contact with the woman following their insertion, although some companies are marketing brands that are unflavored and unscented. Nonoxynol-9 especially has the added advantage of providing some protection against STDs, including AIDS.

The contraceptive sponge, introduced in 1983, is a round, thick, polyurethane disc with a dimple that fits over the cervix. The sponge holds a gram of spermicide and is moistened with water before insertion. Attached to it is a woven loop that is used to pull the sponge out of the vagina. While it acts as a barrier to sperm, so that they cannot enter the uterus, the main function of the sponge is to release its spermicide and kill sperm. It must be left in place for at least 6 hours following intercourse and can be left for up to 24 hours. This long period of protection represents a significant advantage of the sponge, although its rate of effectiveness is somewhat lower than several other methods (see Table 5.1 on pp. 111–113). While research on the sponge is continuing, its effectiveness seems to be similar to that of spermicides when used alone (Edelman, McIntyre, & Harper, 1984). A few women have difficulty removing the sponge, sometimes tearing the device, and some women have complained that it causes vaginal dryness by absorbing secretions (see Fig. 5.3). The sponge may provide some protection against sexually transmitted disease. A study done in Thailand with prostitutes showed that the spermicide in the sponge lowered the women's risk of acquiring gonorrhea by 69 percent and chlamydia by 33 percent (see chapter 14, "Sexually Transmitted Diseases and Other Physical Problems").

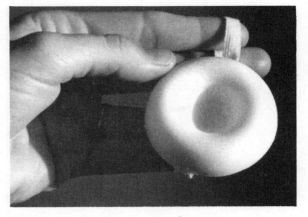

FIGURE 5.3 Contraceptive Sponge

A popular method of birth control, because of its availability and ease of use, is the sponge. It carries a spermicide that is activated by moistening the sponge with water before inserting it into the vagina. Some women complain it causes vaginal dryness.

Contraceptive suppositories are designed to melt or foam in the vagina to distribute the spermicide contained in them. However, this takes between 10 and 30 minutes, necessitating the postponement of intercourse. Some suppositories do not always liquefy completely. Their effectiveness is the same as other forms of spermicide.

BARRIER METHODS

The barrier methods are those contraceptives that prevent sperm from entering the uterus, thus preventing conception. Their effectiveness is enhanced when used in conjunction with a spermicide, although directions should always be followed carefully so that the proper spermicide is chosen and so that it is used correctly with the barrier. Additional use of a condom also increases the effectiveness rate of barrier methods, and helps prevent the spread of sexually transmitted diseases.

Diaphragms and Cervical Caps A diaphragm is a latex rubber cup with a flexible rim that is placed in the

spermicides: chemicals that kill sperm; available as foams, creams, jellies, or implants in sponges or suppositories.
sponge: a thick polyurethane disc that holds a spermicide and fits over the cervix to prevent conception.
suppositories: contraceptive devices designed to distribute their spermicide by melting or foaming in the vagina.
diaphragm (DY-a-fram): a latex rubber cup, filled with spermicide, that is fitted to the cervix by a clinician; the woman must learn to insert it properly for full contraceptive effectiveness.

117

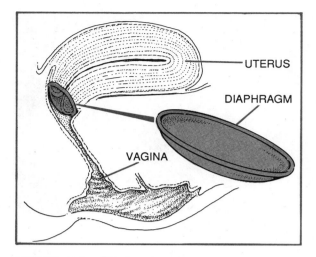

FIGURE 5.4 Diaphragm

The diaphragm is a mechanical barrier to sperm that comes in different sizes and must therefore be fitted to a woman by a clinician or physician. Because it may be dislodged during lovemaking, it is best to combine its use with a condom. Its reliability rate is fairly high when used properly and with a spermicide.

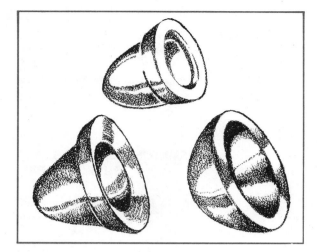

FIGURE 5.5 Cervical Caps

Similar to the diaphragm, the cervical cap must be fitted by a clinician. It stays in place by suction and can be worn for several weeks at a time. It may be uncomfortable for some males during intercourse and can be easily dislodged. They are not approved for use in the United States.

vagina in such a way as to cover the cervix (see Fig. 5.4). Spermicidal jelly or cream is placed inside the diaphragm and around its rim to help hold it in place and kill sperm. A clinician must fit the diaphragm to the woman, and the woman must learn how to insert it properly. Once learned, insertion of a diaphragm becomes a quick and simple matter. It should not be inserted more than 2 hours prior to intercourse. After this time period, if intercourse has not yet occurred, a diaphragm should be removed and more spermicide added before intercourse takes place. The diaphragm is left in place for at least 6 to 8 hours after intercourse, after which it is removed and washed. It can be used for many months, although it should be checked by a doctor from time to time to ensure that it still fits over the cervix properly and isn't damaged. The diaphragm has been in use since the end of the nineteenth century.

Because the diaphragm is comparatively inexpensive, can be used for years, and presents few risks to health, it has seen an increase in popularity in recent years. It is not an ideal contraceptive for a woman who might feel uncomfortable touching her own genitals or inserting something into her vagina.

The cervical cap looks like a large thimble with a tall dome (see Fig. 5.5). As its name implies, it is designed to fit over the cervix. While cervical caps have been used in Europe for several years, they were not approved for marketing in the United States until 1988. Since relatively few companies are manufacturing them, they are still quite difficult to obtain in the United States. Like the diaphragm, caps must be fitted

by a clinician, inserted properly, and used with a spermicide. They can dislodge fairly easily during intercourse, and they have been implicated in some scratching of the vagina and cervix.

Diaphragms, cervical caps, and contraceptive sponges may increase the risk of a woman experiencing toxic shock syndrome (TSS). This is an infection caused by *Staphylococcus aureus* bacteria that are normally present in the body, and which multiply if something is left in the vagina for long periods of time. Toxic shock syndrome has been associated with tampons as well. It is not a common disease, and resulting deaths are rare. Nevertheless, when using a diaphragm, sponge, or cervical cap, it is advisable not to leave the device in place for more than 24 hours. Use should be avoided during menstruation, for a few months following the birth of a baby, or if a vaginal infection is present.

spermicidal jelly (cream): sperm-killing chemical in a gel base or cream, used with other contraceptives such as diaphragms.

cervical cap: a device that is shaped like a large thimble and fits over the cervix; not a particularly effective contraceptive because it can dislodge easily during intercourse.

toxic shock syndrome (TSS): an acute disease characterized by fever and sore throat, and caused by normal bacteria in the vagina that are activated if tampons or some contraceptive devices such as diaphragms or sponges are left in for long periods of time.

Staphylococcus aureus (staf-a-low-KAK-us): the bacteria that can cause toxic shock syndrome.

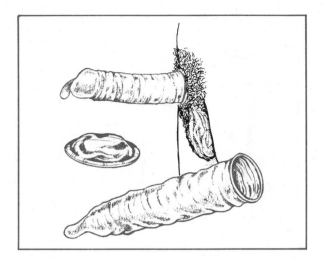

FIGURE 5.6 Condoms

A birth control device for men, the condom is made of latex rubber or animal skin. It is unrolled onto the erect penis before intercourse begins and collects the semen ejaculated. Care must be taken so that the penis doesn't lose its erect state while in the vagina. Latex rubber condoms are also important in preventing many STDs, including AIDS.

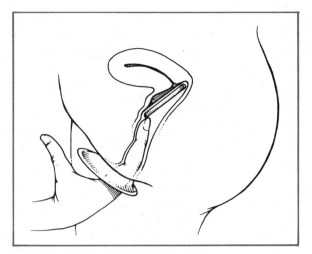

FIGURE 5.7 Female Condom

The diagram above shows one "female condom" design that is currently being tested and should become available soon. The ring at the bottom end is closed and is inserted into the vagina to cover the cervix. The top open ring covers the vulva.

Condoms The condom is a sheath worn over the penis during intercourse that collects the semen when the male ejaculates (see Fig. 5.6). Most condoms today are made of latex rubber (hence the name rubbers) and are available inexpensively in drugstores, supermarkets, convenience stores, and some college bookstores. Rubber condoms may be purchased dry or lubricated, and some have a small nipple at the tip, providing a semen-collection area. Some new condoms contain a spermicide that has been shown to be effective in killing sperm within a minute or two after ejaculation, thus providing more contraceptive effectiveness. Condoms made of animal membrane are also available and cost slightly more than rubber condoms. These skin condoms purportedly allow for more sensation on the penis, although they fit more loosely than rubber condoms and should be checked from time to time during intercourse to make certain that slipping has not occurred. Skin condoms are *not* acceptable as a preventive against transmitting the AIDS virus, whereas latex rubber condoms are considered to offer substantial protection (Centers for Disease Control, 1988).

The condom should be unrolled onto the erect penis before intercourse begins, leaving an empty (not air-filled) space at the tip for semen. This is best accomplished by pinching the tip of the condom while unrolling it onto the penis. More specific directions and suggestions for condom use are found in chapter 15, "The AIDS Crisis and Sexual Decisions." Rubber condoms should never be stored in wallets or automobile glove compartments, since warm temperatures

deteriorate rubber. Petroleum jelly (such as Vaseline), mineral and vegetable oils, and some moisturizing lotions or creams will also weaken rubber and cause tearing (Contraceptive Technology Update, 1988). After ejaculation has occurred, the man or his partner should hold on to the base of the condom when removing the penis from the vagina so that the condom does not slip off or semen does not seep out of the open end of the condom.

Three pharmaceutical companies have been testing a condom that is designed for women. The "female condoms" are polyurethane pouches that may be inserted into the vagina. One female condom design (Fig. 5.7) consists of a ring at both ends, one of which is sealed closed. The closed ring is inserted into the back of the vagina, and over the cervix, much as a diaphragm would be fitted into place. The open-ended ring then rests outside on the vulva. Another version is held in place by a G-string worn by the woman.

The availability of female condoms will fill a crucial need, offering women a new method of birth control under their control that also provides protection against sexually transmitted diseases. Initial testing results suggest that the female condom will be highly effective, and that there is less likelihood of leakage than there is with male condoms. However, actual failure rates are not yet available (Bruce, 1990).

condom: a sheath worn over the penis during intercourse that collects semen and helps prevent disease transmission.

There are two features of female condoms that may prove to be drawbacks. One is the fact that part of the condom will be visible outside the vagina, covering the vulva. An early study has shown that a small percentage of men and women dislike this feature aesthetically (Hosansky, 1990). Another potential problem could be its price, expected to range from $1.60 to $3.00 each. For some users, especially those with a high frequency of intercourse, such costs could be prohibitive (Hatcher et al., 1990).

The barrier methods must all be inserted or put on sometime prior to sex. While some people find this inconvenient, there is also the possibility of integrating the use of a contraceptive into the sexual activities. For example, if a couple is using condoms and foam, the man can insert the foam into the woman's vagina, and the woman can unroll the condom onto the man's penis. Birth control methods, like any other aspect of a responsible sexual relationship, require communication and cooperative effort.

Effectiveness of the vaginal barrier methods is heavily influenced by the age of the user. Younger women are apparently more fertile, and may have a greater frequency of intercourse. The failure rate for women under 30 is approximately twice that of women over 30 when using barrier methods (Hatcher et al., 1990).

INTRAUTERINE DEVICES (IUDS)

Intrauterine devices have been used since the beginning of this century and were particularly popular in the 1960s and 1970s. Two types of IUD are currently marketed in the United States. One is called the progestasert and includes the hormone progestin that is gradually released from the device. Copper T 380 A, a new IUD that contains copper, went on the market in the United States in early 1988. It carries specific warnings about its risks. IUDs are made of plastic and have a nylon thread attached to one end. The contraceptive is inserted into the uterus by a clinician, with the thread left protruding into the vagina so that the woman can check regularly to make certain the IUD is still in place (see Fig. 5.8). If pregnancy is desired, it must be removed by a clinician.

While the actual mechanism by which an IUD prevents pregnancy is not known for certain, there are several hypotheses. One suggests that the device interferes with implantation of the blastocyst into the lining of the uterus. Newer studies have tended to discount this hypothesis. IUDs probably do not interfere with implantation (Alvarez et al., 1988). It has also been

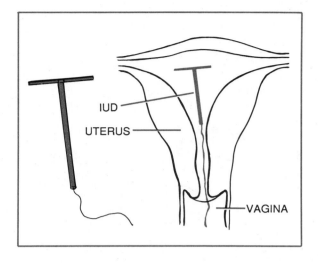

FIGURE 5.8 IUD

The IUD, or intrauterine device, is a small plastic object inserted into the uterus by a trained physician or clinician and left in place for long periods of time. It can be a highly effective form of birth control but there have been serious side effects caused by some types of IUD. Only two types of IUDs remain available in the United States as of 1991.

suggested that IUDs may interfere with the movement of an egg through the fallopian tube or with the mobility of sperm, or in some way inhibit fertilization (Hatcher et al., 1990).

It is now believed that IUDs may facilitate the migration of bacteria up into the uterus and that they may make women more prone to internal infections. This can lead to a chronic infection called pelvic inflammatory disease (PID). If untreated for a long enough time, PID can cause damage to the fallopian tubes, resulting in sterility. The disease may escalate and in rare cases become life-threatening. Since IUD manufacturers have been sued because of these side effects, all types of IUDs, except for the progestasert and Copper T 380 A, have been withdrawn from the market. Because of the risk of infertility, many family planning specialists no longer feel that the IUD represents a suitable method for younger women who may eventually want children. Cost has become another factor in the declining popularity of IUDs. The manufacturer must now charge more for IUDs because of increased liability, and clinicians must pass higher costs along to patients. For these reasons, private physicians are, for the most part, reluctant to recommend its use.

intrauterine devices (IUDs): birth control method involving the insertion of a small plastic device into the uterus.
pelvic inflammatory disease (PID): a chronic internal infection associated with certain types of IUDs.

NATURAL FAMILY PLANNING/ FERTILITY AWARENESS

This method, also known as the rhythm method, relies on awareness of a woman's menstrual-fertility cycle so that intercourse can be avoided when it is likely that the ovum might be available for fertilization. Since it does not require any chemical or manufactured device, it is considered more "natural"; in another sense it certainly isn't natural if a couple must avoid intercourse just when they naturally want to have it. It is also a method that takes a great deal of planning and daily attention and therefore is associated with a high rate of failure as a contraceptive method. Since the rhythm method provides awareness of when the ovum is most likely to be present for fertilization, it may also be used by couples who are attempting to get pregnant.

Natural family planning actually combines three fertility awareness methods. To use it effectively, the woman or couple should receive careful and complete instruction from a trained specialist in the method. Various charts must be made for 6 or more successive months before the method should actually be tried as a contraceptive. The *calendar method* charts the beginning and length of the menstrual cycle. The *basal body temperature (BBT) method* charts the resting body temperature of the woman throughout the menstrual cycle (see Fig. 5.9). Usually the temperature drops slightly just before ovulation and rises thereafter. A special oral thermometer must be used to take these readings. Finally the *mucus method* keeps track of the appearance and consistency of the woman's cervical mucus during the menstrual cycle. Women can learn to recognize that cervical mucus becomes clearer and more slippery during ovulation.

By combining information from these three methods, the woman should be able to predict with accuracy about when ovulation will take place. During several days prior to ovulation and up until 4 days after, either intercourse should be avoided or an alternative birth control method used. This is a method that requires a great deal of cooperation and communication between the partners.

There are some over-the-counter tests available that can help a woman determine when ovulation is most likely to occur. The tests involve measuring the amount of luteinizing hormone (LH) in the urine once a day for about a week during the middle part of the menstrual cycle. Like other predictive techniques, these tests may be used to avoid pregnancy or to increase the likelihood of becoming pregnant. Continued development of accurate, easy-to-use indicators of ovulation may well improve the effectiveness of natural family planning significantly (Djerassi, 1990).

VOLUNTARY STERILIZATION

Sterilization, or surgery to render a person permanently infertile, has become the most common method

rhythm method: a natural method of birth control that depends on an awareness of the woman's menstrual-fertility cycle.
sterilization: rendering a person incapable of conceiving, usually by interrupting passage of the egg or sperm.

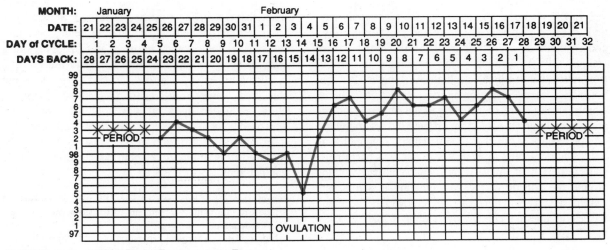

FIGURE 5.9 Basal Body Temperature Record

The woman's resting body temperature is taken each morning immediately upon waking. Just prior to ovulation, there is a noticeable drop in the temperature. Then, for up to 3 days after, the temperature rises. It is usually recommended that the basal body temperature be charted for 3 or 4 successive months so that any peculiarities in the woman's cycle may be noted. After it has become obviously predictable, the information may be used as part of the natural family planning method of birth control, or for determining the best time for conception to occur.

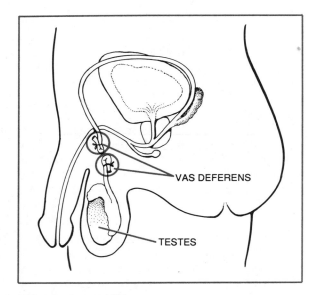

FIGURE 5.10 Vasectomy

A permanent form of male contraception, vasectomy is a surgical procedure in which the vas deferens is cut and tied. This blocks the passage of sperm from the testes to the upper part of the vas deferens. It is a simple and safe form of birth control and doesn't interfere with erection or ejaculation.

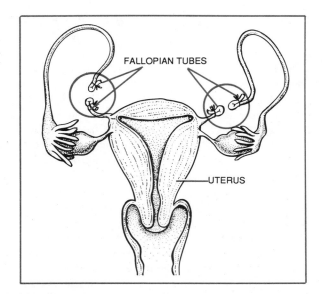

FIGURE 5.11 Tubal Ligation

A permanent form of female sterilization, tubal ligation is a surgical procedure, somewhat more complicated than a vasectomy, in which the fallopian tubes are tied and cut. This prevents the egg from traveling into the uterus and joining with sperm.

of contraception for married couples. It is accomplished either by cutting the vas deferens in the male, the tube through which sperm travel, or by tying or clamping off the fallopian tubes in the woman so an ovum can no longer travel through them.

Male sterilization, called vasectomy, is a simple procedure in which a small incision is made in each side of the scrotum, and each vas deferens is cut and tied (see Fig. 5.10). It is one of the most frequently chosen methods of birth control in the United States (Jarrow, 1987). The operation is usually an office procedure that requires less than 30 minutes. It does not affect sexual functioning or ejaculation. There simply are no more sperm cells in the semen. Studies are currently under way to investigate the reversibility of a procedure in which a flexible silicon plug called a SHUG is implanted in each vas to act as a barrier to sperm. It is held in place by a nylon thread wound around the outside of the vas, creating less internal scar tissue. The SHUG can be removed if the man wishes to attempt conceiving a child ("SHUG Device," 1987).

Tubal ligation is the method of sterilization used for women. It may be performed through an operation called a laparotomy, which requires a hospital stay, or the more simple laparoscopy, in which a small fiber optic scope is inserted into the abdomen through a tiny incision, enabling the physician to see the fallopian

tubes clearly. Through either method, the fallopian tubes are located and sealed (see Fig. 5.11).

Tubal ligations and vasectomies can sometimes be reversed, restoring fertility. However, attempts at reversal are complicated, expensive, and only 40–70 percent effective, so sterilization should be chosen as a contraceptive method only when a decision has been made that a permanent method is desired. Some physicians require the consent of a spouse before performing sterilization, or they refuse to sterilize individuals who do not have any children, but there are no laws requiring either of these qualifications prior to being sterilized. Newer, more reversible methods of sterilization are under study but have not yet been FDA-approved. One includes the *tubal plug,* a silicone plug inserted into each fallopian tube that could later be removed. It is similar to the plug inserted into the male vas deferens.

vasectomy (va-SEK-ta-mee *or* vay-ZEK-ta-mee): a surgical separation of the vas deferens to induce permanent male sterilization.

tubal ligation: a surgical separation of the fallopian tubes to induce permanent female sterilization.

laparotomy: operation to perform a tubal ligation, or female sterilization, involving an abdominal incision.

laparoscopy: simpler procedure for tubal ligation, involving the insertion of a small fiber optic scope into the abdomen, through which the surgeon can see the fallopian tubes and close them off.

Case Study

MARK: MAKING A DECISION ABOUT STERILIZATION

At age 35, Mark was married and had two children. He and his wife had decided that they would not have more children, and she suggested that he have a vasectomy. She had used birth control pills and, more recently, a diaphragm. Both of them were tired of worrying about contraception, but they were equally concerned about chancing another pregnancy.

While voluntary sterilization sounded like the ideal solution, Mark had some doubts about vasectomy. He wondered if it would affect his sexual response and had read somewhere that men with vasectomies were more prone to heart disease.

Several months went by without any action, until Mark's wife complained that she was tired of having the primary responsibility for contraception. She insisted that Mark at least investigate the surgery. He made an appointment with a counselor at a family planning clinic to talk over his concerns.

The counselor showed Mark diagrams that explained the procedure and reassured him that it would not affect erection or ejaculation in any way. He also learned that research was continuing to confirm that the surgery had no negative effects on health. Mark was also able to admit that the idea of having a surgeon handle his genitals and cut into his scrotum was making him squeamish.

After further talks with his wife and one more visit to the counselor, Mark decided to go ahead with his vasectomy. The surgeon set up an office appointment for Friday afternoon, explaining that Mark should just take it easy for the following day or two and would be ready to go back to work by Monday.

The procedure was simpler than Mark had expected, although afterward he went through what he called a brief "what if" stage. He wondered how he would feel if he or his wife changed their minds and decided they wanted more children. That stage passed quickly, and 2 years later he reported that he was very comfortable with having been sterilized.

NEW CONTRACEPTIVES FOR MALES?

Condoms and vasectomy are the only birth control methods available for use by males. Some research in this country has investigated possible methods of male contraception, but still there is an imbalance in the contraceptive field. This may have resulted from marketing studies conducted by pharmaceutical companies that indicate men are reluctant to use methods that might alter their internal chemistry in some way. Many women resent the fact that contraception seems to rest more with their bodies and decision-making.

The World Health Organization has sponsored research into the contraceptive effectiveness of weekly injections of a synthetic testosterone. For many years, it has been known that elevated levels of this substance in men causes a reversible and pronounced reduction in sperm production. Taking the drug by mouth carries an unacceptable risk of liver damage, but weekly injections have been shown to be very effective. In 157 couples who used the method for an entire year, there was only one pregnancy. Research and development of testosterone injections for males will continue. Cost and aversion to injections may well prove to be deterrents for some potential users of the method if it eventually is approved for widespread use.

Probably by the year 2000 research will have progressed on methods of male contraception (Hatcher et al., 1990). One is an antifertility vaccine that would be injected. The other possibilities are chemicals that would either interfere with the maturation of sperm cells in the testes or in some way destroy the sperm or render them immobile. One of these chemicals is gossypol, derived from cottonseed oil. It has been used in China and has been shown to cause reversible infertility in men. It carries with it the side effect of depleting potassium in the body, a condition that can lead to rhythm problems in the heart and other medical difficulties (Mastroianni et al., 1990). Chemicals that are similar to luteinizing hormone (LH) also disrupt the formation of sperm, but seem to reduce interest in sex as well. Research is being done to determine if adding male hormones to such a preparation can prevent the reduction in sex drive.

123

A new technique is being studied to block the passage of sperm through the vas deferens. It involves the injection of a liquid plastic into the inner cavity of the vas, blocking the tube and also lowering the pH within it so that any stray sperm cells are immobilized. So far, this technique has been tested only in monkeys, but it has been shown to render them infertile for up to a year. Finally, the use of ultrasound has been shown to suppress the development of sperm in some animals and in humans, without serious side effects. In time, this and other potential male contraceptive methods will be more thoroughly explored and developed.

POSTCOITAL CONTRACEPTION

Since contraceptive technology is imperfect, and people continue to experience sexual intercourse, or coitus, without birth control, there continues to be a demand for "morning-after" birth control. Women who have experienced unprotected intercourse have traditionally used a variety of methods to avoid pregnancy, such as douching (washing out) the vagina, wiping out the vagina with their fingers, or moving their bodies in an attempt to expel the semen. There are folk remedies that recommend insertion of objects or special concoctions into the vagina. However, there is no evidence that such techniques in any way reduce the likelihood of conception. Sperm cells will still make their way into the woman's reproductive system, and if an ovum is present, fertilization may well occur.

Strictly speaking, the postcoital contraceptive methods now available do not prevent fertilization. Instead, they act as "interceptors," preventing implantation of a fertilized ovum in the uterine wall. For this reason, postcoital contraceptives are a controversial issue. Some view them to be abortifacients, suggesting that they are substances that cause termination of pregnancy. However, the American College of Obstetricians and Gynecologists technically defines pregnancy as implantation, and interceptors do not allow this process to occur. Therefore, proponents of postcoital contraception claim instead that it prevents abortions, since there is no need for terminating a pregnancy. While these may simply represent semantic distinctions, the fact remains that the U.S. Food and Drug Administration (FDA) has not approved postcoital contraceptive techniques as such. Nevertheless, physicians are not prohibited by the FDA from using drugs for purposes other than those specifically indicated in their labeling. Many physicians and clinicians therefore prescribed certain postcoital contraceptive methods throughout the 1980s, especially for rape victims. Since these methods have a relatively high failure rate, they are usually used for emergency situations in which unprotected intercourse was unexpected, and the medication can be administered within 72 hours of exposure (Hatcher et al., 1990).

One of the earliest morning-after pills was diethylstilbestrol (DES), but this chemical is also known to produce a variety of adverse side effects. A more widely accepted approach today involves taking two doses of oral contraceptive pills containing ethinyl estradiol and dl-norgestrel. One study indicated that the treatment averted 70 percent of pregnancies that might otherwise have occurred, although about half of the women experienced side effects such as nausea or vomiting (Percival-Smith & Abercrombie, 1987). Women who are given this postcoital pill should also be alert to the other danger signs (see p. 116) of contraceptive pill use.

A new chemical that has been tested in European countries for several years has been attracting attention as a postcoital contraceptive. The drug RU-486 is a progesterone antagonist. It blocks the hormone progesterone from preparing the uterine lining for pregnancy, causing earlier menstruation. Implantation is therefore prevented, or if it has already occurred, the fertilized egg is sloughed off with the uterine lining (Baulieu, 1989). RU-486 may be administered within six weeks after unprotected intercourse, although after the first three days it would clearly be acting as an abortifacient. While studies have continued to conclude that RU-486 has fewer side effects and risks than other postcoital approaches, some health advocates have advised caution and further research to test its degree of safety.

The development of RU-486 and its approval as a drug to prevent or terminate pregnancy is a good example of the clash between biomedical research and public policy. During the first 11 months after it became available in France, over 25,000 women chose it over surgical abortion. The World Health Organization sees the drug as an important option to be offered to Third World countries. There are indications that it not only is safer than surgical abortion, but that it may have other applications in medicine and research. However, antiabortion groups in the United States have called RU-486 the "death pill," and have threatened to boycott any pharmaceutical company who gets approval to market the substance in this country. It may be, however, that its other uses in the treatment of certain tumors and other diseases will win its eventual approval in the United States. If so, it may well become the most significant form of postcoital contraception available (Palca, 1989; Hublitz, 1990).

abortifacients: substances that cause termination of pregnancy.
RU-486: a progesterone antagonist used as a postcoital contraceptive.

SELF-EVALUATION

Contraceptive Comfort and Confidence
Scale

Method of birth control you are considering using: _____

		YES	NO
1.	Have you had problems using this method before?		
2.	How long did you use this method?		

Answer YES or NO to the following questions: YES NO

3. Am I afraid of using this method?
4. Would I really rather not use this method?
5. Will I have trouble remembering to use this method?
6. Have I ever become pregnant while using this method?
7. Will I have trouble using this method correctly?
8. Do I still have unanswered questions about this method?
9. Does this method make menstrual periods longer or more painful?
10. Does this method cost more than I can afford?
11. Could this method cause me to have serious complications?
12. Am I opposed to this method because of any religious beliefs?
13. Is my partner opposed to this method?
14. Am I using this method without my partner's knowledge?
15. Will using this method embarrass my partner?
16. Will using this method embarrass me?
17. Will I enjoy intercourse less because of this method?
18. If this method interrupts lovemaking, will I avoid using it?
19. Has a nurse or doctor ever told me NOT to use this method?
20. Is there anything about my personality that could lead me to use this method incorrectly?
21. Am I at any risk of being exposed to HIV (the AIDS virus) or other sexually transmitted infections?

Total number of YES answers: _____

Most individuals will have a few "yes" answers. "Yes" answers mean that potential problems may lie in store. If you have more than a few "yes" responses, you may want to talk to your physician, counselor, partner, or friend. Talking it over can help you to decide whether to use this method, or how to use it so it will really be effective for you. In general, the more "yes" answers you have, the less likely you are to use this method consistently and correctly.

Source: R. A. Hatcher et al., *Contraceptive Technology, 1990–1992* (15th edition), p. 150, 1990, New York: Irvington Publishers. Reprinted by permission.

Unintended Pregnancy: The Options

The statistics on unintended pregnancies among adults are inconclusive and largely unavailable. However, it has been established that one in ten women aged 15–19 in the United States become pregnant each year, and that over 80 percent of those pregnancies are unintended (Hatcher et al., 1990). Some teenage women have dropped out of school prior to becoming pregnant, while many others drop out after becoming pregnant or having their babies. Many young mothers are poor even before they become pregnant. For others, however, pregnancy and young motherhood render them less able to compete in the job market (Hofferth, 1990).

Regardless of age or circumstances, an unintended pregnancy can create anguish and the necessity for careful decision-making.

125

It should not be forgotten that the fathers involved in unintended pregnancies often experience a great deal of conflict and psychological distress. They sometimes feel resentful that they have little or no part to play in deciding what to do about the pregnancy and yet can be held financially responsible for the baby. They may experience guilt and eventual distress if they have little access to their babies or if the woman chooses abortion. The problems and concerns of fathers in these cases have been largely ignored.

There are basically three alternatives from which to choose (see Table 5.2): keeping the baby, adoption, or termination of the pregnancy.

KEEPING THE BABY

This is a typical option for married couples or those in established relationships. For unmarried young people there may be a decision about whether or not to enter into marriage. Some teenaged parents allow their children to be cared for by other relatives until they have completed their educations or are otherwise more ready to assume parenting responsibility themselves.

In cases of unintended pregnancy, one of the first

TABLE 5.2

The Options for
Unintended Pregnancy

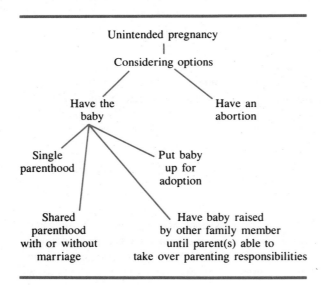

This chart reminds us that whenever an unintended pregnancy occurs, some decision must be made. There is no such thing as not making a decision. To not consider abortion as an option constitutes a decision to have the baby. The choices may not be comfortable or easy, but in one way or another they must be faced and made.

issues to be considered is if the mother can accept all of the emotional and physical implications of the pregnancy and birth process. Depending on his degree of involvement in the situation, the father's reactions and needs may also need to be considered with care. If other family members will in any way be involved in caring for the child, their feelings about the situation must be weighed. For any individual who is intending to keep a baby, there should be a clear commitment to and adequate preparations for effective prenatal care, the learning of appropriate parenting skills, and planning for the financial requirements of child rearing.

ADOPTION

Up until about 1970, the majority of young women who had unintended pregnancies placed their babies for adoption. Today the situation is very different in that only about 5 percent of mothers relinquish babies for adoption. Presently, agencies that handle adoptions are finding it difficult to provide newborn babies for the many childless couples who hope to adopt one. This reflects a generally negative attitude toward putting children up for adoption that is prevalent today. Many young women have learned to think of this option as "giving up your child," the connotations of which are mostly negative. In fact, adoption can represent a viable alternative, and in some cases, the mother is allowed to have contact with the child and its adoptive parents (Lindsay & Monserrat, 1988).

Most adoptions are handled through social agencies, but private arrangements involving physicians and/or lawyers are sometimes arranged. It is helpful to talk with adoptive parents and adults who were adopted as children, to get a realistic and complete perspective. The degree to which adopted children should be allowed to find or contact their birth parents, and vice versa, has been a matter of recent controversy. Nonetheless, adoption is a very real option, and often leads to positive outcomes (Boston Women's Health Collective, 1984).

Adoption represents a reasonable option for unintended pregnancies when the mother chooses to continue the pregnancy—or it is too late to do otherwise—and yet she does not feel ready for the responsibilities of parenthood. Mothers and fathers who choose to have their child adopted often feel that the child will have a chance for a better life with another family. As with any choice that is made in cases of unintended pregnancy, there are emotional consequences to be weighed. Yet there will usually be the option available of becoming pregnant again at a later time in life when circumstances lend themselves more fully to accepting the responsibility for parenting.

TERMINATION OF PREGNANCY

If a pregnancy terminates naturally, it is called a miscarriage or spontaneous abortion. Some women who experience an unintended pregnancy choose to seek ways of terminating it, also known as induced abortion. There are over a million and a half abortions performed in the United States each year, and about one-third of all pregnancies are terminated by induced abortion (Henshaw, 1990). There are many moral and political issues being debated both for and against abortion. An essential difference between "right-to-life" antiabortion forces and "pro-choice" supporters is in their belief concerning when human life begins. Abortion foes believe that life begins at the moment of conception, and that abortion is tantamount to murder since it involves the ending of another human life. The Roman Catholic church and several fundamentalist religious sects hold this as a basic teaching of their faiths. The issue of abortion incites strong emotional reactions, and small factions have even felt justified in burning or bombing abortion facilities. They are exerting political and social pressures to eventually declare abortion illegal again.

While most proponents for the availability of abortion feel that it should not be a decision made lightly, they see it as a necessity in an overpopulated world where many families cannot adequately care for the children they have. They tend not to hold to the idea that life begins at conception and instead feel that the potential quality of life for the unborn child and its parents is a primary issue. Pro-choice advocates insist that women should have the right to determine what happens to their own bodies, including whether or not to proceed with a pregnancy.

The issues are complex and have focused on the rights of pregnant women to choose for themselves versus the rights that an unborn fetus might be assumed to have. For the most part, the two sides of the struggle have found little common ground on which to compromise.

The Supreme Court has itself struggled with the continuing debate. The historic *Roe vs. Wade* decision in 1973 legalized a woman's right to obtain an abortion from a qualified physician. In 1989 the Supreme Court again ruled on the issue of abortion. While not overturning *Roe vs. Wade*, the new ruling *(Webster vs. Reproductive Health Services)* did uphold a restrictive Missouri abortion law, essentially giving states the right to decide on abortion as they see fit. It further restricted the use of taxpayer-supported facilities for abortions and denied public health employees the right to perform or assist at them. Finally, the ruling insisted that medical tests be performed on fetuses if they are thought to be 20 weeks old to determine their viability.

In the late 1980s the Department of Health and Human Services also restricted family planning agencies that receive federal Title X funding from being able to provide or even discuss abortion as an option in unintended pregnancies. While a U.S. Court of Appeals in Massachusetts struck down this "gag rule" as being unconstitutional (Swirling, 1990b), in 1991 the U.S. Supreme Court upheld the right of DHHS to restrict federally funded agencies from dealing with abortion issues in any way. Congress then attempted to override the restriction with legislation. The legislative and judicial fights over abortion are now largely concentrated in individual states. The country's toughest antiabortion legislation was passed in Utah in 1991. It bans all abortions except in cases of rape or incest, when the mother's life is endangered by the pregnancy, or when the fetus is known to suffer from serious birth defects. Opponents of the statute have argued that not only does such a law interefere with a woman's right to choose, but that it will lead to false reports of rape and incest and place a burden of subjective decision-making on medical professionals.

With the increase in restrictive legislation and vocal negative opinion, abortions are becoming increasingly difficult to obtain in the United States, even though they are still legal. This is particularly true for women who do not live in metropolitan areas. In rural areas, the number of abortion providers has decreased by over 50 percent since the late 1970s.

Illegal, risky, or self-induced abortions still occur often with dangerous—even fatal—results. During the 1980s the accessibility of abortion in hospital settings has decreased, presumably largely because of the pressure put on those institutions by antiabortion groups. The number of private physicians being trained to perform abortions, or willing to perform them, has also decreased (Henshaw, 1990). During the next few years the abortion controversy is likely to continue. Efforts will be made to limit and outlaw abortion procedures, while countering moves will attempt to ensure that the choice of abortion remains.

METHODS OF ABORTION

There are several medical procedures that can be employed to terminate pregnancy. The particular method chosen usually depends on the stage of pregnancy. An abortion can be legally performed by a doctor through the 24th week of pregnancy (measured

miscarriage: a natural termination of pregnancy.
spontaneous abortion: another term for miscarriage.
induced abortion: a termination of pregnancy by artificial means.

Case Study

MARIA: FACING AN UNINTENDED PREGNANCY

Beginning her junior year in college, Maria felt totally unprepared to deal with pregnancy. As the summer had ended, she tried to ignore the symptoms; stress, she told herself. But when she missed a second period and she was feeling tired and nauseated much of the time, Maria knew it was time to visit the student health clinic. A pregnancy test was done and confirmed that she was pregnant.

Maria told the nurse that she felt as though her whole world was falling apart. The nurse scheduled two appointments for Maria to return and talk about the options available to her. Her first reaction was to say that she had no choice; she would have to have an abortion. The nurse reminded her that having an abortion was indeed a choice and should be seen as such. She told Maria that any choice she made should be based on having accurate information and sorting through all of the implications for her future and her own feelings.

The next two days were filled with emotional turmoil for Maria. She confided her dilemma to two close friends and called her boyfriend at his college. He told her that he would make the trip to be with her for a few days. She also called her mother, worried about the reaction she would get. While upset, Maria's mother said that she would support whatever decision Maria made.

Maria ultimately did decide to terminate her pregnancy, and her boyfriend took her to the clinic for the abortion. The counselor who talked with her prior to the abortion suggested that she pursue follow-up counseling at her college to resolve any reactions she might have later.

A year after having her abortion, Maria wrote, "It seemed as though there was not any ideal solution for me. After weighing how I felt about the alternatives, I chose abortion. I still feel as though there was a lot of selfishness in that choice, but there would have been some selfishness in any choice I made. I think there has to be. Anyway, if I had to do it all over, I would still choose the abortion. I'll always have the experience in the back of my mind, and I'll wonder where other choices would have taken me. But it was the right choice for me."

from the first day of the last menstrual period). The earlier it is performed, the simpler the procedure and the lower the risks to the woman.

Vacuum Curettage   About 90 percent of abortions in the United States are performed within the first trimester, or first 12 weeks of pregnancy. The method most often used during this stage is vacuum curettage, sometimes called vacuum aspiration or the suction method. First, the cervical opening is dilated through the use of graduated metal dilators. Another more gentle approach to cervical dilation involves the earlier insertion of a cylinder made from a dried seaweed called laminaria. The laminaria insert slowly absorbs moisture from the cervix, and as it expands the cervical os opens wider. This procedure is more comfortable for the woman and carries less risk of abrasions to the uterus.

After the cervical opening is dilated, a thin plastic tube is inserted into the uterus and is connected to a suction pump. The uterine lining, along with fetal and placental tissue, is then suctioned out. This part of the procedure usually takes 10 to 15 minutes.

Dilation and Evacuation or Dilation and Curettage
Beyond the first trimester, the uterus has enlarged and its walls have as a result become thinner. The contents of the uterus cannot be as easily removed by suction. Therefore, vacuum curettage is no longer considered as safe and suitable for abortions in the second trimester of pregnancy. During the 13–16 week period, the usual method employed is dilation and evacuation (D & E). After cervical dilation, a suction tube is still

vacuum curettage: (kyur-a-TAZH): a method of induced abortion performed with a suction pump.

laminaria (lam-a-NER-ee-a): a dried seaweed sometimes used in dilating the cervical opening prior to vacuum curettage.

dilation and evacuation (D & E): a method of induced abortion in the second trimester of pregnancy; it combines suction with a scraping of the inner wall of the uterus.

used, but this procedure is followed by the scraping of the inner wall of the uterus with a metal curette to ensure that all fetal tissue is removed. This is a variation of dilation and curettage (D & C), which omits the initial vacuum aspiration of the uterus and is sometimes used to terminate pregnancy.

Procedures Used Later in Pregnancy For abortions later in pregnancy (16–24 weeks), procedures must usually be employed that render the fetus nonviable and induce its delivery through the vagina. These approaches are more physically uncomfortable and often more emotionally upsetting for the woman, since she experiences uterine contractions for several hours and then expels a lifeless fetus. The two most commonly used procedures at this stage of pregnancy are prostaglandin-induced or saline-induced abortions. Prostaglandins are injected directly into the amniotic sac through the abdominal wall, administered intravenously to the woman, or inserted into the vagina in suppository form. Prostaglandins are hormone-like chemicals that stimulate uterine contractions leading to delivery. Saline (salt) solution is injected into the amniotic fluid and has a similar effect. Some clinicians have also substituted a substance called urea for saline. Sometimes, various combinations of prostaglandins, saline, and urea are used to terminate later pregnancies (Hatcher et al., 1990).

USE OF FETAL TISSUE

An issue related to abortion has recently surfaced among the other controversies. It is the use of fetal tissue in research and medical treatment. In the late 1980s several researchers were transplanting tissues from aborted fetuses into humans in an attempt to cure certain diseases. These tissues are particularly valuable since they grow faster, are more adaptable to a variety of environments, and are less likely to be rejected by the recipient's immune system than tissues transplanted from other adults. Work has been done to investigate the value of fetal tissue transplants in treating Parkinson's disease, Alzheimer's disease, epilepsy, and a variety of neuromuscular disorders. The outcomes of the research have been encouraging.

As the result of pressure from antiabortion forces, the federal government imposed bans on federal funding for any research involving fetal tissues. Those in favor of permitting such research argued that as long as abortion is legal, it made no sense to destroy fetal tissue that could be put to use in ways that might save lives. Congress established subcommittees to study governmental policy on this issue, and in mid-1991 a panel in the House of Representatives voted to over-

turn the ban and permit the funding of fetal tissue research. This debate, along with other abortion-related controversies, will surely continue.

SAFETY OF ABORTION FOR THE WOMAN

All studies have indicated that legal medical abortions have fewer risks to the woman than carrying a pregnancy to full term and giving birth. While in both cases the risk of the woman's death is extremely low, the chance of a relatively healthy woman dying from a legal abortion in the United States is slightly more than one in 100,000 abortions. That compares to nearly 20 deaths per 100,000 pregnancies and births (Atrash et al., 1987).

First-trimester abortions are simplest and safest, and have few complications other than some excessive bleeding or subsequent infection that can be treated with antibiotics. If all of the fetal tissue is not removed, this can cause infection and require further scraping of the uterine wall, usually through a D & C procedure. Later abortions have somewhat higher risks of bleeding or infection since labor is induced, but the risk of fatal complications is still minimal. The surgeon general of the United States was asked in 1987 to review research data and report on the physical and psychological effects of abortion on women. In early 1989 he refused to release the report, saying that the evidence was inconclusive and most major studies were methodologically flawed. It was stated at the time that a 5-year comprehensive controlled study was needed to investigate the effects of abortion (Holden, 1989).

While having two or more abortions has been linked with a higher incidence of miscarriage in later pregnancies, abortion does not reduce fertility, the ability to conceive (Stubblefield et al., 1984).

PSYCHOLOGICAL CONSIDERATIONS

The psychological effects of abortion for a woman depend a great deal on her own beliefs and values and the degree to which she has made the decision with care. She needs to consider her own feelings and the

---

dilation and curettage (D & C): a method of induced abortion in the second trimester of pregnancy that involves a scraping of the uterine wall.

prostaglandin- or saline-induced abortion: used in the 16th–24th weeks of pregnancy, prostaglandins, salt solutions, or urea is injected into the amniotic sac, administered intravenously, or inserted into the vagina in suppository form, to induce contractions and fetal delivery.

reactions of others close to her. Few people see abortion as an easy option but view it instead as a necessary choice given their personal circumstances.

While serious emotional complications following abortion are quite rare, some women and their male partners experience a degree of depression, grieving, regret, or sense of loss. These reactions tend to be even more likely in repeat abortions. Support and counseling from friends, family members, or professionals following an abortion often help to lighten this distress, and it typically fades within several weeks after

the procedure. Counseling often helps in cases where the distress does not become alleviated in a reasonable time (Armsworth, 1991). A review of the wealth of data gathered in studies conducted for the American Psychological Association suggests that most women will not suffer lasting psychological trauma following an abortion. There does not seem to be any evidence to support the existence of a "postabortion syndrome" proposed by some antiabortion groups, and severe negative reactions following abortions are rare (Adler et al., 1990). ■

CHAPTER SUMMARY

1. Distribution of information about birth control was limited in the United States by the Comstock Laws, passed in the 1870s. Activist Margaret Sanger was influential in winning the rights of women to learn about and use contraception in the early part of this century, although laws prohibiting the sale of contraceptives existed until the 1960s.

2. In making decisions about contraceptive use, people are influenced by several factors. These include ethical/moral/religious beliefs; possible effects on the woman's health; and psychological and social factors.

3. Women who have guilt, anxiety, or other negative feelings about their sexuality do not tend to be reliable users of contraception.

4. Each person must sort through personal values and concerns about birth control, understand his or her personal reactions to sexual feelings and activities, and learn how to communicate with a partner effectively in order to prepare fully for contraceptive decision-making.

5. There is no "best" method of birth control for all individuals. Each couple must consider several factors in making a choice: age and amount of protection required, how long the method will be used, what might hinder the method's use, and cost.

6. Birth control methods have varying degrees of effectiveness. The theoretical failure rate assumes the method is being used correctly and without technical failure. The actual use failure rate is the more realistic rating of the method, considering human error, carelessness, and technical failure.

7. Even though most methods of contraception are designed for women, there are many ways for the responsibility to be shared by both partners: application of the method, open communication about birth control, and cost.

8. For summary information on methods of contraception, their rates of effectiveness, potential advantages, possible causes of failure, and possible negative side effects, see Table 5.1, pages 111–113.

9. For couples who choose abstinence from intercourse for birth control, there are many alternatives for sexual and nonsexual intimacy. While withdrawal is better than no method at all, it is not one of the more reliable forms of contraception.

10. Hormones that prevent ovulation and change the consistency of cervical mucus can be administered in the form of pills (combination estrogen and progestin at constant dosage, progestin-only mini-pill, or triphasic pill with varying dosages of estrogen and progestin), Norplant implants under the skin, or injections.

11. Spermicides kill sperm and are available without prescription as foams, jellies, and creams. They may also be purchased in vaginal suppository form or implanted in a sponge that covers the cervix.

12. Barrier methods of contraception prevent sperm from entering the uterus and are most effective when used with a spermicide. They include the diaphragm, cervical cap, and condom. Female condoms may be available soon.

13. The intrauterine device (IUD) is inserted into the uterus and apparently prevents implantation by the embryo. It has been implicated in a high risk of pelvic inflammatory disease (PID) and its use has been declining. The progestasert and Copper T 380 A are the only IUDs still on the market.

14. Natural family planning/fertility awareness allows the woman to become more aware of her fertile period during the menstrual cycle by charting the length of her cycles, basal body temperature, and consistency of cervical mucus.

15. Voluntary sterilization is the most common birth control method among married couples. Vasectomy involves cutting and tying the male vas deferens. Tubal ligation uses one of two methods to seal off the fallopian tubes. Studies are being done on more reversible forms of sterilization, such as the tubal plug.

16. New forms of contraception for males are being researched, including testosterone injections. They will probably interfere with sperm production or viability.

17. When an unintended pregnancy occurs, one of several options must be chosen: keeping the baby, placing it for adoption, or abortion.

18. Some pregnancies terminate naturally, and this is called miscarriage or spontaneous abortion.

19. Induced abortion has been legal in the United States since 1973, but a Supreme Court decision in 1989 placed several restrictions on it. There are still conflicts between right-to-life and pro-choice groups about whether abortion should be continued as a legal option.

20. First-trimester abortions are usually done by vacuum curettage. Later abortions may be done by dilation and evacuation (D & E) or dilation and curettage (D & C) or induced by injection of prostaglandins, saline, or urea.

21. The use of fetal tissue transplants in medical research has become part of the abortion controversy.

22. Abortion is statistically safer for the woman than pregnancy and giving birth. Some women experience a degree of guilt, loss, or other psychological reactions. The availability of supportive counseling before and after an abortion is important.

ANNOTATED READINGS

Boston Women's Health Collective (1984). *The new our bodies, ourselves.* New York: Simon & Schuster. A general and comprehensive book on women's health issues, this volume also provides a balanced presentation on methods of birth control. It is particularly useful in deciding which method to employ.

Bullough, V. L., & Bullough, B. (1990). *Contraception: A guide to birth control methods.* Buffalo: Prometheus Books. A comprehensive source book on reproduction, the history of birth control, and all methods of contraception currently available.

Daniels, P., & Weingarten, K. (1982). *Sooner or later: The timing of parenthood in adult lives.* New York: W. W. Norton. Helps the reader examine the most crucial issues relating to family planning, including one's degree of readiness for parenthood. With careers and material goods becoming increasingly important in couple's lives, this book focuses on how children can fit into the picture.

Everett, J., & Glanze, W. (1987). *The condom book: The essential guide for men and women.* Complete coverage of condoms as a birth control and disease-prevention device. The book includes a buyer's guide that lists condoms by trade name, and offers reactions from users.

Feldman, S. (1985). *Making up your mind about motherhood.* New York: Bantam Books. A sensible guide to decision-making about having children. It covers all of the major issues that need to be considered.

Goldstein, M., & Feldberg, M. (1982). *The vasectomy book: A complete guide to decision making.* Los Angeles: J. P. Tarcher (distributed by Houghton Mifflin). A book that can inform readers about vasectomy, while helping them sort through the issues involved in making a decision about voluntary male sterilization.

Hatcher, R. A., et al. (1990). *Contraceptive technology, 1990–1992,* (15th ed.) New York: Irvington Publishers. Updated every 2 years, it is the most comprehensive and reliable book on contraception available. Reasonably technical, but easy to use in finding information about specific methods.

Hatcher, R. A., et al. (1991). *Safely sexual.* New York: Irvington Press. Realistic advice on preventing unplanned pregnancy and transmission of diseases, written in clear, down-to-earth language.

Lindsay, J. W. (1988). *Pregnant too soon: Adoption is an option.* Buena Park, CA: Morning Glory Press. Surveys the many issues and options relating to adoption as a choice for unintended pregnancies. The book examines the different types of adoption, and the emotional issues in making the choice.

Mastroianni, L., et al. (1990). *Developing new contraceptives: Obstacles and opportunities.* Washington: National Academy Press. Provides an overview of contraceptive research and the political, financial, and legal issues involved in the development of new methods of birth control.

PART III

SEXUALITY, PERSONALITY, AND RELATIONSHIPS

Beyond its biological and reproductive aspects, human sexuality plays a crucial role in determining who we become and how we relate to others. One of the first ways in which its influence is felt is through our realization of our gender. At the moment of conception, a complex series of events is put into motion that will help determine our degree of "masculinity" and "femininity." Many questions still remain about the interactive effects of genetics, hormones, and social influences on the development of each individual's gender-identity/role, or sense of self as a man, woman, or some ambivalent position in between. Chapter 6 surveys all of these issues, and raises questions about the ways in which human females and males may be different or alike. The similarities between the sexes were emphasized during the 1970s and 1980s; but we are beginning to recognize again that there may be differences worth accepting and celebrating. These differences, however, have often led to political and personal oppression in the past, and as we consider the role of gender in human sexuality we must not ignore the social and political issues that are involved as well.

No one has been able to explain satisfactorily or thoroughly how we become the sexual people we become, and what role sexuality plays in the human personality. Chapter 7 focuses on the stages of human development and the unfolding of one's sexual nature as one makes the passages through these life stages. There are many theories of how we learn to be sexual from childhood, through adolescence, to old age. Each stage has its own particular hurdles to be faced. Adult sexuality often involves relating to another person intimately, and establishing long-term bonds such as marriage. Relating sexually within the context of lasting relationships carries its own set of complications and needs.

The complexities of sexuality within relationships become even greater when sexuality is not backed by effective means of communication. Experts agree that intimacy between people is based on the ability to communicate about a whole range of feelings and issues, including the hurtful and difficult ones. Chapter 8 looks at sex and loving, and how people need to learn the ground rules for communicating about them. There is no such thing as *not* communicating, because the avoidance of talking or other sharing represents a message in itself. The most important thing is the quality of the communication, and whether it fosters a more positive interchange and lessening of tension, or instead creates new roadblocks and stresses that drive people further apart. This chapter includes guidelines for improving patterns of communication.

CHAPTER SIX
GENDER-IDENTITY/ROLE AND SOCIETY

Our gender-identity/role—the sense of ourselves and our outward expressions as masculine or feminine—is determined by a complex interaction of genetic, physiological, and sociocultural factors. The normal pairing of sex chromosomes is XX for a female and XY for a male. The hormone testosterone promotes the development of male sex organs. Children are usually raised with traditional expectations of masculine or feminine behavior. Both women and men are beginning to rebel against what they consider restricting roles in their personal lives and relationships.

CHAPTER SEVEN
SEXUALITY THROUGH THE LIFE CYCLE

Our development as sexual beings continues throughout our lives. Psychoanalytic, conditioning, and social script are three theories attempting to describe this sexual development. Adolescents explore their sexuality through relationships with others and develop their sexual values. Adult sexuality involves establishing intimacy with others. The older person may remain sexually active depending on physical health and partner availability.

CHAPTER EIGHT
SEXUALITY, COMMUNICATION, AND RELATIONSHIPS

A healthy and lasting relationship requires open lines of communication. Only too often, couples assume that the best way to stay happy together is to avoid conflict. In fact, good communication means that there is an openness to dealing with hurtful and difficult issues as well as the joyful aspects of relationships. Building sexual intimacy, and keeping a sexual relationship fresh and dynamic, depend on effective communication as well. There are many myths about communication that can create misunderstandings and difficult feelings. Following some step-by-step approaches can keep relationships and sexual interactions on a satisfying and committed course.

CHAPTER SIX

GENDER-IDENTITY/ROLE

SEPARATING WOMEN AND MEN
Prenatal Factors
Factors of Infancy and Childhood
Factors at Puberty
Adult Gender-Identity/Role

EXPRESSING GENDER-IDENTITY/ROLE

MASCULINITY AND FEMININITY TODAY
Learning Sex Roles
Women Rebel—The Feminist Movement

Growing Up Female and Male
Men React
Gender Aware Therapy
Androgyny: Bridging the Gap?

**SELF-EVALUATION: MASCULINITY AND FEMININITY
IN YOUR LIFE**

CHAPTER SUMMARY

I now work in a small town as a secretary. Almost nobody in the town knows I was previously a male, and I'm just beginning to fit into my new, right life-style.

When I was little, I would look around at my mother, my father, my sister, and people that we knew, and I just sort of wondered how I would fit in because I certainly didn't feel like I was going to grow up like the men around me. I didn't even feel like I was going to grow up like the women around me. I felt like a whole different person, although if I had to fit into one role or the other, it would have definitely been female. None of my perceptions or understandings were anything like the way I was being taught they would have to be if I were to be male.

—Statement from a postsurgical male-to-female transsexual

GENDER-IDENTITY/ROLE AND SOCIETY

There are still many aspects of being female or male yet to be explored: How is our sex determined and what factors influence the development of male and female genitals before birth? What factors lead to our awareness of ourselves as girl or boy, feminine or masculine? What determines how we behave as men and women in the context of our society? These are some of the questions to be explored in this chapter.

For the most part, traditional theories of sexual development have emphasized either the genetic-physiological influences or the psychological-social influences—the old nature-versus-nurture controversy. The results of recent research suggest that our development as men and women is determined by a complex interaction of genetic, physiological, and environmental factors. Rather than viewing the development of masculine or feminine traits as either a biological phenomenon or the result of social influences, most scientists now agree that it is best understood as a combined biosocial process (Ehrhardt, 1987).

Gender-Identity/Role

All human beings have a persistent inner sense of themselves as female, male, or some ambivalent position between the two. People also outwardly demonstrate to others the degree that they are male, female, or ambivalent through what they say and do, often including sexual attractiveness and behavior. This combination of private, inner experience and public, outward expression is now collectively termed gender-identity/role (G-I/R), since they represent two sides of the same gender coin (Money, 1987).

The qualities that individuals use to assess and understand their own gender are partly physical (such as body shape and sex organs) and partly sociocultural (such as hair length, clothing, and accepted standards of masculine and feminine behavior in a particular

gender-identity/role (G-I/R): a person's inner experience and outward expression of maleness, femaleness, or some ambivalent position between the two.

135

society). Ambivalence in G-I/R can have physical or sociocultural roots, or both. On the physical level, for example, people are occasionally born with poorly defined sex organs, so that their anatomical identity as male or female is uncertain. A genetic male may be born with an incompletely developed penis and resemble a girl. A genetic female may have an enlarged clitoris at birth and be mistaken for a boy. Either case could lead to confusion about physical identity regarding gender. A male who gains sexual pleasure from dressing in women's clothing—a transvestite—would be exhibiting ambivalence of a sociocultural type, since he would not be demonstrating behavior considered socially appropriate for men in our culture.

Separating Women and Men

The process of defining gender-identity/role begins at the moment of conception when a sperm enters an ovum. At that moment a program is set into motion that will lead eventually to the establishment of an adult gender identity. The factors that can exert influences along the way are incredibly varied and complex. These factors have been well documented by John Money (1977a, 1987); Money and Anke Ehrhardt (1972); and Tom Mazur and Money (1980). The model that follows is largely based on their work.

It is useful to group determinants of gender identity into three categories: prenatal factors, factors of infancy and childhood, and factors at puberty.

1. Prenatal Factors   Before an infant is born, a variety of genetic, hormonal, and developmental factors interact with one another to set the stage for later identification as female or male. Even before a baby is seen, much of the groundwork for her or his gender identity has been established.

2. Factors of Infancy and Childhood   As soon as a baby is born, its sex is assigned by the outward appearance of its genitals. While that may seem to be a simple task, there are sometimes anomalies of fetal development that lead to the incorrect assignment of a baby's sex. In any case, once anatomical sex has been established, the infant is reared as a girl or a boy. Eventually the child begins to develop distinct impressions and perceptions of her or his own body and sex organs. All of these factors, in conjunction with the structure and function of the brain, determine the "core" gender-identity/role of the child.

3. Factors at Puberty   Every day the child continues to receive confirmation of his or her G-I/R from other people. At puberty new hormonal changes occur in the body that lead to further growth of the genitals and the appearance of secondary sex characteristics. There is also an increase in sexual interests around the time of puberty. These developments—if they proceed in the usual way—further confirm the individual's G-I/R in the move toward adulthood. If the pubertal changes do not occur as expected—if the gender identity program has some built-in errors—and the child's G-I/R is not confirmed, the result is often confusion and emotional crisis.

Now we can take a closer look at some of the details in each of these categories.

PRENATAL FACTORS

Chromosomes   The earliest factor that determines a human being's sex and initiates the program for determining gender identity is the combining of chromosomes at conception. Typically, human gametes—the ovum (egg) and sperm—each contain 23 chromosomes, one of which is a sex chromosome. The sex chromosome carried by the sperm may either be an X chromosome or a Y chromosome. The egg contains

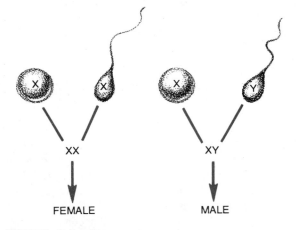

FIGURE 6.1 Chromosomes

Chromosomes are the genetic material in the nucleus of every cell. The sex of the offspring is determined at fertilization by the type of chromosome in the sperm. All egg cells and half the sperm cells contain an X sex chromosome, while the remaining sperm have Y sex chromosomes. A zygote with two X chromosomes will become a female and a zygote with one X and one Y will become a male.

combining of chromosomes: occurs when a sperm unites with an egg, normally joining 23 pairs of chromosomes to establish the genetic "blueprint" for a new individual. The sex chromosomes establish its sex: XX for female and XY for male.

TABLE 6.1

Human Sex Chromosome Anomalies

Abnormal Chromosome Combination	Medical Name	Characteristics of Individual
XXY	Klinefelter's Syndrome	Male genitals, but with female secondary sex characteristics. Scrotum and testes are small; enlarged breasts. Sometimes timid and withdrawn; some level of mental retardation; sterile.
XO (no Y present; only one X)	Turner's Syndrome	Female external genitals; ovaries lacking; lack of menstruation, pubic hair, and breast development. Stunted growth, with several body abnormalities. Sense of direction and spatial relationships may be abnormal; may be mentally retarded.
XO/XY	Mixed Gonadal Dysgenesis	May have female or male genitals, or a combination of the two. Usually no other bodily abnormalities, except may not mature sexually without treatment.
XYY	XYY Syndrome	Appearance of normal male. Tend to be large in stature and have large male genital structure. May show some lack of control over impulsive behaviors. Usually normal to low normal intelligence.
XXX	Triple-X Female	Appearance of normal female. Usually infertile. Occasional mental deficiency.
XX/XY	May be a true hermaphrodite	Variable. Have some combination of both ovarian and testicular tissues. Usually have uterus. External genitals may be distinctly masculine or feminine, or may be an ambiguous combination of both. At puberty, most experience breast enlargement, and the majority menstruate.

only an X chromosome. If an X-bearing sperm fertilizes an egg, the resulting XX combination of sex chromosomes establishes a genetic program to produce a female. If the egg is fertilized by a Y-bearing sperm, the resultant XY combination is destined to become a male. If the genetic mechanisms function normally, the program is well under way toward producing the appropriate female or male child (see Fig. 6.1). In 1991, the single gene that triggers the development of male organs was pinpointed on the Y chromosome. It has been labeled SRY, for sex-determining region of Y, because it is the presence or absence of this section, or gene, of the Y chromosome that determines whether testes or ovaries will develop in the fetus (Cherfas, 1991).

However, things can go wrong with chromosomes, especially during the process that forms the sperm and eggs. For example, there are some "sex-reversed" individuals who are XX males or XY females. This has led researchers to speculate that occasionally the SRY can be attached to an X chromosome or be missing from a Y chromosome. The actual mechanisms by which this gene operates to develop male characteristics are not yet understood (Roberts, 1988). Sometimes a fertilized egg has only one X chromosome. This will develop into a female body, but the ovaries will not develop normally and the adult woman will be unable to produce children (Turner's syndrome). A fertilized egg left with only a Y sex chromosome and no X apparently cannot survive. No human being has ever been found with only a Y sex chromosome. Other erroneous sex chromosome combinations in humans are XXX (triple-X syndrome), XXY (Klinefelter's syndrome), and XYY. Individuals born with these conditions are usually afflicted with conditions such as abnormal development of the sex organs, unusual body shape, behavioral disorders, or mental and emotional retardation as summarized in Table 6.1.

Fetal Gonads or Sex Glands Up until the 8th week of development, it is impossible to determine the sex of a human embryo by the appearance of external genitalia (sex organs). Yet the genetic plan contained within

137

the sex chromosomes carries the necessary information to produce sex glands and genital organs. At first a pair of tiny, sexless gonads form internally, having the potential of becoming testes or ovaries. There are also two pairs of duct systems present in the embryo: the Müllerian ducts that represent potential female reproductive organs and Wolffian ducts that represent potential male reproductive structures. Research has shown that it is the presence or absence of the Y chromosome that determines whether the gonads differentiate into testes or ovaries. As long as at least one Y and one X chromosome are present, testes are produced. Any combination of sex chromosomes lacking a Y produces ovaries. If testes are to be formed from the gonad, they appear during the 6th week of development. Ovaries develop at a later stage, but appear by the 12th week. Variations may occur in these patterns, but they are rare (see Fig. 6.2).

Fetal Hormones   Fetal gonads that are programmed by the chromosomes to produce a female will automatically develop into ovaries. However, if the gonads are programmed to produce a male, another process, controlled by the SRY normally carried on the Y chromosome, is required. First, a substance called H-Y antigen begins the transformation of the fetal gonads into testes (Haseltine & Ohno, 1981). When testes are produced they also begin secreting two hormones. Testosterone promotes development of the Wolffian ducts into internal male sexual and reproductive structures, and Müllerian Inhibiting Substance, as the name implies, suppresses the development of the Müllerian ducts into the female organs. The fact that for a male to be produced, substances must be added to the embryo in the form of these hormones, has sometimes been termed the "Adam Principle."

Development of female sex and reproductive organs does not depend on the production of any hormones, which conversely is termed the "Eve Principle." If the SRY gene is not present, so that male hormones are not produced, the fetal gonads become ovaries and the Müllerian ducts develop into the uterus, fallopian tubes, and part of the vagina. Without testosterone to stimulate their development, the Wolffian ducts simply disintegrate.

There are a number of rare problems that can arise at these stages of sexual differentiation. For example, if a male (XY) fetus' new testes produce testosterone, but lack Müllerian Inhibiting Substance, the external male sex organs may develop normally, but the boy will also be born with a uterus and fallopian tubes as well as internal male organs. The term *hermaphrodite* describes the rare individual who is born with both testicular and ovarian tissue. In another condition, the chromosomal male fetus lacks

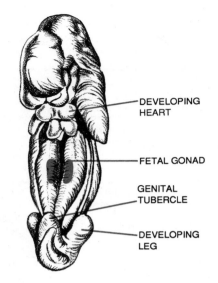

DEVELOPING HEART

FETAL GONAD

GENITAL TUBERCLE

DEVELOPING LEG

FIGURE 6.2   Fetal Gonads in a Developing Fetus

During the first weeks of development male and female embryos are anatomically identical. Two primitive gonads form during the 5th and 6th weeks of pregnancy. An H-Y antigen is necessary if the gonads are to develop into testes. Without H-Y antigen the gonads develop into ovaries.

an enzyme necessary for normal synthesis of male hormones. Affected babies usually die, but those who live have a very small penis and may at birth be mistakenly identified as females. If testosterone or related androgenic hormones somehow enter the bloodstream of a developing female (XX) fetus—usually because of some medical condition such as a testosterone-producing tumor in the pregnant mother—the baby girl is born either with an enlarged clitoris or a normal-appearing penis and empty scrotum. These and related conditions can lead to the erroneous assignment of the girl as a male at birth.

Development of Male or Female Genitals   As described in the preceding section on the fetal gonad, until the 8th week of fetal life, the external genitals are indistinguishable as male or female. Microscopic ex-

Müllerian ducts (myul-EAR-ee-an): embryonic structures that develop into female sexual and reproductive organs unless inhibited by male hormones.
Wolffian ducts (WOOL-fee-an): embryonic structures that develop into male sexual and reproductive organs if male hormones are present.
H-Y antigen: a biochemical produced in an embryo when the Y chromosome is present; it causes fetal gonads to develop into testes.
Müllerian Inhibiting Substance: hormone produced by fetal testes that prevents further development of female structures from the Müllerian ducts.

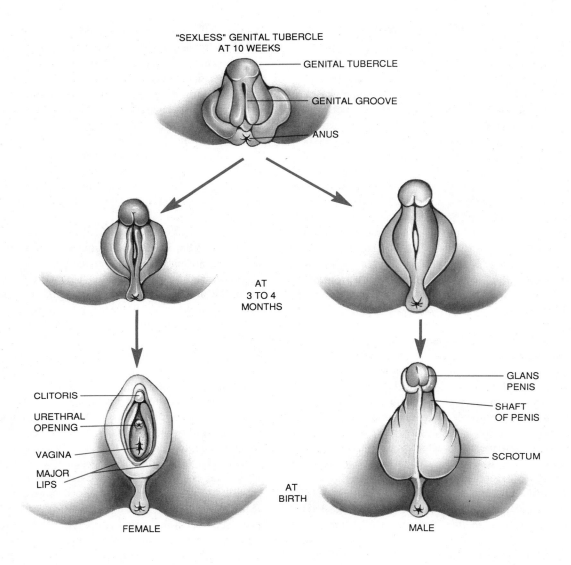

"SEXLESS" GENITAL TUBERCLE
AT 10 WEEKS

GENITAL TUBERCLE

GENITAL GROOVE

ANUS

AT
3 TO 4
MONTHS

AT
BIRTH

CLITORIS

URETHRAL
OPENING

VAGINA

MAJOR
LIPS

FEMALE

GLANS
PENIS

SHAFT
OF PENIS

SCROTUM

MALE

FIGURE 6.3   Differentiation of Male and Female Genitals

From the 10th week of fetal development, sexual differentiation occurs at three different levels—internal sex organs, external sex structures, and the brain. The development of the male is largely controlled by the hormone testosterone. Both the ovaries and the testes first develop in the abdomen; later the ovaries move into the pelvis and the testes descend into the scrotum.

amination of fetal tissue in the gonad could help predict what sex the fetus will become, but genitals are not yet developed enough to permit identification. There is a tiny, sexless genital tubercle on the lower part of the fetus. By the 12th week of development, the male or female sex organs begin to be distinguishable. Gradually the penis and scrotum, or clitoris and vulval lips, become distinct and grow as the fetus develops (see Fig. 6.3). Chromosomal and hormonal abnormalities can cause the external genitals and their inner ducts to develop abnormally, as we have already seen in the section on fetal hormones.

Fetal Hormones and the Brain   One of the most exciting newer advances in animal sex research is the discovery that fetal hormones not only control the development of the fetus' sex organs, but may also affect development of parts of the brain and pituitary gland. Differences have been found in the number and location of nerve synapses in the hypothalamuses of male and female brains. There is speculation that such differences could lead to different behavior patterns later in life (Rubin, Reinisch, & Haskett, 1981). In many lower mammals, predictably different behavior is observed in the male and female of the species.

It was originally assumed that hormones had little to do with the determination of differing behavior in the sexes. The work of William Young (1961) and other researchers has led to the hypothesis that the presence of testosterone in the fetus of many mammals affects the structures and pathways of the brain in such a way as to produce masculine behavior in the adult mammal. If testosterone is not present, the adult behavior becomes feminine. This phenomenon has been identified in monkeys, for example. In many mammals there is apparently a critical period at some point before or after birth when the presence of male hormones has a definite "masculinizing" effect on the development of the brain, resulting in later behaviors that are limited to males of the species (Ehrhardt, 1977). However, since the human brain is structurally different from, and more highly developed than, animal brains, it is risky to extrapolate the findings of animal research to human beings.

Fetally Androgenized Females   Very little has yet been done to determine the effects of fetal hormones on the human brain. Researcher John Money (1987) believes that there are also critical periods in human development during which the interaction of biological (for example, hormonal) and environmental (for example, learning behavior from others) factors may establish some permanent characteristics of the individual. It is believed that human feminine and masculine behavior is determined more by learning during childhood than by prenatal hormonal influences on the brain. A medical mistake made in the 1950s has led to some interesting findings that may well support the idea of biological and environmental factors interacting at a critical period in development. Several pregnant women were given hormones to prevent miscarriages. Later it was discovered that the hormones had a masculinizing effect on the developing fetuses. This resulted in the birth of several *fetally androgenized females* with enlarged clitorises and a few genetic females having a penis.

During 1965–67, Ehrhardt and Money (1967) made a detailed study of 10 of these girls, all of whom had received early corrective surgery and had been raised as girls. They ranged in age from 4 to 16 years, and each was matched with a girl who had normal fetal development as a control. The startling result of their survey was that 9 of the 10 girls considered themselves to be tomboys and that they showed significantly more traditional boyish traits than the control group. These traits included a high level of energy expenditure during play; wearing practical clothing; lack of interest in dolls and infants; and a preference for a future career outside the home rather than homemaking. There were no indications of homosexual tendencies.

Although the study was a limited one, Ehrhardt and Money felt that the most likely explanation was that the male hormones present during these girls' fetal development had created a masculinizing effect on their brains, predisposing them to boyish behavior in later life. It has also been argued, however, that the congenital condition of these children may well have produced concern and ambiguity on the part of their parents. Consequently, the parents may have transmitted some of these feelings to the children, and this may have created the behavioral variations that Ehrhardt and Money observed (Ramey, 1973).

Androgen Insensitivity Syndrome   A similar study has been made of 10 genetic males (XY) who were born with normal-appearing female genitals and were raised as girls. Their anatomical condition resulted from the inability of their body cells to respond normally to the testosterone their testes were secreting. This is called *androgen insensitivity syndrome*. Their bodies failed to develop male sex organs, and internal female structures developed incompletely. It has been speculated that they may also have lacked a process to masculinize brain pathways. These "girls" and "women" exhibited traditional feminine traits. Most showed a preference for being homemakers rather than having a career, and had played with dolls in their younger years. All 10 had dreamed of raising a family even though they were resigned to their inability to bear children. All 10 were heterosexual in their adult sexual preferences, desiring male sexual partners (Masica, Money, & Ehrhardt, 1971). The researchers proposed that in this case, absence of male hormones during these genetic males' fetal development not only led to feminization of their genitals, but also prevented any masculinization of their brains. This may have produced conditions that led to distinctly feminine behavior in later life. Of course, it could also be argued that the socialization process of being raised as girls developed these traditionally "feminine" characteristics.

DHT-Deficiency Syndrome   There is another disorder that has provided interesting insights into the roles of hormones and socialization in the development of gender-identity/role. It is a genetic problem in which genetic males lack an enzyme, dihydrotestosterone (DHT), which is necessary for the normal development of external male sex organs. While his internal organs are normal, a boy with *DHT-deficiency syndrome* is born with undescended testes and an underdeveloped penis that may easily be mistaken for a clitoris. Sometimes, there is also a partially formed vagina, and the scrotum may be folded in such a way that it resembles labia. Researchers identified 18 genetic males in the Dominican Republic who had been misassigned as females at birth, and then had been raised as girls (Imperato-McGinley et al., 1982).

At puberty, these children suddenly began to develop male secondary sex characteristics including increase in muscle mass, deepening of the voice, and growth of the penis. They did not develop any breasts or other female characteristics. These girls-becoming-boys were subjected to a great deal of ridicule and name-calling in their communities. Sixteen of them eventually adopted male gender patterns and seemed to be sexually interested in women. It has been hypothesized that since these boys apparently had testosterone secreted by their fetal gonads during prenatal life, and only the development of their external genitals had been affected by the disorder, it was easier for them to make the transition to a masculine gender-identity/role. In other words, whatever masculinizing effects fetal testosterone might have on brain pathways would still have taken place. Others have questioned that conclusion, suggesting instead that social pressures may well have led to the more culturally acceptable choice of behaving as men. There was a similar case of inherited DHT-deficiency syndrome among five males in New Guinea. They, too, were raised as girls until pubertal changes masculinized them, and they began living as men. Since they lived in a male-dominant society, it meant an increase in social status to be identified as men instead of women (Herdt & Davidson, 1988).

The effects of fetal hormones on the human brain are still mostly a mystery. There is no doubt that learning after birth is a primary factor in determining masculine or feminine behavior and that society largely determines what is thought to be appropriate behavior for girls and boys (Ehrhardt, 1987). What remains to be shown is how much prenatal chromosomal and hormonal influences may predispose an infant to a particular type of behavior and which behaviors tend to be innately a part of maleness or femaleness. Recent attention has focused on the significance of the hypothalamus, pituitary gland, and gonads and how they interact during various stages of development. There has been some suggestion that differences in this neuroendocrine system may even influence human sexual orientation (Gladue, Green, & Hellman, 1984).

Except for reproductive behavior, there are no behaviors that are absolutely either male or female. Instead it may be that although all behaviors are found in some proportion in all humans, the threshold for eliciting a particular behavior may tend to be lower in either females or males. This would mean that a combination of prenatal hormonal influences and postnatal factors might tend to elicit the behavior in a

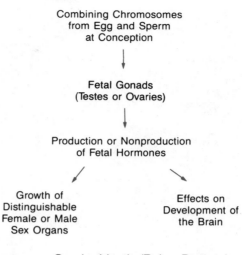

FIGURE 6.4 Gender-Identity/Role—Prenatal Factors

This is a portion of a larger figure (Figure 6.9, p. 146) detailing the factors in the development of adult gender-identity/role. Here we see the prenatal biological factors involved in determining male and female sex organs.

higher proportion of one sex than the other. According to such a hypothesis, the threshold for eliciting aggression, for example, might be lower for males than for females. It has also been proposed, however, that biological theories concerning differences in behavior between women and men are constructed on research studies that are far from objective or well controlled. It has been claimed that social and political values have in fact colored the work behind these theories and led to the development of many gender myths (Fausto-Sterling, 1985).

It can be seen that prenatal factors set the stage for the development of later gender-identity/role. The relationship of those factors is summarized in Figure 6.4. Now we can consider social and environmental factors in determining how humans become mature women or men.

FACTORS OF INFANCY AND CHILDHOOD

Sex Assignment at Birth Usually there is no question about a baby's sex when it is born. A quick glance at the genitals determines whether the child is classified as a female or male. The earlier sections of this chapter have demonstrated, however, that unusual combinations of chromosomes or the presence of inappropriate hormones can cause ambiguous development of the sex organs. For this reason some babies have been mistakenly assigned the wrong sex. Sometimes

FIGURE 6.5 Gender Characteristics

While some effort has been made in recent years to change society's stereotypical view of gender roles, Western culture still tends to reinforce in children the traditional differences between boys and girls.

the mistake is noticed very soon and corrected, but other times the error is not discovered until puberty when the secondary sex characteristics begin to develop. Regardless of the accuracy of the assignment, it is clear that male infants are treated differently than female infants, and that this difference plays an important part in the development of G-I/R. As soon as the physician announces "It's a girl!" or "It's a boy!" the social mechanism that will help shape the individual's adult gender identity has been set into motion.

Rearing a Child as Girl or Boy Girls and boys are treated differently as they are growing up. Parents and others in Western society react differently to boys and to girls (Tavris & Wade, 1984). For example, immediately after sex assignment, there may be the distinctive use of pink or blue colors, the choosing of an appropriately sexed name, and reference to the child as "he" or "she." Even as babies, girls tend to be treated more gently and with greater protectiveness, while

boys are treated more roughly and encouraged to be more independent. As the child grows older, further characteristics considered appropriate for girls or boys are built in by the manner in which she or he is treated. In the United States some people have been questioning the traditional standards of masculinity and femininity, believing them to be inhibiting to an individual's personal development. This is discussed later in this chapter. What effects this trend may have on the G-I/R of future generations—or even whether the traditional standards can be rejected on a widespread basis—remain to be seen.

The Child's Own Body Image Before long, as the child's self-awareness increases, he or she begins to respond to the influences of other people and has a distinct self-concept that includes a sense of being a girl or a boy. The child gradually becomes aware of its male or female sex organs and identifies them as part of her or his sexual nature.

All of these factors (summarized in Fig. 6.6) lead to the evolution of a child's core gender-identity/role. In fact, that gender identity becomes established so early that—with few exceptions—any attempt at sex reassignment (as in the case of a child erroneously

core gender-identity/role: a child's early sense and expression of its maleness, femaleness, or ambivalence, established prior to puberty.

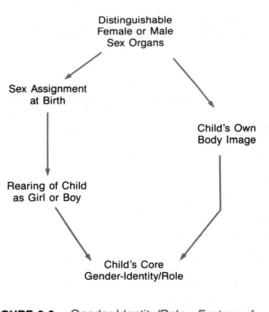

FIGURE 6.6 Gender-Identity/Role—Factors of Infancy and Childhood

This portion of the larger figure (Figure 6.9, p. 146) details the environmental and cultural factors that influence the child's development of his or her gender-identity/role.

Case Study

BILLY: A GENETIC FEMALE MISASSIGNED AT BIRTH AS A BOY

When Billy was born there was no question about his being male. He had a penis and scrotum. His father died when he was quite young, and his mother—with four other children to raise—had only a small income from public assistance. The children received little attention, and Billy had never required medical attention after the age of 2, except for routine inoculations at public health clinics.

At age 11, a school physician examined Billy as part of a routine physical examination and discovered some inconsistencies. The boy's breasts were beginning to enlarge, the penis had not grown much, and what had originally been thought to be a scrotum now appeared to be more like the major lips of the vulva. Upon gentle questioning, Billy told the doctor that urine came out of the underside of his penis and that he had noticed a small amount of bleeding a few times from beneath his penis. Arrangements were made for Billy to see a specialist in endocrine disorders. Upon thorough examination it was confirmed that Billy was indeed a genetic female whose clitoris had enlarged to the extent that it resembled a penis. Menstruation had already begun. A complete female reproductive

system was present internally: vagina, uterus, fallopian tubes, and ovaries.

Although it was now clear that Billy was actually a girl, his gender identity was that of a boy. He thought of himself as a male, talked of being a father someday, and had what were considered boyish traits and interests. He had romantic and sexual attractions to girls. The situation was carefully explained to Billy and his mother, both of whom were shocked and upset. There was no doubt as to how the case was to be handled, however. Everyone agreed—including Billy—that he should be made into a boy as much as possible. His female organs were removed, and some cosmetic surgery was performed to make the penis more prominent and functional. A false scrotum was created and prosthetic "testes" were inserted. Treatment with male hormones was begun to produce the secondary sex characteristics of a male.

Although the period of adjustment was a painful one, Billy now feels reasonably comfortable with himself, and his male identity. He knows he will never have children of his own, but he still hopes to marry and adopt children.

assigned at birth) can be very difficult psychologically beyond the age of 18 or 20 months. So, in childhood, gender identity is for the most part well established. The changes at puberty constitute the next major advance.

FACTORS AT PUBERTY

There is a good deal of evidence to support the contention that even young children have romantic, sensual, and sexual feelings, although they may be vague in some youngsters (see chapter 7, "Sexuality Through the Life Cycle"). As stated above, the individual's core G-I/R is established during childhood. Puberty is the time when the gonads (testes or ovaries) begin producing large amounts of hormones, causing G-I/R to declare itself—both in bodily changes and in deepened sexual feelings.

Hormones at Puberty Following their secreting activities during fetal life, the testes largely cease their production of testosterone just before or just after birth. In both males and females, the onset of puberty is characterized by marked increases in various hormonal secretions. Pubertal development involves two distinct processes. The first stage is *adrenarche,* or the secretion of androgenic hormones by the adrenal glands. This usually happens between the ages of 6 and 8. The exact role of this stage is uncertain, and the only identifiable physical result is some early growth of a small amount of pubic hair. Adrenarche may well set the stage for the more profound stage of puberty, characterized by *gonadarche,* occurring between the ages of 9 and 13. There is an increase in gonadotropin hormone from the pituitary gland, which stimulates the gonads (testes or ovaries) to secrete sex hormones (Nottlemann et al., 1990). It is these hormones that result in the development of secondary sex characteris-

143

Case Study

CHRISTOPHER: DELAYED PUBERTY LEADS TO SEXUAL WORRIES AND CONFUSION

Christopher was an 18-year-old college freshman who sought counseling for sexual problems. He reported that he was embarrassed by the small size of his penis and worried by what he called impotence. On further questioning it became clear that he was not impotent, but that when he experienced orgasm during masturbation or intercourse, there was no ejaculation of semen. This signaled that the problem might be an organic one.

Although Chris was reasonably tall, he looked more like a 14- or 15-year-old than his actual age. His voice had not deepened and he reported no appreciable growth of pubic, facial, or body hair. He described very little development of the scrotum and penis. He had been very worried about his lack of physical maturity, and his girlfriend—with whom he regularly had sexual intercourse—often criticized the size of his penis. He was gradually becoming more nervous and depressed as he increasingly doubted his masculinity. He avoided the shower room in physical education classes and never allowed himself to be nude in front of other men. His parents had never seemed to notice anything unusual about his growth patterns, nor had anyone else.

Since there was an obvious physical problem, Chris was referred to a physician for further examination. The doctor confirmed that he had not matured normally and referred Chris to an endocrinologist for a full diagnosis. All of these developments created mixed feelings for Chris. He was relieved that he was finally working on the problem, but he was also frightened by the fact that something was wrong with his body.

Eventually a pituitary gland disorder was diagnosed and hormonal treatment was begun. Chris was resentful that other physicians who had examined him during his lifetime had never noticed any abnormalities and that other adults had never thought his lack of development unusual. He continued in counseling as he sorted through his many conflicting feelings about his body and sexuality.

tics. The renewed secretion of testosterone and dihydrotestosterone from the testes masculinizes boys' bodies, and the ovaries begin their secretion of estrogens that feminize girls' bodies (Hopwood, 1990). The hormones of puberty probably also begin to exert influences on personality development, all of which are significant in the clearer delineation of G-I/R.

Physical Changes During Puberty and Adolescence

After the important differentiation of male or female genitals in the fetus, there is relatively little further physical differentiation between the sexes until puberty. Except for their genitals, the bodies of young girls and boys are quite similar. The pubertal hormones begin to generate the distinct physical characteristics of a man or a woman. Preliminary research has indicated that the hormonal influences of puberty may exert a clear effect on personalities, including some tendencies toward differences in females and males (Udry, 1990).

In boys the onset of puberty is typically around the age of 13. The penis begins to enlarge, pubic hair starts to grow, and the growth spurt in height is initiated. The testes and scrotum have usually begun to enlarge about a year earlier. Eventually the voice becomes lower as the larynx grows, ejaculation of semen occurs, and pubic and body hair spread to some degree. The appearance of a moustache and beard usually occurs 3 to 5 years later.

In girls puberty typically begins around the age of 11 or 12. The first signs are usually the budding of the breasts, the growth of pubic hair, and the beginning of growth spurts. The first menstruation generally does not occur until after these initial signs have appeared. For several years many books have discussed a purported decrease in the age of first menstruation over the past 150 years. It has now been demonstrated that this is a myth, based on misinterpretation of historical data. In fact girls experience menarche, or first menstruation, today at about the same ages they did in the mid-nineteenth century (Bullough, 1981).

Beginning at puberty, the sex glands of girls and boys actually produce both female and male hormones. However, in the normal male, the male sex hormones

FIGURE 6.7 Sex Drive in Adolescents

Adolescents experience the sex drive in different degrees depending on physical as well as emotional factors. Their families, religious background, peers, and the media all influence how adolescents learn to deal with love and the sex drive. This young couple enjoys an affectionate hug.

are in higher concentration, and their influences override those of the female sex hormones. This is reversed in the normal female. Things can go wrong with these hormone balances during puberty and adolescence, producing conditions such as slight breast enlargement in males (gynecomastia) or deepened voice and unusually enlarged clitoris in the female. The onset of hormonal puberty can sometimes be either premature or delayed. Any of these conditions can shake the

stability of a young person's gender identity and lead to confusion and unhappiness.

Changes in Sexual Drive and Behavior at Puberty
Of particular significance during puberty and adolescence is an increase in interest in sexual behavior. One of the important ways in which gender-identity/role is confirmed during this period is through imagery and fantasy. Boys and girls begin to imagine sexual acts and fantasize about desirable romantic or sexual partners. Adolescents are sometimes upset to find themselves imagining or dreaming about homosexual encounters, sadistic behavior, being a prostitute, or other behaviors they may have learned to consider "abnormal" or inconsistent with their assumed sexual orientation. Yet all of these developments may signal some of the minor alterations that will be made in the achievement of an adult gender-identity/role.

There is great variation in the strength of sexual interest that develops during adolescence. Some youngsters experience frequent fantasies about sex and a strong drive that demands to be put into action. Other adolescents display little interest in sex. Either degree of strength may be subject to change in later life. The factors that determine strength of sex drive are not known. The levels of sex hormones in the blood may exert some effect, but research into that question is incomplete.

The amount of experience with sex and love gained during adolescence also varies a great deal among different individuals (see chapter 7). It is affected by factors such as social class, degree of interest in sex, peer group attitudes, religious background, parental influences, exposure to the media, and so on.

The new factors of puberty interact to confirm the core gender-identity/role begun in childhood (see Fig. 6.8). By this time in an individual's psychosexual

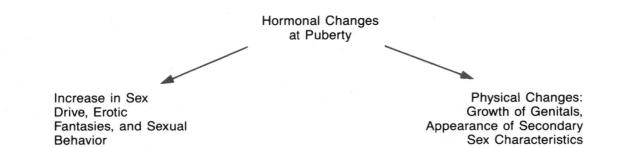

FIGURE 6.8 Gender-Identity/Role—Factors at Puberty

This portion of Figure 6.9 (overleaf) details the elements that confirm gender-identity/role in the adolescent. The increase in hormone production produces mature male and female physical characteristics as well as heightened interest in sexual fantasies and sexual behavior.

development, gender identity is firmly established. There may be a few alterations as time goes on, but the fundamental patterns are apparently unalterable.

ADULT GENDER-IDENTITY/ROLE

Generally, adult G-I/R becomes distinguishable as mostly masculine for males, and mostly feminine for females. It is probably reasonable to view gender identity on a continuum between the two extremes of "totally masculine" and "totally feminine." There may be elements of the masculine and elements of the feminine in all of us, even though our predominant identity leans toward one or the other. It should also be understood that many of what are considered to be appropriate masculine and feminine traits are determined by society and culture. There are certain physiological male-female characteristics or functions that cannot be changed on any large scale by culture: females menstruate, bear children, and produce milk from their mammary glands, while males do not. The differences in sex organs, and their roles in reproduction, and—to a lesser degree—differences in secondary sex characteristics are also easily distinguishable. Beyond these basics, there is very little information on any other inborn characteristics that may be identified

as distinctly female or male. At this point we can only present the rough outline of sequences involved in the establishment of G-I/R, from conception to adulthood. An overall summary is presented in Figure 6.9.

Expressing Gender-Identity/Role

As mentioned earlier, there seems to be a continuum of femininity and masculinity, just as there is for most parts of our sexual individuality (see chapter 9, "Sexual Individuality and Sexual Values"). We sort through the standards and scripts for behavior that our society has identified as "feminine" or "masculine," struggling to live up to the expectations of others while feeling comfortable with ourselves. The expressions of masculinity and femininity come in clothing styles, ways of walking and talking, mannerisms, hobbies, and all sorts of behaviors. Figure 6.10 suggests a way of visualizing this continuum.

We expect males to fall on the "masculine" side of the continuum and females to fall on the "feminine" side. We also expect one's sexual orientation and behaviors to be governed by one's place on the continuum. Even a cursory examination of human gender-identity/role and sexuality shows that such assumptions

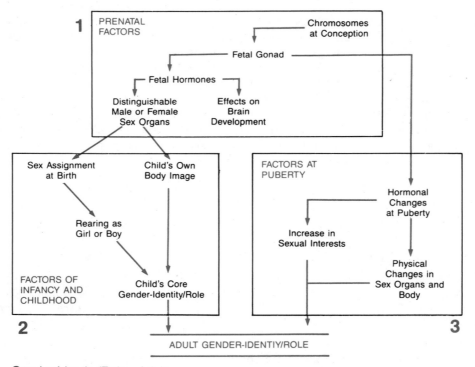

FIGURE 6.9 Gender-Identity/Role—Adult

This figure integrates the three stages of gender-identity/role and summarizes the prenatal factors (1), factors of infancy and childhood (2), and factors at puberty (3) that influence the development of a mature adult gender-identity/role.

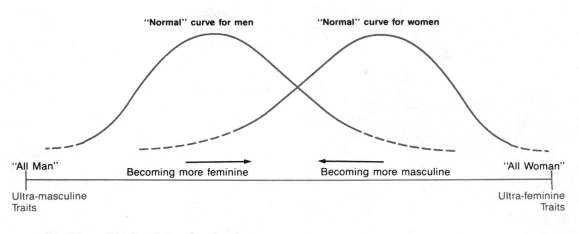

FIGURE 6.10 Masculine-Feminine Continuum

The definition of masculine or feminine behavior is based primarily on environmental influences and cultural expectations. These curves represent the variations possible in what society expects of "normal" or typical feminine or masculine behavior.

and generalizations do not hold up well. The man-woman, masculine-feminine dichotomy is as artificial and blurred as any other.

For example, while nonconformity of G-I/R is typical for at least a proportion of homosexuals, it is not found in all. About half of the homosexual men in one study were typically "masculine" in their personal identities, interests, and activities while growing up. Nearly a quarter of the heterosexual men were nonconforming in these same respects. Only about a fifth of the lesbians studied and about a third of the heterosexual women were highly "feminine" while they were growing up (Bell, Weinberg, & Hammersmith, 1981). The stereotypes of the male homosexual as an effeminate, high-voiced, lisping man and the lesbian as a masculinized, deep-voiced, gruff woman simply are not widely borne out by reality. Some homosexuals fit such stereotypes, sometimes by choice as a bold social statement of their "difference," but most do not (see also chapter 11, "Homosexuality and Bisexuality").

Neither does the presence of female or male genitals seem to determine an individual's place on the masculine-feminine continuum. The majority of men fall toward the masculine side, and the majority of women toward the feminine side, but few of us are located at one extreme end or the other. However, there are some individuals who cross the usual boundaries that delineate "appropriate" sex roles for women and men. Professionals who have sought to classify such gender states often refer to them as gender dysphorias or gender transpositions, occurring in varying degrees (Money & Wiedeking, 1980). Here are some of the most typical examples, with a gradually increasing degree of transposition:

Occasional Cross-dressing Some people enjoy putting on clothes usually limited to members of the other sex just for an occasional joke or thrill. A minority of homosexuals sometimes dress up in clothing of the opposite sex and are said to be "in drag."

Transvestism This term refers to a stronger need, and more deliberate and frequent cross-dressing. Often the person also adopts the sex-role mannerisms and a name consistent with the clothing (Fig. 6.11). There may also be sexual arousal associated with the cross-dressing. In daily life, however, the person supports the sex-role expectations deemed appropriate for his or her genital anatomy (see chapter 12, "The Spectrum of Human Sexual Behavior"). Transvestism is apparently more common in cultures where there are marked sex-role distinctions, leading some observers to speculate that it is a culturally defined phenomenon.

Transgenderism (or Cross-genderism) Transgenderists live portions of their lives cross-dressed and with additional characteristics stereotypically associated with the other sex. The degree of transgenderism may range from the occasional weekend or vacation period during which the individual dresses and acts as a member of the other sex, all the way to individuals who do so consistently for long periods of time, even establishing an identity to friends and co-workers as a member of the "imitated" gender (Freund, Steiner, & Chan, 1982).

gender dysphoria (dis-FOR-ee-a): term to describe gender-identity/role that does not conform to the norm considered appropriate for one's physical sex.
gender transposition: gender dysphoria.

147

FIGURE 6.11 Transvestites

Transvestism is the persistent need to dress as a member of the opposite sex for the purposes of sexual excitement. Most transvestites are heterosexual males who may cross-dress partially or completely. Females who dress in masculine clothes usually do not do so for sexual excitement and are thus not considered transvestites.

Transsexualism This is the most extreme of the gender transpositions. Transsexuals usually feel from an early age as if they had been born into the wrongly sexed body. They feel as though they possess the personality of a member of the opposite sex, and usually strongly desire being hormonally and surgically transformed into that sex (see chapter 12).

It should be emphasized that there are no clear-cut boundaries between these various categories, but much blending and overlap. There are many subtleties of gender transposition that have never been categorized

or labeled. The most obvious conclusion is that gaining feminine and masculine traits and roles is no less complicated and no better understood than the development of the other aspects of our sexuality. Figure 6.12 shows how some specific transpositions of gender identity fit onto the masculine-feminine continuum.

It should again be noted that one's "position" on the masculine-feminine continuum is not necessarily related to sexual orientation. Many male transvestites, though they dress in women's clothing, are heterosexual in orientation and prefer female sexual partners. There are cases of transsexuals who wanted to be surgically changed to the other sex so they could be "homosexual," then interacting sexually with members of the sex to which they were reassigned.

Very little is known about the causes of gender identity incongruencies. There are some who believe that learning after birth is the exclusive cause of conditions such as transsexualism or transvestism. Others believe that they result from a complex interaction of hormonal and learning influences, both before and after birth. It may be, for example, that genes and prenatal hormones lead to variations in brain structures, and that these variations predispose an individual to incongruencies. Only further research into the factors which determine gender-identity/role and our sexual orientations can provide reliable answers to these puzzles.

Masculinity and Femininity Today

How much are women and men alike, and how much are they different? The answer to that question is influenced by social attitudes and historical trends. The scientists who have attempted to clarify the matter over the years have been influenced by these attitudes and trends as well. For example, a survey of the literature on men and women has shown that in the nineteenth century sexologists tended to focus on the many differences between men and women. It was generally assumed that women were weaker and more

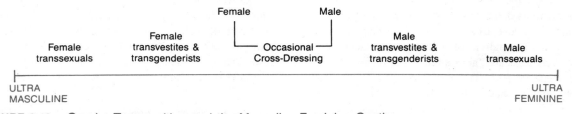

FIGURE 6.12 Gender Transposition and the Masculine-Feminine Continuum

Gender transposition is not necessarily related to sexual orientation but rather to an emotional or psychological attitude that both men and women may have about their own sexual natures.

passive than men. Twentieth-century researchers such as Alfred Kinsey and Masters and Johnson began to reflect a new perspective of male-female similarities that de-emphasized the differences between sexes. Questions are now being raised about the rationale behind the new emphasis on similarity. Are social scientists searching for greater acceptance within their culture? Is scientific methodology being swayed by political agendas? Are social inequities between the sexes being ignored? These issues will be receiving further examination during the decade of the nineties (Irvine, 1990).

Increasingly, it is being recognized that there may be some built-in tendencies, inclinations, or probabilities for women to feel and behave in certain ways, and for men to feel and behave in certain other ways. These are not absolutes; they do not apply to every man and woman, but simply represent predispositions or propensities toward characteristics that tend to be different between males and females. Political systems have often used differences as excuses to exploit or oppress women and ethnic minorities. Any differences that exist in "average" women and men can be acknowledged, honored, and enjoyed without the introduction of exploitation or oppression (Wilber, 1991).

The shaping of sex differences involves an interplay between the individual's biology and social environment. During fetal life, chromosomes and hormonal influences differentiate female or male genitals and probably establish some preliminary gender differences in the brain. While these sex differences are relatively minor at birth, they begin to shape how the infant responds to the environment, *and* how the environment responds to the infant. As a child grows and develops, there is a *multiplier effect* between these two dimensions of the individual's life. The physical differences increase, thus magnifying even more the differences in the ways in which males and females react to their surrounding social environment, and the ways in which the social environment reacts differently to them because of gender. This multiplier effect between biological and social factors results in a period of greatest difference between the sexes during the reproductive years of human life (Sanders & Reinisch, 1990).

It should be evident so far that becoming a man or a woman is not as simple as it might appear on the surface. The differences that are assumed to exist between the sexes—differences in temperament, abilities, values, and other personality characteristics—continue to create conflict, misunderstanding, and distrust between men and women (Tavris & Wade, 1984). You may have noticed that I have been unable to present you with a clear picture of what being a woman or a man really means—what femininity and mas-

FIGURE 6.13 Changing Traditional Roles

Both men and women may feel that the characteristics traditionally assigned to them are biased and unfair. Several theories indicate that social, cultural learning is responsible for the acquisition of roles and that therefore a culture might be able to change the roles it teaches its young.

culinity are all about in today's world. This is because ideas about men and women have been changing, especially as the result of new attitudes toward women (or old attitudes revived). Some of the traditional, stereotypical traits follow.

Traditionally Masculine Traits Independence, aggression, competitiveness, leadership, task orientation, outward orientation, assertiveness, innovation, self-discipline, stoicism, activity, objectivity, analytic-mindedness, courage, unsentimentality, rationality, confidence, and emotional control.

Traditionally Feminine Traits Reliance, trust, passivity, cooperativeness, supportiveness, inner orientation, interpersonal orientation, empathy, sensitivity, nurturance, subjectivity, intuitiveness, creativeness, yieldingness, fragility, receptivity, cautiousness, and emotional fluidity (Ruble, 1983).

These are the characteristics that have been traditionally viewed as masculine and feminine, and until recently they were accepted without much question. Today, however, there are many who insist that these traits have been invented by our culture, and that they are taught to boys and girls as they grow up. A further

149

contention is that, for many boys and girls who live up to these "ideals," the result is a sapping of individuality. There are women who think the traditional qualities are biased against them, and men who are convinced that they are the unlucky ones. There are other people who insist that the traditional male and female roles are set forth in the Bible and they must not be altered in any way. As a result of the controversy, many men and women are confused about their sex roles, especially in partnerships such as marriages.

Data collected over the years that actually compare behavioral and personality traits of males and females have sometimes identified true differences, and sometimes not. For example, while one widely held stereotype contends that men are more intelligent than women, there is no research showing any gender differences in IQ. It is also crucial to note that any differences that have been identified are only true as statistical generalizations; they do not apply to *all* women or men. In one survey of available data, it was pointed out that there is substantial evidence that males are generally somewhat more aggressive and self-confident than females. While the evidence for differences in other traits is far more ambiguous, research does show that boys are more active than girls and less easily influenced by others. There is also suggestive research evidence that girls and women are at least more willing to admit to fears and anxieties, and tend to be more empathic than boys and men, meaning that they are more sensitive to and able to identify with the feelings of others. Although conventional wisdom holds that females are also more "sociable" than males, research demonstrates that there are no gender differences in this trait (Hyde, 1985).

LEARNING SEX ROLES

Another of the unresolved controversies that was implied earlier in this chapter is the following: Are females and males essentially the same at birth, both with the same potentials for developing any personality traits, or are there some prenatal factors that predispose males and females to different personality characteristics as they mature? A rigid position on either side of the controversy cannot be justified in light of present research.

A number of theories concerning the formation of women's identities received wide attention during the 1980s. We must be cautious not to oversimplify the nature of either women or men. An inclusive view of what men and women are all about must take into consideration individual differences, the situations in which people live, and the social forces that influence them (Enns, 1991).

We are just beginning to understand the many variables that determine femininity and masculinity, and to devise means of studying and measuring them. It has been suggested that focusing attention on differences between women and men distracts us from the impressive similarities that are evident in the two sexes. Even for those characteristics where gender differences can be demonstrated, such as a higher level of aggression in males, those differences are not large (Hyde, 1985).

For now it seems safe to assume that a large part of establishing masculine and feminine sex roles results from a learning process—our socialization as women and men. Again, there is controversy over how sex roles are learned, and several different theoretical positions have emerged. Detailed description of these positions is outside the scope of this book, but a brief summary follows.

Psychoanalytic Tradition Founded by Sigmund Freud, this holds that children are confused about anatomical differences between females and males, and that children tend to attribute superior power and value to the male genitals. Thus the view of maleness as having more aggression, leadership, and strength gradually emerges. As children grow and identify with adult women or men, they must cope with their castration anxieties, Oedipal wishes, and Electra complexes (see chapter 7, p. 167).

Social Learning Theory This theory is especially popular and assumes that sex roles are perpetuated by each culture, which promotes those behaviors and values that are biologically easiest to establish in both sexes. These include aggression and dominance for men, passivity and dependence for women. It is believed that sex-role differences are learned by observation and imitation from three main sources: the parent of the same sex with whom the child identifies, the peer group, and the sexual interactions of adolescence. As children develop there is increasing influence on their ideas and behaviors relating to gender from school and the media. The emphasis is placed on identification with same-sexed people, particularly the father or mother (Block, 1983).

Cognitive-developmental This position puts forth the belief that the primary organizer of sex-role attitudes is the early gender-identity/role of the child. The child categorizes itself as girl or boy relatively early in its life, and then develops masculine or feminine values out of the need to value things consistent with or like itself. After feminine or masculine values are acquired, the child tends to identify with the same-sexed parent and deepens its attachment to the feminine or masculine model. The unique feature of this theory is the idea that the child acquires basic male or female values on its own, and then because of its acquired desire to be feminine or masculine, identifies with a woman or man as a model. All of this follows a regular course of development largely determined by cognitive, or intellectual, maturity (Kohlberg, 1966; Maccoby, 1990a; Slaby, 1990).

Gender Schema Theory This concept of how people come to define themselves as masculine or feminine emphasizes the pressures inherent in social attitudes that assume the need for differences between females and males, even in situations where sex has no particular relevance (Bem, 1987). In most cultures maleness and femaleness are defined by a vast gender schema, or complex network of associations, ranging from anatomical differences to the sorts of work people engage in to religious symbolism. A developing child gradually learns to bring the associations of the society's gender schema into her or his thinking processes in order to evaluate and assimilate any new information. In time everything becomes interpreted through this dualistic, male-female schema, and the individual models his or her behaviors and life choices according to those interpretations. Sandra Bem feels that many characteristics of what we have come to classify as femininity or masculinity only exist in the mind of the perceiver:

> Look through the lens of gender and you perceive the world as falling into masculine and feminine categories. Put on a different pair of lenses, however, and you perceive the world as falling into other categories. (Bem, 1987, p. 309)

Although there is still disagreement as to how sex roles are learned, it is generally agreed that learning to be a man or woman is an important part of growing up. As Matthew Arnold noted: "Not a having and a resting, but a growing and a becoming is the character of perfection as culture conceives it."

WOMEN REBEL—THE FEMINIST MOVEMENT

Feminists are women and men who reject prejudices that imply any inferiority of either sex as compared to the other. They advocate equality of women and men in every way and work for recognition of that equality culturally, politically, legally, and in the job market. There is generally a recognition that women have been subject to discrimination because of their sex. Among contemporary feminist groups there is a spectrum of positions. On the more moderate side are women's

rights groups that work for "true equality for all women in America in fully equal partnership with men"—a position of the National Organization for Women (NOW). In using the word *equality,* they are not implying that women and men are the same, but rather that they deserve equal opportunities and rights. Some feminist groups are working to reduce the social importance of gender, and questioning the effects of traditional marriage on women. While married men seem to be happier and healthier than unmarried men, the same cannot be said for women.

The feminist movement in the United States is not new. There have been several waves of activity throughout American history (see Fig. 6.14, overleaf).

The first major public outcry for women's rights came in 1848 when Elizabeth Cady Stanton, Susan B. Anthony, and several other women wrote their "Declaration of Sentiments" and presented it at the first U.S. women's rights convention in Seneca Falls, N.Y. As the move to abolish slavery grew in the nineteenth century, women began to liken their position to that of slaves and began to fight for their own rights. After women gained the right to vote in 1920, the movement subsided somewhat until the mid-1960s.

Then, partly due to the atmosphere of protest occasioned by the Vietnam War, and partly due to a new awareness of inequality in society that was fueled by mass media communication, the modern feminist movement gained momentum. Terms such as "women's liberation" and "sexism" became part of everyone's vocabulary. Unfortunately, some people have developed an inaccurate image of feminists as bra-burning, screaming women who picket sexist issues and hate men. In fact, discrimination against women is evident in our society in a variety of ways, and feminists are working to reduce inequality between the sexes. In the early 1970s most feminists supported the passage of an amendment to the U.S. Constitution that would affirm the equality of the sexes. However, this Equal Rights Amendment (E.R.A.) failed to achieve ratification by a sufficient number of states. Some feminist groups continue to work toward its acceptance.

Contemporary feminist thought has created a renewed awareness that women can be equal participants in sexual activity, as well as other aspects of human life. Traditional stereotypes held that women were less interested in sex and less easily aroused than men. This also meant that men were expected to be the primary initiators of sex, wooing and seducing their female partners until they finally gave in. Modern feminism has raised our consciousness about female sexuality, showing that women want to enjoy and be full participants in sex. It has become clear that women can desire sexual intimacy in all of its dimensions, and it is now socially permissible for them to initiate sexual

151

FIGURE 6.14 Active Feminists

Early feminists campaigning for suffrage were in for a hard fight, but in 1920 they won the right to vote with the passage of the Nineteenth Amendment. At this time the size of the eligible voting population nearly doubled. But it was not until the latter half of the century that the turnout of women at the polls reached the level of male turnout.

encounters. Sex is no longer something to which women are expected to submit as an obligation to a male partner. Instead it is part of the human experience that can be negotiated, discussed, and actively enjoyed by both women and men if and when they choose to do so.

GROWING UP FEMALE AND MALE

One of the major social criticisms that feminists have is the way in which girls and women are socialized. They feel that the traditional feminine sex role places women at a distinct disadvantage in comparison to men. Judith Bardwick (1971) ventured a hypothesis to explain how the whole discriminatory process begins. She believed that our society permits a wider range of behaviors for girls, from the very frilly to the tomboy.

For boys neither the extreme of the sissy nor the too-aggressive bully is acceptable. For these reasons, parents and other adults are typically less disturbed by the behavior of girls than by that of boys. As a result,

more demands are placed on boys to behave in the appropriate way. Bardwick believes that because of their own impulses and the social sanctions exerted by adults, boys are pressured to become more independent and self-controlled. Early in their lives they develop a sense of self-worth, relatively independent of others' responses. At the same time, female roles are devalued, and boys are criticized for stepping out of their role boundaries by being called "girls" or "sissies" in a derogatory way. Girls, on the other hand, are not as pressured to become independent and self-controlling, so they remain more dependent on others for physical comfort and a sense of self-worth, often experiencing no strong pressures until puberty. As children, girls are rewarded for their compliant good behavior by good grades, parental love, teacher acceptance, and acceptance into peer groups; this leaves them generally more passive and conformist.

There is growing evidence that psychological studies of human beings have been fundamentally biased by a male-centered perspective through which research data are analyzed and interpreted (Hyde,

Case Study

PEG: BALANCING CAREER, MARRIAGE, AND FAMILY

Peg was 32, and had just had her third child, when she began to feel dissatisfied with the roles she had chosen for her life. After getting her college degree, she had married, and she and her husband had agreed that Peg would remain home during her children's early years. Parenthood and caring for her home had occupied most of her time, and Peg had been active in community and school volunteer work. She finally reached a point, however, where she longed for the stimulation of an outside, paid position, and decided to pursue a career. Her husband was successful in his career, although he worked long hours and spent little time with the family except on weekends. He was supportive of Peg's desire to begin working, but uneasy about the implications such a move would have for him and the children.

As Peg looks back on this transition period in her life, she recounts the sense of humiliation she sometimes felt as she searched for a job. "Somehow, I had fooled myself into thinking that everything would be put on hold out in the world while I was a mother and homemaker. I assumed that I could just come back with my college degree any time I wanted and pick up where I left off. I was faced with some real shocks as I went to employment agencies and interviews, only to find that I was competing for jobs against people with years of experience and credentials, while about all I could claim was organizing car pools and bake sales for the parent-teacher association. On the one hand, I was angry that my years of dedicated service at home seemed to mean nothing; on the other, I felt humiliated and discouraged."

Eventually, Peg secured a position as an administrative assistant in a small but growing business firm. The pressures she felt then were magnified even more: "I never realized how difficult it was going to be to balance out the demands and responsibilities of a job with those of home. My husband wasn't geared up to take over household duties, and my new job took nearly all of my energy. I felt tremendous guilt every morning when I left my youngest child at day care, even though he seemed to be having a wonderful time there. Before long, it seemed as though my life was a hectic mess, scheduled so tightly that anything that might take a little extra time or deviate from the expected would throw everything into chaos.

"After about a year, I was afraid I was headed for a nervous breakdown. My husband and I were always hurrying, and were usually tired and irritable. Finally, we sat down and talked about how miserable we had become. Our marriage was strong enough so that we both wanted to make the situation better, and we were both willing to compromise. He was in a position to be able to make his hours more flexible and help more with the children. He even started doing some of the cooking. I finally decided that the job I had taken demanded more of my time and energy than I could afford if I wanted to have any family life at all. So I found another position that allowed me to have more flexibility and more vacation time. I felt as though I had been cheated along the way by some of the choices I had made, but I also realized that being able to relax sometimes with my family was more important than anything. As the kids get older, I may well devote an increasing amount of time to my career, but I'm not sure. My husband and I both have enjoyed the time we spend with our family and each other and I have given up on being something beyond my capacities—superwoman."

1985). It has been suggested that, among children, behavioral differences between the sexes may be influenced by the ways in which the children are observed or tested. When children are tested individually, sex differences in behavior tend to be minimal. However, when children are placed in groups, the social situation seems to cause different gender behaviors to emerge (Maccoby, 1990b). When they are told that a particular task is meant for one sex or the other, children also perform better on those tasks that are labeled as appropriate for their gender (Davies, 1990). It has also been argued that so-called "scientific" pronouncements about women are nothing more than biased statements about their social and political roles, made

Is the "Gender Gap" Narrowing?

Do males and females have different kinds of intellectual abilities? That notion, which has probably prevailed through most of recorded history, has undergone sharp alterations as a result of both scientific and political developments in the last 3 decades.

● ● ●

The starting point for this debate is a large body of evidence, accumulated over many decades, suggesting that there are some differences in cognition and perception between men and women. Generally speaking, test results show that females are somewhat better at verbal expression, while males have a persistent advantage in certain quantitative and spatial abilities.

● ● ●

But are these differences "real"? And are they diminishing? Both questions are currently being fiercely debated.

● ● ●

Within this supercharged atmosphere, there's something of a polarity between biologically and socially oriented researchers. Those at the biological end of the spectrum, such as behavioral neuroscientist Sandra Witelson of McMaster University in Ontario, think it's obvious that biology has a role in cognitive sex differences. "The neurobiological evidence is continuing to mount . . . there are too many incontestable findings—things that have to have consequences in behavior and thinking." In fact, she says, "if one didn't observe these sex differences, one would hypothesize that they must exist."

But more socially oriented investigators—such as psychologist Janet Hyde of the University of Wisconsin—flatly disagree. "We've constructed theories of sex differences in the brain to account for differences in abilities," says Hyde. But now, she argues, the gender gap in test scores is waning. "We've come to question the very existence of the phenomenon the brain theories were constituted to explain."

Getting a grip on the available data is not easy: Male-female differences in cognition are often subtle, they change according to age and ability level, and standardized tests are crude tools for resolving questions about sex differences they weren't designed to measure. As a result, even a slight change in a test question can result in a big change in "effect size"—the proportion of a standard deviation by which the sexes differ. Furthermore, generalization about "verbal ability" obscures the fact that this category

by men who claim to speak the scientific truth. A whole new context for research and analysis is developing that recognizes and eliminates the built-in sexism now coloring so much research (Fausto-Sterling, 1985).

For example, early studies on moral reasoning suggested that males generally tend to reach a higher level of moral development than females, implying that women have a less well-developed sense of morality than men. Researcher Carol Gilligan (1982) claimed that much of this research is biased against females. She found that while men make their moral choices with a view toward laws and prevailing social standards, women tend to approach ethical decision-mak-

ing with a sense of caring for others and a desire to alleviate basic human and world problems. Gilligan has been a leading scholar in demonstrating that men and women tend to approach their moral reasoning from different perspectives, and that scientific studies have tended to be male-centered in their analysis of research data. In other words, even in science, there has been a fundamental bias that the man's approach is the "better" and more acceptable way.

In the mid-1980s Gilligan and her research team began to study girls aged 6 through 18 over a 5-year period. They found that young girls seem to feel very good about themselves, and care deeply for others. Up until about the age of 11, girls are assertive, speak includes a variety of skills: verbal fluency (where females excel), analogies (where males do better), spelling, writing, and comprehension. Similarly, the typical male advantages in "visual-spatial ability" vary widely depending on test population and the subskill being measured.

But in spite of such subtleties and confusions, at least one general trend has become apparent in the past decade: Increasing attention is being focused on the question of whether the "gender gap" is narrowing.

• • •

It's clear that the whole question of the gender gap in cognition is still a hotbed of dispute. Nonetheless, some investigators believe enough data have been gathered to start zeroing in on the essence of male-female differences—including the differences in spatial reasoning that seem to persist over time and across cultures. As stated by psychologist David Lohman of the University of Iowa, the hypothesis is that the core difference has to do with what he calls the "visual-spatial scratchpad"—the mental ability to retain and manipulate spatial and numeric data that cannot be solved verbally.

Lohman describes several tests that seem to rely on just such an internal scratch-pad. . . . Males not only perform these tasks better than females, they do them more quickly. When females get a correct result, says Witelson, they seem to get it by reasoning. "Men just look at it and know that's the way it is . . . it's almost as if they look at it without trying to analyze or process it."

Even those researchers who believe that intrinsic factors underlie sex differences in cognition don't believe that these differences alone are sufficient to make females less suited for scientific careers.

• • •

Just as researchers differ on the causes of these discrepancies, so do they place different emphasis on what to do about them. Researchers such as Hyde want more resources put into environmental interventions such as "girl-friendly science class-rooms." Others . . . think it's necessary to do more fine-grained research on cognitive abilities.

But ultimately everyone agrees: The country should be doing whatever works to get more women into science.

—Constance Holden, *Science,* Vol. 253, August 30, 1991

about their feelings, and accept conflict as a natural part of healthy relationships. However, during adolescence they are much more hesitant to express their feelings out of fear that they will anger others. These researchers have concluded that adolescence tends to be a time of repression for girls. Some girls resist the repression by becoming rebels, while others become extremely cautious about what they will say publicly. Often, they resort to "I don't know" as a safe response (Winkler, 1990).

A study sponsored by the American Association of University Women (AAUW, 1991) seems to reinforce this perception of how girls and boys grow up. Three thousand students in grades 4 through 10 were surveyed in 12 locations throughout the United States. Up to 70 percent of both the boys and girls at age 9 tended to reflect positive attitudes toward themselves and willingness to be assertive as needed. The researchers developed a self-esteem index from the questions they asked the children. By age 16, only 29 percent of high school girls indicated they were happy with themselves, while 46 percent of boys retained a sense of self-confidence. Interestingly, the drop of self-esteem was particularly true for white and Hispanic girls. Black girls tended to be better able to maintain their self-esteem during adolescence. In the study, girls who had difficulty with particular academic subjects tended to blame themselves and assume they were not competent to do the work. Boys, on the other hand, were more likely to blame the course's subject matter than themselves. During adolescence, there was also more of an increase in concern about appearance and body image among girls. Boys were more able to gain confidence in themselves from their talents and abilities to do things, and had fewer messages from their culture that their worth was dependent on their appearance.

The media play a major role in how women and men are portrayed in our culture. A study of how gender roles are represented on television found that not only are women underrepresented on television, but that the images of both men and women tended to be stereotypical and traditional (Signorielli, 1990). An analysis has also been done of 62 children's readers that were in use in schools. It found that while girls are now portrayed in a wider range of activities than they once were, women do not appear in the stories as often as men, and are not shown in as wide a range of occupations (Purcell & Stewart, 1990). It is clear that some cultural messages emphasizing inequalities between men and women are still being given to children as they grow up.

Many feminists claim that masculinity has become the societal yardstick against which everything is measured. The characteristics we have traditionally attributed to men are seen as being much more desirable than those we have attributed to women. Therefore many women have internalized self-destructive, demoralizing values about their own worth in comparison to men. This is believed to be a central reason behind the fact that, until recently, very few women could succeed in traditionally male occupational roles; they were not equipped in earlier life to do so.

Research evidence confirms that the traditional roles can lead to lower self-esteem in adult women as well. One group of 112 women was first tested when they were college seniors in the late 1950s. Those women who ultimately chose more traditional homemaking roles as they went through adult life tended to have more adverse changes in both their physical and psychological health by age 43 (Helson & Picano, 1990). Numerous studies have shown that people with more attributes traditionally associated with masculinity tend to have higher self-esteem and higher levels of psychological adjustment than those with more feminine attributes (Harris & Schwab, 1990).

The bias favoring the masculine perspective may infiltrate the workplace as well. While many institutions and employers are trying to create equal employment opportunities for women, there is little evidence of complete success. In fact, in the American workplace, there is still a great deal of job segregation by sex. The possibilities for promotion are greater for men than for women. Parenting and household responsibilities still often fall to women who are married, and may limit the time and energy available for their careers. The facts suggest that women tend to find fewer chances for reaping the rewards, advancement, and benefits in jobs than do their male counterparts (Baron & Bielby, 1985).

The old stereotyped ways are slowly changing. Over two-thirds of American women now hold paying jobs, and many men are rejecting occupational success as their major source of self-esteem. Yet with the change comes confusion and fear. Some people react by clinging even more tightly to traditional sex roles. When the criteria for measuring femininity and masculinity are unclear, and the focus shifts between differences and commonalities, the freedom to alter one's own role can become a frightening responsibility. Yet many people are now accepting that responsibility and finding new levels of personal growth in doing so.

MEN REACT

The women's movement has made it clear that women in our society have been victims of injustice and discrimination. Yet it has also brought into focus the fact that men have been enslaved by certain roles and stereotypes as well. The plight of men is more elusive, since their struggle is more subtle and legislative changes are less likely to produce results. Men have been caught in a vicious circle of proving their strength, invulnerability, and effectiveness as providers, yet, because of social attitudes, are also taught to be dependent on women—first their mothers, then often their romantic partners. Consequently, the liberation of women sometimes pushes men into a frightening state of autonomy and loneliness (Long, 1984).

In this way, the new feminism has generated a reaction among men; it has become as necessary for men to examine and reevaluate their own sexuality as it has been for women to examine theirs (Hutchinson & Schechterman, 1990). This reevaluation has many aspects—interpersonal relationships, love, sexual performance and adequacy, the double standard, and career competencies.

There has been somewhat of a men's movement as well. The first national men's conference was held in Knoxville, Tennessee, in 1975. There is a National Organization for Changing Men (NOCM) that addresses men's issues such as ending men's violence, fathering, gay rights, and male-female relationships, and offers workshops about them. Men's groups have sprung up around the country. Men in our society often report feeling restricted and pressured by the expectations placed on them. Three main aspects of the traditional male role seem especially to make men uncomfortable: (1) the male as competent worker and provider; (2) the male as the emotionally controlled stoic; and (3) the male as sexual aggressor and sex educator of the female (Rupple, 1983).

Traditionally, the responsibility for financial support of the family fell to the man. The centrality of occupation in a man's life has caused many men to rate their own self-worth on the basis of success—or lack of it—in their work. This is psychologically dangerous in a highly technological society in which there is high unemployment. Many male providers feel powerless, meaningless, and isolated in their jobs; and work under constant fear and tension as they strive for promotion and success (Pleck, 1981).

An additional problem is that when men feel certain emotions, they are frequently unable to express them. Many males are taught from the time they are very young not to show certain kinds of emotions—particularly those that reflect fear, unhappiness, anxiety, dependency, or gentle loving. The stereotyped sex role encourages self-control and rationality. "Real men" should not weep, giggle, scream, or coo; these responses are reserved for women. This traditional male role can become destructive—perhaps even lethal—for many men who gradually become discouraged with the inner tensions and feelings of meaninglessness that result from repressing emotion.

The traditional sexual double standard establishes men as the ones to be sexually experienced and to be able to instruct their partners in the ways of sex. Men have been expected to be the sexual aggressors, the initiators of sexual activity in partnerships, and the ones responsible for the success of sexual encounters. As sex therapists can testify, it is these very pressures that often lead to the deterioration of a sexual relationship between a man and his partner, and often produce dysfunctional problems such as erectile difficulty and lack of ejaculatory control (see chapter 16, "Sexual Dysfunctions and Their Treatment").

These are but a few of the pressures that many men feel in their sex roles. It is in the feminist movement that some of these men see real hope; for in the move toward equality, men are also freer to break away from stifling stereotypes. Today, many men feel secure with women financially supporting their families, wholly or in part. These men also express a full range of emotional response and see sex as a product of equal initiation and sharing. They rebel against sex roles and values that do not allow them to be individuals (Julty, 1979).

Most men, regardless of their place in the male scheme of things, have experienced some turmoil and problems during this important period of change and

FIGURE 6.15 Changing Masculine Roles

The feminist movement, in fighting for equal rights for women, has at the same time given men the right to change their expected roles as well. Many men in the 1990s are more comfortable than they ever have been in caring for their children, sharing the role of wage-earner, and expressing a full range of emotions.

growth. Men must share in the constant struggle to learn how to communicate thoughts and feelings and how to balance with their sexual partners the degree of exclusivity they wish to maintain in relationships.

Some men are calling for more rights in such issues as termination of pregnancy. They argue that since the cause of pregnancy is a shared phenomenon and responsibility, the decision of whether or not to terminate the pregnancy through abortion should also be shared, and that women should not be allowed to have an abortion without the male partner's concurrence. In a divorce or separation many men are requesting and getting custody or joint custody of their children. Somewhat less radical is the view that men should no longer be viewed as being attractive to women because of their status, income, or power.

157

Case Study

RUSS: TAKING ANOTHER LOOK AT MANHOOD

Russ grew up with three brothers in a household where the parents took great pride in each son who was "all boy." Like his brothers, he excelled in sports and was also an outstanding student. After attending a university, he got a position as an engineer and soon married. At age 35, he wrote about his re-evaluation of himself as a man.

"I never expected I would marry what I used to call a 'woman's libber.' In fact, when we first married, she had the same attitudes about our relationship as I did. I just assumed, and so did she, that I would provide money and shelter for my family, and she would tend hearth and home. The only problem was, after a couple of years of that routine, she was bored and feeling pretty useless.

"When my wife first started talking about sharing our responsibilities differently, I got mad. I blamed it on her feminist friends. The more we talked about it, and the more I began to take a look at my own background, the more I realized how locked in I was with the way of life I had learned from my family. Not that there was anything wrong with it. But I had never even considered that there might be other ways of doing things that could be just as right and sensible.

"For one thing, I realized that I had always been taken care of by women. My mother and older sister did all the housework, cooking, and laundry. I never had to lift a finger inside the house, although I was expected to help Dad with lawn work and gardening outside. Then my wife took over where my mother left off. For all my supposed male independence, I really didn't know how to operate the washing machine, clothes dryer, iron, or food processor. Big man!

"The more we got into all this, and after we had two kids, I began to feel more and more as if I didn't like how things had balanced out. They seemed unfair to both of us. I didn't want all of the provider-protector responsibilities, and my wife was sick of doing all the household and childcare work. Not that I wasn't a "good" father—I spent lots of time with the kids—but I didn't do much of the diaper-changing, bathing, feeding, or bedtime work.

"Gradually we've worked out more sharing of all the responsibilities of family life. I'm not one of those guys who wants to try being a house-husband, but I don't want to feel like a house-wimp who can't handle anything in the house either. My wife is teaching now, something I didn't expect to happen, and I feel a lot less pressure to bring home all the bacon. She feels a lot less pressure to cook all of it!

"I especially feel good about the examples we're setting for our two kids. There isn't much of anything you have to do just because you're a female or a male. And there are lots of 'fair' ways of being a family. The funny thing is that now I feel more like what I think a man should be all about. I am independent now—and free to be whatever I want to be. I haven't put myself in a box that somebody else built for me."

GENDER AWARE THERAPY

Regardless of what differences actually exist between women and men, gender has become one of the central organizing principles in society and in interpersonal relationships. Many cultural regulations and expectations are systematically related to gender. The stresses and problems that men and women encounter during their lifetimes are often the result of these social and cultural requirements and demands. It has been found that certain types of psychological and behavioral problems are more typical of one gender than of the other. For example, while men are more likely to have difficulties with alcohol and illicit drug abuse, antisocial behaviors, and suicide, women exhibit a higher incidence of phobias, anxiety disorders, prescription drug abuse, and depression. In fact, depressive syndromes are more than twice as common in females than in males.

It has been speculated that the causes of depression in women and men may differ because of sociocultural factors. Women may become depressed when they feel incompetent in or disappointed with their relationships. They sometimes struggle to save their relationships at the expense of expressing their own anger, needs, and wishes. In contrast to this pattern, men may get depressed when they fail to attain their personal and career goals. Eating disorders such as anorexia and bulimia are also far more common in women, probably because of sociocultural pressures that cause women to be more conscious of their appearance.

Men and women cope with their stresses and problems differently too. Men are more apt to become aggressive, become involved in some distracting activity, or be with a group of people without admitting they are upset. Women are more likely to blame themselves, cry, eat, confront their feelings, and seek help from their support groups. Women who have been sexually abused will tend to react by withdrawing from others and becoming more passive, while sexually abused males often react with exaggerated aggressiveness and attempts to control or dominate others (Cook 1990).

The fact that women and men may manifest psychological distress in different ways is one of the reasons why some mental health professionals have called for *gender aware therapy,* sometimes called feminist therapy, an approach to counseling and psychotherapy that takes into consideration and legitimizes these differences (DeVoe, 1990). Another reason is the evidence that has been building over the past 20 years indicating that traditional approaches to counseling have often been sexist. In the 1970s a task force of the American Psychological Association found that therapy tended to foster traditional sex roles, devalue women, make use of outmoded theories that were sexist in nature, and only too often treat women as sex objects (Good, Gilbert, & Scher, 1990). Men may also be viewed in certain ways by therapists because of their gender. One research study indicates that marriage and family therapists tended to assume that men who adopted nontraditional roles were more troubled and had more domestic unrest than men who had adopted traditional roles (Robertson & Fitzgerald, 1990). In contrast, gender aware therapy incorporates the following principles in order to raise consciousness about gender-related issues for counselors and therapists (Good, Bilbert, & Scher, 1990):

1. Gender should be regarded as an integral aspect of counseling and mental health because of the important role it plays in people's lives.
2. Personal problems must be considered within their social and political contexts.
3. Gender injustices experienced by women and men should be actively changed, and counselors can actively encourage clients to look at options that might involve such changes.

4. In therapy, there should be an egalatarian, collaborative relationship between therapist and client, in which the client is freed to explore and discover optimal solutions, rather than a traditional paternalistic approach of therapist "helping" client.
5. People have the right and freedom to *choose* attitudes, feelings, and behaviors that are most congruent for them, despite the gender scripts that have been prescribed for them.

Gender aware therapy is particularly appropriate for dealing with certain issues. As women consider career paths, especially in areas such as science and technology, it is crucial that a full range of opportunity be open to them. Treatment of eating disorders must carefully consider the relevant gender-related pressures and issues. Sexual abuse of women cannot be treated outside of the oppressive social situations in which many women find themselves. Men may be reluctant to seek help for their problems or deal realistically with their feelings, out of fear of being perceived as unmasculine. Therapists who work from a gender aware point of view can bring to their clients a broader context that can change how the clients deal with their lives and perceive themselves as individuals (Good, Gilbert, & Scher, 1990). However, there may also be dangers in these approaches to counseling and therapy if professionals stray too far from some of the traditional ground rules of practice that take theory into consideration, set limits on the counseling process, and realize the power inherent in the counselor's feelings and reactions toward the client (Margolies, 1990).

Gender aware therapists may be either women or men who work with either women or men. While there is suggestive evidence that the dynamics of the counseling process vary with the type of gender pairing between counselor and client, there is not a great deal of solid research data to back up the suggestions (DeVoe, 1990). It has been hypothesized that male counselors may be uncomfortable about showing too much concern for male clients, and that male clients might be resistant to becoming dependent on the counselor's warmth and caring, because of underlying fears of homosexual feelings. It has also been hypothesized that since women are more comfortable with their emotions, a counseling process between a female counselor and female client may be more emotionally intense and empathic (Mintz & O'Neil, 1990). However, the gender of the counselor picked by a client seems to be a very individual matter, and sometimes is simply a matter of chance.

It seems clear that gender aware therapy, or feminist therapy, will become an increasingly prevalent context within which both women and men can work on their personal concerns. As we approach the twenty-first century, professionals will be called upon to an even greater extent to help individuals and society adapt to changing conceptions of gender. We can no longer look at gender simply as a determiner of roles and expectations, but instead it may be recognized as a primary foundation on which we build our perception of the world (Scher & Good, 1990). It remains to be seen whether gender aware therapy is all that much different from what effective forms of counseling and therapy have always been. However, it will now be possible for counseling clients of either sex to find professional counselors who consider the issues of gender to be a significant part of individuality and the counseling process.

ANDROGYNY: BRIDGING THE GAP?

Since it is unusual for any one human being to be "totally" masculine or feminine, most of us have some degree of combination of the traditional feminine and masculine characteristics (Kaplan & Sedney, 1980). This combination of traits in a single individual is called androgyny, coming from the Greek roots *andro,* for male, and *gyn,* for female. Psychologist Sandra Bem (1974) was one of the first researchers to develop a paper-and-pencil inventory to measure the degree to which people might be androgynous. She considered anyone who had both a high femininity score and a high masculinity score to be androgynous. Her study, and others since, have indicated that the term can be applied to about one-third of teenagers and college students.

Bem's research also suggested that androgynous people are more adaptable than traditionalists—a characteristic that has been equated with psychological health. Adaptability in androgynous persons would seem predictable. The traditional male is more adept at aggressive behavior and less able to share feelings and be gentle. The traditional female is more comfortable with showing warmth, concern, and gentleness but less willing or able to demonstrate assertiveness or independence. Bem believes the androgynous person feels at ease being independent and forceful or warm, nurturing, and kind, depending on the situation, and is thus more flexible in adapting to a range of situations.

More recently, Bem (1987) has emphasized that she believes there are biologically based differences in behavior between males and females, and that she does not recommend changing societies in an attempt to eliminate such differences. She does want to see our

cultural restrictions on behavior lifted so that men and women can be free to exercise the full range of individual differences that she believes biology allows for both sexes. Some have hailed androgyny as the ultimate resolution to the unfairness and inequality that traditional sex-role stereotypes have created. This perspective calls into question the notion that highly masculine men and highly feminine women are necessarily well adjusted (Taylor & Hall, 1982).

There is some evidence to suggest that androgynous people have fewer psychological problems than those who adopt traditional sex roles. There are also research findings indicating that androgynous men and women are more comfortable with sex and report a greater degree of satisfaction with their sexual relationships (Garcia, 1982). There is conflicting evidence, however, that androgyny may lead to greater work stress and poorer overall emotional adjustment (Lee & Scheurer, 1983).

It is too early in the research with androgyny to see whether or not it represents a desirable, or even possible, goal for people to attain. Androgyny may represent a way to transcend the roles that have often proved restricting to both women and men.

Some people believe that the old standards by which masculinity or femininity were judged are beginning to fade and are being replaced by the freedom to explore all parts of one's personality—including the parts not once considered appropriate for one's sex. Yet others are calling for a return to the simplistic order of clearly defined sex roles. The sexual double standard still survives on many levels of our society. Author George Gilder (1987) is one of many individuals who maintain that differences between women and men are a fundamental fact of human society, and to deny those differences is a recipe for sexual suicide.

To a large extent, the picture of what makes us women and men and what factors determine our femininity or masculinity is still a muddled one. Yet in spite of all the current confusion, new attitudes have created an atmosphere where the old male and female stereotypes are much easier to break through. This allows young and old who feel stifled by traditional sex roles to give vent to their ideas and feelings and offers new potentials for individuality in human life. ■

---

androgyny (an-DROJ-a-nee): combination of traditional feminine and masculine traits in a single individual.

SELF-EVALUATION

Masculinity and Femininity in Your Life

It seems that attitudes toward masculinity and femininity are in a state of flux. While some people are attempting to blur the stereotyped differences between men and women, others are trying harder than ever to establish definite, identifiable standards of masculinity and femininity. The exercises that follow may help you to clarify your present attitudes toward men and women and how you view your own role as a sexual human being.

1. On a sheet of paper, list two men, by name, who for you exemplify ideal manhood; list two women, by name, who for you exemplify ideal womanhood. Then proceed with the following:

   a. Under the men's names and under the women's names, list the characteristics of these people that have made them your choices as representative of the ideal.

   b. Note which of the characteristics, if any, are listed for both the men and women.

   c. Check those characteristics from either list that you believe you exhibit.

2. Would you ever consider dressing up in clothing generally identified as being appropriate for members of the opposite sex? If not, why not? If so, consider the following:

   a. Under what circumstances would you wear clothing of the opposite sex? Only in private? In front of one other highly trusted person? In front of a small group of friends? At a masquerade party? In public places?

   b. If possible and you're willing, go ahead and dress up in some clothes of the opposite sex, and look yourself over in a full-length mirror. (Note: In some areas it is illegal to cross-dress and be seen in public.) As you look at yourself, how do you feel? Silly? Sexy? Curious? Happy? Sad? Why do you feel that way? Examine the following list of qualities and check those that you feel are most important for you to have as a person. (Add other words of your own if you wish.)

honest	physically strong	responsible
brave	dominating	emotional
athletic	delicate	persuasive
caring	intelligent	protective
competitive	successful	shy
gentle	submissive	reliable
sensitive	manipulative	flighty
aggressive	thoughtful	sincere
considerate	confident	sexy

   c. Now read through the list of qualities again and pick out those that have been traditionally considered masculine and those traditionally considered feminine. Make two separate lists on a sheet of paper. Some words may appear on both lists or on neither. Include any words you have added to the list.

   d. Finally, note where the qualities you checked for yourself fall in your two lists. Think about them. This should help to show how your goals for your own femininity or masculinity relate to traditional ideas about men and women, as you view them.

3. This exercise should be done with a member of the opposite sex, or with a group of people of both sexes. The men should make two lists on a sheet of paper: The advantages of being female and the disadvantages of being female. Likewise, the women should also make two lists: The advantages and disadvantages of being male. When the lists are complete, everyone should compare them and discuss the characteristics.

4. As you are watching television, or leafing through the pages of a magazine, note how men and women are portrayed in advertisements. Note which of the men and women appeal the most to you and which are unappealing to you, asking yourself "why?" in each case. Especially note how women and men in the advertisements are shown in traditional or in nontraditional roles.

5. Think about each of the following, and attempt to get in touch with your gut reactions—how you feel. Try not to intellectualize and react in the manner in which you think you should. Instead, look carefully at how you are reacting and at what your reactions mean in terms of attitudes toward manhood and womanhood.

   a. An unmarried woman who insists on being referred to as Ms.

   b. A married woman who insists on being referred to as Ms.

   c. An all-male organization that refuses to consider admitting women as members.

   d. An all-female organization that refuses to consider admitting men as members.

   e. A board of education that passes a school policy requiring that in all courses, "traditional family values are to be upheld, with the feminine role of wife, mother, and homemaker, and masculine role of guide, protector, and provider."

161

   f.   In considering an equally qualified married man and unmarried woman for a position, a company personnel director hires the woman because the company needs to fulfill its affirmative action quota.

   g.   After a couple has a new baby, the mother wants to continue working, so the father decides to quit his job and stay home with the child.

CHAPTER SUMMARY

1. The development of our gender-identity/role (G-I/R)—the sense of ourselves and our outward expressions as masculine, feminine, or some position in between—is determined by a complex interaction of genetic, physiological, and sociocultural factors.

2. During prenatal life (before birth), the combining of chromosomes sets into motion a genetic program for producing a male, female, or some ambivalent anatomical structure. While the pairing of sex chromosomes is normally XX for female and XY for male, there can be abnormal combinations (for example, XXX, XXY, XYY) that produce unusual characteristics.

3. After about a month of embryonic development, an undifferentiated set of fetal gonads appear, along with Müllerian ducts (potential female organs) and Wolffian ducts (potential male organs).

4. If the Y chromosome is present, with its SRY gene, HY-antigen is produced that transforms the gonads into testes, which in turn produce testosterone and Müllerian Inhibiting Substance. They promote development of male organs from the Wolffian ducts and suppress further development of Müllerian ducts.

5. If the Y chromosome is absent, the fetal gonads automatically become ovaries and the Wolffian ducts disintegrate.

6. Male and female genitals and inner reproductive structures then develop. Some evidence suggests that the presence or absence of the male hormones may affect development of the nervous system and therefore create predispositions toward certain behavior patterns in later life.

7. During infancy and childhood, boys and girls are treated in particular ways, and social influences along with anatomy begin to help the child form a core gender-identity/role.

8. Researchers have gained clues to the effects of hormones on the brain and behavior by studying fetally androgenized females and males with androgen insensitivity syndrome or DHT-deficiency syndrome.

9. At puberty the testes or ovaries begin secreting male or female hormones, triggering the development of secondary sex characteristics and further confirming or disconfirming the individual's G-I/R. Sexual feelings and fantasies also become more pronounced.

10. Adult G-I/R can lie anywhere on a continuum between the "totally masculine" and "totally feminine," although how these definitions and roles are determined is a subject of continuing debate.

11. Gender dysphoria or transposition refers to the crossing of the usual boundaries of sex-role behavior. It includes occasional cross-dressing, transvestism, transgenderism, and transsexualism.

12. There are four basic theories about how sex roles are learned in human development: psychoanalytic, social learning, cognitive-developmental, and gender schema.

13. The feminist movement has existed at various times in American history, beginning with an outcry for women's rights in 1848 by Elizabeth Cady Stanton and Susan B. Anthony.

14. Scientific data on the differences between girls and boys and how they are raised are scant. Girls seem to be more prone to losing self-esteem as they reach adolescence than are boys.

15. Modern-day feminists often believe that traditional male roles have become the standards by which human success is measured. Feminists want to see men and women treated, and compensated, equally and without discrimination.

16. Men have also begun to examine the limiting and unhealthy effects of the roles expected of them in our culture. Many men are beginning to react against these restricting roles in their personal lives and relationships.

17. Gender aware therapy is an approach to dealing with people's personal concerns with a full awareness of how gender affects reactions to stress, perceptions of self and the world, and how people view their choices in life.

18. Androgyny represents a combination of traditionally feminine and masculine traits in one person and has been seen as one way of freeing people from having to conform to sex roles that do not fit them personally.

ANNOTATED READINGS

Cassell, C. (1984). *Swept away*. New York: Bantam Books. This book examines the ways in which women sometimes confuse issues relating to romance and sex. A very readable text, it helps women to take responsibility for the sexual choices they make.

Doyle, J. A. (1983). *The male experience*. Dubuque, IA: William C. Brown. Explores the breaking away from traditional male stereotypes that has resulted from changing social attitudes toward women and men.

Fausto-Sterling, A. (1985). *Myths of gender: Biological theories about women and men*. New York: Basic Books. This book examines biological theories about behavioral differences between women and men, noting that the research behind these theories is often rooted in social and political bias. The author calls into question these biological theories and presents alternative perspectives.

Hoff, J. (1990). *Law, gender and injustice: A legal history of U.S. women*. New York: New York University Press. Examines the legal status of women from the American Revolution to the present, portraying a political system in which laws have been used to disempower women, and arguing for a full emancipation of modern women.

Hyde, J. (1985). *Half the human experience: The psychology of women*. Lexington, MA: D. C. Heath. An informative survey of contemporary ideas and work concerning female psychology.

Kolbenschlag, M. (1988). *Kiss Sleeping Beauty goodbye*. San Francisco: Harper & Row. Examines some of the myths that are a pervasive part of women's roles and choices. It provides a fresh and eye-opening perspective on women and men in our society.

Money, J., & Tucker, P. (1975). *Sexual signatures*. Boston: Little, Brown. A basic treatment concerning the development of gender identity.

Rossi, A. (1974). *The feminist papers*. New York: Bantam Books. A collection of readings by important historical leaders in the feminist movement, this work traces the evolution of feminist thought.

Rossi, A. S. (1985). *Gender and the life course*. Hawthorne, NY: Aldine. A collection of readings that surveys gender and its development from a variety of perspectives: historical, social, biological, and developmental. Political implications are included.

CHAPTER SEVEN

PSYCHOSEXUAL DEVELOPMENT
  Inborn Sexual Instinct Theory
  Psychoanalytic Theory
  Integrated Social Factors Theory
  Conditioning and Social Learning Theory
  Social Script Theory
  A Unified Theoretical Model of Sexual Development

SEXUALITY IN INFANCY AND CHILDHOOD
  Sexual Curiosity Grows in Childhood
  Love and Romance in Childhood

SEXUALITY IN ADOLESCENCE
  Sexual Behavior in Adolescence
  Self-Centered Early Adolescent Sex
  Adolescent Homosexual Activity
  Masturbation in Adolescence
  Adolescent Heterosexual Activity
  Social Relationships

ADULT SEXUALITY AND RELATIONSHIPS
  Intimacy and Sexuality
  Marriage, Cohabitation, Singles, and Sex
  Monogamy Versus Non-monogamy
  Trends in Marriage
  Divorce

SEXUALITY AND AGING
  Myths and Attitudes About Sex and Aging
  Institutional Prohibitions on Sexual Expression
  Special Sexual Problems and Patterns of Aging
  Masturbation and Heterosexual Intercourse in Old
    Age
  Maximizing Sexual Expression During the Later Years

**SELF-EVALUATION: LOOKING AHEAD: SEX IN LATER
  YEARS**

CHAPTER SUMMARY

As I look back over my life, I can recognize how much my sexual feelings and responses have changed over the years—I'm now approaching 72. But the changes were so gradual I never really felt them happening. Nor does it matter to me that they've happened. I'm very comfortable with myself sexually and with the relationship I have with my wife, who is 8 years younger. I can remember the urgency I always felt about sex when I was a young man. It was all fire and agitation. And whatever satisfaction I got never seemed to hold me for long. I think I've enjoyed sex more in the last 20 years than I ever did before that, because I've been able to take my time with it— savor it—and then feel completely satisfied, not just with the orgasm but the whole experience.

—From a letter to the author

SEXUALITY THROUGH THE LIFE CYCLE

I described in earlier chapters how the field of human sexuality is full of issues open to debate. Here I will focus on the ways in which we grow sexually and express our sexual natures in different stages of the life cycle. How do our sexual feelings develop and grow? What are the important ways in which children, adolescents, and adults become acquainted with their sexual needs and drives? How does sex fit with different types of human relationships? What effects does the aging process have on our sexuality? As we look at some answers to these questions, you will again see that there is disagreement and controversy.

The possibility was raised in chapter 6, "Gender-Identity/Role and Society," that chromosomes and hormones may—even before birth—predispose human beings to certain patterns of sexual development. Thorough clarification of how important such physical factors may be is a long way off. For the most part experts seem to agree that human infants are essentially sexually nonspecific. In other words, although most humans have the capacity for sexual arousal and gratification, how they exercise that capacity—or even if they exercise it—is heavily influenced by learning. People probably learn many of the specifics of their sexual arousal. Some disagreement exists over whether sexual behavior is motivated more by biological forces, innate psychological influences, or cultural and social pressures. It is widely accepted that there is a complex interaction of all these factors, but controversy develops over which is most important.

Psychosexual Development

One way or another you gradually develop your own individualized way of thinking and feeling about sex, along with your own patterns of sexual orientation and behavior. This complex process is called psychosexual development, and it involves a great deal of learning.

Learning does not just happen in schools; it is a constant, informal process that results from all sorts of stimuli, from the obvious to the very subtle. For example, parents who choose not to discuss sex with their children are conveying a clear statement that sex

psychosexual development: complex interaction of factors that form a person's sexual feelings, orientations, and patterns of behavior.

FIGURE 7.1 Infant Sexuality

Infants develop an awareness of their bodies and their sexuality first through a bonding with the parents and the sensuous physical contact involved in cuddling and holding, and second by exploring their own bodies, including their genitals.

should not be talked about. There may well be critical periods in the learning process, too. These are times in a person's development when all of his or her capacities are at a maximum, and conditions are ideal for a particular kind of learning to take place. There may be critical periods in child development when sexual attitudes and preferences are established, although there is still little research in this area. Additionally, we know that what is learned and incorporated into the depth of one's being exerts some influence on later life and behavior. However, we need not be saddled indefinitely with learnings that produce negative or self-destructive outcomes. There can always be personal change and relearning.

In the remainder of this section I discuss six main ways in which psychosexual development has been explained. I make no attempt to decide which are the most reliable and accurate. Instead I ask you to find elements in each approach that make sense to you. The truth is that the factual information available, based on sound research, is very limited when we try to find good explanations of how we develop sexually at the different stages of life.

INBORN SEXUAL INSTINCT THEORY

The origins of sexual behavior in the individual have been a source of curiosity that people have been trying to understand for centuries. Among the earlier at-

tempts to explain psychosexual development was the idea that humans have an inborn "sexual instinct." Human beings are born with sex organs that become increasingly functional during their early years, and these organs are necessary for the propagation of the species. It was quite simple to assume, then, that nature had also built into each of us instincts for putting those sex organs into operation.

It is from these assumptions about human sexuality that ideas about the "naturalness" or "unnaturalness" of sexual behaviors developed. Whatever sexual behavior led to potential propagation of the species (i.e., heterosexual intercourse) could easily be classified as natural, while other forms of behavior (i.e., masturbation or homosexual acts) could be considered unnatural by default. Many people carried this concept even farther into moral value judgments of good and bad or healthy and sick. Behind it all was the idea that as children grew and developed, their sexual instincts gradually emerged and unfolded according to nature's plan.

Research gradually began to show that it was a mistake to assume that some behavior could be explained solely on the basis of inborn instincts. It became increasingly evident that environmental factors after birth could exert important influences on behavior. Throughout the years the concept of instinct has become quite muddled, and there is disagreement as to what constitutes an instinct, if indeed such a thing even exists. The theories of psychosexual development that follow put varying degrees of emphasis on the importance of inborn influences and the influences of learning; the nature-versus-nurture controversy continues.

PSYCHOANALYTIC THEORY

The contributions of Sigmund Freud formed the basis for psychoanalytic theory. One of the most controversial aspects of Freud's work has been his theory of infantile sexuality. Relying heavily on the concept of instincts, he postulated the existence of the libido, a word used to describe the sexual longing or sex drive that was a part of the sexual instinct. He also realized that in addition to this psychological aspect of the sexual instinct there was the physical aspect, involving bodily responses and behaviors. Another crucial aspect of psychoanalytic theory is the concept of the unconscious mind, purported to control much of human development and behavior even though its thought processes are outside conscious awareness. The libido

libido (la-BEED-o or LIB-a-do): a term first used by Freud to define human sexual longing, or sex drive.

and unconscious thought processes are essential elements in the psychoanalytic approach to psychosexual development, although there have been modifications made since Freud's early formulations.

The major assumption of this theory is that infants are born with a store of sexual energy in the form of the libido. At first, the energy is completely undifferentiated and indiscriminate. It can be directed at anything. For this reason, Freud said that infants were "polymorphously perverse." This energy gradually becomes associated with different pleasurable areas of the body until it finally localizes in the sex organs. Freud believed that it was variations in this process that molded not only the individual's sexual nature but the entire personality. Therefore, psychoanalysis believes psychosexual development to be at the root of all emotional health and illness.

Classical psychoanalytic theory states that the libido is invested in bodily parts that are important in a child's physical development. Hence sexual energies of the infant become centered in the mouth, important to gratification of the young child. This is referred to as the oral stage. As a child then begins to be toilet trained

and learns how to control pleasurably the retention and elimination of the bowels, her or his libido moves to the anus, a transition to the anal stage. It is then believed that by the age of about 3 years, children begin to be aware of their genitals, and the libido becomes centered in the penis or clitoris. Psychoanalysis teaches that it is in this phallic stage that children form an erotic attachment to the parent of the opposite sex and feel a rivalry toward the parent of the same sex. This is the Oedipus complex in boys and Electra complex in girls. Gradually, the child should resolve this conflict and identify with the parent of the same sex. Then there is the latency period, during which the sexual energies lie dormant while intellectual and social growth continues. The final stage, when sexual feelings are reawakened in the sex organs, begins at puberty and is called the genital stage (Roazen, 1991).

Psychoanalytic theory includes the idea that there are many things that can go wrong as the libido gradually becomes focused into the genitals. It holds that adult emotional and mental problems are the result of difficulties during some stage of psychosexual development. Ideally, according to this theory, young women and men should integrate genital orgasm with loving heterosexual relationships, leading toward healthy life-styles of satisfying sex, reproduction, and work. Needless to say, the emphasis on orgasm in this theory has often created undue concern for many women and their partners.

Modern psychoanalysis has modified many of the classical Freudian views. Critics have reminded us that Freud's work took place with his patients, an unrepresentative sample, and that his period in history was one of sexual repression and restriction, and male dominance. Feminists have taken issue with his work because he suggested that women tend to be inherently passive and that they face a lifetime of "penis envy," never fully resolving their feelings of inferiority and jealousy for lack of a penis. They hold that psychoanalysis is male-centered and discriminatory toward females. There is also evidence from recent research that the latency period does not exist, and that children remain in touch with their sexual and romantic feelings throughout childhood.

FIGURE 7.2 Freud's Oral Stage

The Freudian theory of sexual development states that in the first year of life the libido, or sex drive, is located in the mouth. This is the reason, according to Freud, that infants enjoy sucking and putting things into their mouths.

INTEGRATED SOCIAL FACTORS THEORY

Psychoanalytic theory tends to place the major emphasis on the inner forces of the individual during

latency period: Freudian concept that during middle childhood, sexual energies are dormant; recent research tends to suggest that latency does not exist.

psychosexual development. Other theories have brought social forces more clearly into the picture. For example, Erik Erikson (1968) made significant revisions to Freudian theory, expanding the psychoanalytic scheme into an eight-stage life cycle of psychosocial development, thus extending it into old age. Although Erikson also assumes that there is a powerful libido built into all of us, he believes that cultural and social influences help to shape our sexual identities, including the types of sexual activities that we prefer. He maintained that at each stage of eight stages of life, there is a crisis of psychosocial development that must be resolved in one of two ways (see Table 7.1). Each crisis can take the individual either in a direction of adjustment, health, and positive self-concept, or in a direction of maladaptation, unrest, and low self-esteem. According to Erikson, for example, during adolescence and young adulthood each individual has the task of achieving a clear understanding of herself or himself as a sexual person and of achieving a sense of intimacy with other human beings. Failure to reach these goals may result in role confusion and isolation that can generate unhealthy methods of sexual functioning for a lifetime. Success in achieving a healthy sexual identity partially hinges on how successfully the earlier stages of the life cycle have been passed. Erikson emphasizes the importance of other people and how they respond to the individual—social factors—in this model of psychosexual development.

The classic research of Harry Harlow and his associates (1971) with monkeys may well support the significance of social factors in psychosexual development. Studies with monkeys have demonstrated the serious effects of isolation on their sexual development. It is clear that monkeys' sexual activity, including the ability to establish intimacy (love) with others, cannot develop without lifetime social interaction with other monkeys. Many scientists feel there is now enough data to generalize this statement to human beings as well. It is likely that learning from other people is a necessary part of psychosexual development.

FIGURE 7.3 Erikson's Psychosocial Development

In Erikson's life-span theory of psychosocial development, young children learn skills as well as identity and values from those around them. Positive values about themselves and their sexuality will aid children in developing intimacy with others.

CONDITIONING AND SOCIAL LEARNING THEORY

Some students of human behavior deemphasize the idea of an inner sexual instinct and believe instead that sexual behavior is the result of complex patterns of conditioning. The Russian scientist Pavlov first demonstrated the principles of conditioning when he sounded a bell while giving dogs food. After several times, the dogs were conditioned to salivate simply at the sound of the bell. Such simple conditioning mechanisms may apply to some human responses in sex. For example, if particular erotic words are heard repeatedly during sexual arousal, eventually the words themselves could become a conditional stimulus that could elicit some degree of sexual arousal, the conditioned response. Later work in psychology clarified more complex principles of operant conditioning. According to these principles, when behavior is reinforced—either through pleasure, reward, or removal of some unpleasant stimulus—it is likely to be repeated. Negative consequences of a behavior through unpleasant results, pain, or the loss of rewarding stimuli tend to decrease the frequency of the behavior. As applied to sexual development in humans, this theory emphasizes the influences of positive and negative consequences over the concept of an internal drive.

psychosocial development: the cultural and social influences that help shape human sexual identity.
reinforcement: in conditioning theory, any influence that helps shape future behavior as a punishment or reward stimulus.

TABLE 7.1

The Crises to be Resolved During Erikson's Stages of Psychosocial Development

Stage in Life Cycle	Crisis
Infancy	Gaining trust in self and environment vs. Feeling mistrust and wariness of others
Ages 1½ – 3	Achieving a sense of autonomy vs. Shame and doubt over one's ability to be independent
Ages 3 – 5½	Learning how to take initiative comfortably vs. Feeling guilty over motivations and needs
Ages 5½ – 12	(The time when school and other external influences gain more significance) Gaining a sense of industry and competence vs. Feeling inferior and inept
Adolescence	Forming a sense of one's own identity vs. Role confusion and self-questioning
Young Adulthood	Achieving intimacy and connection with others vs. Isolation and loneliness
Adulthood	Building a feeling of generativity and accomplishment vs. Feeling stagnant and unfulfilled
Maturity	Achieving ego integrity and relative peace with one's life vs. A sense of despair and wastedness

Source: E. Erikson, *Identity: Youth and Crisis*, 1968, New York: W. W. Norton. Reprinted by permission.

Conditioning theorists emphasize that the development of modes of sexual functioning is a complex phenomenon, influenced by many different sources. They also use the concept of generalization to explain how specific, learned sexual responses might be generalized to other, similar circumstances. For example, an individual who is conditioned to become sexually aroused by seeing female breasts may generalize that experience to other things associated with breasts: bras, other underwear, blouses, other parts of a woman's body, perfume, and so on. The generalization process is kept in check by discrimination, which enables the individual to avoid responding to one stimulus while responding to similar stimuli.

Conditioning theory then holds that we learn our sexual preferences and behaviors through observational learning, a complex pattern of reinforcement, and the pairing of stimuli with the sexual reflex. As human beings grow up, social cues are picked up that help determine what is considered "acceptable" sexual behavior. Gradually the set of stimuli to which the individual responds sexually is narrowed. If sexual behaviors or needs that the person does not consider socially acceptable remain, then conflicts and emotional disturbances may develop.

An extension of conditioning theory has been offered by a model called social learning theory (Bandura & Walters, 1963). This model suggests that the learning process is influenced by cumulative observation of and identification with other people. This cumulative learning process is a crucial one, as people's perceptions are shaped by the impressions and attitudes they have formed in their early development. For example, children and adolescents are prone to imitate and adopt the behaviors they see in other people whom they admire and identify with. This theory demonstrates the potential power of television and movies, as well as of parents, friends, and others in the modeling of sexual behaviors.

generalization: application of specific learned responses to other, similar situations or experiences.
discrimination: the process by which an individual extinguishes a response to one stimulus while preserving it for other stimuli.
social learning theory: suggests that human learning is influenced by observation of and identification with other people.

169

FIGURE 7.4   Bandura's Social Learning Theory

According to this theory, children learn attitudes and values by observing and imitating the behavior of others. What they learn depends partly on the power and prestige of the person observed. Television, movies, and music can be powerful influences on the sexual values and behavior of children and adolescents.

SOCIAL SCRIPT THEORY

John Gagnon and William Simon (1973) developed another theory of psychosexual development that emphasizes learning from the society and culture. They took issue with psychoanalysis and many other models on two major counts. First, they questioned the existence of an intense, biologically generated sex drive. They felt instead that sexual energy may not be very intense at all, at least in many individuals. Second, they felt that too much emphasis had been placed on the effects of childhood sexual patterns on later development. Many novel factors come into play at the beginning of adolescence that can exert significant influence on sexual development, quite independent of childhood experience.

According to their theory, almost all human behavior is controlled by <u>social scripts</u>. They believe that very little behavior can truly be called spontaneous, since we learn complex scripts for how we are sup-

posed to behave under various circumstances. In terms of sexual behavior, this would mean that various social situations are not sexually oriented in themselves, but that we are programmed to view some situations as sexual. Because of the social scripts that we learn, we organize the elements of a situation—for example, an available partner, privacy, sexual desire—in such a way that they become sexual; they are not inherently so. Since social scripts are learned, new learning experiences during each new stage of an individual's physical development help to contribute to that individual's sexual development. The foundation of this theory is that sexual behavior—rather than pouring forth from an inner libido or being conditioned—is invented for the individual by psychological, social, and cultural interactions. The social scripts that are learned for sexual behavior not only determine the relative importance of sex in a person's life, but help to mold his or her specific sexual needs and preferences.

Sexual scripts have three different levels, reflective of different levels of functioning for the individual. In the broadest context, scripts have *cultural scenarios,* referring to the messages and instructional guidance about sexual behavior offered by one's culture. It is widely accepted that social and cultural imperatives play a significant role in determining what sexual choices people will make within their society or culture. On an intermediate level, there are the *interpersonal scripts* determined by the expectations from other people about conduct within interpersonal relationships. Then, at the level of the individual's own mind, are the *intrapsychic scripts.* The person takes all of the information from the cultural and interpersonal contexts, and processes it internally. As individual men and women make sense of what the surrounding sexual messages mean for them, they begin to develop their own sets of sexual scripts. These three levels of scripting are constantly interacting with one another, and scripts may be modified over the course of a person's life span (Gagnon, 1990a).

A UNIFIED THEORETICAL MODEL OF SEXUAL DEVELOPMENT

Researcher John Bancroft (1990a) has proposed a unified theory of how sexual development takes place. It considers the various stages of physical and psychological development through which human beings pass, and identifies three principal "strands" that are part of each person's developmental framework. These three strands tend to develop in parallel during the

social scripts: a complex set of learned responses to a particular situation that is formed by social influences.

childhood years, but relatively independent of one another. Then, during adolescence, the strands come together and become more integrated as they form the foundations of a sexually mature adult. These strands have been identified as follows:

1. Gender identity. The inner sense of oneself along the continuum of masculinity and femininity plays a crucial role in sexual development. During childhood, the basic identity is established, and during adolescence, sexual behaviors serve an important function in reorganizing the specifics of one's gender identity. This begins to establish the sense of oneself as man, woman, or in between.

2. Sexual response and understanding one's sexual orientation. Puberty triggers a variety of physical and emotional changes within the individual, and usually leads to a greater awareness of and urge toward sexual arousal. The coming to terms with these needs and responses plays an important part in figuring out who one really is sexually.

3. Capacity for intimate dyadic relationships. In later adolescence and early adulthood, people begin exploring their sexuality within the context of partnerships or dyads (pairs). How effective the individual is in handling the complexities of dyadic relationships is a significant part of later sexual development.

Part of sexual development is gaining a deeper understanding of one's own sexual orientation, a process that unfolds as people negotiate the various stages of their physical and psychological development. There are three distinct steps to this process, that seem to bring together different aspects of the theories of psychosexual development discussed earlier (Bancroft, 1990a):

Children go through a *prelabeling* process, and they begin to identify what is expected of them sexually. Their behavior is mostly subject to the effects of social learning, as their various behaviors are reinforced one way or the other by social expectations and pressures.

Adolescents then begin to categorize their own sexual orientations according to the labels that their social groups provide. This is the *self-labeling* stage of identifying sexual orientation. The adolescent privately compares her or his own feelings and responses to those that are prescribed in the prevailing social scripts. How adolescents react to the sexual orientation labels they give themselves at this point depends on the progress they have made in their three developmental strands; that is, what degree of confidence and conformity they feel with their gender identity, when and how their sexual desires actually developed, and what sort of capacity they have developed for coping with intimacy. If self-labels are out of step with what the

adolescent has learned is expected and desired by the society and culture, a great deal of personal conflict and confusion may result.

Finally, sexual orientation is defined through *social labeling*. The person's perceptions of self are subject to validation by what is known about the society's labels for various sexual orientations and preferences. Again, social scripts are important in determining the sorts of judgments that are made about various orientations.

Sexuality in Infancy and Childhood

Little research data is available concerning the sexual responsiveness of infants. There is evidence from ultrasound images of fetuses still in the uterus that a male fetus can experience erection of the penis even before birth (Calderone, 1983). This reinforces a concept that most sexologists accept today: That the physiological responses of human sex organs occur regardless of whether they are deliberately sought out or even desired. Very early in development, infants seem to show interest in exploring their own bodies and seeking whatever pleasure they can gain from that exploration.

There is ample evidence to suggest that baby boys experience genital responses. Their penises are exposed and parents often report that a boy baby's penis becomes erect easily and that the infant seems to enjoy any penile stimulation. Erection has even been observed within the first few minutes after birth.

A number of male infants seem to have orgasms, as evidenced by sequences of tension-building, rhythmic muscular contractions, and pelvic thrusting, culminating in what appears to be pleasurable sensations and relaxation. The capacity for orgasm is reached at different ages by different boys. Kinsey (1948) reported that in a small sample of males (317), orgasms had been observed in 32 percent of those under 1 year of age and in 57 percent of those between the ages of 2 and 5.

There is less substantial evidence to demonstrate the sexual responsiveness of baby girls, and their sexually responsive organs are not as easily observed. It is known that for about a month after birth a girl's genitals may be somewhat swollen and inflamed because of maternal hormones still present in her bloodstream from her fetal stage. This seems to cause a temporary early "maturation" of the girl's sex organs. The vagina temporarily has secretions and cell maturation typical of adults. This would tend to suggest that girls may well have vaginal sensations immediately

171

after birth. Again, observations by parents and professionals suggest that many infant females are also capable of experiencing some form of orgasmic release (Langfeldt, 1981).

While it is not likely that these early patterns of physical arousal represent an awakening of social levels of eroticism, they do demonstrate the extreme sensitivity of infants. Austrian researcher Ernest Borneman (1983) has suggested that the entire surface of the skin in a newborn infant is a single erogenous zone, meaning that it is sensitive to sensual stimulation that can lead to arousal.

The foundations for sensuality, intimacy, and relationship to other people are established during infancy. Bonding between infants and their parents is an important part of this process. Infancy may also be a time when small children begin to notice differences in how they are treated by their fathers and mothers. Research shows that even though there has been some movement in recent years toward a greater parenting role for fathers, it is mothers who generally assume most of the responsibility for infant care. Fathers will occasionally help out with the caretaking or with household responsibilities when the mother is tired or unavailable, but the routine care typically falls to women (Burns, Mitchell, & Obradovich, 1989). Men tend to become increasingly involved when their children begin to talk and walk.

There are several significant developmental tasks accomplished during infancy. Immediately after birth there is a period when the baby seems very alert and a bonding process goes on between it and its parent(s). The holding, touching, and cuddling given to an infant are part of the evolution of its ability to relate to and be intimate with others (Bensel, 1984). Between 6 months and 1 year of age, babies begin to touch their genitals, if they are not prohibited from doing so. This represents a rehearsal of genital exploration and stimulation, and how adults react to these activities sets the stage for the development of later sexual values. As we have seen in the preceding chapter, infancy is also the time when the baby begins its period of "training" to become masculine or feminine, and its gender identity begins to become clearer (Higham, 1980).

SEXUAL CURIOSITY GROWS IN CHILDHOOD

Very young children are often observed fondling their genitals, sometimes seeming to produce sexual excitement and orgasm. There is some disagreement as to whether this genital play should be considered masturbation, since it does not usually represent a deliberate seeking of sexual gratification. Whatever the motivations, children begin to gain a sense of what their

FIGURE 7.5 Sexual Curiosity

Most children around the age of 2 or 3 are curious about their own bodies as well as the bodies of others. Any sexual activity usually involves a fondling of the genitals. Since children tend to respond to each other affectionately at these ages, touching, hugging, and kissing may extend to the genital area.

bodies are and the capacities for pleasure that their bodies have. This can be seen as a beginning period of potentiation, when vague awareness of sexual feelings and early ranges of sexual responsiveness are established. Most of the specifics of sexual orientations and interests are probably established later in life. Children also learn more and more about sex and reproduction as they progress through childhood, with a spurt of knowledge and understanding occurring around the age of 11 (Goldman & Goldman, 1982).

By the age of 2 or 3, many children begin to explore the genitals of their playmates, as well as continuing to have an interest in their own. Before long many become involved in games, basically nonsexual in context, that permit mutual body exploration. Games such as "doctor" or "nurse" are old standbys.

Self-manipulation of the genitals and exhibiting genitals to other children are the most common forms of childhood sex play. In later childhood some youngsters experiment with other forms of behavior—including oral-genital contact and attempts at anal or vaginal intercourse. These activities may be with a same-sex

erogenous zone (a-RAJ-a-nus): any area of the body that is sensitive to sexual arousal.

potentiation: establishment of stimuli early in life that form ranges of response for later in life.

Case Study	**KAREN AND HER CHILDREN: A MOTHER DEALS WITH HER CHILDREN'S SEX PLAY**

Karen always attempted to answer her two children's questions about sex and where babies come from. At ages 4 and 6 respectively, Bobby and Anne were bright, cheerful youngsters who were relatively well informed about sex.

Another mother in the neighborhood telephoned Karen one afternoon to tell her that Bobby and Anne had been discovered in a bedroom with her child and two other children, all naked and apparently engaged in some sort of "hospital" game. She was sending Anne and Bobby home and suggested that Karen should reprimand them for their involvement in the incident. She also implied that Bobby and Anne might have been the primary instigators of the nude game. Karen, however, was not particularly upset by the incident and considered such play to be normal and healthy sex exploration. She talked about the game with her children briefly and concentrated primarily on soothing their hurt feelings caused by the neighbor's anger.

Several months later Karen happened to enter Anne's room where her two children were play-ing. She discovered both children on the bed in the nude, Bobby lying on top of Anne and apparently imitating the thrusting motions of sexual intercourse. Both children were giggling. Much to her own surprise, Karen reacted to the scene with shock and anger. She yelled at the two to stop and told Bobby to leave the room. She then decided to take some time alone herself to think the situation over. After her own anger had subsided, she talked with the two and explained that their actions had upset her. She also told them that although she knew they had only been playing, she did not like their pretending to have sex with each other. Without going into detail about incest, she said that it would not be "right" for a brother and sister actually to have sex. Anne and Bobby seemed to accept their mother's ideas and said that they would not play that game again.

Although things seemed settled, Karen still had doubts over whether or not she had handled the incident properly. Like all parents she would simply have to wait and see.

partner or one of the opposite sex. Repeated aggressive sexual behavior in younger children toward other children such as coercive oral sex, insertion of objects into the rectum, or attempted rape, may well represent signs of previous sexual abuse of the child (Gale et al., 1988). This is discussed in greater detail in chapter 13.

How parents respond to sex play in children begins to set the stage for later sex-related values. If a parent constantly punishes a child's attempts at genital exploration or sex play, the child may rapidly learn that her or his sex organs and exploratory behaviors are bad. At times the reactions of anxious adults can transform an innocent, natural phase of sexual exploration into a traumatic event with lasting negative consequences for the child. Children often begin to see their sexuality in very clearly defined terms, resulting from parental attitudes toward anything sexual. If parents accept sexual exploration as a natural, positive part of growing up and help children to understand what will be socially acceptable in later life, they may

contribute enormously to the development of a healthy sexuality in their children.

One of the concerns that parents sometimes have is the degree to which nudity should be allowed or encouraged within the family's setting. Most professionals agree that when nudity within the home is permitted, and that provided there is no sexual abuse, there do not seem to be negative consequences. Children themselves may well reach stages in their development when they signal some discomfort with being seen naked by other family members or with seeing their parents nude. It is important for parents to respect these needs, making as little fuss as possible, and avoiding inflicting any embarrassment on the child. A study of 210 college students found that childhood exposure to nudity in the home did not adversely affect adult sexual adjustment or functioning. In fact, men in the study who had regularly seen their parents naked tended to be the ones most comfortable with physical contact and expressions of affection (Lewis & Janda, 1988).

LOVE AND ROMANCE IN CHILDHOOD

Largely because of the Freudian concept of latency, it has generally been assumed that children between the ages of roughly 6 and 12 have little interest in sexual feelings or relationships with the opposite sex. Instead it was believed that the sexual energies were dormant and that children tended to reject members of the opposite sex in favor of same-sexed friends. Researchers who have studied children and their sexual development have generally expressed skepticism about the existence of a latency phase, instead finding evidence that children tend to be in touch with sexual and romantic feelings throughout childhood (Borneman, 1983; Goldman & Goldman, 1982).

One study found that among 9- to 11-year-olds—the age group that was supposed to be the least interested in the opposite sex—90 percent claimed to have a "special" boyfriend or girlfriend. It clarified what seems to happen during the period called latency. The number of youngsters who actually reject relationships with the opposite sex is quite small. Far more children begin to develop heterosexual romantic attachments as the first step in a "sequence of events

leading to full-fledged adolescent heterosexuality" (Broderick, 1972, p. 20). The next step is gradually recognizing the attachment, and the feelings associated with it, as "love." Children appear to take their love very seriously and begin to move toward more concrete wishing and planning. A final step is arranging a "date" with the boyfriend or girlfriend, among those 10- to 12-year-olds who have the courage to do so. During adolescence nearly everyone begins to get involved in romantic attachments, but it is clear that many preadolescent children have already experienced significant development in that area.

There are also same-sexed romantic attachments during childhood. Because of social pressures, children are less inclined to label these attachments "love," and instead describe them as friendships.

It appears that, in our culture, girls who seem interested in romance and sex during childhood create more anxiety and alarm in adults than do boys with such orientations. Early sexual awakening in girls is often interpreted as unnatural precociousness. As the inequities of the double standard shift, perhaps the sexuality of young girls will be accepted with less concern.

FIGURE 7.6 Preadolescent Sexuality

Freud's concept of latency in which he stated that interest in sex declined around the age of 9 or 10 has now been discredited. Rather, preadolescents form close relationships with others that may or may not involve sexual activity, but which they view as special and romantic.

Sexuality in Adolescence

Puberty is that time when youngsters become capable of reproducing and their bodies begin to take on distinctly male or female secondary sex characteristics. It is a biological and physiological phenomenon.

Girls typically experience puberty sooner than boys, so there is often a period around ages 11 to 13 when boys' physical maturation lags behind that of girls. This can be an awkward time, when new relationships between the sexes are just beginning and yet girls have moved into young adolescence and boys feel the need to "catch up" (McCaffree, 1989). Girls' maturation may also cause some difficulty for fathers who find themselves somewhat attracted to their daughters' developing bodies. Their guilt and concern about their own reactions may cause them to be less affectionate to their daughters, and the girls may in turn feel hurt and confused by their fathers' apparent withdrawal. Good communication can often resolve the difficulties (Goulston, 1988).

Adolescence, that period of social and emotional development that moves young people toward adult-

puberty: time of life when reproductive capacity develops and secondary sex characteristics appear.

adolescence: period of emotional, social, and physical transition from childhood to adulthood.

hood, is mostly a social and cultural phenomenon. In North America, the adolescent is caught between new biological forces and the demands of society (Potts, 1990). Although it is generally acknowledged that sexual development during adolescence is significant in the evolution of adult sexual orientations and behaviors, its boundaries are poorly defined in Western societies. In many primitive cultures there are rites of passage in which a youthful individual participates, declaring that she or he is no longer a child. Along with that passage into young adulthood come carefully prescribed (and proscribed) modes of sexual behavior. Youngsters in Western culture usually must deal with growth into adulthood in a much more vague and gradual way. In their sexual development, as in many other aspects of their growth, adolescents often experience confusion, fear, and misunderstandings about their bodies and emotions. Adolescence is an especially important phase in learning to be sexual (Selverstone, 1989).

Adolescence is sometimes portrayed by writers as a period during which the sex drive reaches almost uncontrollable peaks. While most adolescents experience an increased level of interest in sex, this phenomenon occurs in varying degrees. There are young people who experience an insistent sexual interest and the need for frequent sexual gratification, but there are others who experience very little in the way of sexual needs. The influence of social attitudes in this picture cannot be ignored. There are adolescents who feel pressured by our sex-oriented culture to show special interest in sex and those who feel guilty or frightened because they do not experience intense sexual drives.

There is at the very least for most adolescents an increased interest in matters sexual. In recent years there has been pressure on adolescents to experiment with sexual activities at a relatively young age, creating conflict for some young people who do not feel ready for such a step (Sarrel & Sarrel, 1979).

SEXUAL BEHAVIOR IN ADOLESCENCE

The development of sexual behavior during adolescence seems to be influenced by several factors. First, there are the biological influences from hormones that have triggered certain sexual arousal capabilities. Boys' automatic sexual responses, such as erections and nocturnal orgasms, increase dramatically as their bodies' secretion of testosterone surges during puberty. Then there are the social factors that on the one hand demonstrate the rewards and good feelings of sexual behavior, while on the other hand establish social controls on behavior through disapproval of sexual activity. A third factor, which cannot be ignored

in the determination of when shared sexual activity begins for an adolescent, and which is also influenced by social standards, is physical attractiveness. For shared sex, the individual must somehow attract a partner (Udry, 1990).

There are several steps or processes that are considered normal and typical during the psychosexual development of adolescents. While these processes may be initiated during adolescence, many of them take a lifetime of unfolding, and offer endless opportunities for growth. They include (Sarrel, 1989):

1. Evolving a body image specific to one's gender.
2. Overcoming, or at least modulating, the guilt, shame, or inhibitions associated with one's childhood sexual thoughts or feelings.
3. Loosening the ties to parents and siblings.
4. Recognizing what is sexually pleasurable and unpleasurable.
5. Resolving most conflict or confusion about sexual orientation.
6. Developing an increasingly satisfying and rich sexual life, free of problematic compulsions or dysfunctions.
7. Growing in awareness of the place sexuality is to have in one's life, and considering various options, including celibacy.
8. Developing a sense of responsibility toward oneself, one's sexual partners, and society.
9. Increasing the ability to experience eroticism as one aspect of intimacy with another person.
10. Experiencing first sexual intercourse, although this is by no means the case for *all* adolescents.

SELF-CENTERED EARLY ADOLESCENT SEX

As the physical changes of puberty occur, the adolescent must begin to integrate new awareness into her or his core gender identity. Boys experience their first ejaculations of semen, and girls begin menstruating. New attention is therefore called to their sex organs. At the same time, parents and others begin to attach new meanings to behaviors and emotions. The adolescent must build these developments into his or her self-awareness as a young man or woman. The ages between 12 and 16 often see the beginning of more specifically sexual behavior. The earlier an adolescent girl has experienced physical sexual maturation, the earlier she may be expected to become involved in dating and sexual intercourse (Phinney et al., 1990). Since social development often has not matched physical maturation, sex in early adolescence tends to be self-centered.

Most boys experience their first ejaculation during masturbation, although they may have previously

175

experienced orgasm without emission of semen. The first ejaculation usually occurs between the ages of 11 and 15, although Kinsey reported cases of the earliest remembered ejaculation occurring as young as 8 years and as old as 21 years. In about 12 percent of boys first ejaculation happened as a nocturnal emission ("wet dream"), and in about 5 percent it occurred during some homosexual activity (Kinsey et al., 1948). Some boys, after puberty, report having "spontaneous" ejaculations from time to time, produced by nonsexual physical activity or psychological influences (for example, viewing pictures, watching an attractive person). By late adolescence the capacity to have "spontaneous" orgasms is apparently lost in nearly all males.

Girls have tended to exhibit less sexual activity and less intensity in sexual feelings during adolescence. There is disagreement currently over whether this is the result of innate differences or cultural influences. Childhood sex play tends to reach a peak in girls around the age of 9. It then drops off considerably. So while boys tend to be getting more involved in sex play at the beginning of adolescence, girls tend to be getting less involved. As adolescence progresses, however, girls gradually become more involved in sexual activity and better acquainted with their sexual responsiveness, a trend that often continues for another 10 to 20 years. Throughout adolescence females exhibit a somewhat lower incidence of masturbation, homosexual activity, and heterosexual experimentation (Kinsey et al., 1953; Sorenson, 1973; Mott & Haurin, 1988). The capacity for "spontaneous" orgasm, without physical stimulation, apparently exists in some girls and even persists in a few women. They can experience orgasm by viewing sexually arousing material or just by thinking about sex.

Another aspect of self-centered sex that often increases during early adolescence is the experiencing of erotic fantasies and dreams. As the body matures and new sexual feelings emerge, an awareness develops of the social significance of sex, and young people begin to daydream about sex. Adolescents may fantasize about loving relationships that involve sexual activity with a particular person or about a wide array of sexual practices with nonspecific partners. The fantasies that accompany masturbation are often quite vivid and add to the pleasure of the masturbatory experience. If the fantasies contain sexual behaviors that the young person has learned to consider "unnatural" or "bad" or "sick," a great deal of guilt may be generated. In any case it is likely that early fantasies not only act as temporarily satisfying substitutes for unavailable sexual acts, but help the young person to become more fully acquainted with her or his sexual preferences. It is also likely that many adolescents use

their fantasy experiences to plan for real sexual encounters later in life.

The new awareness that comes with experiencing sexual feelings, orgasm, and erotic fantasies is an important step in learning to be sexual.

ADOLESCENT HOMOSEXUAL ACTIVITY

Early adolescence is a period when girls and boys tend to associate more with members of their own sex. Sexual preferences are also relatively nonspecific at these ages. Consequently, it is not surprising that as youngsters experience pronounced physical changes in their sex organs and begin to become more aware of their sexual feelings, they experiment with sex in encounters with same-sexed peers.

The statistics on adolescent homosexual activity are inconclusive and mostly focus on males. Because of the stigma that young people often attach to homosexual behavior, it is assumed that some would be hesitant to admit to any homosexual experiences they may have had. The lowest incidence of adolescent homosexual behavior was reported in a study by Sorensen (1973). In that study, 11 percent of adolescent boys and 6 percent of adolescent girls reported having participated in some sort of homosexual act. Boys tended to report more frequent homosexual experiences in later adolescence (ages 16 to 19), while girls reported less frequent experiences in the later age levels. Another study indicated that 11 percent of teenage girls and 14 percent of boys reported having had at least one sexual experience with someone of the same sex (Hass, 1979).

The figures of the Kinsey studies (1948, 1953) indicate that 60 percent of males and 33 percent of females report having had at least one homosexual experience by the age of 15. Since these were adults reporting experiences during their youth, it might be expected that there was less tendency to avoid the truth.

However, the significance of the statistics comes clearer only with closer analysis. Many of the males reporting some homosexual experience actually had only one such encounter. About half of the males reporting homosexual activity had no further homosexual contact after the age of 15 and another 33 percent never had any further homosexual contact after the age of 17 or 18. Also much of what is classified as homosexual behavior in these statistics is apparently little more than sex play, rather than intense sexual intimacy (Gagnon & Simon, 1973).

So it is clear that while many adolescents, particularly boys, may participate at least once in some sexual contact with a same-sexed partner, overt homosexual activity during adolescence is not a predominating form of sexual behavior. It is also true, however, that some adolescents begin to get in touch with their homosexual inclinations during adolescence. Adult male homosexuals report that their first homosexual experience generally occurred by the age of 14, while adult lesbians report that their first experiences tended to occur in the late teenage years.

For adolescents who have clearly identified themselves as being primarily homosexual in orientation, there are some very real social obstacles to their sexual development. Not the least of these obstacles is a society that tends to expect heterosexuality and tends to fear and dislike same-sexed orientations (Friedman, 1989). Homosexual adolescents have to achieve self-acceptance of their sexual orientation in the face of pressures not to accept or act upon that orientation. They also face the task of developing intimate emotional attachments with members of their own sex, when there are many social prohibitions for doing so. Nevertheless, attitudes in recent years toward differing sexual orientations have been changing, and there is more information and support available for people with homosexual orientations. Some homosexual teenagers have been able to surmount the extra measure of social difficulty with resilience and self-acceptance while others have continued to wrestle with their sexual identity issues into adulthood (Remafedi, 1989).

It is difficult to assess the full meaning of adolescent sexual behavior. For most people, adolescent sexual experiences appear to have little significance for their adult lives. Most professionals agree that it is usually not childhood or adolescent sexual activity that leads to predominantly homosexual or heterosexual preferences in later life (see chapter 11, "Homosexuality and Bisexuality"). It is likely that adolescent experimentation with either sex represents another way in which people learn about their sexuality.

MASTURBATION IN ADOLESCENCE

The most prevalent form of sexual activity in adolescence is masturbation. Most males and many females begin to learn about their bodies' sexual responses through masturbation. Adolescent boys have tended to discuss masturbation among themselves—often in a joking way—more than adolescent girls. Consequently, a great many slang terms have evolved to describe male masturbation (jerk off, jack off, whack off, beat off, beat the meat). In comparison there are almost no slang terms for female masturbation (except for rubbing off, rolling the pill, and fingering), and it seems to be a more taboo topic for discussion among adolescent girls.

Statistics also indicate that at all age levels, masturbation is more common among males than females. In the Sorensen study, 58 percent of adolescent boys and 39 percent of adolescent girls admitted to having masturbated at least once. Only 36 percent of the boys questioned and 21 percent of the girls admitted to masturbation once or more during the preceding month. Many professionals have contended that these figures are too low and that the actual incidence of masturbation among adolescents is higher. Other studies have supported that contention. The Kinsey statistics (1948, 1953) showed that by the age of 15, 82 percent of boys and 20 percent of girls had masturbated. By age 20, the figures rose to 92 percent and 33 percent respectively. In later life the statistics go even higher. Another study of over 1,100 high school youth (Gagnon et al., 1970) showed that 77 percent of high school males and 17 percent of high school females reported masturbating twice a week or more. Another 12 percent of the boys and 23 percent of the girls admitted to masturbating at least once, to as often as once per month. A smaller percentage of the boys (11 percent) and the majority of girls (60 percent) said they had never masturbated. There may be a slight decline in frequency of masturbation during the years when young people are in college (Atwood & Gagnon, 1987).

It is clear that adolescent boys masturbate more than adolescent girls and more boys than girls seem to enjoy it (Sorensen, 1973). It is unclear whether these differences between the sexes are the result of innate psychological differences or learned attitudes toward sexual behavior. There is more information on masturbation in chapter 10, "Solitary Sex and Shared Sex."

ADOLESCENT HETEROSEXUAL ACTIVITY

Experimentation with heterosexuality is an important step for many adolescents in learning to be sexual. Actual sexual contact with a member of the opposite sex is often preceded by fantasies about such contact. These fantasies, sometimes accompanying masturbation, constitute a rehearsal for the "real thing." Most adolescents are hesitant to begin carrying out their fantasies in real life. Many become convinced, often mistakenly, that their friends are more knowledgeable and experienced when it comes to sex, and they fear that their own lack of experience will be exposed by their initial awkwardness. Additionally, many young people have strong feelings of guilt over their new sexual feelings and desires. Eventually, most adolescents manage to find someone with whom they try some form of heterosexual experimentation. For some the period of awkwardness and embarrassment passes

177

FIGURE 7.7　Adolescent Sexuality

Adolescents in contemporary industrial societies acquire adult status much later than they acquire biological maturity. This accounts for some of the confusion in adolescent sexual behavior. Adolescence is a time of awkward experimentation in sexual behavior and the acquisition of adult sexual attitudes involving commitment, intimacy, and fidelity.

quickly, and they soon become more comfortable with their sexuality. For others the awkwardness persists, or else other factors lead to lack of interest in sex, and they do not become sexually experienced until later in their lives.

Terms such as necking, petting, and heavy petting have been used for years to describe various sorts of sexual activity. In recent years young people have used these terms less, partly because their meanings are vague and more specific terms have come along to take their place (masturbation, blow job, deep kissing), and partly because today's young people view them as being unsophisticated.

Heterosexual contact usually seems to proceed through stages of progressive intimacy or what has been called levels of sharing (Kelly, 1986). How rapidly a particular couple progresses through the stages depends, of course, on many factors, including the type of relationship involved. Gagnon (1990a) believes that the sequence is another social script by which we learn to live. In any case the first level of intimacy is kissing and tongue ("French") kissing. Bodily contact below the neck usually begins with hand-holding and the male touching the female's breasts, first through

the clothing and then inside the clothing. Both partners begin to touch one another's genitals through the clothing and then directly. It is quite common during this level of intimacy for the two individuals to bring their genitals close together while clothed. It is not uncommon for males to have the experience of ejaculating with their clothes on at some time in this process (thus, the expression "creaming your jeans").

Research studies have offered some insights about adolescent heterosexual activity. Eighty-five percent of adolescents report having had a boyfriend or girlfriend, and close to 90 percent report having kissed someone of the opposite sex. At age 13, 20 percent of males say they have touched a girl's breasts, and 25 percent of females indicate they have had their breasts touched. Twenty-three percent of boys at this age, and 18 percent of girls, report having participated in vaginal play. In the older teenage brackets, these figures increase to 61 percent of males and 60 percent of females (Bigler, 1989).

Although many adolescent couples stop at this point, the typical sequential pattern is then to bring the nude genitals together. These latter stages of sexual exploration can lead to intercourse. There may also be some oral-genital contact either preceding intercourse or instead of it. Oral sex has become more common among adolescents in the past two decades. In one study of high school students, 25 percent of males and 15 percent of females who reported never having had intercourse did indicate that they had participated in oral-genital sex (Newcomer & Udry, 1985).

We are only beginning to understand how adolescents learn about sex, and much of the information we do have comes from questioning college students about their earlier sources of sex information. Over the years, research has tended to confirm that families are not a primary source of sex information, although in general, children are far more confident about asking sex questions of their mothers than they are of their fathers (Goldman & Goldman, 1982). Primary sources of sex information for the majority of young persons are friends of the same sex and independent reading. Teachers and the mass media are becoming increasingly important to adolescents in learning about issues such as sexual biology, sexually transmitted diseases, abortion, and homosexuality (Trost, 1990).

Fathers, siblings, teachers, and doctors have relatively little influence on most adolescents' types and frequency of premarital sexual behavior. Mothers tend to regard their daughters' premarital sexual activity in a negative manner, whereas the daughters' male friends and the media tend to support such activity in a positive way. Premarital sexual behavior for men is more positively accepted by both their male and female friends and by attitudes in most print and media

Case Study | ## JOE: A TEENAGER EXPLORES HETEROSEXUALITY

Joe first experienced sexual intercourse at the age of 16. He enjoyed the experience and continued to search for new sexual encounters. By the age of 20, he had had 10 different sexual partners and considered himself quite a connoisseur of sex. He had contracted gonorrhea once but none of his partners had ever experienced a pregnancy scare. More recently, he became worried by the AIDS scene, and sought testing, which proved negative.

For all of his sexual activity, Joe was dissatisfied with sex. He felt no guilt and believed that he had never exploited any of his partners. However, he had the distinct sense that something was missing. His relationships had all been casual, and he longed for something more than friendship. Yet Joe was afraid of getting trapped into something too serious.

Toward the end of his second year in college, he began seeing a young woman on a regular basis. Early in the relationship they began having sexual intercourse. After several months Joe decided that this was the sort of relationship he had been wanting. He and his girlfriend decided to maintain sexual fidelity, and he gave up looking for other sexual partners. Soon after that, the woman transferred to a different college, and they have made tentative marriage plans for after college. During their temporary periods of separation, they suspend their fidelity agreement, and Joe and his girlfriend are free to have sex with other partners. So far they have each had several sexual partners, yet they both feel committed to their future together.

material; the clergy still generally tend to exert negative influence (Mancini & Mancini, 1983).

Several studies in recent years have confirmed that adolescents are becoming sexually active much earlier now than they did in the late 1940s. Nonintercourse activities have increased, and there has been an associated increase in heterosexual intercourse as well. In the United States, nonwhite teenagers have consistently shown a higher incidence of sexual intercourse than white adolescents. However, during the 1980s those ethnic statistical differences were diminishing and becoming less significant (Wyatt, 1990). Data suggest that sexual experience for white teens increased during the 1970s and then leveled off at new higher levels between 1979 and 1982. For nonwhite adolescents, however, the incidence of sexual experience leveled off between 1976 and 1979, and then declined somewhat during the early eighties (Hofferth, 1990). The most typical reasons that teenagers cite for not choosing to have sexual intercourse are parental disapproval, fear of pregnancy, or not feeling as though they are mature enough. For women who have chosen to have intercourse prior to the age of 18, the top reasons cited were curiosity, partner pressure, love for a partner, or simply wanting to have sex (Wyatt, 1990).

The Kinsey research (1948, 1953) suggested that only about 20 percent of adolescent girls and 45 percent of adolescent boys had experienced intercourse by the age of 19. These figures had risen to 68 –69 percent of females and 77–78 percent of males by the 1980s (Zelnik & Kantner, 1980; Mott & Haurin, 1988). To put these figures in a broader perspective, among the 9 million adolescent women in the United States in 1988, about 4.9 million, or 52 percent, had experienced sexual intercourse. In fact, from 1985 through 1988, the proportion of teenage women reporting sexual activity increased 7.4 percentage points, accounting for one-third of the increase in teenage women between the entire period from 1970 to 1988.

From 5 percent to 17 percent of girls under the age of 15 have had intercourse, as have 19 percent to 38 percent of boys under age 15 (Gordon & Gilgun, 1987). Research also indicates that once adolescents have had intercourse, it is relatively likely they will participate more than once. This is especially true for the older teenage brackets. Of the teenagers between 15 and 17 who have had intercourse, only about 10 percent experienced it just once (Hofferth, 1990). Fifty-eight percent of sexually active teenage women aged 15 to 19 have reported having intercourse with two or more partners (Singh & Forrest, 1990).

Adolescents who are involved in longer-term relationships with members of the opposite sex are more likely to have intercourse on a regular basis.

Although heterosexual contact during adolescence is often sporadic, there can be no doubt that it plays a significant role in learning how sex will be shared and in discovering how important that sharing will be to the individual.

The sharp increase in sexual activity among adolescents has surprised and alarmed some experts. It is particularly significant when there have been so many efforts to provide AIDS education and prevent unintended pregnancies among teenagers. Nevertheless, the United States continues to have one of the highest rates of unintended pregnancy and abortion among developed countries of the world, and the least accessibility to contraception for teenagers (Forrest, 1990). It is interesting to note that with increased awareness of the disease AIDS has come a higher incidence of condom use among teenaged males. In 1989, 58 percent of sexually active males aged 15 to 19 reported having used a condom during their last intercourse, as compared with only 21 percent in 1979 (Sonenstein & Pleck, 1989). Girls are also having their partners use condoms more consistently. Forty-seven percent of females in a 1988 study indicated their partners had used a condom during intercourse, as compared to 23 percent in 1982 (Singh & Forrest, 1990).

Ours is a culture that continues to demonstrate great ambivalence toward sexual activity among the young. While on the one hand young people hear many negative messages about sex from adults, the media are increasingly depicting sexual themes in more explicit ways (Brown, Childers, & Waszak, 1990). The statistics have led some experts to conclude that we may be at a point in human history where we must accept that adolescent sexual activity is inevitable, and that adults can no longer afford to fool themselves into thinking that teenagers can be scared out of making the choice to have sex (Wyatt, 1990; Fisher, 1990). If our society is to help adolescents develop into sexually healthy adults, there are several steps that must be taken (Haffner, 1990). We must begin educating children openly and honestly about sexuality from the time they are born, and promote in them a healthy and positive self-concept. Young people also need to understand the range of values and experiences that will be open to them as they grow up in a pluralistic society such as ours, and be prepared for the realistic work that must go into maintaining a long-term relationship. On many different levels, we will have to address issues of poverty and political obstacles that prevent some of the population from having equal opportunity for education and a hopeful future. These issues affect self-esteem and therefore the sex-related decisions that young people make. Adolescent sexuality can no longer be ignored. There are too many health and social issues at risk (Cross, 1991).

SOCIAL RELATIONSHIPS

During adolescence most people become involved in social relationships with members of both sexes. Self-concept can play a major role in how comfortable the person is with these relationships. Some research has indicated that there is often a lowering of one's conception of oneself during adolescence, especially in females (Bryan & Petrangelo, 1989).

Important steps in personal development occur within the context of teenage romances and relationships. In recent years traditional patterns of dating and going steady have given way to more informal ways of relating (Murstein, 1980). With the privacy available to most adolescents, a close relationship can easily progress to sexual exploration if they want it to. Learning how to deal with the new intimacy is essential to becoming comfortable with sharing one's sexuality.

How far the sexual intimacy proceeds is important. Many sexual activities may be viewed as part of sex play behavior. Intensive sexual sharing takes on extra meaning for most individuals, however. For one thing, to manage intense sexual activity successfully, the two people usually have to cooperate in a number of ways. For another, the two are opening themselves to each other more fully—and with more vulnerability—than ever before. These factors, along with the emotional reactions of intense physical intimacy, often lead to a deepening of the relationship. If this is desired and expected, things may go well, but if it is a surprise or undesirable, conflicts may develop between the partners. Whatever the consequences of intensive sex, after their initial experiences many adolescents begin to clarify the place sex will have in their adult relationships.

Adult Sexuality and Relationships

It has been claimed that, as the culture that invented the term *adolescence,* we have placed great importance on prolonging the youthful period of the life span, delaying adulthood longer than ever before in history. The life-styles, expectations, and responsibilities of adult life tend to be approached gradually in North America and often with considerable delays to provide time for advanced education. Our society often asks sexually mature young adults to fit their sexual interests and behaviors into life-styles more appropriate to people much younger.

The college years represent a transitional phase for young adults. They are often still bound to home and parents financially and as a permanent address, and yet they have a great deal of freedom to choose their own relationships and sexual activities. During the 1970s and 1980s the in loco parentis role of American colleges and universities faded, and dormitory curfews and visitation rules for the most part disappeared. All recent research indicates that shared sexual activity among college students increased during those decades as well (Daher, Greaves, & Supton, 1987). Studies in the mid-1980s reported that two-thirds of college students had experienced intercourse, as compared to less than half during the 1960s (Hildebrand & Abramowitz, 1984).

A study done in the late 1980s indicated that 89 percent of college males surveyed and 70 percent of college women had engaged in sexual intercourse (Rubinson & DeRubertis, 1990). While the double standard was once rampant on college campuses, it would now appear that the disparity between levels of sexual permissiveness in males and females has been decreasing (Sprecher, 1989). As might be expected, attitudes of college students toward premarital sexual intercourse have continued to be relatively accepting. In 1972, 87 percent of males and 80 percent of females tended to approve of premarital intercourse, and by 1987 these figures had increased to 91 percent of males and 84 percent of females (Rubinson & DeRubertis, 1990). Other research indicates that although the amount of sexual activity remains relatively high among college students, they have not modified their sexual practices significantly in response to the threat of AIDS and other sexually transmitted diseases (De-Buono et al., 1990).

There also has been an increase in the incidence of unplanned pregnancies and sexually transmitted diseases (STDs) among college populations. Many experts believe that this is the result of young people not coming to terms with their own sexuality during the confusing transition years of college. They often have not been encouraged by their families to deal with sexual issues or their own sexual feelings, but have been implicitly expected to ignore or deny such things. This pattern may make it difficult for college students to feel comfortable planning ahead to avoid a pregnancy or STD, because it also means they are planning to have sex. This can create guilt, or make them question their own moral character.

The young adult years provide a transition to adulthood, but it would be a mistake to view adulthood as a time when all of the loose ends are tied up, all spontaneity and fun are left behind, and life-style patterns are established that will take people through the rest of their lives. Rather, like all other stages of human life, it is a dynamic time filled with transitions, new decisions, inner journeys to be undertaken, and

problems to be resolved. One's sexuality weaves its way through all of these twists and turns of adult life.

INTIMACY AND SEXUALITY

Erikson (1968) indicated that one of the major tasks of early adulthood is to achieve intimacy with others. But what does the term intimacy really mean, and how does one go about establishing it? Intimacy is for the most part the ability to open oneself to others in a way that permits mutual sharing and caring. It is therefore an essential quality in the deeper forms of human relationships, whether we call them friendships or love (Rubin, 1983).

Intimacy is something most people long for. They want that opportunity to build the sort of trust with another human being that allows deep levels of openness and sharing (Avery, 1989). It is also a primary basis for relating to another person sexually. To share some form of sex without a foundation of intimacy can only be an experience of the senses.

When people have difficulty establishing intimate relationships, they may well display behaviors that make it difficult for others to relate to them: shyness,

in loco parentis: a Latin phrase meaning "in the place of the parent."

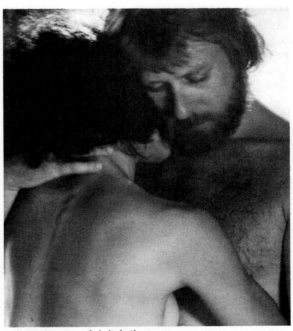

FIGURE 7.8 Adult Intimacy

Early adulthood is a time of establishing sexual identity and acquiring sexual intimacy. The cultural freedom to enjoy premarital sex and cohabitation, however, presents its own set of problems, not the least of which is the transmission of sexual diseases.

hostility, self-centeredness, or insensitivity. The result can be a life of loneliness and isolation. Their relationships tend to stay at superficial levels. Sexual sharing, in such a nonintimate context, may be physically satisfying, but in time often loses the deeper feelings of fulfillment and commitment that help a relationship to flourish and last. There is more about intimacy and the role of effective communication in chapter 8, "Sexuality, Communication, and Relationships."

MARRIAGE, COHABITATION, SINGLES, AND SEX

In Western culture, romantic love and sexual attraction have become the most important bases for marriage, along with the expectation that they will be continuing parts of any marriage. This is apparently unique in the world's history and cultures. As Keen (1983) has pointed out, in many other societies "marriage is far too serious a social institution to be left to the whims of individual passions" (p. 9). In some cultures marriages are arranged by the parents. The partners are expected to build their relationships and learn how to love and care for one another after they are married. To maintain a loving relationship over a long period of time takes attention, work, and commitment. Married couples must invest their relationships with sharing, energy, and communication if a healthy and growing marriage is to continue.

A recent survey of college student attitudes indicated that 96 percent of the students intended to marry eventually, and that 95 percent intended to have children (Rubinson & DeRubertis, 1990).

The U.S. Bureau of the Census figures show that 90 percent of all people in the United States marry by their late thirties, with another 5 percent marrying by the time they are 55. Sexual activity is one of the expected parts of a marital relationship, and research studies indicate that a wide variety of sexual behaviors are shared by married people. There is some indication of changes in the types of sex in which married couples participate since the Kinsey studies of the late 1940s and early 1950s. The majority of couples apparently include oral-genital sexual activity in their sexual repertoires, and about half have at least tried anal intercourse. Couples also seem to be more adventurous with the positions they are using for sexual intercourse (Kinsey et al., 1948, 1953; Hunt, 1975; Gebhard & Johnson, 1979). One may speculate that these changes in marital sexuality are the result of increased openness about sex in recent years and the tremendous amount of media attention given to sex-related topics.

Married couples, on average, try a variety of positions for sexual intercourse. The average frequency for intercourse gradually declines with age, with two to three times per week being typical for couples in their twenties and thirties (Doddridge et al., 1987). However, frequency of intercourse should not be construed as a measure of happiness in marriage. Different couples find different levels of sexual interaction appropriate and pleasing for them.

More than ever before, women and men are also choosing to live together in loving and sexual relationships without marrying. This is called cohabitation. It is believed that over 2.6 million people in the United States are cohabiting, about half of whom have been previously married and close to half of whom are college students. The majority of young people who cohabit do not see the relationship necessarily as a long-term commitment. Cohabitation has gained increased acceptance as a form of close relationship and for many couples has become a first stage of marriage. How cohabitation may affect the success of eventual marriage remains unclear. One study has shown that less than 25 percent of people ultimately marry the partner with whom they are cohabiting. There is also mounting evidence that couples who lived together prior to marriage have a substantially higher divorce rate (up to 80 percent higher) than those who did not live together (Browder, 1988) and a lower level of marital satisfaction in general. Other research has suggested that cohabitation was not a significant factor one way or the other in terms of the marital adjustment of couples over the first few years of marriage (Watson & DeMeo, 1987).

In their study of both married and cohabiting American couples, Blumstein and Schwartz (1983) investigated several aspects of sexual relationships and sexual satisfaction. Among both married and cohabiting couples, the degree of satisfaction expressed with sex was directly correlated with the frequency of sex. Close to 90 percent of men and women who had sex 3 or more times each week expressed satisfaction with their sex lives, while only half or less expressed satisfaction when the frequency of sex was between once a week and once a month. On the average the frequency of sex tends to decline in a long-term relationship. We must interpret such information with caution. While these statistics could suggest that people are more satisfied with sex simply because they have it more frequently, they could also tell us that the couples who had sex less frequently did so because it tended to be somehow less pleasurable and satisfying for them. Other research has shown that sexual satisfaction in marriage is closely connected with how satisfied couples are with their communication about

cohabitation: living together and sharing sex without marrying.

Adult Sexual Behavior in 1989

Questions on sexual behavior that were added to the National Opinion Research Center's 1988 and 1989 General Social Surveys reveal that 97 percent of adult Americans have had intercourse since age 18. Respondents report having an average of about 1.2 sexual partners during the year preceding the survey and nearly 7.2 partners since age 18; men claimed to have had considerably more partners than did women. About one-fifth of adult Americans had no partners during the previous year. Moreover, over a year's time, only 1.5 percent of married people reported having had a sexual partner other than their spouse. On average, adults report engaging in intercourse 57 times per year.

—Tom W. Smith, *Family Planning Perspectives,* May/June 1991

sex and their relationship (Cupach & Comstock, 1990). This tends to confirm what marital therapists have been insisting for a long time: that having a happy and healthy sexual relationship requires working at effective communication.

MONOGAMY VERSUS NON-MONOGAMY

Not all married or cohabiting individuals remain monogamous, sharing sexual relations only with their spouses. Nonetheless, Blumstein and Schwartz (1983) found that monogamy is still held as the proper and moral life-style even by those who do not practice it. They found that 71 percent of husbands and 57 percent of wives admitted to having had sex with at least one person other than their spouses. Their extramarital sexual activity did not seem to be related in any clear-cut way to the degree of happiness in the marriage or attitudes about religion. Often the activity was simply a search for sexual variety and excitement. Sometimes it was motivated by a need for stronger emotional involvement and intimacy than what they seemed to be able to achieve with the spouse.

Some couples have insisted that a healthy loving relationship need not preclude love for or sex with others outside the primary relationship. Nena and George O'Neill (1975) were among the first of the new wave of writers to explore the concepts of open marriage and open relationships. They studied experimental relationships ranging from the group marriage of three or more persons to shared sex in communal life-styles and polygamy. They saw new patterns of relationships offering necessary options for couples who did not accept traditional concepts of monogamy. Adultery is nothing new. What is new is consensual adultery—being honest about extramarital sex and having one's spouse know about and approve the activity.

Three subtypes of consensual adultery have been described. The first is group marriage, in which three or more persons are linked not only by shared sex, but by a commitment toward a future together. Another form is open-ended marriage, in which there is a primary relationship, but each partner grants the other the freedom to become emotionally and sexually involved with others. The third type of consensual adultery is recreational adultery, in which the extramarital sex has a relatively low level of emotional commitment and is primarily done for variety and fun. Recreational adultery is also called swinging or mate swapping (Clanton, 1977).

Some social commentators are claiming that there is a growing antipathy toward the institutions of marriage and the nuclear family. Some have attacked monogamous marriage as being more important as a stabilizer of a particular social system than as a beneficial relationship for two partners and their children. From this perspective, monogamy is seen basically as a system of mutual ownership that may inhibit individual needs and potentials for growth.

It has been suggested that although monogamous marital relationships are not fading as an ideal for which couples may strive, the sexual realities make it generally impossible for the ideal to work in practice

monogamous: sharing sexual relations with only one person.

polygamy: practice, in some cultures, of being married to more than one spouse.

consensual adultery: permission given to at least one partner within the marital relationship to participate in extramarital sexual activity.

group marriage: three or more people in a committed relationship who share sex with one another.

open-ended marriage: each partner in the primary relationship grants the other freedom to have emotional and sexual relationships with others.

recreational adultery: extramarital sex with a low level of emotional commitment and performed for fun and variety.

183

(Raphael, 1987). Others hold that given the religious and ethical foundations on which marriage is built in our culture, monogamy represents the most viable context for a continuing sexual relationship (Schumm & Rekers, 1984; Rimmer, 1987).

Some observers of social trends believe that future modifications will permit the survival of happy, satisfying monogamous relationships, but in nontraditional ways. These modifications might include the further legitimization of premarital sex; living together as a trial period prior to marriage; and some degree of freedom following marriage so that the partners may express themselves sexually outside the marital relationship (Chilman, 1984; Myers, 1987).

The studies on sexually open marriages and nonmarital relationships have been inconclusive. Research throughout the 1960s and 1970s suggested that more women were seeking extramarital sex and at younger ages than in the 1950s. However, there are data suggesting that during recent years married people have been maintaining their monogamous sexual relationships rather faithfully. Questions asked in the yearly General Social Surveys indicated that 96 percent of married people said they had only had one sexual partner during the previous 12 months. It has been speculated that the new high annual rates of marital fidelity reflect concern about exposure to the AIDS virus (Greeley, Michael, & Smith, 1990).

Professional therapists are also still debating the issues. Some mental health workers (Myers, 1987) are proposing guidelines for sexually open relationships; others (Davis, 1987) are advocating the need for caution in exploring alternative forms of sex in relationships. One fact seems to emerge from the research and discussions: some couples seem to be able to cope with sex outside of a primary relationship quite positively, while other couples do not seem ready or able to deal with it (Rimmer, 1987).

TRENDS IN MARRIAGE

There has been a trend toward delaying marriage until somewhat later in life than in the past, and younger professional women and men sometimes want to establish themselves in careers before they pursue committed relationships. Census Bureau statistics show the extent of this trend. Among 20- to 24-year-olds in 1970, 54.7 percent of men and 36 percent of women were still single. By 1988, the percentages had risen to 77.7 percent of men and 61.1 percent of women. For people in their late twenties and early thirties, the proportion who have never married has doubled since 1970. Women are getting married later now than at any time in the past century. In 1990 the median age for

women to first get married was 24. The median age for men marrying for the first time was just over 26, an age that has remained relatively stable. The apprehension created by rising divorce rates, economic pressures, and the availability of sexual relations outside of marriage all seem to have contributed to the fact that the average age for marriage has been increasing (Hofferth, 1990).

However, some social scientists are predicting that this trend will be changing. Already there has been a change in the birth and death ratios between younger males and females. In 1970, for every 100 men in their twenties, there were 107 women. In 1990, there were only 92 women in that age bracket for every 100 men. Historically, population trends of this sort lead to earlier marriage and higher birth rates. During the last 3 years of the decade of the eighties, there were indications that such trends were already in effect (Guttentag & Secord, 1989).

Regardless of marriage trends, there is no longer a strong stigma attached to remaining single. If we include the numbers of never-married single people with those who have been divorced or have not remarried, we find that single adults comprise about 25 percent of American households. Single people, however, often find it difficult to meet with others outside a social structure such as in college where dating is widely accepted and encouraged. Some singles pursue casual sexual relationships via singles bars or other social settings, some live together and share sex, and some remain celibate. Singlehood, though not the long-term choice of a major portion of our population, has become an accepted life-style in Western culture.

DIVORCE

It has been reported that 20 percent of those who marry today will be divorced within 5 years; one-third may be divorced within 10 years; and 40 percent will be divorced before they might have celebrated their 15th anniversary.

During the late 1980s there was a slight reduction in the national divorce rate, and then a leveling off at the lower rate (National Center for Health Statistics, 1989). Recent studies have found a serious underreporting of divorce and a lack of statistics about marriages that end in separation without a legal divorce. There is a possibility that close to two-thirds of first marriages may eventually break up (Bumpass & Martin, 1989). It is unclear to what extent sexual incompatibility and dissatisfaction are factors in divorce. Couples who are having marital difficulties often experience sexual problems, yet these problems are just as frequently the effect as they are the cause.

Seventy percent of divorced people try marriage again, hoping that things will be better the second time around (Norton & Moorman, 1987). However, close to half of these second marriages also end in divorce. There is some evidence that sexual problems present in a first marriage reappear in a second marriage. Although the reasons behind the trend are not clear, a review of surveys conducted by the National Opinion Research Center has shown a decline in the happiness of married people. Compared to 1972, when 43 percent of married women and 32 percent of married men reported being "very happy," by the mid-1980s only 34 percent of women and 25 percent of men who were married said their lives were very happy (Glenn & Weaver, 1988).

Adjusting to divorce can be a traumatic experience, and involves the grieving experiences typical of any major loss (Gove & Shin, 1989). Divorced people often experience upheavals in their life-styles that create new stresses and pressures. They may feel depressed or anxious, and feel a loss of self-esteem. Women are more likely to see a decline in their standard of living following divorce, and are typically left with more of the parenting responsibilities if children are involved (Clarke-Stewart & Bailey, 1989). It seems clear that divorce represents a significant change for anyone's life, and that the psychological stresses it creates must be considered within the context of each person's gender and patterns of socialization. Everyone reacts to divorce in different ways, and divorce therapists need to address these issues individually (Lund, 1990).

Most divorced people go on to sexual relationships with others. More than half report an increase in their sexual activity (Simenauer & Carroll, 1982), probably the result of a renewed sense of freedom following their divorces.

Sexuality and Aging

The sharing of sex is usually viewed as something for lustful and passionate youth and for the earlier years of marriage. As the collective imagination would have it, there is a general decline in sexual interests and potencies as we age, until old age finds us politely asexual. There are anecdotes and jokes about the occasional "dirty old man," an object of ridicule and disgust. In a youth-oriented culture such as ours, being old is equated with giving up sex. Yet studies have revealed that the elderly are indeed sexual beings. Older people not only retain sexual desires but enjoy the pleasures of the same sexual activities they knew as younger people. In fact, sometimes they apparently even enjoy them more (Walz & Blum, 1987).

FIGURE 7.9 Old Age and Sexuality

Patterns of sexual activity vary greatly among the elderly. Cultural, social expectations of sexual behavior as well as the state of health of both partners may play a part in the frequency and type of sexual activity engaged in by elderly couples.

One cross-cultural study examined data relating to sexual activity in 106 traditional societies. In 70 percent of those societies, continuation of sexual activity was expected among the aging. Men were not expected to have much, if any, loss of their sexual capabilities until they were very old. In the majority of these societies, women were also expected to maintain their sexual interests and activities. In fact, women frequently reported signs of stronger sexual interests and fewer inhibitions toward discussing sex after they had passed their childbearing years. A significant finding of this research was that whether expressions of sexuality among the aged were encouraged or discouraged seemed to depend on the cultural attitudes of a particular society (Winn & Newton, 1982).

Larger proportions of our population than ever before are now in middle and older age groups. In this sense we are becoming an older society. Improved

50 Years of Sex: From Oppression to Obsession

Next week, 16 members of our family will gather in the Adirondacks to celebrate the day 50 years ago when a green girl promised to "love, honor, and obey" (obey?) a young blade fresh from Harvard. Neither he nor I had any clue what we were getting into.

Exactly nine months after the wedding, our first child was born, as was customary. I admired birth control pioneer Margaret Sanger but I had no idea what she was recommending. We did our bit for the population explosion: five children, seven grandchildren, so far.

When I was growing up, solid information on sex was difficult to come by. A friend's mother slipped her a book called "Marjorie May's Thirteenth Birthday." We were stunned by its message: women were made to have babies, thanks to something called "a monthly cleansing," and from now on we couldn't be too careful.

Our sex-related vocabulary was meager. Even if we knew the correct word for anything, we would not utter it. We said "bust" for breast and wouldn't say "bra" in mixed company. Who could imagine going without a bra?

Sex was a mystery to be solved by matrimony; we got married first and then lived together. After the wedding it was learning by doing. "Marriage itself was sexy," states the writer Michael J. Arlen. "Imagine sharing your bed with a female every night!"

Some mothers dispensed a little sex instruction before the ceremony; others left that to the bridegroom. The classic British mother is supposed to have told her daughter, "Just close your eyes, dear, and think about England."

In my family, sex was too serious to discuss. To obtain a marriage license in Virginia, you had to pass a Wasserman test proving you had no venereal diseases. Our wedding was almost derailed because my husband-to-be sent me a wisecracking telegram that was delivered by mistake to my father. It read: "How did you ever make out on your Wasserman test?" My father did not laugh. But I side with Malcolm Muggeridge who said, "Sex is a funny thing and the older I get, the funnier it gets." You might as well laugh.

---

medical care and increased emphasis on good health habits are helping many of us to have a longer life span than we might have once expected. At the same time, economic conditions and greater access to a range of birth control methods are reducing the birth rate. The children of the post–World War II baby boom are entering middle age. Over 11 percent of the American population are now over the age of 65; by the year 2020 that proportion is expected to rise to 13 percent or more. By the year 2000, there will be about 31 million older Americans. All of these factors have created a considerable interest and awareness about aging. Many dread the presumed loss of sex to the aging process and do not know that things will not be so bad.

When college students were asked recently to assess the sexual activity of people in various age groups from 20 to 80, they answered that as individuals reach their seventies and eighties their sexual needs and behaviors have disappeared. It also became evident that students were very uncomfortable about estimating the frequency of sexual activities of their own parents. These findings are unsurprising in a culture that prefers to ignore and discourage sexual expression among aging women and men (Zeiss, 1982).

MYTHS AND ATTITUDES ABOUT SEX AND AGING

I mentioned some of the physiological effects of aging on sexual functions in chapter 3, "Human Sexual Response." Here are some myths and attitudes that lead to misunderstandings about the sexuality of older people:

Loving and Sexual Feelings Are Experienced Only During Youth In fact, human beings retain a full range of emotions—including romantic and sexual ones—throughout the life cycle. A major reason behind the suppression of these feelings in many older people

Laughing or not, my generation has zoomed with the speed of light from the era of the chaperone to the era of the pill. Today, 5-year-olds know the correct word for everything. When my classmate spilled hot coffee in her lap, her little granddaughter lisped, "Gwanny, did you burn your wagina?"

A few years ago, I had the word vagina deleted by an editor from a piece I published in The New York Times. Such delicacy is as out of date as a five-cent newspaper. Today, the Times reports on Madonna, the sexibitionist, masturbating or simulating oral sex with a bottle of soda. Without batting an eye, this newspaper quoted a female college student: "A year ago, I wouldn't be caught dead with a condom, but now it's like an American Express card—you can't leave home without it." When I was in college I had never heard the word condom, and I thought oral sex meant talking a good game.

In 50 years we have gone from a sex-oppressed to a sex-obsessed society. Make that a sex-drenched society. It's refreshing when someone suggests the whole thing is a bit overblown. In a Monty Python movie, John Cleese shows us where we may be headed. A naked Cleese and his naked wife are demonstrating sexual intercourse for a class of adolescents. Suddenly he explodes in anger. Instead of watching the copulating couple, the students are sneaking peeks at copies of Virgil hidden in their laps.

My generation deserves a medal for just surviving the sexual revolution. Who can guess what lies ahead? Why not cling to the adage, "When you stop learning it's time to die." I must say enlightenment took a long time. As one who is still learning, I'm happy to discover that although people age, emotions do not. After half a century, that young blade from Harvard still delights me.

On our 60th anniversary I hope we won't be like the deaf couple, fictitious I hope, I heard about. At their party celebrating their 60 years of wedded bliss, he patted her hand and said, "I'm proud of you." She looked into his eyes and replied, "I'm tired of you, too."

—Nardi Reeder Campion, *New York Times,* June 27, 1991

is the societal attitude that such reactions are indeed lost with age. To the contrary, a study of 202 healthy retirement-home residents, aged 80 to 102, found that 88 percent of the men and 72 percent of the women fantasized about being intimate with a partner (Bretschneider & McCoy, 1988).

Sex Is Primarily for Reproduction This is an attitude that negates a spectrum of nonprocreative sexual experiences and obviously sets aside those who are past the age of reproductive capability or interest. Yet for older people who have held this value during their lifetimes, it may become a factor in discouraging sexual expression.

Remarriage After Loss of a Spouse Should Be Discouraged There is often pressure on a widow or widower to remain "faithful" long after a spouse has died. Sometimes children discourage the possibilities of remarriage out of loyalty to the deceased parent or out of fear of losing some inheritance. However, many older people can be enriched by the companionship and continued sexual involvement that remarriage offers (Kuhn, 1976).

Older Men Remain More Sexually Interesting to Younger Partners Than Do Older Women There is a distinct double standard when it comes to the sexual desirability and attractiveness of older people. While the graying hair and bodily changes of an aging man are often perceived as being distinguished, women are more likely to be viewed as becoming less and less attractive with aging (Rosenthal, 1990). Such attitudes only foster further negative attitudes in aging women about their own sexuality. The pairing of older men with younger women happens relatively frequently; while the reverse situation is still not as common, it seems to be gaining increased acceptance and popularity today.

Aged People Lose Interest in Sex It is normal for even very old people to retain their sexual needs and to

Case Study

GARRETT: DEALING WITH THE SEXUALITY OF GRANDPARENTS

When Garrett returned home from college for spring vacation, he sensed there was a good deal of tension. Finally his father explained that he was very upset because *his* father—Garrett's grandfather—was contemplating marriage. He had been a widower for 5 years and had met a woman at a senior citizens' center in their town.

Garrett's father told him how the grandfather had actually spent several nights recently with his new companion. Garrett was particularly struck by one of his father's statements: "He ought to know how that must look to everybody!"

"But Dad," Garrett had said, "if Grandpa were my age, you wouldn't think anything about it. Why shouldn't he have the right to his own relationships?"

"Because he is 73 years old, that's why," his father had answered.

Before the end of the vacation, Garrett sought out his grandfather and told him how happy he was about the new relationship.

The older man was very touched by his grandson's sensitivity. "You know," he said, "You are the only one who has bothered to let me know that you can still see me as a real person with real feelings, even though I'm getting old."

Several months later Garrett reported that his grandfather had indeed remarried and that his family had gradually come to accept his new wife.

engage in sexual behavior as the opportunity exists (White, 1982). While aging sometimes changes the frequency or intensity of sexual feelings and activities, they do not become nonexistent.

INSTITUTIONAL PROHIBITIONS ON SEXUAL EXPRESSION

All of these sex-negative myths and attitudes add up to policies or attitudes that prohibit sexual expression among the aged. Nowhere is this more evident than in nursing homes and other institutions that provide care for older men and women. Not only are outward expressions of sexual interest seen as inappropriate and therefore discouraged, there is often a lack of privacy for any sort of personal or shared sexual activity (Cross, 1989). Even when nursing home personnel are aware of the facts about the sexuality of the aged, appropriate policy changes may be hindered by lack of support from administrative personnel, physicians, and the families of older patients.

Attempts at changing such conditions have generally been met with positive results. At one geriatric institution (Silverstone & Wynter, 1975) 62 elderly residents (mean age of 87 years) of an all-male floor and all-female floor were integrated, following some resistance to the proposal by the staff. The increased opportunity for physical and emotional interaction resulted in a healthier and more cheerful atmosphere

and led to significant improvements in the social behavior of the residents. Only too often, institutional staffs forget that their clients are adults with rights to privacy and social interaction. Providing older people with opportunities for choice and a sense of personal autonomy can enhance sexual identity and adjustment (Cross, 1989).

SPECIAL SEXUAL PROBLEMS AND PATTERNS OF AGING

In addition to the psychological stresses that may inhibit sexual activities, there are a number of illnesses and physical infirmities that interfere with sexual abilities. Fifty percent of the sexual dysfunctions of individuals over 40 may well be due to physiological changes and illnesses (Schiavi, 1990). It is sometimes the treatment of such problems that produces negative sexual consequences. Since the elderly are usually not recognized as being sexual, medications for conditions such as arthritis or high blood pressure may be prescribed without any explanation of potential sexual side effects. The older person may simply assume that the change in sexual function is a natural outcome of aging, perpetuating a downward spiral in sexual activity.

Likewise, certain surgeries can have effects on sexual behavior that should be thoroughly explained to the elderly patient. Prostate surgery, for example, is very common in older men and may in a few cases inhibit the capability to have an erection and ejaculate. However, with reassurance, encouragement, and education, many men who have had prostatic surgery can resume satisfactory sexual activity (Whitbourne, 1990).

Similarly, hysterectomy (removal of the uterus and cervix) need not adversely affect the sex lives of women. For some women there are many psychological stresses to be faced following hysterectomy, but with appropriate education and adjustment counseling, the majority of women can emerge feeling healthier, sexier, and more self-confident than before (Johnson, 1990).

Diabetes, a common disorder of older individuals, is also known to be associated with a variety of sexual problems. Some of these respond to medical treatment and others the patient must learn to cope with. Heart disease, lung disease, stroke, arthritis, Parkinson's disease, and a variety of other chronic disorders can lead to disruption of one's sex life that eventually produces complete lack of sexual activity. Effective counseling services for older people can provide the necessary incentive and instructions to reestablish their sexual functioning even in the face of such difficulties (Capuzzi, 1982).

While there is a distinct decline in levels of sexual interest and behavior as people age, many elderly people remain active—or at least capable of sexual activity—until very old age. One study asked a group of people aged 60 and over to record weekly data on their sexual behaviors. Their reports showed that a significant proportion of these older people desired a sexual partner, were stimulated by reading materials, kissed and caressed their partners, and participated in sexual intercourse (Taylor, 1980). There are several life factors that influence sexual potentials in old age:

The Individual's or Couple's Sexual History A very significant factor is the degree of importance and priority the individual or couple has placed on sex throughout the life cycle. There is a high correlation between the amount of sexual interest shown in the young adult years and that shown in older adult years (Steinke & Bergen, 1986). Those who have tended to see sex as an important part of their lives, and who have sought frequent sexual outlets, tend to continue these patterns into old age. Likewise, letting it become a low priority of life may well lead to a complete absence of sexual interest as one ages.

Partner Availability How much shared sexual activity is pursued by an older individual depends a great deal on the availability of a sexual partner. Several studies have indicated, for example, that older women

tend to be less sexually active than older men in general. This reflects the fact that older heterosexual women are often left without sexual partners due to the shorter life expectancies of their male partners and a high incidence of illness and erectile difficulty in the older male partners. Because of higher mortality rates in older men, single women outnumber single men by 4 to 1 in the higher age brackets (Cross, 1989). Masters and Johnson (1981) discussed the "widow's/widower's syndrome," which in turn can lead to difficulty with sexual functioning. After the death of a beloved sex partner of long duration, many people go through a lengthy period of avoiding serious relationships with others (Huntley, 1988).

Sexual Values and Attitudes Throughout the life cycle sexual behaviors are influenced by attitudes and values. People who are old today grew up in times during which negative and repressive sexual codes were taught, and many have carried these values with them into old age, where they may become self-fulfilling prophecies. Research confirms that among older people negative attitudes toward sex correlate with relative sexual inactivity (Kaplan, 1990). Unfortunately, opportunities for older people to discuss, explore, or even change their value systems are often neglected, because it is assumed that their values are too entrenched.

Knowledge About Sexuality Ignorance about sex is rampant; this is no less true among the old as it is among the young. Older people often labor with myths and misinformation about sex and sexual behaviors, leading them to further conflicting attitudes and values about their own sexual lives. At the same time, older people often want more information about sexuality (Smith, 1981).

Maintenance of Self-Esteem and a Sense of Identity Older people must adapt to many physical, emotional, social, and economic changes in their lives. There may be loss of companionship, loss of role status after retirement, and some losses of physical and cognitive functioning. The individual's perception of her or his sexuality is a crucial part of her or his adjustment to a new stage of life. Dissatisfaction with sexual activity relates to depression and feelings of worthlessness, which in turn can discourage further activity.

MASTURBATION AND HETEROSEXUAL INTERCOURSE IN OLD AGE

For many older people who have lost their sexual partners, masturbation becomes their sole means of

189

sexual gratification. There are few statistical data concerning masturbation among the aged (Berezin, 1975). In their first study on human sexual response, Masters and Johnson (1966) reported that most of the older people in their study had tended to continue masturbating into old age if they had masturbated previously.

As might be expected, negative social attitudes toward masturbation affect not only its practice among older people but their willingness to admit to it. The frequency of reported masturbation among the elderly is largely determined by sexual attitudes and knowledge. Those individuals who feel comfortable making their own decisions and who have more sexual knowledge tend to masturbate more than those who are easily influenced by external social attitudes and who have less knowledge (Catania & White, 1982). A recent study of 202 people over the age of 80 indicated that 72 percent of the men and 40 percent of the women said they currently masturbated. Again, however, there were indications that they did not feel fully comfortable about the behavior (Bretschneider & McCoy, 1988).

Research on the sexual behavior of older people has usually concentrated on heterosexual intercourse. There is one generalization that every study supports: the frequency of intercourse steadily declines with age (Cross, 1989). A particularly significant factor here is whether the older person has been married and, if so, whether the spouse is still alive. In a survey of 4,246 men and women ages 50 to 93, more than three-quarters of married women in their sixties reported having intercourse with their husbands on an average of once each week. Of the married people in their seventies, 60 percent were having regular intercourse, averaging once every 10 or 11 days. Not surprisingly, these figures were less for unmarried people in the same age groups (Brecher et al., 1984). Another study of people aged 80 to 102 reported that 30 percent of the women and 62 percent of the men were still experiencing sexual intercourse (Bretschneider & McCoy, 1988).

Recent research suggests that our preoccupation with intercourse as a standard of measurement does not do justice to the sexuality of the aging. When we broaden our definition of "sexually active" to mean a spectrum of sexual and sensual behaviors, older people fare quite well. This may signal the maturation of older people away from the narrow, limiting genital focus of intercourse, toward a fuller and more complete sense of what it means to be a sexual human being. The unwarranted emphasis on intercourse as the "right way to have sex" poses unfortunate restrictions. In this sense, younger generations may well have lessons to learn from older generations.

MAXIMIZING SEXUAL EXPRESSION DURING THE LATER YEARS

It is clear that while the aging process makes an indelible mark on the ways in which the human body responds sexually, older people can remain in touch with the sexual part of their lives if they wish. There are some considerations in maximizing the sexual potentials of the elderly.

Some nursing homes and health-care clinics have offered various types of sexual enhancement programs for the elderly. One such effort included educational sessions about sex and aging and instruction on the improvement of communication and sexual enjoyment (Rowland & Haynes, 1978). Another program conducted in a nursing home offered thorough education on the physiological effects of aging on sex and a stimulation exercise for the participants (White & Catania, 1982). Following both programs, there were significant increases in sexual satisfaction, frequency of sexual activities, and positive sexual attitudes in the participants. Appropriate counseling services for elderly people can also lead to greater sexual satisfac-

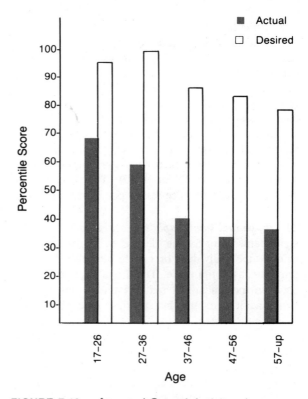

FIGURE 7.10 Age and Sexual Activity—I

A study by Arthur L. Foster (1979) of 100 married men between the ages of 17 and 74 confirmed that there was some decline in both actual and desired amounts of sexual activity as they aged. The disparity between the actual and the desired sexual activity also varied with age.

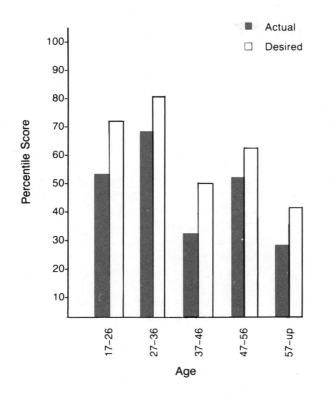

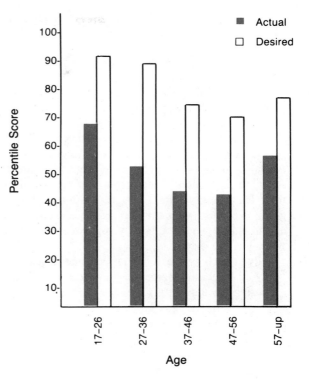

FIGURE 7.11 Age and Sexual Activity—II

FIGURE 7.12 Age and Sexual Activity—III

Foster also concluded that how much and in what way sexual activity changed depended on how it was measured. When the same men reported on the amount of pleasure they derived from their marital sexual interactions, the picture was quite different. There was a perceptible drop in pleasure for the 37–46 age group, and an increase for the 47–56 age group.

When the groups were asked about nongenital sexual activities, such as caressing, there was actually an increase in both actual and desired amount in the oldest (57 and up) age group.

tion, and with increased proportions of older adults in the population, these services are more crucial than ever. Only too often counselors are unaware of the special sexual concerns and needs of older people (Woody, 1989). The sensitivity of those who work with the elderly can be a crucial factor in the enhancement of their sexuality.

The revolution in openness about human sexuality has reached older people. Contemporary literature is helping to overturn many of the myths and conventions once associated with their sexual behavior (Laughman, 1980). A revealing study by Foster (1979) has suggested that older individuals not only participate in more sexual behavior than suspected but that they find it highly pleasurable. Again, Foster adds the qualification that sexual activity be defined in nongenital terms.

Ernest Borneman (1983) believes that infants find sexual and sensual pleasure over the entire surface of

their bodies, only focusing those pleasures on the sex organs later in their development. However, Borneman has also suggested that as adult human beings age and become less genitally oriented once again, they have the potential of rediscovering the sensuousness of their entire bodies. Older people consistently report the sexual satisfaction they gain from kissing, caressing, holding, cuddling, and other types of lovemaking that involves both spiritual and physical intimacy.

In a sense, elderly people can be freed from many of the concerns that interfere with sexual intimacy in younger age groups: risks of pregnancy, the need to "prove" oneself with sex, obsessions with performance and orgasms, balancing work and personal time, and having children to care for. All of us could stand to learn from those older people who have come to value sexual intimacy in its holistic sense, they who have come to realize that sex is far more than only what genitals do together. They know the meaning of a cherished touch and the sense of intimacy that shared bodies can enjoy. ■

SELF-EVALUATION

Looking Ahead: Sex in Later Years

In recent years there has been a recognition that older people are often discriminated against. Some of the strongest misconceptions and prejudices about the aged relate to their sexuality. It is assumed that older people lose their sexual feelings, needs, and behaviors. Actually, many of elderly people are still aware of sexual feelings and still seek physical sexual gratification. This questionnaire is designed with two primary goals: to evaluate your attitudes about sex and the aged and to clarify what you hope your sexual life will be when you are older.

1. Read each of the following statements and rate your level of agreement or disagreement to each, using the following scale:

   5 = Strongly agree
   4 = Agree somewhat
   3 = Neutral
   2 = Disagree somewhat
   1 = Strongly disagree

   a. A widowed man of 73 confided to his physician that he enjoyed masturbating occasionally but wondered if this practice might cause any ill effects. The physician encouraged him to masturbate as frequently as he wished—the more the better. _____

   b. A man and woman whose spouses have died, both in their late seventies, have decided to live and sleep together. For reasons of fi-

nances and distribution of estates, they have decided against marrying. _____

   c. A 67-year-old woman announces that she is in love with a 40-year-old man and that they are planning to marry. _____

   d. A 70-year-old widower announces that he is planning to marry a 37-year-old woman. They have been dating for several months and he has bragged about how the relationship has restored his sexual potency. _____

   e. An elderly man and woman meet in the recreation room of the nursing home where they both reside. The staff at the home will not allow them to spend time alone in privacy, even though the older couple has asked for this privilege. _____

2. Now go back to all of the above situations and imagine how you would feel if the older person in each instance were your father or mother. Also consider how you would feel if the older person were you.

3. Are you frightened of how aging will affect your sex life? Or doesn't it really matter that much how sexually active you remain in your later years?

4. Ideally, how would you like to see yourself functioning as a sexual human being at the age of 60? 70? 80? 90? Do you have any plan in mind for working toward these ideals?

CHAPTER SUMMARY

1. Individual patterns of sexual orientation and behavior probably develop through the interaction of biological, social, cultural, and psychological factors. The process is called psychosexual development.

2. Some theories of psychosexual development hold that there is a natural, instinctual drive toward sexual behavior.

3. Psychoanalytic theory has taught that the sexual instinct, or libido, becomes invested in different bodily areas through stages in human development: oral, anal, latency, and genital. This theory has seen much opposition in recent years.

4. Many theories emphasize the importance of socialization, interaction with other people, in psychosexual development. Erik Erikson has described eight stages of development, each of which has a crisis to be resolved.

5. Conditioning theorists believe that positive and negative reinforcement play a role in shaping people's sexuality, generalizing learned patterns from specific experiences to other experiences. Social learning theory sees identification with other people as a key in psychosexual development.

6. Social script theory teaches that human behavior is controlled by complex social scripts that integrate sexual behavior. Sexual scripts have cultural, interpersonal, and intrapsychic dimensions.

7. A unified model of sexual development considers three crucial strands that eventually integrate to form adult sexuality: gender identity, sexual response and orientation, and the capacity for dyadic intimacy.

8. Identifying one's own sexual orientation involves prelabeling, self-labeling, and social labeling.

9. In infancy and childhood the sex organs respond to many stimuli. Babies are sensitive over the entire surface of their bodies. Children become more curious about their bodies and sex-related matters.

10. Children are capable of strong romantic attachments and varying levels of sexual interaction.

11. Adolescence is the period of life between childhood and adulthood. At puberty the body becomes capable of reproduction and develops its secondary sex characteristics. It is a time for exploring masturbation and relationships.

12. Adolescents learn more about sex and develop their sexual values and attitudes through interaction with peers, by contact with the media, and in their sexual experimentation. Dating, going steady, and less formal relationships develop during this period of life.

13. Sexual activity among adolescents has been on the increase in recent years, even with the concerns about unintended pregnancy and AIDS.

14. Adult sexuality involves establishing intimacy with others.

15. Most people in the United States eventually marry, and some 2.6 million people are cohabiting, or living together. While monogamy is still accepted as the most appropriate type of relationship, some level of extramarital sexual activity has been reported by substantial numbers of husbands and wives.

16. Up to 60 percent of marriages may end in divorce or separation.

17. Even though older people retain their interests and physical capacities for sexual expression, our youth-oriented culture often fails to recognize it.

18. In nursing homes and institutions for elderly people, lack of privacy and policies of sex segregation may prevent expression of sexual needs.

19. How sexually active an older person is depends on past activity, partner availability, physical health, and knowledge and attitudes of sexuality.

ANNOTATED READINGS

Brecher, E. M., & Editors of Consumer Reports Books (1984). *Love, sex, and aging.* Boston: Little, Brown. Reporting on a study of 4,000 men and women aged 50 to 93, this book includes the most comprehensive view of sexuality and aging presently available. It includes both statistical and anecdotal material.

Butler, R. N., & Lewis, M. (1988). *Love and sex after sixty.* New York: Harper & Row. Offers insights about, and specific advice for, sexual expression in middle and old age. Worth reading at earlier stages of adulthood.

Gale, J. (1989). *A parent's guide to teenage sexuality.* New York: Henry Holt. This book not only serves as a guide for parents to the typical sexual issues of adolescence, but deals with special situations and needs such as single parenthood, sexual trauma, and teenagers who are gay or lesbian. It provides suggestions for improving communication within families.

Hammond, D. B. (1989). *My parents never had sex: Myths and facts of sexual aging.* Buffalo, NY: Prometheus Books. Surveys the changes that affect sexuality during the aging process, reminding readers that human beings remain sexual throughout their lives.

Lawson, A. (1988). *Adultery: An analysis of love and betrayal.* New York: Basic Books. One of the few resources available that examines the effects of extramarital or extrarelational sex on individuals and relationships. It recounts the findings of a research study done with 600 volunteers, taking into consideration their reasons for the adultery and their reactions to it.

Myers, M. F. (1989). *Men and divorce.* New York: Guilford Press. Looks at the impact of divorce on men's sexuality and relationships. The book includes a wealth of case study material that covers why men divorce, how they interact with children after divorce, and how they may be helped to deal with the conflicts and anxieties of the experience.

Olds, S. W. (1985). *The eternal garden: Seasons of our sexuality.* Westminster, MD: Random House. Surveys the various phases of adult sexual development, from young adulthood to old age. It is a highly readable, thorough book that examines the impact of typical life events on one's sexuality.

Rosenthal, E. (1990). *Women, aging and ageism.* Binghamton, NY: Haworth Press. A collection of papers examining aging in women, and how social attitudes affect women during the aging process. It is a sensitive book in addition to being highly informative.

Sarnoff, I., & Sarnoff, S. (1989). *Love-centered marriage in a self-centered world.* New York: Hemisphere. A basic guide to establishing a healthy, lasting relationship in the face of many social pressures that exist today. Includes sections on sexual intimacy and functioning.

Sarrel, L., & Sarrel, P. (1984). *Sexual turning points: The seven stages of adult sexuality.* New York: Macmillan. Discussing all of the stages of sexual development from puberty onward, this book is particularly readable and filled with facts.

Schover, L. R. (1984). *Prime time: Sexual health for men over fifty.* New York; Holt, Rinehart & Winston. A thoroughgoing book, offering advice and factual information on sexuality for older men and their partners.

193

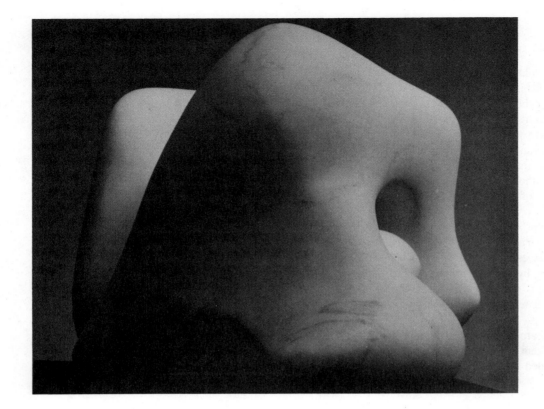

CHAPTER EIGHT

COMMUNICATING ABOUT SEX
    The Communication Process
    The Words We Use to Talk About Sex
    Contemporary Myths About Communication
    The Sexual Games We Play

EFFECTIVE COMMUNICATION
    The Ground Rules
    Making it Happen
    The Pros and Cons of Quarreling
    Resolving Conflicts Effectively
    People Have Different Personality Types for
      Communicating
    Communication Differences Between Women and
      Men

LOVING RELATIONSHIPS AND SEXUALITY
    The "Other" Risks of Sex
    What Is Love?
    Infatuation and Being in Love
    Sternberg's Triangular Theory of Love
    Establishing Sensual and Sexual Intimacy
    Confusion About Love and Sex in Relationships
    Friendship and Sexuality
    Jealousy and Possessiveness
    Dealing With the Loss of a Loving Relationship

SELF-EVALUATION: COMMUNICATING ABOUT SEX

CHAPTER SUMMARY

I just couldn't bring myself to tell him how I felt about him sometimes. I knew he didn't really mean some of the things he said, and he could make a fool of himself when we were around other couples, especially at parties. I would feel irritated and disgusted, but I was always afraid of hurting his feelings. I guess I was also scared of losing him. I just let it all build up inside until it got in the way of our love. I think he did a lot of the same things with his feelings. Anyway, the final outcome was what I had been trying to prevent all along: we both got hurt, and we lost each other.

—Written by a student following the breakup of a relationship

SEXUALITY, COMMUNICATION, AND RELATIONSHIPS

Most people long for close relationships with others. They long for the intimacy, companionship, sharing, and contentment that we associate with friendship and loving relationships. Sometimes, sexual sharing is also part of what a relationship brings. Keeping any relationship on an even keel can be complicated enough; bringing sexual feelings or activities into the picture often only makes things more complex and confusing.

One of the major foundations for a healthy, lasting relationship is effective communication between people who feel relatively comfortable and confident with themselves. As any counselor can testify, relationships typically experience tension and crisis when the communication process has become blocked or muddled. This chapter deals with that process, its role in relationships, and how to keep lines of communication open.

Communicating about Sex

Communication is an ongoing, dynamic process. It has been said that "one cannot *not* communicate." Even silence and avoiding another person convey certain messages, often very powerful ones. Unfortunately, many people do not realize the importance of communication in building a healthy sexual relationship. As a male student once stated to me, "Sex is something you *do* with each other; you shouldn't have to *talk* about it." That philosophy might work fine if people were just walking sex organs who slipped in and out of sexual encounters. Instead, we human beings have a range of thoughts, feelings, fantasies, and needs that must be shared with one another if we are to maintain relationships within and beyond the bedroom. A great many sexual problems could be prevented or resolved through open, honest communication. Yet people are often discouraged from pursuing such communication.

From the time most of us were very young, we learned that sexuality was not a subject to be brought up in "polite" company. Traditionally, girls learned that they should not appear interested enough in sexual issues to talk much about them. Boys learned that sex was all right to joke about, but that to talk seriously and sensitively about it might betray some ignorance or insecurity. Fortunately, these stereotypical attitudes have begun to change, but there are still many people who find it difficult or impossible to communicate about sex.

195

THE COMMUNICATION PROCESS

Many things can be communicated: ideas, feelings, attitudes and values, needs and desires. There is also a diversity of ways in which people communicate. Our eyes, facial expressions, and body language convey a great many messages for us. The tone and intonation of voice we use in speaking are crucial in communicating subtle aspects of our message. And of course, words are an important ingredient in any communicative interaction between people. However, words are also imperfect and often imprecise and in our society we tend to be caught between terms that are either too scientific or too vulgar to be appropriate in all circumstances. Their meanings may be interpreted differently by different people. One party to the communication process may not be paying as close attention as the other, or may be swayed by internal moods or mindsets. The process of communication is filled with subtleties and opportunities for misinterpretation. It is not surprising, then, that human communication may sometimes be fraught with complications and misunderstandings.

Figure 8.1 illustrates the basics of any process of communication. Someone, the sender, has some thought that she or he wishes to convey to someone else, who will become the receiver. However, there are many factors that influence the way in which the sender's message is formed. It is made up of specific understandings of certain words and is also filled with beliefs, attitudes and values, and emotions. The sender may well hope to fulfill a particular agenda or accomplish some objective. As the thought to be conveyed is filtered through this interpretive system, the message takes shape and is "sent" to the receiver. At this point, it must be filtered through the receiver's own very individualized interpretive system, from which that person then draws his or her own understanding of the message. Obviously, the process is complicated enough that the message intended by the sender may not at all be the message understood by the receiver. Figure 8.2 shows how misunderstandings can take place.

Communication works best when there is a well-developed feedback system through which the receiver may ask for clarification and check out the assumptions that have been made in understanding the message. As with most shared human processes, good communication takes a committed effort from everyone involved, so that misinterpretations and misunderstandings are kept to a minimum.

THE WORDS WE USE TO TALK ABOUT SEX

In our culture, people are not encouraged to talk openly about sexual issues. Such discussions are often avoided altogether or at the very least approached with some discomfort and embarrassment. For some people, and in some contexts, the "proper" scientific terminology may seem more inappropriate or embarrassing than slang terms. This is probably one of the reasons why so many slang terms exist for the description of sex-related body parts and sexual activities.

Research on speech communication reveals that men and women often have different sets of behavior

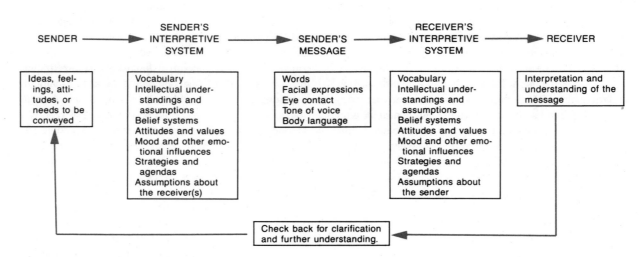

FIGURE 8.1 The Process of Communication

Whatever is to be conveyed from one person to another is filtered through each person's individualized interpretive system. Therefore, the message intended by the sender may be quite different from the message that is picked up and understood by the receiver. An active feedback system is one of the best ways to keep communication on track.

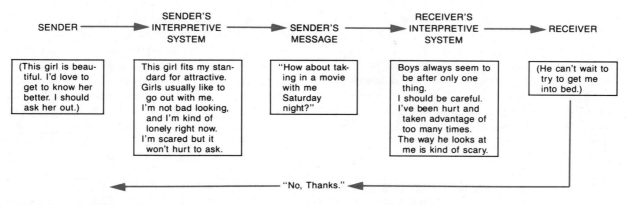

FIGURE 8.2 Misunderstood Communication

The process of communication yielding a misunderstanding between sender and receiver.

patterns for communicating and they use words in predictably gender-specific ways. These may cause misunderstanding between couples attempting to communicate intimately. I have asked students to make lists of slang terms for sexual words in classrooms. When it comes to some things such as masturbation, there are far more slang terms used to describe male masturbation than female masturbation. When it comes to talking about sex in private, there seem to be rather predictable norms for the terms that women and men use with each other. For college students, these norms are determined by the immediate peer group.

Research conducted in 1978 (Sanders, 1978) showed that men were most likely to refer to their own sex organ as a "dick" (26 percent) or "penis" (25 percent) when talking with a lover, or to avoid using any term at all (17 percent). However, only 8 percent of women used the term "dick." Nearly half of the women would say "penis," and 18.5 percent used no term for the male organ. In data gathered a decade later with another sample of college students, these trends again become clear, but with a significantly greater number of men and women reporting that they would use no term at all in reference to the penis (Fischer, 1989).

In 1978 women were even less likely than men to name their own sex organs in intimate conversations, with nearly 25 percent avoiding the use of any term. Those who did use some term were most likely to say "vagina" (32 percent). Men were more likely to use the term "pussy" (22 percent) to describe the partner's genitals than they were the term "vagina" (19.4 percent). The term "cunt" was more frequently used by men (14 percent) than by women (1 percent), who apparently are more apt to find the term offensive. In the 1989 study, women were still much less likely to use slang terms to describe the vagina than were men.

Again, both sexes showed a much higher number of individuals who would use no term at all to describe the female genitals.

The act of sexual intercourse was called that by over 10 percent of both men and women in 1978, although the term "make love" was far more popular for both women (56 percent) and men (32 percent). Men used the term "fuck" in their intimate conversations more than women did, although men were more likely to use this word in the presence of other men than they were with women. Fischer (1989) showed that the term "having sex" had become a more popular term in recent years, with "intercourse" being used much less frequently. Students in the more recent study were less likely to use terms such as "fuck" or "screw" and again more likely to use no term at all to describe sexual intercourse.

Sanders (1978) found that in describing the penis, men were more likely to use what she called "power slang," with such labels as "rod," "womp," and "pistol." Women tended toward "cute" euphemisms such as "penie," "oscar," or "baby-maker." Gender differences were also noted for the female genital terminology. Whereas males tended to use very specific terms, women tended more toward nonspecific personal terms such as "me," "mine," "she," or "my body."

Research also has suggested that after taking a college course in human sexuality, students are likely to use some term to describe the male or female genitals, and the term is likely to be "penis" or "vagina." There is still a tendency not to use a term for intercourse even following participation in a sexuality course, and the term "intercourse" is almost never used; "making love" and "having sex" seem to be the currently popular terms for talking with a lover about sexual intercourse. One study has shown that gay

197

men and lesbian women are more likely to use sexual slang with a partner than either heterosexual males or females (Wells, 1990).

Every relationship will evolve its own vocabulary for the intimate discussions of sex. The important thing is that both partners feel comfortable with the terms used. Neither should employ words that seem offensive, insensitive, or insulting to the other. Working out the details of acceptable terminology may itself require some careful communication and negotiation.

CONTEMPORARY MYTHS ABOUT COMMUNICATION

Different societies and different times in history have always had their mythology surrounding communication and relationships. Unwritten rules evolve from that mythology and make their way into most human interactions. Our society is no exception. There are several myths that govern how we communicate (Kelly, 1980). Consider how many of them have played a role in your own interactions with others.

Myth 1: You should have a confident opinion on every issue. We live in opinionated times. Media news quite often focuses its attention on gathering people's opinions. One of the stereotyped images of men would have them be filled with confidence and assertiveness on any issue, speak with a strong, unwavering voice and look others directly in the eye. If you listen carefully to the disagreements that people have with one another in everyday life, however, you will notice that this is only an image. Many individuals argue their points without much solid information to back them up. Even when it comes to sex, many people feel they must have all the answers, never appearing uncertain or insecure. The truth of the matter is that nearly everyone feels somewhat shy and scared in new situations, meeting new people, and forming new relationships. Whenever we come face-to-face with a stranger and need to communicate, there is usually an initial, tense period during which we begin evaluating what we will have to offer each other. And when we find ourselves in a position where we think we have to offer an opinion about some subject about which we know very little, it can be perfectly acceptable to say "I'd really have to think that through and learn more about it before I could have much of an opinion about it."

Myth 2: An impressive conversationalist never permits any dead air. For most people, the most uncomfortable part of any conversation can be silence. Their eyes search around trying to avoid the other person's gaze. They begin to fidget, or shift their weight from one foot to the other. They vainly hunt in their minds for some fresh topic to talk about. Unfortunately, it is this fear of silence that often forces people to fill the air with words. Silence forces a kind of intimacy when two people have to look at one another momentarily, simply and quietly sharing each other. That intimacy can often make us feel vulnerable, and so we search for topics that will help us keep each other at "words length." However, when we want to become closer to someone, and develop a deeper relationship, being able to be quiet—and being able to listen carefully—can be important elements of communication.

Myth 3: Mapping out strategies ahead of time makes for better communication. A young man who was once a counseling client of mine told me about the advice a friend had given him before a date at a fraternity party. It went something like this: "Stay loose. Keep three or four things in mind to talk about, but only use them when the conversation lags. Don't look too interested. Smile a lot to yourself and look a little bored. When you look hard to get, women chase even harder. When you're ready to get things really moving, tell her you're sick of the party but she's welcome to come back to your room with you. But don't look too anxious." My client tried to carry out this strategy at the party, only to end up feeling foolish and having his date indicate that she preferred to stay at the party and go home alone. Planned communication strategies set up games to which only one person knows the rules. Sometimes they work, but then a relationship has been established on the basis of manipulation, or even dishonesty. Usually the best "strategy" is to work at being yourself.

Myth 4: Using the right line will convince a partner to have sex. Rarely are relationships that simple. While one partner is rehearsing the line to carry out a seduction, the other partner may well be rehearsing the best way to turn down the proposition. Sexual relationships that grow out of invented lines can rarely be effective or lasting, and enticing someone into sex in this manner is ethically objectionable.

Myth 5: The rational mind is the only basis for effective communication. People often make the mistake of assuming that logical, rational thought processes are the only basis of good communication. There is a common misconception that "feelings only get in the way." In fact, emotional reactions are a legitimate part of what human beings need to communicate, especially in close relationships. To work only with one aspect of human nature during communication is to ignore crucial parts of oneself that need to be shared.

These myths can form the basis for a surefire prescription to stifle good communication. They stimulate the development of games, phony conversation, manipulative sexual seduction, and shallow relationships. When effective communication is lacking, even minor sexual problems are more likely to turn into major ones.

THE SEXUAL GAMES WE PLAY

Contemporary modes of thought tend to emphasize cause-and-effect relationships. Scientific approaches to human psychology imply that human behavior may be predicted and even controlled. These perceptions of human nature have led to the development of systematic approaches to communication that sometimes accomplish preestablished goals, but may also yield a somewhat stilted, artificial quality to human interaction. When it comes to romantic and sexual relationships, there can be a dynamic tension between two people that results in posturing and attempts at "reverse psychology" to achieve certain ends. We live with the illusion that if we always do X and Y, we will automatically get Z as the result. However, human relationships are simply more complicated than mathematical equations or generalized scientific predictions. They must be approached in very individualized ways.

Nevertheless, people are forever playing games with one another when it comes to sex and relationships. Here are some of the most common ones:

The Power Games   Sex is a common place for people to express their struggles for power over one another. Most relationships have their share of such struggles. A man who is fearful of appearing vulnerable may always want to be in a dominant position during sexual activity, quite literally needing always to be "on top." A woman who resents something about her partner might show little interest in sex to punish the other person through the withholding of sexual activity.

Some men and women use power games to spoil sex by being unavailable at the "right" time. Being drunk may sometimes be a handy way either to avoid sex or to justify a sexual failure. Some people play "hard to get" by being too busy, too tired, or emotionally detached. Power games can turn into a sort of sexual sabotage, in which one partner manages to ruin a sexual encounter without looking like the "guilty party." Dropping some subtle criticisms about the other person's sexual performance may sometimes lower that individual's level of sexual interest considerably. As long as these power struggles proceed, sexual sharing will have its difficulties.

The Relationship Games   There are many different ways in which partners play games within their relationships. For example, some men and women bring unresolved conflicts and emotional problems with them to their sexual relationships. A stormy relationship with a parent that has resulted in certain patterns of reaction may affect one's present relationship if some of the old feelings are lingering inside. Mutual trust is a crucial factor in building intimacy and a satisfying sex life. When trust is lacking, the inner barriers stay up, holding a partner away. People who feel as though significant others in their lives have always left them may test how much a partner will put up with. The partner is in a sense being called upon to prove his or her love and devotion by sticking by the other person no matter what. Such games can create great strain in relationships, and are often the cause of their destruction.

The Communication Games   One of the most common communication games is to push for the resolution of a conflict as quickly as possible. One partner, wanting the problem to be over, comes up with what seems the most logical solution to her or him, then tries to impose the solution on the other. Statements

Cathy   by Cathy Guisewite

may be made such as "You shouldn't feel that way," or "Come on, cheer up," or "You're blowing this all out of proportion." In the face of such seemingly logical suggestions, the other person may end up feeling guilty for having some reaction, and then pretend that all is resolved. Many communication games are designed to avoid confronting potentially hurtful feelings or situations. Yet when truly effective communication happens, both partners feel that they have permission to feel and express whatever they need to. Sexual and relational difficulties often grow out of situations where two people fool themselves into thinking that some rough spots have been logically resolved, but in actuality, their differences are still simmering under the surface.

Most sex therapists agree that a primary cause of sexual problems is inadequate communication. An essential key to a full and satisfying sexual relationship is knowing how to communicate effectively with a partner. That does not mean that you have to be an extrovert or well versed in the social graces. Neither does it mean that you have to be a great conversationalist, or even talk a great deal. What it does mean is that you care enough about yourself, your partner, and the relationship you share to put some effort and energy into communicating.

Effective Communication

For the most part, people do not find it easy to communicate about the more intimate aspects of their lives such as their sexuality. The opinion or "idea" topics may be discussed with some ease—issues such as how society should deal with homosexuals, or values concerning sex and marriage, or which form of birth control is most effective. But when it comes right down to talking about one's own sexual orientation, or a preferred sexual activity, or the form of birth control the individual wants to use, the conversation may not flow quite so smoothly. This section of the chapter presents some basic guidelines for facilitating good lines of communication.

THE GROUND RULES

There are some preliminary steps to opening up channels for effective communication between two people about sex or any other sensitive topic. Here are some ground rules for getting started:

1. *Think about the degree of commitment you hold for each other and the relationship.* Not much will happen with two-way communication unless *both* part-

ners really want it to happen. This may well depend on the quality of the relationship you are sharing. Communicating honestly about sex takes energy. You may begin to feel tired, frustrated, or hopeless at times, and it will take a solid commitment from both people to see you through the more difficult steps. Relationships in which sex is discussed may exist on many different levels. On one end of the scale is the casual encounter in which two people barely know one another. On the other end is the long-term loving involvement where discussing sex is continually necessary to assure mutual satisfaction.

2. *Know your own values.* Before you try communicating about sex, it is a good idea to have thought through where you stand on some of the value issues that may be involved. Know your own beliefs, while letting yourself be open to the attitudes and values of the other individual.

3. *Keep yourselves on equal ground.* A sense of equality between two people is usually essential to their communicating well. If someone is always feeling in the "one-down" inferior position, it is not likely that he or she will be able to communicate very openly or confidently.

4. *Build trust for one another.* When there is a lack of trust between two partners, there is likely to be not only a strain in their sexual interactions, but also a tendency toward reserved and uncomfortable communication. A sense of trust is fundamental to honest, genuine dialogue.

5. *Pick the right location for talking.* Where you talk may be very important. You will both want to feel as relaxed and comfortable as possible, and have adequate privacy. Sometimes bed is the ideal place to talk, but it may also produce an emotionally charged situation for some kinds of communication. Beware of atmospheres that encourage superficial conversations and games. Ask your partner where she or he would feel most comfortable talking, and be certain you feel all right there as well.

MAKING IT HAPPEN

A central message of this chapter is that the process of making good communication happen takes some deliberate effort. There are several qualities that have repeatedly been shown through research to facilitate open and honest communication between people:

Demonstrate an Attitude of Warmth, Caring, and Respect In order to feel enough trust to open up to another person and share on more than a superficial level, there has to be some sense of mutual positive regard. However, it is not enough to feel a sense of caring for another person; the feelings need to be demonstrated or communicated in some way. Sometimes it may be a simple willingness to be quiet and listen attentively; other times, it will require overt expressions of love or kindness.

Avoid Making Snap Judgments and "All-ness Statements"

One of the greatest problems in human communication is the tendency of some to jump to premature conclusions and make snap judgments about others. Most people open up best to those who are not judgmental. Because sex is one of those areas of life about which people have strong opinions, intimate communication would be improved if we set assumptions aside and allow other points of view to be expressed openly. In a more technical sense, it is also valuable to avoid using "all-ness" words such as *always* or *never*. When referring to another person, use of statements including these words is rarely fair or accurate.

Listen Carefully and Really Hear

Often when people appear to be listening, they are actually thinking ahead, formulating their response to what the other person is saying. It is all too easy for ideas and concepts to become garbled and misunderstood unless one listens carefully. Let yourself hear the other person out, then think through your reactions and responses. Listening is not just a passive state of resting the senses; it is an active process of being attuned to the words and nonverbal messages someone else is conveying to us.

Empathize and Understand That Feelings Need to Be Felt

Empathy is the ability to identify with what another person is feeling and to experience, in a sense, "walking a mile in their shoes." All of us have experienced a full range of emotions, although for different reasons. When listening to another, listen for their feelings too, and try to recall the experience of your own emotions so you can better understand where they're coming from. Two people who want to communicate about personal things must be willing to share emotions, even hurtful ones, and empathize with each other. It is also important to allow one another to express feelings. Sensing that your feelings are being heard and understood is one of the most crucial aspects of good communication.

Be Genuine

Research shows that hidden agendas make communication more difficult and problems harder to resolve (Krokoff, 1990). Most people can sense superficiality and deceptiveness and respond much more positively to genuineness and honesty. Effective communication about sexual matters must be

FIGURE 8.3 Genuineness

Loving relationships depend on attitudes of warmth, caring, and a genuine respect for each other.

based on such openness. However, sometimes the issues are often subtle and difficult. Shades of meaning may cloud the truth. No lasting relationship can escape the need to communicate about difficulties and misunderstandings. Otherwise, they accumulate under the surface and create problems later. For these reasons, you must work at being honest and being yourself in personal communications.

Make Sense and Ask for Clarification

It is all too easy for words or mannerisms to be misunderstood in the communication process. We often make assumptions about what the other person means, without ever bothering to check those assumptions out with that individual. It takes work to listen carefully, understand what is being said, and then clarify if your understanding is correct. In order to do this, it is a good idea occasionally to feed back your understanding to your partner by saying, "So what I hear you saying is . . ." or "Do you mean . . . ?" You have clarified your interpretation of their words, and they are then able to correct any misconceptions. When formulating a reply to any message, take the time you need to think it through, choose your words carefully, and give a focused response. The response may not always be verbal, but may be made through expressions of the face, eyes, or body.

Don't Let Silence Scare You

As pointed out earlier in this chapter, gaps in conversation often make people feel uneasy and vulnerable. They may rush to fill the gap with words. Instead, it is more important to take your time, allowing silence to be a part of communication at times. It can be intimate and calming as well.

Beware of the "I Don't Want to Hurt You" Copout In relationships, hurtful things must be shared. That sort of confrontation is not always easy, but in the long run will help get tension-producing conflicts resolved. It is not unusual for counselors to hear one partner explain that they avoided dealing with painful topics because they were afraid of hurting someone's feelings. Of course, they were also avoiding their own discomfort that comes from having to talk about hurtful issues.

Use Self-Talk Effectively How we talk to ourselves can have a profound effect on the ways we relate to other people. The things we say inside our own minds can color our emotions and our reactions both positively and negatively. For example, if during sex you are worrying about how you look or sound, or are thinking negatively about your own body, it is not likely to be a very positive experience. However, if you work at positive self-talk, emphasizing how good the experience seems, and how much you are enjoying being with your partner, it is much more likely the experience will be enjoyable and fulfilling.

Sex is a difficult topic for many people to communicate about, especially if there is concern over one's own sexual feelings or relationships. Sex is deeply personal to most of us and to discuss it with someone else represents a special degree of vulnerability. Yet in a partnership where sex is shared, words and feelings must also be shared. There are always decisions to be made, signals to be checked, worries to be resolved, and feelings to be discussed. Communication about sex takes effort and practice, but the results can be worth it.

THE PROS AND CONS OF QUARRELING

Even the happiest of couples are bound to have disagreements, some of which will become arguments. Conventional wisdom, even among some marital therapists, has held that quarreling is a sign of dissatisfaction and unhappiness in the relationship, and that it ultimately is destructive for the partnership. However, recent research has shown that things are not that clear-cut. In fact, certain kinds of quarreling can actually improve relationships. Even couples who describe themselves as unhappy, but who are able to express their anger and resentment in constructive ways, have been shown to be much happier 3 years later than they previously had been (Gottman & Krokoff, 1989).

Fighting in relationships is most likely to begin after an initial romantic period has passed (Hendrix, 1988). Many couples fear that when tensions and conflicts begin to develop, it means that the relationship is in serious trouble. They may even go out of their way to avoid arguments, under the assumption that no fighting is the equivalent of relational bliss. Actually, lack of arguing may signal trouble in the relationship, because it may mean that disagreements are not getting resolved.

The key here is whether the mode of arguing is constructive or destructive (see Table 8.1). In the most destructive kinds of fights, anger is expressed in vicious and attacking ways, with blaming and character assassination (Beck, 1988). The two people are defensive, accusatory, and stubborn, while resorting to insults, contemptuous remarks, and whining complaints (Goleman, 1989). A more constructive and hopeful pattern is found in couples who feel free to express their anger to one another, but without allowing the anger to escalate until it gets out of control. They make a concerted effort to acknowledge their differences, be open to one another's points of view, and listen to each other. Eventually, they work toward arriving at some resolution to their differences, often involving negotiation and compromise.

Women and men typically play different roles in fights. It is more common for males to want to avoid

FIGURE 8.4 Quarreling

Quarreling in a relationship can be constructive or destructive. Anger expressed in a violent or accusatory manner is destructive. Rather, couples should make an effort to express their views openly, listen to the other person, and learn to compromise.

TABLE 8.1

Anatomy of a Lovers' Quarrel

Helpful and destructive arguments differ in each of their three major phases.
Here are some of the typical differences:

FIRST PHASE: Picking the Fight and Stating Its Agenda.

Helpful: Even as the couple are beginning to disagree, one partner at least partly acknowledges the other's point of view, even by such subtle cues as carefully listening to a charge and nodding to show it might have some validity.	**Destructive:** Every complaint of one partner is matched by a countercharge by the other; neither gives the least indication that there may be some validity to the other's views.

SECOND PHASE: The Argument at Its Most Heated.

Helpful: Even during the stormiest time, one partner accurately feeds back what she or he thinks the other is feeling about the issue.	**Destructive:** One partner makes mistaken assumptions about how the other feels, and then attacks those inaccurate thoughts or feelings.

THIRD PHASE: Negotiation or Wind-Down.

Helpful: The partners agree to modify their views.	**Destructive:** Every proposed compromise is met by a counterproposal, with no accommodation on either side.

Source: John Gottman, University of Washington. Adapted from *New York Times*, February 21, 1989, p. C6.

conflict with their partners, and they may at first withdraw or become defensive. Women, on the other hand, are often the "emotional managers" of relationships. They are more likely to bring up some issue about which there is disagreement, wanting to confront the problem with their partners. It is sometimes crucial for the woman to present her anger in such a way that does not drive her partner away. Likewise, it is important for a man to work at listening to the other point of view and recognizing that there is a problem in need of resolution (Gottman & Krokoff, 1989).

RESOLVING CONFLICTS EFFECTIVELY

People have different styles of conflict resolution. Some prefer to give in quickly and avoid unpleasant encounters altogether. Some jump in with full force and try to coerce others into accepting their points of view. While some people place the most significance on principles, others place more value on maintaining the relationship. One person may want to confront conflicts head-on, and another may want to smooth over ruffled feelings as quickly as possible.

An important beginning step to working out solutions to conflicts is realizing and admitting that people and their points of view are indeed different. Everyone has his or her own perceptions of any

situation. And all of us tend to see ourselves as more correct in our perspectives than others.

In most conflicting situations in relationships, one partner is more affected by the problem than the other. A second step in conflict resolution is clarifying who really has the problem. This will be the individual who is suffering apparent consequences, is more unhappy or frustrated about the situation, and whose needs are not being met.

Once someone has effectively claimed ownership of a particular problem, it is crucial for the person to explain in clear terms what the problem is and what its consequences have been. This third step involves formulating "I" messages. That means taking responsibility for communicating about the problem to a partner. For example:

Instead of attacking: "You are such a bastard for doing that."
Use an "I" message: "I feel really hurt whenever this happens."
Instead of making assumptions about another's motives: "You deliberately set out to make a fool of me."
Use an "I" message: "I am really angry and embarrassed about how this situation makes me look."
Instead of dwelling on past offenses: "This is another example of the way in which you show no consideration for me. Last week, you . . ."
Use an "I" message: "I often feel demoralized and frustrated by the way you treat me."

TABLE 8.2

Useful Strategies for Improving Communication in a Loving Relationship

Here are some ways of keeping your relationship open, honest, and caring:

1. If you must criticize, focus on specific behavior rather than criticizing the person. For example, say something like *"That* irritates me," rather than *"You* irritate me." Your partner will feel less "attacked."

2. Don't make assumptions and judgments about your partner, so you end up telling him/her what he/she is thinking or feeling. We cannot be mind readers.

3. Avoid using "all-ness" words such as "always" and "never." They typically represent unfair generalizations. Again, try to be more specific.

4. Try to see gray areas in issues, rather than strictly black-and-white, good-bad dichotomies. Remember our own "truths" often depend on our individual perceptions.

5. Use "I feel . . ." messages rather than "You are . . ." statements. No one can dispute what you feel. However, your partner may well be offended by judgments about his or her character that are perceived as being unfair or untrue.

6. Be direct and honest, avoiding games, power plays, and attempts at using reverse psychology.

7. Work toward a sense of equality. An "I'm OK–You're OK" feeling is fundamental to good communication.

8. Positive reinforcement is preferable to negative reinforcement. Compliment and thank the other person when she/he pleases you. When she/he does something that displeases you, try making a positive suggestion for a change ("Could you try doing . . .") rather than a negative prohibition ("Stop doing that . . .").

And remember:
Whether the issue is pleasant or hurtful, don't put it off. Communicate about it as soon as possible.

The other communication strategies discussed in this chapter may assist in resolving many conflicts. A fundamental principle is to be assertive, stating clearly and in a personalized way how *you* feel. This is in contrast to aggressive behavior, in which you attack, blame, and accuse others, making assumptions and judgments about their motives. Some useful suggestions for assertive communication are given in Table 8.2.

PEOPLE HAVE DIFFERENT PERSONALITY TYPES FOR COMMUNICATING

Psychologists have many ways of describing various characteristics of the human personality. Two things remain quite clear as we study personality: 1) it may be demonstrated that people really are different in the ways they perceive and approach life; and 2) most people tend to view their own perceptions and approaches as the "right" ones. It is no wonder, then, that when people attempt to establish an intimate partnership, their differences sometimes create tensions, disagreements, and arguments. It can help if you have a clearer picture of your own personality and its characteristics.

In recent years, one of the most popular tests to be used for evaluating personality traits has been the Myers-Briggs Type Indicator (MBTI) (Myers & Mc-Caulley, 1985), and its modified version, the Kiersey Temperament Sorter (Kiersey & Bates, 1984). These tests are based on a model that portrays the human personality as a combination of varying balances between four main pairs of traits. While any such model is bound to oversimplify the complexities of being human, the MBTI can also offer some general insights into one's personality. Most counseling centers have this test available, and are willing to interpret and explain its results.

Everyone is familiar with the pair of personality traits known as extraversion and introversion, although these terms are frequently misused and misunderstood. Extraverted individuals tend to be energized by other people and the external environment. They connect with others easily and enjoy group situations. Introverted people prefer being their own company, but being introverted does not necessarily imply that they are shy or antisocial. They simply tend to draw their energy more from inside themselves. They need more time and privacy for processing their inner experience, and often prefer one-to-one interactions with others.

The Myers-Briggs typology also makes a distinction between people who are specific and concrete in their approach to life, and those who rely on their abstract, intuitive natures. It suggests too, that while some individuals make their judgments through logical, step-by-step analysis and reasoning, others are more oriented toward messages they take from their feelings and wanting to maintain harmonious relationships. In the final pair of MBTI characteristics, people are viewed either as punctual, decisive, scheduled, and orderly, or as unstructured, open-ended, and spontaneous.

It is these various combinations of personality traits that must come together in any relationship between two people, sometimes creating difficulty in understanding one another (Kiersey & Bates, 1984). The extravert may be miffed that an introverted friend is more content to stay at home and avoid large parties. The individual who pays attention to feelings and wants to preserve harmony between people may be frustrated by a partner who prefers approaching problems in a highly rational manner, only wanting to arrive at the most logical conclusion.

Personality differences in relationships only underscore the need for good communication skills and a commitment to using them. The differences may also be expressed through an individual's sexual preferences and styles. While it is certainly not always true that opposites attract, or that it is easy for them to get along well, human differences—sexual and otherwise—can be managed and even enjoyed. They sometimes provide the spice of a loving relationship.

COMMUNICATION DIFFERENCES BETWEEN WOMEN AND MEN

Women and men sometimes express frustration with their shared communications. Deborah Tannen (1990) is a sociolinguist who has been studying the intricacies of communication patterns in males and females. Her work has revealed some fascinating differences in the ways the two sexes are taught to communicate. She began by studying the videotapes of people in different age groups having conversations with best friends of the same gender. She noticed that girls tended to face each other squarely, look directly at each other, and enjoy talking together. Boys seemed much more uncomfortable having to make conversation with a friend, and were more likely not to face one another or look at each other directly.

Boys seem to grow up in a much more hierarchical social order than girls do. When they play in large groups, the group usually has a leader who tells others what to do. An elaborate system of rules filters down through the group, and there is a struggle to maintain one's status within the group. Girls are more apt to play in small groups or in pairs, and focus on maintaining intimacy and a sense of community. They want to get along with their friends so that everyone can have a

turn, and there often are no "winners" or "losers." When they encounter conflict, both boys and girls want to get their own way, but they will try to achieve that in different ways. Boys resort to insistence and threats of physical violence, while girls usually try to mediate the situation and preserve harmony through compromise and avoidance of confrontation (Taylor, 1990).

Tannen has suggested that the differences in communication style between adult men and women are rooted in the fact that they have practically grown up in different cultures when it comes to communicating. Women place a premium on being agreeable and congenial, while men have a tendency to resist doing what they are told because they do not want to feel dominated or in a "one-down" position in their social interactions. There are several different ways in which these differences cause confusion and turmoil in male-female relationships.

Talking Over Problems   A man is much less likely to tell a woman about his difficult feelings or life problems because he does not want to worry her or seem helpless. Men also feel more obligated to offer solutions when someone tells them about a problem, even if the other person is just looking for an empathetic ear. For women, not being told about something such as personal feelings or troubles seems like a rejection from a partner. They value the intimacy in telling secrets and worries, whereas men are more likely to feel too vulnerable in doing so. In fact, men do live in a social milieu where other men may indeed be trying to put them down, and they therefore have to be somewhat self-protective. The social atmosphere for women is very different, and so misunderstandings develop.

Asking for Directions   In the same way, men are more resistant to asking for directions when they are trying to find or do something. For them, it is putting yourself "one down" with someone else. Women welcome the chance to connect with another person, and are not bothered by seeming to need help.

Expressing Needs   One of the areas of communication that often causes trouble for women and men is how they express various needs. For example, Tannen (1990) cites a typical situation in which a woman asks her husband if he would like to stop in somewhere for a drink. He truthfully answers "No," and nothing more is said for the moment. It eventually becomes evident that the wife was hurt and angered by his response. While he had seen the interaction as a simple statement of fact—he did not want to stop for a drink—she had felt that her wishes had not been considered. The wife had not realized that he would have been open to

Internal/External Consistency in Communication

Using assertive communication skills can reduce misunderstandings and conflicts in relationships. The more consistency there can be between the thoughts and feelings going on internally with what is being expressed externally, the more likely that minor concerns may be resolved before they become major problems. Note these hypothetical interactions between a couple: how things were said, and how they could have been expressed more effectively.

THE SETTING: AFTERPLAY

	What was said:	What was being thought and felt:	What could have been said:
Man	"You haven't seemed very into sex lately. Is there anything wrong?"	Something is wrong. She just lies there. I guess I'm not much of a lover.	"I'm embarrassed to bring this up, but I've been worried lately that I'm not pleasing you much during sex."
Woman	"No, I'm fine."	Oh my God, he doesn't think I'm much good in bed.	"I've been worrying that you would think I'm not much good in bed."
Man	"Was it good for you this time?"	Maybe she doesn't love me anymore. Or maybe I'm just not doing something right.	"I really love you a lot, and I've been scared that either you don't feel the same about me or that my sex techniques just aren't working for you."
Woman	"Yes, it was fine, I said."	He must know that I'm not reaching orgasm. This is so embarrassing.	"It's not you. I love you so much. I haven't wanted to admit this to anybody, but I've never been able to have an orgasm. I'm really embarrassed."
Man	"Come on, are you sure? You just don't seem very turned on."	She just doesn't want to admit that she doesn't feel the same about me anymore. I've never been able to hold on to a relationship.	"I was afraid that things were falling apart between us. It must be a real let-down not to be able to come. Maybe we can work on it together."
Woman	"Do we really need to talk about this? I don't really like analyzing our sex life. I've told you everything is okay. Okay?"	I'm going to lose him if I don't find a way to fake having an orgasm. I love him so much.	"It's not easy for me to talk about this, but I would sure like to do something about it."

further negotiation, and in fact could have been easily persuaded to follow her lead had she made it clear that it was an important issue for her. Because of how they learn to communicate, men are more likely to start any sort of negotiation with a clear statement of where they stand, but understand that there will be further discussion. Women, on the other hand, are likely to accept any such statement as a clear indication of a man's position and see it as immovable unless she presses the communication into some form of unpleasantness.

Another variation on this theme is that when women are trying to focus on intimacy and connection by expressing needs, men tend to view such expression as a demand they must resist. Male socialization causes them to be cautious about one-down positions. So when a woman suggests to her male partner that she would like to know when he is going to be late because otherwise she feels upset, he may see it as a challenge to his freedom and rebel against the suggestion.

Talking and Listening Research shows that, contrary to popular opinion, men tend to talk more than women in public situations such as meetings, group discussion, or classrooms. When questions are asked

THE SETTING: AFTER CLASS

	What was said:	What was being thought and felt:	What could have been said:
Chris	"How about joining me at the snack bar so we could go over these notes? I'm getting confused."	I'm really attracted to him/her. If there was only a way to strike up a relationship.	"I've been noticing you in class, and I was wondering if you might be interested in going to the snack bar to talk."
Jan	"I'm pretty busy right now. Maybe another time."	What's going on here? S/He has been watching me in class for weeks.	"I've noticed you watching me. You just want to talk?"
Chris	"How about this afternoon? We could meet around 4:30 and then catch a bite to eat."	If I let her/him get away now, there'll never be another chance. Maybe if I press it a little further.	"I'd like a chance to get to know you better. How about it?"
Jan	"I've got another commitment for dinner time, okay?"	This person doesn't know when to give up. I wish I knew what he/she was really looking for. I've got enough problems.	"I don't know. I'm feeling a little uncomfortable. My life is kind of complicated right now, and I'm hesitant to make any new commitments."
Chris	"Well, how about Friday after class?"	I think I'm making a jerk of myself. S/He thinks s/he's pretty hot stuff, apparently. What's so wrong with me?	"I don't want to look like a jerk, but I really hope you'll consider it. We'll just talk; I'm not so bad."
Jan	"Look, I may not be here Friday. Maybe you could find somebody else to go over the notes with you."	I just want to get out of here. Won't this person take no for an answer?	"I appreciate the invitation, but this just isn't a good time for me. I don't mean to hurt your feelings, but I'd really rather not."
Chris	(sarcastically:) "Sorry I asked. I won't trouble you again. See you around."	I really blew it. I always have to push too hard.	"Well, if you ever change your mind, I'll be sitting in the same seat in this class. Keep me in mind."
Jan	"Fine."	Maybe I was too hard on him/her. But he/she wouldn't let up. I feel like a heel.	"Look, it was really nice of you to ask. I just don't want any more complications right now. But I will keep you in mind. Thanks for understanding."

As this example shows, effective and assertive communication may not always change the ultimate outcome of people's behavior. However, it can change how people end up feeling about the interaction, themselves, and each other.

in a group meeting, men tend to ask the first question, more questions, and longer questions. Not unexpectedly, in the listening process women tend to show frequently that they are listening to another person, while men focus more on the literal content and react only when they agree or disagree (Tannen, 1990).

At home, however, the talking roles seem reversed. Women see talking as a way to foster intimacy with their partners at home. Men view talking as a way to negotiate status, and therefore do not fit it into the private home context as much as women do. When women talk about their feelings and problems, and see

that as a way to work on them, men tend to perceive the communication as wallowing in complaints. They tend to be more solution-oriented, and want to resolve the difficulty with definitive action (Taylor, 1990).

Even though men have more difficulty with it, intimate talking seems to be a healthier mode of communication. The sooner people talk out problems, the sooner they tend to get over them and feel better. Talking in the manner described earlier in this chapter is a learnable skill, even for men. What Deborah Tannen's work has demonstrated, however, is that when communication behavior frustrates a partner of the other sex, it may represent a normal expression of gender rather than some individual failing. To understand the gender differences in communication, rather than assigning blame and becoming lost to disappointment, is the first step toward changing the behavior or learning how to live with some of the differences.

Loving Relationships and Sexuality

Building any worthwhile relationship takes effort and commitment. When sexual sharing is part of the relationship, things become that much more sensitive and complicated. To share sex is to share a deep level of intimacy and the strong feelings that usually accompany such intimacy. Positive sexual relationships do not just fall into place from one encounter in bed; they evolve from a deliberate process of communicating together and working to be responsive to one another.

THE "OTHER" RISKS OF SEX

There have always been highly publicized risks of sex, such as unplanned pregnancy or sexually transmitted disease. Recently, AIDS has come to represent another serious threat in indiscriminate sexual activity. However, there are other risks of sex too, risks that are associated with the relational aspects of human interaction (Kelly, 1988). Here are some examples:

Risk: Modeling Your Sexuality Only After External Standards Rather Than Your Own Of course we must pay attention to socio-cultural standards relating to sexuality. That constitutes responsible, civilized sexual behavior. But we must also accept our complete sexuality, regardless of whether we ever act on it. Each of us has his or her very individualized aspects of sexuality, a unique blend of needs, orientations, fantasies, attractions, and behaviors. We must find ways of bringing that sexual individuality into some sort of balance and harmony with our society, which is always circumscribed by its cultural, political, and historical boundaries. Not to achieve that harmony is to be alienated from ourselves, perhaps playing some sexual role that is inconsistent with the core of our being. That can create a remarkable degree of personal pain and confusion.

Risk: Confusing Romantic Attachments and Sexual Attractions Most people have learned to say that sex is only "right" and justified within the context of a loving or "meaningful" relationship. While that is a

perfectly desirable value, it often engenders some confusion between romantic attachment and sexual attraction. There may be a tendency to rush toward saying "I love you" in order to justify sex. Or sexual interaction may mistakenly be construed as evidence of love. In many cultures other than our own, especially in Eastern countries, there has been far less confusion over these matters. Love is not allowed to become an excuse for sex. Sexual passion and infatuation are not considered legitimate bases from which to embark on major life adventures such as marriage. People in our society sometimes have difficulty distinguishing between their loving emotions and their sexual turn-ons. To perceive them as the same thing is risky business, indeed.

Risk: Not Allowing Yourself to Be Vulnerable Enough to Accept the Risks Inherent in Loving Relationships Almost everyone has bought into the typical scenario of relationships: partners meet; they "fall in love"; there is a growing closeness and exciting sense of intimacy until some misunderstandings, miscommunications, and conflicts begin to generate some hurt and tension; as the partners struggle to protect themselves, their process of loving becomes filled with blocks and barriers, and the relationship deteriorates. I am increasingly convinced that fear of dealing with hurt—in oneself or in a partner—is one of the leading causes of broken relationships. We must encourage people to be willing to be vulnerable to the fears of being hurt or of hurting someone else. Without vulnerability, relationships and their sexual components eventually become sterile, brittle, and empty.

However, before we can deal with vulnerability in a healthy, positive manner, we must also know and accept ourselves. We have to develop a level of self-esteem and self-confidence that will help us to feel worthwhile and validated as individuals. When we depend too heavily on others to make us feel good, we give up a great deal of personal power in the relationship. This can exaggerate the risks of vulnerability, as well as robbing ourselves of the right to accept ourselves as we are and feel good about who we are. There is even some research evidence to indicate that college students who have a clear sense of their own identity are more able to establish intimacy in their relationships (Dyk & Adams, 1990).

Risk: Being in a Situation in Which You Feel Bound to Do Something Sexual That Just Doesn't Feel Quite Right to You People often model their sexual standards on their perceptions of what other people are doing, and these perceptions are often not terribly accurate. This is then integrated with the fact that our society does not encourage much sense of "ownership" over our genitals until we reach some arbitrary age of passage when we are suddenly expected to become sexually responsible. This results in a good deal of confusion about sexual values and behaviors, and often leads us to engage in sexual activities out of a sense of obligation rather than a conviction that they are right for us.

We need to be open to our sexuality so that we can think and plan ahead. We never have to be at the mercy of whims or urges, whether our own or those of others. It takes introspection, time, and even some experimentation to know where we stand with sexual values and what we want for our lives sexually. Nearly everyone makes some sexual mistakes during their lives. But the key to facing and dealing with such mistakes is talking them through, experiencing the range of emotions they have generated, making whatever changes in ourselves that we must, and then moving on. Not to be open to our sexual selves, not to find ways of accepting all aspects of that sexuality, is to risk stagnating in a set of standards that may well lead to sex by obligation.

WHAT IS LOVE?

Love, intimacy, and sex seem to be parts of a singular, confusing package that writers, poets, priests, and scientists have been trying to understand and explain for centuries. Love is a quality and an experience that somehow has seemed more comfortable in the hands of artists than it has with scientists, but it has also lent itself to historical exploration. In his book *About Love,* author Robert Solomon (1989) insists that romantic love the way we perceive it today is the result of a synthesis of beliefs about human nature and behavior. All too often, explanations and descriptions of love have tended toward one extreme of being seen as mysterious and somehow divine, or the other extreme of being reduced to a set of simple skills, a commodity to be acquired. Solomon suggests that love lies somewhere between these two poles, and that sex has a crucial and positive place in the picture. Love and sex seem to be primary ingredients that bring people together in intimate relationships. Every loving partnership also has its own unique history and configuration. Each relationship has its own identity, just as do the two individuals who make it up (Douglas & Atwell, 1988).

Love between people represents a challenge to go beyond the single-minded pursuit of personal gratification and to break down some of the habitual patterns of behavior that have been a part of being non-partnered. It has been said that love and relationship have a transformative power, in that they bring two people together who then have to sort through the many complications of being together. Until recently, the social regulations that prescribed the form and functions of relationships, particularly formalized ones such as marriage, were clearly and carefully delineated. Couples had defined roles within an extended family that existed within a broader, close-knit community. This also constituted a stabilizing influence for relationships. We now live in a mobile, more disconnected culture and a time in history where the rules about love and relating are much more vague and confusing. The external pressures and reasons for people to come together and form a partnership are far less convincing than they once were. Now it is internal reactions and the intrinsic qualities of two individuals' personal connection that will keep a relationship going (Welwood, 1990). It has been suggested that creating and sustaining a relationship constitute a whole new frontier in the human journey. Whenever we enter into a loving connection with another person, it is largely unexplored territory, with all sorts of new things to discover—within ourselves and within the dynamics of what we are sharing as a couple.

INFATUATION AND BEING IN LOVE

A number of years ago, psychoanalyst Erich Fromm (1970) maintained in his book *The Art of Loving* that love is indeed an art. He went on to explain that, like any form of art, love is something to be practiced, perfected, and worked at if its full potential is to be realized. Only too often in our culture, the impression is created that love just happens; either you have it or you don't. But Fromm and others have stated that things are not that clear-cut.

Some close relationships begin with a process of "falling in love" or *infatuation*. This kind of loving involves an intense desire to be close to another person, and strong emotions may surface as well as intense sexual attraction. Infatuation can be exciting and exhilarating but it can have its difficult side, since such strong emotions are involved, and may be particularly painful when the other person is unable to feel mutually attracted and loving. On the other hand, when two people fall in love, they typically want to spend a great deal of time together, gradually let down their usual barriers and become more and more vulnerable to one another. Their sense of shared intimacy deepens, and they may eventually progress to sexual sharing. Often there is a sense of never wanting things to change, never wanting to be apart. It is typical at this point for partners to make promises to each other such as "I'll always love you," or "I'll never leave you," or "I'll never hurt you."

As Erich Fromm has pointed out, however, the

209

FIGURE 8.5 Infatuation

Infatuation, the process of falling in love, is emotionally and physically exhilarating, but must inevitably end. A couple may decide either to end the relationship or to commit more fully to each other.

process of falling in love must always come to an end. It is often at this point that relationships end too, largely because people in our society have been led to believe that infatuation is the only kind of loving worth having. This intense phase may also evolve into the more stable and deeply committed stage of *being* in love.

Being in love involves a conscious choice on the part of both partners to be together. They care about one another and trust each other enough to commit themselves to working at the relationship. They recognize that their love is more than just a passionate emotion. They see it as a process of communicating, negotiating, and compromising when differences get in the way, and agreeing to struggle through the more difficult times together. Being in love also means that two people are struggling to accept and love each other, even in the face of their individual differences and idiosyncrasies. They may eventually find ways of celebrating their mutual differences instead of finding them to be obstacles.

STERNBERG'S TRIANGULAR THEORY OF LOVE

Even though love would appear to be one of the most significant human experiences, it has not been subjected to much objective study. However, Yale researcher Robert Sternberg has studied the dynamics of loving relationships for several years, and has developed a model that accounts for three distinct components of love (Trotter, 1986). These components may be viewed as the three sides of a triangle, with the area of the triangle representing the amount and style of loving.

1. *Intimacy* is the emotional component, and involves closeness, mutual support, and sharing. In relationships, intimacy tends to increase gradually but steadily at first, naturally leveling off as two persons become more comfortably knowledgeable about each other. In well-established, healthy relationships, intimacy may not even be particularly noticeable on the surface, but it will quickly become evident during some crisis that the couple must face together (see Fig. 8.6).

2. *Passion* provides a motivational component to love. It is manifested in a desire to be united with the loved one, leading to sexual arousal and sharing. It is the aspect of some loving that tends to increase most rapidly at first. Sternberg has likened passion to an addictive substance, since people are so drawn to its stimulation and pleasure. If one person abruptly ends the relationship, suddenly withdrawing the outlet for passion, the other person may have to suffer all of the depression, irritability, and emotional pain of the withdrawal process. In time, even in a lasting relationship, passion levels off, simply not providing the stimulation and arousal it did at first. That does not mean that passion necessarily becomes unimportant or lacking. It simply loses some of its importance as a motivating force in the relationship (Fig. 8.6).

3. *Commitment* represents the cognitive side of love, in both its short- and long-term senses. The development of commitment in a relationship is easy to understand, as Figure 8.6 demonstrates. When you first meet another person, there is no particular commitment to a loving process. As you get to know each other better, however, the commitment begins to grow. As with all other components of love, commitment eventually levels off, and if the relationship fails, it will then decline.

(continued on page 212)

210

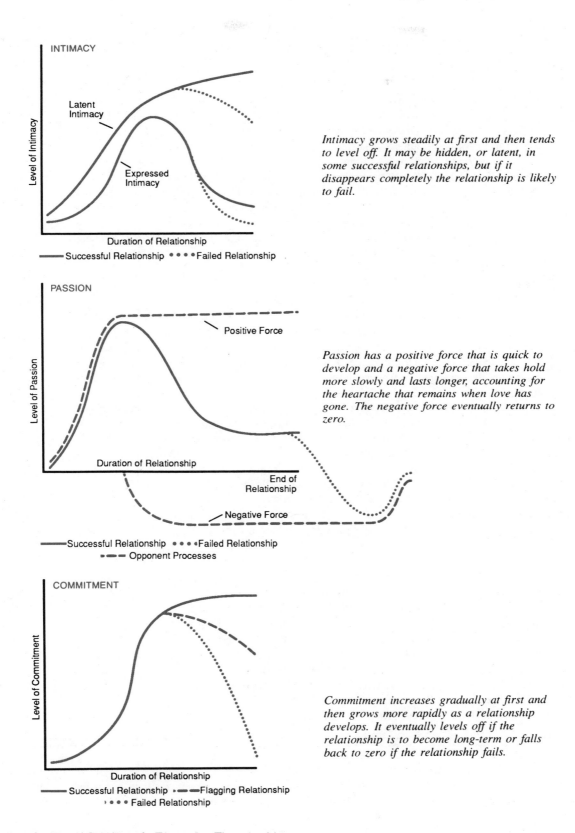

Intimacy grows steadily at first and then tends to level off. It may be hidden, or latent, in some successful relationships, but if it disappears completely the relationship is likely to fail.

Passion has a positive force that is quick to develop and a negative force that takes hold more slowly and lasts longer, accounting for the heartache that remains when love has gone. The negative force eventually returns to zero.

Commitment increases gradually at first and then grows more rapidly as a relationship develops. It eventually levels off if the relationship is to become long-term or falls back to zero if the relationship fails.

FIGURE 8.6   Sternberg's Triangular Theory of Love

Yale researcher Robert Sternberg has developed one model for the complicated emotion of love. In the model, he describes intimacy, passion, and commitment as love's basic components.

How Do I Love Thee?

Intimacy, passion, and commitment are the warm, hot, and cold vertices of Sternberg's love triangle. Alone and in combination they give rise to eight possible kinds of love relationships. The first is nonlove—the absence of all three components. This describes the large majority of our personal relationships, which are simply casual interactions.

The second kind of love is liking. "If you just have intimacy," Sternberg explains, "that's liking. You can talk to the person, tell about your life. And if that's all there is to it, that's what we mean by liking." It is more than nonlove. It refers to the feelings experienced in true friendships. Liking includes such things as closeness and warmth but not the intense feelings of passion or commitment.

If you just have passion, it's called infatuated love—the "love at first sight" that can arise almost instantaneously and dissipate just as quickly. It involves a high degree of physiological arousal but no intimacy or commitment. It's the 10th-grader who falls madly in love with the beautiful girl in his biology class but never gets up the courage to talk to her or get to know her, Sternberg says, describing his past.

Empty love is commitment without intimacy or passion, the kind of love sometimes seen in a 30-year-old marriage that has become stagnant. The couple used to be intimate, but they don't talk to each other any more. They used to be passionate, but that's died out. All that remains is the commitment to stay with the other person. In societies in which marriages are arranged, Sternberg points out, empty love may precede the other kinds of love.

Romantic love, the Romeo and Juliet type of love, is a combination of intimacy and passion. More than infatuation, it's liking with the added excitement of physical attraction and arousal but without commitment. A summer affair can be very romantic, Sternberg explains, but you know it will end when she goes back to Hawaii and you go back to Florida, or wherever.

Passion plus commitment is what Sternberg calls fatuous love. It's Hollywood love: Boy meets girl, a week later they're engaged, a month later they're married. They are committed on the basis of their passion, but because intimacy takes time to develop, they don't have the emotional core necessary to sustain the commitment. This kind of love, Sternberg warns, usually doesn't work out.

Companionate love is intimacy with commitment but no passion. It's a long-term friendship, the kind of committed love and intimacy frequently seen in marriages in which the physical attraction has died down.

When all three elements of Sternberg's love triangle come together in a relationship, you get what he calls consummate love, or complete love. It's the kind of love toward which many people strive, especially in romantic relationships. Achieving consummate love, says Sternberg, is like trying to lose weight, difficult but not impossible. The really hard thing is keeping the weight off after you have lost it, or keeping the consummate love alive after you have achieved it. Consummate love is possible only in very special relationships.

—R. J. Trotter, "The Three Faces of Love," *Psychology Today*, September, 1986

Sternberg's research has also shown that the best predictor of happiness in a loving relationship is the degree of similarity between how an individual wants the other person to feel about him or her, and how the individual thinks the partner actually feels. If one person believes that the other doesn't feel enough love, there can be disappointment and conflict (Trotter, 1986).

Everyone recognizes that love is one of the more complex human emotions, and that it cannot be adequately explained by any single research model. Through objective studies such as Sternberg's, we can only hope to be able to glimpse a few aspects of that part of the human personality that can create so much joy and pain.

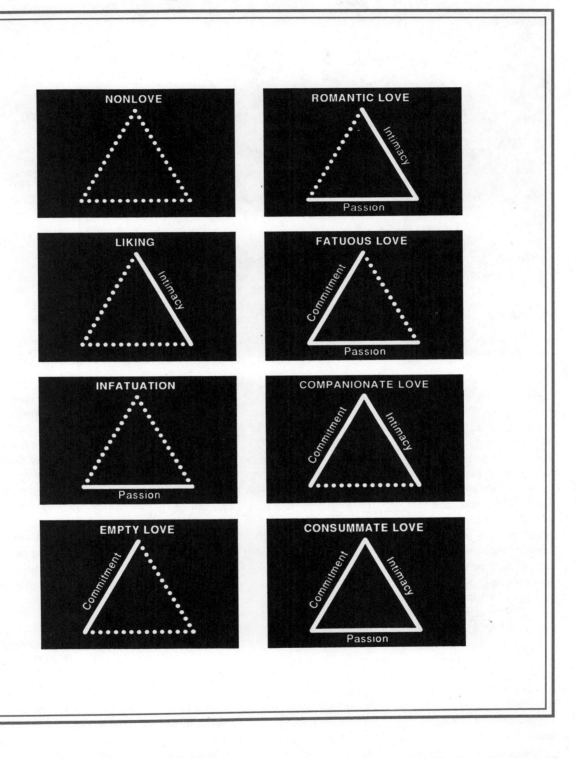

ESTABLISHING SENSUAL AND SEXUAL INTIMACY

We hear a great deal about intimacy in relationships, and the term seems to mean different things to different people. Intimacy usually describes a special kind of closeness between people, a deep connection that feels more special than the superficial interactions that tend to dominate our lives. But how do people go about building the kind of intimacy that they seem to crave at some deeper level within themselves?

1. *Touching* can establish a crucial foundation for intimacy. Skin sensitivity is apparently the first of the senses to develop in fetal life. We feel with the nerve

FIGURE 8.7 Intimacy

Developing intimacy in a relationship involves touching in a caring, loving, manner; learning to reduce tension by physically and psychologically relaxing; and being fully aware of the need to communicate.

endings of our skin before we make use of any other sense organs. The sensations of touch then remain at the forefront of our conscious experience (Montagu, 1986). Sensual touching is gratifying to the senses, but does not necessarily lead to sexual interaction. Only too often, people's sensual needs are ignored or starved. The need to be touched in caring, loving ways—to be taken care of through touching—is an important one for both women and men. Only too often, if such touching leads to sexual arousal, the sensual aspects are hurried along so that genital sexual activity may be initiated (Cohen, 1987). Like being in love, touching is an art, to be developed, worked at, and perfected through time and practice.

2. *Relaxation* is another important factor in intimacy. People need to be able to feel relaxed together in order to be open to one another. Physiologically, the term relaxation refers to a relatively low level of tension in the muscles. While it is possible to use relaxation techniques and other stress control methods to reduce tension, psychological factors are often an important part of the picture. Anxiety, depression, anger, hostility, or even subtle disagreements between people can create tension. Even subtle tension may block intimacy and interfere with sexual enjoyment. While sexual arousal involves a buildup of body tensions, it paradoxically is most effective within the context of a relaxed atmosphere between the partners. The more people have to work at sex, the more tension may destroy the sense of intimacy (Patrick, 1986).

3. *Being a participant* in a relationship is necessary to intimacy. Only too often, people allow themselves to become spectators, in a sense standing outside themselves and watching what is going on. Or they may escape into the withdrawal of daydreams and inattention. It is far better to be fully in touch with one's own inner reactions and with one's partner at the moment (Wright, 1986). To be preoccupied only with future goals, or how sex is going to go, is a distraction from experiencing and dealing with how things are actually going *right now*. That is what participating in an intimate relationship is all about—being fully aware of what is going on and taking responsibility to communicate or act as necessary.

CONFUSION ABOUT LOVE AND SEX IN RELATIONSHIPS

Issues of love and sex have become blurred in our culture. In fact, romantic love is a fairly recent development historically, and a century ago was not associated with sexual feelings. Love was meant to be a pure feeling, expressed through the idealization of the loved one. The modern period has witnessed the uniting of love with sex (Crosby, 1985), but this has not occurred without confusion.

One of the complications of this perspective is that we have come to expect intense feelings of love and the passion of sex to be a continuing part of lasting relationships such as marriage. Author John Crosby (1985) has called this the "grand illusion." It is an illusion that sees individuals using sex to hold on to their partners, or pretending that having sex must mean that you are in love.

People often assume that if they have chosen a partner well, the love and the relationship should last forever, and the love will never change. In fact, loving feelings and levels of interest in sex change over time. The important thing is how well the couple keeps up with the process of change (Wright, 1986). It is also assumed that when people love each other, sex will just happen. However, most couples have busy lives; as they spend time together, their priorities may change. Sometimes, they will have to create the opportunity for sex to happen, but without making it seem too contrived (DeAngelis, 1987).

Love may be abused in relationships as well (Crosby, 1985). It may be used as a justification for controlling others: "I only did it because I love you." Or it may be cited as the reason for some imperative being imposed on a partner: "If you really loved me, you would _____." The blank in this imperative could be completed in any number of ways, including:

. . . want sex as often as I do.
. . . have eyes for no one else but me.
. . . trust me without question.
. . . have sex with me now.
. . . know how to turn me on.
. . . never hurt me.

Such imperatives can place the receiver in a situation sometimes called the "double bind." In other words, you are "damned if you do and damned if you don't." The sender of the message has created a no-win situation in which if you go against the grain of the statement, you are only demonstrating your lack of caring. On the other hand, if you follow through as dictated by the imperative, you may be accused of only trying to please the person but not really meaning it (Crosby, 1985).

The confusions over love and sex are best resolved through effective communication methods, based on a real commitment to work together on having a dynamic and caring relationship.

FRIENDSHIP AND SEXUALITY

In many ways, friendships represent intimate and important life relationships. It is not always an easy matter to distinguish between what we call "love" and what we label "friendship." Certainly, many people would say they love their friends, but would not be referring to a romantic or sexual attachment. Studies on friendship show that, in general, people tend to prefer friendships with members of their own sex, and get less intimacy and support from other-gender friendships. Research has also demonstrated that individuals who have close friendships tend to be less anxious and depressed than those who do not, and that mental health is particularly associated with having friends of the other sex.

Other-gender friendship has been called the "final frontier in human relationships" (Cassel, 1989, p. 18), because it is confusing and largely uncharted territory in social relationships. Single men and women are far more likely than married people to have friends of the other gender. This probably reflects confusion over what friendship between the sexes should be all about. For men and women who see their gender in traditional terms, there may be an assumption of dominance and submissiveness in male-female relationships, while friendships are expected to be founded on mutuality and a sense of equality. Beyond that barrier, however, it seems clear that there is a great deal of suspicion about close friendships between women and men, and an assumption that there may be something more to the relationship than just being friends.

For people who are married or part of a committed relationship, it may be threatening to know that a partner has a close friendship with someone else. There may be a fear that the friendship will lead to deeper intimacy or sexual sharing. Therefore, friendships outside the primary relationship are often considered acceptable only to a point that clearly distinguishes them as auxiliary and secondary to that primary relationship (Cassel, 1989).

Friendships also appear to be more acceptable between men and women who work together, and therefore see each other within the more protected social confines of the workplace or business lunches. In fact, many people do seem to maintain friendships that they consider to be loving, though nonsexual, at work. In a survey of 1,050 managers, 22 percent reported that they had been involved in nonsexual love relationships with colleagues, as compared to 5 percent who indicated they had experienced sexual involvement with coworkers. The researchers who conducted the survey identified two types of deep friendships, involving mutual respect, support, open communication, and a sense that the two people constitute a "couple." One was called an Agape or altruistic relationship, and was based on a deep trust and respect for one another's qualities and skills. It was not defined by gender and did not have a clear sexual component. A second pattern was the Eros relationship, in which there was a feeling of romance, excitement, and sexual attraction. Both types of couples chose not to have

215

(continued on p. 217)

Sexual Etiquette 101

Today's sexual world is dramatically different from that of the past. The changes that have occurred during the past 25 years—the sexual revolution, the development of the birth control pill, the legalization of abortion—have resulted in unprecedented sexual freedom. American youth are becoming sexually active with more partners at younger ages: 65 percent of 19-year-olds engage in sexual intercourse.

This sexual freedom has brought about greater acceptance of our sexuality, but it also has created a need for increased responsibility. Recent patterns of sexual behavior on university campuses, for example, suggest that significant problems exist regarding students' consideration of these issues. It is possible that more responsible sexual decision-making may only occur through greater awareness of sexual etiquette, methods of contraception, and sexually transmitted diseases.

Guidelines, therefore, are clearly needed that take into account the fact that all students are sexual beings, that each has individual feelings about sexual intimacy, and that sexual intercourse often has serious consequences. Such guidelines can be effective tools in making responsible sexual decisions.

10 Guidelines of Sexual Etiquette

1. Never use force. It is never appropriate to use force in sexual relationships. Regardless of whether you have previously agreed to have sex, are in a monogamous relationship, or are under the influence of alcohol or other drugs, force is not fun.

2. Respect the word "No." At any point in a sexual relationship, either individual has the right to say "No" to physical contact. When a woman says "No," she does not mean "Try harder so I can be swept away." When a man says "No," it is not an invitation to be seduced.

3. Avoid potentially difficult situations. Taking necessary precautions can increase your safety. While attending a party, make sure you have a trusted friend to accompany you to and from the place. Be aware of your alcohol and other drug intake: it can impair your ability to effectively say "No," and reduce your inhibitions to the use of force.

4. Be prepared. If there is a possibility that you will engage in sexual activity, carry a form of contraception. If you are not prepared, do not do it.

5. There is shared responsibility in a sexual relationship. Contraception is a shared responsibility. The consequences of a sexual encounter, pregnancy, or sexually transmissible disease (STD) affect *both* partners.

6. Communicate openly about contraception. Master the art of talking about contraceptives and your sexual history. Talking about these issues shows that you care about your partner's feelings and health. It is difficult, but actively asking questions about contraception, infection, and previous risk factors is essential to your sexual health.

7. Sexual privacy should be respected. It is inappropriate to talk about specific sexual experiences with a third party. Respect for privacy need not, however, restrict communication about sexuality.

8. Be considerate of others. Public expression of sexual intimacy may embarrass or offend other people. Sexual expression is an individual choice. Be sensitive to the feelings of others.

9. Sexual harassment is not a joke. Sexual harassment is intrusive, thoughtless, insensitive, and a violation of personal privacy.

10. Most importantly, do unto others as you would have them do unto you. Treat a sexual partner with the care and respect that you would expect in return.

Source: Adapted from R. A. Hatcher, C. A. Sanderson, and K. L. Smith, "A Special Supplement for Contraceptive Technology Update Readers," *SIECUS Report*, September, 1989. Used by permission.

Case Study

WHIT: A RELATIONSHIP PLAGUED WITH JEALOUSY

Whit admitted that he had never before been so upset with another person or himself. His relationship with Susan was the first in which he had experienced intense loving feelings. Susan had never felt quite the same intensity of emotion as had Whit, but had agreed to date him occasionally. She liked him, and found him attractive. Eventually, she also chose to share sexual activity with him. She made it clear, however, that she was not interested in a long-term relationship. Whit was elated, and convinced himself that Susan would eventually fall in love with him too.

As the relationship progressed, Whit became increasingly obsessed with Susan. He telephoned her several times a day and tried to arrange his schedule so that he would see her as much as possible. She tried several times to explain to him that she felt smothered, and needed more room for her own life. She also began seeing another man. When Whit pro-

tested, she reminded him that she had never made any promises to him, and had no intention of doing so. Whit felt so desperate that he began following Susan and her new date when they went out together. After one of these incidents, she confronted him angrily, threatening to have him arrested if he did not leave her alone. She also asserted that she no longer wished to date or see him.

Whit was crushed, but he also felt frustrated with his own actions. He told a counselor that he had realized how his possessiveness had in a sense driven Susan away, and was afraid that the intensity of his feelings might interfere with future relationships as well. As they worked together, Whit began to uncover some deep feelings of personal insecurity that seemed to play a role in his possessiveness. The counselor helped him to practice some new strategies that might help him to prevent clinging behaviors in the future.

sexual contact—the Agape types because of other moral commitments and less focus on sexual attraction, and the Eros types because of concerns about consequences to that relationship or others in their lives. People in both kinds of relationships seemed to be experiencing personal benefits, including feeling more creative, motivated, and competent at their work (Quinn et al., 1990).

Close, intimate friendships are a domain where there seem to be few clear social rules. As social commentator Carol Cassel (1989) has pointed out, the sexual aspect of friendships may well exist and have to be sorted through. What may distinguish some nonsexual friendships from other relationships is not the absence of sexual attraction so much as the decision not to become sexually involved. The reasons behind such a decision can be varied, and may include differences in life-style or temperament, the wish not to complicate the friendship, or commitment to another sexual or romantic relationship. To deny sexual attraction within the relationship may prove unhealthy and unproductive to open communication. Of course, another largely unexplored territory is the friendship which include sex. An obvious risk here is that one of the partner's expectations and emotions will

shift and more will be wanted than what is being called friendship (Walthers, 1988).

As people explore intimate friendships and the place that sexual attraction is to have in such friendships, they may well run into the difficulty of making clear distinctions between friendship and love. Sometimes, it may be that friendship is simply a safer word that allows couples to remain comfortable with a relationship that has actually become loving, but the term love will represent more of a dilemma for their lives. Perhaps there are fewer differences between love and friendship than most people want to accept.

JEALOUSY AND POSSESSIVENESS

When we become highly attached to something—whether it be a material object we have paid dearly to own or another person whom we dearly love—there is often a growing fear that we could end up losing what we had originally longed to possess. Loving relationships can have elements of territoriality and fear. We want the object of our affection to love us in return and, frequently, to love only us. We fear rejection by that person and especially fear the loss of his or her love to someone else. If there is some inkling, even an imagined one, that a partner's interests might be straying, it is quite natural to feel jealous.

A reasonable amount of jealousy can be expected in any relationship. It is one of those issues about which couples need to communicate openly. It is important to remember that even those individuals who are happy and comfortable in a loving and sexual relationship will still occasionally find themselves attracted to others. This does not have to threaten the relationship, nor does it signal that there is some sort of difficulty between the partners (Mullen, 1990).

Sometimes, jealousy gets out of control and becomes possessiveness. One partner seems always worried about losing the other, and may even imagine that there is something more going on in other relationships. There may be an unreasonable degree of anger over the partner's casual and innocent social interactions. Such possessiveness can have many roots. Feelings of inferiority often play a role, and may be accompanied by some basic insecurity and immaturity in the individual (Hawkins, 1990). Some people who become overly possessive expect complete and utter devotion from a partner, and have difficulty seeing that individuals always need room for personal growth, even within a committed relationship.

Possessiveness usually signals some fundamental insecurities in the person's personality that may well deserve some attention. Professional counseling can be a viable option for consideration (Timmreck, 1990). It is also often true that overly jealous people are not willing to take much responsibility for changing their behavior. They may even assume that their possessiveness is perfectly justified.

There are several ways for dealing with a situation in which your partner is being unreasonably jealous (Hauck, 1981):

1. *Don't fall into the trap of trying to answer unreasonable questions.* A jealous lover may be convinced of your unfaithfulness and grill you with questions. As rules for good communication suggest, focus on how the questions are making you feel and stick with the truth.

2. *Encourage your partner to work on the jealousy with you.* You may want to suggest seeking out a counselor together. In any case, act with assertiveness. Don't simply give in to keep the peace for the time being. The jealousy may be signs of trouble in the relationship that should not be ignored.

3. *Don't be ruled by pity for the other person.* Even if you feel that you understand the unfortunate reasons why your partner is so desperately jealous, don't feel that they should justify unfair accusations or suspicions. It is your partner's responsibility to find a way to work on her or his problems. When you hear

threats of suicide or violence, you are being subjected to the most extreme forms of relational coercion and manipulation. They represent serious problems for which you should seek professional advice.

4. *Take a close look at whether this is a relationship that is healthy for you.* If the jealousy and possessiveness begin to seem hopeless, it may simply be that you will be unable to find much relaxed fulfillment in the relationship. Even if you love the other person, it may be important to sort through whether it is wise to remain in the relationship. Again, talking the situation over with a trained counselor can represent a significant step toward maintaining your own psychological balance.

DEALING WITH THE LOSS OF A LOVING RELATIONSHIP

As you look around at loving relationships, it is clear that many of them ultimately fail. Does that mean that people are picking out the wrong partners for loving? Not necessarily. Relationships typically begin with

FIGURE 8.8 Loss of a Relationship

Being open to loving means being vulnerable to being hurt. Those best able to deal with the hurt are those who enter the relationship with a good sense of self, an understanding and appreciation of their own personalities.

attention being given to what matters to the partners in the short run. Like all things, people and their relationships change. The long-range issues may be quite different. Therefore, as relationships grow, it becomes increasingly important for partners to be willing to change in their response patterns toward one another. What first seemed to be a charming idiosyncrasy may in time become a grating nuisance. What once was sexual turn-on may become boring and humdrum. Couples must be open to these changing patterns in relationships and learn how to tolerate the changes (Trotter, 1986).

However, with time and change, it may also become evident that there are too many differences between two people to allow for a comfortable and fulfilling loving relationship. The long-run issues may be so different from those that were a part of the beginning relationship that it no longer makes sense for the two to remain together. The uncoupling process is almost always a painful one, but it may also represent a viable choice for a failing relationship in which one or both of the partners lack the desire and motivation to move to a new level of commitment.

The bottom line here is that love holds no guarantees. No matter how much lovers promise to be true to each other forever, there really are no guarantees against the possibility of one or both eventually choosing to end the relationship. Loving leaves one vulnerable, so to choose to enter a loving relationship is to choose the risk of being hurt (Kelly, 1981). This is one reason why knowing, understanding, and feeling good about oneself can be so crucial before entering a relationship.

The initial reactions that follow the breakup of a relationship may be quite varied. If the final days of the relationship have been troubled and full of turmoil, there may even be a sense of relief. There are often intense feelings of loneliness and grief, accompanied by the sense of having been rejected or by guilt at having initiated the breakup. Anger is also a common emotional reaction, and can represent a very healthy response. If anger is expressed in ways that are not harmful, it is prevented from turning inward, where it can become depression and self-deprecation. Crying may also be a healthy release of emotion (Fisher, 1983).

Some people rush to put the pain of their loss behind them. They may even hurry into a "rebound" relationship to soothe their wounds. However, like any grieving process, the aftermath of a broken relationship must be given its time, and the painful reactions are best resolved by allowing them to be experienced. If you hurry them, or try to escape from them so that the breaking-up process remains incomplete, the reactions will eventually find new outlets in your life. They may make it difficult for you to be trusting and intimate in new relationships that eventually develop for you.

Therefore, recognize that losing a love is as much a part of life and loving as the joyful experience of falling in love. If you allow yourself to have that process fully, and seek whatever help and support you may need to get through it, you will be able to put the painful aspects behind you eventually and get on with your life and new relationships. ■

SELF-EVALUATION

Communicating About Sex

One of the most necessary human processes, and yet one of the most complex and difficult, is communication. Many difficulties in relationships—including many sexual problems—are at least partly the result of lack of communication or misunderstood communications. Thoughts, ideas, feelings, values, attitudes, opinions, needs, and desires are not only communicated verbally but also through eye contact, facial expressions, and body language. The questions and exercises in this section are designed to help you evaluate and facilitate your communication about sex with someone who is important to your life and

therefore worth the effort. You may find some of the suggestions difficult to carry out, but good communication does take work.

WORKING ON COMMUNICATION: AN EXERCISE FOR TWO

The following exercise can help you and your partner improve your patterns of communication. Start by rating each other, using the Rating Scale of 1–4 below on the qualities listed in the next column. Write your answers on separate sheets of paper without first discussing the rating scale or qualities with each other.

Rating Scale:

4 = Tops. He/she does a great job of showing this quality to me.

3 = Okay. Most of the time I feel this from him/her.

2 = Fair. I could really stand to have more of this quality from her/him.

1 = Poor. I rarely, if ever, feel this from her/him.

*Rating
of Your
Partner*　　*Qualities in Your Partner*

_____	Caring and consideration toward me.
_____	Ability to show warmth and love.
_____	Sensitivity and understanding toward my emotions.
_____	Lets me feel whatever I need to feel, without trying to talk me out of it.
_____	Seems to listen and really hear what I mean.
_____	Acts real and honest with me so that I can feel that he/she is being genuine.
_____	Seems to feel on an equal level with me in the areas that are important to me.
_____	Doesn't jump to conclusions or make snap judgments about me or others.
_____	Treats me with respect.
_____	Is trustworthy.
_____	Seems to trust me and shares inner feelings and thoughts with me.

When you have both finished your ratings, exchange them so that you each may take a look at how you were rated by the other. However, you both should agree to the following:

1. Do not talk about your reactions to the ratings for *15 minutes,* during which time you should:

   a. Think about why your partner might have rated you as he or she did. Assume that the ratings represent honest reactions.

   b. Think about which ratings made you feel best and which made you feel worst.

   c. Ask yourself if you were surprised by any of the ratings. Why or why not?

   d. Look beneath any anger you might feel or any need to "defend" yourself against a rating. If you are hurt, be ready to admit it. Keep in mind that your partner had a right to rate you in any manner that seemed honest to her or him. It can lead to a deeper understanding.

2. When you are ready to start talking together about your mutual ratings:

   a. You should agree on the most comfortable location.

   b. Share only your own feelings and reactions, being careful not to make assumptions and judgments about your partner's feelings or motivations.

   c. After one of you has had a chance to make a point, the other should spend some time summarizing what was heard, so you can be sure that you are hearing each other accurately. Clear up any misunderstandings that your partner has about anything you have said. Give each other time to do this.

Now, where do you go from here? If this exercise has shown you ways to improve your ability to communicate, are you ready to work toward this goal? Decide whether or not you think the two of you could work on particular areas.

WORKING ON THE FUNDAMENTALS

There are certain basic qualities that underscore good communication. Here are some ways to evaluate them:

1. *Lack of manipulation.* In healthy, two-way communication, there is no need for games or manipulations. Before proceeding any further, answer the following questions. Write down your answers.

   a. Why are you working on this section concerning sexual communication?

   b. What are your short-term and long-term goals for improving communication with your partner?

   c. Do you have any ulterior or exploitive motives in pursuing communication about sex? If so, what are they?

   d. Do you really think you can face the vulnerability that comes with honest, two-way communication? Before answering, you may want to look through the remainder of this section. When you answer in the affirmative, proceed.

2. *A desire to involve your partner in communication.* There is no point in waiting. Communication takes at least two people. Now allow your partner to read this section, and share with him or her your answers to the questions above. If your partner is willing, have him or her answer those same questions and share the answers with you. If you are both willing, proceed with the remainder of this section. It is designed for use by two people who together want to improve their communication about sex.

3. *Sense of equality.* Both of you should write your own answers to the following questions of separate sheets on paper. Do not compare any answers until both of you are finished answering all questions.

   a. Do you feel there is any difference in the

general common sense possessed by you and your partner? If so, which one of you do you think has more of this quality?

b. Does one of you tend to give in more to the other when there are disagreements? If so, who?

c. Generally in your relationship, does one of you seem to emerge as the dominant partner and the other as the submissive partner? Which of you is which?

d. Which one of you tends to initiate sexual contact most often?

e. Are there any other factors that seem to lead to continuing feelings of inequality between the two of you?

After each of you has written answers to all questions, exchange papers and read them. Make the following agreement: do not make any comments for 10 minutes. Read one another's answers and silently think about them and how you feel about them.

Both of you should also read the following two paragraphs:

As you are thinking about your partner's responses, and comparing them to your own, can you detect that one or both of you see certain inequalities in your common sense, willingness to stick by points of view, degree of dominance, and/or willingness to initiate sex?

Two-way communication seems to work best when there is a sense of equality between both partners. Otherwise, there is the danger of one person feeling inadequate to deal with conflicts and disagreements in communication. With this in mind proceed with part 4.

4. *Working at it.* Your answers to the questions in part 3 can provide some beginning topics for discussion.

a. If both of you answered questions in such a way that reflects nearly complete equality, perhaps you will want to move on to the next section of this communication questionnaire. If not, try part b below.

b. Go through the answers to your questions one by one, following these rules:

1. State only what you feel or think, without making any judgments or assumptions about what the other person is feeling or thinking, or about the other person's accuracy.

2. After one of you has made *I feel . . .* and *I think . . .* statements about the answers to one question, the other person should take time to summarize what has been heard.

Then the first partner should clarify any misunderstandings. Do this with each of the questions. If anger or hostility develops, consider the following:

3. If you are feeling angry or resentful, try to pause, look beneath your negative feelings, and see what is at their roots. Perhaps you are really feeling some hurt or sense of threat. Look honestly at what you are feeling and share it with your partner.

4. Persist with this process until you both feel some real sense of resolution about the differences of opinion that have arisen. If you feel stumped by this, you may even want to consider consulting an outside person to talk over some of these issues.

5. When you both feel ready, go on with the remaining parts of this communication exercise.

SHARING SEXUAL ATTITUDES AND VALUES

An important part of communication is letting your partner know your personal attitudes and values about sex. The following exercises may help you get started:

1. Turn back to the sexual attitude questionnaire in chapter 1, "Historical and Research Perspectives on Sexuality." If you have not already done so, both of you should complete your ratings for each of the attitude statements on separate sheets of paper. Go through the questionnaire item by item, and compare your present ratings. On those items where you show a difference of opinion, talk about those differences. If either of you begins to feel anger or tension during the discussion, you may want to try using the approaches in exercise 4b. Remember, it is perfectly all right to have different attitudes. The essential thing is to be able to accept these differences in one another. The key to acceptance is full understanding of one another.

2. Now continue going through the sexual history section of the questionnaire in chapter 1, "Historical and Research Perspectives on Sexuality." Share as many of your answers with your partner as you can feel comfortable with. If both of you already feel very well acquainted with one another's backgrounds, you might try going through the questions one at a time, answering for your partner in the ways you feel are most accurate. Your partner can then clear up any inaccuracies or misconceptions you seem to have concerning his or her sexual history. When you are finished with

221

this process, summarize any new understandings that you have gained about your partner.

3. Here are some other issues that might be worth discussing with one another. You may skip any questions you prefer not to answer. Again, you may either share your answers with one another, or try answering each question in the way you think your partner would.

    a. What is your opinion on abortion? Should it be legal and available to those women who wish to have an abortion? To what degree should the man be allowed to participate in the decision-making process about abortion?

    b. Which positions for sex do you like the best? Why?

    c. Would you (or do you) like being watched while engaged in some sexual activity? Which activities in particular?

    d. What are some of your wildest sexual fantasies? How do you feel about them?

    e. How do you feel about your partner's nude body? What parts of his or her body do you like most? least?

    f. Would you consider (or have you considered) having sex with a stranger? Would you pay for sex or have sex for money?

    g. What precautions do you consider essential in reducing the risk of contracting the AIDS virus?

NONVERBAL COMMUNICATION

Very often more can be communicated without words than with them. The following is a list of suggestions for nonverbal communication between you and your partner, each step becoming progressively more intimate. At any step, some verbal communication may be necessary to sort through difficult feelings that may surface. Before proceeding with each new stage of intimacy, there should be complete mutual agreement and willingness between the two of you. Each step should continue until one of you feels ready to stop.

Even if you both feel that your relationship has already reached deep levels of intimacy, it would be best to spend at least some time with even the earliest steps of the nonverbal communication process.

Activity 1. In comfortable positions, sit facing one another and look at each other's faces. Spend plenty of time looking into one another's eyes and attempting to express positive feelings to each other. You may feel a little foolish and feel like laughing; go ahead and get it out of your system.

Activity 2. Take turns touching and caressing each other's faces. The person being touched should close his or her eyes and fully enjoy the sensations. The person doing the touching should make an effort to convey warm, caring messages with the touches.

Activity 3. Take turns feeding one another a piece of fruit or some other food.

CHAPTER SUMMARY

1. Communication is a key to healthy sexual relationships. It involves not only words, but eyes, facial expressions, and body language.

2. Any communicated message is filtered through the interpretive systems of both the sender and the receiver. There is a strong likelihood of misinterpretation and misunderstanding unless a feedback system is part of the process.

3. People often use slang terms, or no words at all, when making sexual references.

4. Communication can be hindered by the myths people believe and the sexual "games" they have learned to play out in relationships.

5. Effective communication grows out of mutual commitment, shared understanding, mutual regard, avoidance of snap judgments, careful listening, empathy, genuineness, clear expression, viewing oneself positively, and appropriate confrontation.

6. Quarreling in relationships is inevitable and can be helpful if partners acknowledge differing points of view, accurately feed back feelings, and are open to negotiation. Conflict resolution involves clear ownership of the problem, and the use of "I" messages to communicate about it.

7. As the Myers-Briggs Type Indicator demonstrates, there are very real personality differences among people that can have important implications for how they get along with one another.

8. Males and females are taught different patterns for communicating as they grow up, and these differences show up in adult communication.

9. Healthy sexual sharing in a relationship involves being comfortable with one's own sexual needs, not confusing romance and sex, knowing how to risk vulnerability, having a clear sense of one's own identity, and avoiding sexual coercion.

10. Today, the rules for love and relationships are vague. Each couple must find their own process for relating.

11. Infatuation or "falling in love" eventually ends; being in love involves a choice and commitment to the process of being together.

12. Sternberg's theory holds that love is a dynamic interaction of three components: intimacy, passion, and commitment.

13. Sexual intimacy involves touching, relaxation, involved participation, and a realistic view of how romantic love and sex fit into relationships.

14. Intimate friendships represent a new area of exploration. Sometimes, friends must work out the place that sexual attraction will have in the friendship.

15. While a degree of jealousy and possessiveness is expected in any loving relationship, these qualities may become destructive if they are rooted in serious insecurities and get out of control.

16. Loss of a loving relationship can be painful, and often needs to be followed by a process of grieving.

ANNOTATED READINGS

Bird, G., & Sporakowski, M. J. (1992). *Taking sides: Clashing views on controversial issues in family and personal relationships.* Guilford, CT: The Dushkin Publishing Group. Presents opposing viewpoints of 34 leading sociologists, psychologists, and family therapists on controversial current issues in family development and personal relationships.

Beck, A. (1988). *Love is never enough.* New York: Harper & Row. A psychiatrist presents a practical discussion of the various dimensions of love in relationships. Many common myths and misconceptions about love are debunked.

Cohen, S. S. (1987). *The magic of touch.* New York: Harper & Row. Reaffirms the significance of sharing the experience of touch, not just the sexual kind but sensual as well. Offers suggestions for experimenting with touch.

Douglas, J. D., & Atwell, F. C. (1990). *Love, intimacy, and sex.* Newbury Park, CA: Sage Publications. A serious, carefully researched examination of how sex and love have evolved during contemporary times. It helps to demysticize love and show how sex fits with love and intimacy.

Fisher, B. (1983). *Rebuilding: When your relationship ends.* San Luis Obispo, CA: Impact Publishers. Examines the stages that are experienced after a relationship has failed, and the factors that can help build a new and more solid one.

Goodman, G., & Esterly, G. (1988). *The talk book: The intimate science of communication in close relationships.* Emmaus, PA: Rodale Press. Presents talking as a skill that can be analyzed, taught, practiced, and improved. This book deals realistically with the improvement of communication skills as a way to improve relationships. It also gives suggestions for detecting and resisting manipulation from others.

Hauck, P. A. (1981). *Overcoming jealousy and possessiveness.* Philadelphia: The Westminster Press. A basic outline of the psychology of jealousy and possessiveness, along with specific strategies for overcoming their destructive effects on individuals and relationships.

Kingma, D. R. (1988). *Coming apart: Why relationships end and how to live through the ending of yours.* Berkeley, CA: Conari Press. Helps readers face the difficult tasks involved in ending a relationship. Includes written exercises to help deal with the different emotional stages involved in ending a relationship, so that one's dignity and self-esteem are left intact.

Mayer, A. (1990). *How to stay lovers while raising your children: A burned out parent's guide to sex.* Los Angeles: Price/Stern/Sloan. Having children typically places new pressures on couples that change the quality of their sex life. This is a realistic guide for becoming more aware of those stresses and finding ways of preserving intimacy and sex for parents.

Solomon, E. C. (1989). *About love: Reinventing romance for our times.* New York: Simon & Schuster/Touchstone. This book traces the development of romantic love from ancient times to the present. It emphasizes the ways in which we seek completion of our own identities through the process of loving.

Vaughan, P. (1989). *The monogamy myth: A new understanding of affairs and how to survive them.* New York: Newmarket Press. A guide to understanding the choice to have an "affair" and dealing with its consequences. An excellent program for honest communication between partners is included.

Vannoy, R. (1989). *Sex without love: A philosophical explanation.* Buffalo, NY: Prometheus Books. Unlike most others, this book argues that there is a place for sex outside the context of traditional love, and that it can, in fact, be very fulfilling.

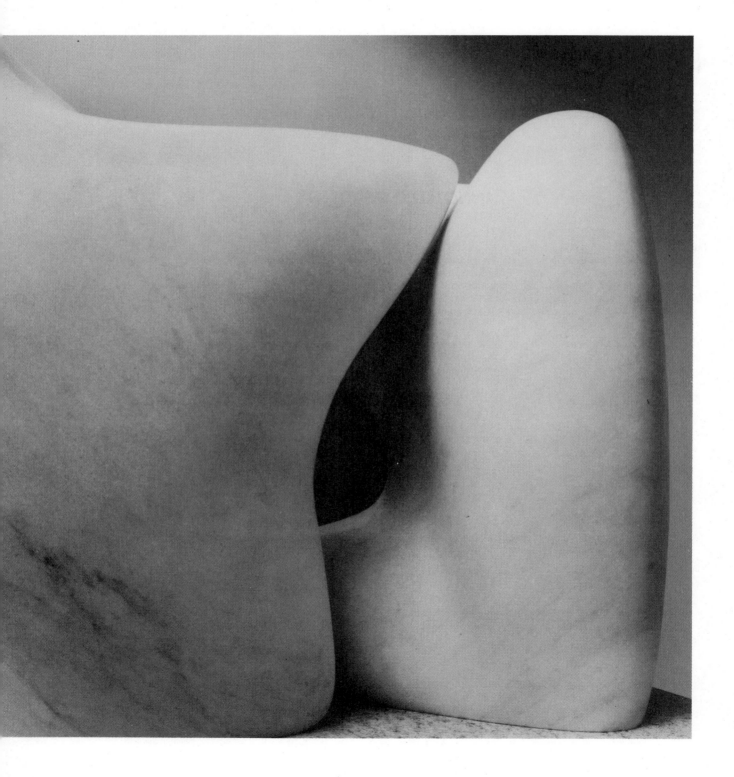

The ways in which human beings are either programmed to behave or taught to behave sexually are matters of conjecture and debate. Certainly the choices we make about how to act sexually are based partly on the sexual attitudes and values that each of us holds. As chapter 9 explains, we develop a very individualized set of sexual needs, orientations, fantasies, turn-ons, turn-offs, and behaviors. The process of developing a sexual individuality is only poorly understood, but it is this individuality that determines much of who we are and what we do sexually. Developing sexual values is a crucial part of our development as people.

The two most common forms of sexual activity are masturbation and heterosexual intercourse. Although masturbation is usually a solitary activity and may involve both positive and negative feelings on the part of the person doing it, intercourse bridges the gap into shared sexual encounters. New responsibilities and complications are involved when we share sexual intimacy with another person. The dynamics of the interaction, whether they relate to technique or how personalities are connecting, become crucial to determining whether a sexual interaction is pleasurable or exploitative. Chapter 10 deals with both solitary and shared sexual activity.

It seems clear from research that throughout history and across diverse cultures of the world a substantial percentage of human beings—probably about 10 percent—have been predominantly sexually attracted to members of their own sex. While many people espouse a live-and-let-live attitude toward homosexual persons and behaviors, ours is essentially a homophobic culture. That means that we view same-sexed preferences as being reflective of abnormalcy, illness, or immorality. Chapter 11 takes a close look at what we know, and do not know, about homosexuality and bisexuality, and tries to dispel the idea that sexual orientation is an either-or phenomenon. Instead, there would seem to be a continuum between the exclusively heterosexual and the exclusively homosexual.

The kinds of sexual activities in which people have chosen to participate seems limited only by the imagination. Chapter 12 focuses on the range of sexual behaviors found in humans. People find ways of expressing their gender and their sexual preferences that sometimes appeal to the rest of us, and sometimes offend. Only in recent years has scientific research begun to give us a clearer picture of human sexual diversity. Acceptance of that diversity by the mainstream can be another matter.

CHAPTER NINE
SEXUAL INDIVIDUALITY AND SEXUAL VALUES

The factors that lead to the development of sexual individuality are highly complex and poorly understood. All types of sexual behavior and values may be considered normal. External social values as well as internal personal values should not conflict with the larger moral and ethical values of human behavior. The sexuality of people who are physically or mentally disabled may challenge our concept of sexual individuality. They, too, define their own limits of sexual normality.

CHAPTER TEN
SOLITARY SEX AND SHARED SEX

Masturbation can occur at all stages of life and can be enjoyed for its own sake rather than as a substitute for other forms of sex. Various forms of fantasy—pictures, films, stories—may be used to stimulate sexual activity both with oneself or with others. Heterosexual intercourse is the most widely accepted of shared sexual behaviors. Knowing the techniques for heterosexual intercourse can make it a more comfortable and pleasurable activity.

CHAPTER ELEVEN
HOMOSEXUALITY AND BISEXUALITY

The term homosexual refers to a sexual attraction between members of the same sex. Several theories attempt to describe the origin of homosexuality, but we still do not understand clearly how sexual orientation develops. Homosexuality exists in all cultures and is treated differently and valued differently according to each society's attitudes. Bisexuality, or ambisexuality, is the term that refers to sexual interaction with members of both sexes. Sexual orientation is an issue that has social and political implications, and people who do not fit accepted norms may be subjected to bigotry and discrimination.

CHAPTER TWELVE
THE SPECTRUM OF HUMAN SEXUAL BEHAVIOR

Human beings are diverse in their sexual orientations and behaviors. Celibacy refers to the choice not to share sexual activity with others. Transvestism refers to some type of cross-dressing, sometimes for sexual arousal. Troilism, group sex, and extramarital sex with the consent of both partners are enjoyed by some. Sadomasochism and frottage are types of sexual activities that may be considered unusual, but not necessarily harmful as long as they don't violate another person's right to privacy.

225

CHAPTER NINE

LABELING SEX: CROSS-CULTURAL AND HISTORICAL PERSPECTIVES
    Sociocultural Standards for Sexual Arousal and Behavior
    Sexual Standards in Other Cultures
    Who is Normal?
    Limits and Misuses of Labels

SEXUAL INDIVIDUALITY
    How Does Sexual Individuality Develop?
    Making Sexual Choices

SEX AND VALUES
    Dealing with Sex as a Moral Issue
    Religion and Sex

    Aligning Yourself with Social and Cultural Values
    Finding Healthy Sexual Values

SEX EDUCATION
    Current Trends in Sex Education
    What Sex Education Can and Cannot Accomplish
    Sex Education for Professionals

SEX AND DISABILITY GROUPS
    Mental Retardation
    Visual and Auditory Disabilities
    Spinal Cord Injuries
    Other Physical and Mental Disabilities
    Institutions

CHAPTER SUMMARY

It's always with me—feeling different I mean—I look around at my friends and their sex lives. It all looks so easy for them. In my eyes they're being really irresponsible with sex, but in their eyes my sex life would be the ultimate perversity. I don't know, it's all so confusing. Who decides what's normal, anyway?

—Based on a college student's counseling session

SEXUAL INDIVIDUALITY AND SEXUAL VALUES

Up until the beginning of this century, Western attitudes regarding sex had remained relatively unchanged for 2,000 years. The Industrial Revolution and a new appreciation for the value of the scientific method brought a fresh perspective to the study of society. The advent of human psychology gave new legitimacy to the study of human sexual behaviors. Gradually a new ethic has emerged, holding that there is real value in a thorough, honest understanding of human nature, regardless of the moral values and attitudes that a particular society may attach to specific sexual behaviors. It has become increasingly legitimized for researchers to find the truths of human sexual diversity without having to judge them in moral terms. As a result, we are now beginning to understand sexual individuality, and sex education has emerged as a legitimate personal and academic pursuit.

A fundamental understanding of this chapter is that humans have the potential to participate in, and find physically pleasurable, a wide spectrum of sexual activities. There may be some inborn factors that determine which of these activities are actually chosen by a particular individual. However, it is largely the cultural and social mores and values that determine the extent and types of sexual behaviors found in any particular human society at any particular time in history. Sex education provides a forum for discussing and examining all of these issues.

Labeling Sex: Cross-Cultural and Historical Perspectives

Until quite recently, the predominating assumption in Western culture regarding human sexuality was as follows: To be normal was to be attracted sexually to members of the opposite sex and to desire penis-in-vagina intercourse as the ultimate expression of that attraction; everything else, in varying degrees, was considered abnormal. Yet there is ample historical, anthropological, and psychological evidence that hu-

normal: a highly subjective term used to describe sexual behaviors and orientations. Standards of normalcy are determined by social, cultural, and historical standards.

abnormal: anything considered not to be normal, that is, not conforming to the subjective standards a social group has established as the norm.

FIGURE 9.1 Ancient Greek Art

The Greeks idealized youth and in their art depicted both male and female bodies in erotic sexual positions. The phallic image was revered in Greek society as a symbol of fertility and immortality.

man beings are—and have always been—extremely diverse and variable in their sexual attractions and behaviors.

While sex has always found its subtle, often disguised, place in human mythology, there is little reliable statistical data concerning the spectrum of human sexual behaviors. Literature and art have portrayed all sexual activities through the ages, but the extent to which they have been expressed and permitted in various societies and times in history is only known in bits and pieces. For some past cultures we know what sexual behaviors were considered unlawful. For some we know the codes of sexual activity that were established by religions and philosophies. For others we know what the practitioners of medicine thought about specific behaviors. However, the extent to which information about a sexual activity was recorded in a society may have depended on the extent to which the activity was tolerated and accepted (Bullough, 1990a). Consider the examples of prostitution and homosexuality. Since prostitution has generally been more accepted over the span of human history than has same-sexed behavior, we have far more historical records about it than we do homosexuality.

One of the jobs of science is to categorize, classify, and label. To organize and name things and phenomena are the only ways for us to continue being able to communicate about them intelligently. The

same has been true for human sexuality, as science has attempted to explain, understand, and classify sexual attractions and activities. However, it is important to remember that scientists are products of their sociocultural environments too. Their conclusions and labels may reflect the agendas of their society (Gagnon, 1990a). Labels can have great power, both positive and negative.

You may recall that Richard von Krafft-Ebing, during the latter part of the nineteenth century, wrote about masturbation in his famous book on sexual behavior, *Psychopathia Sexualis* (see chapter 1, "Historical and Research Perspectives on Sexuality," p. 8). He condemned the practice as depraved and identified it as a source of mental contamination, weakened sexual desire, and all manner of physical and sexual problems. His book eventually became one of the most widely accepted medical textbooks on human sexuality, thus helping to promulgate the view that masturbation was one of the most damaging of sexual acts. Hence, it was given labels such as secret sin, self-

FIGURE 9.2 Female Prostitute

Although prostitution has existed throughout history, attitudes toward it have depended on the sexual values of the time: Greek courtesans were held in high esteem; American prostitutes are traditionally looked down upon.

FIGURE 9.3 Black-figure Cup

The Greek Amasis Painter (530–520 B.C.) portrayed figures masturbating on this black-figure cup.

abuse, and self-pollution. Generations of young people grew up viewing masturbation with fear and frustration.

Krafft-Ebing did not invent prohibitive social attitudes regarding masturbation. He simply reflected the values of his place and time, reinforcing and perpetuating them. It was not a time when science could see the description of behavior as being unrelated to moral implications and teachings. As we know, the twentieth century has seen a very gradual shift in attitudes toward masturbation. Medical science has yielded accurate information about its effects and its frequency. While some religious prohibitions against masturbation remain, the general opinion in the professions of medicine and psychology is that the practice is a widespread and generally harmless form of sexual expression. It is interesting that books about sex have now shifted to using labels such as self-gratification and self-pleasuring to describe masturbation. It has become, like heterosexual intercourse, one of the norms against which other behaviors are compared and standardized.

For years sexologists have been struggling to come up with general terms to describe the more atypical of behaviors such as sadomasochism or cross-dressing for gratification. They continue to face the issue of how to judge whether or not some sexual activity truly is atypical. Most statistical studies show the majority of sexual behaviors are far more common than was previously realized. Psychoanalysis first gave us the term deviation, which of course implies that one has strayed from some defined, normal pathway. It may be a pathway determined by statistics, so the deviant is one who is located on one of the ends of a

bell curve (Brown, 1983). Or it may be established simply by prevailing values. In any case the label "deviation" has taken on so much emotional content and vagueness that it is no longer widely used to describe sexual behaviors.

A more recent label has been variation or variance, also implying that an individual is somehow different or aberrant sexually. The question remains of how the standard for determining the norm is established. One might ask, "A variation on what?" or "Different from what?" These terms have come to have negative connotations, even though originally they were not meant to have any particular value implications.

A more scientific label has emerged within the last decade. The term paraphilia, loosely meaning "a love beside," is considered to be sexual attachment or dependency on some unusual or typically unacceptable stimulus, either in actuality or in fantasy, in order to initiate or maintain sexual arousal and to achieve or facilitate orgasm (Money & Werlwas, 1982). So far this label has been less subject to negative implications.

self-gratification: giving oneself pleasure, as in masturbation; a term typically used today instead of more negative descriptors.

self-pleasuring: self-gratification; masturbation.

deviation: term applied to behaviors or orientations that do not conform to a society's accepted norms; it often has negative connotations.

variation: a less pejorative term to describe nonconformity to accepted norms.

paraphilia (pair-a-FIL-ee-a): a newer term used to describe sexual orientations and behaviors that vary from the norm; it means "a love beside."

SOCIOCULTURAL STANDARDS FOR SEXUAL AROUSAL AND BEHAVIOR

It is easy to see that labels such as deviation, variation, and paraphilia all imply some aberration from an accepted sexual standard. There are several standards that permeate the values of Western culture today. In an informal—and sometimes quite formalized—way, they tell us how we are supposed to feel and act sexually. They are as follows:

The Heterosexual Standard   We are supposed to be sexually attracted to members of the opposite sex and desire therefore to be sexually involved with them.

The Coital Standard   We are supposed to view sexual intercourse between woman and man, or coitus, as the ultimate sexual act. Most other forms of shared male-female sexual activity have come to be labeled as foreplay, with the implication that rather than being enjoyed for their own sake, or as sexual goals and ends in their own right, they represent steps toward intercourse. They prepare the couple for coitus.

The Orgasmic Standard   We are supposed to experience orgasm as the climax of any sexual interaction. This standard has been particularly prevalent among males in Western culture, although in recent years it has been predominating among women as well.

The Two-Person Standard   We are supposed to view sex as an activity for two. While masturbation has gained in legitimacy as an acceptable behavior, it is still typically viewed as a substitute for shared sexual activity, especially intercourse. It is still better, according to this standard, to experience sex as a duo. And any sexual activity involving more than two is considered distinctly kinky.

The Romantic Standard   We are supposed to relate sex to love. Romance and sex have become inseparably intertwined, and it is certainly true that the intimacy generated by one may enhance the other. But it is also true that love and sex can be subject to very different interpretations and values. In Victorian times, healthy and positive loving relationships were supposed to be unspoiled by the desires of the flesh. Today, according to this new standard, it would seem that romantic love without sex would be incomplete and sex without love would be emotionally shallow and exploitive (Kelly, 1984).

All of these current standards are determined by the prevailing cultural values and mores with which we live. That is not to imply that they are inconsequential or should not be respected, for we are all products of

FIGURE 9.4   Heterosexual Standard

The form and meaning of behavior are influenced by the culture and the time in which one lives. Thus, in North American society in the 1990s, heterosexuality is the standard form of sexual behavior. The cultural standard, however, should not be confused with a moral and ethical standard that is individualistic and flexible.

and integral parts of our society and culture. Yet at the same time we cannot ignore the fact that such standards shift and alter with time. Neither can we deny the fact that significant proportions of the human population simply do not live their sexual lives according to these standards.

The sexual attitudes and values that are adopted in personal development are influenced by many factors in people's lives, including ethnic background, socioeconomic status, and whether one grows up in a rural, suburban, or urban setting. For example, it has been noted by several researchers that working-class people tend to view sex in more traditional, genital terms, while those in higher socioeconomic groups are more likely to see sexuality within a broader context of love and relating, and to be more accepting of a variety of sexual behaviors (Francoeur, 1991a). To examine the

coitus (KO-at-us *or* ko-EET-us): heterosexual, penis-in-vagina intercourse.
foreplay: sexual activities shared in early stages of sexual arousal, with the term implying that they are leading to a more intense, orgasm-oriented form of activity such as intercourse.

Case Study

LUCILLE: A WOMAN DOUBTS HER SEXUAL NORMALCY

Lucille came to a sex therapist out of concern over whether or not she was normal. She told the therapist that she felt as though she were different from most women and believed that she might be in need of treatment.

In taking a routine and thorough sex history, the therapist found nothing unusual about Lucille's past or present sexual activities or interests. It was clear from the woman's reactions, however, that she perceived several aspects of her sexuality to be different or unusual in comparison to what she assumed to be typical of other women.

Lucille had started masturbating to orgasm at about the age of 7 and had continued to do so to the present time on a regular basis. She believed that since she was married and had what she described as a "good sex life" with her husband, masturbation must represent an abnormal practice. She also found herself aroused by erotic magazines and videotapes that she and her husband obtained from time to time. Her impression was that other women found such materials offensive, and this again left her feeling somehow unusual.

The sex therapist found herself more in the position of being an educator for Lucille, letting her know of the wide range of behaviors and orientations found in human beings. Lucille did not seem to have a strong set of religious values that were determining her reactions, nor did she seem particularly concerned about others' judgments. She had simply assumed, based on her limited information, that her needs were out of the normal range. She seemed comfortable with the new level of information that the therapist provided, although there was no follow-up to determine how the information may have affected her attitudes or behaviors.

evolution of sexual values in the United States over the past 75 years is to see that we have gone through a period of increased sexual liberation, along with movements countering what is seen by some as unfettered sexual permissiveness (Money, 1991).

One thing that this evolutionary process has generated is a greater focus on how people develop their attitudes, and the dangers of buying into social values that are unrealistic for the individual. For example, there is a growing emphasis on sexual abstinence as the safest course of action for unmarried people. Statistics are continuing to demonstrate that significant numbers of young people are not choosing to abstain from sex, even though they may believe the prevailing social standard that it would be better for them to do so. This may reflect an internal conflict for some people that will prevent them from preparing for safer sex through the use of condoms, choosing alternatives to penetrative sex, or using contraception. The United States is clearly a pluralistic nation, in that it approaches such things as politics, religion, education, and occupational choice with an acceptance of a whole range of differences. However, the country has been slower to accept the possibility that a spectrum of sexual orientations and behaviors might also be legitimate (Reiss, 1991).

SEXUAL STANDARDS IN OTHER CULTURES

Sociologist John Gagnon has said that "sexual life is like all social life: an activity elicited by social and cultural circumstance and an activity that differs from one historical era to another or from one culture to another" (Gagnon, 1990a, p. 3). Anthropologists usually classify cultures on the basis of their subsistence patterns, which reflect how the people produce and distribute food and other goods. Reproductive patterns and gender roles are closely tied to social structures within a culture, and anything that impinges on the subsistence pattern will influence reproduction as well. Therefore, sexuality has a place at the center of any culture (Hotvedt, 1990).

In smaller, homogeneous cultures in which a great deal of effort is spent on maintaining conformity among people, individuals tend to conduct their sexual lives in accordance with accepted social roles. Larger, heterogeneous cultures that do not work toward producing or stabilizing conformity will have many different patterns of sexual conduct. These include not only sexual subcultures based on sexual orientation or behavioral preferences, but more highly individualistic patterns of behavior within particular people. The United States is an example of such a culture. There

231

are many ethnic and immigrant groups, each with its own viable sexual culture. There is little direct training in "appropriate" sexual conduct, and no consensus of opinion about what constitutes appropriateness. There are also many conflicting messages about sex. Therefore, it is a culture in which there are high levels of sexual variability, and sporadic conflicts about what should be considered proper sexual conduct (Gagnon, 1990a).

All cultures have their own particular instructions about sex—whether they are rigid and specific, or flexible and ill defined—imbedded in the very structure of their social institutions: families, religions, the military, businesses, educational systems, medicine, and laws.

There are wide variations in the kinds of sexual behaviors that are forbidden, tolerated, or encouraged in various cultures. A former director of the Kinsey Institute for Sex Research, Paul Gebhard (1971), has pointed out that anthropological data on various sexual activities are scanty as well. He indicates that there are clear differences between sexual practices in smaller, preliterate societies and the larger, more complex societies of developed countries. For example, while voyeurism—gaining sexual gratification from seeing others nude or involved in sexual acts—is not at all uncommon in Europe and North America, it is almost unheard of in preliterate cultures. Likewise, while exhibiting the genitals to another person may be used to solicit sexual activity in more primitive societies, exhibitionism as an end in itself is apparently absent among preliterate people. Even in those cultures where sexual contact between adults and children is permitted, it is apparently rare for adults to have a strong sexual preference for children. Gebhard hypothesizes that in large, literate societies it is easier for people to avoid social sanctions through anonymity, and that this may indeed encourage them to participate in sexual activities that would be avoided in other social contexts.

There have been many societies in which the prevailing standards of sexual conduct are very different from our own. For example, homosexual behavior is tolerated, and even expected, to a greater extent in those cultures that place strong restrictions on marriage. Early in this century, among the Aranda in Central Australia, men were initiated into sex homosexually before becoming eligible to marry. Until marriage became possible, these men would take a boy of 10 or 12 to live with them as sexual partners (Bullough, 1976). It is not at all unusual for boys in such cultures to have been initiated into sexual practices by older men. Boys among the East Bay Melanesians in the Southwestern Pacific are forbidden to have contact with girls until they marry. In the meantime,

they are expected to have sex with an older male and a boy who is of the same age (Francoeur, 1990a). Among the Ngonda tribe in Africa through the 1950s, boys were confined to "boys' villages," and homosexual activity was permitted for them until marriage. The only standard was that such sex must be voluntary, never forced (Wilson, 1959). Homosexuality before marriage still occurs among the Sambia of New Guinea (Gerdt, 1981).

Sexual behavior on the Polynesian island of Mangaia (Marshall, 1971) has been studied in great detail. In this society sex is a very open topic for discussion, and children are instructed at early ages in the techniques of various sexual activities. Both boys and girls begin to have sexual intercourse regularly around the age of thirteen or fourteen. Mangaian males, through the age of thirty, average two to three orgasms nearly every day. In addition to copulating in all varieties of positions, Mangaians regularly practice oral sex; anal intercourse; insertion of the penis between the breasts, thighs, or other body parts; and mutual genital stimulation. In any sexual activity, these people place a great deal of emphasis on lengthy and enjoyable sexual experiences. While orgasm is enjoyed, it is not viewed as the sole goal of sex. Interestingly, in this society where there is less emphasis on orgasm as an achievement, everyone seems to reach orgasm easily.

On the island of Mangaia, there is no strong cultural connection between feelings of affection and the willingness to have sexual relations with a person. The degree of passion in sex is apparently not related to emotional involvement but instead to attention paid to sexual techniques. Mangaian couples who marry seem eventually to share affectionate feelings, but this is not seen as being related to sexual intimacy.

Neither intercourse nor love finds a prominent place among the Ik hunting group of East Africa (Turnbull, 1972). They are a very individualistic people who deemphasize interpersonal relationships and affection. Masturbation is the primary sexual outlet, with intercourse being accepted as somewhat of an extension of self-centered sex. A cardinal social teaching of the Ik "is not to love anyone" (Turnbull, 1972, p. 125).

Examination of Balinese cultures has provided an excellent look at how general cultural mores are reflected in a society's sexual customs and standards (Bateson, 1972). The Balinese are always struggling to achieve a steady state of balance and interpersonal stability, rather than building cumulative interactions between people that have some goal or climax. Even their arguments tend not to be resolved or concluded,

voyeurism (VOI-yur-izm): gaining sexual gratification from seeing others nude or involved in sexual acts.

and meetings go on with much happening but little developing with clarity. This ethos of balance is expressed in Balinese sexual relationships as well. Sexual intercourse is seen as one more thing that is part of the intense interpersonal balance, rather than an isolated act in itself. It is not viewed as something that begins with foreplay and ends with orgasm.

All of this is in contrast to the typical Western values that determine most of our sexual standards. It is not surprising that in Europe and North America sexual activity is most frequently a part of a context of competition—even conquest—and goal orientation. Our standards question the worth of sex without orgasm and the legitimacy of sex without the justifications of love.

WHO IS NORMAL?

Anthropologists speak of ethnocentricity, the quality of assuming that one's own culture is the right one, superior to all others. Our ethnocentricity finds us surprised, amused, and shocked by the beliefs and customs of others, who of course are just as taken aback by ours. In their classic anthropological study, *Patterns of Sexual Behavior,* Ford and Beach (1951) concluded that there is such a wide variation in sexual behaviors across cultures that no one society can even be regarded as representative. Yet a type of ethnocentricity that might be called *erotocentricity* causes us to assume that our own—either cultural or individual—sexual values, standards, and activities are right and best.

Ours is a culture of dichotomies and categories. Everything must fit into some classification. If something is not right, it must be wrong. If some behavior is not bad, it must be good. In the viewpoint of modern psychology, the normal–not-normal dichotomy is often strongly held, and people constantly worry about whether their feelings and behaviors are indeed normal. Every society must, with good reason, set sexual standards and regulate sexual behaviors. These standards are passed from one generation to the next, sometimes being modified as they go along. Boundaries therefore arise, distinguishing the good from the bad, the acceptable from the unacceptable. They become the criteria that are used to establish the concepts of normal and not normal. We have already seen how definitions of normalcy are relative to cultures, but there are other specific ways in which they are formulated.

Statistical Normalcy   One of the most common ways of deciding the relative normalcy of some sexual behavior is based on how widespread and frequent it is in a particular population. If most people do it, then it is considered normal. If it is practiced by only a small minority, it is not considered normal.

Normalcy by Expert Opinion   Every society has its experts, either by choice or by default. Our society venerates educational and professional credentials and listens to the opinions of those who possess what are perceived to be expert credentials. For example, members of the psychiatric profession's associations may decide, by vote, to consider a certain sexual orientation healthy or unhealthy, normal or abnormal (as in 1974, when the American Psychiatric Association decided, by polling their members, that homosexuality would no longer be considered an illness). Such opinions are typically widely accepted.

Moral Normalcy   Religions usually have standards regarding sexual morality. The predominant religions in a particular society therefore establish the norms for morality. These standards are perpetuated in laws and social sanctions. In most societies, behaviors and values that are seen as morally acceptable are also defined as normal.

A Continuum of Normalcy   In Western societies there has recently been increased acceptance of concepts such as situation morality, reality as a matter of perception, and nonjudgment. As a result, there has been an increased willingness to view sexual attraction and activities in relative terms, by asking such questions as: Is a behavior healthy and fulfilling for a particular person? Does it lead to exploitation of others? Does it take place between responsible, consenting adults? In this manner, normal and abnormal are part of a continuum that considers numerous individual factors.

Nevertheless, societies must establish sexual norms and make decisions about what is to be done with people who violate them. They may be treated by medical practitioners with anything from witch doctor spells to modern drugs, depending on the culture. They may be banished from the society, or forced to live in a kind of special sexual exile. Or they may be subject to legal sanctions and even imprisoned. They also may be ignored or tolerated.

LIMITS AND MISUSES OF LABELS

Labels for various forms of sexual behavior can really only provide a very general category of definition. However, whatever defines groups of people can sepa-

ethnocentricity: the tendency of the members of one culture to assume that their values and norms of behavior are the "right" ones in comparison to other cultures.

FIGURE 9.5 A Homosexual Male Couple

Society has formulated a means of classifying homosexual relationships into categories such as open-coupled and closed-coupled, yet the definition of homosexual continues to be questioned. This couple is pictured with the collages they both make.

rate them as well (Elshtain, 1991). Consider, for example, the term *homosexual*. Most people believe that they understand what is meant by the term. Closer examination might call the use of such a label into question. Here are some of the issues to be clarified in deciding whom to label a homosexual:

1. Must the person participate in actual sexual activity with another of the same sex, or is it enough to just want it?
2. If a person has had one sexual experience with a same-sexed partner, should he or she automatically be considered homosexual?
3. Should only those who have been involved exclusively with members of their own sex be called homosexual? Or what percentage of same-sexed experience is required?
4. Should people who have been attracted sexually to members of their sex all of their lives but have married and led an exclusively heterosexual existence be considered homosexual?

Similar questions arise with other sex-related labels. A man who dresses in women's clothing is often labeled a transvestite. And yet there are all sorts of different motivations for such behavior. Terms such as *sadism* and *masochism* are so general and ill-defined that they have little meaning at all in talking about the

behavior of individuals (see chapter 12, "The Spectrum of Human Sexual Behavior").

Of special concern is the use of specific sexual labels to define the entire person. Only too often an individual's entire identity seems to be summarized in a single description of his or her sexual orientation. We say "Isn't she a lesbian?" or "There goes a transvestite," instead of recognizing these orientations and behaviors as only one small part of an individual's personality. Yet we never label anyone a heterosexual or with other terms for what we consider normal behavior. Such misuses of terminology are disservices to individual human beings.

Sexual Individuality

At birth, human beings are typically assigned to a sex category: female or male. Our societal standards immediately create certain expectations for each person's sexual life at that very moment. For most of us, some of those expectations will be met, some not. For one thing, all of us develop a particular sense of ourselves as male or female, man or woman, or something in between. As I explained in chapter 6, it is our gender identity and the gender roles we fulfill as part of that identity that form a major portion of our sexuality.

As we grow and develop, we take on the very specific parts of what becomes our sexuality. One of those parts is usually some degree of sexual attraction toward other human beings: male, female, or some proportion of both sexes. However, there is far more to being a sexual person than that. There are certain characteristics about other people we may find sexually attracting and arousing: facial features, body types and builds, hairstyles, age, certain parts of their bodies (for example, legs, buttocks, genitals, breasts), styles of clothing, or complete lack of clothing. When we interact with others sexually, there are usually specific sexual acts that we prefer. We have our own particular frequencies and techniques for masturbation. And there are activities and things that some people find sexually exciting that have little to do with other people.

Most people have a sexual life of the mind, too, consisting of sexual fantasies and dreams, as well as sensations of sexual need, desire, and attraction. Only some of the time are these inner experiences expressed in physical responses or actual sexual behaviors. Since performing some sexual act involves a degree of

transvestite: an individual who dresses in clothing considered appropriate for the opposite sex, and adopts similar mannerisms, often for sexual pleasure.

FIGURE 9.6   Inner Sexual Life

Fantasy gives people the opportunity to escape from the frustrations and drudgeries of their lives. It may provide excitement in a safe environment, promote feelings of self-confidence, or release inner tensions. Some sexual fantasies may promote sexual desire, while some may mirror sexual desire.

decision-making, our inner sexual reactions and needs are not always consistent with our outward expressions of sexual behavior.

All of these aspects of a person's sexuality are intimately intertwined with all other aspects of the personality. Like classifying fingerprints by loops, whorls, and other configurations, it is possible to find general categories for some parts of everyone's sexual nature. But, taken together, the aspects of our sexualities are as individualized and specific as our fingerprints. They constitute our sexual individuality.

HOW DOES SEXUAL INDIVIDUALITY DEVELOP?

One of the most common questions asked of sexologists is, what causes homosexuality? The classic answer is that we won't know how one gets to be homosexual until we understand how one gets to be heterosexual. If we examine all aspects of one's collective sexual individuality, the picture becomes even more complex. Sex research into the origins of sexual attractions, orientations, preferences, and behaviors is still in a very primitive state. At this point, the most honest statement would be that we really do not know how human beings take on the specific characteristics of their sexuality. However, we do have some hypotheses that may form a foundation for eventual understanding.

Since homosexuality has been the most noticed and publicized of the nonstandard sexual orientations in our culture, more research has gone into seeking its origins than those of any other sexual phenomenon. Although the evidence is highly tentative, it begins to suggest the complexity of building sexual individuality. A study from the Kinsey Institute for Sex Research titled *Sexual Preference* (Bell, Weinberg, & Hammersmith, 1981) has offered some especially valuable insights. I give a detailed discussion of homosexuality in chapter 11, "Homosexuality and Bisexuality," but here are some conclusions of the Kinsey Institute researchers that may well help us to generalize about other forms of sexual orientation and behavior:

1. The importance of the relationship with parents and identifying with a parent in determining a child's sexual orientation have been overestimated by traditional psychoanalysis. Parents may influence the development of sexual attractions to some extent, but there are few generalizations to be drawn and the influences are not profound.

2. An individual's basic sexual orientation is usually determined by adolescence, even though the person has not been particularly sexually active.

sexual individuality: the unique set of sexual needs, orientations, fantasies, feelings, and activities that develops in each human being.

235

Adult expressions of sexual orientation and preference tend to be a continuation and confirmation of earlier sexual feelings. For example, people who are predominantly homosexual as adults usually were aware of their inclinations in childhood and adolescence and even then found their romantic and sexual contact with the opposite sex to be less gratifying than those with the same sex.

3. Developing patterns of sexual feelings and responses within children and young people cannot be traced back to a single social or psychological root. They are instead the result of many factors that are a part of any human being's life, too numerous, complex, and poorly understood at this time to be predictable or controllable.

4. There may be some biological bases for the development of sexual orientation. If such inborn factors do in fact exist, they most likely establish sexual predispositions that may then be influenced in various ways by psychological and social factors. Thus, it is likely that the *interaction* between nature and experience, rather than one or the other, influences our sexual development, along with most other facets of human development.

As we saw in chapter 7, "Sexuality Through the Life Cycle," there are persuasive arguments on both sides of the nature/nurture debate.

There is a growing body of research evidence to indicate that the development of sexual orientations and preferences is a complex process, involving many different dimensions. Both biological and social-environmental factors seem to be involved (Sanders & Reinisch,

1990). Klein (1990) was one of the first researchers to develop a model showing many different components of sexual identity, all relating to one another but having a degree of independence from each other at the same time. He initially developed a list of seven variables that needed to be considered when describing a person's sexual orientation or identity: sexual attraction, sexual behavior, sexual fantasies, emotional preference, social preference, self-identification, and actual life-style. He soon realized, however, that these dimensions of a person's life often change with time. Where people are today in terms of their sexual identities is not necessarily where they were in the past or where they will be, or would like to be, in the future. Therefore, he developed a grid system, the Klein Sexual Orientation Grid (KSOG) that considers this time factor along with each of the seven variables (see Fig. 9.7).

Building on the work of Klein and earlier researchers, Coleman (1990) defined sexual orientation in terms of nine different dimensions of people's lives:

1. Their life-style and current relationship status.
2. How they identify themselves in terms of sexual orientation.
3. Their ideal picture of what they would like their sexual orientation to be.
4. Their degree of comfort with and acceptance of their orientation.
5. Their physical sexual identity.
6. Their gender identity: how they perceive themselves as male or female.
7. Their sex role identity: how they behave in accordance with their gender.

(continued on p. 238)

FIGURE 9.7 Klein Sexual Orientation Grid (KSOG)

Variable	Past	Present	Ideal
Sexual attraction			
Sexual behavior			
Sexual fantasies			
Emotional preference			
Social preference			
Self-identification			
Life-style			

Source: Fritz Klein, *Bisexualities: Theory and Research* (p. 280), 1985, Binghamton, NY: Haworth Press.

Where people are today in terms of their sexual identities is not necessarily where they were in the past or where they will be, or would like to be, in the future.

Sexual Pluralism

Pluralism in any area of life asserts that there is more than one morally acceptable way for people to behave. The heart of pluralism is to tolerate a broad range of choices by others and try not to impose one's personal choices on all others. Pluralism is the way Americans approach religion and politics, marriage partners, and occupational and educational choices. We freed ourselves far quicker from the narrow perspectives of past centuries in these areas, but many still believe that, in sexuality, there is but one moral path.

Let us be clear. Sexual pluralism does not assert that all forms of sexuality are legitimate—that anything goes. Or, that if it feels good, do it. No, not at all. Sexual pluralism is a moral concept; it is not an invitation to an orgy. Sexual pluralism totally rejects the use of force or manipulation, as in rape and sexual exploitation of children by adults. The best way to ensure that pressure and deception are avoided is to encourage a concern for one's sexual partner; pluralism promotes this by asserting that honesty, equality, and responsibility (HER) are essential ingredients in any sexual relationship. Advising people to "just say no" does not do this. Pluralism offers choices to people, but demands that they take responsibility for making those choices in line with HER principles. Such principles promote *honesty* about each person's sexual goals for the relationship; ask that we treat the other person as having *equal* rights to choose what sexual acts will occur, if any; and insist that both partners take *responsibility* for avoiding unwanted outcomes, like pregnancy and disease. Only if a sexual relationship is honest, equal, and responsible is it acceptable. This should hold, whether one is 26 or 16, and whether one is seeking pleasure, love, or both.

• • •

The parents of today's teenagers are the older baby boomers, who led the sexual revolution which began in the late 1960s. These baby boomers, because of their sexual experiences and higher levels of education, have found it easier to move toward sexual pluralism. They know that they changed our society during the last sexual revolution, but they are also aware that they did not discard enough of their Victorian past to permit them to put in place a new workable sexual ethic. As parents, they want to protect their children, and know from their personal experience that compulsory abstinence does not do that. The inner conflict they feel will spur them on to support a movement toward sexual pluralism, because this will aid in the completion of the sexual revolution begun by them a generation ago.

Our fears of HIV/AIDS, rape, teenage pregnancy, and child sexual abuse are major motivations for discarding failed dogmatic approaches to sexuality, and for promoting HER sexual pluralism. In spite of this, the supports of traditional, male-dominated societies have powerfully opposed such changes. For example, over the past 20 years herpes 2 has spread in America at the rate of more than 500,000 cases a year. Also, millions of women each year have become infected with chlamydia, which for many will mean an inability to bear children. Yet, no one suggested advertising condoms as a preventive measure before the advent of HIV/AIDS, and our television networks, to date, have not accepted condom brand advertisements.

This dogmatic blockage of our own safety and happiness has been in place too long. The cost is immense in human suffering in all sexual problem areas. In the interest of all, we must clearly point out the great harm promoted by our lack of a sexual ethic appropriate for today's society. Old sexual dogmas help produce the sexual problems we face; they do not offer realistic guidance. Conflicts about how to handle our sexual problems could be resolved by working to accelerate the acceptance of sexual pluralism.

—Ira L. Reiss, "Sexual Pluralism: Ending America's Sexual Crisis," 1991, *SIECUS Report,* Vol. 19 (3)

8. Expressions of their orientation through sexual behavior, fantasies, and emotional attachments.
9. Their perceptions of past and idealized future sexual identity.

These researchers have reinforced the concept that sexual individuality is a combination of many life dimensions and includes many facets of the personality and patterns of behavior. It would be too narrow to define a person's sexual orientation on the basis of any one activity or fantasy. Surely to label a whole person in terms of the name given to one sexual category cannot do justice to the complexity of human sexual identity or orientation. The development of sexual individuality takes place over a lifetime, and includes many different components. How all of these components relate to one another, and what causes each of them to develop in certain ways, are aspects of human sexuality that remain largely unknown at this time.

MAKING SEXUAL CHOICES

Most sexologists have moved away from the concept that there is some natural sexual way for human beings to be, that there is an inborn sexual instinct to guide our behaviors. The diversity of sexual individuality provides ample evidence that there is no representative human sexuality.

There is increasing support, too, for the concept of sexual decision-making. Regardless of how we develop sexually, and regardless of the sexual fantasies, needs, attractions, and orientations that become part of every human being, each of us must make choices about his or her sexual behaviors. The standards and scripts of our society are important factors to be weighed in the decision-making. It is by dealing with sexual choices that we fulfill some of the other expectations of being civilized human beings: to be responsible, to develop self-respect, and to be nonexploitive toward others.

Sex and Values

Consider your reactions to the following situations:

Susan, a sophomore in college, goes with some friends to a favorite bar just off campus. She meets Alan for the first time and they spend 2 hours together, sharing drinks and conversation. He invites her back to his dorm room, and after some kissing and mutual fondling he asks her to have intercourse. Susan agrees and spends the night in Alan's room. The next morning they agree that neither is looking for a heavy relationship, although both would enjoy remaining friends.

+ + +

Mike has just entered college and has agreed to maintain an exclusive relationship with his girlfriend at home, some 600 miles away. He feels strongly about their commitment and is determined to make it last. He decides that he will not date at all and that his only sexual outlet will be masturbation.

+ + +

Worried about his grades in English, Derek pays a visit to the office of his instructor, an attractive woman in her late twenties. They discuss his recent papers and examinations, with Derek admitting that English has never been his strongest subject. To Derek's surprise, the professor hints that one sure way to earn an A would be to spend some time alone with her at her apartment. At first he thinks she is joking, but she touches his hand and makes it clear that she is being very serious.

+ + +

Lucy returns to her dorm room following a shower and begins to dress. Her roommate Karen seems to be watching her rather intently, and Lucy is trying to hide her discomfort. Karen asks her to sit down for a moment and is soon telling her about how attracted she has been to her. She expresses fear of Lucy's rejection but explains that she just couldn't hide her feelings any longer. Lucy is somewhat surprised but not at all angry. In fact she finds the idea of sex with Karen a bit intriguing.

+ + +

Now try to think about why you had the reactions and thoughts you did in relation to these sex-related situations. What were the specific aspects that made you feel positively or negatively about the people? Would there be any difference in your reaction if Susan and Alan had been dating for several months before having sex? If they were engaged? What if Mike had decided that what his girlfriend doesn't know won't hurt her? What if he had decided not to masturbate either? What if Derek's instructor had been a man? What if the instructor were a man and the student a woman? What if Lucy and Karen had been two men instead? What if Lucy had been disgusted by Karen and immediately sought to change rooms?

How you as an individual view these and other sex-related situations is determined by your values. It is not simply based on your sexual values but also your values about relationships, coercion, responsibility, and a long list of other issues. Our sexual values are weighed in our sexual decision-making, along with

---

values: system of beliefs with which people view life and make decisions, including their sexual decisions.

other related values. However, it is also clear that many people decide to participate in sexual activities that are inconsistent with their values. This decision can create conflict and guilt.

DEALING WITH SEX AS A MORAL ISSUE

From the time human beings are born, they begin learning how their culture and how the people closest to them feel about sexual matters. They learn what is right and what is wrong. It is these external value systems that give individuals their ideal values according to the society. As people mature, however, and begin examining these externally imposed values, they begin to develop their own internal values. The more conflict between external and internal values, the more potential for personal problems.

Moral values deal with the ethics, or rights and wrongs, of life situations. Theories of morality assume that humans are capable of making choices based on rational thought, thus making them responsible for their decisions and actions (Darling & Mabe, 1989). Since sexuality is such a pervasive and powerful aspect of human nature, all societies have sought to control and regulate it. Religion is the social institution usually concerned with ethics, so moral values related to sex have often been rooted in religious teachings. Most sexual morality today is founded in one of the following ethical traditions:

Adherence to Divinely Established Natural Laws
This is a legalistic view of sexual ethics that establishes clear and unwavering absolute boundaries between right and wrong. It is usually based on the idea that there is one correct interpretation of holy books such as the Bible, and is accompanied by a long list of do's and don'ts for followers. Today this approach to sexual morality is basic to the official positions of the Roman Catholic hierarchy, Eastern Orthodox churches, Orthodox Judaism, and fundamentalist or evangelical Protestant churches. Some of the most common teachings from this tradition are:

- Heterosexuality is natural and good; homosexuality or other variations are unnatural and bad.
- Sexual intercourse is good when practiced within marriage.
- Procreation is good and the major purpose of sex.
- Adultery is bad.
- Masturbation is bad and unnatural.

The Existence of a Religious Covenant Between Humankind and a God Jesus, Moses, and some of the other prophets spoke of a covenant of love and

FIGURE 9.8 Religious Attitudes Toward Sexuality

Religion may play an important role in establishing the sexual standards of a society. People may face conflicts if their personal values contradict the established morality.

hope between human beings and their god. Some religions have interpreted this to mean that moral principles can change as societies and human behavior patterns change. Within this approach to sexual ethics, there is a recognition that social values may change with time, rather than being bound to rigid traditional standards. New information from science, medicine, psychology, and sociology may be incorporated into new moral perspectives. This approach is quite common in Protestant churches, non-Orthodox Jewish groups, and among less formalized Roman Catholics (Francoeur, 1982).

This more flexible approach to morality still calls for establishment of moral codes of behavior, often by delegations of people in the governing body of some

external values: the belief systems available from one's society and culture.
internal values: the individualized beliefs and attitudes that a person develops by sorting through external values and personal needs.
moral values: beliefs associated with ethical issues, or rights and wrongs; they are often a part of sexual decision-making.

239

religious group. They may still decide that homosexuality or adultery is bad, but there is room for the issues to be discussed, debated, and then decided upon. Many Protestant churches, for example, have in recent years stated that masturbation and premarital sexual intercourse can be positive and good, provided they are practiced in a context of self-respect, love/caring, responsibility, nonexploitiveness, and other nonhurtful conditions.

Situation Ethics This is a system of morality that sees every situation as a unique collection of considerations and conditions. Therefore, moral decisions must be made only in the context of a particular situation, with a view toward all of the people involved. Situation ethics does not attach moral judgments to any sexual orientations or acts per se. The key to whether some form of sex is right or wrong lies in the human motivations behind it and the foreseeable consequences it might have (Fletcher & Wassmer, 1970).

From this ethical perspective, adultery might be considered wrong in one context, but right in another. Obviously it gives much more responsibility to the individual for making such judgments in arriving at sexual decisions. The disease AIDS and all of its implications raise entirely new issues that now must be considered in sorting through the ethics of sexual situations.

Hedonistic and Ascetic Traditions These moral perspectives represent opposite ends of the ethical spectrum. Hedonists hold that pleasure is the highest good, outweighing religious dogma or situational context. This point of view can be crystallized by the phrase, "If it feels good, do it." The sex drive is viewed as an appetite to be satisfied with a maximum amount of physical and emotional pleasure. There are few people who manage a purely hedonistic life-style, since the complications of relationships can easily get in the way. Some psychologists see hedonism as a self-centered way of life that may indeed represent what they would define as a sociopathic, or socially irresponsible, emotional disorder. It should be noted, however, that even this kind of professional judgment can reflect the professional's moral beliefs.

Asceticism has been a part of some religious and philosophical traditions and is characterized by celibacy. The goal is to rise above base physical pleasures and instead emphasize self-denial, self-discipline, and the life of the mind or spirit. Asceticism is often characterized by the teaching that denial of sexual pleasure helps one be closer to spiritual needs and to God, and is part of the celibate life-style expected of priests, nuns, and monks.

RELIGION AND SEX

Judeo-Christian-Muslim religious values have traditionally constituted the moral backbone for various prohibitions against sexual behaviors in Western culture, typically taking a rather sex-negative position in which the emphasis is on the repression of sexual desire. In contrast to this perspective, the Eastern traditions—Hindu, Buddhist, Tantric, and Taoist—have tended to view sexuality in terms of its creative potential and its power in spiritual development. Eastern thought places more emphasis on the harmony of body and spirit rather than the opposition of the two (Francoeur, 1990).

Religions influence child-rearing practices and often significantly determine a culture's world view. Within all major religious traditions, there are two basic ways in which the world tends to be perceived: one is a fixed world view, in which it is assumed that the universe was created by a deity and is now completely finished. This is the fundamentalist perspective that finds followers within every tradition. The other point of view is more process-oriented, seeing the world and human nature as constantly changing and evolving (Francoeur, 1991a). These two viewpoints are usually associated with differing attitudes toward sexuality as well. The fundamentalist view is that there is a constant battle between good and evil, and that sex is a major source of temptation and sin. Those with a more evolutionary world view tend to see the essential goodness of the human body and sexual desire, and place the emphasis on people choosing sexual behaviors that are healthy, responsible, and considerate of others (Speas, 1990).

Within religious circles, attitudes toward sex changed during the late 1960s and 1970s. Many religious groups began to examine more carefully their teachings regarding sex. In doing so they considered appropriate new evidence on human sexuality. Most Protestant churches began to adopt less oppressive positions on issues such as masturbation, homosexuality, and premarital sexual activity, although fundamentalist sects have taken strong antisexuality stands.

During the 1990s the religious controversies continue. The Presbyterian church recently faced a nationally publicized debate about sexual teachings. One faction within the church was advocating a position that would sanction sexual relations between unmarried people as long as they were involved in a loving relationship. This was to be extended to same-sexed

hedonists: believers that pleasure is the highest good.
asceticism (a-SET-a-siz-um): usually characterized by celibacy, this philosophy emphasizes spiritual purity through self-denial and self-discipline.

couples as well. However, at their 1991 General Assembly, church representatives defeated this attempt at liberalizing church doctrine.

One of the most significant areas of impact on religion in recent years has been feminism. There has been a reshaping of some religious symbolism to recognize the feminine images of God that are a part of religious history. Some religious groups have attempted to eliminate what they have come to see as sexist language within their books—including the Bible—and hymns. Women are taking stronger leadership roles in many religious groups, moving away from the patriarchal structures that have dominated Western religion for centuries. These changes are having a profound effect on the inclusiveness of many religions and will continue to change the very structure of many religious groups for years to come (Stackhouse, 1990).

The Roman Catholic church has met with inner turmoil as a result of its declarations on human sexual behavior. In an encyclical letter titled *Humanae Vitae,* Pope Paul VI restated the church's rejection of all forms of birth control other than planned abstinence from intercourse. In 1975 the Church's Sacred Congregation for the Doctrine of the Faith issued a "Declaration on Certain Questions Concerning Sexuality" condemning masturbation, homosexual behavior, and premarital sex. This statement did not carry the weight of an encyclical letter but did create a great deal of publicity and controversy. In recent years the Vatican has reaffirmed strong stands against most forms of nonheterosexual behavior within the context of marriage and has condemned the use of reproductive technology (Maguire, 1987). There are many Roman Catholic laypersons and clergy who are experiencing serious conflict between these religious teachings and their personal values. More liberal members of the church have adopted their own sexual values and have called for more open debate and discussion on the issues. Professor Charles Curran was fired from his faculty position at Catholic University of America because of his advocacy of freedom of choice in the matter of birth control, an end to required celibacy in the priesthood, and other controversial issues. Twenty-four Catholic nuns were reprimanded by the church for expressing the opinion that the abortion issue should be discussed as a morality question from various points of view.

Judaism encompasses a wide spectrum of beliefs but has generally held tolerant attitudes toward sexual activities. Ancient Jewish texts affirm the goodness of the sex organs and intercourse, although strict rules of conduct have often been established. Modern Judaism integrates changing social values into its teachings about sex (Brickner, 1987).

Religious ideology is controversial in sexology. Christianity has been denounced as the major source for the majority of Western culture's antisexual attitudes and sexual oppression (Stackhouse, 1990) and hailed as the source of a fundamental ethic for gender equality and sexual pleasure (Gardella, 1987). Research conducted with one group of unmarried men and women, aged 17–25, showed that regular church attendance did not seem to affect sexual behavior one way or the other. Instead, the degree of permissiveness within individuals' sexual values had the most influence (Jensen, Newell, & Holman, 1990). While many people have become confused or disillusioned by the diverse religious values on sexuality, religions continue to represent a source of guidance to which many will continue to turn.

ALIGNING YOURSELF WITH SOCIAL AND CULTURAL VALUES

Every person must find a comfortable balance and harmony between the external sexual values he or she has learned and the internal values that have evolved during maturation. There is now a fair amount of evidence that moral and ethical development proceeds in predictable stages as a child grows and develops.

The two primary theorists on the moral development of children have been Jean Piaget and Lawrence Kohlberg. While there are some differences in how these two researchers saw ethical concepts forming in children, there are enough similarities to summarize some of their major points together. Both agree, for example, that children essentially lack any sense of right or wrong when they are born. As they develop physically and intellectually, they are gradually able to understand moral values. That understanding deepens and becomes incorporated into their ways of dealing with other people as they become older.

In their first few years of life, children gradually pick up the rules of behavior expected of them, learning to some degree that they must obey parents (or other adult authorities) or risk disapproval and punishment. Their basic approach to life, however, is to satisfy their own needs. They react to their environment reflexively.

By the time children are 8 to 10 years old, they usually are beginning to adapt to the moral codes imposed on them by their environment. They realize that they are expected to behave in particular ways and often conform in order to be seen as good boys and girls. As adolescence and young adulthood progress, they gradually define their own standards of morality and the ethical principles they want to guide their lives. There is always incorporation of societal values into

241

Case Study

WENDELL: CONFLICTS WITH PERSONAL RELIGIOUS VALUES

When Wendell committed himself to fundamentalist Christianity in high school, it was a profound decision in his life. He had felt lacking in moral direction and often unhappy with the life choices he had made. His new dedication to religion was exciting and comforting to him.

During his first year at college, he associated himself with a Christian fellowship group on campus and drew most of his social contacts from that group. In one of his classes he met a young woman to whom he eventually felt romantically attracted. They soon began to date. She did not consider herself a fundamentalist Christian, although she respected the choice that Wendell had made.

In time Wendell began to experience inner conflicts because of the strong sexual feelings he was experiencing toward the young woman. He believed that it would be immoral for him to masturbate or share any form of sexual behavior with her. Yet he often felt distracted and upset by his frustrating arousal and interest.

In talking with a counselor at his college, Wendell admitted that he did masturbate occasionally, always feeling guilty and uncomfortable because of doing so. He also expressed feelings

of guilt about the many sexual fantasies he was having about the woman he loved. She seemed open to going further with him sexually and in fact had encouraged him to be more demonstrative about his sexual needs. She told Wendell that she thought such feelings to be natural and good.

Realizing that the conflicting issues were related mostly to his religious values, the counselor advised Wendell that one way or another he would have to reconcile the conflicts and find a way to reduce the turmoil he felt inside. Since the counselor was not a religious counselor, it was suggested that Wendell sort through some of the issues with his pastor or others in the fellowship group.

After several weeks of turmoil and discussion with others, Wendell decided that the only viable choice for him was to end his relationship with the woman. He first reported back to the counselor and then explained to the young woman that although he loved her deeply, his sexual passions would have to be brought back under control in order for him to feel that he was being faithful to his religion. He ended the relationship at that point.

---

this personal system, but these external values are now weighed and considered more carefully.

Our values are important motivational forces that influence our life choices. They do not form by accident or by luck, but instead by some sort of internal process. Sometimes people form their sexual values in a very intentional manner. They weigh their ideas and needs carefully, selecting and cultivating those values that seem to be in harmony with their other life choices. Other values emerge in people's lives as a result of developmental influences such as family of origin, cultural background, or religious training. It has been suggested that sexual health will best be maintained when the formation of sexual values is able to be an ongoing process, so that value systems evolve for the individual that are appropriate to his or her various developmental stages of life (Richards, 1990).

We live in confusing times when it comes to

sexual values. Some observers feel that sex has become too important and that we have overemphasized the importance of sexuality in defining human existence. We are realizing, however, that sex is not so simple either. AIDS, increasing sexual violence, and soaring rates of unintended pregnancy are thought by some to signal the need for new limits on sexual behavior (Elshtain, 1991). Others insist that it is not necessary to view everything sexual in terms of problems. AIDS does not have to be viewed as a reason to discourage sex as much as a disease to be conquered by medical science. Those on this side of the controversy believe that sexual liberation has been worth fighting for, that sexual pleasure is a legitimate goal, and that hysteria and overemphasis on the negative aspects of sex should be discouraged (Levine, 1991).

In a pluralistic society such as our own, it is impossible to find general agreement with any particular approach to sexual morality and values. However, several widely accepted moral principles seem to be in effect today, and would be supported by most religious teachings as well (Darling & Mabe, 1989; Reiss, 1991):

1. *The principle of noncoercion:* People should not be forced to engage in sexual expression. Sexual expression should occur only when there is voluntary consent to do so.

2. *The principle of nondeceit:* People are not to be enticed into sexual expression based on fraud or deception.

3. *The principle of treatment of people as ends:* People are not to be treated as a means only; they must be treated as ends. In the sexual realm, this means that another person should never be viewed solely as a means to one's own sexual satisfaction.

4. *The principle of respect for beliefs:* People must show respect for the sexual values and beliefs of others. This means that one person should not pressure another to act in a way not in accord with his or her sexual values and beliefs. However, this does not prevent someone from attempting to persuade others rationally that they are mistaken in their beliefs.

A person's religion can play a significant part in determining specific details of sexual morality, although many individuals do not accept their religion's sexual values without question or conflict. If people continually violate the sexual moral codes taught by their religions and believe that those codes are essentially right they can develop a good deal of guilt and personal conflict. The balance between highly regarded values and behavior can be a delicate one, requiring careful thought and deliberation (Richards, 1990).

The transition from home to college or some other away-from-home context can be filled with new stimuli and new choices. There is often greater freedom to have sex and to experiment with sexual values (Daher, Greaves, & Supton, 1987). Even making mistakes with sex can serve a useful purpose in clarifying the individual's personal code of sexual morality (Committee on the College Student, 1983). However, the balancing act between satisfying one's own sexual needs and living up to the moral principles that are demanded by one's society and oneself may actually last a lifetime. Every stage of life offers new sets of sexual decisions and questions to be resolved. In addition, society's values are always shifting. One limited study of several hundred students showed significantly less tolerant attitudes toward abortion and extramarital sexual intercourse among college students in 1982 than in 1972. The dynamic nature of external values may necessitate continuing reexamination of internal value systems (Lawrance, Rubinson, & O'Rourke, 1984).

FINDING HEALTHY SEXUAL VALUES

There is general agreement among counselors and other helping professionals that achieving a healthy sexuality must involve a level of consistency between a person's behavior and a person's moral values. In former times, society's moral codes about sex were often clearly stated and generally agreed upon by the majority. A number of factors in recent years have produced a plurality of sexual values in today's society. There is less tendency to see the issues in strictly black-and-white terms. This can make it even more confusing to arrive at a personal set of values.

The unfortunate result of this confusion for many people is choosing not to choose. Instead of thinking through their values and deciding in advance how they will want to behave in certain sexual situations, they wait until they are swept away by passion or a persuasive partner (Cassell, 1985). This then becomes a handy way to deny responsibility for sex or its consequences.

In order to establish your own set of moral values regarding sex, there are several steps that you can take:

1. Know yourself and work toward acceptance of your sexual needs and orientations. Basic to the success of any code of values is feeling good about yourself. Even if you find some aspects of your sexuality that you would not feel comfortable acting on, it is important that they be accepted as part of you. Whether you ever act on them or not is up to you. That is what choice and personal decision-making are all about.

2. Try not to let yourself be bound by popular sexual standards that you are uncomfortable with. Popular songs, television programs, advertising, and other media presentations often promulgate specific values about sex and sexual attractiveness. You may receive pressure from peers at times about what is currently in vogue sexually. You will need to weigh all this information carefully, decide how much you want and need to fit in with a particular group, and then choose how you want to become involved sexually. Be cautious about going along with any aspects of sex that don't seem quite right to you. Give yourself as much time as you need to think; after all, your goal is to feel good about yourself.

3. Examine your feelings about religion and find out what your religion has to say about sexual matters. You may be surprised. Many religious groups have given careful consideration to human sexuality and have devised written guides to help with personal decision-making. You will need to consider just how important your religious background and your current feelings about religion are to you. Agnostics and

atheists also develop their own codes of moral behavior that emphasize responsibility to others.

4. Think ahead. It is a good idea to think carefully about various sexual situations and issues and anticipate how you might react to them. This is an excellent way to clarify your personal values about sex. For example, when do you think it is all right for two people to share a sexual relationship? If heterosexual intercourse will be involved, how should decisions about contraception be made? What are some of the possible consequences of various sexual activities, and how would you deal with those consequences?

5. Consider what level of responsibility you have toward other people. Most forms of sex involve interaction between people. Whenever interpersonal relationships are involved, the issue of responsibility to others comes up. How do you think you should treat others? What degree of responsibility do you have not to put others in exploitative or potentially hurtful situations?

6. Remember that you are not a mind reader. This is where good communication comes in. Part of sexual values must be to know how a potential sexual partner thinks and feels about the sex before you get involved. It is dangerous to make assumptions about the values and feelings of others. You will need to spend time and energy communicating in order to find out what they are.

7. Decide what role you want loving relationships to play in your life. Loving and sex are often intertwined in relationships, though not necessarily so. An important part of establishing your own sex-related values is to know how you feel about the place of loving relationships in your life.

8. Take opportunities to clarify your sexual values on an ongoing basis. Sex education books, classes, and discussion groups provide opportunities for participation in values clarification exercises. These may challenge you to think through your values more clearly and to understand the bases for holding them. Over time, such exercises may help you to rethink values or to realize that your attitudes have changed. Using opportunities to clarify values can keep your personal code of moral behavior clear and workable for everyday life.

Sex Education

Little attention was given to sex education until the 1960s. It was during that decade that two professional groups began to highlight the need for improved sex education efforts and to work toward the establishment of sex education programs. Those groups were the Sex Information and Education Council of the United States (SIECUS) and the American Association of Sex Educators, Counselors, and Therapists (AASECT). Public opinion polls consistently demonstrate that over three-fourths of adult Americans favor the teaching of sex education in schools, and that over 80 percent of teenagers favor such courses.

The fact remains, however, that young people still gain most of their sex information from their peers, and that the information is usually laden with myths and misconceptions (Cross, 1991). Sex education programs in schools are still the exception rather than the rule, even though over half the states have mandated sex education in public schools, and two-thirds are requiring that AIDS education be offered to students (de Mauro, 1990).

As states have mandated sex and AIDS education programs, it has also become clear that many sex educators lack professional training in those fields. Experts are concerned that not only are many teachers underprepared, they are also being forced to teach material with which they do not feel personally comfortable. It has been suggested that compulsory teacher training be part of any legislation mandating sex education. Both undergraduate and graduate degree programs will need to increase their course offerings in the area of human sexuality (Krueger, 1991). There is also a need for some specialization in sex education efforts.

It is now recognized that special groups in our society—the mentally retarded, the aged, and adolescents, for example—need sex education that addresses their special concerns. This will continue to be part of the trend toward helping each individual live the most comfortable, problem-free sexual life possible.

There are a number of attitudes that have hindered sex education efforts. One, certainly, is a general reluctance and embarrassment about discussing sex openly. At the same time, adults often mistakenly assume that with the new availability of sex information, young people already know everything about sex.

Another prevalent attitude is that if people are given information about sexuality, they will then experiment with sex. However, research continues to indicate that sex education does not seem to encourage sexual behavior and in some cases may even discourage it (Haffner, 1989).

Finally, many fundamentalist religious groups object to the kind of sex education that allows for differing values concerning issues such as masturbation, sex outside of marriage, same-sex behavior, birth control, and other controversial topics. Some opponents have objected to the use of values clarification techniques, encouragement of sexual tolerance, or discussion of contraceptive methods, preferring in-

FIGURE 9.9 Sex Education Class

To dispel sexual ignorance and the problems that ignorance can cause, attention is being given to sex education in some of our nation's schools. Discussing contraceptive methods can be a controversial part of sex education.

stead that sex education be restricted to reproductive anatomy, physiology, and reminders to students that they should abstain from any sexual activity (Flax, 1990).

There are plenty of reasons why sex education should be a viable option. We live in a time when people are encouraged to be more expressive and individualistic. Old biases about sex and traditional sex roles are being challenged and reexamined. At earlier ages than before, children are being exposed to confusing messages about sex from the media and have more freedom to experiment with sex themselves. Sex education can be a significant way of helping young people deal with the stresses that accompany these changes (Cross, 1991).

Sex educators have generally felt that it is irresponsible to isolate the physical and reproductive aspects of sex from the broader emotional, social, and psychological aspects of human sexuality. Often sex education is included in courses called "family life education" or "human relations," to emphasize the interrelatedness of sexuality with these other aspects of human life (Moglia, 1990).

CURRENT TRENDS IN SEX EDUCATION

Never in the history of humankind has so much effort been devoted to the understanding of sexuality. Since the studies of Alfred Kinsey in the late 1940s and early 1950s, new findings have led to a new view of sex.

Sexology has emerged as an academically respected field suitable for scholarly work. It is increasingly clear that to study any aspect of human life adequately, sexuality cannot be ignored. This trend has also meant that we can no longer omit sexual issues as a part of any educational process.

Technical Advances   Television and computers have revolutionized the flow and distribution of information. They are and will continue to be powerful tools in education. There are already computer-accessed databases of sex information and computer networks for the sharing of sex-related resources and news.

Distinguishing Sexual Expression From Procreation   The once–widely held value that sex should be primarily for producing children has become distinctly less prevalent. As concerns about overpopulation and world economy have grown, so has emphasis on limiting the number of children conceived. Contraceptive education and services have expanded markedly. Gradually there has been a separation of sex's procreative function from its potential for pleasure and communication. This has been hastened by the advent of sex therapy, which emphasizes the fulfillment of sexual needs and feelings. This trend is being reflected in sex education offerings as well.

It is this sex-positive view that offends and concerns many of those who oppose sex education, because they fear it will lead to sexual permissiveness. They feel that permissiveness is exactly what sex education should be combatting. Again, however, there is no evidence that current sex education efforts are leading to increased levels of sexual activity. There have been social trends since the 1960s that seem to have produced this effect over time, and most sex educators believe that it has been their job to help young people cope with the confusion that has resulted and to help them find a healthy, comfortable place for sexuality in their lives. Sex has been gradually seen as part of an integrated whole rather than as an isolated appendage of human nature. More and more, sex education is emphasizing that to be human is to be sexual, and that to learn how to manage and enjoy that sexuality is an important responsibility (Cross, 1991).

Debating the "Just Say No" Philosophy Because of the increase in rates of adolescent sexual behavior, and because of fears about AIDS and other STDs, many people would like to see sex education emphasize abstinence. Aside from fears of promiscuity, pregnancy, or disease, some simply feel that chastity is a value to be promoted. Several sex education curricula have emerged that place their emphasis on the "Just Say No" philosophy. The central theme behind these curricula is that if we can persuade young people to practice sexual abstinence until they marry, many social problems would be solved.

Opponents of this approach maintain that it is no longer realistic, given how sexuality has been opened to consideration and choice in recent years. These opponents remind us that even when chastity was taught as the highest virtue, there were still many sexual problems. People simply suffered with them in private. Two sex educators have analyzed one curriculum that stresses abstinence, called *Sex Respect*, written by a woman who has also written guides on Christian morality. These educators concluded that the curriculum would represent a problem for public school settings, since it substitutes opinion for fact, conveys incomplete information, relies on scare tactics, reinforces gender stereotypes, does not consider cultural and economic differences, and has not been adequately evaluated for effectiveness (Trudell & Whatley, 1991). Nevertheless, sex educators have been feeling the pressure to make sure they present abstinence as a desirable choice in all curricula.

Increased Emphasis on Developing Decision-Making Skills and Loving Relationships Sex educators learned early in their work that it is impossible to conduct good sex education by imposing specific codes of moral behavior on students. Instead, there is growing emphasis on helping students understand the process of moral or ethical decision-making for their own lives. In sex education, students are helped to clarify their

FIGURE 9.10   Loving Relationships

Rather than the permissive attitude toward sexual encounters that was popular in the 1960s and early 1970s, a trend in the 1990s has been toward the establishment of a meaningful relationship prior to sexual intimacy.

own values and to understand the responsibilities they have toward others in making decisions about sex.

The 1990s have seen a continued return to discussions of loving relationships. Sex without some other meaningful human connection now tends to be seen as shallow and ultimately unfulfilling. Sex education is increasingly including love education and skills for the improvement of human relationships.

Recognizing the Need for Sex Education as a Coordinated Effort Research continues to indicate that parents are not providing adequate sources of sex education for most young people. Parents often have difficulty admitting to themselves that their children are sexual beings and may feel inadequately prepared to be sex educators. Nevertheless, educators are in general agreement that the home can be the most significant environment for sex education. Training programs to help people with this aspect of parenting are becoming increasingly available. This can be one of the best ways for parents to convey to their children the information and sexual values that they consider important to a happy life.

To expect all parents to be able to handle the long and complicated job of sex education may have its unrealistic aspects, however. There may also be times when involvement of other people in a child's life can be the most valuable direction to take. Probably the best sex education is represented by a concerted effort on the part of many different people: parents, teachers, religious leaders, counselors, youth organizations, and the media. In this way, young people receive messages and skills from a variety of individuals and are helped to integrate sexual feelings and decisions into their lives more realistically (Haffner, 1989).

The Necessity of Dealing With the AIDS Crisis
Currently much discussion about sex education has been focusing on the need to alert people of all ages to the dangers of HIV, the AIDS virus. Sex educators are now wrestling with the many issues of when and how to inform young people about AIDS and the safer sex measures that can be taken to reduce the risks.

WHAT SEX EDUCATION CAN AND CANNOT ACCOMPLISH

It has often been said that sex education is a lifelong process, beginning at the moment one is born. We learn many sexual lessons from how we are handled as babies, from the toys we are given to play with, and from how we are taught to feel about our bodies. Many of the fundamental values about sexuality that any individual holds are well established before she or he enters a school environment.

Most often, sex education programs grow out of a school's or community's concerns about teenage pregnancy. The implied goal, then, is to prevent such pregnancies. Often it is assumed that this will be accomplished by persuading teenagers to stop having sexual intercourse. There has been no strong evidence to indicate that sex education causes people to alter their sexual behaviors (Kirby, 1985). There is evidence, however, that a coordinated sex education effort can reduce teen pregnancy rates (Haffner, 1989).

A large body of research evidence indicates that people can gain significant increases in knowledge about sexuality as the result of sex education courses. It has been extrapolated from this evidence that gaining sex information can lead to more informed, perhaps more responsible, decision-making about sexual behavior. There may also be some changes in values concerning sex roles, responsibility, and acceptance of one's own body (Cross, 1991; Krueger, 1991).

While there is still far more research to be done on sex education and its outcomes, most professionals today feel that adequate sex education is one of the most important ways of preventing sexual problems. However, this means sex education in its broadest terms. Comprehensive sex education provides thorough coverage of the body's sexual anatomy and how it functions. It also examines the relationship of sexuality to the whole person—feelings, values, decisions—and to the society in which the person lives. It will still be a long time before this sort of educational experience is available to everyone.

SEX EDUCATION FOR PROFESSIONALS

It was in the early- and mid-1960s that the sexual revolution began to catch up with the medical profession. Several studies began to suggest that medical students brought to medical school a great many sexual misconceptions and anxieties and a great deal of sexual misinformation, and that the medical schools were doing very little to provide these students with better information or new attitudes. Only three medical schools offered any formal training in the area of human sexuality in 1960. By 1975 well over 100 medical schools were including courses on sexuality (Lief, 1981). In their training of counselors, psychologists, and social workers, most graduate schools now offer coursework in human sexuality. However, such courses for professionals are not always required and may, alas, be condensed into brief workshop formats.

Studies continue to show that the ability of professional workers to perceive sexual problems in their patients or clients, and then pursue these problems once they have been noticed, depends on the degree of comfort the professionals feel toward sexuality. The more anxious physicians are about dealing with sexual issues, the less apt they will be to pursue a patient's sexual history. Some doctors will also avoid discussing sex because they are uncertain of how to alleviate patient anxiety about the topic (Schnarch, 1982). While exposure to sex education has increased physicians' knowledge base relating to sex, it does not necessarily reduce their anxiety about dealing with sexual issues (Calamidas, 1987). This is an issue that medical schools and other professional training institutions must continue to address.

Sex and Disability Groups

People with physical and mental disabilities represent another facet of our sexual values and the concept of sexual individuality. As with older people, it can be difficult for others to accept their sexuality, and this has led to sex-related prejudice. The fact that people with disabilities might have to approach their sexual decisions differently, or make some special arrangements in order to participate in sex, has often led them to be viewed as somehow asexual. To perceive disabled individuals as having the full range of sexual interests, orientations, and activities simply makes many people uncomfortable. Yet there is new awareness of the special sexual concerns and problems of disabled individuals and a new acceptance of their rights to be sexual (Francoeur, 1991b).

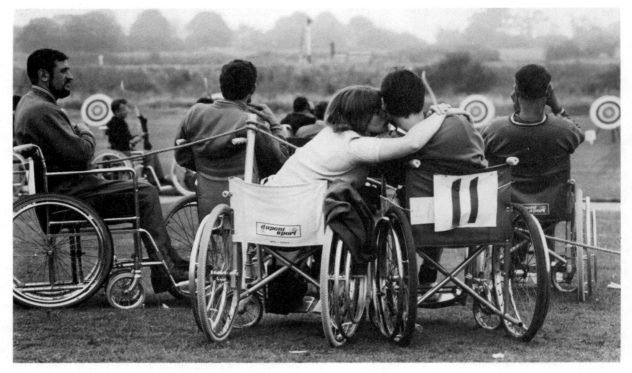

FIGURE 9.11 Sexuality and People With Disabilities

People with physical and mental disabilities have as much a right to intimacy and sexual pleasure as anyone else. The quality of the sexual relationship will depend, as in any relationship, on the quality of the total care and respect each partner has for the other.

Most physical handicaps do not directly affect the sex organs or their ability to function. Nor do they affect the individual's sexual feelings, need for sex, or the desire to be physically and emotionally intimate with others. However, they may have a great effect on how people with disabilities view their attractiveness and the degree to which they seek sexual relationships. Consider a man with a serious skin disease that causes unsightly blotches all over his body, or the woman born with cerebral palsy who has difficulty controlling her arm movements and speech. While these individuals have the same sexual drives and interests as anyone else, they may find themselves limited by prejudice and misunderstanding.

Our culture has acquired specific, rather stereotypical attitudes about sexual attractiveness. At the same time we have also developed prejudices about disabilities; these prejudices tend to dehumanize people. Often when individuals with disabilities are young, there is a reluctance on the part of adults even to deal with any special sexual concerns. This is often a misguided attempt to protect the person from being hurt. It arises out of the belief that if the issue is never raised, temptation and negative consequences can be avoided (Leyson, 1991).

From a more positive perspective, recent trends in sexual attitudes have de-genitalized sex somewhat, legitimizing the idea of "sexual celebration" in a broader context. No longer does sex need to be viewed solely as an act of sex organs, but instead as an intimate emotional and physical connection between two human beings that may involve a variety of behaviors. This broadened view of sexual interaction is particularly valuable for people with disabilities, who may have to make special accommodations for their sexual practices. It is crucial for them to accept the notion of their sexuality themselves, rejecting assumptions about being unattractive to others. Then they must work to find ways of expressing that sexuality in ways that fit their personal values and needs (Francoeur, 1991b).

In recent years there has been a growing awareness of the needs and rights of disabled persons. Architects and builders have been obliged to consider the accessibility of buildings to people in wheelchairs; school districts are required to provide specially designed educational programs for people who need them. Last but not least, sex educators are beginning to realize that those with disabilities have the right to be sexual too.

MENTAL RETARDATION

Probably no other group of people who are handicapped has been as oppressed sexually as those with mental retardation. One of the historical roots of this problem has been the fear that sexual activity among the mentally disabled would lead to pregnancies and risk passing on genetic defects to children. Another fear was whether or not such parents could care properly for their children. While these are legitimate concerns, the age-old solution was to create conditions where the sexual feelings of and interaction between people with mental retardation could be ignored or denied. Many parents once institutionalized their retarded children primarily because of these fears or the concern that their children might be vulnerable to sexual exploitation by others. In those institutional settings people who were mentally retarded were often discouraged from masturbating or from showing affection openly. But when people with mental retardation are denied access to appropriate information about their bodies, sexual responses, and sexual behavior, they actually become even more vulnerable, because they may not learn the rest of the world's basic rules of social propriety. They may attempt to masturbate in public places or may be overly physically demonstrative in their affections; thus their bodies may be exploited by nonretarded people (Kempton, 1977).

There is growing recognition that children and adults with mental retardation are particularly vulner-

FIGURE 9.12 Sexuality and the Mentally Disabled

With the proper instruction in meeting their own sexual needs and following the rules and ethics of a given society's sexual behavior, some people with mental disabilities can lead fulfilling lives in a mutually supportive relationship.

TABLE 9.1

Sexual Rights of People With Mental Retardation

1. The right to receive training in social sexual behavior that will open more doors for social contact with people in the community.
2. The right to all the knowledge about sexuality they can comprehend.
3. The right to enjoy love and be loved by the opposite sex, including sexual fulfillment.
4. The right to the opportunity to express sexual impulses in the same forms that are socially acceptable for others.
5. The right to marry.
6. The right to have a voice in whether or not they should have children.
7. The right for supportive services that involve those rights as they are needed and feasible.

Source: W. Kempton, "The Mentally Retarded Person," in *The Sexually Oppressed*, edited by H. L. & J. S. Gochros, 1977, New York: Association Press.

able to sexual abuse and exploitation by others, often needing special counseling help with the emotional and social insecurities that foster this vulnerability. Even professionals often do not thoroughly understand the emotional development and health problems of people with mental disabilities. Researchers in this field have recommended that professionals who work with those with mental retardation receive more education about the rights of these individuals and ways of preventing and reacting to situations where sexual abuse has taken place (Tharinger, Horton, & Millea, 1990).

Concern over reproduction by people with mental retardation has received greater attention in recent years. In the early 1900s, when there was a strong eugenics movement that advocated careful genetic selection in human reproduction, people with mental retardation were usually considered unfit to reproduce and were often involuntarily sterilized in institutions. Now it is clear that many mentally disabled people are able to learn enough about birth control methods to choose and use them effectively. The issue of informed consent for sterilization continues to be a difficult one because individuals with mental retardation may not fully understand the procedure and its outcome. They may be too easily influenced by authority figures to give consent to sterilization (Hall, 1975).

Gradually, those with mental retardation have been helped to articulate their sexual rights, and educational efforts have been improving (see Table 9.1). The principle of <u>normalization</u> came to the United States in

normalization: integration of mentally retarded persons into the social mainstream as much as possible.

the 1960s from Scandinavia: simplified programs in social skills and sex education are now available for use with those who have mental retardation to help them adapt to the norms and patterns of mainstream social life (Tharinger, Horton, & Millea, 1990). Some couples who are mentally retarded have been able to marry and learn how to manage their social and sexual lives very effectively as the result of these new efforts.

VISUAL AND AUDITORY DISABILITIES

In addition to the prejudices to which individuals with visual or hearing impairments are usually subjected, there are two major sources or problems in developing sexual awareness. The first is gaining an understanding of sex and sexuality. One recent study demonstrated that women who are visually impaired had significantly less knowledge about human sexuality and had received their information at a later age than women who are not visually impaired (Welbourne et al., 1983). People who are blind cannot see diagrams that could help them understand anatomy and physiology. People who are hearing impaired are limited in how information can be presented to them as well. Both groups may experience delays in the total education process, including learning to read, because of their respective disabilities.

A second major difficulty lies in their socialization process. Those who are visually or hearing impaired are often hindered in contacts with others because those others are uncomfortable with their disabilities. Those others may feel afraid or embarrassed about even attempting to communicate with people with visual or hearing impairments. In addition, usual routes for communication are undermined. Blind people cannot read the subtleties of facial expressions and body language. Deaf people might miss words in lipreading or might risk being misunderstood when using sign language with someone who is unfamiliar with it.

Sex educators for the sensorially impaired are beginning to challenge some of the problems. In Sweden they have provided blind people with life-size plastic models of the human sexual anatomy and in some cases even with real-life models. Sex educators for the deaf make special use of visual materials such as models, charts, photographs, slides, and transparencies. They have provided captioning services for commercially available sex education filmstrips, for example. Several studies have indicated that blind and deaf young people are anxious to have sex education, and their parents support this attitude (Love, 1983). It is again crucial, however, that such curricula include a spectrum of topics such as communication skills, values, decision-making, and responsibility.

SPINAL CORD INJURIES

The spinal cord, running through the vertebrae that make up the backbone, is the nervous system's major link between the brain and the body's various organs. Injuries to the back or neck can cause damage, or even complete severing, of the spinal cord. If an injury does not prove fatal, there may be interruption of nerve messages to the parts of the body below the injury. This results in partial or total paralysis of those organs and muscles. There is little or no sensation, and the muscles can no longer be directed by the brain to contract. Typically, the spinal cord does not heal and repair itself, so the paralysis is permanent. If only the legs are paralyzed, the person is said to be paraplegic; if the arms are involved as well, the term used is quadriplegic.

Not long ago, it was assumed that paraplegics and quadriplegics were incapable of sexual response. More recently, spinal cord injury patients are being encouraged to enjoy sexual expression. The degree of interference with sexual functions depends on the exact location and extent of the injury to the spinal cord. When paralysis of the pelvic region exists, thinking sexy thoughts or having sexual needs no longer has any effect on the genitals, because the connection with the brain has been lost. However, erection of the penis and lubrication of the vagina are also partially controlled by a localized spinal reflex. Many paralyzed men and women can experience arousal of their sex organs, and sometimes even orgasm, through direct stimulation. There may also be small areas of skin in the pelvic area where feeling remains intact.

Each case of spinal cord injury is unique, but any patient and his or her partner can learn new forms of sexual expression. Often, intercourse is still possible, with adjustments in position. Some paraplegics and quadriplegics have a bladder catheter (tube) in place to carry urine out of the body to a storage bag. While the catheter may be an inconvenience during sex, a couple committed to maintaining their sexual relationship can learn how to accommodate it (Dahlberg & James, 1991).

Often, the partners of people whose spinal cords have been injured are left out of the adjustment and rehabilitation process. They too have many emotional issues to resolve as they face a very stressful time in

paraplegic: a person paralyzed in the legs, and sometimes pelvic areas, as the result of injury to the spinal cord.
quadriplegic: a person paralyzed in the upper body, including the arms, and lower body as the result of spinal cord injury.

Case Study

SAM AND MARSHA: A PARAPLEGIC REDISCOVERS SEX

As the result of a diving accident Sam was paralyzed from the waist down. He had been married to Marsha only a few months before the accident. During her first few visits with Sam in the hospital Marsha found him to be aloof and depressed. Several times, he indicated that it might be best for them to consider a divorce. Marsha urged him to join her in talking with a rehabilitation counselor at the hospital. Eventually, Sam's fears of sexual inadequacy emerged, and he stated that he didn't see how he could be much of a husband in his condition.

The counselor referred Sam and Marsha to a special group that helped paraplegics and quadriplegics explore and develop whatever levels of sexual functioning they retained. Before long the two were reporting that Sam could still maintain full erection and, with Marsha's cooperation in

finding suitable positions, still have intercourse. He was especially thrilled to discover that he could still experience a pleasurable orgasm, even though there was no ejaculation of semen. As their marriage and sex continued, it became clear that both Sam and Marsha wanted to maintain their relationship. Sam gradually emerged from his depression and became self-sufficient enough to return home in a wheelchair. He now occasionally returns to the hospital to talk with other spinal cord injury victims about their sexual worries. He firmly believes that anyone can find sexual pleasure with a little exploration, regardless of the severity of their injury. Sam and Marsha are now investigating the possibility of adopting children or of Marsha becoming pregnant through artificial insemination.

---

adjusting to the changes that occur in the relationship, including its sexual dimensions. For married couples in which one of the partners is injured after they were married, the relational difficulties frequently lead to marital disharmony or divorce. Again, however, with appropriate and skilled professional help, couples may be helped to learn how to recapture a viable emotional and physical relationship following the devastating effects of spinal injury (Neumann, 1991).

Increasingly, institutions involved in the rehabilitation of spinal cord injury patients are dealing with their sexual concerns, and providing techniques to assist with their sexual readjustments. It may be that women's concerns in this area have been less clearly addressed than men's, since their sexual interactions are not as closely linked with a physiological response such as penile erection (Zwerner, 1982).

OTHER PHYSICAL AND MENTAL DISABILITIES

Many chronic physical conditions and mental illnesses can affect sexual functioning and the place of sex in relationships. These may be diseased or damaged sex organs, general physical debilitation that lowers interest and energy for sex, difficulty in socializing, or lowered feelings of self-worth.

Cerebral palsy can cause spastic conditions in various parts of the body. Victims of heart attacks or strokes may be physically debilitated and may worry about how much physical exertion they can withstand during and after their recovery. A variety of neuromuscular conditions, such as multiple sclerosis and muscular dystrophy, can result in gradual loss of bodily control. Chronic lung disease makes exertion during sex difficult and uncomfortable. Cancer can affect sexual organs and/or general body fitness. Mental and emotional illnesses, ranging from depression to schizophrenia, can rob patients of a sense of security and well-being basic to fulfilling sex (Sha'ked, 1978).

Terminally ill patients often experience sexual disruption because of internal stress, which, in turn, affects relationships. They may feel guilty about experiencing sexual arousal, and their lovers may find it difficult to desire intimacy when experiencing anticipatory grief or fear of their partner's fatal illness. However, open communication and, when available, counseling and the opportunity for privacy in hospital settings can all help with the sexual adjustments of long-term illness (Waxberg & Mostel, 1980).

When people approach the special sexual problems associated with their disabilities and illnesses honestly, they can make new adaptive approaches to sex. It is important to recognize that sexual needs remain even when there is a health crisis, disability, or

251

in the aftermath of a serious injury or illness. To help maintain one's involvement in sexual activities can also help maintain one's sense of integrity and personal self-worth. The English historian Arnold Toynbee wrote, "Love cannot save life from death, but it can fulfill life's purpose."

INSTITUTIONS

Some people with disabilities and chronic illnesses require long-term institutional care, in which sexual problems may multiply. Where the sexes are segregated, institutional residents may be limited to homosexual contact. There may be little privacy for masturbation or shared sex. The key to preventing desexualization in institutions is the attitude of the staff. Often, in-service training on sex-related issues, along with establishment of humane administrative policies regarding sex, can help. The first step in preventing sexual problems relating to those who are disabled, ill, or institutionalized is being able to admit that all human beings are sexual and that they have a right to find the best ways for them, as individuals, to express that sexuality (Shore & Gochros, 1981). ■

CHAPTER SUMMARY

1. Human beings have the potential for participating in and being drawn to a range of sexual activities.

2. Heterosexual attraction and intercourse have often represented the standards by which other orientations and activities have been judged. The words and labels applied to sexual matters frequently reflect socially influenced judgments about their degree of normalcy.

3. General labels such as deviation, variation, and paraphilia have been applied to sexual activities and preferences that fall outside of the accepted norm.

4. In present-day Western culture, sex is still judged by several fundamental standards: two-person heterosexuality, a focus on coitus, and expectation of orgasm and romantic feelings.

5. Other historical periods and cultures have seen different prevailing standards of sexual conduct. Ethnocentric attitudes that one's own culture has the right standards includes sexuality in what can be called erotocentricity.

6. The concept of normalcy can be determined by statistical norms, prevailing expert opinion, moral standards perpetuated by religion and law, or as part of a more flexible continuum. Normalcy is a relative concept.

7. Labels represent generalities and are inadequate to a full understanding of a particular person's sexuality.

8. The factors that lead to the development of sexual individuality are highly complex and only poorly understood. Patterns seem to be fairly well estab-

lished by adolescence and probably develop through a combination of learning experiences, possibly superimposed on some biological predispositions.

9. Everyone faces the need to make decisions about the sexual choices faced in life. In doing so, moral values, religious teachings, and the ethics represented in a particular situation are weighed.

10. Religions exert strong influences on social sexual attitudes, from either fixed or evolutionary world views. In recent years religions have been debating and changing their positions with regard to sexuality.

11. In developing sexual values that are right for you, it is necessary to see how you will align yourself with the values of your society and culture. Self-examination and introspection are necessary to making decisions that will be healthy and nonhurtful for yourself and others.

12. Sex education represents one of the major ways in which sexual problems may be prevented. The attitude among the general public has tended to be favorable toward sex education in schools, although studies show that young people still get most of their sex information from peers or the media.

13. Several new trends, including research, technical advances, teaching of decision-making skills, changing sexual values, the "just say no" approach, the need for more coordinated efforts, and the AIDS crisis are shaping the future of sex education in the United States.

14. Some professional groups, such as medical stu-

dents, social workers, and counselors in training, have been receiving education to assist them in dealing with sexual concerns of future patients/clients.

15. People with physical and mental disabilities have sexual feelings and needs, although they may need to learn how to manage and cope with their sexual expression in special ways. People who are disabled have the right to recognition of their sexuality.

16. Mentally retarded people need special approaches to sex education, including how to express their sexuality in private and how to employ appropri-

ate methods of birth control. They are particularly vulnerable to sexual abuse.

17. Visually and hearing impaired individuals may require special sex education and help in learning how to manage their loving and sexual relationships.

18. Spinal cord injuries may affect physical aspects of sexual response. Most paraplegics and quadriplegics can find levels of sexual functioning that will be satisfying to themselves and their partners.

19. Many other handicaps and illnesses may have sex-related implications to which personal adaptations can be found.

ANNOTATED READINGS

Caplan, P. (Ed.) (1987). *The cultural construction of sexuality.* New York: Tavistock Publications. Offers a cross-cultural perspective on human sexuality, examining sexual mores and behaviors in several different cultures. Some historical implications are also covered.

Goldenson, R. M., & Anderson, K. N. (1986). *The language of sex from A to Z.* New York: World Almanac/Walter D. Glanze. A comprehensive dictionary that defines nearly 5,000 sexological terms. Not for leisure reading, but an excellent resource.

Kempton, W., Bass, M., & Gordon, S. (1985). *Love, sex, and birth control for the mentally handicapped.* Philadelphia: Planned Parenthood of Southeastern Pennsylvania. Covers the crucial issues relating to sexuality for mentally handicapped persons, with suggestions for sex education.

Mooney, T. O., Cole, T. M., & Chilgren, R. A. (1975). *Sexual options for paraplegics and quadriplegics.* Boston: Little, Brown. An explicitly illustrated guide to sexual activities for people who have varying degrees of paralysis. It is a factual and reassuring book.

Rabin, B. J. (1980). *The sensuous wheeler: Sexual adjustment for the spinal cord injured.* (Available from the author at 5595 E. 7th St., Long Beach, CA 90804 for $6.95.) A down-to-earth and sensitively written book to help people with spinal cord injuries sort through their sexual feelings, needs, and activities.

Williams, W. (1986). *The spirit and the flesh: Sexual diversity in American Indian culture.* Boston: Beacon Press. A fascinating look at sexual customs and practices of Native American cultures. A good reminder of how sexual customs are strongly influenced by cultural and societal imperatives.

CHAPTER TEN

SOLITARY SEX: MASTURBATION
How Girls and Women Masturbate
How Boys and Men Masturbate
Fantasy and Pictures in Masturbation
Facts and Fallacies About Masturbation
Masturbation and Morality

SHARED SEXUAL BEHAVIOR
Nongenital Oral Stimulation
Stimulation of Erogenous Zones
Oral-Genital and Oral-Anal Sex
Mutual Manual Stimulation and Masturbation
Interfemoral and Anal Intercourse
Vibrators, Pornography, and Fantasies
Chemical Aphrodisiacs

HETEROSEXUAL INTERCOURSE
Sexual Intercourse and AIDS
Intromission
Intercourse
Positions for Intercourse
Reclining Face-to-Face
Other Variations on Face-to-Face
Rear Vaginal Entry
After Sexual Relations
Intercourse and Marriage

CHAPTER SUMMARY

After the first time I had sex, I was flooded with all sorts of conflicting thoughts and feelings. It suddenly hit me that after all the years of wondering, planning, avoiding, and wanting, I was no longer a virgin. Then I wondered why I had made such a big deal out of the whole thing. For one thing, I felt relieved that the "big step" had been taken. But I also felt a little sad, as though I had left something of myself behind that I could never have back. One minute I'd feel thrilled and excited, and the next I'd feel sad or angry with myself. Sometimes it seems to me that we've blown this whole business of sex way out of proportion.

—From a student's essay

SOLITARY SEX AND SHARED SEX

This chapter examines closely some of the most common sexual behaviors in which human beings participate. Although masturbation and sexual intercourse constitute primary parts of the discussion, many other forms of sexual experiences that can be shared by partners are also examined.

The Kinsey research studies (1948, 1953) were the first to collect statistics on sexual behavior from a large sample of the population. They represented the first attempt at gathering reliable information on the sexual activities in which people engage. Although Kinsey emphasized that the statistics gained from his sample of about 16,000 individuals could not be generalized to the total human population, they represent the most reliable figures on which to base at least some ideas concerning human sexual behavior. As I have said in earlier chapters, no surveys of sexual behavior have the depth or the reliability of the Kinsey studies. But it is dangerous to generalize on the basis of available data concerning sexual behavior. It is advisable to interpret statistics on behavior cited in this and other chapters with caution. They can be considered approximations of what people are doing and only that.

Perhaps we also ought to examine the relative usefulness of our numbers. While statistics can give us interesting information and establish certain statistical norms for human sexual behavior, we must be cautious not to assume that such data represent standards for behavior. Just because most males masturbate does not mean that males should masturbate or that nonmasturbating males are abnormal. Just because the majority of females have not experienced intercourse by the age of 17 does not mean that 15-year-old females who have intercourse are immoral.

Statistics are just that—numbers that summarize the activities of a group of people. The chapters in this book that describe human sexual behaviors consider the statistical evidence. However, the most significant fact is that these behaviors exist. They are a part of what human beings can experience sexually. How many humans experience them, and how often, are secondary considerations. Each of us possesses his or her own specific sexual interests, values, preferences, needs, and behaviors. These aspects of our sexuality may change many times during our lifetimes, since sexual individuality as a dynamic process is always in a

255

state of flux. I hope the information in these chapters can help you gain a clear understanding of your own sexuality as it is now and inform you of the spectrum of sexual behaviors open to human beings.

Solitary Sex: Masturbation

Masturbation is apparently one of the commonest ways in which human beings seek sexual pleasure. I will use the term masturbation to refer to deliberate, rhythmic stimulation of the sex organs—often along with other parts of the body—to produce pleasurable sexual sensations and (usually) orgasm. Genital self-stimulation in early childhood is often too nonsexual to be considered masturbation, although some children do masturbate. Masturbation is not confined to the human species; it is common among many mammals, especially the primates. No other form of sexual behavior has been subject to as much misunderstanding, folklore, religious attention, moral analysis, and ignorance on the part of professionals as masturbation. Although the wild tales of the evils of masturbation have gradually died away, some misconceptions remain for many people.

The Kinsey statistics (1948, 1953) indicated that at least 92 percent of men and 62 percent of women reported having masturbated at some time in their lives, and these findings have been closely substantiated by other studies (Hunt, 1975; Atwood & Gagnon, 1987). While research with representative samples is generally lacking in this area, some recent questionnaire studies have suggested that more women are masturbating today than previously. The figures may now indicate that between 75 percent and 82 percent of women have masturbated (Hite, 1977; Levin & Levin, 1975). It is also clear that men masturbate more

frequently than women, and that they experience more personal guilt about the practice (Darling & Davidson, 1987).

However, exact statistics are of little importance. The fact is that many individuals have masturbated, and many of them have done so on a regular basis. Each of these individuals has found her or his own meaning for masturbation—ranging from the guilt-ridden, hurriedly finished, hidden act to the fully enjoyed, unhurried, luxuriously sensual experience which can even be shared with someone else. The techniques that one uses in masturbation are also highly individualized.

HOW GIRLS AND WOMEN MASTURBATE

Masturbation is one way in which many women become acquainted with their own sexual responsiveness and learn how to have an orgasm. This may serve them well as they develop their responsiveness with a partner. Masters and Johnson (1966) reported on the results of observing hundreds of women masturbating, an act which those researchers have termed auto-manipulation. Although no two women were observed to masturbate in exactly the same way, very few of them seemed to use direct stimulation of the glans clitoris. The tissues of the clitoral glans are apparently too sensitive for any prolonged direct stimulation, just as the glans of the penis is. Women who stimulate the clitoris tend to stroke gently only the shaft. Right-handed women usually manipulate the right side of the shaft and left-handed women the left side.

A more common way for females to masturbate is by manipulation of the entire mons area, and this exerts less direct stimulation to the clitoris. The minor lips or other areas surrounding the clitoris are also frequently stimulated. It is important to note that

FIGURE 10.1 Female Masturbation

immediately following orgasm, the clitoral glans is especially sensitive to touch or pressure, and most women avoid touching it at that time.

While use of the hands is the most common method of masturbation, many girls and women find other means of stimulating their genitals. Rubbing the mons or other parts of the vulva against a pillow, bed, doorknob, or some other object is quite typical. It is also not unusual for a female to insert a finger or some suitably shaped long object into the vagina during masturbation. Cylindrical electric vibrators or flexible plastic devices (often called dildos) may also be used during masturbation (Hite, 1977). Some women are able to produce sexual arousal and orgasm by creating muscular tension in the pelvic region through the tightening of leg and abdominal muscles. Others may cross their legs and apply rhythmic stimulation to the vulva by contracting and relaxing the thigh muscles.

An oriental invention, recently introduced to Western culture, can also be used by women for self-stimulation. It consists of two hollow metal spheres, called ben-wa balls, one of which contains small pellets. They are inserted into the vagina and held in place by a tampon. Movement of the body causes the two balls to vibrate and that is reported to produce pleasurable vaginal sensations. Women sometimes find that running a stream of warm water over the vulva, and especially the clitoris, or sitting in a whirlpool bath can create sexual stimulation. Many women stimulate other parts of their bodies while masturbating. Stimulation of the breasts and nipples is very common, and some women enjoy stroking the anal region. There are many individual differences in the ways people stimulate themselves for sexual pleasure. No one pattern needs to be considered the only right way of doing so.

Common sense dictates that cleanliness should be observed during masturbation and that women should not insert sharp, pointed, or rasping objects into their vaginas. It is also important not to introduce bacteria from the anal region into the genital area, since infection may result.

HOW BOYS AND MEN MASTURBATE

Masters and Johnson (1966) also found highly individualized methods of masturbating in the hundreds of men they observed. Some type of stimulation of the penis almost always occurs in male masturbation. Typically the penis is grasped by the hand and stroked until orgasm takes place. How the penis is grasped and stroked varies with different males.

The most common method is for the man to stroke the shaft of the penis, just touching the top edge of the corona around the glans and the frenulum on the underside where the glans and shaft join. The amount of pressure used, number of fingers employed on the penis, how rapidly the stroking proceeds, and how far up and down the hand moves, all vary from man to man. Some men—particularly those with circumcised penises—stimulate just the glans by pulling at it or rubbing its entire surface. As men get closer to orgasm, the stroking or rubbing of the penis tends to become more rapid, then usually slowing or stopping during actual ejaculation. This is in direct contrast to most women, who continue stroking the clitoris during orgasm.

During manual masturbation, many men enjoy occasionally using both hands to stroke the penis, or using their free hand to fondle the scrotum or anal region. Some men insert a finger or object into the anus during masturbation. It is also not unusual for a male to use some sort of lubricating jelly or liquid on his hand during masturbation to create intense sexual sensations.

It seems safe to assume that most boys and men

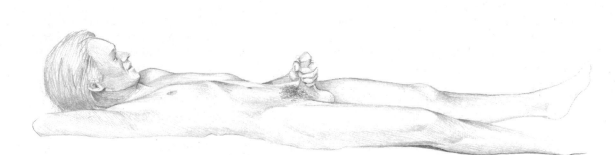

FIGURE 10.2 Male Masturbation

experiment with a variety of ways of producing orgasm. Many males enjoy rubbing their penises on blankets, pillows, beds, and other suitable objects. Kinsey (1948) reported that a significant proportion of men attempt autofellatio at one time or another; that is, they try to put their penises into their own mouths, a feat which very few have the acrobatic capability to achieve.

There are also masturbation aids that are marketed for men. These include rubber pouches into which the penis can be inserted, artificial vaginas made of plastic and often showing the external organs of the vulva, and full-sized inflatable dolls that have built-in pouches at the location of the vagina, mouth, and/or anus.

A few boys and men enjoy inserting objects into the urethra at the end of the penis, especially those who find pain sexually arousing. There are obvious dangers to this practice, since injury or infection in the urethra could result. Physicians occasionally see boys or men who have inserted some small object into their urethras, only to have it become lodged there. Again, it is common sense that masturbation should be done with attention to basic cleanliness and safety, so that genito-urinary injury or infection will not result.

FANTASY AND PICTURES IN MASTURBATION

Many people fantasize about other sexual activities while masturbating. The most common fantasies are about sexual activity with a loved partner, although fantasies about sexual involvement with acquaintances and strangers are also very typical. Additionally there is the whole gamut of fantasies about group sex, being forced to have sex, raping another person, and every other imaginable form of behavior (Hunt, 1975). The Sorensen (1973) data show the similarity of these fantasy patterns during adolescence as well.

Some people occasionally view erotic photographs or videotapes or read erotic literature as an accompaniment to masturbation, or are stimulated to masturbate by such materials. Pornography seems to hold more appeal for men than women, although the studies cited in chapter 6, "Gender-Identity/Role and Society," suggest that this difference could be the result of socialization. It is probably safe to assume that erotic pictures, videos, and literature help to generate fantasies in many individuals during masturbation and that people often project themselves into the subject matter of the erotic material.

FACTS AND FALLACIES ABOUT MASTURBATION

It is surprising how many myths and misconceptions about masturbation persist. The next few paragraphs attempt to separate the fallacies from the facts. Each of the following italicized statements is a fact.

autofellatio (fe-LAY-she-o): a male providing oral stimulation to his own penis, an act most males do not have the physical agility to perform.

Case Study

LAURA: GUILT OVER MASTURBATION

Laura grew up in a family that displayed relatively liberal attitudes toward sex. She began masturbating at the age of 9 and continued to masturbate occasionally throughout her teenage years. She accepted the normalcy of her practice and enjoyed it.

At the age of 22, Laura had a long-standing relationship with a young man she met in her sophomore year at college. They were planning on marriage, and they shared sexual intercourse regularly. She enjoyed their sexual relationship and felt no guilt because of it. However, she did feel some guilt because she continued to masturbate from time to time. Laura confided to a counselor that she felt as though she was cheat-

ing on her boyfriend by masturbating. She had always had the impression that when people established adult sexual relationships they should no longer masturbate.

The counselor discussed with Laura the possibility of her telling the boyfriend about her worries concerning masturbation. Eventually she did so and was surprised to learn that her boyfriend felt similar guilt, for he, too, had been masturbating quite regularly and had experienced strong concerns about cheating on Laura. After talking the matter over, both lost their guilty feelings and understood one another better.

Fact: Masturbation is not confined to childhood and adolescence or to single persons. Many adult men and women—including married individuals—continue to masturbate throughout their lives. There is solid evidence to indicate that the majority of adult males and over half of adult females masturbate from time to time. Their frequency of masturbation decreases with age, and single adults tend to masturbate more than married individuals. The average frequency of masturbation for unmarried adult men up to the age of 45 is roughly once or twice a week, with some decline in frequency for older age groups. The rates for married men are lower, usually closer to once or twice a month. Unmarried women who masturbate average once every 2 or 3 weeks up to the age of 55. Married women average slightly less, closer to once a month. It should be emphasized that these averages are obtained by including those who masturbate very seldom (once or twice a year) and those who masturbate more frequently (once a day or more). All of these patterns are found in normal, healthy, happy individuals.

Fact: Masturbation is not necessarily a substitute for sex with a partner. It is certainly true that masturbation is often used as a substitute for sexual activity with a partner. For people of all age groups who do not have an available partner—those who have chosen to postpone intercourse, individuals who are separated from their partners, and many others—masturbation is frequently used as a substitute source of sexual outlet. However, masturbation can also be viewed as a form of sexual expression in itself, regardless of what other sexual activities the individual has available. Many people who have very fulfilling sexual lives and have access to shared sexual activity whenever they wish still enjoy masturbating. Some people may actually prefer masturbation over other forms of sexual behavior. This should not be considered a sign of immaturity or sexual dissatisfaction. These individuals have simply integrated masturbation into their lives as one means of sexual gratification.

Fact: Masturbation can be shared. In my counseling and sex therapy practice, I never cease to be surprised by the number of couples who share sex but who never even discuss masturbation. Even though both partners may be masturbating regularly, it is often impossible for them to admit that fact to one another. Being able to surmount this communication barrier and talk about masturbation can be an important step toward better sexual communication. Some couples find that masturbating together or watching one another masturbate can be an enjoyable form of sexual sharing.

Fact: There is no such thing as excessive masturbation. For years books on sex for young people have implied that there is nothing wrong with masturbation, so long as it is not practiced to excess. The fact is that there is no medical definition of what excessive masturbation might be. There are apparently no dangers of physical harm, regardless of the frequency of masturbation. For the most part it seems to be a self-limiting practice, and when the individual is sexually satiated, he or she loses interest in being sexually aroused. The number of orgasms necessary to reach satiation will vary among individuals and their circumstances. Of course, if a person has masturbated to satiation, she or he may not be interested in other forms of sex for a while. Masters and Johnson (1966) reported that most men they questioned expressed vague concerns over excessive masturbation but consistently established the frequency which they considered excessive to be greater than their own masturbatory frequency. A man who masturbated once a month stated that once or twice a week would be excessive; while a man who masturbated 2 or 3 times a day thought that 5 or 6 times a day might be excessive.

Fact: Masturbation can be as physically sexually satisfying as intercourse. From a purely physical standpoint, masturbation can offer full sexual satisfaction for some people. Of course, if physical and emotional intimacy with another person is important to an individual's full experiencing of sexual feelings, masturbation will leave some gaps. Particularly in women, however, masturbation often provides the opportunity for the kind of self-regulated stimulation that produces a more intense orgasm than can be obtained with coitus (Masters & Johnson, 1966). Some of that effective stimulation can be transferred to shared sex when the partners have good communication about sex.

Fact: Masturbation does not hinder the development of social relationships or create problems in a relationship. Masturbation usually is a very private form of sex, but most sexual behavior requires some degree of privacy. It is also true that some individuals, who are too shy to establish meaningful relationships with others or to pursue sexual relationships, may masturbate as an alternative way of getting sexual gratification. But there is no evidence that masturbation causes further shyness or social alienation. In fact it may constitute good self-preparation for later sexual experiences involving other people. Neither is there evidence to support a contention that masturbation inevitably creates problems in a relationship. Some couples talk about masturbation together, and find it to be an acceptable practice for both partners.

Fact: Masturbation is a good way to learn about one's own sexual feelings and responsiveness. Among sex therapists and educators today, the attitude is quite prevalent that masturbation is not only healthy and normal, but that it can be a very useful learning experience. In males it is likely that patterns of sexual functioning may be influenced by early patterns of masturbation. For the boy who learns to masturbate to orgasm in the shortest possible time, the pattern may well carry over into later intercourse as premature ejaculation (Kaplan, 1974). Men who have learned to prolong the time it takes to ejaculate during masturbation often can transfer that ability into intercourse. When discussing masturbation with young men, I often encourage them to use masturbation as a learning experience that will prepare them to be effective sexual partners by developing their control over the orgasmic process. For women masturbation is recognized as an important way to learn first what orgasm feels like and how to produce it. Various masturbation exercises are commonly used as a preliminary step toward orgasmic response and full enjoyment in shared sexual activity (Barbach, 1980).

Fact: Masturbation does not lead to weakness, mental illness, or physical debilitation. Even within the past century, masturbation was blamed for all sorts of mental and physical maladies. There was a long-standing belief that a male's semen was a vital body fluid related to strength and that it must be conserved at all cost. It is now clear that there are no medical conditions caused by masturbation, regardless of frequency. Coaches often have warned athletes to avoid masturbation, or other forms of sex, especially the night before the big game, because they see it as an energy-sapping practice. While orgasm may indeed release tension and lead to relaxation, many athletes claim that this can be a real help to their performance. Masturbation does not drain the body of energy.

Fact: Males do not eventually run out of semen if they masturbate frequently. It has been a common misconception that the male body is granted the potential of producing only a certain amount of semen and that each ejaculation leads a man closer to the bottom of the barrel. In actuality the glands that produce sperm and semen tend to be active from puberty into old age. They do not cease production after a certain number of orgasms. In fact evidence shows that the more sexually active an individual is in earlier life, the more active he or she will be in later years. The more semen a male ejaculates, the more his body produces.

Fact: Masturbation does not lead to homosexuality. In many people's minds masturbation is associated with homosexuality. Apparently the idea of a person seeking pleasure from her or his own genitals is interpreted as sexual attraction to same-sexed genitals. This is not true. Heterosexuals masturbate and so do homosexuals. The practice does not change the sexual preferences of either.

Fact: Masturbation is not physically essential. Some people—particularly men—believe that it may be harmful to abstain from having orgasms. They fear that storing sperm and semen may eventually be harmful to the body. Actually, the body adjusts its production of semen to the amount of sexual activity, and "extra" semen can be released through nocturnal emissions. While masturbation can be a pleasurable learning experience and important to a persons' sexual life, it is not essential for physical or mental well-being.

MASTURBATION AND MORALITY

As with all other forms of sexual behavior, various cultures and religions have attached many different moral implications to masturbation. The Judeo-Christian-Muslim position has predominantly been anti-masturbation. The story of Onan has often been cited as evidence of the sinfulness of masturbation. The Old Testament tells that while having sexual intercourse with his deceased brother's wife, Onan withdrew before ejaculation and "spilled his seed on the ground." God was angered and struck him dead. Actually, of course, Onan was not masturbating but practicing what we now call coitus interruptus or withdrawal as a means of birth control. In any case, masturbation has also been called onanism and condemned by some religions. Very few religious groups continue to prohibit masturbation today.

It is clear that each individual—considering the religious, parental, and peer values of his or her background—must decide whether or not to masturbate. Long-term guilt or worry about masturbation can cause negative feelings about oneself. If such feelings are intense, talking with a professional counselor may be advisable.

Shared Sexual Behavior

In our culture when two people encounter one another for sexual expression, there is a reasonably predictable progression through levels of increased intimacy. Generally, the pattern proceeds from kissing and caressing to fondling of the genitals—first outside the clothing and then inside—to various states of nudity and varying degrees of direct genital contact. At what point the progression ceases and whether or not it leads to orgasm depends on the relationship between the two

---

onanism (O-na-niz-um): a term sometimes used to describe masturbation, it comes from the biblical story of Onan, who practiced coitus interruptus and "spilled his seed on the ground."

individuals, their sex-related values, and a variety of other factors.

The kinds of physical contact described in this section are often sexually arousing and constitute what many couples consider a prelude to activities that may or may not involve intercourse and that may include orgasm. (It is important to recognize that intercourse is only one of a number of behaviors that can lead to orgasm; and for a significant number of women, intercourse often is not the behavior most likely to result in orgasm.) These kinds of physical contact are often collectively termed foreplay. As in many other aspects of a continuing sexual relationship, there is a gradual learning process between the partners concerning their own individual preferences for various activities. Conflicts may arise when one partner finds a particular activity to be appealing and desirable while the other partner finds it to be offensive or unappealing. Such conflicts may have to be accepted as a part of the relationship and appropriate compromises made, but it is also quite typical for people to experiment with new activities as a relationship progresses, sometimes even learning to enjoy them more than before.

NONGENITAL ORAL STIMULATION

The lips, tongue, and oral cavity are often associated with intimate, sexually arousing activity. The oral areas are highly innervated, moist, and associated with pleasurable sensations of taste and food consumption. The movability of the tongue and lips affords them versatility and allows them to be voluntarily controlled by the individual. All of these factors are probably involved in the various uses of the mouth in pleasurable sexual sharing.

Although there exist a few small societies where it is not practiced, kissing is used to express affection in most parts of the world. Kissing usually carries with it important messages concerning the depth of intimacy in a relationship. The least intimate kind of kissing is the simple peck on the cheek. Lengthy lip contact, gentle rubbing of another person's lips, and insertion of the tongue into the partner's mouth (French kissing or soul kissing) are considered to be more deeply intimate and sexually arousing. Kissing, licking, or nibbling at other parts of the body—such as the abdomen, breasts, ears, or genitals—is also considered to be particularly intimate by many.

STIMULATION OF EROGENOUS ZONES

There are certain areas of the body that almost always generate sexual arousal when they are touched. The glans penis and the clitoris are two examples of

FIGURE 10.3 Kissing

In most parts of the world, kissing is a sign of affection. This young couple in Germany share a warm and loving moment.

particularly sexually sensitive organs. However, it seems that almost any area of the body can become conditioned to respond erotically to tactile stimulation in particular individuals. If touching a particular part of a person's body leads to sexual arousal, the area is called an erogenous zone for that person. Typical nongenital erogenous zones are the mouth, earlobes, breasts, buttocks, lower abdomen, inner thighs, and the anal-perineal area. In a fulfilling sexual relationship, it is important for both partners to learn about the most pleasurable kinds of stimulation to exert on the zones.

In devising methods for the treatment of sexual dysfunctions (see chapter 16), Masters and Johnson (1970) recognized that touch is a vital part of the experience that gives meaning to sexual responsiveness for women and men. Their therapy program

261

encourages couples to spend time together in the nude, gently massaging, fondling, and tracing one another's bodies in pleasurable ways. Both partners are encouraged to accept and enjoy being stimulated to the fullest possible extent. Most people in our culture find some degree of sexual arousal in having their bodies close to another naked body and having the opportunity to share touching experiences. The sense of touch is usually an essential part of sexual arousal.

Some people find an element of sexual arousal in more aggressive forms of touch. Sexual contact can have its aggressive, even violent, sides. Light scratching, pinching, and biting are considered enjoyable by some. It is not unusual for one partner to bite and suck the other during strong sexual passion, even to the extent of producing a bruise. Such a bruise on the neck is commonly called a hickey, and it seems to represent a badge of experience for some individuals.

ORAL-GENITAL AND ORAL-ANAL SEX

Some individuals report deriving intense pleasure from being orally stimulated, partly because they can relax and enjoy it, and because the partner can provide intense, localized stimulation. Oral sex is a popular form of pleasuring between same-sexed partners, but it is by no means limited to homosexual couples. Many heterosexual couples include oral sex in their repertoire of sexual behaviors. While using the mouth to stimulate the genitals of a sexual partner can be highly exciting for some people, it can be distinctly disgusting for others. The term fellatio refers to kissing, licking, or sucking on the penis or allowing the penis to move in and out of the mouth. Some men particularly enjoy oral stimulation of the frenulum on the underside of the penile head, one of their most sensitive genital areas. Cunnilingus involves kissing, licking, or sucking the clitoris, labia, and vaginal opening or inserting the tongue into the vagina. Sometimes partners perform oral sex on one another simultaneously, the position called, in slang, "sixty-nine," due to the relative positions of the bodies.

The Kinsey studies (1948, 1953) indicated that attitudes toward oral-genital sex varied with educational level. About 50 percent of college-educated men and only 5 percent of those with grade school educations reported having stimulated their female partners by cunnilingus. Only about 40 percent of all the women in the sample had orally stimulated their male partners, and in most cases it was done infrequently. The study by Hunt (1975) suggests that oral-genital sex is either becoming more prevalently practiced or that people are less reluctant to admit to the practice. This survey reported that 80 percent of single males and

females between the ages of 25 and 34 had engaged in oral-genital sex during the previous year, and 90 percent of married persons under the age of 25 had done so. One study indicated that over 80 percent of college students had participated in oral-genital sex in the mid-1980s, only a slight increase in figures for 1974 (Story, 1985). The statistics also suggest that the most significant increases have taken place in the groups with less education, particularly males. Oral-genital stimulation has apparently increased in acceptability for the general population, but especially for those with lower educational levels.

Oral-genital sex has been considered a relatively safe practice, providing that rules of basic hygiene are followed. Some partners fear that the male will ejaculate semen into their mouths during fellatio because of the mistaken notion that the substance is, in itself, dangerous to ingest. If the male is known to be free of sexually transmitted diseases and prostate infection, and the partner wishes to do so, there is no particular danger in swallowing semen (Fiumara, 1975). It is simply digested.

There are new concerns about the spread of AIDS through oral sex, however, and unless there is absolute certainty about a partner's lack of exposure to this disease, a condom should be worn during fellatio or a rubber dam (the kind used in dental work) placed over the vulva during cunnilingus. As yet there have not been any studies concerning the actual effectiveness of rubber dams in preventing transmission of the AIDS virus, but experts have reasoned that any barrier to the mixing of body fluids certainly reduces the risks. How practical the rubber dam can be in even acting as such a barrier is particularly debatable. Other infections can be transmitted through oral-genital contact, including most sexually transmitted diseases, throat infections from the genital bacteria, and urethral or vaginal infections transmitted from the mouth. It is unsafe to blow on the penis during fellatio (even though a common slang term is "blow job") or to blow into the vagina during cunnilingus, since bacteria may be forced in or actual injury can result. There are some indications that air blowing into the vagina, particularly during pregnancy, can lead to air embolisms in a woman's blood vessels that are potentially fatal.

Sometimes the anal region is stimulated orally, but strict hygienic measures are crucial to prevent transmission of bacteria. Even with thorough washing, there is a chance of some rectal bacteria being in-

fellatio: oral stimulation of the penis.
cunnilingus (kun-a-LEAN-gus): oral stimulation of the clitoris, vaginal opening, or other parts of the vulva.
rubber dam: a piece of rubber material, such as used in dental work, placed over the vulva during cunnilingus.

gested. This practice would again be considered dangerous if there were any chance that the AIDS virus were present in the person being stimulated anally. A rubber dam can be placed over the anal region to protect against transmission of AIDS, other STDs, and bacteria.

MUTUAL MANUAL STIMULATION AND MASTURBATION

Most sexually active couples use some form of mutual manual stimulation of the genitals. The clitoris may be manipulated with a finger, although direct stimulation of the glans can be uncomfortable for some. One or more fingers might be inserted into the vagina and moved. The penis may be grasped and stroked and the scrotum fondled. These techniques are often used by sexual partners to stimulate each other to orgasm. Mutual manual stimulation of genitals and the anal region is also one of the most common forms of foreplay.

Although some couples find it difficult to discuss their masturbatory practices and even more difficult to masturbate in each other's presence, others report that they find enjoyment in watching one another masturbate and in being so observed. Masturbation is still considered a relatively taboo subject, and to break through these barriers apparently often represents a level of intimacy even deeper than sharing other forms of sex. Masturbation is usually a very private experience and sharing it can generate extreme sexual excitement. Many couples at least occasionally incorporate manual stimulation of the partner or masturbation into their sexual activities.

INTERFEMORAL AND ANAL INTERCOURSE

Many sexual partnerships including at least one male make use of various forms of nonvaginal penile intercourse. The penis is versatile and may be inserted into the partner's hand, between female breasts, between the buttocks, or between the thighs (interfemoral intercourse), or it may be rubbed on the partner's abdomen or any other body area. These forms of sexual activity are often accompanied by pelvic thrusting.

It is wise for heterosexual couples who practice interfemoral intercourse to know that if semen is ejaculated near or at the vaginal opening, there is some risk of pregnancy. Even a small amount of semen entering the vagina will carry sperm, and though the chances are minimal, it is possible for some of those sperm to travel into the fallopian tubes and fertilize an ovum.

A type of sexual sharing that seems to wax and wane in popularity is anal intercourse, insertion of the penis into the partner's rectum. Hunt (1974) reported that about 50 percent of the married men and over 25 percent of the married women between the ages of 18 and 34 in his sample had attempted anal intercourse at least once. The anal sphincter muscles tend to resist penile entry, and it usually takes appropriate lubrication (such as K-Y surgical jelly), gentle prodding by the penis, and concentrated relaxation of the anus by the partner to permit penetration. Physicians occasionally see rectal or anal injuries resulting from anal coitus, although the dangers of these occurring are not great (Swerdlow, 1976). There is a danger that the tissue damage that can occur with anal intercourse may increase the chances of transmitting the AIDS virus if the man is infected. Again, unless there is absolute certainty that the man is not infected, a condom should be worn, which affords substantial—but not absolute—protection. Semen should not be ejaculated into the rectum (see chapter 15, "The AIDS Crisis and Sexual Decisions"), and it is unsafe to insert the penis into the mouth or vagina following anal intercourse, since bacteria are easily transferred and may cause infection.

VIBRATORS, PORNOGRAPHY, AND FANTASIES

Any aids that are used for sexual stimulation by individuals can be shared and probably often are. Electric vibrators that are typically used in masturbation may be used by couples to provide intense sexual pleasuring for one another. Some couples enjoy viewing pornographic materials together, such as magazine photographs or movies showing a variety of sexual acts. Others enjoy reading books that portray sexual scenes in explicit language.

It has long been recognized that fantasy can be an integral part of sexual experiences. As some recent books have dealt openly with the sexual fantasies of individuals, many people seem more willing to talk about their own fantasies. Some couples enjoy acting out their sexual fantasies together and find them sexually stimulating. Fantasies that involve the inflicting of pain or humiliation on a partner are stimulating to some people. Behavior that leads to sexual stimulation through pain or humiliation is termed sadomasochistic and is discussed in more detail in chapter 12, "The Spectrum of Human Sexual Behavior."

anal intercourse: insertion of the penis into the rectum of a partner.

CHEMICAL APHRODISIACS

Some foods and chemicals have been purported to act as sexual stimulants for those who consume them. Substances that create erotic stimulation are called aphrodisiacs. A wide variety of exotic substances have been labeled aphrodisiacs, including powdered rhinoceros' horn, powdered stag's horn, dried salamanders, and dried beetles, along with some common foods, such as eggs, olives, peanuts, oysters, venison, and bananas.

Some individuals report increased interest in sex under the influence of alcohol or marijuana. Both of these drugs lead to relaxation and lowered inhibitions and therefore when used in moderation enhance sexual activities. Used in larger amounts, however, they may inhibit sexual desire and lead to impotence in males. In some individuals another group of chemicals, the volatile nitrites, are reported to enhance response to sexual stimulation and orgasm. These chemicals, especially amyl nitrite and isobutyl nitrite, have been marketed as room deodorizers. They are volatile, and are absorbed quickly by inhalation, causing immediate dilation of blood vessels, with a resulting rush. They are also highly flammable and must be kept away from flames. While most users have suffered no ill effects other than headache and temporary pounding pulse, these chemicals have been implicated in some fatal cerebral hemorrhages (Lowry, 1979). One study reported that in males who are heavy users of marijuana (who smoke four or more joints a week) there is a decrease in testosterone and sperm production by the testes. There were no indications that sexual functioning was impaired, however (Kolodny et al., 1974), and the findings remain largely unconfirmed.

A widely touted aphrodisiac is "Spanish fly," the slang name for cantharides, a chemical extracted from a certain species of southern European beetle. Taken internally the drug produces inflammation of the urinary tract and dilation of blood vessels in the genital area. This can lead to prolonged, often painful, erection of the penis. Cantharides is considered to be a dangerous chemical that can cause serious illness and even death.

Available research would suggest that there are no surefire aphrodisiacs available. Many purported aphrodisiacs are dangerous. It is probably true that so-called aphrodisiacs work because their user believes in their effectiveness. Whenever an individual desires sexual stimulation, looks for it, and expects it, it is not surprising that it may be generated. Masters and Johnson have said that one of the most effective aphrodisiacs is an interesting and expressively interested partner. Certainly one's own inner fantasies may also be sexually invigorating.

Heterosexual Intercourse

In most cultures the act of sexual intercourse, or coitus, is surrounded by a variety of moral and social values. Most societies and religions have sought to place some restrictions on coital behavior in order to regulate which heterosexual couples have babies, to prevent people from enjoying bodily pleasures which some may consider sinful, and to regulate sexual forces that may be considered too powerful to be indulged in casually.

Sexual intercourse takes on different meanings in different circumstances, as do all forms of sex. It may be a perfunctory, hurried experience with little communication, or a lengthy, sensual experience involving the exchange of love and other warm emotions between the partners. The personal needs and characteristics that each partner brings to coitus help to determine the depth and degree of pleasure that results. Factual knowledge about sex, the capacity to accept differences in needs and responses, and personal attitudes all play a part in determining the enjoyment and meaning of coitus for each individual and each couple.

SEXUAL INTERCOURSE AND AIDS

When acquired immunodeficiency syndrome (AIDS) began to receive worldwide publicity, it was viewed mostly as a concern for special populations such as male homosexuals, drug users, and certain ethnic groups. However, it is now spreading among heterosexuals in the United States and is apparently most likely transmitted from person to person by blood (as in contaminated needles) or by semen, through ejaculation into the vagina, mouth, or rectum.

While there are certainly factors that can increase the risk of contracting AIDS, such as the part of the country where one lives and the number of sexual partners one has, if your partner has had sex with anyone else since about 1981 there could be at least some risk that he or she carries the AIDS virus. While this advice is indeed extreme, it would always be safest for a male partner to wear a condom containing nonoxynol-9 during intercourse unless there is absolute certainty that there could never have been any exposure to the AIDS virus. Much remains to be learned about the virus and how it is transmitted. See chapter 15 for more information on AIDS and its prevention.

aphrodisiacs (af-ro-DEE-zee-aks): foods or chemicals purported to foster sexual arousal; they are believed to be more myth than fact.
cantharides (kan-THAR-a-deez): a chemical extracted from a beetle that, when taken internally, creates irritation of blood vessels in the genital region; it can cause physical harm.

INTROMISSION

Sexual intercourse, by definition, involves the insertion of the penis into the vagina. Comfortable intromission requires a suitable degree of penile erection, lubrication, relaxation of the vaginal opening, and cooperation between the two partners. Erection of the penis is a natural part of male sexual arousal, and the vagina usually produces enough lubricant to permit easy movement of the penis in the vagina. If there is insufficient vaginal lubrication, external lubricants may be applied to the penis and the vaginal opening. Water-soluble lubricants such as K-Y jelly or saliva are generally satisfactory. Petroleum-based jellies are not recommended.

The vaginal opening is sometimes tense, and gentle patience is necessary to give time for it to relax. If the outer vaginal muscles cannot relax to the point where intromission can take place comfortably, the woman may be experiencing vaginismus, a problem discussed in chapter 16. Actual insertion of the penis can represent an awkward time for both partners and active mutual cooperation is helpful. Either partner may part the minor lips to expose the vaginal opening and then guide the penis into the vagina. The position of the couple also helps to determine the ease of intromission. The first few coital thrusts of the male may be progressively more forceful as the penis is pushed gradually deeper into the vagina. Depth of penetration depends on the size of the penis and vagina, the coital position, and the relative comfort for both partners.

As discussed in chapter 2, "Sexual Systems," if the hymen is still present at the opening of the vagina, prodding by the penis may be necessary to rupture it and the female should expect some discomfort or pain. Cooperation and understanding on the part of both partners can lead to easy, unembarrassing intromission. Some males feel awkward in attempting to find the opening and the best angle for inserting the penis; the female partner can minimize such difficulties. Frequently difficulties or discomfort in intromission during early coital experiences generate performance fears in both males and females. These fears can lead to problems in later experiences such as lack of erection or lack of vaginal lubrication. After several sexual contacts, intromission is usually accomplished with more ease. Entry is easier if the woman raises her legs widely apart.

INTERCOURSE

Intercourse usually involves movement of the penis in and out of the vagina, resulting from pelvic movements of both partners. Different coital positions afford different amounts of control over these movements to both partners. The rate and vigor of thrusting depend to a large degree on the mood of the couple and how long they wish to prolong coitus. The factor that usually determines duration of intercourse is the length of time required for the male to reach orgasm. Since erection of the penis almost always subsides following orgasm, intercourse can rarely continue. Rapid, forceful movements of the penis generally bring males to orgasm quite quickly, and the amount of precoital stimulation also plays an important role. Intercourse is often not effective in generating orgasm for women, and additional clitoral stimulation is necessary for orgasm to occur.

It is very possible for couples to learn how to modulate the amount of stimulation required for both of them to obtain maximum enjoyment. By occasionally slowing his pelvic thrusting, making shallow thrusts of the penis, and even temporarily ceasing coital movements, the male may exert a great deal of control over the amount of time required to reach orgasm. Certain positions also enhance this control. Kinsey and his associates (1948) estimated that 75 percent of males ejaculated within 2 minutes after intromission. The Hunt (1974) study suggests that couples may now be more concerned with prolonging intercourse, listing a median duration of about 10 minutes and even longer for people under the age of 25. Women vary a great deal in the amount of time required to reach orgasm but often require more than 2 or 3 minutes. It is up to each couple to work on developing the duration of intercourse most suitable for them. Open and specific communication can be an important help in this process.

The movements used by both partners during intercourse may be varied a great deal, and finding the most pleasurable movements can be an exciting learning process in a growing sexual relationship. Alternating shallow and deep thrusts of the penis is often recommended, and the penis may also be rotated or moved from side to side in the vagina. According to most research, including that reported in this textbook, penis size has no bearing on the amount of sexual pleasure derived by the female during intercourse. It is usually assumed that women prefer penises of a particular size out of psychological biases. Although some women do contend that size of the penis makes a difference to them, it is more typical for them to report that this is not a crucial factor in their pleasure. Clitoral stimulation by some means is often important for women during intercourse. Many couples caress one another and use their hands to give added pleasure to each other. One of the commonly sought-after accomplishments in intercourse is simultaneous orgasm of both partners. While some couples enjoy having orgasm at the same time and can accomplish this with relative ease, others find that trying for orgasm at the same time detracts from their sexual pleasure. Some people enjoy experiencing their partner's orgasm without being preoccupied with their own.

Couples usually have intercourse in bed, but many at least occasionally experiment with other locations, including the out-of-doors. While some people prefer coitus in the dark or in dim lighting, others enjoy bright light. Finding ways to enhance the pleasure of sexual intercourse continues to be a human concern.

POSITIONS FOR INTERCOURSE

There are a variety of body positions in which the penis may be comfortably inserted into the vagina. Many couples enjoy experimentation with different positions and find that sex can be made more interesting by changing positions during intercourse, often several times. Some changes of position can be accom-

plished by rolling over or other slight movements, without any interruption of coitus. Other changes require that the penis be withdrawn until the new position is assumed. Which positions a couple finds the most enjoyable, comfortable, and manageable will depend on their own individual characteristics such as body size and weight, degree of physical fitness, length and diameter of the erect penis, personal attitudes about particular positions, and their moods during the sexual encounter. Different positions may place more physical strain on one or the other and afford one of them more ability to control the rate and vigor of coital movements. For each of the 10 basic positions discussed below, there are myriad variations.

RECLINING FACE-TO-FACE

Positions in which the two partners face each other are most commonly used, since the two are more free to look at one another, kiss, and communicate in these positions. Reclining positions are preferred since they usually require less physical energy than does supporting the body in some upright posture.

FIGURE 10.4   A, B Man on Top, Woman Supine

Man on Top, Woman Supine (Fig. 10.4A, B) This position is the most common one used in European and American societies and is erroneously considered by some couples to be the only normal way to have intercourse. Kinsey (1948) reported that 70 percent of the males in his sample had never used any other position for coitus, but recent studies show that most people now at least experiment with other positions. The position seems particularly compatible from an anatomical standpoint, considering the usual angles of the erect penis and the vagina in a reclining position. The male often supports part of his weight on his arms and knees, although this may place real strain on some men. Women sometimes find it suitable in this position to hold their legs up somewhat or to wrap them around the male's waist or even over his shoulders, the latter variation requiring more of a kneeling position from the man. Some couples insert a pillow under the woman's buttocks for greater ease. These positions give the male partner maximum control over the coital thrusting, since the female's pelvis is relatively immobile, and allow deep penetration by the penis. Conversely, they may also make it somewhat more difficult for the woman to have the sort of stimulation neces-

sary to achieve orgasm. Women, or their partners, may want to increase manual stimulation of the clitoris during intercourse to assist in producing the orgasmic response.

Woman on Top, Man Supine (Fig. 10.5A, B) This is the second most commonly used coital position. There are many variations, since the woman may lie on the man with her legs fully extended, or may straddle him in a sitting, crouching, or kneeling position. The position provides the woman more opportunity to control the coital movements and leaves the male's hands more free to caress her body. Some men experience some difficulty keeping the penis in the vagina in this position, and some women experience discomfort with the deep penile penetration that is possible.

However, this position reportedly is more likely to result in orgasm for the female partner, likely due to the fact that she can exert more control over the movements, leading to better stimulation for her.

Side-by-Side (Fig. 10.6) There are many advantages to coital positions in which both partners are lying on their sides, and the lateral position is recommended by

FIGURE 10.5   A, B Woman on Top, Man Supine

FIGURE 10.6   Side-by-Side

Masters and Johnson (1970) in the treatment of several sexual dysfunctions. They found that the majority of couples used a side-by-side position consistently after having given it a try. Since both partners are lying down and need to worry less about supporting their bodies, there is less strain on both of them. They are able to share in controlling their thrusting motions, and both are free to use their hands for touching and caressing. Deep penetration by the penis is sometimes more difficult in the side-by-side positions, and some couples find it less comfortable than do others.

OTHER VARIATIONS ON FACE-TO-FACE

Woman on Edge of Bed or Chair   (Fig. 10.7) When the woman positions herself on the edge of a bed or chair, her back reclining and her feet resting on the floor, the man may either stand or kneel on the floor in

a manner that enables him to enter her. The male is in control in these positions. The male's position on the floor gives him a good deal of leverage for controlling movements and giving powerful thrusts. He is also easily able to vary the angle at which the penis enters the vagina.

Both Partners Seated   (Fig. 10.8) Seated intercourse with the partners facing each other is easier for some couples to achieve than it is for others. The typical manner is for the male to sit in a chair or on the edge of the bed; a reasonably solid support is usually more desirable. The female then lowers herself onto his erect penis, either keeping her feet on the floor or placing her legs around his waist. The woman usually has greater control over the coital movements in this position, although the degree of control varies with the positioning of her legs and feet. The man's hands are relatively free, and he may help to move the female's body up and down on his penis. Usually, deep penile penetration is possible in seated positions.

FIGURE 10.7   Woman on Edge of Bed or Chair

FIGURE 10.8   Both Partners Seated

Both Partners Standing   (Fig. 10.9) Coital positions in which both partners stand are generally the most difficult to manage and sustain. Attention must be given to maintaining balance and stability, along with keeping the penis comfortably inside the vagina. Although many couples experiment with standing intercourse and some use the position occasionally, it is not

a popular one. Deep penile penetration is difficult while standing, since the angles of the penis and the vagina are not particularly complementary. For couples who find comfortable standing intercourse positions, they are apparently exciting for occasional variation.

REAR VAGINAL ENTRY

Most mammals use a rear entry position for copulation. It may be for precisely this reason that many people do not choose such positions. The Kinsey studies reported that a relatively small number of couples had even tried rear entry intercourse. Yet those who do employ these variations often find them comfortable and exciting. Although some intimacy may be lost without face-to-face contact, natural body contours afford especially close body contact during many rear entry positions.

Both Partners Kneeling, Rear Entry   (Fig. 10.10) In this position the woman may hold the upper part of her body up on her arms while kneeling or lower her shoulders and head downward. The man kneels behind her and inserts his penis into the vagina from behind. He may also assume a higher crouched position. Deep penile penetration is usually achieved in this position. The man's hands are generally free to offer stimulating contact for the woman, including contact with the clitoris. Another variation is the wheelbarrow position, in which the male stands behind the female and holds her legs while having intercourse.

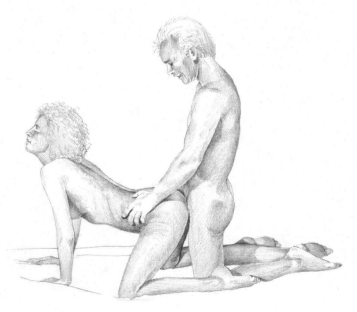

FIGURE 10.9   Both Partners Standing

FIGURE 10.10   Both Partners Kneeling

FIGURE 10.11   Man on Top, Woman on Abdomen, Rear Entry

Man on Top, Woman Lying on Her Abdomen, Rear Entry   (Fig. 10.11) This position is difficult for some couples to manage but can be enjoyable. The man may lie on top of the woman with his legs fully extended or straddle her body in a crouched or seated position. If the woman arches her back somewhat, pushing her vulva backwards, penile entry is usually easily accomplished. This can be a relatively comfortable position, although deep penetration may be difficult.

Side-by-Side, Rear Entry   (Fig. 10.12) In the side-by-side position, intromission is quite easily accomplished, and this position is often recommended during pregnancy. Both partners are lying down and neither is placed under any strain. Their hands are generally quite free to touch one another, although since the man is behind, his hands have easier access to his partner, for example, her breasts and clitoris.

Both Partners Seated or Standing, Rear Entry   (Fig. 10.13) Rear entry is also possible when both partners are seated or standing. The seated position is the easiest and is a comfortable way for the woman to sit on the man's lap while participating in intercourse. She can exercise a good deal of control over coital movements. Standing rear entry is not as easily managed, although it is generally easier than in face-to-face standing intercourse.

It should be reemphasized that sexual intercourse need not be a series of acrobatics to be pleasurable for

FIGURE 10.12   Side-by-Side, Rear Entry

FIGURE 10.13   Both Partners Seated or Standing, Rear Entry

both partners. Yet if both partners are willing and able, varying coital position from time to time can be an exciting part of an ongoing sexual relationship.

AFTER SEXUAL RELATIONS

Many couples find that the period during which they are together following sexual relations is significant to their relationship. If the sexual experience has been satisfying to both partners and they both are feeling relaxed or even drowsy, this may be a time for communicating quiet, gentle, loving feelings. Women in general seem to take longer than men in the resolution phase of the sexual response cycle, although this phenomenon may be the result of lack of satiation because of an inadequate number of orgasms.

When sex has been unsuccessful in any way or has generated some negative feelings, the period following orgasm may be especially valuable for two-way communication. Many couples store up fears, resentments, and feelings of inadequacy because of sexual problems, only to find that these tensions eventually catch up with the relationship and place strains on it. Talking out the negative feelings while they are fresh—

in an atmosphere of mutual warmth, caring, and reassurance—can often be a strengthening influence on any relationship. If one partner has not reached orgasm during coitus and wishes to do so, it is very appropriate for the other to employ suitable techniques to help the partner to achieve orgasm.

After a suitable length of time (see chapter 3, "Human Sexual Response," on the male's refractory period), some couples proceed to orgasm for a second time. Whether or not a second orgasmic experience takes place depends on many factors, such as age, level of sexual arousal, arousing aspects of the surroundings, newness of the relationship, and desire for further sex on the part of both partners.

INTERCOURSE AND MARRIAGE

The social mores related to sexual intercourse are often intimately associated with a particular society's marriage customs. In many societies, including most Western societies, marriage represents a legitimization of coitus. This attitude is apparently rooted in the reproductive aspects of sex. Since the family is the basic unit of most societies, it has often been decided that a child is best raised and cared for in a secure nurturing atmosphere created by the continuing relationships within its family. Hence sex, with its risk of pregnancy, has often been discouraged outside the context of such a committed, long-term relationship. Social institutions, such as religion, school, and family, are charged with the enforcement of these rules. Premarital and extramarital sex are more permissible in some societies than in others.

There can be no doubt that in North America sex is a significant part of marriage—some people believe to an exaggerated extent. Sexual problems can lead to severe marital difficulties and even divorce, and all sorts of publications are available to spice up and renew sex within marriage. It is also true that communication problems in marriage are often reflected in sexual difficulties between the partners. Sex is a potential source of marriage enrichment, reinforcing the interdependence of husband and wife, unifying them through shared enjoyment, symbolizing their shared life, and helping to resolve episodes of alienation. Sexual activity can exert these same positive factors on relationships other than those involving marriage.

For most married individuals, sexual intercourse with the spouse constitutes the major, though not the only, form of sexual outlet (Kinsey, 1948, 1953). In more recent years married couples have been having intercourse more frequently than when the Kinsey

271

studies were published (Hunt, 1975). Frequency of coitus varies with age group. The median is 3.25 contacts a week among 18- to 24-year-old married people and about 2 contacts a week in the 35-to-44 age group. Of course individual couples show wide variations away from the median, and the frequency of intercourse can be affected by many factors.

Our society has a mixture of values concerning premarital and extramarital sexual activity. On the basis of present evidence, it seems safe to state that among young adults the amount of premarital sex has been increasing. Not only have more people been experiencing coitus before marriage and at a younger age, they have been doing so more often and with fewer inhibitions than in the past. There is a possibility that with the AIDS scare is affecting sexual decision-making, and with a shift back to more conservative attitudes and values generally, these trends may gradually reverse themselves as we near the end of the twentieth century.■

CHAPTER SUMMARY

1. Masturbation, or self-stimulation of the genitals, is a sexual activity in which most people participate at one point or another, usually throughout their lifetimes.
2. There are a variety of ways in which people masturbate, although most commonly women stimulate their clitoral area and men stroke or otherwise stimulate the penis.
3. The use of fantasy or erotic pictures, videos, and stories serves as an enhancement for masturbation in many people.
4. Masturbation can occur at all stages of life and can be enjoyed for its own sake rather than as a substitute for other forms of sex. Medically speaking, there is no such thing as excessive masturbation, and it does not produce physical weakness or illness.
5. There are many forms of shared nongenital stimulation that are considered intimate and arousing. Kissing and massaging of erogenous zones may be highly erotic. → arousing sex. feeling
6. The mouth can be used to stimulate the sex organs. Fellatio is oral stimulation of the penis, and cunnilingus is oral stimulation of the clitoris and other areas of the vulva.
7. The hands are often a part of shared sexual stimulation, and the penis may be inserted between a partner's legs, breasts, or buttocks, or into the anus. Anal intercourse is one of the ways in which the AIDS virus is transmitted.
8. Vibrators, erotic pictures and films, and personal sexual fantasies may be integrated into sexual sharing.
9. There are many myths about foods or chemicals leading to sexual arousal. Substances that create erotic stimulation are labeled aphrodisiacs, although they are believed to operate largely on suggestion and imagination.
10. Heterosexual intercourse is the most widely accepted of shared sexual behaviors, although it is often subject to strict moral, social, and relational codes of behavior. It is also one possible mode of transmitting the AIDS virus.
11. The techniques and timing of intercourse are extremely variable, as are the positions in which a woman and man can share penile-vaginal penetration.
12. The time following the end of intercourse can serve as a quiet, warm, and comfortable time for communication between partners, or it can become a time of tension and further misunderstanding.
13. Intercourse is closely associated with marriage customs in most cultures. In North America sex is considered to be a significant part of the marital relationship.

ANNOTATED READINGS

Barbach, L. G. (1982). *For each other: Sharing sexual intimacy.* Garden City, NY: Anchor/Doubleday. A guide to enhancing aspects of a relationship that lead to increased intimacy and sexual satisfaction. Includes step-by-step exercises.

Levine, L., & Barbach, L. (1983). *The intimate male: Candid discussions about women, sex and relationships.* Garden City, NY: Anchor/Doubleday. Anecdotes and quotes from men about their sexual relationships, along with suggestions from the authors for enhancing partnerships.

Levine, S. B. (1988). *Sex is not simple.* Columbus, OH: Ohio Psychology Publishing Co. Offers a blend of personal essays, scholarly information, and practical suggestions for enhancing one's sexual life or working on sexual problems. The book takes a very positive and helpful look at sexual functioning.

McCarthy, B., & McCarthy, E. (1984). *Sexual awareness.* New York: Carroll and Graf Publishers. Written for individuals and couples who want to enhance their sexual pleasure. There are chapters on overcoming specific sexual dysfunctions and problems.

Nowinski, J. (1988). *A lifelong love affair: Keeping your sexual desire alive in your relationship.* Goes beyond the "technical" aspects of a sexual relationship to the important ways in which we can maintain and foster real intimacy and desire throughout a long-term relationship.

Wright, J. (1986). *Survival strategies for couples.* Buffalo, NY: Prometheus Books. Suggestions for improving communication in partnerships, with special sections on sexuality.

CHAPTER ELEVEN

PERSPECTIVES ON HOMOSEXUALITY
    The Kinsey Scale and Its Limitations
    Incidence of Homosexuality
    Cross-Cultural Comparisons
    Studying Homosexual Behavior
    Homophobia

MODELS OF HOMOSEXUALITY
    Moral Model
    Biological Determinants Model
    Psychoanalytic Models
    The Normal Variant Model
    The Bell, Weinberg, and Hammersmith Study on
      Sexual Preference
    Finding the Facts
    Perspectives on Therapy

HOMOSEXUAL IDENTITY FORMATION
    Stages of Homosexual Identity Formation
    Male-Female Differences in Identity Formation
    Bisexual People
    Comparing Same-Sex Behavior in Males and Females
    Same-Sex Relationships
    Aging and Homosexuality

MYTHS AND FALLACIES ABOUT HOMOSEXUALITY

HOMOSEXUALITY AND SOCIETY
    Homosexual Subculture
    AIDS and Homosexuals
    Homosexuality and Religion
    Homosexuality and the Law
    Homosexuality and Marriage

CONCLUSION

CHAPTER SUMMARY

My high school years were confusing, as I tried to pretend to the world, and to myself, that I was a great lover of women. My main regret now is that I really hurt a lot of girls who didn't understand why I lost interest eventually. I "came out" to some close friends during my junior year in college, and things have been much better in my life since then. While I don't find much need to broadcast my sexual orientation to very many people, I feel as though I am true to myself, and far more secure and happy about who I am as a person. Ken and I met nearly seven years ago (our "anniversary" is March 26), and we are still together and quite happy.

—From a letter to the author

HOMOSEXUALITY AND BISEXUALITY

Heterosexual behavior, within fairly narrow boundaries of expression, has been considered the norm against which other sexual orientations and behaviors have been judged. It is often misleading to label and compartmentalize sexual behaviors, for example, homosexual, heterosexual, bisexual. Yet sexologists have been reluctant to give up these "discrete" categories. It has been suggested that this is the first generation to recognize the myth of the "heterosexual assumption," that misconception that everyone we know and see is heterosexual in orientation. The facts of human sexual behavior reveal a very different perspective (Selverstone, 1989).

Perspectives on Homosexuality

This chapter focuses on homosexuality and bisexuality, often at the center of the sexual behavior controversy. Because of the prevalence of sexual behavior shared by members of the same sex, it has been a convenient focus of attention for sex researchers. Same-sex behavior also provides a clear example of how strongly perceptions of human sexuality are influenced by so-

cial and historical attitudes. In ancient and medieval Europe, for example, sexual activity was not judged within what we would call a psychological framework, because little attention had been given to the workings of the individual human mind. Psychology, as we know it, had not yet been "invented." There was no thought given to what a person's sexual orientation might be, or what sexual activities might fit that person's needs best. It has only been in very recent times that we have focused on people's sexual choices as being reflective of some inherent characteristic that somehow defines them and their personalities. In premodern times, norms for human behavior were established by social codes that clearly established what people could and could not do, regardless of what their inner inclinations might be. For example, marriage was typically a duty of every citizen, and marriage and parenthood were not thought to have anything in particular to do with sexual attraction.

Historically, there seems to have been great ambiguity about what today we label homosexuality (Bullough, 1990b). Historical norms for sexual behavior were governed more by ethical ideals than by the sex of one's sexual partner. Records suggest that ancient Greco-Roman people thought of sexuality as neutral or good, so long as it was "responsible." In those times, responsibility was measured by such things as whether the behavior interfered with one's duties to the state or involved an abuse of freeborn (nonslave) children or married women. Opportunities for sex were organized more around issues of class, age, and marital status than they were around one's gender. A wealthy, powerful male could penetrate anyone with his penis without loss of social status, but he might be judged more harshly were he to be penetrated by another male of lower class (Boswell, 1990a).

Today, we have come to conceive of heterosexual attraction and behavior as being the norm. For this very reason, it is left relatively unmarked and unnoticed. The term *heterosexual* is not really used to define a person, behavior, or life-style, since it is accepted that there is a great deal of diversity among those people considered to be heterosexual. The term *homosexual* is quite a different story. It is usually understood to be a distinct and permanent category, a defining characteristic that implies a great deal beyond some occasional sexual behavior of the person who has been labeled. This conceptual difference between heterosexuality and homosexuality seems to be much greater in today's way of thinking than it was in ancient times. A consequence of our modern concept is the creation of a sense that homosexuals constitute a minority, often provoking disapproval, fear, or loathing because of their perceived "abnormalcy" or "unhealthiness" (Boswell, 1990a).

With modern science's penchant for labeling things, there has been an unfortunate tendency to categorize sexual activities by the sex of the people involved, and then draw inferences about the people who fit into the categories. The fact that people have had a sexual experience with someone else of their own sex does not constitute much data with which to group them together into a category. One researcher has raised the interesting possibility that we might eventually find out that knowing that certain people are homosexuals would not permit us to infer anything about their psychological adjustment, hormone balances, masculinity or femininity, childhood development, or any other characteristic. In fact, the research data continue to indicate that people who have sex with members of their own sex are remarkably similar to any other people. It could be that science has been trying to invent categories and commonalities where there just are not any (Koertge, 1990).

Another problem with the term *homosexual* is that its definition has tended to focus only on sexual activity and ignore the individual's preferences. In actuality, one's sexual behavior does not necessarily wholly reflect inner orientations and inclinations. It is quite possible for individuals who find

themselves strongly sexually attracted to members of their own sex never to participate in homosexual acts and to function effectively in their heterosexual contacts. It is also possible for those with a primarily heterosexual orientation to experiment with homosexual behavior. Although sex has traditionally been viewed as either heterosexual or homosexual, research evidence shows that such dichotomous categories fail to reflect the complex realities of sexual orientation.

THE KINSEY SCALE AND ITS LIMITATIONS

Concepts of sexual orientation have been evolving much as our views of masculinity and femininity did when these traits came under scientific scrutiny (Sanders & Reinisch, 1990). Instead of conceptualizing masculinity and femininity as polarized entities in themselves, we now see them as representing clusters of relatively independent traits that may coexist within the same individual, regardless of whether that individual is male or female. Masculinity and femininity are now viewed as multidimensional sets of characteristics, existing to varying degrees within both men and women.

When Alfred Kinsey began his research on sexual behavior in the 1930s and 1940s, he faced the great ambiguity of the times about what constituted homosexuality. Sexual acts between women were often ignored altogether, and no consideration was given to the frequency with which sexual acts took place. If one had a sexual experience with someone of the same sex, one might well be defined as a homosexual. Social scientists of that day had not given much consideration to making a distinction between behavior and inner inclinations. What one did sexually was assumed to define what he or she wanted most to do sexually.

Kinsey recognized early on in his research that substantial numbers of people had experienced both homosexual and heterosexual activity. For use in his studies he devised a seven-category sexual behavior rating scale by which individuals could be classified (Fig. 11.1). On the scale he used the numbers 0 to 6, with 0 representing exclusively heterosexual behavior, and 6 representing exclusively homosexual behavior. Those individuals who showed some combination of both heterosexual and homosexual behavior were classified somewhere between these two extremes, in categories 1 through 5. Categories 1 and 5 were for those who showed predominantly heterosexual or homosexual behavior, respectively, but had experienced at least some of the other type of behavior. Category 2

affectional: relating to feelings or emotions, such as romantic attachments.

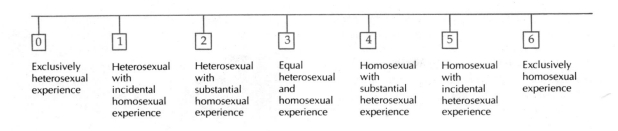

FIGURE 11.1 Kinsey Scale of Sexual Behavior

Kinsey recognized that for some people the strict dichotomy between homosexual and heterosexual behavior didn't exist. In order to classify his clients into appropriate categories for study, Kinsey devised a rating scale based on behavior.

included people who had experienced more than incidental homosexual behavior, but still leaned more toward the heterosexual; while category 4 was for those who leaned more toward the homosexual but had experienced more than incidental heterosexual behavior. Category 3 included people with approximately equal amounts of heterosexual and homosexual behavior (Kinsey, 1953). While this continuum represented the most reasonable approach to classifying sexual behavior at the time, it still did not adequately reflect the inner interests and needs of individuals. Although behavior may often reflect inner orientation, it may not represent an adequate measure of a person's degree of heterosexual or homosexual preference.

Kinsey's scale has been called a "stroke of political genius," since it offered some resolution to issues that had been troubling researchers for many years, and opened up a whole new way of understanding human sexual behavior (Bullough, 1990b). The scale and the behavioral statistics that accompanied it clearly demonstrated that sexual behavior between people of the same sex was widespread in the U.S. population, and was a particularly common aspect of growing up. This was comforting not only to persons who perceived themselves as homosexual, but also to predominantly heterosexual people who had experienced some same-sex activity. Since there was now a continuum of sexual behavior, people no longer had to see themselves at one pole of experience or the other. The middle ground of the scale clarified the idea that there is a range of behavior that could not fall neatly into heterosexual or homosexual categories, and so the concept of bisexuality was also legitimized.

Kinsey's approach is believed to have played a major role in allowing American society to begin coming to terms with homosexuality. His scale permitted individuals to identify themselves as homosexual, and any social movement must begin with people distinguishing themselves in some way from others. While there has been a negative and oppressive side to being labeled homosexual, as homosexual persons

began to feel a greater sense of identity and realize that their numbers were larger than previously thought, they had a new impetus for activism to reduce bigotry and discrimination.

Research since the time of Kinsey's work has shown that the more we know about the complexities of human sexuality, the less valuable his bipolar scale is in offering a thorough understanding of sexual orientation as part of the human personality. One of the problems with the scale is its implication that the more homosexual one is, the less heterosexual one can be, and vice versa. It has been proposed instead that these characteristics are relatively independent. Some people may exhibit high levels of both homoeroticism and heteroeroticism, low levels of both, or differing levels of each. Across people's life spans, there may be changes and discontinuities in sexual behavior patterns and identities. For example, in a Kinsey Institute study of 262 self-identified homosexual women, 75 percent had had sex with men since the age of 18 (Sanders & Reinisch, 1990).

As described in chapter 9, newer models of sexual orientation take into consideration many different variables, including behavior, self-identification, life-style, frequency of sex with different partners, and changes over time (Whalen, Geary & Johnson, 1990). The present state of knowledge about human sexuality no longer permits us to identify the term homosexual as anything very specific. The term should only be used as a very general way of referring to same-sex behavior and affectional preference.

The slang term gay is sometimes used to describe homosexual persons or behaviors. The word lesbian is used specifically in reference to a female homosexual. The term heterosexual refers to opposite-sex behavior

homosexual: term applied to romantic and sexual attractions and activities between members of the same sex.
gay: slang term referring to homosexual persons and behaviors.
lesbian (LEZ-bee-un): refers to female homosexuals.
heterosexual: attractions or activities between members of opposite sexes.

or affectional preference. The slang term straight applies to heterosexuals. The term bisexual is used to describe some level of sexual activity with or affectional interest in both sexes. On Kinsey's scale the bisexual person would be rated behaviorally in categories 2, 3, or 4. Another term used for bisexual is ambisexual. It is worth noting that Kinsey never intended for the intermediate numbers on his scale to be treated as a social type called bisexuals. He felt it was more accurate to view them as persons with a mixture of homosexual and heterosexual acts during their lives. However, over the years people who have experienced desires for both men and women, and/or have shared sexual activity with both men and women, have come to label themselves bisexual. The term has gradually gained more acceptance in common usage (Gagnon, 1990b).

The term bisexual may be confusing as a description of behavior. If an individual were having sex with both a man and woman at the same time, the behavior might legitimately be called bisexual. More typically, however, behavior is either homosexual or heterosexual, but not both at the same time.

A survey of some research and theory on homosexuality follows in this chapter. However, the discussion should be prefaced with a warning that very little of this research can be considered to be of a truly unbiased, scientific nature. The same could probably be said of most research published on the variations of sexual activity. One study that examined the reports of psychological research on homosexuality done during an 8-year period from 1967 to 1974 found a large amount of heterosexual bias reflected in that research. Predictably, the most startling biases were found in the work of researchers who viewed homosexuality in a framework of pathology (Morin, 1977).

We are again reminded that scientists are products of their cultures. Their perceptions and values become part of the conclusions they draw from their research. Studies of homosexuality or other erotic experiences cannot be "treated as merely the results of disinterested inquiry but represent moral and political acts in larger dramas of liberation and repression" (Gagnon, 1990b, p. 180).

An unfortunate consequence of the limited and biased research on homosexuality, and the behavioral focus of the research, is that we seldom examine the implications of loving relationships between members of the same sex. While heterosexuality is often intricately entwined with male-female romance and love, homosexuality is usually viewed in terms of sexual behavior. This is a distorted view, since strong loving relationships can develop between people of the same sex as well, and the nonsexual intimacy is as important to them as it is to heterosexual couples.

FIGURE 11.2 Intimate Relationships

It is erroneous to view homosexual relationships strictly in terms of sexual behavior. As with heterosexual relationships, same-sexed intimacies are based primarily on warmth and caring.

INCIDENCE OF HOMOSEXUALITY

There are no truly reliable statistics on the numbers of predominantly homosexual men and women in the United States or any other location. The only large-scale study that has investigated the degree of homosexuality and heterosexuality in large samples of women and men was conducted by Kinsey and his coworkers (1948, 1953). Using the seven-point rating scale on page 277, they gathered some statistics on the amount of homosexual behavior since adolescence described by several thousand individuals.

When these statistics first appeared many people were shocked by the percentages of men and women who reported at least some involvement with homosexual behavior. Some people have declared that the

straight: slang term for heterosexual.
bisexual: refers to some degree of sexual activity with or attraction to members of both sexes.
ambisexual: alternate term for bisexual.

MICHELLE: A YOUNG WOMAN TRIES TO DECIDE ABOUT HER SEXUALITY

Case Study

Michelle was an attractive 21-year-old college student who had been very sexually active with men. She went through a 3-month period of feeling disillusioned and dissatisfied with sex and decided to abstain from sexual contact until she felt more positively toward it. During her period of abstention, she began to have vivid fantasies about being sexually involved with other women. She found her fantasies exciting and appealing and decided that she might be bisexual.

She eventually had opportunities to have separate sexual encounters with two women about her own age, one of whom was her roommate. She enjoyed both experiences, but also found herself missing intercourse with men. She decided to allow herself to become sexually involved with men again, but also wished to be open to possible future homosexual contacts. In talking about her sexuality, Michelle spoke of herself as bisexual and maintained that she had no idea where her future sexual practices might take her.

---

percentages were too high, while others insist they are on the conservative side. The average figures most frequently cited from Kinsey, often without much explanation, are that 37 percent of men and 20 percent of women have had at least some homosexual experience to the point of orgasm since adolescence. This information requires examination, since it may have created the impression of a higher incidence of same-sex behavior in humans than is actually the case. There was a reanalysis of the cases of 2,900 college-educated men who had been interviewed by the Kinsey team. The reexamination of the files indicated that in their homosexual experiences, either the interviewee or his male partner had reached orgasm, but not necessarily both—a definition different from Kinsey's. The retabulation also showed that in 25 percent of all males interviewed, the homosexual experience was confined mainly to adolescence or isolated experiences before the age of 20 (Gagnon & Simon, 1973). Data from surveys conducted in 1970 and 1988 show that over 20 percent of adult men in the United States had sexual contact with another male at some time in their lives. Nearly 7 percent of them had such contact after age 19, and about 2 percent reported same-sex activity within the previous year. The researchers recognized factors in the research that may well have resulted in figures that were below the actual rates of such behavior (Fay et al., 1989).

In any case, the statistics suggest that there are millions of people who are predominantly homosexual in their behavior. The Kinsey criteria indicate that 13.95 percent of males and 4.25 percent of females, or a combined average of 9.13 percent of the total population, have had either extensive homosexual experience (21 or more partners or 52 or more experiences) or more than incidental (5–20 partners or 21–50 experiences) homosexual experience (Gebhard, 1977; Voeller, 1990a). It has also been suggested that the percentage of homosexual persons in the population is relatively consistent among different cultures and that there are also many similarities in their behaviors (Whitam & Mathy, 1986).

In most studies the proportion of females who are homosexual is usually about one-third the number of males. There are several theories concerning this lower incidence of female homosexuality, none of which is supported by scientific evidence. One hypothesis is that women in our society have been less experimental in sex and have been generally less in touch with their sexual feelings than have men. If these ideas are true, it would seem likely that the women's movement might in time increase the percentages of women who will be aware of their homosexuality.

CROSS-CULTURAL COMPARISONS

Although it is outside the scope of this book to dwell on anthropological findings, some cross-cultural comparisons of homosexual behavior are in order. Anthropologically, generalizations about homosexual behavior are difficult to make. It is particularly ineffective to try to interpret or understand the sexual behaviors of other cultures using the psychological, sociological, or biological theories developed within the context of our own culture. Even applying our terms to those behaviors may not make much sense, since these terms carry with them the assumptions of the time and place in which they were first coined (Gagnon, 1990b).

Different rates of homosexual behavior do not seem to bear any particular relationship to a society's climate, race, affluence, typical family structure, or state of development. Rules and social sanctions seem to have some effect at least on the visibility of homosexual behavior, since in societies where it is approved or praised, it tends to be more frequently observed, and in societies where it is condemned, homosexuality tends to be less frequently observed (Herdt, 1990).

Some preindustrial societies use homosexual behavior, particularly between males, in their religious rites. It is sometimes believed that an older male giving semen to a young boy orally or anally strengthens the boy and helps make him into a man. This age-structured homosexuality is more common among males than among females, and is typically viewed as a stage of an individual's development. It occurs in 10 to 20 percent of Melanesian societies in the Southwest Pacific. In these societies, the rule is that a man must engage in homosexual activity until he is married; then he must adopt heterosexual behavior. Most men make the transition without trouble. In societies where homosexual behavior is accepted prior to marriage and there are no strong social prohibitions against continuing it after marriage, it is usually continued.

In some cultures, homosexual behavior is accompanied by reversals in normal sex roles. Not only does the individual interact sexually with members of the same sex, but dresses and acts as someone of the other sex would. This may reflect one way in which discontinuities in gender-identity/role are adapted to in these cultures. The *berdache* tradition among American Indians is an example of this gender-reversed homosexuality. There are also societies in which same-sex activity is recognized as legitimate only for people who hold a certain status role. If an Indian shaman were told in a vision to engage in homosexual activity, it might well be considered acceptable for the individual's status. In societies where men take more than one wife, it is quite common for women to form permanent bonds that involve same-sex activity. In contemporary Western societies, the gay/lesbian movement has taken on political and cultural dimensions that have enabled homosexual people to have more than a specialized role in the society. Instead, they are more or less integrated into the larger social framework, often with little attention paid to them as being different from other members of the society (Herdt, 1990).

Homosexuality apparently exists to varying degrees in other cultures. It is sometimes accepted or tolerated, sometimes condemned or punished. Nevertheless, homosexual subcultures seem to appear in all societies, and social norms apparently have little effect on whether homosexual orientations emerge. Norms can determine, of course, how open people dare to be about their homosexuality. Also found in all societies is a continuum ranging from very masculine male homosexuals to the very effeminate (Whitam & Mathy, 1986).

STUDYING HOMOSEXUAL BEHAVIOR

Homosexual behavior is difficult to study objectively, as are other forms of sexual expression. The research that has been published tends to focus on homosexual males, but our objective knowledge of homosexual behavior in both sexes is extremely limited. The available research is often of questionable value, since the scientific methodologies used are often inadequate. Many researchers have approached the study of homosexuality with built-in biases that are reflected in their results.

One major research deficiency has been the small samples of study subjects usually employed. Generalization from inadequate samples is impossible, and the study subjects tend to be chosen from biased groups such as the patients of a practicing clinician or a population of prisoners. Another deficiency is the lack of adequate control groups of heterosexual people in most studies of homosexuality. Even in those studies where controls are used, they are often not sufficiently well matched with the study subjects to make comparisons valid. An additional problem is that most research on homosexuality is culture-bound. Insufficient work has been done in comparing cross-cultural influences; and, even in the anthropological studies that have been done, analyses and interpretations are often made with models and labels that are more applicable to contemporary, developed Western societies (Gagnon, 1990b).

Homosexual experience may be studied from three general perspectives. The most commonly used research perspective looks at the sexual behaviors of the *individual*. For example, the Kinsey scale was an attempt to provide a framework for judging where an individual might fit on the spectrum of experience between exclusively heterosexual and exclusively homosexual activity. Other individualistic approaches examine personality characteristics, psychological adjustment, or life histories of gay men and lesbians.

A second general standpoint for research has been *sociocultural* analysis. This approach focuses on the patterns of homosexual behavior within cultures and societies, attempting to examine and explain societal reactions to homosexuality and the variations on homosexuality within particular societies. Studies that examine public attitudes toward homosexuality or the ways in which social institutions deal with same-sex behavior are examples of this research perspective.

A third, and less commonly applied, viewpoint for research is the *relationship* perspective. In this approach, the sexual and romantic attachments that occur between same-sexed partners constitute the central issues for study. This form of research shifts away from examining isolated individuals or group dynamics to what is going on between two human beings. It looks at the characteristics of relationships between members of the same sex, including such things as the extent of commitment, balances of power between partners, how sex is expressed between partners over a long-term relationship, and how same-sex partnerships change with time. The relationship perspective in studying homosexuality is one of the newest approaches to be used; and, as later sections of this chapter will show, has afforded us whole new conceptual frameworks for understanding persons who have entered into homosexual partnerships (Peplau & Cochran, 1990).

Until recently, psychiatry and psychology tended to study homosexuality in the contexts of deviance and pathology. Using a medical model for the understanding of homosexuality, psychologists and psychiatrists have often pursued research on the causes and effects of same-sex orientations, in hopes that new methods of treatment and cure would emerge—without even questioning whether the concepts of "treatment" and "cure" were at all appropriate. Some of the theoretical stances that have emerged from their research are discussed later in this chapter. Very few researchers have concerned themselves with the cause-and-effect relationships in heterosexuality, assuming its normalcy or naturalness for the human personality. Sociological aspects of homosexuality were largely ignored until the Kinsey studies provided impressive data on homosexual behavior. Since then, many researchers have begun to move away from the medical model, viewing homosexual behavior as an alternate form of expression within the normative continuum, rather than as a sickness.

HOMOPHOBIA

Public attitudes toward homosexuality tend to be negative; and several studies have reflected this public negativism over the past 2 to 3 decades. In the mid-1980s the Roper Center for Public Opinion Research reported that 78 percent of Americans believed sexual relations between two adults of the same sex to be always (73 percent) or almost always (5 percent)

wrong (Davis & Smith, 1984). Studies of attitudes among college students have shown widespread hostility toward lesbians and gay men, and have demonstrated that men tend to have a lower level of acceptance for same-sex behavior and affectional preference than women do (D'Augelli & Rose, 1990). It may well be because of such attitudes that homosexual men in one study found their college environment less emotionally supportive and less tolerant of change and innovation than did a heterosexual comparison group (Reynolds, 1989). Several research studies have suggested that college courses in human sexuality can have a significant effect on promoting more tolerant attitudes toward homosexuality, but other work has suggested that students who enroll in such courses are already more accepting of their own sexuality and more liberal in their sexual attitudes. Therefore, it may not be that courses in human sexuality have all that much to do with modifying student attitudes (Stevenson, 1988, 1990).

Irrational fear of homosexuals, and strongly held negative attitudes about them, have been labeled homophobia. Sex education classes and textbooks are usually based on an underlying set of heterosexual assumptions, leading to the claim that they are unfairly biased in heterosexist directions. Cultural heterosexism fosters individual antihomosexual attitudes by providing a system of values and stereotypes that seem to justify prejudice (Herek, 1990). Homophobia may also be expressed through jokes or derogatory terms concerning gay persons, in banning known homosexuals from particular jobs, or by actual physical attacks. Gay and lesbian college students have frequently been subjected to harassment, misunderstanding, and discrimination. The Justice Department has claimed that homosexual people are subjected to physical violence more than any other minority community, and there are indications that antigay violence has been increasing (Wertheimer, 1988). It has frequently been suggested that the homophobic reactions of some may rest in their own confusion or uncertainty about sexual identity.

Homophobia and its resultant prejudices take their toll on people's lives and attitudes toward themselves. Even among boys who are not attracted to other males, there is a fear of behaving in any way that might give an appearance of being gay. Homophobia has been called the "disease of suspicion," since it creates an atmosphere of mistrust and curiosity about people's sexual lives (Friedman, 1989). A report from the federal Task Force on Youth Suicide (1989) pointed out that gay and lesbian youth are at a higher risk of

homophobia (ho-mo-PHO-bee-a): strongly held negative attitudes and irrational fears relating to homosexuals.

281

suicide, and that this is the leading cause of death among young people who see themselves as part of some sexual minority. They are also more prone to self-destructive behaviors such as alcohol and drug abuse. Some high schools and many colleges are attempting to establish support programs to help lesbian and gay young people cope with the pressures of a homophobic society (Flax, 1990).

Several groups of professionals have taken new public stands with regard to homosexuality. In late 1973 the American Psychiatric Association's board of trustees voted unanimously to remove homosexuality from its list of mental illnesses, declaring that it does not constitute a psychiatric disorder. Individuals who are either disturbed by or in conflict with their homosexuality are considered to have a sexual orientation disturbance. While many members of the American Psychiatric Association originally objected to the decision of their trustees and forced a referendum on the question, the vote of the membership, though far from unanimous, upheld the trustees' move to no longer consider homosexuality an illness. The American Psychological Association soon took a similar stand. Professional groups have formed, such as the Association of Gay Psychologists and the Gay Caucus of the American Psychiatric Association. The Board of Directors of the Sex Information and Education Council of the United States, most of whom are professionals in the field of human sexuality, adopted the following position statement on sexual orientation in 1990:

> The Sex Information and Education Council of the United States believes that an individual's sexual orientation—whether bisexual, heterosexual, or homosexual—is an essential quality of humanness and strongly supports the right of each individual to accept, acknowledge, and live in accordance with his or her orientation.
> SIECUS advocates laws guaranteeing civil rights and protection to all people regardless of their sexual orientation and deplores all forms of prejudice and discrimination against people based on their sexual orientation.

It is clear, then, that many professionals have adopted a more accepting attitude toward homosexual behavior. While it seemed for a time that this would filter through the general public as well, some new factors have been influencing public opinion. In addition to a general trend toward increased conservatism in sexual values, the prevalence of AIDS among homosexual males led to even more negativism toward gay people.

There is a growing recognition among American corporations that homophobia is bad for business, since gay and lesbian workers cannot function optimally if they have to be constantly concerned about the

FIGURE 11.3 Homosexual Rights

Social discrimination against homosexuals is declining at least at the professional level. SIECUS (the Sex Information and Education Council of the United States) has declared that sexual orientation is an essential quality of humanness. These homosexual women (lesbians) enjoy a close and caring moment.

attitudes and behaviors of their colleagues. Some businesses have begun to offer workshops to their employees, with the aim of reducing homophobic attitudes (McNaught, 1989). In the corporate environment, as well as on college campuses, these attitudes will not change until an effort is made to educate people about sexual orientation, and break through some of the stereotypical beliefs about gay, lesbian, and bisexual persons.

Models of Homosexuality

Homosexual concerns are frequently brought to physicians, psychiatrists, psychologists, and counselors. The manner in which professionals deal with the issue of homosexuality will differ according to their theoretical framework. Those professionals who accept an illness-oriented theory, although they are now in a definite minority, will attempt either to "cure" a homosexual person through a reorientation to heterosexuality, or to help the person adjust to the "malady" as well as possible. Professionals who believe homosexuality to be an alternate means of sexual expression within the limits of normalcy will help homosexual persons become more comfortable with and accepting of their orientation in the face of homophobic social attitudes. This section will present a variety of hypotheses that have attempted to explain the causes and meanings of homosexuality. Each hypothesis has its proponents and opponents, all quite sincere in their opinions and values.

Theories about the origins of sexual orientation have focused on both biological and socioenvironmental factors. In weighing the issues, it is crucial to keep in mind that there is a great deal of diversity among individuals who identify themselves as homosexual. Again, it is very possible that same-sex behavior and attraction may be about the only thing these individuals have in common. The possibility exists that there are many different pathways to a common sexual orientation—whether homosexual, bisexual, or heterosexual (Sanders & Reinisch, 1990). It used to be that researchers believed sexual orientation to be rooted in either nature *or* nurture. Recent research has changed that view in favor of a more comprehensive approach including both factors. It seems increasingly likely that sexual orientation develops through a complex interaction of innate biological and external social influences. Some of the "programming" that results in an individual's sexual orientation may take place during "critical periods" of development when nature and nurture interact with each other, either in prenatal life or after birth (Money, 1990).

One of the most comprehensive systems for understanding the many different variables that play a part in one's sexual orientation is the Klein Sexual Orientation Grid (Klein, Sepekoff, & Wolf, 1990). As described in chapter 9, this approach takes into consideration several different variables—sexual attraction, sexual behavior, sexual fantasies, emotional preference, social preference, self-identification, and lifestyle—and examines how they applied to the person in the past, how they apply to the person in the present, and what they would ideally be, in the person's opinion. This kind of model makes it clear that simple labels for one's sexuality can only be incomplete and inadequate.

MORAL MODEL

The attitudes and teachings of some religions toward homosexuality have traditionally played an important role in the formation of public opinion. Sex not intended for the purpose of reproduction may be viewed by some as lustful and therefore sinful (Darling & Mabe, 1989). Furthermore, sexual behavior that cannot be conducted within the bond of heterosexual marriage is sometimes viewed as sinful.

People who view homosexuality as immoral tend to approach homosexual individuals with contempt, pity, offerings of salvation, calls for repentance, or tolerance. Homosexual people who hold this view of homosexuality often feel guilt, self-condemnation, and generally low self-esteem. Because sexual orientation is such a significant aspect of the personality, they may experience guilt and frustration if they continue to judge themselves within a rigidly restrictive moral model that permits only heterosexual expression. All of the major Judeo-Christian religious denominations have theologians who argue that neither the Torah nor the Bible condemns homosexuality as we know it (Boswell, 1990a). There are a number of religious groups studying the moral implications of same-sexed orientation and behavior. Many religiously oriented counselors help gay people sort out these issues in relationship to their own lives.

BIOLOGICAL DETERMINANTS MODEL

In one of the last revisions of his famous work, *Three Essays on the Theory of Sexuality,* Sigmund Freud speculated that the roots of homosexuality might eventually be found in the effects of hormones on mind and body. Since that suggestion was made in 1920, theories emphasizing a physiological basis for homosexuality—either hormonal or genetic—have waxed and waned. Research studies have approached the question from four different angles: (1) examining hormonal differences between adult homosexuals and heterosexuals; (2) studying the sexual orientations of adolescents and adults whose normal hormonal balances have been upset by some medical condition; (3) attempting to discover any prenatal genetic or hormonal factors that might be involved in the determination of later sexual orientations and activities; and (4) examining anatomical differences between the brain structures of homosexual and heterosexual persons.

A few studies have attempted to compare testosterone levels in homosexual men with those of heterosexual men, in an effort to show that homosexual males had less testosterone than heterosexual males. However, very small research populations were used, and the studies were difficult to control well. Their results, therefore, have been inconclusive.

In one research study the hormone estrogen was administered to a group of heterosexual females, heterosexual males, and homosexual males. The researchers believed that various physiological responses might differ in the three groups, since the estrogen would become part of biochemical processes mediated by a system made up of the brain's hypothalamus, the pituitary gland, and the gonads. It is presumed that this system responds differently in men and women, and

283

may even be linked to sexual orientation. Estrogen is known to increase the amount of luteinizing hormone (LH) in men, but not in women. It also can depress the amount of testosterone. The study found that LH was produced in the homosexual men, in amounts intermediate between those found in heterosexual women and men, and also found that their testosterone level stayed depressed for a significantly longer period than that of the heterosexual men (Gladue, Green, & Hellman, 1984). This research has now been replicated by other workers, and no statistically significant differences in LH response were found between homosexual and heterosexual persons (Gooren, 1990).

Another way of studying hormonal influences on sexual orientation is to observe what happens to adolescents or adults whose hormonal balances are disturbed in some way. It seems clear that in males who are exposed to increased levels of female hormones and in females who are exposed to high levels of male hormones there is no change in sexual orientation. The bodily changes resulting from hormone imbalances may upset the affected persons, but their sexual preferences apparently remain intact. Sometimes hormone injections have been used experimentally in attempts to change sexual orientation, but these attempts have failed. Far more research will be necessary to clarify how much—if at all—hormones might influence sexual orientation in adolescents or adults.

The third avenue of study concerning biological determinants of homosexuality has focused on possible prenatal influences. Chapter 6 dealt with the chromosomal and hormonal factors before birth that may affect the development of gender identity in later life. The evidence suggests that certain brain structures may be masculinized by male hormones produced in the fetal testes. It is believed that these influences on the brain lead to a predisposition toward masculine-identified behavior after birth. Conversely, if the fetus is female and no male hormones are produced, the brain pathways are not masculinized, and the behavior of the child is feminine-identified. So far, there has been no clearly demonstrated relationship between such prenatal factors and the development of homosexuality or heterosexuality in humans; but prenatal hormones have been shown to affect later sexual behavior in certain animals. There is currently much speculation regarding the possible part played by the early prenatal hormones in influencing later sex partner preferences in humans.

We might expect that by studying twins we could gain some insight into possible genetic or biological links to homosexuality. While one researcher (Kallman, 1952) reported several decades ago that identical twins tended to have the same sexual orientation, later researchers have not been able to confirm that finding.

Some research data have suggested that homosexuality does tend to run in families. Gay males have a significantly higher likelihood of having a brother, uncle, or male cousin who is homosexual, but no significant likelihood of having a female homosexual relative. Lesbian women also have a greater likelihood of having a homosexual or bisexual sister, although this tendency is less pronounced than the trend among males is. No one is yet sure what these findings mean, but they could indicate some sort of familial connection in the development of sexual orientation, especially in male or female lineages (Pillard, 1990). A controversial study done in Canada showed that homosexual women and men might have a higher incidence of left-handedness, suggesting again some sort of genetic or biological connection (McCormick, Witelson, & Kingstone, 1990).

During the early 1990s, two scientific studies found anatomical differences between the brains of homosexual and heterosexual men. While the findings were preliminary and based on a relatively small number of subjects, they have opened up a new area of research into the possible biological foundations of sexual orientation. The first study found that a part of the brain that governs daily rhythms, the suprachiasmatic nucleus, is twice as large in homosexual men as it is in heterosexual men (Swaab & Hofman, 1990). However, this brain region has not been associated with sexual behavior.

The brain's hypothalamus, on the other hand, is known to play a role in determining sexual behavior in some mammalian groups. The development of the hypothalamus is influenced by hormones, and how it develops then determines sexual behaviors in those animals. It is also known that the anterior part of the human hypothalamus plays some role in human sexuality. A highly compelling research study was published in 1991 that found that a particular collection of cells typically found in the anterior hypothalamus of heterosexual men is missing in homosexual men and in women (LeVay, 1991). These findings will still need to be confirmed by further research, and their implications will be further debated (Barinaga, 1991).

What might be emerging is a view of the brain as a mosaic of different areas that may respond to sex hormones at various stages of fetal and childhood development. Average or usual levels of female or male hormones would produce the typical female or male brain. However, unusual hormone levels present at some critical period in brain growth may affect the development of susceptible areas. This could mean that different regions of the same brain might undergo various kinds of sexual differentiation. Depending on hormone levels and the timing of their exposure to the developing brain, there could be influences on a wide range of characteristics, including handedness and sexual orientation (Witelson, 1991).

All of the conclusions about a possible biological basis for sexual orientation are speculative at this point. When specific biological differences have been discovered, they have increased the danger that homophobic people may react by claiming that the difference in homosexual persons is clearly a "defect." On the other end of the spectrum are those who would insist that it offers evidence that same-sex orientation is as natural a variation from the average brain as something such as left-handedness (Barinaga, 1991). Much more work remains to be done before we can offer solid conclusions about any biological correlates of homosexuality (Gooren, 1990).

PSYCHOANALYTIC MODELS

Many hypotheses concerning homosexuality have viewed it as some sort of psychological problem resulting from unhealthy influences on personality development. Psychoanalysts in particular have contributed numerous hypotheses on the psychodynamics behind the development of homosexuality. Freud believed that homosexuality could result from a variety of difficulties in passing through the various stages of development—oral, anal, latency, and genital. Late in his life, Freud stated that he did not consider homosexuality to be an illness, but instead a sexual function produced by arrested sexual development. Nevertheless, many psychoanalysts have continued to assert that homosexuality is a malady that should receive psychiatric treatment (Isay, 1990).

Irving Bieber and his associates (1962) conducted a study of 106 male homosexual patients, comparing them to 100 heterosexual patients. This study supported the traditional psychoanalytic view that family interactions caused homosexuality—the most typical background consisting of a close-binding, overprotective mother, and a detached, absent, or openly hostile father. The hypothesis claimed that such parents inhibit the expression of heterosexual feelings in the son and do not provide for adequate masculine identification, thus leading to homosexuality. The study subjects were all drawn from patients undergoing psychoanalysis—hardly a representative population. Other studies that attempted to explore Bieber's hypothesis found contradictory results, and more recently it has been concluded that there are no reliable data to support the dominating mother–ineffectual father model for male homosexuality.

The theoretical models typically used to explore women's issues, including lesbianism, have been rooted in psychoanalytic theory. This has led to problems: it has limited the creation of new theories that more accurately reflect the experience of women (Sang, 1989).

Modern psychoanalysts have come to believe that attempts to change people's sexual orientation through therapy may cause severe anxiety, depression, and other symptoms. Such attempts may also reflect the heterosexual biases of the psychoanalyst (Isay, 1990).

THE NORMAL VARIANT MODEL

An increasingly large and powerful group of theorists and researchers believe homosexuality to be a normal variation within the continuum of human sexual behavior. They recognize that homosexual behavior is less common than heterosexual behavior, but do not see any grounds for classifying same-sex behavior as pathological, deviant, perverse, or abnormal. Instead, they view homosexual behavior as a natural, but less prevalent, form of sexual expression. As early as 1951, Ford and Beach noted that among mammals sexual contacts between members of the same sex are quite common. These contacts may be playful and casual or overtly sexual. This information has led some theorists to conclude that a degree of homosexual activity is quite typical for mammals, including humans. Others have claimed that comparison of humans to other animals has no validity. In any case, here are some of the hypotheses that fit into this model.

Judd Marmor, a Los Angeles psychiatrist, has been a primary advocate for considering homosexuality to be a valid, nonpathological form of human sexual expression. He has cited the Ford and Beach work as evidence of homosexual activity in mammalian species. Marmor accepts that parental influences may play a role in the development of sexual preference. Homosexuals, like heterosexuals, come from a variety of backgrounds. He emphasizes that many homosexual people are happy, productive, and apparently well adjusted, and that their sexual orientations can hardly be considered illness (Marmor, 1980, 1985).

In England during the late 1950s a special committee was formed to study homosexual offenses and prostitution. The committee studied many homosexual people and concluded that most of them were well-adjusted individuals. The committee's report drew wide attention because of its recommendations for repeal of British laws prohibiting homosexual acts between consenting adults (Wolfenden, 1963).

Another important British study compared lesbian women and heterosexual women who had been matched by age, education, and intelligence. Both groups were administered a series of personality tests,

FIGURE 11.4 Same-Sex Orientation

Researchers believe that homosexual behavior is simply a variant of the predominant sexual orientation of most humans. The psychological health of both heterosexuals and homosexuals appears to be, statistically, about the same.

and the homosexual and heterosexual women were found to be equally healthy psychologically (Hopkins, 1969). In the United States, Evelyn Hooker was one of the most influential researchers to propose that homosexuality is a normal behavioral variant. She has studied well-adjusted homosexuals living in the gay community. Hooker's findings tend to confirm that in terms of psychological health, homosexual and heterosexual people are indistinguishable. She has reported that many gay men and lesbians are living happy, productive lives (Hooker, 1965, 1967).

Researchers at the Kinsey Institute for Sex Research conducted a carefully designed study of homosexual people, recruiting them from a variety of environments. They reported that in light of the evidence gathered it is difficult not to agree with the conclusion that homosexuality is a sexual variation within the normal range of psychological functioning (Bell & Weinberg, 1978).

THE BELL, WEINBERG, AND HAMMERSMITH STUDY ON SEXUAL PREFERENCE

While this ground-breaking study on the development of sexual preference has already been discussed in chapter 9, "Sexual Individuality and Sexual Values," it

is worth noting again here because lesbians and gay men were such a crucial part of the research population. Representing the Kinsey Institute, Alan Bell, Martin Weinberg, and Sue Kiefer Hammersmith (1981) designed and carried out important research into the possible causes of homosexuality. It was a controlled study, involving interviews with 979 homosexual men and women and a comparison sample of 477 heterosexual men and women. In examining any difference found between the homosexual and heterosexual samples, the researchers controlled for the possible effects of age, education, and social status to make sure any differences between the two groups were not due to such factors.

A tremendous amount of data was gathered in the 3- to 5-hour, face-to-face interviews conducted with each person. The questions in the interview were drawn from a variety of theoretical stances concerning the development of homosexual orientations. The data were then subjected to a complex statistical technique known as path analysis.

On the basis of their research, the most scientifically sound work ever done on this particular issue, Bell, Weinberg, and Hammersmith drew the following conclusions concerning sexual preference:

1. Sexual preference appears to be largely determined prior to adolescence, even when youngsters have not been particularly sexually active.
2. Homosexual behavior emerges from homosexual feelings typically experienced for about 3 years prior to any overt homosexual activity. Such feelings play more of a role in becoming homosexual than any particular activities with others.
3. Homosexual women and men tend to have a history of heterosexual experiences during childhood and adolescence. Unlike the control group heterosexuals, however, they report these experiences as being relatively unsatisfying.
4. Identification with a parent of either sex appears to play no significant role in the development of sexual orientation.
5. There is no support for the hypothesis that any particular type of mother produces homosexual children. In the study there was a slightly higher proportion of homosexuals that had poor relationships with their fathers. However, it was impossible to determine if this was a causative factor in their sexual orientation or simply a reflection of the difficulty that sexually different sons or daughters might have in relating with their fathers.

The findings of the Bell, Weinberg, and Hammersmith study provide little support for the models that emphasize psychoanalytic or learning theories as determinants of homosexual orientation. Although these researchers did not study genetic or hormonal characteristics, they did state that their "findings are not inconsistent with what one would expect to find if, indeed, there were a biological basis for sexual preference" (p. 216). They further speculated that such a biological mechanism would probably account for gender identity as well as sexual orientation (see chapter 6, "Gender-Identity/Role and Society") and that it might well be operative in varying degrees. That is to say, it would operate more powerfully in individuals who are exclusively homosexual or heterosexual than it would for bisexual people.

This crucial study has shed new light on the development of sexual orientation. Most importantly of all, it has demonstrated the complexity of this issue and the research that attempts to study it. We are still a very long way from having a comprehensive model explaining how any of us become homosexual, heterosexual, or any other variation on the sexual preference theme. Until then, the only factually supportable answer to the question "What causes sexual orientation?" is "We don't know."

FINDING THE FACTS

There are many questions about homosexuality that remain unresolved. Hypotheses and therapies abound, a few supported by careful research and investigation, many concocted from opinion and personal bias. As a result of their research, Bell and Weinberg (1978) proposed that the terms *homosexual* and *homosexuality* are imprecise and misleading. They emphasized that there are as many different kinds of homosexuals as there are heterosexuals and that it is impossible to predict the nature of one's personality, social adjustment, or sexual functioning on the basis of one's sexual orientation. Instead, they recommended that homosexuality be defined in terms of several variables: the degree to which one is sexual, the level of sexual interest and activity, the nature of sexual stimulation, the extent of sexual problems, the nature of one's sexual relationships and partnerships, and the attitudes one has toward homosexuality. In this sense there is no such thing as the homosexual but instead several homosexualities.

The confusion over homosexuality is particularly difficult for the person who is concerned about his or her own homosexual feelings. Whether such individuals consider themselves sick or healthy, normal or abnormal, will depend largely on the attitudes of the people around them and what information is available to them. The essential aim for all human beings, regardless of their sexual orientations, must be to find

FIGURE 11.5 Homosexual Stereotyping

Perhaps because homosexual behavior is not predominant in this society, many people have stereotyped ideas about homosexuals that are not based on fact. One of the most common myths is that gay men act and dress in an effeminate manner and gay women act and dress in a masculine manner.

the sexual life-style that is most satisfying, peaceful, and comfortable for them, without being hurtful or exploitative of others.

PERSPECTIVES ON THERAPY

Among those professionals who have viewed homosexuality as a disorder, a great deal of attention has been given to therapy and cure. As is appropriate for any illness model, these practitioners hope that as many individuals as possible can be helped to achieve a state of health—in this case assumed to be heterosexuality. The psychoanalytic models have usually recommended that the homosexual individual face the conflicts and problems left over from childhood, resolve them in some manner, and thereby be left free to pursue heterosexuality.

Some psychotherapists claim that they have "cured" or changed homosexuals. This usually seems

homosexualities: a term that reminds us there is not a single pattern of homosexuality, but a wide range of same-sex orientations.

287

to mean that the patient has stopped participating in homosexual behavior and has begun functioning sexually with members of the opposite sex. The people who have made this change were apparently unhappy with and guilty over their homosexual activities and wished very much to give them up. There are other professionals who debate that a behavioral shift simply represents a conscious choice to act in a way that both the homosexual and the therapist consider more appropriate.

One model of homosexual identity formation (which we will look at further in the next section) suggests that people probably have some personal latitude in choosing particular sexual activities, regardless of how they identify their sexual orientations (Cass, 1990). Inherent in this concept are the ideas that people may choose or avoid whatever sexual behaviors they want for whatever reasons and that those behaviors may change at different points in people's lives. From this perspective, then, the change from homosexual to heterosexual behavior could result from an individual's realization of her or his freedom of choice regarding sexual behavior.

It is clear that some counselors and therapists have homophobic attitudes that may be detrimental to gay or lesbian clients. Of particular concern are those professionals who are not aware of their own prejudices, but bring their negative sentiments in subtle ways to the counseling process. Some surveys have shown a greater degree of dissatisfaction with counseling among gay and lesbian persons, and this often seems to be the result of negative messages from professional counselors (Rudolph, 1988). Homosexual people must therefore select their counselors and therapists with great care; they frequently prefer to select a professional who also has a homosexual orientation, avoiding those who might hold homophobic attitudes (McDermott, Tyndall, & Lichtenberg, 1989).

In the 1960s, when behavior modification was gaining in popularity among psychologists, a number of techniques were developed to eliminate homosexual behavior and condition the individual to find heterosexual stimuli appealing. One approach, called aversion therapy, involved showing pictures of male nudes to male homosexuals while administering painful electrical shock at the same time. Then pictures of female nudes would be shown without the shock and with encouragement to feel sexually aroused. Studies began to appear indicating that long-range effects were limited and that most patients reverted to homosexual behavior in a relatively short time. The techniques came under fire for their inadequacies, oversimplifications, and barbaric treatment of clients. For the most part, aversion therapy has been dropped as a treatment for homosexuals.

Homosexual Identity Formation

Until recently, very little attention had been given to the process by which a person comes to adopt a homosexual identity. While categories and labels represent generalizations, and are often used as excuses for bigotry or oppression, they also provide a way of making sense out of an immense array of information. Sometimes people need a label or category into which they can fit themselves, and thus have a greater sense of who they are. This inner sense of personal identity can have important implications for the way an individual experiences herself or himself. It was not until the late 1960s and early 1970s that the notion of homosexual identity began to emerge. It was an important transition time socially, since it began to draw attention away from specific sexual behaviors and more toward an understanding of sexual orientation as it becomes integrated into the personality. Becoming able to identify oneself as gay or lesbian and disclosing that orientation to selected others seem to be important in the formation of a comfortable homosexual identity. This, in turn, is important to promoting the person's psychological adjustment (Miranda & Storms, 1989).

Australian psychologist Vivienne Cass (1983/84, 1990) has emphasized the need to pay attention to people's self-perceptions in understanding the experience of homosexuality. This perspective assumes that sexual orientation is not so rigidly fixed that it cannot be modified. People's perceptions of their sexuality may shift with time, even during the adult years, and such shifts may result in new patterns of sexual behavior or relationships. In other words, homosexual identity is not something that is necessarily permanently fixed, even though it may be long-lasting and relatively unswerving for many people. This model of sexual orientation assumes that individuals may consciously alter their sexual behaviors to a degree, depending on the ways in which they have come to see themselves.

STAGES OF HOMOSEXUAL IDENTITY FORMATION

Cass's theory holds that in order for the process of homosexual identity formation to begin, the individual must experience some degree of sexual interest in, or attraction for, someone of the same sex. This does not necessarily have to be expressed through any overt sexual behavior, but may instead take the form of fantasies or daydreams. Cass has elucidated six stages in the process of homosexual identity formation, and maintains that there may be many individual variations in how different people progress through these stages.

Case Study

STEVEN: A YOUNG MAN'S SEXUAL IDENTITY UNFOLDS

Steven had realized that he was somewhat attracted to other boys by the time he was 8 years old. He had his first sexual experience with another boy about his age when he was 13, and found it extremely enjoyable. He maintained a close bond and sexual relationship with the other boy for about a year, at which time the boy told Steven that he did not wish to continue having sex. This was a difficult time for Steven, but he eventually coped with the end of the relationship.

While in high school, Steven came out to several carefully selected friends and to his parents. Most of these individuals were quite accepting of his orientation, particularly his mother. Although his father said he would always love him, he told Steven that he was not particularly comfortable discussing the matter further. In his school, he helped form a small support group for gay and lesbian students, and he became politically active with a group of gays in a nearby city.

When Steven moved away to college, he was uncertain of how open he wanted to be about his sexual orientation. However, within a month of his arrival, he had talked about his orientation with his straight roommate, and had joined a lesbian and gay student organization on campus. When he ran for office in the student senate of

his college, he received some telephoned threats. This led Steven to seek help from college administrators to deal with homophobia on the campus; in turn he worked with them for the creation of a new support group for gay and lesbian students in the counseling center. Steven continued to offer advice and encouragement to other students who were coming out at the college. During this time he maintained a close relationship with another young man, and they eventually chose to room together in one of the dormitories.

When Steven was a senior, he talked with a counselor about clarifying his relationship with his father. During visits home, he felt increasingly as though he were being called upon to pretend that he was not gay. A strategy for communicating with his father emerged, and he put it into action at the next opportunity. He was pleased to discover that his father had done a great deal of thinking and reading about homosexuality, and was ready to permit more openness on Steven's part about his sexual orientation. He affirmed for Steven that he would be happy to talk with other relatives or family friends if Steven wanted him to. Being able to establish more open communication with his father seemed to help Steven feel more comfortable about his own life.

She believes that movement through the stages is motivated by the persistent need to maintain some sort of consistent image of oneself in relationship to sexual orientation, and the need to maintain a sense of self-esteem—or positive feelings about oneself—relevant to one's sexual orientation. A summary of the six stages of homosexual identity formation follows (Cass, 1990):

Stage I: Identity Confusion   This stage occurs when people begin to realize that information about homosexuality somehow relates to them and their reactions. As they realize that the personal relevance of this information cannot be ignored, they begin to experience a sense of inconsistency and incongruency in their view of their sexual selves. This period of confusion may go on for some time, during which there may be an attempt to avoid homosexual behavior even in the

face of persistent dreams and fantasies about members of the same sex. Individuals may attempt to find more information about homosexuality as the question "Am I homosexual?" is addressed. This moves them along toward the second stage of identity formation.

Stage II: Identity Comparison   It is during this stage that people begin to examine the broader implications of being homosexual, as they begin to feel different from family members and peers. Everyone grows up with certain heterosexual expectations and behavioral guidelines. As people's homosexual identities develop, those expectations and guidelines are gradually given up, and there may be a profound sense of loss and grieving. Individuals who are experiencing this sense of social alienation may react in a variety of ways. They may react positively to being different, and begin devaluing the importance of heterosexuality in their lives. However, they may still need to "pass," or pretend heterosexuality, in order to avoid negative confrontations about their homosexuality that they are not prepared to deal with. Many people react by rejecting a homosexual identity at this point, even though they may recognize their behaviors and inclinations as homosexual. They may define their same-sexed behavior as the result of a particular relationship, of having been innocently seduced, of being bisexual, or as only a temporary state. Another possible reaction is to fear negative reactions from others so much that homosexuality is devalued. Some people at this stage undoubtedly turn their own personal identity confusion into antihomosexual attitudes and exaggerated heterosexual behavior, even though they may be covertly indulging in homosexual activities or fantasies.

Stage III: Identity Tolerance When individuals come to accept their homosexuality and begin to recognize the sexual, social, and emotional needs that go with being homosexual, an increased commitment to and tolerance for the identity emerges. Typically, there is increased involvement with other homosexual people. At this stage, involvement with the gay or lesbian community may have advantages, since there will be a support group that understands the person's concerns, more opportunity to meet partners and see positive role models, and a chance to begin feeling more at ease with the identity. This stage may be more difficult for people who are shy and lacking in social skills, or who have low self-esteem and fears of having their sexual identity known by others. People whose experiences are largely negative during this stage may never progress any further in the development of a homosexual identity. However, those who perceive their experiences as more positive will eventually develop enough commitment to a homosexual identity to be able to say, "I am a homosexual."

Gay men and lesbians are found in every community, all walks of life, and on every socioeconomic level. They often share little in common except their sexual orientation, and even that has many different variables. It seems likely that most homosexual people blend into their environments without being noticed for their sexual inclinations or behaviors. Most of the people around them—particularly those who react adversely to homosexuality—undoubtedly assume them to be heterosexual and give their sexuality little thought. Those who wish to blend in often become quite adept at making gestures toward and about the opposite sex that create an impression of heterosexual interest.

Since there are still many forms of discrimination and homophobic sentiment, lesbians and gay men face

decisions about how open they wish to be about their sexual orientation. Being secretive about one's homosexuality has been called being in the closet. The process of allowing oneself to acknowledge homosexual attractions and then express them to others has been called coming out of the closet. How far a gay man or lesbian individual will come out, and to whom, depends on a variety of factors, one of the most crucial being her or his degree of self-acceptance. Some homosexual persons feel that it is crucial to share this important aspect of their personalities with friends and family members, while others feel that it is more a personal matter that is irrelevant to others. Decisions about coming out must be weighed with care, and the possibility of negative or hurtful consequences considered. Many homosexual people have found, however, that others can accept their orientation comfortably.

Stage IV: Identity Acceptance This stage occurs when people accept a homosexual self-image, rather than simply tolerating it, and when they have continuing and increased contact with the gay and lesbian subculture. There is a positive identification with other homosexual persons. The attitudes and life-styles of other homosexual people can play a significant role in determining how comfortable individuals are in ex-

(continued on p. 292)

coming out: to acknowledge to oneself and to others that one is sexually attracted to others of the same sex.

FIGURE 11.6   Self-Acceptance

Many homosexuals need to decide when and if they will make their sexual orientation known to others. The primary factor in the ability to make this decision is the homosexual female or male's degree of self-acceptance.

Coming Out Requires Support and Understanding

Coming out is the process whereby lesbians, bisexuals, and gay men reveal their sexual orientation to themselves and/or others. Coming out can be both a rewarding and a difficult process whether you are the person coming out or the person who is come out to. It can be rewarding by bringing a new level of openness and honesty into relationships with family, friends, and roommates. But it can also be difficult.

Because most people tend not to discuss homosexuality and bisexuality as general issues very frequently, it's often hard for gays, lesbians, and bisexuals to know how someone they might otherwise know very well will respond, much less someone they've only known a short while.

"Hi. What's your name? What college are you in? I'm a lesbian. What's your major?"

Coming out involves sharing an important and personal part of yourself and risking being rejected for it.

"Will she hate me? Beat me up? Move out? Kick *me* out?" "Should I even tell him? If I don't tell him, will he find out? Not trust me? Can my boyfriend ever visit?"

Coming out can also be hard if you are the person who is come out to. Suddenly someone shares this "important and personal part of themselves" with you and you're supposed to respond. You may feel pressured to say the right thing, and at the same time be confused about the way you feel. "Is she attracted to me? Will people think I'm a lesbian too? Is it moral? Do I have to be supportive?" "Will he bring all his gay friends over? Am I closed-minded? Will he *think* I'm closed-minded?"

The best advice I have to offer people, whether you're coming out or someone is coming out to you, is to try to understand what the other person is feeling without denying your own feelings.

If you come out to someone, don't expect him/her to be 100 percent supportive right away. I don't mean you should accept intolerance, but that a certain amount of uncertainty when you first come out is understandable, especially if you're the first openly non-straight person he/she has known.

If someone comes out to you, be as supportive as you can. Recognize that it may have been very difficult for him or her to share this with you. And even if you are uncomfortable with someone's sexuality, you can still be supportive.

The best way I've found for working through the discomfort of coming out is to talk about it. If you're not ready for this right away, wait. But don't avoid the subject forever.

When you do talk, be honest and listen to what the other person says. If you've come out to someone, remember that, "I'm a little uncomfortable with this. I've never known anyone gay before," is *not* the same thing as, "I hate all Queers." It's honest, it's not an attack, and it can express a willingness to try to become more comfortable. In the same way, "I wish you were more comfortable with my sexuality," is *not* the same thing as, "I think you are a homophobic idiot." It's honest, it's not an attack, and it can express an attempt to understand the discomfort.

Finally, if you have to be untrue to yourself to accommodate another, don't. If someone is homophobic, call them on it. If your roommate expects you to devote your life to gay-supportive activism—and you don't want to—don't.

Even though we may approach issues and events from different perspectives, we're all people, no matter what label (if any) we use for our sexualities. Keeping in mind the things we have in common makes it easier to mediate our differences.

—Karla Westphal, *Yale Herald,* September 20, 1991

pressing their identity. If they associate with others who feel that homosexuality is fully legitimate, then this is the attitude that will most likely be adopted. Then they must deal with finding homophobic attitudes offensive; and, as self-acceptance increases, move toward Stage V.

Stage V: Identity Pride By this point in their identity formation, homosexual people are not as likely to be using heterosexuality as the standard by which they judge themselves and the behavior of others. As they identify more with the gay and lesbian community, pride in the accomplishments of that community deepens. Sometimes people in this stage become activists in political movements to fight discrimination and homophobia, and there may be more confrontations with the heterosexual establishment. For many, this is an angry stage. Efforts to conceal one's sexual orientation are increasingly abandoned, and selected family members and coworkers may be informed.

Because of prevailing social attitudes toward homosexuality, people are often alarmed to discover that a spouse, parent, child, sibling, or friend is a homosexual. Some people react to such a discovery with fear and loathing, others with blame and guilt, still others with tolerance, understanding, and sensitivity. It is quite typical for parents, upon discovering that a son or daughter is homosexual, to blame themselves and wonder "what we did wrong." Yet, as earlier sections of this chapter have demonstrated, there is no solid evidence to support the belief that parental influences are important in the formation of sexual orientation. Coming out to parents and other family members remains one of the greatest challenges to young gay men as they consolidate their personal identity during the college years (D'Augelli, 1991). There is an organization called Parents and Friends of Lesbians and Gays (PFLAG), through which parents and others can learn more about homosexuality and deal with their feelings. Eventually many parents come to accept the homosexuality of their child. There are other unfortunate cases in which the homosexual daughter or son is excluded from the family. This reaction usually only intensifies feelings of guilt and rejection.

Whether individuals move to the final stage of identity formation is often determined by the reaction of significant others to the disclosure of homosexuality. If there are mostly negative reactions, the person may only feel more confirmed that heterosexuals represent the opposition and are not to be trusted. If the reactions tend toward the positive and accepting, individuals may well be able to move on.

Stage VI: Identity Synthesis In this final stage of identity formation, people realize that the world is not divided into us (homosexuals) and them (heterosexuals). Not all heterosexuals need to be viewed negatively, and not all homosexuals positively. The anger that is so often experienced in Stage V is reduced, and the gay or lesbian aspects of one's identity may be fully integrated with other aspects of the self and personality. The identity formation process is complete.

MALE-FEMALE DIFFERENCES IN HOMOSEXUAL IDENTITY FORMATION

Different patterns of socialization between women and men lead to differences in the ways that homosexual identity is acquired by the two sexes. Up until the 1980s most research on homosexuality focused on males. It has only been since about 1980 that lesbian-centered models have emerged, and so we have been able to view lesbians within new and more positive contexts (Sang, 1989).

It is often stated that male homosexuals tend to be more promiscuous than lesbians. The word *promiscuity* has been given a variety of definitions—the most general and workable one being lack of strict monogamy; that is, seeking more than what a single (sexual) partner has to offer. This definition includes those individuals who have frequent casual sexual contacts, often with complete anonymity between the partners. The evidence does seem to suggest that more male homosexuals seek contact from a variety of sexual partners than do lesbians or heterosexual males, in general. This is probably in part because men in our society are taught to behave more promiscuously than women are. Extreme promiscuity, involving anonymity between partners, is almost unknown among female homosexuals.

Several research studies indicate that most homosexual males become aware of their same-sex orientation during childhood or adolescence. Whitam (1977) reports that of 107 exclusively homosexual men, 67 percent indicated having been aware of their sexual attraction to males by age 13, and 91 percent by age 17. These results are supported by Dank (1971) who showed that 93 percent of homosexual men had been aware of their orientation by age 19. A study of 789 male homosexuals in West Germany indicates that 86 percent of them had realized they might be homosexual by the age of 19 (Reiche & Dannecker, 1977). The Whitam study also showed that many gay men were aware of their same-sex interests at an early age. When asked, "In childhood sex play were you more interested in and excited by playing around with other boys than with girls?" 77.6 percent of the exclusively homosexual men answered yes and 19.6 percent answered no. In contrast, among the exclusively heterosexual men who were asked the same question, only 11.8 percent answered yes and 82.4 percent said no. It is evident that at least among many homosexual males an awareness of their sexual orientation emerges early in their lives.

Because of the early awareness of homosexual feelings and attractions, males are more likely to enter the identity formation process earlier than is typical for females. They often fantasize sexually about other males relatively early in their lives. Males are also more likely than females to enter the process of homosexual identity formation on the basis of sexual stimulation, while at the same time adjusting to male stereotypical roles by dressing and acting in the traditional male manner. This is probably because there is less incentive for gay men to reject male sex roles, since these roles are more highly valued in our culture than traditional female sex roles, which tend to be given a lower status (Cass, 1990).

It may be that people have less negative reaction to the idea of lesbian contacts. Gagnon and Simon (1973) suggested that heterosexual men probably fantasize about lesbians more than heterosexual women do and that these men may simply assume that lesbians are really heterosexual women who haven't yet found the right man. In fact, research tends to show that lesbianism is not associated with either a lack of past heterosexual experience or a history of negative sexual interactions with men (Bell, Weinberg, & Hammersmith, 1981; Brannock & Chapman, 1990). Loving contacts between women are certainly less noticeable than those between men, since Western culture generally permits more demonstration of affection between women.

Lesbians are less likely to use sexual stimulation as a route into the homosexual identity formation process. Instead, that process is more typically initiated when a woman falls in love with another woman. Again, because this often occurs later in life for women than for men, it is not uncommon for a woman in midlife to experience homosexual love for the first time. In the earlier stages of homosexual identity formation, women are more likely to reject the passive, nurturing aspects of the traditional female sex role. Sometimes, women begin adopting a homosexual identity as the result of their association with feminist groups and philosophies, which may have also put them in touch with loving feelings for other women (Cass, 1990). Other times, a woman may first begin to have fantasies and feelings for other women only after having first experienced pleasurable sex with a woman. For these reasons, it may also be that the lesbian experience of sexual orientation may not fit the more sexual behavior-oriented Kinsey scale particularly well. Women generally seem to show less

consistency than men over time in their sexual fantasies, emotional attractions, and behaviors (Nichols, 1990).

BISEXUAL PEOPLE

What of those men and women whose behavior and/or preferences do not reflect a clear predominance of either heterosexual or homosexual behavior or attraction? At least a small percentage of human beings experience relatively equal amounts of homosexual and heterosexual behavior. Slang terms such as *AC-DC* and *switchhitter* have been applied to these individuals. It is likely, however, that they are often identified as homosexual. It has even been suggested that research on homosexuality has been confounded by the inclusion of large numbers of bisexuals in studies (MacDonald, 1984).

The term *bisexual* has come under attack for its implicit assumption that the bisexual person makes a distinct separation between men and women, and that sexual activity must be involved. It has been suggested that terms such as *bisensual* or *bigenderist* be employed to describe people who have the ability to be sensual and intimate with both women and men (Geller, 1990).

In one study of gay men and lesbians, aged 25 to 40, few of the men showed a substantially bisexual orientation (2–4 on the Kinsey scale), and they seemed to see themselves as either homosexual or heterosexual. Even those whose behavior was a fairly even mix of same- and opposite-sex activities tended to say they knew they were really homosexual or heterosexual, but behaved differently because of social expectations or other reasons (Pillard, 1990). It has also been suggested that people who fit into Kinsey categories 1–5 have been tacitly told by those on both ends of the scale to make up their minds and make a choice (Voeller, 1990). There is even a level of what has been called *biphobia* within lesbian and gay communities, and bisexual persons are sometimes considered to be fence-sitters, traitors, and cop-outs politically (Udis-Kessler, 1990).

It was Sigmund Freud who first suggested that human beings are essentially bisexual at birth, but that most often the homosexual component is blocked during psychosexual development and by social pressures. Since Freud put forth his hypothesis, people have argued for and against it. Some professionals have maintained that some persons go through a period of bisexuality when they are in transition from heterosexual behavior to homosexual behavior.

Several circumstances seem to be especially conducive to homosexual activity among people who may

293

otherwise have considered themselves primarily heterosexual. For example, any group sexual behavior may lead to some sexual interaction among members of the same sex. Sexual experimentation can also occur between two close friends of the same sex. Sometimes, sharing closeness in political philosophies or personal belief systems leads to physical closeness and sharing as well (Blumstein & Schwartz, 1977).

One hypothesis suggests that many bisexuals respond to particular human qualities that are not exclusive to either women or men and therefore permit the bisexual to respond erotically to women and men who have those particular qualities. Much more work must be done before we fully understand bisexuality and the development of all sexual preferences. For individuals who exhibit both heterosexual and homosexual behavior or preference over an extended period of time, the following categories could be considered definitive:

1. Those who see sexual participation as a stage in the evolution of intimacy between individuals who are striving to deepen the meaning of their relationship, regardless of their sex.
2. Individuals who are truly confused with regard to their sexual identity and—through diverse experience—are attempting to define a more distinct sexual role.
3. Essentially hedonistic, or sociopathic, individuals whose primary goal is their own sensual pleasure and sexual release. The sex of their partners is immaterial.
4. Individuals with a primarily homosexual orientation who make attempts to affirm a heterosexual identity and/or to reduce the guilt that they associate with exclusive homosexuality through heterosexual participation (MacDonald, 1981).

The phenomenon of bisexuality remains confusing. Rarely is it considered separately from homosexuality, and most often it is viewed as one form of homosexuality. There is still much to be learned about its many aspects.

COMPARING SAME-SEX BEHAVIOR IN MALES AND FEMALES

To approach an understanding of different persons' life-styles from the perspective of their shared sexual orientation is constricting and limiting. For some predominantly homosexual individuals, their homosexuality is a central and important theme of their lives; for others, it is a relatively insignificant sidelight. In terms of sexual activity, it should be emphasized that except for penis-in-vagina intercourse, same-sexed couples share a full range of sexual activity and can find great joy and satisfaction in this sharing. Their

physiological responses to sexual arousal are the same as those of heterosexuals (Masters & Johnson, 1979). Two books that are available describing the spectrum of sexual and sensual activities for homosexual men and women are: *Intimacy Between Men* (Driggs & Finn, 1990) and *Lesbian Passion: Loving Ourselves and Each Other* (Loulan, 1987).

Many people wonder what sexual activities two men can share. As described in chapter 10, "Solitary Sex and Shared Sex," there is a full range of sexual intimacy in male homosexual contact (Driggs & Finn, 1990). Some men fondle one another's genitals or masturbate each other. There often are gentle, loving gestures such as kisses, embraces, and body stroking. Oral-genital contact is common, and many homosexual males practice fellatio. Simultaneous mouth-genital contact of both partners (sometimes called sixty-nine) is not always easily accomplished and may not be as common as many believe (Tripp, 1975). Anal intercourse is practiced by some male couples, although not as frequently as fellatio (Bell & Weinberg, 1978). It is likely that gay men will approach both fellatio and anal intercourse with increased caution, since both may transmit the AIDS virus. Wearing condoms can reduce, though not eliminate, the dangers.

Men who share sex have definite preferences, and there are some who are not at all interested in oral-genital sex or anal intercourse. Many gay males apparently have a strong preference for manual manipulation of one another's genitals or lying together in such a way that the genitals may be rubbed together. It is also common for one partner to insert his penis between the other's thighs (interfemoral intercourse) or to rub his penis on the other's abdomen (Tripp, 1975). There have been some reports of brachioproctic activity, commonly called fisting or handballing, in which the hand of one partner is inserted into the rectum of the other, producing an intense sexual experience (Lowry & Williams, 1983). There are risks of damage to the anal or rectal tissue with such practices.

To view male homosexual relations only in terms of sexual behavior would be unfair. Homosexual people love one another, seek out one another for companionship, and share a full range of nonsexual activities. In a sex education group I once attended, several homosexuals were asked what they did together. One of them answered, "We watch TV, go to the theater, go for walks, travel, play baseball, go to the beach, and a lot more."

It is often assumed that since women lack a penis their sexual interactions with one another must either

brachioproctic activity (brake-ee-o-PRAHK-tik): known in slang as "fisting"; a hand is inserted into the rectum of a partner.

Case Study

ROXANNE: A WOMAN FINDS HER IDENTITY AS A LESBIAN

When Roxanne and her husband were married, he was fully aware of her homosexual background. Although she had been a sexually active lesbian since the age of 17, Roxanne had fallen in love with Leonard and wanted a family very much. The first 5 years of their marriage went well, and the couple had two children, a boy and a girl. Roxanne reports that she enjoyed the sexual relationship with her husband, although she was still fully aware of her homosexual interests. She then began to develop a relationship with a lesbian who worked in the same office. Eventually they began to share sexual activity. This relationship continued sporadically for about 3 years, without the knowledge of Roxanne's husband. Then the other woman moved away, and Roxanne refrained from further homosexual contact for a 4-year period.

It was when her children were aged 10 and 12 that Roxanne confronted her husband with the fact that she was in love with a woman and no longer felt that it was fair for her to continue in the marriage. She also admitted her lesbian affair of former years. The husband immediately sought legal advice and left their apartment with the children. During the divorce proceedings that ensued, Roxanne fought for custody of her children, maintaining that her sexual orientation did not hinder her capabilities as a mother. The social worker who investigated the case reported that Roxanne appeared to be a competent parent and recommended to the court that her sexual orientation not be considered a relevant issue. The court granted a shared custody arrangement, although eventually the children spent most of the year with Roxanne and her female partner.

---

make use of an artificial phallus (dildo), or be relatively uninteresting. This view reflects a mistaken preoccupation with the phallic necessities of sex. Female homosexuals have a wide range of intimate activities to share (Loulan, 1987). It is true that many women almost exclusively use petting techniques such as kissing and general body contact with one another—especially those women who are less experienced with homosexual activity. Manual manipulation of one another's genitals and finger penetration is the most frequently used form of stimulation among lesbians, with oral-genital contact (cunnilingus) being the preferred technique for reaching orgasm. The use of dildos or other objects to be used in vaginal insertion is less common.

Women involved in a sexual encounter usually spend a longer period than male couples in gentle and affectionate foreplay, also giving more attention to caressing and nongenital stimulation (Masters & Johnson, 1979). One study indicated that lesbian couples shared genital sexual activity less frequently than married heterosexual couples (Blumstein & Schwartz, 1983), while another study found that lesbian women reported more frequent orgasms and a greater degree of sexual satisfaction than did heterosexual women (Coleman, Hoon, & Hoon, 1983). Research does indicate that "single" lesbians have sex less frequently than "single" gay men, and that lesbians have relatively low levels of sexual activity when they are involved in a long-term committed relationship. They often seem to prefer hugging and cuddling to more genitalized forms of sexual sharing. Research also suggests that lesbian women have a lower rate of sexual activity in their relationships than gay men do, and that women have somewhat less social freedom in our culture to live out homosexual life-styles with one another (Nichols, 1990).

In the homosexual community and subculture, it is clear that lesbians have a very low profile in comparison to male homosexuals. They are less detectable, arrested less frequently, and suffer less from adverse public opinion. They can be subjected to discrimination in jobs and housing. Exploration of female homosexuality and lesbian relationships should be a major priority of future sex research, since there is such a lack of information at present.

SAME-SEX RELATIONSHIPS

Heterosexual relationships have usually served as the prototype by which relationships between members of the same sex have been judged and labeled. In any relationship between human beings, two people are interdependent, and each partner influences the other to some extent. In a close relationship, the partners

295

interact and influence each other frequently and strongly. Even when they are apart, they think of one another. Their mutual influence spans a range of activities and domains in their lives, and the relationship is of relatively long duration. In conceptualizing homosexual relationships, it has been typical to single out shared sex between the partners as the distinguishing factor. However, there are nonsexual loving relationships between members of the same sex, too.

There are also situations in which two same-sexed individuals share a lengthy sexual affair, but do not consider themselves to be lesbian or gay. They simply have chosen to have sex with this one particular partner. Therefore, in examining some relationships, we must also take into consideration how the partners identify themselves. As we have seen, sexual self-identification can change over time. It is also crucial to point out that physical sexual attraction is not always the central basis for homosexual relationships. Partners may also be drawn together for social and psychological reasons other than sex (Peplau & Cochran, 1990).

Unfortunately, there has been little research on same-sex relationships, particularly those involving women. Yet it may be that studying lesbian relationships can tell us a great deal about women. In the last century, romantic friendships were apparently common among upper-middle-class women. These women were often single, childless, and career-oriented. They would sometimes live together, although the scarce evidence available would suggest that their relationships, sometimes called "Boston marriages," may not have included genital sexual activity. Around the turn of the century in America, some women dressed as men, adopted male names, and "passed" for men. Sometimes they established marriage-like relationships with other women. Women in this time and culture had fewer life options than men did, and it may be that these relationships represented ways of escaping from the limited social roles available to them. More recently, as the lesbian-feminist culture expanded in the 1970s and 1980s, women became more able to recognize their same-sex attractions, although lesbianism is often perceived among women more as a choice of life-style than it is a sexual identity (Nichols, 1990).

In a survey of research on gay and lesbian relationships in the United States, Peplau & Cochran (1990) found several trends. Most gay men and lesbian women want to have an enduring close relationship. About 75 percent of lesbians and 40 to 60 percent of gay men report being in an ongoing intimate relationship at present, and most perceive those relationships as stable. Not surprisingly, satisfaction tends to be highest when both partners are equally committed to and involved in the relationship. Factors such as age,

education, income, religion, and race do not seem to be significant in determining relational satisfaction between homosexual persons. In general, people involved in relationships are also satisfied with their sex lives, and value a sense of power equality between themselves and their partners.

There are three primary patterns of relationships that develop between gay men and between lesbian women. One pattern employs the heterosexual model for dating and marriage as a basis for determining roles within the relationship, with one partner adopting more of the traditional masculine functions and the other adopting more of the feminine roles. Another common pattern sees a marked age difference between the partners, with an older individual paired with a younger person of the same sex. A third pattern seems to be modeled after friendships, with emphasis on sharing and equality between partners who are similar in age and social status.

Significant others may have an impact on the lives of homosexual individuals in relationships. Studies tend to show that "coming out" to parents and other significant relatives and friends, and being honest about homosexual relationships, seem to be generally desirable steps to take for the individuals, even if there is some degree of disapproval. The whole issue of parents can be complicated, and some same-sexed couples even sleep separately when one partner's parents are visiting. In a long-term relationship, the kinds of issues and problems encountered may be very much the same as those surrounding in-laws within heterosexual relationships (Murphy, 1989; Berger, 1990).

AGING AND HOMOSEXUALITY

There is a commonly held belief that since the homosexual subculture seems to value youth, aging is particularly difficult for gay men and lesbians. In actuality, older homosexual persons do not exhibit any significant increase in loss of self-acceptance, depression, or loneliness. In fact, there is evidence that they must recognize and manage role conflicts earlier in their lives, since their sexual life-style is unconventional and socially less accepted. Older gay men and lesbians actually have better self-concepts and tend to be more stable than those who are younger. There is even some evidence that the friendship support systems of gay men and lesbians, along with their greater sex-role flexibility, promote a healthier and more successful outlook on aging than is typically held by heterosexual individuals (Lee, 1990).

Very little research has been done concerning the effects of aging on the sexual activities of homosexual

FIGURE 11.7   Homosexuality and Aging

Most homosexuals solve conflicts about their sexual preference relatively early in life. There is some evidence, therefore, that they are more adept at problem-solving and thus may accept the aging process with more equanimity than their heterosexual counterparts.

people. They face the same physiological changes as everyone else, and the frequency of sexual outlets for homosexuals does indeed decrease with age. The information that is available suggests that gay men and lesbians must face essentially the same adjustment problems of aging as heterosexuals. In all age groups homosexual persons experience the most stress from the societal stigmas and prejudices to which they are subjected (Miranda & Storms, 1990).

Myths and Fallacies About Homosexuality

It often seems that there is more misinformation about homosexuality than almost any other aspect of human sexuality. Perhaps because so little accurate information has been available, a variety of myths and fallacies

have evolved over the years. Some of these mistaken ideas are outlined in this section, each myth or fallacy being italicized.

Myth: It is relatively easy to identify a homosexual; male homosexuals are effeminate and female homosexuals are mannish. This is one of the most persistent myths about homosexuality. In sections of cities where homosexuals congregate, there are some who fit the stereotyped view of the gay male as a swishy, limp-wristed man and the lesbian as a tough, butch woman. Some homosexuals adopt such mannerisms to call attention to themselves or to shock outsiders. However, homosexual people are generally indistinguishable from heterosexual people, and there are no characteristics that can be used to positively identify either type of individual. There are men with effeminate mannerisms and women with masculine mannerisms who are exclusively heterosexual; there are macho men and delicate women who are exclusively homosexual. It has been reported that 90 percent of homosexual men dislike effeminacy and are not sexually aroused by it.

Only about 5 percent of male homosexuals show effeminate walk, clothing styles, or speech with any consistency, and probably less than 3 percent of lesbians show stereotyped masculine behavior and style consistently. So, very few homosexual people can be identified by their appearance or mannerisms (Sonenschein, 1975; Voeller, 1980). However, there is some evidence to indicate that among children and adolescents who show gender nonconformity in appearance and mannerisms, there is indeed a somewhat greater likelihood of homosexual feelings and behaviors later on in their lives (Bell, Weinberg, & Hammersmith, 1981).

Myth: Homosexual people really wish that they were members of the opposite sex. People who feel trapped in the body of the wrong sex and want very much to be members of the opposite sex are called <u>transsexuals</u> (see chapter 12, "The Spectrum of Human Sexual Behavior"). This is very different from homosexuality. Homosexual persons are attracted to members of their own sex and enjoy sexual intimacy with same-sexed partners. They are generally very happy with their own sex organs and have no desire to have the body of a member of the opposite sex.

Myth: Homosexual individuals are prone to dressing in the clothes typical of the opposite sex. This misconception is more commonly directed to gay men, since a female dressing in male clothing is more accepted and therefore less conspicuous in our society than a male dressing in female clothing. A few men, especially in a

transsexuals: people who feel as though they should have the body of the opposite sex.

city homosexual subculture, may occasionally dress in drag (in women's clothing), but this is usually done for fun to amuse or shock others. Most homosexual men have no interest in cross-dressing. Dressing in drag should not be confused with transvestism.

Transvestites are men who periodically dress in women's clothing and adopt feminine mannerisms, sometimes receiving sexual gratification from this practice. Research has shown that many transvestites are heterosexual and have no interest in homosexual behavior.

Myth: Gay men and lesbians dislike members of the opposite sex. Homosexual males are usually not woman-haters and lesbians are usually not man-haters. In fact, homosexuals often feel very comfortable in their social interactions with the opposite sex and greatly enjoy these friendships. Again, it should be emphasized that homosexual behavior is usually not an all-or-nothing phenomenon, and many predominantly homosexual persons also participate in heterosexual activity from time to time. It has been found that at least one-fifth of gay men and one-third of lesbian women marry at least once, and many others date members of the opposite sex occasionally (Bell & Weinberg, 1978; Masters & Johnson, 1979).

Myth: In homosexual partnerships one individual assumes the traditional male role and the other assumes the traditional female role. A few years ago, when a greater stigma was attached to homosexual behavior and little information was available, homosexual couples had little to model their relationships after except heterosexual couples. Today, however, homosexual people who live together often share the household and financial responsibilities equally. This is increasingly true for heterosexual couples as well. In their sexual behavior it is quite typical for same-sex couples to share a great variety of activities, rather than one partner always assuming the stereotypical male role and the other always assuming the stereotypical female role. The dominant-passive dichotomy in homosexual partnerships is not typical, and only a minority of homosexuals show any special preference for one of those roles (Jay & Young, 1979).

Myth: Gay men and women are likely to molest same-sexed children. This fear seems to be one of the reasons why admitted homosexuals are sometimes not allowed to hold jobs in which they will be in contact with children. Most adult homosexual persons, as well as heterosexuals, abhor and condemn sexual involvement between adults and children. Adults who seek out children for sexual contact generally have problems in their social relationships and may also have serious emotional difficulties, and they certainly are not representative of typical homosexual or heterosexual individuals. In any case, heterosexual seduction of

children—usually an adult male seeking sexual contact with a young girl—is far more common than homosexual seduction of either sex (Jay & Young, 1979; Sorensen, 1973).

Myth: All people who are violently opposed to homosexuality are most likely latent homosexuals themselves. The concept of latency has been significant in psychoanalytic thought. The purported latent homosexual has homosexual tendencies but manages to repress them to some degree and attempts to deny them. It has been assumed that in some latent homosexuals their feelings are so deeply repressed that they are pushed into the unconscious mind. It has been proposed that the unconscious guilts and fears thus produced manifest themselves in anxiety, depression, exaggerated attempts to prove their own heterosexuality, and hostility toward homosexuals. In actuality, there is no empirical evidence to support the existence of latent homosexuality.

Myth: Gay men and lesbians are more artistic and creative and tend to choose occupations where their creativity can be expressed. There has been no research evidence to indicate that homosexuals tend to be more artistic or creative than heterosexuals or that they have special talent in decorative arts. There are those who point out the great artists, writers, and composers who have been homosexual, but there are many other creative persons who have been heterosexual. Until quite recently, occupations in the arts and decorating trades were the only ones where homosexuals could be open about their sexual orientation, and this may be the source of myths about these occupations. From evidence presently available, it may only be concluded that homosexuals probably have no special claim on creativity and that vocationally they are very ordinary people, dispersed through all occupational areas.

Myth: When exposed to a happy heterosexual experience with a good lover, most homosexual people realize that homosexuality isn't so great after all. Many homosexual men who are somewhat open about their sexual orientation discover that some women are quite convinced that they can convert them to heterosexuality. Likewise, many lesbians are confronted by men who are prepared to show them what they are missing. Homosexual people react to such self-appointed saviors with a mixture of tolerance, amusement, and anger. Some are insulted by this heterosexist egotism. In any case, homosexual orientation is not changed by a pleasant heterosexual experience, and in fact most homosexual persons report having experienced some heterosexual behavior.

transvestism: dressing in clothes considered appropriate to the opposite sex, usually for sexual gratification.

Case Study

RICHARD: A YOUNG GAY MAN COMES OUT IN THE CITY

Although Richard had recognized his homosexual orientation during his small-town high school days, he had never talked about it with others. He had not developed any strong negative attitudes toward homosexuality, however. He dated girls frequently and had sexual intercourse occasionally. Following high school, he secured a job in a nearby city and moved into a boarding house. He became friends with an ex-marine who lived in the same house. One night while they were drinking and talking together, the other man made sexual advances toward Richard that were accepted somewhat reluctantly. He was then persuaded to share oral sex with the man. He enjoyed the experience and for the first time felt able to admit his homosex-

uality. The two men continued to live together and share sex until Richard was transferred to another city by his employer.

After having relocated, Richard frequented meeting places where gay men tended to congregate in the city. He was very active in homosexual life and eventually began to do volunteer office work and counseling for a local gay organization. His homosexual contacts tended to be mostly casual one-night stands until concern about AIDS in the homosexual community caused him to exercise greater caution. At age 32, Richard was happy and satisfied with his life, successful in his job where his homosexuality was known, and active in community affairs.

Homosexuality and Society

Homosexual behavior has always received attention from our social institutions and developed subcultures. Judeo-Christian-Muslim religions have taken firm stands on sexual behavior and usually exhibit negative stances toward homosexuality. There are often laws that prohibit or restrict homosexual behavior. Families frequently face major crises when they discover that one of their members is a homosexual. Admitted homosexual and bisexual persons are not allowed to hold positions with the CIA, FBI, or American military. The reason once given for this discriminatory practice was that they would be more subject to blackmail and extortion. This would be difficult to substantiate for homosexuals who have been open about their orientation. This section will deal briefly with some of these aspects of homosexuality and society.

HOMOSEXUAL SUBCULTURE

It is often assumed that homosexual persons who wish to be sexually active have little chance to do so in small towns and must seek out the anonymity of city life. While there are many small communities that would find open homosexuality difficult to accept, attitudes regarding sex are not necessarily correlated with the size of a community. There are small towns that

provide a great deal of personal liberty and freedom, and there are large cities that are rigidly conformist. In any case, where the atmosphere permits, it is quite typical for some homosexual people to group together as a gay and lesbian community. The size and structure of such a community varies with many circumstances. Colleges and universities often have gay and lesbian organizations; towns and cities often have gay and lesbian organizations, meeting centers, bookstores, restaurants, bars, etc., sometimes located in specifically gay sections or streets. The majority of homosexual people, on the other hand, may never associate themselves with a gay or lesbian community.

Gay and lesbian communities have changed significantly since the early 1970s. They were formerly dominated by males, and many members remained closeted out of fear of exposure. They were also the main way in which homosexual persons could find their way to friendships and loving relationships with others of their own sex. No longer are communities within urban areas sexual marketplaces, although they still provide a place for people to meet. There are specialized institutions for both lesbians and gay men, including restaurants, newspapers and magazines, political groups, counseling services, bookstores, health services, and housing cooperatives. There are now many more possibilities for "being out" as a gay or lesbian person, and this has changed the population that is attracted to life in the homosexual subculture. Likewise, the larger population no longer has such a

Personal Politics: A Lesson in Straight Talk

I'll begin at the beginning, when you and I first meet. Maybe we'll talk about our work, or the weather. But my antennae are out, and if it's a particularly delicate situation (someone I'm interviewing, say, or another parent at school), I may even have a knot in my stomach. I haven't had a casual conversation in nearly a decade, because I know what's coming: any minute now we'll hit the topic that to most Americans seems innocuous, friendly, getting-to-know-you. *The Family.*

Are you married? "Not legally," I may answer, "but I've been in a relationship with Pamela since 1978." I've learned to say things like this in a perfectly natural tone of voice and to burble on a bit while you regain your composure. I've even started to refer to Pamela as my Life-Partner—even though I think it sounds like we run an insurance agency together—since I know that "lover," while an honorable term in the gay world, often falls upon straight ears as a synonym for someone I've had sex with a few times.

But unless you already have lesbian friends in your life (or you're gay yourself), chances are that you're incredibly uncomfortable. At worst, you think I'm saying something hostile—or dirty. Sometimes you think I'm confiding a deep secret. If by some fluke it takes a few conversations before we get to this point, you might even feel vaguely betrayed, as if you'd been getting to know me under false pretenses (although this can still coexist with the thought that I should have kept my "private life" private). If you're a man, you might tell me that you're "disappointed" or that I don't "seem the type," and expect me to be flattered. If you're a woman, your first thought might be to wonder if I'm coming on to you (by mentioning my long-term committed relationship?). If you're basically a nice, liberal person—a potential friend—your impulse will be to want to do the right thing. But maybe you're not sure what that is—so you quickly change the subject.

My straight friend Jane says I'm usually silly to tell the truth, especially to men. "He's really asking if you're available," she says. "So say yes, you're married." The problem with this, as Adrienne Rich has pointed out, is that whether you're dark-skinned or disabled or a lesbian, when someone "describes the world and you are not in it, there is

---

skewed and negative view of what the homosexual community is all about (Gagnon, 1990b).

The homosexual subculture is dispersed throughout every other cultural milieu. It takes on special meaning in those areas where homosexual people gather together and interact with one another. The community in the homosexual subculture seems to serve several important functions, one of which is bringing homosexual people together socially. The community also provides a supportive atmosphere in which they can share mutual concerns and experiences and be met with understanding. In this way, gay people may fully realize their sexuality and learn to affirm it. Another important function of the community is to provide a language and ideology that accept homosexuality as a valid form of sexual expression rather than condemning it as depraved or shameful.

In every large city and some smaller cities, there are bars, restaurants, hotels, sports clubs, political groups, and religious organizations that cater to gay people. There are bookstores with hundreds of volumes published each year, along with magazines, newspapers, and sexually explicit films available to gay men and lesbian women.

There are some homosexuals and bisexuals who do not live in the gay community but visit it for occasional sexual encounters. Humphreys (1970) studied men who frequented public restrooms for the purpose of casual homosexual encounters, finding that over half of them were married to women and lived apparently very straight lives.

Some people who visit the homosexual community are willing to pay for a homosexual encounter, and homosexual prostitution has been commonplace. What effect the AIDS crisis has had on homosexual prostitution is still unclear. Prostitution has been far more common among males than among females. There is further information about homosexual prostitution on page 327.

The homosexual subculture should not be pora moment of psychic disequilibrium, as if you looked into a mirror and saw nothing." To collaborate and agree that there's no one in the mirror—that we *do not exist,* are not real—is what legions of closeted lesbians do, and it's a vicious cycle: how can a group of phantoms ever hope to change anything?

Lesbians have a serious visibility problem, which is one of the reasons you were surprised when you first met me. And it's not getting better: although "gays" have surfaced all over the map lately because of AIDS awareness, my own sense is that lesbians are even *less* visible than before—and if anything we've been subsumed. (How many times have you read that "homosexuals" are the major risk group?) Because of the times we live in, more of us also seem to be hiding who we are. For all the most sexist reasons, this is distressingly easy: a single man of a certain age might be presumed to be gay, especially if he has a roommate, but a woman is simply assumed to be saving her (underpaid) pennies and waiting for Mr. Right.

So what I would hope you would do, first of all, is to remember that any woman you meet might be a lesbian. By the same token, remember that any lesbian you meet probably wants to be treated pretty much like any other woman. When I mention Pamela, understand that she is as dear to me as any boyfriend or husband, and if you would have asked me about *him,* don't change the subject: ask about *her.*

But beyond that, I'm asking you not only for an awareness of the ways our lives are alike, but the ways they're different. Please don't feel that you have to pretend that my relationship is a clone of yours, exactly the same but with Veronica instead of Archie. Lesbians *do* exist in a context of discrimination, and like all minority groups, we have a culture of our own. Not only am I not offended if you've thought or even just wondered about this; I'm relieved.

After all, if we're going to be friends, isn't it because we're interested in each other's lives?

—Lindsy Van Gelder, *Ms,* November 1987

trayed as a cold, unfeeling world of casual sex and prostitution, or as a world only of men. Homosexual people seek fulfilling, loving relationships, both short-term and long-lasting. They fall in love with one another and share intimate relationships, just as heterosexual people do. There are, of course, social pressures exerted on homosexual couples that may create external strains with which heterosexual couples do not have to cope.

AIDS AND HOMOSEXUALS

The sexually transmitted disease called acquired immunodeficiency syndrome, or AIDS (see also chapter 15, "The AIDS Crisis and Sexual Decisions"), first began to be recognized in the United States among male homosexuals who had shared sex with numerous partners. While the disease is known not to be limited to homosexuals, and in fact is now spreading among

heterosexuals, it brought a great deal of negative attention to the gay community. Some cities closed down gay baths, where homosexual men shared sex, in the interests of public health. For the same reason, education efforts have been directed at helping gay men to change some sexual practices. Research data indicate that casual sexual encounters among gay men are declining because of the AIDS scare. Educational efforts in San Francisco have apparently generated results, since risky sexual behavior had changed more in San Francisco by the end of the 1980s than anywhere else it had been studied in the United States. Among the gay male population, the incidence of AIDS transmission, along with that of other sexually transmitted diseases, has decreased (McKusick, 1990).

As fear of this fatal disease spreads, so do misconceptions and myths about how it can be transmitted. AIDS education efforts have had their share of homophobia, with blaming, hostility, and misinformation about homosexuality and AIDS (Wright &

301

FIGURE 11.8 AIDS and the Homosexual Community

While not exclusively a homosexual disease, in the United States AIDS has, so far, primarily affected the gay community. To call attention to the need for more research to combat AIDS, the Names Project sponsored the creation of the AIDS Quilt, a 150- by 450-foot memorial consisting of individual squares of cloth, each one representing someone who has died of AIDS.

Thompson, 1990). People mistakenly fear that even casual social interaction with an infected person could be dangerous. In fact, it has been recommended that those sexual activities in which bodily fluids are exchanged be avoided. This applies particularly to semen. Anal intercourse has been shown to be a primary means of transmitting the AIDS virus, and there is some possibility that oral sex can transmit the virus as well. Wearing a condom can substantially reduce, but not eliminate, the risks. The risks of woman-to-woman

transfer of the virus are less certain at present, although experts are warning about exchange of vaginal fluids. Probably the likelihood of transmission of AIDS between women is less than between men (Reinisch, Ziemba-Davis, & Sanders, 1990), but women should also guard against contact with internal bodily fluids until more is known about the phenomenon. Rubber dental dams can be used to cover the vulva and vaginal opening during oral sexual contact, and rubber gloves could be worn when inserting a finger into the vagina or anus. Safer sex practices are gradually being adopted within the gay community, and sexual behavior will surely be modified in years to come, so long as the threat and spread of AIDS continue (Leviton et al., 1990).

HOMOSEXUALITY AND RELIGION

Many Judeo-Christian-Muslim denominations have sought to judge and regulate various forms of sexual behavior, including homosexuality. Passages from the Bible and other religious texts are often cited as evidence for the sinfulness of homosexual behavior. In the mid-1950s a British clergyman researched the Bible carefully, concluding that references to homosexuality were very occasional and that many of them had been subject to misinterpretation (Bailey, 1955).

In the ancient world, no religions apart from Judaism categorically prohibited homosexual behavior, although some did advocate celibacy. Around A.D. 400 Christianity began to introduce a new sexual code that focused on maintaining "purity" and equated some sexual behaviors with the "fallen" state of the human soul (Boswell, 1990). Over the centuries, homosexuality has been variously accepted and condemned within religious traditions.

During the past 3 decades, many theologians have called for increased understanding and acceptance of homosexual individuals by the Christian churches. Some Protestant groups have decided to be tolerant of homosexual behavior and not consider it a sin, but still maintain that it is a kind of illness. The Roman Catholic church seems to be facing some crucial conflicts concerning the issue, but has reaffirmed its position that homosexual behavior is immoral and unnatural. Gay men and lesbians themselves have suggested that a new religious ethic could develop from what they have to offer. This is an ethic that would allow for human diversity, acknowledge variant sexual orientations, honor the concept of mutual sharing by consent, and affirm the freedom to grow and change (Uhrig, 1986). Many religious groups are still debating the issue of how to view homosexuals and how to treat them.

FIGURE 11.9   Sexuality and Religion

Religious groups increasingly find it necessary to address a wide range of sexual issues. In June, 1991, the delegates shown here at a meeting of the General Assembly of the Presbyterian Church (U.S.A.) debated proposed changes in their church's attitude toward sexual relations among homosexuals and unmarried heterosexuals. Many other religious groups have recently debated similar questions.

HOMOSEXUALITY AND THE LAW

One of the dilemmas that faces homosexuals in some areas of the United States is the existence of sodomy laws. These do not outlaw homosexuality or homosexual acts per se, but instead vaguely prohibit certain noncoital behaviors such as oral or anal sex. However, although the sodomy laws render illegal a variety of sexual behaviors typically engaged in by heterosexual couples, the laws are enforced almost entirely against homosexuals, particularly males.

In 1962 Illinois became the first state to decriminalize homosexual behavior practiced in private between consenting adults. About half of the other states gradually followed suit. Many of the laws that still exist are often vague and could be interpreted as prohibitions of just about any form of sexual behavior other than heterosexual intercourse. In some states the penalties may be extremely harsh, including possible maximum penalties of several years of imprisonment. These laws are rarely enforced, and maximum sentencing is rarely given. Most often, homosexuals are charged with misdemeanors such as disorderly conduct, lewd behavior, and vagrancy.

An important test of sodomy laws came in 1986 when two men in Georgia were arrested after being observed in the home of one of the men, by a policeman who had come to the house on another matter. The men were convicted of sodomy, but the case was appealed to the Supreme Court on the basis of the couple's right to consensual sex in private. The court upheld the conviction, ruling in effect that even consenting adults have no constitutionally protected right to homosexual acts, even in private.

Although thorough enforcement of sodomy laws is practically impossible, legal authorities use several

303

FIGURE 11.10 Homosexuality and the Law

Organizations such as the National Gay Task Force were founded to educate the public about homosexuality. Through organized lobbying of Congress and planned marches, they hope to prevent discrimination against homosexuals and achieve equal rights.

methods to aid in that enforcement. Police decoys sometimes loiter in areas where homosexual men gather, arresting those men who solicit sexual activity. Solicitation laws are separate from sodomy laws, however. Many gay men claim that the police decoys use entrapment by enticing the gay men to become sexually involved. Police sometimes arrest people through direct observation of their homosexual acts in public places, such as restrooms. Police surveillance of known homosexual bars, private clubs, and baths was once quite common, although with the AIDS crisis many of the more public meeting places for casual sex have now closed.

The U.S. government continues to exhibit signs of homophobia. Each year, about 1,400 men and women are discharged from the Armed Forces for violating a directive that says "persons who engage in homosexual conduct" or "demonstrate a propensity" to do so, "adversely affect the ability of the Armed Forces to maintain discipline, good order, and morale." Lesbian women are discharged at a much greater rate than are gay men. In 1989 the Secretary of Health and Human Services disavowed the report of a national Task Force on Youth Suicide because it demonstrated the need for special suicide prevention efforts for lesbian and gay youth. The secretary felt that this recommendation was inconsistent with the advancement of traditional family values (Haffner, 1991).

For a time, the impetus seemed to be toward elimination of legal sanctions for victimless crimes. In the mid-1950s the American Law Institute's Model Penal Code and the Wolfenden Committee Report in England recommended reform of the statutes and decriminalization of homosexual acts between consenting adults. The Criminal Code of Canada and several states have agreed with that recommendation. Yet the issues surrounding homosexuality can often become politically charged, stirring strong public sentiments, and the evolution of new laws reflects such pressures (see also chapter 17).

HOMOSEXUALITY AND MARRIAGE

Many people with a predominantly homosexual orientation marry members of the opposite sex. Homosexuality does not seem to affect so much whether one marries, but whom one has sex with (or would like to) outside of marriage (Weinrich, 1990). In choosing heterosexual marriage, the individual may have decided to live as an exclusive heterosexual or may still expect to maintain some level of homosexual activity. Gay men and lesbian women sometimes marry each other—presenting a straight image to the world yet continuing with their gay life-styles.

FIGURE 11.11 Homosexual Marriage

Marriage between same-sexed people is not recognized as a legal contract in any state. Many gay couples, however, wish to formalize their relationship. This couple is shown outside San Francisco's City Hall, having just registered as domestic partners under a new city ordinance allowing them to do so.

The married homosexual individual expecting to have some homosexual contact is not much different from the heterosexually adulterous spouse, and many of the same kinds of problems may arise in the marriage relationship. Homosexuals marry for a variety of reasons, although it is clear that some do not become fully aware of their sexual inclinations until after they have married. Some see marriage as a way to achieve social respectability, as an escape from their homosexual tendencies, or as a way to avoid the loneliness they may stereotypically associate with homosexual life-styles. Others want children, and still others feel strong loving feelings toward their spouses. Yet these marriages often face sexual conflicts of various sorts. There are some couples who can deal with such conflicts honestly and with sensitivity, enriching their marriage. There are others who cannot handle such conflicts and can no longer continue their marriage (Coleman, 1983).

Homosexual marriage—the marriage of members of the same sex—has received attention in recent years. Jack Baker, a student at the University of Minnesota, sought a marriage license in 1970 so that he could marry another man. He felt that he should have the same right as heterosexuals to the legal advantages of marriage. The civil government denied the request, however. If one of the two men had undergone a sex-change operation, the marriage would have been permitted, leading Baker to charge that the government considers marriage to be a union between a penis and a vagina rather than between two human beings. Some members of the clergy have sanctioned homosexual marriages. The Metropolitan Community Church was founded by a homosexual preacher; it now has branches in numerous cities, especially aimed at members of the gay community. Unitarian-Universalist ministers will also conduct gay unions. Holy Union ceremonies are performed between homosexuals in these churches and in some others, but they are still not legally binding in the United States. Most gay rights organizations are not focusing their efforts on changing the marriage laws. Rather, they are working for legal changes to ensure that all couples who have formed committed relationships—homosexual or heterosexual—have the same rights and privileges as those who have chosen to formalize their commitment in marriage. In 1989 New York State's Court of Appeals ruled that a long-term gay relationship could qualify as a family, and therefore be eligible for rent-control assistance in New York City. Gay rights activists consider this a major step toward recognition of the legal rights of couples who are not heterosexual.

FIGURE 11.12 Lesbian Family

Some homosexual couples are beginning to form their own families and raise children. Many couples adopt children or bring their own from a previous heterosexual marriage to the new union.

305

Conclusion

It is obvious that there is much we do not understand about homosexual, bisexual and heterosexual feelings, behaviors, and life-styles. We still do not know how sexual orientation develops in human beings. Social institutions face many unresolved issues concerning sexual orientations that do not fit the standard heterosexual expectations. Attitudes are always changing and evolving, and social attitudes toward homosexual persons may be expected to shift as time goes by. ■

CHAPTER SUMMARY

1. The terms *homosexual* or *gay* refer to people or acts relating to romantic or sexual attractions between members of the same sex. The term *lesbian* refers to homosexual women.

2. Kinsey developed a scale demonstrating that there is no one pattern of homosexual orientation, but different degrees between the heterosexual (opposite-sexed) and homosexual (same-sexed) orientations.

3. Traditionally, homosexual orientation and behavior were viewed in the context of pathology (illness), but that perspective has changed in recent years.

4. Homosexuality has been difficult to study because of the difficulty in finding representative samples of the population.

5. Large proportions of people in the United States have a negative feeling and discriminatory attitude about homosexual people. This is called homophobia.

6. There are several models from which homosexuality has been viewed. The moral model tends to base its view on religious or other morally based values regarding sexual orientation and behavior.

7. There is much speculation about the possible biological determinants of sexual orientation, including hormonal influences at various stages of life. Some researchers believe that hormonal factors during prenatal life may predispose people to particular sexual orientations.

8. Psychoanalytic theories focus on the different stages of psychosexual development in creating sexual orientation. The normal variant model sees homosexuality as one form of expression within a range of sexual orientations and behaviors.

9. The Bell, Weinberg, and Hammersmith research represents one of the most thorough studies on the development of sexual preference to date.

10. Among professionals who have viewed homosexuality within a model suggesting illness or abnormality, attempts have been made to change the homosexual behavior or orientations. Current professional opinion is more oriented toward seeing homosexuality as one of several orientations that needs no particular intervention or cure. There is still a startling lack of research information about homosexuality and its implications for people's lives.

11. Homosexual identity forms through a series of up to six stages. Different people proceed through these stages differently, and a person's perceptions of his or her sexual orientation may shift over time.

12. There are apparently different motivations behind behaviors or orientations that are called *bisexual* or *ambisexual*. These terms are used in reference to people who have some level of sexual interaction with members of both sexes.

13. Gay men and lesbian women can share a spectrum of sexual behaviors, although reducing the risks of AIDS transmission must now be a part of their sexual decision-making.

14. Same-sex relationships should not be judged by the heterosexual model. Most gay men and lesbian women want long-term close relationships, and over half are involved in such relationships. Sexual activity is not always involved.

15. Aging among homosexual people leads to the same physiological effects on sexual functioning as with any other group. Social supports within the homosexual community can be strong.

16. There are many myths and misunderstandings about homosexuality. Gay and lesbian individuals are found in all walks of life, do not dislike members of the opposite sex, sometimes marry, and are not readily identifiable unless they choose

to be. They appear to have no more emotional difficulties than the nonhomosexual population.

17. Most cities and some rural areas have well-developed homosexual subcultures that permit communication and support for lesbian women and gay men.

18. AIDS was first identified in the United States among homosexual men, and the virus has spread rapidly among gay men. This may lead to increased negativism toward homosexuality and increased homophobia.

19. There are proportions of the population that fall into all categories of Kinsey's scale measuring experience between the exclusively heterosexual and the exclusively homosexual. Studies continue to support that close to 10 percent of the population (about 14 percent of the men and over 4 percent of women) have had substantial sexual involvement with members of their same sex.

20. Homosexuality exists in all cultures and is treated differently and valued differently according to each society's attitudes.

21. In the United States, different states have laws that may to some degree be used to restrict homosexual behaviors. Sodomy laws are enforced primarily against gay males. The Armed Forces prohibit homosexual contact.

22. Many homosexuals marry heterosexual partners and raise families. Their homosexual orientation may or may not be known by their partners. Homosexuals have also been fighting for the right to marry between members of the same sex, since there are financial and legal implications for this. While homosexual marriage is not yet sanctioned by law, some churches will perform Holy Union ceremonies between same-sexed persons.

ANNOTATED READINGS

Berzon, B. (1988). *Permanent partners: Building gay and lesbian relationships that last.* New York: E. P. Dutton. Shows how gay men and lesbian women can realistically establish lasting intimate relationships without necessarily imitating the heterosexual model. Explains the development of homosexual identity, and how people then initiate relationships.

Curry, H., & Clifford, D. (1990). *A legal guide for lesbian and gay couples.* Berkeley, CA: Nolo Press. Deals with current information concerning relationship agreements, planning for medical emergencies, estate planning, raising children together, buying real estate, and relating to former spouses and children of former marriages.

Eichberg, R. (1990). *Coming out: An act of love.* New York: Penguin Books. A how-to book for the coming out process, it explains how to tell the truth about one's sexual orientation and create an honest, open life-style.

Fairchild, B., & Hayward, N. (1989). *Now that you know: What every parent should know about homosexuality.* San Diego, CA: Harcourt Brace Jovanovich. A guide for parents who want to understand a gay son or lesbian daughter more completely. It explains how to remain supportive while dealing with one's full range of reactions and emotions.

Geller, T. (1990). *Bisexuality: A reader and sourcebook.* Ojai, CA: Times Change Press. One of the only guidebooks on the topic of bisexuality, this book provides several readings, and a list of references and resources that cannot be found in any other source.

Isensee, R. (1990). *Love between men: Enhancing intimacy and keeping your relationship alive.* New York: Prentice-Hall. This guide teaches intimacy skills and offers help with the coming out process. It deals realistically with issues of safer sex in gay male relationships.

Lee, J. A. (Ed.). (1991). *Gay midlife and maturity: Crises, opportunities, and fulfillment.* Binghamton, NY: Haworth Press. A collection of readings that break through the stereotyped views of older gay men and lesbians as sad and lonely people. Discusses the adjustment issues of midlife and aging, especially for those whose sexual orientation is primarily homosexual.

Loulan, J. (1990). *Lesbian erotic dance: Butch, femme, androgyny, and other rhythms.* San Francisco: Spinsters Book Co. Examines lesbian eroticism and feminine images over the years, and describes the results of a survey of over 1,000 lesbian women concerning how they feel about their bodies and sexuality.

McNaught, B. (1988). *On being gay: Thoughts on family, faith, and love.* New York: St. Martin's Press. A collection of personal essays designed for gay people coming out, their families, and those who want to learn more about them.

McWhirter, D. P., Sanders, S. A., & Reinisch, J. M. (Eds.). (1990). *Homosexuality/heterosexuality: Concepts of sexual orientation.* New York: Oxford University Press. An outstanding collection of papers from international experts on a wide range of topics relating to homosexuality.

Sang, B., Warshow, J., & Smith, A. J. (Eds.). (1991). *Lesbians at midlife: The creative transition.* San Francisco: Spinsters Book Co. An anthology of essays and poems by and about lesbians as they go through midlife. Practical issues are covered, as well as the more personal aspects of aging for lesbians.

CHAPTER TWELVE

VARYING DEGREES OF SEXUAL INTEREST AND ACTIVITY
    Celibacy as a Choice
    The Variability of Sexual Individuality

EXPRESSING GENDER-IDENTITY/ROLE
    Cross-dressing: Transvestism
    Transgenderists
    Transsexualism
    Sex Reassignment
    Implications of Treating and Predicting Gender
      Transpositions

THE NEED TO ENHANCE SEXUAL AROUSAL
    Use of Erotica and Pornography
    Sexual Devices and Gadgets
    Sexual Fantasy: Our Internal Pornography

    Fetishism
    Varying the Numbers

ATYPICAL AND POTENTIALLY PROBLEMATIC SEXUAL CONNECTIONS
    Extramarital Sex
    Paying For Sex
    Close Encounters
    Sadomasochism
    Sex With Animals
    Sex With the Dead
    The Emergence of Casual Sex and Pansexualism

CONCLUSION

SELF-EVALUATION: YOUR SEXUAL FANTASIES

CHAPTER SUMMARY

I grew up in a small town. In high school, I heard things about different kinds of sex, but I mostly assumed they were exaggerations or myths. It wasn't until I got to college and experienced a few late night bull sessions that I began to realize that there was a whole wide world of sex out there that was practically beyond my imagination. After a few visits to the city, I had that picture confirmed. I have always lived a pretty conservative sexual life-style, although my fantasies can get pretty wild sometimes, but that doesn't mean I feel the need to judge other people for what they might want to do in sex.

—From a student's essay

THE SPECTRUM OF HUMAN SEXUAL BEHAVIOR

Alfred Kinsey's work in the 1940s and 1950s established many of the fundamental assumptions on which later research into human sexual behavior would be based. One of those assumptions is that research should focus on the physical nature of sexuality, with emphasis on anatomy, physiology, and numbers of orgasms. Another assumption is that human sexual orientations and preferences are acquired as a product of learning, just as other mammals learn mechanistically to respond to certain stimuli. What sex research has tended to ignore is the distinction between *sexual performance*, which might be measured objectively by things such as numbers of orgasms or types of behavior, and the more *subjective erotic experience* going on in a person's mind and emotions. This latter experience includes *desire*, or the ways in which one might be emotionally drawn to people and things.

Subjective eroticism also includes what has been termed *sensuosity*, or that inner enjoyment of the whole sensual experience of sex, not just orgasm (DeCecco, 1990).

One of the most basic assumptions about human sexuality has been that there is a true, unchanging sexual "core" that has developed by the time one is an adult, and that sexual behavior and orientation emerge from this core set of desires. This assumption is now being challenged. Cross-cultural studies certainly demonstrate that cultures impose many guidelines for how people should feel and act about sex. There is also increasing evidence that sexuality can be quite situational and changeable, and that people's sexual needs and behaviors may be modified by day-to-day life circumstances (Blumstein & Schwartz, 1990). The research that has been done so far has not made it clear how individualized preferences for seeking sexual arousal and orgasm are formed, or how they may be modified over time.

It has been suggested that in addition to the most often-cited motivations for sexual behavior—recreation, procreation, and as an expression of emotional connectedness—there are personal and public political expressions that are made with our sexuality as well. Sometimes, sex is used as a symbol of power or control. Sexual behavior may also represent an expression of one's self in the world, one form of assertion for one's identity and personal sense of meaning (Mays & Cochran, 1990). These motivations have implications for how we see the role of sexuality in our lives.

Most human beings at least occasionally want to experience sexual arousal and orgasmic release. We know that the spectrum of human sexual preferences and behaviors is broad indeed, and the varieties of these activities have been subject to many medical, legal, and moral judgments. One form of heterosexual intercourse—man on top, woman underneath—has most often been deemed as the healthy, legally permissible, and morally acceptable mode of sexual behavior between a married couple in Western culture. Masturbation and homosexual activity have been recognized as being common in our society. In various societies and at different times in history, these and every other form of sexual behavior have been classified as unhealthy, illegal, and/or immoral. With heterosexual intercourse established as the norm, other behaviors are often labeled abnormal, a term that may have statistical validity but often carries emotional overtones and implications of illness or perversion. Yet no sexual behavior, whether it is uncommon or atypical, should automatically be considered unhealthy or wrong.

While some professionals still use words such as "aberrant," "deviant," "abnormal," and "perverse" to describe some sexual preferences and acts, the terms *variant* and *paraphilia* seem to have gained in acceptance. They imply that a particular sexual phenomenon varies from what is considered typical, or that it exists in addition to those more mainstream sexual behaviors. This chapter deals with sexual preferences and behaviors that are not as common as masturbation and heterosexual and homosexual activity. We will look at less typical variations that are part of the extensive repertoire of feelings and activities from which components of any person's sexual individuality can be drawn.

It is important to note that there are varying degrees to which the "different" sexual orientations and behaviors may play a role in a person's life. This spans the continuum from a mild degree of interest that would not violate norms of social acceptability, all the way to a strong compulsion that excludes nearly every other form of sex. As noted in chapter 13, "Sexual Abuse and Other Sexual Problems," such compulsions can become serious sexual problems. Although we lack studies that can tell us how common different sexual variations really are, we can assume that public opinion holds some behavior to be more startling than others. While most people are not completely shocked by the idea of a man slipping into panty hose for sexual kicks, they are decidedly upset by the prospect of someone becoming sexually involved with a dead person.

A recent review of the paraphilias, or unconventional sexual variations, pointed out several criteria for determining when a problem exists. In order to be considered a paraphilia in the problematic sense, the sexual attraction must be a long-standing, highly arousing preoccupation. The person must feel a need to act on the sexual fantasy and be unable to have a "conventional" sexual or loving relationship. To a degree, there must be a problem with self-regulation of behavior; in other words, there must be a gap between how the individual wishes to behave and how he or she actually chooses to behave. It has been suggested that the paraphilias are frequently confused with compulsive behavior or acting out of inner conflicts (Levine, Risen, & Althof, 1990).

Varying Degrees of Sexual Interest and Activity

It is evident that different people have different degrees of interest in sex, pursue sexual activity with different amounts of energy, and participate in sex with varying frequencies. Traditionally, these variations have been explained as differences in the strength of one's sex drive or the intensity of what Freud called the libido. It has also been generally assumed that the sex drive of human males is greater than that of females. Today these concepts are being questioned and reexamined. For one thing, some people are now doubting whether there is really any part of the personality that can be legitimately termed a sex drive. There is no evidence to support any generalized conclusion that physiological factors, such as hormones, have any direct or conclusive influence over a person's degree of need for sex. There has been speculation that observed differences in sex drive between males and females may be the result of childhood learning during the socialization process. This reasoning might be carried a step further, suggesting that not only what a person finds sexually interesting, but how strongly he or she is interested, might be learned during socialization.

Because the concept of a physiologically based sex drive is open to controversy, this section will examine different degrees of sexual interest and sexual activity as parts of the human personality. Some people report thinking about sex and being interested in sexual matters most of the time, while others report that they seldom even think about sex. It is logical to conclude that the more interested one is in sex the more one becomes sexually aroused and seeks sexual gratification. Yet there are some individuals who feel guilty or anxious about their sexual preferences and interests; therefore they tend to engage in sexual activity as seldom as possible. There are others who have relatively low interest levels in sex but feel obligated by social or personal pressures to participate in a great deal of sexual behavior. Therefore, levels of sexual activity do not necessarily reflect levels of sexual interest.

Consistently responding positively to sexual cues has been called *erotophilia,* while responding negatively has been termed *erotophobia* (Fisher et al., 1988). The degree to which any individual is erotophilic or erotophobic obviously depends on a great many factors, including learning during childhood and adolescence. Erotophilia-erotophobia has been shown to affect many dimensions of a person's sexual responses. Erotophobic individuals tend to react more negatively to sexual images, be less interested in sexual activities, be less likely to use contraceptives during intercourse, and experience more guilt about sexual behaviors and fantasies (Byrne & Schulte, 1990).

Society has persisted in determining that some individuals possess an exaggeratedly high level of sex drive, hypersexuality, while others have an abnormally low level of sexual interest, hyposexuality. These might also be considered the extremes on the bipolar scale of erotophilia and erotophobia.

There are physical and emotional factors that can cause a drop in sexual interest and activities. Some people appear to have been fundamentally asexual throughout their lives (Kaplan, 1987). Until recently, hypersexuality always seemed to generate more attention than hyposexuality; it was the extremely sexually active person that society seemed to have the most trouble understanding and accepting. However, current media attention has focused more specifically on low sexual desire and how it might be overcome. In a society that has placed such a high premium on sexual performance and a high level of interest in sex, such a shift in attitudes is not surprising.

Promiscuity is a term that is applied to those who have sexual contact with several different partners on a relatively emotionally uninvolved, casual basis. It is an emotionally and morally loaded label that has also been applied to those who have had more than one sexual partner. Because of the double standard of our society, it is a term more often applied negatively to women than to men. While promiscuous men are often praised and admired for their impressive records, promiscuous women tend to suffer more guilt, self-abasement, and social ostracism.

There are some who believe promiscuity, by definition, to be a problem. There is no reliable research evidence to support or negate such a stance. However, it seems likely from clinical evidence that some people simply enjoy sex with a variety of partners, perhaps for a period during their lives, and prefer to avoid emotional involvements for various reasons. If the individual approaches these encounters in a responsible, nonexploitative manner, taking appropriate steps to reduce the risks of transmitting STDs and HIV (the AIDS virus) and emerges from them without negative feelings or inner conflict, there is no particular reason to judge the behavior as problematic.

Sometimes, however, having multiple sex partners may be motivated by more questionable, or unhealthy, factors. These include unsatisfactory personal relationships, antagonism toward members of the opposite sex, or lack of self-respect. The individual feels a need to prove himself or herself. There are some men whose image of themselves as men is supported by living up to a macho image of having a long list of sexual "conquests." There are some women who use sex to experience a sense of power or control in their lives (Kasl, 1989). A high level of sexual activity may also represent a response to some stressful situation such as separation from parents upon entering college, the onset of early menopause, or experiencing some traumatic loss. Multiple sexual contacts may also represent a means of escape, compensation, or retaliation for a troubled partnership or unhappy family. Obviously these motivations hold the potential for creating serious stresses and further problems for the individual and his or her partners.

The more compulsive form of hypersexuality, purportedly characterized by uncontrollable sexual drives as part of various mental illnesses, has been called nymphomania in females and satyriasis in males. Again, the double standard seems to rate a far

hypersexuality: exaggeratedly high level of interest in and drive for sex.

hyposexuality: an especially low level of sexual interest and drive.

promiscuity (prah-mis-KIU-i-tee): sharing casual sexual activity with many different partners.

nymphomania (nim-fa-MANE-ee-a): compulsive need for sex in women; apparently quite rare.

satyriasis (sate-a-RYE-a-sus): compulsive need for sex in men; apparently quite rare.

Case Study

LAUREN AND CASSIE: A COUPLE WITH DIFFERING LEVELS OF SEX INTEREST

Lauren, a 25-year-old construction worker, first consulted a counselor with the complaint that his wife Cassie, a 26-year-old electrician, was "some sort of nymphomaniac." He was seeking advice on how to cope with what he called an "oversexed woman." Further discussion clarified a situation in which Lauren was interested in having sexual intercourse once or twice a week, while his wife expressed a desire for coitus more frequently. From the beginning of their 4-year marriage, Lauren had resented what he perceived as his wife's pressuring him to have sex. He criticized her aggressiveness often, and she had eventually ceased being the sexual aggressor. Lauren continued to sense her dissatisfaction with their coital frequency, however. The final event that caused Lauren to seek professional help came when he entered their bedroom unexpectedly and found his wife masturbating. His anger precipitated anger on Cassie's part, and she began a tirade in which she berated Lauren's sexual adequacy.

Cassie agreed to come with Lauren for the second counseling session. Detailed questioning promptly indicated that neither of them had unusual sexual backgrounds, but that Cassie had always shown a higher level of sexual activity than Lauren. She had been very comfortable with her sexuality and enjoyed sex. She experienced orgasms easily, often several during a single sexual encounter. Yet there did not seem to be anything compulsive about her sexual needs. Except for their conflict about different levels of interest in sex, their marriage seemed to be relatively stable and happy. This conflict had indeed been a serious source of friction and resentment, however.

During several counseling sessions, Lauren and Cassie opened up new avenues of communication about sex and their mutual negative feelings. They gradually began to accept their differences as healthy, manageable aspects of each other's personality. They realized that their typical pattern of harboring resentments and unspoken frustrations was destructive, and they began building new ways of communicating their needs and concerns to one another. Lauren also began to explore the ways in which he could participate with Cassie in sexual activities between times of coitus, even to the extent of enjoying her masturbating with him present. She worked to communicate her needs without blaming her husband or pressuring him to feel responsible for always satisfying them.

greater interest in women's compulsive sexual needs than in men's. Nymphomaniac is a term often used rather lightly and applied mistakenly to women who show any level of interest in sex. Yet nymphomania is actually difficult to define and has been subjected to a great deal of interpretation rooted in prejudice, a double standard, and male chauvinism. The term is so vague and outmoded it should be dropped altogether. Such forms of hypersexuality are also extremely rare, if they even exist at all. Very few people seek help for excessive sexual desire, and even for those who do, it is doubtful if any of those cases could truly have been classified as nymphomania.

We have no way of accurately measuring degrees of sexual interest. Subjective reports indicate that there are certainly differences in sexual interests among people, but those differences have not been correlated with any other psychological or physiological factors.

There is anecdotal evidence that some women experience cyclical changes in sexual interest during different stages of their menstrual cycles. Yet this is apparently not true of all women.

Kinsey and his associates (1948, 1953) provided some objective information on differences in sexual activity and demonstrated a remarkably wide range among humans. More than 7 percent of adult males in the Kinsey study averaged 7 or more orgasms per week, and another 10 percent of those males up to the age of 30 averaged 1 orgasm every 2 weeks. A small percentage of males had only 1 orgasm in about 10 weeks. Some of the women in the Kinsey samples were as sexually active as the most active males, and some others were as sexually inactive or even more inactive than some of the least active males. Most individuals tended to fall at some intermediate point between these two extremes in the spectrum. However, as noted earlier, Kinsey's work placed an inordinate amount of emphasis on physical factors such as orgasm. We have continued to carry the assumption that a higher frequency of orgasm is a sign of strength, health, and robustness, while a lower frequency is associated with poorer health, sexual apathy, or physical incapacitation (DeCecco, 1990).

People often worry about having too much or too little sexual interest and activity, especially if their degree of interest or activity differs significantly from that of a continuing sexual partner. In Western society, one who displays high levels of sexual interest and behavior may be branded with a name such as nymphomaniac or satyr. Actually these conditions of uncontrollable sexual desire (discussed in chapter 13, "Sexual Abuse and Other Sexual Problems") are extremely rare. The individual with low levels of sexual interest and behavior is often made to feel dull and uninteresting, or as if there must be something wrong with him or her. Available evidence would suggest that wide individual variations in sexual interest and activity are a part of the normal human sexual continuum. There is nothing inherently dangerous or harmful in thinking about sex and having sexual activity very often, and there is no harm or danger, per se, in a lack of sexual interest or activity.

CELIBACY AS A CHOICE

In a culture that places such a high premium on sexual gratification and enjoyment, celibacy, or not engaging in any kind of partnership sex, might be viewed with suspicion and surprise. Celibacy can be the result of life circumstances, such as imprisonment or death of a partner, or it may be the result of normal asexuality, characterized by a very low interest in sex. Erotophobic individuals may be celibate because of guilt or fear about sexual issues (Fisher et al., 1988). The term asexuality is sometimes used, although it can be misconstrued as suggesting that celibate individuals have no sexual interest or arousal, which is usually not the case. In a *Psychology Today* survey (Rubenstein, 1983), 1 percent of 12,000 respondents reported little or no interest in sex. Some priests and nuns vow to be celibate because their church demands it. In this section we will be considering voluntary, secular celibacy, a conscious choice not to become involved with others sexually.

An increasing number of young to middle-aged adults in Western culture are choosing to be celibate (Brown, 1989). Some of these individuals are reacting to having tried various sexual life-styles that turned out to be unfulfilling or destructive. They are looking for alternatives to the new pressures brought about by the

sexual revolution. They have sometimes found that the intensity of sex created tensions in their relationships. The term *sexual burnout* has been coined to describe the fatigue resulting from such sexual pressures, and some professionals and celibates themselves feel that celibacy has become a workable alternative for many who have experienced such burnout (Whelehan & Moynihan, 1982). In addition, as concern over the spread of AIDS becomes more acute, it may well be that celibacy will be viewed as a less risky, healthier, and more acceptable choice of life-style as well.

The most important thing to remember about celibacy is that it is not necessarily a symptom of a problem or of feelings of inadequacy. Some marriages become sexless eventually, but this is not necessarily a difficulty. Often a deep affection and respect between the partners provides adequate fulfillment for the couple, and sex is not a necessary component. It is important to be reminded that sexuality is far more than an act of sexual intercourse. Caressing, kissing, and other forms of noncoital physical sharing may be deeply satisfying to some couples (Brown, 1989).

THE VARIABILITY OF SEXUAL INDIVIDUALITY

Statistical evidence highlights an interesting fact that many have observed about human sexuality: men seem more prone to participating in atypical sexual activities, to straying more from established societal sexual norms and standards, than do women. All available statistics on the frequency of various nonstandard forms of sexual orientation and behavior show them to be much more common in men, usually at least three times so or more than in women.

Attempts have been made to explain this by both social and biological theories. Sherfey (1972), for example, proposed that our culture has feared the expression of female sexual potentials for implications of political and individual power and perhaps other ego-enhancing reasons, and therefore has tended to establish various mores that discourage most women from getting in touch with their sexuality and all of its ramifications. For whatever social or political reason, there has always been a double standard with regard to sexual behavior in our culture: it has been more permissible, even expected, for men to be more sexually active than women. Such an attitude offers one explanation for less involvement on the part of women in a variety of sexual practices, but it may not be the only one.

celibacy (SELL-a-ba-see): choosing not to share sexual activity with others.
asexuality: a condition characterized by a low interest in sex.

It has also been suggested that there may be some inborn biological propensities that cause males to behave with greater sexual diversity, although most biologically based hypotheses about sexual preference have not withstood rigorous scientific examination as yet (Gooren, Fliers, & Courtney, 1990). It has been proposed that because of prenatal developmental differences, males become more responsive than females to visual stimuli in learning sexual cues (Money, 1989). Men may establish images of erotic arousal in response to early life experiences at certain critical periods of development. If the visual image does indeed hold greater importance for causing sexual arousal in males, they would be far more vulnerable to diverse and variable kinds of visual learning than females. Only further research will provide the final explanation for this sexually differentiated phenomenon.

Expressing Gender-Identity/Role

In chapter 6, theories concerning the development of gender-identity/role (G-I/R) were discussed. It is clear that an individual's inner experience of oneself as a woman, man, or some ambivalent position between the two sexes is a significant part of the human personality. That inner experience then typically becomes expressed outwardly in some form of gender-related and sexual behavior on the masculine-feminine continuum. The following behaviors and states of mind represent expressions of transpositions in gender identity.

CROSS-DRESSING: TRANSVESTISM

The definitions of cross-dressing behavior are variable. The term *transvestite* has been applied to anyone who cross-dresses, or wears clothes of the opposite sex, for any reason. More specifically, it has been applied to individuals who feel driven to cross-dress and often associate it with sexual arousal. Cross-dressing is certainly not a new phenomenon, and has been identified in most cultures from earliest recorded history through the Greco-Roman, Judeo-Christian-Muslim, and Renaissance periods (Steiner, 1981).

In anthropological literature the term berdache is used to describe the practice of cross-dressing in other cultures. Most often these are men who dress in women's clothing and adopt behaviors considered feminine in the society. In many cultures berdache is considered acceptable or even a sign of spiritual specialness to be respected and revered. Among American Plains Indians individuals who felt compelled to

FIGURE 12.1 Transvestism

Those who dress in clothes of the opposite sex seem to derive sexual pleasure from doing so. Anthropologist Robert Monroe has noted that transvestism occurs more frequently in cultures where the male assumes more of the economic burden than does the female.

wear women's clothing were consulted by tribal councils because they were considered to have unique insights.

It can also be difficult to distinguish transvestism from the kind of fetishism in which a person is sexually attracted to some object of clothing usually worn by the opposite sex (see Fetishism, p. 323). For example, a man may become sexually aroused by viewing and touching various objects of women's underwear. He may find that it is even more exciting to actually wear the garments, usually as an accompaniment to masturbation or other sexual activity. The heterosexual transvestite usually becomes aroused by completely dressing up in women's attire and makeup and adopting effeminate mannerisms. Usually cross-dressing behaviors begin in childhood and become well established by adolescence. Sometimes it disappears by adulthood, but most often does not (Buhrich & Beaumont, 1981).

berdache (bare-DAHSH): anthropological term for cross-dressing in other cultures.

There are no reliable statistics on the incidence of cross-dressing phenomena, but they are probably more common than generally believed. One expert has estimated that 3 to 5 percent of the male population in the United States wears women's clothing at least occasionally (Allen, 1989). The evidence would suggest that cross-dressing is almost exclusively limited to men. However, there are studies of women who have an erotic attachment to men's garments (Stoller, 1982). At least for the limited number of female examples available, the drive toward cross-dressing seems less demanding than it typically is for male transvestites. Again, there are plausible sociological explanations for a lower incidence of transvestism in women. Western society permits a wider range of fashion for women than for men. There are few, if any, male outfits that now would be deemed inappropriate on a woman. Conversely, men are quite specifically restricted from wearing most articles of female attire unless they are willing to risk ostracization and name-calling. This establishes a very different social context for male cross-dressing, one demanding privacy and often subterfuge.

The world of the heterosexual transvestite is a fascinating underground subculture (Allen, 1989). There are organizations and magazines designed for these men who experience a need to wear women's clothing to relieve tension and anxiety. There are occasional regional gatherings for such individuals, with meetings on fashion and makeup techniques. Typically the participants are married. Some hide their transvestism from their wives and cross-dress away from home; some inform their wives of their preference. One limited study of the partners of transvestites (Wise, Dupkin, & Meyer, 1981) indicated that those women in the study were generally of low self-esteem and had to tolerate many difficulties in their relationships. There is certainly other clinical evidence that some wives integrate their husbands' cross-dressing behaviors into their lives with less difficulty.

There is one ongoing study of boys ranging in age from 4 years through adolescence who have shown a preference for dressing in girls' clothing (Green, 1987). When denied access to such garments, these boys would fashion their own dresses from blankets, T-shirts, and other materials. They have also tended to

---

Case Study

ARTHUR: TRANSVESTISM INTEGRATED INTO A SEXUAL RELATIONSHIP

Now 27 years old, Arthur can remember that he enjoyed dressing in girls' clothing even in early childhood. Throughout his adolescence and adulthood his sexual preferences were distinctly heterosexual. He had several girlfriends and had experienced sexual intercourse with three of them. He was not sexually attracted to other men. From time to time, however, he dressed in women's clothing, a wig, and cosmetics, then paraded before a mirror with very feminine mannerisms. He found this activity sexually arousing and would usually masturbate before removing his female garb. He occasionally purchased new garments for his feminine wardrobe and kept the entire collection in a locked closet. He never left his apartment while cross-dressed.

Until he was 24 and began developing a continuing relationship with a woman, Arthur never told anyone about his transvestism. When he began to consider marriage, he thought it would be fairer to the woman to inform her of his occasional practice of cross-dressing. At

first, she was somewhat alarmed by his revelation and decided to talk to a counselor. As she began to understand his transvestism more completely and it became clear that he sought sexual pleasure in this manner only occasionally, she decided that it would not interfere with their relationship. Arthur had no desire to cease cross-dressing and did not see the practice as sick or immoral, although he was somewhat embarrassed by it. After nearly 3 years of marriage, his transvestism seems to have had no negative effects on the couple's sexual relationship. They are both pleased by the quality and frequency of their sexual contacts. Arthur reports that he occasionally wears some articles of women's clothing during intercourse and that his wife is very accepting of this. He does not dress in full costume as often as he did before marriage. He is a successful young businessman, and the marriage appears to be a happy and productive one.

315

assume female roles during play and exhibit distinctly feminine mannerisms. Research is still in its early stages, and it is as yet impossible to predict which of these behaviors represent simple play activity and which are expressions of gender transpositions (Money & Russo, 1981).

It should be emphasized that transvestites are generally productive citizens whose gender role preferences do not harm others. While personal concerns and relational problems associated with the transvestism may lead transvestites to therapy, many professionals feel that transvestism, per se, does not require any intervention or treatment. One study of 70 male members of cross-dressing clubs found few differences between those who had received treatment and those who had not. The same research did not find any significant degree of "illness" in the behavior (Croughan, Saghir, Cohen, & Robins, 1981).

TRANSGENDERISTS

In this book I identify separately those individuals who seem to fall between transvestites and transsexuals. They may be called transgenderists or cross-genderists. Rather than cross-dressing to relieve an accumulating inner urge and tension to do so, these people—usually men—become comfortable with sustained cross-gender identity (Freund, Steiner, & Chan, 1982; Pauly, 1990). They may remain in their cross-dressed and cross-gender role for days or even months at a time, depending on their life situations. They may also maintain separate lives that are more consistent with their anatomical gender for varying periods of time. These individuals, however, do not exhibit the dissatisfaction with their anatomy of birth that is found in transsexuals, and they generally do not have a strong urge to undergo a sex reassignment process. There are some cases, however, in which this sort of transgenderist behavior represents a precursor of transsexualism.

An interesting historical example of this phenomenon is found in the English writer William Sharp, who lived from 1855 to 1905. Over a period of some years, he created for himself the personality of a woman whom he called Fiona MacLeod. He began to spend increasing proportions of time as Fiona, and she emerged as a leading writer in the Scottish Celtic literary movement. In the later years of his life, very little of the male William Sharp identity was left (Bullough, 1976). It is possible, of course, that someone such as Sharp was actually a transsexual, but that lack of medical treatment techniques rendered it impossible for him to do any more than cross-dress on a consistent basis.

TRANSSEXUALISM

Transsexuals are anatomically normal males or females who express a strong conviction that they actually have the mind and personality of a member of the opposite sex. They usually are aware of these feelings at a very young age, long before they know very much about sexuality or about the possibility of sex change procedures. Eventually, however, the transsexual may become convinced of wanting to change his or her sex legally and through hormonal and surgical sex reassignment (Pauly, 1990).

One of the earliest instances of sex change through surgery was the case of Sophia Hedwig in Germany who, with the help of physicians in 1882, was transformed into Herman Karl. Very little remains

transgenderists: people who live in clothing and roles considered appropriate for the opposite sex for sustained periods of time.

cross-genderists: transgenderists.

FIGURE 12.2 Transsexualism

Transsexuals are people who are one sex biologically but who feel an identity with the opposite sex. Renée Richards faced many legal battles when she attempted to compete as a female tennis player after male-to-female surgery in the 1970s.

Case Study

LILLIAN/GRANT: A FEMALE-TO-MALE TRANSSEXUAL

Lillian, at 18, was referred by her family physician to a clinic that dealt with gender identity problems. From the time she was very young, she had felt she was a boy and had enjoyed behaving in ways that she felt were boyish. She found herself sexually attracted to other girls. In high school she had avoided wearing dresses, instead wearing jeans and mannish shirts. Although Lillian had cultivated her manner of walking and talking to be masculine, others had never seemed to notice anything particularly extraordinary about Lillian. At the clinic she poured out a long story of depression and torture at having been trapped in the body of a woman. She had often prayed at night that she would awaken the next day as a man. She had considered suicide many times but finally decided to seek help. She had never heard the word transsexual and was somewhat surprised to learn that she was not the only person experiencing such feelings.

After a thorough evaluation and several months of psychotherapy, it was decided that

Lillian was indeed a transsexual and a good candidate for sex reassignment. Within a short time she moved to another city and began living as a man. She adopted the name of Grant, dressed in men's clothing, dated women, and got a job as a cook in a small restaurant. For the 2 years Grant remained in this job, saving money for his sex change, no one ever questioned his masculine identity. Eventually, the team of physicians who worked with Grant decided to begin their medical procedures.

Presently Grant is undergoing hormonal treatments as a prelude to the surgical procedures that will construct an artificial penis and scrotum for him. Like most transsexuals he is most anxious to have the surgery and has no dread at all of the pain and discomfort that may be involved. As he has said, "all that surgery is just a way of showing to others what I've known all my life—that I am a man. I can't wait."

on how the transformation actually was accomplished, but Herman Karl grew a beard and was given genitals that at least mimicked a penis, testes, and scrotum (Bullough, 1976). There were occasional attempts at surgically changing sex organs over the next 70 years, but the case that attracted most attention was that of Christine Jorgensen, who in 1952 became a woman after having lived until that time as George Jorgensen. As a result of the publicity, her doctor was deluged with requests for sex changes, and the science of sex reassignment was off and running.

At this time the cause of transsexualism is unknown, and there continues to be debate about inborn influences from prenatal life versus theories of social learning. There is agreement, however, that whatever the cause, the inner gender transposition is sensed by the individual at a young age. There are also no solid statistics on the incidence of transsexualism. It has been estimated that postoperative transsexuals in the United States number in the thousands but probably not in the tens of thousands. Of course, these figures do not take into consideration those transsexuals who have not been able to undergo sex reassignment,

certainly numbering more than those who have. The number of transsexuals in the United States has been estimated to be 1 transsexual per 50,000 people over the age of 15. The estimates for female-to-male transsexuals have sometimes been lower than those for male-to-female, but that is now believed to represent cultural values more than actual numbers (Pauly, 1990).

SEX REASSIGNMENT

Transsexuals, in their years of feeling trapped in the wrongly sexed body and wishing for a completely different anatomy, are often troubled and unhappy people. They are prone to depression and thoughts of suicide. There are case studies of male transsexuals who have actually removed their own penises or testes (Krieger, McAninch, & Weimer, 1982). Psychotherapy has not proven to be especially effective with transsexuals. One recognized form of rehabilitative therapy has been the hormonal and surgical transformation of the individual's external features into a form

317

resembling the anatomy of the other sex. As one might expect, this process of sex reassignment has been fraught with clinical and ethical complications. First has been the difficulty of diagnosing the true transsexual, as distinguished from a frustrated homosexual or transvestite whose desire to change sex will eventually wane, or from the schizophrenic who has deeper personality disturbances (Burns, Farrell, & Brown, 1990). Once diagnosed as a transsexual, the individual must face the huge medical expenses of reassignment, possibly reaching $30,000 or more; most health insurance companies consider such processes elective and cosmetic and do not cover them. Sometimes if a physician such as a psychiatrist is willing to indicate that reassignment is absolutely necessary to the person's future well-being, health insurance will cover part of the costs.

There are the unethical physicians who will agree to treat anyone desiring reassignment, so long as the money is paid up front. But anyone who desires advice about these matters should go to a medical center. In North America most gender clinics are designed to diagnose and treat gender transpositions, as well as sex reassignment procedures. Typically an individual is given a psychiatric evaluation, a series of psychological tests, and counseling. Then, if sex reassignment emerges as the most reasonable course of treatment, it begins with a trial period real-life test lasting up to 2 years. Usually, it is during this time that the person dresses and lives as a member of the desired sex, receiving adjustment counseling and appropriate legal advice concerning a name change, a new birth certificate, and a new driver's license (Pauly, 1990).

It is also during the real-life test that hormonal treatment begins. The changes brought about by hormone therapy are reversible, with the exception of a deepened voice in the female-to-male transsexual, should a decision be made not to continue the reassignment process. Female hormones administered to men cause breast enlargement and a feminine redistribution of fat. While the growth of facial and body hair may be somewhat retarded, it is necessary to remove permanently unwanted beard and body hairs by electrolysis. Hormonal masculinization of the female, in addition to deepening the voice, suppresses menstruation and promotes growth of some facial and body hair.

Practitioners have assumed that this period of the real-life test would be reversible if the individual had a change of mind. However, it has also been argued by others that once the new roles and hormonal treatment are set in motion it may be very difficult for the person to move out of the sex reassignment path, even when doubts are serious or even if there has been a complete shift in attitude (Oppenheim, 1986).

While a detailed description of sex change sur-

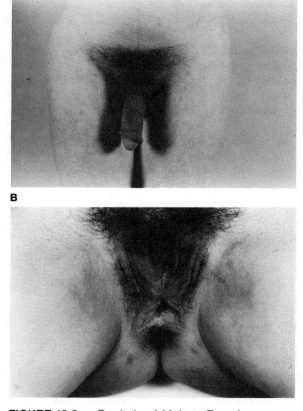

FIGURE 12.3 Genitals of Male-to-Female Transsexual

The penis (A) of a transsexual prior to surgery. The vulva (B) and vagina are constructed of the sensitive penile tissue.

gery is beyond the scope of this text, a summary follows. In male-to-female surgery, the testes are removed and an artificial vagina and labia are constructed from the sensitive skin of the penis and scrotum (Fig. 12.3). Breasts are fashioned through the use of mammary implants (Fig. 12.4). Following reassignment, male-to-female transsexuals usually report some moderating of their orgasmic response, but they still enjoy their sexual activities. In female-to-male surgery the breasts, uterus, and ovaries are first removed and artificial penis and scrotum are constructed, partially using tissue from the vagina and labia (Fig. 12.5). The clitoris is usually left intact beneath the new penis and is still part of sexual arousal. There are several techniques being tried to simulate penile erection, ranging from the insertion of a plastic rod into a special canal within the constructed penis to surgical implantation of a special hydraulic system. Of course, postsurgical transsexuals cannot reproduce, ejaculate, or menstruate (Noe, Laub, & Schulz, 1976; Ryan, 1976).

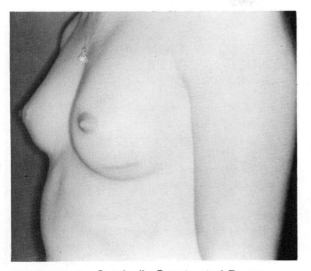

FIGURE 12.4   Surgically Constructed Breasts

In male-to-female transsexual surgery the breasts may respond to hormone treatment, but, if not, are generally augmented with implants.

A controversy emerged for a time, questioning some of the original assumptions concerning transsexuals and sex reassignment. A major study of 526 patients concluded that, in a 5-year comparison of those transsexuals who received intensive psycho-

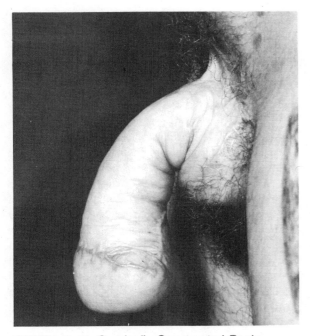

FIGURE 12.5   Surgically Constructed Penis

In female-to-male transsexual surgery the penis is constructed from abdominal tissue or from labial and perineal tissue. The penis is not capable of erection in response to sexual arousal but several artificial devices are available that produce an erection for intercourse.

therapy with those who underwent surgery, the degree of improvement in mental attitude was the same for both (Meyer, 1982). This, of course, called into question the sensibility of expensive and risky sex reassignment procedures, to the extent that some medical centers at least temporarily halted these procedures. The standard medical attitude has been that surgical intervention should be restricted to highly selective criteria. There is now clinical evidence and research suggesting that sex reassignment can indeed lead to improved psychological and social adjustment for many individuals. Reviews of the world literature on this surgery indicated only a 10 to 15 percent failure rate with patients. In general, people seem subjectively satisfied with their sex reassignments. Dissatisfaction with the results was more common as the age of patients increased, and in cases where the person was not a carefully diagnosed, confirmed transsexual (Green & Fleming, 1990). As with many newer medical treatments, there are many issues of prognosis, cost effectiveness, and ethics yet to be resolved.

IMPLICATIONS OF TREATING AND PREDICTING GENDER TRANSPOSITIONS

When terms such as "treatment" are used in conjunction with gender transpositions, there obviously is an implied assumption that something is wrong, that indeed something requires therapy. This is a situation that many transvestites and transsexuals resent. They believe that since their gender-related expressions and preferences do not harm or exploit others, the decision over whether any kind of therapy is indicated, and what type, should be left to them. Since sex reassignment is a complicated medical process, the medical profession has assumed the right and responsibility of deciding who will receive various alternatives of treatment. Our society has not as yet questioned this mode of decision-making to any great degree, but transsexuals do not always feel that the present system is fair to them.

Another complicated issue involves the prediction and differentiation of various gender transpositions during childhood or adolescence. It has been suggested, for example, that for children who exhibit symptoms of gender transposition, early intervention could prevent these patterns from extending into adulthood (Bradley & Zucker, 1990). Again, serious ethical questions can be raised concerning of such intervention. What if transsexualism could be identified prior to puberty? If hormonal and surgical reassignment happened prior to the development of secondary sex characteristics at puberty, the process would be far simpler and more effective. However, there would be

319

Case Study

KENT: CONFUSION OVER GENDER IDENTITY

Kent was a high school senior when his older sister brought him to a counselor. He had confided to his sister that he thought he was a transsexual and that he wanted to have a sex-change operation. The counselor found him to be depressed and confused about his sexuality.

For 2 years Kent had been sexually attracted to a male artist in his high school class. He felt that he was deeply in love with the other young man, although he knew that the other man did not have any similar attraction for him. As the discussion proceeded, Kent explained that he had often felt that if his own body (which was very stocky, masculine, and hairy) had a softer, more feminine appeal, the other boy might be attracted to him. As the details of sex-reassignment procedures were further discussed with Kent, it became quite clear that he was not at all certain he would ever want to lose his penis and testes or to possess a woman's genitals. He freely admitted that if he could have the love and sexual attentions of the young man he so ad-

mired, he would be content to keep his body the way it was. He also recognized that his reasons for desiring a sex change were not well-founded.

As his sexual history was discussed with the counselor, it seemed clear that Kent's gender identity had been predominantly male. He had never experienced continuing feelings of being trapped in the wrong body or of wanting to be a girl. He did see himself as having stereotypical feminine interests, since he preferred art and music over sports. The counselor spent several sessions dealing with Kent's views of masculinity and femininity before referring him to a psychiatrist for further evaluation.

After several months Kent had decided that he really did not want to pursue any sex reassignment, and the psychiatrist concurred that he was not actually a transsexual. Following this period, Kent was more content to pursue a predominantly homosexual life-style in the city where he attended college.

---

obvious ethical objections to such steps for young people.

The research in this area is still very new. One study examined men aged 23–29 who as children stated that they wanted to be girls and who acted out their wishes through dress and play activities. None of these men had carried their desire to be female into adulthood, leading the researchers to conclude that transpositions such as transsexualism and transvestism cannot yet be predicted in childhood (Money & Russo, 1981).

The Need to Enhance Sexual Arousal

Being a sexual human being, expressing that sexuality, and experiencing the physiological reactions of the sexual response cycle involve far more than our sex organs. Human senses, especially sight and touch, play a major role in sexual individuality. Our sensory input,

emotions, and thought processes blend in our brains to promote or inhibit sexual feelings and arousals in ways that are only poorly understood at this point. One neurological fact is known: the sensations of sexual stimulation and orgasm are controlled by the pleasure centers in the limbic system of the brain.

Human beings whose personalities are on the erotophilic side of the spectrum may spend a great deal of time and energy perfecting and enhancing their sexual experiences. The consumption of food provides sensual pleasure and gratification that might be second only to sex. It is not surprising, then, that in developed areas of the world much effort is given the preparation of dishes that will delight the senses, particularly the palate, and be sumptuously satisfying. Just as some people become good cooks and connoisseurs of great food, so some take pride in learning the sexual techniques that will provide the optimal levels of enjoyment and satisfaction for them and their partners. As men and women learn the very individualized triggers and enhancers for their own sexual arousal, they find many different avenues to explore.

USE OF EROTICA AND PORNOGRAPHY

Nudity and a variety of sexual acts have been depicted in statuary, pottery, and paintings since ancient times. It is estimated that in the United States today the sale of sexually explicit media—magazines, still pictures, films, and videotapes—is a $5 to $8 billion a year business. This means that for millions of people, such materials incite sexual arousal. They also have become extremely controversial, as we will explore further in chapter 17, "Sex, Art, the Media, and the Law."

SEXUAL DEVICES AND GADGETS

While sexual enhancement gadgetry is nothing new, its availability to the general public has increased since the 1960s. Some locations have sex shops that sell a variety of devices designed to heighten sexual arousal and pleasure. Mail-order advertisements and catalogs are easily found. The gimmicks vary in their effectiveness; each device will have advocates who have found it satisfies their tastes and needs. While most individuals who give gadgets a try use them only occasionally or as an experiment, a few people come to rely on them as constant aids to sexual satisfaction. This, of course, can become inconvenient and might eventually be considered a fetish, discussed on p. 323.

Vibrators are probably the most common of the sexual aids, providing an intense vibration to the genitals or other sensitive body parts. There are battery-operated and plug-in models. Some are cylindrical or penis-shaped, in a variety of lengths and widths. Others come with several attachments to be used for stimulating different sex organs. Vibrators are sometimes recommended for people who have trouble reaching orgasm, especially women. The rapid, localized vibration is often helpful in triggering the orgasmic reflex. Vibrators can, of course, be used for masturbation or integrated into shared activities.

Cylindrical dildos, made of everything from ivory to clay, have existed for at least 2,500 years. Today they are usually made of soft flexible plastics. Although they may be used for solitary masturbation, for vaginal or anal insertion, dildos are also used in some partnership sex. Plastic penis extenders are designed to fit over the head of a man's penis, supposedly to make it seem longer during sex. Actually such devices rarely yield much extra pleasure for either partner and may even reduce sexual sensations for the man.

FIGURE 12.6 Popular Culture

Many forms of pornography may be found in popular culture. Such material may produce sexual stimulation and pleasure in some people, but may be the source of aggressive and hostile behavior in others.

Case Study

MAXINE: A YOUNG WOMAN CONCERNED ABOUT HER USE OF PORNOGRAPHY

In discussing her sexual behavior with a counselor, Maxine—a college sophomore—explained that she was concerned about whether or not one of her activities was normal. She reported that she very much enjoyed viewing explicit pornographic pictures, particularly of couples engaged in heterosexual intercourse. She often masturbated while viewing her collection of pornography. Maxine was aware that many males sought sexual arousal from pornographic pictures, but had never heard of a woman who enjoyed this type of stimulation.

Maxine maintained a continuing sexual relationship with a male student. She said that there were no long-term commitments in the relationship and that masturbation had always been an essential part of her sexual expression. She seemed to have a realistic attitude toward sex and understood the varieties of sexual activities quite thoroughly. She did not feel any special guilt or disgust because of her use of pornography, but her mild concern about it had persisted until she decided to seek counseling. Since it did not seem to be interfering with her sexual activity or to be creating negative feelings toward herself, the counselor assured Maxine that there was apparently nothing harmful about her finding pornographic materials appealing. Follow-up visits indicated that this assurance helped her to feel more comfortable with her sexuality and removed the doubts about her normalcy.

Some men enjoy wearing various bondage or pressure devices, including metal, leather, or rubber rings that fit around the base of the penis and scrotum. While these "cock rings" are advertised to help maintain erection, there is no particular evidence that they do so, and in fact if they are too tight they can cause some damage. A variation on this theme is the clitoral or French tickler, worn at the base of the penis and having projections on the top surface. The projections are supposed to press on the female's clitoris during heterosexual intercourse, providing extra stimulation (Kelly, 1980).

There are a number of other sexual gadgets available. Increasing in popularity are oriental ben-wa, or ba-wa balls, two spheres that are inserted into the vagina and vibrate against each other (see chapter 10, "Solitary Sex and Shared Sex," p. 257). One company that manufactures sex toys encourages women to hold house parties for other women, at which questions about sex are answered. A representative from the company is available to display and take orders for vibrators, lotions, lingerie, and other sensuous aids. It is estimated that about one million women have attended such parties. There is a paucity of objective information about all such sexual enhancement devices, but their availability is another reflection of the constant search for new sexual pleasure.

SEXUAL FANTASY: OUR INTERNAL PORNOGRAPHY

Mental images, daydreams, and fantasies seem to be a significant part of most people's sexual individuality. Such imagery may be fleeting and incomplete or lengthy and detailed. Sexual fantasy is not necessarily connected with one's sexual behavior. For example, most men who fantasize about forcing a partner to have sex with them would never carry out such an action. Studies indicate that human beings fantasize about many sexual practices in which they would actually never participate in real life. A study of 171 men, mostly in their twenties, indicated that about one-third at least occasionally fantasize about having sex with other men (Ellis, Burke, & Ames, 1987). On the other hand, fantasies may also reflect areas of sexual longing and frustration in a person's life. Some research has indicated that sexual fantasies can be an important source of information in designing treatment approaches for those who have sexual problems and dysfunctions (Zimmer, Borchardt, & Fischle, 1983).

Earlier studies found some sex differences in the typical fantasy lives of males and females. For example, men's fantasies tended to be more active, impersonal, and visually oriented, while women's fantasy themes were generally more passive and romantic

(McCauley & Swann, 1978). Another study also suggested that sexual fantasies often play different roles in the lives of women and men (Wilson, 1980), with men's fantasies tending to reflect some degree of frustration, of sexual needs not completely fulfilled. Women were found to fantasize more when their sexual lives were most satisfying, and their fantasies seemed to reflect intimacy with a particular partner. More recent research has found no particular differences in female and male fantasies, and suggests that when men and women are exposed to similar environments and sexual experiences, they learn to prefer similar erotic imagery (Rokach, 1990).

Sexual fantasies have been categorized into four main groups: exploratory, including themes such as group sex, mate-swapping, and homosexuality; intimate, with the themes of passionate kissing, oral sex, making love outdoors, and mutual masturbation; impersonal, which includes sex with strangers, looking at pornography, watching others engage in sex, and fetishism; and sadomasochistic, including themes such as whipping, spanking, and forceful sex. Men tended to have more fantasies in all four of these categories, but the greatest proportion for both sexes was in the intimate category. Both men and women had the fewest number of fantasies reflecting impersonal or sadomasochistic themes (Wilson, 1980). The kinds of sexual fantasies people experience—their length and degree of explicitness—seems to be determined to a large degree by the amount of sex guilt they experience and how they feel about sex. As might be expected, the

FIGURE 12.7 Sexual Fantasy

Many people use internal images to fantasize about sexual encounters and behaviors. Fantasy may be used to enhance sexual arousal or may reflect sexual frustration.

less guilt people experience, and the more liberal their attitudes about sex, the longer and more explicit their fantasies tend to be (Gold & Chick, 1988).

For most people, sexual fantasies seem to be part of masturbation activities. They may also be present in shared activities and do not necessarily reflect any dissatisfaction with one's partner or the particular sexual activity. One study of 178 university undergraduates, faculty, and staff found that 84 percent at least sometimes fantasized during intercourse. Most of these people experienced little guilt or concern about their sexual fantasies. However, those who did report significant levels of guilt also tended to be more sexually dissatisfied and to experience more sexual problems (Cado & Leitenberg, 1990). There is also research indicating that people who suppress their sexual fantasies and thoughts may experience a backlash effect in which the fantasies become even more persistent (Wegner et al., 1990). Different people have different levels of imaginative ability and use it in very individualized ways to enhance sexual arousal and gratification. Sexual fantasies can be one of the most powerful avenues to sexual arousal. Sex therapists often encourage people to make use of their "inner erotica."

FETISHISM

Fetishism is defined as finding sexual excitement in objects, parts of the body, articles of clothing, or the textures of particular materials that are not usually considered to be sex-related, per se. Sometimes the definition is expanded to include sounds (such as a particular song) or scents (such as perfume). Taken in its broadest sense, there would seem to be an element of fetishism in most people. For a man to be aroused by seeing a woman in a satin nightgown, and by caressing her hair and smelling her perfume, is in a sense fetishism. For a woman to be turned on by a man's muscular abdomen or by his style of clothing is also fetishism. There are all degrees of fetishism, ranging from these mild preferences that accompany most sexual relations, to an intense drive and complete substitution of the fetish for any other forms of sexual gratification (Gebhard, 1976).

There are certain things that are very commonly held as fetishes, including the feet, women's breasts, underwear, soft and silky clothing, rubber, and leather. The inner mechanisms by which sexual fetishism develops are unknown, but it is typical for the fetishist to have experienced sexual arousal in association with

fetishism (FET-a-shizm): sexual arousal triggered by objects or materials not usually considered to be sexual.

323

Case Study

CRAIG: A HARMLESS FETISH WORRIES A YOUNG GROOM

Following a class in human sexuality, a male graduate student named Craig asked for an appointment for counseling, explaining that he had a sexual problem to talk over. During the counseling session, he nervously described his plans for marriage in 2 months and said that there was an aspect of his sexuality that bothered him. He went on to explain that he became sexually aroused by touching soft blankets and often enjoyed lying on a blanket during masturbation or intercourse. He was also quite certain that his partiality to blankets resulted from his earliest masturbatory experiences, in which he would rub his penis against a blanket.

Craig was told that the fetish did not seem particularly troublesome, and some further questioning elicited other important facts about his preference. Basically he had very open and positive attitudes toward his sexuality and felt concern only about his mild blanket fetish. Of special importance was the fact that he did not feel compelled or driven to become sexually aroused by blankets, and they instead were employed only when convenient. His fiancée not only had been told about his inclinations but found the whole situation humorous. She had assured Craig that she would be happy to cooperate in the use of blankets in their sexual experiences whenever he wished. They were both highly satisfied with their present sexual relationship. On the basis of this information, it was concluded that if Craig could come to accept his blanket fetish as a desirable, harmless part of his sexual responsiveness, there was no reason to see it as a problem or sign of sexual disturbance. Before leaving the counseling session, he sighed with great relief and said that he felt confident he could feel very positively about the fetish as long as he did not have to view it as sick or abnormal.

the fetished object at some point in her or his life. Use of the fetish during masturbation is most typical, in which the object is fondled, rubbed on the genitals, viewed, or used for direct stimulation of sex organs. Some males ejaculate in or on the fetished object. Sometimes fetishes are integrated into shared activities as well, but this may create some emotional discomfort for the partner.

Most fetishes are harmless and inoffensive to others. However, they sometimes are carried to extremes that may have negative implications for others. It is not uncommon to read newspaper accounts of an adolescent male who has entered someone's home to touch the feet of a sleeping girl or to steal some of her undergarments. True kleptomania, involving sexual excitement when stealing, and pyromania, in which the individual derives sexual arousal from setting fires, are considered to be forms of fetishism.

Fetishes are a poorly understood facet of sexual individuality. Since they are usually socially innocuous, they have not generated much attention among sex researchers. It could be suspected that someone who is inordinately sexually attached to a fetish, to the exclusion of other forms of sex, may be exhibiting some signs of emotional insecurity or stress worthy of professional consultation.

VARYING THE NUMBERS

Partly because of the social standards that place sex within the context of an intimate and romantic one-to-one relationship, sex for more than two has generally been considered decadent and meaningless in Western culture. In other cultures large orgies are sometimes a part of rites or religious ceremonies. In our culture, sexual involvement for more than two is more typically done as an experiment that develops unplanned out of some other social activity. It may be seen as a way to enhance the usual arousal patterns.

Group sex can apply to a variety of situations, ranging from threesomes (troilism or ménage à trois) to large groups. One study analyzed data from 50 situations in which a married couple was involved sexually with another male. It found that these troilistic liaisons often grew out of inhibitions in sexual functioning or out of the enjoyment of watching others have sex. The group sexual situation could be considered a

kleptomania: extreme form of fetishism, in which sexual arousal is generated by stealing.
pyromania: sexual arousal generated by setting fires.
troilism (TROY-i-lizm): sexual activity shared by three people.
ménage à trois (may-NAZH-ah-TRWAH): troilism.

FIGURE 12.8 Mate Swapping in Films

The topic of mate swapping was the light-hearted focus of the 1969 film *Bob & Carol & Ted & Alice*. A chic, trendy activity of the 1960s sexual revolution, mate swapping is not, generally, regularly practiced in the 1990s. This is a photo of the famous bedroom scene in the film.

way of creative problem solving in some relationships (Wernik, 1990). The activity may involve one or more persons simply observing a couple engage in sex, or actual physical interaction among all present. Probably the most common form of group sex occurs when more than one couple engage in sexual activity, but each couple remains quite separate from the other(s). Groups in which everyone participates with one another may be called an <u>orgy</u>. The incidence of such behavior is still uncertain. Available evidence suggests that it is rarely a continuing or regular form of sexual behavior and instead usually represents a once-in-a-lifetime experience or an occasional episode.

There are, of course, other implications to group sex. There are the elements of exhibitionism, voyeurism, and homosexuality that are natural by-products of group activities, sought by some participants and upsetting to others. There is always the risk of generating discord among participants, since it is difficult to devise shared activities that will help everyone feel involved, cared for, and satisfied. Feelings of possessiveness and jealousy may easily arise, or feelings of spontaneity may be destroyed by the individual who becomes too autocratic or ritualized. As with any kind of shared intimacy, later nonsexual social contacts may feel awkward and strained. Group sex may also accompany mate swapping, also called swinging, and other variations on extramarital sex.

Atypical and Potentially Problematic Sexual Connections

Current sociosexual scripts and standards aside, penis-in-vagina intercourse is only one of the many different ways in which human beings connect sexually. Freud's original theory of psychosexual development held that mature sexuality was characterized by the final genital phase, in which the libido, or sex drive, became focused in the sex organs. Hence, it is a simple matter to extrapolate that mature sex would involve the matching up of sex organs to interact together. More recent research is suggesting that this view may be too limiting.

Ernest Borneman (1983), an Austrian sexologist, directed one of the most ambitious studies of childhood sexuality ever conducted in Europe. His work has led him and his associates to conclude that, at birth, infants' entire skin surface constitutes a single erogenous zone. Furthermore, they have suggested that sexually mature people are indeed sexually and sensuously sensitive over their entire bodies. Such a perspective not only broadens the view of what stimuli might be considered legitimately sexual but helps to explain the many different forms of sexual enjoyment enjoyed by humans.

orgy (OR-jee): group sex.

325

Case Study

JACQUELINE AND DONALD: A MARRIED COUPLE TRIES MATE SWAPPING

Jacqueline and Donald talked regularly with a counselor as part of an effort to improve their lines of communication. Donald was a college professor and Jacqueline was a dean of the college. The couple had three teenage children. As part of their discussions in counseling, they mentioned that they had often considered the question of sexual exclusivity and had wondered about the possibilities of mate swapping. Both were somewhat interested in exploring swinging, but they were also fearful about the potential problems involved. During counseling they sorted through the many pros and cons of the issue.

Eventually a situation developed in which they experimented with mate swapping. One evening at a party they danced with a neighboring couple. In previous social gatherings they had discussed the issues of sexual nonexclusivity in a theoretical sense with this couple, and the four had agreed that if the appropriate opportunity arose, it might be worth a try. At the party they enjoyed dancing with swapped spouses, and eventually someone suggested that they swap and retire to separate bedrooms. During a counseling session following this experience, Jac-

queline and Donald seemed enthusiastic about the encounter and both reported having enjoyed the sexual activity. They were uncertain if they would pursue further sexual contact with the other couple.

In the weeks that followed they did share sex in the mate-swapping situation several times. After each encounter the four would discuss their feelings, both positive and negative. There was general agreement that if any situation developed that might prove to be a threat to either primary relationship, the swapping activity would be halted. After about 6 months the other couple moved to a distant city, and everyone seemed quite satisfied to see the mate-swapping activity end. During the following year the four got together for a weekend visit and exchanged mates for a single sexual encounter. Jacqueline and Donald reported that it was a pleasurable experience but that no definite plans had been made for the future. They maintained that they did not expect to seek out other couples deliberately for mate swapping, but if such a relationship were to develop again, they would be open to the possibilities.

EXTRAMARITAL SEX

The term extramarital sex refers to those situations in which a married individual has sexual intercourse with someone other than his or her spouse. It is also known by the morally biased term infidelity, implying a breach of a marriage vow for faithfulness, and the somewhat more legalistic term adultery. In Western society adultery is prohibited or condemned, and committing adultery is typically considered immoral and illegal. Yet a double standard has been operative in some times and places as well. For example, in ancient Roman law and in English common law, adultery was defined as intercourse with a married woman. A married man having intercourse with a single woman was not considered to be an adulterer. Even in recent times, men having extramarital sexual relations have been more accepted than women doing the same. With increased emphasis on the equality of women and men, that double standard is beginning to fade, and evidence

suggests that the number of women involved in extramarital sex now nearly equals the number of men (Lawson, 1988).

The traditional pattern has been that of conventional adultery, in which the extramarital sex has occurred without the knowledge of the spouse. More recently another form of adultery has increased in popularity. It is consensual adultery, in which there is no deception, and the spouse knows about and consents to the extramarital sexual encounter. There are two different forms of consensual adultery: adultery toleration, in which the marriage partners simply

extramarital sex: married person having sexual intercourse with someone other than her or his spouse; adultery.

conventional adultery: extramarital sex without the knowledge of the spouse.

consensual adultery: extramarital sex in which the spouse is informed and has agreed to allow it.

adultery toleration: marriage partners extend the freedom to each other to have sex with others.

extend to each other the freedom to have sex with others; and comarital sex (also called swinging or mate swapping), in which both partners participate as a dyad in sexual sharing with others. Mate swapping became more common during the 1960s and early 1970s. Two studies demonstrated that of the married adults questioned, 5 percent admitted to having participated at least once in some sort of comarital sexual experience (Athanasiou et al., 1970; Johnson, 1971). These couples were usually middle- and upper-middle-class individuals, many of them well educated, affluent, and engaged in professional or semiprofessional occupations. Not much is known concerning the motivations behind comarital sex. There can be no doubt that some seek extramarital activity out of frustration or boredom with their marital sex. Many professionals find, however, that couples often do not handle the emotional aspects of sexual nonexclusivity as well as they handle the intellectual concepts.

Sociologist Annette Lawson (1988) has studied data provided by 600 volunteers who had been involved in extramarital sex. The reasons individuals gave for their adultery included boredom and restlessness; wanting a wider view and broader range of sexual and relational experience; needing more control in sex or lacking self-control in themselves; and searching for a stronger sense of self-worth. Of those couples who had been married prior to 1960, almost none had discussed extramarital sex before they married. For those married after 1970, almost all had talked about the issue, indicating that a significant degree of consciousness-raising about extramarital sex took place during the intervening decade, which has been touted as the beginning of the sexual revolution. Lawson contends that as women have gained an increased sense of entitlement to make decisions about their bodies in recent years, and as they have entered the workplace in increasing numbers, they have been more likely to consider the choice of extramarital sex and more likely to find partners with whom sex is available.

It is difficult to generalize about the dangers or benefits of extramarital sexual activity. Conventional adultery, with its deceit and dishonesty, can lead to disastrous results for some marriages. Consensual adultery probably runs the gamut from being a negative, destructive force to enhancing and enlivening a marriage. For many contemporary married couples, communication is considered a crucial part of their intimate relationship. Therefore, any deceit or dishonesty involved in extramarital sex may now be perceived as more of a betrayal than the sexual activity itself (Lawson, 1988). Interestingly enough, the most commonly kept sexual secret in marriage is the fact that one masturbates. Many people hide this behavior from their spouses out of fear of rejection, much as they might hide extramarital sex with another partner (Klein, 1989). Couples must make their own decisions concerning the limits of their exclusivity and nonexclusivity for love and sex. In times when the risks of contracting the AIDS virus increase for nonmonogamous individuals, the pressures on that decision-making process are greater than ever.

PAYING FOR SEX

Like anything that can provide people with pleasure, sex has often become a commodity. Prostitutes participate in sexual activity for money. Often facetiously called the world's oldest profession, prostitution has met with varying degrees of tolerance throughout history and in various societies. In contemporary Western culture, there has been a growing attitude that prostitution represents an exploitation and subordination of women (Basow & Campanile, 1990). There are both male and female prostitutes, of course, although far more research is available on the latter.

Male prostitutes who serve women have been known as gigolos, or more recently as escorts. However, sometimes escorts are just that—companions to some social event. Almost no empirical data have been gathered on this group. More typically, male prostitutes engage in homosexual activity with other males. There are boys and young men who have discovered that older men will pay them for sex. Usually the client or "john" wishes to perform fellatio (oral sex) on the prostitute. Some young male prostitutes consider themselves heterosexual and view their same-sexed involvement purely as a business venture. The longer they work as prostitutes the more likely they are to think of themselves, and be identified by their peers, as homosexual. Male hustlers tend to work full-time as prostitutes on the street or in other locations. Some of the particularly good-looking and well-mannered male prostitutes may eventually become attached to an older affluent man or become more highly paid call boys.

While female prostitutes are usually hired to give their clients an orgasm, male prostitutes are typically hired to have an orgasm themselves through stimulation by their clients (Gagnon, 1990a). Given the realities of male sexual response, particularly the refractory period, this limits the numbers of clients a male may serve in one day. Female prostitutes, by contrast, are not limited by this physiology and typ-

comarital sex: also called mate-swapping, in which a couple swaps sexual partners with another couple.
hustlers: male street prostitutes.
call boys: highly paid male prostitutes.

FIGURE 12.9   Prostitution

Female prostitutes are commonly called hookers, street-walkers, or call girls. Male prostitutes are referred to as gigolos, hustlers, or call boys. Both female and male prostitutes use their bodies as commodities to exchange sexual favors for money.

ically do not experience orgasm in their paid encounters. A study that surveyed 46 street prostitutes found that nearly three-fourths of them did enjoy intercourse and oral sex with their customers. The study also found that all of these women reported enjoying sex with their boyfriends or husbands as well (Savitz & Rosen, 1988).

The most common street name given to female prostitutes is <u>hookers</u>. While <u>brothels</u>, or houses of prostitution, can still be found, they have largely been replaced by <u>streetwalkers</u> who work for <u>pimps</u> and by <u>massage parlors</u>. <u>Call girls</u> tend to be the higher paid prostitutes who cater to a more exclusive clientele.

The sexual acts requested of female prostitutes seem to vary with the times, as do costs. Prior to World War II prostitutes usually had sexual intercourse with their clients. In 1973 Winick and Kinsie reported that oral sex had become the most popular request. A

more recent study of requests made to prostitutes by 530 men showed intercourse to be the top choice in men aged up to the mid-to-late thirties, but in older age groups, oral sex became a more popular request (Robinson & Krussman, 1983). While men who seek sex from female prostitutes cross all social boundaries and occupational categories, the majority tend to be white, middle-class men with no history of pathological behavior (Holzman & Pines, 1982).

There is much debate over prostitution being a victimless crime. However, research shows that the majority of prostitutes have a background of sexual abuse and other forms of physical abuse that has damaged their feelings of self-worth (Silbert & Pines, 1983). Also, ample evidence indicates that prostitution is a dangerous job in which the women are frequently raped, beaten, robbed, and forced to perform various sexual acts against their will (Winick, 1991). Another increasingly serious concern is the spread of the AIDS virus or other sexually transmitted diseases by prostitutes. Preliminary testing shows a substantial proportion of female prostitutes already infected with the AIDS virus. In some cities well over half of the prostitutes tested had a positive result for the virus. However, it is also claimed that a relatively small amount of disease transmission actually comes from prostitution, and that this would be reduced if prostitution were decriminalized and regulated (Almodovar, 1991). While absolute protection cannot be guaranteed for the prostitute or the client, any man seeking sex with a prostitute should wear a condom throughout the sexual activity. Clients of male prostitutes should insist that the prostitute wear a condom in order to somewhat reduce the risks of AIDS transmission.

An increasing concern among professionals is the number of prostitutes who are adolescents, ranging in age from 13 to 18. Girls are particularly susceptible to becoming prostitutes if they have a poor self-image, have run away from home, have friends who are already prostitutes, or are seeking an adult on whom they need to depend. Pimps quite often fill this need by showering a girl with attention and gifts, developing a romantic attachment with her, then using the relationship to entice the girl into prostitution. Studies have shown that most men who hire adolescent prostitutes are over age 25, and often have families of their own. They tend to frequent prostitutes during their lunch

hookers: street name for female prostitutes.
brothels: houses of prostitution.
streetwalkers: female prostitutes who work on the streets.
pimps: men who have female prostitutes working for them.
massage parlors: places where women can be hired to perform sexual acts under the guise of giving a massage.
call girls: highly paid prostitutes who work by appointment with an exclusive clientele.

hours or immediately after work, so that they may continue home life and relationships without interference. Most experts in this area feel that one ideal way to reduce or eliminate adolescent prostitution is to solve the social problems that lead girls to the activity in the first place. Then information should be provided about how they may be influenced by pimps. It may also be necessary to use law enforcement agencies to separate the girl from her pimp. Finally, she should be provided with appropriate social services and housing that would create an alternative environment to prostitution (Baizerman, Thompson, & Stafford-White, 1979).

CLOSE ENCOUNTERS

Nonphysical or nonintimate forms of sexual connection with other human beings involve several forms of behavior and an unwilling partner. The unknowing person who is sought out for such a sexual connection is a victim in the sense of having been an unwilling participant in someone else's sexual activity. The degree of victimization may range from feeling some petty annoyance to being seriously traumatized by the experience.

Obscene Telephone Calls   Men who have strong feelings of insecurity and inadequacy have a tendency to engage in obscene telephone calls. Their phone calls to women, or occasionally other men, represent ways of anonymously asserting their sexuality to women without having to face a frightening social contact. Since their calls are usually spiced with sexual obscenities, designed to shock or surprise women, the behavior may also reflect some negative attitudes toward women (Nadler, 1975). Sometimes such calls surely represent a prank, but they may also become a continuing form of sexual release, often accompanied by masturbation. It is very rare for an obscene telephone caller to follow up the call with any sort of actual contact with the victim. The best way to react to such a call is to hang up immediately, without comment, and then to report the call to the local telephone company.

Consensual Telephone Sex   A relatively new form of sexual encounter is represented by the "900" telephone numbers that can reach people who are willing to talk in a sexually provocative way over the phone. These services automatically bill a charge to the caller's telephone, depending on the amount of time involved, and sometimes the minute-to-minute charge is quite substantial. Most callers to dial-for-sex services are apparently men who share fantasies over the telephone. It is believed that they typically are mastur-

bating during their phone call. Some evidence suggests that the majority of callers are married, and want to talk with someone who will not be offended by their behavior or fantasies. There is very little research on telephone sex at this point, but it may well represent a relatively harmless, and certainly safe, form of sexual encounter. Sometimes the need to make such a call may indicate problems within a relationship, but there is no indication that this is always the case. It has been suggested that telephone services cater to couples as well, so that partners may use telephone sex as a shared experience (Cooper, 1990).

Frottage   A term that applies to gaining sexual enjoyment from pressing or rubbing against another person in some anonymous setting is frottage. Crowded places, such as elevators, subways, or theaters, are common locations in which the frotteur may operate, since the close contact will usually go unnoticed. Little is known about frottage, but professionals assume again that this is a way for insecure people to seek out minimal physical contact with someone who is sexually appealing to them. Probably the act is often followed by masturbation in private.

Exhibitionism   Exposing the genitals to someone else for sexual pleasure is called exhibitionism. Usually the one who commits this act is a man who exposes his penis to children or to an adult woman, although women sometimes gain sexual pleasure from exposing their breasts. The exhibitionist may go to great pains to make it seem as though he was caught undressing or urinating, so that the victim will be less prone to reporting it as a crime. People who are arrested for such behavior are charged with indecent exposure or public lewdness. The repeating male exhibitionist usually gains pleasure from shocking others with the sight of his penis, thereby gaining some sort of confirmation of his male power.

It is apparent that many people display some degree of exhibitionism in their attempts to appear and feel sexy. Bikinis for women and men, see-through clothing, tight trousers and blouses all attest to that fact. Some women add extra padding to their bras to emphasize their breasts, and some males admit to adding extra padding to their genital areas occasionally. These are subtle forms of exhibitionism. Nudity is obviously a form of exhibitionism, although

---

frottage (fro-TAZH): gaining sexual gratification from anonymously pressing or rubbing against others, usually in crowded settings.
frotteur: one who practices frottage.
exhibitionism: exposing the genitals to others for sexual pleasure.

"You don't often see a real silk lining, these days . . ."

it may have few, if any, sexual connotations. People shower together in gym shower rooms, and at least some of them report a feeling of enjoyment in being nude together with other people. Nude beaches are becoming increasingly popular. There seem to be few sexual implications of nudity in actual nudist camps, and, in fact, attaching sexual meanings to nudism in these settings is generally frowned upon (Story, 1987). It can be expected, however, that in a society that typically requires the sex organs to be covered, a real sense of liberation and sexual pleasure might sometimes accompany the uncovering of these organs in the presence of other people.

A study of men who masturbate in public places (Maletsky & Price, 1984) found that men who lose their sexual pleasure and erections when they become aware of being observed by a female are unlikely to become exhibitionists later. However, those men whose sexual pleasure was enhanced by being observed during masturbation were highly likely to display subsequent exhibitionistic behavior. Since such behaviors are generally considered antisocial, there are various treatment programs designed to help these individuals channel their sexual energies into more acceptable directions.

The motivations behind exhibitionism vary among individuals. It seems that a typical motivation stems from the exhibitionist's feelings of inadequacy and inferiority. In exposing his penis to a woman, he seeks reassurance of his maleness and masculinity. There are probably some aggressive motives as well, since the victim may react strongly to the situation that the exhibitionist creates and experience a degree of emotional distress. If a woman does not react with any particular surprise or fear upon being confronted by an exhibitionist, she destroys his primary source of gratification. Public exhibitionism can be offensive to the individual who, without consenting to do so, is confronted with having to see someone else's sex organs. This is not necessarily a seriously harmful event, but it still can be emotionally exploitative. A study of 846 women found that 18 percent of those who had encountered exhibitionists found the experience severely distressing. An additional 25 percent had their attitudes about men, sex, or themselves affected in some way by the experience (Cox, 1988). Whenever possible, the best response is probably to ignore the exhibitionist. The police or other authorities may also be contacted and asked to take action. Exhibitionism is often found in the criminal and sexual histories of rapists and abusers of children.

Voyeurism   The gaining of sexual pleasure from observing nudity in others or by watching others engage in sexual acts is voyeurism. There is certainly an element of voyeurism in most of us, and it is quite natural to be interested in other people's genitals and body form. The prevalence of pornography provides ample evidence of the voyeuristic needs of the public. This behavior becomes more offensive when the voyeur, or Peeping Tom, goes out of his or her way to peer in windows of bedrooms or spy on people in public bathrooms to satisfy his or her needs. Voyeurs tend to be younger males in their early twenties, usually unmarried or separated. About 25 percent of these young males are married. Very few seem to have any serious mental disorders but most have had unsatisfactory sexual relationships. Voyeurs are usually interested in viewing strangers and usually do not interact physically with their victims. Nonetheless, the act is an obvious violation of another's right to privacy. Again, it may not harm the victim, and in fact the voyeur's presence may never be known, but it is an exploitative act.

It is certainly true that men are implicated in these forms of sexual connection far more often than women, and the scanty statistics available seem to confirm that males do indeed find such behaviors sexually arousing, more so than females. However, social attitudes and values may also be operative here. It has been suggested, for example, that if a man is

voyeurism (VOYE-yu-rizm): sexual gratification from viewing others who are nude, or who are engaging in sexual activities.

Case Study

GLENN: A YOUNG HUSBAND'S PROBLEM WITH VOYEURISM

Glenn was a 34-year-old business manager in a small town. He was a well-respected member of the community and had a wife, Lisa (a 33-year-old real estate agent), and three school-age children. Twice he had been reported to local police for lurking around homes. He had not been arrested and the incidents had been hushed up. Eventually, however, he was brought to the state police by the security forces from a college in a neighboring city. He had been caught peeping in the first-floor windows of a women's dormitory. This time he was arrested and required to appear at a hearing before a judge. The judge recognized that Glenn was repentant and wished to change his behavior, and Glenn's lawyer asked that Glenn be given a chance to seek professional psychological help. Glenn was required to see a sex counselor with Lisa.

The first visit with the counselor was painful for both Glenn and Lisa. Glenn was depressed, embarrassed, and ashamed, claiming that he was ready to be put away. Lisa was feeling confused about their relationship and afraid that her own sexual inadequacy had led her husband into his activities. They both spent much of the time venting their many emotions. Glenn begged

Lisa's forgiveness, insisting that he now only wanted to preserve their marriage. He said that he felt helpless to control the need to see young women undressing, and admitted that he had "peeped" many times without being discovered—usually masturbating while doing so.

Over a period of about 5 months, the couple were helped to increase their levels of communication about sex and other aspects of their marriage. Glenn reported that being able to talk about his voyeuristic needs seemed to lessen their intensity. With some building of skills to help deal with his sexual impulsiveness, he began to develop a sense of self-control and feel that he could choose not to peep in windows. The counselor encouraged him to talk about his voyeuristic sexual fantasies with his wife as well. She began to accept them more easily, and as his sexual nature became more fully shared, he began to feel more positive about himself and his marriage. Three years after his arrest his marriage seemed to be on stable ground, he had not repeated any illicit voyeuristic acts, and he no longer felt compelled to give in to his voyeuristic needs.

standing outside of an open window watching a woman undress, he would be arrested for being a voyeur. However, if the situation were reversed, with the woman watching the man undress beyond the open window, it would still be the man who would be arrested for exhibitionism.

SADOMASOCHISM

Sadomasochism is probably the least understood of the relatively common routes to sexual arousal and connection. The term includes a whole range of sexual behaviors involving discomfort, pain, humiliation, excretion or excrement, dominance and submission, and bondage (tying all or parts of the body). It has been traditional to define the sadist as the partner who derives sexual pleasure from inflicting a form of some usually negative stimulus on another person, the masochist being the individual who is aroused by receiving

such negative treatment. These are surely simplistic definitions, since many people seem to be able to enjoy either role. Sadism and masochism are opposite sides of the same coin and tend to accompany one another, even though one may dominate the other at any given time (Gebhard, 1976).

Sadomasochism is always a matter of degree. For most people shared sexual activity has its share of urgency and rapid movements, with tightly gripping hands, hard sucking movements, and the possibility of mild pinching, scratching, and biting. Such behaviors are part of the intensity of sex. For the sadomasochist, variants of such stimuli have become an important part

sadomasochism (sade-o-MASS-o-kiz-um): refers to sexual themes or activities involving bondage, pain, domination, or humiliation of one partner by the other.

sadist: the individual in a sadomasochistic sexual relationship who takes the dominant role.

masochist: the individual in a sadomasochistic sexual relationship who takes the submissive role.

331

of sexual arousal. The intensity of the stimulation desired may vary from scratching or biting through spanking, whipping, and severe beating. Occasionally, cutting to draw blood or to mutilate may be involved. People who pair up for sadomasochistic sex usually make careful agreements ahead of time concerning how far the activities should go. There are always risks of such contracts being broken, of course. It is also true, ironically, that the person in the submissive or masochistic role often wields more power and control over the interaction because it will be his or her reactions that largely determine the eventual direction of the encounter.

The acting out of fantasies in which one individual plays a dominant role is a very common sadomasochistic activity. Often the dominant person plays the role of a severe parent, teacher, or police officer who demands compliance from the submissive partner. The scenario often ends with some mock forced sexual activity. Urination and defecation sometimes are included in the sexual acts, and some individuals find sexual interest and arousal in urine (urophilia) or feces (coprophilia). Bondage, tying or restraining parts of the body, seems to be a variant of sadomasochism. Wearing a hood is often a part of such shared activities (Bronski, 1991). Adult sex shops sell all sorts of devices for binding the body or genitals. Most common are rings, straps, and other pressure devices used by males to bind the penis and/or testicles to generate or heighten sexual pleasure.

A very dangerous variation on the bondage theme is autoerotic asphyxiation. Some people, usually boys or men, have found that inducing a state of near asphyxiation by wearing a noose around the neck can enhance erotic pleasure and orgasm. They often devise various sorts of hanging techniques from which they can cut themselves loose prior to losing consciousness. What these individuals do not realize is how easy it is to lose consciousness when pressure is placed on the carotid artery in the neck. The Federal Bureau of Investigation estimates that between 500 and 1,000 people die accidentally each year from this sort of sexual activity. Families of victims are often confused about the sexual nature of the death and are embarrassed about reporting it as such. Partly for the same reason, the dangers of this kind of bondage have not been widely publicized to young men (Saunders, 1989).

There are few statistics on the frequency of sadomasochistic preferences and activities. One study indicated that 7 percent of 65,000 men questioned and 8 percent of over 15,000 women reported that they had at least tried sadomasochistic sexual acts (Lowe et al., 1983). In a survey done on over 2,000 students in the United States, Canada, and European countries, 8 percent of U.S. male students and 5 percent of female students reported that they had engaged in "whipping or spanking before petting or other intimacy." These percentages were markedly higher among British students (17 percent of males; 33 percent of females), where spanking is a prevalent form of childhood punishment. There is a well-developed network of gay male and lesbian sadomasochists within the homosexual subculture as well (Bronski, 1991; Stamps, 1991).

In sex-oriented tabloids available in some cities, sadomasochists advertise for sexual partners, making it clear which role is preferred. Some typical advertisements follow:

DISCRIMINATING MASTER, 32, Caucasian, very controlled but strict, desires applications from obedient, attentive slaves. T.J.M., Box 172.

FEMALES AND FEMININE MALES only. Have you had a good cry lately, or are you too grown up for that? Have you disciplined yourself so much that you mask your real feelings? Well, if you wear that mask in front of me, I'll slap you right out of it! I'm an attractive, imaginative black female, late 20s, and will give you highly private teachings in freeing your emotions. Send phone and fantasies to: Josa, P.O. Box 82.

One theorist suggests that masochistic behavior may represent an escape from the usual burdens and responsibilities of one's normal identity. In a masochistic role, the individual is spared the anxiety of making decisions, asserting control, or maintaining a favorable image. The role may also deter feelings of guilt and insecurity. A variety of other theories have attempted to explain how sexual orientations of a sadomasochistic nature develop, but there is little solid evidence to support any of them.

SEX WITH ANIMALS

Since before recorded history, humans have lived in close association with a variety of domesticated animals. Folklore and the literature of mythology contain many examples of humans having sex with animals, often portraying a woman who has become enamored of the large genitals and sexual prowess of some animal. The half-bull, half-human Minotaur of Greek mythology was the offspring of Pasiphae, wife of the King of Crete, and a bull whom she purportedly seduced.

urophilia: sexual arousal connected with urine or urination.
coprophilia: sexual arousal connected with feces.
bondage: tying, restraining, or applying pressure to body parts as part of sexual arousal.
autoerotic asphyxiation: accidental death from pressure placed around the neck during masturbatory behavior.

Cross-cultural studies have reported many cases of humans having sex with animals, usually called bestiality or zoophilia. There are cases of sex between humans and dogs, cattle, sheep, burros, horses, and chickens. There was even the suggestion that some animals may make sexual advances toward humans (Ford & Beach, 1951). The Alfred Kinsey studies reported that in his sample of the general population, 8 percent of adult males and 3 percent of adult females admitted having had at least some sexual contact with animals. Among men raised on farms, 17 percent reported having had at least one orgasm through contact with an animal, after puberty.

It appears likely that sex with animals usually represents sexual experimentation and the frustration of lacking an available sexual partner. It does not necessarily reflect serious psychological disturbance and seldom becomes a continuing pattern of sexual activity. What humans actually do with animals is as varied as any other aspect of human sexuality. Kinsey found masturbation of the animal and actual intercourse to be more common among men. General body contact with the animal is more common among women. Oral-genital contacts with animals were reported by both women and men.

Sex with animals is a topic usually met with abhorrence and disgust. Judeo-Christian-Muslim tradition carries strong prohibitions about humans having sex with animals, which may have grown out of fears that monstrous hybrids might be formed by such unions. In fact, no offspring can be formed by sexual intercourse between human and animals because of the genetic differences between species. The behavior is illegal in most areas today, covered by various types of laws concerning sodomy and lewd behavior. There is also the additional issue of possible injury or pain being inflicted on the animal, especially if restraints have been used to keep it from moving during the sexual activity.

SEX WITH THE DEAD

Probably no form of sexual behavior stirs negative reactions in quite the same way as necrophilia, or sexual relations with a corpse. It has been said that in ancient Egypt women of high rank and women of particular beauty were not given to embalmers until they had been dead for 3 or 4 days, to prevent the embalmers from having intercourse with them (Bullough, 1976).

There are no statistics concerning the incidence of necrophilia, and almost nothing written about people who participate in sex with the dead. It is believed to be a rare phenomenon, since few people have access to cadavers. It is likely that necrophilic sex acts are committed primarily by people who work with corpses, as in mortuaries or morgues, and have therefore become desensitized to them. Case studies of necrophiles show them taking jobs where they will be able to have such contact (Klaf & Brown, 1958). This behavior is prohibited under laws regarding the handling of bodies.

There are apparently some people who fantasize about sex with the dead and who then masturbate to these fantasies. They typically never carry through with the actual act of having sex with a dead body. This obsession has been termed pseudonecrophilia (Lazarus, 1977).

THE EMERGENCE OF CASUAL SEX AND PANSEXUALISM

It is generally agreed that there has been more permissiveness and tolerance toward sex in the past few decades than had existed at any time in the previous century. As we look toward the future, some people fear that we have entered a period during which people may share sex too casually. Others who view the changes more positively see the trend as a way for human beings to become more fulfilled sexually.

It is certainly true that now that the procreative emphasis has been reduced in sex, people are freer to enjoy sexual activities that are not intended to produce children. These include body touching, group sex, homosexual activity, masturbation, transvestism, sadomasochism, and other noncoital behaviors. Pornographic materials and sexual aids designed to enhance sexual pleasure have become commonplace. Our changes in values have led to the emergence of both recreational and casual sex. Proponents of recreational sex claim that shared sexual emotion can be a creative human force that can solve many problems. Those who advocate casual sex go even further, claiming that sex can be fun even when shared without any depth or structure in the relationship, as long as no one is hurt. If recreational and casual sex were to become even more acceptable, we could expect that more people would experiment with pansexual alternatives. The term *pansexual* has been used to describe individuals

---

bestiality (beest-ee-AL-i-tee): a human being having sexual contact with an animal.
zoophilia (zoo-a-FILL-ee-a): bestiality.
necrophilia (nek-ro-FILL-ee-a): having sexual activity with a dead body.
pseudonecrophilia: a fantasy about having sex with the dead.
pansexual: lacking highly specific sexual orientations or preferences; open to a range of sexual activities.

who see their sexual capacities as transcending human objects of attraction. They find a variety of behaviors and inanimate objects, or even concepts, sexually exciting (Geller, 1990).

Beginning in the mid-1980s, some trends began to develop that would tend to mitigate against the proliferation of casual approaches to sex. There has been a gradual shift toward more conservative values about sexual behavior. Even more significantly, the growing concern over AIDS has discouraged casual sexual encounters. The risks are now simply too great for many people to chance having sex with a partner whom they do not know. Until a vaccine or effective treatment for AIDS emerges, it seems likely that people will be cautious about casual sex.

Conclusion

We are living in a time unmatched for its diversity of sexual values. This also means that it is a period of confusion for many individuals and for society as a whole. Our culture has attempted to reconcile a plu-rality of value systems within a democratic political framework. A continuing fundamental question for such a society is how wide a latitude of values can be permitted. The same may be said for a spectrum of sexual preferences and activities. Never has there been such freedom to accept and live out nearly any aspect of one's sexual individuality. At the same time, debate will continue over which behaviors will be accepted and tolerated, and to what degree.

There are now groups calling for strict legislation to regulate any sexual activity that is not guided by their own sexual standards. Such groups typically have religious overtones and believe that only those forms of sex that fit into the contexts of marriage and procreation should be permitted. This belief system is certainly being given a boost by the deepening threat and spread of AIDS. As this chapter has shown, sexual individuality does not always fit into such a moral framework very easily. The spectrum of human sexuality raises issues that cannot be ignored. These issues are multifaceted, with social, political, health, and personal implications. And they are issues that affect all of us. ■

SELF-EVALUATION

Your Sexual Fantasies

It seems that nearly everyone experiences a rich sexual life in his or her imagination. Yet we react to our sexual fantasies in different ways. We may feel aroused, amused, frightened, ashamed, proud, or guilty, depending on how we have learned to think of our sexual fantasies. They may give us clues to what we like and dislike about sex, help us plan future sexual encounters, put us in touch with the richness of our imaginations, and provide interesting accompaniments to our sexual activities. Sexual fantasies are just that—fantasies. There is no particular need to fight or deny them. In fact, sometimes the more we try not to think about something, the more it plagues us. Keep in mind that it is our sexual actions for which we must accept responsibility; our fantasies need only be accepted as very personal parts of our minds. The following questions and exercises may help you take a closer look at your fantasy life and its meaning.

1. Take some time to think about your most common sexual fantasies in some detail. It may help to close your eyes and relax. Write down each fantasy if you wish.
   a. What are the predominant feelings generated in you by each fantasy? Start by deciding whether it gives you mostly positive feelings that make you glad to indulge in it, or whether it generates negative feelings that make you wish the fantasy would go away.
   b. More specifically, what feelings does each fantasy generate? Write down a list of all feelings that you experience during each fantasy.
   c. Have you ever told another person about any or all of your sexual fantasies? Why or why not? If so, what conditions helped you to feel able to share such a personal aspect of your life?
2. Here is a list of some typical topics of sexual fantasies. They may be simply fleeting thoughts or

rich in detail. For each fantasy you can remember experiencing, assign it a number, using the following scale as a way of noting the relative intensities of your fantasies.

0 = I have not experienced this fantasy.
1 = An appealing, arousing enjoyable fantasy.
2 = Most aspects of the fantasy were enjoyable and positive.
3 = A mixture of positive and negative aspects.
4 = Most aspects of the fantasy were unenjoyable and negative.
5 = A disgusting, guilt-producing, unenjoyable fantasy.

TYPICAL FANTASIES (YOUR RATING)

a. Having sex with someone to whom you are attracted but who is unavailable to you or uninterested in you. _____

b. Kissing or hugging someone of your own sex or admiring his or her nude body. _____

c. Having quick, uninvolved sex with a stranger whom you will never see again. _____

d. Having sex with someone of your own sex. _____

e. Watching a couple you know having sex with one another. _____

f. Forcing another person to have sex with you._____

g. Being forced to have sex with someone against your will. _____

h. Seeing the nude body and genitals of someone you judge to be attractive. _____

i. Having sexual contact with your brother or sister. _____

j. Being watched while you masturbate. _____

k. Being watched while engaging in some sexual activity with a partner. _____

l. Inflicting or being subjected to pain or humiliation during sexual activity. _____

m. Paying a female or male prostitute to have sex with you. _____

n. Having sex with someone under the legal age of consent. _____

o. Being tied up during sex or tying up someone else during sex. _____

p. Participating in oral-genital sex with a desirable partner. _____

q. Being part of a group sexual experience or an orgy. _____

3. Are there any sexual fantasies that you enjoy using as an accompaniment to masturbation? If so, try to sort out the unique features of each fantasy that contribute to your sexual enjoyment.

4. Do you sometimes find yourself fantasizing while engaging in masturbation or sexual activity with a partner?

a. If so, how does this make you feel?

b. Do you consider such fantasizing unusual? (It's not.)

c. Have you ever discussed these fantasies with your sexual partner? If so, did your partner share any of his or her sexual fantasies with you?

d. Have you ever acted out a sexual fantasy with a partner or considered doing so? (Some couples find this to be an occasional source of enjoyment and mutual arousal.)

5. Have you been able to give yourself permission to experience, accept, and enjoy your sexual fantasies? If not, is this a goal toward which you would like to work? If your fantasies are giving you problems, perhaps you would like to consider talking with a qualified professional about your concerns.

335

CHAPTER SUMMARY

1. Contemporary sex research has emphasized the physical, orgasmic aspects of sex. There is also the subjective erotic experience that includes sensuosity and desire.

2. Sexual orientation and objects of sexual desire may change with circumstances and time.

3. Human beings are extremely diverse in their sexual orientations and activities. Behaviors that differ from whatever is considered the norm may be classified by terms such as deviant, variant, or paraphilia.

4. There is a wide range of levels of interest in sex and amounts of actual sexual activity among people, ranging from the erotophilic to the erotophobic. An exaggeratedly high level of sexual interest or drive is called hypersexuality, while an especially low level is called hyposexuality. While either may reflect a normal pattern for a particular person, they may also signal deeper emotional distress. Compulsive sex, although apparently rare, is called nymphomania in females and satyriasis in males.

5. Celibacy refers to the choice not to share sexual activity with other people. It sometimes is a reaction to sexual burnout or can represent a choice based on ethical or religious issues. Noncoital sharing is fully satisfying to some couples.

6. Diverse sexual behaviors are more common among men than among women, at least according to reports of behavior. The reasons for this are unknown, although theories cite both biological and sociological possibilities.

7. Gender-identity/role (G-I/R) may be expressed along a continuum of male to female, masculine to feminine.

8. Transvestism refers to some type of cross-dressing, sometimes for purposes of sexual arousal.

9. Transgenderists live for periods of time as if they were members of the other sex.

10. Transsexualism applies to those individuals who feel strongly that their personalities do not fit their anatomical sexuality. They may desire to undergo sex reassignment procedures, which involve hormonal and surgical interventions.

11. There is controversy over what treatments or counseling should be made available to young people whose G-I/R may not fit the conventional expectations.

12. People use a variety of ways to enhance their own sexual arousal, including erotic pictures, devices to stimulate the genitals, and internal fantasy. Fetishism is the term used to describe sexual arousal by objects or materials not usually considered sexual.

13. There are several forms of sexual interaction for more than two persons. Troilism and group sex are examples.

14. Extramarital sexual activity may occur with or without the knowledge of the spouse. Another term used to describe this is comarital sex. There are many potential complications for any relationships involved.

15. There are both female and male prostitutes, and particular social structures have developed around prostitution. Legal debates over prostitution continue, and the AIDS issue has raised new concerns for this kind of casual sex.

16. Among the sex-related behaviors that have unwilling or unwitting victims are obscene telephone calls and frottage, or rubbing up against the other person.

17. Consensual telephone sex has become more available through "900" numbers that offer an opportunity for sex-related talk.

18. Exhibitionism is exposing the genitals or breasts to others, usually for sexual arousal. It is sometimes accepted as an innocent gesture but may also be offensive and involve police intervention.

19. Voyeurism refers to finding sexual arousal in viewing others in the nude or engaged in sexual activity. It most often violates another's right to privacy.

20. Sadomasochism encompasses a range of behavior involving inflicting pain or humiliation, tying parts of the body (bondage), or acting out of dominant-submissive fantasies, all for sexual arousal.

21. Sex with animals has been reported in a small percentage of humans, although most often it does not represent a continuing pattern of behavior.

22. Sex with the dead (necrophilia) is probably a rare phenomenon. Fantasizing about such an act has been called pseudonecrophilia.

23. There has been an increase in casual sex. The term pansexual refers to people who are open to a wide range of sexual activities.

24. We have been living in times when there is more freedom to exercise one's own sexual individuality than ever before. Social codes and legal statutes will continue to regulate behavior.

ANNOTATED READINGS

Allen, M. P. (1989). *Transformations: Crossdressers and those who love them.* New York: E. P. Dutton. Explores the private stories of men who dress and act as women. The book is profusely illustrated with photographs of these men in both male and female identities, and shows a diversity of age groups. One of the more enlightening books available on this complex theme.

Brown, G. (1989). *The new celibacy: Why more men and women are abstaining from sex—and enjoying it.* New York: McGraw-Hill. Approaches celibacy through interviews with women and men who have made that choice. The book emphasizes the importance of celibacy as a consciously chosen alternative rather than a rejection or fear of sexual expression.

Bullough, V., & Bullough, B. (1988). *Women and prostitution: A social history.* Buffalo, NY: Prometheus Books. Examines sex for money within the context of the role of women in society. This is a comprehensive historical, sociological, and cross-cultural study.

Haeberle, E. J. (1982). *The sex atlas.* New York: Continuum Publishing. A compendium of general topics on human sexuality, this book is organized somewhat like an encyclopedia and includes pertinent photographs.

Money, J. (1989). *Lovemaps: Clinical concepts in sexual/erotic health and pathology, paraphilia, and gender transposition.* Buffalo, NY: Prometheus Books. Introduces the concept of "lovemap" as the template that shapes an individual's erotic and sexual needs and preferences, and explains a theory for how lovemaps develop.

Weinberg, T., & Kamel, G. W. (Eds.). (1983). *Studies in sadomasochism.* Buffalo, NY: Prometheus Books. One of the most comprehensive recent books on sadomasochism available.

PART V
DEALING WITH SEXUAL PROBLEMS

t is likely that most people face some sort of sex-related problem sometime during their lives. The individual who faces a sexual problem may be forced to cope with a wide range of emotions, including guilt, anxiety, depression, self-doubt, and feelings of inadequacy. Yet, in seeking professional help, it is important to find a professional person who is well equipped to deal with sex-related matters. The four chapters in this part explore a variety of sexual problems, the different perspectives from which these problems may be viewed, and the ways in which professionals approach them. Chapter 13 reminds us that there has been an increase in awareness in recent years about exploitative sexual behaviors, including rape, child sexual abuse, and sexual harassment. People are now more willing to report such incidents to appropriate authorities and talk about the problems they have experienced as victims.

Sexual interaction has always been associated with the transmission of certain diseases, and that is one of the reasons that many social and religious codes of conduct have been established to regulate sexual behavior. For a time, however, it seemed that antibiotics would save us from the disease threats that came with sex. First herpes, and then AIDS, represented cruel reminders that there are still some health risks associated with shared sex. Chapters 14 and 15 examine the range of sexual diseases and disorders that are part of human sexuality, and offer up-to-date information on the AIDS crisis currently facing our world.

People's bodies do not always function sexually the way people expect or want, or the way a partner might prefer. Sometimes, that can mean that the person is experiencing a sexual dysfunction. Several common dysfunctions are discussed in chapter 16, along with some of the approaches to treating them that have been developed in the relatively new field of sex therapy. Most sexual problems do not have to remain problems forever. The chapters in this section of the text provide helpful suggestions for preventing and seeking help with problematic sex.

CHAPTER THIRTEEN
SEXUAL ABUSE AND OTHER SEXUAL PROBLEMS

All types of sexual behavior need to be considered in the context of an individual's life-style. There is controversy over what constitutes a sexual problem. Sexual addiction represents another area of current controversy. Rape, child sexual abuse, and incest are very serious problems that affect other people in society. There are ways of coping with and preventing sexual problems.

CHAPTER FOURTEEN
SEXUALLY TRANSMITTED DISEASES AND OTHER PHYSICAL PROBLEMS

Part of responsible sexual decision-making is to take appropriate measures to prevent the transmission of STDs. Syphilis and gonorrhea continue to infect large numbers of people. A new penicillin-resistant strain of the gonorrhea bacterium has worried officials. Chlamydia and genital herpes have become prevalent in the 1980s. Prostate infection, Peyronie's disease, and testicular cancer are of concern to men, while cystitis, prolapse of the uterus, and cervical cancer affect women. Prompt treatment and informing partners are important in controlling STDs.

CHAPTER FIFTEEN
THE AIDS CRISIS AND SEXUAL DECISIONS

AIDS destroys the body's immune system so that opportunistic infections eventually weaken the victim. It is fatal. The people most at risk for the disease are homosexual men and intravenous drug users who share needles, but it is spreading among heterosexuals. The crisis has raised many social and ethical issues, such as care for AIDS patients, costs, and safety to others. Safe sex can prevent the spread of AIDS. Using condoms with spermidical foams and jellies containing nonoxynol-9, using rubber dams, and limiting the number of one's sexual partners are ways of practicing safe sex.

CHAPTER SIXTEEN
SEXUAL DYSFUNCTIONS AND THEIR TREATMENT

Sexual dysfunctions may be caused by physical problems or psychological stress. Female vaginismus and post-ejaculatory pain involve involuntary muscle spasms that interfere with sexual activity. Poor communication and difficulties in a relationship can cause pressures that may contribute to sexual dysfunction. Behavioral sex therapy attempts to help couples learn positive, effective patterns of sexual interaction.

CHAPTER THIRTEEN

WHEN AND HOW DOES SEX BECOME A PROBLEM?
Negative Self-Attitudes
Self-Destructive Behavior
Harm or Exploitation of Others
Results of Prejudice and Ignorance
When the Body Does Not Function as Expected or
Desired
The Sexual Addiction Controversy

SEXUAL HARASSMENT

SEXUAL ABUSE BY PROFESSIONALS

RAPE
Acquaintance Rape
Marital Rape
Rape of Men
The Aftermath of Rape

SEX BETWEEN ADULTS AND CHILDREN
Effects of Child Sexual Abuse

SEX BETWEEN FAMILY MEMBERS

**PREVENTING AND DEALING WITH PROBLEMATIC
SEX**
Learning About Sex
Knowing How to Communicate
Having Realistic Expectations
Being Cautious and Responsible
Finding Sex Counseling and Therapy

CONCLUSION

**SELF-EVALUATION: YOUR SEXUAL CONCERNS AND
PROBLEMS**

CHAPTER SUMMARY

I think the hardest part for me was that my father never actually forced me to do anything with him, I mean physically forced me. He always made me feel like it was up to me. But I knew how much he wanted to do those things, and I didn't want to let him down or something. I always felt so awful about myself afterward, and I would feel sort of sorry for him. It has taken me a long time to realize how much I really was forced into sex with him, even though it was subtle and nonviolent.

—From a counseling session

SEXUAL ABUSE AND OTHER SEXUAL PROBLEMS

This chapter examines sexual problems, including various forms of sexual abuse. It begins with an overview of the elements that define what a "problem" may be. The chapter deals with several forms of sexual exploitation and abuse that have received wide attention recently. Finally, there is an emphasis on the many approaches that people can use to cope with and prevent sexual problems in their lives. One of the major difficulties is establishing what constitutes problematic sex. Behavior and feelings that are troublesome for one person may be pleasurable and enjoyable for another. In one sense, any kind of sexual activity may become a problem if someone is feeling worried, guilty, fearful, or ashamed about it. However, another issue then arises: Are the negative feelings justified in terms of present knowledge and attitudes, or do they simply stem from ignorance and misinformation? The answer is not clear-cut, but is rooted in other complex social issues. Sexual behaviors and feelings become problems because of the social values that surround them and the social judgments that are made about them. *Clearly, any sexual activity that involves the abuse, exploitation, or coercion of someone else is a serious problem.*

When and How Does Sex Become a Problem?

Consider the following case study of a 34-year-old lawyer who consulted a professional sex therapist. She complained of her lack of interest in sex and expressed hope that the therapist could help her become a more sexually active partner for her husband. She explained that her husband, a 36-year-old accountant, had a stronger sex drive than did she.

On the surface of things, this could seem to be a relatively straightforward problem of sexual incompatibility—one partner wanting sexual involvement more frequently than the other. Sex counselors and therapists encounter such discrepancies in relationships often and use various techniques that may help to resolve the difficulties.

However, as the therapist gathered a thorough history of the woman's situation, a much more complex picture emerged. She reported that her husband desired and expected to have sexual intercourse 2 or 3 times every day. He wanted coitus after going to bed and frequently upon awakening in the morning. It was not unusual for him to rouse his wife out of sleep in the

341

FIGURE 13.1 Miscommunication

Miscommunication over sexual expectations can result in confusion, frustration, and self-doubt. This is when a professional sex therapist can help. Counseling sessions can help people open communication pathways to try to deal with their complex sexual problems.

middle of the night for sex. If they both came home for lunch during their afternoon breaks, he often wanted sex. At times she had protested, only to have him coerce her emotionally or even physically into intercourse. The woman felt that her husband had a right to as much sex as he wanted and she wanted only to find ways of becoming a more willing and interested partner for him.

The therapist was now in somewhat of a dilemma, finding issues other than the woman's level of sexual interest to represent more serious concerns. The therapist felt that she probably exhibited normal levels of sexual arousal, and that the constant excessive sexual demands and pressures of the husband had quite predictably led to sexual boredom, depression, and burnout on her part. The therapist was also concerned about the continuing patterns of noncommunication and coercion evident in the couple's relationship.

What should the therapist do? Should she attempt to fulfill the woman's request and try to help her become more interested in sex? Redefine the problem in different terms and try to help the woman to see it that way? Tell the woman that she does not have a problem but that her husband does? Encourage marriage counseling for the couple?

This case study illustrates some fundamental difficulties in considering problematic sex. For example,

who is to define whether a problem actually exists at all? And to what degree does a problem exist? What problems are worthy of professional treatment? What are the standards by which problematic and nonproblematic behaviors are to be distinguished from one another? The following are a few scenarios that may signal the development of sex-related problems.

NEGATIVE SELF-ATTITUDES

The young man unprepared for his first emission of semen and the young woman shocked by her first discharge of menstrual blood are bound to experience some fear and worry. Those who have been encouraged to have negative feelings about the sex organs and sexual activities are bound to experience guilt over masturbation and sexual fantasies.

Society has perpetuated some rather specific stereotypes of sexual attractiveness through popular myths and advertising. Boys and men are most prone to be concerned about their height, muscularity of their bodies, and size of their penises. Girls and women are most prone to be concerned about their weight, breast size, and curvaceousness of their bodies. Those who end up feeling inadequate, who do not perceive themselves as living up to the prevailing standards of sex appeal, often experience negative feelings, a lowered self-concept, and even social isolation. For those who have been subjected to jokes or malicious criticism about their bodies, the pain may be even greater.

Personal conflict is a frequent result of the struggles to understand and fulfill our sexual needs. Most people have experienced their share of remorse, guilt, and self-hatred over sexual mistakes and misconceptions. At times the negative self-attitudes become troublesome enough to warrant counseling or other professional help.

SELF-DESTRUCTIVE BEHAVIORS

Those people who find themselves continuing to participate in some sexual activity they view as unhealthy or immoral can certainly experience self-destructive reactions with time. Those who choose sexual acts in which they risk arrest and prosecution are certainly not reflecting very positive or self-protecting attitudes. They may also enter into certain situations with a false sense of invulnerability, believing "it won't happen to me." Most professionals agree that such behavior may well represent personal problems worthy of attention. This is particularly true of some sadomasochistic activities in which there is the risk of bodily harm, or even death.

The issue becomes more clouded when the practitioner of some risky sexual act does not feel that there is anything to be concerned about. An example of this is autoerotic asphyxiation, discussed in chapter 12, "The Spectrum of Human Sexual Behavior," p. 332. Several other masturbatory activities that may have life-threatening aspects include wrapping oneself in plastic bags, use of electrical devices for stimulation, or insertion of objects into the penile urethra. Numerous theories have been proposed to explain such behaviors, but the most straightforward may be the connection of sexual arousal with the excitement of risk-taking (Saunders, 1989).

There is another paraphilia that may be related to masochism and also to some forms of sexual identity disturbances; it is the strong desire to have a limb amputated. This need has been labeled apotemnophilia, literally meaning "amputation love." Apotemnophiles are erotically obsessed with getting a limb amputated and who attach sexual significance to the stump. Money, Jobaris, and Furth (1977) have reported case studies of men who attempted to find surgeons who would amputate one leg, and cited other cases where men had self-inflicted injuries that led to actual amputation. These men apparently feel that their sexual identity (as amputees) can be fulfilled only through amputation.

apotemnophilia (a-POT-em-no-FIL-ee-a): a rare paraphilia characterized by the desire to function sexually after having a leg amputated.

FIGURE 13.2 Stereotypes of Attractiveness

One of the great myths about sexuality in our modern culture is that sexual prowess and satisfaction are mostly available to the young. The beach-going, tanned, firm-bodied youth, such as those shown here in Fort Lauderdale, Florida, are a stereotype in American society and a standard by which many young people measure themselves.

343

HARM OR EXPLOITATION OF OTHERS

When sex is used for selfish gratification, it may end up being hurtful or traumatic for others. Although there are elements of mutual seduction in most forms of shared sex, there may also be physical or emotional coercion in persuading a partner to become sexually involved. In a relationship one person may be interested in sex before the other and may begin using various forms of pressure to convince the reluctant partner to get involved. Emotional blackmail, such as saying, "You would have sex with me if you really loved me," or hinting that the relationship will end if sex does not improve, certainly constitutes sexual exploitation and a relational problem.

There seem to be some common characteristics among people who tend toward sexually exploitative behavior. For example, they typically felt isolated within their families when young. They also had often been subjected to violence or sexual abuse. They may show serious personality disturbances, have difficulty maintaining social relationships, and have a propensity toward depression, loneliness, and personal rigidity (Milner & Robertson, 1990).

RESULTS OF PREJUDICE AND IGNORANCE

The price of being openly different sexually in any society can be high. On the other hand, a narrowly restricted, inhibited pattern of sexual living is not without its costs either. While we have made great inroads in fighting racial and ethnic prejudice in recent decades, prejudice about sexual differences remains deeply ingrained in our society's values. Keep in mind that prejudice is holding strong attitudes that are seen as truth, even though they have no basis in fact. Prejudice grows out of exaggerated stereotypes and lack of information.

As any sex counselor can confirm, prejudice takes its toll. People with unconventional sexual orientations or life-styles often feel forced into secret relationships and deception. They may end up feeling as though they live double lives, struggling to exhibit a socially acceptable image while quietly maintaining a very different life-style in private. The stress of such an existence can have serious consequences in a person's life. There may be a growing lack of self-respect and self-esteem. Some enter into socially acceptable relationships in hopes that they will be able to pass as acceptable, only to experience instead a period of interpersonal conflict and unhappiness. Constantly being made to feel wrong or as if you don't fit in as the result of prejudice can lead to years of self-denigration and lack of self-acceptance.

WHEN THE BODY DOES NOT FUNCTION AS EXPECTED OR DESIRED

Most of us have some expectations and hopes about how our sexual encounters with others should go. We just expect that our sex organs will go along too, cooperatively and excitedly. It can be quite a shock when that does not happen. Men and women may find difficulty in becoming sexually aroused: a man may not achieve erection of his penis, a woman may not produce lubrication in her vagina. Or there may be difficulty in reaching orgasm. Orgasm may happen too quickly or not quickly enough. There may be pain, or tightness, or dryness. For a variety of reasons our bodies simply may not function sexually the way we want or expect them to.

These are the sexual problems that fall into the category of dysfunctions. While they may have physical roots, most often the sexual dysfunctions are caused by psychological blocks and stresses. These problems are discussed in detail in chapter 16, "Sexual Dysfunctions and Their Treatment."

THE SEXUAL ADDICTION CONTROVERSY

Sometimes, sexual behavior is defined as problematic by expert opinion. What has come to be called sex addiction is an example of this. It has been recognized that sexual activity becomes compulsive for some people, and regulating their sexual behavior is difficult or impossible for them. In 1983 author Patrick Carnes published a book in which he compared compulsive sexual behavior to alcoholism or other chemical dependencies. He maintained that sex addiction was characterized by typical symptoms of other forms of addiction, such as an inability to stop the behavior even in the face of serious consequences. These could include physical consequences, such as self-mutilation, disease, or unwanted pregnancy; occupational consequences, such as losing one's job or being charged with sexual harassment; and complications within relationships. Carnes has come up with a model to explain sex addiction, in which compulsive sexual behavior is followed by feelings of despair that then lead back to ritualized repetition of the behavior for relief of stress (Carnes, 1991).

A National Association of Sexual Addiction Problems has been formed, which encourages the

---

dysfunction: when the body does not function as expected or desired during sex.

sex addiction: inability to regulate sexual behavior.

development of a 12-step treatment program for sex addiction, similar in its philosophy and practice to the 12-step approaches for alcoholism and drug abuse. One survey estimated that about 17,000 individuals had joined sex addiction programs based on this approach to treatment (Avasthi, 1990). In his treatment program, Carnes has reported a high rate of improvement among the sex-addicted patients, and has also found that a high proportion of these people had observed addictions of various sorts (sex, alcohol, food, drugs) among their parents and siblings (Carnes, 1990).

Other workers have taken exception to the sex addiction model, believing it to be misleading and even dangerous. Therapist Marty Klein (1991) insists that this approach has encouraged people to diagnose themselves as "sex addicts" when they may actually just be ignorant or misinformed about normal sexual behavior, and that the treatment approaches have been developed and operated largely by people who are not trained in the fields of human sexuality. Again we face the difficulty of defining what is problematic. Some people might feel that masturbation once a week would be a behavior to be brought under control, while most sexologists would consider it very normal. Klein also feels that the sex addiction philosophy is basically antisexual, because it emphasizes specific negative values about such things as masturbation, pornography, fantasy, and choosing to have sex outside of a loving, committed relationship. In this sense, the sexual addiction movement has been seen as having a missionary zeal that might be dangerously oversimplified.

Of even greater concern for some sexologists is the possibility that individuals who have come to consider themselves sex addicts will use their "illness" as an excuse for their sexual affairs or other exploitative sexual choices. Most sex therapists emphasize the need for clients to take full responsibility for their choices and behaviors rather than excusing them. A final argument against the sex addiction model is that people whose compulsive sexual behaviors stem from more serious underlying psychiatric disorders may not be getting the intensive treatment they should have. Instead, they are relying on a simplistic 12-step program that may not be sufficiently rooted in psychotherapy or treatment of serious illnesses such as manic depression or psychosis (Mosher, 1991).

It is too early to tell where the controversy over sex addiction will go. It would appear that many people feel they have been helped by treatment programs for sex addicts (Earle & Crow, 1990). Potential negative outcomes are only beginning to be publicized and debated. It is certainly a controversy that will continue to be hotly debated during the 1990s.

Sexual Harassment

There is a form of sexual exploitation that can be very subtle—even confusing to identify—and yet be highly upsetting to the victim. It is the unwanted sexual advances, suggestiveness, or coercion that can occur in academic settings or the workplace. The term most often used to describe such behavior is sexual harassment. While the incidence of sexual harassment has not been investigated widely, and definitions vary among people, it would appear to be widespread. Even conservative estimates would suggest that about 30 percent of women are victims of sexual harassment. Studies have suggested that during their college years 50 to 60 percent of women are subjected to some sort of treatment that would clearly be defined as sexual harassment (Hotelling, 1991). Although studies have tended to focus on harassment of women, it is certainly not rare for men to be victims of sexual harassment. Results of a Pentagon survey of Armed Forces personnel released in 1990 showed that 82 percent of the women and 74 percent of the men had felt sexually harassed by teasing, jokes, remarks, or questions. Sixty percent of women and 51 percent of men reported having been victims of physical forms of ha-

sexual harassment: unwanted sexual advances or coercion that can occur in the workplace or academic settings.

FIGURE 13.3 Sexual Harassment

National attention was focused on the issues surrounding sexual harassment when law professor Anita Hill's accusations of inappropriate behavior were aimed at Supreme Court nominee Clarence Thomas. Ultimately, the Senate Judiciary Committee decided there was insufficient evidence to indicate that Thomas had harassed Hill. The case dramatized the complications of situations in which one person's word is pitted against another's.

345

Sexual Harassment: It's About Power, Not Sex

Consider the case of a male supervisor who, in the midst of a conversation with a female employee about an assignment, asked her out of the blue, "Are you wearing panties?" and then blithely continued the conversation seemingly pleased that he had left her rattled.

Years later, the woman says she is still outraged by the incident, though she said nothing at the time. . . . The story underscores a picture that is emerging from extensive research on such harassment: it has less to do with sex than power. It is a way to keep women in their place; through harassment men devalue a woman's role in the work place by calling attention to her sexuality.

● ● ●

While sexual harassment may on first glance be taken as simple social ineptness or as an awkward expression of romantic attraction, researchers say that view is wrong and pernicious because it can lead women who suffer harassment to blame themselves, believing that something in their dress or behavior might have brought the unwanted attention.

In fact, only about 25 percent of cases of sexual harassment are botched seductions, in which the man "is trying to get someone into bed," said Dr. Louise Fitzgerald, a psychologist at the University of Illinois. "And in less than 5 percent of cases the harassment involves a bribe or threat for sex, where the man is saying, 'If you do this for me, I'll help you at work, and if you don't, I'll make things difficult for you.' " The rest, she said, are assertions of power.

All the Signs of a Tactic

The use of harassment as a tactic to control or frighten women, researchers say, explains why sexual harassment is most frequent on occupations and work places where women are new and are in the minority. In fact, no matter how many men they encounter in the course of their work, women who hold jobs traditionally held by men are far more likely to be harassed than women who do "women's work."

● ● ●

The style of harassment is likely to differ among professionals and blue-collar workers. "In the blue-collar work place there's often a real hostility to women," said Dr. Fitzgerald. "Men see women as invading a masculine environment. These are guys whose sexual harassment has nothing whatever to do with sex. They're trying to scare women off a male preserve."

Dr. Fitzgerald added, "Professional men don't go around putting used condoms in your desk, as can happen in a blue-collar setting. It's more likely to be something like what happened to a woman lawyer I know at a large international firm. As she was sitting

rassment, including being leaned over, being touched, or being cornered, pinched, or being brushed against in a deliberately sexual manner. Fifteen percent of Armed Forces women and 2 percent of the males indicated that they had actually been pressured for sexual favors.

Scenarios in the civilian world are similar; they involve, for example, the worker who is subjected to intimate touches or sexual innuendos from a superior. The worker often feels trapped in an uncomfortable situation, resenting the uninvited attention, but fearful that reporting it will create embarrassing confrontations or even jeopardize further employment. In colleges and universities, sexual harassment is often evident in situations where a faculty member suggests to a student that a grade might be improved in exchange for sexual favors. The student may feel caught in the dilemma of being subjected to inappropriate and at a conference table with other executives, all men, she said, 'I have two points,' and one of the men interrupted, 'Yes you do, and they look wonderful.' "

[Dr. Fitzgerald also said,] "She felt humiliated that the men were laughing at her as a way to avoid taking her seriously."

* * *

Perhaps the most startling finding on the gulf between men and women in awareness about sexual harassment came in a study by Dr. Michelle Paludi, a psychologist at Hunter College who coordinates a committee there on sexual harassment. In the study men and women in college were presented with hypothetical scenarios and asked to say when sexual harassment occurred.

In one scenario, a woman gets a job teaching at a university and her department chairman, a man, invites her to lunch to discuss her research. At lunch he never mentions her research, but instead delves into her personal life. After a few such lunches he invites her to dinner and then for drinks. While they are having drinks, he tries to fondle her.

"Most of the women said that sexual harassment started at the first lunch, when he talked about her private life instead of her work," said Dr. Paludi. "Most of the men said that sexual harassment began at the point he fondled her."

Dr. Paludi added, "There is a difference between intent and impact. Many may not intend it, but some things they do may be experienced by women as sexual harassment. A touch or comment can be seen very differently."

* * *

Few Women Complain

Several studies have found that only 3 percent of women who have been sexually harassed make a formal complaint. "We find that close to 90 percent of women who have been sexually harassed want to leave, but can't because they need their job," said Dr. Paludi.

Despite company policies forbidding harassment, many victims say they believe that reporting it will simply lead to more trouble. In a study of 2,000 women working at large state universities, Dr. Fitzgerald found that most had not reported sexual harassment because they feared they would not be believed, that they would suffer retaliation, would be labeled as troublemakers, or would lose their jobs. Some women say they stay silent because they fear that reporting an incident may cost the harasser his job or his marriage.

Another reason most women who are sexually harassed remain silent is that "women feel a responsibility to be emotional managers of relationships and often want to keep things friendly," said Antonio Abbey, a psychologist at Wayne State University.

—Daniel Goleman, *New York Times,* October 22, 1991

unethical treatment while at the same time feeling that there is no tangible proof to offer others, and fearing that attempts to take action could lead to serious academic consequences if the offender were to seek retribution.

Victims of sexual harassment often minimize the importance of the event in their own minds, or they may react with shock and disbelief. They may feel ambivalent toward the offender, and sometimes even blame themselves for not having prevented the situation from developing. In this sense, the injuries of harassment may be subtle and emotional, calling the victim's own sense of self into question. Only too often, these reactions lead victims to ignore the incident and not report it to anyone in authority.

In sexual harassment cases, there is usually an imbalance in power through which the offender tries to take unfair advantage of the victim. The result of such

TABLE 13.1

How Women Deal With Harassment

INTERNALLY FOCUSED STRATEGIES

Detachment. Minimizing the situation, treating it like a joke or deciding it was not really important.

Denial. Pretending nothing is happening, trying not to notice, hoping it will stop, trying to forget about it.

Relabeling. Offering excuses for the harasser or interpreting the behavior as flattering.

Illusory control. Attributing harassment to one's behavior or attire.

Endurance. Suffering in silence, either through fear of retaliation, blame or embarrassment, or in the belief no one will help.

EXTERNALLY FOCUSED STRATEGIES

Avoidance. Quitting a job, dropping a class, etc.

Assertion/Confrontation. Confronting the harasser, making it clear the behavior is unwelcome.

Seeking Institutional Help. Reporting the incident.

Social Support. Seeking support and acknowledgment of the reality of the occurrence.

Appeasement. Attempting to placate the harasser.

Source: Dr. Louise Fitzgerald, *New York Times*, October 22, 1991, p. C12.

---

a trap for the individual being harassed is often a sense of helplessness that can lead to depression, other emotional upsets, and physical illness (Hotelling, 1991). Victims have often been known to quit their jobs or leave school as a result of continuing sexual harassment that they feel at a loss to cope with.

Most colleges and corporations now have specific policies defining what sort of conduct constitutes sexual harassment and outlining procedures for dealing with cases. Title VII of the Civil Rights Act of 1964 and Title IX of the Education Amendments of 1972 both clearly prohibit sexual harassment of employees and students. However, even with such policies in place, sexual harassment can be a difficult issue to resolve (Stringer et al., 1990). People in administrative positions may not agree on how to define the problem, and may have a stake in trying to protect the offender. It is also one of those offenses for which there is usually little tangible evidence to substantiate the victim's claims. It then becomes a situation of one person's word against another's.

One of the issues being debated in academia is whether even consensual relationships between faculty and students should be prohibited, because of the power imbalance and all of the potential for harass-

ment. On one side of the argument are the issues of personal privacy and freedom for legal adults to make choices about their relationships. Colleges and universities are no longer expected to exercise the same in loco parentis role that they once fulfilled. On the other side of the debate lie concerns about how imbalances of power, even when unintended, may lead to exploitation or sexual coercion. It is for these reasons that educational institutions need to develop sexual harassment policies with great care, and educate both students and faculty about the dangers and concerns. Any such policy must provide for grievance procedures, so that an individual who feels unfairly charged will be offered an opportunity for defense (Howard, 1991).

Recommendations to those encountering sexual harassment tend to emphasize the need to take as much control over the situation as possible. There are several specific suggestions for steps that can be taken:

1. *Seek sources of personal support.* Find an individual or small support group with whom you can share your fears and frustrations. This can provide support and encouragement through a difficult time, put the incident(s) and your concerns in clearer perspective, and give you guidance in making decisions about how you want to proceed.

2. *Find out which authorities or administrators are designated for the reporting of sexual harassment.* Some forms of harassment can be considered violations of law, and you might consider reporting them to police authorities. Most institutions have an affirmative action officer or other administrator designated to handle reports of sexual harassment. Even if these individuals feel that a lack of substantive evidence may make pursuit of a particular case difficult, they may have good suggestions for putting an end to the offensive behavior. Remember too, that if a person in authority receives more than one complaint about a particular employee, he or she will have more evidence with which to act. In the case of a student who is being harassed by a professor, reporting the incident may be useful in rectifying a situation in which an unfair grade is eventually given by the teacher as retribution. Keeping careful records of classroom performance would, of course, be necessary in arguing such a point.

3. *Be clear about your needs.* One common reaction of many victims of sexual harassment is to feel guilty that they may have somehow precipitated the sexual advances. Regardless of any ambivalence you may have once felt about the offender, if you now feel certain that you do not appreciate the behavior, be firm in your resolve to end the harassment and be assertive about it.

4. *Write a letter to the offender.* This is considered one of the best approaches to ending sexual

harassment (Sandler, 1983). It is a clear and direct statement to the offender that can often avoid formal charges and public confrontation. It may also provide the harasser with a new perspective on the behavior. Not all offenders have realized how negatively their actions have affected others. A copy of the letter should be kept and used as supportive evidence later if the harassment does not cease. Such a letter should clearly and directly state: a) specifically what actions have taken place, giving as many details, dates, and times as possible, but without evaluation; b) the feelings and reactions that have been generated by the actions; and c) a very short statement that you want the harassment to stop and also want your relationship to return to an appropriate professional, or student-teacher, level. Such letters are usually quite useful in placing a harasser on warning, and typically lead to quick cessation of the behavior.

Institutional policies and recent court decisions continue to confirm that everyone deserves to work or pursue an education in an environment that is free from inappropriate sexual overtures. If you find yourself subject to such behavior, take action promptly to avoid escalation in the tensions and consequences that may result.

Sexual Abuse by Professionals

Closely related to the sexual harassment issue is a growing concern about professionals—physicians, therapists, clergy, lawyers, social workers—who take advantage of their patients or clients sexually. In one survey of literature on patient-therapist sexual contact, about 10 percent of male therapists, and 2 to 3.5 percent of female therapists, admitted to having engaged in intimate contact with their patients. It is fairly common for therapists to justify their conduct as either innocuous or as being beneficial to the patient (Carr & Robinson, 1990). Most professions in which one individual is placed in a one-to-one helping role for another have seen their share of reports about sexual abuse. Unfortunately, these professions have often been slow to acknowledge the scope of the problem, sort through the complex problems of who was responsible for the actions, and develop mechanisms for handling cases where sexual abuse is alleged (Pope, 1990).

Psychiatrist Peter Rutter (1990) has highlighted the dynamics behind the abuse of female clients by male professionals. He sees the status and power of men in the helping professions to be key factors in sexual exploitation. Women come to these men in a highly vulnerable state. They may perceive the men as being warm, caring, and helpful. At the same time, men who have achieved professional status may sometimes see themselves as being above ordinary rules of ethical conduct, and may also see vulnerable women as potential sources of help for their own stresses, depressions, and relational problems. These perceptions conspire to create a situation where the patient is vulnerable to sexual abuse.

It has become increasingly clear that helper-client sexual exploitation often has disastrous consequences. The client may end up feeling used and angry, and whatever trust had been established for the professional is destroyed. Again, there is a tendency for clients who have been sexually exploited to blame themselves and assume that they should have prevented the behavior. The professional, too, suffers serious consequences: his or her career can be jeopardized because of the exploitation, and with good reason. Experts agree that it is up to the professional worker to establish and maintain appropriate boundaries in the helping relationship. For these reasons, it is crucial that physicians, lawyers, therapists, and others in these professions pay attention to their feelings and reactions, and work to prevent situations where unethical, exploitative actions might be likely (Sanderson, 1989). A number of states have enacted legislation providing civil and criminal penalties for professionals who violate ethical standards and participate in sexual or other inappropriate contact with their clients (Appelbaum, 1990). Sexual abuse by professionals is a problem that has been continuing to gain attention in recent years, and it will surely become even more visible as a problem in years to come.

Rape

In general usage, the term *rape* refers to any form of sex in which one person forces another person to participate. When used as a verb, it means making an individual engage in a sexual act without that individual's consent or against that individual's will. Men and children can be subjected to rape, as well as adult women. In many states rape is legally defined as forced sexual intercourse between a man and a woman. In these cases penetration of the vagina by the penis is essential if the crime is to be called rape. However, in about one-third of attempted rapes, penile-vaginal contact never occurs; but a variety of other forms of forced sex, including oral and anal penetration by the penis or vaginal penetration by fingers or objects, may occur. Traditionally these acts have been legally prosecuted as less serious offenses under most penal codes. Recognizing that these acts may be just as physically

349

(continued on bottom of p. 350)

Sexual Harassment on Campus: A Growing Issue

Once a hidden issue on campuses, sexual harassment is becoming a pervasive concern at colleges and universities nationwide, college officials say.

A recent letter from the American Council on Education reminded its 1,700 members that courts could hold them responsible for allowing a "hostile" or "offensive" environment if they failed to establish and enforce policies against sexual harassment.

One result is that institutions are developing a variety of grievance procedures in response to increasing reports of harassment that range from lewd remarks to bribes of higher grades in return for sex.

The complaints come from students and from faculty and staff members. The incidents include harassment by teachers, employees and other students.

Bernice R. Sandler, executive director of the Project on the Status and Education of Women of the Association of American Colleges, a Washington-based organization, said that, based on several thousand responses to more than two dozen campus questionnaires, 20 to 30 percent of undergraduate women nationwide had experienced some form of sexual harassment. Among graduate students, she said, the rate is even higher: 30 to 40 percent.

From Winks to Seduction

Miranda Massie, who recently graduated from Cornell University, says she thinks the rate of sexual harassment for undergraduate women is much higher. "Of all the women I am close to," she said, "I would say there are only one or two who haven't experienced sexual harassment—from either a series of winks that make it uncomfortable to go to class to actual seduction."

Ms. Massie said that when she was a sophomore her faculty adviser invited her to his house for dinner, and she became increasingly uncomfortable during the evening when the middle-aged professor told her how lovable she was. Finally, she said, he grabbed her, pulled up her skirt and tried to kiss her.

"I dashed out, absolutely in shock," she said. "It just grossed me out."

While unwanted sexual advances are not new on campus, experts say there is an enlarged perception now of what constitutes harassment and an increased willingness and assertiveness, mainly by women, to report abusive incidents.

"Quid pro quo" arrangements—good grades in exchange for sex—apparently account for a minority of cases among undergraduates. Dr. Sandler's research indicates, for example, that only 2 percent of undergraduate women experience direct threats or bribes for sexual favors.

Other forms of harassment include sexist comments, personal remarks and unwelcome touching. Sexual harassment today is generally defined as unwanted sexual attention that interferes with a person's ability to work.

Nearly all experts on the subject say their experience is limited to cases of men harrassing women. And while many said they knew of reports of homosexual and lesbian harassment, they said they knew of no comparable studies of such cases.

and psychologically damaging to the victim as intercourse, the American Law Institute has recommended that violent and forced sexual acts all be prosecuted under the more general label of "rape and related offenses." Statutory rape is a legal term used in a situation where an adult or adolescent has sexual intercourse with a younger partner who is under the age of consent, even if that partner was willing to have sex. Age of consent varies in some states, but is usually the age of 18.

statutory rape: a legal term used to indicate sexual activity when one partner is under the age of consent; in most states that age is 18.

Verbal Harassment Cited

Harassment can be verbal as well as physical. Anne Truax, director of the women's center at the University of Minnesota, tells of an undergraduate at a large Midwestern university who was speaking in front of the class when she was interrupted by the professor, "Tell me," he said, "do you have freckles all over your body?"

Although women are increasingly speaking out about such incidents, "most women still don't tell anyone and a lot of them blame themselves," Dr. Sandler said. "When someone brings a formal complaint, people say, 'But she isn't even that pretty.' It has nothing to do with attractiveness. It has to do with power and vulnerability. It's the professor using his power over the student."

In 1986 the Supreme Court ruled in *Meritor Savings Bank v. Vinson* that sexual harassment in a workplace that creates a hostile or offensive job environment is subject to action under Title VII of the Civil Rights Act of 1964. Since *Meritor,* an institution of higher learning that receives complaints of such incidents is required to take prompt action to determine the facts in the case.

Moreover, guidelines issued recently by the Equal Employment Opportunity Commission say an institution will be held responsible for a hostile work environment if it has failed to establish an explicit policy against sexual harassment and does not have a reasonably available way for victims to get someone in authority to investigate the complaints.

Reluctant to File Charges

As a result, colleges and universities are setting up advisory committees, drawing up grievance procedures and publicizing their efforts through workshops, seminars and brochures. But the process is complicated by the fact that many victims are reluctant to file formal charges.

Sanctions against offenders can involve a reprimand, loss of pay, a letter of censure, a change in the student's grade, a written apology to the victim or, in extreme cases, dismissal.

In most procedures, the accuser does not face the accused. The complaint is related to someone in authority who then talks to the accused to determine the facts.

Most sexual harassers turn out to be repeat offenders. "You never hear of a guy who has just harassed one woman unless he has just arrived on campus," Dr. Sandler said.

Ms. Truax of the University of Minnesota said the typical response from men was: "Yes, I did do that. I just thought I was being nice and friendly."

"Sexual harassment has to be understood within a context of unequal power relations," Ms. Peters said in an interview. "Professors should not be involved with students over whom they have grade power."

She added, "I hate to know that year after year, freshmen can come to an institution starry-eyed, walk into classes and then have this happen to them."

—Deirdre Carmody, *New York Times*, July 5, 1989

Determining the incidence of rape is difficult, since it is assumed that reported rapes represent only the tip of the iceberg. It has been estimated, however, that between 15 and 25 percent of women will be raped in their lifetimes. It is believed that as few as 10 percent of those rapes will be reported, and less than 5 percent of the rapists will end up in prison (Gibbs, 1991). The most recent Justice Department statistics indicate that from the mid-1970s to the late 1980s attempted rapes declined by 46 percent. Completed rapes, by contrast, held at a steady rate over that period. It was suggested that the decrease in rape attempts was the result of heightened consciousness about women's concerns and about what constitutes rape.

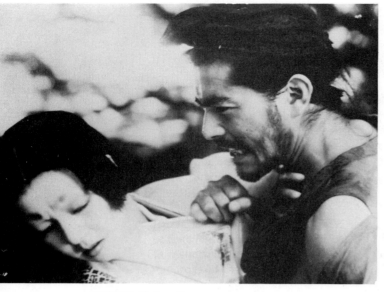

FIGURE 13.4   Rape

Rape is forced sexual participation, as depicted in the film *Rashomon*. Rape is not limited to women: men and children are also potential rape victims.

Fear of rape or other forms of sexual victimization is prevalent among women and affects their lives profoundly. They grow up learning to limit and restrict their behavior in various ways, such as never walking alone in certain locations or at night. Studies have shown that the fear of rape often makes women feel vulnerable and weaker than men. While it is recognized that protecting oneself through cautious behavior is absolutely essential, many women also resent having to live with the fears and limitations of their activity (Riger & Gordon, 1989).

The stereotyped rape scenario is that of a stranger accosting a woman in some secluded location at night and forcing her through threats and violence to have sex. Far more commonly, however, the victim knows the assailant. About 60 percent of women know the man who commits the rape, and among adolescent victims, closer to 90 percent are acquainted with the rapist (Hughes & Sandler, 1987). This form of sexual abuse is called acquaintance rape, or date rape.

acquaintance (date) rape: when a sexual encounter is forced by someone who is known to the victim.

Case Study

PATTY: A PERSONAL ACCOUNT OF RAPE

Following a traumatic rape experience, 30-year-old Patty writes about the attack and the aftermath as follows:

"I never dreamed anything like it could really happen to me. He just slipped into the car as I was getting in, right in broad daylight. He pushed me over to the passenger's side of the front seat and grabbed the keys. He showed me a knife and told me to be calm and quiet and he wouldn't hurt me. He said he only wanted to go for a little drive. He was so big and looked so strong, that I just sat there terrified and couldn't say anything.

"He drove us to a deserted dirt road and pulled me out of the car. Then he pulled me off into some bushes and raped me. I was so scared I hardly knew what was happening. It hurt, but I kept my eyes closed and just kept whispering, 'Please don't kill me, please don't kill me.' When he ejaculated, he grabbed me very tightly and yelled. Then, before I knew what was happening, he was running toward my car, and I

think he yelled back something about being sorry before he got in my car and drove away. I stumbled up the road to a farmhouse and they called the state police.

"I never have felt so dirty and humiliated in my life. I answered all their questions and was examined by a doctor, but then I couldn't wait to shower and douche.

"It took me months to really feel back to normal. I was in a women's support group for survivors of rape, and that helped a lot, just being able to talk about the awful feelings. Even now [3 years later], I feel dirty and sick just remembering it; I shake all over. Worst of all, they never caught him. Even though I now live over 200 miles from where it happened, I still worry about seeing him.

"I'm also married now, and my husband knows about it. It angers him, but that's all. But if I think about it while we're making love, I lose the good feelings and have to stop. It was all like a nightmare."

TABLE 13.2

What Constitutes Rape?

Do you believe a woman who is raped is partly to blame if:			
	AGE	YES	NO
She is under the influence of drugs or alcohol	18–34	31%	66%
	35–49	35%	58%
	50+	57%	36%
She initially says yes to having sex and then changes her mind	18–34	34%	60%
	35–49	43%	53%
	50+	43%	46%
She dresses provocatively	18–34	28%	70%
	35–49	31%	67%
	50+	53%	42%
She agrees to go to the man's room or home	18–34	20%	76%
	35–49	29%	70%
	50+	53%	41%
Have you ever been in a situation with a man in which you said no but ended up having sex anyway?	ASKED OF FEMALES	YES	NO
		18%	80%

Would you classify the following as rape or not?		RAPE	NOT RAPE
A man has sex with a woman who has passed out after drinking too much	FEMALE	88%	9%
	MALE	77%	17%
A married man has sex with his wife even though she does not want him to	FEMALE	61%	30%
	MALE	56%	38%
A man argues with a woman who does not want to have sex until she agrees to have sex	FEMALE	42%	53%
	MALE	33%	59%
A man uses emotional pressure, but no physical force, to get a woman to have sex	FEMALE	39%	55%
	MALE	33%	59%
		YES	NO
Do you believe that some women like to be talked into having sex?	FEMALE	54%	33%
	MALE	69%	20%

Source: From a telephone poll of 500 American adults taken for TIME/CNN on May 8 [1991] by Yankelovich Clancy Shulman. Sampling error is plus or minus 4.5%. "Not sures" omitted.

The issue of rape is a complicated one, partly because people define sexual acts in different ways. A survey conducted for *Ms.* magazine of 7,000 students on 32 college campuses found that over half had been subjected to sexual victimization, and one in every 8 women had been victims of rape. One in every 12 men admitted that they had forced a woman to have intercourse through physical force or coercion, or had attempted to. Yet, only 57 percent of the women who had been subjected to sexual acts against their will actually labeled the experience as rape. The rest had not acknowledged to themselves that they had indeed been raped. Almost none of the men said that they had committed rape. (Sweet, 1985).

The differences in perception between men and women have also been observed in a survey conducted for *Time* magazine and the Cable News Network (see Table 13.2). Men tended to place more responsibility for the sexual victimization on the women themselves than did women who were asked the same questions. The survey also demonstrated differing opinions about what sort of behaviors and situations actually constitute rape, with women always more likely than men to perceive scenarios as rape (Gibbs, 1991). These perceptual differences between the sexes have been confirmed by research as well (Harrison, Downes, & Williams, 1991). It is this very confusion and difference in opinion that may lead to miscommunication and ultimately to sexual abuse.

Research has not yielded a particularly clear

Even the Victim Can Be Slow to Recognize Rape

A reporter from the New York Times *interviewed several women who had been sexually assaulted. Their comments reflected the confusion, and frequent feelings of self-blame, that accompany the aftermath of acquaintance rape.*

Several women described men who ignored their resistance and tears before and during sexual intercourse and acted afterward as if nothing untoward had happened. Typical was Jenifer W., an undergraduate . . . who said she had been raped by a medical student. Jenifer met the man while studying the bulletin board in the student union in search of an apartment. She was impressed by his English accent and flattered by his attention.

Alternately charming and hectoring in a series of telephone calls, the man persuaded her to invite him to her dormitory. When he arrived, the girl said she told him, "I have no desire to have sex with you." During the attack, she cried, pushed him away and begged him to stop, "but that didn't faze him." Afterward, apparently immune to her distress, the man said, "I'll give you a call," as he headed out the door.

Jenifer, who came to the realization that she had been raped over the next several days, then notified the police about the attack but law-enforcement officials told her there was not enough evidence to pursue a case. Most of the women did not notify the authorities, saying they doubted anyone would believe them since they were willingly in the company of the men who attacked them.

But counselors encourage women to take the position that sex without an explicit "yes" is not consensual, even between people who have had sexual intercourse in the past. That was the case with K. Kaufman, a 38-year-old free-lance writer, who allowed a man to sleep in the same bed after he promised not to "bother" her. Later that night, he forced her to have sex, she said.

Ms. Kaufman noted that calling what happened to her rape was likely to prompt disdain. "But what people don't understand is powerlessness," she said. "They don't understand the amount of sex women submit to because it's easier than saying no."

Several of the women said they were assaulted by men who were very drunk and subsequently passed out, thus enabling them to flee. Ms. Serena[another victim], for instance, recalled pulling the man's limbs off her and inching to the door, terrified that her footsteps or the click of the latch would rouse him. At home she said she "showered and showered but couldn't get clean, no matter how hot the water or how stiff the brush."

Ms. Serena said that people who hear her story often inquire if the man had a weapon. "They ask, 'Did he have a knife? Did he have a gun?' I guess you had to be there to understand."

—Jane Gross, *New York Times,* May 28, 1991

profile of the "typical" rapist. In fact, adult rapists are extremely varied in their personality characteristics, motivations, and tendencies to commit other crimes. Studies on the characteristics of imprisoned rapists have suggested that there are at least five basic profiles common among these men. One group fits the profile of people who tend to commit other crimes and are quite apt to know their victims. Two groups are characterized by highly antisocial and aggressive behavior and a great deal of hostility. Another group tends to commit the rape in the course of committing some other crime, and they also tend toward mental

disturbances and unconventional sexual behaviors. A fifth group of rapists is prone to more serious psychiatric problems, substance abuse, and social maladjustment (Kalichman, Craig et al., 1989; Kalichman, Syzmanowski et al., 1989).

Rapists usually have lacked the experiences to help them develop a sense of responsibility and caring toward others, feelings of self-worth, and positive attitudes toward sexuality. They are often products of unhealthy home and family environments, characterized by conflicts with siblings, continual arguing, rigidly repressive religious training, lack of parental

Acquaintance Rape

Women

- **Know your sexual desires and limits.** Believe in your right to set those limits. If you are not sure, STOP and talk about it.
- **Communicate your limits clearly.** If someone starts to offend you, tell them firmly and early. Polite approaches may be misunderstood or ignored. Say "No" when you mean "No."
- **Be assertive.** Often men interpret passivity as permission. Be direct and firm with someone who is sexually pressuring you.
- **Be aware that your nonverbal actions send a message.** If you dress in a "sexy" manner and flirt, some men may assume you want to have sex. This does not make your dress or behavior wrong, but it is important to be aware of misunderstanding.
- **Pay attention to what is happening around you.** Watch the nonverbal clues. Do not put yourself in vulnerable situations.
- **Trust your intuitions.** If you feel you are being pressured into unwanted sex, you probably are.
- **Avoid excessive use of alcohol and drugs.** Alcohol and drugs interfere with clear thinking and effective communication.

Men

- **Know your sexual desires and limits. Communicate them clearly.** Be aware of social pressures. It's OK not to "score."
- **Being turned down when you ask for sex is not a rejection of you personally.** Women who say "No" to sex are not rejecting the person; they are expressing their desire not to participate in a single act. Your desires may be beyond your control but your actions are within your control.
- **Accept the woman's decision.** "No" means "No." Don't read other meanings into the answer. Don't continue after "No!"
- **Don't assume that just because a woman dressed in a "sexy" manner and flirts that she wants to have sexual intercourse.**
- **Don't assume that previous permission for sexual contact applies to the current situation.**
- **Avoid excessive use of alcohol and drugs.** Alcohol and drugs interfere with clear thinking and effective communication.

—From a brochure published by the American College Health Association

affection, and little sex education. Rapists frequently have fears about women and were often sexually abused themselves during childhood. To the rapist, the act of rape often seems to represent a way of proving his masculinity by attacking and dominating a woman (Fuller, Fuller, & Blashfield, 1989).

ACQUAINTANCE RAPE

Being raped or forced into any sort of sexual activity against your will, and by someone known to you, is an upsetting crisis and may leave you with a variety of complicated issues to consider. Women may be concerned that by being alone with a man they will look as if they had unwisely placed themselves in a compromising situation; they may be reluctant to report someone they have considered a friend, or even a lover, to the authorities. And yet they may be left feeling used, angry, fearful, and powerless.

Acquaintance rape happens on all college campuses and in many other nonacademic settings. One survey of 6,000 American college women found that 25 percent had been victims of rape or attempted rape,

FIGURE 13.5 Rape Prevention

Antirape talks are an important part of educating the public about avoiding situations that might lead to rape. Here, male students at Hobart College in Geneva, New York, attend a rape-prevention workshop.

and that 84 percent of these women knew their attackers. Other studies have shown that 1 in 10 young women have experienced forced sexual encounters while dating (Bateman, 1991). When close to 200 college males were questioned, 42 percent of them admitted to having engaged in verbal sexual coercion, using emotional pleas, threats, or guilt-producing mechanisms to pressure others into having sex (Craig, Kalichman, & Follingstad, 1989). On college campuses, sexual victimization has often been associated with male athletes and fraternity members. It has been suggested that the elevated status of these campus constituencies, and the sense of power they gain from being identified as a closely bonded group, conspire to make them more likely to be sexually coercive toward women (Sanday, 1990). Other researchers, however, have claimed that the incidence of rape and other forms of sexual coercion are not any higher among athlete groups than they are among nonathletes (Jackson, 1991).

Statistics aside, it is clear that acquaintance rape continues to affect the lives of many people and deserves careful attention by anyone involved in relationships where the possibility of such coercion exists. It is one of the most difficult sexual abuse situations to predict or avoid, since most women have dated or befriended a man partly because they have assumed they could trust him. The rape usually occurs in the room of either the man or the woman and often happens in a place, such as a dormitory, where there may be many other people close by. Use of alcohol or drugs often plays a role in the situation.

Misunderstandings and lack of communication between partners are crucial issues in acquaintance rape. Mixed signals can confuse both individuals. There is a common myth, often substantiated by movie scenarios and other media, that even when women say no, they mean yes. Men sometimes think that it is their task to persuade women into sex until the woman finally realizes how good it is and ceases her protest. Research indicates, for example, that many college students, both male and female, do not consider a simple "no, I don't want to" sufficient reason to define subsequent sex as rape. How much physical force was used, how much the woman protested, and when in their interactions the woman's protest began seem to be important in making that determination (Harrison, Downes, & Williams, 1991).

Because of social pressures on women concerning their sexual expression, they may be truly confused about what they want and how far they should go. If a woman begins to place limits on a man in the midst of other sex play, she may not be prepared to deal with his anger or expressed frustration. All of this can add up to an uncomfortable situation, filled with risks for trouble. While most men are not potential rapists, this kind of setting can trigger violence and power issues in those men who are basically insecure, who need to prove their manhood to women, or who are simply used to getting and taking what they want (Gibbs, 1991).

Acquaintance rape cannot always be prevented. In fact, research indicates the most frequent acquaintance rapists are men who are considered to be well known by their victims. However, there are several ways in which both women and men can reduce the risks for trouble. The most important steps involve developing the kind of relationship that is based on mutual trust, respect, and understanding. That takes work on many aspects of the relationship but especially on open and honest communication and clearly letting each other know about needs and feelings.

There are some warning signals to which women should pay attention in their relationships. They do not mean that a man is a rapist for certain, but they represent characteristics that can warn that a man has a greater likelihood of sexual aggression (Hughes & Sandler, 1987; Gray, et al., 1990):

- Lack of respect for women, as evidenced by his not listening well or ignoring what you say.
- Tendency to become more physically involved and invasive than makes you feel comfortable, and yet refusal to respect your discomfort.
- Expression of generally hostile or angry reactions to women.
- Disregarding your wishes, and doing as he pleases. Tendency to make decisions about dating and other issues without consulting you.
- Tendency to act jealous and possessive, or to make you feel guilty if you resist sexual overtures.
- Attitudes and values about women that are negative (such as "women are supposed to serve men").
- Tendency to drink heavily and to get abusive when drunk.

If you are subjected to acquaintance rape or other forms of forced sexual abuse, *it is important not to blame yourself.* Many women feel that they should have been forceful in their resistance or that they may have somehow encouraged the rape. This can be especially confusing if your body responds sexually during the assault. That does not automatically mean that you enjoyed the experience, nor does it mean that you really wanted it to happen.

MARITAL RAPE

Traditionally, it was impossible in the eyes of the law for a woman to be raped by her husband. It was apparently assumed that it was a wife's duty to submit to sex. In recent years that assumption has been challenged, and the concept of marital rape has been accepted. The most recent studies estimate that 1 in 7 married women will be raped by their husbands or ex-husbands, often accompanied by other sorts of physical violence. Some husbands have even been convicted for raping their wives. Between 1978 and 1985, only 118 cases of marital rape went to trial, but husbands were convicted in 104 of these cases (Gibbs, 1991). The evidence suggests that marital rape is more likely to occur in relationships where there is continued disagreement, alcohol or drug abuse, and nonsexual violence (Bowker, 1983). There is little evidence to support the stereotype that wives provoke such acts by refusing to have sex with their husbands, and in fact one study indicated that husbands who raped their wives appeared to enjoy violent sex (Frieze, 1983).

Because of increased awareness of marital rape, most states have reassessed their laws that would deal with such a crime. Twenty states have completely eliminated any preferential treatment for husbands when it comes to rape. A few still allow statutes that exempt husbands from being charged with raping their spouses, and about 25 other states require extenuating circumstances—such as gross brutality—to be present before a husband could be so charged (Small & Tetreault, 1990).

Wives may be even less likely to report rape by their husbands to authorities because of potential consequences for themselves, their children, or the marriage. They sometimes still believe that it is their duty to give their husbands sex. This often leaves women feeling trapped, helpless, and fearful. Their feelings of self-worth and self-respect may plummet, with resulting depression and anxiety (Russell, 1982). In most cities and many rural areas, centers are springing up to help such victims of marital violence. They sometimes offer temporary housing for women and children who must leave a potentially violent home situation, along with counseling to help with decision-making for the future.

RAPE OF MEN

Rape of men is considered by some to be a paradoxical concept, especially if rape is defined narrowly as

marital rape: a woman being forced to have sex by her husband.

Case Study

RODNEY: A SEXUALLY ASSAULTED MALE

In counseling, Rodney told his story of sexual abuse. He had always felt embarrassed and uncomfortable about the event in his life, and during counseling as a senior in college became more fully in touch with the deep feelings he still attached to the incident. He agreed to write about it:

"I was seventeen when it happened, and thought I was pretty hot stuff. I was going to bars with my fake ID, and every once in awhile, I'd get lucky with a woman there. They were always older.

"This one night there were two women at the bar who had come in together. After a while, they called me over and soon suggested that we go somewhere together. One of them ran her hand along the inside of my thigh. It looked like it was turning into some evening. I was pretty drunk, but the prospect of getting it on with two women at the same time made me really horny.

"They took me to the apartment where one of them lived. I can still see the bedroom in my head. They both seemed really playful, and before long I was letting them tie my hands to the head of the bed and take my pants off. We were all laughing and kidding. But as soon as I was tied up, things just seemed to change, and I realized I'd been had. They started acting mad and bossy like they were going to take all their hatred for men out on me. One of them got a kitchen knife, and I started getting scared. I lost

my erection, and one of them grabbed hold of the knife and said I'd better get the erection back or else. I tried to start joking again, but they weren't even smiling.

"I got hard again, and they did a lot of stuff with me that I'd rather not go into. Sometimes I would start getting into the feelings, but then I would feel used and dirty. They kept calling me wimp and boy.

"The thing I'm most embarrassed about as I look back is that I finally ejaculated. They smeared it on my face, and I felt completely humiliated. They untied me after that and told me I could go. They even seemed more playful again, as though they thought I had really enjoyed myself. I tried to get into it again and pretended that I had. The truth was, though, that I felt completely disgusted and lacking in self-respect.

"It's still hard for me to admit that I was raped, but I was. I even felt as though it was all my fault—I had asked for it. I carried those feelings around for a long time, and certainly didn't feel very proud of myself. It seemed like a guy ought to be able to take care of himself and not let something like that happen.

"I saw one of the women a few weeks later somewhere, and I couldn't even look her in the eye. I ducked out as soon as I could. For that matter, I couldn't look myself in the eye for quite awhile."

penile-vaginal contact. However, there are increasing reports of men who have been subject to sexual abuse either by other men or by women. Anal intercourse is the usual sexual act committed in male-male rape, and it is quite common for two or more attackers to be present. Physically beating the victim is even more common in male rape than in female rape. Male rape is commonplace in prison settings, although it seems to be increasingly common in nonprison situations too. Cathy Atwell (1987), a college security officer who has developed student programs for the prevention of sexual assault, reports that hospital sexual assault centers are reporting an increased incidence of male college students being raped by groups of other men. There are estimates that 10 percent of sexual assault

victims are male, although they rarely report the crime (Gibbs, 1991). Rapists of males are usually heterosexual men who are finding a way to humiliate and degrade their victims. It seems to be more an issue of power than of sex, which is typical of heterosexual rape as well.

Rape of men by women has received barely any attention in the sexological literature and has never been taken particularly seriously by the general public. The assumption is made that men would simply not be able to respond with erection unless they were willing to participate in sexual activity. In what has become a classic paper on sexual abuse of men by women, Sarrel and Masters (1982) cite evidence that males can be quite capable of erection and ejaculation in situations where they are afraid or anxious. In fact, anxiety may even heighten the potential for physical response, even when the man is an unwilling victim. Sarrel and Masters have cited 11 cases of sexual assault in which women have restrained, threatened, and stimulated men until they have responded sexually against their will. One study of sexually active college students found that 62.7 percent of men had engaged in unwanted sexual intercourse. At the very least, then, peer pressure and coercion lead many men into sexual experiences they later regret (Gibbs, 1991).

Men appear to react to sexual violence in the same essential ways as women, feeling a tremendous loss of control. Because it can be viewed as such a humiliating assault, men feel de-masculinized and embarrassed. This probably prevents many men from ever reporting such abuse to authorities. Yet they require the same sorts of support and counseling as women do to deal with the emotions, conflicts, and loss of self-esteem that follow a rape (Smith, Pine, & Hawley, 1988).

THE AFTERMATH OF RAPE

Rape victims experience a variety of negative reactions that can disrupt the physical, sexual, social, and psychological aspects of their lives. The majority of victims report feeling permanently changed by the experience (Nadelson, 1990). The psychological pain that follows a rape may vary in its intensity, depending on a variety of circumstances, although the reactions are generally difficult and unpleasant. For example, women who are of reproductive age and who are married tend to be more severely traumatized than older or younger women, or those who are unmarried. As might be expected, rape by a stranger is more psychologically upsetting than other forms of assault (Thornhill & Thornhill, 1990). Because of the AIDS crisis, female rape victims are likely to be concerned about having contracted the AIDS virus during the assault (Baker et al., 1990). Post-rape trauma also tends to be heightened for those survivors who somehow blame themselves for their situations. Those who are more able to focus the blame on the offender tend to experience less depression during the aftermath (Frazier, 1990).

The rape trauma syndrome is divided into two phases. The first (acute or disruptive) phase is characterized by stress and emotional reactions, such as anxiety and depression. The victims may be anxious to deny the experience, insisting they just want to put it all out of their minds. The second (recovery) phase may last many months and involves a long-term reorganization to regain a sense of personal security and control over one's environment. Relationships with a partner or family members may be seriously disrupted and need to be resolved over a period of time (Thornhill & Thornhill, 1990). Many rape victims feel a great deal of anger, and that anger needs to be expressed outwardly, rather than allowed to turn to inner guilt, depression, or self-hatred. Some women eventually feel the need to move residences, change jobs, and change their telephone listings.

Treatment for rape, likewise, usually proceeds in two phases. Early crisis intervention aims at helping the individual see herself as a survivor rather than as a victim. She needs to accept the consequences of the rape and begin to reestablish a sense of personal competence and control. Often, it takes time to regain a sense of continuity and meaning in life (Sorenson & Brown, 1990). Over the longer run, treatment focuses on sexual and relational problems that have resulted from the rape, as well as reactions such as depression or physical symptoms of coping with stress. With proper follow-up and treatment, survivors of rape can make a complete recovery, and live their lives with a comfortable sense of security and self-respect (Nadelson, 1990).

There are two consequences of rape that have received only minimal attention in the literature. One is the effect on women's sexual functioning. Many women experience lack of interest in sex and specific sexual dysfunctions after having been subjected to rape. Close to half of the women may completely abstain from sexual activity for 6 months or more following the incident. Some victims are reluctant to talk about such issues, and it has been recommended that counselors who work with rape victims take the time to bring up these sensitive subjects during the counseling process (Gilbert & Cunningham, 1987). Another, though less common, result of rape is pregnancy. One survey of research done on this issue showed pregnancy rates from rape ranging from less than 1 percent up to 10 percent. As some abortion funding becomes limited to rape or incest cases, some women may misrepresent their circumstances in order to be able to qualify for an abortion, which complicates the tallying of pregnancy rates due to rape. There may be many factors that increase the risk of pregnancy from rape, including whether or not the rapist ejaculates intravaginally, and the possibility that stress or coitus might induce ovulation on the woman's part. In any case, pregnancies resulting from rape represent a very real issue that deserves further attention from researchers (Krueger, 1988).

rape trauma syndrome: the predictable sequence of reactions that a victim experiences following a rape.

FIGURE 13.6   Self-Defense

Self-defense courses are offered in many cities to teach men and women the skills needed to defend themselves in the event of an attack.

Police agencies are becoming better equipped to deal with reports of rape of women. Officers have been trained to interview victims in a sensitive way that minimizes their humiliation and discomfort. Most rape counselors agree that women should report rapes even if they are not yet certain they want to proceed with prosecution of the rapist. The victim should receive a medical examination prior to showering or douching, in order to gather important evidence such as semen samples.

The courts have often had to wrestle with difficult issues relating to rape survivors' privacy. Many states have enacted what are called rape-shield laws that protect a victim from having any details of a former romantic relationship with the rapist, or other information about former sexual behaviors, admitted as evidence during the rapist's trial. In 1991 the Supreme Court upheld these laws as constitutional. Another conflict has arisen over protecting the victim from

publicity in the media. There has been general agreement among the media that the names of victims will not be released. However, some accused offenders have declared this to be unfair to them, since their names may be released before they have been tried, and issues about freedom of the press have been raised. Decisions about these matters continue to be made in favor of protecting the victim.

Individual and group counseling are the most commonly used approaches for helping rape victims cope with their traumas. Most cities and larger communities have rape crisis centers that are equipped to help women deal with all aspects of the aftermath of rape. There are also a number of programs designed to help prevent rape and help ward off potential attackers.

Sex Between Adults and Children

In the past 2 decades, there has been increased awareness of sexual abuse of children, often referred to as child molesting or pedophilia. Once thought to be a rare occurrence, we now realize that a substantial percentage of children and adolescents are subjected to sexual abuse by adults. Several studies have revealed startlingly high proportions of adults reporting instances of sexual abuse when they were children. In one national telephone poll of 2,627 randomly selected adults, 27 percent of the women and 16 percent of the men confided that they had been subjected to experiences as children that they would now label sexual abuse (Kohn, 1987). Another study of 1,145 men and 1,481 women over the age of 18 confirmed these figures, with 27 percent of the females and 16 percent of the males again reporting histories of sexual victimization as children. The abuse tended to occur when the child was between the ages of 9 and 10. The abuse of members of both sexes was almost always perpetrated by males. Girls were more likely to be abused by family members and boys were more likely to be abused by non-relatives. Abuse by strangers is not particularly common, but is somewhat more likely for boys than for girls.

Such statistics would suggest that as many as 40 million people in the United States, or one person in six, have been sexually victimized as children.

There is evidence that abuse of boys is less likely to be reported than abuse of girls, and the phenomenon

child molesting: sexual abuse of a child by an adult.
pedophilia (peed-a-FIL-ee-a): another term for child sexual abuse.

has been researched to a much lesser extent. These facts need to be understood within the context of our culture's views of maleness and masculinity. Our society may at some level feel that boys really do not need or deserve the same protection from and reaction to sexual abuse as do girls. It may also be that reporting an incident of sexual abuse would be viewed by the boy himself, or by someone close to him, as an admission of being a powerless victim, not a role that is respected for males (Hunter, 1990).

It is difficult to determine whether or not child sexual abuse has been on the increase. There is no particular evidence to suggest that the rates of abuse have gone up markedly since the days of the Kinsey studies in the 1940s and 1950s. However, the definitions of what constitutes sexual abuse have varied with different researchers, making this an issue about which it is difficult to generalize (Friedman, 1990). A five-component model has been proposed that considers several different dimensions of a potentially abusive situation. First, the type of sexual behavior is considered, particularly whether physical contact has oc-

curred (as in fondling, intercourse, or oral sex), or not (as in exhibitionism). The age of the subject of sexual contact is considered, as is the age of the perpetrator. Some workers do not automatically assume the situation to have been abusive unless the perpetrator is at least 5 years older than the subject. Most workers agree that if the subject is under 12 and the perpetrator is older, then the situation may be assumed to be abusive. The relationship of the perpetrator to the subject is also considered, and so is the rather complex issue of the subject's degree of willingness to participate in the activity. When the victim is between the ages of 13 to 17, the issue becomes somewhat more complicated, and definitions of abuse will typically depend on the age of the perpetrator and whether the subject wanted the sexual contact (Wyatt, 1990).

In our culture, children are taught to respect and obey adults, and children are given little direct information about sex and their own sex organs. Children are easily manipulated, both physically and psychologically, and often easily frightened into silent compliance. As with rape of women and men, child

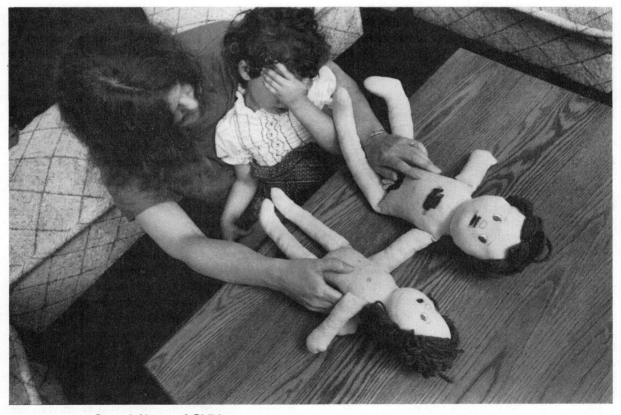

FIGURE 13.7   Sexual Abuse of Children

In order to prosecute someone involved in child pornography and/or the sexual abuse of children, the court must often depend on the testimony of children. The very young often don't understand what has happened to them, or are reluctant to talk about it. Anatomically correct dolls help children to explain to authorities the nature of the abuse they may have suffered.

Case Study

AARON: CONTINUING SEXUAL ENCOUNTERS WITH CHILDREN

Aaron, a college senior, came to a counselor with what he termed a "serious sexual problem." He explained that for about 8 years he had been primarily sexually interested in prepubescent boys. He had participated in a variety of sexual activities with numerous boys, but he hastened to add that he had never physically forced any of the boys to do anything against their wills. He told the counselor that he realized he might get in serious trouble because of his actions or that one of his young sexual partners might become "psychologically upset" by an encounter. Therefore, he wanted to be helped to cease his actions.

With the counselor Aaron explored many aspects of his sexuality. It became clear that he felt no homosexual attraction to men his own age or older and that he had no interest in a homosexual life-style. With women he felt awkward and lacking in confidence. Except for a few dates during high school, his fears had kept him from exploring relationships with them. He felt at least some sexual interest in women, even though he had had little opportunity to explore its place in his life.

The counselor further emphasized the unethical and dangerous aspects of his present sexual functioning and suggested that he begin to explore more socially acceptable forms of behavior. It was also made clear to Aaron that it would be up to him to stop his pedophilic behavior if he truly wished to do so, and he was taught some skills to gain some control over his impulsiveness. Yet the counselor did not try to convey to Aaron that he was sick, immoral, or deserving of condemnation. Instead, the counselor continually emphasized that he was a good person who was capable of finding a satisfying life-style without exploiting or endangering himself or others.

As the counseling progressed, Aaron began to explore heterosexual dating and eventually developed a sexual relationship with a woman. His homosexual interests in children did not vanish, but he did begin to feel that he could no longer choose such behavior. Instead he felt happy about not choosing such activity and confident that he could live with his choice. There was no follow-up of Aaron's progress once he had graduated from college.

molestation is as much an act of power as it is a sexual act.

We are just beginning to understand the psychological dynamics of perpetrators of child sexual abuse. Most professionals believe that such behavior may well be rooted in the perpetrator's own treatment as a child, with at least some evidence suggesting that abusive adults were themselves sometimes sexually abused as children. However, preliminary research has also suggested that other factors are crucial in the development of sexually abusive behavior. For example, child abusers tend to lack confidants during their own childhoods, and be emotionally isolated. They also use sex as an escape from and solution to emotional pain. As adults, they tend to attribute sexual meanings to the normal behaviors of children, and to view their victims as sexual objects. While many of the same characteristics were noted in a control group of people who had not abused children, this control group did not tend toward seeing sexual meanings in the behaviors of children (Gilgun, 1988).

Again the stereotypes would have us believe that pedophiles are degenerate men who lurk in trenchcoats near schools and parks, waiting to accost youngsters. Actually the majority of sexual abuse victims are molested by a family member or someone known to the child. Teenage babysitters, or their friends, are common offenders. It has also been recognized that not all sexual abusers of children are men. In fact, estimates based on recent surveys show that 24 percent of male victims and 13 percent of female victims were sexually abused by women, either acting alone or with a partner. Approximately 14 percent of the boys and 6 percent of the girls were sexually victimized by a woman acting alone.

Little is known about women who sexually abuse children. A study of nine convicted female child molesters showed them generally to be of marginal intelligence, to have a long history of sexual activity, and to have a tendency to commit the assault in the company of a dominant male (Rowan, Rowan, & Langelier, 1990). It has been proposed that since we traditionally view women as nonviolent and nurturing, professionals and law enforcement personnel fail to ask victims the right questions, and victims themselves may find it difficult to acknowledge or express the role a woman has played. Similarly, female offenders may be particularly reluctant to admit to the abuse, since it is seen in our society as a particularly abhorrent and unexpected role for a woman. It may also be that the sexually abusive behavior of women is more covert than that of men, making it a less visible phenomenon (Family Sexual Abuse project, 1987).

One recent study found that there may actually be some hormonal differences in men who sexually abuse children. When 133 men who had been convicted of sexually abusive behavior were compared with control subjects, the child abusers were found to have elevated levels of certain sex hormones other than testosterone. It is not yet known if these findings might reflect the stressful situation in which these men found themselves, or if the findings indicate some biological phenomenon that predisposed the men to being abusive (Lang, Flor-Henry, & Frenzel, 1990).

Increased attention has been given to sex offenders who are themselves only adolescents. There has been an increase in reported sex crimes perpetrated by adolescents, usually involving the abuse of younger children. Adolescent sex abusers are usually males. These young men often come from dysfunctional family backgrounds and have serious developmental and psychological difficulties (Porter, 1990). In a study of 169 adult sex offenders, 21 percent of the men admitted to having committed sexual crimes during their adolescent years (Hindman, 1988).

Children are often reluctant to report sexual abuse, and they sometimes lack the verbal development to explain clearly what happened. They sometimes communicate directly to a close adult or professional person, either in language or by demonstrating what happened on an anatomically correct doll (see Figure 13.7, p. 361). However, information gained from children's use of anatomically correct dolls has not been found all that reliable for deciding whether a child has been sexually abused (Realmuto, Jensen, & Wescoe, 1990). The communication may be more indirect, as in cases where children are showing sexualized behavior or play that would be considered inappropriate for their age. They may hint at what has happened through ambiguous statements. Children who are unable to communicate about the sexual abuse to which they have been subjected may show symptoms of reaction to trauma and stress, including fearfulness, moodiness, sleep disorder, depression, phobias, and other emotional disturbances (Elliott & Tarnowski, 1990). Some experts recommend that a medical examination be done whenever physical sexual abuse is a possibility, since the genitals or anal region of the abused child may show signs of trauma. In one study of girls, it was shown that twice as many cases of sexual abuse were identified when a physical examination of the vagina was included in an assessment of the girls' condition (Cantwell, 1983).

Unfortunately, when children report sexual abuse, they sometimes are not taken seriously, or adults want to avoid confrontations with relatives or friends. When sexual abuse of children has been uncovered, it is not at all uncommon for the adult to be referred for professional counseling, with no formal legal conditions being imposed. Yet the fact remains that many child molesters do not respond well to counseling and indeed eventually repeat the act even after being discovered, sometimes with the same child.

Our society expects adults to be responsible for the well-being of children and not to exploit them sexually. Current guidelines suggest that police always be involved in child sex abuse cases and that the offender be processed through the judicial system. Experts in this field believe that this provides essential leverage to force the offender to obtain necessary treatment or face a prison sentence to prevent further such behavior (Sgroi, 1982).

EFFECTS OF CHILD SEXUAL ABUSE

Longitudinal studies about the effects of child sexual abuse suggest that symptoms of stress and trauma in the child gradually decline in the months following the abuse. Two controversies have emerged in studying effects of child sexual abuse. One is the finding that a substantial number of sexually abused children do not seem to show any measurable symptoms, and the other involves the question of whether the post-traumatic stress disorder model is applicable in these cases (Finkelhor, 1990). There is certainly evidence to indicate that among many adult psychiatric patients, substance abusers, and people with eating disorders, there is a history of sexual abuse that is higher than in the general population (Beckman & Burns, 1990; Surrey et al., 1990).

Some observers have argued that it is society's automatic condemnation of intergenerational sexual contact that may contribute to the confusion and harm that a child experiences. It has been suggested that all sexual behavior, regardless of the age of the partners, be considered on a continuum from violent rape to nurturing lovemaking, with the amount of harm done being paramount to understanding where on the continuum a sexual act belongs (Nelson, 1989). Others insist that problems resulting from adult-child sex may not be evident until much later in the child's life, and

363

that children cannot truly consent to sexual contact. They feel that, by definition, sex with minors is exploitative and represents a betrayal of the trustworthiness and protection adults should provide for children (Maltz, 1989).

Based on present research evidence, it is difficult to generalize about the short-term or long-term effects on children and adolescents of sexual contact with an adult. There are highly publicized accounts linking sexual abuse to a variety of emotional and behavioral problems, and there are cases where few or no negative effects seem to result (Conte, 1985). One model has been proposed that categorizes the sorts of ill effects that may be generated (Finkelhor & Browne, 1985):

1. *Traumatic sexualization* means that the child's feelings, attitudes, and behaviors relating to sex may be brought into focus in a way that is inappropriate to the child's age and stage of development. For example, a recent study demonstrated that inappropriate sexually aggressive behavior on the part of young children is frequently linked to past sexual abuse of these children (Gale et al., 1988).

2. *A sense of betrayal* may also result in children who find that someone they trusted and on whom they depended has caused them harm. This is particularly true when the perpetrator of the abuse is a family member. This sense of betrayal may be intensified if the child's report of sexual abuse is disbelieved, or if the child is blamed for the event (Berliner & Conte, 1990).

3. *Disempowerment* results when a child feels that his or her will or desires have been ignored and deliberately violated. The more physical force or coercion the perpetrator has used in the sexual activity, the greater the child's sense of powerlessness (Conte & Schuerman, 1987).

4. *Stigmatization* is particularly problematic when the child is expected to react with feelings of shame and guilt to the event. Such negative connotations may come directly from the abuser, who may want the victim to take the blame for the activity, or be reinforced by others in the family or community who hear of the abuse. This dynamic may play a significant role in the reason that one study found 73 percent of female runaways and 38 percent of male runaways to have been victims of prior sexual abuse.

We are just beginning to understand the effects that sexual abuse may have on later adult life. It has recently been found that early sexual abuse is a profound risk factor in suicidal feelings in women (Van Egmond, 1988). Women who suffer from chronic pelvic pain and depression often have a history of sexual abuse, although the cause-and-effect relationship has not been established. While it has been widely

accepted that adults who were abused as children are likely to become abusive to their own children, recent reviews of the literature indicate that unqualified acceptance of that belief is unfounded. There are other factors associated with such later behavior, including the social supports available while growing up, the extent of emotional isolation, and the effects of poverty and stress (Kaufman & Zigler, 1987).

There is very little empirical evidence about the effects of sexual abuse during a boy's childhood on his later development and adult sexual behavior. The studies that have been done suggest that these men may have confusion about their male identity or some difficulties in maintaining healthy, intimate relationships. Again, male socialization patterns appear to play a role in how men eventually perceive themselves in the aftermath of childhood sexual abuse (Finkelhor, 1990; Schacht, Kerlinsky, & Carlson, 1990).

One study indicates that victims often feel guilty and believe somehow that the incident was their fault. They often harbor fears and lack of trust for the offender and other grownups. Some become more fearful of later sexual relationships and marriage (Gilgun, 1984). It would appear that the effects of sexual abuse can be quite subtle, but often long-lasting. The most serious effects are usually the result of violence or severe coercion inflicted by the adult. Professionals agree that an important determinant of these effects is how the child is treated by authorities and then how much counseling help the child is given to deal with his or her own confusion and fear. Many victims of incest do not confront their feelings and reactions until adulthood, and there are now support groups that can help such adults deal with their experiences.

Sex Between Family Members

Strictly defined, the term incest refers to sexual intercourse between close blood relatives. It tends to be used in a broader context these days, referring to any sort of sexual contact between close blood relatives, stepparents, or others who live together in a family-like system (McCarthy, 1990). Confusion concerning definitions of incest has created difficulty in researching the extent of the problem. It has been estimated that as many as 250,000 children in the United States are sexually molested in their own homes each year, across all socioeconomic groups. In the study of 930 adult women, 16 percent reported at least one incident

incest (IN-sest): sexual activity between closely related family members.

of intrafamilial sexual abuse prior to the age of 18. Twelve percent reported such abuse before the age of 14 (Russell, 1983). Eighty-five percent of incest victims are female, and girls tend to be at greater risk with stepfathers than with their biological fathers. Father-daughter incestuous relationships tend to begin when the girl is between 6 and 11 years old and last for 2 years or more. It has been estimated that only about 20 percent of sexual abuse of boys and 5 percent of the abuse of girls is perpetrated by adult females (Stark, 1984). While there are few reliable statistics to support contentions about the incidence of various forms of incest, it is believed that father-daughter sexual contact constitutes slightly less than 25 percent of incest cases. Stepfather-daughter incest accounts for about 25 percent of cases. The remaining 50 percent of cases involve brothers, uncles, in-laws, grandfathers, step-family members, and live-in boyfriends of mothers (McCarthy, 1990). It is generally believed that brother-sister incest is the most common. A study of sibling incest cases showed some dynamics that the families tended to have in common. The parents were often emotionally distant, inaccessible, and controlling; they tended to stimulate a sexual climate at home; and there were often family secrets, such as one parent having an affair (Carson et al., 1990).

Virtually every society has strong prohibitions against sexual relationships within families. This is often called the incest taboo. There are many theories about why the incest taboo exists, one of the most common involving the desire to avoid disruption of the family system. There are exceptions to the taboo, however. In the Trobriand Islands, a girl who has intercourse with her mother's brother is committing incest. If she has intercourse with her father, she is not. Among the Kubeo Indians of South America, boys come of age only after having sexual intercourse with their mothers. It certainly is true that incest often results from unhealthy family interactions and that its discovery causes reverberations throughout the family's entire structure. Families in which the relationship between the father and mother is weak, and in which a daughter takes on many household responsibilities, are susceptible to incestuous contact between father and daughter. Abuse of boys by their fathers is known to be more common in households where the father is very dominating, has alcohol and marital problems, and is physically abusive toward other family members (VanderMey, 1988). Families in which there is a great deal of chaos, role confusion, and blurring of boundaries between generations are also frequently involved in incest (Rucker & Lombardi, 1990).

A good deal of attention has focused on the role of the mother in cases where a child, especially a daughter, has been sexually abused by the father. It has often been suggested that the mother acts within the family system in a way that consciously or unconsciously pushes the daughter into the incestuous act. Mothers of incest victims have variously been described as passive, dependent, or masochistic, and are also suspected of knowing about the sexual behavior. Closer examination of the literature, and newer studies of mothers, have indicated that such assumptions are not well founded. There is usually no clear evidence to indicate that a mother failed to take protective action once she had discovered that her daughter had been incestuously involved. A significant number of these mothers, however, have also been subjected to sexual and physical violence themselves from their childhood families or husbands (Kaplan, Becker, & Martinez, 1990). It is important for professionals who deal with incest cases to be cautious about assuming that the mother was knowledgeable about the activity or in any way colluded to make it happen.

Incest is usually a confusing interaction for a child. Youngsters may be quite passive during the relationship and may even exhibit a kind of seductive behavior that encourages the sexual activity. As a result of the experiences, they may become highly erotic and more interested in sex than would be expected for their age. Victims of incest may exhibit self-destructive and aggressive forms of behavior, apparently representing their guilt, resentment, and low feelings of self-worth (German, Habenicht, & Futcher, 1990). However, there are also cases where the disruption following discovery of incest is even more upsetting to the younger victim than the incest itself. One research study found that over 20 percent of victims reported that being questioned during investigations or in court was a harmful experience for them, while 53 percent found it helpful (Tedesco & Schnell, 1987).

A primary goal in helping victims of incest has been to convince them that they are not to blame for the incestuous relationship. However, this approach may have its negative side as well. Even though such reassurances may be well-intentioned, they may intensify the sense of powerlessness and lack of control the child has already felt because of the incident. It is usually the therapist's or social worker's own anger toward the perpetrator that leads to this protective response toward the child. It has been suggested that therapists work with children in a way that will help them see a spectrum of choices in sexual situations and help them understand the complexity of emotional reactions that may be involved. While providing empathy and support through any traumatic responses they

incest taboo: cultural prohibitions against incest, typical of most societies.

365

may have encountered, children are thus empowered to see future situations as at least potentially controllable (Lamb, 1986).

The therapist treating an abused child must anticipate a variety of possible reactions in the child. Many children express anger during the early stages of therapy, and they need to know that limits will be placed on this anger. Later, feelings of guilt, loss, neglect, and depression may emerge. In particularly violent sexual abuse cases, children may experience personality dissociation that can well lead to disturbances involving multiple personalities. The therapist may also be called on to deal with the highly sexualized nature that has been stimulated in a young child, helping the child to learn more age-appropriate responses to adults and other children. Many victims live with the secret well into adulthood and then seek therapy to deal with their conflicting feelings about the offender and themselves. It is not unusual for psychiatric patients or alcoholics to admit during therapy that they were once victims of incest. They still may be struggling to understand how and why the incest occurred. Research indicates that being able to deal with these unresolved feelings can help people gain a new sense of mastery over their lives (McCarthy, 1990). Group counseling is one of the more common therapeutic approaches for incest victims, although one-to-one counseling is often used as well. Therapists must often help adult survivors of incest deal with relationship difficulties. These adults also need assurances that they are worthwhile and strong. They may need to deal with years of shame and anger, being helped to accept and express their strong emotions (Jackson et al., 1990).

FIGURE 13.8 Learning About Sex

There are many ways to gather information about human sexuality. These teenagers are listening to a sex education lecture on The Floating Hospital in New York City.

Preventing and Dealing With Problematic Sex

Sexual problems and concerns need not be devastating, or permanently disruptive. Several lessons may be drawn from this chapter concerning how each of us may work to prevent sexual problems in our own lives and to deal with them should they arise. Consider each of the following points with care, and think about how you might want to apply them in your own life.

LEARNING ABOUT SEX

It is a good idea to learn about your own body, its sexual parts, and what they are called. You should also understand the patterns of sexual response that are part of your body's repertoire. Gradually, with time and experience, you begin to understand your own sexual orientations and preferences—the things that turn you on. However important sexual self-knowledge is, it is not enough. We also need to take time to understand the many individual sexual differences found in human beings. These range from different sizes of sex organs to different sexual orientations. Accepting the fact that we are all different from one another can be an important step toward preventing sexual difficulties.

There are numerous ways today to gather knowledge about the broad area of human sexuality. There are books, magazines, films, television documentaries, professional journals, college courses, conferences, lectures, and many other opportunities. Yet, we need to weigh sources of sex information with care. It is a field that is filled with controversy and new research. There are far more questions left unanswered than there are answered. Therefore, different opinions and all sides of any issue need to be explored and debated.

Conversation

You didn't know what to say, when I called you on Father's Day. The conversation floated away into thin air, and you asked that I speak to your wife.

There was a long pause before she got on the phone. I am sure that she objected to you ordering her to speak to me.

How does she know about the beatings? You've spent your money on her. You've taken her around the world so many times I can't count. You've bought her whatever she desired.

She wouldn't believe that my mother went threadbare. That you didn't give her enough for groceries.

She wouldn't believe that you slept with me until I was fifteen, and then you found someone else whom you told me you loved more. She was seventeen. Her name was Ruth.

Does your wife know that I aborted your child? That I had a spontaneous miscarriage? That I told no one until now?

You are afraid. You don't know what I remember. I didn't recall for a long, long time. I carried the pain next to my heart. I carried the tears there, too.

How devastating for a father to violate his own flesh! How devastating to be part of a conspiracy of silence!

I live with the scars and the screams of yesterday. I live with the threats and beatings. I can still see your face crazy and mad and perverted, distorted into some sort of non-creature called you.

And now, it's Father's Day. Do I rejoice that you were my father? That you sired me?

And why do I call? There is nothing to say but empty words. You can tell all your glorious friends that your darling daughter did her noble duty. You can continue to pretend that the madness never happened.

But I learned not to pretend. I learned to live in the real world. Not the world of brightly colored cards and streamers. Not the world of false smiles and fantasy.

The attempts on my life were real. Your disturbed mind is real. Your asocial behavior is real. Your pedophilia is real.

Why do I call? Because I have compassion for you. You have lied to yourself. You have to live with this somewhere in your reality. And because you didn't go for help, you will die the same way.

Sir, I pity you. I pity my sisters and brother who keep on pretending, who keep on wondering why they have a perpetual sadness, a continuing anxiety and distrust.

I call, because I have been forced to forgive you, or quit. I call because I have compassion. You are so lost, undone, and you do not know it.

I call because you sired me. Because you were the first man in my life. Because I have found much better than you. Because I am as free as possible with these scars.

Not for Father's Day, but for you, Dad. I can play your game, but you will never know mine.

It's real. It's called LIFE.

—"Norma," *Survivor,* Fall 1990

KNOWING HOW TO COMMUNICATE

Communication is fundamental to a continuing, healthy sexual relationship. Counselors who work with couples find that flaws in communication are one of the most common roots of sexual problems. There are many different things that must be communicated between people: thoughts, ideas, feelings, values, opinions, needs, and desires. Not only are they communicated verbally but also through eye contact, facial expressions, and body language. Communication is far more difficult than often believed, and most people are given very little help in learning how to communicate effectively. See chapter 8, "Sexuality, Communication, and Relationships," for a more complete discussion of communication and sexuality.

HAVING REALISTIC EXPECTATIONS

People are prone to compare themselves to others sexually. "Am I normal?" is one of the most commonly asked questions when it comes to sex. The media provide models of sexual attractiveness and imply standards of sexual prowess. All of this can create unrealistic expectations that people then struggle to live up to.

Sexual problems often stem from setting expectations for one's attractiveness or level of sexual activity that simply cannot be met. It is important to know oneself sexually and to work toward sexual goals that are comfortable, attainable, and consistent with personal values. To live with unrealistic goals is to invite sexual problems.

BEING CAUTIOUS AND RESPONSIBLE

Shared sex always has some consequences, potentially positive or negative. It is important to approach sexual decision-making with an awareness of possible consequences, knowledge about sex, and open communication between the partners. Sexual problems such as guilt, unwanted pregnancy, contracting a sexually transmitted disease, and feelings of having been exploited can usually be prevented with a cautious attitude toward sexual choices.

Responsible sexual decisions are made by keeping the other person in mind as well as oneself. Only too often, people shirk their sexual responsibility with excuses such as: "I didn't mean to go so far"; "It just happened"; or "I was so drunk I didn't know what I was doing." Responsibility means approaching relationships with an awareness of how powerful sexual emotions can be and how complicated the aftermath of sex can sometimes be. Responsible sexual decision-making can prevent problematic sex more so than any other step.

FINDING SEX COUNSELING AND THERAPY

A part of being a healthy, sexually fulfilled person is knowing when you've exhausted your own resources. Sometimes, we can cope with a problem ourselves, sometimes not. Often it helps just to talk things out with another person, pulling thoughts and feelings into a more manageable perspective. It can be important to have the objectivity that an outsider can bring to one's situation. Sometimes specific suggestions and strategies are in order that only someone with professional training can offer. Best friends seldom make the best counselors, regardless of how good their intentions may be.

Usually the best time to seek professional help is when you realize you need it and feel ready to seek it, even if you are nervous about it. Early intervention can prevent further complications. There is always one important point to keep in mind, however. No professional counselor or therapist can wave a magic wand and make the problem disappear. No treatment can be successful unless there is a sincere motivation to change. You will have to want to work on the problem and be willing to expend some energy doing so. If it is a shared partnership problem, then usually both people will have to be committed to working together on it.

Here are some specific guidelines to be considered when trying to decide whether to seek professional help, and then when looking for an appropriate counselor or therapist:

1. *Make a preliminary assessment of the seriousness of the problem.* This has implications for the type of help you may want to seek. Problems with disease or pain generally need to go to medical professionals. Concern over sexual orientation, decision-making, and sexual behaviors may be handled by sex counselors. Sexual dysfunctions (see also chapter 16) are best dealt with by a specially trained sex therapist.

2. *Locate a qualified professional.* You may want to ask a trusted doctor, minister, or teacher to suggest a professional whom he or she would recommend for dealing with sexual problems. The yellow pages of telephone directories often list people who specialize in treating sex-related concerns. Counseling centers or health centers in larger colleges and universities offer sex counseling and therapy services for students. Large medical centers usually offer a variety of sexual health services.

3. *Investigate and ask questions.* It is always advisable to be an informed consumer. Do not be hesitant or embarrassed about checking out professionals' qualifications and inquiring about their background preparation. Asking questions during an initial visit, or even prior to a first visit, is a good way to find out what to expect. A true professional will not be offended or insulted by such questions. Here are some areas you might consider finding out more about:
   • What does the service cost, and how frequent are visits?

- What sort of education, training, and other credentials does the person have?
- What records are kept, and are they treated in a completely confidential manner? How long are records kept on file?
- Is the professional appropriately licensed or certified by the state or by any professional society?

4. *Know what you are looking for.* You should be able to feel comfortable and relatively relaxed with a counselor or therapist. Look for the kind of atmosphere in which you are free to discuss sex openly and express your feelings without being judged, put down, or made to feel embarrassed. You should sense a degree of trust, caring, and respect between yourself and the therapist. Any counseling process has its ups and downs, but you should be able to feel eventual progress so long as you are working for it. If you feel discouraged, you should be able to discuss it with the counselor or therapist.

5. *Know what you are not looking for.* Be skeptical about anyone who promises quick and easy solutions. If the person seems to have personal values that might interfere with her or his objectivity in assessing your situation, think about changing to another professional. Also watch out for any seductiveness or sexual aggression from the professional. This is considered unethical behavior and may be grounds for taking action against the offender (Hotelling, 1988). Be cautious, too, about people who seem overly anxious to persuade you to adopt their sexual values when you are not particularly anxious to change your ways of looking at things. And finally, unless the professional is a physician who must conduct a legitimate physical examination, reject any suggestions that you should remove your clothing or submit to some sort of sexual touching. Codes of professional ethics consider such behavior inappropriate (Rutter, 1990).

Professional help can often resolve sexual concerns and problems and help individuals and couples feel better about themselves. To seek such help is not a weakness but instead constitutes a sign of maturity, strength, and personal responsibility.

6. *Check with people who are familiar with the counselor's or therapist's work.* Word-of-mouth recommendations or condemnations are also worth taking into consideration. People who have had professional contacts with a counselor or therapist, either as a client or a colleague, may be able to offer especially valuable insights. On the other hand, such opinions cannot always represent the final word. Some people can be persuaded into an overly positive view by a professional who knows how to sound well-informed; and some may gripe about the therapist who cannot perform miracles on demand.

Conclusion

A primary message of this chapter is that problematic sex need not be allowed to become a sexual catastrophe. Help is now available for any sexual problem, and it can be obtained easily and confidentially from well-qualified professionals.

Preventing and dealing with sexual problems is largely a matter of personal responsibility. We must take responsibility for accepting our sexuality and admitting that we are indeed sexual human beings. We must be ready to accept that any sexual act has a variety of potential consequences, both positive and negative. Most of all, we must be responsible enough to recognize that anyone may experience a sexual problem, and then to *do something about it.* ■

SELF-EVALUATION

Your Sexual Concerns and Problems

Most of us do not feel fully comfortable with or relaxed about all aspects of our sexuality all of the time. It is difficult to say when discomfort becomes concern or when concern becomes a problem. However, this questionnaire may help you to evaluate your particular sex-related worries and what you want to do about them. Before proceeding with the questionnaire, take the following two preliminary steps:

Step 1. Ask yourself if you really need to proceed with this questionnaire. If you have had or now have some area about sex about which you have experienced a continuing sense of unrest or worry, it probably will be worth your time to go ahead with the questions. If you feel fully comfortable with your sexual needs, feelings, orientations, and activities all the time, skip this questionnaire.

Step 2. If possible, make certain that you have all the facts about the sexual areas that are of special concern to you. Before going on with this questionnaire, read the earlier parts of this book pertaining to those areas. The table of contents and index can help you find appropriate information. You may even want to read some of the reference articles or books that are listed at the end of each chapter. Some worries and problems fade with appropriate, accurate sex education.

1. Mentally, or on paper, list the sexual concern(s) or problem(s) that are presently most worrisome for you. Do not list more than three.

2. For each concern you have listed, answer the following questions:
   a. For how long has this worried you?
   b. Can you identify the particular incident or time in your life when it started to become a real concern? If so, think it over in as much detail as you can recall:
      1. What were your feelings at the time?
      2. What are your feelings now as you think back?
      3. Is there anything that you wish you could change about the origins of your concern?
      4. If another person was involved in the origins of your concern, how do you feel about that person now?

   c. Is there another person directly involved in (or affected by) the problem now? If so, how would you summarize your present relationship with that person?

3. Evaluate your concerns:
   a. For each concern you have listed, read through the following categories and decide which category best describes your concern. Note whether it is labeled with number I, II, III, or IV.

Category Number	Types of Concerns
I	Body appearance, lack of sex appeal
	Size or shape of genitals or breasts
	Sexual things you have done in the past, but no longer care about doing
II	Sexually transmitted disease or other infection of sex organs
	Concern about having been infected with the AIDS virus
	Pregnancy or difficulty with birth control methods
	Fear of sexual exertion following a heart attack or other illness
	Other medical problems relating to sex organs
III	Masturbation
	Sexual fantasies
	The things or people to whom you feel sexually attracted do not fit the typical socially acceptable male-female standard
	The sexual interests and/or activities of your partner or another important person in your life are upsetting to you in some way
	Lack of information about sex
	Lack of communication with a sexual partner

IV   Deep, long-term guilt, dissatisfaction, or unhappiness with your sexuality

A history of sexual abuse as a child that you have not dealt with completely or effectively

You worry about your body image to the extent that you avoid eating, or binge on food and then vomit or take laxatives

Sexual activities in which you now engage are unusual, illegal, or not generally accepted socially

Problems with sexual functioning; e.g., impotence, premature ejaculation, lack of sexual arousal, difficulty reaching orgasm (in yourself *or* your partner)

b. Do you feel discouraged, depressed, and hopeless about your sexual worries and problems? Do not give up on yourself, because for others to be able to help you, you must be willing to work on your problem. There may be many things that will help. Also, be careful of blaming someone else for your problem. Regardless of the type of problem or who has it, you are responsible for how it affects you and what you do about it—keep reading.

c. Now what are you going to do? First go back and note the category of your concern, chosen in part 3a. Regardless of the category, it might be worth considering talking with a professional counselor who has a good understanding of human sexuality. Here are some specific comments about each category; note the category you have chosen:

Category I for the most part includes problems that you cannot do very much about. One way or another, you are probably going to have to try to become more comfortable with what you've got or what you've done. Counseling could help you do that.

Category II consists of medical problems. If you haven't already consulted a physician, do so. If you already have, but are unsatisfied, try to find another physician who can help. Your city or county medical society might be able to help. Most cities also have STD and family planning clinics, and AIDS-testing services.

Category III includes some of the most common types of sexual problems. Although many people learn to live with them, some form of sex counseling can often do wonders. See part d.

Category IV includes problems that might easily fit into category III, but that also sometimes require more intensive kinds of sex therapy or psychotherapy. In seeking a professional to help you deal with such problems, choose carefully and check credentials.

d. Now, if you decide to seek professional help, consider the following:

1. Should your spouse or sexual partner be involved in the counseling? If you are having difficulty communicating, see chapter 8.

2. Try to gain a clear idea of what your goals are in dealing with your sexual concern(s), and express them to the person from whom you seek help.

CHAPTER SUMMARY

1. The definition of when some sexual orientation, preference, or behavior becomes a problem can be highly subjective. It often needs to be viewed within the context of an individual's life-style.

2. Negative attitudes about the self, or lack of accurate information as related to sexuality can become a problem.

3. Some sexual behaviors, such as certain sado-masochistic activities or autoerotic asphyxiation, represent obvious physical dangers to individuals, sometimes reflective of self-destructive qualities.

4. Sexual violence or exploitation of others can be a serious sexual problem.

5. Ignorance about human sexuality can generate prejudice toward those who in some way are different sexually.

6. There has been an ongoing controversy about whether people can become addicted to sex, and whether sex "addiction" treatments are adequate.

7. Sexual harassment is a growing problem on campuses and in the workplace. There are steps that may be taken to address these difficult situations. Sexual abuse by professionals is prohibited by ethical standards.

8. Rape is believed to be far more common than generally realized. It often represents an attempt to humiliate someone and exercise power over them. In many cases, the rapist is known by the victim, and so it is called acquaintance rape. In female-male relationships, there are several early warning signals that suggest that a man has negative or disrespectful attitudes toward women and could potentially rape.

9. A small percentage of wives admit to having been raped by their present or former husbands. Many states have removed laws that exempt husbands from the possible rape of their spouses.

10. Men can be raped, too. Rape of men by other men is becoming increasingly common and seems to represent an attempt to humiliate and gain power over the victim. There are a few case studies of men who have been sexually abused by women under force.

11. Rape victims go through various phases of the rape trauma syndrome as they adjust to the event, cope with a range of emotions, and attempt to reestablish a sense of control and safety back into their lives. Counseling and support are necessary during these phases of adjustment.

12. Sexual abuse of children by adults, called pedophilia or molestation, is now seen as a common and serious problem. We are only beginning to learn about the later emotional difficulties that such abuse can create.

13. The term incest applies to sexual activity between closely related family members. Incestuous relationships usually stem from unhealthy family patterns and create serious confusion for the developing child or adolescent. Victims must learn how not to blame themselves for what has happened.

14. The best ways to prevent and deal with sexual problems are to be knowledgeable about human sexuality, develop communication skills based in qualities that facilitate good relationships; keep realistic expectations about sex; and exercise caution and responsibility.

15. Sometimes it makes sense to seek out professional help for dealing with sexual problems. As a consumer you have the right to check out such professionals with great care and be suspicious about behavior that makes you uncomfortable or that seems to be unethical.

ANNOTATED READINGS

Bart, P. B., & O'Brien, P. H. (1985). *Stopping rape: Successful survival strategies*. Elmsford, NY: Pergamon Press. This book surveys a range of techniques, with careful explanation, that may help prevent rape.

Benedict, H. (1985). *Recovery: How to survive sexual assault*. Garden City, NY: Doubleday. An excellent guide for anyone who has been subjected to any sort of forced or coerced sexual encounter; it includes sections for men, teenagers, homosexuals, and older adults.

Crewdson, J. (1988). *By silence betrayed: Sexual abuse of children in America*. New York: HarperCollins. A comprehensive examination of child sexual abuse in the United States, this book discusses effects on children; how law enforcement officials treat cases; therapy; and preventive education. An excellent sourcebook for anyone wanting a clearer picture of all dimensions of the problem.

Dziech, B. W. & Weiner, L. (1990). *The lecherous professor: Sexual harassment on campus*. Champaign, IL: University of Illinois Press. An overview of sexual harassment on college campuses, including guidelines for institutional policy statements and for students who are subjected to harassment. This is a scholarly and yet sensitive treatment of the subject.

Hunter, M. (1990). *Abused boys: The neglected victims of child abuse*. Lexington, MA: Lexington Books. One of the few full-length works to focus on the special issues relating to sexually abused boys.

Kasl, C. D. (1989). *Women, sex, and addiction: A search for love and power*. New York: Ticknor and Fields. This is an insightful look at women who become obsessed with sex. The book presents a model that explains how poor self image and a need for power may conspire to create compulsive sexual behaviors in some women.

Levy, B. (1991). *Dating violence: Young women in danger*. Seattle, WA: Seal Press. A collection of readings concerning the growing problem of courtship violence and acquaintance rape. The book provides insights into the dynamics of the problem and guidelines for prevention.

Lew, M. (1990). *Victims no longer*. New York: Perennial Library. A book for survivors of sexual abuse and incest which provides specific suggestions for dealing with inner pain and finding productive new directions in life. This is a helpful guide for anyone who needs to let go of inner pain connected with a history of sexual abuse.

Maltz, W. (1991). *The sexual healing journey: A guide for survivors of sexual abuse*. New York: HarperCollins. A book that helps sexual abuse survivors learn that sex can be healthy and pleasurable. It provides specific suggestions for coping with the sexual and relational problems that may result from sexual abuse.

Riger, S., & Gordon, M. T. (1990). *The female fear*. New York: Free Press. Based on interviews with nearly 300 women and 68 men, this book focuses on the fear of rape with which women must constantly live. The authors take a critical look at the legal system and how it treats victims of sexual assault. Much of the discussion relates to college settings.

Rutter, P. (1990). *Sex in the forbidden zone: When men in power betray women's trust*. Los Angeles: Jeremy P. Tarcher. An examination of the dynamics behind sexual abuse of women by professional men, particularly therapists. The book opens issues for discussion that have largely been ignored or hidden in the professional community.

Sanday, P. R. (1990). *Fraternity gang rape: Sex, brotherhood, and privilege on campus*. New York: New York University Press. There has been an increase in publicity given to sexual abuse by groups of fraternity men. This book examines the conditions that seem to make such abuse more likely, including the sense of special status and power that some fraternities foster.

Warshaw, R. (1988). *I never called it rape*. New York: HarperCollins. Results of a survey of 6,000 American college students, offering startling statistics on the extent of sexual victimization. The book also deals with the confusing feelings that women experience following acquaintance rape.

CHAPTER FOURTEEN

SEXUALLY TRANSMITTED DISEASES AND THEIR PREVENTION
    Gonorrhea
    Syphilis
    Chlamydia
    Nongonococcal Urethritis (NGU) in Males
    Vulvovaginal Infections
    Genital Herpes
    Genital Warts
    Viral Hepatitis
    Pubic Lice
    Other Sexually Transmitted Diseases
    Preventing Sexually Transmitted Diseases
    Legal Aspects of Sexually Transmitted Diseases

OTHER SEX-RELATED MEDICAL PROBLEMS
    Disorders of the Male Sex Organs
    Disorders of the Female Sex Organs
    Sexual Effects of Debilitating Illnesses

SELF-EVALUATION: EXAMINING YOUR ATTITUDES TOWARD STDS

CHAPTER SUMMARY

When I found out that I have genital herpes, I thought my sex life was over. My first outbreak of the sores was very painful, and I felt completely disgusted with myself. That was 5 years ago, and I haven't had another outbreak since. I was completely honest with the next man I had sex with, and he didn't mind using a condom. It seems like a strange thing to say, but I was glad to find out that my present partner has herpes too, so we don't have to worry about infecting each other. I still get a little concerned when I think ahead to having children, but my doctor has been pretty reassuring. Getting herpes changed my life to an extent, but didn't end it.

—Based on a counseling session

SEXUALLY TRANSMITTED DISEASES AND OTHER PHYSICAL PROBLEMS

The human body can experience a variety of diseases that either are transmitted by the intimate physical contact of sexual activity or have direct and indirect effects on sexual functioning. In recent years medical science has been paying more attention to these sex-related conditions. Many sexually transmitted diseases are continuing to spread rapidly among some populations. Physicians and other health professionals also have a heightened awareness of the need to help patients understand and adapt to the sex-related effects of other illnesses. This chapter provides an overview of these topics. AIDS as a sexually transmitted disease is discussed in chapter 15, "The AIDS Crisis and Sexual Decisions."

Sexually Transmitted Diseases and Their Prevention

At various times in history some sexually transmitted diseases (STDs), such as syphilis, have represented scourges that attacked societies. They were feared and often assumed to represent retribution from the gods. When soldiers of the French army were garrisoned in Naples in the winter of 1495, they suffered syphilitic sores on the genitals, followed by skin eruptions. The Italians called it the "French sickness," while the French blamed it on the Italians. The Turkish people would come to call it the Christian disease, and the Chinese dubbed it the Portuguese disease. Nearly every major country and religion would eventually be blamed for the scourge of syphilis (Bullough, 1976). Gonorrhea and syphilis were significant problems among United States troops during World War II, and extensive educational efforts were launched to prevent their spread. However, effective and rapid medical treatments for the venereal diseases (VD)—as they were once called—were generally lacking, and their incidence increased at alarming rates.

When penicillin and other antibiotics began to appear in the late 1940s, it seemed as though VD had finally been conquered. By 1957 the number of cases of both gonorrhea and syphilis had dropped to an all-time low. However, as public concern began to fade and assurances of quick cure increased, the incidence

syphilis (SIF-uh-lus): sexually transmitted disease (STD) characterized by four stages, beginning with the appearance of a chancre.

of sexually transmitted diseases began to rise again. During the same period, new strains of STD-causing organisms began to appear that were more resistant to some antibiotics. New diseases, such as chlamydia and AIDS, now have been added to the list of infections that can be transmitted by intimate bodily contact.

While the STDs discussed in this chapter are transmitted mostly through direct sexual activity, some of them may occasionally be spread in nonsexual ways. In recent years the definition of what constitutes an STD has been expanded to include several diseases that have alternate means of transmission. The newest and most lethal of the STDs, acquired immunodeficiency syndrome (AIDS), is covered in the following chapter, "The AIDS Crisis and Sexual Decisions." It is known, however, that infection with other STDs can increase the risk of contracting the AIDS virus. Presumably, an already existing infection causes weakness and breaks in tissue that permit easier entry of the AIDS virus into the bloodstream.

The incidence of many sexually transmitted diseases continues to be high. People under the age of 25 account for the majority of STD cases (Hatcher et al., 1990). Educational efforts and antibiotic treatments have failed to eliminate STDs and in many cases have not even significantly reduced their transmission. Many people are mistakenly convinced that they could not contract STD because of their care in choosing sexual partners or because they maintain high standards of personal hygiene. They may also be embar-

rassed to seek treatment once they realize their symptoms are suggestive of an STD. One of the difficulties with most STDs is that their symptoms may be relatively mild at first, especially in women. Gonorrhea, syphilis, and chlamydia are particularly known for the inconspicuousness of their symptoms in the early stages. They may progress into full-blown infections with potentially serious consequences before they have been recognized. Pelvic Inflammatory Disease (PID) in women often results from untreated STDs (see chapter 5, "Birth Control and Unintended Pregnancy"). It is now estimated that there are 125,000 new cases of infertility each year because of STDs (Reproductive Health, 1988).

The following sections outline basic information on STDs. For quick and accurate answers to any personal questions you might have, try calling the STD National Hotline on weekdays at their toll-free number between 8:00 A.M. and 11:00 P.M. Eastern Standard Time. The number is 1-800-227-8922 anywhere in the United States.

GONORRHEA

With over 700,000 cases of gonorrhea (in slang, called "clap" or "the drip") reported each year in the United

gonorrhea (gon-uh-REE-uh): bacterial STD causing urethral pain and discharge in males; often no symptoms in females.

Case Study

Vivian, a college student, writes about her reactions to learning that her partner was infected with gonorrhea:

"We didn't have any sort of agreement to be monogamous, but I was still shocked to have him tell me that he might have given me a disease. We never talked about his love life, and I had just assumed—or wanted to believe—that I was the only one in it. First I felt betrayed. Then I felt dirty. And then I got scared that I might have gonorrhea, even though I didn't feel sick or have any symptoms.

"They tested me at health services, and it turned out that I had it. A shot of penicillin took care of it, but I was even more scared by what one of the nurses told me.

VIVIAN: DISCOVERING A CASE OF GONORRHEA

"She said that since I had one sexually transmitted disease, I should realize that I had also risked getting others—even AIDS. She told me about protecting myself in the future and gave me a Safer Sex Kit, which contained condoms, foam, and two brochures. I read them both from front to back and realized how careless I'd been.

"I broke up with him after all that. I just felt disgusted by him. Later, I even got tested for AIDS, because I was so scared. Fortunately that turned out negative. I haven't had sex with anybody since, but when I do, you can be sure I won't risk catching *any* disease. If I can get gonorrhea, I've got to face the fact that I could get something even worse."

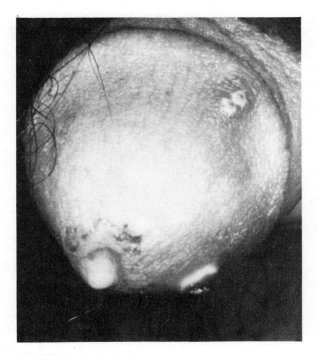

FIGURE 14.1 Gonorrhea

States, it is the most commonly reported communicable disease. The National Centers for Disease Control estimate that if unreported cases are included, there are probably closer to 2 million cases of the disease annually. There has been a gradual decline in the incidence of the disease throughout the 1980s, after an increase in the 1970s. However, the statistics on most STDs tend to show periodic fluctuations, the reasons for which are difficult to explain.

Caused by the bacterium *Neisseria gonorrhoeae* (named after Dr. Albert Neisser, who discovered the bacterium in 1879), gonorrhea seems to be transmitted almost exclusively through sexual contact. Sexual activity—intercourse, oral sex, or anal sex—with an infected partner is riskier for women than for men. There is over a 50 percent chance of women contracting the disease on a single exposure, while for men the risk is about 25 percent (Platt, Rice, & McCormack, 1983). Bacteria migrate less easily into the male urethra than into the female vulva, where they have more moist locations in which to multiply. Of course the risk increases for both men and women with each repeated exposure.

Babies may pick up the bacteria during the birth process if the mother is infected. Their eyes are particularly vulnerable to gonorrheal infection, and blindness can result. It is a routine precaution in most hospital obstetrical units to put a few drops of silver nitrate into the eyes of newborns in order to kill bacteria.

Symptoms   Probably one of the major reasons that gonorrhea is the most commonly reported STD is that its symptoms tend to appear quite quickly and be decidedly unpleasant for men. However, it is also possible for the infection to be mild and relatively asymptomatic. In men, within 2 weeks after infection, burning and itching sensations develop in the urethra, especially during urination. There is also a thick, puslike discharge from the urethra, often showing up on underwear. Although up to 80 percent of women do not detect gonorrhea in its earlier stages, its most typical early symptom is a green or yellow discharge from the cervical area, where the bacteria tend to strike first. There may then be some vaginal irritation. Gonorrheal infections in the throat tend to create soreness and some mucus in the throat; rectal infection causes soreness, itching, rectal discharge, and bowel abnormalities.

If gonorrhea is not treated in its early stages, the initial symptoms usually disappear on their own but the bacteria often move to other organs, causing more serious infections and complications. In men it may affect the bladder, prostate, kidneys, or epididymis of the testes. Left untreated in either sex, the disease can cause sterility. In women the infection often moves into the reproductive organs such as the uterus, fallopian tubes, and ovaries, and may eventually result in pelvic inflammatory disease. Rarely, in either sex, the bacteria create systemic infections throughout the body, with generalized symptoms, arthritis, and complications in major organs such as the heart or brain.

Diagnosis   There are three main ways in which gonorrhea bacteria are identified. First, a smear is made of the discharge, taken from the penile urethra, cervix, throat, or rectum, depending on where infection most likely took place. The material is stained and examined microscopically for evidence of the bacteria. A culture may also be made, with bacteria grown on a nutrient medium and then examined for the gonorrhea bacterium. The culture method has been most widely used with women. More recently a new enzyme-sensitive immunoassay test has been developed that can detect the bacteria with great accuracy. A substantial proportion of women and men with gonorrhea are also infected with chlamydia.

Treatment   Gonorrhea is treated with a large dose of injected penicillin, usually followed by doses of oral tetracycline or an alternate antibiotic, such as erythromycin, for a week. In the mid-1970s, a strain of

chlamydia (kluh-MID-ee-uh): now known to be a common STD, this organism is a major cause of urethritis in males; in females it often presents no symptoms.

N. gonorrhoeae was found that is resistant to penicillin. The new strain of the bacterium produces an enzyme that destroys the antibiotic's action. It is a persistent bacterium, and during the late 1980s health officials became concerned as infection by the strain continued to increase. This strain is usually treated with spectinomycin. Since some gonorrhea bacteria may not be completely eliminated by typical treatment, follow-up checks should be made about a week after treatment has ended. Treatment would include antibiotics that destroy chlamydia organisms as well.

As with any STD, sexual partners of a patient with gonorrhea should be notified of their risk, so that they may seek appropriate diagnosis and treatment.

SYPHILIS

Intermittently throughout history, syphilis has been considered a scourge. Some historians have speculated that some of the "leprosy" present in biblical times may actually have been syphilis. An epidemic of the disease spread through Europe at the end of the fifteenth century, leading to further speculation that a virulent form of the disease was brought back to Europe by Christopher Columbus and his crew. In 1905 the spiral-shaped organism, or spirochete, that causes syphilis was identified and named *Treponema pallidum.*

The number of reported syphilis infections in the United States has traditionally been lower than reported cases of gonorrhea, and now averages about 40,000 reported cases per year. The incidence of the disease has seen an alarming increase in recent years, with the early 1990s having the highest rate of syphilis infection in 40 years. While some of this increase might be attributable to increased concern over and attention to STDs because of AIDS, it is another reminder that diseases such as syphilis cannot be dismissed as minor medical concerns even today. Most states require a blood test for syphilis as a prerequisite to obtaining a marriage license.

Symptoms Syphilis can progress through four major stages, beginning 2 weeks to a month after infection. The first stage, or *primary syphilis,* is nearly always characterized by the appearance of a painless sore wherever the spirochete entered the body. The sore, called a chancre, begins as a reddish bump that develops into a pimple. It then opens and ulcerates, often oozing pus until a scab develops. The chancre is sometimes surrounded by a pink border. This sore is infested with the treponema organism, and so the individual is highly infectious at this stage. Usually the chancre appears on the genitals, although it can appear

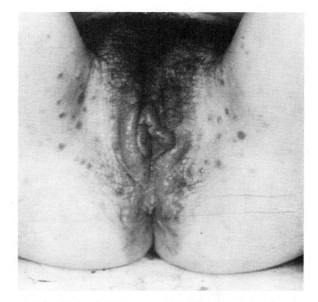

FIGURE 14.2   Primary syphilis chancre

on the mouth, anal area, and on fingers or breasts. In women it frequently occurs on the inner vaginal wall or cervix and sometimes in the rectum. Since it is relatively painless, it may not be noticed there. Within 4 to 6 weeks, the chancre heals even without treatment and there may be no further symptoms for up to 6 months (Fitzgerald, 1984).

The next stage, *secondary syphilis,* usually begins with some degree of a bumpy skin rash, accompanied by general symptoms of illness such as fever, swollen lymph nodes of the neck, nausea, headache, sore throat, loss of scalp hair, and loss of appetite. More moist sores may appear around the genitals or anal region. Again, even without treatment, the symptoms eventually abate within a few weeks, and the disease enters its *latent stage.* It is estimated that slightly more than half of untreated syphilis victims remain in this latent stage for the rest of their lives.

People who progress to the *tertiary syphilis* stage usually face serious complications resulting from the spirochete infecting inner tissues and organs. It may attack the heart, brain and spinal cord, eyes, joints, and numerous other areas, leading to life-threatening disease, blindness, insanity, or paralysis. Although modern medical treatment has greatly reduced the number of syphilis cases progressing to the tertiary stage, they still occur. In latent tertiary stages the disease typically cannot be transmitted to others.

Congenital syphilis refers to an unborn fetus being infected by its mother's bloodstream. It can result in significant birth defects, especially of the bones, blood, and kidneys. If a pregnant woman with

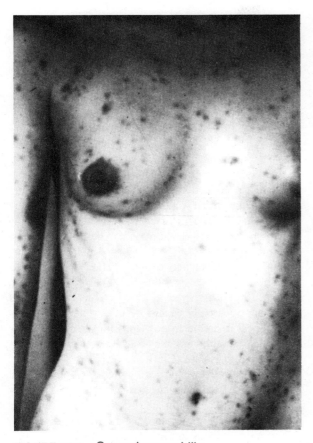

FIGURE 14.3 Secondary syphilis

syphilis is treated prior to the 16th week of pregnancy, congenital syphilis can be averted. It is important that a pregnant woman have a blood test for syphilis before the fourth month of pregnancy.

Diagnosis and Treatment The two main ways in which syphilis can be identified are through one of several blood tests or by microscopic examination of fluid from the chancre, in which the spirochete may be seen. Once diagnosed, it is usually treated in its primary and secondary stages by a single injection of penicillin. Tetracycline and erythromycin may also be used. Latent and tertiary syphilis require larger doses of antibiotics over a period of several weeks.

CHLAMYDIA

It has long been known that the organism *Chlamydia trachomatis* is a frequent cause of inflammation in the urinary and genital systems. Only recently in the mid-1980s, however, was chlamydia recognized as a very widespread sexually transmitted disease that has a range of serious complications. The Centers for Dis-

ease Control estimate that there are close to 4 million chlamydial infections each year in the United States, although others believe the actual number to be closer to 10 million. The chlamydia organism invades the cells it attacks and multiplies within those cells. It therefore can create a variety of symptoms and can be resistant to some antibiotics. It is a particularly common infection on college campuses, where up to 10 percent of the students may typically be infected (Schachter, 1989).

Like gonorrhea, chlamydia offers special risks to the eyes of newborns. *Conjunctivitis,* an inflammation of the eye, can be contracted at birth as the baby passes through the vagina, or birth canal. If it is not treated thoroughly and promptly, blindness can result. Throughout the world, it may well be the most widespread preventable cause of blindness (Crum & Ellner, 1985). Babies may also develop chlamydial pneumonia during their first few months of life.

Although the disease is spread primarily through sexual contact, once the infection is established it can be spread to other areas of the body or other people by hand contact, insects, or contact with human excretions. These modes of transmission are particularly prevalent in underdeveloped countries where there is overpopulation and inadequate sanitation (Bowie, 1984).

Symptoms The symptoms of chlamydial infection are often vague or nonexistent, and they can masquerade as symptoms of other diseases as well. This is one of the reasons that many such infections go unnoticed or are inaccurately diagnosed. In about 70 percent of all cases, there are no early symptoms, and it may take more serious later complications to alert the infected individual that something is wrong (Holmes, 1981).

In males there is often a burning sensation during urination and discharge of pus from the penis. If the organism moves further into the body, swelling and discomfort in the testicles may result. Untreated, it can cause infertility in men. In females the early symptoms are often mild but can involve itching or burning of the vulva, some discharge, and irritation during urination. In its later stages the disease may cause pelvic inflammatory disease, with fever, nausea, abdominal pain, and abnormal patterns of menstruation. It can also damage the fallopian tubes and is now known to be a common cause of infertility and ectopic pregnancy (Crum & Ellner, 1985).

Diagnosis and Treatment Until recently, tests for chlamydia were time-consuming and expensive, requiring the growing of the organism in a laboratory culture for identification. There are now several tests available that can render a quick, inexpensive, and relatively accurate diagnosis.

379

CHLAMYDIA IS NOT A FLOWER.

It's a Sexually Transmitted Disease with Devastating Effects.

FIGURE 14.4 Chlamydia

Once diagnosed, the disease can usually be cured with a week-long treatment of tetracycline, doxycycline, or erythromycin. Penicillin is not an effective treatment (Bowie, 1984). As with any antibiotic treatment, it is crucial that the entire dosage of the prescribed medication be taken. Otherwise the infection may continue in more persistent forms. Ointments containing tetracycline or erythromycin may also be applied to the eyes of newborns to prevent the development of chlamydial conjunctivitis.

Health workers continue to emphasize that chlamydia is a serious STD, now of vast epidemic proportions. Medical costs relating to the disease are approaching $2 billion each year in the United States. We should pay attention to and seek appropriate medical checkups for any unusual sensations or discomforts

in the genital or urinary tracts. Because of the prevalence of this infection, it is a good idea to include a chlamydia culture test in the routine pelvic exams of young women who are having sexual intercourse (Joffe, 1988).

NONGONOCOCCAL URETHRITIS (NGU) IN MALES

Sometimes called *nonspecific urethritis (NSU)*, nongonococcal urethritis (NGU), refers to any inflammation of the male urethra that is not caused by gonorrhea. NGU is a much more common infection than gonorrhea and has been on the increase. The most common cause of NGU is chlamydial infection, accounting for about half of the cases. Another 20–25 percent are caused by the mycoplasmic bacterium *Ureaplasma urealyticum*. The remainder of NGU cases are apparently caused by other microorganisms or by local irritation from soap, vaginal secretions, or spermicides, although the exact cause is sometimes impossible to isolate (Clark, 1985a).

While the symptoms are often less pronounced than those associated with gonorrhea, there is usually some degree of burning and itching during and after urination. There may also be some discharge of pus, often more evident in the morning.

Prompt treatment of NGU is crucial, even though the symptoms typically subside and disappear on their own within a few weeks, because the organism causing the inflammation will usually persist somewhere in the body. This can increase the likelihood of a repeat infection or of more serious complications at a later time.

Again, antibiotics such as tetracycline or erythromycin are most frequently used to treat NGU, although they are not always effective. Regardless of the cause, it is advisable for any sexual partner of a man with NGU to seek examination to determine the possible presence of infection as well.

VULVOVAGINAL INFECTIONS

Vulvovaginitis, or infection within the vulval region and vagina, is extremely common and often not caused by a sexually transmitted disease. Almost every woman will experience a vulvovaginal infection some-

---

nongonococcal urethritis (NGU) (non-gon-uh-KOK-ul yur-i-THRYT-us): infection or irritation in the male urethra caused by bacteria or local irritants.

vulvovaginitis (vaj-uh-NITE-us): general term for inflammation of the vulva and/or vagina.

Case Study

JOHN: SEEKING TREATMENT FOR AN STD

A month after his first sexual intercourse, at the age of 16, John began to experience itching and burning in his penis. He was alarmed that he might have gonorrhea but was also embarrassed and afraid that his parents might find out. Finally he told an older friend about the problem, and the older boy suggested he visit a doctor in the neighborhood who would treat the disease confidentially.

At the physician's office John explained his symptoms. The doctor did not take a bacterial culture or examine John's penis. He did give him an injection of penicillin and assured John that the antibiotic should take care of the symptoms. Over the next few weeks, the symptoms subsided, although John experienced occasional burning and itching. He avoided sexual intercourse.

A year later he again began to have discomfort and yet had not had further sexual relations. He had read about a sexually transmitted disease clinic and visited the facility. This time he was diagnosed as having nongonococcal urethritis, and tests confirmed that his infection was being caused by chlamydia. The clinician told John that even his original symptoms had not been typical for gonorrhea, and that penicillin had not been the appropriate treatment. He was given a prescription of tetracycline capsules and told to be certain to take all of the medication. A follow-up test a month later confirmed that the infection had been cured.

---

time. The lining of the vagina has a carefully balanced system for cleansing itself. Fluids from the tissues in the lining and the cervix and discarded cells from the uterus form a discharge that cleanses the vagina and protects it from infection by hostile bacteria. However, the balance of this cleansing mechanism may change during various stages of the menstrual cycle, during pregnancy, or with the use of birth control pills, antibiotics, or other medications. The pH of the vagina, usually slightly acidic, may become more alkaline. Any such upset can make the vagina more vulnerable to infection (Clark, 1985b).

Symptoms All types of vulvovaginitis are usually characterized by some discharge, the color, thickness, and odor of which varies with the type of infection. There are often sensations of burning and itching in the vulval region and outer vagina.

Types There are four main types of vulvovaginitis, as determined by their causes. The first three may be transmitted by sexual activity, although their microorganisms are found naturally in the environment or in the body and may develop into an infection without sexual contact if the conditions present themselves.

1. *Bacterial vaginosis* is most often caused by the bacterium *Gardnerella vaginalis*. Men apparently can carry gardnerella, but often do not experience any symptoms of disease. Occasionally it causes urethritis, bladder infection, or infection of the penile foreskin in males. Vaginal gardnerella is treated with oral antibiotics such as penicillin, ampicillin, amoxicillin, or tetracycline and with a drug called metronidazole, commonly known as Flagyl. Sexual partners are usually treated at the same time to reduce the risks of reinfecting one another.

2. Yeast infection* in the vagina is sometimes called *monilial vaginitis*. It occurs when conditions within the vagina permit an overgrowth of a fungus that normally is found there, *Candida albicans*. Such infections can sometimes mask the presence of other sexually transmitted diseases, and so it is often important to check for other STDs whenever a yeast infection is found. This disease is treated with fungicides that are used within the vagina in cream or suppository form, such as miconazole or nystatin.

3. Trichomoniasis is an infection caused by a one-celled protozoan organism, *Trichomonas,* that can take up residence within the vulva and vagina and

*Note: Yeast infections can also affect males, in the form of an itchy rash on the penis and scrotum.

yeast infection: a type of vaginitis caused by an overgrowth of a fungus normally found in an inactive state in the vagina.
trichomoniasis (trik-uh-ma-NEE-uh-sis): a vaginal infection caused by the *Trichomonas* organism.

can be carried in the male urethra as well. Frequently there are no noticeable symptoms. Again it is necessary to treat sexual partners as well as the woman, to prevent reinfection. The drug used is metronidazole (Flagyl), which is not considered safe for use during pregnancy or when a woman is nursing a baby.

4. *Atrophic vaginitis* is caused by low estrogen levels and occurs almost exclusively after menopause. It is not a sexually transmitted disease, although it can lower resistance to vulvovaginal infection by other microorganisms that are.

Prevention of Vulvovaginal Infections One of the best ways to prevent sexually transmitted vaginosis is for the male to use a condom during sexual intercourse. There are several simple hygienic measures that can at least reduce the risk of vaginal infection through nonsexual contamination. These include daily washing of the vulva with mild soap and water, followed by thorough drying, since dampness heightens the risk of infection. For this reason too, underwear made of nonabsorbent synthetic fibers such as nylon are not recommended. Experts also recommend against the use of vaginal sprays and douches unless they have been specifically prescribed for some medical condition. They are often implicated in upsetting the balance of the vagina's natural cleansing mechanisms, increasing the likelihood of infection (Hasselbring, 1983).

GENITAL HERPES

Genital herpes is caused by the *Herpes simplex* virus. There are two strains of the virus, *Herpes simplex* virus type 1 *(HSV-1)* and type 2 *(HSV-2)*. Cold sores on the mouth are usually caused by HSV-1, while lesions in the genital area are caused most often by HSV-2. It is now known, however, that up to 20 percent of genital herpes is linked to the HSV-1 virus. Although it is not clearly understood why this is the case, it has been proposed that an increase in oral-genital sexual activities may play a role (Peter, Bryson, & Lovett, 1982).

While it seems likely that the genital herpes epidemic of the early 1980s may now be subsiding, an estimated 30 million people in the United States have been infected with the virus, with another quarter million contracting the disease each year. Research indicates that students tend to have unreasonable fears and misconceptions about herpes, leading to negative stereotypes regarding herpes sufferers (Bruce & Bullins, 1989). HSV-2 is transmitted almost exclusively by sexual contact, although the virus can survive

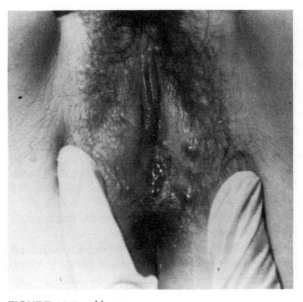

FIGURE 14.5 Herpes

externally for several hours if the conditions are right (Neinstein, Goldenring, & Carpenter, 1984).

Once the herpes simplex virus has been contracted, it may continue to live in the body, even if no symptoms of the disease are present. There are no vaccines to prevent infection nor any medications to eradicate the virus from the body. The actual appearance of the painful herpes blisters seems to be associated with periods when disease resistance might be weakened by other illnesses, stress, exhaustion, or inadequate nutrition. It may also be triggered by irritation to the susceptible regions of the skin, such as by overexposure to the sun or irritation from clothing.

Symptoms Like cold sores, genital herpes is characterized by the appearance of what may be painful or itchy clusters of blisters on the sex organs. During the first outbreak women usually have blisters on the cervix as well as externally on the vulva. Within a few days the blisters open and ulcerate, leaving wet, open sores that are highly contagious. Care is especially crucial during these outbreaks to prevent transmission of the virus to other individuals or even to other parts of the infected person's own body. Exposure of the eyes to the virus is particularly dangerous, since a severe eye infection called *herpes keratitis* may develop that can cause serious damage to the cornea. The sores should be touched as little as possible and only when followed by thorough washing of the hands. Sometimes outbreaks of the blisters are accompanied

genital herpes (HER-peez): viral STD characterized by painful sores on the sex organs.

by other symptoms of illness, such as fever, achiness, or pain in the groin or thighs. It usually takes another 2 weeks for the sores to crust over and heal.

Up to 70 percent of people who have had a genital herpes infection will experience at least one recurrence of the disease. This usually begins with prickling or burning sensations in the skin where the blisters are about to appear. It is during such outbreaks that sexual contact, or any direct contact with the infected area, is particularly risky. It is advisable to avoid such contact until at least 10 days after the sores have healed completely (Bernstein, Lovett, & Bryson, 1984). However, the risk of infection remains, even when the blisters are not present. Use of a condom reduces the chance of infection (Mertz et al., 1988). Up to 30 percent of infected people never have a further outbreak of the herpes sores.

Most men do not experience any complications from a herpes infection, although herpes may increase the risks of being vulnerable to infection by the AIDS virus. Although relatively rare, there are two possible complications for women. There is a higher incidence of cervical and vulval cancer among women who have had genital herpes, even though the cause-and-effect

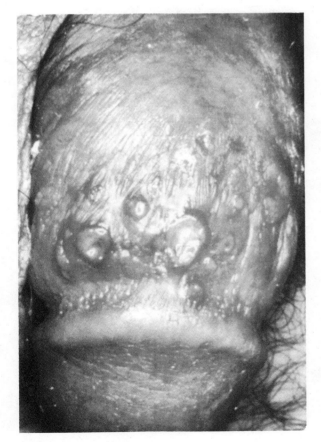

FIGURE 14.6 Herpes corona

mechanism for this phenomenon is not understood. For this reason, women with HSV-2 are advised to have an annual pelvic examination and Pap smear to detect any abnormal cells in the cervix. The second danger is to a baby during the birth process, in which the presence of HSV-2 can lead to seriously damaging infection or even death. This is called congenital herpes. In women with a history of genital herpes, cultures are taken from the cervix, vagina, and vulva several times during the final weeks of pregnancy to detect a possible recurrence of the disease. If there is a risk of infection to the baby during birth, the delivery may be accomplished by caesarean section.

Diagnosis and Treatment   Genital herpes is usually diagnosed by direct observation of the blisters, although a variety of tests are available that use cultures of the virus for positive identification. While there is no cure for the disease, an antiviral drug called *acyclovir* can help relieve some symptoms and may be used to suppress recurrences of the disease (Wilbanks, 1987). It can be applied to the blisters in ointment form during the initial outbreak, although it proves less useful in this manner with recurrent outbreaks. Orally administered acyclovir has been shown to reduce recurrent infections in those who are susceptible to frequent outbreaks and also to reduce the duration and severity of the infection. The drug has not been tested in pregnant or nursing women (Hatcher et al., 1990). Other antiviral drugs are presently being tested for possible use with herpes infections, the most promising being called *intervir.*

Health-care professionals offer some suggestions for relieving the painful symptoms of a herpes outbreak. They suggest keeping the infected area as clean and dry as possible. Baby powder or cornstarch may be used to absorb moisture. Aspirin or other pain relievers can help, as well as direct application of an ice pack (Straus, Seidlin, & Takiff, 1984).

GENITAL WARTS

These warts are caused by the *human papilloma virus (HPV),* a virus similar to the one that causes warts in other bodily regions. There are over 50 known strains of the virus. The condition is also known as *condyloma acuminata* or *venereal warts.* This disease is now the most common sexually transmitted viral disease in the United States, with an estimated 3 million cases diagnosed annually. Genital warts occur more frequently in people who began sexual activity comparatively early

genital warts: small lesions on genital skin caused by papilloma virus; this STD increases later risks of certain malignancies.

FIGURE 14.7 Genital warts

in their lives and have had multiple sexual partners and casual sexual relationships. Women with the disease are likely to have had male sexual partners with warts on the penis or partners who are carrying the virus (Hatcher et al., 1990).

Symptoms Warts usually do not appear on the genitals for about 3 months after exposure to an infected partner. Their color and texture can vary with location; with soft, pinkish lesions occurring in moist areas and harder, greyish-white warts in dry areas. They have irregular surfaces. The warts usually grow on the penis, vulva, anal area, or urethra. If they grow inside the urethra, they can cause difficulty in urinating and lead to other infections. For the most part they are not particularly painful or dangerous in themselves. This virus, however, has been increasingly associated with a high incidence of cancerous or precancerous cells in the cervix, a condition called *cervical intraepithelial neoplasia (CIN)*. It is believed that certain strains of the papilloma viruses can cause abnormal cell division in cervical tissues. More recent evidence is indicating that these viruses may also be implicated in a variety of other cancers, including those on the genitals or other bodily organs. It also appears that they can produce anal cancers, and some cases have been identified in gay males (Schmeck, 1987).

Treatment Genital warts can be removed by laser surgery, electrosurgery (using an electrical current), freezing with liquid nitrogen, or surgery with scissors. For external warts, chemicals such as podophyllin may

be applied over a period of 3 or 4 weeks, often causing the lesions to heal. However, since the virus remains in the body, the warts can recur until immunity develops.

VIRAL HEPATITIS

There are two potentially sexually transmitted viruses that can cause the liver infection known as viral hepatitis. They have been designated as *Hepatitis A* and *Hepatitis B*. The B form of the virus is more common, with close to 150,000 new cases reported each year in the United States. This disease is frequently transmitted through food that has been contaminated by the virus or by sharing intravenous needles for illicit drug use. Hepatitis B is most likely to be transmitted sexually, since the virus is found in bodily fluids such as saliva, semen, vaginal secretions, and blood. Its transmission is especially likely with various forms of anal sex, and the disease is far more prevalent among homosexual men than among the rest of the population. Hepatitis A is usually contracted through the mouth and is carried by fecal material. Therefore it is sexually transmitted by oral-anal contact (Francis et al., 1984).

Symptoms Hepatitis occurs within a range of degrees of severity. It may have no symptoms at all or may cause complications serious enough to be fatal. Hepatitis A is typically a milder infection with fewer complications than Hepatitis B. The typical symptoms of both types include loss of appetite, lethargy, headache, joint achiness, nausea, vomiting, diarrhea, yellowing of the skin (jaundice), darkening of the urine, and some enlargement of the liver. Usually hospitalization is unnecessary. Infection with Hepatitis B may increase later risks for developing liver cancer (Zuckerman, 1982).

Treatment As with all viral infections, there is no treatment for hepatitis presently. Some medications can provide relief of symptoms, and a period of bed rest and heavy fluid intake is usually required. Gradually the body's immune system conquers the disease, although in more severe cases this process can take several months.

PUBIC LICE

The STD commonly called "crabs" is caused by a tiny (1–4 mm) parasitic louse with the scientific name *Phthirus pubis*. Health workers often refer to an infestation of these lice as *pediculosis pubis*. The lice

viral hepatitis: inflammation of the liver caused by a virus.

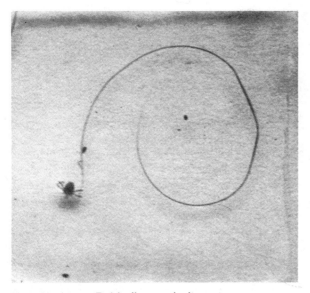

FIGURE 14.8 Pubic lice and nits

have claws that allow them to hold tightly to hairs, usually in the pubic, anal, and perineal areas. Occasionally they spread to armpits, or even the scalp. The lice found in head hair are usually of a different species, however, and are not spread by sexual contact.

Pubic lice bite into the skin to feed on blood from tiny blood vessels. This creates tiny little papules on the skin that cause intense itching. They lay their eggs, or nits, on hairs to which they are tightly attached. These eggs could drop onto sheets or bed clothes and survive for several days. The lice also can live away from the body for about one day in clothing, sheets, towels, and even furniture, making their way to other people if the opportunity presents itself. Both the whitish nits and the adult lice themselves can be seen upon close examination.

Treatment Any treatment must be thorough to ensure complete eradication of the lice. The best medication to use is a 1 percent lindane lotion or cream, which is applied to the infested area, then washed off after 8 hours. Lindane shampoo, applied for 4 minutes, is also available. The brand name of lindane is Kwell, and it is only available by prescription. Other shampoo treatments can be purchased without a prescription, including A-200 Pyrinate and *Triple XXX*. A repeat treatment is recommended after 7 days to take care of any eggs that may have been missed the first time. It is also crucial that all potentially exposed bedclothes, underwear, towels, or other materials be thoroughly washed or dry-cleaned. An insecticide spray is available to treat furniture as well. Close physical contact with others should be avoided until treatment is completed.

OTHER SEXUALLY TRANSMITTED DISEASES

There are several other STDs that are more common in tropical climates but have recently been on the increase in temperate-zone countries such as the United States. Lymphogranuloma venereum (LGV) is caused by several strains of *Chlamydia* and produces painless, pimplelike ulcers on the genitals or rectum. There may be other symptoms, such as fever, hives, or swollen lymph nodes in the groin. If left untreated, it can cause blockage of lymph vessels, resulting in swollen limbs or bodily organs. In the tropics this condition is called "elephantiasis." LGV is treated with antibiotics such as tetracycline or erythromycin, or sulfa drugs.

Chancroid is caused by the bacterium *Hemophilus ducreyi*. Within a week after infection, several small sores appear on the genitals. They are filled with pus, and may rupture to form painful open sores that bleed easily. Antibiotics and sulfa drugs are effective in curing the disease; if it is left untreated it can cause swelling, pain, and rupture of lymph tissue at the surface of the skin.

Granuloma inguinale is a rare infection caused by *Calymmatobacterium granulomatis*. It also involves the appearance of small blisters and swelling of lymph nodes. The sores often do not heal easily unless treated and can become infected, eventually causing permanent damage and scarring of tissue. It can be cured with antibiotics such as tetracycline, streptomycin, or erythromycin.

Since cases of LGV, chancroid, and granuloma inguinale only number in the thousands annually in the United States, they are diseases less commonly seen by physicians and STD clinics. This makes them harder to diagnose, which may result in dangerously delayed treatment (Leary, 1988).

There are two skin diseases in the United States that are transmitted by direct bodily contact, not

perineal areas (pair-a-NEE-al): the sensitive skin between the genitals and the anus.
pubic lice: small insects that can infect skin in the pubic area, causing a rash and severe itching.
lymphogranuloma venereum (LGV) (lim-foe-gran-yu-LOW-ma va-NEAR-ee-um): contagious STD caused by several strains of *Chlamydia* and marked by swelling and ulceration of lymph nodes in the groin.
chancroid (SHAN-kroyd): an STD caused by the bacterium *Hemophilus ducreyi* and characterized by sores on the genitals, which, if left untreated, could result in pain and rupture of the sores.
granuloma inguinale (gran-ya-LOW-ma in-gwa-NAL-ee *or* -NALE): STD characterized by ulcerations and granulations beginning in the groin and spreading to the buttocks and genitals.

385

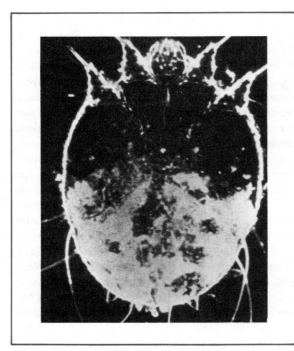

FIGURE 14.9   Scabies mite

necessarily sexual. One is <u>molluscum contagiosum</u>, a pox virus that causes small papules to appear on the skin. They often look similar to whiteheads and have a hard seed-like core. They usually do not create any discomfort or pain. Occasionally they may become infected by other bacteria and ulcerate. Molluscum blisters often heal by themselves, although they may be removed by scraping, freezing, or treatment with chemicals. If all of the lesions are not removed, they will often recur.

<u>Scabies</u> is caused by a tiny mite that burrows under the skin to lay its eggs. It causes redness and itching and may lead to secondary infections. Epidemics of scabies often spread throughout schools, hospitals, or other institutions where people interact closely. Obviously sexual contact also provides an easy mode of transmission for the disease. The same chemical lotions and creams used for pubic lice are effective with scabies as well.

PREVENTING SEXUALLY TRANSMITTED DISEASES

Many STDs have reached epidemic proportions. Some strains of STD-causing bacteria may actually be showing signs of greater resistance to the antibiotics that have constituted standard treatments for years. AIDS is a disease that has no cure at this time (see the following chapter). For these reasons, the possibility

of contracting or transmitting disease should be weighed as part of everyone's decision-making regarding sex. It must be part of sexual responsibility. Here are some specific suggestions for minimizing the chances of getting or transmitting a sexually transmitted disease:

1. *Recognize that abstinence from sex represents a rational choice in the face of the evidence about STD.* There are plenty of pressures to have sex. Our sexual feelings may be strong and difficult to resist. However, each individual must make his or her own decisions about how sexually involved to get with others. Especially with the AIDS crisis, abstinence will become even more of a viable alternative in the years ahead; it is a rational choice.

2. *Remember that sexual sharing does not have to involve internal penetration.* Most of the serious STDs are transmitted by penetration that involves mingling of bodily secretions (oral-genital, anal-genital, penile-vaginal, or finger insertion). The transmission of these diseases could be sharply reduced by emphasis on forms of sexual sharing that do not require such penetration. These include massage, most forms of mutual masturbation, and some degree of external mutual genital contact. Unfortunately, social values have often led us to believe that some form of penetration is necessary to legitimize a sexual experience. Given the prevalence of STDs, alternative values may well begin to filter into our social systems.

3. *Avoid multiple partners and partners who are not well known to you.* The more partners you have and the less well known they are to you, the greater the risks of contracting an STD. This is a fact that has been confirmed by research. Casual sex is simply riskier sex. There is less chance that partners' sexual histories will be known, that suspicious symptoms will be noticed in a partner, and that partners will be notified if a disease is eventually diagnosed.

4. *Take responsibility for yourself and your own protection.* There are several measures that you can take to protect yourself and reduce the risks of getting a sexually transmitted disease. They may not always be easy steps to take and may require

molluscum contagiosum (ma-LUS-kum kan-taje-ee-O-sum): a skin disease transmitted by direct bodily contact, not necessarily sexual, that is characterized by eruptions on the skin that appear similar to whiteheads with a hard seed-like core.

scabies (SKAY-beez): a skin disease caused by a mite that burrows under the skin to lay its eggs, causing redness and itching; transmitted by bodily contact that may or may not be sexual.

some degree of assertiveness, but they are part of sexual responsibility. First, it is important to talk with a partner about sex, and even to ask about possible infections. You might want to ask if he or she has ever had a herpes infection or any recent symptoms of infections. Second, it can be important to observe your partner's genitals, checking for any sores, warts, discharge, lice, or rashes. And finally, take responsibility to wash your genital area with soap and water before and promptly after sex. While these suggestions may not be conducive to sexual intimacy, they are worth considering as precautionary measures in preventing STDs.

5. *Use condoms and spermicides.* Whenever there is a risk of an STD infection, condoms can reduce the chances of transmission (see chapter 5, "Birth Control and Unintended Pregnancy," for more information, and chapter 15, "The AIDS Crisis and Sexual Decisions," for instructions on the proper use of condoms). They do not offer total protection but certainly reduce the risks substantially. Likewise, spermicidal foams and creams, especially nonoxynol-9, placed in the vagina kill some bacteria and offer a partial barrier for microorganisms. A recent study of prostitutes in Thailand showed that use of a contraceptive sponge containing nonoxynol-9 reduced the women's risks of acquiring gonorrhea by 67 percent and chlamydia by 33 percent.

6. *Seek medical treatment promptly if symptoms develop.* Whenever you have any suspicious or uncomfortable symptoms in the genital area or urinary tract, seek medical advice and treatment right away. Most cities have sexually transmitted disease clinics, staffed by workers who have expertise in this area. Clinical workers are nonjudgmental and the tests are nearly always painless. Unfortunately, many physicians are not well equipped and trained to deal with STDs.

7. *Inform sexual partners.* Whenever an STD is diagnosed, it is crucial for sexual partners of the infected person to be notified and to have a physical examination. Remember, many STDs do not have obvious symptoms in the earlier stages but still require prompt treatment to prevent complications.

LEGAL ASPECTS OF SEXUALLY TRANSMITTED DISEASES

Most of us assume that a person would not knowingly or deliberately transmit a disease to another person. For the most part, such assumptions are probably

warranted. However, sexual behavior is an area of life about which people can be extremely private and secretive. They may feel uncomfortable with certain aspects of their past sexual activities and may worry that to discuss their sexual histories will jeopardize present relationships. People also tend to choose to ignore the riskier aspects of sexual behavior, especially when they are caught up in powerful romantic or sexual feelings.

In recent years, more attention has been focused on the legal responsibilities of sexual partners as they relate to sexually transmitted diseases. Individuals who have contracted an STD after being assured that there was no danger of doing so, or without being informed of potential risks, have resorted to legal action. Multimillion-dollar lawsuits have been brought against celebrities for infecting sexual partners with diseases such as genital herpes. Legal experts warn that the law expects people to be responsible in their sexual behaviors and to protect others from potential harm that might come from sexual activity. In the years ahead, as STDs reach epidemic proportions, legal precedents are likely to be established that will demand even higher levels of responsibility during sexual encounters. Margaret Davis, a lawyer, and Robert Scott, a physician, (Davis & Scott, 1988) worked together to develop guidelines that are of increasing importance when considering sexual involvement. These guidelines are presented in the box on pages 388 and 389.

Other Sex-Related Medical Problems

There is a long list of other medical problems that can directly or indirectly affect one's sex organs and sexual functioning. While detailed discussion of these problems is beyond the scope of this text, this section will briefly describe some of the more common sex-related medical disorders.

DISORDERS OF THE MALE SEX ORGANS

Several organic problems can affect the internal organs of the sexual and urinary systems. In men the bladder may become infected, and various parts of the testes may occasionally become inflamed. Epididymitis, or inflammation of the epididymis at the top of each testis, is relatively common and can be treated with antibiotics. It can be caused by many different types of

epididymitis (ep-a-did-a-MITE-us): inflammation of the epididymis of the testis.

A Lover's Legal Checklist

Before engaging in sexual intimacy, consider these points to avoid both legal liability and the risk of infection. These questions may seem tough to handle in a romantic setting, but they are necessary to an exchange of genuine promises. They are the heart of your commitment to a healthy, meaningful relationship for you and your sexual partner.

Adapt this checklist to your own particular needs. Whether you use all of it or a part of it depends on you and your partner, your sexual history, and your personal concerns.

1. Share Your Medical History

Exchange with your lover:

- When you've each last had a medical checkup.
- What, if anything, that checkup showed.
- Whether either of you has had any recent STD symptoms.
- Whether previous lovers exhibited any of these symptoms.
- If either of you has a medical condition, whether it has been treated and cured. If it is recurrent or chronic, when were dates of occurrences?
- Information about blood transfusions received before 1985 (when effective blood screening for AIDS began).

Consider a joint visit to the doctor.

2. Share Your Sexual History

- Discuss your recent sex life.
- Is either of you bisexual?
- Were any partners in a high-risk group?

3. Act With Integrity

- Make your promises genuine. Get all the secrets out.
- Don't let passion cloud your better judgment. Make sure that any risk you take is full and informed—not under the influence of drugs or alcohol.
- Be practical: Suggest a condom or spermicide.
- Be careful: Exchange letters with your partner, so that you have some written records of your communications.
- Make a physical examination part of your foreplay.
- If you have an STD, make sure you have met your legal responsibility to your partner through full and complete disclosure. Your legal duty can be met with three simple words—for example, "I have herpes."
- Be trustworthy: Keep the information about your partner confidential.

bacteria that make their way into the urethra and eventually back through the vas deferens to the epididymis. In severe cases surgical intervention may be necessary. A large proportion of men at one time or another suffer from prostatitis, or inflammation of the prostate gland. The symptoms may include some thin discharge from the penis, pain in the lower abdomen and scrotum, or painful ejaculation. In acute cases there is a sudden onset of fever, chills, and urinary discomfort. Antibiotics are used for prostatitis, al-though it can be difficult to cure completely in its more chronic forms.

In older men enlargement of the prostate gland is also common, and is sometimes the result of malignant tumors. There are close to 70,000 new cases of prostatic cancer each year; if detected early, the chances of complete cure are good. If the prostate

prostatitis (pras-tuh-TITE-us): inflammation of the prostate gland.

4. Trust Your Feelings

- Don't underestimate your inner voice. If you feel insecure about your partner, practice caution.

A LAWYER'S LEGAL CHECKLIST

If you should get an STD, you may need a lawyer. Here are some of the questions your attorney will want you to weigh before deciding whether you should and want to sue.

- History of relationship with the defendant
- Medical history of plaintiff and defendant
- Sexual history of plaintiff and defendant
- The actual injury:
  Date, time, and place
  Medical evidence
  Mental and physical condition of both partners
  Use of condoms or spermicide
- Plaintiff's efforts to question or examine the defendant
- Representations of the defendant:
  Did plaintiff assume any risks?
  Were they full and informed?
- Defendant's reputation in the community
- Defendant's financial status:
  Employment
  Homeowner's insurance
  Other assets
- Plaintiff's motive for legal action:
  Revenge
  Compensation
- Plaintiff's willingness to submit to intense scrutiny of his or her private life.

Thoughtful use of the Lover's Legal Checklist could make the Lawyer's Legal Checklist obsolete. When it comes to safe sex, selfishness is a virtue. Your partner should appreciate it as much as you do.

Lovers must ask questions *before* they engage in sexual intimacy. Use the Lover's Checklist as a resource for better communication. Don't be afraid to use it. It can preserve your good health and peace of mind.

—Margaret Davis and Robert Scott, *Lovers, Doctors, and the Law,*
1988, New York: Perennial/Harper & Row

enlarges too greatly, urination may become difficult, or eventually impossible, since the urethral passageway may be pinched by the swollen prostate. This increases the susceptibility to bladder and prostate infections. Surgical treatment, including removal of the prostate (prostatectomy), or parts of it, may become necessary. If there is a malignancy present, surgery is often followed by radiation or chemical therapy. Even in radical prostate surgery, newer techniques usually do not interfere with later erectile function or ejaculation. Occasionally surgery can produce *retrograde ejaculation,* sometimes called *dry ejaculation.* Orgasmic sensations remain intact, but no semen is emitted (Goldsmith, 1983).

It is generally recommended that men over the age of 35 have regular prostate examinations to detect any possible enlargement or tumors. The physician, using a rubber glove and lubricant, inserts a finger into the rectum, where the surface of the prostate may be felt through the rectal wall. While such an examination is not particularly pleasant, it represents an important health-care measure. Recently an ultrasound technique has been developed for more accurate checking of prostate problems.

Disorders of the penis are relatively uncommon, but a few are worth mentioning here. There are two disorders that relate to the erection of the penis. One is priapism, a condition that involves continual, painful, undesired erection of the penis. It can be caused by circulatory disorders or abuse of certain drugs, including cocaine. If the erection cannot be relieved within an hour or two, there can be eventual destruction of the corpora cavernosa so that future erection becomes impossible. Peyronie's disease occurs primarily in older males and involves the development of tough, fibrous tissue around the corpora cavernosa within the penis. There may be eventual calcification of this tissue. The disease results in curvature of the penis and painful erection, both of which can make intercourse impossible (Horton & Devine, 1975).

Particularly vigorous stimulation to the penis during sexual activity can sometimes inflame lymphatic vessels, creating a swollen band around the penile shaft, just behind the glans. While this condition may be alarming to men, it is not dangerous, and generally the swelling gradually subsides over a few weeks (Sieunarine, 1987). Use of ringlike devices to maintain erection can damage penile tissues and blood vessels, especially if they are left on too long. If damage occurs, extensive surgical treatment may be required (Stoller, Lue, & McAninch, 1987).

Cancer of the penis is quite rare, and there is a possibility that it is even less common in circumcised males. Although the hypothesis is open to debate, it has been suggested that the accumulation of secretions and impurities under the foreskin of uncircumcised males may predispose them to malignant growth on their penises. Careful attention to cleanliness and personal hygiene is, therefore, particularly important to uncircumcised males. Testicular cancer is also relatively rare and is usually noticeable as a bump or irregularity on the surface of one testis. In about half of the cases there is some pain. For directions on testicular self-examination, see chapter 2, "Sexual Systems."

There are a number of congenital conditions of the penis. Occasionally a male child is born with agenesis (absence) of the penis, in which the phallus is very tiny and nonfunctional. In such rare cases it is not unusual to have the child surgically modified to have femalelike genitals and then raise it as a girl. There is little research to indicate how these individuals feel about themselves, or if they experience confusion in their gender-identity/role. For the nonsurgically treated boy with penile agenesis, counseling may be necessary to aid in the sexual adjustments of adolescence and adulthood. There are two congenital conditions resulting from difficulties in fetal development of the penis: hypospadias and epispadias. Hypospadias is an incompletely fused penis, with an open "gutter" extending along the underside of the penis instead of an internal urethra. In epispadias the urinary bladder empties through a large opening in the abdomen, and the penis is split open along its upper length. Both hypospadias and epispadias require surgical repair, although the penis may not be fully functional for intercourse following the surgery (Anhalt & Carlton, 1973). Sometimes a child is born with an abnormally long foreskin covering the end of his penis, a condition called phimosis. This can make retraction of the foreskin back from the glans painful or impossible, and circumcision of the foreskin is necessary to correct the phimosis.

There are also several disorders of the testes. In very rare cases both testes are completely lacking at birth, a disorder known as anorchism. A more common problem is cryptorchidism, in which the testes have not descended into the scrotum before birth. This condition usually corrects itself within a few years, but if not, it must be corrected by the time of puberty through hormonal or surgical treatment. If only one testis is present in the scrotum, the condition is termed monorchidism. However, one testis can easily handle the work of two, producing sufficient quantities of male hormones and sperm. Occasionally a male suffers from testicular failure, in which the testes do not produce male hormones and/or sperm. The condition usually responds to some form of hormonal therapy.

If a man experiences prolonged sexual arousal without having an orgasm, the testes may become

---

priapism (pry-AE-pizm): continual, undesired, and painful erection of the penis.

Peyronie's disease (pay-ra-NEEZ): development of fibrous tissue in spongy erectile columns within the penis.

testicular cancer: malignancy on the testis that may be detected by testicular self-examination.

agenesis (absence) of the penis (ae-JEN-a-ses): a congenital condition in which the penis is undersized and nonfunctional.

hypospadias (hye-pa-SPADE-ee-as): birth defect caused by incomplete closure of the urethra during fetal development.

epispadias (ep-a-SPADE-ee-as): birth defect in which the urinary bladder empties through an abdominal opening, and the urethra is malformed.

phimosis (fye-MOE-sus): abnormally long, tight foreskin on the penis.

anorchism (a-NOR-kiz-um): rare birth defect in which both testes are lacking.

cryptorchidism (krip-TOR-ka-diz-um): condition in which the testes have not descended into the scrotum prior to birth.

monorchidism (ma-NOR-ka-dizm): presence of only one testis in the scrotum.

testicular failure: lack of sperm and/or hormone production by the testes.

swollen, tender, and painful due to their long-term congestion with blood. The vas deferens may also become irritated, causing pain that extends up through the pubic area and lower abdomen. In slang this condition is often called "lover's nuts," "blue balls," or "stone ache." It is not dangerous or permanently damaging—only uncomfortable. It is also much less common than usually believed.

DISORDERS OF THE FEMALE SEX ORGANS

The female sex and urinary organs may be the sites of infection not transmitted in sexual ways. Bladder infection, or cystitis, is a common complaint and is a recurrent problem for 10–15 percent of women. The symptoms include frequent urge to urinate, burning or pain on urination, and possibly severe pain during sexual intercourse or when the bladder is placed under pressure. Medical professionals frequently fail to recognize bladder disease as the cause of such symptoms, and may assume that the woman is imagining the problem (McCormick, 1990). Antibiotics and other medications may be used for treatment. Since one of the most common bacteria to cause cystitis is *E. coli* (short for *Escherichia coli*), the organism that lives in the colon and is found in feces, good personal hygiene is the best preventative measure. Wiping from front to back after a bowel movement is always advisable, as is frequent washing of the vaginal and anal areas. Drinking plenty of liquids and urinating frequently is another good precaution. Washing and urinating after sexual activity is important in cleansing the urethral area of any bacteria that might cause cystitis. Of particular concern is the possibility of a bladder infection spreading to the kidneys, where the condition can be far more serious and even life-threatening (Nelson, 1984).

The vagina can be subject to several disorders. It can undergo vaginal atrophy, in which the inner surfaces of the vagina shrink and narrow; this occurs more often in older women as the result of lowered estrogen levels (Rayner, 1986). Sometimes during pregnancy varicose veins can develop in the vulva, surrounding the vagina; this leads to an aching, heavy sensation in the pelvis. The hymen present in the vaginal opening may cause problems. Occasionally the hymen is imperforate, meaning that there are no openings in it. When a woman begins to menstruate, the menstrual flow builds up in the vagina and uterus, causing pain and swelling. If a physician makes an incision in the imperforate hymen, the condition is quickly relieved. Occasionally, too, the hymen is especially thick and tough, a condition called fibrous hymen. This will interfere with sexual activity and must be treated surgically. Many women who experi-

ence pain during sexual activity may have problems with the hymen. Such difficulties are often not diagnosed by physicians, and the pain may be dismissed as psychosomatic (Brashear & Munsick, 1991).

There are several congenital abnormalities that may affect female sex organs. Vaginal atresia is the absence or closure of the vagina, often not discovered until puberty. In such cases there can be a surgical construction of a vaginal passageway to permit sexual intercourse or other sexual activity, although the constructed passageway does not usually permit vaginal delivery when giving birth. Sometimes two vaginas may be present at birth. There are also a number of conditions that involve a malformation or absence of the uterus, fallopian tubes, or ovaries, all variably treatable by surgery or hormones. There are sometimes vaginal fistulae—or abnormal openings—that connect the bladder, urethra, or rectum with the vagina; all of these usually require surgical treatment. Hypospadias and epispadias involving incomplete closure of the urethra and urinary tract during fetal development occur in females as in males, but usually do not require surgical correction unless they are associated with an inability to retain urine or feces (Anhalt & Carlton, 1973).

Cancer of the cervix is a common type of malignancy in women, second in frequency only to cancer of the breast. Uterine cancer occurs with about half the frequency of cervical malignancies. These cancers are particularly dangerous because there may be no symptoms for several years. The Pap smear test, which should be a routine part of a woman's annual physical examination, microscopically examines a smear of cervical mucus. It can detect cancerous or precancerous cells, indicating that the condition should be surgically treated or kept under observation. There are two stages of cancer that may be detected in a Pap smear. One is cervical intraepithelial neoplasia (CIN),

cystitis (sis-TITE-us): a nonsexually transmitted infection of the urinary bladder.

E. coli: bacteria naturally living in the human colon, often causes urinary tract infection.

vaginal atrophy: shrinking and deterioration of vaginal lining, usually the result of low estrogen levels during aging.

varicose veins: overexpanded blood vessels; can occur in veins surrounding the vagina.

imperforate hymen: lack of any openings in the hymen.

fibrous hymen: unnaturally thick, tough tissue composing the hymen.

vaginal atresia (a-TREE-zha): birth defect in which the vagina is absent or closed.

vaginal fistulae (FISH-cha-lee *or* -lie): abnormal channels that can develop between the vagina and other internal organs.

cervical intraepithelial neoplasia (CIN) (ep-a-THEE-lee-al nee-a-PLAY-zhee-a): abnormal, precancerous cells sometimes identified in a Pap smear.

391

(continued on p. 394)

Causes of Pain in Sexual Intercourse

When sexual intercourse causes pain . . . , the effects on the partners and the relationship can be devastating. The partner who is in pain is likely to avoid sexual activity, and the other partner is likely to feel guilty and reluctant to inflict pain by attempting intercourse. Both partners may end up frustrated and resentful as well as confused when an activity purported to bring joy to so many turns out to be so discomforting. . . .

In decades past, both the public and professionals widely believed that pain in sex, medically termed dyspaneuria, was rooted in a person's psyche. Consciously or subconsciously, the person was thought to be resisting sexual pleasure. Among the explanations proffered were long-standing parental or religious proscriptions that were difficult to overcome, a lack of interest in or dislike for one's partner, and unspoken resentments about the relationship.

But in recent years studies of human sexual response and the development of scientific sex therapy have revealed otherwise. It is now known that in more than half of the people who find sexual intercourse painful, there is an underlying anatomical cause or physical illness that can usually be treated. In perhaps 30 percent, sexual pain is the indirect result of sexual ignorance or ineptitude, most often reversible through education or sex therapy. Even when emotional factors—in the remaining 15 to 20 percent of cases—are the sole problem, most can be resolved through sexual, marital or psychological therapy.

It is also now widely recognized—among professionals, at least—that pain in intercourse is not just a woman's complaint but also afflicts men, though much less frequently. Sex therapists estimate that 15 percent of women experience pain during sex at varying times, and for 1 to 2 percent it is a chronic problem. The following are the most common causes of sexual pain:

Vaginal Dryness

This is the most common, and most easily corrected, problem for women. Though most frequent in postmenopausal women who have lost the vaginal stimulation of natural estrogen, vaginal dryness can afflict women of all ages for varying reasons.

Ordinarily, during sexual arousal, the walls of the vagina sweat, providing lubrication that eases penile penetration. However, sufficient lubrication may not occur when arousal is inhibited by fear, for example, or by inadequate precoital stimulation. Lubrication may also be inadequate when a woman is nursing, immediately after a menstrual period, during or after menopause (natural or surgical), after pelvic radiation therapy, during treatment with antihistamines or other decongestants, while a woman pursues a grueling exercise regimen or when she is under undue stress.

For women lacking sufficient hormonal stimulation, estrogen replacement therapy usually solves the problem. When the cause of vaginal dryness cannot be corrected, there are a number of water-soluble lubricants sold over-the-counter. The most effective are products that can be inserted into the vagina, either as a suppository or through a plunger-type applicator. Use of lubricated condoms also helps. If a particular product causes an allergic reaction or irritation, try another. However, avoid oil-based lubricants like baby oil or petroleum jelly, which can only make the problem worse by clogging the pores of the vagina.

Infection and Irritation

The explosive increase in sexually transmitted diseases, including vaginal yeast (candida), trichomonas, chlamydia and herpes, many of which can be passed back and forth between a symptom-free man and a woman, have made this a prominent cause of sexual discomfort. Women with vaginal infections commonly experience burning, irritation and even bleeding as a result of intercourse. Men with penile lesions also find sexual contact and friction painful.

Other causes of vaginal irritation can include medicated douches, feminine hygiene sprays, deodorant tampons, contraceptive foams and creams, and rough objects used for stimulation. Use of superabsorbant tampons or removal of a dry tampon can also cause vaginal irritation.

When intercourse irritates the urethra or bladder, a change in coital position may help. If a urinary tract infection is present, it should be treated with antibiotics. Many women find it helpful to empty the bladder just before and immediately after intercourse and to increase their fluid intake. In some men, the tip of the penis may be irritated during intercourse by the tail of an intrauterine device.

When a genital infection is present, both partners should be treated simultaneously with appropriate antibiotics. Men with prostate infections or enlargement, which can cause pain in arousal or orgasm, are often helped by antibiotics, warm sitz baths and periodic prostatic massage by a physician. Increasing the frequency of sexual activity and avoiding overly long arousal or frequent arousal without release may also reduce prostatic congestion.

Other treatable disorders that can cause painful intercourse include pelvic inflammatory disease, skin problems affecting the vulva, endometriosis (abnormal growth of uterine tissues) and ovarian cysts. In men, the treatable disorders include infections of the seminal vesicles, diseases of the testicles and dermatological problems or shingles that may cause penile lesions.

Other Problems

The problem of an inpenetrable hymen in a woman has received a great deal of attention. This tissue may cover most of the vaginal opening and may not tear open easily or may leave behind a tag of tissue, causing pain when penetration is attempted. These problems can be corrected with minor surgery. In some women, a vagina may not have properly formed, necessitating surgical correction.

Injuries may occur in childbirth that interfere with a woman's sexual comfort. Among them are tender scars from an episiotomy (an incision of the vulva), perianal tears (around the anus), and a dropping, or prolapse, of the uterus too far into the vagina. A hysterectomy may leave scar tissue that causes pelvic pain during intercourse. For women with a bladder that protrudes into the vagina, causing pain during intercourse, estrogen therapy and perineal squeeze exercises (Kegel's exercises) may bring relief.

Anatomical problems in men that can interfere with sexual pleasure include fracture of the penis and sickle cell disease, both of which could cause painful erection, and Peyronie's disease, a hardening of penile blood vessels that may result in a permanent erection at a distorted angle. Men may also experience pain or distress during intercourse if they suffer from back problems or arthritis of the hip, or if sexual erection causes chest pains or respiratory difficulties.

Perhaps the most widely known cause of sexual pain is spasm of the vaginal muscles (vaginismus), once incorrectly labeled frigidity. In fact, these spasms can occur in women who are highly stimulated and desirous of sex. Sometimes vaginismus occurs only after a woman develops a problem that causes sex to hurt. In nearly all cases, the condition can be corrected by therapy in which the woman learns to relax the muscles.

Men, too, may experience genital muscle spasms, causing pain during or after ejaculation. The pain, which can be so intense that it is disabling, may last for minutes, hours or even days. As with vaginismus in women, this problem is usually emotional in origin and responds well to therapy.

—Jane E. Brody, "New Understanding on Dealing With Problems of Pain in Sexual Intercourse," *New York Times,* March 10, 1988.

Case Study

AMANDA: LIVING WITH ENDOMETRIOSIS

From the time she was 14 years old, Amanda had experienced cramping with her menstrual periods. Her mother had reassured her that the discomfort was a normal part of her monthly cycle. During her college years, it seemed to her that the pain was worsening. She would sometimes be unable to attend classes because of her cramps. She continued to assume that it was something she would just have to put up with. Her boyfriend sometimes became annoyed with her and felt that she must be exaggerating.

During a particularly difficult bout with menstrual cramping, she visited the student health clinic. The physician told her that one possibility was a chlamydial infection and did the appropriate testing. When the test was negative, and a complete history of her symptoms taken, a tentative diagnosis of endometriosis was made. She was given a prescription for a medication called a prostaglandin inhibitor and another prescription for birth control pills. Both were known to reduce pain and slow the progress of endometriosis. Amanda was also told that a surgical examination using a laparoscope would be the only way to make a definitive diagnosis, but the

physician recommended that she give the medications a try for several months. The doctor indicated that if Amanda actually had endometriosis, and hoped to have children eventually, she should consider pregnancy as early in her life as would be practical. The complications of the disease increase with age and can eventually make conception and pregnancy difficult or impossible.

Amanda continued to have regular checkups with the student health service and later with her own gynecologist. The symptoms of cramping were greatly relieved by the medication. In her early thirties, she began to have increasing difficulties and finally had a laparoscopic procedure. This confirmed the presence of endometriosis, and several areas of thick endometrial growth were removed by electrical cauterization at that time. Amanda had two pregnancies after this procedure and then decided she would have no more children.

While her endometriosis is under control for the time being, she has been told there is a possibility that further and more extensive surgery might be necessary in the future.

in which precancerous or early cancer cells are found. They are still confined to the cervix and can be treated easily. Pap smears of about 15 percent of teenage girls who have had sexual intercourse show evidence of CIN (Hillard, 1988). The more advanced and dangerous malignancy is invasive cancer of the cervix (ICC), which must be treated promptly and with whatever techniques necessary to reduce the risk of its spreading to other organs. Early treatment of uterine and cervical cancer is highly successful, but if the cancer is allowed to invade other surrounding tissues it may be far more dangerous. Studies show that there is a higher incidence of cervical cancer among women who have been sexually active with several men and have had children than among those who have not. The reasons for this correlation are not well understood at present. Cervical cancer and other abnormalities have been found to be more common in women whose mothers were given the synthetic estrogen compound diethylstilbestrol (DES) during pregnancy. DES was used from the 1940s through 1971 in pregnancies where

miscarriage was a high risk. Women whose mothers were administered DES during pregnancy should receive frequent pelvic examinations to detect any potential problems (Meyers, 1983).

Tumors of the ovaries—both malignant and benign—are also common in women. Nonmalignant growths in the uterus are often found as well.

The uterus can be the site of numerous disorders. Hormonal imbalances may lead to abnormal and profuse bleeding from the uterus. Often such conditions are accompanied by excessive growth of the inner uterine lining (endometrium), a condition called endometrial hyperplasia. It may have a variety of causes. A

invasive cancer of the cervix (ICC): advanced and dangerous malignancy requiring prompt treatment.

diethylstilbestrol (DES) (dye-eth-a-stil-BES-trole): synthetic estrogen compound given to mothers whose pregnancies are at high risk of miscarrying.

endometrial hyperplasia (hy-per-PLAY-zhee-a): excessive growth of the inner lining of the uterus (endometrium).

similar disorder is <u>endometriosis</u>, occurring in 10–15 percent of premenopausal women in which the uterine lining grows outward into the organs surrounding the uterus. This typically causes pain, abnormal menstrual bleeding, and sometimes sterility (Nelson, 1985). The cervix may also become irritated or infected, leading to a gradual erosion of cervical tissues.

The uterus is sometimes displaced from its usual position in the abdomen, often called "tipped uterus." Unless there is pain connected with the displacement, there is no particular need for surgical intervention. Uterine displacement apparently has no effect on the woman's ability to become pregnant or give birth naturally.

Occasionally the ligaments that support the uterus become weakened to the extent that the uterus drops down and protrudes too far into the vagina. This is called <u>prolapse of the uterus</u>. Prolapse may cause serious discomfort and require surgery.

When women experience prolonged sexual arousal without having an orgasm, their ovaries may become swollen and congested, leading to pain and feelings of fullness. The vulva may also become congested and painful by such activity. In former times this discomfort was often called "engagement ovaries." Like testicular discomfort following prolonged arousal, ovarian and vulval discomfort is not particularly common.

SEXUAL EFFECTS OF DEBILITATING ILLNESSES

Because sexuality is a part of the whole person, anything that affects physical or psychological health and well-being can have implications for sexual functioning as well. Unfortunately, health professionals often fail to assess the sexual implications of various illnesses and discuss these aspects with their patients. They may feel personally uncomfortable talking about sex with patients or be concerned about creating undue embarrassment in them. Especially in long-standing chronic illnesses, or in acute illnesses that create serious debilitation, careful sexual assessment should be an integral part of total health care (Hanson & Brouse, 1983). The partners of patients often are dealing with difficult emotional issues as well, which may affect their sexual attitudes and functioning. It has been recommended that partners be included in sexual assessment and counseling procedures when a serious illness is being treated (Schover, Evans, & Von Eschenbach, 1987).

Treatments for some illnesses, such as medication for blood pressure or chemotherapy for cancer, can have direct effects on sexual functioning. A study of

100 patients hospitalized for a variety of illnesses examined their degree of satisfaction with the level of sex-related information given them. About half of the patients felt that their illnesses might interfere, or already had, with their sexual lives, and the majority of them expressed worry and frustration about that possibility. Yet only 30 percent of the patients had heard any mention of sexual issues from their doctors or the hospital staff (Young, 1984).

Among the diseases most frequently found to have adverse effects on sexual functioning are neurological disorders such as multiple sclerosis or stroke, diabetes, cardiovascular disease and heart attacks, chronic lung disease, cancer and its treatments, and arthritis (Hanson & Brouse, 1983).

Cardiac patients, for example, often are concerned about the amount of physical exertion that is safe for them during sexual activity. This can lead to psychological pressures that can in turn produce sexual dysfunctions. Erection problems are particularly common in men who have heart disease. Health workers can gradually encourage post–heart-attack patients to get back in touch with their sexual feelings, even suggesting masturbation when the individual is physically ready for any exertion. Later, specific suggestions can be given for shared sexual activity, at first using positions requiring a lesser degree of physical strain and energy. With reassurance and education, most cardiac patients can reestablish full sexual lives (Pachtman & Southern, 1984).

Diabetes is known to cause some physical complications that can directly interfere with sexual activity. Two of the most commonly reported problems are difficulty having an erection in men and some degree of vaginal dryness and its associated discomfort in women. Physically based complaints of this sort then have their psychological spinoffs as well. People begin to feel sexually inadequate and fear failure during their sexual interactions. In turn, new pressures are created on communication within their relationships. Often, these difficulties can be alleviated by intervention from health professionals who are sensitive to the sex-related implications of diabetes (Pieper et al., 1983; Whitley & Berke, 1983).

Mental illness may also adversely affect one's sexual activities. The emotional disruption of mental illness often leads to lack of interest in sex and loss of the ability to be sexually responsive. However, it has also been noted that many mentally ill people still have sexual needs and wish to pursue sexual activity. In

endometriosis (en-doe-mee-tree-O-sus): growth of the endometrium out of the uterus into surrounding organs.
prolapse of the uterus: weakening of the supportive ligaments of the uterus, causing it to protrude into the vagina.

institutional settings, it may be that mentally ill persons who seem especially preoccupied with sex simply are searching for human warmth and closeness. Activities such as masturbation may become ways for mental patients to control anxiety, affirm the existence of their bodies, or safely act out their sexual fantasies (Skopec, Rosenberg, & Tucker, 1976).

Increasingly, health professionals are realizing the importance of exploring sex-related issues with their patients. It is to be hoped that assessment of potential sexual effects of various illnesses will soon become a standard and accepted part of medical evaluation and treatment. ■

SAFE SEX

SELF-EVALUATION

Examining Your Attitudes Toward STDs

The following scale will give you an opportunity to explore some of your own beliefs, feelings, and intentions with regard to sexually transmitted diseases. The scale was developed by Yarber, Torabi, and Veenker (1989) and has been tested with hundreds of college and secondary school students. The evaluation is for your own use only.

Directions: Please read each statement carefully. *STD* means sexually transmitted disease, once called venereal disease. Record your first reaction by marking an "X" through the letter that best describes how much you agree or disagree with the idea.

USE THIS KEY: SA = Strongly Agree
A = Agree
U = Undecided
D = Disagree
SD = Strongly Disagree

Example: Doing things to prevent getting an STD   SA A U D SD
is the job of each person.

396   REMEMBER: STD means sexually transmitted disease, such as gonorrhea, syphilis, genital herpes, or AIDS.

	(Mark "X" through letter)

1. How one uses his/her sexuality has nothing to do with STD.   SA A U D SD

2. It is easy to use the prevention methods that reduce one's chances of getting an STD.   SA A U D SD

3. Responsible sex is one of the best ways of reducing the risk of STD.   SA A U D SD

4. Getting early medical care is the main key to preventing harmful effects of STD.   SA A U D SD

5. Choosing the right sex partner is important in reducing the risk of getting an STD.   SA A U D SD

6. A high rate of STD should be a concern for all people.   SA A U D SD

7. People with an STD have a duty to get their sex partners to medical care.   SA A U D SD

8. The best way to get a sex partner to STD treatment is to take him/her to the doctor with you.   SA A U D SD

9. Changing one's sex habits is necessary once the presence of an STD is known.   SA A U D SD

10. I would dislike having to follow the medical steps for treating an STD.   SA A U D SD

11. If I were sexually active, I would feel uneasy doing things before and after sex to prevent getting an STD.   SA A U D SD

12. If I were sexually active, it would be insulting if a sex partner suggested we use a condom to avoid STD.   SA A U D SD

13. I dislike talking about STD with my peers.   SA A U D SD

14. I would be uncertain about going to the doctor unless I was sure I really had an STD.   SA A U D SD

15. I would feel that I should take my sex partner with me to a clinic if I thought I had an STD.   SA A U D SD

16. It would be embarrassing to discuss STD with one's partner if one were sexually active.   SA A U D SD

17. If I were to have sex, the chance of getting an STD makes me uneasy about having sex with more than one person.   SA A U D SD

18. I like the idea of sexual abstinence (not having sex) as the best way of avoiding STD.   SA A U D SD

19. If I had an STD, I would cooperate with public health persons to find the sources of STD.   SA A U D SD

20. If I had an STD, I would avoid exposing others while I was being treated.   SA A U D SD

21. I would have regular STD checkups if I were having sex with more than one partner.   SA A U D SD

22. I intend to look for STD signs before deciding to have sex with anyone.   SA A U D SD

23. I will limit my sex activity to just one partner because of the chances I might get an STD.   SA A U D SD

24. I will avoid sex contact anytime I think there is even a slight chance of getting an STD.   SA A U D SD

25. The chance of getting an STD would not stop me from having sex.   SA A U D SD

26. If I had a chance, I would support community efforts toward controlling STD.   SA A U D SD

27. I would be willing to work with others to make people aware of STD problems in my town.   SA A U D SD

Scoring: Calculate total points for each subscale and total scale, using the point values below.

For items 1, 10–14, 16, 25

Strongly Agree = 5 points
Agree = 4 points
Undecided = 3 points
Disagree = 2 points
Strongly Disagree = 1 point

For items 2–9, 15, 17–24, 26, 27

Strongly Agree = 1 point
Agree = 2 points
Undecided = 3 points
Disagree = 4 points
Strongly Disagree = 5 points

Total Scale: items 1–27
Belief Subscale: items 1–9
Feeling Subscale: items 10–18
Intention to Act Subscale: items 19–27

Interpretation: The higher your score, the higher your risk of behavior that can spread sexually transmitted diseases.

CHAPTER SUMMARY

1. Sexually transmitted diseases have caused much human misery throughout the centuries and continue to represent serious health problems today. The development of penicillin was a major step in conquering some STDs, but several of these diseases are spreading in epidemic proportions.

2. Gonorrhea can be spread through vaginal, anal, and oral sexual contact, and infects around 2 million people each year. The eyes of babies are vulnerable to infection during birth and are routinely treated to prevent gonorrheal blindness. A new penicillin-resistant strain of the gonorrhea bacterium has worried health officials.

3. Syphilis can be particularly dangerous in its later stage, and the prevalence of the disease tends to vary over time. Throughout the 1980s it infected an average of 40,000 people each year in the United States.

4. The large proportion of the population infected with the *Chlamydia* organism was not recognized until the mid-1980s. It is the cause of many different forms of genital and urinary tract infections in both men and women, and can cause infertility.

5. Nongonococcal urethritis has been steadily increasing as an STD problem in males. Even though its symptoms may be mild, and disappear without treatment, the causative organisms can persist in the body. Therefore, seeking prompt medical treatment for NGU is essential.

6. Vaginal inflammation may be caused by bacteria, yeast organisms, or trichomonads. Taking proper hygienic measures and keeping the vulval area dry can reduce the risk of contracting vaginitis.

7. Genital herpes reached epidemic proportions during the 1980s and probably has infected at least 30 million people. Once the virus has infected the body, it can cause recurrent outbreaks of the lesions. The disease has been associated with a higher incidence of cervical and vulval cancer in women and can be dangerous to newborn infants.

8. Genital warts (condylomata acuminata) may also be associated with a higher incidence of cervical cancer. The warts infect up to 3 million people annually in the United States.

9. Viral hepatitis can be a serious liver infection, although it is not always transmitted sexually.

10. Pubic lice must be thoroughly treated to ensure that all insects and their eggs have been eliminated from bodily hairs.

11. Lymphogranuloma venereum, chancroid, and granuloma inguinale are sexually transmitted diseases that are more common in tropical climates. They can generally be effectively treated with antibiotics.

12. Two skin diseases that may be transmitted by the intimate bodily contact of sex are molluscum contagiosum and scabies.

13. Part of responsible sexual decision-making is to take appropriate measures to prevent the transmis-

sion of STDs. Considering abstinence, avoiding penetration, avoiding multiple partners, knowing partners, and using condoms and spermicides are among the best preventative precautions. If infected, prompt medical treatment is essential, as is telling any potentially infected partners.

14. Epididymitis is an inflammation of the epididymis in the testes.

15. Prostatitis, or prostate infection, can be either acute or chronic. A common problem in older men is prostate enlargement, sometimes caused by malignant tumors. Since enlargement can restrict urinary flow, it must be corrected, usually by surgery.

16. Some diseases that can affect the penis are priapism (painful, continuous erection); Peyronie's disease (calcification of erectile tissue); cancer; and phimosis (too-tight foreskin). Testicular cancer can often be detected early by regular self-examination.

17. Cystitis, or bladder infection, is common in women, often caused by the *E. coli* bacterium.

18. The vagina is subject to several medical conditions, including atrophy because of lowered estrogen levels, varicose veins, and fistulae (openings between the vagina and other organs).

19. The hymen may cause sexual difficulties if it is imperforate (having no openings) or tough and fibrous.

20. Pap smears offer the possibility of early detection for cervical cancer or precancerous cells in the cervix, called cervical intraepithelial neoplasia (CIN). Untreated cervical cancer may become invasive cervical cancer (ICC). Women whose mothers were given DES during pregnancy have a higher risk of cancer and other cervical abnormalities.

21. The uterus may be affected by hormonal imbalances, leading to abnormal bleeding, overgrowth of its lining either in the form of endometrial hyperplasia or endometriosis, or prolapse into the vagina.

22. Any disease that affects general physical health or mental well-being can affect sexual functioning. The medical profession is becoming more aware of the need to evaluate possible sexual implications of diseases.

23. Neurological disorders, diabetes, heart disease and heart attacks, chronic lung disease, cancer, and arthritis often affect the way patients view themselves sexually and their sexual functioning.

ANNOTATED READINGS

Davis, M., & Scott, R. S. (1988). *Lovers, doctors and the law*. New York: Harper & Row. A practical guide to legal issues relating to the transmission of STDs, this book details individuals' rights and responsibilities in sexual matters.

Holmes, K. K., et al. (1990). *Sexually transmitted diseases*. New York: McGraw-Hill. One of the most comprehensive texts available on STDs, this book provides detailed information about all such diseases. It is one of the best references available.

Langston, D. P. (1983). *Living with herpes*. Garden City, NY: Doubleday. A comprehensive book about the causes, symptoms, and treatment of herpes illnesses. It dispels many myths and offers reassurance.

Lumiere, R., & Cook, S. (1983). *Healthy sex and keeping it that way*. New York: Simon & Schuster. A handy guide to the sex organs and their health, including the various diseases that can affect them. While it was published when AIDS was just appearing, the other information is excellent.

Ortiz, E. T. (1989). *Your complete guide to sexual health*. Englewood Cliffs, NJ: Prentice Hall/Simon & Schuster. A basic reference work on common concerns about sexual and reproductive health that includes lists of resources and references.

Schover, L., & Jensen, S. B. (1988). *Sexuality and chronic illness*. New York: Guilford Press. A comprehensive guide to the effects chronic illnesses can have on sexual feelings and functioning. It deals with many issues that are often ignored or avoided by health-care professionals.

CHAPTER FIFTEEN

THE EVOLUTION OF A NEW DISEASE
  The Origin of AIDS
  Discovery of HIV
  Statistics on the Prevalence of AIDS and HIV
    Infection
  Risks of Infection

HIV: THE INFECTION AND THE VIRUS
  Mechanism of HIV Action
  How HIV Is Spread
  Does Infection With HIV Mean AIDS?

HIV TESTING, TREATMENT, AND VACCINES
  Controversy Over HIV Testing
  Treatment for HIV-Infected Persons
  Vaccines for HIV

AIDS AND SOCIETY
  Individual Freedom vs. Public Health Interests
  Other Ethical Issues and AIDS
  Witch-Hunting Mentality

AIDS AND PERSONAL DECISIONS ABOUT SEX
  AIDS and HIV Education
  Can Sex Be Safe and Satisfying?
  Minimizing the Sexual Risks of Contracting HIV

CONCLUSION

CHAPTER SUMMARY

It's real hard for me to trust a lot of men enough to have sex with them right now. Most of them seem to think they could only have been exposed to AIDS if they were gay. I know that's not true. I'm a twenty-three-year-old woman, and I don't think there are too many male virgins around in my age bracket. I'm going to be a lot more careful about my sexual partners, if I have any at all for awhile.

—Statement made in a human sexuality course

THE AIDS CRISIS AND SEXUAL DECISIONS

The AIDS epidemic has now entered its second decade. More than any new disease to appear in recent history, it is lethal and it continues to spread. Some public health officials are quietly concerned; others are predicting serious consequences in years to come. Everybody who knows anything about acquired immunodeficiency syndrome, better known as AIDS, is taking the threat of the disease seriously. Not since Jonas Salk developed a vaccine in 1955 for the dreaded paralytic poliomyelitis have we felt so threatened by a disease. Although there was a scare about the outbreak of swine influenza in 1976, it did not manifest itself; we had been lulled into a sense of calm and complacency about epidemic diseases until now.

Human immunodeficiency virus (HIV), the virus that eventually produces AIDS when it infects humans, has raised political and economic issues; it has unleashed prejudice, especially homophobia and racism. HIV is also changing how people approach their sexual activities and decision-making. A sexual revolution is in the making that may dwarf any changes in attitudes and values that came about in the 1960s and 1970s.

Science is only beginning to piece together the many puzzles that HIV and AIDS present. I have tried in this chapter to bring together the best information available, but since research into this disease is one of the most active areas in science today, new information is continually replacing old. Therefore, it is crucial for you to inform yourselves of any new findings. This is now, more than ever before, an essential component of being a sexually responsible individual. It may be your health and well-being, or your very life, at stake.

The Evolution of a New Disease

It was in the summer of 1981 that a newsletter published by the U.S. Public Health Service's Centers for Disease Control (CDC) ran a brief story about an outbreak of rare cancers and lung diseases in five

acquired immunodeficiency syndrome: fatal disease caused by a virus that is transmitted through the exchange of bodily fluids, primarily in sexual activity and intravenous drug use.
AIDS: acquired immunodeficiency syndrome.
human immunodeficiency virus: the virus that initially attacks the human immune system, eventually causing AIDS.
HIV: human immunodeficiency virus.
homophobia: irrational fear of homosexuals.

401

Source: *HIV/AIDS Surveillance*, August 1991, Rockville, MD: U.S. Department of Health and Human Services, Centers for Disease Control.

FIGURE 15.1   Incidence of AIDS in the United States (through July 1991)

AIDS is a global epidemic. Although underreporting continues to be a problem in developing countries, the World Health Organization estimates there have been about 1 million cases worldwide. In the United States, the total number of cases reported as of mid-1991 was just over 180,000, with New York, Los Angeles, and San Francisco having the highest incidence of the disease.

youthful homosexuals in San Francisco. Similar reports soon started to appear in other cities. The *New England Journal of Medicine* carried several articles later that same year describing symptoms that appeared in a number of homosexual men and users of intravenous drugs who shared needles. One of the things that all of these individuals seemed to have in common was an apparent weakness in their immune systems, the collection of mechanisms with which the body wards off disease. The patients experienced long periods of ill health while their bodies struggled to fight various bacteria, protozoa, and viruses. Eventually, the infections would become more tenacious and rare, finally resulting in death (Nelkin et al., 1991). The CDC soon labeled the new and puzzling disorder acquired immunodeficiency syndrome. Before long, it became clear that AIDS could be transmitted between people and that it was frighteningly lethal.

No one knows for certain how long this disease has been around. It may be that in earlier years, people who actually died of AIDS were diagnosed as having died of one of the many infections that the disease produces, or that medical personnel simply had no way of knowing what they were dealing with. A case

recently came to light in England of a sailor who had died in 1959 of symptoms we would now connect with AIDS. Physicians had been confounded by the case, and kept preserved tissue samples from the sailor's body in hopes that they might eventually understand his disease more thoroughly. In 1990 tests of these tissues confirmed that the sailor had AIDS, making this the oldest documented case of the disease. It has been suggested that many other such cases probably exist, but it is unusual for tissue or blood samples to be kept for an extended length of time (Altman, 1990).

While it has generally been believed that the AIDS virus did not reach the United States until the mid-1970s, another historical case has interested medical investigators. In May, 1969, a 15-year-old boy died in St. Louis after a year-long decline in his health. Doctors were so puzzled by his illnesses that they kept samples of his blood and tissues. In late 1987 tests showed the presence of the AIDS virus in his blood. Although a complete sexual history was not taken from the boy, there was evidence that he could have been a homosexual prostitute. This development has further confused experts about how and when the virus made its way to this country.

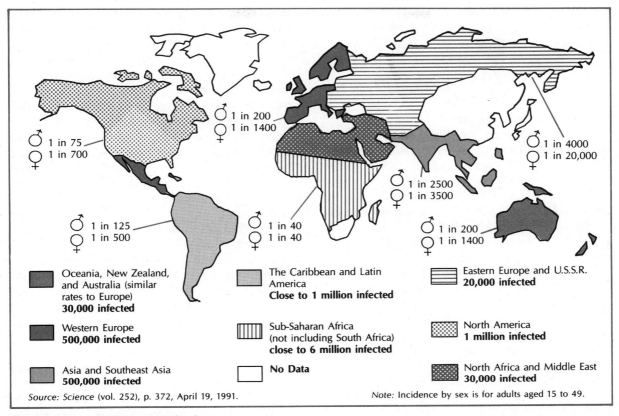

♂ 1 in 75
♀ 1 in 700

♂ 1 in 200
♀ 1 in 1400

♂ 1 in 4000
♀ 1 in 20,000

♂ 1 in 125
♀ 1 in 500

♂ 1 in 40
♀ 1 in 40

♂ 1 in 2500
♀ 1 in 3500

♂ 1 in 200
♀ 1 in 1400

Oceania, New Zealand, and Australia (similar rates to Europe)
30,000 infected

The Caribbean and Latin America
Close to 1 million infected

Eastern Europe and U.S.S.R.
20,000 infected

Western Europe
500,000 infected

Sub-Saharan Africa (not including South Africa)
close to 6 million infected

North America
1 million infected

Asia and Southeast Asia
500,000 infected

No Data

North Africa and Middle East
30,000 infected

Source: Science (vol. 252), p. 372, April 19, 1991.

Note: Incidence by sex is for adults aged 15 to 49.

FIGURE 15.2 Global HIV Infections

Although sub-Saharan Africa still has the most HIV infections, other regions of the world appear to be catching up.

THE ORIGIN OF AIDS

When a new disease appears on the scene, there is always interest in determining how it originated. Although it is often impossible to trace the origins of any illness, speculating on its evolution may sometimes have important implications for seeking a treatment and cure. The predominant theory—although it remains only a theory—about the origin of HIV is that the virus first attacked humans in central Africa sometime between 20 and 100 years ago. It may have remained isolated in small, remote societies for years until changing ways of African life brought it to urban centers, from which it was then transported to the rest of the world by infected persons (Potts, 1990).

There is evidence to support this theory, based on research that turned up a very similar virus in wild African green monkeys. It has been suggested that the virus somehow crossed the species barrier and mutated so that it became infectious to humans. In support of this theory, blood samples taken from prostitutes in Senegal in West Africa contained a virus that was more closely related to the one infecting monkeys than it was to the HIV present in eastern and central Africa and

the rest of the world. This virus has been labeled HIV-2, and so far has tended to produce less serious symptoms than the originally discovered, more prevalent strain of HIV (Ndinya-Achola et al., 1990).

About 20 sub-Saharan African countries have reported AIDS cases, the hardest hit being Uganda, Rwanda, Tanzania, Zambia, the Central African Republic, the Ivory Coast, Kenya, and Zaire. In urban centers of these countries, it has been estimated that from 5 to 20 percent of the sexually active population has already been infected with HIV. In the Zambian capital of Lusaka, 18 percent of blood donors were infected. Among prostitute populations, the rate of infection is even higher, ranging from 27 percent to 88 percent in some African cities (Ndinya-Achola et al., 1990). In one area of West Africa, AIDS has become the leading cause of adult deaths (DeCock et al., 1990). Countries in other parts of the world are closely watching what happens in Africa, where the epidemic first appeared, because they may expect a similar scenario.

We will never completely understand the routes by which HIV has spread throughout the world. Once a pool of infected people was established in a popula-

403

tion center that interacted with outside areas, it was only a matter of time before the virus would make its way into larger segments of the human population.

DISCOVERY OF HIV

The human immunodeficiency virus has proved to be elusive and complex for researchers to study. Controversy over its discovery took on international proportions, as millions of dollars in eventual royalties turned out to be at stake. The two virologists who finally agreed to share credit for the discovery of the virus, and thus also share patent rights for test kits to detect the presence of the virus, were Robert C. Gallo of the United States National Cancer Institute and Luc Montagnier of the Pasteur Institute in France.

Controversy over the discovery of HIV flared again in the 1990s, when it was suggested that Gallo might have deliberately or inadvertently grown the French virus and claimed it as his own. Eventually, evidence emerged from both laboratories suggesting that both researchers had experienced contaminations in their viral cultures, but there had not been any deliberate falsification of data. Nevertheless, there were criticisms leveled concerning Gallo's management of his research laboratory (Palca, 1991b).

Dr. Gallo's research, first reported in 1983, held that the virus that caused AIDS was a variant of viruses isolated earlier in his laboratory that were known to cause human T-lymphotropic leukemia. These had been named HTL viruses or HTLVs. Since there were two strains of the virus that caused leukemia, Gallo named the AIDS virus HTLV-III. In Montagnier's laboratory, during the same year, the AIDS-causing virus was isolated and identified. Because it was found in a patient suffering from lympho-adeno-pathy syndrome, the virus was named LAV. For a time, the U.S. Department of Health and Human Services adopted the double name of HTLV-III/LAV for the virus. It soon became clear that they were actually the same virus, and that they constituted an entirely new class of human viruses. Therefore, a formal nomenclature committee recommended that they be grouped together under the generic term *human immunodeficiency virus* or *HIV*.

STATISTICS ON THE PREVALENCE OF AIDS AND HIV INFECTION

Epidemiological studies are being conducted to determine the extent of HIV infection in the U.S. population. One method is surveillance data concerning the number of AIDS cases reported by hospitals, clinics,

physicians, and medical-record systems. It is believed that in the United States, at least 90 percent of AIDS cases are actually reported, a very high rate when compared with the reporting of other diseases.

During the early 1990s the estimates concerning rates of HIV infection in the United States were reduced somewhat. However, tracking the infection and making predictions about the future of the epidemic have been difficult problems for statisticians and epidemiologists (Culotta, 1991). Current estimates suggest that from 500,000 to nearly 1 million Americans had already been infected with HIV by the end of 1991, with another 20,000 to 80,000 new infections occurring each year in the United States (Brookmeyer, 1991; Kolata, 1991a). By mid-1991 more than 180,000 actual cases of AIDS had been reported to the Centers for Disease Control, and it has been predicted that the number of new cases will level off at between 40,000 and 67,000 per year through 1995. However, there may also be a substantial increase in the numbers of individuals with serious HIV-related diseases who have not yet been officially diagnosed as having AIDS. In addition, a second wave of the AIDS epidemic could conceivably sweep through the populations that were hardest hit in the beginning of the crisis (Brookmeyer, 1991). A few epidemiologists believe that the disease has crested in the United States and will begin leveling off, but others say that it is too soon to make such predictions (Kolata, 1991a).

At first the virus spread most rapidly through the male homosexual population and in intravenous drug abusers who shared needles. Many hemophiliacs and some surgical patients who received transfusions prior to the routine checking of donated blood for the virus were infected, and over 4,000 have developed the disease. Slowly the virus spread to other groups as well. The number of AIDS cases in the United States that presently can be traced to heterosexual transmission is on the increase, with men transmitting the virus to women much more often than women to men. That may reflect the fact that this country began with a larger pool of infected men, or it may mean that male-to-female transmission of HIV is more efficient than female-to-male transmission (Osborn, 1991).

One of the the fastest growing groups of AIDS patients now is children under the age of 13. Children seem to become infected perinatally, meaning during

epidemiology (e-pe-dee-mee-A-la-jee): the branch of medical science that deals with the incidence, distribution, and control of disease in a population.
hemophiliac (hee-mo-FIL-ee-ak): someone with the hereditary sex-linked blood defect hemophilia, affecting males primarily and characterized by difficulty in clotting.
perinatally: a term used to describe things related to pregnancy, birth, or the period immediately following the birth.

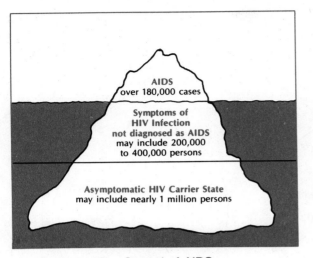

FIGURE 15.3   The Spread of AIDS

Close to 1 million people in the United States are believed to have been infected by the HIV virus that causes AIDS, but they don't have any symptoms of the disease. It is estimated that 25 percent of those infected will develop symptoms of infection within 3 years and one-third will develop AIDS within 6 years. By 1995 authorities project that over 400,000 people will have developed AIDS.

pregnancy, the birth process itself, or soon after birth. The number of diagnosed AIDS cases among adolescents aged 13 to 19 also doubled between January 1990 and June 1991.

The evidence is clear that the AIDS virus continues to spread rapidly in Africa, with 85 percent of cases occurring among the age group that is most sexually active, men and women in equal numbers between the ages of 15 and 40. It is clearly a disease of heterosexuals there.

HIV infection represents a serious global threat. It is estimated that about a million AIDS cases have already occurred throughout the world, and that between 8 and 10 million people are infected with the virus. The predictions from the World Health Organization have been grim. Originally, it had been estimated that between 15 and 20 million people worldwide would be infected with HIV by the year 2000. Because of the alarming spread of the infection in many areas of the world, officials now believe that level will be reached slightly after the mid-1990s (Palca, 1991a).

Remember that statistics on reported cases of AIDS represent only the tip of the iceberg (Fig. 15.2). There are many more individuals who have been infected with HIV, but as yet have no symptoms of disease. There are several hundred thousand others who are experiencing various stages of infection, but are not yet officially diagnosed as having AIDS. Additional epidemiological studies are underway to deter-

mine more accurately the extent of HIV infection in the U.S. population by checking blood samples.

Studies conducted on U.S. college campuses have found that about 2 of every 1,000 blood samples of students showed evidence of being infected with HIV. Although this did not represent a random sample of the student population and simply used blood drawn at college health centers for other reasons, two studies have clearly demonstrated that HIV infection is a very real and active problem on the campuses of U.S. colleges and universities (Leary, 1989). However, these results also show that the infection is not yet rampant on college campuses, and therefore may be prevented and controlled by careful choices of behavior.

RISKS OF INFECTION

Anyone may be potentially at risk of being exposed to bodily fluids in which HIV is present, if they choose to engage in risky behaviors. Since semen and blood are the fluids most often implicated in transmission of HIV, certain kinds of sexual activity and people who exchange blood are at highest risk.

In some areas of the world, such as Africa, heterosexual activity has been the primary mode of HIV transmission. Recent studies in Africa have also found that uncircumcised men may be 5 to 8 times more likely to contract HIV during heterosexual intercourse than circumcised males. There has now been a high correlation shown in 37 countries between areas of no circumcision and a high prevalence of AIDS. The fact that the United States has a high proportion of circumcised adult men may help to explain why HIV has spread more slowly through the heterosexual population there (Marx, 1989). In any case, for reasons that are not fully understood, the AIDS virus took hold first in the United States among homosexual males. The disease was first noticed among gay men who had shared sex with large numbers of partners, presumably increasing their risks of contracting and transmitting the disease. Their risks may have been increased by sharing anal intercourse (Detels et al., 1990). The virus from the semen enters the bloodstream through the many small tears in the colon. The possibility also exists that cells of the colon are particularly vulnerable to infection by HIV. Since a substantial number of women engage in anal intercourse with men, it should be recognized as a potentially risky sexual behavior for them as well (Voeller, 1990b).

The other group in which HIV spread rapidly was the population of intravenous (IV) drug abusers, through sharing of needles. In New York City alone, it is believed that 60 to 70 percent of IV drug abusers are infected with the virus (Des Jarlais et al., 1990).

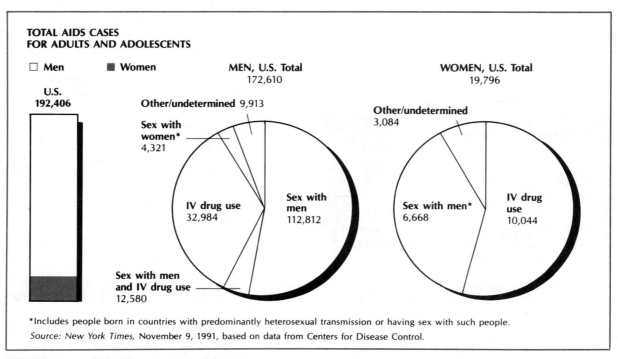

FIGURE 15.4 Risk Patterns for AIDS: An Emerging Picture

The rate of AIDS transmission through heterosexual intercourse is the subject of some debate. One indication is the number of cases diagnosed in people whose only known risk factor is heterosexual sex. Because people are often infected years before they become ill, and because the epidemic first appeared among drug users and gay men, the share of heterosexual infections may rise as the disease spreads.

IV drug abusers represent the largest heterosexual population in the United States infected with HIV, and therefore also represent the most significant vehicle for heterosexual transmission of the virus. They have accounted for over 70 percent of the HIV cases transmitted heterosexually. Bisexual men account for another 8 percent of the infections between men and women. During the first decade of the HIV epidemic, the actual number of infections transmitted by heterosexual contact has been steadily rising, although proportionately these cases continue to represent about 5 percent of all HIV infections (Greenspan & Castro, 1990). What is particularly alarming is that women are now the fastest growing population segment in the AIDS epidemic. The disease has become one of the five leading causes of death for women between the ages of 15 and 44 (Byron, 1991). In studies that have been done on heterosexual couples in which one partner had already been infected with HIV, it is clear that the risk of women contracting HIV from men is 10 to 18 times greater than the risk of men getting the virus from women. It has been suggested that the problem of HIV infection among women may well represent a "silent epidemic," the magnitude of which will be seen in the next decade as the proportion of AIDS cases in females rises dramatically (Osborn, 1991). The risks of trans-

mission become even greater when there is another sexually transmitted disease already present. Inflammation of tissues from STDs may well make it easier for HIV to enter the body (Greenspan & Castro, 1990).

In the United States, people of color are 3 to 21 times more likely than whites to become HIV-infected, depending on their gender, geographic region, and history of drug use. It has been suggested that sexual behavior is regarded in a much more serious light within the communities of people of color. It often has political implications and may be seen as an assertion of the self or as a way of gaining personal power. Therefore the approaches to AIDS prevention often used in white communities, with their emphasis on sex as "fun" or recreation, may not be effective with minority cultures (Mays & Cochran, 1990).

Hemophiliacs and others requiring transfusions were at high risk until the problem was recognized, and donated blood began being tested prior to use. Donated blood is now routinely tested for HIV, and has been considered relatively safe. Several units of HIV-contaminated blood recently were used by error, and the American Red Cross is converting to a central management system that should further guard against such accidents. People who are preparing for surgical procedures are often encouraged to have their own

FIGURE 15.5 AIDS Family

AIDS can devastate a family. An example is the Burke family, shown above. The father, a hemophiliac, had contracted HIV, and, before he was aware he had the infection, had passed it to his wife who then transmitted the disease to their son. The father and son have since died. The daughter was not infected. This tragedy underscores the fact that AIDS does not discriminate against age, sex, or sexual orientation.

blood saved ahead of time, thus eliminating the risks of infection from others. The one problem that remains is that HIV antibodies may not show up in blood until several months after infection, allowing for a small possibility of infection. The chances of being infected with HIV from donated blood are now placed at about 1 in 60,000. When evidence of HIV is discovered in donated blood, the donor is asked to report to a counselor who provides information on the infection in person. It is believed that some people are using blood donation as a way of getting tested for HIV that will not necessitate their going to a clinic.

AIDS cases among infants have been on the rise in the United States and globally. It is now believed that by the end of 1992 one million children in the world will be HIV-infected. While there are still many unanswered questions about HIV infection in infants, the evidence suggests that HIV may be transmitted to the fetus from the mother's blood system or during the delivery process; and there is now conclusive evidence that it may be transmitted in breast milk during nursing (Hilts, 1991). Babies born to HIV-infected mothers have at least a 30 percent chance of contracting the virus. Of those infants who become infected, there is a 20 percent chance of their dying by the age of 5 (Gillespie, 1991).

There has been growing controversy over transmission of HIV between health-care workers and their patients. At first, the concern was clearly for the safety of medical professionals who have to work with infected patients. By early 1991, cases had been reported of about 40 health-care workers who had become infected by accidental exposure to patients' blood. Until that year, there had been no reported cases of a patient being infected by a medical worker. In fact, if health-care workers use proper aseptic techniques, the risk of infection in either direction should be nil. However, concern for patient risk began to grow in 1991 when reports emerged of 5 individuals who had apparently all been infected by the same Florida dentist, who himself had died of AIDS the year before. It may never be completely clear how these infections occurred, but officials at the Centers for Disease Control suspect that the dentist did not always dispose of or sterilize his equipment properly, and probably the HIV transmission resulted from use of contaminated instruments. He was known to have treated about 10 patients whom he knew to have been HIV-infected (DePalma, 1991).

One of this dentist's patients, Kimberly Bergalis, made embittered public attacks on legislators and health officials for not requiring health-care providers to notify patients if they knew they were HIV-infected. This led to public outcries for more regulation of the health professions, and proposals for legislation that would require notification of patients by infected health-care workers. Organizations for medical professionals have gone on record as opposing such laws, calling instead for stronger enforcement of medical protocols that assume any patient could be infected, and advocating appropriate procedures for preventing any transmission of the virus. There have also been counterproposals requiring that patients notify medical personnel if they know they are infected with HIV, since statistics demonstrate that it is the professionals who are at greater risk than patients. In late 1991 a surgical technician filed suit against an infected patient from whom she had contracted the virus, since the patient had known she was HIV-infected. The patient's lawyer countered that the surgical team had not used proper techniques that would have prevented any infection. All of these issues remain open for debate, and have generated a great deal of controversy. Statutes and judicial precedents will surely establish clearer guidelines in the next few years.

407

The Public Health Service and Centers for Disease Control continue to promulgate regulations and recommendations for various occupational groups to prevent the spread of HIV. The facts available at present, however, strongly suggest that aside from intravenous drug abuse, it is sexual activity that is the greatest threat for transmitting the virus today.

HIV: The Infection and the Virus

The focus of discussions on HIV originally was on AIDS. We now know that the emphasis should be on the entire course of infection by the human immunodeficiency virus, and not just the late stage of that process that has become known as AIDS. This is crucial, because when HIV infection is diagnosed in its earlier stages, the patient is able to get treatment that may well delay certain aspects of the infection and prevent some complications. Researchers at Walter Reed Army Institute of Research in Washington, D.C. have shown that HIV infection passes through predictable stages, during which the body's immune system is gradually undermined. Although the duration of the infection varies, depending on other factors in the infected person's health and behavior, there is a gradual depletion of cells in the body that are crucial to its defense against disease-causing agents.

Once a laboratory test has shown HIV to be present in the body, the person is considered to be in the first stage of infection. There may or may not be any symptoms of disease at that time. Soon after contracting HIV, some people develop a fever, swollen glands, fatigue, and perhaps a rash. These early symptoms usually disappear within a few weeks as the body first manages to ward off the infection with its immune defenses. Most people infected with HIV first notice that something is wrong when they begin to experience chronically swollen lymph nodes, although they may have few other symptoms. It is important to note that there are other diseases that can create any of these symptoms as well, most of which are not nearly as serious as HIV infection.

As the infection progresses, there is a continual drop in the number of important immune cells in the body. The individual becomes increasingly vulnerable to opportunistic infection, meaning that disease-causing organisms normally present in the environment become able to attack the person by taking advantage of the weakened resistance. One of the most common diseases in the earlier stages of HIV infection is a yeast infection of the mouth called thrush (again, however, this disease in itself is not necessarily a sign of a serious disorder). There may also be infections of the skin and moist inner membranes of the body. There may be general feelings of discomfort and weakness, accompanied by sustained fevers, drenching night sweats, weight loss, and frequent diarrhea.

Within a year or two after these earlier stages appear, HIV infection typically progresses to its more serious stages, characterized by much more severe diseases. It is usually at this point in HIV infection that the person is considered to have acquired immunodeficiency syndrome, or AIDS. The term syndrome refers to a collection of disease symptoms that tend to cluster together. Unlike most syndromes, AIDS can have a spectrum of symptoms, and the disease can progress in many different ways.

There is controversy over the precise diagnosis of AIDS. The Centers for Disease Control define AIDS in terms of a list of particular life-threatening illnesses that may develop as the disease progresses. That definition was developed some time ago as a means of tracking the disease, and was based largely on the manner in which the disease typically progresses in gay males. It is now known that women and intravenous drug abusers often develop different symptoms in the earlier stages of the disease. However, because of the CDC definition being used at present, many of these people are not officially counted as having AIDS, and they cannot qualify for disability payments or other benefits available to AIDS patients. The American Medical Association and some national AIDS activist groups have been working to revise the definition of AIDS so that seriously ill people who do not meet the present criteria would still be eligible for benefits and proper medical treatment. It has been estimated that if the definition of AIDS is broadened, up to 140,000 more Americans might be added to the official numbers of people with AIDS.

In about 30 percent of cases there is an appearance of purplish skin lesions that accompany a previously rare form of cancer called Kaposi's sarcoma. Or the victim may begin to develop pneumocystic pneumonia caused by microorganisms that were formerly rarely seen as the cause of disease and are resistant to treatment. In its final stages, HIV attacks the nervous system, damaging the brain and spinal cord. This can lead to eventual memory loss, depression, and the inability to make decisions, or result in gradual loss of coordination and bodily control. Partial paralysis can

opportunistic infection: a disease resulting from lowered resistance of a weakened immune system.

thrush: a disease caused by a fungus and characterized by white patches in the oral cavity.

syndrome (SIN-drome): a group of signs or symptoms that occur together and characterize a given condition.

Kaposi's sarcoma: a rare form of cancer of the blood vessels, characterized by small, purple skin lesions.

TABLE 15.1

Evidence That HIV Causes AIDS

Type of Evidence	Description
ANIMAL SYSTEMS	Several types of retroviruses can cause severe immune deficiencies in animals. For example, the feline leukemia virus (FeLV) can cause either immune deficiency or cancer, depending on slight genetic variations in the virus.
	A virus related to HIV, the simian immunodeficiency virus (SIV), can cause AIDS in macaque monkeys. The second AIDS virus, HIV-2, may also cause AIDS in macaques.
EPIDEMIOLOGY	In every country studied so far, AIDS has appeared only after the appearance of HIV.
	Using the most recent technology, HIV can be isolated from almost 100 percent of the people with AIDS.
	Earlier in the epidemic, the virus was present in the groups at risk for the disease and in almost no healthy heterosexuals.
BLOOD-TRANSFUSION DATA	A study of people who received blood transfusions in 1982–83 (when the fraction of blood donors infected with HIV was about 1 in 2,000) showed that of 28 people who got AIDS, the virus could be found in all 28. Furthermore, for each recipient who got AIDS an infected donor could be found. Today most of those infected donors have also developed AIDS.
	Elimination of HIV in blood transfusions by antibody screening has drastically reduced the number of AIDS cases resulting from transfusions.
TEST-TUBE STUDIES	In the laboratory the virus kills the very T-4 cells whose depletion is the hallmark of AIDS. It also infects and alters the function of cells of the monocyte-macrophage lineage, which may serve as a reservoir of infection in AIDS patients.

Source: R. C. Gallo and L. Montagnier, "AIDS in 1988," *Scientific American,* October 1988, p. 44.

also follow. Ultimately, there will be months of debilitating illness until the body can no longer prevail, and the victim dies (Redfield & Burke, 1988).

No one fully understands yet why HIV infection progresses so slowly. It may be that the virus replicates itself very slowly, and so initially does not represent a serious threat to the body. Or it may be that the body's immune system is simply able to do its job for a time, managing to ward off the toxic effects of the virus. Only further research will clarify the answer to this question that continues to puzzle scientists.

There is now general agreement that HIV is the virus that eventually leads to the development of AIDS. See Table 15.1 for a summary of this evidence.

MECHANISM OF HIV ACTION

Viruses are among the tiniest of microorganisms to infect human tissues. Typically, they attach themselves to the outside of a cell and inject their genetic material inside, where it takes over the DNA of its host cell to produce new viruses. These viruses then spread to other cells, disrupting or killing them as new viruses are produced. It is the destruction of tissue that causes the symptoms of the viral infection. Usually various elements of the body's immune system are eventually able to develop antibodies to a particular virus, so immunity develops and the disease abates. Often this natural immunity remains and thus makes the host permanently immune to infection by the specific virus. Antibiotics and other known medications are not effective against viral infections, although they may be extremely useful in combatting bacterial infection. Many vaccines have been developed that help the human body produce antibodies to particular viruses, thereby preventing infection before it occurs. Polio, whooping cough, measles, smallpox, certain strains of influenza, and a variety of other diseases have been kept in check by such vaccines.

In the early 1970s a new mechanism of viral action was discovered in the cells of research animals.

409

Because of how they functioned, these viruses were called retroviruses. The HTLVs isolated by Gallo and his coworkers were of this type. Retroviruses take their name from a method of reproduction that is different from the more typical viral infections.

In all living things, it is the hereditary code stored in the DNA of each cell's genes that determines the characteristics of the organism; the complex biochemical processes of life are governed by that code. The DNA passes its messages to another chemical found in all cells, RNA, which then plays many roles in helping the cell manufacture all of the products it requires to live and function as it is programmed to do.

The retroviruses are unique in that their genetic code is instead carried in the form of RNA. They also carry a special combination of enzymes called reverse transcriptase. When a retrovirus attacks a cell, this chemical orders the cell's RNA to translate the genetic blueprints of the virus into the cell's DNA, thus instructing it to make a whole new crop of virus particles. It is because this mechanism is the reverse of the usual order of things that these viruses are called retro (Jackson, 1992).

To complicate matters, HIV seems to have extremely complex genetic codes. Although most animal retroviruses have only three genes, the AIDS virus has at least nine, and probably more. Researchers are just beginning to understand the various functions of these genes, information essential to developing effective vaccines or cures for AIDS. It is also likely that HIV varies its genetic code when replicating itself, creating new variations that make it even more difficult to pin down an exact structure of the virus (Kolata, 1991b).

The reason that the AIDS virus is so lethal is that it directly attacks some primary cells of the immune system. To reproduce itself and multiply in the body, it destroys the very cells that are essential in helping the body produce immunity to all disease. These cells are the T-4 lymphocytes, a type of white blood cell that plays a major role in bringing together the body's immune defenses. These cells are coated with a special protein that acts as a receptor for the virus. Molecules on the virus particles link up with molecules in the protein, much like a key in a lock, completing the infection process. It appears likely that the AIDS virus only attacks cells that have this particular protein on their surfaces (Angier, 1990).

However, HIV is now being seen as even more insidious than previously believed. Not only can it attack several human tissues, but it also seems to have a potential for hiding itself away in certain cells. The virus is known to infect monocytes and macrophages, two other blood cells that migrate about in the body, engulfing and destroying germs. It also may attack the neuroglial cells of the brain and central nervous sys-

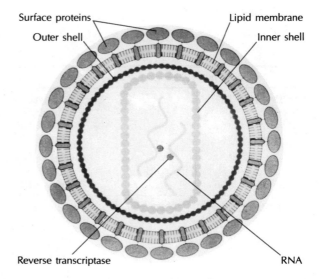

Surface proteins • Lipid membrane
Outer shell • Inner shell
Reverse transcriptase • RNA

Source: NIAID, National Institutes of Health.

FIGURE 15.6   Schematic Diagram of HIV Virus

AIDS is caused by the human immunodeficiency virus (HIV), a retrovirus that converts RNA into a DNA copy using an enzyme called reverse transcriptase.

tem, the endothelial cells that line various body organs and internal body cavities, and perhaps the lining of the colon. With so many potential places for hiding and multiplying, it is no wonder that the human body has such difficulty in defending itself against infection by HIV.

A major effort has identified the structure of the receptor protein on cell surfaces that seems to provide a link-up site for the virus. New research emerging from the French laboratories that originally discovered HIV is suggesting that bacteria-like organisms called mycoplasmas may work together with HIV to attack the T-4 cells, thereby contributing to the eventual development of AIDS (Balter, 1991). These findings may lead to new understandings of how the body falls victim to AIDS, and eventually how the disease may be treated or prevented.

HOW HIV IS SPREAD

It is now clear that HIV is transmitted by the direct transfer of certain bodily fluids from one infected individual to another. HIV is usually present in peo-

retrovirus (RE-tro-vi-rus): a class of viruses that reproduces with the aid of the enzyme reverse transcriptase, which allows the virus to integrate its genetic code into that of the host cell, thus establishing permanent infection.

ple's bodies for years before disease symptoms actually develop. *However, the virus still may be transmitted by infected people who have not developed any symptoms.* People with AIDS or who are experiencing other symptoms of HIV infection are even more likely to transmit the virus. HIV enters the body through internal linings of organs (such as the vagina, rectum, urethra within the penis, or mouth) or through openings in the skin, such as tiny cuts or open sores.

Researchers have shown that the most typical fluids to be involved in transmission of the virus are blood, semen, and vaginal secretions (Jackson, 1992). The virus can be transmitted perinatally, and there is evidence that it can be transmitted to an infant through breast milk. Additionally, there is documentation of HIV being found in saliva, tears, urine, and feces, but no direct evidence that the virus has actually been transmitted by these secretions and excretions.

Several routes of HIV infection have been clearly documented:

1. Anal or vaginal intercourse.
2. Contact with semen; transplanted organs; or blood, such as on contaminated needles and syringes shared by drug users, or used for tattooing, ear piercing, or injection of steroids.
3. Transfer from mother to child.

The evidence on the risks of oral-genital sex is still inconclusive and confusing, partly because this behavior is usually practiced in conjunction with other sexual activities that may be highly risky (Simon, Kraft, & Kaplan, 1990).

Although ordinary kissing appears to pose no particular threat of transmission, experts have not ruled out the possibility that prolonged, wet, deep kissing (French-kissing) might transfer the virus. Theoretically, viruses carried in saliva could enter the body through tiny breaks or sores within the mouth.

There is no evidence at this time that casual contacts with infected persons—even in crowded households, social settings, schools, or the workplace—are dangerous. There are no documented cases of HIV being transmitted through food, water, toilets, swimming pools, or hot tubs, shared drinking or eating utensils, telephones, or used clothing. Several research studies have demonstrated that the virus is not transmitted by insects.

DOES INFECTION WITH HIV MEAN AIDS?

So far, not all people who are infected with HIV have actually developed symptoms of infection or progressed to a stage that is considered to be AIDS. It is not known as yet what proportion of infected persons will actually become ill with the disease. While it has been shown that a large enough dose of HIV can cause AIDS on its own, there are a number of other factors that influence the progression of the disease over time. For example, a person whose immune system is already impaired prior to HIV infection will tend to develop AIDS more rapidly than someone whose immune system is strong. Similarly, the more other infections an individual's immune system must fight, the more readily HIV can take hold and do its damage. Research is also indicating that HIV can interact with certain other viruses, such as one of the human herpes viruses, so that cellular infection by both virus particles becomes more efficient and rapid (Jackson, 1992).

The risk of developing symptoms of disease, and eventually AIDS, increases with time after infection with HIV. It is important to emphasize, however, that the longer-term statistical models on the progress of the infection have been based largely on gay male populations. There is growing evidence that women may develop AIDS more quickly than men do, and children may react differently. There is a group of gay men whose progress with HIV infection has been followed for over 10 years now. They orginally were participating in a hepatitis study, and so some of their blood samples were drawn prior to the development of the AIDS crisis. Of these men, 345 are known to have been infected in 1977; of those 345, 61 percent have developed AIDS, and three-fourths of those have died. Another 18 percent have developed early indications of the disease. Twenty-one percent of the HIV-infected men remain symptom-free. Several explanations have been offered to explain why one-fifth of the men have not developed AIDS. They may have especially strong immune symptoms, or they may have been infected with a weaker strain of the virus. Some of them have been taking medications used to treat HIV infection, but not all of them have. Only time will tell whether everyone who becomes infected with HIV will eventually develop full-blown AIDS (Lambert, 1990). Once diagnosed with the disease, about 75 percent of patients die within 2 years.

It had been believed that there was a milder form of the disease, in which only some AIDS-related symptoms appear. This has been called AIDS-related complex, or ARC. However, it now appears that these symptoms represent the earlier stages of HIV infection, and are sometimes collectively termed HIV disease.

It is important to counteract the notion that being infected with HIV constitutes a death sentence. Even after 10 years, some infected individuals remain free of disease symptoms. Health experts advise that changing health habits to keep the immune system strong is a wise idea for anyone who has been diagnosed with HIV infection.

411

How Can This Be? How Can Alison Gertz Have AIDS?

Alison L. Gertz wasn't supposed to get AIDS.

She has never injected drugs or had a blood transfusion, and she describes herself as "not at all promiscuous." But she does say she had a single sexual encounter—seven years ago—with a male acquaintance who, she has since learned, has died of AIDS.

Though AIDS has hit hardest among gay men and poor intravenous drug users, it also afflicts people like Ms. Gertz.

"People think this can't happen to them," she said in an interview at her Manhattan apartment. "I never thought I could have AIDS."

She is 23 years old, affluent, college-educated and a professional from a prominent family. She grew up on Park Avenue.

Now Ms. Gertz and her family are going public because they have a message. A message for heterosexuals who could make a potentially fatal mistake if they dismiss the threat of AIDS. A message for doctors who may miss a diagnosis; she spent three weeks undergoing exhaustive hospital tests for all other conceivable causes of her illness before AIDS was discovered. And a message asking for greater public support on AIDS issues.

"I decided when I was in the hospital I would give as much time as I can to help people who are going through this, and warn others of the danger," she said. "I want to make a condom commercial, do speaking engagements, whatever I can.

"All the AIDS articles are about homosexuals or poor people on drugs, and unfortunately a lot of people just flip by them," she said. "They think it doesn't apply to them."

But she added: "They can't turn the page on me. I could be one of them, or their daughter. They have to deal with this."

• • •

"I want to talk to these kids who think they're immortal," Ms. Gertz said. "I want to tell them: I'm heterosexual, and it took only one time for me."

Ms. Gertz is certain how it happened. "It was one romantic night," she said. "There were roses and champagne and everything. That was it. I only slept with him once."

Ms. Gertz has since learned that the man was bisexual and has died of AIDS. She said that had she known his past she doubts it would have made a difference. "At that point they weren't publicizing AIDS," she said. "It wasn't an issue then."

• • •

When AIDS struck, Ms. Gertz said, "I was just, as they say, starting out in life." Her goals had been simple: "I wanted a house and kids and animals and to paint my paintings."

She had recently signed on with an art agent, embarking on a career as an illustrator. She had also quit her pack-a-day smoking habit and joined a health club "to get really healthy," she said.

HIV Testing, Treatment, and Vaccines

When HIV infects people, their bodies begin the natural process of combatting the disease. Antibodies begin to form that will attempt to destroy the reproducing viruses. The blood tests that are most frequently used to confirm the presence of the virus can actually detect the antibodies that a body is producing, although the antibodies may not be detectable for several months after the virus has entered a body. It has been generally accepted that such antibodies show up within 6 months following infection. However, a study of 133 homosexual men showed that a few of them actually took close to 3 years to develop the antibodies (Imagawa, 1989). These results have raised new concerns

412

FIGURE 15.7 AIDS Patient

Alison Gertz is an AIDS patient who never injected drugs or had a blood transfusion. Through a single sexual experience, she now faces the consequences of this deadly disease. She is working hard to warn heterosexuals who are not drug users about the dangers of unprotected sexual behavior.

Then fever and a spell of diarrhea hit last summer. A doctor told her it was "probably just a bug," she said. But the symptoms persisted, so she checked into Lenox Hill Hospital.

When her doctor told her the diagnosis, he had tears in his eyes. "I said: 'Oh, my God. I'm going to die,' " she recalled. "And as I said it, I thought to myself, 'No I'm not. Why am I saying this?' I thought my life was over. 'I'm 22. I'm never going to have sex again. I'm never going to have children.' "

From that initial shock, Ms. Gertz bounced back with the ebullience so well known to her friends—they call her Ali for short—and the fervor of activism that runs in the family. Recovering from her first treatment, she returned to her apartment, her pets (a dog, Saki; a cat, Sambucca, and tropical fish) and a new course in life.

"It's a dreadful disease, but it's also a gift," she said. "I've always been positive, optimistic. I thought, 'What can I do with it?' I like to think I'm here for a purpose. If I die, I would like to have left something, to make the world a little bit better before I go, to help people sick like me and prevent others from getting this. It would make it all worthwhile."

—Bruce Lambert, *New York Times*, March 11, 1989

about the accuracy of HIV testing. Pharmaceutical companies continue to research new and more accurate methods of testing for HIV.

The test currently in greatest use is an enzyme-linked immunosorbent assay—ELISA. It is inexpensive, can be completed in up to 5 hours, and is not technically difficult to interpret. However, the ELISA test tends to give a high percentage of false positives, so the results may signal the presence of HIV antibodies when in fact none are present. A positive result is then further tested with the Western blot or immu-

ELISA: the primary test used to determine the presence of HIV in humans.

Western blot: the test used to verify the presence of HIV antibodies detected first by the ELISA.

413

noblot test. It is more accurate than ELISA, but because it is lengthy and expensive and must be interpreted by trained and experienced technicians, it is not suggested as a primary test in large-scale screening.

A serious difficulty with HIV testing is the fact that the body may be quite slow to develop measurable quantities of antibodies following infection. Blood tests conducted in the early phases of infection may have false negative results, incorrectly signaling that HIV is not present. Obviously, this could mean that an infected individual proceeds under the assumption that he or she is free of the virus, does not seek appropriate medical help, and may endanger others. Some laboratories are now able to culture viruses from infected blood, or to identify chemicals from HIV in blood or tissue samples. While such tests are much more expensive and time-consuming, they do improve the chances of detecting infection at an early stage.

New generations of HIV tests are extremely sensitive and can distinguish between different strains of HIV. These tests will be especially valuable to developing countries because they are only one-step procedures, require less sophisticated laboratory facilities, and can detect strains more common in those areas. There is a new test that may be used to detect HIV in infants as young as 3 to 6 months. This is an especially positive development, because early detection can lead to earlier treatment and a potentially longer period of survival (Altman, 1991).

Given the present state of HIV-testing technology, testing can have three possible outcomes: 1) clear confirmation of the presence of HIV antibodies; 2) clear confirmation that the antibodies are absent; or 3) an uncertain result that leaves patients frighteningly unsure. When there has been a high risk of recent infection, physicians often recommend repeat testing after several weeks if testing has proved negative or uncertain. HIV testing centers are typically staffed by trained counselors who can deal with the range of personal reactions prior to testing or when the outcome of tests is positive.

CONTROVERSY OVER HIV TESTING

Since HIV infection is so dangerous and is spreading at such an alarming rate, there has been a great deal of controversy over who should be tested and whether testing should be mandatory or voluntary. Most experts recommend that testing efforts should be expanded, but they are divided on how strongly the tests should be required. Some believe mandatory tests are unfair so long as effective treatment for the disease does not exist. Others say that mandatory testing for

the public welfare has been used with other sexually transmitted diseases, such as syphilis, and that the seriousness of HIV infection certainly warrants similar intervention. They also advocate tracking down sexual partners of known infected people so that they too may be tested. Mandatory testing for STD has already been implemented among applicants for marriage licenses in some states, immigrant visas, and for those who wish to enter the armed forces. Enlistees in the U.S. armed forces are also tested for the presence of HIV antibodies.

The Immigration and Naturalization Service screens would-be immigrants for HIV infection. Foreigners who are HIV-infected are not permitted to enter the United States. This is a policy that has angered many in the international community. In early 1991 the Secretary of Health and Human Services indicated that these prohibitions would be lifted, to bring the United States "in line with the best medical thinking, here and abroad." However, political pressures caused officials to back away from this proposed change, and the restrictions banning infected foreigners remain in place. As a protest to these policies, the International AIDS Society refused to hold their International AIDS Conference in the United States in 1992.

One of the most hotly debated issues about HIV testing has been the concept of mandatory testing for health-care workers, or for patients in hospitals. While there have been a few cases of accidental infection of medical workers, and the one case of the dentist who apparently infected five of his patients through contaminated instruments, there has been increasing pressure for both health-care workers and patients to be required to inform the other if they know they are HIV-infected.

In a few rape cases, alleged rapists have been asked to submit to HIV testing, so that the victim may know if the risk of infection exists. Increasingly, the testing has been included in plea-bargaining arrangements for the rapist. It has been suggested, however, that this information may not be as useful as it seems on the surface of things, and that there can be a negative side. There is always a chance that the rapist was infected after the rape actually occurred. There is also a relatively small chance of becoming infected with HIV after one incident of intercourse, about 1 chance in 300 to 500. Therefore, the rape survivor may be left not knowing for sure if actual infection has taken place, or even if the rapist was infected at the time of the rape. There is also a possibility that the willingness of the rapist to submit to testing has earned him a lighter sentence in the plea bargaining. No matter what the outcome of the testing, it will still be important for the victim to be tested immediately, and then about a year later. Therefore, it may well be that information gained through forced testing of accused rapists may not be all that useful to anyone, particularly the victim (deLeon & Lebow, 1991).

A basic issue in the testing question is one of civil rights. To what degree does government have the right to require individuals to submit to physiological tests? How confidential can the results be kept? What happens to the lives of people who are presently healthy but who find out they are infected with the virus? These are ethical issues with which society must continue to wrestle.

Some states have already required their family planning and STD clinics to offer free, voluntary testing for HIV. The Centers for Disease Control have made the following recommendations concerning HIV testing:

1. Couples planning marriage should be provided "ready access" to testing and to information about HIV and AIDS.
2. People should have the "right to choose not to be tested" and be given appropriate counseling prior to testing. They should also give explicit consent, orally or in writing, before being tested.
3. Anyone seeking treatment for other sexually transmitted diseases should be encouraged to undergo HIV testing.
4. People with a history of intravenous drug use, who have shared equipment with others, and their sexual partners should be encouraged to have tests.
5. Pregnant women who are at high risk of infection or "live in a geographic area or community with a high prevalence of infection" should be tested.
6. Women seeking family planning services should be routinely counseled about HIV infection and have testing made available to them.

As states deal with the issues of HIV testing in their legislatures, there is another controversy that has arisen. It involves the need for counseling prior to and following the test. AIDS has created many fears, and people approach HIV testing with a great deal of trepidation. It is crucial that they be helped through the early phase of making a decision about getting tested, and then sorting through their reactions to the possible results of the testing. There is also a waiting period of several days before test results can be made available, and this period may create high levels of anxiety. While some insurance companies do not want to require pre-testing counseling because it adds to the expense, experts generally agree that such counseling should be considered a requirement for HIV testing.

Most state health departments also require that an individual come in person to find out the results, rather than be told over the telephone or by mail. Obviously, there is a degree of trauma and anguish connected with learning that the test results were positive. However, counseling can not only provide support for the anxiety, but reassurance and advice about the future. HIV infection does not necessarily mean that disease symptoms will develop in the near future, or perhaps at all. Only further studies will tell. The infected person may continue to make behavioral choices to enhance the strength of his or her immune system, and to prevent the spread of the virus to others. Even if the test results are negative, counseling can be important to providing the person with information to avoid infection in the future, along with other education about HIV and AIDS.

Anyone who is worried about the possibility of having been infected with HIV can seek advice and voluntary testing through STD clinics or private physicians. Such testing will undoubtedly become a more routine part of health examinations and screenings in years to come.

TREATMENT FOR HIV-INFECTED PERSONS

Whenever a new disease appears on the scene, there are predictable stages through which medical science must pass as it approaches cure or prevention. At first, physicians must describe and analyze the symptoms, using whatever treatments are available and beneficial. Eventually, they develop an understanding of the causes of the disease, and the course it tends to follow. Then these physicians can diagnose and assess patients more quickly. Next they develop and refine treatments until a cure is finally found. We are still in the early stages of understanding HIV infection. We are beginning to understand the mechanisms by which the virus wreaks havoc with the immune system. While there is still a long way to go toward finding a cure, most experts feel that this will only be a matter of time (Redfield & Burke, 1988).

Even though the final stage of HIV infection, AIDS, is a fatal disease, appropriate medical treatment during the course of the illness can prolong a patient's life and improve its quality. Adequacy of treatment is one of the primary reasons that testing for the virus is crucial. The strategy for treatment varies with the stage of the infection. When it is known that someone is infected, experienced physicians can monitor progress of the virus and provide appropriate interventions. As opportunistic diseases develop, carefully selected medications may be used to relieve symptoms or to help the body fight the infections. For example, the drug Famsidar has proved effective in warding off the

415

type of pneumonia that is particularly persistent among AIDS patients, providing that HIV infection is diagnosed early.

Although the development of antibiotics brought a variety of bacterial infections under control, antiviral therapies have generally lacked success. The antiviral drugs that have been developed have numerous side effects, in some cases life-threatening ones. Although cures for viral infections have been almost nonexistent, HIV presents even more problems because it can attack the brain and spinal cord. Most drugs cannot penetrate the blood-brain barrier that protects the central nervous system, making it unlikely that all of the viruses could be reached and destroyed. The genetic complexity of HIV generates further concern. There is a possibility that it will be able to mutate easily to variant forms, thus evading any drug that might be developed. Other researchers believe that the complexity of the virus may be its downfall, since all of its genes must operate together. Each stage of its functioning can represent a point of attack at which to destroy the virus's action. Researchers have identified about 15 vulnerable spots in the life cycle of HIV, any of which may eventually provide help in destroying the virus.

Since research with HIV treatments began, a remarkable number of new anti-viral preparations have gone into testing stages. There are now so many, in fact, that the clinical testing system has become overloaded. One system that is being investigated is targeted drug design. This refers to the development of drugs that will target HIV at some very specific stage of its replication process. One of the most promising approaches in this realm so far has been attacking one of the enzymes involved in the reproduction of retroviruses (Palca, 1991c).

The most widely used drug at present is azidothymidine or AZT, although it can have severe side effects. Studies of the drug's longer-term effectiveness have been disappointing, and its potency for a particular patient may actually fade over time. Other drugs are being tested that may be stronger and less toxic for AIDS patients. AIDS activist groups have complained that because of one pharmaceutical company's monopoly on the production of AZT, its cost of $2,000 to $3,000 per year has become prohibitive for many AIDS patients. The National Institutes of Health have recently decided that licensing agreements for manufacturing AZT should be given to a generic drug manufacturer. It is expected that this competition will bring down the drug's price and make it more widely available (Palca, 1991d).

In 1991 the Federal Food and Drug Administration approved a second drug for the treatment of HIV-infected people. It is dideoxyinosine, or DDI. Like AZT, DDI produces uncomfortable or risky side effects in some patients, but it also may provide an extra boost for those patients in which AZT is losing its effectiveness over time. It will also be about 20 percent less costly than AZT, and has been cleared for use with children as well as adults. There has been a "grass roots" movement among AIDS patients to try experimental drugs. Federal guidelines were changed to permit patients to use some of these medications under the supervision of their own physicians.

Treatment strategies have involved combining a range of antiviral drugs in an attempt to interfere with multiple stages of the virus's life cycle, stopping the infection and preventing the virus from reproducing. Another side of the treatment issue is the need to get a patient's immune system operating more effectively again. Bone marrow transplants have been tried with some success, as have drugs to stimulate action of the immune system. Unfortunately, these drugs may also have the effect of stimulating production of the viruses. Another complication has been the discovery of drug-resistant strains of HIV. Already, AZT-resistant forms have emerged. A truly reliable antiviral treatment for HIV is still a long way off. Until then, prevention of infection is the most viable alternative, and vaccines offer some hope for accomplishing this end.

VACCINES FOR HIV

The best way to combat HIV infection is to prevent it. When it comes to viral infections, one of the safest and most effective means of prevention is vaccination. Vaccines take advantage of the body's ability to "remember" a disease-causing agent. They involve introducing a harmless form of the germ into the body, so that the immune system develops necessary antibodies to ward off later infections. This strategy has worked in controlling such diseases as smallpox and polio.

The search for an HIV vaccine has been a top priority since 1984, and a number of experimental vaccines are currently undergoing testing in humans. There have been three major complications that make the search a difficult one. First, HIV seems to be able to "hide" in cells by installing its genes within the genes of the cell. Neither is there a particularly good animal model for the disease, and this is where testing would normally begin. Since HIV infection is so dangerous, experimental trials for a vaccine with humans have had to proceed with the utmost caution. In such trials, a substantial number of at-risk people are given the vaccine, and their rate of infection is compared to a control group of persons who have not received the vaccine.

Since there are different strains of HIV, there is

some concern over whether several vaccines will have to be developed to protect people from AIDS. Some virologists believe that enough weak spots can be found that are common to most of the strains, so that a single vaccine can produce immunity to them. Animal testing with vaccines had shown enough success by 1991 that the search began for the best method to conduct experiments with humans. However, a number of concerns were being raised by the international team that is monitoring such research. It is uncertain, for example, whether vaccines developed with one population will still be effective with other populations, which might in fact be subject to infection by a different strain of HIV. There is also concern that because of the inevitable costs of its development, the vaccine might not be accessible to developing countries. While preliminary tests on humans have shown experimental vaccines to be safe, there is still great concern about how safe they will turn out to be when tested on large groups of people (Cohen, 1991).

Jonas Salk, who developed the polio vaccine, is one of a group of scientists who believe that vaccines might also be used to promote immunity in people who are already infected with HIV. This would prevent them from actually developing disease symptoms, but might not reduce the risks of their transmitting the virus to others. This strategy did not gain much support from the scientific community. However, research reported in 1991 confirmed that vaccines can indeed give the immune system a boost, and this information bolstered Salk's proposals.

The experts seem to be in general agreement that it will take several more years of painstaking research and clinical testing before reliable treatments or preventative vaccines for HIV become available. There is an international group, composed of scientists from 10 countries, who are working on the development of a vaccine. In the meantime, society must continue to face the many issues that this disease has created.

AIDS and Society

Whenever epidemics have swept through populations, crises of morality have accompanied the disease. Should victims of the disease be cared for or isolated so they cannot infect others? Should there be a social stigma for those with the disease and those who live with them? How much energy and what resources should be diverted from finding cures and preventative measures toward caring for victims who seem surely doomed? These are ancient questions that still catch us off guard. We must examine the applicability of time-tested solutions today and sort through new ethical insights that may help with the AIDS dilemma.

FIGURE 15.8 International Concern for Public Health

Many countries around the world are seeking to inform people about AIDS and how the disease can be prevented. In Denmark, the focus on posters to encourage condom use is not only on the beauty and delight of sexual experiences, but also on the need to prevent the transmission of sexual disease. The last line translates "Protect yourself . . . also against another's ignorance."

The epidemic of HIV infection has touched every aspect of society. It has led to courageous and generous actions, and it has led people to be irrational and mean-spirited. Most of all, it will not be ignored. The National Commission on AIDS made its first report in late 1991, calling for increased governmental action on AIDS. They reiterated that it is time to stop blaming any group of people for the disease and instead to mount a concerted effort to fight the virus. They charged that the greatest threats in the AIDS crisis at present are public complacency and governmental inaction.

417

INDIVIDUAL FREEDOM vs. PUBLIC HEALTH INTERESTS

Whenever societies have been faced with epidemic diseases, they have also been called upon to make decisions regarding the degree of freedom infected individuals should be afforded. Historically, individual rights have been subordinated—often to cruel dimensions—to protect the general population. Lepers were forced into exile; victims of bubonic plague were jailed or forced into confinement, often along with their healthy relatives.

In the nineteenth century, legal systems began to develop more rational principles for protecting the public from infected individuals. Quarantines of various degrees of severity were imposed for certain infectious diseases. Many of those guidelines are being reinterpreted in light of emphasis during recent times on the rights of individual citizens.

There are four general rules that now determine how many restrictions are to be imposed on individual freedom when serious illness threatens. It is assumed that each point can be supported with valid scientific data.

1. A serious threat to public safety must be clearly defined and verified. Suspicion is not considered a valid reason.
2. The actual means by which the disease will be spread must be specific and recognizable.
3. Carriers of the disease must be able to be identified with certainty. Again, suspicion is not considered sufficient.
4. Any restrictions imposed must be effective in preventing spread of the infection.

How far present-day society will be willing to go in restricting individual freedom over HIV infection remains to be seen. In San Francisco, a city noted for its tolerance of a large gay population, there seems to be evidence that AIDS patients are being treated with sensitivity and impartiality. That city, however, and New York City have placed restrictions on bath houses, locations of a great deal of casual sexual conduct among gay males.

In a number of cases, people have been denied certain rights because they were known to carry the virus or have the disease. One hemophiliac boy who contracted HIV through blood transfusions was for several weeks denied admittance to his school because of fear that his presence would place classmates at risk. Some office workers have threatened to quit rather than work with infected people. New York City has an AIDS Discrimination Unit to monitor such cases, and its director feels that HIV infection represents a dis-

ability for which discrimination is prohibited by the state's Human Rights Law.

Some experts feel that as concern over the spread of AIDS grows, so will calls for involuntary quarantining and testing. Already, a number of states are considering premarital HIV testing. Officials of the Centers for Disease Control fear that such moves may drive infected people underground to protect themselves from discrimination. There is also fear that HIV and AIDS will be used as an excuse to discriminate against and criminally prosecute homosexuals or other groups. Others insist, however, that society has used mandatory quarantines, tests, and legal sanctions during epidemics before, and that indeed these represent legitimate approaches to protecting the public health.

OTHER ETHICAL ISSUES AND AIDS

There are a number of other ethical issues that have arisen concerning AIDS. There will be more in the years ahead. Here is a summary of some of the more pressing issues:

1. *The issue of confidentiality.* Traditionally in the field of medicine, patient confidentiality has been afforded the utmost respect. Yet some information from health records is subject to disclosure, with the patient's permission, for a variety of purposes. The question remains: Who should be allowed access to information about an individual's sexual life-style or infection with HIV? Such information can affect reputation, employment, and insurance coverage. Yet, if that information were crucial to protecting others from contracting the virus, how and under what circumstances would it be legitimate for it to be revealed? Several states have passed legislation giving physicians the discretion to decide about releasing information about HIV-infected people. Other states are expected to consider similar moves.

2. *The dilemmas of treatment.* There are always ethical dilemmas posed in treating terminal illnesses. Often, in order for AIDS patients to survive one of their many opportunistic infections, aggressive, intensive medical measures are required. The choice for the patient may be between accepting death quickly or putting it off and experiencing prolonged deterioration and discomfort. Surgery may be required, and yet may not be suitable for patients not expected to survive, especially given the risks of infection for the surgical workers. Since many AIDS patients suffer early deterioration of the central nervous system and may not be competent to make decisions relatively early in the disease, medical personnel, friends, and relatives may be forced to make difficult choices about life-and-death issues themselves. Several states now have laws allow-

Do physicians have a duty to treat AIDS patients?

Have you been provided with sufficient information from professional and public health organizations to permit optimal treatment of AIDS?

Should we institute quarantine measures for HIV-positive patients in general?

Especially for sociopathic drug abusers?

If HIV-positive patients are unwilling to inform their sex partners, do physicians have any further obligation in the matter?

Does the government?

Source: Science, November 23, 1990

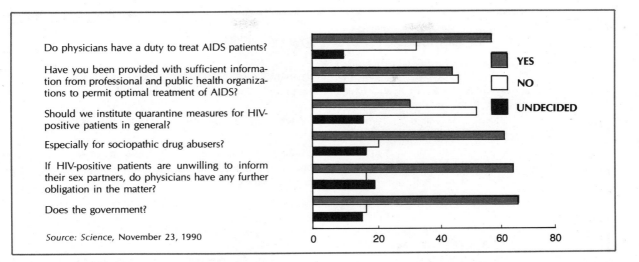

FIGURE 15.9 The Ethics of AIDS Care

A poll of 317 physicians shows that "doctors are far less certain about the nature of [AIDS] and the threat it poses than are other segments of our population," reports the November issue of *MD* magazine. The poll found that 64% of respondents now have AIDS patients, but many doctors don't feel they know enough about the disease. Nonetheless, 58% think the danger of AIDS infection to physicians has been understated. There is also considerable division of opinion and uncertainty regarding ethical and privacy issues.

ing people of sound mind to designate others to make health-care decisions for them in case they eventually become mentally disabled, including what forms of resuscitation are to be attempted in the event of cardiac failure. Other states are considering similar legislation. Nevertheless, as the numbers of AIDS patients increase, there will be even more confusion over how far to carry their treatment.

3. *The dangers of caring for HIV-infected patients.* Workers in the health-care professions have begun to realize that they carry some special risks in caring for AIDS patients or even working with those still-healthy individuals who are infected with HIV. Physicians are reporting various levels of anxiety with regard to these risks, and one-fourth of 258 doctors surveyed in New York City indicated they would *not* consider it unethical to refuse to care for people infected with the AIDS virus. It has been proposed that young physicians have more difficulty dealing with these patients because they are frustrated by their inability to cure the disease, and they are made uncomfortable by identifying with large numbers of people in their own age group suffering from an incurable disease. Figure 15.9 summarizes the conflicting attitudes of 317 physicians and demonstrates the dilemmas they face. These attitudes are creating a crisis in a profession that has been founded on a tradition of caring for anyone in need, even if one's own life must be risked.

4. *The costs of caring for HIV-infected patients and supporting research.* The costs of AIDS and

earlier stages of HIV infection are proving to be staggering, and there is already a marked shortage of facilities to care for HIV-infected patients. The federal government in the United States is now spending over $800 million annually on AIDS research. States, particularly California and New York, are contributing over $100 million each year on efforts to contain the infection. The increasing number of HIV-infected patients is raising the issue of where the money will come from to care for them. The direct cost of caring for patients, and indirect costs, including lost wages and earning power of patients, are costing the nation billions of dollars.

A number of people have inadequate health insurance coverage, which means that governments will soon be faced with an enormous financial burden of coping with the costs—both direct and indirect—of HIV-infected patients. The insurance companies of those who do have health insurance will find it increasingly difficult to keep up with the cost of providing care for these patients. The HIV epidemic points out some crucial ethical issues of health care. Is it time for a system of national medical insurance that will provide adequate and just treatment for anyone affected by acquired immunodeficiency syndrome, or will governments find it necessary to turn their backs on the suffering of thousands?

5. *Legal ramifications of AIDS.* As ethical problems multiply, the judicial system is increasingly being called upon to resolve disputes revolving around AIDS. Already several criminal and civil cases have

419

The Search for Romance in the Shadow of AIDS

Last spring, George K., a 43-year-old family therapist from Brooklyn, placed a personal ad, describing himself as heterosexual, white, professional, spiritual, healthy and infected with HIV, the virus that causes AIDS.

"If you love warm sandy beaches, pure white snow and fireplaces, let's connect," the ad read.

A 34-year-old woman from Connecticut, also infected with the virus, was one of six to respond. "I view HIV as a challenge, and not as the end of my life," she wrote.

They met in April, and plan to get married next year.

● ● ●

They are among the one million Americans, gay and heterosexual, estimated to carry the deadly virus usually transmitted by sex. . . .

And as they learn to live with the virus, many of the infected are striving for companionship, sexual intimacy and even marriage.

Still, many people suffer rejection, struggle in vain to keep marriages together or withdraw into the loneliness more commonly experienced in old age or widowhood, psychotherapists and support groups for the HIV-positive [say]. Yet there are relationships that survive, couples that become closer and people who fall in love, sometimes with uninfected partners.

"Many people are very concerned about not ever wanting to transmit this to anyone else," said Alison M. Deming, a psychotherapist in Syracuse who works with an HIV-positive support group. "Yet the need for a relationship and someone to care about is so important. It's basic."

Telling, or Not

A key question for HIV-positive people—most of whom are between the ages of 25 and 44—is when and how to disclose their infection to a romantic interest. For some the decision is even harder, because they are also forced to disclose intravenous drug use or bisexuality.

Some say they tell straightaway. But others say that as long as they keep the risk of transmission to a minimum—by using condoms and avoiding any exchange of blood or semen, as health experts advise—they think that they pose little threat and feel they can withhold the information.

There are HIV-positive people who engage in sex without revealing their infection or

reached the courts in which people are accused of deliberately or carelessly exposing others to HIV. Charges have stemmed from situations in which people who knew they carried the virus continued to have unprotected sexual relations. In Los Angeles in 1989, a jury awarded Rock Hudson's former lover over $5 million because he had been exposed to HIV. More than half of the states have statutes that make it a criminal offense to knowingly transmit a sexually transmitted disease, but most states have been hesitant to give HIV infection that particular classification. Some states have already enacted legislation that makes willful exposure of another to HIV a crime.

Many experts feel that legal precedents are being established based on hysteria and misunderstanding rather than rational scientific and legal principles. They suggest that getting a conviction in such cases will be extremely difficult, given the complications of proving that someone was actually infected with the virus, knew it, and wantonly spread it to someone else. It would also be difficult to prove that the plaintiff was indeed infected solely by the defendant, especially given the long incubation period of the disease. In the climate of fear that surrounds AIDS, public opinion polls show that more than half the populace would support legislation criminalizing willful transmission of the disease. Litigation on issues regarding HIV and AIDS will be on the rise in years to come.

taking precautions. Four states have passed laws that make a failure to inform a sexual partner of HIV-infection before sex a crime, and 15 others have made it a crime to knowingly expose a partner to the virus.

But experts say that most people with the virus feel compelled to tell, or at least to practice preventive measures. George K.'s fiancée said she previously had a simple rule—she would keep quiet unless there was the possibility of a long-term relationship. . . .

"I felt no HIV-negative man would want to sleep with me if he knew," said the woman, a physical therapist who tested positive in 1989. "My feeling was that if I was going to practice safe sex, why should I put myself on the line while there are people who do not know they are infected and are not practicing safe sex?"

• • •

Many people with the virus find it easier to be with someone who is also HIV-infected. Many AIDS organizations arrange social gatherings for HIV-positive people to meet, and workshops on dating and sex.

George K., who found his fiancée in the personal ads of *The Body Positive,* a magazine for people with the virus published by a group of the same name, said the couple share both fears and a desire to enjoy each day. A former intravenous drug user, he learned of his infection in 1988.

"We live now. We don't wait," he said. "The new car next year is not as important as what we can do now."

The only disadvantage in their relationship, they said, is a temptation not to practice protected sex since both are HIV-positive, despite the possibility that they could reinfect each other with different strains of the virus and further weaken their immune systems.

"For us," his fiancée said, "part of it is denial and that we can pretend for a short time that we're like regular people."

• • •

George K. does not count on his HIV-positive fiancée to see him through his illness. Her own health might falter first, he said, or she might not be able to handle the stress.

All he wants, he said, is to enjoy a rewarding relationship, even in the shadow of AIDS. "It's all attitude," he said. "You have to be thankful for what you have."

"I have a career. I have health. I have a wonderful woman in my life. I'm alive."
—Mireya Navarro, *New York Times,* October 10, 1991

WITCH-HUNTING MENTALITY

When a disease crisis faces a society, the people often search for a group on which to focus the blame. Since HIV spread first among homosexuals and a few other identified high-risk groups, many have speculated about the degree of responsibility these groups have for bringing the disease to others. Some have claimed that AIDS is a clear indication of God's disapproval of gay people or as evidence of the inherent evil of sex (Boswell, 1990b); others have used the AIDS issue to encourage new forms of discrimination against homosexuals.

It is crucial that we maintain a level of rationality and good sense with regard to this disease. No group must accept the blame for HIV or AIDS. The virus took hold first in some parts of the population and will spread to others. It is more important that we find ways of reducing the spread of the virus, developing effective treatments and preventions, and educating people thoroughly about the risks. There is nothing to be gained by succumbing to a witch-hunting mentality that can only foster attitudes of mistrust and discrimination.

As the next section demonstrates, each individual can take measures in his or her sexual decision-making and other aspects of life to minimize the risks of contracting HIV.

421

My brother is HIV positive. He is exactly like me in many ways. Our birthdays are eight days and four years apart; we look and sound alike.

When I visit him he often makes me answer the phone as a joke, knowing that his friends can't tell the difference. One time the first person to call was his boyfriend (now dead), who simply said, "Hi, Tiger." We are more alike than we admit, and certainly more alike than different.

There is one difference between us: Peter is gay and I am not. But that is not important in how we get along or in who we are. We have such a history together as brothers with a common life that his choice of sexual partner means nothing to me compared with everything in life we must now confront together.

And why is that important? Because too much of the public and the media believe (implicitly or explicitly) that a person's sexuality defines or characterizes who he or she is. My brother will almost certainly die of AIDS. It doesn't matter that he is gay. He is my brother. It's not too far to say that he is I.

And he is as beautiful and significant as Alison Gertz. He just won't get the same treatment. *Esquire* won't ever call my brother "Man of the Year," *People* won't put him on the cover, and few local columnists will see his life as anything special.

My criticism is tied to a personal reason. But I am not alone. I am a member of the so-called general population, whose health must be imperiled before this epidemic takes real shape in the public eye.

Yet I also belong, vicariously, to the world of people whom the media just can't get as worked up about. Because of that I know that all the "other" people with AIDS are just that: people. People with brothers and sisters and mothers and fathers and friends who know them as just that, and who have been fed up for a long time with most of the media's inability to capture what is happening to their lives.

When gay people have AIDS they are thought of as gay. When people who use drugs get AIDS they are depicted as drug users. When heterosexual people get AIDS they are depicted as people. Feeling especially sad for Alison Gertz because she is young, beautiful and heterosexual is as wrong as not feeling sad for gay men such as my brother because they are gay. We have to think of all people with AIDS as the children of sad parents, as brothers and sisters with terrified families, as the friends and relatives of everyone. As people.

—Tom Ehrenfeld, *New York Times,* August 17, 1990

AIDS and Personal Decisions About Sex

In an abrupt and dramatic way, the spreading epidemic of HIV infection is beginning to change human sexual behavior. We have made far more progress in understanding the biological aspects of the AIDS virus and the disease than we have the social and behavioral aspects. The problems inherent in this epidemic will only be brought under control through a multidisciplinary approach involving both the biomedical and behavioral sciences (Voeller, Reinisch, & Gottlieb, 1990). If the spread of HIV is to be brought under control before cures or preventative vaccines are developed, it is the behavior of people that will have to change.

AIDS AND HIV EDUCATION

Everyone seems to agree that educational efforts regarding AIDS must receive a high priority, especially for young people. A number of states already require their schools to offer AIDS education. However, there is controversy over at what age such education should begin and what its content should be. In many ways these controversial factors are extensions of debates

TABLE 15.2

Degree of Safety in Types of Sexual Activity

Safest	Less Safe	Risky	Least Safe
Dry kissing	Vaginal or anal intercourse using a condom	Cunnilingus without a dam*	Fellatio without a condom*
Body-to-body contact and embracing	Wet kissing	External skin contact with semen, if break or sore is present on skin	Vaginal intercourse without a condom
Massage	Cunnilingus using a dam		Anal intercourse without a condom
Mutual masturbation (with care in avoiding contact with semen)	Fellatio using a condom		Other anal contact, orally or manually

*As of 1991, there was still no definitive answer concerning the likelihood of HIV transmission through oral sex. Until the degree of risk can be more accurately assessed, using a condom or rubber dam during oral sex is highly recommended.

Source: G. Jacobs and J. Kerrins, *The AIDS File,* 1987, Woods Hole, MA: Cromlech Books.

that have been raging in the field of sex education for years. Some experts recommend beginning AIDS education with 9-, 10-, and 11-year-olds; others oppose starting at such early ages. Some groups claim that it is unrealistic to expect all youth to abstain from shared sexual activity because of the AIDS scare, and advocate the teaching of safer sex practices that will at least minimize the risks of contracting HIV. Critics of this approach feel that teaching about preventative measures condones casual sex. Among schools that have mandated AIDS education, some have also required that the emphasis be placed on sexual abstinence. Local communities are now being faced with decisions about these issues, and the evidence suggests AIDS education is only being incorporated into school systems half-heartedly (Calamidas, 1990).

Most experts agree that, in the general population, older teenagers and young adults tend to be the most sexually active and therefore at higher risk than some other groups. At school, students are surrounded by a population of their peers who come from diverse places and backgrounds, some of whom may be carriers of HIV. Reports from college campuses suggest that many students have been slow to accept the potential risks of HIV and AIDS around them and are slower still to modify their sexual behaviors. College students are still often neglecting to use condoms in their sexual activities (Crawford, 1990). Since few of those who may be infected have yet shown advanced symptoms of the disease or died from it, the threat may not yet seem real.

There have been debates in the media about the advertising of condoms as an AIDS-preventative measure, although most magazines and television networks are now willing to accept condom ads. In New York City, local television stations recently began a campaign of advertisements encouraging the use of con-

FIGURE 15.10   Distribution of Condoms to High School Students

While safe-sex kits and brochures have been available on many college campuses for some time, high schools are now also becoming involved in distributing condoms to students. Above, Jose Guzman, 18, and his girlfriend, Mary Matus, 16, hold condoms that they were given at John Dewey High School in Brooklyn, New York.

423

FIGURE 15.11   Condom Advertisement

The New York City Department of Health AIDS Program Services has sponsored several kinds of advertisements to encourage the use of condoms in sexual intercourse, particularly between male homosexuals.

doms. The advertisements focused on women and their insistence that their sexual partners use condoms. In San Francisco, poster advertisements for condoms have been displayed in public buses. In New York City, judges have offered condoms to convicted prostitutes and the Board of Education voted to give condoms to students on request (Flax, 1991).

The issue of AIDS education is new and will surely take us in new directions and encourage further debates on sex education. One thing is certain: no one grows up in today's world without hearing a great deal about HIV, AIDS, and their connections to sex.

CAN SEX BE SAFE AND SATISFYING?

Each human being has to make his or her own decisions about sex. In order to make these decisions, consideration must be given to the spread of HIV. A survey of 1,422 college students, aged 18 to 19, suggests that more than ever before in recent history,

male virginity and sexual inexperience are being viewed in a positive light. Twenty-two percent of the women surveyed indicated that they wanted their next lover to be a virgin, up from 9 percent 10 years before (Blotnick, 1987).

Although more individuals than in recent years will surely postpone sexual contact until they find lasting, monogamous relationships, others will choose to share sex now. How seriously they will consider the risks of contracting HIV, or what sorts of practices they will employ to decrease those risks, will depend on a variety of psychological and social factors, including the following:

1. *The degree of willingness to prepare ahead for sex.* The fear of condemnation from parents, religious leaders, and society has often made it difficult for young people to plan ahead and prepare for sexual activity. Many have therefore preferred to have sex be regarded as accidental or spontaneous in order to bear less sense of having been responsible for a bad deci-

sion or immoral behavior. Such attitudes can only interfere with the kind of mutual questioning and preparation that can render a sexual encounter at lower risk of spreading HIV.

2. *Self-esteem and assertiveness.* To protect oneself against HIV infection will require enough self-esteem and sense of self-worth to remember that one's health must be protected. It will also mean having enough self-confidence and assertiveness to make it clear that certain rules must govern a sexual encounter. This sort of behavior is often difficult for people who feel that their popularity, attractiveness, or even an entire relationship may be in question.

3. *Overcoming peer pressures about use of condoms.* As birth control devices, condoms have often been given a bad name. Some claim they reduce sexual sensations. They may be embarrassing to purchase. For such a simple device, they are frequently not used completely correctly. The fact remains, however, that for now latex condoms represent one of the best protections against HIV transmission in sexual encounters. Those that are lubricated with nonoxynol-9 provide even more protection, since spermicidal chemicals destroy HIV on contact. People will have to relearn that sex with condoms can not only be safer, but still be pleasurable and satisfying.

4. *Understanding that it can happen to you.* At various times in life, people are prone to feeling relatively invincible. Or they may believe that any consequence, even a negative one, is reversible. It will be crucial for everyone to realize that not only is HIV infection a threat to anyone, but for the time being it is irreversible. If you get the virus, there is no way to get rid of it. If you get the disease, there is no cure.

5. *Accepting the struggles of establishing a sexual identity.* Even people who consider themselves heterosexual sometimes have homosexual encounters. Because such choices may be personally difficult to accept psychologically, there may also be a tendency not to pay attention to proper protection during sex. For males, in particular, who share homosexual activity there must be careful consideration about the risk involved and precautions should be taken to prevent contracting HIV. Many young men who identify themselves primarily as gay are also having sex with women (Pollner, 1990).

In spite of the threat of HIV, couples should regard sex in a positive way as an enhancer of life. The new threat should force potential sexual partners to think more carefully about their sexual decisions, open up channels of communication, and protect themselves more deliberately from the spread of the disease. These new approaches to sex should prove of real value in reducing a spectrum of negative sexual consequences.

MINIMIZING THE SEXUAL RISKS OF CONTRACTING HIV

From the information now available about AIDS, there are particular guidelines for having safer sex:

1. Know your sexual partners and their sexual histories. You risk contracting HIV if you have sex with someone who has had sex with someone else previously. The more sexual partners an individual has had, the greater the risk, although it can take only one infected partner to get the virus. One rather disturbing study found that in a sample of 422 sexually active 18- to 25-years-olds, 34 percent of the males and 10 percent of the females admitted to having lied about their sexual histories in order to have sex. When asked if they would lie to a partner about having a negative AIDS test when they actually had not had such a test, 20 percent of the men and 4 percent of the women said they would (Cochran & Mays, 1990). This points up a sinister type of risk that exists.

2. If you are contemplating having sex with a new partner and there is no absolute guarantee that the virus is not present, it is crucial to make some agreements and live up to them:

- Agree not to share sex with any other partners for the duration of the relationship.
- Agree to be tested for HIV regularly after any sexual contact that could have transmitted it. It can take up to 6 months, or perhaps longer, for the antibodies to develop and show up on the blood test.
- Agree either to wait 6 months to share sex, after tests for HIV, or to use protection for that period of time.

3. The best form of protection is the use of a latex condom throughout a sexual encounter, being careful not to allow semen to spill out of it. There are newly designed condoms that have adhesive around the shaft to prevent slippage and leakage. A new "female condom" that would be inserted into the vagina should be marketed soon (see p. 119).

4. During vaginal intercourse, a spermicidal foam containing nonoxynol-9 should be used in addition to the condom, because spermicides appear to help kill HIV on contact.

5. Avoid direct contact with any bodily fluids or excretions from a partner.

6. Use a rubber "dam" during oral contact with the vulva or anus. Oral contact with sites where the virus could be harbored is considered risky. Some experts have recommended that small, square latex

rubber dam: small square sheet of latex used to cover the vulva, vagina, or anus to help prevent transmission of HIV during sexual activity.

FIGURE 15.12 Think About It First

AIDS knows no boundaries. This advertisement by the New York City Department of Health is an effort to get young heterosexual couples to think about the consequences of unprotected sexual behavior before they become emotionally involved in it.

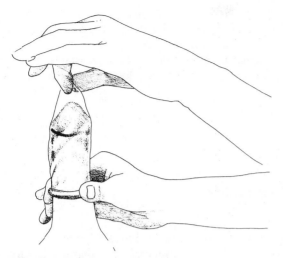

FIGURE 15.13 How to Use the Condom

Do not allow the penis to make sexual entry or contact before putting on the condom. Semen and sperm can escape from the penis at any time.

sheets, of the sort dentists sometimes use in the mouth, can be placed over the vulva, vagina, or anus. This would allow for some oral stimulation without direct contact from the tongue or lips. There is no research to date that can show how effective or necessary such a dam might be in preventing the transmission of HIV, but it represents the best precaution, given the present state of our knowledge. The latex dams are not widely available, but could be obtained at medical/dental supply stores. Some dentists might be willing to provide them. Use of a dam would represent a reasonable precaution for lesbian women to use in their oral-genital contacts. A rubber glove or individual rubber fingercots that fit over a single finger might also be considered for either sex if a finger is to be inserted into the vagina or anus, to offer protection from the virus entering through a break in the skin from either partner.

These practices cannot provide a guarantee of safety against HIV transmission. They can minimize your risks of contracting the virus. They also represent the most responsible ways of approaching sexual activity in a world where AIDS exists and is becoming increasingly prevalent.

Conclusion

The HIV epidemic has mobilized the forces of science, medicine, and society in unprecedented ways. Never in history have human beings moved so quickly from recognition of a medical problem to comprehensive understanding of the problem. Never in recent history have human beings faced a disease epidemic of the proportions that HIV is now threatening. At the foundation of all the issues is the matter of personal sexual decision-making. It is through safe and sane approaches to sex that the spread of this disease can effectively be slowed.

It will take a well-coordinated effort on the part of every facet of society for the HIV/AIDS crisis to be brought under control. When the National Commission on AIDS released its report in 1991, it reminded us that the government must take a strong and active role in responding to the problem. The report was critical of the nation's leadership for not having taken more initiative in dealing with AIDS. At a press conference when the report was released, the commission's director, Dr. June Osborn, dean of the Univer-

FIGURE 15.14 Magic Johnson

In November 1991, Los Angeles Lakers star Magic Johnson announced that he was retiring from his basketball career because he was infected with HIV. He indicated that he would devote his attention to educating people about AIDS and safer sex. Observers agreed that his courageous disclosure will have a more profound effect on AIDS education, and perhaps on AIDS research funding, than any development in the AIDS crisis so far. Some AIDS activists expressed their concern that it had taken Johnson's tragedy to focus political and public attention on the magnitude of the problem, after so many thousands of AIDS patients have already succumbed to the disease.

427

sity of Michigan's School of Public Health, said, "We're not talking about business as usual. We're talking about an extraordinary event in human evolution. The denial phase of the last decade must go away. . . . We're lagging behind our own information. We really need a national commitment to deal with this."

The second decade of HIV/AIDS will be filled with more tragic human loss and the staggering costs of dealing with the infection. The need for changes in human behavior will become increasingly clear as HIV infection hits everyone closer to home.■

CHAPTER SUMMARY

1. Acquired immunodeficiency syndrome (AIDS) was first identified in 1981. It is a disease that progressively destroys the body's immune system so that opportunistic infections eventually weaken the victim. It is eventually fatal.

2. While the origins of the disease are uncertain, it may have begun in Africa, when an animal virus mutated. HIV infection has now been identified in 149 countries, and it is believed that up to 1.5 million Americans are infected with the virus.

3. A retrovirus causes AIDS, and several strains have been identified. They have been given the general name human immunodeficiency virus (HIV). The virus can probably attack several human tissues, but particularly affects the T-4 lymphocytes that are crucial in the immune system.

4. Anyone who has been infected with HIV, even if he or she has not developed symptoms of disease, may spread the virus to others. Semen and blood have been most widely implicated in the transmission, but vaginal secretions and breast milk also transmit the virus. Saliva and other bodily secretions or excretions may hold some risk.

5. HIV infection spread first among homosexual men and intravenous drug abusers who share needles. HIV infection is spreading among heterosexuals. Women are at higher risk in heterosexual activity than men are. Once symptoms appear, the infection progresses through predictable stages,

with AIDS being the final, terminal stage. It is not yet known if everyone who contracts the virus will become ill, but the percentage of those infected developing the disease increases with time.

6. Tests to detect HIV in the blood are quite reliable, although there is controversy over how strongly such testing should be required.

7. There is no cure for HIV infection. Treatment focuses on prevention and control of opportunistic infections. Research is focusing on the development of a vaccine to produce immunity to the virus, thus preventing infection. Such a vaccine will not be available for some time.

8. Social and ethical problems surround any epidemic, and HIV has generated many such issues. Individual freedoms can be jeopardized by overreaction to the crisis. Caring for AIDS patients raises issues of confidentiality, cost, and safety. Legal conflicts about HIV infection are becoming increasingly common.

9. HIV requires some new approaches to sexual decision-making. Some sex should be avoided; use of condoms and other protective measures can reduce the risks of contracting HIV if certain sexual behaviors are chosen.

10. Sex can still be pleasurable and a safe part of relationships if approached responsibly and with appropriate precautions.

ANNOTATED READINGS

A number of excellent books on HIV and AIDS are in various stages of preparation and publication. Watch your bookstores and consult with instructors who can keep you up to date on the latest references.

Alyson, S. (Ed.). (1990). *You can do something about AIDS.* Boston, MA: The Stop AIDS Project, Inc. Suggestions for people who want to become personally involved in making a contribution to the battle against AIDS.

Blake, J. (1990). *Risky times: How to be AIDS-smart and stay healthy.* New York: Workman Publishing Co. Focusing on behaviors and their implications, this book provides guidelines for protecting oneself against HIV infection. In addition to suggestions for safer sex practices, it offers a perspective on people who are infected that is empathic and encouraging. Many myths and misconceptions about AIDS are dispelled.

Hatcher, R. A. (Ed.). (1991). *Safely sexual.* New York: Irvington Publishers. A practical and sensible guide to a safer sexual life-style, with suggestions for satisfying sexual encounters in which the partners are protected against AIDS and other sexually transmitted diseases. This book also includes discussion of contraceptive methods and how to make a choice of a method for personal use.

Jackson, J. K. (1992). *Wellness: AIDS, STD, & other communicable diseases.* Guilford, CT: The Dushkin Publishing Group. Provides an overview of HIV and its mechanisms of action, as well as specific guidelines for prevention and treatment.

Miller, H. G. (1990). *AIDS: The second decade.* Washington, DC: National Academy Press. An update on the AIDS crisis, offering information on how the disease has progressed and how it may progress in the future. This volume reminds us that there is no magic cure or vaccine in sight, and that the second decade of AIDS will see much greater problems than did the first decade.

Nelkin, D., Willis, D. P., & Parris, S. V. (Eds.). (1991). *A disease of society: Cultural and institutional responses to AIDS.* New York: Cambridge University Press. An excellent collection of articles that examines the impact that AIDS has had on families, social institutions, medical science, prisons, and the health-care system. This is a scholarly work, filled with useful information and insights.

Perrow, C., & Guillen, M. F. (1990). *The AIDS disaster: The failure of organization in New York and the nation.* New Haven, CT: Yale University Press. Examines the ways in which society has responded to the AIDS epidemic, often finding the reactions of governments and cultural institutions to be inadequate. The book provides information that will be helpful in framing new, more effective approaches for the future.

Preston, J., & Swann, G. (1987). *Safe sex: The ultimate erotic guide.* New York: New American Library/Plume. This is an explicit guide to integrating measures for protecting against AIDS infection into a full and active sex life.

Turner, C. F., et al. (1989). *AIDS, sexual behavior, and intravenous drug use.* Washington, DC: National Academy Press. A scholarly work examining the relationships between IV drug abuse and the spread of HIV infection. Studies of sexual behavior are detailed.

United Hospital Fund (1991). *Simple acts of kindness: Volunteering in the age of AIDS.* New York: United Hospital Fund. Descriptions of several model programs in which volunteers have made a difference in the lives of persons with AIDS. The writing is highly personal, and dispels many of the negative perceptions about working with AIDS patients.

Voeller, B., Reinisch, J. M., & Gottlieb, M. (Eds.). (1990). *AIDS and sex: An integrated biobehavioral approach.* New York: Oxford University Press. A collection of papers from a conference of AIDS experts sponsored by the Kinsey Institute. Summarizes research and social commentary relating to sexuality and HIV infection. One of the most comprehensive resources available on information up to 1990.

Whipple, B., & Ogden, G. (1989). *Safe encounters: How women can say yes to pleasure and no to unsafe sex.* New York: McGraw-Hill. Practical, down-to-earth advice for women on sex in a dangerous time. Suggestions for dealing with partners while protecting oneself. Reflects the changing times in sexual behavior.

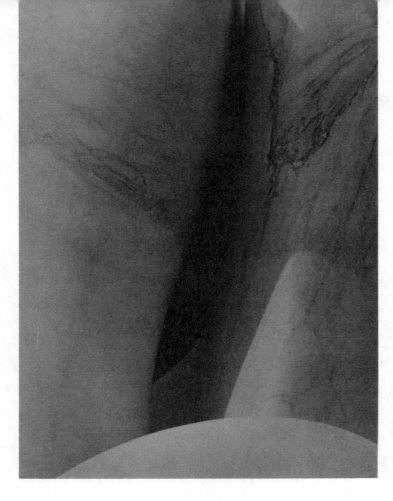

CHAPTER SIXTEEN

UNDERSTANDING SEXUAL DYSFUNCTIONS
When Is a Dysfunction a Dysfunction?
What Labels Tell Us
The Sexual Response Cycle
Desire Phase Problems
Arousal Difficulties
Vaginismus
Orgasmic Dysfunctions
Lack of Ejaculatory Control
Post-Ejaculatory Pain
Sexual Problems of Homosexuals

CAUSES OF SEXUAL DYSFUNCTIONS
Ruling Out Physical Causes
Drugs and Alcohol
The Pressure to Perform
Relationships and Sexual Functioning
Other Causes

TREATING SEXUAL DYSFUNCTIONS
Folk Remedies
Modes of Treatment
What Is a Sex Therapist?

BEHAVIORAL APPROACHES TO SEX THERAPY
Basic Goals of Behavioral Sex Therapy
Self-Help Approaches
Partnership Approaches
Some Specific Behavioral Methods

A CRITICAL LOOK AT SEX THERAPY
Is Sex Therapy Effective?
Ethical Issues in Sex Therapy

CONCLUSION

CHAPTER SUMMARY

I suppose I thought it would never happen to me. I had never had any problems getting an erection since I started getting interested in sex. Then this one night when my girlfriend and I were just starting to have intercourse, I just lost it. Now I've had it come and go sometimes, but a little stimulation would always bring it right back. This time—nothing. I never felt so embarrassed and unmanly. As I look back on it now after seeing the therapist, I can see how I set myself up for the whole problem.

—Statement written by a college student

SEXUAL DYSFUNCTIONS AND THEIR TREATMENT

Workers in the helping professions—physicians, psychologists, counselors, social workers, and clergy, for example—have always been presented with the sexual concerns and complaints of their clients. Until the publication of *Human Sexual Inadequacy* by Masters and Johnson in 1970, these professionals rarely received any specialized training in dealing with sexual problems. Instead, they were left to muddle through their own discomfort in discussing sexual topics and to dole out a vague blend of reassurance, moralizing, and poorly researched suggestions for living up to the performance standards. There were few accepted terms with which to label sexual dysfunctions. Words such as impotence, frigidity, and premature ejaculation could create a hush in any room, and even the professionals only partially understood their meanings.

Understanding Sexual Dysfunctions

With the publication of *Human Sexual Inadequacy*, the field of sex therapy began expanding rapidly, and the systematized treatment of sexual problems was legitimized. For the first time, dysfunctional symptoms were given labels that could be used in both professional and popular communication. There was new hope for those who were experiencing dissatisfaction in their sexual encounters. However, before long there were also many new questions to be answered and new ethical issues to be resolved.

WHEN IS A DYSFUNCTION A DYSFUNCTION?

In a British study on sexual functioning of 436 women in their thirties, about one-third of the women responded in ways that led the researchers to conclude that the women were experiencing some sexual dysfunction. However, only 23 percent of those women believed to be dysfunctional regarded themselves as having a sexual problem (Osborn, Hawton, & Gath, 1988).

Traditionally, men who experience difficulty controlling their ejaculations are said to suffer from premature ejaculation. Women who never experience orgasm are said to be experiencing orgasmic dysfunction. However, the situation may be more complex than these handy labels might suggest. Who is to define

431

whether or not some phenomenon of sexual response is a problem—a dysfunction? If the woman enjoys her sexual encounters without feeling any need for orgasm, should she be treated for a dysfunction? If the rapidly ejaculating man and his partner are perfectly comfortable with his pattern of response, should they be made to feel they have a problem?

Sex therapy and sex research face many such troublesome ethical issues. Effective sex therapy is based on several basic assumptions (discussed later in this chapter) concerning the removal of barriers to normal sexual functioning, and the values of both therapists and patients are involved. Treatment of sexual problems cannot be reduced to a series of mechanical steps, although there are specific skills that may help a great deal. It has been suggested that helping people with sexual dysfunctions requires human sensitivity, creativity, openness to new directions, and well-honed skills. One cannot attempt to change sexual functioning without being prepared also to examine sexual values, the quality of relationships, and other highly subjective life issues (Mosher, 1991).

Since we do not yet have reliable and valid norms for human sexual behavior, we must use whatever statistical and clinical evidence is available, in order to establish ranges of sexual behavior that can then be used to make practical judgments about sexual dysfunctions. The individual's own sexual history and feelings are particularly important in arriving at any diagnosis. Perhaps it is sufficient to assume that if some functional difficulty with sex prompts an individual or couple to seek professional help, it is a dysfunction. However, this definition would leave out the many millions of others for whom sex is unsatisfactory but who are reluctant to seek treatment. A workable definition of dysfunction would, above all, allow the therapist room for professional judgment in reassuring clients that they should not be fooled by unrealistically high sexual standards into believing they have a problem where none exists.

Most cultures through the ages have established certain mythical standards and expectations regarding sexual performance. The performance standards for women have been more vague and mysterious, while those for men have been fairly rigid. When people's bodies do not function sexually as expected and desired, they often feel frustrated, inadequate, and unhappy. In a society such as our own, which places a premium on being successful in sexual endeavors, to fail in a sexual encounter is perceived as tantamount to being a failure at manhood or womanhood. Whether or not the performance standards have some basis in the realities of human physiology or are simply the inventions of a sex-obsessed culture, many of them persist today and are perpetuated by the media.

Mythical Performance Standards for Men   Men have always been plagued by the standard that successful sex requires an erect penis. It is even assumed by most males that their partners cannot be expected to find sexual pleasure unless an erection is achieved and maintained. Closely allied to this standard is the standard of postponing ejaculation or orgasm. Since a penis tends to lose its erection following ejaculation, the longer a man can postpone ejaculation, the better sexual performer he will be considered. A third standard might better be stated as the unquestioned assumption it has always been: that men reach orgasms without difficulty and find in this peak experience the ultimate pleasure of sex. It was not until very recently that men's difficulties in reaching orgasms became recognized as a fairly common complaint.

Mythical Performance Standards for Women   Historically, the sexual performance standards for women have focused on issues of sexual attractiveness and availability rather than desire. Women traditionally were viewed by heterosexual men as passive, nonperforming sex partners. More recent attitudes encourage women to take a more active role in sex. However, women have also become more bound by new standards of sexual performance. Women are under pressure today to become intensely aroused and ready for sexual contact, and to reach orgasm without difficulty. Another expectation for women is the ability to have more than one orgasm during a single sexual encounter.

These become the standards on which men and women pin their sexual hopes, play out their roles in bed, and judge their performances afterward. It is little wonder, then, that so many people end up feeling inadequate, dissatisfied, and disillusioned by what is actually happening in their sexual lives. When individuals experience some functional problem during sex, or their bodies fail to perform as expected and desired with some consistency, they are said to be experiencing sexual dysfunction. Today, more than ever before, such problems need not signal a lifetime of unfulfilled sexual needs. As this chapter will demonstrate, most dysfunctions can be eased and corrected.

WHAT LABELS TELL US

Scientific communication demands that a terminology be available, and each of the sexual difficulties has been given a general label. However, it is important not to lose sight of the fact that such labels may have profound implications for the individual sufferer. Consider the term impotence, which conjures up images of

impotence (IM-pa-tens): difficulty achieving or maintaining erection of the penis.

failure and powerlessness, hardly reassuring concepts for the impotent man with erectile difficulties. A more positive term, preorgasmic, was coined to describe women who had never been able to reach orgasm. This is a more upbeat hopeful label because it implies that, although it has not yet been reached, a potential for orgasm still exists. I shall use terms in this chapter that minimize negative implications.

There are certain modifying terms that are employed in diagnosing and describing sexual dysfunctions. The term primary dysfunction means that the problem has always existed and the person has never functioned normally or as desired. The term secondary dysfunction is used in describing a dysfunction that has appeared after a period of normal function. Thus, a woman with primary orgasmic dysfunction has never been able to reach orgasm, while the woman with secondary orgasmic dysfunction is no longer able to be orgasmic, but once was.

Dysfunctions may also be *total* or *partial,* such as in the cases of men who are totally unable to achieve erections or who are able to experience at least partial erection. The term *absolute* is used in referring to a dysfunction that occurs in all of an individual's sexual encounters, while the label *situational* means that it happens only under specific conditions.

Labels can tell us a great deal about a person's sexual difficulties. At the same time, as noted earlier, they must be used with caution because they can influence people's attitudes about themselves.

THE SEXUAL RESPONSE CYCLE

In chapter 3, "Human Sexual Response," various models were described for understanding the predictable sequence of physiological events that constitute the human sexual response cycle. The Masters and Johnson (1966) model includes four phases: excitement, plateau, orgasm, and resolution. A three-phase model was also discussed on pages 62 and 63 that is of greater value in understanding the relationship of sexual dysfunctions to sexual response (Kaplan, 1979). This model demonstrates that sexual response consists of three distinct components:

1. A desire phase, having to do with one's degree of interest in and desire for sexual gratification. Sexual desire is probably controlled by centers of the limbic system in the brain—centers that seem to activate sexual desire, and centers that seem to inhibit desire. This phase precedes the more profound physiological changes in the sex organs and throughout the body. The desire phase may be influenced by emotion, memory, and conditioning.

2. A buildup of blood in the genital areas that causes the typical signs of sexual arousal, such as penile and clitoral erection and lubrication of the vagina. This phase is accompanied by increased muscular tension and arousal throughout the body. It is controlled primarily by the parasympathetic division of the autonomic nervous system.

3. Reversal of the genital blood flow and muscular relaxation, triggered by the orgasm. This phase is mostly controlled by the sympathetic division of the autonomic nervous system.

Things can go wrong in any of these phases of sexual response. Table 16.1 (overleaf) summarizes the relationship of various sexual dysfunctions to the three-phase model. Each is described in more detail in the next few sections.

DESIRE PHASE PROBLEMS

Although most people can identify and describe inner feelings of needing or desiring sexual gratification, it is not yet known whether these feelings represent strictly an innate biological drive associated with species survival, a learned way of seeking physically pleasurable sensations, or some combination of both. Nor is it well understood why the reported levels of interest in sex vary a great deal among people, as do the frequencies with which they choose to have sexual activity. We do know, however, that these differences in sexual response, whatever their causes, are an important concern to a great many people: a discrepancy in level of sexual desire between two partners is the most common complaint brought to sex therapists (Goleman, 1988).

It might be that low levels of sexual desire result from lack of activity in the brain centers that control sex drive, and this may in turn affect the levels of hormones that mitigate sexual desire. But diagnosing desire phase dysfunctions is subjective and difficult because no standard has yet been set to describe the normal human sexual appetite. Some researchers have suggested that there is no absolute scale of sexual desire, but only discrepancies between people's sexual styles and interests (Weeks, 1987). Some people seem to have very infrequent needs for sex and are not

preorgasmic: a term often applied to women who have not yet been able to reach orgasm during sexual response.

primary dysfunction: a difficulty with sexual functioning that has always existed for a particular person.

secondary dysfunction: a difficulty with sexual functioning that develops after some period of normal sexual functioning.

433

TABLE 16.1

The Sexual Response Cycle and Sexual Dysfunctions

Desire Phase Dysfunctions:	Arousal (Vasocongestive) Phase Dysfunctions:	Orgasmic (Reversed Vasocongestive) Phase Dysfunctions:
Normal asexuality: the individual who naturally has low levels of need for sexual gratification (not necessarily a dysfunction) Inhibited sexual desire (ISD) Sexual avoidance: caused by anxiety and phobias relating to sexual activity	Problems in achieving a suitable level of sexual arousal *In men:* erectile dysfunction *In women:* lack of vaginal lubrication, general sexual dysfunction Involuntary spasm of outer vaginal musculature in women: vaginismus	Problems in triggering orgasm, creating an inordinate orgasmic delay or a complete inability to reach orgasm *In men:* called delayed (or retarded) orgasm or ejaculatory incompetence *In women:* called orgasmic (or orgastic) dysfunction, preorgasmia, anorgasmia Lack of ejaculatory control in men; often called premature ejaculation Post-ejaculatory pain in men

Source: Information from *The New Sex Therapy* by H. S. Kaplan, 1974, New York: Brunner/Mazel; and *The Evaluation of Sexual Disorders* by H. S. Kaplan, 1983, New York: Brunner/Mazel.

bothered by this. Even in a sex-saturated society, it is possible to maintain feelings of well-being and self-worth with minimal levels of sexual interest. It is also possible for some people to choose a celibate or sexually inactive life-style that represents a mature, responsible approach to life and is manifested by a suppressed sexual desire or at least suppressed expression of the desire. Priests and nuns, for example, are often successful in maintaining a life-style that includes

FIGURE 16.1   Sexual Phobias

An aversion to or fear of sexual intimacy is considered one form of sexual dysfunction. A real or imagined physical problem or psychological stress might cause someone to sabotage an otherwise satisfactory relationship in order to avoid sexual contact.

very little expression of sexual needs. This non-pathological way of life is called normal asexuality and need not be considered a problem or dysfunction.

Sometimes, however, low sexual desire is viewed as a problem, and desire phase complaints are being brought to therapy clinics in increasing numbers (Spector & Carey, 1990). As a dysfunction, it takes two distinguishable forms: the milder inhibited sexual desire (ISD) and the more severe sexual phobias and aversions (Kaplan, 1987). ISD may be characterized by a loss of attraction to formerly exciting stimuli and a lack of pleasure even in direct stimulation of the sex organs. Dysfunctional individuals may not be particularly aroused by seeing attractive people and rarely seek sexual activity. They may still function normally when sexual stimulation is permitted, but the physical pleasure they derive from it is limited and fleeting. ISD is often rooted in other difficulties within a relationship that need to be resolved before sexual interactions can improve or become more frequent (Hotchner, 1991).

Sexual phobias and aversions are generated by anxiety about sexual contact. Some men and women develop fearful reactions toward sex or its possible consequences and eventually become unreasonably afraid of becoming sexually involved. These reactions can stem from psychological stress resulting from inhibiting or punitive upbringing, rigidly religious

normal asexuality: an absence or low level of sexual desire, considered normal for a particular person.

inhibited sexual desire (ISD): loss of interest and pleasure in what were formerly arousing sexual stimuli.

sexual phobias and aversions: exaggerated fears toward forms of sexual expression.

backgrounds, health concerns, or a history of physical and/or sexual abuse. Often such individuals become involved in close relationships and are successful in making themselves attractive to others. As the levels of intimacy and commitment deepen, however, there usually comes a point where they become fearful about sex. They may then find ways of sabotaging the relationship or finding fault with their partner, so they will not feel obligated to go any further with sex. They may, for example, become increasingly irritable or critical so that arguments are constantly developing. It is often difficult for therapists to distinguish these desire phase dysfunctions from problems with arousal, since individuals with ISD and sexual phobias and aversions may also experience trouble in becoming sexually aroused. It will be up to the sex therapist to seek specific information about a particular person's level of sexual desire in order to make valid judgments about a proper course of treatment.

AROUSAL DIFFICULTIES

Whenever something interferes with blood flow into the sex organs, the human body fails to exhibit the preliminary signs of sexual arousal. In men the penis fails to become erect or loses some of its erection. This has traditionally been called impotence but is better called erectile dysfunction, as I refer to it in this chapter. In women, lack of arousal is characterized by the vagina remaining dry and tight. The term *frigidity* was once widely used to describe these symptoms, but it is no longer used by professionals because it is such a vague and seemingly negative label. The term general sexual dysfunction will be employed here.

erectile dysfunction: difficulty achieving or maintaining penile erection (impotence).

general sexual dysfunction: difficulty for a woman in achieving sexual arousal.

Case Study

KRISTIN AND MARK: LACK OF SEXUAL AROUSAL INTERFERES WITH A RELATIONSHIP

Kristin and Mark sought help from a male sex therapist for a long-standing problem. They had been living together for 2 years, while Mark finished earning his doctorate. Kristin, a graphic artist, was supporting them both. They planned to be married in another year, although their sexual difficulties were beginning to create some doubts in their minds. They explained to the therapist that Kristin rarely was interested in sex. She might become sexually aroused once every month or two, but most of the time she participated in sexual activity only to please Mark. He was often left with a feeling of having coerced her into sex, and this made him feel guilty and anxious. They both seemed committed to their relationship and to staying together.

In discussing their sexual histories, Kristin explained that she masturbated frequently to orgasm and had many sexual fantasies. It also became apparent that she had grown up with some highly negative attitudes toward sex. Mark's sexual background was not particularly unusual, and he apparently had no problems with his own sexual functioning. Both of them did feel that sex had become a very anxiety-producing subject for both of them. Further discussions with the therapist brought out some other fears

and doubts. Kristin admitted that she often did not find Mark particularly sexually attractive and felt that he did not pay enough attention to expressing romantic and loving feelings. Mark explained that her lack of sexual responsiveness made him angry, and that he often felt she regretted having broken up with a particular former boyfriend. The therapist encouraged them to talk out and resolve these conflicts and began assigning structured behavioral exercises.

The sensate focus exercises (see page 450), which they did in a dimly lighted room with music playing, immediately began to make a difference. They both felt emotionally closer, and Kristin felt real warmth and caring from Mark. Much of the time during sensate focus, Kristin felt aroused and interested in sex. As the therapy process continued, a need for sexual compromise arose. There was some difference between their levels of interest in sex. Kristin saw sex as a special experience to share occasionally, while Mark viewed it as a constant source of relief from physical tension. The therapist helped them to work out some compromise agreements to help govern their sexual contacts in the future.

Since the control mechanisms in the brain and nervous system for the arousal phase of sexual response are different from those that control orgasm, it is possible—though unusual—for those who show few characteristics of arousal to be orgasmic. A man with erectile dysfunction may achieve orgasm, ejaculating with a flaccid (nonerect) penis. Likewise, some women who do not manifest the usual signs of sexual arousal such as vaginal lubrication and clitoral erection may still have an orgasmic response.

Although penile erection seems to be controlled primarily by spinal reflexes, and can even occur in a male whose spinal cord has been severed above the erectile reflex center, the phenomenon is highly susceptible to input from the brain. Not only can thoughts, fantasies, and sensory stimuli trigger erection, but they can inhibit it as well. Most men will experience some instances of erectile difficulties during their lifetimes, typically as a result of fatigue, from having consumed too much alcohol, or simply from not being in the mood for sex. A common pattern for the dysfunction is for erection to take place easily for masturbation, but to be lost during shared activities such as intercourse. Recent research is making it increasingly clear that erection problems may be the result of physical disorders more frequently than was once believed. This makes a thorough physical examination all the more crucial in evaluating erection problems (Diokno & Hollander, 1991; Batra & Lue, 1990).

Men in our culture place a great deal of importance on their penises and often consider erection to be one of the trappings of masculinity. They typically have adopted the unwarranted performance standard that good sex requires an erect penis. Therefore, experiencing erectile dysfunction can be devastatingly embarrassing and frightening for most men. They feel as if they are not whole men.

It is not unusual for men to experience trouble having an erection after experiencing some other sexual problem for a period of time. If, for example, a man continually has trouble reaching orgasms or constantly feels he is disappointing a partner by ejaculating too rapidly, he may begin to feel frustrated and discouraged. He may eventually feel anxiety about any sexual involvement, and his body begins to fail in becoming aroused (Buvat et al., 1990).

Women have experienced less pressure toward proving their womanhood by being able to become sexually aroused, primarily because they are at least physically capable of participating in sexual intercourse even without arousal. Traditionally, women were viewed as reproductive human beings more than sexual ones. Since they could conceive without ever becoming sexually excited or having enjoyed sex, little notice was given to their arousal patterns. With increased attention given to female sexual response in recent times, however, some women have felt the need to fake arousal and orgasm to meet performance standards. Some women with general sexual dysfunction report that they still enjoy the physical intimacy of sexual contact. More often, unresponsive women eventually come to think of sex as something to be endured: they become trapped between their lack of physical arousal and their desire to live up to social standards of eroticism.

The partners of individuals with general sexual dysfunction vary in their reactions to the problem. Some are unconcerned because they care primarily

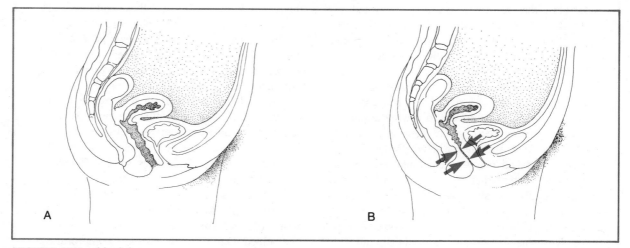

FIGURE 16.2 Vaginismus

Vaginismus is an involuntary constriction of the outer vaginal muscles prohibiting intercourse. Vaginismus might be caused by ignorance of bodily functions or might be considered a physical manifestation of a psychological fear. The drawing on the left (A) illustrates the relaxed vagina, while the drawing on the right (B) illustrates vaginismus.

Case Study

GEORGIA AND AL: VAGINISMUS FRUSTRATES SEXUAL ACTIVITY

Georgia and Al, married for 2 years, were referred to a sex therapy clinic by Georgia's gynecologist. They were assigned to work with a therapy team consisting of a female physician and a male psychologist. Because of difficulty with vaginismus, their marriage had never been consummated. They had developed other forms of sexual activity, but both remained frustrated by the inability to have coitus. Georgia often become highly sexually aroused and wanted very much to share intercourse with her husband.

After their initial therapy session, the physician suggested that Al try inserting a finger into Georgia's vagina, at home and with her permission, to feel the muscular contractions of vaginismus. Al could immediately feel the contraction of her muscles. He admitted to being somewhat surprised at the reaction and said during their next session that he had secretly suspected that the reaction was more under his wife's control than it actually was.

During the second session, the therapy team assigned exercises to be used over a period of several weeks. These exercises involved helping Georgia feel more comfortable with insertion of her own fingers into her vagina, then with the insertion of Al's fingers. After four weekly therapy sessions, the therapy team recommended that coitus be attempted. All indications were that Georgia was sufficiently relaxed to have intercourse. At the next session, the couple reported that there had been some discomfort at first, but that they had successfully completed two acts of intercourse. They both were thrilled by their progress and were quite determined to improve their sexual relationship even more.

During a follow-up visit 1 year after therapy had ended, Georgia and Al reported that during a brief period 3 months before, she had experienced two instances of vaginismus. They were apparently associated with some tension in the relationship at that time. However, the couple used some of their former dilation techniques, and the problem disappeared almost immediately. Other than the two brief relapses, their sexual relationship was very happy and fulfilling.

about their own satisfaction. Others feel somehow responsible for the dysfunction and perceive it to be a function of their own unattractiveness or sexual inadequacy, and may therefore feel hurt or disappointed (Carroll & Bagley, 1990). Others recognize that such difficulties often do not signal any negative feelings toward them and simply accept incidents of this sort as temporary and transitory.

VAGINISMUS

The woman with vaginismus may occasionally enjoy sexual arousal and be capable of orgasms with clitoral stimulation. However, when an attempt is made to introduce a penis or other object into the vagina, the muscles surrounding its opening contract involuntarily (see Fig. 16.2). This holds the vaginal entrance closed and makes intromission impossible or painfully difficult. Many women with this dysfunction are also fearful about sexual intercourse or other forms of vaginal penetration or are very concerned about the possibility of pregnancy. They often express miscon-

ceptions about the delicacy of the vaginal lining, believing that it can be easily injured.

Vaginismus is the major cause of unconsummated marriages (marriages in which sexual intercourse has not taken place). Because it interferes with sexual intercourse so blatantly, it is one of the sexual dysfunctions for which heterosexual couples are more prone to seek treatment (Hawton & Catalan, 1990). On the other hand, some heterosexual couples adopt alternative methods of sexual expression that are mutually pleasurable and go on for many years without experiencing intercourse. There are even documented cases of pregnancy resulting from semen being deposited near the vagina of women with vaginismus, without coitus actually having taken place (Moynihan & Whelehan, 1983). This should serve as a further warning to those who rely on withdrawal as a method of birth control.

It is quite typical for women who experience vaginismus to have had an unpleasant early sexual experience. For those who have not been told that first intercourse may generate some pain and bleeding if a hymen is present, the experience may be traumatic.

437

There are other organic conditions that can result in painful sex as well. These include dryness of the vagina caused by antihistamines or other drugs, infection of the clitoris or vulval area, injury or irritation in the vagina, and tumors of the internal reproductive organs. Such negative stimuli can easily establish fears of sex that are expressed through contractions of the vaginal musculature. Women with vaginismus often lack accurate information about their own sexual anatomy and physiology.

ORGASMIC DYSFUNCTIONS

Primary orgasmic dysfunction, in which an individual has never been able to achieve an orgasm, is far more common in females than in males. It has been estimated that up to 10 percent of women are unable to reach orgasm through any form of stimulation. There

are very few documented cases of men who have never been able to reach orgasm, even through masturbation, although 4 to 10 percent of males experience some level of difficulty in reaching orgasm (Spector & Carey, 1990). Difficulty of this sort in males has been labeled retarded ejaculation. There has been some confusion about what happens to men who are experiencing this dysfunction. One theory is that these men are so focused on their partners' pleasure, or have so many conflicting feelings about sexual pleasure, that they have what might be called a "numb" erection. In other words, even though they have no difficulty with erection, they do not experience many of the subjective sensations of sexual arousal and stimulation associated with orgasm (Apfelbaum, 1989).

retarded ejaculation: a sexual dysfunction in which a male has difficulty reaching an orgasm.

Women Becoming Orgasmic

Female orgasm. There have been more articles written and more talk about it than any other area of human sexuality in the past decade. "The Big O." Are you less of a woman if you don't have an orgasm each time? Are multiple orgasms better than single orgasms? Is simultaneous orgasm the ideal? Is there a difference between vaginal and clitoral orgasm? Is the "G" spot orgasm the best? Is it the man's responsibility to give the woman an orgasm? Old myths are replaced by new myths.

Let us begin by giving our perspective on orgasm. Orgasm is not something separate from the comfort, pleasure, arousal cycle. Orgasm is the natural culmination of involved, effective sexual stimulation. Orgasm is a psychophysiological response which is a positive, integral part of a woman's sexuality. Physiologically, orgasmic response is basically the same, whether obtained through masturbation, intercourse, oral stimulation, vibrator stimulation, or manual stimulation. The woman's subjective experience of satisfaction can vary, depending on a number of factors, including her values, partner response, involvement in the sexual interaction, emotional mood, trust in the relationship, and intensity of stimulation. Each woman develops her own style of being orgasmic. Setting a criterion of good or bad styles of orgasm is self-defeating. It is not better or worse to have multiple orgasms; it's a question of the woman's pattern of arousal and orgasmic response. Focusing on the G spot orgasms or deep vaginal orgasms or simultaneous orgasms is the perfect example of making sex a performance goal rather than an experience of shared pleasure. You need not fall into the traditional male trap of pressuring yourself to be orgasmic each time (and if not, feeling the experience was a failure); you need not have the "right" kind of orgasm. Orgasmic response with your partner is a function of being comfortable with and responsible for your sexuality, being aware of and receptive to arousing stimulation, and letting go and allowing yourself to be orgasmic. Your responsibility includes making sexual requests and guiding your partner. Your partner cannot "make" you have an orgasm nor is he responsible for your orgasm, but he does need to be caring, cooperative, and sharing with you.

Sexual Awareness: Enhancing Sexual Pleasure, 1984, New York: Carroll & Graf

Case Study

LYNDA: A PREORGASMIC WOMAN DISCOVERS HER POTENTIAL

Lynda was a 22-year-old college student when she sought counseling from a female therapist in the college's sex therapy unit. She explained that although she became sexually aroused easily, she was never able to reach orgasm. Until recently she had not been particularly upset by the problem, but since becoming involved with a woman in a committed, loving relationship, she found the difficulty even more frustrating. During manual stimulation or oral sex she would feel herself building sexual tension, but then it would seem to dissipate just prior to orgasm. She would be left feeling angry and resentful with herself, and her partner would also express frustration.

In taking a sexual history, the therapist learned that, although Lynda masturbated occasionally, she never reached orgasm in this manner either. The first homework exercise was for Lynda to remove her clothes in private and examine her body carefully before a full-length mirror, noting her feelings and reactions. Gradually, she was encouraged to stroke and massage all of her body, including her genitals. At a later stage of

therapy, the therapist recommended that she try more deliberate genital stimulation and eventually actual massaging of the clitoral area. Lynda was told to try distracting her thoughts by fantasizing, listening to music, and concentrating on her breathing. Yet she continued to report that even after 30 minutes or more of stimulation, she was still unable to have an orgasm. The therapist then recommended that she try using a battery-operated vibrator to increase the degree of clitoral stimulation. The second time she used the device, she experienced orgasm.

By this time Lynda's partner was also involved in the treatment process, and they began applying some of the techniques together. Very soon the partner was able to bring Lynda to orgasm through manual and oral stimulation, and she was reaching orgasm much more rapidly. After 2 more weeks, she was occasionally experiencing more than one orgasm during a single sexual experience. Follow-up visits indicated that she was fully orgasmic in her further masturbatory and shared sexual experiences.

Women, however, have not generally been given as much social legitimization as men for developing and enjoying their sexual responsiveness. As a result, a much more substantial percentage of women are preorgasmic. Orgasmic dysfunctions are among the most common problems that women bring to therapists, and there is a far greater range of variability in women's experience of orgasm than in men's. Orgasmic dysfunction may well be a culturally determined phenomenon. It has been demonstrated that women with orgasmic dysfunction tend to have more negative attitudes toward sex, greater discomfort in communicating about sex, and higher levels of guilt over sexual matters (Kelly, Strassberg, & Kircher, 1990). In societies where sexual expression is permitted, and even encouraged, women are less likely to be nonorgasmic.

LACK OF EJACULATORY CONTROL

In their study of male sexual behavior, Alfred Kinsey and his associates (1948) found that nearly three-quarters of men ejaculated within 2 minutes of beginning sexual

intercourse. Yet it would not be scientifically acceptable to assume that a substantial number of those men were dysfunctional, experiencing what has usually been termed premature ejaculation. Between 36 and 38 percent of men in the United States probably now experience what they consider to be premature ejaculation (Spector & Carey, 1990). But premature to what? As with much sexual behavior, the lines between normal and abnormal are not absolute. They are largely culturally determined. For example, in East Bay, Melanesia, if men take more than 30 seconds to ejaculate after intromission, they are considered to have a problem (Reiss, 1986). Clinical textbooks in the United States have variously defined premature ejaculation as orgasm occurring within 30 seconds of intromission, within 2 minutes, or prior to the man's accomplishing 10 pelvic thrusts—arbitrary diagnoses, to be sure. Masters and Johnson (1970), acknowledg-

premature ejaculation: difficulty that some men experience in controlling the ejaculatory reflex, resulting in rapid ejaculation.

439

ing the arbitrary nature of their statement, chose to label a heterosexual man as a premature ejaculator if he reaches orgasm prior to his partner in 50 percent or more of their coital experiences. This presumes that the partner is orgasmic within a reasonable length of time. In this chapter it will be considered a dysfunction whenever the male reaches orgasm too rapidly for his own or his partner's sexual enjoyment, and is so consistently unable to exert voluntary control that one or both of them consider it a problem.

Lack of ejaculatory control is not related to timing so much as it is to a lack of voluntary control over the ejaculatory reflex. This is not surprising if we consider some typical ways in which males learn about their sexual responses. Most boys have begun masturbating with some regularity by the age of 15. Yet they usually have done so with little accurate sex information and with a measure of guilt. Therefore, they usually develop a pattern of stimulating themselves relatively rapidly, reaching orgasm in a hurry. For the majority of men, this rapid response becomes habitual. Because of the intense arousal typical of their first shared sexual experiences, most males ejaculate quickly in these instances too (Kaplan, 1989).

The end result of this conditioning is a linear approach to their own sexual responsiveness. Men progress from the absence of arousal, through the stages of sexual excitement, and directly to orgasm, with little hesitation or modulation along the way. There is also evidence that anxiety plays a role in initiating rapid ejaculatory response (Strassberg et al., 1990). Men may feel disappointed and frustrated by their lack of control, but since they are still experiencing the pleasure of orgasm, they may not be urgently motivated to seek help with the problem. Often it is their partners, who are just building their own sexual arousal when these men ejaculate, who suffer the most. Continuing problems with lack of ejaculatory control in a sexual partnership can generate conflicts and further sexual dysfunctions between the two people. Women who become angry and disillusioned by continuing patterns of rapid ejaculation in their male partners may begin experiencing loss of interest and arousal for sex themselves.

POST-EJACULATORY PAIN

This condition is an example of a muscle spasm problem that can occur in males either at the moment of ejaculation or immediately after. Although little is known about the difficulty, it is apparently caused by involuntary contraction of the ejaculatory musculature and some other associated muscles (Kaplan, 1983). Occasionally the cremasteric muscles that help control

suspension of the testes in the scrotum are also involved. The result is intense pain following ejaculation. It usually subsides within a few minutes, but can last longer.

Men who experience post-ejaculatory pain often develop a pattern of general sexual avoidance. Since their sexual activities end unpleasantly and uncomfortably, they may begin developing problems with erection or orgasm.

SEXUAL PROBLEMS OF HOMOSEXUALS

Most research on sexual dysfunctions has been done with heterosexuals. The literature on sex therapy focuses predominantly on the problems associated with heterosexual intercourse. Masters and Johnson (1979) eventually opened their sex therapy clinic to homosexual couples as well, employing treatment techniques similar to those used with heterosexuals. Although modifications in the therapy methods were made to accommodate anatomical and social differences, sex therapy proved to be as useful and successful with homosexuals as it had with heterosexuals. Homosexual persons experience the same kinds of dysfunctions as heterosexual persons.

Causes of Sexual Dysfunctions

The causes of any one person's sexual problems may be quite complex and involve the overlapping of physical, emotional, and relational components. They, however, may be grouped into some meaningful categories.

RULING OUT PHYSICAL CAUSES

Prior to beginning behavioral and psychological treatment for a sexual dysfunction, a sex counselor or therapist must be certain there are no physical causes for the problem such as an illness or anatomical problem. This may include an examination by a physician, including relevant laboratory testing. In most large clinics where sexual dysfunctions are treated, physical examinations are considered routine procedure.

Many sex therapists, especially those working in private practice, only require a physical examination by a physician when a client's symptoms raise some suspicion of possible organic disorders. In such cases,

---

organic disorder: physical disorder caused by the organs and organ systems of the human body.

TABLE 16.2

Organic Conditions That Can Cause Sexual Dysfunctions

Sexual Dysfunction	Potential Organic Causes
Inhibited Sexual Desire	Diseases, abnormalities, or tumors of the pituitary gland Diseases of the immune system Infections, abnormalities, or tumors of the testes Chronic kidney or liver disease, adrenal insufficiency, diabetes, hypothyroidism, Parkinson's disease, certain types of epilepsy, and strokes
Erectile Dysfunction	Congenital abnormality of or later injury to penis Multiple sclerosis or spinal cord injury Arteriosclerosis or blockage of blood vessels in penis Endocrine gland disease, especially if there is a testosterone deficiency Diabetes (probably impairs circulatory and neurological mechanisms of erection)
Impaired Sexual Arousal in Women	Estrogen deficiency, causing lack of vaginal lubrication Injury or disease of the central nervous system Multiple sclerosis, amyotrophic lateral sclerosis, alcoholic neuropathy Endocrine gland insufficiency, especially thyroid, adrenals, or pituitary
Lack of Ejaculatory Control (Premature Ejaculation)	No known organic causes, except the anxiety that may accompany various physical complaints
Orgasmic Dysfunction in Women	Severe malnutrition, vitamin deficiencies Disease or injury of the spinal cord Diabetes Deficiency of thyroid, adrenals, or pituitary
Delayed (or Absent) Orgasm in Men	Injury to nervous system Parkinson's disease, multiple sclerosis, diabetes, alcoholism, uremia

Source: Information from *The New Sex Therapy* by H. S. Kaplan, 1974, New York: Brunner/Mazel; and *The Evaluation of Sexual Disorders* by H. S. Kaplan, 1983, New York: Brunner/Mazel.

referral would be made to a physician who possesses specialized knowledge of what conditions to look for.

The fact remains that many sexual dysfunctions are not caused by physical problems. Lack of ejaculatory control, for example, is rarely rooted in organic conditions. Only if the onset of the dysfunction was abrupt, following a long period of good functioning, would various potential neurological or urological disorders be investigated (Reckler, 1983). The same may be said for vaginismus. It rarely has a direct organic cause. However, there are many diseases that can cause pain during sex, and pain is often the original stimulus that plays a part in the development of vaginismus. In treating vaginismus, it must be determined if there are any painful conditions present that could further aggravate the spastic muscular contractions of the vagina (Hawton & Catalan, 1990).

Sexual arousal seems to be more susceptible to interference by physical problems. Any sort of illness characterized by general malaise, fever, or exhaustion can cause erectile dysfunction in men and general sexual dysfunction in women. Since rather complex

circulatory and neurological mechanisms are involved in arousal, any disorder that interferes with these mechanisms will inhibit arousal. Spinal cord injury and blocked or diseased arteries leading to the genitals are common causes of arousal dysfunctions. It has been found that many men experiencing continuing erectile difficulty have leakage of penile veins, so that blood fails to be trapped in the erectile tissues (Rajfer, Rosciszewski, & Mehringer, 1988). Diabetes often leads to the development of conditions that affect arousal, particularly erection of the penis (Turner et al., 1990).

Any painful condition in the body can interfere with the sexual response cycle, including heart conditions, lower back pain, sexually transmitted disease or other infection, and specific genital conditions such as cysts. Painful adhesions around the clitoris, for example, make it difficult for a woman to reach orgasm. Delayed ejaculation in males has few organic causes, although again general systemic illness can interfere with orgasmic capacity.

In the past few decades, there has been some

441

evidence that the pubococcygeus (PC) muscle, deep in the pelvis, must have good tone to permit a full orgasmic experience, particularly in women. Kegel (1952) published data to support this contention and prescribed exercises designed to strengthen the PC muscle, now called Kegel exercises. He and subsequent researchers have claimed that women who strengthen this muscle are more able to build voluntarily the muscular tension that helps trigger orgasm. Some books on male sexuality have suggested that men's orgasmic responses can be heightened by strengthening the PC muscle as well.

Multiple sclerosis, brain disorders, endocrine gland diseases, lung disease, kidney disorders, and cancer are a few of the other illnesses that can be at the root of sexual dysfunctions (Stenager et al., 1990; Kaplan, 1983). Sometimes it is the individual's psychological reaction to a disease that actually causes the dysfunction. For example, those who have suffered a heart attack may be fearful of the exertion connected with sexual activity. More work is in process to determine the limits of activity for various types of cardiac diseases. It has also been found that sexual dysfunction often occurs in men with kidney disease who have to undergo regular dialysis treatment. Erectile dysfunctions were traditionally thought to be rooted mostly in psychological causes. Recent work has shown that many men who have problems with erection may have an underlying physical problem. The difficulty can be compounded by psychological stress and worry. It is therefore often simplistic to view psychological and physical causes as excluding each other. Often, it is a combination of the two (Buvat et al., 1990). Table 16.2 summarizes some of the possible sexual consequences of various physical conditions that may produce sexual dysfunctions.

DRUGS AND ALCOHOL

Many men experience their first erectile problems after having drunk too much alcohol. As with other depressant drugs, such as barbiturates and narcotics, alcohol may at first lower inhibitions and cause people to feel an increased sexual desire. As concentration of the drug builds in the body, the physiological responses of sexual arousal are inhibited, leading to poor sexual performance.

Many mood-altering or hallucinogenic drugs seem to have unpredictable effects on sexual functioning. Some—such as marijuana, LSD, and cocaine—are often reported to enhance sexual experiences when taken in highly erotic situations with positive expectations. However, the same drugs are capable of compounding negative moods as well and may even

FIGURE 16.3 Marijuana and Sexual Functioning

Sensations of touch and taste are generally enhanced by smoking marijuana, but increase in sexual desire may be as much a function of psychological expectation as of the drug. Testosterone and sperm levels may be reduced in some men by smoking marijuana, but the total effect on sexual functioning is not completely known.

magnify preexisting sexual problems. The placebo effect—the drug's perceived effect being generated by the consumer's expectations—undoubtedly plays a major role here.

Many chemical substances affect people's sexual lives, either by producing changes in the level of interest in sex, diminishing general erotic pleasure, or altering the reactions of the genitals. Prescribed medications can exert profound influences over sexual desire and functioning and can be useful in treating serious dysfunctions. Some men who take phenothiazine tranquilizers are alarmed to find that they no longer experience ejaculation of semen at the time of orgasm. Other antipsychotic drugs may interfere with the triggering of orgasmic responses. The adverse sexual effects are usually reversed with a change in dosage or if the drug is discontinued. Some medications used to treat high blood pressure can cause erectile dysfunction. Stimulant drugs, such as amphetamines, sometimes enhance sexual awareness in small dosages but interfere with sexual responsiveness when consumed in larger quantities.

THE PRESSURE TO PERFORM

Societally imposed standards of sexual performance reach almost mythological proportions for some people. The media add to this myth by suggesting that everyone is physically attractive and having sex all the time. People become convinced that all normal men get rock-hard erections on demand and have sexual intercourse for hours in every imaginable position without reaching orgasm, while their female partners writhe about in the throes of one orgasm after another. They become convinced that all women must have size 5 bodies and full heads of flowing wind-blown hair. Women may become so concerned about their body image that they are too preoccupied to experience the pleasure of sexual touch and intimacy. Even for those with less exaggerated sexual expectations, the pressures to perform well are usually enormous.

Stage fright is not an uncommon reaction to any situation in which a good performance is expected. It is just this kind of anxiety that can generate the typical vicious circle of sexual dysfunction that is shown in Figure 16.4. It is this pattern that can escalate what would have been an isolated sexual failure into a continuing cycle of sexual dysfunction.

Another potential result of performance pressure is what Masters and Johnson (1970) referred to as spectatoring. Instead of being able to relax and lose themselves in the sensual delights of the sexual experience, individuals may constantly seem outside themselves, wondering how they are doing and judging their sexual expertise, as if they were spectators at someone else's sexual event. They may also be especially conscious of their partner's degree of involvement and enjoyment in the sexual encounter.

Performance pressure is often rooted in an excessive need to please a partner. It is not unusual for a heterosexual man to assume that he is responsible for bringing pleasure to a woman, while heterosexual women are prone to believe they must serve a man's sexual desires and whims (Mostel, 1990). One may also have a nagging insecurity generating continual worry that one's partner will become sexually bored or interested in someone else. All of these sources of anxiety are likely to interfere with sexual responsiveness at some level.

RELATIONSHIPS AND SEXUAL FUNCTIONING

Many dysfunctions are rooted in problems that have developed in the partners' relationship. Lack of communication is one of the most widespread of these problems. Communication difficulties may be relatively uncomplicated at first, such as a failure to let one's partner know what types of stimulation are particularly enjoyed and which might better be avoided. Left to fester, these minor relational irritants may turn into more serious and lasting conflicts. Communication problems may also originate at much deeper levels and be symptomatic of severe disturbances and lack of compatibility between the two people involved.

Loving relationships have complex dynamics, and both the joys and discord in any relationship usually get played out in the sexual arena. When power struggles result in two people trying to gain control from one another, sex will be affected. If one partner is having trouble trusting in the other, or if some pattern of outright rejection has emerged, the possibilities of sexual dysfunction are enormous. Sometimes, subtle games of sexual sabotage, which result in turning off one's partner, will mask some of the deeper relational problems in couples. These factors may be important in determining the outcome of therapy for sexual problems as well. It is likely that the happier and more stable a couple's relationship is, the more positive and satisfactory the outcome of therapy.

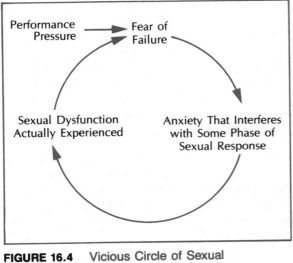

FIGURE 16.4 Vicious Circle of Sexual Dysfunction

Some people may be more prone than others to feel the pressure society exerts to perform sexually. These real or imagined pressures may result in fear of performing adequately and ultimately produce sexual dysfunction.

spectatoring: term used by Masters and Johnson to describe self-consciousness and self-observation during sex.

Case Study

DAVID AND MARIA: A VICIOUS CIRCLE OF SEXUAL DYSFUNCTION

David and Maria had been dating since the second semester of their freshman year in college. A year later they were having sexual intercourse on a regular basis, and both seemed comfortable and happy with their relationship.

After an evening at a fraternity party, they returned to Maria's room. The two of them had consumed a fair amount of alcohol and were looking forward to an exciting sexual encounter.

The couple's foreplay activities proceeded in their normal patterns, and Maria pulled David over on top of her for intercourse. He entered her and they began thrusting their bodies together.

Suddenly, David realized that he was losing his erection. He moved more rapidly in an attempt to provide extra stimulation, but to no avail. His penis soon slipped out of Maria's vagina, and he rolled over on his back.

Maria asked if there was anything wrong, and he answered that he was just tired. They said little more, and eventually both fell asleep. But David was actually feeling very embarrassed and somewhat alarmed. He had never before experienced any difficulty with erection and was bewildered by what had happened. By the next morning he had put the entire incident out of his mind.

Two nights later they went to bed together again. During foreplay some doubts crossed David's mind several times, but he tried to ignore them. Again, he lost his erection soon after beginning sexual intercourse.

This time Maria pressed with more questions, sounding a little worried. He knew she was wondering if his feelings toward her were changing, and even he was beginning to wonder if something was wrong between them. He searched for an explanation of what was happening to him.

After two more sexual failures, Maria insisted they talk about what was happening. With some prodding, David told her how scared and frustrated he was about his erectile difficulty. She assured him that it did not matter to her so long as he still loved her. After further sharing of feelings, they decided to visit the college counseling center that had advertised sex counseling services.

The counselor helped them understand the vicious circle of anxiety that had been set into motion by David's first alcohol-induced erectile problem. They were able to communicate more openly about their mutual reactions, and the counselor gave them specific suggestions for working on the problem together. When the counselor advised that they avoid intercourse for a period of time, David felt very relieved. His relief gave him very clear evidence of just how tense he had become about sex.

After another three counseling sessions, David and Maria had resumed sexual intercourse without further erectile difficulties. They also had learned new patterns of communication that enhanced their overall relationship.

OTHER CAUSES

There are many other possible roots for sexual dysfunction. Recently, for example, fear of AIDS has interfered with some people's sexual functioning. Some theorists place a great deal of emphasis on the role of childhood learning, influences of the unconscious mind, and other intrapsychic factors. There is mounting evidence that prior experiences with acquaintance rape or childhood sexual abuse may play a significant role in causing later sexual problems. Every individual troubled by a sexual dysfunction will have his or her own set of interacting causes. Sometimes therapy can proceed without spending time elucidating all of these causes. Other times, an effective therapeutic outcome depends on the untangling of a complex web of physical, psychological, and relational causes.

Treating Sexual Dysfunctions

The early work of Masters and Johnson (1966) that investigated the various physiological events of human sexual response established the basis for understanding what they originally called sexual incompatibility. Their research on the sexual response cycle was largely intended to provide a rational basis for treating these functional difficulties with sex. To proceed beyond those initial stages, they had to face a fundamental paradox of their work: while they had discovered the physiological bases of sexual response, most of the sexual dysfunctions had psychological roots. Therefore, they were faced with the challenge of modifying psychological and cultural factors that were interfering with the physiological expression of the human body.

As they worked on developing a model for the effective treatment of sexual dysfunctions, it became clear to Masters and Johnson that they needed techniques to help patients relax and restructure their behavior. However, it was also clear they would have to use methods that encompassed all of the complexities of human communication and relationships. Eventually, it became clear that sexual dysfunctions could not be considered the problem of an individual and instead must be viewed—and treated—as a problem for a couple. They also knew that their treatment methods would have to provide ample opportunity for sexually dysfunctional couples to learn more about their own sexual feelings and responses.

There have now been a great many new approaches that represent variations on the techniques of Masters and Johnson. There has been a continuing controversy over whose "turf" sex therapy belongs on. Medical professionals have tended to keep some ownership over the field, since physical assessment of patients is often indicated. Yet psychological professionals, with their knowledge and skills relating to the mind and relationships, have often received the most training in the treatment of sexual problems. It has even been suggested that the term *sex therapy* should now be modified to be "psychosexual" therapy, since its emphasis has become so psychotherapeutic. However, there is always the need to use medical personnel to rule out potential organic causes. The fact remains that good sex therapy cannot be carried out solely in a step-by-step, mechanical way. Therapists still need to design and improvise their treatments for particular clients. It takes a therapist who can recognize the intricacies behind each individual and each relationship to do this well. It is, in a sense, an art to be practiced with skill and creativity (Mosher, 1991).

FOLK REMEDIES

In the past, neither the medical profession nor other potential helpers had much to offer in the way of reliable help for sexual problems. Not surprisingly, home remedies and patent medicines were developed to create at least an illusion that there was some hope. In the United States, males seem most concerned about their lack of ejaculatory control. As a result, a variety of sprays and creams to be applied to the penis are advertised. They contain a mild anesthetic that dulls sensation in the head of the penis. There is no evidence that these substances prolong sexual response at all. Men also invent their own techniques for delaying ejaculation, such as wearing more than one condom or masturbating just prior to shared sex. They may try to distract themselves by thinking about other things, clenching their fists, or biting themselves to produce pain, or may devise a number of other techniques. Unfortunately, such home remedies may only intensify the problem. There are also pills available and various types of rings to fit around the penis, all purported to help maintain erection. There is no basis for such claims. It always seems that the placebo effect is an important factor for those who use these methods.

Most cultures have their folk remedies to allay men's concerns about sexual adequacy. (Women's sexual dysfunctions are rarely addressed by these techniques, further evidence of the performance pressures

---

Curing an Impotent Male Patient in the Mid-1700s

I told him that he was to go to bed with this woman but first promise himself that he would not have any connection with her for six nights, let his inclinations and powers be what they would: which he engaged to do. About a fortnight after, he told me that this resolution had produced such a total alteration in the state of his mind that the power soon took place, for instead of going to bed with fear of inability, he went with fears that he should be possessed with too much desire. And when he had once broken the spell, the mind and powers went on together.

—John Hunter, *English physician*

felt by men in most parts of the world.) In Africa, for example, impotent men drink potions made of bark or resort to ritual ceremonies. Hashish is used in Morocco by dysfunctional males, while nonorgasmic women are encouraged to take a young lover or have a lesbian relationship. In Thailand, men drink the bile of a cobra and the blood of a monkey, mixed in a local liquor. In India, men apply to the penis an herb that is a potent urinary irritant. Wives of impotent men in the West Indies may serve them a soup made of ox penis and testes, or the penis of a turtle marinated in wine. European men usually treat their dysfunctions with various alterations in diet (Jordheim, 1983). Lest we be too quick to dismiss the remedies of other cultures—or even those of our own—as superstitious and ineffective, it should be emphasized that modern sex therapy methods have yet to be fully tested by rigorous scientific standards, as discussed in the final section of this chapter.

MODES OF TREATMENT

One of the issues in treating sexual dysfunctions is the number of therapists to be involved. Masters and Johnson maintained that therapists of both sexes are essential if the couple in therapy is to glean the full supportive benefit of the therapeutic relationship. Their clinic will only accept couples for treatment. There are other models used, however. Most sex counselors or therapists in private practice work alone and feel able to deal with couples. Lesbian or gay male couples may seek a solo therapist of the same sex. Some counselors and therapists will also agree to work with clients who do not have a partner available or whose partners are unwilling to participate in therapy. Certain types of problems are amenable to self-help approaches and do not necessarily require the cooperation of a partner.

Clients in sex therapy without partners raise the additional issue of using sexual surrogates, or paid partners, for the purpose of practicing therapeutic exercises. In the early phases of their work to develop treatment strategies, Masters and Johnson used female surrogates for single men. These women were not prostitutes but instead were well-trained, sexually responsive women who were culturally matched with patients and who were able to cooperate in all of the behavioral exercises designed to improve sexual functioning. There have also been a few male surrogates who work with female partners. As might be anticipated, ethical difficulties arose with the use of paid surrogate partners, since sex for pay is usually considered illegal and/or immoral. Masters and Johnson soon discontinued the use of surrogates, although some

FIGURE 16.5   Co-therapist Counseling Session

Masters and Johnson developed a technique for dealing with sexual dysfunction that involved counseling the couple involved, not just the individual. This gives the therapists an opportunity to gain the cooperation of both people in solving their problem. The co-therapy team, such as this one from the Masters and Johnson Institute, consists of a man and a woman and brings a balanced approach to the therapy sessions.

other clinics continue to feel they are the only viable option for single patients.

While some dysfunctions are clearly rooted in negative emotional states such as anxiety, fear, guilt, or depression, others seem to be generated by deep-seated or unconscious psychological conflict. *Psychotherapy* is a term that applies to any one of a number of techniques that may help people resolve psychological problems. Psychoanalysis, which originated with the theories of Sigmund Freud, is usually a long-term form of therapy involving analysis of childhood factors and other psychodynamics in producing unpleasant symptoms. In recent years short-term forms of psychotherapy have gained in popularity. The success rate for treating sexual dysfunctions solely by these verbal therapies, without incorporating some of the specific treatment exercises developed in behavioral therapy, has been rather low.

There has been a resurgence of interest in hypnosis as a therapeutic approach for sexual problems. Hypnosis may be considered a form of psychotherapy that makes use of relaxation and suggestion in helping

sexual surrogates: paid partners used during sex therapy with clients lacking their own partners; only rarely used today.

susceptible, or willing, individuals to change. There are case studies dealing with the successful use of hypnosis in treating a variety of sexual problems and dysfunctions (Hammond, 1991). The hypnotic treatment is often used as an adjunct to other treatment techniques. An extensive review of published reports on the outcome of hypnotherapy for sexual dysfunctions found that many reports were anecdotal in nature and that larger studies tended to be methodologically unsound. There are few generalized conclusions to be drawn at this time about the effectiveness of such methods.

Group therapy has been successfully used with some sexual dysfunctions as well. Behavioral techniques are usually prescribed for individual patients within the course of treatment, and the group setting provides the support, information, and sharing of feelings necessary to a successful outcome. Barbach (1975) was one of the first sex therapists to employ group methods and developed a successful mode of treatment for women with orgasmic dysfunctions. Groups have also been successful for men with erectile difficulties and problems with ejaculatory control.

Use of medication and prosthetic devices has been increasing in the treatment of dysfunctions. Erectile difficulties, for example, can sometimes be treated with hormone injections or use of a muscle relaxant (Carani et al., 1990). In extreme cases, where some organic damage makes erection impossible, special tubular devices that can produce an artificial erection are surgically implanted into the penis (Leyson, 1991).

Some 30,000 of these prosthetic devices are now being implanted annually. The ultimate success of the surgery, however, has been found to depend greatly on the quality of the relationship between the man and his partner (McCarthy & McMillan, 1990). In cases of sexual aversion and phobia, antidepressant medications or anxiety-reducing drugs may prove effective (Kaplan, 1987).

Behavior therapy was predominant sex therapy for a number of years. Behavioral approaches typically involve the use of systematic desensitization, through which the patient gradually unlearns the tension-producing behaviors that are causing problems. Then more desirable behaviors are learned to replace the old dysfunctional patterns. Behavior therapy techniques provide the basic structure for most sex therapy today. When used to treat sexual problems, behavior therapy entails physical activities that are practiced at home by the couple, or in some cases as self-help approaches by single clients.

Most counselors and therapists are somewhat eclectic in their treatment of sexual dysfunctions, meaning that they combine therapy techniques in a variety of ways to meet the needs of individual patients as effectively as possible. While they may draw meth-

behavior therapy: therapy that uses techniques to change patterns of behavior, often employed in sex therapy.
systematic desensitization: step-by-step approaches to unlearning tension-producing behaviors and developing new behavior patterns.

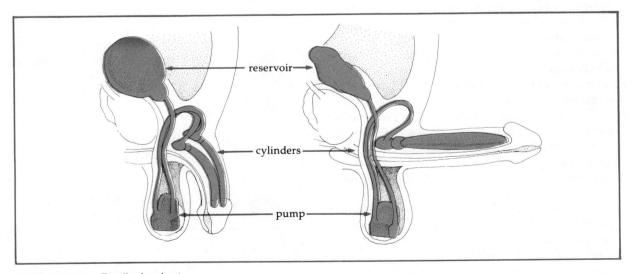

FIGURE 16.6 Penile Implant

If impotence cannot be cured, particularly if it is caused by an organic physical condition such as damage to the spine, intercourse can become possible by the implantation of a mechanical device. A reservoir filled with fluid is implanted in the abdomen. It is connected by tubes to a pump that is inserted into the scrotum, and this is connected to two cylinders that are slipped into the penis. To cause an erection, the man pumps the fluid into the cylinders; to reverse the procedure, he releases a valve in the pump, returning the fluid to the reservoir.

ods from some primary school of thought, they recognize the need to be flexible and to keep pace with changing techniques and a growing body of research knowledge (Mosher, 1991).

WHAT IS A SEX THERAPIST?

The term sex therapist is relatively new, entering our popular usage only since the early 1970s. The title seems to have achieved an almost romantic status, even though many people have little idea of what sex therapists actually do. Defined narrowly, the term refers to professionals who have been trained to treat male and female sexual dysfunctions. Counselors are now being trained to treat sexual problems as well. However, there is usually a broader context in which they work. Sex therapists and counselors attempt to restore sex to its natural context so that it can be a spontaneous human function, and to reestablish the positive pleasurable sensations and attitudes naturally present in childhood. They can help people enrich their sex lives, overcome lack of interest in sex, improve communication about sex between partners, and overcome specific sexual problems.

Since human sexuality is such a multidisciplinary field, professionals enter sex therapy from a variety of backgrounds. Some have had medical training as physicians or nurses. Some hold degrees in psychology, counseling, or social work. A few come from a background of pastoral counseling and hold degrees in religion. In the mid-1970s, a national organization called the American Association of Sex Educators, Counselors, and Therapists (AASECT) took the lead in establishing criteria with which to certify individuals who have met appropriate training standards as sex therapists. These criteria include not only degrees in one of the helping professions but specialized coursework in human sexuality and many hours of practical therapy work, under the supervision of an already certified sex therapist. AASECT was also the first organization to formulate specific ethics statements concerning how therapists were to conduct their work (see "Ethical Issues in Sex Therapy," p. 19).

While the members of the sex therapy profession continue to call for strictly established guidelines to govern their work, state legislatures have been slow to enact regulations concerning licensing of sex therapists. This increases the risks for the consumer, since in most states anyone, regardless of training or other professional credentials, can lawfully call himself or herself a sex therapist and set up a private practice. Any new profession has its share of quacks and charlatans, and sex therapy has been no exception. One hint for finding a good sex therapist is to ask

one or two trusted professionals whom they would recommend for help with a sexual problem. Sometimes an individual's name will come up more than once, probably a good sign. It is always appropriate to check out a sex therapist's qualifications directly as well. Consumers may wish to ask about degrees and training, the therapy model used, the kinds of records kept, the costs of therapy, and whether or not the therapist is certified to practice sex therapy by any professional group. It is important to watch out for any sort of unethical behavior, such as a suggestion by a sex therapist that nudity or sexual relations with the therapist might be appropriate. It should be expected, however, that a therapist will ask rather specific and intimate questions about sexual functioning in evaluating the problem and deciding about a course of treatment.

The American Association of Sex Educators, Counselors, and Therapists (435 N. Michigan Avenue, Suite 1717, Chicago, IL 60611) can provide a list of certified counselors and sex therapists by mail for a slight charge. The most crucial advice of all to anyone consulting a sex therapist is to expect treatment that is conducted in a respectful, caring, and dignified manner. It is even appropriate to set some tentative deadlines by which certain goals are to have been met. If the results are not forthcoming, reevaluating the worth of the therapy process is certainly in order.

Behavioral Approaches to Sex Therapy

As discussed earlier in this chapter, behavior therapy techniques, involving the learning of tension-reduction techniques and more effective approaches to sharing sexual activity, are the mainstay of sex therapy. This section will provide an overview of how such techniques are employed in therapy.

BASIC GOALS OF BEHAVIORAL SEX THERAPY

Behavior therapy essentially involves the unlearning of ineffective, dysfunction-promoting sexual behavior and its replacement with more positive and healthy patterns. Sex therapists attempt to move their clients toward the following major goals:

Gaining a Sense of Permission to Value One's Sexuality   Those suffering from a sexual dysfunction often

sex therapist: professional trained in the treatment of sexual dysfunctions.

have long-standing problems in accepting and feeling good about their sexuality. Whether it stems from social pressures, religious training, parental attitudes, or previous negative experiences, sexually dysfunctional individuals may feel guilty and uncomfortable about their sexual feelings, attractions, and behaviors. Therefore, a primary principle of therapy is to lend a sense of permission that it is all right to be sexual, that sexuality is a natural and healthy aspect of the human personality. Sex therapists encourage their clients to place a higher priority on sexual enjoyment, including saving time to work on sexual activities. Many sex therapy exercises are designed to help clients get in touch with their bodies, their sexual sensations, and their emotional reactions in more positive ways than ever before.

Taking More Time to Make Sexual Activity a Priority We live in busy times, and in many relationships both partners have careers. Sexual activity may eventually take a back seat to other priorities in a couple's life together (Gelman et al., 1987). In sex therapy, time is saved specifically for working on sexual problems. Therapists usually assign suggested activities and recommend a time frame for their completion. All of this helps the couple to develop a higher priority for improving sexual functioning.

Eliminating Elements That Are Blocking Full Sexual Response The human sexual response cycle—starting with sexual desire and proceeding through sexual arousal, higher levels of excitement to orgasm, and then resolution—is a normal part of every human being. People seek out therapy when some factor has interfered with all or a part of that cycle. Sex therapists, then, must work to eliminate whatever elements are necessary to restore full and satisfying sexual functioning. This means tracking down the causes of a dysfunction and then mapping out a realistic plan for correcting them. This can be a simple matter of teaching new relaxation and communication techniques, or it may necessitate in-depth counseling for deep-seated personal or relational conflicts. If drugs or alcohol are part of the problem, they will have to be eliminated or reduced. Guilt reactions or other emotional blocks must also be overcome.

Reducing Performance Pressures Sex therapy clients must learn how to stop focusing on their own sexual performance, instead relaxing and letting sex happen. Behavior therapy provides techniques to distract people from this spectatoring and to keep their bodies as relaxed as possible. Partners are helped to change their emphasis on feeling responsible for giving one another pleasure toward working on their own sexual satisfaction.

Using Specific Sexual Exercises to Develop More Positive Ways of Functioning Sexually Over the years sex therapists have devised activities that can actually help a sexually dysfunctional person overcome the dysfunction. These exercises are done at home in private and must be prescribed in a very systematic manner, with opportunity to talk about reactions after each stage. The sex therapist makes decisions about how quickly to move through increasingly intimate stages of therapy depending on how both partners are progressing and feeling. These sexual exercises constitute the most significant route to behavioral change in this form of treatment.

SELF-HELP APPROACHES

Many sex therapists feel there is enough clinical data to justify prescribing self-help approaches to overcoming sexual dysfunctions, although there is little evidence to demonstrate the long-term effectiveness of such approaches. A number of self-help guides are listed at the end of this chapter. Although the low cost and complete privacy of self-directed sex therapy are obvious advantages, it is also clear that many sexual dysfunctions can only be effectively treated by professional therapists. Self-help approaches cannot reach some of the more complex personal and relational factors that are at the root of most dysfunctions. The self-help guides may provide solid information, offer a positive beginning for many who want to improve their sexual functioning, and help people feel more relaxed in discussing sexual matters. Rarely can they effect a total cure.

Many therapists do suggest techniques for individuals to try at home on their own, not involving a partner. The two most common self-help themes make use of body exploration and masturbation. Many sexually dysfunctional men and women have never taken the time to become acquainted with their sex organs or even other parts of their bodies. Body exploration exercises involve viewing one's own body in a mirror and touching oneself to elicit emotions and physical sensitivities. Sometimes very specific directions are given to discover how various parts of the genitals respond to stimulation.

Masturbation exercises have proven especially useful in treating orgasmic dysfunctions in women and lack of ejaculatory control in men. A program of masturbation is often recommended for women who are attempting to trigger their orgasmic responses. Once the orgasmic capability is well established through these self-help techniques, the woman gradually integrates her partner into the activities, teaching that partner the best approaches for bringing her to orgasm.

Long-standing patterns of hurried masturbation are a common cause of ejaculatory control difficulties in men. Self-help techniques that encourage men to slow down in masturbation have been effective in establishing more modulated forms of male sexual response that can carry over in the form of better orgasmic control with partners.

There are other self-help techniques that can be used to reorient negative thought patterns about sex, rehearse fantasized situations with partners ahead of time, or learn patterns of distraction to prevent excessive focusing on one's own sexual functioning. There is general agreement among sex professionals that self-awareness, along with an ability to interpret one's own sexual needs and idiosyncrasies to a partner, are important aspects of good sexual adjustment.

PARTNERSHIP APPROACHES

Most behavioral techniques used in treating sexual dysfunctions are prescribed for couples to use together. Therapists view the partnership therapeutic experience as being important in the couple's growing ability to communicate and function together sexually. Partnership approaches are used in graduated steps, designed to accomplish the following results. Therapists usually need to be satisfied that each stage of treatment has been mastered successfully before moving on to the next:

1. Learning how to enjoy and relax with one another's bodies while providing nonsexual touching and massage.

2. Providing each other with light genital stimulation, designed to be pleasurable, but without any pressure to respond with arousal or orgasm.
3. Learning how to communicate and physically guide one another toward the most effective forms of sexual stimulation.
4. Using specific exercises to reverse dysfunctional patterns and establish a pattern of sexual interaction that is pleasing and satisfying to both partners.

To accomplish the first three goals outlined, sex therapists prescribe various types of mutual body pleasuring exercises, often called sensate focus since they provide couples with an opportunity to develop and appreciate physical sensations generated by one another. They bring a physically pleasurable dimension into a relationship that has been troubled by physical and emotional distress because of some sexual dysfunction. An added positive outcome of sensate focus can be the reduction of power imbalances in the sexual relationship that may make one partner feel pressured, untrusting, coerced, or misunderstood (see Fig. 16.7).

The first phase of sensate focus activities involves nongenital touching. The partners are instructed by the therapist to be together nude, in as warm and relaxing a private setting as possible. They take turns giving and receiving gentle physical pleasuring that is not overtly sexual. With a minimum of talking, the giver

sensate focus: early phase of sex therapy treatment, in which the partners pleasure each other without involving direct stimulation of sex organs.

FIGURE 16.7 Mutual Pleasuring or Sensate Focus

provides caring touches to the partner in the form of massaging, tracing, and rubbing. The receiver has only to relax and enjoy the pleasant sensations, giving positive verbal suggestions for changing the form of touching if anything is in any way uncomfortable or irritating. After an agreed upon length of time, the partners switch sensate focus roles. For many couples these exercises represent the first time they have experienced physical intimacy and pleasure without the tensions and pressures of performing sexually. Obviously such activities can be an important step in overcoming some dysfunctions.

In the second phase of sensate focus, light genital stimulation and teasing are encouraged, but without the goal of generating sexual arousal. The couple is in fact instructed not to allow sensate focus activities to lead to sexual overtures. Instead, they are told simply to enjoy and accept whatever sexual arousal may occur and then to let it dissipate. Again, sexual sensations are made a part of a relaxed, nonpressured context that is nonetheless pleasurable.

A final phase of mutual pleasuring typically involves some form of guiding procedure, in which one partner carefully shows the other how to give her or him optimum sexual stimulation. This will involve some mutually comfortable position, in which the one partner can place a hand directly on top of the other's hand, carefully guiding it in genital stimulation. Figure 16.8 shows a position that is often used for women who are teaching their partners how to provide clitoral stimulation to produce orgasm.

The number of times that a couple participates in the various phases of sensate focus may depend on how well and how rapidly they seem to be proceeding. Therapists watch for potential resistance or other difficulties in the therapy process and try to assure that positive results have been achieved at each stage before moving on.

Sex therapists who employ behavioral therapy understand that it is crucial for couples to build a pattern of successful sexual experiences, reversing the series of failures they have been experiencing with the dysfunction. Therefore, during the early stages of treatment, therapists usually ask their clients to avoid sexual intercourse or other forms of sexual interaction that have been beset with problems. Gradually, as confidence and relaxation are achieved with each new goal, a couple will begin to attempt intercourse again.

It is also important to have a graduated strategy for bringing the couple back into sexual intercourse. Based on the assumption that most heterosexual couples in Western cultures use—and perhaps prefer—an intercourse position with the man on top and the woman on the bottom, the typical strategy usually begins with a woman in the top position. It seems to be effective

FIGURE 16.8 A Guiding Position for Clitoral Stimulation

in treating women's dysfunctions because it affords women a greater sense of control over the sexual experience. On the other hand, it is useful in dealing with male dysfunctions because they are more able to relax while their partner takes more of the responsibility for controlling the sexual action. This constitutes an interesting commentary on some typical causative factors behind female and male dysfunctions: women often feel somewhat compromised by male-dominant intercourse positions; while men feel threatened by the weight of responsibility for sexual expertise usually assigned to them.

An excellent intermediate step on the way to developing confidence with man-on-top intercourse is a face-to-face, side-by-side position that enables both partners to be more physically relaxed (see chapter 10, "Solitary Sex and Shared Sex"). Neither is called upon to support his or her full weight (see Fig. 16.9), resulting in a greater sense of shared responsibility. Sex therapists find that many heterosexual couples enjoy this position so much that they begin to use it on a more regular basis than their former man-on-top intercourse position.

The final therapeutic step, providing it is the desired goal of the couple, is to succeed in their usual intercourse position, with all sexual functioning proceeding as desired. Coital position may play a role in improving sexual functioning other ways as well. One study showed that both women and men experienced

451

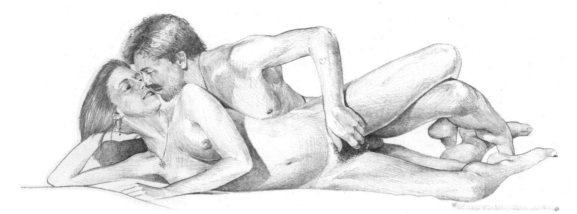

FIGURE 16.9 Side-by-Side Position for Relaxation

more "complete and satisfying" orgasms when using a position in which the penis moves higher on the mons and clitoris and presses on this area (Eichel, Eichel, & Kule, 1988). Women who experience painful intercourse are often helped by positions where they are on top (Mira, 1988). Again, the process of overcoming a couple's sexually dysfunctional patterns involves a systematic process of desensitizing them to the tension-producing difficulties of the past, conditioning them instead to new, more mutually comfortable and enjoyable behaviors.

SOME SPECIFIC BEHAVIORAL METHODS

Aside from the general techniques already described, there are specific behavioral exercises used in treating each of the sexual dysfunctions. An exhaustive survey of these techniques is not appropriate to this text, but some examples will be explored.

Vaginismus involves the involuntary contraction of vaginal muscles, making entry of the penis difficult or impossible for heterosexual intercourse. Since this dysfunction is almost always caused by fears and earlier negative experiences, it is crucial to help the woman learn how to develop a positive pattern of relaxation and pleasure with insertion into her vagina. The behavioral exercises used in therapy are therefore designed to reduce tension and permit this to happen. They might begin with the suggestion that the woman privately examine the opening of her vagina with a mirror, using some relaxation technique at the same time. Gradually, over a period of time, she will insert her little finger (or a small dilator made of plastic or rubber) into her vagina, also using relaxation. Eventually, the partner's fingers will be used in the same manner, but under the complete control and direction of the woman. In the final phases of treating va-

ginismus, the man's penis will be slowly and gently inserted, again with the woman having full control over how deeply and for how long this takes place. The ultimate goal is to achieve relaxed and pleasurable intercourse.

In the past, men tended to try to delay ejaculation by focusing on anything but their pleasurable sexual sensations. In treating lack of ejaculatory control in males today, the emphasis is on helping the man to become aware of the inner subjective sensations that signal when his ejaculation is imminent. Men have pelvic sensations just prior to ejaculating that need to be identified, so that they may take some action to prevent orgasm before they have passed the "point of no return." There is a simple behavioral technique that many sex therapists suggest. Known as the stop-start method, it asks men to stop any stimulation when they feel the sensation of imminent orgasm. The sensations completely disappear quite rapidly, and stimulation may then be resumed. Most sex therapists recommend that the partner use slow manual stimulation on the man's penis at first, in a convenient position (see Fig. 16.10). The man gives a prearranged signal to halt the stimulation when he feels orgasm approaching. Some therapists recommend that the partner add the squeeze technique at this point, giving a firm squeeze to the head of the penis (see Fig. 16.11). This further diminishes the sensation of imminent orgasm (Kaplan, 1989). Over a period of time the man learns better control over his ejaculatory reflex and feels increased confidence in his sexual abilities. These behavioral exercises lead to the development of sexual patterns in which the man knows how to slow down and modulate his stimulation so that he takes longer to reach orgasm. In the intercourse sequence described earlier, he gradually integrates his control into sexual relations with his partner. During intercourse, the squeeze technique may also be applied at the base of the penile shaft so

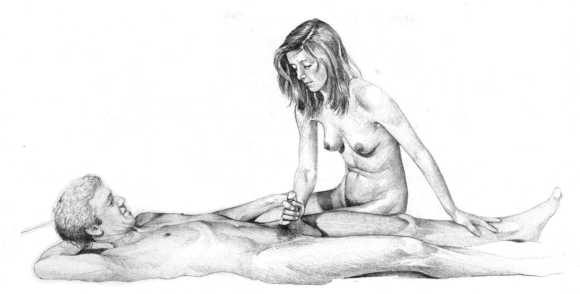

FIGURE 16.10   Manual Stimulation of the Penis

that the penis need not be withdrawn from the vagina (Berger & Berger, 1987).

There are various specific behavioral methods used in the treatment of the other sexual dysfunctions. They help couples unlearn the conditions that have led to their sexual dissatisfaction and learn how to function normally and happily. Sometimes sex therapy aids people in saying no to sex when they are not in the mood or to particular sexual activities that they do not enjoy. Thus sex therapists attempt to meet the specific objectives of their clients as realistically as possible.

A Critical Look at Sex Therapy

As a new field, sex therapy has only begun to be subjected to rigorous scientific studies of its effectiveness. Progress and success in changing human behavior are difficult variables to quantify. Criteria for measurement are usually highly subjective, and researchers must rely on the self-reporting of clients, always subject to distortion and misunderstanding. Yet sex therapy is now considered a professional field that attracts more practitioners and clients all the time.

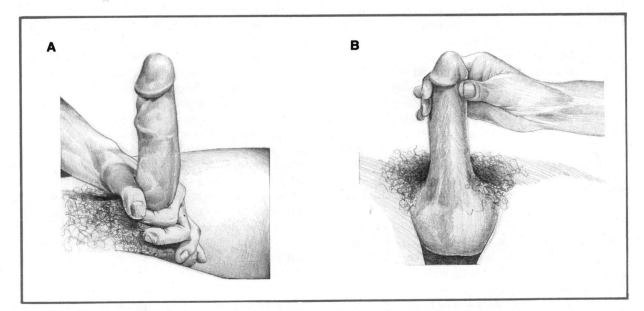

FIGURE 16.11   The Squeeze Technique: Base of Penis (A) and Head of Penis (B)

453

IS SEX THERAPY EFFECTIVE?

Valid scientific research must always be replicable. That is, the researcher must outline all of the experimental and control variables and analyze the results with statistical care, so that another researcher could repeat the same procedures and expect similar results. Sex therapy has not been widely studied in this manner. Masters and Johnson's (1970) early work appeared scientifically sound on the surface and included follow-up contacts with treated couples to check on their progress. They reported percentages of failures for treating the various sexual dysfunctions.

A decade following the publishing of Masters and Johnson's *Human Sexual Inadequacy,* the book that actually sparked the sex therapy revolution, the soundness of their methodology and statistical analysis was called into question. After finding that many sex therapists did not seem to be getting as good results as Masters and Johnson had claimed, Zilbergeld and Evans (1980) began to feel that a second look at their report was warranted. Zilbergeld and Evans concluded from their look at Masters and Johnson's work that it was "so flawed by methodological errors and slipshod reporting that it fails to meet customary standards—and their own—for evaluation research." These critics were particularly concerned because so much of sex therapy seemed to have evolved directly from Masters and Johnson's work. Masters and Johnson (1983) publicly defended their work and outlined more specifically the criteria for determining if treatment was a failure. They also indicated that, with sex therapy advances in recent years, they no longer considered their original criteria adequate.

Case Study

RONALD AND CAROL: PREMATURE EJACULATION CAUSES OTHER SEXUAL PROBLEMS

Ronald and Carol were students when they sought counseling at the university's counseling center. They were assigned to a male-female team of co-therapists. They had been involved in a relationship for nearly a year and had been having intercourse for 8 months. Their mutual complaint was that Carol never reached orgasm during intercourse, although she was fully orgasmic in masturbation, petting, or postcoital stimulation. Upon further questioning about their sexual relationship, the therapists discovered that Ronald rarely took more than a minute to ejaculate during intercourse. Carol gradually admitted that she felt it impossible for her to reach orgasm in such a brief period of time and indeed felt somewhat cheated and resentful about the situation. Fearing that she would hurt Ronald's feelings and make the problem even worse, she had not dared tell him about her feelings.

In the counseling process, as Carol's feelings emerged, Ronald admitted that he had been feeling guilty and anxious about "not being able to satisfy Carol." He went on to explain that he had been bothered by premature ejaculation in previous relationships and had tried many ways

of postponing his orgasms. None of the methods had worked.

The therapists asked the couple to agree not to have intercourse for the time being and assigned the stop-start technique for them to use as a homework exercise. They were seen by the therapists twice each week over a period of 6 weeks. By the end of the 3rd week, Ronald felt much more confident about his ability to exert some control over his ejaculation, the result of using the stop-start method. The therapists then recommended they begin including intercourse in their treatment program.

During their first two coital attempts, Ronald was disappointed by not having lasted more than 5 minutes before ejaculating. In subsequent attempts, however, he was able to have intercourse for 10 or 15 minutes before reaching orgasm. Carol was happy with his new levels of control and often experienced two or three orgasms during their intercourse.

Two years following therapy, and after both had graduated from college, Ronald and Carol married. A year later they reported to one member of their therapy team that their sexual relationship was still a very happy, fulfilling one.

FIGURE 16.12 Mutual Understanding

Sex therapists emphasize that communication and understanding are very important factors in solving sexual problems and developing a relationship that is complete and fulfilling for both partners.

There is much to be done in determining the actual effectiveness of sex therapy. How is success in therapy to be judged: by the patient, the therapist, or an objective outsider? And by what criteria should it be judged? What methods are the most successful, and for what types of individuals? How are patients to be selected, and by whom? How long should sex therapy last, and how long should successful sexual functioning last before it is called a successful treatment? How expensive should therapy be?

At this point, it certainly can be stated that based on a wealth of clinical data, sexual dysfunctions can be treated. It must also be said that there is much yet to be learned about the reliability of such treatment. It is not unusual for the pioneers in any field eventually to face attack by those who begin to notice the shortcomings of their pathfinding work. However, therapy for alleviating the anguish of sexual dysfunctions has been markedly different after Masters and Johnson from what was available before.

ETHICAL ISSUES IN SEX THERAPY

Human sexual conduct is interwoven into our sociocultural values. Sex has become associated with a variety of moral issues. When professionals intervene in the sexual lives and decision-making of their clients, there are also many ethical issues to be confronted. Work in sexology demands the highest standards of professionalism, confidentiality, and informed consent.

Yet professionals also bring their own sets of values to their work, and these values help determine the decisions they make about ethical behavior.

Sex therapists face their share of ethical dilemmas that simply cannot be ignored. For example, if, in the course of treating a married couple for some sexual dysfunction, one of the partners privately admits having contracted a sexually transmitted disease during a recent extramarital affair, the therapist must make some decisions. Confidentiality has been promised, and yet the other partner may be at risk of catching the disease. The extramarital affair may have implications for the entire treatment process that cannot be explored so long as it is kept secret. The therapist may feel as though she or he has been drawn into a dishonest alliance with the partner who had the affair. There are a number of courses of action that could be taken. Making the decisions about how to proceed is an exercise in professional ethics for the therapist.

There are all of the day-to-day questions in sex therapy that raise ethical points as well. Who decides whether or not there is actually a problem at all? What methods will be used to treat the problem? Should masturbatory exercises be assigned to a client whose religion sees masturbation as immoral? Should sexual intercourse be prescribed for an unmarried client?

The American Association of Sex Educators, Counselors, and Therapists (AASECT), has promulgated its own code of ethics. It deals with several basic issues, designed to protect clients from exploitation or incompetence. The main points of this code are as follows:

1. Sex therapists must receive adequate training and have a strong sense of integrity.
2. Strict standards of confidentiality must govern a sex therapist's work, and there should be no disclosure of information about a client without the individual's written consent.
3. Since clients are always in a somewhat vulnerable position, their welfare is to be protected and respected at all times by the therapist.

In making this final point, the AASECT Code of Ethics places strict limitations on nudity of clients and therapists and on the use of sexual surrogates as partners during therapy. Sexual contact between therapists and their clients has been a major concern in sex therapy ethics and has been the subject of some lawsuits.

All helping professions face their share of ethical dilemmas to be resolved. Codes of ethics establish general guidelines but can never offer hard and fast advice to be used in a specific complicated case that presents some confusing dilemma. It is crucial for sex

455

therapists, as well as others in the helping professions, to understand their own value systems regarding sexuality and to sort through all of the moral and ethical issues involved (Vasquez, 1988).

Conclusion

Sex therapy is experiencing its share of growing pains. No other profession deals so directly with some of the most sensitive and intimate questions of human nature. Therefore, while still in its infancy, sex therapy has been delegated a great deal of power and responsibility. People look toward sex therapists to provide them with the sexual thrills and happiness their culture has led them to believe are rightfully theirs. Can sex therapy predictably accomplish these goals? Does the new awareness of sexual dysfunctions create as many new questions as sex therapy solves? These questions, and many others, remain to be answered.

It does seem clear that sex therapists must be cautious not to isolate the functioning of human sex organs too completely from the psychodynamics of each partner's personality or the more complex issues of a couple's relationship. Since human sexual response depends on an interaction of biological, psychological, relational, sociological, and cultural factors, the treatment of problems in responsiveness cannot proceed in a vacuum that focuses only on one factor.

Sex therapy has often been restrictive, available only to heterosexual couples who could afford the luxury of full sexual enjoyment (Mosher, 1991). Only recently have some therapists begun to treat other groups. There are individuals who desire treatment for sexual dysfunctions alone, either because the dysfunction has prevented them from finding partners or because their partners are unwilling to participate. There are homosexual couples who want to improve their sexual interactions. And there are those who lack the funds to pay for therapy and find insurance companies are reluctant to help them.

As professional organizations and state legislatures continue to examine these issues and to clarify standards for the training and licensing of sex therapists, the efficacy, methods, and ethical standards of the therapy process will also be clarified. ■

CHAPTER SUMMARY

1. There must be careful evaluation of any problem with sexual responsiveness to determine if a true dysfunction is present.
2. Every culture sets standards of sexual performance that may become debilitating pressures and unfair expectations for men and women.
3. Individuals who have impaired need for sexual gratification may be experiencing inhibited sexual desire (ISD) or sexual avoidance.
4. Arousal problems are expressed as erectile problems in men and as lack of vaginal lubrication in women.
5. Female vaginismus and male post-ejaculatory pain are difficulties involving involuntary muscular spasms that interfere with sexual activity.
6. Both men and women can experience a complete lack of orgasmic response or difficulty in achieving orgasm.
7. Lack of ejaculatory control is the most common sexual dysfunction in men.
8. While psychological stresses are the most common cause of sexual dysfunctions, possible physical causes must be investigated. Performance pressures and difficulties in relationships (such as poor communication) are often at the root of sexual dysfunctions.
9. Drugs and alcohol can also play a role in causing dysfunctions such as lack of arousal.
10. Every society has developed its own folk remedies for improving sexual function.
11. Of the variety of treatment approaches that have emerged, behavioral techniques are the most widely used.
12. Sex therapy is a relatively new field, and the ethics, training standards, and certification standards for sex therapists are still being debated.
13. Behavioral sex therapy helps dysfunctional individuals to unlearn ineffective behaviors and replace them with positive, effective patterns of sexual interaction.
14. Specific homework exercises are assigned to those in therapy, using both self-help and partnership approaches. Improved sexual communication is essential.
15. There is still debate about the actual effectiveness of sex therapy methods, and further research is needed to settle the remaining questions.
16. Because of its sensitive subject matter, sex therapy is faced with ethical issues that national professional organizations are continuing to try to resolve.

ANNOTATED READINGS

Barbach, L. G. (1976). *For yourself: The fulfillment of female sexuality*. New York: New American Library. A classic in its field, this book outlines a program for women who want to enhance their capacity to reach orgasm. It provides basic information about female sexual anatomy and physiology.

Castleman, M. (1989). *Sexual solutions: An informative guide*. New York: Touchstone/Simon & Schuster. A practical guide to lovemaking that includes valuable suggestions for dealing with a range of sexual problems. The book does not ignore the importance of the relationship in working on sexual difficulties.

Cole, E., & Rothblum, E. D. (Eds.). (1989). *Women and sex therapy*. Binghamton, NY: Haworth Press. A collection of papers that deals with feminist views of sexuality and sex therapy, this volume challenges readers with points of view that are often ignored or dismissed.

Kaplan, H. S. (1989). *How to overcome premature ejaculation*. New York: Brunner/Mazel. Offers specific suggestions that men and their partners may use to slow down ejaculatory response. It discusses obstacles that may be encountered in a realistic and sensitive manner.

Levine, S. B. (1989). *Sex is not simple*. Columbus, OH: Ohio Psychology Publishing. A realistic, down-to-earth discussion of sexual problems and interactions between people. As the title suggests, this book helps give a sensible perspective to one's sex life.

Lieblum, S. R., & Rosen, R. C. (Eds.). (1989). *Principles and practices of sex therapy: Update for the 1990s*. New York: Guilford Press. This is a thorough collection of papers from experts in the field of sex therapy. It is largely a textbook for therapists, but contains useful information for anyone with specific concerns about sexual functioning.

Mason, T., & Norman, V. G. (1988). *Making love again: Renewing intimacy and helping your man overcome impotency*. Chicago: Contemporary Books. While this book is written largely for women who are working with a partner experiencing erectile dysfunction, it provides helpful suggestions for both partners. Its emphasis is on improving and maintaining intimacy as they work toward resolution of the sexual dysfunction.

PART VI
SEX AND CONTEMPORARY SOCIETY

T hroughout this book, a predominant theme has been the social implications of human sexuality. Sex is indeed a pervasive aspect of contemporary society. The chapter that follows concentrates on several issues of sociosexual significance. What is pornography and what are its effects on people of various ages? How have sexual themes become a part of art, literature, films, and television? To what extent should laws regulate erotic themes in the media and the sexual activities of human beings? These are major issues facing society today, and courts and legislative bodies are struggling to grapple with their complicated natures. This is another reminder that human sexuality is a permeating influence in every aspect of human life. As we untangle all of the issues that help explain what sexuality is all about, there may be many sexual revolutions yet to come, and there may be threads of continuity and stability through them all.

CHAPTER SEVENTEEN
SEX, ART, THE MEDIA, AND THE LAW

Erotica is sexually explicit material that is portrayed in an artistic manner or in the context of a broad range of human emotions. Pornography portrays raw lust with aspects of violence or aggression. Some films, television programs, advertising, and other media use pornography to sexually arouse its audience or to sell a product. Research into the effects of pornography on individuals and society has often yielded conflicting results. Presidential commissions on pornography in 1970 and in 1986 reached different conclusions about the effects of pornography and made recommendations for laws to support their positions.

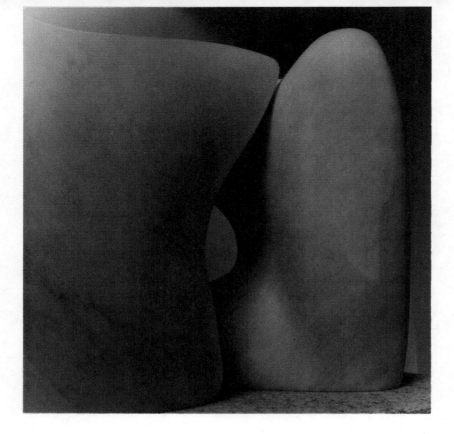

CHAPTER SEVENTEEN

PORNOGRAPHY: A DEFINITION

NUDITY AND SEX IN ART
    Historic Foundations of Erotic Art

SEX AND THE PRINTED PAGE
    The Evolution of Literary Pornography
    Victorian Pornography
    Themes in Contemporary Literature
    Magazines and Tabloids

SEX IN THE MEDIA
    Films
    Video
    Telephone
    Computers and Sex Information
    Television
    Advertising
    Child Pornography

EFFECTS OF PORNOGRAPHY

PORNOGRAPHY, THE COURTS, AND THE LAW
    Presidential Commission on Obscenity and
        Pornography, 1970
    United States Attorney General's Commission on
        Pornography, 1986

LEGAL ASPECTS OF SEXUAL BEHAVIOR
    Sex and the Constitution
    Special Issues and the Law

CONCLUSION

CHAPTER SUMMARY

The first time I saw a triple-X-rated video was at a fraternity party. Everybody was cheering and clapping. I guess I was naive, but I never knew that movies would show everything. This one was showing sexual activity that I had never even fantasized about! I must admit I was turned on by it. But I didn't feel good about the whole thing. It just seemed as though something this personal shouldn't be viewed by an audience. The people having sex in the film didn't even look like they were enjoying themselves much. I've seen more skin videos since then, but they just get boring in a hurry as far as I'm concerned.

—From a student's essay

SEX, ART, THE MEDIA, AND THE LAW

Depictions of human sexuality have been abundant in many cultures and periods of history, from the figures on a Greek urn to the billboards on Times Square; from the couples on a television soap opera to the advertisements for Calvin Klein jeans; from the videos of Madonna to the lyrics of the 2 Live Crew or Guns N' Roses. These images, implicitly or explicitly, reflect the attitudes of the society in which they appear. Our society has witnessed a great deal of freedom to portray sexuality graphically. However, the more tolerant a society becomes, the more it invites criticisms from certain factions within it. Thus, conflicts have arisen about the nature of sexual portrayals and their effects on others.

Pornography: A Definition

The terms pornography and obscenity are often used interchangeably. Both terms are subject to multiple definitions and interpretations, and both have become emotionally charged. Typically however, pornography refers to any visual or literary portrayal that may be sexually arousing to some people. Legal definitions of obscenity usually include the phrase "appeals to pru-

rient interests," a somewhat vague and all-inclusive description.

Pornography is commonly defined as material in which the primary goal is to sexually arouse viewers or readers by portraying raw lust, and obscenity as that which may be offensive to public taste and morals.

Erotically realistic art or fiction, sometimes called erotica, is seen as distinguishable from pornography because sex is portrayed as part of the broad spectrum of human emotions present in intimate relationships. The people involved are shown to be complex human beings with a variety of nonsexual feelings in addition to sexual ones. The sex may be depicted in just as graphic a way as in pornography; it is the overall context that differs. It has also been suggested that pornography has aspects of violence, aggression, or the degradation of another human being, while erotica reflects a balance of mutual respect, affection, and pleasure (Davis, 1991).

pornography: photographs, films, or literature intended to be sexually arousing through explicit depictions of sexual activity.

obscenity: depiction of sexual activity in a repulsive or disgusting manner.

erotica: artistic representations of nudity or sexual activity.

461

Nudity and Sex in Art

In recent times in Western culture, art has been a relatively uncensored means of expression, in which nudity at least has been considered quite permissible. That is not to say, however, that paintings or sculptures of nudes have not incurred the ire of some viewers.

HISTORICAL FOUNDATIONS OF EROTIC ART

The prehistoric representations of the human body and sexual activities were very likely fertility symbols with magical and religious significance. Representations of the sex organs themselves probably became objects of worship with great symbolic meaning. Penis-shaped monuments and adornments have been found in the ruins of many ancient cultures. Religious erotic art tended to portray the aspects of sex that were seen as important and necessary to the survival and well-being of the human species: intercourse for procreation, for example. Other forms of erotic art, mostly three-dimensional, were used to ward off evil spirits or improve the harvest of crops.

Nearly every culture has seen its share of erotic art that departs from such religious intent. There have always been those artists who violated the limits of "acceptable" moral values and sexual tolerance and portrayed aspects of the body or sexual behavior that were considered to be shameful, obscene, or very private. It is this form of erotic art that was often treated with great secrecy, used for sexual titillation, or strictly limited to a select group of privileged viewers. There are many Greek and Etruscan paintings that show sexual intercourse, fellatio, orgies, pedophilic behavior, and a variety of other sexual activities. There are examples of pre-Columbian pottery from Mexico and Peru that represent male masturbation and fellatio, often with great exaggeration of phallic size (see Fig. 17.1). Some oriental art also portrays especially large genitals, so that the viewer's attention is drawn to them (Reinisch, Ziemba-Davis, & Sanders, 1990).

Some erotic art has been used for special educational functions. In Japan there was a tradition of "bride scrolls" and "position pictures," or shunga, which were passed on from mother to daughter upon the daughter's betrothal. Their dual purpose apparently was to instruct and to encourage the daughter's erotic interest in her husband-to-be. This duality reflects a purpose of most erotic art—to make us think as well as respond with feeling, including sexual arousal. Erotic art is also of great use in helping to foster a deeper understanding of the sexual values and mores of both historic and present-day cultures.

Nudity in art is often directly affected by cultural

FIGURE 17.1 Pre-Columbian Pottery

The ancient Peruvians from the southern coast of Mochica were famous for their stirrup-spout jars. They were molded without the aid of a potter's wheel and featured a large flat bottom with a dominant sculptured form. This jar shows an act of fellatio.

attitudes. Ancient Greek artists portrayed the nude male and female figures without hesitation (see Fig. 17.2). Gradually, however, as their attitude toward nakedness changed, they began to include gestures of modesty, with the genitals at least partially covered.

Probably the roots of modern, commercial pornography can be found in the sixteenth century, when engraving, etching, and woodcutting made reproduction of erotic scenes simpler and much less expensive. Eventually there was a resurgence of a more Puritan attitude that discouraged artistic representations of nudity and sex. In the repressive movement, we probably find the roots of modern censorship and suppression of erotic images.

The first 2 or 3 decades of the twentieth century saw some new approaches to erotic art. Surrealism, for instance, often relied on sexual fantasy and free

shunga: ancient scrolls used in Japan to instruct couples in sexual practices through the use of paintings.

FIGURE 17.2 Greek Sculpture

The Greek sculpture of a kouros, or young warrior, c. 600 B.C. was significant because it glorified man and gave him a godlike scale and presence. It differed from the Egyptian style in that it was freestanding, had a dynamic stance, and its nude form was molded in an anatomically correct way.

association borrowed from psychoanalysis. Contemporary art has created some fresh erotic themes in Western culture. Yet it seems that photography and films have taken over many of the important functions that painting, drawing, etching, and sculpture once provided and have elicited their share of controversy as well.

In the summer of 1989 Andres Serrano exhibited a photograph of a crucifix in urine that he called "Piss Christ," and Robert Mapplethorpe's exhibit contained several photographs of homoerotic and sadomasochistic subjects. While, by themselves, the photographs might not have caused a stir, the fact that both artists had received federal grants from the National Endowment for the Arts (NEA) caused both Congress and the Corcoran Gallery of Art in Washington, D.C., to question the advisability of using federal funds for the creation of what some judged to be obscene and indecent art. Senator Jesse Helms proposed that all federal funding be banned for obscene work, and the

Corcoran canceled its Mapplethorpe exhibit (Hyde, 1991).

The Helms proposal was ultimately defeated because of the difficulty in defining obscene and indecent art. At the Corcoran, the situation became more complicated as some artists boycotted the gallery, deciding not to show their works. Several staff members resigned and museum membership dropped. Other art galleries in the country decided to show the exhibit. In Cincinnati, Ohio, the director of the Contemporary Arts Center was arrested in 1990 and placed on trial for exhibiting obscenity in the gallery when he opened the Mapplethorpe show. It was the first obscenity trial in the United States involving an art gallery, and represented an important test of issues such as freedom of expression and artistic freedom. A crucial legal precedent was set when the art gallery director was found not guilty.

The controversy about use of federal grant money erupted again in 1991 when NEA funds helped produce

FIGURE 17.3 Embrace, 1982

This photograph by Robert Mapplethorpe is one among several that some people found objectionable because of its homoerotic subject matter. The exhibition caused Congress to question the grants of federal funds to artists who create works considered by some to be obscene. © *1982 The Estate of Robert Mapplethorpe*

463

Mike Luckovich ATLANTA CONSTITUTION

Nice touch, Michaelangelo. We decided to grant you an arts endowment..

Congress

a film by New York City filmmaker Todd Haynes. The film, called *Poison,* included scenes of a young thief being brutalized and raped in prison. While opponents claimed the film depicted homosexuals involved in anal sex, officials of the NEA countered that the award-winning film illustrated the destructive effects of violence. They also said the film was not sexually graphic.

The major controversy in these cases was the use of taxpayers' money for what some taxpayers would consider objectionable art. On the other hand, without government support many art projects would not be completed. Thus, the controversy continues, and will not be easily resolved. Federal agencies such as the National Endowment for the Arts are walking a difficult line between encouraging artists and not exerting undue censorship. It is clear that they are being cautious about the projects that are awarded grants. Critics charge that this is a fundamental violation of the freedom of expression (Davis, 1991).

Sex and the Printed Page

Just as erotic themes have universally found their way into visual art, so have they always been a part of literature. The explicitness of the sexual descriptions varies with the cultural and sexual mores of the times. In some societies and periods of history, little more than a romantic embrace is described, with participants fully clothed. The rest is left to the reader's imagination. In other societies and times, minute and graphic details of a sexual encounter are discussed; the reader needs no flight of the imagination. As with other erotic art forms, pornographic literature has often been available only as costly contraband.

THE EVOLUTION OF LITERARY PORNOGRAPHY

It seems that because sex was viewed as joyous and pleasurable in ancient times, authors were permitted to write about it openly and unashamedly. In most languages, including English, some of the oldest writings are the most ribald. One of the most ancient love songs known comes from a Sumerian civilization about 4,000 years ago. It was sung at the annual ritual marriage of the king. Some of its verses are more explicit than love songs of today:

> You have captivated me, let me stand
>   trembling before you.
> Bridegroom I would be taken by you
>   to the bedchamber;
> You have captivated me, let me stand
>   tremblingly before you.
> Lion, I would be taken by you to the
>   bedchamber.
> Your place, goodly as honey, pray lay
>   your hand on it,
>   Bring your hand over it like a
>   gishban-garment,
> Cup your hand over it like a gishban-
>   sikin-garment.
>
> (Loth, 1961)

Ancient Greek writers drew much of their eroticism from the fertility rites of Dionysian festivals. These rites developed into wild orgies in some communities, occasionally to the dismay of Greeks who preferred more staid and formal ceremonies. The plays and songs that emerged were the mass media of the times, often glorifying the phallus and retelling stories about the sexual activities of the gods. Many of the masters of Greek tragic and comedic writing created plays with central sexual themes. The erotic literature of the ancient Romans was more lighthearted than that of the Greeks, although there is evidence to indicate that their sexual behaviors surpassed whatever excesses the Greeks may have had. One of the most famous Roman "pornographers" was Ovid, whose *Art of Love* and *Heroides* are erotic classics. Another Roman, Caius Petronius, wrote the *Satyricon,* a work that is filled with sexual themes.

VICTORIAN PORNOGRAPHY

The nineteenth century brought a rise in prudery, during which ladies could be offended not only by sexual references but by any sort of indelicate statement made in writing. Nevertheless, erotic literature flourished even though sexual feelings became increasingly repressed, and sexual attitudes, at least superficially, became models of propriety (Kendrick, 1987). By 1834, 57 pornography shops had opened on one London street.

THEMES IN CONTEMPORARY LITERATURE

Although sexuality has never been totally repressed in literature, the kind of exuberance and acceptance of erotic themes that was prevalent in Greek and Roman literature did not manifest itself again until the twentieth century. In the early years of this century some writers rebelled against the notion that sex must be accompanied by feelings of shame and guilt. Undoubtedly the writings of Sigmund Freud, Havelock Ellis, and others influenced the emergence of new sexual attitudes.

D. H. Lawrence's *Lady Chatterley's Lover* (1929) stirred controversy over its explicitness for decades. Lawrence is now recognized as a literary genius who was a pioneer in the sensitive treatment of erotic themes. James Joyce's *Ulysses* was not accepted in the United States for years. In 1933 John Woolsey, a district judge for New York, wrote a landmark decision that redefined the limits of pornography and allowed *Ulysses* to be admitted into the United States. Woolsey's basic attitude was that the redeeming artistic value of an entire book needed to be considered before it would be banned as obscene because of any given passage. *Ulysses* is now recognized as a modern masterpiece. While it contains passages about masturbation, prostitution, voyeurism, and adultery, it uses them to tell the story of Stephan Dedalus, a young student; Leopold Bloom, an advertising salesman; and Molly, his adulterous wife. Joyce uses an innovative style that has little or no paragraph indentation or punctuation; intended to duplicate the way we think, it is called stream of consciousness.

Modern themes of homosexual love emerged in the works of Marcel Proust, *Remembrance of Things Past* (1923–27); André Gide, *Corydon* (1924); and American author James Baldwin, *Giovanni's Room* (1956). While many books have at least touched on homosexuality, some contemporary books have dealt with homosexual themes sensitively and thoughtfully. Two examples are Patricia Warren's book *Front Runner* (1974) and Isabel Miller's story of two nineteenth-century women, *Patience and Sarah* (1969). Notable, too, was the description of gay life in New York in David Feinberg's novel, *Eighty-Sixed* (1985).

Other sexual themes have been written of as well. The sadomasochistic themes that gained prominence in the late eighteenth century through the works of the

FIGURE 17.4 Victorian Pornography

In the nineteenth century the nude figure was often represented in the romantic neoclassical style. This photograph of a woman reading a letter in bed is characteristic of that style. She reclines on a divan or couch and is seminude, with the lower half of her body draped.

Marquis de Sade still continue in literature. Two books by Hubert Selby Jr., *Last Exit to Brooklyn* (1964) and *The Room* (1971), have sadistic themes. One of the best known contemporary books relating to sadomasochism is Anne Rice's *Exit to Eden* (1985). Masturbation has found its way into a great deal of erotic literature including some autobiographical accounts. A modern novel that used masturbation as a central theme was Philip Roth's *Portnoy's Complaint* (1967).

Since the early 1970s there have been hundreds of books published on many different levels of literary quality that treat sex openly and frankly. Sometimes the erotic themes are interwoven with other themes of literary importance. In other cases the author's intent seems to be to crowd as many pornographic scenes onto the pages as possible. Although there have been no recent attempts to censor erotic themes in literature, the rising tide of antipornography sentiment may well be felt in literary circles and publishing houses again.

MAGAZINES AND TABLOIDS

Magazines with stories about sex have been available for more than a century. It has only been within recent times that they have been so readily available and openly displayed. When *Esquire: The Magazine for Men* appeared in 1933, a new precedent was set for

465

(continued on p. 468)

Demi Moore, Postcards, and Topless Dancers

As you walked through New York this summer, Demi Moore's eight-month-pregnant and nude body stared back at you from every newspaper kiosk. The July cover of *Vanity Fair* stimulated news coverage, radio talk shows, and debates. Several major chain stores decided not to carry this issue, claiming that the image should not be seen by children.

I personally think the cover and the inside photographs by acclaimed photographer Annie Leibovitz are beautiful. How wonderful it is to see a model of a pregnant woman who is healthy and sexy. How affirming it is to see a pregnant woman who clearly feels that in her pregnancy she is beautiful and sexually arousing. And what a wonderful way to break the taboos about sexuality and pregnancy. And yet, several of my women friends find the cover offensive and exploitative, seeing it as pandering and without value. One, siding unknowingly with Phyllis Schafley, said that she thought it was vaguely pornographic.

My friend's comment brought to mind some of the feelings I had just a few weeks ago while visiting Amsterdam. I was in Amsterdam in June at the World Congress of Sexology biannual meeting and spent some time visiting with colleagues throughout the Netherlands. The Netherlands is a society that is wonderfully open about sexuality. In her opening address to the Congress, the Dutch Minister for Welfare, Health and Cultural Affairs, Ms. H. d'Ancona, told the participants: "We remain convinced that continuing openness and attention to the subject [sexuality] are the habits best calculated to enable people to exploit their sexual potential and enjoy their sex lives, as well as avoiding frustration and trauma. It seems reasonable to assume that satisfying sexual contacts and relationships will have a beneficial effect on the mental and physical health of the people concerned and will consequently help them to function better both as individuals and as members of society." There are laws protecting the civil rights of gay men and lesbians, and a beautiful monument in central Amsterdam is dedicated to the gay men and lesbians who were killed in World War II. Sexuality education programs for adults appear on television, along with explicit advertisements for HIV prevention.

But there was another side to the openness that I found disquieting and uncomfortable. The red light district features blocks of live sex shows, explicit book stores, and female sex workers in small, red-lit windows who negotiate with passersby. Materials are not limited to this section of the city; in the postcard stores found throughout Amsterdam, one can buy postcards depicting couples having intercourse; painted, mutilated, and distorted genitals; and other sexual scenes. To me, many of these images were offensive, without artistic or social merit, and distasteful. In my view, the live sex shows and the pictures of floating genitals were not an affirmation of sexuality, but sexist and exploitive.

It was indeed ironic to learn, in an Amsterdam hotel lobby one night, catching up on news with CNN, that the U.S. Supreme Court had decided *Barnes v. Glen Theater,* ruling that states may ban nude dancing in the interest of "protecting order and morality." The 5–4 decision upheld an Indiana law requiring female performers in night clubs and adult bookstores to wear at least pasties and a G-string. Chief Justice Rehnquist wrote that "nude dancing of the kind sought to be performed here is expressive conduct within the outer perimeters of the First Amendment, though we view it as only marginally so." He then went on to say that "the perceived evil that Indiana seeks to address is not erotic dancing, but public nudity. . . . Indiana's requirement that the dancers wear at least pasties and a G-string is modest, and the bare minimum necessary to achieve the State's purpose."

Justice Souter wrote a separate opinion to "rest my concurrence in the judgment, not on the possible sufficiency of society's moral views to justify the limitations at issue, but on the State's substantial interest in combating the secondary effects of adult entertainment establishments. . . ." These effects, as described later in his opinion, are "prostitution, sexual assault, criminal activity, degradation of women, and other activities which break down family structure." Justice Souter seems painfully ignorant that there is no scientific basis for these connections, instead allowing his own perception of what a viewer might feel to override his legal judgment. I could not help but wonder, as I read his opinion, if Justice Souter had ever been in such an establishment and what the effects on him had been!

Justice White, writing for the four dissenters, chided his colleagues for obfuscating their real intent. He wrote, "the purpose of forbidding people from appearing nude in parks, beaches, hot dog stands, and like public places is to protect others from offense. But that could not possibly be the purpose of preventing nude dancing in theaters and barrooms since the viewers are exclusively consenting adults who pay money to see these dances. The purpose of the proscription in these contexts is to protect the viewers from what the State believes is the harmful message that nude dancing communicates." He went on to say, "that the performances in the Kitty Kat Lounge may not be high art, to say the least, and may not appeal to the Court, is hardly an excuse for distorting and ignoring settled doctrine. The Court's assessment of the artistic merits of nude dancing performances should not be the determining factor in deciding this case."

The implications of this case are chilling. The case sends a clear message that in the words of *The New York Times,* "freedom of speech must bow to protecting public order" and conservative visions of morality. Conservative groups hailed the decision as a victory. A spokesperson for the Free Congress Foundation was quoted in *The Washington Post* as saying, "It is a green light for communities to aggressively enforce basic community standards of decency." And, as many of you know, that means that there will be more attacks on bookstores, video stores, and college and high school classrooms, as opposition groups work to abridge the First Amendment in order to promote *their own version* of order and morality.

And that brings me back to Demi Moore and the Amsterdam postcards. It is unacceptable to use our own personal judgments to decide whether sexually explicit materials or content are appropriate or acceptable to others. As sexologists, we need to support the informed use of sexually explicit materials for educational and therapeutic purposes and affirm the rights of adults to have access to sexually explicit materials for personal use. We must object to sexually explicit materials that condone or promote violence and exploitation, and we must protect minors from exploitation, while working to protect the rights of freedom of speech and freedom of the press. And we need to be concerned with the rights of topless dancers because the abridgement of their rights to expression can quickly lead to abridgement of the rights of educators, counselors, researchers, and therapists.

—Debra W. Haffner, 1991, *SIECUS Report,* Vol. 19(6)

BEST FOOT FORWARD—Athletic, professional SWM, 28, seeks footloose SWF for exciting barefoot adventures. I've always been attracted to a woman with pretty featues, so if the shoe fits, let's get to the sole of the matter. Send letter and phone.

BiWM (30's), seeks occasional contact with trim, white males, 18-25. Inexperienced, curious, OK. Reply with descriptive letter, age,, how to contact, phone, photo.

BiWM, 41, seeks young, trim males, 18+.

D.M. Hamden—You like to act. I see you most Sundays, as you work (FIC). I live No. Haven. Interested in some fun?

DEAR O—I have moved from P.O. Box 511. I am now at P.O. Box 740.

DOMINANT MALE seeks submissive people. Friendship/good times.

DWM, 40, slim, handsome, professional, wishes to meet an attractive, slender, caring WF.

DWM, 37, looking for attractive female, active, outgoing, down-to-earth, for relationship.

IF YOU ANSWER one ad, then try this one. Uncommon GWM, 27, 130 lbs., cute and good looking, successful, athletic and bright. Into sports, music, theater, NYC on Sundays, and living life to the full. Looking for a possible relationship with one special, similar guy. Photo appreciated, but not necessary. Send letter with ph.#.

M OF MIDDLEFIELD (5'8", 125). Met June and Aug '90. You called recently, nothing since. Why? You were No. 295. Gave you some mags, the view was "awesome." Please call anytime, OK! Let's meet again. Have not seen anyone since you. On vacation, 11-22-29. Ride?

MWBiF, 40, seeks same for friendship and romantic interludes.

N—Love you, but can't write back. Send address.—T

SBF, 34, great personality, fun-loving, enjoys romance, quiet evenings, music, movies, and reading. Seeks companionship/friendship of (straight) SWM (preferably Italian) with similar interest. Photo please.

SMB, 30 y.o., light skin, attractive, lonely. Likes nature, video, eating out, reading. Seeks female for romance. Age, race, unimportant.

FIGURE 17.5 Classified Advertisements

Advertisements for social connections that may or may not involve sexual activity appear regularly in some magazines and newspapers that are sex-oriented. The number of personal advertisements has declined, probably due to the AIDs crisis.

sophistication in erotic magazines. Twenty years after *Esquire's* beginnings, *Playboy* appeared on the newsstands. This magazine attempted to strike a balance among offering sex information, advice on male attire, an open philosophy toward sex, and photographs of nude women and titillating fiction. The *Playboy* approach was adopted by a large number of other magazines for men. As women began to ask for a more balanced view of sex, magazines such as *Cosmopolitan* and *Playgirl* began printing photographs of nude men and stories with special erotic appeal for women. This trend is continuing.

By the late 1960s other magazines began to appear that were more blatantly sex-oriented and included hard-core pornography. *Penthouse, Hustler,* and *Oui* were among the first to deal openly with sex. In 1968 *Screw* scored a resounding commercial success and was followed by a number of other sex tabloids with provocative titles such as *Smut, Ball, Stud, Hot Stuff,* and *Sex.* Not only did the sex tabloids publish photographs of male and female nudes showing genitals, there were usually pictures of people engaged in a variety of sexual activities, some fiction, articles relating to new developments in the study of sex, and a classified section in which people advertised their sexual services or requested sexual partners for all sorts of activities.

Sex in the Media

Film, television, video, and computers represent modern mass media. They have undergone—and continue to undergo—an evolutionary process that parallels, reflects, and often stimulates the evolution of social attitudes. The integration of nudity and sex into films and television has been gradual and careful, yet because of their mass audiences, reaction to nudity and sex in these media has been more visible than any responses to erotic art or literature ever were.

FILMS

From the earliest days of film there were some moviemakers who made use of the medium to photograph sexual activity. Until very recently, however, such films were available only through the underground market. However, the movies that were offered to the public for the first 50 years were almost totally lacking in anything that would today be judged as sexually explicit. There were innuendos and seductive women even in silent films; Greta Garbo's first talking picture, *Anna Christie* (1930), was about a prostitute. But whatever people did together sexually was left strictly to the viewer's imagination. Movie actors were never seen wearing less than a bathing suit considered appropriate for the times; a man and woman were never shown in bed together; kisses rarely betrayed any sense of real passion. This was partially due to the producers' code established by the movie industry itself as a response to several sexual themes that appeared in a few movies in the 1920s. The prohibitions in the producers' code included such topics as prolonged passionate lovemaking, white slavery, and anything that would instruct the audience in committing a crime. It also restricted the portrayal of such topics as nudity, drug use, childbirth, and ridicule of the clergy. The Roman Catholic church instituted the Legion of Decency in 1930 and its standards were soon adopted by Hollywood producers. The Anglo-Saxon

FIGURE 17.6   Tootsie

In this film Dustin Hoffman stars as an actor who discovers that he can get more work as a female than as a male. The role reversal engaged in by the character gives a perspective to the female sexual identity/role that is neither deliberately stereotypical nor obviously feminist, but sympathetic and humorous at the same time.

Protestant conservative attitude in the late nineteenth and early twentieth century also opposed alcohol, drugs, equality for blacks, women's rights, prostitution, communism, and other themes that did not fit into the general prevailing mode of behavior or thought. That is not to say that "sex symbols" did not emerge from among the movie stars. Actors such as Mae West, Jean Harlow, Clark Gable, Humphrey Bogart, James Dean, and Marilyn Monroe undoubtedly drew theatergoers who were romantically attracted to their filmed images. In the 1990s Kim Basinger, Madonna, Michelle Pfeiffer, Julia Roberts, Tom Cruise, Kevin Costner, Mel Gibson, and Patrick Swayze are such sex symbols.

In 1965 *The Pawnbroker* became the first American film to show bare female breasts. Today they are a standard part of a great many movies. Overtly erotic themes began to emerge in films that lacked explicitly sexual scenes. *Midnight Cowboy* (1969) dramatized the story of a male prostitute, and *Klute* (1971) dealt with some intimate details of a female prostitute's life. One of the most popular films of its day, *The Graduate* (1967), portrayed a brief sexual encounter between a young man and an older woman. Mate-swapping couples and group sex were important themes of *Bob &*

Carol & Ted & Alice (1969) and *I Love My Wife* (1970). *Myra Breckinridge* (1970) and *The Christine Jorgensen Story* (1970) dealt with sex-change operations. Yet these films appeared in a time when filmmakers were still not completely free to deal fully with sex. More explicit was Marlon Brando's brilliant portrayal of an aging, aggressive, domineering American male in Bernardo Bertolucci's *Last Tango in Paris* (1972). In 1975 the British spoof, *The Rocky Horror Picture Show*, showed scenes of transvestites, as did the light-hearted *Victor, Victoria* (1982). The 1986 film *9¹/₂ Weeks* had many explicitly sexual scenes, showing a pliant seductress and her partner.

Educators, philosophers, and psychologists have engaged in a good deal of debate concerning the significance of sex-related themes in films. As a society evolves, does its art reflect its changing values, or do artists and filmmakers form the avant-garde in effecting these changes? As a society becomes more tolerant and breaks down the barriers of its stereotypical attitudes toward groups of people and sexual behaviors, how does the art of that society reflect these changes? There are no definitive answers to these questions, but perhaps a discussion of some cinematic themes will provide a clue.

There has, for example, been controversy over how women have been depicted in American films. One study compared male and female roles from 1927 through the late 1980s, finding that women's roles were generally rather rigidly stereotyped (Levy, 1990). Women have frequently been portrayed as self-destructive, manipulative, and sexually seductive. A common cinematic scene over the years has involved a forceful man pulling a woman into his arms and forcing kisses on her. At first, the woman pushes and fights against the aggressor with clenched fists, but eventually her body softens, her hands open and slide around his neck, and she surrenders herself to him passionately. Although such scenes still occur in movies, there have been other, more positive themes as well. There have been several films in recent years in which intense friendships between women have been depicted, such as *Beaches* (1988) and *Steel Magnolias* (1989). A *Time* movie critic said of *sex, lies, and videotape* (1989), "It is about men who use women by watching them, and women tired of being the object of satyric attention." The film *Thelma and Louise* (1991) shows two women on the run after murdering a man who was trying to rape one of them, and, while escaping, they punish other male characters for their abusive behaviors. There have been films that have examined political issues relating to gender, including *The Color Purple* (1986) and *The Handmaid's Tale* (1990). It has also been suggested that there has been a backlash to these positive depictions of women in film. There have been movies about deranged, murderous women, such as *Fatal Attraction* (1985), *Presumed Innocent* (1990), and *Misery* (1991), and Cinderella stories whose heroines are rescued by strong male figures, such as *Pretty Woman* (1989). Some observers believe that there is a long history of woman-hatred in the movies, and that many of the glamorous female stars of the past had histories of sexual abuse and mistreatment at the hands of the moviemakers themselves (Steinem, 1991).

Homosexuality Prior to 1960 homosexuality was avoided as a cinematic theme. Some European films were frank about homosexual relationships, but American films tended to obscure even suggestions of same-sex attractions. When plays such as *Streetcar Named Desire* (1952), *Tea and Sympathy* (1957), and *Cat on a Hot Tin Roof* (1958) were made into movies, their significant allusions to homosexuality were lost. In the early 1960s, however, Hollywood became less hesitant about using homosexual themes. Tennessee Williams's 1960 film, *Suddenly Last Summer,* was reasonably straightforward about the topic.

As society has become tolerant of homosexual/lesbian relationships, these themes have been depicted

FIGURE 17.7 Homosexuality in Films

Homosexuality is treated with respect and dignity in the 1985 film *Kiss of the Spider Woman.* Two prisoners in a South American jail, one homosexual and one heterosexual, become involved in a sexual relationship with each other that is complicated by the fact that the prisoners have different political affiliations.

in a variety of ways. In Robert Aldrich's 1969 film *The Killing of Sister George,* a rather sad and brutal relationship is depicted between a mannish middle-aged woman and a younger, somewhat childish woman. A very different approach was used in *The Lickerish Quartet* (1970), in which the director implies that only a lesbian relationship can satisfy a woman. *The Boys in the Band* emerged in 1972 as the first film to explore the problems of the homosexual subculture, although some people have objected to the stereotyped image that is presented. The French film *La Cage Aux Folles* (1978) received acclaim for its treatment of a gay male partnership. In the 1980s, the film *Making Love* (1982) dealt frankly with a married man who eventually left his wife to establish a gay relationship with another man. *Kiss of the Spider Woman* (1985) focused on the touching relationship of two male political prisoners, one openly homosexual and one heterosexual. Another filmed tale of homosexual obsession in prison is told in *Homo,* one of three stories derived from Jean Genêt in *Poison* (1991), mentioned earlier (p. 464). The 1982 film *Personal Best* dealt with the relationship between two women athletes, one older than the other. It showed the many conflicts experienced as two women attempted to sort out their loving and sexual feelings for each other in a relationship that could not be highly visible or public.

The impact of AIDS on the gay community, and on personal relationships, became a cinematic theme in the 1990 film *Longtime Companion*. This critically acclaimed film was one of the first to examine how HIV infection affects partnerships, and how ignorance and discrimination affect people with AIDS. Dealing with AIDS has been a difficult issue among filmmakers, because issues such as homosexuality and other forms of sexual behavior often must be part of the theme.

Hard-Core Pornography Films whose main purpose is to show lengthy scenes of genitals and/or persons engaged in any form of sexual activity are considered hard-core pornography. The earliest such films were made before 1925, mostly by professionals who had access to 35mm movie camera equipment. As 16mm and 8mm film became available, amateurs began producing hard-core films for private use and sale. Popular from the 1950s through the early 1980s, these movies were 10 to 20 minutes in length and were sold for amounts that far exceeded the costs of production. In Great Britain they were called blue movies, and in the United States they were often labeled as stag films. The latter term reflects the fact that such films were generally used at all-male (stag) parties.

As explicit sex began to become permissible in theaters, the underground porno film business suffered. The picture quality of "stag films" was often poor and they were expensive, so many viewers chose to pay less for what could be seen more clearly. Such films as the Swedish import *I Am Curious (Yellow)* (1967) and *Deep Throat* (1972) depicted intercourse and various types of explicit sexual activity and were allowed to be shown in theaters, presumably because of their redeeming social value and a more liberated social attitude.

Eventually, "X" ratings on films became box-office liabilities. Regular theaters were reluctant to run these films, and the public generally did not show up in great numbers to see them. Pornographic films were for the most part relegated to adults-only theaters, usually found in sections of cities where prostitution and strip shows were concentrated. With the advent of home videos, the adult movie business in theaters has gone steadily downhill.

Some special television stations have attempted to offer adult movies as a service to subscribers. One home satellite dish station that broadcast adult movies to its paid subscribers from New York found itself violating community standards in an Alabama county where 22 subscribers lived. The state of Alabama asked for extradition of the officers of the satellite station, and eventually the threats of legal action brought their showing of adult movies to a halt. The president of the American Civil Liberties Union saw these actions as a danger to the rights of others, since one prosecutor in Alabama was having an impact on what people throughout the country might be able to watch in the privacy of their own homes (Dorsen, 1990). Makers of adult films have indicated that it is becoming increasingly difficult to produce and market their movies (Royalle, 1989).

VIDEO

The age of the home videocassette recorder (VCR) has brought another revolution to the pornography business in the United States. Video shops often have sections of full-length adult films that show explicit sexual acts. Although there has been little scientific study of this phenomenon, it appears that hard-core videos are rented by couples in many cases, and are considered stimulants and enhancers for their sex lives. The relatively low rental fees allow for a great deal of pornographic variety on home VCRs, and have given rise to a new set of conflicts involving the availability of such videos to adolescents and children.

Evidence suggests that about 70 percent of the adult movies rented in video stores are signed out by women. They often rent an X-rated video to watch with their husbands after the kids have watched their PG films and gone to bed. Adult videos are rented most frequently on weekend nights. Some chains of video stores have asked sexologists for guidelines in choosing sexually explicit materials for their outlets. These experts discourage use of films in which children are portrayed in any way, even if by adults, and they seek to avoid scenes in which sex is associated with violence or blood. Some believe that explicit videos represent a significant source of sex education to many people, and therefore should be regulated to provide as positive a sexual message as possible (Mooney & Siefer, 1991).

TELEPHONE

An entirely new phenomenon of the 1980s and 1990s has been "telephone sex." Although these services have now come under federal regulation concerning the hours during which they can operate and age

hard-core pornography: pornography that makes use of highly explicit depictions of sexual activity or shows lengthy scenes of genitals.

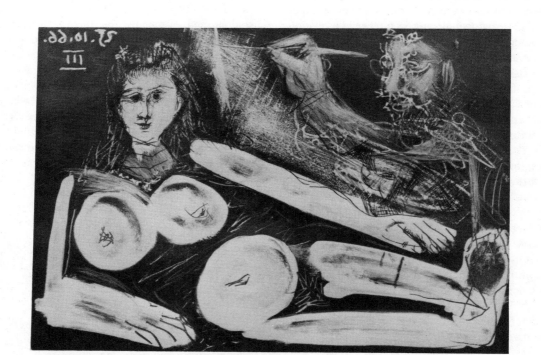

FIGURE 17.8   Pablo Picasso (1881–1973)

Picasso used many styles and innovative techniques to become the predominant artist of the twentieth century. This simple sketch featuring the nude female figure prompted the Orlando, Florida, police department to want to destroy it, along with pieces of confiscated pornography.

It's Not Porn, It's Picasso

Orlando, Fla.—The people in the evidence room at Orlando police headquarters hated the charcoal-colored picture of the naked woman and the bearded man.

They stuck it on the floor facing the wall. They planned to have it burned with the rest of the seized pornography.

The city's property control manager rescued the dusty picture, but only because he thought the frame was salvageable.

It was only after property manager Phil Edwards wiped it clean and examined the abstract image and pencil markings in a bottom corner [that he] realized it was more significant than the unicorn-on-velvet pictures he often ends up junking.

The penciled signature says Picasso.

The portrait, which appears to be an original aquatint etching prepared in 1966 by the prolific and innovative Pablo Picasso, could be worth $2,000 to $9,500, said some New York art dealers.

Orlando police Thursday said they couldn't pinpoint where the print came from. It was either unclaimed stolen property or material seized in a drug raid, said police spokesman Mike Wenger.

The print had been collecting dust in the police evidence room for at least a year. "It was horrible," said one of the evidence caretakers. "When we first pulled it, we all laughed about it."

The print shows a dark-haired nude with large breasts and a pregnant-looking belly lounging for a bearded artist at an easel with a paintbrush in his hand.

—*Orlando Sentinel,* November, 1987

groups they can serve, there are numbers that can be dialed to hear a woman or man talking explicitly about sexual acts or making suggestive sounds. Some services provide a recorded message for which a flat amount is automatically billed to the caller's telephone. Other services offer customers whatever live "performance" they desire, charging it to a credit card.

There have been many concerns about "dial-a-porn" because it is so easily accessed by minors. In 1989, however, the U.S. Supreme Court ruled that telephone sex could not be outlawed. The Court did uphold stricter controls to prevent calls from minors. When stiffer regulations were imposed in 1991, federal judges blocked them with an injunction. However, the general public and state legislatures are placing increasing amounts of pressure on telephone companies that allow these services to use their networks. Some of these companies are beginning to withdraw their sex phone services as a result of this pressure.

COMPUTERS AND SEX INFORMATION

Computers represent the newest medium for transmitting information, and computer software has been adapted for a variety of sex-related uses ranging from computer dating services to sex education. Not only can people at some distance from one another carry on sensual conversations on their keyboards or play X-rated computer games with each other, there are services that can provide the most recent information on a variety of sexual topics. Computer bulletin boards, available through some networks, allow people to leave sexual messages for one another. Software is available that offers self-help for the diagnosis and treatment of sexual dysfunctions.

For an annual fee and hourly charges for use of the service, subscribers to commercial computerized "information utilities" can type in one of several hundred keywords and receive information about the latest findings in some sex-related field. The first on-line computer service to provide sex information was *AMSEX,* for *American Sexology,* offered by the Delphi computer network in 1984. Several others have since appeared, including the Human Sexuality Information and Advisory Service (*GO HSX* on Compuserve network) and *Sexuality Today* on NewsNet (Greenwald, 1990).

Like any medium, computers have potential for abuse in sex-related matters. As yet, there are few controls to prevent young people from making use of communications inappropriate to their ages. At the same time, computers represent an impressive way to get the most recent information about human sexuality quickly and privately.

TELEVISION

Sexual themes on television have been subject to more controversy than sex in films. There is an element of control over who views films in theaters. The rating system, enforced by conscientious theater owners, can help control the age groups allowed to view movies. Television is another matter, however. Television comes into the home, and adults usually feel that although some control over who watches what programs is possible, complete control is not. Some young people will be able to watch any television program that is aired; some adults will be offended by any sexual theme that becomes a part of a program. Therefore, balancing new attitudes toward sexuality in movies and television against what the viewing public wants or will tolerate is a major problem for the television networks and federal regulatory agencies.

Some attempt at control is becoming evident on television. Networks permit local stations to preview controversial programs, so the local managers may have the option of not airing a program that appears to violate prevailing community attitudes about sex. In addition, programs that have sexual themes are preceded by suggestions to parents that they use their discretion in allowing children to view the program. Movies originally made for theaters are popular television offerings, although there are standards that determine what dialogue and scenes will have to be cut before airing on television. Nudity, explicit sexual scenes, scenes suggestive of the sexual act, and words of sexual slang are almost always eliminated.

The most blatantly sexually suggestive material on television screens in the 1990s (apart from cable stations that show adult movies) comes from music videos. There are television networks that specialize in showing rock music videos, and many of these videos have erotic themes. Scantily clad women and men are often seen moving and dancing in erotic ways. Rock star Madonna is probably best known for explicitness in her music videos; the MTV network refused to air her "Justify My Love" video. Paula Abdul's "Cold Hearted" is known for its sexy dancing. Among male rock singers, Prince is clearly sexual in his lyrics and in the dancing evident with such videos as "Cream" and "Get Off." George Michael left one rock group so that he could become more erotic with his video material, and has produced sexy rock videos such as "Careless Whisper" and "Father Figure." Billy Idol's "Cradle of Love" represents another example of a video where the emphasis is on seductiveness and partial nudity. The blending of erotic lyrics and rhythms with visual images has become one of the newest media art forms, and television has provided the vehicle that makes it accessible.

473

While explicit material usually does not show up on television, it is increasingly common for sex-related themes to become part of the scripts for TV dramas and situation comedies. Television talk shows have a reputation for dealing with every conceivable sexual variation and relationship, even during daytime hours. The television viewing public is arguably the most widely sex-educated public in history. How much of an impact that exposure to sexual themes has on the lives of people in all age brackets is yet to be fully understood.

ADVERTISING

More than any other medium in today's American society, advertising uses and exploits sex to sell a product. Calvin Klein advertisements for jeans, featuring Brooke Shields, caused a sensation in the 1970s, and in the 1980s the Calvin Klein print advertisements for Obsession perfume showed a tangle of naked bodies not clearly male or female, in rather subdued romantic lighting. It is the young, attractive male and the beautiful female who predominate in advertisements for liquor, perfume, jewelry, cars, and jeans, because the basic idea behind using sex to sell a

product is something advertisers call "identification." If the consumer uses a certain perfume, wears a certain pair of jeans, or drives a certain car, he or she will be as glamorous and attractive as the model and will have the kind of excitement and romance in her or his life as that implied in the advertisement.

If the advertisement is not blatantly sexual, then it may be subliminally so. As Vance Packard described in his book *Hidden Persuaders* (revised in 1981), advertisers may use a technique called embedding, in which they deliberately hide emotionally or sexually charged words or pictures in the background of an advertisement. The hidden persuader may be a word as simple as "sex" or "ass," or the subtle visual suggestion of male or female anatomy artfully concealed in the ripple of a jacket or the shadows of an ice cube in a drink. The power of the message is in the fact that it is not available to conscious awareness. Precisely because of this fact, it has also caused consternation among the critics, since some of them view these messages as a type of mind control.

One might ask why the sexual message is such a powerful one, especially in this country. Why does everyone want to identify with a symbol of sex? One possible answer is that in our culture, sex is synonymous with youth, attractiveness, and desirability,

FIGURE 17.9 Exploitation of Sex in Advertising

Advertising is a medium that traditionally has exploited the female body to sell products. The male figure is increasingly used for the same purpose. This billboard appeared in San Diego, California, with feminist grafitti spray-painted over it.

and implies wealth and power. However, whether the media have created that image identification or simply mirror it is still a debatable point.

CHILD PORNOGRAPHY

One of the most secretive, most lucrative, and most damaging types of pornography is that involving children. Children are emotionally unable to give true consent to sexual behavior and thus are the innocent victims of adult greed. Kiddie porn, as it is more popularly known, involves everything from children simply posing in the nude, to suggestive movement, to actual intercourse with others their own age and with adults. While statistics on child pornography can only be estimates, United States customs officials believe that up to 20,000 pieces of such material are smuggled into this country each week, primarily from Scandinavia.

The vast majority of children who become involved with prostitution and pornography are runaways. Over a million youngsters under the age of 18 leave their homes each year in the United States. Since they have no skills or money, some of them may find the pornography business a way to support themselves. At the same time, they may have the false security of the adult pimp or sex-ring organizer who gives the appearance of protecting and caring for them. In some cases parents themselves force their children into pornography.

The most devastating effect of child pornography is the emotional toll it takes on the children themselves. Put in a compromising and confusing situation and faced with conflicting emotions about their part in the film or photo, the children soon learn to distance themselves emotionally from the event. Eventually all sexual activity becomes to them a business, and as these children grow into adulthood these same feelings will carry over, perhaps damaging permanently their ability to have truly intimate relationships with anyone. Victims of child pornography are particularly subject to guilt, anxiety, depression, and self-destructive behavior. They may learn to distrust all adults, all sexual activity, and to bear their own burden of guilt for the rest of their lives (Burgess et al., 1984).

Courts in the United States continue to support the contention that child pornography lies outside First Amendment protection. The Child Protection and Obscenity Enforcement Act of 1988 supports stiff penalties for those who involve children in sexual exploitation through the making and distribution of pornography. Some photographers, book distributors, and librarians believe that parts of that law are too restrictive and counter to constitutional guarantees of freedom of speech.

Effects of Pornography

Many people have conflicting attitudes about pornography. They may be reluctant to admit that they enjoy reading or seeing erotic material, perhaps because they are embarrassed about finding it sexually arousing. And perhaps because pornography makes very private acts seem very public, various groups in society have been concerned with the effect pornographic material is likely to have on those who read and see it.

The prevailing evidence through the early 1980s had suggested that the amount of pornography depicting violence toward women or degradation of them had been increasing for a number of years. But Donnerstein and Linz (1984) refuted that idea. They cited a study by sociologist Joseph E. Scott of Ohio State University, who examined the cartoons in *Playboy* magazine from 1954 to 1983. He found that around 1977 the violence in these cartoons peaked, and that since then the violence had decreased; violent material seemed to occur on about 1 page in 3,000 and in fewer than 4 pictures of 1,000, a hardly noticeable amount. More recently, two long judicial studies of pornography found no increase in violence in either homosexual or heterosexual explicit material (Duncan, 1990a). The fact remains, however, that in other magazines and in videotape formats, violent pornography does exist.

Perhaps a more crucial issue is the effect that violent pornography may have on its viewers. Donnerstein and Linz conclude that it is violence per se, rather than sex, that is likely to cause aggressive behavior. Several researchers, Malamuth, Haber, and Fesbach (1980) among them, found that motivation to rape was not influenced by exposure to pornography; rather pornography reinforces already-existing beliefs and values about rape. Yet the idea of pornography causing contempt for women and encouraging their being treated as sexual objects is one that deserves much more concern and study (McKenzie-Mohr & Zanna, 1990).

In 1989 Ted Bundy was executed after being found guilty of a series of murders in which the victims had been sexually abused and then sadistically and brutally killed. Just prior to his execution, Bundy granted an interview in which he stated that he had been influenced by violent pornography. He was careful to say that he had no way of knowing if such pornography could affect others in this way, but that his own peculiar personality makeup had been subject to the influences of such pornographic material. This disclosure created a renewed debate in the media about

kiddie porn: term used to describe the distribution and sale of photographs and films of children or younger teenagers engaging in some form of sexual activity.

pornography. There were those who claimed that this information should motivate citizens to oppose pornography of all kinds. Others felt that the eleventh-hour confessions of a psychopathic killer should be kept in context. Again, available research has suggested that for people with propensities toward violent sexual acts, pornography depicting violence may well have some influence on their behavior. No solid evidence exists, however, to suggest that violent pornography actually creates a sadist or murderer.

Conflicts over the positive and negative features of pornography are based in two major theoretical camps. The modeling theory holds that when people are exposed to sexual acts through pornography, there is a greater likelihood that they will copy this behavior in their own lives—with violent and antisocial results. Another point of view, sometimes called the catharsis theory, is that pornography actually prevents violence or unconventional sexual behavior by releasing sexual tension in the viewer or reader.

Research into the effects of pornography on behavior has tended to concentrate on the immediate and the short-term effects, especially on men. The conclusions drawn have been considered limited in value, since the research settings tend to be artificial and the people studied tend not to be a representative sample of the general population (Green, 1985). The immediate effects of pornography fall into three main categories: (1) exposure to pornography may generate emotional reactions, both positive and negative, including sexual excitement; (2) sexual fantasies may be elicited, which are either brief and transitory or persistent and recurring; or (3) the person may respond with some form of sexual behavior such as masturbation, approaching an available sex partner, or approaching an unwilling sex partner. If the person carries out some sexual activity following exposure to pornography, there may be some imitation of behavior portrayed in the pornographic material, or already-established patterns of behavior may simply be activated (Duncan, 1990b).

In the 1948 Kinsey study of male sexual behavior, several thousand men were questioned about the types of erotic materials that sexually aroused them. Seeing portrayals of nudity, observing genitals and sexual acts, and reading erotic materials were reported to be arousing by large percentages of these men. More than 20 years later, Levitt (1969) investigated the relationship of specific pornographic content to the degree of sexual arousal more systematically. For male graduate students, the pictures that were rated as most often sexually arousing were those of heterosexual intercourse, heterosexual petting, oral-genital sex, and a nude female. These studies suggested that for heterosexual males, the more explicit the portrayal of hetero-

sexual coitus, the more apt the pornography was to be sexually arousing.

In studying female sexuality, Kinsey (1953) showed that women did not seem to experience quite the degree of interest in and sexual arousal through pornography as men did. Somewhat later studies (Mosher & Greenberg, 1969; Schmidt & Sigusch, 1970) tended to show that men and women experienced equal sexual arousal to many forms of pornography, but that women also experienced more negative emotions—such as guilt or disgust—along with the arousal. In another study (Heiman, 1977) both males and females were tested after listening to taped erotic stories; both found erotic-romantic stories more arousing than non-erotic-romantic and nonerotic control ones. Women found the erotic tapes more arousing than did men, and both men and women found stories in which women initiated erotic activity most arousing. Most studies seem to have suggested that women are in the process of redefining themselves as sexual beings, and this includes an increased awareness of responsiveness to erotic materials, formerly attributed or admitted to only by men. Heiman also reported that some women were not aware their bodies were responding to pornography with arousal, even though measuring devices were demonstrating physiological arousal. Because erection is such a noticeable response in men, men did not show the same lack of awareness.

One of the more exhaustive studies on longer-term effects of pornography was done by Goldstein and Kant (1973), who developed a carefully structured research questionnaire to evaluate exposure to pornography over one's lifetime, and the possible effects of the exposure on sexual attitudes and behaviors. They were particularly concerned with how exposure to pornography might relate to antisocial or criminal sexual behavior in males. Earlier research had suggested that sex offenders reported less exposure to erotic stimuli than nonsexual offenders. Goldstein and Kant conducted detailed interviews with institutionalized sex offenders, self-defined homosexuals, transsexuals, pornography users who frequented "adult" bookstores and cinemas, minorities, and a carefully matched sample of individuals in a control group. It was found that the controls—the average, nonoffender heterosexuals—had been exposed to more pornography during adolescence than all of the other groups surveyed, and to more explicit forms of pornography as well. Some interesting findings emerged concerning the sex-offender group. Unlike the

modeling theory: suggests that people will copy behavior they view in pornography.
catharsis theory: suggests that viewing pornography provides a release for sexual tension, thus preventing antisocial behavior.

controls, they reported responses to pornography typical of people who had a great deal of emotional guilt about sexual thoughts and behaviors, and at the same time had less frequent exposure to pornographic materials. It also seemed that the sex offenders' reactions to pornography during adulthood was more typical of what one might expect of adolescents—especially because arousal so often led to masturbation. The controls tended to seek heterosexual outlets after being aroused by erotic materials.

This was one of several studies emerging in the 1960s and 1970s that suggested pornography might be relatively harmless, even having some educational and tension-releasing effects that could reduce antisocial behavior. The conclusions of Donnerstein and Linz (1984) on the effects of pornography seem to indicate that (1) we don't know if any detrimental effects are long-lasting or fleeting, (2) depictions of women "enjoying" rape are the most harmful, but it isn't clear if all men are affected in the same way, and (3) it is not conclusive that attitudes about women and rape revealed in small-scale studies have any applicability to large-scale aggressive behaviors.

In the 1990s the controversy has centered on whether pornography may have some positive benefits. One study demonstrated that men may find pornography to be a source of sex information (Duncan, 1990b). One sex therapist has been critical of the idea of couples using sexually explicit videos as a way of enhancing their sexual lives, maintaining that pornography places too much emphasis on sexual intercourse, and suggesting that videos may actually impede the development of sexual intimacy (Offit, 1990). Other therapists have countered that viewing erotic material can stimulate erotic fantasy, provide a starting point for sexual enjoyment, and enhance intimacy, so long as films are chosen with care (Hoffman, 1991; Kircher, 1991).

Nevertheless, there is continuing concern about the more general impressions that pornography may create about sexuality, especially among younger people. It may generate attitudes of callousness or lack of interpersonal concern that are not positive influences in sexual relationships. With the spectre of HIV infection and AIDS looming over our society, no one cares to see sexual interaction trivialized or portrayed as completely carefree. The majority of people believe that pornography can have both positive and negative effects, and that the availability of sexually explicit materials to younger people should be regulated. However, they also generally feel that pornography should be protected by freedom of speech and of the press (Hevener, 1990; Thompson et al., 1990). The next few years are certain to see more debate about the effects of pornography on people's attitudes and behavior.

Pornography, the Courts, and the Law

The pornography issue is intimately associated with the role of the courts and the law in our democratic society based on principles of freedom of speech and freedom of the press. While some persons crusade for lack of censorship and the freedom to read or view whatever sexually oriented matter that one wishes, others argue that "trash" can be distinguished from "art" and that there should be liberal rights for censorship even in a democracy (Johnson, 1987; Vance, 1987).

Legislation, state courts, and the United States Supreme Court have reflected this confusion and the role that individual biases play in the decision-making process. In 1868 a basic legal definition of obscenity was established as any material whose tendency was to "deprave and corrupt those whose minds are open to such immoral influences, and into whose hands a publication of this sort may fall." It was illegal to purvey obscenity to the public. In the 1957 landmark Supreme Court case of *Roth v. the United States,* obscenity was redefined as matter appealing to prurient interest ("a shameful or morbid interest in nudity, sex, or excretion, which goes beyond customary limits of candor"). The Court further ruled that censorship of obscene material would not be allowed if the material had some "socially redeeming significance." In 1969, in the case of *Stanley v. Georgia,* the Court ruled that a person is entitled to possess pornography in the privacy of his or her own home and to use that pornography to satisfy whatever intellectual or emotional needs he or she desires. However, the public dissemination of pornographic material through the mails, over broadcast airwaves, or across state borders has been heavily regulated by numerous federal laws.

In 1973 the Supreme Court took a different position on pornography. It decided that a connection between pornography and antisocial behavior could be neither proved nor disproved. On this basis, the Court ruled that state legislatures themselves may adopt their own limits on commerce in pornography, placing more of the responsibility for judgments about pornography on local governments. The Court also dropped the obscenity standard of lack of "redeeming social value," in favor of a new standard that says the work, taken as a whole, must lack serious literary, artistic, political, or scientific merit. The Court limited the standard to works that depict or describe sexual conduct. The vagueness of these definitions and the apparent reversals in Supreme Court positions continue to create confusion in other court decisions, and lead to widely disparate attitudes toward pornography in different communities around the country.

477

Position Statements From the Sex Information and Education Council of the United States (SIECUS) on the Media and Sexually Explicit Materials:

Sexuality and the Media

SIECUS urges the media to present sexuality as a positive aspect of the total human experience, at all stages of the life cycle. Because of the media's powerful influence on all aspects of society, and particularly upon children, SIECUS believes the media has a responsibility to present matters relating to sexuality with accuracy, without exploitation, and with sensitivity to diversity. SIECUS particularly condemns gratuitous sexual violence and all dehumanizing sexual portrayals.

Sexually Explicit Materials

SIECUS supports the use of a variety of explicit visual materials as valuable educational aids, to reduce ignorance and confusion, and to contribute to a wholesome concept of sexuality. Such visual materials need to be sensitively presented and appropriate to the age and developmental maturity of the viewer.

SIECUS supports the informed use of sexually explicit materials for educational and therapeutic purposes and also affirms adults' right of access to sexually explicit materials for personal use. SIECUS opposes legislative and judicial efforts to prevent the production and/or distribution of sexually explicit materials, insofar as such efforts endanger constitutionally guaranteed freedoms of speech and press. Furthermore, such actions could be used to restrict the appropriate professional use of such materials by sexuality educators, therapists, and researchers. SIECUS supports the legal protection of minors from exploitation in the production of sexual materials.

SIECUS deplores violence, exploitation, and human degradation in our society and objects to the use of sexually explicit materials that condone or promote these negative values.

—*SIECUS Report,* January 1990 Vol. 18(2), p. 11

PRESIDENTIAL COMMISSION ON OBSCENITY AND PORNOGRAPHY, 1970

This commission's majority report recommended the repeal of legislation prohibiting the sale, exhibition, or distribution of sexual materials to consenting adults. The report further stated that the recommendation was based on the commission's finding "no evidence to date that exposure to explicit sexual materials plays a significant role in the causation of delinquent or criminal behavior among youth or adults." Additionally, the commission stated that pornography did not cause "social or individual harms such as . . . sexual or nonsexual deviancy or severe emotional disturbance" (pp. 32, 58). A minority of commission members did not concur with the report, however, and the U.S. Senate and President Richard Nixon rejected the commission's recommendations.

Many criticisms of the work done by the commission and its conclusions soon emerged. There were several limitations in the commission's research, such as the lack of longitudinal studies to assess long-term effects of pornography, or any in-depth clinical studies of the effects of pornography on the sexuality of particular individuals. Some critics maintained the commission should have considered more thoroughly evidence about the connections of violence and sex, and about how people sometimes imitate the behavior they observe in others. Neither were there any studies done with young people. Instead, the conclusions about youth were drawn from retrospective reports by adult research subjects (Cline, 1974).

UNITED STATES ATTORNEY GENERAL'S COMMISSION ON PORNOGRAPHY, 1986

In 1984 President Ronald Reagan called for the establishment of a new commission to assess more recent evidence on the effects of pornography. Attorney

General Edwin Meese appointed an 11-person advisory commission a year later, and they held hearings in six cities across the country. From its inception, the Meese Commission, as it became known, was clearly charged with making recommendations on how "the spread of pornography could be contained." Its work was governed by a stated premise that pornography was a "serious national problem." Commission members were chosen for their recognized antipornography stances. The only two members who had not demonstrated preconceived notions about pornography, Ellen Levine and Judith Becker, would eventually write a dissenting opinion about the commission's report, claiming that many of the group's conclusions were simplistic and not justified by scientific data. The commission had neither the funds nor time to support new research studies, and relied instead on the testimony of witnesses (Lynn, 1986; Mosher, 1986).

In any case, the commission concluded in its majority report that violent pornography causes sexually aggressive behavior toward women and children and fosters accepting attitudes toward rape. There were mixed opinions on pornography that the commission deemed "nonviolent and nondegrading." Consistent with its charge, the commission made nearly 100 recommendations for the control and elimination of pornography, including stricter law enforcement and stiffer penalties for offenders, particularly of child pornography, and the recommendation that possession of pornography depicting children be made a felony.

The American Civil Liberties Union (1986) opposed these recommendations as being unconstitutional and as intrusions on "civil liberties values like due process, privacy, and choice." Legislative bodies have been slow to enact new laws, and future court cases may help to clarify the many entanglements that remain with the pornography issue.

It is clear that governmental commissions fulfill the political agendas of a particular administration (Mould, 1990). To a degree, however, they may also reflect the attitudes of a society. Comparing the conclusions of the 1986 commission report with the one that appeared in 1970 provides interesting speculation about how social attitudes and values regarding pornography and individual freedom have been shifting.

Legal Aspects of Sexual Behavior

Lawmakers and law enforcers seem to fall into two major philosophical camps. Some believe that the law has a responsibility to enforce private morals publicly, and to prohibit whatever the community or society deems to be morally wrong or offensive. The other philosophical camp holds that the purpose of the law is to protect rather than to prohibit. They are not concerned about laws against sexual activities that involve consenting adults, and believe that government should stay out of the bedrooms of private citizens.

It seems that in the area of sexual behavior, for every activity that some people find disturbing or worthy of moral disapproval, a law has appeared to prohibit the activity. There have been laws that have attempted to regulate the permissible degree of consent in sex, the nature of the sexual act, the object to which it is directed, and where the act takes place. Although the laws concerning sexual behavior differ among the states, it is likely that a great many adults in the United States have performed sexual acts considered criminal under the law. There are only three types of sexual behavior that are usually not potentially subject to criminal prosecution: petting not involving intercourse; solitary masturbation in private; and intercourse between husband and wife. About half the states in the United States have statutes prohibiting homosexual activity, intercourse between unmarried persons, extramarital sex, oral-genital sex, and anal intercourse. These are called sodomy laws, the term *sodomy* being applied rather freely to many forms of sex other than heterosexual intercourse. Even for those activities not specifically prohibited by law, police often give stiff warnings or use intimidation in attempts to preserve their criteria for moral conduct (Press et al., 1986).

There is another understanding vital to our discussion of legal aspects of sexual behavior. It is that the social context in which a particular behavior occurs may determine its degree of offensiveness, and therefore whether or not law enforcement agencies become involved. A truck driver's pass at the waitress in a roadside cafe may be viewed as harmless. However, if the same man were to attempt the same pass with a strange woman on a city street, he might well be charged with sexually motivated assault.

In their classic book, *Sex Offenders: An Analysis of Types* (1965), Gebhard and his associates struggled with the legal, cultural, and psychiatric factors involved in defining what a sex offense actually is. They eventually decided that a vital criterion to incorporate into their definition was that the act results in the person's being legally convicted. They hastened to point out that the conviction may not be for a specifically sexual charge. Often charges of a sexual nature

sodomy laws: prohibit a variety of sexual behaviors in some states, that have been considered abnormal or antisocial by legislatures. These laws are often enforced discriminatorily against particular groups, such as homosexuals.

Pee Wee Herman

"Paul Reubens is living out every man's and every boy's worst nightmare. He is alleged to have been seen touching himself." —The Washington Post

Though much of the press found it difficult to write dispassionately about the arrest and disgrace of Pee Wee Herman, his case is both an indication of the success and the failure of sexuality education.

First the good side. Sexuality educators have, over the last few years, emphasized the importance of safer sex, and the dangers of picking up a casual sex partner, and many have encouraged masturbation as an alternative. Paul Reubens, professionally known as Pee Wee Herman, engaged in safer sex, albeit in a XXX-rated movie theater: he did not pick up a prostitute; . . . he did not proposition anyone.

However, Reubens was arrested in the lobby of a XXX-rated movie theater in Sarasota, Florida. The arresting officers apparently went into the theater—which was featuring heterosexually-oriented films, *Tiger Shark, Turn Up the Heat,* and *Nancy Nurse*—only after a drug case they had been working on did not pan out. Maybe, wanting to have something to show for their shift, they decided to check out the theater for sex offenders. They alleged they saw Reubens with an exposed penis in his left hand. Since the theater was dark and Reubens had a coat on his lap, it [is] difficult to say what they saw; in short, it is their word against his. The point is that the officers knew ahead that they could charge almost anyone in the theater with indecent exposure—if they chose to do so. If Herman had rented the same films at a video store and masturbated at home, there would be no issue today; Reubens, however, was staying at his parents' home where he, most likely, would not feel comfortable viewing explicit sexual materials. Sexuality researchers, therapists, and educators know that masturbation is often done to some kind of visual fantasy, and that many people use explicit sexual materials as an aid to their visualizations. Gay men use gay male sexually explicit films, heterosexuals use heterosexual sexually explicit films, etc.

The failure of sexuality education lies in the public's immediate reaction to masturbation *per se,* which became further confused when Reubens was charged with

---

are disguised under broader charges such as disorderly conduct, vagrancy, loitering, disturbing the peace, or trespassing.

The American Law Institute, composed of law professors, judges, and practitioners, faced these issues in developing their Model Penal Code, approved in 1962. It did not contain any prohibitions against any kind of sexual behavior among consenting adults in private. Although state legislatures used many aspects of the Model Penal Code in the reevaluation of laws, the provisions dealing with sexual behavior had less impact. By 1975 only eight states had adopted the institute's recommendations fully, although several others had reduced their punishments for sexual offenses. By 1986, 26 states had enacted legislation permitting consenting adults to share private sexual acts of their choosing. At the same time, the Supreme Court upheld the Georgia conviction of two gay males

who were noticed having oral sexual contact in their bedroom. This represented one of many signals that legislation concerning sexual behavior, along with stricter enforcement of existing laws, was on the way (see the section in chapter 11, p. 303, on Homosexuality and the Law).

The debate continues over whether sex laws should be for prohibition or protection. Those who are in favor of legal reforms argue that laws prohibiting sexual behavior between consenting adults are attempts to impose specific moral and religious standards on citizens. To speed up the adoption of reforms, proposals have called for the United States Congress to legislate a nationwide uniform criminal code that would include sexual offenses. The proponents of this approach claim that with present-day mobility, it is senseless to have a situation where a person may engage in some form of sexual activity in one state indecent exposure. Such a charge immediately conjures up a picture of a devious man in a raincoat who exposes himself to children; such a picture probably helped to fan the hysteria. Our failure as sexuality educators is that we have not effectively informed the American public that fantasy masturbation is common. Some people fantasize by using visual images; some rely solely on their imagination, some seek still other ways. Educators need to emphasize that masturbation is a normal activity; that it is often achieved through fantasizing; and that Reubens was doing nothing wrong.

Theaters that specialize in XXX-rated films anticipate and expect that their patrons will masturbate. XXX-rated theater owners know this, and so do the police; such behavior is generally ignored or tolerated—unless the vice officer needs to make some arrests. Since such theaters are legal, society, in effect, has said that such behavior is acceptable. Periodically, however, perhaps to discourage too many patrons, police make sweeps through the theaters and use catch-all laws to arrest the patrons. The night Reubens was arrested, three other men, who were spotted allegedly doing the same thing, were arrested as well. There is usually a small fine, both the police and the officer know the client will be back, and everyone, except the arrested client, feels better. (In some cases, the client may even feel better, since he may have guilt feelings about what he has done.) Generally, the officers do what they can to keep a *public nuisance* under control, society applauds them, and things return to normal—*except when a prominent person is discovered*. Then there can be a tragedy.

Did we help put Pee Wee Herman's career in jeopardy? Have we failed as sexuality educators, in our campaign for safer sex, by not emphasizing that masturbation is often practiced using explicit fantasy/sexual materials? While masturbation is only one aspect of human sexuality education, it is an aspect about which the public needs better education. Sexuality educators also need to come to grips with their ambivalence toward XXX-rated theaters. Personally, I think that they serve a purpose by encouraging some people to practice safer sex.

—Vern L. Bullough, 1991, *SIECUS Report,* Vol. 19(6)

without worrying about the legal implications, then cross state lines and become a criminal for engaging in the same activity.

SEX AND THE CONSTITUTION

The legal aspects of sexual behavior cannot be fairly considered without examining some of the constitutional implications. Since the United States Constitution was written, there has been a conflict over the extent to which it guarantees personal liberty, providing other people are not harmed. The debate has sometimes focused on the laws governing, or attempting to govern, sexual behavior.

One scholarly report has charged that lawmakers have overstepped the Constitution and that laws prohibiting consensual sexual activity between adults—particularly homosexuals—are indeed unconstitutional. Most such laws have vague wording and may label many different sexual behaviors under the catchall term of "crimes against nature." Courts have often declared laws "void for vagueness," and this doctrine may well apply to sex laws.

Two other doctrines have been used to fight laws about sex. One is the "independent rights" doctrine, which holds that the Constitution imposes certain restrictions on state laws that might interfere with personal liberty. The other is the "right of privacy" doctrine, which has in many courts been used to uphold the concept that what people do in private should not be the concern of prohibitive laws, unless someone is being harmed. The Constitution requires states to apply their laws equally to all people and not to allow discrimination within laws—part of the "equal protection" doctrine. Sodomy laws, however, are of-

481

"Obviously been too long in the making. What was obscene enough when you started isn't obscene enough now."

ten not applied equally, and they are used particularly against homosexuals.

The debates over laws concerning consensual sexual behavior and other victimless crimes will continue. Yet these issues should be of concern to all citizens, since they often have implications for our freedom in other areas. In recent years, the makeup of the Supreme Court—the primary governmental branch to interpret the Constitution and set precedents about legal interventions—has taken a more conservative trend that may well change a variety of perspectives on sexual behaviors as we approach the year 2000.

SPECIAL ISSUES AND THE LAW

Sex Education   A number of issues seem to receive more legal attention than others. Sex education has not been subject to much court action, but it has been met with a great deal of controversy. In the late 1960s groups throughout the United States were waging heated battles over sex education in the public schools. A landmark court case was initiated in 1970 against the Topeka, Kansas, Board of Education, alleging that the school district's sex education program was unconstitutional because it violated the parents' personal liberty to determine what subjects are taught. It was further alleged that the authority to instruct children in sex education is reserved for the parents. At the conclusion of the trial, the judge found for the defendant, permitting the schools to continue their sex education program.

Although the teaching of sex education topics has now been left to the jurisdiction of state laws and local boards of education, there has been a resurgence of anti–sex-education sentiment. Citizen groups, often with religious affiliations, have attacked sex education in public school settings, pressuring boards of education into reversing previous decisions. The issues of AIDS and the spread of the AIDS virus have become a new focus of groups that maintain sex education only condones sexual activity among the young. Nevertheless, studies consistently demonstrate that two-thirds or more of all adult Americans favor sex education in public schools (see also chapter 9, "Sexual Individuality and Sexual Values").

Rape   Historically women were not considered equal under the law and were instead treated as possessions of men. Therefore rape was not viewed as a crime against the female victim, but as a property crime against the man who "owned" her, either her father or her husband. Among ancient Hebrews and Assyrians, raping the women of enemy tribes was often considered a legal form of retribution. William the Conqueror reduced the punishment for a rapist from death to castration. Under Henry II, a raped virgin could bring suit against the attacker, and a conviction could result in his being blinded or castrated. However, the victim could "save" her rapist from punishment by marrying him! In the United States in 1868, laws required that rape be corroborated by evidence of actual penetration, the use of force, and identification of the rapist. In the 1970s corroboration laws were generally repealed, so that the burden of proof was lessened for the victim. Nonetheless, conviction still depends on being able to provide tangible evidence that sexual assault has occurred.

A landmark decision emerged in 1979 when a Massachusetts court found a man guilty of raping his wife. During the previous year, there had been a trial in Oregon involving a case in which a husband was accused of raping his wife, but there was no conviction. In the Massachusetts case, the couple had been separated for several months when the man forced himself into his wife's apartment and threatened to kill her if she did not have intercourse with him. A jury of eight men and four women found him guilty, and he was sentenced to 3 to 5 years in prison, along with several years of probation.

Many states have been reevaluating their legislation that applies to the investigation and prosecution of rape cases. For example, in 1987 the New York State Assembly's Task Force on Sexual Assault proposed several legislative measures to help rape victims and increase conviction rates (Assembly Task Force, 1987). They proposed that evidence of symptoms of the rape trauma syndrome be admissible as evidence in rape trials (see chapter 13, "Sexual Abuse and Other Sexual Problems"). Other recommendations included increased police training with respect to sexual assault and extensive training for those who deal with rape victims. Lie-detector tests for victims were restricted. Penalties for conviction of rape have been increased in recent years as well. Some local agencies provide rape-victim counselors who act as advocates and sources of support throughout the criminal justice system. The Task Force also recommended third-party reporting of rape in case a victim is reluctant to come forward. This at least informs authorities that a rape has occurred, and this may be valuable if the victim later decides to proceed with a report.

It would appear that after centuries of neglect and mistreatment by most judicial systems, rape victims are finding the prospects of having their attackers prosecuted and convicted more probable. Legislative bodies are taking increased responsibility for treating rape as a serious crime, with the convicted perpetrators given full prosecution and severe sentencing. For more information see chapter 13, "Sexual Abuse and Other Sexual Problems."

Prostitution and Nude Dancing Legal reforms are difficult in the area of prostitution. It is often considered a victimless crime and usually constitutes sexual activity between two consenting adults. Two types of laws attempt to control overt prostitution: (1) those that prohibit loitering with the intent to commit an act of prostitution; and (2) those that prohibit either offering or agreeing to an act of prostitution. Again, the basic philosophy behind such laws is concerned with regulation of private morality. However, many groups insist that it is a social necessity to attempt legal control of prostitution. Police claim that the street environment generated by prostitutes breeds crime of other sorts. Public health officials say that prostitutes are responsible for much of the increase in rates of sexually transmitted diseases and are now being implicated in the transmission of the AIDS virus. Moralists attack prostitution on religious grounds (Winick, 1991).

Some people favor the decriminalization of prostitution, which would lead to regulation of the trade. Under such a plan, there would be certain age requirements, taxation rules, and standards of hygiene. Prostitutes would be required to obtain a license. Decriminalization would protect the civil rights of both the prostitute and his or her client. It would free the prostitute from the system of arrests, bail, and release to the street; the abuse of pimps; and the harassment of society (Almodovar, 1991).

The Supreme Court has also been called on to decide on the constitutionality of nude dancing and

stripping in bars. The owners of the Kitty Kat Lounge in South Bend, Indiana, had been convicted of violating a state law prohibiting nude dancing. G-strings and "pasties" over the nipples were considered to be minimum attire for a dancer. A federal Court of Appeals first overturned the conviction, maintaining that nude dancing is "inherently expressive," and therefore constitutionally protected. However, in 1991 the Supreme Court ruled that states may ban nude dancing in the interest of "protecting order and morality." The requirement for G-strings and pasties was considered appropriate because it combated what the Chief Justice called the "evil" of public nudity without suppressing the "erotic message" of the expressive dancing.

Birth Control, Sterilization, and Abortion Three controversial issues that have found their way into courts and laws are birth control, sterilization, and abortion (see also chapter 5, "Birth Control and Unintended Pregnancy"). Until the mid-1960s, in the states of Connecticut and Massachusetts it was illegal to use contraceptives during sexual intercourse. The Supreme Court, however, declared such bans to be unconstitutional. Sterilization has been a more complicated issue. There have been several cases in which black women or people with mental retardation have been sterilized without their consent. Such actions seem to rest on the assumption that judges and physicians know best and have the right, and privilege, to decide whether or not an individual will be a fit parent and whether or not the individual's children are apt to be "suitable" for society. This notion is beginning to be met by challenges.

During the 1990s several states have attempted to pass laws that would prohibit abortion and even limit the use of certain kinds of contraceptives. It is likely that as the abortifacient drug RU-486 (see p. 124) makes its way to the United States, there will be many legislative attempts to curb its use. The next few years will represent a critical time for abortion and contraceptive rights, since the Supreme Court is expected to hand down decisions concerning several cases that will have impact on these issues.

The Rights and Responsibilities of Sexual Partners The AIDS crisis has created a whole new awareness of the dangers of sexual activity shared with someone who is unwilling to be open and honest about his or her sexual history. It is possible to contract a fatal disease, or a nonfatal sexually transmitted dis-

decriminalization: reducing the legal sanctions for particular acts while maintaining the possibility of legally regulating behavior through testing, licensing, and reporting of financial gain.

ease, from someone who does not reveal his or her physical condition or who fails to provide appropriate protection such as use of a condom.

Most states are passing, or at least considering passing, statutes that would make the rights and responsibilities of sexual partners clear. The individual who is aware of carrying genital herpes or HIV, but fails to inform a sexual partner and fails to use adequate protection to prevent transmission of the disease, will most probably be prosecuted for criminal behavior. These suits or civil penalties are bound to become more common as the risks of contracting AIDS and other STDs become greater. The outcome of these suits will set legal precedents by which future relationships may well be governed.

Conclusion

The legal aspect of human sexual behavior will probably always be in conflict with the personal emotional aspect. The public has a right to protection from dangerous behavior, and the individual has a right to behave in any way she or he chooses as long as the behavior doesn't hurt anyone else. In some cases it isn't possible to separate public and private rights. Then, a legal interpretation must be made of the situation and a judgment passed on whose right has priority. As the historical cycle moves from liberalism to conservatism, the judgment may be made in favor of what courts and legislatures consider the public good rather than private freedom. ■

CHAPTER SUMMARY

1. Graphic depictions of human nudity and sexual behavior have been a part of every society and historical period. Pornography is generally considered to be material that is meant to sexually arouse. Erotica is a name given to erotically realistic art or fiction.

2. In many ancient cultures, erotic art was used for purposes of instructing people in sexual behaviors. Today erotic themes have a range of purposes.

3. Writing about sex can be traced back 4,000 years. There have been cycles of acceptance and repression about erotic writings over the centuries.

4. Even in Victorian nineteenth-century literature, there were frank accounts of sexual behavior. Contemporary literature has explored all sex-related themes. Illustrations are now often used to enhance the impact of erotic material.

5. Since the mid-twentieth century, sexuality has become increasingly open in films, television, and other media. The video pornography market has expanded significantly. Hard-core pornography is widely available today in North American and European countries.

6. Computer networks now distribute up-to-date information on sexuality.

7. Advertising frequently makes use of sexual themes to popularize and sell products.

8. Child pornography represents a lucrative market and has been shown to have a devastating effect on children who have been forced to act in it.

9. Research on the effects of pornography has often yielded conflicting results. Some research indicates that effects on adults are minimal and that it might relieve sexual tensions, thus preventing antisocial behavior. Other research claims that pornography can increase negative attitudes toward women, especially if it depicts sexual aggression or violence.

10. Both men and women may experience sexual arousal in response to viewing pornography.

11. Pornography has been subject to various laws throughout recent history. Since 1973, individual states have been allowed to develop their own legislation, although there are often challenges because of constitutional rights to freedom of speech and the press.

12. The Presidential Commission of the 1960s found no particular evidence that pornography caused criminal behavior or contributed to emotional problems. The pornography commission established in the 1980s made sweeping recommendations about limiting pornography because of its negative effects. These differences reflect changing social and political attitudes.

13. Societies always regulate sexual behaviors, often through laws. In the United States, sodomy laws have prohibited those behaviors considered to be deviant from the norm.

14. More liberal proponents have argued that any sexual behavior between consenting adults should be considered legal.

15. There are sometimes constitutional issues raised by the regulation of sexual behavior, especially if laws are enforced in a discriminatory manner.

16. State legislatures and courts are sometimes called upon to determine whether sex education should be allowed in public schools.

17. Rape has been considered illegal in recent history, although victims were often subjected to humiliating and difficult treatment in order to prosecute the rapist. Convictions in rape cases have been proportionately small. Newer laws are being developed to deal with rape, including marital rape.

18. Prostitution, often considered a "victimless" crime, has presented difficult issues to lawmakers. In most states it is prohibited by law. Nude dancing may be regulated by state laws.

19. Birth control in some states was prohibited by laws until the mid-1960s. Sterilization of people without their consent has been challenged in the courts. States are increasingly placing restrictions on abortion.

20. Increasingly, statutes are appearing to clarify that sex partners have certain legal rights and responsibilities.

ANNOTATED READINGS

Chaneles, S. (ed.). (1984). *Gender issues, sex offenses and criminal justice: Current trends*. New York: Haworth Press. Focuses on the special issues of legality and criminal justice as they relate to sexual behaviors.

Copp, D. & Wendell, S. (eds.). (1983). *Pornography and censorship*. Buffalo, NY: Prometheus Books. Explores the complexities of balancing freedom of the press, research on effects of pornography, and judicial decision-making.

Davis, M. & Scott, R. S. (1988). *Lovers, doctors and the law*. New York: HarperCollins. Outlines the current state of legal affairs relating to the individual rights and responsibilities surrounding sexual activity. Provides useful suggestions for protecting oneself and one's partner from disease and legal complications.

Francoeur, R. T. (ed.). (1991). *Taking sides: Clashing views on controversial issues in human sexuality*. Guilford, CT: The Dushkin Publishing Group. A collection of essays debating many controversial issues in human sexuality. Many of the articles relate to freedom of expression or choice and legal matters concerning sex-related issues.

Kendrick, W. (1987). *The secret museum: Pornography in modern culture*. New York: Viking/Penguin. One perspective on the roles and regulation of pornographic materials in society.

Lederer, L. (ed.). (1980). *Take back the night: Women on pornography*. New York: William Morrow. A collection of essays about pornography from a feminist point of view.

Paglia, C. (1991). *Sexual personae: Art and decadence from Nefertiti to Emily Dickinson*. New York: Random House. A highly controversial book, in which a scholar takes on prevailing feminist attitudes about gender, sexuality, pornography, and restrictive legislation. The author examines sensuality and sexuality in art.

APPENDIX

APPENDIX: RESOURCES ON HUMAN SEXUALITY

Here you can find sources of further information about sex, help for various personal concerns, support groups of people with whom you can discuss sex, and organizations from which sex education materials may be ordered. To find other resources in your locality, consult the yellow pages, local medical society, area sex educators, the education department of your local Planned Parenthood agency, counselors, campus groups, or social service agencies.

National Organizations and Clearinghouses

Sex Information and Education Council of the U.S.
(SIECUS)
130 West 42nd Street, Suite 2500
New York, NY 10036
(212) 819-9770
This organization continually updates lists of selected books and resources in a variety of areas relating to sexuality. They also maintain the Mary S. Calderone Library, open to individuals researching topics in human sexuality.

American Association of Sex Educators, Counselors and Therapists (AASECT)
435 North Michigan Avenue, Suite 1717
Chicago, IL 60611
(312) 644-0828
This organization certifies qualified educators, counselors, and therapists in the fields of human sexuality. AASECT can provide a directory of certified professionals in the United States and other countries.

American Board of Sexology
1929 18th Street, NW, Suite 1166
Washington, DC 20009
(202) 462-2122
Also provides lists of certified diplomates in the fields of sex therapy and sex education.

Association for Voluntary Surgical Contraception
79 Madison Avenue
New York, NY 10016

Centers for Disease Control
Division of Sexually Transmitted Diseases
1600 Clifton Road
Atlanta, GA 30329

The Center for Population Options
1025 Vermont Avenue, NW, Suite 210
Washington, DC 20005
(202) 347-5700

Kinsey Institute for Research in Sex, Gender, and Reproduction
Morrison Hall
Indiana University
Bloomington, IN 47405

Masters and Johnson Institute
24 South Kingshighway
St. Louis, MO 63108

National Abortion Rights Action League
1101 14th Street, NW (5th floor)
Washington, DC 20005
(202) 408-4600

National Center for the Prevention and Control of Rape (NCPCR)
National Institute of Mental Health
5600 Fishers Lane, Room 6C-12
Rockville, MD 20857

Planned Parenthood Federation of America
810 Seventh Avenue
New York, NY 10019
(212) 541-7800

Society for the Scientific Study of Sex
P.O. Box 208
Mt. Vernon, IA 52314

Journals and Newsletters

AIDS Education and Prevention (quarterly)
Guilford Publications
72 Spring Street
New York, NY 10012

Annals of Sex Research (quarterly)
Juniper Press
P.O. Box 7205
Oakville, Ontario L6J 6L5
Canada

Annual Review of Sex Research (annual)
Society for the Scientific Study of Sex
P.O. Box 208
Mt. Vernon, IA 52314

Archives of Sexual Behavior (bimonthly)
Plenum Publishing Corporation
233 Spring Street
New York, NY 10013

Bisexuality: News, Views, and Networking (monthly newsletter)
Gibbon Publications
P.O. Box 20917
Long Beach, CA 90801-3917

Contemporary Sexuality (monthly newsletter)
American Association of Sex Educators, Counselors and Therapists
435 North Michigan Avenue, Suite 1717
Chicago, IL 60611

Family Life Educator (quarterly)
Network Publications
P.O. Box 1830
Santa Cruz, CA 95060–1830

Journal of Sex Education and Therapy (quarterly)
Guilford Publications
72 Spring Street
New York, NY 10012

Journal of Homosexuality (quarterly)
Haworth Press
10 Alice Street
Binghamton, NY 13904-1580

Journal of Sex Research (quarterly)
Society for the Scientific Study of Sex
P.O. Box 208
Mt. Vernon, IA 52314

Journal of Sex and Marital Therapy (quarterly)
Brunner/Mazel, Inc.
19 Union Square West
New York, NY 10003

Journal of Gay and Lesbian Psychotherapy (quarterly)
Journal of Psychology and Human Sexuality (biannual)
Journal of Social Work and Human Sexuality (biannual)
Haworth Press
10 Alice Street
Binghamton, NY 13904-1580

Medical Aspects Human Sexuality (monthly)
Hospital Publications, Inc.
500 Plaza Drive
Secaucus, NJ 07094

Sex Over Forty (monthly newsletter)
DKT International
P.O. Box 1600
Chapel Hill, NC 27515

Sex Roles: A Journal of Research (monthly)
Plenum Publishing
233 Spring Street
New York, NY 10013

Sexual and Marital Therapy
Carfax Publishing
P.O. Box 25
Abingdon, Oxfordshire OX14 3UE
England

Sexuality and Disability (quarterly)
Human Sciences Press
233 Spring Street
New York, NY 10013

SIECUS Report (bimonthly)
130 West 42nd Street, Suite 2500
New York, NY 10036

Women and Health (quarterly)
Haworth Press
10 Alice Street
Binghamton, NY 13904-1580

Telephone Hotlines for Information on Sex and Sexually Transmitted Diseases

Los Angeles Sex Information Helpline
(213) 653-1123
 (Telephone information: Mon.–Thurs.,
 3:30–9:30 P.M. PST)

National STD Hotline
 National toll-free telephone (for anywhere in USA):
 1-800-227-8922
 Call for STD information or referral to local clinics
 for treatment. Hours: 8 A.M.–11 P.M. (EST) weekdays.

Organizations for Information on AIDS

AIDS Action Council
729 8th Street, SE, Suite 200
Washington, DC 20003
(202) 547-3101

AIDS Information
U.S. Public Health Service
Office of Public Affairs, Room 721-H
200 Independence Avenue, SW
Washington, DC 20201
(202) 245-6867

American Red Cross
Contact your local chapter.

AIDS-Related Discrimination Unit
American Civil Liberties Union
132 West 43rd Street
New York, NY 10036
(212) 944-9800 (ext. 545)

American Foundation for AIDS Research
1515 Broadway, Suite 3601
New York, NY 10036
(212) 719-0033

Gay Men's Health Crisis
129 West 20th Street
New York, NY 10011
(212) 807-6655

National AIDS Information Clearinghouse
Box 6003
Rockville, MD 20850
1-800-458-5231

National AIDS Network
2033 M Street, NW, Suite 800
Washington, DC 20036
(202) 293-2437

National Hemophilia Foundation
110 Greene Street, Room 406
New York, NY 10012
(212) 219-8180

National Lesbian and Gay Health Foundation
P.O. Box 65472
Washington, DC 20035
(202) 797-3708

National Association of People with AIDS
P.O. Box 65472
Washington, DC 20035
(202) 483-7979

AIDS Telephone Hotlines

AIDS Crisisline 1-800-221-7044

National AIDS Hotline 1-800-342-AIDS, operated by
the U.S. Health Service
 Most state departments of health have now established AIDS hotlines. Consult your yellow pages, or
 call the headquarters of your county or state health
 department.

National AIDS Information Clearinghouse
1-800-458-5231

For Information and Support Relating to Homosexuality and Bisexuality

Bisexual Information and Counseling Service
599 West End Avenue, Suite 1-A
New York, NY 10024
(212) 496-9500

Center for Research & Gay Education in Sexuality
(CERES)
Psychology Building, Room 503
San Francisco State University
San Francisco, CA 94132
(415) 338-1137

Coalition for Lesbian and Gay Civil Rights
P. O. Box 611
Cambridge, MA 02238
(617) 828-3039

International Gay and Lesbian Archives
Box 38100
Los Angeles, CA 90038-0100
(213) 854-0271

Lesbian and Gay Youth Helpline
(202) 483-9585
(Available for telephone counseling and advice,
Mon. & Wed., 7:00–10:00 P.M.; Sat. 3:30–6:30
P.M., EST)

National Bisexual Network
584 Castro Street, Box 422
San Francisco, CA 94114
(415) 775-1990

National Federation of Parents & Friends of Lesbians
& Gays (P-FLAG)
1012 14th Street NW, 6th Floor
Washington, DC 20005
(202) 638-3852

National Gay and Lesbian Crisis Line
1-800-221-7044

National Gay and Lesbian Task Force
1734 14th Street, NW
Washington, DC 20009-4309
(202) 332-6483

For Information and Support Relating to Sexual Abuse

The National Child Abuse Hotline/Referral Service
1-800-422-4453

National Center on Child Abuse and Neglect
P.O. Box 1182
Washington, DC 20013
(202) 245-2858

National Resource Center on Child Sexual Abuse
106 Lincoln Street
Huntsville, AL 35801
1-800-543-7006

National Coalition Against Sexual Assault
8787 State Street
East St. Louis, IL 62203

Adults Molested as Children United
P.O. Box 952
San Jose, CA 95108
(408) 280-5055

Incest Survivors Anonymous
P.O. Box 21817
Baltimore, MD 21222
(301) 282-3400

Incest Recovery Association
6200 North Central Expressway, Suite 209
Dallas, TX 75206
(214) 373-6607

Incest Resources, Inc.
Cambridge Women's Center
46 Pleasant Street
Cambridge, MA 02139
(617) 354-8807

Incest Survivors Resource Network International
P.O. Box 911
Hicksville, NY 11802
(516) 935-3031

Women's and Men's Issues

Boston Women's Health Collective
465 Mt. Auburn Street
Watertown, MA 02172

National Organization for Women
1000 16th Street, NW, Suite 700
Washington, DC 20036
(202) 331-0066

National Organization for Changing Men
P.O. Box 451
Watseka, IL 60970
(815) 432-3010

For Help With Infertility Problems

Resolve, Inc.
P.O. Box 474
Belmont, MA 02178

GLOSSARY

GLOSSARY

Page references indicate where term is first defined.

A

abnormal anything considered not to be normal, that is, not conforming to the subjective standards a social group has established as the norm. 227

abortifacients substances that cause termination of pregnancy. 124

acquaintance (date) rape when a sexual encounter is forced by someone who is known to the victim. 352

acquired immunodeficiency syndrome fatal disease caused by a virus that is transmitted through the exchange of bodily fluids, primarily in sexual activity and intravenous drug use. 401

activating effect the direct influence some hormones can have on activating or deactivating sexual behavior. 73

actual use failure rate a measure of how often a birth control method can be expected to fail when human error and technical failure are considered. 114

adolescence period of emotional, social, and physical transition from childhood to adulthood. 174

adultery toleration marriage partners extend the freedom to each other to have sex with others. 326

affectional relating to feelings or emotions, such as romantic attachments. 276

afterbirth the tissues expelled after childbirth, including the placenta, the remains of the umbilical cord, and fetal membranes. 98

agenesis (absence) of the penis (ae-JEN-a-ses) a congenital condition in which the penis is undersized and nonfunctional. 390

AIDS acquired immunodeficiency syndrome. 401

ambisexual alternate term for bisexual. 278

amniocentesis a process whereby medical problems with a fetus can be determined while it is still in the womb; a needle is inserted into the amniotic sac, amniotic fluid is withdrawn, and its cells examined. 93

amnion (AM-nee-on) a thin membrane that forms a closed sac around the embryo; the sac is filled with amniotic fluid that protects and cushions the embryo. 84

anal intercourse insertion of the penis into the rectum of a partner. 263

androgen a male hormone, such as testosterone, that affects physical development, sexual desire, and behavior. It is produced by both male and female sex glands and influences each sex in varying degrees. 73

androgyny (an-DROJ-a-nee) combination of traditional feminine and masculine traits in a single individual. 160

anejaculation lack of ejaculation at the time of orgasm. 52

anorchism (a-NOR-kiz-um) rare birth defect in which both testes are lacking. 390

aphrodisiacs (af-ro-DEE-zee-aks) foods or chemicals purported to foster sexual arousal; they are believed to be more myth than fact. 264

apotemnophilia (a-POT-em-no-FIL-ee-a) a rare paraphilia characterized by the desire to function sexually after having a leg amputated. 343

areola (a-REE-a-la) darkened, circular area of skin surrounding the nipple of the breast. 37

artificial embryonation a process in which the developing embryo is flushed from the uterus of the donor woman 5 days after fertilization and placed in another woman's uterus. 90

artificial insemination injecting the sperm cells of a male into a woman's vagina, with the intention of conceiving a child. 88

asceticism (a-SET-a-siz-um) usually characterized by celibacy, this philosophy emphasizes spiritual purity through self-denial and self-discipline. 240

asexuality a condition characterized by a low interest in sex. 313

autoerotic asphyxiation accidental death from pressure placed around the neck during masturbatory behavior. 332

autofellatio (fe-LAY-she-o) a male providing oral stimulation to his own penis, an act most males do not have the physical agility to perform. 258

B

Bartholin's glands (BAR-tha-lenz) small glands located in the opening through the minor lips that produce some secretion during sexual arousal. 30

495

behavior therapy therapy that uses techniques to change patterns of behavior, often employed in sex therapy. 447

berdache (bare-DAHSH) anthropological term for cross-dressing in other cultures. 314

bestiality (beest-ee-AL-i-tee) a human being having sexual contact with an animal. 333

birth canal term applied to the vagina during the birth process. 97

birthing rooms special areas in the hospital, decorated and furnished in a nonhospital way, set aside for giving birth; the woman remains here to give birth rather than being taken to a separate delivery room. 99

bisexual refers to some degree of sexual activity with or attraction to members of both sexes. 278

blastocyst the morula, after 5 days of cell division, that has developed a fluid-filled cavity in its interior; it has entered the uterine cavity. 84

bond the emotional link between parent and child created by cuddling, cooing, physical and eye contact early in the newborn's life. 99

bondage tying, restraining, or applying pressure to body parts as part of sexual arousal. 332

brachioproctic activity (brake-ee-o-PRAHK-tik) known in slang as "fisting"; a hand is inserted into the rectum of a partner. 294

brothels houses of prostitution. 328

bulbourethral glands also called Cowper's glands. 50

C

call boys highly paid male prostitutes. 327

call girls highly paid prostitutes who work by appointment with an exclusive clientele. 328

cantharides (kan-THAR-a-deez) a chemical extracted from a beetle that, when taken internally, creates irritation of blood vessels in the genital region; it can cause physical harm. 264

case study an in-depth look at a particular individual and how he or she might have been helped to solve a sexual or other problem. Case studies may offer new and useful ideas for counselors to use with other patients. 18

catharsis theory suggests that viewing pornography provides a release for sexual tension, thus preventing antisocial behavior. 476

celibacy (SELL-a-ba-see) choosing not to share sexual activity with others. 313

cervical cap a device that is shaped like a large thimble and fits over the cervix; not a particularly effective contraceptive because it can dislodge easily during intercourse. 118

cervical intraepithelial neoplasia (CIN) (ep-a-THEE-lee-al nee-a-PLAY-zhee-a) abnormal, precancerous cells sometimes identified in a Pap smear. 391

cervix (SERV-ix) lower "neck" of the uterus that extends into the back part of the vagina. 35

cesarian section a surgical method of childbirth in which delivery occurs through an incision in the abdominal wall and uterus. 98

chancroid (SHAN-kroyd) an STD caused by the bacterium *Hemophilus ducreyi* and characterized by sores on the genitals, which, if left untreated, could result in pain and rupture of the sores. 385

child molesting sexual abuse of a child by an adult. 360

chlamydia (kluh-MID-ee-uh) now known to be a common STD, this organism is a major cause of urethritis in males; in females it often presents no symptoms. 377

chorion (KOR-ee-on) the outermost extraembryonic membrane, essential in the formation of the placenta. 84

chorionic villi sampling (CVS) a technique for diagnosing medical problems in the fetus as early as the 8th week of pregnancy; a sample of the chorionic membrane is removed through the cervix and studied. 94

cilia microscopic hairlike projections that help move the ovum through the fallopian tube. 37

circumcision in the male, surgical removal of the foreskin from the penis; in the female, surgical procedure that cuts the prepuce, exposing the clitoral shaft. 31, 48

climacteric mid-life period experienced by both men and women when there is greater emotional stress than usual and sometimes physical symptoms. 53

climax another term for orgasm. 62

clinical research the study of the cause, treatment, or prevention of a disease or condition by testing large numbers of people. 18

clitoridectomy surgical removal of the clitoris; practiced routinely in some cultures. 32

clitoris (KLIT-a-rus) sexually sensitive organ found in the female vulva; it becomes engorged with blood during arousal. 31

clone the genetic-duplicate organism produced by the cloning process. 91

cloning a process involving the transfer of a full complement of chromosomes from a body cell of an organism into an ovum from which the chromosomal material has been removed; if allowed to develop into a new organism, it is an exact genetic duplicate of the one from which the original body cell was taken; the process is not yet used for humans, but has been performed in lower animal species. 91

cohabitation living together and sharing sex without marrying. 182

coitus (KO-at-us or ko-EET-us) heterosexual, penis-in-vagina intercourse. 230

coitus interruptus (KO-at-us or ko-EET-us) a method of birth control in which the penis is withdrawn from the vagina prior to ejaculation. 115

comarital sex also called mate-swapping, in which a couple swaps sexual partners with another couple. 327

combining of chromosomes occurs when a sperm unites with an egg, normally joining 23 pairs of chromosomes to establish the genetic "blueprint" for a new individual. The sex chromosomes establish its sex: XX for female and XY for male. 136

coming out to acknowledge to oneself and to others that one is sexually attracted to others of the same sex. 290

Comstock Laws enacted in the 1870s, this federal legislation prohibited the mailing of information about contraception. 104

condom a sheath worn over the penis during intercourse that collects semen and helps prevent disease transmission. 119

consensual adultery permission given to at least one partner within the marital relationship to participate in extramarital sexual activity. 183, 326

controlled experiment research in which the investigator examines what is happening to one variable while all other variables are kept constant. 18

conventional adultery extramarital sex without the knowledge of the spouse. 326

coprophilia sexual arousal connected with feces. 332

core gender-identity/role a child's early sense and expression of its maleness, femaleness, or ambivalence, established prior to puberty. 142

corona the ridge around the penile glans. 47

corpus luteum cell cluster of the follicle that remains after the ovum is released, secreting hormones that help regulate the menstrual cycle. 40

Cowper's glands two small glands in the male that secrete an alkaline fluid into the urethra during sexual arousal. 50

cross-genderists transgenderists. 316

cryptorchidism (krip-TOR-ka-diz-um) condition in which the testes have not descended into the scrotum prior to birth. 390

cunnilingus (kun-a-LEAN-gus) oral stimulation of the clitoris, vaginal opening, or other parts of the vulva. 262

cystitis (sis-TITE-us) a nonsexually transmitted infection of the urinary bladder. 391

D

decriminalization reducing the legal sanctions for particular acts while maintaining the possibility of legally regulating behavior through testing, licensing, and reporting of financial gain. 483

deoxyribonucleic acid (DNA) (dee-AK-see-rye-bow-new-KLEE-ik) the chemical in each cell that carries the genetic code. 82

desire phase Kaplan's term for the psychological interest in sex that precedes a physiological, sexual arousal. 63

deviation term applied to behaviors or orientations that do not conform to a society's accepted norms; it often has negative connotations. 229

diaphragm (DY-a-fram) a latex rubber cup, filled with spermicide,

that is fitted to the cervix by a clinician; the woman must learn to insert it properly for full contraceptive effectiveness. 117

diethylstilbestrol (DES) (dye-eth-a-stil-BES-trole) synthetic estrogen compound given to mothers whose pregnancies are at high risk of miscarrying. 394

dilation and curettage (D & C) a method of induced abortion in the second trimester of pregnancy that involves a scraping of the uterine wall. 129

dilation and evacuation (D & E) a method of induced abortion in the second trimester of pregnancy; it combines suction with a scraping of the inner wall of the uterus. 128

discrimination the process by which an individual extinguishes a response to one stimulus while preserving it for other stimuli. 169

dysfunction when the body does not function as expected or desired during sex. 344

dysmenorrhea (dis-men-a-REE-a) painful menstruation. 42

E

E. coli bacteria naturally living in the human colon, often causes urinary tract infection. 391

ectopic pregnancy (ek-TOP-ik) the implantation of a blastocyst somewhere other than in the uterus, usually in the fallopian tube. 84

ejaculation muscular expulsion of semen from the penis. 51

ejaculatory inevitability the sensation in the male that ejaculation is imminent. 71

ELISA the primary test used to determine the presence of HIV in humans. 413

embryo (EM-bree-o) the term applied to the developing cells when, about a week after fertilization, the blastocyst implants itself in the uterine wall. 84

endometrial hyperplasia (hy-per-PLAY-zhee-a) excessive growth of the inner lining of the uterus (endometrium). 394

endometriosis (en-doe-mee-tree-O-sus) growth of the endometrium out of the uterus into surrounding organs. 395

endometrium interior lining of the uterus, innermost of three layers. 35

epidemiology (e-pe-dee-mee-A-la-jee) the branch of medical science that deals with the incidence, distribution, and control of disease in a population. 404

epididymis (ep-a-DID-a-mus) tubular structure on each testis in which sperm cells mature. 45

epididymitis (ep-a-did-a-MITE-us) inflammation of the epididymis of the testis. 387

episiotomy (ee-piz-ee-OTT-a-mee) a surgical incision in the vaginal opening made by the clinician or obstetrician if it appears that the baby will tear the opening in the process of being born. 97

epispadias (ep-a-SPADE-ee-as) birth defect in which the urinary bladder empties through an abdominal opening, and the urethra is malformed. 390

erectile dysfunction difficulty achieving or maintaining penile erection (impotence). 435

erection enlargement and stiffening of the penis as blood engorges the columns of spongy tissue and internal muscles contract. 47

erogenous zone (a-RAJ-a-nus) any area of the body that is sensitive to sexual arousal. 172

erotica artistic representations of nudity or sexual activity. 461

estrogen (ES-tro-jen) hormone produced abundantly by the ovaries; it plays an important role in the menstrual cycle. 40

estrogen replacement therapy (ERT) controversial treatment of the physical changes of menopause by administering dosages of the hormone estrogen. 54

ethnocentricity the tendency of the members of one culture to assume that their values and norms of behavior are the "right" ones in comparison to other cultures. 233

excitement the arousal phase of Masters and Johnson's four-phase model of the sexual response cycle. 62

exhibitionism exposing the genitals to others for sexual pleasure. 329

external values the belief systems available from one's society and culture. 239

extramarital sex married person having sexual intercourse with someone other than her or his spouse; adultery. 326

497

F

fallopian tubes structures that are connected to the uterus and lead the ovum from an ovary to the inner cavity of the uterus. 36

fellatio oral stimulation of the penis. 262

fetal alcohol syndrome (FAS) a condition in a fetus characterized by abnormal growth, neurological damage, and facial distortion caused by the mother's heavy alcohol consumption. 96

fetal surgery a surgical procedure performed on the fetus while it is still in the uterus. 94

fetishism (FET-a-shizm) sexual arousal triggered by objects or materials not usually considered to be sexual. 323

fetus the term given to the embryo after 2 months of development in the womb. 84

fibrous hymen unnaturally thick, tough tissue composing the hymen. 391

follicles capsules of cells in which an ovum matures. 36

follicle-stimulating hormone (FSH) pituitary hormone that stimulates the ovaries or testes. 40

foreplay sexual activities shared in early stages of sexual arousal, with the term implying that they are leading to a more intense, orgasm-oriented form of activity such as intercourse. 230

foreskin fold of skin covering the penile glans; also called prepuce. 47

fraternal twin a twin formed from two separate ova that were fertilized by two separate sperm. 82

frenulum (FREN-yu-lum) thin, tightly-drawn fold of skin on the underside of the penile glans; it is highly sensitive. 47

frottage (fro-TAZH) gaining sexual gratification from anonymously pressing or rubbing against others, usually in crowded settings. 329

frotteur one who practices frottage. 329

G

G spot a vaginal area that some researchers feel is particularly sensitive to sexual stimulation. 69

gamete intra-fallopian transfer (GIFT) direct placement of ovum and concentrated sperm cells into the woman's fallopian tube to increase the chances of fertilization. 90

gay slang term referring to homosexual persons and behaviors. 277

gender dysphoria (dis-FOR-ee-a) term to describe gender-identity/role that does not conform to the norm considered appropriate for one's physical sex. 147

gender transposition gender dysphoria. 147

gender-identity/role (G-I/R) a person's inner experience and outward expression of maleness, femaleness, or some ambivalent position between the two. 135

general sexual dysfunction difficulty for a woman in achieving sexual arousal. 435

generalization application of specific learned responses to other, similar situations or experiences. 169

genetic engineering the modification of the gene structure of cells to change cellular functioning. 88

genital herpes (HER-peez) viral STD characterized by painful sores on the sex organs. 382

genital warts small lesions on genital skin caused by papilloma virus; this STD increases later risks of certain malignancies. 383

glans in the male, the sensitive head of the penis; in the female, the sensitive head of the clitoris, visible between the upper folds of the minor lips. 31, 47

gonadotropin releasing hormone (GnRH) (go-nad-a-TRO-pen) hormone from the hypothalamus that stimulates the release of FSH and LH by the pituitary. 40

gonorrhea (gon-uh-REE-uh) bacterial STD causing urethral pain and discharge in males; often no symptoms in females. 376

granuloma inguinale (gran-ya-LOW-ma in-gwa-NAL-ee *or* -NALE) STD characterized by ulcerations and granulations beginning in the groin and spreading to the buttocks and genitals. 385

group marriage three or more people in a committed relationship who share sex with one another. 183

H

hard-core pornography pornography that makes use of highly explicit depictions of sexual activity or shows lengthy scenes of genitals. 471

hedonists believers that pleasure is the highest good. 240

hemophiliac (hee-mo-FIL-ee-ak) someone with the hereditary sex-linked blood defect hemophilia, affecting males primarily and characterized by difficulty in clotting. 404

heterosexual attractions or activities between members of opposite sexes. 277

HIV human immunodeficiency virus. 401

homophobia (ho-mo-PHO-bee-a) strongly held negative attitudes and irrational fears relating to homosexuals; irrational fear of homosexuals. 281, 401

homosexual term applied to romantic and sexual attractions and activities between members of the same sex. 277

homosexualities a term that reminds us there is not a single pattern of homosexuality, but a wide range of same-sex orientations. 287

hookers street name for female prostitutes. 328

hot flash a flushed, sweaty feeling in the skin caused by dilated blood vessels, often associated with menopause. 54

human chorionic gonadotropin (HCG) a hormone detectable in the urine of a pregnant woman. 96

human immunodeficiency virus the virus that initially attacks the human immune system, eventually causing AIDS. 401

hustlers male street prostitutes. 327

H-Y antigen a biochemical produced in an embryo when the Y chromosome is present; it causes fetal gonads to develop into testes. 138

hymen membranous tissue that can cover part of the vaginal opening. 31

hypersexuality exaggeratedly high level of interest in and drive for sex. 311

hyposexuality an especially low level of sexual interest and drive. 311

hypospadias (hye-pa-SPADE-ee-as) birth defect caused by incomplete closure of the urethra during fetal development. 390

I

identical twin a twin formed by a single ovum that was fertilized by a single sperm before the cell divided in two. 82

imperforate hymen lack of any openings in the hymen. 391

impotence (IM-pa-tens) difficulty achieving or maintaining erection of the penis. 432

in loco parentis a Latin phrase meaning "in the place of the parent." 181

in vitro fertilization (IVF) a process whereby the union of the sperm and egg occurs outside the mother's body. 89

incest (IN-sest) sexual activity between closely related family members. 364

incest taboo cultural prohibitions against incest, typical of most societies. 365

induced abortion a termination of pregnancy by artificial means. 127

infertility the inability to produce offspring. 94

infibulation surgical procedure, performed in some cultures, that seals the opening of the vagina. 32

informed consent the consent given by research subjects, indicating their willingness to participate in a study, after they are informed about the purpose of the study and how they will be asked to participate. 19

inhibited sexual desire (ISD) loss of interest and pleasure in what were formerly arousing sexual stimuli. 434

internal values the individualized beliefs and attitudes that a person develops by sorting through external values and personal needs. 239

interstitial cells cells between the seminiferous tubules that secrete testosterone and other male hormones. 45

interstitial-cell-stimulating hormone (ICSH) pituitary hormone that stimulates the testes to secrete testosterone; known as luteinizing hormone (LH) in females. 51

intrauterine devices (IUDs) birth control method involving the insertion of a small plastic device into the uterus. 120

introitus (in-TROID-us) the outer opening of the vagina. 31

invasive cancer of the cervix (ICC) advanced and dangerous malignancy requiring prompt treatment. 394

K

Kaposi's sarcoma a rare form of cancer of the blood vessels, characterized by small, purple skin lesions. 408

kiddie porn term used to describe the distribution and sale of photographs and films of children or younger teenagers engaging in some form of sexual activity. 475

kleptomania extreme form of fetishism, in which sexual arousal is generated by stealing. 324

L

labor uterine contractions in a pregnant woman; an indication that the birth process is beginning. 97

lactation production of milk by the milk glands of the breasts. 37

Lamaze method (la-MAHZ) a birthing process based on relaxation techniques practiced by the expectant mother; her partner coaches her throughout the birth. 98

laminaria (lam-a-NER-ee-a) a dried seaweed sometimes used in dilating the cervical opening prior to vacuum curettage. 128

laparoscopy simpler procedure for tubal ligation, involving the insertion of a small fiber optic scope into the abdomen, through which the surgeon can see the fallopian tubes and close them off. 122

laparotomy operation to perform a tubal ligation, or female sterilization, involving an abdominal incision. 122

latency period a stage in human development characterized, in Freud's theory, by little interest in or awareness of sexual feelings; recent research tends to suggest that latency does not exist. 14, 167

lesbian (LEZ-bee-un) refers to female homosexuals. 277

libido (la-BEED-o or LIB-a-do) a term first used by Freud to define human sexual longing, or sex drive. 166

lumpectomy surgical removal of a breast lump, along with a small amount of surrounding tissue. 39

luteinizing hormone (LH) pituitary hormone that triggers ovulation in the ovaries and stimulates sperm production in the testes. 40

lymphogranuloma venereum (LGV) (lim-foe-gran-yu-LOW-ma va-NEAR-ee-um) contagious STD caused by several strains of *Chlamydia* and marked by swelling and ulceration of lymph nodes in the groin. 385

M

major lips two outer folds of skin covering the minor lips, clitoris, urethral opening, and vaginal opening. 30

mammography sensitive X-ray technique used to discover small breast tumors. 38

marital rape a woman being forced to have sex by her husband. 357

masochist the individual in a sado-masochistic sexual relationship who takes the submissive role. 331

massage parlors places where women can be hired to perform sexual acts under the guise of giving a massage. 328

mastectomy surgical removal of all or part of a breast. 39

ménage à trois (may-NAZH-ah-TR-WAH) troilism. 324

menarche (MEN-are-kee) onset of menstruation at puberty. 39

menopause (MEN-a-poz) time in mid-life when menstruation ceases. 39

menstrual cycle the hormonal interactions that prepare a woman's body for possible pregnancy at roughly monthly intervals. 39

menstruation (men-stru-AY-shun) phase of menstrual cycle in which the inner uterine lining breaks down and sloughs off; the tissue, along with some blood, flows out through the vagina; also called the period. 41

midwives medical professionals, both women and men, trained to assist with the birthing process. 99

minor lips two inner folds of skin that join above the clitoris and extend along the sides of the vaginal and urethral openings. 30

499

miscarriage a natural termination of pregnancy. 127

modeling theory suggests that people will copy behavior they view in pornography. 476

molluscum contagiosum (ma-LUS-kum kan-taje-ee-O-sum) a skin disease transmitted by direct bodily contact, not necessarily sexual, that is characterized by eruptions on the skin that appear similar to whiteheads with a hard seed-like core. 386

monogamous sharing sexual relations with only one person. 183

monorchidism (ma-NOR-ka-dizm) presence of only one testis in the scrotum. 390

mons cushion of fatty tissue located over the female's pubic bone. 30

moral values beliefs associated with ethical issues, or rights and wrongs; they are often a part of sexual decision-making. 239

morula (MOR-yul-a) a spherical, solid mass of cells formed after 3 days of embryonic cell division. 83

Müllerian ducts (myul-EAR-ee-an) embryonic structures that develop into female sexual and reproductive organs unless inhibited by male hormones. 138

Müllerian Inhibiting Substance hormone produced by fetal testes that prevents further development of female structures from the Müllerian ducts. 138

myometrium middle, muscular layer of the uterine wall. 35

N

National Birth Control League an organization founded in 1914 by Margaret Sanger to promote use of contraceptives. 104

natural childbirth a birthing process that encourages the mother to take control, thus minimizing medical intervention. 98

necrophilia (nek-ro-FILL-ee-a) having sexual activity with a dead body. 333

nongonococcal urethritis (NGU) (non-gon-uh-KOK-ul yur-i-THRYT-us) infection or irritation in the male urethra caused by bacteria or local irritants. 380

normal a highly subjective term used to describe sexual behaviors and orientations. Standards of normalcy are determined by social, cultural, and historical standards. 227

normal asexuality an absence or low level of sexual desire, considered normal for a particular person. 434

normalization integration of mentally retarded persons into the social mainstream as much as possible. 249

Norplant implants contraceptive method in which hormone-releasing rubber containers are surgically inserted under the skin. 116

nymphomania (nim-fa-MANE-ee-a) compulsive need for sex in women; apparently quite rare. 311

O

obscenity depiction of sexual activity in a repulsive or disgusting manner. 461

onanism (O-na-niz-um) a term sometimes used to describe masturbation, it comes from the biblical story of Onan, who practiced coitus interruptus and "spilled his seed on the ground." 260

oocytes (OH-a-sites) cells that mature to become ova. 36

open-ended marriage each partner in the primary relationship grants the other freedom to have emotional and sexual relationships with others. 183

opportunistic infection a disease resulting from lowered resistance of a weakened immune system. 408

organic disorder physical disorder caused by the organs and organ systems of the human body. 440

organizing effect manner in which hormones control patterns of early development in the body. 73

orgasm (OR-gaz-em) a rush of pleasurable physical sensations associated with the release of sexual tension. 51, 62

orgasmic release reversal of the vasocongestion and muscular tension of sexual arousal, triggered by orgasm. 63

orgy (OR-jee) group sex. 325

os opening in the cervix that leads into the hollow interior of the uterus. 35

osteoporosis (ah-stee-o-po-ROW-sus) disease caused by loss of calcium from the bones in postmenopausal women, leading to brittle bones and stooped posture. 54

ova egg cells produced in the ovary. One cell is an ovum; in reproduction, it is fertilized by a sperm cell. 36

ovaries pair of female gonads, located in the abdominal cavity, that produce ova and female hormones. 36

ovulation release of a mature ovum through the wall of an ovary. 40

ovum transfer use of an egg from another woman for conception, with the fertilized ovum then being implanted in the uterus of the woman wanting to become pregnant. 90

oxytocin pituitary hormone that plays a role in lactation and in uterine contractions. 37

P

pansexual lacking highly specific sexual orientations or preferences; open to a range of sexual activities. 333

Pap smear medical test that examines a smear of cervical cells, to detect any cellular abnormalities. 36

paraphilia (pair-a-FIL-ee-a) a newer term used to describe sexual orientations and behaviors that vary from the norm; it means "a love beside." 229

paraplegic a person paralyzed in the legs, and sometimes pelvic areas, as the result of injury to the spinal cord. 250

partial zona dissection (PZD) a technique used to increase the chances of fertilization by making a microscopic incision in the zona pellucida of an ovum. This creates a passageway through which sperm may enter the egg more easily. 94

pedophilia (peed-a-FIL-ee-a) another term for child sexual abuse. 360

pelvic inflammatory disease (PID) a chronic internal infection associated with certain types of IUDs. 120

penis male sexual organ that can become erect when stimulated; it leads urine and sperm to the outside of the body. 47

perimetrium outer covering of the uterus. 35

perinatally a term used to describe things related to pregnancy, birth,

500

or the period immediately following the birth. 404

perineal areas (pair-a-NEE-al) the sensitive skin between the genitals and the anus. 385

Peyronie's disease (pay-ra-NEEZ) development of fibrous tissue in spongy erectile columns within the penis. 390

phimosis (fy-MOS-us) a condition in which the penile foreskin is too tight to retract easily. 49, 390

pimps men who have female prostitutes working for them. 328

placenta (pla-SENT-a) the organ that unites the fetus to the mother by bringing their blood vessels closer together; it provides nourishment and removes waste for the developing baby. 84

plateau phase the stable, leveled-off phase of Masters and Johnson's four-phase model of the sexual response cycle. 62

polygamy practice, in some cultures, of being married to more than one spouse. 183

pornography photographs, films, or literature intended to be sexually arousing through explicit depictions of sexual activity. 461

potentiation establishment of stimuli early in life that form ranges of response for later in life. 172

pregnancy-induced hypertension a disorder that can occur in the latter half of pregnancy, marked by a swelling in the ankles and other parts of the body, high blood pressure, and protein in the urine; can progress to coma and death if not treated. 99

premature birth a birth that takes place prior to the 36th week of pregnancy. 99

premature ejaculation difficulty that some men experience in controlling the ejaculatory reflex, resulting in rapid ejaculation. 439

premenstrual syndrome (PMS) symptoms of physical discomfort, moodiness, and emotional tensions that occur in some women for a few days prior to menstruation. 44

preorgasmic a term often applied to women who have not yet been able to reach orgasm during sexual response. 433

prepuce (PREE-peus) in the female, tissue of the upper vulva that covers the clitoral shaft. 30

priapism (pry-AE-pizm) continual, undesired, and painful erection of the penis. 390

primary dysfunction a difficulty with sexual functioning that has always existed for a particular person. 433

progesterone (pro-JES-ter-one) ovarian hormone that causes the uterine lining to thicken. 40

progestin injection use of injected hormone that can prevent pregnancy for several months; not yet approved for use in the United States. 116

prolactin pituitary hormone that stimulates the process of lactation. 37

prolapse of the uterus weakening of the supportive ligaments of the uterus, causing it to protrude into the vagina. 395

promiscuity (prah-mis-KIU-i-tee) sharing casual sexual activity with many different partners. 311

prostaglandin hormonelike chemical whose concentrations increase in a woman's body just prior to menstruation. 44

prostaglandin- or saline-induced abortion used in the 16th–24th weeks of pregnancy, prostaglandins, salt solutions, or urea is injected into the amniotic sac, administered intravenously, or inserted into the vagina in suppository form, to induce contractions and fetal delivery. 129

prostate gland located beneath the urinary bladder in the male; it produces some of the secretions in semen. 50

prostatitis (pras-tuh-TITE-us) inflammation of the prostate gland. 388

pseudonecrophilia a fantasy about having sex with the dead. 333

psychosexual development complex interaction of factors that form a person's sexual feelings, orientations, and patterns of behavior. 165

psychosocial development the cultural and social influences that help shape human sexual identity. 168

puberty time of life when reproductive capacity develops and secondary sex characteristics appear. 174

pubic lice small insects that can infect skin in the pubic area, causing a rash and severe itching. 385

pubococcygeus (PC) muscle (pyub-o-kox-a-JEE-us) part of the supporting musculature of the vagina that is involved in orgasmic response and over which a woman can exert some control. 34

pyromania sexual arousal generated by setting fires. 324

Q

quadriplegic a person paralyzed in the upper body, including the arms, and lower body as the result of spinal cord injury. 250

R

random sample a representative group of the larger population that is the focus of a scientific poll or study in which care is taken to select participants without a pattern that might sway research results. 17

rape trauma syndrome the predictable sequence of reactions that a victim experiences following a rape. 359

recreational adultery extramarital sex with a low level of emotional commitment and performed for fun and variety. 183

refractory period time following orgasm during which a man cannot be restimulated to orgasm. 72

reinforcement in conditioning theory, any influence that helps shape future behavior as a punishment or reward stimulus. 168

resolution phase the term for the return of a body to its unexcited state following orgasm. 62

retarded ejaculation a sexual dysfunction in which a male has difficulty reaching an orgasm. 438

retrograde ejaculation abnormal passage of semen into the urinary bladder at the time of ejaculation. 52

retrovirus (RE-tro-vi-rus) a class of viruses that reproduces with the aid of the enzyme reverse transcriptase, which allows the virus to integrate its genetic code into that of the host cell, thus establishing permanent infection. 410

Rh incompatibility condition in which a blood protein of the infant is not the same as the mother's; antibodies formed in the mother can destroy red blood cells in the fetus. 100

Rho GAM medication administered to a mother to prevent formation of antibodies when the baby is Rh positive and its mother Rh negative. 100

501

rhythm method a natural method of birth control that depends on an awareness of the woman's menstrual-fertility cycle. 121

rubber dam small square sheet of latex used to cover the vulva, vagina, or anus to help prevent transmission of HIV during sexual activity. 262, 425

RU-486 a progesterone antagonist used as a postcoital contraceptive. 124

S

sadist the individual in a sado-masochistic sexual relationship who takes the dominant role. 331

sadomasochism (sade-o-MASS-o-kiz-um) refers to sexual themes or activities involving bondage, pain, domination, or humiliation of one partner by the other. 331

sample a representative group of a population that is the focus of a scientific poll or study. 17

satyriasis (sate-a-RYE-a-sus) compulsive need for sex in men; apparently quite rare. 311

scabies (SKAY-beez) a skin disease caused by a mite that burrows under the skin to lay its eggs, causing redness and itching; transmitted by bodily contact that may or may not be sexual. 386

scrotum (SKROTE-um) pouch of skin in which the testes are contained. 45

secondary dysfunction a difficulty with sexual functioning that develops after some period of normal sexual functioning. 433

selective reduction use of abortion techniques to reduce the number of fetuses when there are more than three in a pregnancy, thus increasing the chances of survival for the remaining fetuses. 83

self-gratification giving oneself pleasure, as in masturbation; a term typically used today instead of more negative descriptors. 229

self-pleasuring self-gratification; masturbation. 229

semen (SEE-men) mixture of fluids and sperm cells that is ejaculated through the penis. 50

seminal vesicle (SEM-un-al) gland at the end of each vas deferens that secretes a chemical that helps sperm to become motile. 50

seminiferous tubules (sem-a-NIF-a-rus) tightly coiled tubules in the testes in which sperm cells are formed. 45

sensate focus early phase of sex therapy treatment, in which the partners pleasure each other without involving direct stimulation of sex organs. 450

sex addiction inability to regulate sexual behavior. 344

sex therapist professional trained in the treatment of sexual dysfunctions. 448

sexual dysfunctions difficulties people have in achieving sexual arousal. 63

sexual harassment unwanted sexual advances or coercion that can occur in the workplace or academic settings. 345

sexual individuality the unique set of sexual needs, orientations, fantasies, feelings, and activities that develops in each human being. 235

sexual phobias and aversions exaggerated fears toward forms of sexual expression. 434

sexual revolution the changes in thinking about sexuality and sexual behavior in society that occurred in the 1960s and 1970s. 4

sexual surrogates paid partners used during sex therapy with clients lacking their own partners; only rarely used today. 446

shaft in the female, the longer body of the clitoris, containing erectile tissue; in the male, cylindrical base of penis that contains three columns of spongy tissue: two corpora cavernosa and a corpus spongiosum. 31, 47

shunga ancient scrolls used in Japan to instruct couples in sexual practices through the use of paintings. 462

Skene's glands secretory cells located inside the female urethra. 69

smegma thick, oily substance that may accumulate under the prepuce of the clitoris or penis. 31

social learning theory suggests that human learning is influenced by observation of and identification with other people. 169

social scripts a complex set of learned responses to a particular situation that is formed by social influences. 170

sodomy laws prohibit a variety of sexual behaviors in some states, that have been considered abnormal or antisocial by legislatures. These laws are often enforced discriminatorily against particular groups, such as homosexuals. 479

sonograms ultrasonic rays used to project a picture of internal structures such as the fetus; often used in conjunction with amniocentesis or fetal surgery. 94

spectatoring term used by Masters and Johnson to describe self-consciousness and self-observation during sex. 443

sperm reproductive cells produced in the testes; in fertilization, one sperm unites with an ovum. 45

spermatocytes (sper-MAT-o-sites) cells lining the seminiferous tubules from which sperm cells are produced. 51

spermicidal jelly (cream) sperm-killing chemical in a gel base or cream, used with other contraceptives such as diaphragms. 118

spermicides chemicals that kill sperm; available as foams, creams, jellies, or implants in sponges or suppositories. 117

sponge a thick polyurethane disc that holds a spermicide and fits over the cervix to prevent conception. 117

spontaneous abortion another term for miscarriage. 127

Staphylococcus aureus (staf-a-low-KAK-us) the bacteria that can cause toxic shock syndrome. 118

statutory rape a legal term used to indicate sexual activity when one partner is under the age of consent; in most states that age is 18. 350

sterilization rendering a person incapable of conceiving, usually by interrupting passage of the egg or sperm. 121

straight slang term for heterosexual. 278

streetwalkers female prostitutes who work on the streets. 328

suppositories contraceptive devices designed to distribute their spermicide by melting or foaming in the vagina. 117

syndrome (SIN-drome) a group of signs or symptoms that occur together and characterize a given condition. 408

syphilis (SIF-uh-lus) sexually transmitted disease (STD) characterized by four stages, beginning with the appearance of a chancre. 375

systematic desensitization step-by-step approaches to unlearning tension-producing behaviors and developing new behavior patterns. 447

T

testes (TEST-ees) pair of male gonads that produce sperm and male hormones. 44

testicular cancer malignancy on the testis that may be detected by testicular self-examination. 390

testicular failure lack of sperm and/or hormone production by the testes. 390

testosterone (tes-TAS-ter-one) major male hormone produced by the testes; it helps to produce male secondary sex characteristics. 45

testosterone replacement therapy administering testosterone injections to increase sexual interest or potency in older men; not considered safe for routine use. 56

theoretical failure rate a measure of how often a birth control method can be expected to fail, when used without error or technical problems. 114

thrush a disease caused by a fungus and characterized by white patches in the oral cavity. 408

toxic shock syndrome (TSS) an acute disease characterized by fever and sore throat, and caused by normal bacteria in the vagina that are activated if tampons or some contraceptive devices such as diaphragms or sponges are left in for long periods of time. 118

transgenderists people who live in clothing and roles considered appropriate for the opposite sex for sustained periods of time. 316

transsexuals people who feel as though they should have the body of the opposite sex. 297

transvestism dressing in clothes considered appropriate to the opposite sex, usually for sexual gratification. 298

transvestite an individual who dresses in clothing considered appropriate for the opposite sex, and adopts similar mannerisms, often for sexual pleasure. 234

trichomoniasis (trik-uh-ma-NEE-uh-sis) a vaginal infection caused by the *Trichomonas* organism. 381

troilism (TROY-i-lizm) sexual activity shared by three people. 324

tubal ligation a surgical separation of the fallopian tubes to induce permanent female sterilization. 122

U

umbilical cord the tubelike tissues and blood vessels arising from the embryo's navel connecting it to the placenta. 84

urethra (yu-REE-thrah) tube that passes from the urinary bladder to the outside of the body. 47

urethral opening opening through which urine passes to the outside of the body. 31

urophilia sexual arousal connected with urine or urination. 332

uterus (YUTE-a-rus) muscular organ of the female reproductive system; a fertilized egg implants itself within the uterus. 35

V

vacuum curettage (kyur-a-TAZH) a method of induced abortion performed with a suction pump. 128

vagina (vu-JI-na) muscular canal in the female that is responsive to sexual arousal; it receives semen during heterosexual intercourse for reproduction. 33

vaginal atresia (a-TREE-zha) birth defect in which the vagina is absent or closed. 391

vaginal atrophy shrinking and deterioration of vaginal lining, usually the result of low estrogen levels during aging. 391

vaginal fistulae (FISH-cha-lee *or* -lie) abnormal channels that can develop between the vagina and other internal organs. 391

vaginismus (vaj-uh-NIZ-mus) involuntary spasm of the outer vaginal musculature, making penetration of the vagina difficult or impossible. 34

values system of beliefs with which people view life and make decisions, including their sexual decisions. 238

variable an aspect of a scientific study that is subject to change. 18

variation a less pejorative term to describe nonconformity to accepted norms. 229

varicose veins overexpanded blood vessels; can occur in veins surrounding the vagina. 391

vas deferens tube that leads sperm upward from each testis to the seminal vesicles. 45

vasectomy (va-SEK-ta-mee *or* vay-ZEK-ta-mee) a surgical separation of the vas deferens to induce permanent male sterilization. 122

villi fingerlike projections of the chorion; they form a major part of the placenta. 84

viral hepatitis inflammation of the liver caused by a virus. 384

voyeurism (VOYE-yu-rizm) sexual gratification from viewing others who are nude, or who are engaging in sexual activities. 232, 330

vulva external sex organs of the female, including the mons, major and minor lips, clitoris, and opening of the vagina. 30

vulvovaginitis (vaj-uh-NITE-us) general term for inflammation of the vulva and/or vagina. 380

W

Western blot the test used to verify the presence of HIV antibodies detected first by the ELISA. 413

Wolffian ducts (WOOL-fee-an) embryonic structures that develop into male sexual and reproductive organs if male hormones are present. 138

Y

yeast infection a type of vaginitis caused by an overgrowth of a fungus normally found in an inactive state in the vagina. 381

Z

zona pellucida (ZO-nah pe-LOO-sa-da) the transparent, outer membrane of an ovum. 82

zoophilia (zoo-a-FILL-ee-a) bestiality. 333

REFERENCES

REFERENCES

A

AAUW. (1991). *Shortchanging girls, shortchanging America*. Washington, DC: American Association of University Women.

Abramson, P. R., Perry, L. B., Seeley, T. T., Seeley, D. M., & Rothblatt, A. B. (1981). Thermographic measurements of sexual arousal: A discriminant validity analysis. *Archives of Sexual Behavior, 10*, 171–176.

Adler, N. E., David, H. P., Major, B. N., Roth, S. H., Russo, N. F., & Wyatt, G. E. (1990). Psychological responses after abortion. *Science, 248*, 41–44.

Alan Guttmacher Institute. (1981). *Teenage pregnancy: The problem that hasn't gone away*. New York: Alan Guttmacher Institute.

Allen, M. P. (1989). *Transformations: Crossdressers and those who love them*. New York: E. P. Dutton.

Almodovar, N. J. (1991). Prostitution and the criminal justice system. In Francoeur, R. T. (Ed.), *Taking sides: Clashing views on controversial issues in human sexuality* (pp. 220–226). Guilford, CT: The Dushkin Publishing Group.

Alpert, H. (1972). Whither the erotic film? *Sexual Behavior, 2*(6), 44–47.

Altman, L. K. (1990, July 24). Puzzle of sailor's death solved after 31 years: The answer is AIDS. *New York Times*, C3.

Altman, L. K. (1991, June 19). Infants' AIDS test is called reliable. *New York Times*, A6.

Alvarez, F., Branche, V., & Fernandez, E. (1988). New insights on the mode of action of intrauterine devices in women. *Fertility and Sterility, 49*, 768–773.

Alzate, H. (1990). Vaginal erogeneity, the "G spot" and "female ejaculation." *Journal of Sex Education and Therapy, 16*(2), 137–140.

American Cancer Society. (1991). *Cancer facts and figures, 1991*. New York: American Cancer Society.

American Civil Liberties Union. (1986). *Polluting the censorship debate*. Washington: ACLU.

Andrews, L. (1981). Removing the stigma of surrogate motherhood. *Family Advocate, 20*(2).

Angier, N. (1990, Nov. 29). Researchers gain in mapping how AIDS virus enters cells. *New York Times*, A1, B16.

Anhalt, M. A., & Carlton, C. E. (1973). Hypospadias and epispadias. *Medical Aspects of Human Sexuality, 7*, 218–226.

Apfelbaum, B. (1989). Retarded ejaculation: A much misunderstood syndrome. In Leiblum, S. R., & Rosen, R. C. (Eds.), *Principles and Practices of Sex Therapy: Update for the 1990s* (pp. 168–206). New York: Guilford Press.

Appelbaum, P. S. (1990). Statutes regulating patient-therapist sex. *Hospital and Community Psychiatry, 41*(1), 15–16.

Armsworth, M. W. (1991). Psychological responses to abortion. *Journal of Counseling and Development, 69*, 377–379.

Assembly Task Force. (1987). *Sexual assault: Research findings and public hearing report*. Albany: The Assembly, State of New York.

Athanasiou, R., Shaver, P., & Tavris, C. (1970). Sex. *Psychology Today, 4*(2), 37–52.

Atrash, H. K., MacKay, H. T., Binkin, N. J., & Hogue, C. J. R. (1987). Legal abortion mortality in the United States: 1972–1982. *American Journal of Obstetrics and Gynecology, 156*, 605–612.

Attorney General's Commission. (1986). *Final report of the attorney general's commission on pornography*. Nashville, TN: Rutlidge Hill.

Atwell, C. (1987). Personal communication from police community relations officer at the University of Maryland, College Park.

Atwood, J. D., & Gagnon, J. (1987). Masturbatory behavior in college youth. *Journal of Sex Education and Therapy, 13*(2).

Avasthi, S. (1990, September 1). Sex addiction: Pros and cons of 12 step treatment fuel controversy. *Guidepost, 33*(3), 1, 20–21.

Avery, C. S. (1989). How do you build intimacy in an age of divorce? *Psychology Today, 23*(5), 27–31.

B

Bachrach, C. (1984). Contraceptive practice among American women, 1973–1982. *Family Planning Perspectives, 16*, 253–259.

Bailey, D. S. (1955). *Homosexuality and the western Christian tradition*. London: Longmans.

Baizerman, M., Thompson, J., & Stafford-White, K. (1979). Adolescent prostitution. *Children Today, 8*(5), 20–24.

Baker, T. C., Burgess, A. W., Brickman, E., & Davis, R. C. (1990). Rape victims' concerns about possible expo-

507

sure to HIV infection. *Journal of Interpersonal Violence, 5*(1), 49–60.

Baldwin, J. D., & Baldwin, J. I. (1988). AIDS information and sexual behavior on a university campus. *Journal of Sex Education and Therapy, 14*(2), 24–33.

Balter, B. (1991). Montagnier pursues the mycoplasma—AIDS link. *Science, 251,* 271.

Bancroft, J. (1984). Hormones and human sexual behavior. *Journal of Sex and Marital Therapy, 10,* 3–21.

Bancroft, J. (1990a). Commentary: Biological contributions to sexual orientation. In McWhirter, D. P., Sanders, S. A., & Reinisch, J. M. (Eds.), *Homosexuality/heterosexuality: Concepts of sexual orientation* (pp. 101–111). New York: Oxford University Press.

Bancroft, J. (1990b). The impact of sociocultural influences on adolescent sexual development: Further considerations. In Bancroft, J. & Reinisch, J. M. (Eds.), *Adolescence and puberty* (pp. 207–216). New York: Oxford University Press.

Bandura, A., & Walters, R. H. (1963). *Social learning and personality.* New York: Holt, Rinehart and Winston.

Barbach, L. G. (1975). *For yourself: The fulfillment of female sexuality.* New York: Doubleday.

Barbach, L. G. (1980). *Women discover orgasm.* New York: Free.

Bardwick, J. M. (1971). *The psychology of women.* New York: Harper and Row.

Barinaga, M. (1991). Is homosexuality biological? *Science, 253,* 956–957.

Barnett, W. (1973). *Sexual freedom and the Constitution.* Albuquerque: University of New Mexico.

Baron, J. N., & Bielby, W. T. (1985). Organizational barriers to gender equability: Sex segregation of jobs and opportunities. In Rossi, A. S. (Ed.), *Gender and the life course* (pp. 233–251). Hawthorne, NY: Aldine.

Baruch, E. H., D'Adamo, A. F., & Seager, J. (1989). *Embryos, ethics, and women's rights: Exploring new reproductive technologies.* Binghamton, NY: Haworth Press.

Basow, S. A., & Campanile, F. (1990). Attitudes toward prostitution as a function of attitudes toward feminism in college students. *Psychology of Women Quarterly, 14*(1), 135–141.

Bateman, P. (1991). In Levy, B. (Ed.), *Dating violence: Young women in danger* (pp. 94–99). Seattle, WA: Seal Press.

Bateson, G. (1972). *Steps to an ecology of mind.* New York: Ballantine.

Batra, A. K., & Lue, T. F. (1990). Physiology and pathology of penile erection. *Annual Review of Sex Research, 1,* 251–263.

Baulieu, E. (1989). Contragestion and other clinical applications of RU 486, an antiprogesterone at the receptor. *Science, 245,* 1351–1357.

Baumeister, R. F. (1988). Masochism as escape from self. *Journal of Sex Research, 25*(1), 28–59.

Beck, A. (1988). *Love is never enough.* New York: Harper and Row.

Beckman, K. A., & Burns, G. L. (1990). Relation of sexual abuse and bulimia in college women. *International Journal of Eating Disorders, 9*(5), 487–492.

Bell, A., & Weinberg, M. S. (1978). *Homosexualities: A study of human diversity.* New York: Simon and Schuster.

Bell, A., Weinberg, M. S., & Hammersmith, S. K. (1981). *Sexual preference: Its development in men and women.* Bloomington: Indiana University.

Bem, S. L. (1974). The measurement of psychological androgyny. *Journal of Consulting and Clinical Psychology, 42*(2), 155–162.

Bem, S. L. (1975). Androgeny vs. the tight little lives of fluffy women and chesty men. *Psychology Today.*

Bem, S. L. (1987). Masculinity and femininity exist only in the mind of the perceiver. In Reinisch, J. H., Rosenblum, L. A., & Sanders, S. A. (Eds.), *Masculinity/femininity: Basic perspectives* (pp. 304–311). New York: Oxford University.

Bensel, R. W. (1984). The needs of children. *Juvenile and Family Court Journal, 35,* 33–39.

Berezin, M. A. (1975). Masturbation and old age. In Marcus, I. M., & Francis, J. J. (Eds.), *Masturbation from infancy to senescence* (pp. 329–347). New York: International Universities.

Berger, R. E., & Berger, D. (1987). *Biopotency: A guide to sexual success.* Emmons, PA: Rodale Press.

Berger, R. M. (1990). Passing: Impact of the quality of same-sex couple relationships. *Social Work, 35*(4), 328–332.

Berliner, L., & Conte, J. R. (1990). The process of victimization: The victim's perspective. *Child Abuse and Neglect, 14*(1), 29–40.

Bernstein, D., Lovett, M., & Bryson, Y. (1984). Serologic analysis of first episode nonprimary genital simplex virus infection. *American Journal of Medicine, 77,* 1055–1060.

Bieber, I., Dain, H. J., Dince, P.R., Drellich, M. G., Grand, H. G., Gunlach, R. H., Kremers, M. V., Wilbur, C. B., & Bieber, T. B. (1962). *Homosexuality: A psychoanalytic study.* New York: Vintage.

Bigler, M. O. (1989). Adolescent sexual behavior in the eighties. *SIECUS Report, 18*(1), 6–9.

Bjorksten, O. J. W. (1976). Sexually graphic materials in the treatment of sexual disorders. In Meyer, J. K. (Ed.). *Clinical management of Sexual Disorders* (pp. 161–194). Baltimore: Williams and Wilkins.

Blakeslee, S. (1991, January 1). Research on birth defects turns to flaws in sperm. *New York Times,* p.1.

Block, J. H. (1983). Differential premises arising from differential socialization of the sexes: Some conjecture. *Child Development, 54,* 1335–1354.

Blotnick, S. (1987, March 16). A survey of college students reported in *USA Today* by N. Hellmich, p. 1.

Blume, E. (1983). Methodological difficulties plague PMS research. *Journal of the American Medical Association, 249,* 2866.

Blumstein, P. W., & Schwartz, P. (1977). Bisexuality: Some social and psychological issues. *Journal of Social Issues, 33*(2), 30–45.

Blumstein, P. W., & Schwartz, P. (1983). *American couples.* New York: William Morrow.

Blumstein, P. W., & Schwartz, P. (1990). Intimate relationships and the creation of sexuality. In McWhirter, D. P., Sanders, S. A., & Reinisch, J. M. (Eds.), *Homosexuality/heterosexuality: Concepts of sexual orientation* (pp. 307–320). New York: Oxford University Press.

Booth, W. (1989a). Asking America about its sex life. *Science, 243,* 304.

Booth, W. (1989b). WHO seeks global data on sexual practices. *Science, 244,* 418–419.

Borneman, E. (1983). Progress in empirical research on childhood sexuality. *SIECUS Report, 12*(2), 1–5.

Boston Women's Health Collective. (1984). *The new our bodies, ourselves.* New York: Simon and Schuster.

Boswell, J. E. (1990a). Sexual and ethical categories in premodern Europe. In McWhirter, D. P., Sanders, S. A., & Reinisch, J. M. (Eds.), *Homosexuality/heterosexuality: Concepts of sexual orientation* (pp. 15–31). New York: Oxford University Press.

Boswell, J. E. (1990b). Social history: Disease and homosexuality. In Voeller, B., Reinisch, J. M., Gottelieb, M. (Eds.), *AIDS and sex* (pp. 171–182). New York: Oxford University Press.

Bowie, W. (1984). Epidemiology and therapy of Chlamydia trachomatis infections. *Drugs, 27,* 459–468.

Bowker, L. H. (1983). Marital rape: A distinct syndrome? *Social Casework, 64*(6), 347–352.

Bradley, S. J., & Zucker, K. J. (1990). Gender identity disorder and psychosexual problems in children and adolescents. *Canadian Journal of Psychiatry, 35*(6), 477–486.

Brannock, J. C., & Chapman, B. E. (1990). Negative sexual experiences with men among heterosexual women and lesbians. *Journal of Homosexuality, 19*(1), 105–110.

Brashear, D. B., & Munsick, R. A. (1991). Hymenal dyspareunia. *Journal of Sex Education and Therapy, 17*(1), 27–31.

Brecher, E. M. (1979). *The sex researchers* (Rev.). San Francisco: Specific.

Brecher, E. M., & Editors of Consumers Reports Books. (1984). *Love, sex, and aging: A Consumers Union report.* Boston: Little, Brown.

Bretschneider, J. G., & McCoy, N. L. (1988). Sexual interest and behavior in healthy 80- to 102-year olds. *Archives of Sexual Behaviors, 17,* 109–129.

Brickner, B. (1987). Judaism and contemporary sexuality. *SIECUS Report, 15*(5), 5–8.

Broderick, C. B. (1972). Children's romances. *Sexual Behavior, 2*(5), 16–21.

Bronski, M. (1991). The mainstreaming of S/M. *Outweek, 89,* 32–37.

Brookmeyer, R. (1991). Reconstruction and future trends of the AIDS epidemic in the United States. *Science, 253,* 37–42.

Browder, S. (1988, June). Is living together such a good idea? *New Woman,* pp. 120–124.

Brown, C. J. (1983). Paraphilias: Sadomasochism, fetishism, transvestism, and transsexuality. *British Journal of Psychiatry, 143,* 227–231.

Brown, G. (1989). *The new celibacy.* New York: McGraw-Hill.

Brown, J. D., Childers, K. W., & Waszak, C. S. (1990). Television and adolescent sexuality. *Journal of Adolescent Health Care, 11*(1), 62–70.

Bruce, G. (1990, November). A woman's guide to birth control. *East West,* pp. 60–67, 88–89.

Bruce, K. E., & Bullins, C. G. (1989). Students' attitudes and knowledge about genital herpes. *Journal of Sex Education and Therapy, 15*(4).

Bryan, A. J., & Petrangelo, G. J. (1989). Self-concept and sex role orientation in adolescence. *Journal of Sex Education and Therapy, 15*(1), 17–29.

Buhrich, N., & Beaumont, T. (1981). Comparison of transvestism in Australia and America. *Archives of Sexual Behavior, 10*(3), 269–279.

Bullough, V. L. (1976). *Sexual variance in society and history.* New York: John Wiley.

Bullough, V. L. (1981). Age at menarche: A misunderstanding. *Science, 213,* 365–366.

Bullough, V. L. (1990a). History and the understanding of human sexuality. *Annual Review of Sex Research, 1,* 75–92.

Bullough, V. L. (1990b). The Kinsey Scale in historical perspective. In McWhirter, D. P., Sanders, S. A., & Reinisch, J. M. (Eds.), *Homosexuality/heterosexuality: Concepts of sexual orientation* (pp. 3–14). New York: Oxford University Press.

Bumpass, L. L., & Martin, T. C. (1989). Recent trends in marital disruption. Research cited in Associated Press story March 13, 1989.

Burgess, A. W., Hartman, C. R., McCausland, M., & Powers, P. (1984). Response patterns in children and adolescents exploited through sex rings and pornography. *American Journal of Psychiatry, 141,* 656–662.

Burgess, A. W., & Hazelwood, R. R. (1983). Autoerotic asphyxial deaths and social network response. *American Journal of Orthopsychiatry, 53*(1), 166–170.

Burns, A., Farrell, M., & Brown, J. C. (1990). Clinical features of patients attending a gender-identity clinic. *British Journal of Psychiatry, 157,* 265–268.

Burns, A. L., Mitchell, G., & Obradovich, S. (1989). Of sex roles and strollers; Female and male attention to toddlers. *Sex Roles, 20,* 309–315.

Buvat, J., Buvat-Herbaut, M., Lemaire, A., Marcolin, G., & Quittelier, E. (1990). Recent developments in the clinical assessment and diagnosis of erectile dysfunction. *Annual Review of Sex Research, 1,* 265–308.

Byrne, D. (1977). The imagery of sex. In Money, J. & Musaph, H. (Eds.), *Handbook of sexology* (pp. 328–350). New York: Excerpta Medica.

Byrne, D., & Schulte, L. (1990). Personality dispositions as mediators of sexual responses. *Annual Review of Sex Research, 1,* 93–117.

Byron, P. (1991). HIV: The national scandal. *Ms. The World of Women, 1*(4), 24–29.

C

Cado, S., & Leitenberg, H. (1990). Guilt reactions to sexual fantasies during intercourse. *Archives of Sexual Behavior, 19*(1), 49–63.

Calamidas, E. G. (1987). Effects of sex education on the sexual anxiety of medical students. *Journal of Sex Education and Therapy, 13*(1).

Calamidas, E. G. (1990). AIDS and STD education: What's really happening in our schools? *Journal of Sex Education and Therapy, 16*(1), 54–63.

Calderone, M. S. (1983). Fetal erection and its message to us. *SIECUS Report, 11*(5/6), 9–10.

Cantwell, H. B. (1983). Vaginal inspection as it relates to child sexual abuse in girls under thirteen. *Child Abuse and Neglect, 7,* 171–176.

Caprio, F. S. (1955). *Variations in sexual behavior.* New York: Grove.

Capuzzi, D. (1982). Sexuality and aging: An overview for counselors. *Personnel and Guidance Journal, 61*(1), 31–35.

Carani, C., Zini, D., Baldini, A., & Della Casa, L. (1990). Effects of androgen treatment in impotent men with normal and low levels of free testosterone. *Archives of Sexual Behavior, 19*(3), 223–234.

Carnes, P. (1983). *Out of the shadows.* Comp Care Publications: Minneapolis.

Carnes, P. (1990). Sex addiction treatment outcome results released. *Contemporary Sexuality, 24*(8), 4.

Carnes, P. (1991). Progress in sex addiction: An addiction perspective. In Francoeur, R. T. (Ed.), *Taking sides: Clashing views on controversial issues in human sexuality* (pp. 18-23). Guilford, CT: The Dushkin Publishing Group.

Carr, M., & Robinson, G. E. (1990). Fatal attraction: The ethical and clinical dilemma of patient-therapist sex. *Canadian Journal of Psychiatry, 35*(2), 122-127.

Carroll, J. L., & Bagley, D. H. (1990). Evaluation of sexual satisfactions in partners of men experiencing erectile failure. *Journal of Sex and Marital Therapy, 16*(2), 70-78.

Carson, D. K., et al. (1990). Family-of-origin characteristics and current family relationships of female adult incest victims. *Journal of Family Violence, 5*(2), 153-171.

Cass, V. C. (1983/1984). Homosexual identity: A concept in need of definition. *Journal of Homosexuality, 9,* 105-126.

Cass, V. C. (1990). The implications of homosexual identity formation for the Kinsey model and scale of sexual preference. In McWhirter, D. P., Sanders, S. A., & Reinisch, J. M. (Eds.), *Homosexuality/heterosexuality: Concepts of sexual orientation* (pp. 239-266). New York: Oxford University Press.

Cassell, C. (1985). *Swept away.* New York: Simon and Schuster.

Cassel, C. (1989). The final frontier: Other-gender friendship. *SIECUS Report, 18*(1), 18-20.

Catania, J. A., & White, C. B. (1982). Sexuality in an aged sample: Cognitive determinants of masturbation. *Archives of Sexual Behavior, 11*(3), 237-245.

Centers for Disease Control. (1988). Condoms for prevention of sexually transmitted diseases. *Journal of the American Medical Association, 259*(13), 1925-1927.

Cherfas, J. (1991). Sex and the single gene. *Science, 252,* 782.

Cherlin, A. J. (1981). *Marriage, divorce, remarriage.* Cambridge, MA: Harvard University.

Chilman, C. S. (1983). *Adolescent sexuality in a changing American society.* New York: John Wiley.

Chilman, C. S. (1984). Sexual relations within and outside of marriage can be equally acceptable. In Feldman, H., & Parrot, A. (Eds.), *Human sexuality: Contemporary controversies* (pp. 140-158). Beverly Hills: Sage.

Clanton, G. (1977). The contemporary experience of adultery. In Libby, R. W., & Whitehurst, N. (Eds.), *Marriage and alternatives: Exploring intimate relationships* (pp. 112-130). Glenview, IL: Scott, Foresman.

Clark, K. (1985a). *NGU: Nongonococcal urethritis* (pamphlet). Santa Cruz, CA: Network.

Clark, K. (1986b). *Vaginitis* (pamphlet). Santa Cruz, CA: Network.

Clarke-Stewart, K. A., & Bailey, B. L. (1989). Adjusting to divorce: Why do men have it easier? *Journal of Divorce, 13,* 75-94.

Clement, U. (1990). Surveys of heterosexual behavior. *Annual Review of Sex Research, 1,* 45-74.

Cline, V. B. (1974). Another view: Pornography effects, the state of the art, and the pornography commission: A case study of scientists and social policy decision making. In Cline, V. B. (Ed.), *Where do you draw the line?* (pp. 203-256). Provo, UT: Brigham University.

Cochran, S. D., & Mays, V. M. (1990). Sex, lies, and HIV. *New England Journal of Medicine, 322*(11), 774-775.

Cochran, W. G., Mosteller, F., & Tukey, J. W. (1953). Statistical problems of the Kinsey report. *Journal of the American Statistical Association, 48,* 673-716.

Cohen, J. (1991). AIDS vaccine trials: Bumpy road ahead. *Science, 251,* 1312-1313.

Cohen, S. S. (1987). *The magic of touch.* New York: Harper and Row.

Coleman, E. (1983). Developmental stages of the coming out process. *Journal of Homosexuality, 7*(2/3), 31-43.

Coleman, E. M., Hoon, P.W., & Hoon, E. F. (1983). Arousability and sexual satisfaction in lesbian and heterosexual women. *Journal of Sex Research, 19,* 58-73.

Coleman, G. (1990). Toward a synthetic understanding of sexual orientation. In McWhirter, D. P., Sanders, S. A., & Reinisch, J. M. (Eds.), *Homosexuality/heterosexuality: Concepts of sexual orientation* (pp. 267-276). New York: Oxford University Press.

Collins, J. A., et al. (1983). Treatment-independent pregnancy among infertile couples. *New England Journal of Medicine, 309,* 1201-1206.

Commission on Obscenity and Pornography, 1970. *Report of the commission on obscenity and pornography.* New York: Bantam.

Committee on the College Student (1983). *Friends and lovers in the college years.* New York: Mental Health Materials Center.

Connell, E. B. (1987, May/June). The crisis in contraception. *Technology Review,* pp. 47-55.

Conte, J. R. (1985). Clinical dimensions of adult sexual abuse of children. *Behavioral Sciences and the Law, 3*(4), 341-354.

Conte, J. R., & Schuerman, J. R. (1987). Factors associated with an increased impact of child sexual abuse. *Child Abuse and Neglect, 11*(2), 201-211.

Contraceptive Technology Update (1988). Advise patients to be wary of lotions when seeking condom lubricants. *Contraceptive Technology Update, 9*(3), 30-31.

Cook, E. P. (1990). Gender and psychological distress. *Journal of Counseling and Development, 68*(4), 371-375.

Cookerly, J. R., & McClaren, K. (1982). Sex therapy with and without love: An empirical investigation. *Journal of Sex Education and Therapy, 8*(2), 35-38.

Cooper, A. (1990). Dialing for sex. *Contemporary Sexuality, 24*(8), 1-2.

Corea, G. (1985). *The mother machine: Reproductive technologies from artificial insemination to artificial wombs.* New York: Harper and Row.

Cox, D. J. (1988). Incidence and nature of male genital exposure behaviors as reported by college women. *Journal of Sex Research, 24*(1), 227-234.

Craig, M. E., Kalichman, S. C., & Follingstad, D. R. (1989). Verbal coercive sexual behavior among college students. *Archives of Sexual Behavior, 18*(5), 421-434.

Crawford, I. (1990). Attitudes of undergraduate college students toward AIDS. *Psychological Reports, 66*(1), 11-16.

Crosby, J. F. (1985). *Illusion and disillusion: The self in love and marriage.* Belmont, CA: Wadsworth.

Cross, R. J. (1989). What doctors and others need to know about human sexuality and aging. *SIECUS Report, 17*(3), 14-15.

Cross, R. J. (1991). Helping adolescents learn about sexuality. *SIECUS Report, 19*(4), 6-11.

Croughan, J. L., Saghir, M., Cohen, R., & Robins, E. (1981). A comparison of treated and untreated male cross-dressers. *Archives of Sexual Behavior, 10*(6), 515–528.

Crum, C., & Ellner, P. (1985). Chlamydia infections: Making the diagnosis. *Contemporary Obstetrics and Gynecology, 25*, 153–168.

Culotta, E. (1991). Forecasting the global AIDS epidemic. *Science, 253*, 852–854.

Cupach, W. R., & Comstock, J. (1990). Satisfaction with sexual communication in marriage: Links to sexual satisfaction and dyadic adjustment. *Journal of Social and Personal Relationships, 7*(2), 179–186.

Curran, J. W., et al. (1985). The epidemiology of AIDS: Current status and future prospects. *Science, 229*, 1350–1357.

D

D'Augelli, A. R. (1991). Gay men in college: Identity processes and adaptations. *Journal of College Student Personnel, 32*, 140–146.

D'Augelli, A. R., & Rose, M. L. (1990). Homophobia in a university community: Attitudes and experiences of heterosexual freshmen. *Journal of College Student Development, 31*, 484–491.

Daher, D., Greaves, C., & Supton, A. (1987). Sexuality in the college years. *Journal of College Student Psychotherapy, 2*(1–2), 115–126.

Dahlberg, J., & James, J. M. (1991). Salvaging one's sexuality. In Leyson, J. F. (Ed.), *Sexual rehabilitation of the spinal-cord-injured patient* (pp. 343–350). Clifton, NJ: Humana Press.

Dalton, K. (1979). *Once a month.* Ramona, CA: Hunter House.

Dank, B. (1971). Coming out in the gay world. *Psychiatry, 34*(5), 180–197.

Darling, C. A., & Davidson, J. K. (1987). Guilt: A factor in sexual satisfaction. *Sociological Inquiry, 57*(3), 251–271.

Darling, C. A., Davidson, J. K., & Conway-Welch, C. (1990). Female ejaculation: Perceived origins, the Grafenberg spot/area, and sexual responsiveness. *Archives of Sexual Behavior, 19*(1), 29–47.

Darling, C. A., & Mabe, A. R. (1989). Analyzing ethical issues in sexual relationships: An educative model. *Journal of Sex Education and Therapy, 15*(4).

Davies, D. R. (1990). The effects of gender-typed labels on children's performance. *Current Psychology: Research and Reviews, 8*(4), 267–272.

Davis, D. (1991). Arts and contradiction: Helms, censorship, and the serpent. In Francoeur, R. T. (Ed.), *Taking sides: Clashing views on controversial issues in human sexuality* (pp. 209–216). Guilford, CT: The Dushkin Publishing Group.

Davis, J. A., & Smith, T. (1984). *General social surveys, 1972–1984: Cumulative data.* New Haven: Yale University/Roper Center.

Davis, L. (1987, November). Vive monogamy. *Forum.*

Davis, M., & Scott, R. S. (1988). *Lovers, and doctors and the law: Your rights and responsibilities in today's sex-health crisis.* New York: Harper and Row.

DeAngelis, B. (1987). *How to make love all the time.* New York: Rawson Associates.

DeBuono, B. A., et al. (1990). Sexual behavior of college women in 1975, 1986, and 1989. *New England Journal of Medicine, 322*(12), 821–825.

DeCecco, J. P. (1990). Sex and more sex: A critique of the Kinsey conception of human sexuality. In McWhirter, D. P., Sanders, S. A., & Reinisch, J. M. (Eds.), *Homosexuality/heterosexuality: Concepts of sexual orientation* (pp. 367–386). New York: Oxford University Press.

DeCock, K. M., Barrere, B., Diaby, L., LaFontaine, M. F., Gnaore, E., Porter, A., Pantobe, D., LaFontaine, G. C., Dago-Akribi, A., Ette, M., Odehouri, K., & Hayward, W. L. (1990). AIDS-the leading cause of adult death in the west African city of Abidjan, Ivory Coast. *Science, 249*, 793–796.

Deedy, J. (1977, February 6). The clergy's revolution in sexual mores. *New York Times,* p. 16E.

de Leon, D., & Lebow, A. (1991, June 3). AIDS and rape suspects: A smart test? *New York Times,* C1.

deMauro, D. (1990). Sexuality education 1990. *SIECUS Report, 18*(2), 1–9.

deMauro, D., & Haffner, D. (1988). *Sexuality education and schools: Issues and answers* (pamphlet). New York: Sex Information and Education Council of the U.S.

Denfield, D. (1973). Sex tabloids. *Sexual Behavior, 3*(3), 18–23.

DePalma, A. (1991, June 26). No conclusion on ways dentist passed on AIDS. *New York Times,* A14.

Des Jarlais, D. C., Friedman, S. R., Goldsmith, D., & Hopkins, W. (1990). Heterosexual transmission of human immunodeficiency virus from intravenous drug users: Regular partnerships and prostitution. In Voeller, B., Reinisch, J. M., & Gottlieb, M. (Eds.), *AIDS and sex* (pp. 245–256). New York: Oxford University Press.

Detels, R., Visscher, B. R., Jacobson, L. P., Kingsley, L. A., Chmiel, J. S., Eldred, L. J., English, P., & Ginzburg, H. (1990). Sexual activity, condom use, and HIV-1 seroconversion. In Voeller, B., Reinisch, J. M., & Gottlieb, M. (Eds.), *AIDS and sex* (pp. 13–19). New York: Oxford University Press.

Devi, K. (1977). *The Eastern way of love: Tantric sex and erotic mysticism.* New York: Simon and Schuster.

DeVoe, D. (1990). Feminist and nonsexist counseling: Implications for the male counselor. *Journal of Counseling and Development, 69*(1), 33–36.

Dickinson, R. L. (1932). *A thousand marriages.* Baltimore: Williams and Wilkins.

Dickinson, R. L. (1949). *Atlas of human sex anatomy.* (2nd ed.). Baltimore: Williams and Wilkins.

Diokno, A. C., & Hollander, J. B. (1991). Diagnosis of erectile dysfunction. In Leyson, J. F. (Ed.), *Sexual rehabilitation of the spinal-cord-injured patient* (pp. 207–219). Clifton, NJ: Humana Press.

Djerassi, C. (1990). Fertility awareness: Jet-age rhythm method? *Science, 248*, 1061–1062.

Doddridge, R., Schumm, W., & Berger, M. (1987). Factors related to decline in preferred frequency of sexual intercourse among young couples. *Psychological Reports, 60*, 391–395.

Doering, C., et al. (1978) Plasma testosterone levels and psychologic measures in men over a two-month period. In Friedman, R. (Ed.), *Sex differences in behavior.* Huntington, NY: Krieger.

Donnerstein, E., & Linz, D. (1984). Sexual violence in the media: A warning. *Psychology Today,* (1), 14–15.

Donnis, S. (1984). Common themes of infertility: A counseling model. *Journal of Sex Education and Therapy, 10*(1), 11–15.

Dorsen, N. (1990). Alabama anti-sexuality forces destroy New York video company. *Contemporary Sexuality, 22*(6), 3.

Douglas, J. D., & Atwell, F. C. (1988). *Love, intimacy, and sex*. Newburg Park, CA: Sage Publications.

Driggs, J. H., & Finn, S. (1990). *Intimacy between men: How to find and keep gay love relationships*. New York: Penguin Books.

Duncan, D. F. (1990a). "Misrepresentation of pornography research: Psychology's role": Comment. *American Psychologist, 45*(6), 778.

Duncan, D. F. (1990b). Pornography as a source of sex information for university students. *Psychological Reports, 66*(2), 442.

Dyk, P. H., & Adams, G. R. (1990). Identity and intimacy: An initial investigation of three theoretical models using cross-lag panel correlations. *Journal of Youth and Adolescence, 19*(2), 91–110.

E

Earle, R. H., & Crow, G. M. (1990). Sexual addiction: Understanding and treating the phenomenon. *Contemporary Family Therapy, 12*(2), 89–104.

Edelman, D. A., McIntyre, S., & Harper, J. (1984). A comparative trial of the Today contraceptive sponge and diaphragm. *American Journal of Obstetrics and Gynecology, 151*, 552–556.

Ehrhardt, A. A. (1977). Prenatal androgenization and human psychosexual behavior. In Money, J. & Musaph, H. (Eds.), *Handbook of sexology* (pp. 246–257). New York: Excerpta Medica.

Ehrhardt, A. A. (1987). A transactional perspective on the development of gender differences. In Reinisch, J., Rosenblum, L. A., & Sanders, S. A. (Eds.), *Masculinity/femininity: Basic perspectives* (pp. 281–285). New York: Oxford University.

Ehrhardt, A. A., & Money, J. (1967). Progestin-induced hermaphroditism: IQ and psychosexual identity in a study of ten girls. *Journal of Sex Research, 3*, 83–100.

Eichel, E. W., Eichel, J. D., & Kule, S. (1988). The techniques of coital alignment and its relation to female orgasmic response and simultaneous orgasm. *Journal of Sex Education and Marital Therapy, 64*(2), 129–141.

Eitner, L. (1975). The erotic in art. In Katchadourian, H. A., & Lunde, D. T. (Eds.), *Fundamentals of human sexuality* (pp. 389–423). New York: Holt, Rinehart, and Winston.

Elliott, D. J., & Tarnowski, K. J. (1990). Depressive characteristics of sexually abused children. *Child Psychiatry and Human Development, 21*(1), 37–48.

Ellis, A. (1990). Commentary on the status of sex research: An assessment of the sexual revolution. *Journal of Psychology and Human Sexuality, 3*(1), 5–18.

Ellis, H. H. (1936). Studies in the psychology of sex (complete in two volumes). New York: Modern Library.

Ellis, L., Burke, D., & Ames, M. A. (1987). Sexual orientation as a continuous variable: A comparison between the sexes. *Archives of Sexual Behavior, 16*(6), 523–529.

Elshtain, J. B. (1991). What's the matter with sex today? In Francoeur, R. T. (Ed.), *Taking sides: Clashing views on controversial issues in human sexuality* (pp. 182–184). Guilford, CT: The Dushkin Publishing Group.

Enns, C. Z. (1991). The "new" relationship models of women's identity: A review and critique for counselors. *Journal of Counseling and Development, 69*, 209–217.

Erikson, E. (1968). *Identity: Youth and crisis*. New York: W. W. Norton.

F

Family Sexual Abuse Project. Female sex offenders. (1987). *Innovation and Inquiry in Family Sexual Abuse Intervention 1*(1), 1–6.

Fasteau, M. F. (1974). *The male machine*. New York: McGraw-Hill.

Fausto-Sterling, A. (1985). *Myths of gender: Biological theories about women and men*. New York: Basic Books.

Fay, R. E., Turner, C. F., Klassen, A. D., & Gagnon, J. H. (1989). Prevalence and patterns of same-gender sexual contact among men. *Science, 243*, 338–348.

Feder, H. H. (1984). Hormones and sexual behavior. *Annual Review of Psychology, 35*, 165–200.

Feldman, S. (1978). *Choices in childbirth*. New York: Grosset and Dunlap.

Ferre Institute. (1988, November 5, 8). In vitro fertilization: Calculating the odds. *Ferre Fax*.

Finkelhor, D. (1990). Early and long-term effects of child sexual abuse: An update. *Professional Psychology: Research and Practice, 21*(5), 325–330.

Finkelhor, D., & Browne, A. (1985). The traumatic impact of child sexual abuse. *American Journal of Orthopsychiatry, 55*, 530–541.

Finkelhor, D., Hotaling, G., Lewis, I. A., & Smith, C. (1990). Sexual abuse in a national survey of adult men and women: Prevalence, characteristics, and risk factors. *Child Abuse and Neglect, 14*(1), 19–28.

Fischer, G. J. (1989). Sex words used by partners in a relationship. *Journal of Sex Education and Therapy, 15*(1), 50–58.

Fisher, B. (1983). *Rebuilding: When your relationship ends*. San Luis Obispo, CA: Impact Publishers.

Fisher, W. A. (1984). Predicting contraceptive behavior among university men: The role of emotions and behavioral intentions. *Journal of Applied Social Psychology, 14*, 104–123.

Fisher, W. A. (1990). All together now. *SIECUS Report, 18*(4), 1–11.

Fisher, W. A., Byrne, D., White, L. A., & Kelley, K. (1988). Erotophobia-erotophilia as a dimension of personality. *Journal of Sex Research, 25*(1), 123–151.

Fitzgerald, F. (1984). The classic venereal diseases: Syphilis and gonorrhea in the '80s. *Postgraduate Medicine, 75*, 91–101.

Fiumara, N. J. (1975). Semen ingestion. In Lief, H. I. (Ed.), *Medical aspects of human sexuality* (pp. 195–196). Baltimore: Williams and Wilkins.

Flax, E. (1990). Special problems of homosexual students need special attention, advocates urge. *Education Week, 9*(20), 1, 10.

Flax, E. (1990, March 14). Sex education plan urging chastity sparks controversy in South Carolina. *Education Week, 9*(25), 1.

Flax, E. (1991). Condom plan for N.Y.C.'s schools prompts debate among educators, health experts. *Education Week, 10*(25), 1, 30.

512

Fletcher, J., & Wassmer, T. (1970). *Hello, lovers: An invitation to situation ethics.* Washington: Corpus Books, World.

Ford, C. S., & Beach, F. A. (1951). *Patterns of sexual behavior.* New York: Harper.

Forrest, J. D. (1990). Cultural influences on adolescents' reproductive behavior. In Bancroft, J., & Reinisch, J. M. (Eds.), *Adolescence and puberty* (pp. 234–253). New York: Oxford University Press.

Fortney, J. (1989). As quoted in Human Sexuality Update, *Journal of Sex Education and Therapy, 15*(2), 134–135.

Foster, A. L. (1979). Relationships between age and sexual activity in marriage. *Journal of Sex Education and Therapy, 5*(1), 21–26.

Francis, D., Hadler, S. C., Prendergast, T. J., Peterson, E., Ginsberg, M. M., Lookabaugh, C., Holmes, J. R., & Maynard, J. E. (1984). Occurrences of hepatitis A, B, and non-A, non-B in the United States: CDC sentinel county hepatitis study. *The American Journal of Medicine, 76,* 69–74.

Francoeur, R. T. (1982). *Becoming a sexual person.* New York: Wiley.

Francoeur, R. T. (1985). Reproductive technologies: New alternatives and new ethics. *SIECUS Report, 14*(1), 1–5.

Francoeur, R. T. (1990). Sexual archetypes in Eastern cultures can be helpful in creating sex-positive views. *Contemporary Sexuality, 22*(2), 6.

Francoeur, R. T. (1991a). Historical and sociocultural perspectives in human sexuality. In Leyson, J. F. (Ed.), *Sexual rehabilitation of the spinal-cord-injured patient* (pp. 1–9). Clifton, NJ: Humana Press.

Francoeur, R. T. (1991b). Sexual attitudes in perspective. In Francoeur, R. T. (Ed.), *Taking sides: Clashing views on controversial issues in human sexuality* (pp. xii–xxi). Guilford, CT: The Dushkin Publishing Group.

Frayser, S. G. (1985). *Varieties of sexual experience: An anthropological perspective on human sexuality.* New Haven, CT: HRAF.

Frazier, P. A. (1990). Victim attributions and post-rape trauma. *Journal of Personality and Social Psychology, 59*(2), 298–304.

Freeman, E. (1990, July 18). Ineffectiveness of progesterone suppositories for premenstrual syndrome. *Journal of American Medical Association, 349.*

Freund, K., Steiner, B. W., & Chan, S. (1982). Two types of cross-gender identity. *Archives of Sexual Behavior, 11*(1), 49–63.

Friedman, J. (1989). The impact of homophobia on male sexual development. *SIECUS Report, 17*(5), 8–9.

Friedman, S. R. (1990). What is child sexual abuse? *Journal of Clinical Psychology, 46*(3), 372–375.

Friedmann, T. (1989). Progress toward human gene therapy. *Science, 244,* 1275–1281.

Frieze, I. H. (1983). Investigating the causes and consequences of marital rape. *Signs, 8*(3), 532–553.

Fromm, E. (1970). *The art of loving.* New York: Bantam.

Fuller, A. K., Fuller, A. E., & Blashfield, R. K. (1990). Paraphilic coercive disorder. *Journal of Sex Education and Therapy, 16*(3), 164–171.

G

Gagnon, J. H. (1990a). The explicit and implicit use of the scripting perspective in sex research. *Annual Review of Sex Research, 1,* 1–43.

Gagnon, J. H. (1990b.) Gender preference in erotic relations: The Kinsey scale and sexual scripts. In McWhirter, D. P., Sanders, S. A., & Reinisch, J. M. (Eds.), *Homosexuality/heterosexuality: Concepts of sexual orientation* (pp. 177–207). New York: Oxford University Press.

Gagnon, J. H., & Simon, W. (1973). *Sexual conduct.* Chicago: Aldine.

Gagnon, J. H., Simon, W., & Berger, A. J. (1970). Some aspects of sexual adjustment in early and late adolescence. In Zubin, J., & Freedman, A. N., *Psychopathology of adolescence* (p. 278). New York: Grune and Stratton.

Gale, J., Thompson, R. J., Moran, T., & Sach, W. H. (1988). Sexual abuse in young children: Its clinical presentation and characteristic patterns. *Child Abuse and Neglect, 12,* 163–170.

Gallup Survey. (1990). Gallup survey points to frequent contraceptive switching. *SIECUS Report, 18*(4), 25.

Garcia, L. T. (1982). Sex role orientation and stereotypes about male-female sexuality. *Sex Roles, 8,* 863–876.

Gardella, P. (1987). Christianity has given us a positive ethic of gender equality and sexual pleasure. In Francoeur, R. T. (Ed.), *Taking sides: Clashing views on controversial issues in human sexuality* (pp. 284–292). Guilford, CT: Dushkin.

Garner, M. (1987, June). Miracle babies: The next generation. *Self,* pp. 129–133.

Gebhard, P. H. (1971). Human sexual behavior: A summary statement. In Marshall, D. S. & Suggs, R. C. (Eds.), *Human sexual behavior* (pp. 206–217). New York: Basic.

Gebhard, P. H. (1976). Fetishism and sadomasochism. In Weinberg, M. S. (Ed.), *Sex research: Studies from the Kinsey Institute* (pp. 206–217). New York: Basic.

Gebhard, P. H. (1977). Memorandum on the incidence of homosexuals in the United States. Personal communication with National Gay Task Force.

Gebhard, P. H., Gagnon, J. H., Pomeroy, W. B., & Christenson, C. V. (1965). *Sex offenders: An analysis of types.* New York: Harper-Hoeber.

Gebhard, P. H., & Johnson, A. B. (1979). *The Kinsey data: Marginal tabulations of the 1938–1963 interviews conducted at the Institute for Sex Research.* Philadelphia: Saunders.

Geer, J. H., & McGlone, M. S. (1990). Sex differences in memory for erotica. *Cognition and Emotion, 4*(1), 71–78.

Geller, T. (1990). *Bisexuality: A reader and sourcebook.* Ojai, CA: Times Change Press.

Gelman D., et al. (1987, October 26). Not tonight, dear. *Newsweek,* pp. 64–66.

Gerdt, G. H. (1981). *Guardians of the flute.* New York: McGraw-Hill.

German, D. E., Habenicht, D. J. & Futcher, W. G. (1990). Psychological profile of the female adolescent incest victim. *Child Abuse and Neglect, 14*(3), 429–438.

Gerrard, M. (1987). Emotional and cognitive barriers to effective contraception: Are males and females really different? In Kelley, K. (Ed.), *Females, males, and sexuality: Theories and research* (pp. 213–242). Albany: State University of New York.

Gerrard, M. (1987). Sex, sex guilt, and contraceptive use. *Journal of Personality and Social Psychology, 42,* 153–158.

Gibbs, N. (1991, June 3). When is it rape? *Time,* 48–55.

513

Gilbert, B., & Cunningham, J. (1986). Women's postrape sexual functioning: Review and implications for counseling. *Journal of Counseling and Development, 65*(2), 69–71.

Gilder, G. (1987, July). Sexual suicide. *Harper's.*

Gilgun, J. (1988). Research results reported at national conference of the Society for the Scientific Study of Sex, discussed in: Sexually abused children believe it's their fault. *Sexuality Today, 7*(14), 1–3.

Gillespie, M. A. (1991). Women and AIDS. *Ms. The World of Women, 1*(4), 16–22.

Gilligan, C. (1982). *In a different voice: Psychological theory of women's development.* Cambridge, MA: Harvard University Press.

Gladue, B. A., Green, R., & Hellman, R. E. (1984). Neuroendocrine response to estrogen and sexual orientation. *Science, 225* 1496–1498.

Glenn, N. D., & Weaver, C. N. (1988). The changing relationship of marital status to reported happiness. *Journal of Marriage and the Family, 50,* 317–334.

Goettsch, S. L. (1987). Textbook sexual inadequacy? A review of sexuality texts. *Teaching Sociology, 15,* 324–338.

Gold, S. R., & Chick, D. A. (1988). Sexual fantasy patterns as related to sexual attitudes, experiences, guilt and sex. *Journal of Sex Education and Therapy, 14*(2), 18–23.

Golden, G. H. (1983). Psychosexual problems in infertility: A preventive model. *Journal of Sex Education and Therapy, 9*(1), 19–22.

Goldman, R., & Goldman, J. (1982). *Children's sexual thinking.* Boston: Routledge and Kegan Paul.

Goldsmith, M. (1983). Modifications in prostate cancer operation preserve potency. *Journal of American Medical Association, 250,* 2897–2899.

Goldstein, M. J., & Kant, H. S. (1973). *Pornography and sexual deviance.* Berkeley: University of California.

Goleman, D. (1988, October 18). Chemistry of sexual desire yields its elusive secrets. *New York Times,* C1, 15.

Goleman, D. (1989, February 21). Want a happy marriage? Learn to fight a good fight. *New York Times,* pp. C1, C6.

Good, G. E., Gilbert, L. A., & Scher, M. (1990). Gender aware therapy: A synthesis of feminist therapy and knowledge about gender. *Journal of Counseling and Development, 68*(4), 376–380.

Gooren, L. (1990). Biomedical theories of sexual orientation: A critical examination. In McWhirter, D. P., Sanders, S. A., & Reinisch, J. M. (Eds.), *Homosexuality/heterosexuality: Concepts of sexual orientation* (pp. 71–87). New York: Oxford University Press.

Gooren, L., Fliers, E., & Courtney, K. (1990). Biological determinants of sexual orientation. *Annual Review of Sex Research, 1,* 175–196.

Gordon, S., & Gilgun, J. F. (1987). Adolescent sexuality. In VanHasselt, V. B., & Hersen, M. (Eds.), *Handbook of Adolescent Psychology.* New York: Pergamon Press.

Gottman, J., & Krokoff, L. (1989). Marital interaction and satisfaction: A longitudinal view. *Journal of Consulting and Clinical Psychology, 57*(1), 47–52.

Goulston, M. S. (1988, January 25). Sexual confusion passes from father to daughter. *Sexuality Today,* pp. 4–6.

Gove, W., & Shin, H. (1989). The psychological well-being of divorced and widowed men and women. *Journal of Family Issues, 10,* 122–144.

Gräfenberg, E. (1950). The role of the urethra. *International Journal of Sexology, 3,* 145–148.

Gramick, J. (1991). Homosexuality and bisexuality are as natural and normal as heterosexuality. In Francoeur, R. T. (Ed.), *Taking sides: Clashing views on controversial issues in human sexuality* (pp. 36–44). Guilford, CT: The Dushkin Publishing Group.

Gray, M. D., Lesser, D., Quinn, E., & Bounds, C. (1990). The effectiveness of personalizing acquaintance rape prevention: *Journal of College Student Development, 31*(3), 217–220.

Gray, S. H. (1982). Exposure to pornography and aggression toward women: The case of the angry male. *Social Problems, 29*(4), 387–398.

Greeley, A. M., Michael, R. T., & Smith, T. W. (1990). *A most monogamous people: Americans and their sexual partners.* Chicago, IL: NORC.

Green, R. (1985, September 12). Exposure to explicit sexual materials and sexual assault: A review of behavioral and social science research. Paper presented at hearing of the Attorney General's Commission on Pornography, Houston.

Green, R. (1987). *The sissy boy syndrome.* New Haven: Yale University Press.

Green, R., & Fleming, D. T. (1990). Transsexual surgery follow-up: Status in the 1990s. *Annual Review of Sex Research, 1,* 163–174.

Green, S. E., & Mosher, D. L. (1985). A causal model of sexual arousal to erotic fantasies. *Journal of Sex Research, 21,* 1–23.

Greenspan, A., & Castro, K. G. (1990). Heterosexual transmission of HIV infection. *SIECUS Report, 19*(1), 1–8.

Greenwald, M. (1990). Help from the sexperts. *CompuServe Magazine, 9*(12), 40.

Greenwood, S., & Margolis, A. J. (1981). Outercourse. *Advances in Planned Parenthood, 15,* 4.

Greenwood, S. (1988). *Menopause, naturally: Preparing for the second half of life.* San Francisco: Volcano Press.

Greer, D., et al. (1982). A technique for foreskin reconstruction and some preliminary results. *Journal of Sex Research, 18,* 324–330.

Griffitt, W. (1987). Females, males, and sexual responses. In Kelley, K. (Ed.), *Females, males, and sexuality: Theories and research* (pp. 141–173). Albany: State University of New York.

Griggs, J. (Ed.). (1987). *AIDS: Public Policy dimensions.* New York: United Hospital Fund.

Guttentag, M., & Secord, P. (1989). As quoted in Traditional sex roles: Re-emerging? *Journal of Sex Education and Therapy, 15*(1), 60.

H

Hacker, S. (1990). The transition from the old norm to the new: Sexual values for the 1990s. *SIECUS Report, 18*(5), 1–8.

Haffner, D. W. (1989). Human sexuality education: Whose job is it anyway? *SIECUS Report, 17*(3), 11–12.

Haffner, D. W. (1990). Moving toward a healthy paradigm of teen development. *SIECUS Report, 18*(4), 12–14.

Haffner, D. W. (1991). Help SIECUS protect sexual rights. *SIECUS Report, 19*(3), 10–12.

Hall, E. (1986, June). New directions for the Kinsey Institute. *Psychology Today*, pp. 33–39.

Hall, J. E. (1975). Sexuality and the mentally retarded. In Green, R. (Ed.), *Human sexuality: A health practitioner's text* (pp. 181–195). Baltimore: Williams and Wilkins.

Hallstrom, T., & Samuelsson, S. (1990). Changes in women's sexual desire in middle life: The longitudinal study of women in Gothenburg. *Archives of Sexual Behavior, 19*(3), 259–268.

Hammond, D. C. (1991). The advantages of hypnosis in sex therapy. *Contemporary Sexuality, 25*(4), 4.

Hanson, E. I., & Brouse, S. H. (1983). Assessing sexual implication of functional impairments associated with chronic illness. *Journal of Sex Education and Therapy, 9*(2), 39–45.

Harlow, H. F., McGaugh, J. L., & Thompson, R. F. (1971). *Psychology*. San Francisco: Albion.

Harris, T. L., & Schwab, R. (1990). Sex role orientation and personal adjustment. *Journal of Social Behavior and Personality, 5*(4), 473–479.

Harrison, M. (1982). Self-help for premenstrual syndrome. Cambridge, MA; Matrix Press.

Harrison, P. J., Downes, J., & Williams, M. D. (1991). Date and acquaintance rape: Perceptions and attitude change strategies. *Journal of College Student Development, 32*, 131–139.

Harrop-Griffiths, J., Katon, W., Walker, E., Holm, L., Russo J., & Hickok, L. (1988). The association between chronic pelvic pain, psychiatric diagnoses, and childhood sexual abuse. *Obstetrics and Gynecology, 71*, 589–594.

Hartman, W., & Fithian, M. (1984). *Any man can*. New York: St. Martin's.

Haseltine, F., & Ohno, S. (1981). Mechanisms of gonadal differentiation. *Science, 211*(4488), 1271–1278.

Haseltine, W. A., & Wong-Staal, F. (1988). The molecular biology of the AIDS virus. *Scientific American, 259*(4), 52–62.

Hass, A. (1979). *Teenage sexuality*. New York: Macmillan.

Hasselbring, B. (1983, Summer). Every woman's guide to vaginal infections. *Medical self-care*, pp. 45–49.

Hatcher, R. A., et al. (1990). *Contraceptive technology 1990–1992* (15th ed.). New York: Irvington.

Hauck, P. A. (1982). *Overcoming jealousy and possessiveness*. Philadelphia: Westminster Press.

Hawkins, R. O. (1990). The relationship between culture, personality, and sexual jealousy in men in heterosexual and homosexual relationships. *Journal of Homosexuality, 19*(3), 67–84.

Hawton, K., & Catalan, J. (1990). Sex therapy for vaginismus: Characteristics of couples and treatment outcome. *Sexual and Marital Therapy, 5*(1), 39–48.

Hedbloom, J. H. (1972). Social, sexual, and occupational lives of homosexual women. *Sexual Behavior, 2*(10), 33–37.

Heiman, J. R. (1977). A psychophysiological exploration of sexual arousal patterns in females and males. *Psychophysiology, 14*(13), 266–274.

Helson, R., & Picano, J. (1990). Is the traditional role bad for women? *Journal of Personality and Social Psychology, 59*(2), 311–320.

Henahan, J. (1984). Honing the treatment of early breast cancer. *Journal of the American Medical Association, 23*, 309–310.

Henderson, B. E., Paganini-Hill, A., & Ross, R. K. (1991). Decreased mortality in users of estrogen replacement therapy. *Archives of Internal Medicine, 151*(1), 75–78.

Hendrix, H. (1988). *Getting the love you want*. New York: Henry Holt and Co.

Hendrixson, L. L. (1989). Care vs. justice: Two moral perspectives in the Baby "M" surrogacy case. *Journal of Sex Education and Therapy, 15*(4), 247–256.

Henker, F. O. (1977). A male climacteric syndrome: Sexual, psychic, and physical complaints in 50 middle-aged men. *Psychosomatics, 18*(5), 23–27.

Henshaw, S. (1990). Major decline in availability of abortion. *Contemporary Sexuality, 24*(8), 6.

Herdt, G. (1990). Developmental discontinuities and sexual orientation across cultures. In McWhirter, D. P., Sanders, S. A., & Reinisch, J. M. (Eds.), *Homosexuality/heterosexuality: Concepts of sexual orientation* (pp. 208–236). New York: Oxford University Press.

Herdt, G. H., & Davidson, J. (1988). The Sambia "Turnim Man": Sociocultural and clinical aspects of gender formation in male pseudohermaphrodites with 5-alpha reductase-deficiency in Papua New Guinea. *Archives of Sexual Behavior, 17*, 33–56.

Herek, G. M. (1990). The context of anti-gay violence: Notes on cultural and psychological heterosexism. *Journal of Interpersonal Violence, 5*(3), 316–333.

Hetherington, S. E. (1988). Common postpartum sexual problems: A management guide. *The Female Patient, 13*(4), 43–53.

Hevener, F. (1990). College students' attitudes toward censorship of sexual explicitness. *College Student Journal, 24*(2), 167–172.

Higham, E. (1980). Sexuality in the infant and neonate: Birth to two years. In Wolman, B., & Money, J. (Eds.), *Handbook of human sexuality* (pp. 15–27). Englewood Cliffs, NJ: Prentice-Hall.

Hildebrand, M., & Abramowitz, S. (1984). Sexuality on campus: Changes in attitudes and behaviors during the 1970s. *Journal of College Student Personnel, 25*, 534–538.

Hillard, P. A. (1988). Dysplasia seen in 15% of Pap smears taken from a group of teens. *Obstetrics and Gynecology News, 23*(12), 1.

Hilts, P. J. (1991, August 29). Study shows passing AIDS in breast milk easier than thought. *New York Times*.

Hindman, J. (1988 July/August). Research disputes assumptions about child molesters. *National District Attorneys Association Bulletin*.

Hingson, R., et al. (1982). Effects of maternal drinking and marijuana use on fetal growth and development. *Pediatrics, 70*, 539–546.

Hite, S. (1977). *The Hite report*. New York: Dell.

Hite, S. (1981). *The Hite report on male sexuality*. New York: Knopf.

Hite, S. (1987). *Women and love*. New York: Knopf.

Hobbins, J. C. (1988). Selective reduction—A perinatal necessity? *New England Journal of Medicine, 318*(16), 1062.

Hoch, Z. (1983). Confusion over the G spot. *Journal of Sex Education and Therapy, 9*(1), 8.

Hoenig, J. (1977). Dramatis personae: Selected biographical sketches of 19th century pioneers in sexology. In Money, J., & Musaph, H. (Eds.), *Handbook of sexology* (pp. 21–43). New York: Excerpta Medica.

Hofferth, S. L. (1990). Trends in adolescent sexual activity, contraception, and pregnancy in the United States. In Bancroft, J., & Reinisch, J. M. (Eds.), *Adolescence and*

Puberty (pp. 217–233). New York: Oxford University Press.

Hoffman, F. P. (1991). Feedback on sexually explicit movies. *Contemporary Sexuality, 25*(3), 7.

Hoffman, M. (1968). *The gay world.* New York: Basic.

Holden, C. (1989). Koop finds abortion evidence "inconclusive." *Science, 243,* 730–731.

Holmes, K. K. (1981). The chlamydia epidemic. *Journal of the American Medical Association, 245,* 1718–23.

Holzman, H. R., & Pines, S. (1982). Buying sex: The phenomenology of being a john. *Deviant Behavior, 4*(1), 89–116.

Hooker, E. (1965). Male homosexuals and their "worlds." In Marmor, J. (Ed.), *Sexual inversion.* New York: Basic.

Hooker, E. (1967). The homosexual community. In Gagnon, J. H., & Simon, W. (Eds.), *Sexual deviance.* New York: Harper and Row.

Hooker, E., & Chance, P. (1975). Facts that liberated the gay community. *Psychology Today, 9*(7), 52–55.

Hopkins, J. (1969). Lesbian personality. *British Journal of Psychiatry, 115,* 1433–1436.

Hopwood, N. J., Kelch, R. P., Hale, P. M., Mendes, T. M., Foster, C. M., & Beitins, I. Z. (1990). The onset of human puberty: Biological and environmental factors. In Bancroft, J. & Reinisch, J. M. (Eds.), *Adolescence and puberty* (pp. 29–49). New York: Oxford University Press.

Horton, C. E., & Devine, C. J. (1975). Curvatures of the penis. *Medical Aspects of Human Sexuality, 9*(9), 167–168.

Hosansky, T. (1990, January/February). Your condom or mine? New *Age Journal,* p. 24.

Hotchner, B. (1991). Desire dysfunctions. In Leyson, J. F. (Ed.), *Sexual rehabilitation of the spinal-cord-injured patient* (pp. 115–130). Clifton, NJ: Humana Press.

Hotelling, K. (1988). Ethical, legal, and administrative options to address sexual relationships between counselor and client. *Journal of Counseling and Development, 67*(4), 233–237.

Hotelling, K. (1991). Sexual harassment: A problem shielded by silence. *Journal of Counseling and Development, 69,* 497–501.

Hotvedt, M. E. (1990). Emerging and submerging adolescent sexuality: Culture and sexual orientation. In Bancroft, J., & Reinisch, J. M. (Eds.), *Adolescence and puberty* (pp. 157–172). New York: Oxford University Press.

Howard, S. (1991). Organizational resources for addressing sexual harassment. *Journal of Counseling and Development, 69,* 507–511.

Hublitz, L. S. (1990). Dispute continues over so-called abortion pill, RU-486. *Contemporary Sexuality, 24*(8), 5.

Hughes, J. O'G., & Sandler, B. R. (1987). *"Friends" raping friends: Could it happen to you?* Washington: Project on the Status and Education of Women, Association of American Colleges.

Humphreys, L. (1970). *Tearoom trade: Impersonal sex in public places.* New York: Aldine.

Hunt, M. (1975). *Sexual behavior in the 1970s.* New York: Dell.

Hunter, M. (1990). *Abused boys: The neglected victims of child abuse.* Lexington, MA: Lexington Books.

Huntley, D. (1988). Sex partner's death causes longstanding grief. As reported in *Sexuality Today, 11*(16), 5–6.

Hutchinson, R. L., & Schechterman, A. L. (1990). Perceived impact of the women's movement: Views of midwestern university men and women. *Journal of College Student Development, 31*(1), 85–86.

Hyde, H. J. (1991). The culture war. In Francoeur, R. T. (Ed.), *Taking sides: Clashing views on controversial issues in human sexuality* (pp. 204–208). Guilford, CT: The Dushkin Publishing Group.

Hyde, J. S. (1985). *Half the human experience: The psychology of women.* Lexington, MA: D.C. Heath.

I

Imagawa, D. T. (1989, June 1). As quoted in AIDS antibodies evade detection. *New York Times,* p. C1.

Imperato-McGinley, J., Peterson, R. E., Gautier, T., Looper, G., Danner, R., Arthur, A., Morris, P. L., Sweeney, W. J., & Schackleton, C. (1982). Hormonal evaluation of a large kindred with complete androgen insensitivity: Evidence for secondary 5-alpha-reductase deficiency. *Journal of Clinical Endocrinology Metabolism, 54,* 15–22.

Institute of Medicine and National Academy of Sciences. (1986). *Mobilizing against AIDS: The unfinished story of a virus.* Cambridge, MA: Harvard University.

Irvine, J. M. (1990). From difference to sameness: Gender ideology in sexual science. *Journal of Sex Research, 27*(1), 7–24.

Isay, R. A. (1990). Psychoanalytic theory and the therapy of gay men. In McWhirter, D. P., Sanders, S. A., & Reinisch, J. M. (Eds.), *Homosexuality/heterosexuality: Concepts of sexual orientation* (pp. 283–303). New York: Oxford University Press.

J

Jackson, J. K. (1992). *Wellness: AIDS, STD, & other communicable diseases.* Guilford, CT: The Dushkin Publishing Group.

Jackson, J. L., Calhoun, K. S., Amick, A. E., & Maddever, H. M. (1990). Young adult women who report childhood intrafamilial sexual abuse: Subsequent adjustment. *Archives of Sexual Behavior, 19*(3), 211–221.

Jackson, T. L. (1991). A university athletic department's rape and assault experiences. *Journal of College Student Development, 32,* 77–78.

Jamison, P. L., & Gebhard, P. H. (1988). Penis size increase between flaccid and erect states: An analysis of the Kinsey data. *Journal of Sex Research, 24*(1), 177–183.

Jancin, B. (1988). Prenatal gender selection appears to be gaining acceptance. *Obstetrics and Gynecology News, 23*(5), 1, 30–31.

Jaroff, L. (1989, March 20). The gene hunt. *Time,* pp. 62–67.

Jarrow, J. P. (1987, December). Vasectomy update: Effects on health and sexuality. *Medical Aspects of Human Sexuality,* 64–67.

Jay, K., & Young, A. (1979). *The gay report.* New York: Summit.

Jenny, C., Huhns, M. L. D., & Arakawa, F. (1987). Hymens in newborn female infants. *Pediatrics, 80*(3), 399–400.

Jensen, L., Newell, R. J., & Holman, T. (1990). Sexual behavior, church attendance, and permissive beliefs among unmarried young men and women. *Journal for the Scientific Study of Religion, 29*(1), 113–117.

Joffe, A. (1988). As quoted in Human Sexuality Update. *Journal of Sex Education and Therapy, 14*(2), 7.

Johnson, B. (1990). Survey reveals male and female differences in sexual behaviors of older adults. *Contemporary Sexuality, 24*(8), 3.

Johnson, H. (1987). Pornography: A humanist issue. In Francoeur, R. T. (Ed.), *Taking Sides: Clashing views on controversial issues in human sexuality* (pp. 236–240). Guilford, CT: Dushkin.

Johnson, R. (1971). A personal communication reported by Smith and Smith, 1973 (see reference).

Jordheim, A. (1983). Non-professional ethnic treatment of sexual dysfunctions. *Journal of Sex Education and Therapy, 9*(1), 57–59.

Julian, T. W., McKenry, P. C., & Arnold, K. (1990). Psychosocial predictors of stress associated with the male midlife transition. *Sex Roles, 22*(11–12), 707–722.

Julty, S. (1979). *Men's bodies, men's selves.* New York: Delta.

K

Kalichman, S. C., Craig, M. E., Shealy, L., Taylor, J., Szymanowski, D., & McKee, G. (1989). An empirically derived typology of adult rapists based on the MMPI: A cross-validation study. *Journal of Psychology and Human Sexuality, 2*(2), 165–182.

Kalichman, S. C., Syzmanowski, D., McKee, G., Taylor, J., & Craig, M. E. (1989). Cluster analytically derived MMPI profile subgroups of incarcerated adult rapists. *Journal of Clinical Psychology, 45*(1), 150–155.

Kallman, F. (1952). Comparative twin study on the genetic aspects of male homosexuality. *Journal of Nervous and Mental Disease, 115,* 283–298.

Kaminer, W. (1980). What the Constitution says: A woman's guide to pornography and the law. *Nation, 230,* 754.

Kaplan, A., & Sedney, M. A. (1980). *Psychology and sex roles: An androgynous perspective.* Boston: Little, Brown.

Kaplan, H. S. (1974). *The new sex therapy.* New York: Brunner/Mazel.

Kaplan, H. S. (1979). *Disorders of sexual desire and other new concepts and techniques in sex therapy.* New York: Brunner/Mazel.

Kaplan, H. S. (1983). *The evaluation of sexual disorders.* New York: Brunner/Mazel.

Kaplan, H. S. (1987). *Sexual aversion, sexual phobias, and panic disorder.* New York: Brunner/Mazel.

Kaplan, H. S. (1989). *PE: How to overcome premature ejaculation.* New York: Brunner/Mazel.

Kaplan, H. S. (1990). Sex, intimacy, and the aging process. *Journal of the American Academy of Psychoanalysis, 18*(2), 185–205.

Kaplan, H. S., & Sager, C. J. (1971). Sexual patterns at different ages. *Medical Aspects of Human Sexuality, 5*(6), 10–23.

Kaplan, M. S., Becker, J. V., & Martinez, D. F. (1990). A comparison of mothers of adolescent incest vs. non-incest perpetrators. *Journal of Family Violence, 5*(3), 209–214.

Karacan, I., Aslan, C., & Hirshkowitz, M. (1983). Erectile mechanisms in man. *Science, 220,* 1080–1082.

Kasl, C. D. (1989). *Women, sex, and addiction: A search for love and power.* New York: Ticknor and Fields.

Kaufman, J., & Zigler, E. (1987). Do abused children become abusive parents? *American Journal of Orthopsychiatry, 57*(2), 186–192.

Keen, S. (1983). *The passionate life: Stages of loving.* New York: Harper and Row.

Kegel, A. H. (1952). Sexual functions of the pubococcygeus muscle. *Western Journal of Surgery, Obstetrics and Gynecology, 60*(10), 521–524.

Kelley, K. (Ed.). (1987). *Females, males and sexuality: Theories and research.* Albany: State University of New York.

Kelly, G. F. (1980). *Good sex: The healthy man's guide to sexual fulfillment.* New York: NAL/Signet.

Kelly, G. F. (1981). Loss of loving: A cognitive therapy approach. *Personnel and Guidance Journal, 59*(6), 401–404.

Kelly, G. F. (1984). Is it time for sexologists to clarify a position on pornography? *Journal of Sex Education and Therapy, 10*(2), 3–4.

Kelly, G. F. (1986). *Learning about sex* (3rd ed.). Woodbury, NY: Barron's Educational Series.

Kelly, G. F. (1986). Some of my pet peeves with sex education. *Journal of Sex Education and Therapy, 12*(1), 3–4.

Kelly, G. F. (1988). The other risks of sex. *Journal of Sex Education and Therapy, 14*(1), 3–4.

Kelly, J. (1977). The aging male homosexual: Myth and reality. *Gerontologist, 17*(4), 328–332.

Kelly, M. P., Strassberg, D. S., & Kircher, J. R. (1990). Attitudinal and experiential correlates of anorgasmia. *Archives of Sexual Behavior, 19*(2), 165–177.

Kempton, W. (1977). The mentally retarded person. In Gochros, H. L., & Gochros, J. S. (Eds.), *The sexually oppressed* (pp. 239–256). New York: Association.

Kendal-Tackett, K. A. (1988). Molestation and the onset of puberty: Data from 365 adults molested as children. *Child Abuse and Neglect, 12,* 73–81.

Kendrick, W. (1987). *The secret museum: Pornography in modern culture.* New York: Viking/Penguin.

Keye, W. R. (1983). Update: Premenstrual syndrome. *Endocrine and Fertility Forum, 6*(4), 1–3.

Kieffer, C. (1977). New depths in intimacy. In Libby, R. W., & Whitehurst, R. N. (Eds.), *Marriage and alternatives: Exploring intimate relationships* (pp. 267–293). Glenview, IL: Scott, Foresman.

Kiersey, D., & Bates, M. (1984). *Please understand me: Character and temperament types.* DelMar, CA: Prometheus-Nemesis Book Co.

Kinsey, A. C., Pomeroy, W. B., & Martin, C. E. (1948). *Sexual behavior in the human male.* Philadelphia: Saunders.

Kinsey, A. C., Pomeroy, W. B., Martin, C. E. & Gebhard, P. H. (1953). *Sexual behavior in the human female.* Philadelphia: Saunders.

Kirby, D. (1985). The effects of selected sexuality education programs. *Journal of Sex Education and Therapy, 11*(1), 28–37.

Kircher, J. (1991). Feedback on sexually explicit movies. *Contemporary Sexuality, 25*(5), 9.

Klaf, F. S., & Brown, W. (1958). Necrophilia, brief review and case report. *The Psychiatric Quarterly, 32,* 645–652.

Klassen, A., Williams, C., & Levitt, E. (1989). *Sex and morality in the U.S.* Middletown, CT: Wesleyan University Press.

Klein, F. (1990). The need to view sexual orientation as a multivariable dynamic process: A theoretical perspective. In McWhirter, D. P., Sanders, S. A., & Reinisch, J. M. (Eds.), *Homosexuality/heterosexuality: Concepts of sexual orientation* (pp. 277–282). New York: Oxford University Press.

Klein, F., Sepekoff, B., & Wolf, T. J. (1990). Sexual orientation: A multivariable dynamic process. In Geller, T. (Ed.), *Bisexuality: A reader and sourcebook* (pp. 64–81)). Ojai, CA: Times Change Press.

Klein, M. (1989). What is the most commonly kept sexual secret? *Contemporary Sexuality, 21*(8), 7.

Klein, M. (1991). Why there's no such thing as sexual addiction—and why it really matters. In Francoeur, R. T. (Ed.), *Taking sides: Clashing views on controversial issues in human sexuality* (pp. 24–31). Guilford, CT: The Dushkin Publishing Group.

Knudsen, D. D. (1987). Sex in childhood: Aversion, abuse or right? *Journal of Sex Education and Therapy, 13*(1), 16–24.

Koertge, N. (1990). Constructing concepts of sexuality: A philosophical commentary. In McWhirter, D. P., Sanders, S. A., & Reinisch, J. M. (Eds.), *Homosexuality/heterosexuality: Concepts of sexual orientation* (pp. 387–397). New York: Oxford University Press.

Kohlberg, L. (1966). A cognitive-developmental model analysis of children's sex-role concepts and attitudes. In Maccoby, E. E. (Ed.), *The development of sex differences* (pp. 82–173). Stanford, CA: Stanford University.

Kohn, A. (1987). Shattered innocence. *Psychology Today, 21*(2), 54–58.

Kolata, G. (1991a, June 3). After decade, many feel AIDS battle just started. *New York Times,* A2.

Kolata, G. (1991b, June 18). Experts debate if AIDS epidemic has at last crested in U.S. *New York Times,* C1.

Kolodny, R. C., Masters, W. H., Kolodner, R. M., & Toro, G. (1974). Depression of plasma testosterone levels after chronic intensive marijuana use. *New England Journal of Medicine, 290*(16), 872–874.

Konner, M. (1988, March/April). Is orgasm essential? *The Sciences,* pp. 4–7.

Krafft-Ebing, R. von (1965). (Trans.). *Psychopathia sexualis.* New York: Bell (Original edition, 1886).

Kremer, E. B., Zimpfer, D. G., & Wiggers, T. T. (1975). Homosexuality, counseling, and adolescent male. *Personnel and Guidance Journal, 54*(2), 95–99.

Krieger, M. J., McAninch, J. W., & Weimer, S. R. (1982). Self-performed bilateral orchiectomy in transsexuals. *Journal of Clinical Psychiatry, 43*(7), 292–293.

Krim, M. (1986). American Foundation for AIDS research statement on the AIDS crisis in the United States. *SIECUS Report, 14*(3), 7.

Krokoff, L. J. (1990). Hidden agendas in marriage: Affective and longitudinal dimensions. *Communication Research, 17*(4), 483–499.

Kronhausen, P., & Kronhausen, E. (1970). *Erotic art 2.* New York: Bell.

Krueger, M. M. (1988). Pregnancy as a result of rape. *Journal of Sex Education and Therapy, 14*(1), 23–27.

Krueger, M. M. (1991). The omnipresent need: Professional training for sexuality education teachers. *SIECUS Report, 19*(4), 1–5.

Kuhn, M. E. (1976). Sexual myths surrounding the aging. In Oaks, W. (Ed.), *Sex and the life cycle* (pp. 117–124). New York: Grune and Stratton.

L

Ladas, A. K. (1989). False information about female anatomy causes great unhappiness. *Contemporary Sexuality, 21*(6), 5, 11.

Ladas, A., Whipple, B., & Perry, J. (1983). *The G spot and other recent discoveries about human sexuality.* New York: Dell.

Lamb, S. (1986). Treating sexually abused children: Issues of blame and responsibility. *American Journal of Orthopsychiatry, 56*(2), 303–307.

Lambert, B. (1990, July 17). Ten years later, hepatitis study still yields critical data on AIDS. *New York Times,* C3.

Lang, R. A., Flor-Henry, P., & Frenzel, R. R. (1990). Sex hormone profiles in pedophilic and incestuous men. *Annals of Sex Research, 3*(1), 59–74.

Langfeldt, T. (1981). Sexual development in children. In Cook, M., & Howells, K. (Eds.), *Adult sexual interest in children.* London: Academic.

Laughman, C. (1980). Eros and the elderly: A literary view. *Gerontologist, 20*(2), 180–187.

Lawrance, L., Rubinson, L., & O'Rourke, T. (1984). Sexual attitudes and behaviors: Trends for a ten-year period, 1972–1982. *Journal of Sex Education and Therapy, 2*(2), 22–29.

Lawson, A. (1988). *Adultery: An analysis of love and betrayal.* New York: Basic Books.

Lazarus, A. A. (1977). A case of pseudonecrophilia treated by behavior therapy. In Fischer, J., & Gochros, H. L. (Eds.), *Handbook of behavior therapy with sexual problems Vol. II* (pp. 581–584). Elmsford, NY: Pergamon.

Leary, W. E. (1988, July 14). Sharp rise in rare sex-related diseases. *New York Times,* p. B6.

Leary, W. E. (1989, May 23). Campus AIDS survey finds threat is real but not yet rampant. *New York Times,* p. C12.

Leboyer, F. (1975). *Birth without violence.* New York: Knopf.

Lee, A. L., & Scheurer, V. L. (1983). Psychological androgyny and aspects of self image in women and men. *Sex Roles, 9,* 289–306.

Lee, J. A. (Ed.), (1990). *Gay midlife and maturity.* Binghamton, NY: Haworth Press.

Leo, J. (1986, July 21). Pornography: The feminist dilemma. *Time,* p. 18.

LeVay, S. (1991). A difference in hypothalamic structure between heterosexual and homosexual men. *Science, 253,* 1034–1037.

Levin, R. J., & Levin, A. (1975, September). Sexual pleasure: The surprising preferences of 100,000 women. *Redbook,* pp. 51–58.

Levine, J. (1991). Thinking about sex. In Francoeur, R. T. (Ed.), *Taking sides: Clashing views on controversial issues in human sexuality* (pp. 185–188). Guilford, CT: The Dushkin Publishing Group.

Levine, M. P., & Troiden, R. R. (1988). The myth of sexual compulsivity. *Journal of Sex Research, 25*(3), 347–363.

Levine, S. B., Risen, C. B., & Althof, S. E. (1990). Essay on the diagnosis and nature of paraphilia. *Journal of Sex and Marital Therapy, 16*(2), 89–102.

Leviton, L. C., Valdiserri, R. O., Lyter, D. W., & Callahan, C. M. (1990). Preventing HIV infection in gay and bisexual men: Experimental evaluation of attitude change from two risk reduction interventions. *AIDS Education and Prevention, 2*(2), 95–108.

Levitt, E. E. (1969). Pornography: Some new perspectives on an old problem. *Journal of Sex Research, 5,* 247–259.

Levy, E. (1990). Stage, sex, and suffering: Images of women in American films. *Empirical studies of the arts, 8*(1), 53–76.

Lewis, R. J., & Janda, L. H. (1988). The relationship between adult sexual adjustment and childhood experience regarding exposure to nudity, sleeping in the parental bed, and parental attitudes toward sexuality. *Archives of Sexual Behavior, 17*(4), 349–362.

Leyson, J. F. (1991). Surgical treatment of impotence. In Leyson, J. F. (Ed.), *Sexual rehabilitation of the spinal-cord-injured patient* (pp. 251–264). Clifton, NJ: Humana Press.

Libby, R. (1990). Review of *Sex and morality in the U.S. SIECUS Report, 18*(5), 14–15.

Lief, H. I. (1981). Sex education in medicine. In Brown, L. (Ed.), *Sex education in the eighties* (pp. 203–216). New York: Plenum.

Lightfoot-Klein, H. (1989). *Prisoners of ritual.* Binghamton, NY: Haworth Press.

Linder, V. (1987, April). Saying no to motherhood. *New Woman,* pp. 57–64.

Lindsay, J., & Monserrat, J. (1988). *Adoption awareness: A guide for teachers, counselors, nurses and caring others.* Buena Park, CA: Morning Glory Press.

Lipman, A. G. (1987). Drugs affecting oral contraceptive efficacy. *Modern Medicine, 55*(5), 189–190.

Long, J. (1984). Nontraditional roles of men and women strengthen the family and provide healthier sexual relationships. In Feldman, H., & Parrot, A. (Eds.), *Human sexuality: Contemporary controversies* (pp. 25–43). Beverly Hills: Sage.

Loth, D. (1961). *The erotic in literature.* New York: Julian Messner.

Loulan, J. (1987). *Lesbian passion: Loving ourselves and each other.* San Francisco: Spinsters Book Co.

Love, E. (1983). Parental and staff attitudes toward instruction in human sexuality for sensorially impaired students. *American Annals of the Deaf, 128*(1), 45–47.

Lowe, W., Kretchmer, A., Petersen, J. R., Nellis, B., Lever, J., & Hertz, R. (1983). The *Playboy* reader's sex survey. *Playboy* (7), 130.

Lowry, T. P. (1979). The volatile nitrites as sexual drugs: A user survey. *Journal of Sex Education and Therapy, 5*(1), 8–10.

Lowry, T. P., & Williams, G. R. (1983). Brachioproctic eroticism. *Journal of Sex Education and Therapy, 9*(1), 50–52.

Loy, P., & Stewart, L. (1984). The extent and effects of the sexual harassment of working women. *Sociological Focus, 17,* 31–43.

Lund, K. L. (1990). A feminist perspective on divorce therapy for women. *Journal of Divorce, 13*(3), 57–67.

Lundstrom, B., Pauly, I., & Walinder, J. (1984). Outcome of sex reassignment surgery. *ACTA Psychiatrica Scandinavica, 70,* 289–294.

Lynn, B. W. (1986). The new pornography commission: Slouching toward censorship. *SIECUS Report, 14*(5), 1–6.

M

Maccoby, E. E. (1990a). Gender and relationships: A developmental account. *American Psychologist, 45*(4), 513–520.

Maccoby, E. E. (1990b). The role of gender identity and gender constancy in sex-differentiated development. *New Directions for Child Development, 47,* 5–20.

MacDonald, A. (1981). Bisexuality: Some comments on research and theory. *Journal of Homosexuality, 6,* 21–35.

MacDonald, A. (1984). Reactions to issues concerning sexual orientations, identities, preferences, and choices. *Journal of Homosexuality, 10*(3–4), 23–27.

Maguire, D. C. (1987). Catholic sexual and reproductive ethics: A historical perspective. *SIECUS Report, 15*(5), 1–4.

Mahlstedt, P. P. (1987). The crisis of infertility: An opportunity for growth. In Weeks, G. R., & Hof, L. (Eds.), *Integrating sex and marital therapy* (pp. 121–148). New York: Brunner/Mazel.

Mahoney, E. R. (1983). *Human sexuality,* New York: McGraw-Hill.

Malamuth, N., Haber, S., & Fesbach, S. (1980). Testing hypotheses regarding rape: Exposure to sexual violence, sex differences, and the "normality" of rapists. *Journal of Research in Personality, 14,* 121–137.

Maletsky, B., & Price, R. C. (1984). Public masturbation in men: Precursor to exhibitionism? *Journal of Sex Education and Therapy, 10*(1), 31–36.

Maltz, W. (1989). Counterpoints: Intergenerational sexual experience or child sexual abuse. *Journal of Sex Education and Therapy, 15*(1), 13–15.

Mancini, J. A., & Mancini, S. B. (1983). The family's role in sex education: Implications for educators. *Journal of Sex Education and Therapy, 9*(2), 16–21.

Mann, D., Sumner, J., Dalton, J., & Berry, D. (1990). Working with incest survivors. *Psychoanalytic Psychotherapy, 4*(3), 271–281.

Mann, J. M., Chin, J., Piot, P., & Quinn, T. (1988). The international epidemiology of AIDS. *Scientific American, 259*(4), 82–89.

Mansfield, P. K. (1986). *Pregnancy for older women: Assessing the medical risks.* New York: Praeger.

Margolies, L. (1990). Cracks in the frame: Feminism and the boundaries of therapy. *Women and Therapy, 9*(4), 19–35.

Marmor, J. (Ed.). (1980). *Homosexual behavior: A modern reappraisal.* New York: Basic.

Marmor, J. (1985). Homosexuality: Nature vs. Nurture. *The Harvard Medical School Mental Health Letter, 2*(4), 5–6.

Marshall, D. S. (1971). Sexual behavior on Mangaia. In Marshall, D. S., & Suggs, R. C. (Eds.), *Human sexual behavior* (pp. 103–162). New York: Basic.

Marshall, E. (1991). Stymied sex survey. *Science, 252,* 497.

Marx, J. L. (1987). Probing the AIDS virus and its relatives. *Science, 236,* 1523–1525.

Marx, J. L. (1989). Circumcision may protect against the AIDS virus. *Science, 245,* 470–471.

Masica, D. N., Money, J., & Ehrhardt, A. A. (1971). Fetal feminization and female gender identity in the testicular feminizing syndrome of androgen insensitivity. *Archives of Sexual Behavior, 1,* 131–142.

Masters, W. H., et al. (1980). *Ethical issues sex therapy and research Vol. 2.* Boston: Little, Brown.

Masters, W. H., & Johnson, V. E. (1966). *Human sexual response.* Boston: Little, Brown.

Masters, W. H., & Johnson, V. E. (1970). *Human sexual inadequacy.* Boston: Little, Brown.

Masters, W. H., & Johnson, V. E. (1979). *Homosexuality in perspective.* Boston: Little, Brown.

Masters, W. H., & Johnson, V. E. (1981). Sex and the aging process. *Journal of American Geriatrics Society, 29*(9), 385–390.

Masters, W. H., & Johnson, V. E. (1983). As reported in: Masters and Johnson dismiss Zilbergeld's charges as "ludicrous." *Sexuality Today, 6*(35), 1–3.

Mastroiani, L., et al. (1990). *Developing new contraceptives: Obstacles and opportunities.* Washington: National Academy Press.

Mayer, A. (1990). *How to stay lovers while raising your children.* Los Angeles: Price-Stern-Sloan.

Mays, V. M., & Cochran, S. D. (1990). Methodological issues in the assessment and prediction of AIDS risk-related sexual behaviors among black Americans. In Voeller, B., Reinisch, J. M., & Gottlieb, M. (Eds.), *AIDS and sex* (pp. 97–120). New York: Oxford University Press.

Mazur, T., & Money, J. (1980). Prenatal and subsequent sexuality. In Wolman, B., & Money, J. (Eds.), *Handbook of human sexuality* (pp. 4–14). Englewood Cliffs, NJ: Prentice-Hall.

McCaffree, K. (1989). Male and female adolescent developmental needs. *SIECUS Report, 18*(1), 3–4.

McCarthy, B. W. (1990). Treatment of incest families: A cognitive-behavioral model. *Journal of Sex Education and Therapy, 16*(2), 101–114.

McCarthy, J., & McMillan, S. (1990). Patient/partner satisfaction with penile implant surgery. *Journal of Sex Education and Therapy, 16*(1), 25–37.

McCary, J. L. (1973). *Human sexuality.* New York: Van Nostrand.

McCauley, C., & Swann, C. P. (1978). Male-female differences in sexual fantasy. *Journal of Research on Personality, 12,* 76–86.

McCormick, C. M., Witelson, S. F., & Kingstone, E. (1990). Left-handedness in homosexual men and women: Neuroendocrine implications. *Psychoneuroendocrinology, 15*(1), 69–76.

McCormick, N. (1990). Under-diagnosed bladder disease makes sex painful for women. *Contemporary Sexuality, 22*(3), 4–5.

McDermott, D., Tyndall, L., & Lichtenberg, J. W. (1989). Factors related to counselor preference among gays and lesbians. *Journal of Counseling and Development, 68*(1), 31–35.

McKenzie-Mohr, D. & Zanna, M. P. (1990). Treating women as sexual objects: Look to the (gender schematic) male who has viewed pornography. *Personality and Social Psychology Bulletin, 16*(2), 296–308.

McKusick, L. (1990). Changing sexual behavior. In Voeller, B., Reinisch, J. M., & Gottlieb, M. (Eds.), *AIDS and sex* (pp. 155–167). New York: Oxford University Press.

McNaught, B. (1989). How to address homophobia in the workplace. *Contemporary Sexuality, 21*(11), 5–6.

Meisler, A. W., Carey, M. P., Krauss, D. J., & Lantinga, L. J. (1988). Success and failure in penile prosthesis surgery: Importance of psychosocial factors. *Journal of Sex and Marital Therapy, 14,* 108–119.

Menninger, K. A. (1951). Contemporary attitudes toward animals. In Wilbur, G. B., & Muensterberger, W. (Eds.), *Psychoanalysis and culture* (pp. 42–74). New York: Wiley.

Mertz, G. J., Coombs, R. W., Ashley, R., Jouden, A. R., Remington, M., Winter, C., Fahnlander, A., Guinan, M., Ducey, H., & Corey, L. (1988). Transmission of genital herpes in couples with one symptomatic and one asymptomatic partner: A prospective study. *Journal of Infectious Diseases, 157,* 1169–1175.

Messe, M. R., & Geer, J. H. (1985). Voluntary vaginal musculature contractions as an enhancer of sexual arousal. *Archives of Sexual Behavior, 14,* 13–28.

Messenger, J. C. (1971). Sex and repression in an Irish folk community. In Marshall, D. S., & Suggs, R. C. (Eds.), *Human sexual behavior* (pp. 3–37). New York: Basic.

Meyer, J. K. (1982). The theory of gender identity disorders. *Journal of the American Psychoanalytic Association, 30*(2), 381–418.

Meyers, R. (1983). *D.E.S.—The bitter pill.* New York: Putnam.

Miccio-Fonseca, L. C., Jones, J. E., & Futterman, L. A. (1990). Sexual trauma and the premenstrual syndrome. *Journal of Sex Education and Therapy, 16*(4), 270–278.

Milner, J. S., & Robertson, K. R. (1990). Comparison of physical child abusers, intrafamilial sexual child abusers, and child neglecters. *Journal of Interpersonal Violence, 5*(1), 37–48.

Mintz, L. B., & 0'Neil, J. M. (1990). Gender roles, sex, and the process of psychotherapy: Many questions and few answers. *Journal of Counseling and Development, 68*(4), 381–387.

Mira, J. J. (1988). A therapeutic package for dyspareunia: A three case example. *Sex and Marital Therapy, 3,* 77–82.

Miranda, J., & Storms, M. (1990). Psychological adjustment of lesbians and gay men. *Journal of Counseling and Development, 68*(1), 41–45.

Moglia, R. (1990). The professional preparation of sexuality educators. *SIECUS Report, 18*(2), 13–15.

Money, J. (1977). Determinants of human gender identity/role. In Money, J., & Musaph, H. (Eds.), *Handbook of sexology* (pp. 57–79). New York: Excerpta Medica.

Money, J. (1987). Propaedeutics of diecious G-I/R: Theoretical foundations for understanding dimorphic gender-identity/role. In Reinisch, J., Rosenblum, L.A., & Sanders, S. A. (Eds.), *Masculinity/femininity: Basic perspectives* (pp. 13–28). New York: Oxford University.

Money, J. (1989). *Lovemaps.* Buffalo, NY: Prometheus Books.

Money, J. (1990). Agenda and credenda of the Kinsey scale. In McWhirter, D. P., Sanders, S. A., & Reinisch, J. M. (Eds.), *Homosexuality/heterosexuality: Concepts of sexual orientation* (pp. 41–60). New York: Oxford University Press.

Money, J. (1991). Sexology and/or sexosophy: The split between sexual researchers and reformers in history and practice. *SIECUS Report, 19*(3), 1–4.

Money, J., & Ehrhardt, A. A. (1972). *Man and woman, boy and girl.* Baltimore: Johns Hopkins University.

Money, J., Jobaris, R., & Furth, G. (1977). Apotemnophilia: Two cases of self-demand amputation as a paraphilia. *Journal of Sex Research, 13*(2), 115–125.

Money, J., & Russo, A. H. (1981). Homosexual vs. transvestite or transsexual gender-identity/role: Outcome study in boys. *International Journal of Family Psychiatry, 2*(1–2), 139–145.

Money, J., & Werlwas, J. (1982). Paraphilic sexuality and child abuse: The parents. *Journal of Sex and Marital Therapy, 8,* 57-64.

Montagu, A. (1986). *Touching: The human significance of skin.* New York: Harper and Row.

Mooney, E., & Siefer, J. H. (1991). Setting standards for sexually explicit material. *Contemporary Sexuality, 25*(5), 5-6.

Mooney, T. O., Cole, T. M., & Chilgren, R. A. (1975). *Sexual options for paraplegics and quadriplegics.* Boston: Little, Brown.

Morin, S. F. (1977). Heterosexual bias in psychological research on lesbianism and male homosexuality. *American Psychologist, 32*(8), 629-637.

Morris, M. (1991). Reproductive technology and restraints. In Francoeur, R. T. (Ed.). *Taking sides: Clashing views on controversial issues in human sexuality* (pp. 129-136). Guilford, CT: The Dushkin Publishing Group.

Mosher, D. L. (1986). Misinformation on pornography: A lobby disguised as an educational organization. *SIECUS Report, 14*(5), 7-10.

Mosher, D. L. (1991). Psychosexual therapy in the 90s. *SIECUS Report, 19*(5), 14-20.

Mosher, D. L., & Greenberg, I. (1969). Females' affective responses to reading erotic literature. *Journal of Consulting and Clinical Psychology, 33,* 472-477.

Moss, A. M. (1978). Men's mid-life crisis and the marital-sexual relationship. *Medical Aspects of Human Sexuality, 13*(2), 109-110.

Mostel, A. (1990). Performance anxiety no longer just a problem for men. *Contemporary Sexuality, 22*(6), 1.

Mott, F., & Haurin, R. (1988). Linkages between sexual activity and alcohol and drug use among American adolescents. *Family Planning Perspectives, 20,* 128-137.

Mould, D. E. (1990). A reply to Page: Fraud, pornography, and the Meese Commission. *American Psychologist, 45*(6), 777-778.

Moynihan, J., & Whelehan, P. (1983). Treating protracted vaginismus: A case study. *Journal of Sex Education and Therapy, 9*(1), 60-62.

Mullen, P. E. (1990). A phenomenology of jealousy. *Australian and New Zealand Journal of Psychiatry, 24*(1), 17-28.

Murphy, B. C. (1989). Lesbian couples and their parents: The effects of perceived parental attitudes on the couple. *Journal of Counseling and Development, 68*(1), 46-51.

Murstein, B. I. (1980). Mate selection in the 1970s. *Journal of Marriage and the Family, 42,* 77-792.

Myers, I. B., & McCaulley, M. H. (1985). *A guide to the development and use of the Myers-Briggs Type Indicator.* Palo Alto, CA: Consulting Psychologists Press.

Myers, L. (1987). Freedom in marriage: It works! In Francoeur, R. T. (Ed.), *Taking sides: Clashing views on controversial issues in human sexuality* (pp. 58-61). Guilford, CT: The Dushkin Publishing Group.

N

Nadelson, C. C. (1990). Consequences of rape: Clinical and treatment aspects. *Psychotherapy and Psychosomatics, 51*(4), 187-192.

Nadler, R. P. (1975). Obscene telephone calls. In Lief, H. I. (Ed.), *Medical aspects of human sexuality* (pp. 296-297). Baltimore: Williams and Wilkins.

National Center for Health Statistics. (1989). *U.S. Department of Health and Human Services, Vol. 38,* No. 12.

National Institute on Aging (1979). Male menopause? The hormones flow but the sex does slow. *Medical World News, 20*(14), 11-12.

Navarro, M. (1991, July 8). Dated AIDS definition keeps benefits from many patients. *New York Times,* A1, B5.

Ndinya-Achola, J. O., Plummer, F. A., Piot, P., & Ronald, A. R. (1990). Acquired immune deficiency syndrome in Africa. In Voeller, B., Reinisch, J. M., & Gottlieb, M. (Eds.), *AIDS and sex* (pp. 185-196). New York: Oxford University Press.

Neaman, H. (1981). Postmenopausal osteoporosis. *Sexual Medicine Today, 5*(6), 6-12.

Neinstein, L., Goldenring, J., & Carpenter, S. (1984). Nonsexual transmission of sexually transmitted diseases: An infrequent occurence. *Pediatrics, 74,* 67-76.

Nelkin, D., Willis, D. P., & Parris, S. V. (Eds.). (1991). *A disease of society: Cultural and institutional responses to AIDS.* New York: Cambridge University Press.

Nelson, J. (1989). Intergenerational sexual contact: A continuum model of participants and experiences. *Journal of Sex Education and Therapy, 15*(1), 3-12.

Nelson, M. (1984). *Cystitis.* Santa Cruz, CA: Network.

Nelson, M. (1985). *Endometriosis.* Santa Cruz, CA: Network.

Neuhaus, R. J. (1991). Renting women, buying babies and class struggle. In Francoeur, R. T. (Ed.), *Taking sides: Clashing views on controversial issues in human sexuality* (pp. 124-128). Guilford, CT: The Dushkin Publishing Group.

Neumann, R. J. (1991). The forgotten others. In Leyson, J. F. (Ed.), *Sexual rehabilitation of the spinal-cord-injured patient* (pp. 351-377). Clifton, NJ: Humana Press.

Newcomer, S. F., & Udry, J. R. (1985). Oral sex in an adolescent population. *Archives of Sexual Behavior, 14,* 41-46.

Newton, N. (1955). *Maternal emotions.* New York: Harper and Brothers.

Newton, N., & Newton, M. (1967). Psychological aspects of lactation. *New England Journal of Medicine, 277,* 1179-1188.

Nichols, M. (1990). Lesbian relationships: Implications for the study of sexuality and gender. In McWhirter, D. P., Sanders, S. A., & Reinisch, J. M. (Eds.), *Homosexuality/heterosexuality: Concepts of sexual orientation* (pp. 350-364). New York: Oxford University Press.

Noe, J. M., Laub, D. R., & Schulz, W. (1976). The external male genitalia: The interplay of surgery and mechanical prostheses. In Meyer, J. K. (Ed.), *Clinical Management of Sexual Disorders* (pp. 252-264). Baltimore: Williams and Wilkins.

Norton, A. J., & Moorman, J. E. (1987). Current trends in marriage and divorce among American women. *Journal of Marriage and the Family, 49,* 3-14.

Nottelmann, E. D., Inoff-Germain, G., Susman, E. J., & Chrousos, G. P. (1990). Hormones and behavior at puberty. In Bancroft, J., & Reinisch, J. M. (Eds.), *Adolescence and Puberty* (pp. 88-123). New York: Oxford University Press.

Nugent, R. (1987). Racism, sexism, and social homophobia—What are the costs of denying civil rights to homosexuals? In Francoeur, R. T. (Ed.), *Taking sides:*

Clashing views on controversial issues in human sexuality (pp. 216–225). Guilford, CT: Dushkin.

O

O'Connor, J. F. (1976). Sexual problems, therapy, and prognostic factors. In Meyer, J. (Ed.), *Clinical management of sexual disorders* (pp. 74–98). Baltimore: Williams and Wilkins.

O'Neill, N., & O'Neill, G. (1975). Open marriage: An synergic model. In DeLora, J. R., & DeLora, J. S. (Eds.), *Intimate life styles* (pp. 150–158). Pacific Palisades, CA: Goodyear.

Offit, A. K. (1990). Sexually explicit movies may impede sexual intimacy. *Contemporary Sexuality, 24*(12), 1.

Oppenheim, G. (1986). The snowball effect of the "real-life" test for sex reassignment. *Journal of Sex Education and Therapy, 12*(2), 12–14.

Osborn, C. A., & Pollack, R. (1977). The effects of two types of literature on measures of female sexual arousal. *Journal of Sex Research, 13*(4), 250–256.

Osborn, J. E. (1991). Women and HIV/AIDS. *SIECUS Report, 19*(2), 1–4.

Osborn, M., Hawton, K., & Gath, D. (1988). Sexual dysfunction among middle-aged women in the community. *British Medical Journal, 296*, 959–962.

P

Pachtman, R., & Southern, S. (1984). Sex counseling for impotence among cardiac patients. *Journal of Sex Education and Therapy, 10*(1), 41–45.

Paddison, P. L., Gise, L. H., Lebovits, A., & Strain, J. J. (1990). Sexual abuse and premenstrual syndrome. *Psychosomatics, 31*(3), 265–272.

Palca, J. (1989). The pill of choice? *Science, 245,* 1319–1323.

Palca, J. (1991a). Finding a new target for AIDS therapy. *Science, 252,* 31.

Palca, J. (1991b). Monopoly patients on AZT challenged. *Science, 252,* 1369.

Palca, J. (1991c). The sobering geography of AIDS. *Science, 252,* 372–373.

Palca, J. (1991d). The true source of HIV? *Science, 252,* 771.

Pasquale, S. (1984). Rationale for a triphasic oral contraceptive. *Journal of Reproductive Medicine, 29,* 560–567.

Patrick J. G. (1986, October 1). Don't let sex myths hurt your marriage: An interview with Masters and Johnson. *Family Circle,* pp. 40, 55.

Pauly, I. (1990). Gender identity disorders: Evaluation and treatment. *Journal of Sex Education and Therapy, 16*(1), 2–24.

Penrod, S., & Linz, D. (1984). Using psychological research on violent pornography to inform legal change. In Malamuth, N., & Donnerstein E. (Eds.), *Pornography and sexual aggression.* Orlando, FL: Academic.

Peplau, L. A., & Cochran, S. D. (1990). A relationship perspective on homosexuality. In McWhirter, D. P., Sanders, S. A., & Reinisch, J. M. (Eds.), *Homosexuality/heterosexuality: Concepts of sexual orientation* (pp. 321–349). New York: Oxford University Press.

Percival-Smith, R. K. L., & Abercrombie, B. (1987). Postcoital contraception with dl-norgestrel/ethinyl estradiol combination: Six years' experience in a student medical clinic. *Contraception, 35,* 287.

Perry, B. L. (1989, October). Bright light used to treat premenstrual mood disorders. *Contemporary Sexuality,* 6–7.

Perry, J. D. (1983). A response to Hoch about the "G" spot (letter). *Journal of Sex Education and Therapy, 9*(2), 6–7.

Peter, J. B., Bryson, Y., & Lovett, M. A. (1982, March/April). Genital herpes: Urgent questions, elusive answers. *Diagnostic Medicine,* pp. 71–88.

Phinney, V. G., Jensen, L. C., Olsen, J. A., & Cundick, B. (1990). The relationship between early development and psychosexual behaviors in adolescent females. *Adolescence, 25*(98), 321–332.

Pieper, B. A., et al. (1983). Perceived effect of diabetes on relationship to spouse and sexual function. *Journal of Sex Education and Therapy, 9*(2), 46–50.

Pillard, R. C. (1990). The Kinsey Scale: Is it familial? In McWhirter, D. P., Sanders, S. A., & Reinisch, J. M. (Eds.), *Homosexuality/heterosexuality: Concepts of sexual orientation* (pp. 88–100). New York: Oxford University Press.

Pillard, R. C., & Weinrich, J. D. (1987). The periodic table model of the gender transpositions: Part I. A theory based on masculinization and defeminization of the brain. *Journal of Sex Research, 23*(4), 425–454.

Platt, R., Rice, P., & McCormack, W. (1983). Risk of acquiring gonorrhea and prevalence of abnormal adnexal findings among women recently exposed to gonorrhea. *Journal of the American Medical Association, 250,* 3205–3209.

Pleck, J. H. (1981). *The myth of masculinity.* Cambridge, MA: MIT.

Pollner, F. (1990, July). Prevention effort misses the mark. *Medical World News,* 14–15.

Pomeroy, W. B. (1972). *Dr. Kinsey and the Institute for Sex Research.* New York: Harper and Row.

Pomeroy, W. B. (1975). The diagnosis and treatment of transvestites and transsexuals. *Journal of Sex and Marital Therapy, 1*(3).

Pope, K. S. (1990). Therapist-patient sex as sex abuse. *Professional Psychology: Research and Practice, 21*(4), 227–239.

Porter, S. (1990). Adolescent sex offenders. *American Journal of Forensic Psychology, 8*(3), 61–73.

Potter, J. (1989). Viewpoint: Circumcision should be stopped. *Contemporary Sexuality, 21*(10), 4.

Potts, D. M. (1990). Adolescence and puberty: An overview. In Bancroft, J., & Reinisch, J. M. (Eds.), *Adolescence and puberty* (pp. 269–279). New York: Oxford University Press.

Potts, M. (1990). Cross-cultural perspectives on AIDS: A commentary. In Voeller, B., Reinisch, J. M., & Gottlieb, M. (Eds.), *AIDS and sex* (pp. 211–218). New York: Oxford University Press.

Press, A., McDaniel, A., Raine, G., & Carroll, G. (1986, July 14). Government in the bedroom. *Newsweek,* pp. 36–38.

Przyyla, D. P., & Byrne, D. (1984). The mediating role of cognitive processes in self-reported sexual arousal. *Journal of Research in Personality, 18,* 54–63.

Purcell, P., & Stewart, L. (1990). Dick and Jane in 1989. *Sex Roles, 22*(3–4), 177–185.

Purdy, S. B. (1975). The erotic in literature. In Katchadourian, H. A., & Lunde, D. T. (Eds.), *Fundamentals of human sexuality* (pp. 425–461). New York: Holt, Rinehart, and Winston.

Q

Quinn, R. E., Lobel, S. A., & Hulik, K. (1990). "Nonsexual" love affairs on the job: New link between men and women. *Contemporary Sexuality, 24*(10), 7.

R

Rajfer, J., Rosciszewski, A., & Mehringer, M. (1988). Prevalence of corporeal venous leakage in impotent men. *Journal of Urology, 140,* 69–71.

Ramey, E. (1973). Sex hormones and executive ability. *Annals of the NY Academy of Sciences, 28,* 237.

Raphael, P. (1987). Sexually exclusive monogamy is unworkable. In Francoeur, R. T. (Ed.), *Taking sides: Clashing views on controversial issues in human sexuality* (pp. 51–54). Guilford, CT: The Dushkin Publishing Group.

Rayner, C. (1986). *Woman: Your body, your health.* Middlesex, England: Hamlyn.

Realmuto, G. M., Jensen, J. B., & Wescoe, S. (1990). Specificity and sensitivity of sexually anatomically correct dolls in substantiating abuse. *Journal of the American Academy of Child and Adolescent Psychiatry, 29*(5), 743–746.

Reckler, J. M. (1983). The urologic evaluation of ejaculatory disorders. In Kaplan, H. S. (Ed.), *The evaluation of sexual disorders* (pp. 139–149). New York: Brunner/Mazel.

Redfield, R. R., & Burke, D. S. (1988). HIV infection: The clinical picture. *Scientific American, 259*(4), 90–98.

Reiche, R., & Dannecker, M. (1977). Male homosexuality in West Germany—A sociological investigation. *Journal of Sex Research, 13*(2), 35–53.

Reinisch, J. M., & Beasley, M. L. S. (1990). *The Kinsey Institute new report on sex: What you must know to be sexually literate.* New York: St. Martin's Press.

Reinisch, J. M., Ziemba-Davis, M., & Sanders, S. A. (1990). Sexual behavior and AIDS: Lessons from art and sex research. In Voeller, B., Reinisch, J. M., & Gottlieb, M. (Eds.), *AIDS and sex* (pp. 37–80). New York: Oxford University Press.

Reiss, I. L. (1986). A sociological journey into sexuality. *Journal of Marriage and the Family, 48,* 233–242.

Reiss, I. L. (1990). *An end to shame: Shaping our next sexual revolution.* Buffalo: Prometheus Books.

Reiss, I. L. (1991). Sexual pluralism: Ending America's sexual crisis. *SIECUS Report, 19*(3), 5–9.

Remafedi, G. (1989). The healthy sexual development of gay and lesbian adolescents. *SIECUS Report, 17*(5), 7–8.

Reproductive Health. (1988). STD-related infertility finds 125,000 victims a year in U.S. *Reproductive Health Digest, 2*(4), 1.

Reynolds, A J. (1989). Social environmental conceptions of male homosexual behavior: A university climate analysis. *Journal of College Student Development, 30,* 62–69.

Richards, D. E. (1990). Values and sexual health. *SIECUS Report, 18*(6), 1–14.

Riger, S., & Gordon, M. T. (1989). *The female fear.* New York: Free Press.

Rimmer, R. (1987). Sexually open marriages rarely succeed. In Francoeur, R. T. (Ed.), *Taking sides: Clashing views on controversial issues in human sexuality* (pp. 62–66). Guilford, CT: The Dushkin Publishing Group.

Ritter, T. J. (1980). The case against circumcision. *Sexual Medicine Today, 4*(11), 41.

Roazen, P. (1991). *Helene Deutsch: Psychoanalysis of the sexual functions of women.* New York: Brunner/Mazel.

Robbins, M., & Jensen, G. D. (1978). Multiple orgasm in males. *Journal of Sex Research, 14,* 21–26.

Roberts, L. (1988). Zeroing in on the sex switch. *Science, 239,* 21–23.

Roberts, L. (1989). Ethical questions haunt new genetic technologies. *Science, 243,* 1134–1136.

Roberts, L. (1991). Does egg beckon sperm when the time is right? *Science, 252,* 214.

Robertson, J., & Fitzgerald, L. F. (1990). Men with nontraditional gender roles may not be getting a fair shake in psychotherapy. *Contemporary Sexuality, 22*(2), 1–2.

Robinson, G., Garner, C., Gare, D., & Crawford, B. (1987). Psychological adaptation to pregnancy in childless women more than 35 years of age. *American Journal of Obstetrics and Gynecology, 156,* 323–328.

Robinson, I. E., & Jedlicka, D. (1982). Change in sexual attitudes and behavior of college students from 1965 to 1980: A research note. *Journal of Marriage and the Family, 44*(1), 237–240.

Robinson, S. E., & Krussman, H. W. (1983). Sex for money: Profile of a john. *Journal of Sex Education and Therapy, 9*(1), 27–31.

Rokach, A. (1990). Content analysis of sexual fantasies of males and females. *Journal of Psychology, 124*(4), 427–436.

Rolker-Dolinsky, B. (1987). The premenstrual syndrome. In Kelley, K. (Ed.), *Females, males, and sexuality: Theories and research* (pp. 101–126). Albany: State University of New York.

Rosenthal, E. (Ed.). (1990). *Women, aging and ageism.* Binghamton, NY: Haworth Press.

Rossi, A. S. (1974). *The feminist papers.* New York: Bantam.

Rowan, E. L., Rowan, J. B., & Langelier, P. (1990). Women who molest children. *Bulletin of the American Academy of Psychiatry and the Law, 18*(1), 79–83.

Rowland, K. F., & Haynes, S. N. (1978). A sexual enhancement program for elderly couples. *Journal of Sex and Marital Therapy, 4*(2), 91–113.

Royalle, C. (1989, October). Filmmaker sees bleak future for pro-sexuality erotica. *Contemporary Sexuality,* 9.

Rubenstein, C. (1983). The modern art of courtly love. *Psychology Today,* (7), 40–49.

Rubin, L. (1983). *Intimate strangers: Men and women together.* New York: Harper Colophon.

Rubin, R., Reinisch, J., & Haskett, R. (1981). Postnatal gonadal steroid effects on human behavior. *Science, 211*(4488), 1318–1324.

Rubinson, L., & DeRubertis, L. (1990). Trends in sexual attitudes and behaviors of a college population over a 15-year period. *Journal of Sex Education and Therapy, 17*(1), 32–41.

Ruble, T. L. (1983). Sex stereotypes: Issues of change in the 1970s. *Sex Roles, 9,* 397–402.

523

REFERENCES

Rucker, N. G., & Lombardi, K. L. (1990). The familial ménage-à-trois: Mother-daughter sexuality and father-daughter incest. *Journal of Contemporary Psychotherapy, 20*(2), 99–107.

Rudolph, J. (1988). Counselors' attitudes toward homosexuality: A selective review of the literature. *Journal of Counseling and Development, 67*, 165–168.

Rupple, T. L. (1983). Sex stereotypes: Issues of change in the 1970s. *Sex Roles, 9*, 397–402.

Russell, D. E. H. (1982). *Rape in marriage.* Riverside, NJ: Macmillan.

Russell, D. E. H. (1983). The incidence and prevalence of intrafamilial sexual abuse of female children. *Child Neglect and Abuse, 7*, 133–146.

Rutter, P. (1990). *Sex in the forbidden zone: When men in power betray women's trust.* Los Angeles: Jeremy P. Tarcher.

Ryan, J. J. (1976). Surgical intervention in the treatment of sexual disorders. In Meyer, J. K. (Ed.), *Clinical management of sexual disorders* (pp. 226–251). Baltimore: Williams and Wilkins.

S

Sanday, P. R. (1990). *Fraternity gang rape: Sex, brotherhood, and privilege on campus.* New York: New York University Press.

Sanders, J. S. (1978). Male and female vocabularies for communicating with a sexual partner. *Journal of Sex Education and Therapy, 4*, 15–19.

Sanders, S. A., & Reinisch, J. M. (1990). Biological and social influences on the endocrinology of puberty: Some additional considerations. In Bancroft, J., & Reinisch, J. M. (Eds.), *Adolescence and puberty* (pp. 50–62). New York: Oxford University Press.

Sanders, S. A., Reinisch, J. M., & McWhirter, D. P. (1990). Homosexuality/heterosexuality: An overview. In McWhirter, D. P., Sanders, S. A., & Reinisch, J. M. (Eds.), *Homosexuality/heterosexuality: Concepts of sexual orientation* (pp.xix–xxvii). New York: Oxford University Press.

Sanderson, B. E. (1989). *It's never O.K.: A handbook for professionals on sexual exploitation by counselors and therapists.* Minneapolis: Minnesota Department of Corrections.

Sandler, B. R. (1983). *Writing a letter to the sexual harasser: Another way of dealing with the problem* (Report from the Project on the Status and Education of Women). Washington: Association of American Colleges.

Sang, B. E. (1989). New directions in lesbian research, theory, and education. *Journal of Counseling and Development, 68*(1), 92–96.

Sarrel, L. (1989). Sexual unfolding revisited. *SIECUS Report, 17*(5), 4–5.

Sarrel, L. J., & Sarrel, P. M. (1979). *Sexual unfolding: Sexual development and sex therapies in late adolescence.* Boston: Little, Brown.

Sarrel, P., & Masters, W. (1982). Sexual molestation of men by women. *Archives of Sexual Behavior, 11*, 117–131.

Sauer, M. V., Paulson, R. J., & Lobo, R. A. (1990). A preliminary report on oocyte donation extending reproductive potential to women over forty. *New England Journal of Medicine, 323*(17), 1157–1160.

Saunders, E. J. (1989). Life-threatening autoerotic behavior: A challenge for sex educators and therapists. *Journal of Sex Education and Therapy, 15*(2), 82–91.

Savitz, L., & Rosen, L. (1988). The sexuality of prostitutes: Sexual enjoyment reported by "streetwalkers." *Journal of Sex Research, 24*, 299–308.

Schacht, A. J., Kerlinsky, D., & Carlson, C. (1990). Group therapy with sexually abused boys: Leadership, protective identification, and countertransference issues. *International Journal of Group Psychotherapy, 40*(4), 401–417.

Schachter, J. (1989). Why we need a program for the control of *Chlamydia trachomatis. New England Journal of Medicine, 320*, 802–803.

Scher, M., & Good, G. E. (1990). Gender and counseling in the twenty-first century: What does the future hold? *Journal of Counseling and Development, 68*(4), 388–391.

Schiavi, R. C. (1990). Sexuality and aging in men. *Annual Review of Sex Research, 1*, 227–249.

Schiavi, R. C., Schreiner-Engle, P., Mandeli, J., & Schanzer, H. (1990). Healthy aging and male sexual function. *American Journal of Psychiatry, 147*(6), 766–771.

Schmidt, G., & Sigusch, V. (1970). Psychosexual stimulation by films and slides: A further report on sex differences. *Journal of Sex Research, 6*, 10–24.

Schmidt, G., & Sigusch, V. (1973). Women's sexual arousal. In Zubin, J., & Money, J. (Eds.), *Contemporary sexual behavior: Critical issues in the 1970s* (pp. 117–142). Baltimore: Johns Hopkins University.

Schnarch, D. M. (1982). The role of medical students' stereotype of physicians in sex education. *Journal of Medical Education, 7*, 992–930.

Schneebaum, T. (1969). *Keep the river on your right.* New York: Grove.

Schoen, E. (1990). The status of circumcision of newborns. *New England Journal of Medicine, 322*, 1308–1312.

Schover, L. R., Evans, R. B., & Von Eschenbach, A. C. (1987). Sexual rehabilitation in a cancer center: Diagnosis and outcome in 384 consultations. *Archives of Sexual Behavior, 16*(6), 445–461.

Schroeder, P., & Snowe, D. (1989). Letter to AASECT on new congressional push for birth control research. *Contemporary Sexuality, 21*, 6.

Schumm, W. R., & Rekers, G. A. (1984). Sex should occur only within marriage. In Feldman, H., & Parrot, A. (Eds.), *Human sexuality: Contemporary controversies* (pp. 105–124). Beverly Hills: Sage.

Seagull, A. A. (1972). Should a therapist have intercourse with patients? *Proceedings, 80th annual convention American Psychological Association,* (2), 855–856.

Selverstone, R. (1989). Adolescent sexuality: Developing self-esteem and mastering developmental tasks. *SIECUS Report, 18*(1), 1–3.

Selverstone, R. (1989). Where are we now in the sexual revolution? *SIECUS Report, 17*(4), 7–12.

Semans, J. H. (1956). Premature ejaculation: A new approach. *Southern Medical Journal, 49*, 353–358.

Sevely, J. L. (1987). *Eve's secrets: A new theory of female sexuality.* New York: Random House.

Sgroi, S. M. (1982). *Handbook of clinical intervention in child sexual abuse.* Lexington, MA: Lexington.

Sha'ked, A. (1978). *Human sexuality in physical and mental illness and disabilities.* Bloomington: Indiana University.

Shea, R. (1980, March). Women at war. *Playboy,* (2), 86.

Shepard, M. (1971). *The love treatment.* New York: Wyden.

Sherfey, M. J. (1972). *The nature and evolution of female sexuality.* New York: Random House.

Shore, D. A., & Gochros, H. L. (1981). *Sexual problems of adolescents in institutions.* Springfield, IL: Charles C. Thomas.

SHUG device may offer safe reversible sterilization for men. (1987). *Contraceptive Technology Update, 8*(1), 1.

SIECUS Report (1987). Decline in circumcision reported. *SIECUS Report, 16*(2), 11.

Siefkes, J. A. (1975). Human rights and sexual orientation. *SIECUS Report, 3*(3), 1-2.

Sieunarine, K. (1987). Non-venereal sclerosing lymphangitis of the penis associated with masturbation. *British Journal of Urology, 59,* 194-195.

Signorielli, N. (1990). Children, television, and gender roles: Messages and impact. *Journal of Adolescent Health Care, 11*(1), 50-58.

Silbert, M. H., & Pines, A. M. (1983). Early exploitation as an influence in prostitution. *Social Work, 28*(4), 285-289.

Silney, A. J. (1980). Sexuality and aging. In Wolman, B. B., & Money, J. (Eds.), *Handbook of human sexuality* (pp. 124-146). Englewood Cliffs, NJ: Prentice-Hall.

Silverstone, B., & Wynter, L. (1975). The effects of introducing a heterosexual living space. *Gerontologist, 15*(1), 83-87.

Simenauer, J., & Carroll, D. (1982). *Singles: The new Americans.* New York: Simon and Schuster.

Simon, W., Kraft, D. M., & Kaplan, H. B. (1990). Oral sex: A critical overview. In Voeller, B., Reinisch, J. M., & Gottlieb, M. (Eds.), *AIDS and sex* (pp. 257-275). New York: Oxford University Press.

Singer, P., & Wells, D. (1985). *Making babies: The new science and ethics of conception.* New York: Scribner.

Singh, S., & Forrest, J. D. (1990). *The sexual and reproductive behavior of American women, 1982-1988.* New York: Alan Guttmacher Institute.

Sivin, I. (1988). International experience with Norplant and Norplant-2 contraceptives. *Studies of Family Planning, 19*(2), 81-94.

Skopec, H. M., Rosenberg, S. D., & Tucker, G. J. (1976). Sexual behavior in schizophrenia. *Medical Aspects of Human Sexuality, 10*(4), 32-47.

Slaby, R. G. (1990). The gender concept development legacy. *New Directions for Child Development, 47,* 21-29.

Slade, J. W. (1975). Recent trends in pornographic films. *Society 12*(6), 77-84.

Small, M. A., & Tetreault, P. A. (1990). Social psychology, "marital rape exemptions," and privacy. *Behavioral Sciences and the Law, 8*(2), 141-149.

Smallwood, K. B., & VanDyck, D. G. (1979). Menopausal counseling: Coping with realities and myths. *Journal of Sex Education and Therapy, 1*(6), 72-76.

Smith, M. M. (1981). Identifying knowledge and attitudes toward sexual expression among selected 65-74-year-olds, utilizing a structured interview. *Dissertation Abstracts International, 42*(5), 1818-B.

Smith, M. S. (1977). The deaf. In Gochros, H. L., & Gochros, J. S. (Eds.), *The sexually oppressed.* New York: Association.

Smith, P. B. (1980). Saving lives with a testicular self-examination. *Sexual Medicine Today, 4*(6), 11-12.

Smith, R. E., Pine, C. J., & Hawley, M. E. (1988). Social cognitions about adult male victims of female sexual assault. *Journal of Sex Research, 24,* 101-112.

Smith, T. W. (1990). A report: The sexual revolution? *Public Opinion Quarterly, 54*(3), 415-435.

Snowden, R. A. (1989). We must emphasize female sexuality in sex education. *Contemporary Sexuality, 21*(7), 7.

Solomon, R. C. (1989). *About love: Reinventing romance for our times.* New York: Simon and Schuster/Touchstone Books.

Sonenschein, D. (1975). Homosexual mannerisms. In Lief, H. I. (Ed.), *Medical aspects of human sexuality* (pp. 278-279). Baltimore: Williams and Wilkins.

Sonenstein, F., & Pleck, J. H. (1989, March 31). Twice as many teen boys use condoms in AIDS scare. As reported by Associated Press from a paper prepared for annual meeting of Population Association of America.

Sorensen, R. C. (1973). *Adolescent sexuality in contemporary America.* New York: World.

Sorenson, S. B., & Brown, V. B. (1990). Interpersonal violence and crisis intervention on the college campus. *New Directions for Student Services, 49,* 57-66.

Spanier, G. B. (1977). Sources of sex information and premarital sexual behavior. *Journal of Sex Research, 13*(2), 73-88.

Speas, R. R. (1990). Sex is sin. *Contemporary Sexuality, 22*(6), 4-5.

Spector, I. P., & Carey, M. P. (1990). Incidence and prevalence of the sexual dysfunctions: A critical review of the empirical literature. *Archives of Sexual Behavior, 19*(4), 389-408.

Sporer, A. (1991). Male sexuality. In Leyson, J. F. (Ed.), *Sexual rehabilitation of the spinal-cord-injured patient* (pp. 39-53). Clifton, NJ: Humana Press.

Sprecher, S. (1989). Premarital sexual standards for different categories of individuals. *Journal of Sex Research, 26,* 232-248.

Sprecher, S., McKinney, K., & Orbuch, T. L. (1987, March). Has the double standard disappeared? An experimental test. *Social Psychology Quarterly,* 24-31.

Stackhouse, B. (1990). The impact of religion on sexuality education. *SIECUS Report, 18*(2), 21-24, 27.

Stadel, B. (1989). Oral contraceptives used in women with a family history of breast cancer. *Obstetrics and Gynecology, 73,* 977-983.

Stamps, V. (1991). S & M girls. *Outweek, 89,* 38-41.

Staples, R. (1975). Sex and racism. *SIECUS Report, 3*(5), 1, 14.

Stark, E. (1984). The unspeakable family secret. *Psychology Today, 18*(5), 38-46.

Steinem, G. (1991). Women in the dark. *Ms., The World of Women, 1*(4), 35-37.

Steiner, B. W. (1981). From Sappho to Sand: Historical perspective on cross-dressing and cross gender. *Canadian Journal of Psychiatry, 26*(7), 502-506.

Steinke, E., & Bergen, B. (1986). Sexuality and aging. *Journal of Gerontological Nursing, 12*(6), 6-10.

Stenager, E., Stenager, E. N., Jensen, K., & Boldsen, J. (1990). Multiple sclerosis: Sexual dysfunctions. *Journal of Sex Education and Therapy, 16*(4), 262-269.

Stevenson, M. R. (1988). Promoting tolerance for homsexuality: A review of research. *Journal of Sex Research, 25,* 500-511.

Stevenson, M. R. (1990). Tolerance for homosexuality and interest in sexuality education. *Journal of Sex Education and Therapy, 16*(3), 194-197.

REFERENCES

Stoller, M. L., Lue, T. F., & McAninch, J. W. (1987). Constructive penile band injury: Anatomical and reconstructive considerations. *Journal of Urology, 137,* 740–742.

Stoller, R. J. (1982). Transvestism in women. *Archives of Sexual Behavior, 11*(2), 99–115.

Story, M. D. (1985). A comparison of university student experience with various sexual outlets in 1974 and 1984. *Journal of Sex Education and Therapy, 11*(2), 35–41.

Story, M. D. (1987). A comparison of social nudists and non-nudists on experience with various sexual outlets. *Journal of Sex Research, 23*(2), 197–211.

Strassberg, D. S., Mahoney, J. M., Schaugaard, M., & Hale, V. E. (1990). The role of anxiety in premature ejaculation: A psychophysiological model. *Archives of Sexual Behavior, 19*(3), 251–257.

Straus, S., Seidlin, M., & Takiff, H. (1984). Management of mucocutaneous herpes simplex. *Drugs, 27,* 364–372.

Stringer, D. M. (1990). The power and reasons behind sexual harassment: An employer's guide to solutions. *Public Personnel Management, 19*(1), 43–52.

Stubblefield, P., et al. (1984). Fertility after induced abortion: A prospective follow-up study. *Obstetrics and Gynecology, 63,* 186–193.

Sultan, F. E., & Chambles, D. L. (1982). Pubococcygeal function and orgasm in a normal population. In Graber, B. (Ed.), *Circumvaginal musculature and sexual function* (pp. 74–87). New York: Karger.

Surrey, J., Sweet, C., Michaels, A., & Levine, S. (1990). Reported history of physical and sexual abuse and severity of symptomatology in women psychiatric outpatients. *American Journal of Orthopsychiatry, 60*(3), 412–417.

Swaab, D. F., & Hofman, M. A. (1990). An enlarged suprachiasmatic nucleus in homosexual men. *Brain Research, 537,* 141.

Sweet, E. (1985, October 4). Date rape: The story of an epidemic and those who deny it. *Ms.,* p. 56.

Sweet, E. (1988, March). A failed revolution. *Ms.,* pp. 75–79.

Swerdlow, H. (1976). Trauma caused by anal coitus. *Medical Aspects of Human Sexuality, 10*(7), 93–94.

Swing, W. E. (1990). AIDS: National policy and education. In Voeller, B., Reinisch, J. M., & Gottlieb, M. (Eds.), *AIDS and sex* (pp. 395–398). New York: Oxford University Press.

Swirling, S. (1990a.) 1980's "decade of disaster" for family planning. *Contemporary Sexuality, 22*(3), 3–4.

Swirling, S. (1990b.) Appeals court strikes down "gag rule." *Contemporary Sexuality, 22*(5), 1.

T

Tannen, D. (1990) *You just don't understand: Women and men in conversation.* New York: William Morrow.

Task Force on Youth Suicide. (1989). *Report of DHHS secretary's task force on youth suicide.* Washington, DC: U.S. Government Printing Office.

Tavris, C. (1977). Men and women report their views of masculinity. *Psychology Today, 10*(8), 34–42, 82.

Tavris, C., & Sadd, S. (1977). *The Redbook report on female sexuality.* New York: Delacorte.

Tavris, C., & Wade, C. (1984). *The longest war: Sex differences in perspective.* (2nd ed.). San Diego: Harcourt Brace Jovanovich.

Taylor, B. G. (1980). Self-recording of sexual behaviors and its effects on the sexual attitudes of senior citizens. *Dissertation Abstracts International, 41*(3), 1096B.

Taylor, M. L., & Hall, J. A. (1982). Psychological androgyny: Theories, methods, and conclusions. *Psychological Bulletin, 92,* 347–366.

Taylor, P. (1990). Can we talk? *New Age Journal, 7*(6), 31–33, 60–64, 107–108.

Taynen, H. (1990). In Freud's defense. *Canadian Journal of Psychiatry, 35*(6), 571.

Tedesco, J. F., & Schnell, Steven V. (1987). Children's reactions to sex abuse investigation and litigation. *Child Abuse and Neglect, 11,* 267–272.

Tharinger, D., Horton, C. B., & Millea, S. (1990). Sexual abuse and exploitation of children and adults with mental retardation and other handicaps. *Child Abuse and Neglect, 14*(3), 301–312.

Thompson, M. E., Chaffee, S. H., & Oshagan, H. H. (1990). *Journal of Communication, 40*(3), 73–83.

Thornburg, H. (1985). Sex information as primary prevention. *Journal of Sex Education and Therapy, 11*(1), 22–27.

Thornhill, N. W., & Thornhill, R. (1990). An evolutionary analysis of psychological pain following rape. *Ethology and Sociobiology, 11*(3), 155–193.

Timmreck, T. C. (1990). Overcoming the loss of a love: Preventing love addiction and promoting positive emotional health. *Psychological Reports, 66*(2), 515–528.

Tripp, C. A. (1975). *The homosexual matrix.* New York: McGraw-Hill.

Trost, J. E. (1990). Social support and pressure and their impact on adolescent sexual behavior. In Bancroft, J., & Reinisch, J. M. (Eds.), *Adolescence and puberty* (pp. 173–181). New York: Oxford University Press.

Trotter, R. J. (1986, September). The three faces of love. *Psychology Today,* 46–54.

Trudell, B., & Whatley, M. (1988). School sexual abuse prevention: Unintended consequences and dilemmas. *Child Abuse and Neglect, 12,* 103–113.

Trudell, B., & Whatley, M. (1991). Sex respect: A problematic public school sexuality curriculum. *Journal of Sex Education and Therapy, 17*(2), 125–140.

Turnbull, C. (1972). *The mountain people.* New York: Simon and Schuster.

Turner, L. A., Froman, S. L., Althof, S. E., Levine, S. B., Tobias, T. R., Kurch, E. D., Bodner, D. R., & Resnick, M. I. (1990). Intracavernous injections in the management of diabetic impotence. *Journal of Sex Education and Therapy, 16*(2), 126–136.

U

Udis-Kessler, A. (1990). Bisexuality in an essentialist world: Toward an understanding of biphobia. In Geller, T. (Ed.), *Bisexuality: A reader and sourcebook* (pp. 51–63). Ojai, CA: Times Change Press.

Udry, J. (1990). Hormonal and social determinants of adolescent sexual initiation. In Bancroft, J., & Reinisch, J. M. (Eds.), *Adolescence and puberty* (pp. 70–87). New York: Oxford University Press.

Uhrig, L. J. (1986). *Sex positive: A gay contribution to sexual and spiritual union.* Boston: Alyson.

U.S. Dept. of Education. (1991). *Youth indicators, 1991.* Washington, DC: U.S. Government Printing Office.

V

Van Egmond, M. (1988). History of sex abuse spurs suicide attempts. As reported in "Human Sexuality Update," *Journal of Sex Education and Therapy, 14*(1), 10.

Vance, C. S. (1987). Ordinances restricting pornography could damage women. In Francoeur, R. T. (Ed.), *Taking Sides: Clashing views on controversial issues in human sexuality* (pp. 241–244). Guilford, CT: Dushkin.

VanderMey, B. J. (1988). The sexual victimization of male children: A review of previous research. *Child Abuse and Neglect, 12*(1), 61–72.

Vasquez, M. J. J. (1988). Counselor-client sexual contact: Implications for ethics training. *Journal of Counseling and Development, 67,* 238–241.

Vivar, M. A. (1982). The new anti-female violent pornography: Is moral condemnation the only justifiable response? *Law and Psychology Review, 7,* 53–70.

Voeller, B. (1980). Society and the gay movement. In Marmor, J. (Ed.), *Homosexual behavior* (pp. 232–254). New York: Basic.

Voeller, B. (1990a). Heterosexual anal intercourse: An AIDS risk factor. In Voeller, B., Reinisch, J. M., & Gottlieb, M. (Eds.), *AIDS and sex* (pp. 276–310). New York: Oxford University Press.

Voeller, B. (1990b). Some uses and abuses of the Kinsey scale. In McWhirter, D. P., Sanders, S. A., & Reinisch, J. M. (Eds.), *Homosexuality/heterosexuality: Concepts of sexual orientation* (pp. 32–38). New York: Oxford University Press.

Voeller, B., Reinisch, J. M., & Gottlieb, M. (1990). An integrated biomedical and biobehavioral approach to AIDS: An introduction. In Voeller, B., Reinisch, J. M., & Gottlieb, M. (Eds.), *AIDS and sex* (pp. 3–10). New York: Oxford University Press.

W

Waldman, S. (1991). Enter Norplant. *Contemporary Sexuality, 25*(1), 1–2.

Wallerstein, E. (1980). *Circumcision: An American health fallacy.* New York: Springer.

Walling, M., Andersen, B. L., & Johnson, S. R. 1990. Hormonal replacement therapy for postmenopausal women: A review of sexual outcomes and related gynecologic effects. *Archives of Sexual Behavior, 19*(2), 119–137.

Wallis, C. (1991, January 14). A puzzling plaque. *Time,* pp. 48–52.

Walthers, R. (1988). *Sexual friendship: A new dynamics in relationships.* San Diego: Libra Publishers.

Walz, T., & Blum, N. (1987). *Sexual health in later life.* Lexington, MA: Lexington Books.

Watson, R., & DeMeo, P. (1987). Premarital cohabitation vs. traditional courtship and subsequent marital adjustment: A replication and follow-up. *Family Relations, 36,* 193–197.

Waxberg, J. D., & Mostel, S. (1980). Sex and the terminally ill. *Sexual Medicine Today, 4*(11), 25, 40.

Weeks, G. R. (1987). Systematic treatment of inhibited sexual desire. In Weeks, G. R., & Hof, L. (Eds.), *Integrating sex and marital therapy* (pp. 183–201). New York: Brunner/Mazel.

Wegner, D. M., Shortt, J. W., Blake, A. W., & Page, M. S. (1990). Suppressing exciting, unwanted thoughts may only make them worse. *Contemporary Sexuality, 22*(4), 2.

Weinberg, M. S., & Williams, C. J. (1974). *Male homosexuals: Their problems and adaptation.* New York: Oxford University.

Weinrich, J. D. (1990). The Kinsey scale in biology, with a note on Kinsey as a biologist. In McWhirter, D. P., Sanders, S. A., & Reinisch, J. M. (Eds.), *Homosexuality/heterosexuality: Concepts of sexual orientation* (pp. 115–137). New York: Oxford University Press.

Welbourne, A., Lifschitz, S., Selvin, H., & Green, R. (1983). A comparison of the sexual learning experiences of visually impaired and sighted women. *Journal of Visual Impairment and Blindness, 77*(6), 256–259.

Wells, J. W. (1990). The sexual vocabularies of heterosexual and homosexual males and females for communicating erotically with a sexual partner. *Archives of Sexual Behavior, 19*(2), 139–147.

Welwood, J. (1990). Intimate relationship as path. *Journal of Transpersonal Psychology, 22*(1), 51–58.

Wernik, U. (1990). The nature of explanation in sexology and the riddle of triolism. *Annals of Sex Research, 3*(1), 5–20.

Wertheimer, D. M. (1988, January). Victims of violence: A rising tide of anti-gay sentiment. *USA Today Magazine,* pp. 52–54.

Wertz, D. C., & Fletcher, J. C. (1991). Fatal knowledge? Prenatal diagnosis and sex selection. In Francoeur, R. T. (Ed.), *Taking sides: Clashing views on controversial issues in human sexuality* (pp. 164–175). Guilford, CT: The Dushkin Publishing Group.

Whalen, R. E., Geary, D. C., & Johnson, F. (1990). Models of sexuality. In McWhirter, D. P., Sanders, S. A., & Reinisch, J. M. (Eds.), *Homosexuality/heterosexuality: Concepts of sexual orientation* (pp. 61–70). New York: Oxford University Press.

Whelehan, P. E., & Moynihan, F. J. (1982). Secular celibacy as a reaction to sexual burnout. *Journal of Sex Education and Therapy, 8*(2), 13–16.

Whipple, B. (1991). Female sexuality. In Leyson, J. F. (Ed.), *Sexual rehabilitation of the spinal-cord-injured patient* (pp. 19–38). Clifton, NJ: Humana Press.

Whitam, F. L. (1977). The homosexual role: A reconsideration. *Journal of Sex Research, 13*(1), 1–11.

Whitam, F. L., & Mathy, R. M. (1986). *Male homosexuality in four societies.* New York: Praeger.

Whitbourne, S. K. (1990). Sexuality in the aging male. *Generations, 14*(3), 28–30.

White, C. B. (1982). Sexual interest, attitudes, knowledge, and sexual history in relation to sexual behavior in the institutionalized aged. *Archives of Sexual Behavior, 11*(1), 11–21.

White, C. B., & Catania, J. A. (1982). Psychoeducational intervention for sexuality with the aged, family members of the aged, and people who work with the aged. *International Journal of Aging and Human Development, 15*(2), 121–138.

Whitley, M. P., & Berke, P. A. (1983). Sexual response in diabetic women. *Journal of Sex Education and Therapy, 9*(2), 51–56.

Wilbanks, G. D. (1987). Update on genital herpes. *Modern Medicine, 58*(8), 37–52.

Wilber, K. (1991). Sex, gender, and transformation. *The Quest, 4*(2), 41–49.

Williamson, M. L. (1990). Feedback: Newborn circumcision has undeniable merit. *Contemporary Sexuality, 22*(1), 7.

Williamson, M. L., & Williamson, P. S. (1988). Women's preferences for penile circumcision in sexual partners. *Journal of Sex Education and Therapy, 14*(2), 8–12.

Willis, J. (1985). *Comparing contraceptives* (from *FDA Consumer*). Rockville, MD: Dept. of Health and Human Services Publication No. (FDA) 85–1123.

Willis, J. (1988). Demystifying menopause. *FDA Consumer, 22*(6), 24–27.

Wilson, G. D. (1980). Sex differences in sexual fantasy patterns. In Forleo, R., & Pasini, W. (Eds.), *Medical Sexology* (pp. 238–243). Littleton, MA: PSG.

Wilson, M. (1959). *Communal rituals of the Nyakyusa.* London: Oxford University.

Wilson, R. A. (1964). *Feminine for life.* New York: Wilson Research Foundation.

Winick, C. (1991). Debate on legalization of prostitution. In Francouer, R. T. (Ed.), *Taking sides: Clashing views on controversial issues in human sexuality* (pp. 227–230). Guilford, CT: The Dushkin Publishing Group.

Winick, C., & Kinsie, P. M. (1973). Prostitution. *Sexual Behavior, 3*(1), 33–43.

Winkler, K. J. (1990, May 23). Scholar whose ideas of female psychology stir debate modifies theories, extends studies to young girls. *The Chronicle of Higher Education,* pp. A6, A7.

Winn, R. L., & Newton, N. (1982). Sexuality in aging: A study of 106 cultures. *Archives of Sexual Behavior, 11*(4), 283–298.

Winton, M. A. (1989). The social construction of the G spot and female ejaculation. *Journal of Sex Education and Therapy, 15*(3), 151–162.

Wise, T. N., Dupkin, C., & Meyer, J. K. (1981). Partners of distressed transvestites. *American Journal of Psychiatry, 138*(9), 1221–1224.

Wiswell, T. E., Enzenauer, R. W., Holton, M. E., Cornish, J. D., & Hankins, C. T. (1987). Declining frequency of circumcision: Implications for changes in the absolute incidence and male to female sex ratio of urinary tract infections in early infancy. *Pediatrics, 79*(3), 338–342.

Witelson, S. J. (1991). Sexual differentiation in brain development. *Psychoneuroendocrinology, 16,* 131.

Wolf, Steven C. (1985). A multi-factor model of deviant sexuality. *Victimology: An International Journal, 10*(1–4), 359–374.

Wolfenden, J. (1963). *Reports of the committee on homosexual offenses and prostitution.* New York: Stein and Day.

Woody, J. D. (1989). Sexual and intimacy problems of older clients. *Journal of Sex Education and Therapy, 15*(3), 175–186.

Wright, B., & Thompson, C. (1990). Homophobia in HIV/AIDS education. *SIECUS Report, 19*(1), 20–22.

Wright, J. (1986). *Survival strategies for couples.* Buffalo, NY: Prometheus Books.

Wyatt, G. E. (1990). Changing influences on adolescent sexuality over the past forty years. In Bancroft, J., & Reinisch, J. M. (Eds.), *Adolescence and puberty* (pp. 182–206). New York: Oxford University Press.

Y

Yarber, W. L., Torabi, M. R., & Veenker, C. H. (1989). Development of a three-component sexually transmitted disease attitude scale. *Journal of Sex Education and Therapy, 15*(1), 36–49.

Young, E. W. (1984). Patients' plea: Tell us about our sexuality. *Journal of Sex Education and Therapy, 10*(2), 53–56.

Young, W. C. (1961). The hormones and mating behavior. In Young, W. C. (Ed.), *Sex and internal secretions* (pp. 1173–1239). Baltimore: Williams and Wilkins.

Z

Zaviacic, M., Zaviacicova, A., Holoman, I. K., & Molcan, J. (1988). Female urethral expulsions evoked by local digital stimulation of the G-spot. Differences in the response patterns. *Journal of Sex Research, 24,* 311–318.

Zeiss, A. M. (1982). Expectations for the effects of aging on sexuality in parents and average married couples. *Journal of Sex Research, 18*(1), 47–57.

Zelnik, M., & Kantner, J. F. (1980). Sexual activity, contraceptive use, and pregnancy among metropolitan-area teenagers, 1971–1979. *Family Planning Perspectives, 12,* 230–237.

Zilbergeld, B., & Evans, M. (1980). The inadequacy of Masters and Johnson. *Psychology Today, 14*(3), 29–43.

Zillmann, D., & Bryant, J. (1982). Pornography, sexual callousness, and the trivialization of rape. *Journal of Communication, 32*(4), 10–21.

Zimmer, D., Borchardt, E., & Fischle, C. (1983). Sexual fantasies of sexually distressed and non-distressed men and women: An empirical comparison. *Journal of Sex and Marital Therapy, 9*(1), 38–50.

Zuckerman, E. J., (1982). Viral hepatitis. *Practical Gastroenterology, 6*(16), 21–27.

Zwerner, J. (1982). Yes, we have trouble but nobody's listening: Sexual issues of women with spinal cord injury. *Sexuality and Disability, 5*(3), 158–171.

INDEX

INDEX

Page references in **bold** indicate glossed terms.

A

AASECT, *see* American Association of Sex Educators, Counselors, and Therapists

abnormal chromosome combination, gender-identity/role determination and, 137, 138

abortifacients, postcoital contraceptives as, **124**

abortion: law and, 483; legalization of, and sexual liberation of women, 5, 7; methods of, 127–129; postcoital contraceptives and, 124; rape and, 359; safety and, 129–130; self-induced, 104, 106, 127; selective, and multiple fetuses, 83; selective, and sex selection, 91

abnormal, **227**

absolute dysfunctions, 433

abstinence: as viable alternative to avoid sexually transmitted diseases, 386; as method of birth control, 111, 115; as only permissible birth control method, 104; lack of reality of, as birth control method, 7–8; Roman Catholic church and, 106, 241; *see also* asexuality; chastity

abuse, sexual, 349–366

academic setting: rape and, 355–356; sexual harassment and, 346–347, 348, 350

acceptance, identity, and homosexual identity formation, 290, 292

acquaintance rape, **352,** 355–357

acquired immunodeficiency syndrome: **401;** *see also* AIDS

activating effect, of hormones in human sexual response, **73**

activity, sexual, variance in degree of, 310–313

actual use failure rate: **114;** of birth control methods, 111–113

acyclovir, 383

Adam Principle, 138

adolescence: **174;** heterosexuality in, 177–180; homosexuality in, 176–177; masturbation in, 176–177; premarital sex and, 20–21; prostitution and,

328–329; self-centered sex in, 175–176; sex among, 7–8, 20–21, 176–180; sexual abuse in, 364; committing sexual abuse in, 363; sexual preference in, 286; sexuality in, 174–180

adoption, unintended pregnancy and, 126

adrenarche, in pubertal development, 143

adult gender-identity/role, 146

adult videos, 471

adultery: 183, 326–327; consensual, 183, 326, 327; conventional, 326, 327; recreational, 183; toleration, 326–327; *see also* extramarital sex

adultery toleration, **326–327**

advertising, sexual messages of, 474–475

affectional preferences, homosexuality and, **276**

Africa, spreading of AIDS, 403, 405

African green monkeys, origins of AIDS and, 403

afterbirth, **98**

Agape relationships, friendship, sexuality and, 215, 217

age: choosing between birth control methods and, 113; birth defects and, 40; effect of, on human sexual response, 74–75; homosexual behavior in preindustrial societies and, 280; *see also* aging

agenesis (absence) of the penis, **390**

age-structured homosexuality, in preindustrial societies, 280

aging: heterosexual intercourse and, 190; homosexuality and, 296–297; masturbation and, 189–190; myths regarding sex and, 186–190; sexual problems of, 188; sexuality and, 185–191; *see also* age

agnostics, 243–244

AIDS (acquired immunodeficiency syndrome): **401;** circumcision and, 405; college students and, 181; condoms and, 7, 263; evolution of, 401–402; fear of, and sexual functioning, 444; in filmmaking, 471; genital herpes and, 383; HIV and, 404; homosexuality and, 301–302; intravenous drug use and, 405–406; oral sex and, 7, 263,

405; origin of, 403–404; pornography and, 477; prevalence of, 403, 404, 405; prostitution and, 328; rights and responsibilities of sexual partners and, 483–484; sex education and, 244, 246, 247, 282; sex research and, 15–16; sexual intercourse and, 7, 263, 405; sexual revolution and, 7; as agent of value change, 7; *see also* HIV

AIDS-related complex, forms of AIDS and, 411

air embolisms, blowing on vagina and, 262

alcohol: as chemical aphrodisiac, 264; during pregnancy, and fetal alcohol syndrome, 96; penile erection and, 436; sexual dysfunction from, 442

allantois, 84

altruistic relationships, friendship, sexuality and, 215, 217

ambisexual: definition of, **278;** *see also* bisexual

American Association of Sex Educators, Counselors, and Therapists (AASECT): attitudes towards sex education and, 24, 244; certification of sex therapists and, 448; ethics in sex therapy, 455

American Association of University Women (AAUW), on gender differences in child development, 155–156

American Law Institute, 480

American Plains Indians, practice of berdache among, 280, 314

American Psychiatric Association, on homosexuality as mental illness, 282

American Red Cross, transmission of HIV through blood products and, 406–407

amniocentesis, **93**

amnion, **84**

amniotic sac: 84; during birth process, 97

ampicillin, effect of, on birth control pills, 116

amputation, sexual identity through, 343

amputation love, 343

AMSEX (American Sexology), 473

anal intercourse: **263,** 349; AIDS and, 7, 263; sodomy laws, 303–304; risk of transmission of AIDS and, 405

anal stage, of psychosexual development, 167

anatomical differences, between heterosexuals and homosexuals in human brain, 284–285

androgen, **73**

androgen insensitivity syndrome, gender-identity/role and, 140

androgenized females, gender-identity/role and, 140

androgyny, gender-identity/role and, **160**

anejaculation, **52**

animal: AIDS virus and, 403, 409; sex with, 332–333; testing of, and HIV vaccine, 417

animal testing, of HIV vaccines, 417

anorchism, **390**

anthropology, on sexual activities, 232

antibiotics: birth control pill and, 116; chlamydia and, 379, 380; for gonorrhea, 377–378; HIV viral infections and, 409–410, 416; sexual revolution and, 7; sexually transmitted diseases and, 376; for syphilis, 378

antigay violence, 281

antihistimes, vaginal lubrication and, 437–438

antiviral drugs, treatment for HIV and, 416

anxiety, ejaculation response and, 440

aphrodisiacs, **264**

apotemnophilia, **343**

Aranda, homosexuality among, 232

ARC, *see* AIDS-related complex

areola, **37**

Armed Forces: homosexuals and, 304; sexual harassment and, 345–346

arousal, difficulties in, 435–437

arousal phase dysfunctions, 434

arrested sexual development, homosexuals as suffering from, 285

art: nudity and sex in, 462–464; portrayal of sexual activities in, 228; visual, 464

art galleries, and obscene and indecent art, 463

Art of Living, The (Fromm), 209–210

Art of Love, 464

artificial embryonation, **90**

artificial insemination: **88–89;** in vitro fertilization and, 88–90

artists' boycott, of art gallery, 463

asceticism, sexual values and, **240**

asexuality: 311, **313;** variance in sexual activity and, 311; *see also* abstinence; chastity

asphyxiation, autoerotic, 332

atheists, 243–244

atrophic vaginitis, 382

attitudes: leisure time and, 6–7; sexual revolution and, 4–5; towards sexuality, 19–24

Attorney General's Commission on Pornography (1986), 478–479

attraction: marriage and sexual, 182; confusing of, with romantic attachments, 208

auditory disabilities, sexuality and, 250

authority, questioning of, and sexual attitudes, 5–6

autoerotic asphyxiation, **332**

autoeroticism: **100;** *see also* masturbation

autofellatio, male masturbation and, **258**

aversions, sexual, 434–435

azidothymidine (AZT), treating HIV and, 416

AZT (azidothymidine), treating HIV and, 416

B

baby boom, 103

"Baby M" case, 92

bacterial vaginosis, 381

bag of waters, *see* amniotic sac

Baldwin, James, 465

Balinese cultures, sexual standards in, 232–233

Bancroft, John, unified theoretical model of sexual development of, 170–171

Bangladesh, access to birth control in, 109

Bardwick, Judith, on discriminatory process of socialization, 152

Barnes v. Glen Theater, 466

barrier methods, of birth control: 117–120; age factors in choosing, 113

Bartholin's gland, **30–31**

basal body temperature (BBT) method, of natural family planning, 121

behavior, sexual revolution and sexual, 4

behavior modification, homosexual behavior and, 288

behavior therapy: goals of, 448–449; treating sexual dysfunctions and, **447**

Bell, Alan, research of, on sexual preference, 286–287

Bem, Sandra: on androgyny, 160; on learning gender-identity/roles, 151

ben-wa (ba-wa) balls, female masturbation and, 257, 322

berdache: **314;** gender-reversed homosexuality and, 280

bestiality, **332–333**

betrayal, effects of child abuse and sense of, 364

Bible, on onanism and masturbation, 9, 260

Bieber, Irving, on parental influences on homosexuality, 285

bigenderist, 293

biological determinants model, of homosexuality, 283–285

biology, of pregnancy, 96–97

biphobia, 293

birth canal, **97**

birth control: cost of, and developing countries, 109; historical perspective of, 103–104; laws and, 483; methods of, 111–124; Roman Catholic church, 241; sharing responsibility for, 114–115; *see also* birth control movement; contraceptives; specific method

birth control movement, 104

birth control pills: 111, 115–116; cost of, and developing countries, 109; health and, 107

birth defects: age of mother and, 40; fetal testing for, 93–94; multiple fetuses

and, 83; incidence of, in United States, 96

birth process, 97–98

birthing alternatives, 98–99

birthing rooms, birthing alternatives and, **99**

bisensual, 293

bisexual, **278,** 293–294

blastocyst, **84,** 85

blended orgasm, 69

blindness, sex and, 250

Bloch, Iwan, 8

blood cells, white, AIDS virus and, 410

blood donors: transmission of HIV and, 403, 406–407; in Zambia and HIV, 403

blood transfusions, transmission of HIV and, 406–407, 409

blue movies, 471

Blumstein, Philip, 15

body exploration, self-help approaches to sex therapy, 449

body image: of child; and gender-identity/role, 142–143; sexuality in adolescence and, 175

body temperature, natural family planning and, 121

bond: **99;** in infant development, 172; parental, and birthing rooms, 99

bondage: **332;** devices of, 322, 332

Borneman, Ernest: on erogenous zones of infants, 172, 325; on sensuousness in old age, 191

"Boston marriages," same-sex relationships and, 296

brachioproctic activity, among homosexual males, 294

brain: fetal hormones and, 139–140, 141; effect of, on homosexual development, 283–285

breakups, dealing with, 218–219

breasts: 37–39; cancer of, 38–39, 55

bride scrolls, 462

brothels, **328**

bulbourethral glands: **50;** effect of age on male sexual response and, 75

Bundy, Ted, 475

C

calendar method, of natural family planning, 121

call boys: **327;** *see also* prostitution

call girls: **328;** *see also* female prostitutes; prostitution

Calymmatobacterium granulomatis, 385

cancer: breast, 38–39, 55; of cervix, 36, 391, 394; estrogen replacement therapy and, 55; Kaposi's sarcoma and, 408; ovarian, 394; of penis, 390; prostate, 388; sexual activity and, 251, 395; of testes, 46–47, 390; uterine, 36, 55, 391

Candida albicans, 381

catharides, as chemical aphrodisiac, **264**

Carnes, Patrick, 344, 345

case studies, conducting sex research and, **18**

Cass, Vivienne, on homosexual identity formation, 288–290, 292

Cassel, Carol, on sexuality and intimate friendships, 217
casual sex: AIDS and, 7; emergence of 333–334
catharsis theory, **476**
cats, AIDS and, 409
CDC, *see* U.S. Public Health Service's Centers for Disease Control
celibacy: variance in sexual activity and, **313;** *see also* abstinence
censorship: federal funding and, 464; freedom of speech and press, 477
Centers for Disease Control, *see* U.S. Public Health Service's Centers for Disease Control
cerebral palsy, sex and, 251
certified nurse-midwives, 99
cervical cap: 112, 117–**118;** age and, 113
cervical intraepithelial neoplasia (CIN), 384, **394**
cervix: **35;** during birth process, 97; cancer of, 36, 391, 394
cesarian section, **98**
chancre, 378
chancroid, **385**
chemical aphrodisiacs, 264
child development, psychosexual, in psychoanalytic theory, 167
child molesting, **360**–366
Child Protection and Obscenity Enforcement Act of 1988, 475
childhood: factors of, in influencing gender-identity/role, 142–143; sexuality in, 172–174
children: AIDS and, 404–405; 407; gender differences in moral development of, 241–242; pornography and, 475, 479; sexuality of, 14; therapy for abused, 366
chlamydia: 7, 376, **377,** 379–380, 385, 392; diagnosis and treatment of, 379–380; nongonococcal urethritis (NGU) and, 380; symptoms of, 379
Chlamydia trachomatis, 379–380
chorion, **84**
chorionic villi sampling (CVS), 93–**94**
chromosomes, influence of, on determining gender-identity/role, 136–137
cilia, **37**
CIN, *see* cervical intraepithelial neoplasia
circumcision: of females, **31,** 32–33; males and, 48–50; risk of transmission of AIDS and, 405
Civil Rights Act (1964), 348
classified advertisements, for social connections, 468
climacteric: **53;** male, 55–56; *see also* menopause
climax: **62;** *see also* orgasm
clinical research, **18**
clitoral hood, *see* prepuce
clitoral orgasms, 69
clitoral stimulation, orgasms in women in, 265
clitoral tickler, 322
clitoridectomy, 31, **32,** 33
clitoris: 30, **31;** clitoridectomies and, 31, 32, 33; infection of, 438; stimulation of, and orgasms, 265–266
clone, **91**
cloning, **91**–92
cock rings, 322

coercion: sexual activity and, 341, 349–366; sexual values and, 243
COGENE (Committee on Genetic Experimentation), 88
cognitive-developmental theory, on learning gender-identity/roles, 150–151
cohabitation, **182**
coital standard, of sexual behavior, 230
coitus, **230**
coitus interruptus, as method of birth control, 111, **115**
college students: acquaintance rape and, 355–357; sexual harassment, 346–347, 348, 350; sexual life of, 181
comarital sex: **327;** *see also* mate swapping
combination type, birth control pill, 111, 115
combining of chromosomes, influence of, on determining gender-identity/role, **136**–137
coming out, of closet, homosexuality and, **290,** 291, 296
commitment, role of, in Sternberg's triangular theory of love, 210, 211, 212, 213
Committee on Genetic Experimentation (COGENE), 88
communication: effective, 200–202; games of, 199–200; gender differences in, 205–208; for healthy sexual relationships, 367–368; language and, 196–198; myths about, 198–199; personality types in, 204–205; process, 196, 197; quarreling and, 202–204; about sex, 195–202; sexual expectations and, 342, 443
companionate love, in triangular theory of love, 212, 213
comparison, identity, and homosexual identity formation, 290–291
complete love, in triangular theory of love, 212, 213
compulsive sexual activity, 344
computers: sex education and, 245; sex information, 473
Comstock Laws, **104**
"conditional" double standard, 22
conditioning, psychosexual development and, 168–169
condoms: 112, **119**–120; AIDS and, 7, 262, 263, 264; cost of, and developing countries, 109; female, 119; use of, during sex and, 7, 262; sexually transmitted diseases (STDs) and, 387
condyloma acuminata, 383
confidentiality, patient, HIV and, 418
conflict resolution, effective, in relationships, 203–204
confusion, identity, and homosexual identity formation, 290
congenital syphilis, 378–379
conjunctivitis, 379
consensual adultery, **183, 326,** 327
consensual telephone sex, 329
conservatives: reaction of, to sexual revolution, 5, 6
Constitution, U.S.: child development and, 475; on order and morality, 467
consummate love, in triangular theory of love, 212, 213
contraceptives: availability of, and sexual liberation of women, 5, 7, 104; cost

of, and developing countries, 109; deciding about, 105–110, 113–114; ethical considerations with, 106–107; factors in choosing, 110, 113–114; health considerations concerning, 107–108; historical perspective of use of, 103–104; legal issues of, 483; postcoital, 124; psychology and, 108–110; religion and, 106–107; society and, 108–110; *see also* birth control; specific method
controlled experiment, **18**–19
conventional adultery, **326,** 327
cooperative delivery, birthing alternatives and, 98–99
Copper T 380 A, 120
coprophilia, **332**
Corcoran Gallery of Art, 463
core gender-identity/role, **142**–143
corona, **47**
corpora cavernosa, 47, 48
corpus luteum, **40,** 41, 42, 43
corpus spongiosum, 47, 48
cost: birth control in developing countries, 109; factors in choosing birth control and, 114
cottonseed oil, new male contraceptives and, 123
counseling, sex: 368–369; *see also* sex therapy
counterculture movement, sexual revolution and, 5–6
Cowper's glands: **50;** effect of age on male sexual response and, 75
crabs, 384
cremasteric muscles, 45
cross-cultural differences, *see* cultural differences
cross-dressing: 147, 314–316; labeling of, 229; myths regarding homosexuality and, 297–298
cross-genderists, 147, **316**
cryptorchidism, **390**
crystitis, **391**
cultural differences: incest taboos and, 365; in sexual behavior, 16, 231–233, 365; in sexual practices and AIDS, 16
cultural perspectives: on homosexual behavior, 232–233, 279–280; labeling of sex terms and, 227–229
cultural scenarios, sexual scripts and, 170
culture, sex-obsessed, 432
cunnilingus: **262;** *see also* oral sex
curiosity, sexual, in childhood, 172–173
CVS, *see* chorionic villi sampling

D

D & C, *see* dilation and curettage
D & E, *see* dilation and evacuation
Dalton, Katharina, on premenstrual syndrome, 44
dancing, nude, and U.S. Supreme Court, 466
d'Ancona, H., 466
date rape, **352;** *see also,* acquaintance rape
DDI (dideoxyinosine), for treating HIV, 416
dead, sex with, 333

dead air, communication and, 198, 201–202

deafness, sex and, 250

decriminalization, of prostitution, **483**

dentists, transmission of HIV and, 407

deoxyribonucleic acid (DNA): fertilization and, **82;** genetic engineering and, 85; mapping of human, structure, 88; retroviruses and, 410

DES (diethylstilbestrol), 124

desire phase, in human sexual response, **63**

desire phase dysfunctions, 433–435

developing countries, cost of birth control and, 109

development: fetal, 83–84, 86–87; moral, of child, 241; psychosexual, 9, 165–171, 285

deviation: 8–9; as sex label, **229**

DHT-deficiency syndrome, gender-identity/role and, 140–141

diabetes: 441; sexual activity and, 395; sexual dysfunction in elderly and, 189

dial-a-porn, 473

diaphragm: 112, **117**–118; age and, 113

Dickinson, Robert Latou, 10

Dick-Read, Grantly, natural childbirth and, 98

dideoxyinosine (DDI), treating HIV with, 416

diethylstilbestrol (DES), 124, **394**

dihydrotestosterone-deficiency syndrome, gender-identity/role and, 140–141

dilation and curettage (D & C): 36; abortion and, **129**

dilation and evacuation (D & E), **128**–129

dildos, 257, 321

Dionysian festivals, fertility rites of, 464

directions, gender differences in asking for, 205

disability groups, sex and sex issues of, 247–252

discrimination: conditioning in psychosexual development and, **169;** sex, 151, 154, 156

disempowerment, effects of child abuse and, 364

divorce: 184–185; cohabitation and, 182

dizygotic twin, *see* fraternal twins

dl-norgestrel, as post-coital contraceptive, 124

DNA, *see* deoxyribonucleic acid

dolls, inflatable, male masturbation and, 258

double bind, 215

double standard: attitudes toward, 22; among college students, 181; premarital sex and, 20; variance in sexual activity and, 34

drug abuse, intravenous, transmission of AIDS and, 405–406

drugs: effect of, on pregnancy, 96–97; prenatal influence of, 15; sexual dysfunction and, 442

dry ejaculation, 389

dyadic relationships, capacity for, and psychosexual development, 171

dysfunction(s), sexual: 63, **344;** absolute, 433; arousal difficulties as, 435–437; causes of, 440; desire phase problems as, 433–435; drugs and alcohol and, 442–443; in elderly, 188–189; folk remedies for treating, 445–446; lack of

ejaculation control as, 439; orgasmic, 438; partial, 433; performance, 443; post-ejaculatory pain as, 440; relationships and, 443; sexual response cycle, 433; situational, 433; stimulation of erogenous zones as therapy for, 261–262; total, 433; treatments for, 444–456

dysmenorrhea, **42**

dyspaneuria, 392

E

E. coli (Escherichia coli), **391**

East Bay Melanesians, homosexuality among, 232

ectopic pregnancy, **84**

Education Amendments of 1972, 348

egg bank, 90

egg cells, *see* ova

ejaculation: **51**–53; arousal difficulties in; in female sexual response, 69–70; mythical performance standards and, 432; premature, 434–440; retarded, 438; sexual dysfunction and, 431–432, 434; spontaneous, 176

ejaculatory control: masturbation to improve, 449–450; treatment for, 439

ejaculatory duct, 50

ejaculatory inevitability, **71**

elderly, *see* aging

Electra complex, in psychosexual development, 167

elephantiasis, *see* lymphogranuloma venereum

ELISA (enzyme-linked immunosorbent assay), test for HIV, **413**–414

Ellis, Henry Havelock, sex research of, 9–10

embedding, as an advertising technique, 474

embryo: development of, 83–**84**, 86; freezing of, 89

emotional blackmail, 344

emotional managers, women as, in relationships, 203

empathy, in communication, 201

empty love, in triangular theory of love, 212, 213

endometrial hyperplasia, **394**

endometriosis, 394, **395**

endometrium, **35**, 40, 53, 84

engagement ovaries, 395

England: laws prohibiting homosexual acts in, 285; *see also* Victorian era

enzyme-linked immunosorbert assay (ELISA), test for HIV, 413–414

enzyme-sensitive immunoassay testing, 377

epidemiology, **404**, 409

epididymis, **45**, 51

epididymitis, **387**

episiotomy, **97**–98

epispadias, **390**, 391

erectile dysfunction, **435**, 441

erection: **47**–48; in male infants, 171

Erikson, Erik, theory of psychosocial development, 168, 169, 181

erogenous zone: of infants, **172**, stimulation of, 261–262

Eros relationships, friendship, sexuality and, 215, 217

erotica, as distinguished from pornography, **461**

erotocentricity, defining normalcy in sexual behavior and, 233

erotophilia, variance in sexual activity and, 311

erotophobia, variance in sexual activity and, 311

ERT, *see* estrogen replacement therapy

escorts, *see* male prostitutes; prostitution

estrogen: 36, **40**, 41, 42, 43; effect of, on homosexual development, 283–284; sexual desire and, 73

estrogen replacement therapy (ERT), **54**–55

ethical standards, of professionals, and sexual abuse, 349

ethics: AIDS and, 418–420; contraceptives and, 106–107; use of fetal tissue and, 120; frozen embryos and, 89; marriage and, 184; in sex research, 19; sex selection and, 91; sexual surrogates and, 446; surrogate motherhood and, 92–93; *see also* morality

ethinyl estradiol, as postcoital contraceptive, 124

Ethiopia, cost of birth control methods and, 109

ethnocentricity, defining, normalcy and, **233**

etiquette, sexual, 216

Etruscan paintings, of sexual activities, 462

eugenics, sperm banks and, 89

Eve Principle, 138

excitement, **62**

excitement phase: in female sexual response, 67; in human sexual response, **62**, 64, 67, 70; in male sexual response, 70

exhibitionism: **329**–330, 361; cultural differences in, 232; group sex and, 325

experimental research, 18–19

expert opinion, defining normalcy in sexual behavior by, 233

exploitation, sexual, 341, 342, 344–349

exploration, sex, of children, 172, 173

external values, **239**

extramarital sex: **326**–327; attitudes toward, and sexual revolution, 4; group sex and, 325, 326, 327; mate swapping and, 325, 326, 327; polygamy and, 183–184; variations of, 183–184, 326–327

extraversion, personality types in communication and, 204, 205

F

face-to-face intercourse, 266–269

falling in love, *see* infatuation

fallopian tubes, **36**–37

family, effect of, on homosexuality, 285

family, sexual: 322–323, 462; in masturbation, 258; as aid in sexual stimulation, 263 family planning: contraceptives and, 105; Roman Catholic church and, 106; natural, as method of birth control, 106, 111, 121

Famsidar, treating HIV and, 415–416

FAS, *see* fetal alcohol syndrome

father-daughter incestuous relationships, 365

fatuous love, in triangular theory of love, 212, 213

feedback effect, of female hormones, 40

Feinberg, David, 465

feline leukemia virus (FeLV), links between animals and AIDS and, 409

fellatio: **262**; *see also* oral sex

FeLV, *see* feline leukemia virus

female condoms, 119

female prostitution: 327–328; historical records regarding, 228; *see also* prostitution

female sex organs, 29–44

female-to-male transsexuals, 316–317, 318

femininity: 12, 147, 148–150; *see also* gender-identity/roles

feminism, gender-identity/roles and, 151–156

feminist therapy, 158–160

fertility awareness approach, *see* abstinence; family planning

fertility rites, of Dionysian festivals, 464

fertilization, 81–83

fetal alcohol syndrome (FAS), alcohol during pregnancy and, **96**

fetal development, 83–84, 86–87

fetal gonads, development of, and gender-identity/role, 137–138

fetal hormones: brain and, 139–140, 141; development of fetal gonads and, 138

fetal surgery, **94**

fetal technology: artificial insemination and, 88–89; cloning and, 91–92; genetic engineering and, 85, 88; in vitro fertilization and, 89–90; sex selection and, 90–91; surrogate motherhood and, 92–93

fetal testing, 93–94

fetal tissue, use of, 129

fetally androgenized females, gender-identity/role and, 140

fetishism: 9, **323**–324; distinguishing transvestism from, 314–315

fetus, **84**, 86–87

fibrous hymen, **391**

fighting, *see* quarreling

films, sexually explicit, 468–471

fimbriae, 36, 37

Fiona MacLeod, William Sharp as, 316

First Amendment: child pornography, 475; on order and morality, 467

fisting, 294

Fitzgerald, Louise, 346, 347

fixed world view, religious tradition, 240

folk remedies, for treating sexual dysfunctions, 445–446

follicles, **36**

follicle-stimulating hormone: **40**, 41, 43; menstruation and, 43; in sperm production, 51

follicular phase, of menstrual cycle, 40, 41, 43

Food and Drug Administration, postcoital contraceptives and, 124

foreplay, **230**

foreskin, **47**, 48, 49, 50

fraternal twins, **82**–83

free testosterone index (FTI), male climacteric and, 55–56

Friedan, Betty, on surrogate motherhood, 92–93

French sickness, 375

French tickler, 322

French-kissing: 261; spreading of AIDS virus and, 411

frenulum, **47**

Freud, Sigmund: on learning gender-identity/roles, 150; homosexual development and, 283; homosexuals and, 285; on personality development, 285; on effect of hormones on psychosexual development, 283; on psychosexual development, 9, 166–167, 283; sexual dysfunctions and, 446; sexual theory of, 8, 9, 14

friendship, types of, and sexuality, 215, 217

frigidity, 431, 435

Fromm, Erich, on love as art form, 209–210

frottage, **329**

frotteur, **329**

frozen embryos, ethical considerations over, 89

FSH, *see* follicle-stimulating hormone

FTI, *see* free testosterone index

fundamentalist perspective, on religion, 240

fundus, 35

G

G spot, **69**, 70

gag rule, and family planning agencies, 127

Gagnon, John: on sexual standards in other cultures, 231; social script theory of, 170

Gallo, Robert C.: discovery of AID virus and, 404; discovery of retroviruses and, 410

games: communication, 199–200; power, 199; relationship, 199; sexual, in adults, 199–200; sexual, in children, 172, 174

gamete intra-fallopian transfer (GIFT), **90**

gametes, storage of, and artificial insemination, 89

Gardnerella vaginalis, 381

gay(s): **277**, 466; gender-identity/roles and, 147; *see also* gay community; homosexual behavior; homosexuals; homosexuality

gay community, 299–301

Gebhard, Paul, on anthropological data on sexual activities, 232

gender aware therapy, 158–160

gender differences: in communication, 205–208; in homosexual identity formation, 292–293; in masturbatory practices, 20; in moral reasoning, 154–155; in quarreling, 202–203; in same-sex behavior, 294–295; in sex with animals, 333; in sexual activity, 311–312, 313–314; in sexual fantasy, 322–333; in transvestism, 314–315; *see also* sex differences

gender dysphorias, **147**–148

gender gap, 154–155

gender schema theory, on learning gender-identity/roles, 151

gender transpositions: **147**–148; cross-dressing in young boys as expression of, 316; prediction, 319–320; treatment of, 319

gender-identity/roles: **135**–136; androgyny and, 160; berdache and, 280, 314; changing of, and sexual revolution, 6; determining, 141–143; drug exposure and, 15; expressing, 146–148, 314–320; feminism and, 151–152; gender aware therapy and, 158–160; growing up and, 152–156; homosexual behavior in preindustrial societies and, 280; infancy and childhood factors in determining, 141–143; learning of, 150–151; men and, 156–157; influence of prenatal hormones and drug exposure on, 15; prenatal factors in determining, 136–141; puberty and, 143–146; in unified theoretical model of psychosexual development, 171

gender-reversed homosexuality, berdache tradition and, 280

gene transfer, 88

general sexual dysfunction, **435**

generalization, conditioning in psychosexual development and, **169**

generation gap, in sexual values, 6

genetic engineering, 85, **88**

genetics, effect of, on homosexuality, 283, 284, 285

genital herpes: **382**, 484; diagnosis of, 383; symptoms of 382–383; treatment of, 383

genital stage, in psychosexual development, 167

genital warts, **383**–384

genuineness, in communication, 201

germ theory of disease, attitudes toward masturbation and, 19–20

Gertz, Allison, 412–413

gestation period, human, 84

gestation surrogacy, *see* surrogate motherhood

Gide, André, 465

GIFT, *see* gamete intra-fallopian transfer

gigolos, *see* male prostitutes; prostitution

Gilligan, Carol, research of, on gender differences in moral reasoning, 154–155

glans, **31**, **47**

GnRH, *see* gonadotropin releasing hormone

Goldman, Juliette, 14

Goldman, Ronald, 14

gonadarche, in pubertal development, 143

gonadotropin releasing hormone (GnRH), **40**

gonorrhea: 7, 375, **376**, 377; diagnosis of, 377; symptoms of, 377; treatment of, 377

gossypol, new male contraceptive and, 123

Gräfenberg, on female sexual response, 69

Graham, Robert, origin of sperm bank and, 89
granuloma inguinale, **385**
Greek: paintings, of sexual activities, 462; sculpture, 463
green monkeys, African, origins of AIDS and, 403
group marriage, **183**
group sex, 324–325
group therapy, treating sexual dysfunctions and, 447
guiding position, for genital stimulation, 451
guilt, sexuality in adolescence and, 175
Gurdon, J. D., cloning and, 91
gynecomastria, 145

H

Hammersmith, Sue Keifer, research of, on sexual preference, 286–287
handedness, incidence of homosexuality and, 285
harassment: sexual, **345**–351; verbal, 351
hard-core pornography, **471**
Harlow, Harry, research of, in support of social forces in psychosexual development, 168
HCG, see human chorionic gonadotropin
health factors, of choosing birth control method, 107–108
health-care workers, risks of HIV and, 407, 414–415, 419
hearing impaired, sexuality of, 250
heart disease, sexual activity and, 395
hedonists, sexual values and, **240**
Hedwig, Sophia, 316–317
Heiman, Julia, on gender stereotypes regarding reading, 66
Helms, Jesse, on federal funding of obscene and indecent art, 463
helper-client sexual exploitation, 349
hemophiliacs, transmission of AIDS and, **404,** 406
Hemophilus ducreyi, 385
Hepatitis A, 384
Hepatitis B, 384
HER principles, sexual pluralism and, 237
hereditary diseases, genetic engineering and, 88
heredity, homosexuality and, 284
Herman, Pee Wee, 480–481
Heroides, 464
herpes: 7, 382, 383; see also *Herpes simplex* virus type 1 (HSV-1); *Herpes simplex* virus type 2 (HSV-2)
herpes keratitis, 382
Herpes simplex virus type 1 (HSV-1), 382
Herpes simplex virus type 2 (HSV-2), 382, 383
heterogenous cultures, sexual standards in, 231–232
heterosexual: definition of, **277**–278; see also homosexuality; homosexuals
heterosexual assumption, 275
heterosexual sex: 264; in adolescents, 177–180; AIDS and, 7, 264, 405; in old age, 190

heterosexual standard, of sexual behavior, 230
heterosexuality, see heterosexual; heterosexual sex
Hill, Anita, 345
historical perspectives: of birth control, 103–104; of homosexuality, 275–276; labeling sexual types and, 227–229; records of existence of prostitution and homosexuality and, 228
Hite, Shere, 13–14
HIV (human immunodeficiency virus): **401,** 466; as agent of value change, 7; discovery of, 404; drugs and, 408–409; education, 422–424; mechanism of, 409–410; prevalence of, 404–405; risks of infection, 405–408; society and, 417–418; spreading of, 410–411; testing for, 412–415; treatment of, 415–416; vaccines for, 416–417; see also AIDS
HIV-2, 403, 409
home birth, 99
homoerotic photographs, 463
homogeneous cultures, sexual standards in, 231
homophobia: **281**–282, 283; AIDS and, 401; among counselors and therapists, 288; treatment for homosexuality and, 288; in United States government, 304; see also gays; homosexuality; homosexuals; lesbians
homosexual(s): AIDS and, 7; attitudes toward, 21; the Constitution and, 481; definition of, **277**; gender-identity/role of, 280; homophobia and, 281–282; labels and, 234; sexual problems of, 440; term of, 276; see also gays; homosexual behavior; homosexual identity; homosexuality; lesbians
homosexual behavior: in adolescents, 176–177; models of, 282–288; studying, 280–281
homosexual identity formation: gender differences in, 292–293; stages of, 288–290, 292; see also gender-identity/role
homosexualities, **287**
homosexuality: aging and, 296–297; AIDS and, 301–302; attitudes toward, and sexual revolution, 4; berdache tradition and, 280; as a cinematic theme, 470–471; cultural differences in, 279–280; cultural differences in attitudes toward, 232; gender-reversed, 280; group sex and, 325; historical perspective of, 275–276; historical records of, 228; identity formation in, 288–290, 292; incidences of, 278–279; Kinsey scale of sexual behavior and, 276–278; the law and, 303–304; marriage and, 304–305; models of, 283–288; myths regarding, 297–298; perspectives on, 275–276; religion and, 302; research on, 13; Roman Catholic church on, 142; society and, 299–325; subculture in, 299–301; see also homophobia; homosexual behavior; homosexual identity formation; homosexuals; human sexual response
honesty, equality, and responsibility (HER) principles, sexual pluralism and, 237

hookers: **328;** see also female prostitution; prostitution
hormones: cycles of, in men, 53; effect of, on homosexual development, 283–285; fetal, 138, 139–140, 141; human sexual response and, 73; at puberty, and gender-identity/role, 143–145; prenatal influence of, 15; see also specific hormone
hot flash, **54**
HTLV, see human T-lymphotropic leukemia virus
human chorionic gonadotropin (HCG), pregnancy tests, **96**
human genome, 88
human immunodeficiency virus: **401;** see also HIV
human papilloma virus (HPV), 383, 384
Human Sexual Inadequacy (Masters and Johnson), 431
human sexual response: 61–62; aging and, 73–75; female, 67–70; hormones and, 73; individual differences in, 63–67; Kaplan's three-phase model, 62–63; male, 70–75; Masters and Johnson and, 13, 62, 64
Human Sexual Response (Masters and Johnson), 13, 62
Human Sexuality Information and Advisory Service, 473
human T-lymphotropic leukemia virus (HTLV), discovery of HIV and, 404
Hunt, Morton, 13
hustlers: **327;** see also prostitution
H-Y antigen, development of fetal gonads and, **138**
hymen, **31,** 34–35, 391
hypersexuality, variance in sexual activity and, **311**
hypertension, pregnancy-induced, 99
hypnosis, for treating sexual dysfunctions, 446–447
hyposexuality, variance in sexual activity and, **311**
hypospadias, **390,** 391
hypothalamus: hormones and, 40; role of, in determining sexual orientation, 283–284
hysterectomy, sexual dysfunction in elderly and, 189

I

ICC, see invasive cancer of the cervix
ICSH, see interstitial-cell-stimulating hormone
identical twins, **82**–83
identification, advertising, 474
identity acceptance, homosexual identity formation and, 290, 292
identity comparison, homosexual identity formation and, 289–290
identity confusion, homosexual identity formation and, 289
identity formation, homosexual: gender differences in, 292–293; stages of, 288–290, 292; see also gender-identity/role
identity pride, homosexual identity formation and, 292

identity synthesis, homosexual identity formation and, 292

identity tolerance, homosexual identity formation and, 290

Ik hunting group, intercourse and love among, 232

imitation, learning gender-identity/roles and, 150

immune system, HIV and, 408, 409-410, 415

immunoblot test, for HIV, 414

imperforate hyman, **391**

impotence, 431, **432**-433

in loco parentis, role of American colleges, **181**

in vitro fertilization, 88, **89**-90

inborn sexual instinct theory, of psychosexual development, 166

incest: abortion and, 359, **364**-366; taboo, 365

incest taboo, **365**

incompatibility, sexual, dysfunctions and, 445

independent rights doctrine, 481

Indians, American Plains, practice of berdache among, 280, 314

individual perspective, of homosexual experience, and studying homosexual behavior, 280

individuality, sexual: 234-235; development of, 235-236, 238; variability of, 313-314

induced abortion: **127**; *see also,* abortion

"inert" pills, birth control pills and, 115

infancy: factors of, in influencing gender-identity/role, 141-142; sexuality in, 171-172

infants: in psychoanalytic theory of psychosexual development, 167; sexuality of, and Freud, 9; transmission of HIV and, 404-405, 407

infatuation, versus being in love, **209**-210

infertility: **94,** 95, 376; female, 94; male, 94

infibulation, **32**-33

infidelity, *see* extramarital sex

inflatable dolls, male masturbation and, 258

information utilities, 473

informed consent, ethics in sex research and, **19**

infundibulum, 36, 37

inhibited sexual desire (ISD), **434,** 441

innate biological drive, and sexual gratification, 433

instinct theory, of psychosexual development, 166

institutions: for mentally and physically handicapped and sex, 252; sexual prohibition in, for elderly, 188

integrated social factors theory, of psychosexual development, 167-168

interceptors, postcoital contraceptives as, 124

intercourse, *see* anal intercourse; interfemoral intercourse; sexual intercourse

interest, sexual, varying degrees of, 310-313

interfemoral intercourse, 263

internal values, **239**

International Council of Scientific Unions, establishment of Committee on

Genetic Experimentation (COGENE) and, 88

interpersonal scripts, as sexual script, 170

interstitial cells, **45**

interstitial-cell-stimulating hormone (ICSH), **51**

interviewing, 17-18

intervir, 383

intimacy: adults and, 181-182; establishment of, 213-214; in infant development, 172; in psychosocial development, 168; relationship games and, 199; sexual, 181-182; in Sternberg's triangular theory of love, 210, 211, 212, 213

intimate friendships, sexuality and, 217

intrapsychic scripts, sexual scripts and, 170

intrauterine device (IUD): 113, **120;** ethical controversy over, 107; health considerations and, 107, 108

intravenous (IV) drug users, transmission of HIV and, 405-406

introitus, 30, **31,** 34

intromission, 265

introversion, personality types in communication and, 204, 205

invasive cancer of the cervix (ICC), **394**

ISD, *see* inhibited sexual desire

IUD (intrauterine device): 113, **120;** ethical controversy over, 107; health considerations and, 107, 108

IV drug users, transmission of HIV and, 405-406

J

jealousy: 217-218; group sex and, 325

Johnson, Virginia E.: 12-13; human sexual response and, 62, 64; on premature ejaculation, 439-440; on sexual dysfunctions, 261-262, 444-445, 446; theory of, on sexual dysfunctions, 261-262; sexual response model phases, 433

Jorgensen, Christine/George, 317

Judaism, sexual values and, 241

"Just Say No" philosophy: for adolescents, 7-8; sex education and, 246; *see also* abstinence; asexuality

K

Kaplan, Helen Singer, and Kaplan's three-phase model of human sexual response, 62-63

Kaposi's sarcoma, HIV and, **408**

Karl, Herman, 316-317

Kegel exercises, 70, 393, 442

Kenya, cost of birth control methods and, 109

Khorana, Har Gobind, genetic engineering and, 85

kiddie porn, **475**

Kiersey Temperament Sorter, personality types for communicating and, 204, 205

Kinsey, Alfred C.: 11, 20; on attitudes toward oral sex, 262; on incidence of homosexuality, 278-279; on masturbation, 255, 256; orgasms in infants and, 171; focus of research of, 309; reliability of research of, 17-18; on sexual behavior, 276-278, 476; scale of sexual behavior, 276-278

Kinsey Institute for Research in Sex, Gender, and Reproduction: 11, 12, 15; models of homosexual development and, 286-287; development of sexual individuality and, 235-236

Kinsey scale: as example of individual perspective on homosexual behavior, 280; of sexual behavior, 276-278

kissing: 261; spreading of AIDS virus and, 411

Klein, Marty, 345

Klein Sexual Orientation Grid (KSOG): development of sexual individuality and, 236; models of homosexuality and, 238

kleptomania, fetishism and, **324**

Klinefelter's syndrome, 137

kneeling, rear entry position, 269

Kohlberg, Lawrence, on moral development of children, 241

Krafft-Ebing, Richard van: attitudes toward masturbation and, 9, 20, 228; sex research of, 8-9

L

labeling, in psychosexual development, 171

labia majora, *see* major lips

labia minora, *see* minor lips

labor: **97**-98; *see also* birthing alternatives

lactation, **37**

Lady Chatterley's Lover (Lawrence), 465

Lamaze method, **98**

laminaria, **128**

laparoscopy, **122**

laparotomy, **122**

latency period: **14;** in psychosexual development, 167

LAV, *see* lympho-adenopathy syndrome

law: homosexuality and, 303-304; homosexual marriages, 304-305

Lawson, Annette, on extramarital sex, 327

Lebanon, cost of birth control methods and, 109

Leboyer, Frederick, birthing rooms and, 99

left-handedness, incidence of homosexuality in, 285

legalistic view, of sexual ethics, 239

Legion of Decency, 468

leisure time, sexual attitudes and, 6-7

lesbians: 466; definition of, **277;** gender-identity/roles and, 147; psychoanalytic model of homosexuality and, 285; *see also* gay community; homosexual behavior; homosexuals; homosexuality

levator ani, 33-34

Leydig cells, 45

LH, *see* luteinizing hormone

libido: in psychoanalytic theory, **166**–167; in psychosexual development, 168

liking, in triangular theory of love, 212, 213

listening: in communication, 201; gender differences in, 206–207

literature: contemporary, 465; portrayal of sexual activities in, 228

living together, 182

love: 209; aging and, 186–187; in childhood, 174; confusing sex and, 214–215; coping with loss of, 218–219; as excuse for sex, 208; marriage and, in Western culture, 182; Sternberg's triangular theory of, 210–212, 213; versus infatuation, 209–210; vulnerability and, 208

lumpectomy, **39**

luteal secretion, 40, 41, 43

luteinizing hormone (LH): **40**; effect of, on homosexual development, 284; in menstruation, 40, 41, 43; in sperm production, 50–51; test for, and natural family planning, 121

lympho-adenopathy syndrome, discovery of HIV and, 404

lymphocytes, AIDS virus and, 410

lymphogranuloma venereum (LGV), **385**

M

macrophages, HIV and, 410

magazines, sex-oriented, 465, 468

major lips, **30**

male menopause: 56; *see also* climacteric

male prostitutes: 327; *see also* prostitution

male sex organs, 44–53

male-male rape, 358

males, *see* masculinity; men

male-to-female transsexuals, 317, 318

mammography, **38**

man on top, woman lying on her abdomen, rear entry position, 276

man on top, woman supine position, 267

Mangaia, sexual behavior on, 232

manual stimulation, 263

Mapplethorpe, Robert, 463

marijuana: as chemical aphrodisiac, 264; use of, during pregnancy, 96, 97; sexual performance and, 442, effect of, on testosterone and sperm production, 264

marital rape, **357**, 482

Marmor, Judd, on normal variant model of homosexual behavior, 285–286

marriage: 182; group, 183; for homosexuals, 304–305; intercourse and, 271–272; open-ended, 183; trends in, 184; unconsummated, 437

masculinity: 12, 147, 148–150; *see also* gender-identity/roles

masochist: 8, **331**–332, 343; labels and, 234; *see also* sadomasochism

massage parlors, **328**

mastectomy, **39**

Masters, William H.: 12–13; human sexual response and, 62, 64; on premature ejaculation, 439–440; on sexual dysfunctions, 261–262, 444–445, 446;

theory of, on sexual dysfunctions, 261–262; sexual response model phases, 433

masturbation: 9, 10, 256; in adolescence, 175–176, 177; changing attitudes towards, 19–20; in young children, 172; clitoridectomies and, 32; devices for, 257, 258; exhibitionism and, 330; use of fantasy in, 258; fetishism and, 324; frottage and, 329; historical attitudes towards, 228–229; language used to communicate about, 197; men and, 257–258; morality and, 260; mutual, 263; myths regarding, 258–260; in old age, 189–190; onanism and, 19, 260; use of pornography in, 258, 476, 477; pseudonecrophilia and, 333; Roman Catholic church on, 241; self-help approaches to sex therapy and, 449–450; two-person standard of sexual behavior, 230; woman and, 256–257

mate swapping, 325, 326, 327

Mead, Margaret, 61

media: portrayal of gender roles in, 156; sex in, 468–475; sexual performance and, 443; sexual values and, 243; *see also* magazines; pornography; television

medical professionals, sex education for, 247

medications: sexual dysfunctions and, 188, 189; *see also* antibiotics; drugs

Meese Commission, on pornography, 479

Melanesian culture, homosexuality in, 233, 280

men: changing roles of, 6; communication and, 204–208; infertility in, 94; masturbation and, 257–258; mythical performance standards for, 432; roles of, in quarreling, 202–203; rape of, 357; reaction of, to women's movement, 156–157, 158; sexual abuse of children and, 360–366; sexuality of, and old age, 185, 188–189; transgenderism in, 316; transvestism in, 314–316; *see also* gender differences; gender-identity/roles; male sex organs; male sexual response; masculinity; sex differences

ménage à trois, 324–325

menarche, **39**, 40

menopause, **39**–40, 53–55

menstrual cycle, **39**–44

menstruation, **41**–42, 43, 44

mental illness: homosexuality as, 287–288; sexual activity and, 395–396

mentally retarded, sex and sexual rights of, 249–250, 251

Meritor Savings Bank v. Vinson, 351

message, communication process and, 196, 197

Metropolitan Community Church, homosexual marriage and, 305

Mexico, pre-Columbian pottery of, 462

midwives, **99**

military, homosexuals and, 304

Miller, Isabel, 465

mind control, advertising as a type of, 474

minipill: 111, 115; age and, 113

minor lips: **30**, 31; in female sexual response, 67; infibulation and, 32

miscarriage, **127**

miscommunication, and sexual expectations, 342

mixed gonadal dysgenesis, 137

Model Penal Code, 480

modeling theory, **476**

molluscum contagiosum, **386**

Money, John: 12, 16; on "sexual reform movement," 4

monilial vaginitis, 381

monkeys: African green, origins of AIDS and, 403; macaques, and AIDS, 409

monocytes, HIV and, 410

monogamous, **183**

monogamy, versus polygamy, 183–184

monorchidism, **390**

monozygotic twins, *see* identical twins

mons, **30**

Montagnier, Luc, discovery of AIDS virus and, 404

Moore, Demi, 466, 467

moral model, of homosexual behavior, 283

moral normalcy, defining sexual normalcy and, 233

moral reasoning, studies of gender differences in, 154–155

moral values, **239**

mores and values, sexual, 462, 464

"morning after" birth control, 124

morula, **83**

mucus method, of natural family planning, 121

Müllerian ducts, development of fetal gonads and, **138**

Müllerian Inhibiting Substance, **138**

multiple births, 82–83

multiple orgasms, men and, 73

multiplier effect, of factors in determining gender-identity/role, 149

music videos, 473

mutual manual stimulation, masturbation and, 263

mutual masturbation, 263

mutual pleasuring, partnership approaches to sex therapy and, 450

mycroplasmas, HIV and, 410

Myers-Briggs Type Indicator (MBTI), personality types for communicating and, 204–205

myometrium, **35**

mythical performance standards: for men, 432; for women, 432

mythology, sexual behaviors portrayed in, 228

myths: about communication, 198–199; "heterosexual assumption" and, 275; regarding homosexuality, 297–298; regarding masturbation, 258–260; of sexuality and aging, 186–188; *see also* mythical performance standards; mythology

N

National Association of Sexual Addiction Problems, 344–345

National Birth Control League, Margaret Sanger and, **104**

National Commission on AIDS, 417

National Endowment for the Arts (NEA), 463, 464
National Institute on Child Health and Human Development, proposed study of sexual behavior and transmission of AIDS by, 15
National Opinion Research Center (NORC) surveys, changing attitudes toward sex and, 4
National Organization for Changing Men (NOCM), 156–157
National Organization for Women (NOW), gender roles and, 151
natural childbirth, **98**
natural family planning, 106, 111, 121
natural law, moral values and, 239
necrophilia, **333**
needs, gender differences in expressing, 205–206
Neisser, Albert, 377
Neisseria gonorrhoeae, 377
New England Journal of Medicine, outbreak of AIDS and, 402
Newton, Michael, 11
Newton, Niles, 11
Ngonda tribe, homosexuality in, 232
NGU, *see* nongonococcal urethritis
nicotine, *see* smoking
nocturnal orgasms, in adolescents, 175, 176
noncoercion, principle of, 243
nondeceit, principle of, 243
nongenital oral stimulation, 261
nongonococcal urethritis (NGU), **380**
nonlove, in Sternberg's triangular theory of love, 212, 213
nonoxydol-9: 117; in condoms, and AIDS, 264; *see also* spermicides
nonspecific urethritis (NSU), 380
nonvaginal penile intercourse, 263
NORC (National Opinion Research Center) surveys, changing attitudes towards sex and, 4
normal: **227;** defining, 233
normal asexuality, **434**
normal variant model, of development of homosexual behavior, 285–286
normalization, sexual rights of mentally retarded and, 249–250
Norplant implants, 111, **116**
NSU, *see* nonspecific urethritis
nudist camps: 22; exhibitionism and, 330
nudity: in art, 462; attitudes toward, 21–22; effect of, on children, 173; as exhibitionism, 329–330
numb erection, 438
nurse-midwives, 99
nursing homes, sexual prohibitions in, 188
nyphomania, variance in sexual activity and, 311–312

O

obscene telephone calls, 329
obscenity, **461**
observation: learning gender-identity/ roles and, 150; *see also* observational research
observational research, 18

octoxynol: 117; *see also* spermicides
Oedipus complex, in psychosexual development, 167
old age, *see* aging
Onan, sin of, and masturbation, 19, 260
onanism, **260**
oocytes, **36**
open relationships, 183, 184
open-ended marriage, **183**
openness, in communication, 201
operant conditioning, in psychosexual development, 168–169
opportunistic infections, HIV and, **408,** 415
oral contraceptive, *see* birth control pill
oral sex: 15, 262–263; adolescent sexuality and, 178; AIDS and, 7, 262, 263; -anal sex, 262–263; married couples and, 182; prostitution and, 328; sodomy laws and, 303–304
oral stage, in psychosexual development, 167
oral-anal sex, 262–263
organic disorders, **440–442**
organizing effect, of hormones in human sexual response, **73**
orgasm: **51;** in childhood, 172; dysfunctions of, 434, 436, 438–439, 441; in female sexual response, 68, 69; G spot, 438; in human sexual response, **62,** 63, 64; male, 51–52, 71–72; mythical performance standards and, 432; sexual performance pressure and, 443; sexual problems and, 344; sexual response cycle and, 433; simultaneous, 265–266; vaginal, 9; women and, 9, 10
orgasmic phase dysfunctions, 434
orgasmic release, **63**
orgasmic response, 67, 68
orgasmic standard, of sexual behavior, 230
orgies, 324, **325**
os, **35**
osteoporosis, 53–54
other-gender friendship, 215
outercourse, 115
ova: **36,** 40; in fertilization, 81–82
ovaries: 36–37
Ovid, 464
ovulation, **40,** 41, 43
ovum transfer, **90**
oxytocin: **37;** in birth process, 97

P

Packard, Vance, 474
pads, during menstruation, 42
Paludi, Michelle, 347
Pap smear, **36**
pansexual, **333**–334
paraphilia: 343; as sex label, **229;** sex theory and, 310
paraplegic(s), sex for, **250**–251
parenthood, choosing, 104–105
parents, role of, on homosexuality, 285, 286
Parents and Friends of Lesbians and Gays (PFLAG), 292

partial zona dissection (PZD), male infertility and, **94**
participation, establishment of intimacy and, 214
partner availability, sex for elderly and, 189
partners kneeling, rear entry position, 269
partners seated position, 268–269
partners seated, rear entry position, 270–271
partners standing position, 269
partners standing, rear entry position, 270–271
partnership approaches, to sex therapy, 450–452
passion, role of, in Sternberg's triangular theory of love, 210, 211, 212, 213
patient confidentiality, 418
PC muscle, *see* pubococcygeus (PC) muscle
pediculosis pubis, 384
pedophilia, 360–366
pelvic examination, for women, 36
pelvic infections, infertility in women and, 94
pelvic inflammatory disease (PID); 376; and intrauterine devices, **120**
pelvic nerves, 69, 72
penile implant, impotence and, 447
penis: **47;** cancer of, 390; disorders of, 390; erection, 430; proving masculinity and, 436; size of, 48, 49
penis captivus, 34
penis envy, in psychoanalytic theory, 167
performance pressure: 443; reducing, 449
perimetrium, **35**
perinatally, transmission of AIDS virus, **404–405**
perineal areas, **385**
permissiveness, toward sex, 19
personality development: psychosexual development and, 166–167, 285; of homosexuals, and psychosexual development, 285
personality types, for communicating, 204–205
Peru, pre-Columbian pottery of, 462
Petronius, Caius, 464
Peyronie's disease, **390,** 393
PFLAG (Parents and Friends of Lesbians and Gays), 292
phallic stage, of psychosexual development, 167
pharmaceutical companies: contraceptives and, 105, 107
phimosis, **49–50; 390**
phobias, sexual, 434–435
phone sex, 329, 471, 473
photographs, pornographic, 463
Phthirus pubis, 384
physically handicapped, sexuality of, 248, 250–252
Piaget, Jean, moral development of children and, 241
Picasso, Pablo, 472
PID, *see* Pelvic Inflammatory Disease
pimps, 328
Piss Christ, 463
pituitary gland: effect of hormones on homosexual development and,

283–284; in menstruation, 38, 40, 41, 42, 43; in sperm products, 50–51
placenta, **84,** 85
plateau phase: **62;** in female sexual response, 67–68; in human sexual response, **62,** 64; in male sexual response, 70–71
play, sex, among children, 172, 173
Playboy, 468, 475
pluralism, 8, 231
PMS, *see* premenstrual syndrome
Poison, 464, 470
polygamy, extramarital sex and, **183**
polymorphously perverse, infants as, in psychoanalytic theory of psychosexual development, 167
population samples, 17, 18
pornography: **461;** attitudes toward, and sexual revolution, 4; Attorney General's Commission on Pornography and, 16; child, 475; contemporary literature as, 465–468; and the courts and the law, 477–484; definition of, **461;** effects of, 475–477; erotic art and, 462–464; films, 468–471; literary, 464; masturbation and, 258; and the media, 468–475; sexual aids and, 263, 321; stereotypical sex differences in response to, 65
Portnoy's Complaint, 465
position pictures, of Japan, 462
positions, for intercourse, 266–270
possessiveness: 217–218; group sex and, 325
postcards, pornographic, 466, 467
postcoital contraception, 124
post-ejaculatory, 440
post-rape trauma, 359
post-traumatic stress disorder model, 363
potentiation: sexual, in young children, **172**
pottery, pre-Columbian, of sexual activities, 462
power games, sex and, 199
pregnancy: 95–96; biology of, 96; breasts during, 37; drug use during, 96–97; fetal testing during, 93–94; rape and, 359; sex during, 97; tests, 96; unintended, options, 125–130; *see also* birth process
pregnancy tests, 96
pregnancy-induced hypertension, **99**
preindustrial societies, homosexuality in, 233, 280
prejudice, and sexual differences, 344
prelabeling process, in psychosexual development, 171
premarital sex: 184; changing attitudes toward, 20; Roman Catholic church on, 241
premature birth: multiple fetuses and, 83; problems during pregnancy and, **99**
premature ejaculation: 431, 434, **439**–440, 441, 454; sex therapy and, 449–450
premenstrual syndrome (PMS), **44**
prenatal factors, of determining gender-identity/role, 136–141
preorgasmic, **433**
preovulatory preparation, 40, 41, 43
prepuce: **30,** 31; *see also* foreskin
Presbyterian church, changing of sexual values in religion and, 240–241

Presidential Commission on Obscenity and Pornography (1970), 478
priapism, **390**
pride, identity, and homosexual identity formation, 292
primary dysfunction, **433**
primary syphilis, 378
privacy, sexual prohibitions in nursing homes and, 188
problematic sex, 341–369
producers' code, of movie industry, 468
professionals, sexual abuse by, 349
progestasert, 120
progesterone, 36, 42, 44, **46**
progestin injections, **116**–117
prolactin, **37**
prolapse of the uterus, **395**
promiscuity: gender differences in homosexual identity formation and, 292; variance in sexual activity and, **311**
prostaglandin, **44**
prostaglandin-induced abortion, **129**
prostate gland, **50,** 388, 389
prostate surgery, sexual dysfunction in elderly and, 189
prostatic cancer, 388
prostatitis, **388**
prostitution: 327–329; children and, 475; historical records regarding, 228; spreading of HIV in Africa and, 403
Protestant, conservative attitude of, and filmmaking, 469
Proust, Marcel, 465
pseudonecrophilia, **333**
psychoanalytic theory: of learning gender-identity/roles, 150; model of homosexual development, 285; of psychosexual development, 166–167; sexual dysfunctions and, 446
psychology, factors in choosing contraceptions and, 108–110
psychosexual development: **165**–166; of homosexuals, 285; theories of, 166–171; theory of Sigmund Freud on, 9
psychosexual therapy, 445
psychosocial development, and psychosexual development, **168,** 169
psychotherapy, for treating sexual dysfunction, 446
pubertal development, 143–146
puberty: **174;** factors of, in influencing gender-identity/role, 143–146; sexuality and, **174,** 175
pubic lice, 384–**385**
pubococcygeus (PC) muscle: **34;** Kegel exercises and, 70; **442**
pudendal nerves, 69, 72
Puritan attitude, on nudity and sex, 462
pyromania, fetishism and, **324**

racial and ethnic prejudice, and sexual differences, 344
random sample, in research, **17**
rape: acquaintance, **352,** 355–357; aftermath of, 359–360; definition of, 351; fear of, 352; incidence of, 351; the law and, 482–483; marital, **357;** of men, 357–359; perceptions of, 353; prevention, 356, 360; and profile of rapists, 354; statutory, **350;** stereotyped scenario of, 352; treatment for, 359
rape trauma syndrome, **359**
rape-shield laws, 360
rapist(s), profile of, 354–355
rationality, communication and, 198
rear vaginal entry intercourse, 269–270
receiver, communication process and, 196, 197
reclining face-to-face position, 266–268
recreational adultery, **183**
Redbook Magazine, sex questionnaire of, 15
refractory period: in male sexual response, **72**–73; age and, 75
reinforcement, conditioning in psychosexual development and, **168**–169
Reinisch, June, 12, 15
Reiss, Ira, on next sexual revolution, 7–8
relationship perspective, of homosexual experience, and studying homosexual behavior, 28
relationships: coping with loss of, 218–219; games of, 199; intimacy and, 181–183; open, 183, 184; risk of, 208–209; same sex, 295–296; and sexual functioning, 443
relaxation, establishment of intimacy and, 214
religion: codes of sexual normalcy and, 233; contraceptives and, 105, 106–107; defining sexual normalcy and, 233; erotic art and, 462; homosexuality and, 302; influence of, on women's sexuality, 15; on masturbation, 19, 229; sexual values and, 239, 240–241
representative sample, in research, 17
reproduction: artificial insemination and, 88–89; cloning and, 91–92; fertilization and, 81–83; fetal development and, 81–84, 86–87; fetal technology and, 84–85, 88–93; genetic engineering and, 85, 88; in vitro fertilization and, 89–90; infertility and, 94–95; sex selection and, 90–91; surrogate motherhood and, 92–93; *see also* birthing; pregnancy
research: sexism in, 154; sexual revolution and, 7
resolution phase: **62;** in female sexual response, 68–69; in human sexual response, **62,** 64; in male sexual response, 72, 75
responsibility, towards others, and sexual values, 244
retarded ejaculation, **438**
retrograde ejaculation, **52,** 389
retrovirus, **410**

540

Reubens, Paul, 480–481
reverse transcriptase, enzyme, retroviruses and, 410
reversed vasocongestive dysfunctions, 434
Rh incompatibility, **100**
Rho GAM, **100**
rhythm method: 121; *see also* family planning
Rice, Alice, 465
right of privacy doctrine, 481
risk-taking, sexual acts and, 343
Roe v. Wade, 127
Roman Catholic church: abortion and, 127; on contraceptives, 106–107; homosexuality and, 302; sexual values in religion and, 241; on standards of movie industry, 468
romance: attitudes toward, 22; in childhood, 174; stereotypical sex differences in, 65, 66; versus sexual attraction, 208
romantic love, in triangular theory of love, 212, 213
romantic standard, of proper sexual behavior, 230–231
Roth, Philip, 465
Roth v. the United States, 477
rubber dam, use of, during oral sex, **262, 425,** 427
Ru-486, as postcoital contraceptive, **124,** 483
Rutter, Peter, 349

S

sadist: 8, **331**–332; labels and, 234
sadomasochism: **331**–332; proper labeling of, 229; sexual stimulation and, 263
sadomasochistic: literature, 465; photographs, 463
Safer Sex Kit, 376
saline-induced abortion, **129**
Salk, Jonas: on development of HIV vaccine, 417; polio vaccine and, 401
Sambia, homosexuality in, 232
same-sex relationships: 295–296; sex in, 294–295
sample, in research, **17**
Sanger, Margaret, birth control movement and, 104, 106
satyriasis, variance in sexual activity and, **311**–312
Satyricon, 464
scabies, **386**
Schwartz, Pepper, sex research of, 15
science, impact of, on sexual revolution, 7
scrotum: 44, **45**–46; cancer of, 47
sculpture, Greek, 463
seated position, of intercourse, 268–269
seated, rear entry position, 270–271
secondary dysfunction, **433**
secondary syphilis, 378
Selby, Hubert, Jr., 465
selective abortion: multiple fetuses and, 83; sex selection and, 91
selective reduction, **83**
self-attitudes, negative, 342–343

self-concept, of child, and gender-identity/role, 142
self-destructive behaviors, 343–344
self-esteem: gender differences in, during child development, 155–156; sex in elderly and, 189
self-examination: breast, 38–39; of genitals, for women, 35; testicular, 46–47
self-gratification, **229**
self-hatred, and sexual experiences, 343
self-help approaches, to sex therapy, 449–450
self-induced abortion, prior to legalization, 104, 106, 127
self-labeling stage, in psychosexual development, 171
self-pleasuring, **229**
self-talk, effective communication and, 202
semen, **50**
seminal vesicle, 45, **50**
seminiferous tubules, **45**
sender, communication process and, 196, 197
Senegal, prostitutes in, and spreading of HIV, 403
sensate focus, as sex therapy treatment, **450**–451
sensual experience, of sex, versus physical orgasm in sex research, 309
sensuosity, 309
Serrano, Andres, 463
sex, confusion of, with love, 214–215
sex addiction, **344**–345
sex assignment, influence of, on gender-identity/role, 141–142
sex chromosomes, influence of, on determining gender-identity/role, 136–137
sex differences: in sexual arousal, 65–66; *see also* gender differences
sex drive, *see* libido
sex education: 244–245, 366; adolescent sex and, 8; AIDS and, 244, 246, 247; attitudes toward, 23–24; court actions on, 482; explicit videos and, 471; "Just Say No" philosophy and, 246; for professionals, 247; technology and, 245; trends in, 245–247
sex exploration, of children, 172, 173
sex flush, 67, 68
sex games: of children, 172, 173; of adults, 199–200
Sex Information and Education Council of the United States, *see* SIECUS
Sex Offenders: An Analysis of Types (Gebhard et al.), 479
sex performance, emphasis of sex research on, 309
sex play, of children, 172, 173
sex predetermination, 91
sex reassignment, transsexuals and, 317–319
sex roles, *see* gender-identity/role
sex selection: 90–91; amniocentesis and, 93
sex symbols, movie stars as, 469
sex therapist, **448**
sex therapy: 4, 368–369; criteria for, 453; defining, 445; effectiveness of, 454; ethical issues in, 455–456
sex-determining region of Y, *see* SRY
sexism: of religion, and women, 241; women's movement and, 152–156

sexology, as term, 16
sex-oriented tabloids, 465, 468
sexosophy, as term, 16
sex-reversed individuals, 137
sexual abuse: of children, 360–366; by professionals, 349; premenstrual syndrome and, 44; rape and, 349–360
sexual activity, variance in degree of, 310–313
sexual attraction: marriage and, 182; *see also* attraction
sexual avoidance, 434
sexual behavior, Kinsley scale of, 276–278
sexual burnout, 313
sexual counterreformation, 4
sexual curiosity, in childhood, 172–173
sexual decision-making, 238
sexual desire, 433
sexual development, *see* psychosexual development
sexual dysfunction(s): **63,** 344; absolute, 433; arousal difficulties as, 435–437; causes of, 440; desire phase problems as, 433–435; drugs and alcohol and, 442–443; in elderly, 188–189; folk remedies for treating, 445–446; lack of ejaculation control as, 439; orgasmic, 438; partial, 433; performance, 443; post-ejaculatory pain as, 440; relationships and, 443; sexual response cycle, 433; situational, 433; stimulation of erogenous zones as therapy for, 261–262; total, 433; treatments for, 444–456
sexual enhancement programs, for elderly, 190–191
sexual etiquette, 216
sexual fantasy: 322–323; in masturbation, 258; pornography and, 476; sexual stimulation and, 263
sexual harassment, **345**–351
sexual incompatibility, sexual dysfunctions and, 445
sexual individuality: 234-**235;** development of, 235–236, 238; variability of, 313–314
sexual instinct theory, of psychosexual development, 166
sexual intercourse: 264, 265–266; AIDS and, 7, 264; with children, 361; marriage and painful, 392–393; positions for, 266–270; during pregnancy, 97
sexual interest, varying degrees of, 310–313
sexual intimacy, *see* intimacy
sexual liberation: sex research and, 10–11; of women, 4–5
sexual orientation: confusion and conflict over, in adolescence, 175; development of sexual individuality and, 235–236, 238; formation of, 286–287; understanding of, and psychosexual development, 171
sexual phobias and aversions, **434**
sexual pluralism, 8, 237
sexual positions: married couples and, 182;
sexual preference, 286–287
Sexual Preference (Bell, Weinberg, & Hammersmith), development of sexual individuality, 235–236

sexual pressure: sexual burnout and, 313; reducing, 449

sexual problem(s): dysfunctions as, 344; and negative self-attitudes, 342; prejudice and ignorance and, 344; preventing and dealing with, 366–369; and self-destructive behaviors, 343; self-evaluation of, 370–371; sexual abuse as, 349–366; sexual addiction as a, 344–345

sexual reflex, in conditioning, 169

sexual reform movement, 4

sexual response, *see* human sexual response

sexual response cycle, 433, 434

sexual revolution, historical perspective of, **4**–**7**

sexual rights, of mentally retarded, 249–250

sexual scripts, in psychosexual development, 170

sexual surrogate, for treating sexual dysfunctions, **446**

Sexuality Today, 473

sexually transmitted disease(s) (STDs): 385–386; among college students, 191; chlamydia as, 379–380; genital herpes as, 382–383; genital warts as, 383–384; gonorrhea as, 376–378; legal aspects of, 387; nongonococcal urethritis as, 380; prevention of, 375–376, 386–387; and pubic lice, 384–385; self-evaluation of attitude toward, 396–398; sexual revolution and, 7; syphilis as, 378–379; vulvovaginal infections as, 380–382

shaft: clitoral, **31;** of penis, 47

Sharp, William, transgenderism and, 316

sheep membranes, condoms made from, 103–104

Sherfey, Mary Jane, 11–12

SHUG, vasectomy and, 122

shunga, **462**

side-by-side position, 267–268

side-by-side, rear entry position, 270

SIECUS (Sex Information and Education Council of the United States): on media and sexually explicit materials, 478; attitudes toward sex education and, 23–24, 244

silence, communication and, 198, 201–202

simian immunodeficiency virus, *see* SIV

Simon, William, social script theory of, 170

simultaneous orgasms, 265–266

sin of Onan, masturbation and, 19

Singapore, access to birth control in, 109

single persons: 183, 184; *see also* premarital sex

situational dysfunctions, 433

situational ethics, sexual values and, 240

SIV, HIV and, 409

Skene's glands, ejaculation in female sexual response and, **69**

skin sensitivity, establishment of intimacy and, 213–214

smegma: on females, **31;** and males, 48

smoking, effect of, on pregnancy, 96

social institutions, sexual instructions and, 232

social labeling, in psychosexual development, 171

social learning theory: on learning gender-identity/roles, 150; on psychosexual development, 168–**169**

social marketing, cost of birth control for developing countries and, 109

social nudists, 22

social script theory, of psychosexual development, 170

social scripts, **170**

society: AIDS and, 417–421; factors in choosing contraceptives and, 108–110; homosexuality and, 299–305

sociocultural analysis, studying homosexual behavior and, 280–281

sociocultural standards, of sexual arousal and behavior, 230–233

sodomy laws, **479,** 481–482; homosexuality and, 303–304

sonograms, fetal testing and, **94**

Spanish fly, 264

spectatoring, **443**

sperm: **45;** effect of marijuana on production of, 264; production of, 50–51

sperm bank, 89

sperm count: infertility and, 94; effect of marijuana on, 264

spermatocytes, **51**

spermicidal jelly (cream): **118;** *see also* spermicides

spermicides, 112, 114, **117;** and STD infections, 387

sperm-separating technique, sex predetermination and, 91

sphincter vaginae, 33–34

spinal cord injuries, sex and, 250–251

sponge, contraceptive: 112, **117;** age and, 113

spontaneous abortion, **127**

spontaneous ejaculations, 176

squeeze technique, 452, 453

SRY, chromosome abnormalities and, 137

stag films, 471

standing position, of intercourse, 269

standing, rear entry position, 270–271

Stanley v. Georgia, 477

Staphylococcus aureus: barrier birth control methods and, **118;** tampons and, 42

statistical normalcy, defining normal sexual behavior and, 233

statutory rape, **350**

Steinem, Gloria, on surrogate motherhood, 92–93

stepfathers, and incestuous relationships, 365

stereotypes, of sexual attractiveness, 342–343

sterility, and gonorrhea, 377

sterilization: as birth control method, **121**–122, 123; the law and, 483; of mentally retarded, 249

Sternberg, Robert, triangular theory of love of, 210–212, 213

stigmatization, effects of child abuse and, 364

straight, **278**

stop-start method, 452, 454

strands, of personal development, 170–171

strategies, for communication, 198

streetwalkers: **328;** *see also* female prostitutes; prostitution

subculture, of homosexuality, 299–301

subjective erotic experience, lack of emphasis on, in sex research, 309

sub-Saharan Africa, spreading of HIV in, 403

suicide, rate of, among homosexuals, 281–282

Sumerian civilization, ancient love songs of, 464

suppositories, spermicidal, 112, **117**

suprachiasmatic nucleus, anatomical differences between heterosexuals and homosexuals, 284

surrogate motherhood, 92–93

surveys, proper methodology for, 17

swinging, 325, 326, 327

syndrome, **408**

synthesis, identity, and homosexual identity formation, 292

syphilis: 7, **375,** 378–379; congenital, 378–379; symptoms, 378

systematic desensitization, **447**

T

tabloids, sex-oriented, 465, 468

taboo(s), incestuous, 365

tampons, 42

Tannen, Deborah, on gender differences in communication, 205, 207–208

technical virgins, 20

technology: sex education and, 245; impact of, on sexual revolution, 7

teenage pregnancy, sex education and, 247

teenagers, *see* adolescents

telephone calls, obscene, 329

telephone sex: 329, 471, 473

television: portrayal of gender roles on, 156; sex education and, 245; sexual themes on, 473–474; sexual values and, 243

tertiary syphilis, 378

testes: **44**–46; cancer of, 46–47, 390; during orgasm, 71

testicular cancer, 46–47, **390**

testicular failure, **390**

testing: for HIV, 412–415; controversy over mandatory, 414–415

testosterone: **45,** 53; development of fetal gonads and, 138; effect of, on homosexual development, 283; male climacteric and, 55–56; effect of marijuana on, 264; replacement therapy, 56; sexual desire and, 73

testosterone replacement therapy, male climacteric, and, **56**

test-tube babies, *see* in vitro fertilization

test-tube studies, HIV and, 409

tetracycline, effect of, on birth control pills, 116

T-4 lymphocytes, AIDS virus and, 420

Thailand, access to birth control in, 109

theoretical failure rate: **114;** of various birth control methods, 111–113

therapy: criterion for, 453; effectiveness, 454; ethical issues in, 455, 456; homosexuality as mental disorder and, 287–288; sex, 368–369; *see also* group therapy; psychoanalytic therapy; psychosexual therapy

Thomas, Clarence, **345**
threesomes, group sex and, 324–325
thrush, early stages of HIV and, **408**
tipped uterus, 395
Title VII, Civil Rights Act (1964), 348, 351
Title IX, Education Amendments (1972), 348
Title X funding, *Webster vs. Reproductive Health Services* and, 127
tolerance, identity, and homosexual identity formation, 290
Tootsie, 469
topless dancing, 466–467
total dysfunctions, 433
touching, establishment of intimacy and, 213–214
toxic shock syndrome (TSS): barrier birth control methods and, **118;** tampons and, 42
transfusions, blood, transmission of HIV and, 406–407, 409
transgenderists, 147, **316**
transsexuals: 148, **297,** 316–320; gender transpositions and, 319–320; myth regarding homosexuals and, 297; sex reassignment and, 319–320
transvestism: **298;** *see also* transvestites
transvestites: 147, **234,** 314–316; distinguishing fetishists from, 314–315; myth regarding homosexuals and, 297
traumatic sexualization, effects of child abuse and, 364
treatment: ethical dilemmas of, and HIV, 418–419; for HIV-infected persons, 415–417; of sexual dysfunctions, 444–456; *see also* sex therapy; therapy
Treponema pallidum, 378–379
triangular theory of love, Sternberg's, 210–212, 213
Trichomonas, 381–382
trichomoniasis, **381–382**
triphasic pill, 111, 115
triplets, 83
triple-X female, 137
troilism, **324–325**
trust: communication and, 199, 200; relationship games and, 199
tubal ligation, 113, **122**
tubal plug, reversible female sterilization and, 122
Turner's syndrome, 137
twelve-step program, for sex addiction, 345
twins, 82–83
two-person standard, of sexual behavior, 230

U

ultrasound, for fetal health, 94
Ulysses (Joyce), 465
umbilical cord, **84**
unconscious mind, libido and, 166–167
unified theoretical model of sexual development, 170–171
unintended pregnancy, options for, 125–130
Ureaplasma urealyticum, 380

urethra: **47;** female, 30, 31; injury to, in menstruation, 258; male, **47**
urethral opening: female, 30, **31;** male, 47
urinary meatus, *see* urethral opening
urinary tract infections, circumcision and, 50
urophilia, **332**
U.S. government, homophobia in, 304
U.S. Public Health Service's Centers for Disease Control (CDC): outbreak of AIDS, 401–402; diagnosis of AIDS and, 408
U.S. Supreme Court: on abortion, 127; on nude dancing, 466–467, 483; on obscenity, 477; on pornography, 477; on sexual behavior, 480, 482; sodomy laws, and, 303; on telephone sex, 473
uterine lining, *see* edometrium
uterine orgasm, 42
uterus: **35;** cancer of, 36, 55; endometriosis, 394, 395; prolapse of the, **395,** tipped, 395

V

vaccines, for HIV, 416–417
vacuum curettage, **128**
vagina: 30, 31, **33–**34; on female sexual response, 67; infibulation and, 32–33; painful, 438
vaginal atresia, **391**
vaginal atrophy, **391**
vaginal fistulae, **391**
vaginal musculature, 438
vaginal orgasm: Masters and Johnson on, 69; Sigmund Freud on, 9
vaginismus, **34,** 265, 393, 434, 436, 437–438, 452
values: social and cultural, 243; sex and moral, **238–241;** sexual, 243–244; sexual revolution and, 4, 5–6
van de Velde, Theodoor, 10
variable, in experimental research, **18,** 19
variation, as sex label, **229**
varicose veins, **391**
vas deferens, **45**
vasa efferentia, 45
vasectomy, 113, **122**
vasocongestion: in female sexual response, 67; in human sexual response, 63; in male sexual response, 70
vasocongestive dysfunctions, 434
venereal diseases (VD), 375
venereal warts, 383
verbal harassment, 351
vibrators, 10, 257, 263, 321
victimization, sexual, 353
Victorian era; attitudes toward contraceptives in, 104; behavior in, 230; pornography, 464–465; romantic standards of, 230; sex codes of, and morality, 5
videocassette recorder (VCR), and pornography business, 471
videos: adult, 471, music, 473
villi, **84**
violence, and pornography, 475–476
viral hepatitis, **384;** symptoms, 384; treatment, 384

viral infections, treating HIV and, 409–410
virginity, attitudes toward, 20
visually impaired, sexuality and, 250
volunteer bias, in research, 17
voyeurism: 330–331; cultural differences in, **232;** group sex and, 325
vulnerability, risks of relationships and, 208
vulva, **30–31**
vulvovaginal infections, prevention of, 382
vulvovaginitis, **380–382**

W

Warren, Patricia, 465
Webster vs. Reproductive Health Services, 127
Weinberg, Martin, research of, on sexual preference, 286–287
West Africa, origins of HIV in, 403
Western blot, HIV test, **413–414**
wet dreams, 175, 176
white blood cells, AIDS virus and, 410
WHO, *see* World Health Organization
withdrawal, as method of birth control, 111, 115
Wolffian ducts, development of fetal gonads and, **138**
woman on edge of bed or chair position, 268
woman on top, man supine position, 267
women: birth control movement, and 104; changing roles of, 6; communication and, 204–208; extramarital sex and, 183–184; feminist movement and, 151–156; Freud and, 9; illness and sexual arousal of, 441; infertility in, 94; marriage and, 184; masturbation and, 20, 256–257; mythical performance standards for, 434; orgasm in, 9, 10, 265; preorgasmic, 439; psychoanalytic model of homosexuality and, 285; rape and, 349–357; roles of, in quarreling, 202–203; sex in old age, 185, 189; sexism in religion and, 241; sexually abused, 364; sexual harassment and, 345–349; sexual liberation of, 4, 10–11; traditional views of sexual response of, 436; transvestism in, 315; working, 153; *see also* female sex organs; female sexual response
Woolsey, John, 465
words, communication about sex and, 196–198
working women, 153
workplace: masculine perspective bias in, 156; other-gender friendship in, 215; sexual harassment in, 345
World Health Organization (WHO), spreading of AIDS and, 15–16
Wright, Helena, 10–11

X

X chromosome, sex determination, gender-identity/role and, 136–137

XO chromosome combination, 137
XO/XY chromosome combination, 137
XX chromosome combination, gender-identity/role and, 137, 138
XXX chromosome combination, 137
XX/XY chromosome combination, 137
XY chromosome combination, gender-identity/role and, 137, 138
XYY syndrome, 137

Y

Y chromosome, sex determination, gender-identity/role, and, 136–137
yeast infection(s), **381**; in mouth, early stage of HIV and, 408
yolk sac, 84

Z

Zambia, HIV and blood donations in, 403
zona pellucida, 81–**82**
zoophilia, 332–**333**

CREDITS & ACKNOWLEDGMENTS

All chapter openers and part title openers have been reproduced by kind permission of the Henry Moore Foundation.

Cover: *Young Moe* by Paul Klee. © The Phillips Collection, Washington, D.C. Cover design by Harry Rinehart.

Chapter 1 3 *Preface to Sexual Variance in Science and History* by V. L. Bullough, 1976, New York: John Wiley and Sons, Inc.; 9 The Bettmann Archive, Inc.; 10 Dellenbach—Institute for Sex Research; 11 Dellenbach, courtesy of the Kinsey Institute, Indiana University; 12 Scott F. Johnson, courtesy Masters and Johnson Institute; 21 The Bettmann Archive, Inc.

Chapter 2 30 Robert Reynolds; Mel Erikson; 31–42 Mel Erikson; 45 Robert Reynolds; 46–52 Mel Erikson.

Chapter 3 67–68, 71–72 Illustrations by Mel Erikson, adapted from *Human Sexual Response* by W. Masters and V. E. Johnson, 1966, Boston: Little, Brown.

Chapter 4 82 Photo Researchers, Inc.; Mel Erikson; 85 Mel Erikson; 92 UPI/Bettmann; 93 Nancy Durrell McKenna, © 1985—Photo Researchers, Inc.; 97 Illustrations from *Williams Obstetrics*, 16th ed., by Pritchard & McDonald, 1980, Norwalk, CT: Appleton & Lange; 98 Doug Baz—The Image Works; 99 Suzanne Szasz—Photo Researchers.

Chapter 5 104 The Bettmann Archive, Inc.; 106–107 "Margaret Sanger" from *Margaret Sanger: An Autobiography* by Margaret Sanger, 1938, New York: W. W. Norton and Co., reprinted by permission of Grant Sanger, M.D.; 108 © Blair Seitz—Photo Researchers, Inc.; 109 "Cost Rules Out Birth Control for Many" by Philip J. Hilts, *New York Times*, July 2, 1991, copyright © 1991 by The New York Times Company, reprinted by permission; 117 Pamela Carley Petersen; 118 Mel Erikson; 119 Mel Erikson; courtesy Wisconsin Pharmacal Company; 120 Mel Erikson; 122 Mel Erikson.

Chapter 6 136–139 Mel Erikson; 142 Sean Connelly; 145 Spencer Grant—The Picture Cube; 146 Figure 6.9 adapted from "Propadeutics of Diecious G-I/R: Theoretical Foundations for Understanding Dimorphic Gender-Identity/Role" by J. Money in *Masculinity/Femininity: Basic Perspectives*, J. Reinish et al., eds., 1987, Oxford University Press; 148 Cathy Cheney—EKM Nepenthe; 149 Dushkin Publishing Group; 152 Library of Congress; 154–155 "Is the 'Gender Gap' Narrowing?" by Constance Holden in *Science*, Vol. 253, August 30, 1991, p. 959, copyright 1991 by the American Association for the Advancement of Science; 157 Spencer Grant—The Picture Cube.

Chapter 7 166–167 Elaine Ward; 168 Pamela Carley Petersen; 170 Elaine Ward; 172 Richard Freiman—Photo Researchers; 174 UN photo by Marcia Weistein; 178 © Kit Hedman—Jeroboam; 181 © Frank Siteman—EKM-Nepenthe; 185 David M. Grossman—Photo Researchers; 186–187 "50 Years of Sex: From Oppression to Obsession" by Nardi Reeder Campion, *New York Times*, June 27, 1991, copyright © 1991 by The New York Times Company, reprinted by permission; 190–191 "Relationship Between Age and Sexual Activity in Married Men" by A. L. Foster, 1979, in *Journal of Sex Education and Therapy*, Vol. 5, No. 1, pp. 21–26.

Chapter 8 201 Mark Antman—The Image Works; 202 © Chester Higgins, Jr.—Photo Researchers, Inc.; 203 "Anatomy of a Lovers' Quarrel" from "Want a Happy Marriage? Learn to Fight" by James Gottman, *New York Times*, February 21, 1989, copyright © 1989 by The New York Times Company, reprinted by permission; 210 © 1981 Mike Murphey—Photo Researchers, Inc.; 211 Figure 8.6 from "The Three Faces of Love" by R. J. Trotter, *Psychology Today*, September 1986, p. 122; 212–213 "How Do I Love Thee?" from "The Three Faces of Love" by R. J. Trotter, *Psychology Today*, September 1986, p. 122; 214 Charles Gatewood—The Image Works; 218 © Richard Hutchings—Photo Researchers, Inc.

Chapter 9 228 The Bettmann Archive, Inc.; © Abraham Menashe—Photo Researchers, Inc.; 229 Museum of Fine Arts, Boston; 230 Sandra Weiner—The Image Works; 234 Rick Grosse—EKM Nepenthe; 235 Charles Gatewood—The Image Works; 236 Klein Sexual Orientation Grid from *Bisexualities: Theory and Research* by Fritz Klein, copyright 1985, Haworth Press, Binghamton, NY, reprinted by permission; 237 "Sexual Pluralism" by Ira L. Reiss, reprinted from the SIECUS Report, Feb./March 1991, Vol. 19, No. 3, copyright © Sex Information and Education Council of the U.S.; 239 © Maureen Fennelli—Comstock; 245 © Bob Daemmrich—The Image Works; 246 Ursula Markus—Photo Researchers, Inc.; 248 Lily Solmssen; 249 Robert Foothorap—Jeroboam, Inc.

Chapter 10 256–257 Robert Reynolds; 261 Lionel J. M. Delevingne—Stock • Boston; 266–271 Robert Reynolds.

Chapter 11 277 Kinsey scale adapted from Kinsey, Pomeroy, & Martin, *Sexual Behavior in the Human Female* (1953), reprinted by permission of The Kinsey Institute for Research in Sex, Gender, and Reproduction, Inc.; 278 Bohdan Hrynewych—Stock • Boston; 282 © Barbara Alper—Stock • Boston; 286 Ira Kirschenbaum—Stock • Boston; 287 © Emilio A. Mercado—The Picture Cube; 290 © Suzanne Arms—Jeroboam, Inc.; 291

"Coming Out Requires Support and Understanding" by Karla Westphal, *Yale Herald,* September 30, 1991, reprinted by permission; 297 Bettye Lane—Photo Researchers, Inc.; 300–301 "Personal Politics: A Lesson in Straight Talk" by Lindsy Van Gelder, *Ms.,* November 1987, reprinted by permission; 302 AP/Wide World; 303 Marty Katz—NYT Pictures; 304 Rose Skytta—Jeroboam; 305 AP/Wide World; © Catherine Allport—The Image Works.

Chapter 12 314 © Chester Higgins, Jr.—Photo Researchers, Inc.; 316 Jaye R. Phillips—The Picture Cube; 318–319 courtesy the Gender Clinic, University of Texas Medical Branch; 321 Spencer Grant—Stock • Boston; 325 Museum of Modern Art/Film Stills Archive; 328 © Robert V. Eckert, Jr.—EKM Nepenthe.

Chapter 13 342 © David Whitbeck—The Picture Cube; 343 The Picture Cube; 345 Reuters/ Bettmann; 346–347 "Sexual Harassment: It's About Power, Not Sex" by Daniel Goleman, *New York Times,* October 22, 1991, copyright © 1991 by The New York Times Company, reprinted by permission; 348 "How Women Deal With Harassment" by Dr. Louise Fitzgerald, *New York Times,* October 22, 1991, copyright © 1991 by The New York Times Company, reprinted by permission; 350–351 "Sexual Harassment on Campus: A Growing Issue" by Deirdre Carmody, *New York Times,* July 5, 1989, copyright © 1989 by The New York Times Company, reprinted by permission; 352 Museum of Modern Art/Film Stills Archive; 353 "What Constitutes Rape?" copyright 1991 The Time Inc. Magazine Company, reprinted by permission; 354 "Even the Victim Can Be Slow to Recognize Rape" by Jane Gross, *New York Times,* May 28, 1991, copyright © 1991 by the New York Times Company, reprinted by permission; 355 "Acquaintance Rape" reprinted from the brochure "Acquaintance Rape: Is Dating Dangerous?" produced by the American College Health Association, 1987; 356 Bob Mahoney for Time; 360 © Spencer Grant—Photo Researchers, Inc.; 361 Mary Ellen Mark/Library; 366 © David M. Grossmann—Photo Researchers, Inc.; 367 "Conversation" reprinted by permission from *Survivor.*

Chapter 14 377 National Audio-Visual Center; 378–379 National Audio-Visual Center; 380 courtesy Abbott Laboratories; 382–286 National Audio-Visual Center; 388–389 "A Lover's Legal Checklist" and "A Lawyer's Legal Checklist" from *Lovers, Doctors and the Law* by Margaret Davis and Scott R. Davis, copyright © 1988 by Margaret Davis and Scott R. Davis, reprinted by permission of HarperCollins Publishers; 392–393 "New Understanding on Dealing With Problems of Pain in Sexual Intercourse" by Jane E. Brody, *New York Times,* March 10, 1988, copyright © 1988 by The New York Times Company, reprinted by permission; 396–397 Sexually Transmitted Diseases Attitude Scale from "Development of a Three-Component Sexually Transmitted Diseases Attitude Scale" by W. L. Yarber, M. L. Torabi, & C. H. Veenker, copyright © 1989 by the American Association of Sex Educators, Counselors, and Therapists, reprinted by permission from the *Journal of Sex Education and Therapy,* Vol. 15, No. 1, pp. 42–43.

Chapter 15 403 "Global HIV Infections" from "The Sobering Geography of AIDS" by J. Palca, *Science,* Vol. 252, April 19, 1991, p. 372, copyright 1991 by the American Association for the Advancement of Science; 406 "Risk Patterns for AIDS: An Emerging Picture," *New York Times,* November 9, 1991, copyright © 1991 by The New York Times Company, reprinted by permission; 407 Frank Fournier—Contact Press Images; 409 "Evidence That HIV Causes AIDS" from "AIDS in 1988" by Robert C. Gallo and Luc Montagnier, copyright © 1988 by Scientific American, Inc., all rights reserved; 412–413 "How Can This Be? How Can Alison Gertz Have AIDS?" by Bruce Lambert, *New York Times,* March 11, 1989, copyright © 1989 by The New York Times Company, reprinted by permission; 413 NYT Pictures; 417 AIDS-sekretariatet Sundhedsstyrelsen; 419 "The Ethics of AIDS Care" by D. Hamilton, *Science,* Vol. 250, November 23, 1990, p. 1085, copyright 1990 by the American Association for the Advancement of Science; 420–421 "The Search for Romance in the Shadow of AIDS" by Mireya Navarro, *New York Times,* October 10, 1991, copyright © 1991 by The New York Times Company, reprinted by permission; 422 "An AIDS Martyr the Media Can Love" by Tom Ehrenfeld, *New York Times,* August 17, 1990, copyright © 1990 by The New York Times Company, reprinted by permission; 423 "Degree of Safety in Types of Sexual Activity" from *The AIDS File* by Joseph Kerrins and George W. Jacobs, 1987, Cromlech Books, Inc., Woods Hole, Massachusetts, reprinted by permission; 423 Sara Krulwich—NYT Pictures, 424 City of New York, Department of Health; 426 City of New York, Department of Health; 427 Robert Reynolds; AP/Wide World.

Chapter 16 434 © Frank Siteman—Stock • Boston; 436 Robert Reynolds; 438 "Women Becoming Orgasmic" from *Sexual Awareness: Enhancing Sensual Pleasure* by Barry and Emily McCarthy, 1984, Carroll & Graft Publishers, pp. 187–188; 442 United Nations; 446 Scott F. Johnson; 447 Robert Reynolds; 450–453 Robert Reynolds; 455 © Barbara Alper—Stock • Boston.

Chapter 17 462 Institute for Sex Research; 463 Metropolitan Museum of Art, Fletcher Fund; © 1982 The Estate of Robert Mapplethorpe; 465 The Bettmann Archive, Inc.; 466–467 "Demi Moore, Postcards, and Topless Dancers" by Debra W. Haffner, reprinted with permission from the SIECUS Report, Aug./Sept. 1991, Vol. 19, No. 6, copyright © Sex Information and Education Council of the U.S.; 469–470 Museum of Modern Art/Film Stills Archive; 472 © Sentinel Communications Co.; 474 © Gerry Howard—Stock, Boston; 478 SIECUS position statements reprinted with permission from the SIECUS Report, Dec. '89/Jan. '90, Vol. 19, No. 2, copyright © Sex Information and Education Council of the U.S.; 480–481 "Pee Wee Herman" reprinted with permission from the SIECUS Report Aug./Sept. 1991, Vol. 19, No. 6, copyright © Sex Information and Education Council of the U.S.

Color Insert
Page 1: © Donald Fawcett—Science Source/Photo Researchers, Inc.; © Petit Format/Photo Researchers, Inc.; © Lennart Nilsson *A Child Is Born.*

Page 2: © Lennart Nilsson *Behold Man;* © Lennart Nilsson *Behold Man;* © Lennart Nilsson *A Child Is Born;* © Junebug Clark—Photo Researchers, Inc.

STAFF

Managing Editor John S. L. Holland
Copy Editor Robert Mill
Production Manager Brenda S. Filley
Designers Harry Rinehart and Charles Vitelli
Art Editor Pamela Carley Petersen
Editorial Assistant Diane Barker
Typesetting Supervisor Libra Ann Cusack
Typesetter Juliana Arbo
Production Assistant Lara M. Johnson
Systems Coordinator Richard Tietjen